EXCHANGE-RATE DYNAMICS

Princeton Series in International Economics

Series Editor
Gene Grossman

Sponsored by the International Economics Section of the Princeton University Department of Economics, the Princeton Series in International Economics includes commissioned works by leading scholars in international trade, international macroeconomics, and international finance. The volumes in the series are intended to span the important policy and research topics in international economics and to help define and direct scholarship in the field. This work is published in collaboration with the International Economics Section of the Department of Economics, Princeton University.

Trade and the Environment: Theory and Evidence
by Brian R. Copeland and M. Scott Taylor

EXCHANGE-RATE DYNAMICS

Martin D. D. Evans

Sponsored by the International Economics Section
Department of Economics
Princeton University

PRINCETON UNIVERSITY PRESS

Princeton and Oxford

Published by Princeton University Press, 41 William Street, Princeton,
New Jersey 08540

In the United Kingdom: Princeton University Press, 6 Oxford Street, Woodstock,
Oxfordshire OX20 1TW

press.princeton.edu

Library of Congress Cataloging-in-Publication Data

Evans, Martin D. D.
Exchange-rate dynamics / Martin D.D. Evans.
p.   cm.—(Princeton series in international economics)
Includes bibliographical references and index.
ISBN 978-0-691-15089-5 (hardcover : alk. paper)   1. Foreign exchange
rates.   2. Foreign exchange market.   I. Title.
HG3851.E77   2011

332.4′56—dc22   2010042504

British Library Cataloging-in-Publication Data is available

Sponsored by the International Economics Section of the Princeton University
Department of Economics

This book was composed in Times Roman and Slimbach using ZzTEX
by Princeton Editorial Associates, Inc., Scottsdale, Arizona.

Printed on acid-free paper.   ∞

Printed in the United States of America

1 3 5 7 9 10 8 6 4 2

Contents

PART II   MICROSTRUCTURE MODELS

Preface

The foreign exchange market lies at the heart of the world economy. Since the demise of the Bretton Woods system in the early 1970s, variations in exchange rates between the world's major currencies have been substantial, affecting household, corporate, and government decision making across the world. Understanding the source and consequences of exchange-rate variations has thus remained a prominent goal in international economics for more than 30 years.

Progress toward this research goal has proved difficult, however. Although initial efforts appeared promising, by the mid-1980s there was growing pessimism among researchers that exchange-rate fluctuations could be systematically explained by macroeconomic conditions. This pessimism continued well into the 1990s. In their 1995 survey, Frankel and Rose summarized the state of research as follows:

> To repeat a central fact of life, there is remarkably little evidence that macro-economic variables have consistent strong effects on floating exchange rates, except during extraordinary circumstances such as hyperinflations. Such negative findings have led the profession to a certain degree of pessimism vis-à-vis exchange-rate research.

Fortunately, with the benefit of hindsight, this view has turned out to be too pessimistic. Since the mid-1990s exchange-rate research has advanced on several fronts: Existing models have been refined and extended, new econometric methods have been applied, and entirely new genres of models have been developed. As a result of these efforts, substantial progress has been made toward the goal of understanding the sources and consequences of exchange-rate variations. In this book I provide an in-depth examination of this recent exchange-rate research.

The book distinguishes among three research areas. Part I reviews research based on macroeconomic models. In the first two chapters I focus on the exchange-rate implications of modern open-economy macroeconomic models. These models extend and refine the ideas first found in the monetary, sticky-price, and portfolio balance models of the 1970s and 1980s to a general equilibrium setting where agents' actions reflect optimal decision making. Here I discuss the exchange-rate implications of recent modeling refinements such as the separation of retail from wholesale goods markets, the accurate characterization of monetary policy, and incomplete risk sharing. Part I also reviews recent empirical exchange-rate research using macroeconomic models.

The models I examine in Part I assume that agents (i.e., households, firms, and central banks) have the same information about the structure of the economy and its current state. As a consequence, everyone holds the same expectations regarding future returns on risky assets, including foreign currency returns, and faces the same degree of uncertainty about those returns. In Part II I move on to examine exchange-rate models with informational heterogeneity. First, I focus on noisy rational expectations models, where the heterogeneous information available to individual investors contributes to exchange-rate dynamics via two new channels: rational confusion and higher-order expectations. I then turn to microstructure models of currency trading. These models consider the exchange-rate implications of heterogeneous information in an environment that replicates the key features of actual currency markets. As such, they provide a rich array of empirical predictions concerning currency-trading patterns that are absent in macro-based models. Importantly, these theoretical predictions are strongly supported by the trading data that have become available to researchers during the past decade.

The empirical success of currency-trading models provides a new perspective on the proximate drivers of exchange rates over short horizons, ranging from a few minutes to a few weeks. However, as the models abstract from the role currency trading plays in the larger world economy, they cannot account for the influence of changing macroeconomic conditions on short-term exchange-rate dynamics. Part III examines micro-based exchange-rate models that take up this challenge. Here I report on recent research that links currency-trading patterns and exchange-rate dynamics to underlying macroeconomic conditions. Although still in its early stages, this research holds the promise of providing the micro-foundations for the exchange-rate dynamics that have been missing from open economy macro models.

Progress on Puzzles

A great deal of research in international economics has been directed toward explaining "puzzles," that is, clearly defined and robust features of the data that are at odds with the theoretical predictions of existing models. A number of these puzzles involve the behavior of exchange rates:

1. The Purchasing Power Parity Puzzle.
2. The Consumption Real Exchange-Rate Puzzle.
3. The Exchange-Rate Disconnect Puzzle.
4. The Exchange-Rate Volatility Puzzle.
5. The Forward Premium Puzzle.

The research discussed in this book makes progress on these puzzles. For example, Chapter 2 examines the behavior of exchange rates in an open economy macro model where the array of financial assets available to households is insufficient to permit complete risk-sharing. Here temporary shocks can permanently affect real exchange rates via their effects on the international distribution of wealth. This model can account for observed persistence in real exchange-rate variations without recourse to an unrealistic degree of price-stickiness in goods prices, thereby providing potential resolution of the Purchasing Power Parity puzzle. The model also makes progress on the Consumption Real Exchange-Rate Puzzle because incomplete risk-sharing introduces a wedge between the variations in real exchange rates and international consumption growth differentials, which accounts for the low correlations observed in the data.

The micro-based models discussed in Part III make progress on the Disconnect, Volatility, and Forward Premium puzzles. In macro models variations in the spot exchange rate are driven either by changes in current macro fundamentals—variables describing the current stance of monetary policy—or by changing forecasts of future fundamentals. By contrast, most short- and medium-term variations in actual exchange rates appear to be unrelated to changes in current or expected future macro variables that should identify fundamentals. In other words, exchange-rate variations appear essentially disconnected from changing macroeconomic conditions over horizons up to several years. One striking symptom of this Disconnect Puzzle shows up in research on the effects of macro data releases. This research shows that exchange rates react to data releases in a manner consistent with the predictions of standard macro models, but the releases account for less than 1 percent of the total variance in exchange rates. In other words, most of the volatility in exchange rates takes place in the absence of macro data releases, periods in which macro models are largely silent.

Micro-based models provide a new view on these puzzles by focusing on the forces driving trading activity in the foreign exchange market. In particular, they explicitly model the spot exchange rate as the price of foreign currency that dealers quote to each other and agents outside the market as part of the trading process. Thus the dynamics of spot exchange rates literally reflects the changes in dealers' quotes. This dealer-centered perspective has two critical implications for exchange-rate determination. First, at any point in time the spot exchange rate can only reflect information known to the dealers making quotes. Second, information known to dealers will only be embedded in the spot exchange rate if they find it optimal from a trading perspective to base their quotes on that information, that is, the information is price relevant. These implications are straightforward, but open up new conceptual space for thinking about exchange-rate dynamics. In particular, they lead us to consider the role played by trading flows (i.e., order flows) in conveying new price-relevant information that dealers use to revise their spot rate quotes. For example, Chapter 9 presents a model where order flows provide dealers with information about current macroeconomic fundamentals, which they then use to revise their spot rate quotes. Here the dynamics of the spot exchange rate is connected to dealers' changing perceptions of current fundamentals rather than to changes in actual fundamentals—an empirically important distinction.

Micro-based models also introduce a new perspective on the Forward Premium Puzzle: the widely documented fact that high interest currencies tend, on average, to appreciate rather than depreciate. One long-standing explanation for the puzzle is that the risk premium investors require to hold foreign currency rises with the interest rate, but it has proved extremely difficult to identify such a premium from investors' preferences in macro models. By contrast, in a micro-based model, the risk premium embedded in dealers' spot rate quotes reflects the risks they face in their role of marketmakers. As Chapter 11 shows, these risks are rather different from the macro risks faced by investors. As a consequence, it is possible to account for the Forward Premium Puzzle without making counterfactual assumptions concerning the behavior of macro risks.

This discussion should not be interpreted as claiming that this book contains *solutions* to any of the exchange-rate puzzles. The models I examine open up new conceptual space for understanding the possible sources of the puzzles that could form the basis for future research. One of my aims in writing the book is to spur this research effort by presenting some new macro- and micro-based exchange-rate models to a wider audience.

Bridging the Gap between Exchange-Rate Models

An arm's-length observer of exchange-rate research in the past decade would have no trouble identifying two distinct modeling approaches: the macro approach, which derives the exchange-rate implications of open-economy macro models, and the microstructure approach, which focuses on the details of currency trading. Moreover, it is hard to miss the fact that the contrasting empirical results from each approach have made little impact on the way researchers formulate exchange-rate models. For example, recent empirical research using macro models stresses that short-run movements in spot rates are primarily determined by changes in expectations, principally expectations concerning the future course of interest rates control by central banks. These models have some empirical success at long horizons, but are completely silent on why order flows appear to be such an empirically important driver of spot rate changes at short horizons. The implicit belief in this line of research seems to be that microstructure factors linking order flow and exchange rates are unrelated to the macroeconomic factors included in the model. In a similar vein, microstructure models are silent on the potential links between the macroeconomy and order flows because they focus on the details of currency trading rather than on the macroeconomic factors that ultimately drive the individual trades. Consequently, they cannot explain why the link between the macroeconomy and spot rate is only discernible at long horizons. Nor do they provide any clear implications for how exchange rates respond to macroeconomic policies.

The micro-based models presented in Part III represent attempts to stake out some middle ground between the macro- and microstructure approaches to exchange-rate modeling. Here I have combined the main features of currency trading from microstructure models with the portfolio decisions agents face in general equilibrium macro models. This is one step short of a general equilibrium macro model that incorporates the micro-foundations of trading in foreign currency and other asset markets. Nevertheless, micro-based models do allow us, for the first time, to investigate the links among macroeconomic activity, currency trading, and exchange-rate dynamics.

The sine qua non of micro-based exchange-rate models is that currency trading is an integral part of the process through which spot exchange rates are determined and evolve. This means, in particular, that foreign exchange dealers continually learn important information from their trades with other market participants, which they then use to revise their spot rate quotes in subsequent trading. Micro-based models show how the information conveyed by trading is linked back to current macroeconomic conditions and why dealers find it optimal to incorporate the information into their quotes.

Clearly, this process only makes sense in a world where some price-relevant macroeconomic information is not publicly known. Micro-based models therefore start from the premise that much of the information about the current state of the economy is initially dispersed across agents. This premise accords well with reality. It also distinguishes the informational structure of micro-based models from the assumptions found in both the macro- and microstructure approaches to exchange-rate modeling. Agents in most macro models are assumed to have the same information, which includes the current state of the economy, whereas many microstructure models include informational asymmetries: some agents (insiders) are endowed with more precise information about future asset payoffs than others (outsiders). In contrast, micro-based models include informational heterogeneity but not asymmetries. Agents and dealers have heterogeneous information about the economy in equilibrium but there are no insiders or outsiders.

Audience and Coverage

This book has two intended audiences. One audience comprises Ph.D. students who intend to write their dissertations in the area of international macroeconomics and finance. More specifically, the three chapters in Part I provide a reasonably comprehensive overview of macro exchange-rate modeling that could be covered as part of a standard Ph.D. field course in international macroeconomics. The discussion of exchange-rate risk in the first part of Chapter 11 would also be appropriate for such a course if time permits. The other material in Parts II and III is more suitable for inclusion in a longer field course in international macroeconomics and finance. Additionally, some of these chapters (e.g., Chapters 4, 6, and 11) could be used in a Ph.D. field course on asset pricing. The book is also intended for use by Ph.D. students beyond their field courses. For example, students who have studied the material in Part I should be able to delve further into exchange-rate research by reading Parts II and III.

The second intended audience comprises researchers in international macroeconomics and finance who are looking for a guide to recent developments in the literature, either to aid their own research or to extend the syllabi of their Ph.D. courses. I should stress, however, that my intent is to provide a guide rather than a comprehensive survey of the literature. Despite the book's length, there was no space to discuss all the relevant papers in the literature. Instead, each chapter ends with a bibliographic discussion that provides the starting point for further in-depth reading. I have also developed a set of PowerPoint lecture notes, an answer key to the end-of-chapter questions, and other materials that may be useful to instructors and Ph.D. students. These materials are available on my website at: http://www9.georgetown .edu/faculty/evansm1/.

Space considerations also forced me to exclude a number of topics related to exchange-rate dynamics. In particular, the models I examine are designed to study the behavior of major currency markets with lots of trading activity, such as the USD/EUR, USD/JPY, and USD/GBP markets. They are less well suited for studying the behavior of exchange rates between currencies that trade with much less liquidity. Since the currencies of most countries fall into this category, adapting micro-based models to these markets is an important priority for future research. I have also omitted any serious discussion of exchange-rate derivatives, such as options. In principle, the micro-based approach to modeling spot exchange rates can be extended to include the market determination of derivatives, but this research has yet to be undertaken. Similarly, micro-based models could also be used to design and analyze different currency-trading strategies, such as variants of the carry trade.

Finally, although part of this book was written in the midst of the 2008 world financial crisis, I have not included a model of how the crisis affected currency markets. Nor is there any discussion of how countries operating under different exchange-rate regimes fared as the crisis developed. That said, many of the models I do discuss provide key theoretical ingredients for studying these and other crises-related issues. For example, Chapter 2 shows how the constraints imposed by international solvency interact with the portfolio choices of investors to drive exchange rates. This linkage is not the focus of traditional macro models, but is clearly relevant in thinking about how global imbalances will be resolved. Similarly, Chapter 6 presents a model in which financial institutions act as marketmakers and trade on their own account. In this instance, the market is the spot foreign currency market, but the mechanisms at play apply to financial institutions participating in debt and equity markets. As such, the model may provide a starting point for analyzing the fragility of the shadow banking system. More generally, the models I discuss are intended to spur research on the behavior of exchange rates and other asset prices in environments where market participants have heterogeneous and imprecise information about the economy. Such information constraints were clearly evident as the crises unfolded in 2008, but may also be important in understanding the role financial markets play in coordinating macroeconomic activity under normal conditions.

Acknowledgments

Many of the topics discussed in this book draw heavily on my research with Richard Lyons at the University of California, Berkeley. For more than a decade I have been fortunate to collaborate with Rich in an effort to understand the micro-foundations of foreign exchange dynamics. Throughout he has been a continuous source of ideas and enthusiasm and deserves much of the credit for the progress we have made. Indeed, had he not been called to serve in the dean's office of the Haas School at Berkeley, we would have collaborated on writing this book. Fortunately, he still managed to provide insightful feedback on many chapters and some much-needed encouragement when the scale of the project seemed particularly daunting. I am also grateful to Charles Engel, Viktoria Hnatkovska, and Eric van Wincoop for their comments on individual chapters and to the small army of Ph.D. students who helped check the mathematical derivations. Of course a project such as this requires an enormous amount of time and energy, so I owe my largest debt of gratitude to my family: Liz, Sophie, and Jeremy.

PART I

MACRO MODELS

CHAPTER 1

Macro Models without Frictions

This is the first of two chapters that examine the exchange-rate implications of macro-economic models. My aim is not to survey all the macro models of exchange-rate determination, but rather to provide a theoretical overview of how exchange rates are linked to macro variables in environments that are familiar to students of macro-economics. This overview serves two purposes. First, it highlights the degree to which the exchange-rate implications of widely used macro models accord with the empirical characteristics of exchange-rate behavior. Second, it establishes a theoretical benchmark for judging the success of the new micro-based exchange-rate models presented in subsequent chapters.

The macro models we study have standard features. There are two countries, each populated by a large number of identical utility-maximizing households. In this chapter we study models where households have access to a rich array of financial assets. More specifically, we assume that they all have access to markets for a complete set of contingent claims. As a result, households are able to share risk completely. This feature has important implications for the behavior of exchange rates in both endowment economies (where output is exogenous) and in production economies (where output is determined optimally by firms). Another standard feature of the models we study concerns the role of money. Here we assume that households derive utility from holding real balances and that central banks have complete control of their national money supplies. This framework has a long tradition in the international macro literature. When combined with the implications of complete risk-sharing, it allows us to characterize the differences between the behavior of real and nominal exchange rates in a straightforward manner.

The final noteworthy feature of the models presented herein concerns the behavior of prices. Although "price-stickiness" plays an important role in many international macro models, in this chapter we focus on models in which all prices are fully flexible. In so doing, our analysis abstracts from the complications caused by the presence of frictions in both financial and product markets. The exchange-rate implications of these frictions are examined in Chapter 2.

1.1 Preliminaries

1.1.1 Definitions

The focus of our analysis is on the behavior of the nominal spot exchange rate, which we refer to as the spot rate. The spot rate, denoted by S, is defined as the home price of foreign currency. Throughout, we take the United States as the home country, so S identifies the price of foreign currency in U.S. dollars. According to this definition, an appreciation in the value of the dollar is represented by a *fall* in S because it corresponds to a fall in the dollar price of foreign currency. Conversely, a *rise* in S represents a depreciation in the value of the dollar. Defining spot rates in this way can be a source of confusion at first, but it turns out to be very convenient when considering the determination of spot rates from an asset-pricing perspective. For this reason it is the standard definition used in the international finance literature.

The spot exchange rate identifies the price at which currencies can be traded immediately. Forward rates, by contrast, identify the price at which currencies can be traded at some future date. The k-period forward rate at time t, $\mathcal{F}_t^k$, denotes the dollar price of foreign currency in a contract between two agents at time t for the exchange of dollars and foreign currency at time $t + k$. Foreign currency is said to be selling forward at a discount (premium) relative to the current spot rate when $S_t - \mathcal{F}_t^k$ is positive (negative). Obviously, spot and forward rates are equal when the maturity of the forward contract, k, equals zero.

Two relative prices play prominent roles in international macro models. The first is the terms of trade. In international finance the convention is to define the terms of trade, $\mathcal{T}$, as the relative price of imports in terms of exports:

$$\mathcal{T} = \frac{P^{\text{M}}}{S\hat{P}^{\text{X}}},$$

where P^{M} is the price U.S. consumers pay for imports and $\hat{P}^{\text{X}}$ is the price foreign consumers pay for U.S. exports. (Hereafter, we use a hat, i.e., "ˆ", to denote foreign variables.) Since S is defined as the price of foreign currency in dollars, $S\hat{P}^{\text{X}}$ identifies the dollar price foreign consumers pay for U.S. exports. Note that a rise (fall) in the relative price of U.S. exports, representing an improvement (deterioration) in the U.S. terms of trade, implies a fall (rise) in $\mathcal{T}$. Once again, this may seem unnecessarily confusing, but the international finance literature adopts this definition to simplify the relationship between the real exchange rate and the terms of trade.

The second important relative price is the real exchange rate. This is defined as the relative price of the basket of all the goods consumed by foreign households in terms of the price of the basket of all the goods consumed by U.S. households:

$$\mathcal{E} = \frac{S\hat{P}}{P},$$

where $\hat{P}$ is the foreign currency price of the foreign basket and P is the dollar price of the U.S. basket. Hence, P and $\hat{P}$ are the U.S. and foreign consumer price indices in local currency terms, and $S\hat{P}$ identifies the foreign price index in terms of dollars.

According to this definition, a depreciation (appreciation) in the real value of the U.S. dollar corresponds to a rise (fall) in $\mathcal{E}$ and represents an increase (decrease) in the price of foreign goods relative to U.S. goods.

1.1.2 Price Indices

The behavior of the real exchange rate plays a central role in macro models, so it is important to relate the behavior of the price indices, P and $\hat{P}$, to the prices of individual goods. For this purpose, macro models identify price indices relative to a particular form for the consumption basket based on either the Constant Elasticity of Substitution (CES) or Cobb-Douglas functions.

To illustrate, suppose there are only two goods available to U.S. consumers. Under the CES formulation, the consumption basket defined over the consumption of goods a and b is given by

$$C = \mathcal{C}(a, b) = \left(\lambda^{\frac{1}{\theta}} a^{\frac{\theta-1}{\theta}} + (1 - \lambda)^{\frac{1}{\theta}} b^{\frac{\theta-1}{\theta}} \right)^{\frac{\theta}{\theta-1}}, \tag{1.1}$$

where $\lambda \in (0, 1)$ and $\theta > 0$. This function aggregates the consumption of the two goods into a single index, C, from which households derive instantaneous utility, $U(C)$, for some concave utility function $U(.)$. The consumption-based price index, P, is identified as the minimum expenditure that buys one unit of the consumption index, C. In other words, P minimizes the expenditure $Z = aP^a + bP^b$, such that $\mathcal{C}(a, b) = 1$, given the prices of goods a and b, P^a and P^b.

The mechanics of solving this problem illustrate several properties of the consumption basket and price index, so they are worth reviewing. Choosing a and b to minimize Z such that $\mathcal{C}(a, b) = 1$ gives

$$\frac{b}{a} = \frac{1 - \lambda}{\lambda} \left(\frac{P^b}{P^a} \right)^{-\theta}. \tag{1.2}$$

Thus, the relative demand for good b depends on its relative price, P^b / P^a, and the ratio of shares in the basket, $\frac{1-\lambda}{\lambda}$. Note, also, that θ identifies the elasticity of substitution between goods a and b.

Combining equation (1.2) with the definition of total expenditure, $Z = aP^a + bP^b$, gives us the total demand for each good:

$$a = \frac{\lambda(P^a)^{-\theta}}{\left(\lambda(P^a)^{1-\theta} + (1 - \lambda) \left(P^b \right)^{1-\theta} \right)} Z$$

and $\tag{1.3}$

$$b = \frac{(1 - \lambda)(P^b)^{-\theta}}{\left(\lambda(P^a)^{1-\theta} + (1 - \lambda) \left(P^b \right)^{1-\theta} \right)} Z.$$

Substituting these expressions into (1.1) and setting the result equal to one gives us the minimum necessary expenditure:

$$1 = \left(\lambda^{\frac{1}{\theta}} \left[\frac{\lambda(P^a)^{-\theta} Z}{\lambda(P^a)^{1-\theta} + (1-\lambda)\left(P^b\right)^{1-\theta}} \right]^{\frac{\theta-1}{\theta}} \right.$$

$$\left. + (1-\lambda)^{\frac{1}{\theta}} \left[\frac{(1-\lambda)(P^b)^{-\theta} Z}{\lambda(P^a)^{1-\theta} + (1-\lambda)\left(P^b\right)^{1-\theta}} \right]^{\frac{\theta-1}{\theta}} \right)^{\frac{\theta}{\theta-1}}.$$

Simplifying this equation and solving for Z produces the equation for the price index:

$$P = \left(\lambda(P^a)^{1-\theta} + (1-\lambda)\left(P^b\right)^{1-\theta} \right)^{\frac{1}{1-\theta}}. \tag{1.4}$$

By definition, an expenditure of Z purchases Z/P units of the consumption index C, so we can use (1.4) to rewrite the expressions in (1.3) as

$$a = \lambda \left(\frac{P^a}{P} \right)^{-\theta} C \quad \text{and} \quad b = (1-\lambda) \left(\frac{P^b}{P} \right)^{-\theta} C. \tag{1.5}$$

These equations identify the demand for the individual goods as a function of the share parameter, λ, relative prices, and the consumption index.

The specification of the consumption basket in (1.1), its implications for the price index in (1.4), and individual demand functions in (1.5) prove very useful in the analyses below. In essence, if instantaneous utility over individual goods, $U(a, b)$, can be written in terms of the consumption basket, that is, $U(C)$ with $C = C(a, b)$, household consumption decisions can be separated into two parts. The first is an intertemporal decision concerning the size of the current basket, C. The second is an intratemporal decision about the consumption of individual goods that make up the current basket. As we shall see, understanding how exchange rates affect both intertemporal and intratemporal consumption decisions lies at the heart of macro exchange-rate models.

Finally, it is worth noting that in the limit as the elasticity parameter θ approaches 1, the CES function in (1.1) becomes

$$C(a, b) = \frac{a^\lambda b^{1-\lambda}}{\lambda^\lambda (1-\lambda)^{1-\lambda}}, \tag{1.6}$$

with the associated price index of

$$P = \left(P^a \right)^\lambda \left(P^b \right)^{1-\lambda}. \tag{1.7}$$

1.1.3 Purchasing Power Parity and the Law of One Price

We can now use the price indices to link the real exchange rate to the behavior of individual prices. This allows us to consider three related concepts: the Law of One Price, Absolute Purchasing Power Parity, and Relative Purchasing Power Parity.

The Law of One Price (LOOP) states that identical goods sell in two locations for the same price. This means that when the local currency price of the good for sale abroad is converted into dollars with the spot exchange rate, it will match the price of the same good available in the United States. Thus, if the LOOP applies to good a, $P^a = S\hat{P}^a$, where $\hat{P}^a$ is the local currency price of good a in the foreign country.

The LOOP has implications for the behavior of the real exchange rate. Suppose there are two goods, a and b, that make up the U.S. consumption basket with share parameters λ and $1 - \lambda$, and the foreign basket with shares $\hat{\lambda}$ and $1 - \hat{\lambda}$. The real exchange rate will then be given by

$$\mathcal{E} = \frac{S\hat{P}}{P} = \left(\frac{\hat{\lambda}(S\hat{P}^a)^{1-\theta} + (1-\hat{\lambda})(S\hat{P}^b)^{1-\theta}}{\lambda(P^a)^{1-\theta} + (1-\lambda)(P^b)^{1-\theta}} \right)^{\frac{1}{1-\theta}}.$$

If the LOOP applies to both goods, we can rewrite this expression as

$$\mathcal{E} = \left(\frac{\hat{\lambda} + (1-\hat{\lambda})(P^b/P^a)^{1-\theta}}{\lambda + (1-\lambda)(P^b/P^a)^{1-\theta}} \right)^{\frac{1}{1-\theta}}. \tag{1.8}$$

Clearly, $\mathcal{E}$ will equal one when $\lambda = \hat{\lambda}$. Thus, if the consumption baskets have the same composition in each country and the LOOP applies to each good, then the price of the consumption basket will be the same across countries: $P = S\hat{P}$. This condition is known as Absolute Purchasing Power Parity (PPP).

Now suppose that $\lambda \neq \hat{\lambda}$ so that good a has a different weight in the U.S. consumption basket than in the foreign consumption basket. In this case, (1.8) implies that $\mathcal{E}$ is a function of P^b/P^a. If this relative price is constant, so too is the real exchange rate, but its value can differ from one. This condition, known as Relative Purchasing Power Parity, implies that the depreciation in the spot rate is equal to the difference between the foreign and domestic rates of inflation,

$$\Delta s = \Delta\hat{p} - \Delta p,$$

where Δ denotes the first-difference and lowercase letters denote natural logs, for example, $p = \ln P$.

If $\lambda \neq \hat{\lambda}$ and P^b/P^a varies, both forms of PPP break down. This case is most easily illustrated by taking a log linear approximation of equation (1.8) around the point where $P^b = P^a$. This form of approximation will prove very useful throughout the book and is fully described in Appendix 1.A.2. Here it produces

$$\ln \mathcal{E} = \varepsilon = (\lambda - \hat{\lambda})(p^b - p^a).$$

Clearly, the correlation between the log real exchange rate and log relative prices depends on the relative weights in the two consumption baskets. One important application of this relationship arises when there is bias in consumption toward domestically produced goods. In particular, suppose that good a is produced in the United States and good b in Europe. Home bias in consumption would then be characterized by $\lambda > 1/2$ and $\hat{\lambda} < 1/2$, so clearly $\lambda - \hat{\lambda}$ would be positive. Furthermore, $p^b - p^a$ now represents the log of the U.S. terms of trade, $\tau = p^M - (s + \hat{p}^X)$: p^b is the log price of imports and p^a is the dollar price of exports, which is equal to $s + \hat{p}^X$ under the LOOP. Thus,

$$\varepsilon = (\lambda - \hat{\lambda})\tau.$$

Home bias in consumption implies that an improvement in the U.S. terms of trade (i.e., a fall in τ) is associated with a real appreciation of the dollar (i.e., a fall in ε).

1.2 Empirical Characteristics of Real Exchange Rates

Any successful model of exchange-rate determination must account for the behavior of both nominal and real exchange rates. This section documents two key empirical characteristics of real exchange rates that the model has to explain. First, we examine how the cross-country relative price variations across different types of goods contribute to real exchange variability. Second, we consider the volatility and persistence of real-exchange-rate variations.

1.2.1 Real Exchange Rates and Relative Prices

Variations in real exchange rates can come from many sources because national price indices are composed of the prices of many different types of goods. Historically, researchers have placed goods into two categories; nontraded and traded. The nontraded good category includes any goods that are produced solely for domestic consumption, whereas the traded category includes goods that can be consumed in any country regardless of where they are produced. With this classification, variations in the real exchange rate can be decomposed into changes in the relative price of nontraded goods across countries and changes in the relative price of traded goods across countries.

This decomposition of real-exchange-rate variations is most easily constructed using log approximations to the consumption-based price indices. In particular, assume that the U.S. consumption basket, $\mathcal{C}(\text{T},\text{N})$, is defined in terms of traded goods, T, and nontraded goods, N, with price indices P^T and P^N. In this case, equation (1.4) implies that the U.S. price level in period t is

$$P_t = \left(\lambda (P_t^T)^{1-\theta} + (1 - \lambda)\,(P_t^N)^{1-\theta}\right)^{\frac{1}{1-\theta}}.$$

Log linearizing this expression around the point where $P_t^N = P_t^T$ gives

$$p_t = p_t^T + (1 - \lambda)(p_t^N - p_t^T). \tag{1.9}$$

Similarly, we can approximate the log price level in the foreign country by

$$\hat{p}_t = \hat{p}_t^T + (1 - \hat{\lambda})(\hat{p}_t^N - \hat{p}_t^T), \tag{1.10}$$

where $\hat{p}_t^T$ and $\hat{p}_t^N$ denote the log foreign currency price indices for traded and non-traded goods, respectively, and $\hat{\lambda}$ is the share parameter for traded goods in the foreign consumption basket.

Combining (1.9) and (1.10) with the definition of the log real exchange rate gives

$$\varepsilon_t = (s_t + \hat{p}_t^T - p_t^T) + [(1 - \hat{\lambda})(\hat{p}_t^N - \hat{p}_t^T) - (1 - \lambda)(p_t^N - p_t^T)]. \qquad (1.11)$$

The first term on the right is the log relative price of foreign traded goods in terms of U.S. traded goods. The second term is a weighted difference between the relative price of nontraded to traded goods across countries. It is convenient to identify these terms respectively by ε_t^T and ε_t^{NT}, so that the depreciation of the real exchange rate becomes $\Delta\varepsilon_t = \Delta\varepsilon_t^T + \Delta\varepsilon_t^{NT}$. The variance of the real depreciation rate is therefore

$$\mathbb{V}(\Delta\varepsilon_t) = \mathbb{V}(\Delta\varepsilon_t^T) + \mathbb{V}(\Delta\varepsilon_t^{NT}) + 2\mathbb{CV}(\Delta\varepsilon_t^T, \Delta\varepsilon_t^{NT}), \qquad (1.12)$$

where $\mathbb{V}(\cdot)$ and $\mathbb{CV}(\cdot, \cdot)$ denote the variance and covariance operators.

Engel (1999) documents the relative contribution of ε_t^T and ε_t^{NT} to the variation in U.S. real-exchange-rate movements. Using monthly data on consumer prices and spot rates, he computed measures of ε_t^T and ε_t^{NT} for Canada, France, Germany, Italy, Japan, and the United States from January 1962 to December 1995. He then calculated the ratio, $\mathbb{V}(\Delta\varepsilon_t^T)/\mathbb{V}(\Delta\varepsilon_t)$, over horizons ranging from 1 month to 30 years. The results of these calculations, which were striking, are reproduced in Table 1.1. Aside from the U.S.-Canada rate, his estimates of $\mathbb{V}(\Delta\varepsilon_t^T)/\mathbb{V}(\Delta\varepsilon_t)$ in panel A are just below one at all horizons for all the other real exchange rates. He also finds that the estimates of $\mathbb{CV}(\Delta\varepsilon_t^T, \Delta\varepsilon_t^{NT})$ are very close to zero, as shown in panel B.[1] Taken together, these results imply that variations in the relative price of tradables at the consumer level account for the lion's share of the variations in real exchange rates over a wide range of horizons.

Engel's results present a challenge to traditional thinking concerning international price dynamics. To see why, let us first suppose that only one good is traded internationally. In this case ε_t^T represents the period-t deviation from the LOOP, so international arbitrage should limit the variations in ε_t^T. For example, when ε_t^T falls below a certain lower bound it becomes profitable to incur the costs of importing the good to the home country, so ε_t^T should fall no further. Likewise, the profitability of exporting the good will limit the rise in ε_t^T above a certain upper bound. Under these circumstances, changes in ε_t^T are more likely to be affected by the presence of the bounds when they are computed over longer horizons. As a result, we should expect to see the variance ratio $\mathbb{V}(\Delta\varepsilon_t^T)/\mathbb{V}(\Delta\varepsilon_t)$ fall as the horizon increases, but Engel only finds this pattern for the U.S.-Canada data.

Of course, Engel's calculations are based on price indices rather than the price of a single traded good, so variations in ε_t^T could reflect variations in the terms of trade. Recall that changes in the relative price of different traded goods can affect the real exchange rate computed from two price indices for traded goods if the weights the goods receive in each index differ. For example, if there are only two traded goods

---

1. Engel (1999) actually reports results for the ratios of mean square errors [i.e., $\mathrm{MSE}(\Delta\varepsilon^T)/\mathrm{MSE}(\Delta\varepsilon)$] rather than the variance ratios, but as he notes, this does not materially affect the results. In fact, he cannot reject the hypothesis that ε_t^T and ε_t^{NT} follow independent random walks.

TABLE 1.1
Sources of Real Exchange Variation

Horizon (months)	Canada	France	Germany	Italy	Japan
A. $\mathbb{V}(\Delta\varepsilon_t^{\mathrm{T}})/\mathbb{V}(\Delta\varepsilon_t)$					
1	1.165	1.000	1.010	1.006	1.069
6	0.977	1.000	0.982	0.996	1.018
12	0.928	1.001	0.969	0.996	0.994
36	0.880	1.000	0.934	0.990	0.956
60	0.829	0.997	0.901	0.987	0.942
B. $\mathbb{CV}(\Delta\varepsilon_t^{\mathrm{T}}, \Delta\varepsilon_t^{\mathrm{NT}})\,(\times 100)$					
1	−0.001	−0.006	−0.001	0.000	−0.003
6	−0.001	0.001	0.003	−0.001	−0.009
12	0.003	−0.042	0.015	−0.002	−0.002
36	0.032	−0.037	0.134	0.009	0.073
60	0.066	0.044	0.361	0.027	0.134
C. $\mathbb{V}(\Delta\varepsilon_t^{\mathrm{T}})/[\mathbb{V}(\Delta\varepsilon_t^{\mathrm{T}}) + \mathbb{V}(\Delta\varepsilon_t^{\mathrm{NT}})]$					
1	0.943	1.000	0.992	0.987	0.981
6	0.954	1.000	0.994	0.993	0.989
12	0.955	1.000	0.993	0.993	0.992
36	0.948	0.999	0.991	0.995	0.990
60	0.919	0.999	0.990	0.997	0.987

Source: Engel (1999).

and the shares of the U.S.-produced good are λ and $\hat{\lambda}$ in the U.S. and foreign price indices, respectively, then

$$\Delta\varepsilon_t^{\mathrm{T}} = (\lambda - \hat{\lambda})\Delta\tau_t,$$

where τ_t is the log U.S. terms of the trade. Thus, variations in $\Delta\varepsilon_t^{\mathrm{T}}$ could reflect volatility in the terms of trade if $\lambda \neq \hat{\lambda}$. Engel finds little support for this explanation in the data. The difference between λ and $\hat{\lambda}$ is just too small to account for the volatility of $\Delta\varepsilon_t^{\mathrm{T}}$ given the observed variation in the terms of trade.

Another possible explanation for Engel's findings involves the construction of the price indices. The index for traded goods is constructed from the food and all goods less food CPI subindexes, whereas the index for nontraded-goods' prices is computed from the shelter and all services less shelter CPI subindexes. These measures are imperfect. They include goods in the traded price index that are not traded (e.g., restaurant meals) and goods in the nontraded index that are traded (e.g., financial services). Nevertheless, it is very unlikely that Engel's findings are solely attributable to misclassifications like these because they appear robust to the use of non-CPI price data, such as output prices on consumption deflators.

Burstein, Eichenbaum, and Rebelo (2006) propose a related, but more far-reaching explanation for Engel's results. They argue that traded consumer goods are really composite goods with both traded and nontraded components, where the latter include distribution costs such as wholesale and retail services, marketing and advertising, and local transportation services. This means that the consumer price of each traded good comprises the price of its pure traded component and the price of the distribution services. As a result, variations in ε_t^T computed from consumer prices could reflect changes in the relative price of distribution costs across countries rather than a failure in the LOOP for pure traded goods.

To illustrate this argument, suppose there is little difference in the size of the distribution component across different traded goods, so the log consumer price indices for home- and foreign-traded goods can be approximated by

$$p_t^T = \gamma p_t^R + (1 - \gamma)p_t^D \quad \text{and} \quad \hat{p}_t^T = \gamma \hat{p}_t^R + (1 - \gamma)\hat{p}_t^D,$$

where p_t^R and $\hat{p}_t^R$ denote the log prices of the pure traded goods and p_t^D and $\hat{p}_t^D$ are the log prices of the distribution components. The parameter γ identifies the share of the pure traded good in the composite consumption good. If the LOOP applies to pure traded goods, $p_t^R = s_t + \hat{p}_t^R$, the change in the log relative consumer price of traded goods becomes

$$\Delta\varepsilon_t^T = \Delta s_t + \Delta\hat{p}_t^T - \Delta p_t^T = (1 - \gamma)\Delta\varepsilon_t^D, \tag{1.13}$$

with $\varepsilon_t^D = s_t + \hat{p}_t^D - p_t^D$. Similarly, if traded consumer goods have the same share parameter in the U.S. and foreign price indices [i.e., $\lambda = \hat{\lambda}$ in equations (1.9) and (1.10)], then

$$\Delta\varepsilon_t^{NT} = (1 - \lambda)\left[(\Delta\hat{p}_t^N - \Delta\hat{p}_t^T) - (\Delta p_t^N - \Delta p_t^T)\right]$$

$$= (1 - \lambda)\Delta\varepsilon_t^N - (1 - \lambda)(1 - \gamma)\Delta\varepsilon_t^D, \tag{1.14}$$

with $\varepsilon_t^N = s_t + \hat{p}_t^N - p_t^N$.

Equations (1.13) and (1.14) show that changes in the relative price of distribution services, $\Delta\varepsilon_t^D$, contribute to variations in both components of the real depreciation rate. Consequently, it is possible that variations in $\Delta\varepsilon_t^D$ and $\Delta\varepsilon_t^N$ could account for Engel's findings. To see how, let $\hat{\psi}$ denote Engel's estimate of the variance ratio, $\mathbb{V}(\Delta\varepsilon_t^T)/\mathbb{V}(\Delta\varepsilon_t)$, which is close to one. Now if $\mathbb{CV}(\Delta\varepsilon_t^T, \Delta\varepsilon_t^{NT}) = 0$, as Engel finds, $\hat{\psi} = \mathbb{V}(\Delta\varepsilon_t^T)/(\mathbb{V}(\Delta\varepsilon_t^T) + \mathbb{V}(\Delta\varepsilon_t^{NT}))$. Panel C of Table 1.1 shows that this ratio is very close to one. Rearranging this expression gives

$$\frac{\mathbb{V}(\Delta\varepsilon_t^{NT})}{\mathbb{V}(\Delta\varepsilon_t^T)} = \frac{1 - \hat{\psi}}{\hat{\psi}}. \tag{1.15}$$

Thus, Engel's results imply that the relative variance of $\Delta\varepsilon_t^{NT}$ must be very small compared to the variance of $\Delta\varepsilon_t^T$. This is possible in the presence of distribution costs provided that the variance of $\Delta\varepsilon_t^D$ is sufficiently large. Specifically, equations (1.13) and (1.14) imply that

$$\mathbb{CV}(\Delta\varepsilon_t^{NT}, \Delta\varepsilon_t^T) = (1-\lambda)(1-\gamma)\left[\mathbb{CV}(\Delta\varepsilon_t^N, \Delta\varepsilon_t^D) - (1-\gamma)\mathbb{V}(\Delta\varepsilon_t^D)\right] \quad (1.16)$$

and

$$\frac{\mathbb{V}(\Delta\varepsilon_t^{NT})}{\mathbb{V}(\Delta\varepsilon_t^T)} = \left(\frac{\mathbb{V}(\Delta\varepsilon_t^N)}{(1-\gamma)^2} + \mathbb{V}(\Delta\varepsilon_t^D) - \frac{2\mathbb{CV}(\Delta\varepsilon_t^N, \Delta\varepsilon_t^D)}{1-\gamma}\right)\frac{(1-\lambda)^2}{\mathbb{V}(\Delta\varepsilon_t^D)}. \quad (1.17)$$

Equation (1.16) implies that $\mathbb{CV}(\Delta\varepsilon_t^N, \Delta\varepsilon_t^D) = (1-\gamma)\mathbb{V}(\Delta\varepsilon_t^D)$ if $\mathbb{CV}(\Delta\varepsilon_t^T, \Delta\varepsilon_t^{NT}) = 0$. Substituting this restriction into (1.17), combining the result with (1.15), and rearranging yields

$$\frac{\mathbb{V}(\Delta\varepsilon_t^D)}{\mathbb{V}(\Delta\varepsilon_t^N)} = \frac{\hat{\psi}(1-\lambda)^2}{(1-\gamma)^2\left(1-\hat{\psi}+\hat{\psi}(1-\lambda)^2\right)}. \quad (1.18)$$

Equation (1.18) shows how large the variance of $\Delta\varepsilon_t^D$ must be compared to the variance of $\Delta\varepsilon_t^N$ in order to account for the values of $\hat{\psi}$ estimated by Engel. Note that when the estimates are close to one, the right-hand side is approximately equal to the inverse of the squared share of distribution costs in the consumer prices of traded goods, $(1-\gamma)^{-2}$. Burstein, Neves, and Rebelo (2003) argue that this share is between 0.4 and 0.5 for the United States, which implies that the variance of $\Delta\varepsilon_t^D$ must be four to six times larger than the variance of $\Delta\varepsilon_t^N$ to account for Engel's results. A priori, it is hard to understand why changes in the relative price distribution services, $\Delta\varepsilon_t^D$, should be so much more variable than changes in the relative price of nontraded goods. Indeed, theoretical models that allow for distribution costs, such as that of Corsetti, Dedola, and Leduc (2008a), do not distinguish between distribution and nontraded sectors, so that $\Delta\varepsilon_t^D = \Delta\varepsilon_t^N$.

The preceding analysis shows that the existence of distribution costs *alone* cannot account for Engel's results unless the volatility of those costs is implausibly large. That is not to say that distribution costs are unimportant. Burstein, Eichenbaum, and Rebelo (2006) find that variations in ε_t^T account for a smaller share of the variance of ε_t when ε_t^T is computed with the prices of goods at the dock rather than consumer prices.[2] It appears, therefore, that some of the variations in the relative price of tradables at the consumer level are attributable to distribution costs. The remainder must come from failures in the LOOP for pure traded goods.

---

2. These results are not directly comparable to Engel's because Burstein, Eichenbaum, and Rebelow compute $\mathbb{V}(\tilde{\varepsilon}_t^T)/\mathbb{V}(\tilde{\varepsilon}_t)$, where $\tilde{\varepsilon}_t$ and $\tilde{\varepsilon}_t^T$ are the cyclical components of ε_t and ε_t^T estimated from the Hodrick-Prescott filter.

1.2.2 Volatility and Autocorrelation

Table 1.2 reports the variance and correlations of monthly real and nominal depreciation rates for the United States versus the United Kingdom and Japan between January 1975 and December 2007; for the United States versus Germany between January 1975 and December 1998; and the United States versus the Euroarea between January 1999 and December 2007. The upper panel shows that real depreciation rates are as volatile as nominal depreciation rates and that the two are very highly correlated. These two features imply that very little of the variation in the real depreciation rate is attributable to changes in the inflation differential. In particular, since $\Delta \varepsilon_t = \Delta s_t + \Delta \hat{p}_t - \Delta p_t$ by definition, the variance of the real depreciation rate can be decomposed as

$$\mathbb{V}(\Delta \varepsilon_t) = \mathbb{CV}(\Delta s_t, \Delta \varepsilon_t) + \mathbb{CV}(\Delta \hat{p}_t - \Delta p_t, \Delta \varepsilon_t).$$

Rewriting this expression in terms of the correlation between the nominal and real depreciation rates, $\mathbb{CR}(\Delta \varepsilon_t, \Delta s_t)$, and dividing by the variance of $\Delta \varepsilon_t$ gives

$$1 = \mathbb{CR}(\Delta \varepsilon_t, \Delta s_t) \sqrt{\frac{\mathbb{V}(\Delta s_t)}{\mathbb{V}(\Delta \varepsilon_t)}} + \frac{\mathbb{CV}(\Delta \hat{p}_t - \Delta p_t, \Delta \varepsilon_t)}{\mathbb{V}(\Delta \varepsilon_t)}.$$

According to the statistics in the first three rows of Table 1.2, the first term on the right-hand side has an average value of 0.97 across all the currency pairs. Consequently, changing inflation differentials account for roughly 3 percent of the variance of the real depreciation rate.

The center panel of Table 1.2 reports the variance and correlations for the monthly change in the log bilateral U.S. terms of trade, $\Delta \tau_t$. These data are computed as $\tau_t = s_t + \hat{p}_t^X - p_t^X$ from the log of the export price indices for the United States and the foreign countries, p_t^X and $\hat{p}_t^X$. A rise in τ_t therefore represents a fall in the relative price of U.S. exports compared to dollar export prices of the foreign country. As the table shows, with the exception of the JPY/USD data, the variance of $\Delta \tau_t$ is higher than the variance of the nominal and real depreciation rates. Changes in the terms of trade are also very strongly correlated with the real depreciation rates. These high correlations are not peculiar to the United States. Obstfeld and Rogoff (2000) show that the correlations between bilateral terms of trade and nominal depreciation rates are strongly positive across 15 country pairings.

One possible explanation for these findings is that household preferences are biased toward the consumption of domestically produced traded goods. To see why, let us approximate the log traded price indices in the United States and foreign country as

$$p_t^T = \mu p_t^X + (1 - \mu)(s_t + \hat{p}_t^X) \quad \text{and} \quad \hat{p}_t^T = \hat{\mu} \hat{p}_t^X + (1 - \hat{\mu})(p_t^X - s_t),$$

where the share parameters μ and $\hat{\mu}$ identify U.S. and foreign household preferences between domestic- and foreign-produced traded goods. (Note that these equations incorporate the assumption that the LOOP applies to the exports of traded goods.)

TABLE 1.2
Real and Nominal Exchange-Rate Statistics

	EUR/USD	DM/USD	GBP/USD	JPY/USD
$\mathbb{V}(\Delta s_t)$	6.89	11.05	8.92	10.40
$\mathbb{V}(\Delta \varepsilon_t)$	6.85	11.20	9.44	10.90
$\mathbb{CR}(\Delta s_t, \Delta \varepsilon_t)$	0.99	0.99	0.98	0.99
$\mathbb{V}(\Delta \tau_t)$	7.59	11.31	10.02	7.54
$\mathbb{CR}(\Delta \varepsilon_t, \Delta \tau_t)$	0.99	0.97	0.90	0.84
$\mathbb{CR}(\varepsilon_t, \varepsilon_{t-1})$	0.97	0.99	0.97	0.98
$\mathbb{CR}(\varepsilon_t, \varepsilon_{t-2})$	0.94	0.98	0.94	0.96
$\mathbb{CR}(\varepsilon_t, \varepsilon_{t-3})$	0.91	0.96	0.91	0.94
$\mathbb{CR}(\Delta \varepsilon_t, \Delta \varepsilon_{t-1})$	0.15	0.01	0.05	0.09
$\mathbb{CR}(\Delta \varepsilon_t, \Delta \varepsilon_{t-2})$	0.03	0.09	0.00	0.05
$\mathbb{CR}(\Delta \varepsilon_t, \Delta \varepsilon_{t-3})$	−0.08	0.03	−0.013	0.09

Notes: The log real exchange rate in month t, ε_t, is computed as $s_t + \hat{p}_t - p_t$, where s_t is the log spot rate (FX/USD), $\hat{p}_t$ is the log foreign consumer price index, and p_t is the log U.S. consumer price index in month t. The bilateral terms of trade, τ_t, are computed as $s_t + \hat{p}_t^{\text{X}} - p_t^{\text{X}}$, where p_t^{X} and $\hat{p}_t^{\text{X}}$ denote the U.S. and foreign price indices for exports. Depreciation rates are calculated as the monthly difference in the log level, i.e., $\Delta s_t \equiv s_t - s_{t-1}$, $\Delta \varepsilon_t \equiv \varepsilon_t - \varepsilon_{t-1}$, and $\Delta \tau_t = \tau_t - \tau_{t-1}$ multiplied by 100.

Combining these expressions with the equation for the log real exchange rate in (1.11) gives

$$\Delta \varepsilon_t = \left(\hat{\mu} + \mu - 1 \right) \Delta \tau_t + \Delta \varepsilon_t^{\text{NT}}.$$

Thus the real rate of depreciation reflects variations in the terms of trade when $\hat{\mu} + \mu \neq 1$ and variations in the relative price of nontraded to traded goods across countries, $\Delta \varepsilon_t^{\text{NT}}$. Using this equation to compute the variance of the real depreciation rate and rearranging the result yields

$$\frac{\mathbb{CV}(\Delta \varepsilon_t^{\text{T}}, \Delta \varepsilon_t)}{\mathbb{V}(\Delta \varepsilon_t)} = \left(\hat{\mu} + \mu - 1 \right) \left\{ \mathbb{CR}(\Delta \varepsilon_t, \Delta \tau_t) \sqrt{\frac{\mathbb{V}(\Delta \tau_t)}{\mathbb{V}(\Delta \varepsilon_t)}} \right\}.$$

According to the results in Engel (1999), the ratio on the left is slightly less than one, whereas the statistics in Table 1.2 imply that the term in parentheses on the right is slightly larger than one. Consequently, the sum of the share parameters, $\hat{\mu} + \mu$, must be a little less than two. Although this represents a strong degree of consumption bias, these calculations oversimplify matters in two important respects: they ignore the presence of multiple trading partners and LOOP deviations for traded goods.

The lower two panels of Table 1.2 report the first-, second-, and third-order autocorrelation coefficients for both the log level and the change in the real exchange rate, ε_t and $\Delta\varepsilon_t$. There is strong autocorrelation in ε_t across all the currency pairs and the autocorrelation coefficients are close to one. At the same time, there is little autocorrelation in $\Delta\varepsilon_t$; the autocorrelations are very close to zero. Taken together, these statistics indicate that variations in real exchange rates are quite persistent.

1.2.3 Unit Roots and Half-Lives

There is a large literature examining the persistence of real-exchange-rate movements. One strand looks at whether the time series process for the real exchange rate contains a unit root. Papers in this strand of the literature first considered the behavior of individual rates over single currency regimes and over longer time spans that cover multiple regimes. More recently, attention has centered on the joint behavior of multiple rates under the post–Bretton Woods floating regime. These studies focus on whether shocks to real exchange rates have *any* permanent effect on their level. The second strand of the literature quantifies the rate at which the effects of a shock on the level of the real-exchange-rate decay. A popular metric for this rate is the half-life of the shock, that is, the time it takes for the effect of the shock to be one-half of its initial impact. Recent research in this strand of the literature investigates whether the rate of real-exchange-rate decay can be reconciled with the characteristics of price-setting found in micro data.

Wold and Beveridge-Nelson Decompositions

We can illustrate the issues in both strands of the literature with the aid of the Wold Decomposition theorem. In particular, if the rate of real depreciation follows a mean-zero covariance-stationary process, the Wold theorem tells us that the time series for $\Delta\varepsilon_t$ may be represented by

$$\Delta\varepsilon_t = n_t + b_1 n_{t-1} + b_2 n_{t-2} + \cdots$$
$$= b(L)n_t, \tag{1.19}$$

where $b(L) = 1 + b_1 L + b_2 L^2 \cdots$ is a polynomial in the lag operator, L, (i.e., $Lx_t = x_{t-1}$), and n_t are the errors in forecasting $\Delta\varepsilon_t$ based on a projection (i.e., a linear regression) of $\Delta\varepsilon_t$ on its past values, $n_t = \Delta\varepsilon_t - \mathbb{P}(\Delta\varepsilon_t | \Delta\varepsilon_{t-1}, \Delta\varepsilon_{t-2}, \ldots)$. These errors are also referred to as time series innovations. The Wold theorem also tells us that the moving average representation in (1.19) is unique (i.e., both $\{b_i\}$ and $\{n_t\}$ are unique) and that $E(n_t) = 0$, $E(n_t \Delta\varepsilon_{t-j}) = 0$ and $E(n_t n_{t-j}) = 0$ for $j > 0$ and $E(n_t^2) = \sigma_n^2$.

The Wold Decomposition in (1.19) allows us to identify the presence of a unit root in a very straightforward manner. Let $b(1) = 1 + \sum_i b_i$ denote the sum of the coefficients in $b(L)$. Then we can rewrite (1.19) as $(1 - L)\varepsilon_t = b(1)n_t + (b(L) - b(1))n_t$. Multiplying both sides of this expression by $(1 - L)^{-1}$ gives

$$\varepsilon_t = \mu_t + y_t, \tag{1.20}$$

where

$$\mu_t = \mu_{t-1} + b(1)n_t \quad \text{and} \quad y_t = b^*(L)n_t, \tag{1.21}$$

with $b^*(L) = (1 - L)^{-1} (b(L) - b(1))$. This representation of a time series is known as the Beveridge-Nelson Decomposition. In this context, it decomposes the log level of the real exchange rate into a trend component, μ_t, that follows a random walk and a cycle component, y_t.

Equations (1.20) and (1.21) imply that the real exchange rate contains a unit root when the variance of shocks to the trend, μ_t, is greater than zero. Note though, that this variance is equal to $b(1)^2 \sigma_n^2$, so ε_t contains a unit root if and only if $b(1) \neq 0$. At the same time, the Wold Decomposition in (1.19) identifies the long-run effect of an n_t shock on the level of ε_t by $b(1)$. Thus, although the presence of a unit root implies that n_t shocks have *some* long-run effect on the level of the real exchange rate, it says nothing about the size of the effect [i.e., the size of $b(1)$]. This is an important point. If $b(1)$ is very close to zero, the process for ε_t will contain a unit root, but the behavior of the real exchange rate over any finite sample period will be indistinguishable from the behavior implied by a process for ε_t without a unit root. This form of near observational equivalence makes it impossible to reliably test for the presence of a unit root in a finite data sample even though the test has desirable statistical properties asymptotically (i.e., as the sample size grows without limit). To address this problem, the econometrics literature on unit roots considers tests on the joint null hypothesis of $b(1) = 0$ plus auxiliary restrictions on $b(L)$ that disappear asymptotically.

Half-Lives

The Wold Decomposition theorem also allows us to identify the half-life of a shock. First, we note from (1.19) that the impact of an n_t shock on the log level of the real exchange rate h periods later is $1 + \sum_{i=1}^{h-1} b_i$. The half-life, $\mathcal{H}$, is then the shortest time period, h, such that $1 + \sum_{i=1}^{h-1} b_i$ is less than one-half the original impact of the n_t shock, which in this case is just one:

$$\mathcal{H} = \min_{h \geq 1} \left(1 + \sum_{i=1}^{h-1} b_i \right) \leq 1/2. \tag{1.22}$$

The length of the half-life depends on the size of any unit root in the real exchange rate. To see why, we first note that $1 + \sum_{i=1}^{h-1} b_i = b(1) - \sum_{i=h}^{\infty} b_i$ for all $h \geq 1$. Substituting this identity in (1.22) implies that

$$\mathcal{H} = \min_{h \geq 1} \left(b(1) + b_h^* \right) \leq 1/2, \tag{1.23}$$

where $b_h^* = - \sum_{i=h}^{\infty} b_i$. It is easy to show that b_h^* are the coefficients in the moving average polynomial $b^*(L)$ governing the dynamics of the cycle component in the Beveridge-Nelson Decomposition. As such, we know that $\lim_{h \to \infty} b_h^* = 0$, because y_t is mean-reverting. Thus, (1.23) implies that the half-life, $\mathcal{H}$, must be finite in the absence of a unit root, that is, when $b(1) = 0$. When a unit root is present, the length of the half-life depends on the pattern of the b_i coefficients. For example, in the case where the real exchange rate follows a random walk, all the b_i coefficients are zero, so the half-life is infinite. Alternatively, if the b_i coefficients are such that $b_h^* = \rho^h$ and $b(1) < 1/2$, then the half-life is $\{\ln (1 - 2b(1)) - \ln(2)\}/ \ln(\rho)$. Thus, the presence of a unit root in the real exchange rate does not necessarily imply that the half-life of a shock is infinite. Nor does the length of the half-life indicate anything about the size of the unit root component, $b(1)$.

Much of the literature on real-exchange-rate persistence has focused on estimates of the half-life implied by a stationary AR(1) process. In this case the log level of the real exchange rate is assumed to follow $\varepsilon_t = \rho\varepsilon_{t-1} + v_t$, with $|\rho| < 1$. This process implies that $b(1) = 0$ and $b_h^* = \rho^h$, so the half-life is $-\ln(2)/(\ln \rho)$.[3] According to Rogoff (1996), consensus estimates of ρ in the literature imply a half-life for the real exchange rate of 3 to 5 years. Although such a slow rate of decay could plausibly reflect the effects of productivity and/or taste shocks on the relative price of nontraded to traded goods across countries, $\varepsilon_t^{\mathrm{NT}}$, Engel's findings suggest that variations in $\varepsilon_t^{\mathrm{NT}}$ contribute very little to the volatility of real exchange rates over short- and medium-term horizons. Thus, we are left to ponder what could account for both the high volatility and slow rate of decay in response to shocks in the relative price of traded goods, $\varepsilon_t^{\mathrm{T}}$. This is often termed the Purchasing Power Parity, or PPP, Puzzle.

1.2.4 Aggregation Bias and the PPP Puzzle

At first sight, stickiness in consumer prices appears to offer a simple explanation for the PPP Puzzle. If firms enjoy some monopoly power in both home and foreign markets and adjust the local currency prices for their products infrequently, changes in nominal exchange rates could induce persistent deviations from the LOOP for individual goods, which in turn are reflected in the behavior of $\varepsilon_t^{\mathrm{T}}$. The key issue here is whether the degree of price-stickiness we observe for individual traded goods is sufficient to account for a half-life for $\varepsilon_t^{\mathrm{T}}$ in the 3- to 5-year range. Rogoff (1996) argued that this was unlikely because the first-order effects should occur while prices are sticky—a time frame far shorter than 3 to 5 years. Chari, Kehoe, and McGrattan (2002) provide formal support for this intuition. They are unable to generate the volatility and persistence of real-exchange-rate variations seen in the data from a calibrated general equilibrium model with sticky prices. Imbs, Mumtaz, Ravn, and Rey (2005), hereafter IMRR, present an alternative view. They argue that the estimated persistence of real-exchange-rate variations can be reconciled with the degree of price-stickiness seen in individual prices once proper account is taken of aggregation and heterogeneity. This argument is far from intuitive, so it is worth considering more closely.

Suppose, for illustrative purposes, that households consume just two traded goods, A and B, with dollar prices P^{A} and P^{B}, and euro prices $\hat{P}^{\mathrm{A}}$ and $\hat{P}^{\mathrm{B}}$. To eliminate any terms-of-trade effects, we also assume that U.S. and E.U. households have the same share parameters in their consumption baskets. Thus, the log real exchange rate equals $\varepsilon_t^{\mathrm{T}}$ and can be approximated by

$$\varepsilon_t = \lambda\varepsilon_t^{\mathrm{A}} + (1 - \lambda)\varepsilon_t^{\mathrm{B}}, \tag{1.24}$$

where $\varepsilon_t^{\mathrm{X}} = s_t + \hat{p}_t^{\mathrm{X}} - p_t^{\mathrm{X}}$ denotes the LOOP deviation for good $\mathrm{X} = \{\mathrm{A,B}\}$. At this point we do not consider the pricing decisions of the two firms in any detail. Instead,

---

3. Following the literature, this calculation ignores the fact that the half-life should be an integer. With this restriction the half-life is the smallest integer at least as large as $-\ln(2)/(\ln \rho)$.

we assume that market segmentation allows firms to choose local currency prices, $\hat{p}_t^X$ and p_t^X, given the behavior of the equilibrium spot rate, s_t, so that ε_t^X follows an AR(1) process,

$$\varepsilon_t^X = \rho_X \varepsilon_{t-1}^X + u_t + v_t^X, \tag{1.25}$$

where u_t and v_t^X are mean zero, mutually and serially independent shocks, with variances σ_u^2 and σ_X^2. Realizations of v_t^X represent firm-specific shocks that arise from the pricing decisions of firm $X = \{A,B\}$. By contrast, realizations of u_t are common across firms. As such, they could represent the effects of a change in the nominal exchange rate when both firms keep their prices fixed. Equation (1.25) allows for two sources of heterogeneity across firms. Pricing policies can generate firm-specific shocks with different variances, σ_X^2, and different rates of mean-reversion via the AR(1) coefficients, ρ_X.

Equations (1.24) and (1.25) allow us to investigate how heterogeneity in the pricing decisions of firms shows up in the dynamics of the real exchange rate. As a first step, we rewrite (1.24) using (1.25) to substitute for ε_t^A and ε_t^B:

$$\varepsilon_t = \left(\rho_A + \rho_B\right) \varepsilon_{t-1} - \rho_A \rho_B \varepsilon_{t-2} + \omega_t, \tag{1.26}$$

where $\omega_t = u_t + \lambda v_t^A + (1 - \lambda)v_t^B - \left(\rho_B \lambda + \rho_A(1 - \lambda)\right) u_{t-1}$

$$- \lambda \rho_B v_{t-1}^A - (1 - \lambda)\rho_A v_{t-1}^B.$$

Note that two lags of the log real exchange rate appear on the right-hand side of (1.26) and that ω_t contains both the current and lagged values of the pricing shocks. Taken together, these features imply that the log real exchange rate follows an ARMA(2,1) process. This is an example of a general result concerning the aggregation of individual time series: An average of N variables that all follow an AR(1) process will generally follow an ARMA(N, $N - 1$) process. Consequently, the half-life of the average process will usually differ from the half-lives of the individual variables. The one exception to this result occurs when the individual variables have the same AR(1) parameter. If $\rho_A = \rho_B = \rho$, equation (1.26) simplifies to $\varepsilon_t = \rho \varepsilon_{t-1} + u_t + \lambda v_t^A + (1 - \lambda)v_t^B$ so the half-life for the real exchange rate provides an accurate measure of the half-life of the relative price for individual traded goods.

Up to this point we have seen how the aggregation of individual heterogeneous time series for LOOP deviations can produce a process for the real exchange rate with different time series properties. We now turn to the question of whether this form of aggregation can reconcile the micro evidence on price-stickiness with a half-life for the real exchange rate of between 3 and 5 years.

The first step is to calibrate the processes for the LOOP deviations. In a recent study of a large cross-section of good prices, Crucini and Shintani (2008) find that LOOP deviations for traded goods have half-lives ranging from 9 to 12 months. These results imply values for the ρ_X coefficients in monthly data between 0.925 and 0.943, so we calibrate ρ_A and ρ_B at these values. The behavior of the real exchange rate also depends on the share parameter, λ, which we set equal to 1/2. Finally, we need values for the three variances: σ_u^2, σ_A^2, and σ_B^2. Since there is no direct micro evidence concerning the appropriate calibration of these parameters, we choose values for σ_A^2,

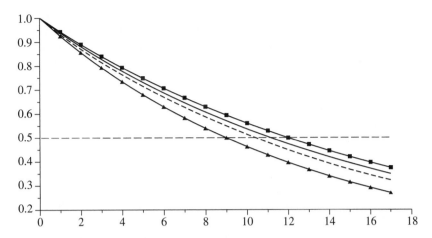

FIGURE 1.1   Impulse response functions (v_t^A shocks, solid triangles; v_t^B shocks, solid squares; u_t shocks, dashed; and n_t innovations, solid).

σ_B^2/σ_A^2, and $\mathbb{CR}(u_t + v_t^A, u_t + v_t^B)$ such that the implied value for $\mathbb{V}(\Delta\varepsilon_t)$ equals 0.11, the estimated variance of the EUR/USD real depreciation rate reported in Table 1.2.

The second step is to compute the parameters of the ARMA(2,1) process implied by (1.26). Without loss of generality, we can write this process as

$$\varepsilon_t = \alpha_1\varepsilon_{t-1} + \alpha_2\varepsilon_{t-2} + n_t + \beta_1 n_{t-1}, \tag{1.27}$$

where n_t are serially uncorrelated mean-zero innovations with variance σ_n^2. We find the values for α_1, α_2, β_1, and σ_n^2 that produce the same autocorrelation pattern [i.e., the values of $\mathbb{CV}(\varepsilon_t, \varepsilon_{t-k})$ for all $k \geq 0$] as the calibrated process in (1.26). With these parameter values in hand, we can compare the impulse response functions from the ARMA(2,1) process against those implied by LOOP deviations and examine the half-life of the real exchange rate with respect to v_t^A, v_t^B, u_t, and n_t.

Figure 1.1 shows the impulse responses of the real exchange rate for the case where $\sigma_B^2/\sigma_A^2 = 2$ and $\mathbb{CR}(u_t + v_t^A, u_t + v_t^B) = 0.2$. The square and triangle plots show the impulse responses to a one unit v_t^A and v_t^B shock, respectively. Note that these plots intersect the 0.5 line at 9 and 12 months, representing the half-lives of the calibrated LOOP deviations. The dashed plot shows the impulse response with respect to a one-unit u_t shock, the shock that is common to both goods. As one would expect, the half-life of this shock lies between 9 and 12 months. Its exact value, $\mathcal{H}$, solves $1/2 = \lambda\rho_A^{\mathcal{H}} + (1 - \lambda)\rho_B^{\mathcal{H}}$, which in this case turns out to be 10.36 months. The impulse response to a unit innovation, n_t, is shown by the solid plot. Once again, this response lies between those for the v_t^A and v_t^B shocks, but it also differs slightly from the response to the u_t shock. It is this difference that represents the effects of aggregation. More specifically, the figure shows that the half-life of real-exchange-rate innovations is slightly longer than the half-life of a common shock to the LOOP deviations. In this sense, there is positive aggregation bias in the half-life.

The distinction between economic shocks and innovations provides the key to understanding the source of aggregation bias. In this example there are three economic

shocks, $\{v_t^A, v_t^B, \text{and } u_t\}$, that represent the effects of nominal-exchange-rate variations and firms' pricing decisions. As Figure 1.1 shows, each of these shocks has a
different dynamic impact on the real exchange rate. By contrast, the innovations, n_t,
are the errors from forecasting the real exchange rate based on a projection of ε_t on its
past values: $n_t = \varepsilon_t - \mathbb{P}(\varepsilon_t | \varepsilon_{t-1}, \varepsilon_{t-2}, \ldots)$. As such, they do not generally represent
the effects of any one economic shock or even a linear combination of shocks. Conse-
quently, it should not be a surprise to find that the exchange rate responds differently
to an innovation than to a particular economic shock.

With this perspective, we can now think about the possible factors affecting the
size of the aggregation bias. In particular, aggregation bias will be greater when the
innovations are poorer approximations to the common shock, u_t. This can occur in
two main ways. First, aggregation bias increases with the variance ratio, σ_B^2 / σ_A^2. In
this case the innovations take on more of the characteristics of the v_t^B shocks, so their
half-life rises. Second, aggregation bias increases as the difference between ρ_B and
ρ_A gets larger. For example, if ρ_B equals 0.955 so that the half-life for v_t^B shocks is 15
months, aggregation bias increases to 2 months. On the other hand, if ρ_B equals ρ_A,
aggregation bias disappears.

This discussion suggests that aggregation bias could offer a potential explanation
for the PPP Puzzle if the half-lives for the LOOP deviations of *some* goods are 2 to
3 years and the innovations to the real exchange rate well approximate the shocks
specific to these goods because their variance is much larger than those for other
goods. For example, the half-life of the real exchange rate rises to 28 months if we
increase σ_B^2 / σ_A^2 to 5 and ρ_B to 0.981. Note though, that even in this case, the half-life
of the real exchange rate is still shorter than the 36-month half-life implied by the new
value for ρ_B. Thus, if LOOP deviations for traded goods have half-lives ranging from
9 to 12 months, as reported by Crucini and Shintani (2008), aggregation bias alone
cannot resolve the PPP Puzzle.

The discussion of aggregation bias to this point omits a key element in the argument
presented by IMRR. They claim that aggregation effects can account for the *estimated*
half-life of the real exchange rate of 2 to 3 years when the estimates are derived
from an AR(1) specification for ε_t. It is important to recognize that this is not a pure
aggregation bias story. It also involves the estimation of the real exchange rate's half-
life. This aspect of IMRR's analysis would not be important if the data on the real
exchange rate spanned a very long time period. Under these circumstances it would
be possible to precisely estimate the parameters of the ARMA(N,$N-1$) process for
ε_t implied by the aggregation of N LOOP deviations. These estimates could then
be used to compute an accurate half-life for the real exchange rate. Unfortunately,
the span of the available data is far too short for IMRR to implement this method.
Instead, they compute the half-life implied by their estimates of ρ from an AR(1)
model: $\varepsilon_t = \rho \varepsilon_{t-1} + \omega_t$. As a consequence, their estimates of ρ have to be corrected
for two problems: (1) finite sample bias induced by the short span of the data, and
(2) misspecification bias that arises when the implied ARMA(N, $N-1$) process for
ε_t does not simplify to an AR(1). As one can imagine, quantifying these biases is
far from straightforward. Indeed, although IMRR claim that they are large enough to
resolve the PPP Puzzle when combined with pure aggregation bias, Chen and Engel
(2005) argue the opposite. At this point, the most we can say is that the question of
whether aggregation and estimation biases resolve the PPP Puzzle remains open.

1.3 Macro Exchange-Rate Models

1.3.1 Overview

We now study the behavior of the nominal exchange rate in a canonical macro model with two countries, the United States and Europe. Each is populated by a large number of identical utility-maximizing households that have access to markets for a complete set of contingent claims. In this setting, households are able to share risk completely, a feature that has important implications for the behavior of exchange rates. To appreciate these implications fully, we first examine the exchange-rate implications of a model where outputs of all the goods are exogenous. We then extend the model to include production. Here, risk-sharing also affects the investment decisions of firms and hence the behavior of output. In the light of Engel's findings concerning the importance of the relative prices of traded versus nontraded goods, there are no nontraded goods in the model. Instead, households consume baskets composed of two traded goods, one produced in the United States and one produced in Europe.

Households

The United States is populated by a continuum of identical households distributed on the interval [0,1/2] with preferences defined over a consumption basket of traded goods and real balances. In particular, the expected utility of a representative U.S. household in period t is given by

$$\mathbb{U}_t = \mathbb{E}_t \sum_{i=0}^{\infty} \beta^i \left\{ \tfrac{1}{1-\gamma} C_{t+i}^{1-\gamma} + \tfrac{\chi}{1-\nu} \left(M_{t+i}/P_{t+i} \right)^{1-\nu} \right\}, \tag{1.28}$$

where γ, ν, and χ are positive parameters and $1 > \beta > 0$ is the subjective discount factor. $\mathbb{E}_t$ denotes expectations conditioned on period-t information and C_t is the consumption index defined over two consumption goods, a U.S.-produced good, C_t^{US}, and a European-produced good, C_t^{EU}. We assume that the index takes the CES form, so $C_t = \mathcal{C}(C_t^{\text{US}}, C_t^{\text{EU}})$ as defined in (1.1) with elasticity parameter θ and share parameter λ for domestically produced goods. P_t is the associated consumption price index and M_t denotes the household's holdings of dollars. The budget constraint for the household is

$$FA_t + M_t = R_t^{\text{FA}} FA_{t-1} + M_{t-1} - P_t C_t, \tag{1.29}$$

where FA_t denotes the dollar value of financial assets held at the end of period t and R_t^{FA} is the (gross) nominal return on assets held between the start of period $t-1$ and t.

Europe is also populated by a continuum of households distributed on the interval [1/2,1]. Here the preferences of the representative E.U. household have an analogous form to those shown in (1.28) except that the consumption index, $\hat{C}_t$, price index, $\hat{P}_t$, and holdings of euros, $\hat{M}_t$, replace, C_t, P_t, and M_t:

$$\widehat{\mathbb{U}}_t = \mathbb{E}_t \sum_{i=0}^{\infty} \beta^i \left\{ \tfrac{1}{1-\gamma} \hat{C}_{t+i}^{1-\gamma} + \tfrac{\chi}{1-\nu} (\hat{M}_{t+i}/\hat{P}_{t+i})^{1-\nu} \right\}. \tag{1.30}$$

E.U. and U.S. households have symmetric preferences with respect to individual traded goods, so $\hat{C}_t = \mathcal{C}(\hat{C}_t^{\mathrm{EU}}, \hat{C}_t^{\mathrm{US}})$, where $\hat{C}_t^{\mathrm{EU}}$ and $\hat{C}_t^{\mathrm{US}}$ denote the consumption of E.U.- and U.S.-produced goods by E.U. households. The budget constraint for the household is

$$\widehat{FA}_t + \hat{M}_t = \hat{R}_t^{\mathrm{FA}} \widehat{FA}_{t-1} + \hat{M}_{t-1} - \hat{P}_t \hat{C}_t, \tag{1.31}$$

where $\widehat{FA}_t$ denotes the euro value of financial assets held at the end of period t and $\hat{R}_t^{\mathrm{FA}}$ is the corresponding period-t (gross) nominal return.

Three features of the household sector deserve comment. First, the presence of real balances in (1.28) and (1.30) generates money demand functions that are reminiscent of traditional models and allow us to examine how exogenous variations in the money supply affect exchange rates. Second, the setup omits any role for labor income; there is no disutility from work and all household income comes from asset holdings. Appendix 1.A.3 shows that household behavior is unaffected by the presence of labor income when markets are complete, so there is no cost attached to this simplifying feature. Finally, the setup leaves the composition of each household's portfolio unspecified. We study this in detail below.

Financial Markets

Both U.S. and E.U. households hold their financial wealth in contingent claims. These primitive financial assets, called Arrow-Debreu (AD) securities, allow U.S. and E.U. households to share their risks perfectly. To understand how households choose among different AD securities, let us assume that there are $\mathcal{Z}$ states of the world indexed by z. Let us also assume that AD securities pay off in dollars. Thus, a household holding one AD security for state z in period t receives \$1 if z is the period-t state and zero otherwise.

Consider the portfolio problem facing the representative U.S. household that has access to a complete set of AD securities. Let $\mathcal{P}_t(z)$ be the price at time t of an AD security that pays \$1 if the state of the world in period $t+1$ is z and zero otherwise. If $\mathcal{A}_t(z)$ denotes the number of type-z AD securities held at the end of period t, the return on last period's portfolio is $R_t^{\mathrm{FA}} FA_{t-1} = \mathcal{A}_{t-1}(z_t)$ and the value of the U.S. household's portfolio at the end of period t is $FA_t = \sum_{\mathcal{Z}} \mathcal{P}_t(z)\mathcal{A}_t(z)$.[4] This portfolio can be decomposed into risky assets and a riskless bond. A riskless bond can be constructed from a portfolio comprising one AD security of each type. This portfolio has a payoff of \$1 next period in all states of the world and has price $\mathcal{P}_t = \sum_{\mathcal{Z}} \mathcal{P}_t(z)$. Thus, the one-period nominal interest rate implied by the prices of AD securities is $r_t = -\ln \mathcal{P}_t$. We can now represent the U.S. household's portfolio as $B_t \exp\left(-r_t\right) + \sum_{\mathcal{Z}} \mathcal{P}_t(s)\left(\mathcal{A}_t(s) - B_t\right)$, where B_t denotes the number of bond-equivalent portfolios of AD assets. Substituting these definitions into the U.S. household's budget constraint in (1.29) gives

---

4. To be clear, $\mathcal{A}_{t-1}(z_t)$ denotes the number of AD securities for the state in period t, z_t, held at the end of period $t-1$, that is, $\mathcal{A}_{t-1}(z_t) = \mathcal{A}_{t-1}(z = z_t)$.

$$\sum_{\mathcal{Z}} \mathcal{P}_t(z) \left(\mathcal{A}_t(z) - B_t \right) + B_t \mathcal{P}_t + M_t = \mathcal{A}_{t-1}(z_t) + M_{t-1} - P_t C_t. \quad (1.32)$$

The budget constraint facing the E.U. household can be derived in a similar manner. The only difference arises from the fact that the available set of AD securities payoff is in dollars rather than euros. To account for this fact, we construct a set of synthetic AD securities that pay off in euros. In other words, we build a portfolio that pays off €1 in state z and zero otherwise. This is straightforward using the contingent spot rate, $S_t(z)$, which is the dollar price of euros in period t when the state is z. Recall that a type-z AD security pays off \$1 in period $t + 1$ if the state is z, so in terms of euros, the payoff is $\in(1/S_{t+1}(z))$ if the state is z and zero otherwise. This means that the dollar cost in period t of purchasing a claim to €1 in state z next period is $\mathcal{P}_t(z)S_{t+1}(z)$ because we have to purchase $S_{t+1}(z)$ of type-z AD securities at price $\mathcal{P}_t(z)$. The cost in euros of putting together this portfolio is $\widehat{\mathcal{P}}_t(z) = \mathcal{P}_t(z)S_{t+1}(z)/S_t$. It is important to recognize that $\widehat{\mathcal{P}}_t(z)$ does not depend upon the actual rate of depreciation between t and $t + 1$. Rather it is a function of the *contingent* rate of depreciation, $S_{t+1}(z)/S_t$ (i.e., the rate if state z is realized in period $t + 1$). Consequently, the value of $\widehat{\mathcal{P}}_t(z)$ for all $z \in \mathcal{Z}$ is known to households in period t.

We are now in a position to write the E.U. household's budget constraint in terms of risky and riskless euro-denominated assets. Recall that $\widehat{FA}_t$ represents the euro value for assets held at the end of period t. Since these assets must be held in the form of AD securities, $\widehat{FA}_t$ must equal $\sum_{\mathcal{Z}} \mathcal{P}_t(z)\mathcal{N}_t(z)/S_t$, where $\mathcal{N}_t(z)$ represents the number of type-z assets held by the E.U. household at the end of period t. Combining this expression for $\widehat{FA}_t$ with the definition of $\widehat{\mathcal{P}}_t(z)$, we can write

$$\widehat{FA}_t = \sum_{\mathcal{Z}} \widehat{\mathcal{P}}_t(z) \frac{\mathcal{N}_t(z)}{S_{t+1}(z)} = \sum_{\mathcal{Z}} \widehat{\mathcal{P}}_t(z)(\widehat{\mathcal{A}}_t(z) - \hat{B}_t) + \widehat{\mathcal{P}}_t \hat{B}_t,$$

where $\widehat{\mathcal{A}}_t(z) = \mathcal{N}_t(z)/S_{t+1}(z)$ and $\widehat{\mathcal{P}}_t = \sum_{\mathcal{Z}} \widehat{\mathcal{P}}_t(z)$. $\widehat{\mathcal{A}}_t(z)$ represents the number of synthetic type-z AD securities that pay off in euros. $\widehat{\mathcal{P}}_t$ is the euro price of a portfolio that pays €1 in all states in the next period, so the one-period foreign nominal interest rate is $\hat{r}_t = -\ln \widehat{\mathcal{P}}_t$. $\hat{B}_t$ identifies the number of foreign bond-equivalent portfolios of AD assets held at the end of period t. Finally, note that $\hat{R}_t^{FA} \widehat{FA}_{t-1} = \widehat{\mathcal{A}}_{t-1}(z_t)$. Thus, using the expression for $\widehat{FA}_t$ above, we can rewrite the E.U. household's budget constraint as

$$\sum_{\mathcal{Z}} \widehat{\mathcal{P}}_t(z)(\widehat{\mathcal{A}}_t(z) - \hat{B}_t) + \widehat{\mathcal{P}}_t \hat{B}_t + \hat{M}_t = \widehat{\mathcal{A}}_{t-1}(z_t) + \hat{M}_{t-1} - \hat{P}_t \hat{C}_t. \quad (1.33)$$

Goods and Money Markets

Recall that in this economy there are just two traded goods, one produced in the United States and the other in Europe. The aggregate demand for each good comprises the sum of the individual demands of U.S. and E.U. households. Let P_t^{US} ($\hat{P}_t^{US}$) and P_t^{EU} ($\hat{P}_t^{EU}$) denote the prices of the U.S. and E.U. good in dollars (euros). Since all households within each country have the same preferences, we can use the demand functions in (1.5) to write the aggregate demand for the two goods as

$$X_t = \frac{\lambda}{2} \left(\frac{P_t^{\text{US}}}{P_t} \right)^{-\theta} C_t + \frac{1-\lambda}{2} \left(\frac{\hat{P}_t^{\text{US}}}{\hat{P}_t} \right)^{-\theta} \hat{C}_t \qquad (1.34a)$$

and

$$\hat{X}_t = \frac{1-\lambda}{2} \left(\frac{P_t^{\text{EU}}}{P_t} \right)^{-\theta} C_t + \frac{\lambda}{2} \left(\frac{\hat{P}_t^{\text{EU}}}{\hat{P}_t} \right)^{-\theta} \hat{C}_t. \qquad (1.34b)$$

The first term on the right-hand side of each equation identifies the aggregate demand from U.S. households and the second the aggregate demand from E.U. households. (Recall that national populations are represented by one-half the unit interval, so aggregate demand from each country is one-half the demand of the U.S. and E.U. representative households.) Note, also, that U.S. demand depends on relative prices in dollars, whereas E.U. demand depends on relative prices in euros. Market clearing requires that the aggregate demand for each good, X_t and $\hat{X}_t$, match the available supply. In the case of an endowment economy, these supplies are exogenous. In the case of a production economy, the supply of each good is endogenously determined by the production decisions of U.S. and E.U. firms.

The aggregate demand for dollars and euros is determined analogously by adding the aggregate national demands. However, in this case, things are further simplified because no household will find it optimal to hold foreign nominal balances when it has access to a complete set of AD securities. As a result, the aggregate demand for dollar balances will be one half the demand of the representative U.S. household. The aggregate demand for euro balances will be similarly just one half the demand of the representative E.U. household. We assume that the aggregate supplies of dollars and euros are completely under the control of the Federal Reserve (FED) and European Central Bank (ECB), respectively.

1.3.2   Equilibrium

Equilibrium in an endowment economy constitutes a sequence for goods prices, $\{P_t^{\text{US}}, P_t^{\text{EU}}, \hat{P}_t^{\text{US}}, \hat{P}_t^{\text{EU}}\}$, interest rates, $\{r_t, \hat{r}_t\}$, AD security prices $\{\mathcal{P}_t(z)\}$, and the nominal exchange rate, $\{S_t\}$, consistent with market clearing in the goods, money, and contingent-claims markets given the optimal consumption and portfolio decisions of households, money supply decisions of central banks, and exogenous output. In a production economy, the output of each good is also determined optimally by firms. Our focus is on the process for the equilibrium exchange rate. Below we lay the groundwork for this analysis in three steps: First, we study households' decisionmaking. Second, we derive two important implications of complete risk-sharing. Third, we examine the implications of market clearing for the links among aggregate consumption, relative prices, and the supplies of traded goods.

Household Decisions

The problem facing the representative U.S. household may be expressed as follows: At the start of each period, the household observes the prices of the $\mathcal{Z}$ AD securities, $\mathcal{P}_t(z)$, and the price index, P_t. On the basis of these prices and real wealth, $W_t = \left(\mathcal{A}_{t-1}(z_t) + M_{t-1}\right) / P_t$, the household then chooses the consumption basket, C_t, the share of wealth in real balances, $\alpha_t^m = M_t / P_t W_t$, and the share of wealth held in each of the AD securities, $\alpha_t(z) = \mathcal{P}_t(z) \left(\mathcal{A}_{z,t}(z) - B_t\right) / P_t W_t$ for all $z \in \mathcal{Z}$, to maximize expected utility (1.28). We can write this problem in the form of the following dynamic programming problem (see Appendix 1.A.1 for details):

$$\mathcal{J}(W_t) = \max_{C_t, \alpha_t^m, \alpha_t(z)} \left\{ \tfrac{1}{1-\gamma} C_t^{1-\gamma} + \tfrac{\chi}{1-\nu} \left(\alpha_t^m W_t\right)^{1-\nu} + \beta \mathbb{E}_t \mathcal{J}(W_{t+1}) \right\},$$

s.t.   (1.35)

$$W_{t+1} = \exp(r_t - \Delta p_{t+1})(ER_{t+1}W_t - C_t),$$

where $\mathcal{J}(W_t)$ is the U.S. value function (i.e., the maximized value of expected utility for the representative U.S. household written as a function of real wealth). The second equation rewrites the budget constraint in (1.32) in terms of real wealth and the excess return on wealth relative to the return on dollar bonds:

$$ER_{t+1} = 1 + \frac{\alpha_t(z_{t+1}) \exp(-r_t)}{\mathcal{P}_t(z_{t+1})} - \sum_{\mathcal{Z}} \alpha_t(z) + \alpha_t^m \left(\exp(-r_t) - 1\right).$$

Note that this excess return depends on the portfolio shares chosen in period t, $\alpha_t(z)$ and α_t^m, and the state in period $t+1$, z_{t+1}.

The problem facing the representative E.U. household is analogously described by

$$\widehat{\mathcal{J}}(\hat{W}_t) = \max_{\hat{\alpha}_t(z), \hat{\alpha}_t^m, \hat{C}_t} \left\{ \tfrac{1}{1-\gamma} \hat{C}_t^{1-\gamma} + \tfrac{\chi}{1-\nu}(\hat{\alpha}_t^m \hat{W}_t)^{1-\nu} + \beta \mathbb{E}_t \widehat{\mathcal{J}}(\hat{W}_{t+1}) \right\},$$

s.t.   (1.36)

$$\hat{W}_{t+1} = \exp(\hat{r}_t - \Delta \hat{p}_{t+1})(\widehat{ER}_{t+1} \hat{W}_t - \hat{C}_t),$$

where $\widehat{\mathcal{J}}(\hat{W}_t)$ is the E.U. value function defined over real wealth, $\hat{W}_t = (\widehat{\mathcal{A}}_{t-1}(z_t) + \hat{M}_{t-1}) / \hat{P}_t$. The excess return on wealth relative to euro bonds is defined by

$$\widehat{ER}_{t+1} = 1 + \frac{\hat{\alpha}_t(z_{t+1}) \exp\left(-\hat{r}_t\right)}{\widehat{\mathcal{P}}_t(z_{t+1})} - \sum_{\mathcal{Z}} \hat{\alpha}_t(z) + \hat{\alpha}_t^m \left(\exp\left(-\hat{r}_t\right) - 1\right),$$

with portfolio shares $\hat{\alpha}_t(z) = \widehat{\mathcal{P}}_t(z)(\widehat{\mathcal{A}}_t(z) - \hat{B}_t) / \hat{P}_t \hat{W}_t$ and $\hat{\alpha}_t^m = \hat{M}_t / \hat{P}_t \hat{W}_t$.

Let $\pi_t(z)$ denote the probability that the state in period $t+1$ is z, conditioned on the current state z_t. Appendix 1.A.1 shows that the first-order conditions from the representative U.S.-household's problem in (1.35) are

$$\alpha_t(z): \quad \mathcal{P}_t(z) = \beta \pi_t(z) \left(\frac{C_{t+1}(z)}{C_t} \right)^{-\gamma} \frac{P_t}{P_{t+1}(z)}, \tag{1.37}$$

$$C_t: \quad C_t^{-\gamma} = \beta \mathbb{E}_t \left[C_{t+1}^{-\gamma} \exp\left(r_t - \Delta p_{t+1} \right) \right], \tag{1.38}$$

and

$$\alpha_t^m: \quad M_t/P_t = \chi^{1/\nu} \left(1 - \exp(-r_t) \right)^{-1/\nu} C_t^{\gamma/\nu}, \tag{1.39}$$

where $C_{t+1}(z)$ and $P_{t+1}(z)$ denote the contingent consumption and U.S. price level in period $t+1$ if the state is z. The corresponding first-order conditions from the representative E.U. household's problem in (1.36) are

$$\hat{\alpha}_t(z): \quad \widehat{\mathcal{P}}_t(z) = \beta \pi_t(z) \left(\frac{\hat{C}_{t+1}(z)}{\hat{C}_t} \right)^{-\gamma} \frac{\hat{P}_t}{\hat{P}_{t+1}(z)}, \tag{1.40}$$

$$\hat{C}_t: \quad \hat{C}_t^{-\gamma} = \beta \mathbb{E}_t \left[\hat{C}_{t+1}^{-\gamma} \exp\left(\hat{r}_t - \Delta \hat{p}_{t+1} \right) \right], \tag{1.41}$$

and

$$\hat{\alpha}_t^m: \quad \hat{M}_t/\hat{P}_t = \chi^{1/\nu} \left(1 - \exp(-\hat{r}_t) \right)^{-1/\nu} \hat{C}_t^{\gamma/\nu}, \tag{1.42}$$

where $\hat{C}_{t+1}(z)$ and $\hat{P}_{t+1}(z)$ are the contingent E.U. consumption and price levels in period $t+1$.

Implications of Risk-Sharing

Access to a complete set of AD securities allows households to perfectly share risks both within and across countries. We now use the first-order conditions to characterize these implications of risk-sharing for the behavior of consumption, the real exchange rate, and the foreign exchange risk premium.

We begin by noting that first-order conditions (1.37) and (1.40) hold for all $\mathcal{Z}$ states. As such, they implicitly define the consumption plan for each household in period $t+1$. In the case of U.S. households, the plan comprises consumption contingent on each state, $C_{t+1}(z)$ for all $z \in \mathcal{Z}$. According to (1.37), these values should be chosen so that the ratio of the marginal utility of \$1 in states z and z' is proportional to the ratio of the AD security prices, with the relative likelihood of states z and z' making up the proportionality factor:

$$\frac{\mathcal{P}_t(z)}{\mathcal{P}_t(z')} = \frac{\pi_t(z)}{\pi_t(z')} \left(\frac{C_{t+1}(z)^{-\gamma}}{P_{t+1}(z)} \frac{P_{t+1}(z')}{C_{t+1}(z')^{-\gamma}} \right).$$

Since all U.S. households face the same AD security prices, $\mathcal{P}_t(z)$ and $\mathcal{P}_t(z')$, and future contingent price levels, $P_{t+1}(z)$ and $P_{t+1}(z')$, their plans for state-contingent consumption, $C_{t+1}(z)$ and $C_{t+1}(z')$, must also be the same. Thus, access to a complete set of AD securities allows U.S. households to share the risk completely within the country. E.U. households also share risks completely within Europe by choosing $\hat{C}_{t+1}(z)$ in a similar fashion based on $\widehat{\mathcal{P}}_t(z)$ and $\hat{P}_{t+1}(z)$.

Equations (1.37) and (1.40) not only identify how the consumption plans of U.S. and E.U. households should be formed across future states, but also show how the contingent consumption decisions are linked internationally. To see this clearly, we combine the identity $\widehat{\mathcal{P}}_t(z) = \mathcal{P}_t(z) S_{t+1}(z) / S_t$ with (1.37) and (1.40) to get

$$
\beta \left(\frac{C_{t+1}(z)}{C_t} \right)^{-\gamma} \frac{P_t}{P_{t+1}(z)} = \frac{\mathcal{P}_t(z)}{\pi_t(z)} = \beta \left(\frac{\hat{C}_{t+1}(z)}{\hat{C}_t} \right)^{-\gamma} \frac{\hat{P}_t S_t}{\hat{P}_{t+1}(z) S_{t+1}(z)}, \quad (1.43)
$$

for all $z \in \mathcal{Z}$. The left-hand side of this equation identifies the nominal intertemporal marginal rate of substitution (MRS) for the U.S. household between t and $t + 1$ when the state in period $t + 1$ is z. The corresponding MRS for the E.U. household measured in dollars is shown on the right-hand side. Equation (1.43) therefore shows that when households construct optimal consumption plans with access to a complete set of AD securities, the implied nominal MRSs measured in terms of a common currency are equalized internationally.

Combining the left- and right-hand sides of (1.43) yields

$$
\frac{\hat{P}_{t+1}(z) S_{t+1}(z)}{P_{t+1}(z)} \frac{P_t}{\hat{P}_t S_t} = \left(\frac{C_{t+1}(z)}{C_t} \right)^{\gamma} \left(\frac{\hat{C}_{t+1}(z)}{\hat{C}_t} \right)^{-\gamma} .
$$

This condition must hold for all period $t + 1$ states, $z \in \mathcal{Z}$. Thus, using the definition for the real exchange rate, $\mathcal{E}_t = S_t \hat{P}_t / P_t$, we can write

$$
\frac{\mathcal{E}_{t+1}}{\mathcal{E}_t} = \left(\frac{C_{t+1}}{C_t} \right)^{\gamma} \left(\frac{\hat{C}_{t+1}}{\hat{C}_t} \right)^{-\gamma} . \quad (1.44)
$$

Equation (1.44) shows that the (gross) rate of depreciation for the real exchange rate must be perfectly correlated with the international ratio of consumption growth. It should be emphasized that this is an *equilibrium* condition that arises from the international risk-sharing properties of the household consumption plans. The equation does not *determine* the real exchange rate any more than it *determines* relative consumption growth; all the variables in (1.44) are endogenous. Nevertheless, this risk-sharing condition plays an important role in determining the equilibrium dynamics of both real and nominal exchange rates.

The presence of a complete set of AD securities also affects the foreign exchange risk premium linking nominal interest rates with the depreciation of the nominal exchange rate. To see this, we start with the identities linking U.S. and E.U. nominal interest rates to the price of AD securities: $1 = \sum_{\mathcal{Z}} \mathcal{P}_t(z) \exp(r_t)$ and $1 = \sum_{\mathcal{Z}} \widehat{\mathcal{P}}_t(z) \exp(\hat{r}_t)$. Combining these identities with the definition of $\widehat{\mathcal{P}}_t(z)$ gives

$$
\exp(r_t) / \exp(\hat{r}_t) = \left(\sum_{\mathcal{Z}} \pi_t^P(z) S_{t+1}(z) \right) / S_t, \quad (1.45)
$$

where $\pi_t^P(z) = \mathcal{P}_t(z) / \mathcal{P}_t$. The term in parentheses identifies the dollar price in period $t + 1$ of a portfolio with a payoff equal to €1 that is set in period t. This is a one-period forward contract for the euro constructed from AD securities:

$\mathcal{F}_t = \sum_{\mathcal{Z}} \pi_t^P(z) S_{t+1}(z)$. Equation (1.45) is therefore nothing other than a statement of Covered Interest Parity (CIP):

$$\exp(r_t)/\exp(\hat{r}_t) = \mathcal{F}_t / S_t.$$

The ratio of returns on one-period U.S. and E.U. bonds equals the ratio of the forward rate relative to the spot exchange rate.

Note, also, that $\sum_{\mathcal{Z}} \pi_t^P(z) = 1$ and $\pi_t^P(z) \geq 0$ for all $z \in \mathcal{Z}$, so the price ratios, $\pi_t^P(z)$, can be interpreted as pseudo probabilities. With this interpretation, we can rewrite (1.45) as

$$\exp(r_t)/\exp(\hat{r}_t) = \mathbb{E}_t^P \left[S_{t+1}/S_t \right]. \tag{1.46}$$

Equation (1.46) links the nominal interest differential to the "expected" rate of nominal depreciation, where expectations are calculated using pseudo probabilities. This expression represents the *exact* uncovered interest parity condition implied by complete markets.

The foreign exchange risk premium is found by comparing (1.46) against the standard expression for Uncovered Interest Parity (UIP). For this purpose we rewrite (1.46) as

$$\exp(r_t)/\exp(\hat{r}_t) = \exp(-\delta_t)\mathbb{E}_t \left[S_{t+1}/S_t \right], \tag{1.47}$$

where $\delta_t = \ln \mathbb{E}_t \left[S_{t+1}/S_t \right] - \ln \mathbb{E}_t^P \left[S_{t+1}/S_t \right]$ identifies the foreign exchange risk premium. When $\delta_t = 0$, equation (1.47) simplifies to become the UIP condition in which the interest differential (on the left) equals the expected depreciation rate (on the right). This condition implies that the expected nominal return on U.S. and E.U. bonds are the same when expressed in terms of a common currency.

UIP fails to hold when the expected rate of depreciation based on the pseudo probabilities, $\mathbb{E}_t^P \left[S_{t+1}/S_t \right]$, differs from the expected rate based on the true probabilities $\mathbb{E}_t \left[S_{t+1}/S_t \right]$. We can examine the source of this difference by returning to the first-order condition governing the portfolio choice of U.S. households. Combining the identity $\mathcal{P}_t = \sum_{\mathcal{Z}} \mathcal{P}_t(z)$ with (1.37) allows us to write the pseudo probability for state z in terms of the true probability:

$$\pi_t^P(z) = \pi_t(z) \frac{C_{t+1}^{-\gamma}(z)/P_{t+1}(z)}{\mathbb{E}_t \left[C_{t+1}^{-\gamma}/P_{t+1} \right]}.$$

Here we see that the pseudo probability associated with state z is distinct from the true probability when the state-contingent marginal utility of \$1 in $t+1$ [i.e., $C_{t+1}^{-\gamma}(z)/P_{t+1}(z)$] differs from the expected marginal utility across all future states. This means that the pseudo expectations, $\mathbb{E}_t^P \left[S_{t+1}/S_t \right]$, will place more (less) weight on state-contingent depreciation rates $S_{t+1}(z)/S_t$ for states z where the marginal utility of \$1 is higher (lower) than is the case when computing standard expectations. Thus, the size of the foreign exchange risk premium depends upon the correlation between $S_{t+1}(z)/S_t$ and $C_{t+1}^{-\gamma}(z)/P_{t+1}(z)$ across period $t+1$ states. For example, when the correlation is positive, $\mathbb{E}_t^P \left[S_{t+1}/S_t \right]$ will be greater than $\mathbb{E}_t \left[S_{t+1}/S_t \right]$ and δ_t will be negative. In this situation, euro bonds provide a consumption hedge to

U.S. households because they offer high dollar returns in states where the marginal utility of \$1 is high. In equilibrium these hedging benefits must be offset by a lower expected dollar return. This is exactly what (1.47) indicates. Indeed, Appendix 1.A.2 shows that if the joint distribution of consumption, prices, and spots rates in period $t + 1$ is approximately log normal, then the risk premium can be expressed as

$$\delta_t = \mathbb{CV}_t \left(s_{t+1}, \gamma c_{t+1} + p_{t+1} \right), \tag{1.48}$$

where $\mathbb{CV}_t(\cdot, \cdot)$ denotes the covariance conditioned on period-t information. This approximation to the foreign exchange risk premium under complete markets will be useful in characterizing the behavior of the spot rate in what follows.

Relative Prices and Output

We next examine the implications of goods market clearing for the behavior of output, aggregate consumption, and relative prices. Equations (1.34a) and (1.34b) show how aggregate demand for U.S. and E.U. goods depends on the aggregate consumption and relative consumer prices in both countries. Our task is to identify how relative prices must adjust to equate aggregate demand for each good with the available supply.

Since aggregate demand for each good and the price indices are nonlinear functions of individual prices, the analysis is greatly simplified if we work with log approximations. Consider the aggregate demand for U.S. goods shown in equation (1.34a). Log-linearizing this expression around the point where $p_t^{US} = p_t$, $\hat{p}_t^{US} = \hat{p}_t$ and $\hat{c}_t = c_t$ gives

$$x_t = \ln(1/2) + \lambda c_t + (1 - \lambda)\hat{c}_t - \lambda\theta(p_t^{US} - p_t) - (1 - \lambda)\theta(\hat{p}_t^{US} - \hat{p}_t). \tag{1.49}$$

The log aggregate demand for E.U. goods is analogously derived from (1.34b) as

$$\hat{x}_t = \ln(1/2) + \lambda\hat{c}_t + (1 - \lambda)c_t - \lambda\theta(\hat{p}_t^{EU} - \hat{p}_t) - (1 - \lambda)\theta(p_t^{EU} - p_t). \tag{1.50}$$

Thus, the aggregate demand for each good is increasing in both U.S. and E.U. log consumption and decreasing in relative prices.[5]

The next step is to relate relative prices to the terms of trade and LOOP deviations. By definition, $p_t^{EU} - p_t^{US} = \tau_t + \varepsilon_t^{US}$ and $\hat{p}_t^{EU} - \hat{p}_t^{US} = \tau_t + \varepsilon_t^{EU}$, where $\varepsilon_t^X = \hat{p}_t^X + s_t - p_t^X$ is the LOOP deviation for good x= {US,EU} and $\tau_t = p_t^{EU} - s_t - \hat{p}_t^{EU}$ is the log terms of trade. Since there are just two traded goods, the U.S. and E.U. log price indices are approximately

$$p_t = \lambda p_t^{US} + (1 - \lambda)p_t^{EU} \quad \text{and} \quad \hat{p}_t = \lambda\hat{p}_t^{EU} + (1 - \lambda)\hat{p}_t^{US}.$$

Combining these approximations with the previous definitions yields

---

5. The log-linearizations in (1.49) and (1.50) are derived from first-order Taylor approximations (see Appendix 1.A.2), so their accuracy depends on how closely the right-hand side variables satisfy the restrictions at the approximation point (e.g., $p_t^{US} = p_t$, $\hat{p}_t^{US} = \hat{p}_t$ and $\hat{c}_t = c_t$). The approximations are quite accurate for the equilibria we study later because shocks to the economy only have temporary effects on $p_t^{US} - p_t$, $\hat{p}_t^{US} - \hat{p}_t$, and $\hat{c}_t - c_t$.

$$p_t^{\text{US}} - p_t = -(1-\lambda)(\tau_t + \varepsilon_t^{\text{US}}), \quad \hat{p}_t^{\text{US}} - \hat{p}_t = -\lambda(\tau_t + \varepsilon_t^{\text{EU}}),$$

and

(1.51)

$$\hat{p}_t^{\text{EU}} - \hat{p}_t = (1-\lambda)(\tau_t + \varepsilon_t^{\text{EU}}), \quad p_t^{\text{EU}} - p_t = \lambda(\tau_t + \varepsilon_t^{\text{US}}).$$

Thus, an improvement in the U.S. terms of trade (i.e., a fall in τ_t) is associated with an increase in the relative price of U.S.-produced goods and a fall in the relative price of E.U.-produced goods in both countries. Variations in the terms of trade also affect the real exchange rate. In particular, combining the identity $\varepsilon_t = s_t + \hat{p}_t - p_t$ with the approximations for the price indices and relative prices gives

$$\varepsilon_t = (2\lambda - 1)\tau_t + 2\lambda\bar{\varepsilon}_t,$$

(1.52)

with $\bar{\varepsilon}_t = \frac{1}{2}(\varepsilon_t^{\text{US}} + \varepsilon_t^{\text{EU}})$. Note that the real exchange rate is unaffected by the terms of trade when $\lambda = 1/2$ because goods' prices receive equal weight in both price indices. Under these circumstances, movements in the real exchange rate only reflect LOOP deviations, $\bar{\varepsilon}_t$. When household preferences are biased toward the consumption of domestically produced goods, $\lambda > 1/2$, so improvements in the U.S. terms of trade are associated with a real appreciation of the dollar.

Finally, we combine (1.49) with (1.50) and (1.51) to get

$$x_t - \hat{x}_t = 4\lambda\theta(1-\lambda)(\tau_t + \bar{\varepsilon}_t) + (2\lambda - 1)\left(c_t - \hat{c}_t\right).$$

(1.53)

This equation shows that the relative demand for U.S. versus E.U. goods depends on the terms of trade, LOOP deviations, and the aggregate U.S. consumption relative to E.U. consumption. More specifically, a deterioration in the U.S. terms of trade (i.e., a rise in τ_t) lowers the relative price of U.S. goods relative to E.U. goods in both countries so ceteris paribus households shift their demand toward U.S. goods via the substitution effect. Similarly, equation (1.51) shows that an increase in $\varepsilon_t^{\text{US}}$ and/or $\varepsilon_t^{\text{EU}}$ lowers the relative price of U.S. goods and raises the relative price of E.U. goods in both countries, which will also shift demand toward U.S. goods. Finally, the last term on the right-hand side of (1.53) shows that a relative rise in U.S. versus E.U. aggregate consumption will increase the demand for U.S. versus E.U. goods when $\lambda > 1/2$, that is, when household preferences are biased toward the consumption of domestically produced goods.

Equation (1.53) plays a key role in macro exchange-rate determination. Market clearing requires that x_t and $\hat{x}_t$ equal the log supply of U.S. and E.U. goods, respectively. These supplies vary exogenously in an endowment economy and endogenously in a production economy, but in either case equation (1.53) allows us to identify how these variations are accommodated by changes in the terms of trade and aggregate consumption.

1.3.3 Exchange Rates in an Endowment Economy

We now study the implications of complete risk-sharing for the behavior of nominal and real exchange rates in an endowment economy, where the supply of traded goods and LOOP deviations are determined exogenously and the national money supplies are controlled by central banks.

The Nominal-Exchange-Rate Equation

We first derive an equation for the equilibrium nominal exchange rate. For this purpose we use the risk-sharing condition in (1.44), the interest parity condition (1.47), and the first-order conditions for real balances in (1.39) and (1.42).

In (1.44) we established that the real depreciation rate must be proportional to relative consumption growth across countries when markets are complete. Without loss of generality, we assume that the world economy is initially in a symmetric equilibrium with $C = \mathcal{E}\hat{C}$ and $\mathcal{E} = 1$. The risk-sharing condition in (1.44) now becomes $\mathcal{E}_t = (C_t/\hat{C}_t)^\gamma$, which we can write in logs as

$$\varepsilon_t = \gamma(c_t - \hat{c}_t). \tag{1.54}$$

Next, we consider the interest parity condition in (1.47). Taking a log-linear approximation around the point where $r_t = \hat{r}_t = r$ and $\Delta s_{t+1} = 0$ gives

$$\mathbb{E}_t \Delta s_{t+1} = r_t - \hat{r}_t + \delta_t. \tag{1.55}$$

This equation says that the expected rate of nominal depreciation equals the interest differential between U.S. and E.U. nominal bonds plus the foreign exchange risk premium, δ_t.

Finally, we derive the log money demand function of U.S. and E.U. households by taking logs of (1.39) and (1.42) and linearizing the resulting term involving nominal interest rates:

$$m_t - p_t = \kappa + \frac{\gamma}{\nu}c_t - \sigma r_t, \tag{1.56}$$

$$\hat{m}_t - \hat{p}_t = \kappa + \frac{\gamma}{\nu}\hat{c}_t - \sigma\hat{r}_t, \tag{1.57}$$

where $\kappa = \frac{1}{\nu}\{\ln \chi + (1 - \gamma\sigma)r + \ln \gamma\sigma\}$ and $\sigma = \frac{1}{\nu}(\exp(r) - 1)^{-1} > 0$. Since national money supplies are exogenous, we can treat (1.56) and (1.57) as log approximations to the money market clearing conditions in each country.

An expression for the nominal exchange rate is easily derived from equations (1.54)–(1.57). First we subtract (1.56) from (1.57) and combine the result with (1.55), (1.54), and the definition of the real exchange rate to get

$$s_t = f_t + \sigma\mathbb{E}_t \Delta s_{t+1}, \tag{1.58}$$

where f_t denotes exchange-rate fundamentals:

$$f_t = m_t - \hat{m}_t + \left(\frac{\nu - 1}{\nu}\right)\varepsilon_t - \sigma\delta_t. \tag{1.59}$$

Next, we rewrite (1.58) as

$$s_t - f_t = b\mathbb{E}_t \left(s_{t+1} - f_{t+1}\right) + b\mathbb{E}_t \Delta f_{t+1}, \tag{1.60}$$

with $b = \frac{\sigma}{1+\sigma} < 1$. Finally, we solve forward under the assumption that $\lim_{h \to \infty} b^h \mathbb{E}_t(s_{t+h} - f_{t+h}) = 0$ to give

$$s_t = f_t + \mathbb{E}_t \sum_{i=1}^{\infty} b^i \Delta f_{t+i}. \tag{1.61}$$

Equation (1.61) links the equilibrium log spot rate to two components. The first is the long-run level implied by the current state of fundamentals, f_t. The second is proportional to the discounted present value of expected future changes in fundamentals. This component appears because expected future changes in fundamentals are reflected in the expected depreciation rate, $\mathbb{E}_t \Delta s_{t+1}$, which, as is shown in equation (1.58), directly affects the current spot rate. Note, also, that fundamentals comprise the relative money supplies and two endogenous variables: the foreign exchange risk premium, δ_t, and the real exchange rate, ε_t. The former depends on the covariance structure of fundamentals, consumption, and prices. In particular, substituting (1.61) into (1.48) gives

$$\delta_t = \mathbb{CV}_t(f_{t+1}, \gamma c_{t+1} + p_{t+1})$$

$$+ \sum_{i=1}^{\infty} b^i \mathbb{CV}_t \left((\mathbb{E}_{t+1} - \mathbb{E}_t) \Delta f_{t+1+i}, \gamma c_{t+1} + p_{t+1} \right). \tag{1.62}$$

The risk premium comprises two elements: The first on the right is the covariance between the log marginal utility of a dollar in the next period (i.e., $-\gamma c_{t+1} - p_{t+1}$) and fundamentals, f_{t+1}. The second is the covariance between the log marginal utility and future news concerning the growth in fundamentals, $(\mathbb{E}_{t+1} - \mathbb{E}_t) \Delta f_{t+1+i} = \mathbb{E}_{t+1} \Delta f_{t+1+i} - \mathbb{E}_t \Delta f_{t+1+i}$.

Two points deserve emphasis here: First, the definition of exchange-rate fundamentals includes both exogenous and endogenous variables. This can be potentially confusing until one understands that equations (1.61) and (1.62) provide representations for the behavior of the nominal exchange rate and the risk premium that apply across a large class of models. As we shall see, the nominal rate and risk premium can always be expressed solely in terms of exogenous variables in a particular equilibrium, but (1.61) and (1.62) apply much more generally. The second point concerns equation (1.62). This is not an *explicit* expression for the risk premium because δ_t is also a component of fundamentals. Instead, the equation represents a complex restriction that links the value of the current risk premium to the second moments of future risk premia, money supplies, and the real exchange rate. These second moments are constant in the equilibria of some models, so the risk premium is also constant and (1.61) alone governs the dynamics of the nominal exchange rate. More generally, equations (1.61) and (1.62) are needed to jointly characterize the behavior of the nominal exchange rate and risk premium in terms of exogenous money supplies and the endogenous real exchange rate.

The Real-Exchange-Rate Equation

We now consider how the real exchange rate is determined. In an endowment economy, the terms of trade must adjust to equate the demand for individual traded goods with the exogenous supplies. More specifically, equation (1.53) implies that the

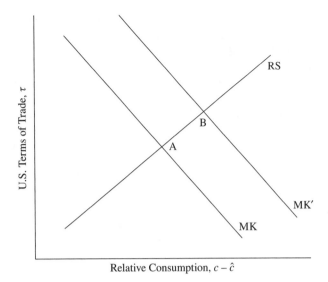

FIGURE 1.2   Goods market equilibrium.

market clearing level for the log U.S. terms of trade is

$$\tau_t = -\frac{2\lambda - 1}{4\lambda\theta(1 - \lambda)}\left(c_t - \hat{c}_t\right) + \frac{1}{4\lambda\theta(1 - \lambda)}(x_t - \hat{x}_t) - \bar{\varepsilon}_t, \qquad (1.63)$$

where x_t and $\hat{x}_t$ now represent the exogenous log endowments of U.S. and E.U. goods. Equation (1.63) says that the U.S. terms of trade improve (i.e., τ_t falls) when U.S. consumption rises relative to E.U. consumption if there is home bias in consumption, that is, when $\lambda > 1/2$. Intuitively, the presence of home bias means that there is a shift in demand toward U.S. goods and away from E.U. goods when U.S. consumption rises relative to E.U. consumption, so the relative price of U.S. goods must rise to clear markets. The MK schedule in Figure 1.2 shows this relation between τ and $c - \hat{c}$ given the endowments of U.S. and E.U. goods, x_t and $\hat{x}_t$, and LOOP deviation, $\bar{\varepsilon}_t$.

When there is home bias in consumption, the terms of trade affect the demand for individual traded goods and cross-country differences in marginal utility. Recall that $\varepsilon_t = (2\lambda - 1)\tau_t + 2\lambda\bar{\varepsilon}_t$ from (1.52), so a deterioration in the U.S. terms of trade induces a real depreciation of the dollar when $\lambda > 1/2$. Combining this equation with the risk-sharing equation (1.54) gives the following relation between the terms of trade and relative consumption:

$$\tau_t = \frac{\gamma}{(2\lambda - 1)}(c_t - \hat{c}_t) - \frac{2\lambda}{(2\lambda - 1)}\bar{\varepsilon}_t. \qquad (1.64)$$

Thus, risk-sharing requires that the U.S. terms of trade deteriorate if U.S. consumption rises relative to E.U. consumption when there is home bias. The RS schedule in Figure 1.2 shows the risk-sharing relation between τ and $c - \hat{c}$ in (1.64) for a given LOOP deviation $\bar{\varepsilon}_t$.

Figure 1.2 identifies the equilibrium terms of trade and relative consumption by the coordinates of point A, where the MK and RS schedules intersect. The figure also illustrates what happens when there is a rise in the endowment of the U.S. good. Under these circumstances, the MK schedule shifts to MK' because relative demand must shift toward the U.S. good via a U.S. terms-of-trade deterioration for a given pattern of aggregate consumption. As the figure shows, this results in a rise in both τ and $c - \hat{c}$ (the coordinates of point B) because the implied real depreciation of the dollar must be accompanied by a rise in $c - \hat{c}$ under complete risk-sharing.

The positive relation between the terms of trade and relative endowments implied by market clearing and complete risk-sharing carries over to the real exchange rate provided $\lambda \neq 1/2$. In particular, combining (1.53), (1.54), and (1.64) gives

$$\varepsilon_t = \xi(x_t - \hat{x}_t) + \frac{4\lambda\theta(1-\lambda)}{2\lambda - 1}\varsigma\bar{\varepsilon}_t, \tag{1.65}$$

where

$$\xi = \frac{\gamma(2\lambda - 1)}{4\gamma\lambda\theta(1-\lambda) + (2\lambda - 1)^2}.$$

There are two noteworthy features of this equation. First, all the effects of changing endowments on the real exchange rate come via variations in the terms of trade, so ξ is positive when there is home bias in consumption (i.e., $\lambda > 1/2$). If there is no home bias, the real exchange rate only varies with LOOP deviations so the RS schedule becomes vertical [see equation (1.64)]. In that case the terms of trade vary with changes in the endowment, but have no impact on the real exchange rate. The second feature concerns the role of risk-aversion. Greater risk-aversion steepens the slope of the RS schedule, so any variation in the relative endowments or LOOP deviations has to be accompanied by a larger change in the terms of trade. For this reason, ξ is increasing in the risk-aversion parameter, γ.

We can gain further perspective on the role of risk-sharing by studying the behavior of aggregate consumption. In particular, if we combine (1.49), (1.50), and (1.51) with (1.52) and (1.65), we find that

$$c_t = \varphi x_t + (1 - \varphi)\hat{x}_t - \varsigma\bar{\varepsilon}_t \quad \text{and} \quad \hat{c}_t = \varphi\hat{x}_t + (1 - \varphi)x_t + \varsigma\bar{\varepsilon}_t, \tag{1.66}$$

where

$$\varphi = \frac{\lambda(2\lambda - 1 + 2\theta\gamma(1-\lambda))}{(2\lambda - 1)^2 + 4\gamma\lambda\theta(1-\lambda)} \quad \text{and} \quad \varsigma = \frac{2\lambda\theta(1-\lambda)}{(2\lambda - 1)^2 + 4\gamma\lambda\theta(1-\lambda)}.$$

Equation (1.66) shows that the log of aggregate consumption in each country is a weighted average of the log endowments across countries plus a term proportional to the LOOP deviation, $\bar{\varepsilon}_t$. The weighting parameter, φ, depends on the degree of home bias and risk-aversion. Recall that LOOP deviations account for all the changes in the real exchange rate when $\lambda = 1/2$. This means that consumption must be perfectly correlated across countries when markets are complete and $\bar{\varepsilon}_t$ is a constant. To achieve this, changes in each endowment must have the same impact on log consumption in each country. Hence, as the preceding definition implies, φ must equal $1/2$ when $\lambda = 1/2$. When household preferences exhibit home bias in consumption, the weighting parameter is decreasing in the risk-aversion parameter, γ. The reason is that variations in endowments have a smaller effect on the terms of trade when risk-aversion is low, so domestic demand must absorb most of any change in the supply of the domestic good. As a result, aggregate consumption is more related to changes in the endowment of domestic goods than foreign goods. Under these circumstances the weighting parameter, φ, is greater than $1/2$. When risk-aversion is high, changes in endowments have larger effects on the terms of trade, so domestic demand responds less to changes in the endowment of domestic goods and more to changes in the endowment of foreign goods. Under these circumstances, the weighting parameter, φ, is smaller, but still larger than $1/2$. In fact, the limiting value of φ as γ approaches infinity is $1/2$. Thus, home bias in consumption has a negligible effect on the cross-country pattern of aggregate consumption at high levels of risk-aversion.

A Volatility Bound for the Real Exchange Rate

Complete risk-sharing has important implications for the cross-country correlation of consumption growth and the relative volatility of the real depreciation rate. To see why, suppose, for simplicity, that the growth in the endowments of each good are uncorrelated [i.e., $\mathbb{CV}(\Delta x_t, \Delta \hat{x}_t) = 0$] and have the same variance. Furthermore, let us assume that the LOOP deviation is constant. Under these conditions, (1.66) implies that the correlation between U.S. and E.U. consumption growth is

$$\mathbb{CR}(\Delta c_t, \Delta \hat{c}_t) = \frac{2\varphi\,(1-\varphi)}{\varphi^2 + (1-\varphi)^2}. \tag{1.67}$$

The expression on the right is a concave function of φ with a maximum of 1 when $\varphi = 1/2$ and a minimum of zero when $\varphi = \{0, 1\}$. Since the weighting parameter, φ, is decreasing in γ, greater risk-aversion increases the correlation between consumption growth across countries via its impact on φ. Greater risk aversion also affects the variance of the real depreciation rate. In particular, the risk-sharing condition $\varepsilon_t = \gamma(c_t - \hat{c}_t)$ implies that

$$\mathbb{V}(\Delta \varepsilon_t) = \gamma^2\left(\mathbb{V}(\Delta c_t) + \mathbb{V}(\Delta \hat{c}_t) - 2\mathbb{CV}(\Delta c_t, \Delta \hat{c}_t)\right).$$

Under our preceding assumptions, the variance of consumption growth is the same in both countries, so we can rewrite this expression as

$$\frac{\mathbb{V}(\Delta \varepsilon_t)}{\mathbb{V}(\Delta c_t)} = 2\gamma^2\left(1 - \mathbb{CR}(\Delta c_t, \Delta \hat{c}_t)\right). \tag{1.68}$$

Equation (1.68) clearly shows that a higher level of risk-aversion raises the relative volatility of the real depreciation rate [i.e., the variance ratio, $\mathbb{V}(\Delta \varepsilon_t)/\mathbb{V}(\Delta c_t)$] given the correlation of consumption growth across countries. However, since higher risk-aversion also pushes the correlation toward one, the relative volatility approaches an upper bound as risk-aversion rises. We can compute this upper bound if we combine the definition for φ with (1.67) and (1.68), and take the limit as $\gamma \to \infty$:

$$\lim_{\gamma \to \infty}\left\{\frac{\mathbb{V}(\Delta \varepsilon_t)}{\mathbb{V}(\Delta c_t)}\right\} = \left(\frac{(2\lambda - 1)}{2\theta\lambda\,(1-\lambda)}\right)^2. \tag{1.69}$$

With benchmark values for λ and θ of 0.85 and 0.74, respectively, the upper bound is approximately 13.8, so the variance of the real depreciation rate must be less than 14 times the variance of consumption growth in a standard model with complete markets. By contrast, the variance of the real depreciation rate for the dollar is approximately 18 times the variance of U.S. consumption growth. This is a large discrepancy. Moreover, it cannot be reconciled by changing the correlation between endowments: It is easy to check that $\lim_{\gamma \to \infty} \mathbb{CR}(\Delta c_t, \Delta \hat{c}_t) = 1$ when $\mathbb{CV}(\Delta x_t, \Delta \hat{x}_t) \neq 0$. In fact, the only way to account for the relative volatility of the real depreciation rate in a model where the risk-sharing condition in (1.54) holds true is to introduce variations in the LOOP deviations, $\bar{\varepsilon}_t$. The upper bound disappears under these circumstances because $\lim_{\gamma \to \infty} \mathbb{CR}(\Delta c_t, \Delta \hat{c}_t) < 1$. We can therefore match the relative volatility of the real depreciation rate and consumption growth with a high level of risk-aversion.

Exchange-Rate Dynamics

Equations (1.59), (1.61), (1.62), and (1.65) provide a complete characterization of the nominal exchange rate in terms of exogenous variables. In particular, we can write the equilibrium log spot rate as

$$s_t = f_t + \mathbb{E}_t \sum_{i=1}^{\infty} b^i \Delta f_{t+i}, \tag{1.70}$$

where fundamentals are now identified by

$$f_t = m_t - \hat{m}_t + \left(\frac{\nu - 1}{\nu} \right) \xi \left(x_t - \hat{x}_t + \frac{4\lambda \theta (1 - \lambda)}{2\lambda - 1} \bar{\varepsilon}_t \right) - \sigma \delta_t,$$

and δ_t is determined by (1.62).

To examine the economic implications of (1.70), we begin with a special case. If $\sigma = 0$ and $\nu = \gamma$, the money market equilibrium conditions in (1.56) and (1.57) become log versions of cash-in-advance constraints:

$$m_t - p_t \cong \kappa + c_t \quad \text{and} \quad \hat{m}_t - \hat{p}_t \cong \kappa + \hat{c}_t.$$

Under these circumstances, the model has the same form as Lucas' (1982) neoclassical exchange-rate model. In particular, since the discount parameter, b, now equals zero, the equilibrium exchange rate in (1.70) becomes

$$s_t = m_t - \hat{m}_t + \left(\frac{\nu - 1}{\nu} \right) \xi \left(x_t - \hat{x}_t + \frac{4\lambda \theta (1 - \lambda)}{2\lambda - 1} \bar{\varepsilon}_t \right).$$

Here the spot rate depends only on the contemporaneous money supplies, endowments, and the LOOP deviations.[6] In the Lucas model there is no home bias in consumption so ξ is equal to zero. Under these circumstances, $\varepsilon_t = 0$, so the spot rate is solely determined by the relative money supplies: $s_t = m_t - \hat{m}_t$.

We now develop some intuition for the exchange-rate behavior implied by equation (1.70) when $b > 0$. First, consider the effects of a permanent positive shock to the U.S. money stock relative to the E.U. money stock, $m_t - \hat{m}_t$. If the real exchange rate is unaffected because the monetary shock has no effect on endowments or LOOP deviations, risk-sharing requires that relative consumption across countries remain constant. As a result, the shock must be accommodated by either a fall in the interest differential, $r_t - \hat{r}_t$, or a relative rise in U.S. prices, $p_t - \hat{p}_t$, to clear the money

---

6. Note that fundamentals do not include the risk premium when $\sigma = 0$.

markets. The former adjustment implies an expected future appreciation of the dollar (i.e., $\mathbb{E}_t \Delta s_{t+i} < 0$), but this is inconsistent with the fact that expected future monetary growth is not affected by the shock. Consequently, adjustment in the money markets requires a one-for one relative rise in U.S. prices, so the dollar must depreciate by the same amount to keep the real exchange rate unchanged. This is exactly what is shown in (1.70). The permanent rise in $m_t - \hat{m}_t$ has no effect on $\mathbb{E}_t \Delta f_{t+i}$ for $i \geq 1$, so the spot rate depreciates one-for-one.

Now suppose that the positive shock to $m_t - \hat{m}_t$ is expected to be temporary but again there is no effect on the real exchange rate. In this case, the dollar will be expected to appreciate in the future (as the effects of the stock dissipate), so the interest differential, $r_t - \hat{r}_t$, falls when the shock hits. As a result, the relative rise in U.S. prices needed to accommodate the immediate effects of the shock on the money markets is smaller and so too is the depreciation of the dollar necessary to maintain the level of the real exchange rate. In terms of equation (1.70), the temporary rise in $m_t - \hat{m}_t$ lowers $\mathbb{E}_t \Delta f_{t+i}$ for $i \geq 1$, so the immediate impact of an increase in fundamentals is partially offset by a fall in the present value term.

Shocks to output and LOOP deviations affect the spot rate via the real exchange rate in a similar manner. A permanent shock to U.S. output, for example, induces an immediate real depreciation of the dollar, but does not affect the expected future rate of real or nominal depreciation. Consequently, the shock increases relative U.S. consumption, $c_t - \hat{c}_t$ (via risk-sharing), but leaves the interest differential unchanged. This means that there must be a relative fall in the U.S. price level, $p_t - \hat{p}_t$, to clear the money markets. When v is greater (less) than one, the fall in $p_t - \hat{p}_t$ is smaller (larger) than the real depreciation of the dollar, so the spot rate depreciates (appreciates). When v is equal to one, the spot rate remains unchanged because the fall in prices $p_t - \hat{p}_t$ required to clear the money markets matches the real depreciation of the dollar necessary to clear goods markets.

Variations in the risk premium, δ_t, provide a further source of variation in the sport rate. Equation (1.48) showed that variations in δ_t must come from changes in the condition covariance between the log spot rate and the log marginal utility of a dollar. If a change in the conditional distribution of future shocks to the economy permanently increases the covariance, there will be no change in the expected future depreciation rate, so the rise in the risk premium is matched by a fall in the interest differential, $r_t - \hat{r}_t$. Under these circumstances, there must be a relative fall in the U.S. price level, $p_t - \hat{p}_t$, to clear the money markets and an immediate appreciation in the spot rate to keep the real exchange rate unchanged. In terms of (1.70), f_t falls, whereas $\mathbb{E}_t \Delta f_{t+i}$ remains unchanged for $i \geq 1$.

Finally, we consider how well the model accounts for the statistical features of exchange rates discussed in Section 1.2. In particular, are the dynamic implications of (1.70) consistent with: (1) the relative volatility of nominal and real depreciation rates, (2) the high correlation between real and nominal depreciation rates, and (3) the lack of serial correlation in real depreciation rates?

These questions are easily addressed once we specify the process for the relative money supplies, endowments, and the LOOP deviations. For example, suppose that the money supplies follow

$$m_t = m_{t-1} + \mu_m + e_t \quad \text{and} \quad \hat{m}_t = \hat{m}_{t-1} + \mu_m + \hat{e}_t,$$

where e_t and $\hat{e}_t$ are i.i.d. mean-zero shocks with a common variance σ_e^2. Further, let us assume that the LOOP holds for both goods, so $\bar{\varepsilon}_t = 0$, and let the endowments of U.S. and E.U. goods evolve according to

$$x_t = \phi x_{t-1} + (1-\phi)\mu_x + \tfrac{1}{2}v_t \quad \text{and} \quad \hat{x}_t = \phi\hat{x}_{t-1} + (1-\phi)\mu_x - \tfrac{1}{2}v_t,$$

with $\phi < 1$, where v_t are i.i.d. mean-zero shocks with variance σ_v^2. Note that the v_t shocks change the *relative* endowments. Under these assumed processes, equations (1.65) and (1.70) imply that the spot and real exchange rates follow[7]

$$\Delta s_t = e_t - \hat{e}_t + \left(\frac{v-1}{v}\right)\left(\frac{1-b}{1-b\phi}\right)\Delta\varepsilon_t \quad \text{and} \quad \varepsilon_t = \phi\varepsilon_{t-1} + \xi v_t.$$

From these expressions we find that

$$\mathbb{CR}(\Delta\varepsilon_t, \Delta\varepsilon_{t-i}) = -\frac{\phi^i(1-\phi)\xi^2\sigma_v^2}{1+\phi} < 0,$$

for $i > 0$, and

$$\mathbb{CR}(\Delta s_t, \Delta\varepsilon_t) = \left(\frac{v-1}{v}\right)\left(\frac{1-b}{1-b\phi}\right)\sqrt{\frac{\mathbb{V}(\Delta\varepsilon_t)}{\mathbb{V}(\Delta s_t)}},$$

where

$$\frac{\mathbb{V}(\Delta\varepsilon_t)}{\mathbb{V}(\Delta s_t)} = \frac{\xi^2\sigma_v^2}{\sigma_e^2(1+\phi) + \left(\frac{v-1}{v}\right)^2\left(\frac{1-b}{1-b\phi}\right)^2\xi^2\sigma_v^2}.$$

We can therefore account for features (1), (2), and (3) if σ_e^2/σ_v^2 is small, ϕ is close to one, and v is very large.

These calculations show that it is not difficult to replicate the statistical behavior of real and nominal exchange rates in the complete markets model *if* we are free to choose the exogenous processes. What they do not show is that the model can simultaneously account for the behavior of exchange rates and other variables. Most importantly, the assumed endowment process implies that the variance ratio $\mathbb{V}(\Delta\varepsilon_t)/\mathbb{V}(\Delta c_t)$ is far smaller than we observe in the data for any values of the risk-aversion parameter γ. Thus, if we choose the variance of the relative endowment shocks, σ_v^2, to replicate the volatility of the real depreciation rate, the implied volatility of consumption growth under complete risk-sharing is much larger than what we observe in the data.

---

7. Since the money supplies and endowments follow homoskedastic processes, the second moments involving all exogenous and endogenous variables are constant. Equation (1.62) showed that the risk premium must also be constant under these circumstances, so it has no effect on the nominal depreciation rate, Δs_t.

1.3.4 Exchange Rates in a Production Economy

We now extend the model to include the production decisions of the firms. This extension does not change the nominal-exchange-rate equation presented in (1.61) because the links among the spot rate, money supplies, risk premium, and the real exchange rate are not affected by firms' decisionmaking. However, these decisions do affect the behavior of the terms of trade, so this is where we concentrate our attention.

In the endowment economy with complete markets, the U.S. terms of trade are proportional to the relative supplies of U.S. to E.U. traded goods. As a result, variations in the terms of trade are directly tied to the relative supplies of traded goods, and so display no intrinsic dynamics (i.e., dynamics generated within the economy). In a production economy, by contrast, the supplies of traded goods are determined optimally by firms taking their current capital stock and the state of current and expected future productivity into account. In an international setting, firms also have to account for both the current and expected future terms of trade. This means that current production decisions not only influence the current terms of trade via their implications for the relative supplies of goods, but are themselves affected by firms' expectations about the future path of the terms of trade. This feedback effect from the terms of trade to production is ruled out in an endowment economy, but is a source of intrinsic terms-of-trade dynamics in a production economy.

Firms

Assume that there is a single industry in each country and that both industries are populated by a continuum of identical firms distributed on the interval [0,1]. A representative U.S. firm owns all of its capital stock, K_t, and produces output, Y_t, according to $Y_t = A_t K_t^{\eta}$ with $1 > \eta \geq 0$, where A_t denotes the exogenous state of productivity. The output of a representative E.U. firm, $\hat{Y}_t$, is given by an identical production function using its own capital, $\hat{K}_t$, and productivity $\hat{A}_t$. At the beginning of each period, firms observe productivity and decide how to allocate their output between investment and consumption goods. Output allocated to consumption is supplied competitively to U.S. and E.U. households and the proceeds are used to finance dividend payments to the owners of the firms' equity. Output allocated to investment adds to the stock of physical capital available for production in the next period. We also assume that both traded goods can be costlessly transported between the United States and Europe, so the LOOP applies to both goods.

Let us first focus on the problem facing a representative U.S. firm. The firm's objective is to choose investment, I_t, so as to maximize its total value to its shareholders, that is, households. Let Q_t denote the ex-dividend dollar price in period t of U.S. equity providing a claim to a dollar dividend payment of D_{t+1} at the start of period $t + 1$. The firm's problem can now be written as

$$\max_{I_t}(D_t + Q_t) \quad \text{s.t.}$$

$$K_{t+1} = (1 - \eth)K_t + I_t \quad \text{and} \quad D_t = P_t^{\text{US}}(A_t K_t^{\eta} - I_t), \tag{1.71}$$

where $\eth > 0$ is the depreciation rate of physical capital. Note that the dividends paid by the firm are equal to the dollar value of goods sold to households, $A_t K_t^{\eta} - I_t$.

To complete the description of the firm's problem, we have to identify how investment decisions affect the price of U.S. equity, Q_t. This is easily accomplished under complete markets because the payout from holding U.S. equity in period $t + 1$, $D_{t+1} + Q_{t+1}$, can be replicated by a portfolio of AD securities. In particular, let $Q_t(z)$ denote the price of a portfolio of AD securities with a payoff of $D_{t+1}(z) + Q_{t+1}(z)$ dollars in period $t + 1$ when the state is z and zero otherwise. Equation (1.37) tells us that the equilibrium price of an AD security for state z is equal to $\beta \pi_t(z) \left(C_{t+1}(z)/C_t \right)^{-\gamma} (P_t/P_{t+1}(z))$. Hence, the price of the portfolio is

$$Q_t(z) = \beta \pi_t(z) \left(\frac{C_{t+1}(z)}{C_t} \right)^{-\gamma} \left(\frac{P_t\{D_{t+1}(z) + Q_{t+1}(z)\}}{P_{t+1}(z)} \right). \qquad (1.72)$$

The price of U.S. equity, Q_t, is nothing other than the price of a claim to a payout of $D_{t+1}(z) + Q_{t+1}(z)$ in all possible states (i.e., for all $z \in \mathcal{Z}$). Thus, Q_t must equal $\sum_z Q_t(z)$. Hence, under complete markets, the price of U.S. equity satisfies

$$Q_t = \beta \mathbb{E}_t \left[\left(\frac{C_{t+1}}{C_t} \right)^{-\gamma} \left(\frac{P_t\{D_{t+1} + Q_{t+1}\}}{P_{t+1}} \right) \right]. \qquad (1.73)$$

The optimal investment decision for the representative U.S. firm is the solution to the problem in (1.71) with the restriction that the equity price, Q_t, satisfies (1.73). Solving this problem produces the following first-order condition:

$$1 = \beta \mathbb{E}_t \left[\left(\frac{C_{t+1}}{C_t} \right)^{-\gamma} \exp\left(\Delta p_{t+1}^{\mathrm{US}} - \Delta p_{t+1} \right) R_{t+1}^k \right], \qquad (1.74)$$

where $R_{t+1}^k = 1 - \eth + \eta A_{t+1} K_{t+1}^{\eta-1}$ denotes the marginal product of U.S. capital.

The problem facing the representative E.U. firm is analogous. Investment, $\hat{I}_t$, is chosen to maximize the value of the firm, $\hat{D}_t + \hat{Q}_t$, where $\hat{Q}_t$ is the ex-dividend dollar price of E.U. equity and $\hat{D}_t$ are dollar E.U. dividends, subject to

$$\hat{K}_{t+1} = (1 - \eth)\hat{K}_t + \hat{I}_t, \qquad \hat{D}_t = P_t^{\mathrm{EU}}(\hat{A}_t \hat{K}_t^{\eta} - \hat{I}_t), \qquad (1.75)$$

and the following restriction on E.U. equity:

$$\hat{Q}_t = \beta \mathbb{E}_t \left[\left(\frac{C_{t+1}}{C_t} \right)^{-\gamma} \left(\frac{P_t\{\hat{D}_{t+1} + \hat{Q}_{t+1}\}}{P_{t+1}} \right) \right]. \qquad (1.76)$$

The associated first-order condition is

$$1 = \beta \mathbb{E}_t \left[\left(\frac{C_{t+1}}{C_t} \right)^{-\gamma} \exp\left(\Delta p_{t+1}^{\mathrm{EU}} - \Delta p_{t+1} \right) \hat{R}_{t+1}^k \right], \qquad (1.77)$$

where $\hat{R}_{t+1}^k = 1 - \eth + \eta \hat{A}_{t+1} \hat{K}_{t+1}^{\eta-1}$ denotes the marginal product of E.U. capital.

Two aspects of these characterizations deserve comment. First, it may appear from equations (1.73) and (1.76) that the price of equity depends only on how U.S. households value future payoffs, because both equations include the MRS for U.S.

households and not E.U. households. This impression is incorrect. In Section 1.3.2, equation (1.43) showed that the nominal MRS for U.S. and E.U. households measured in terms of a common currency are equalized internationally when markets are complete. This means that the dollar value of a claim to a future dollar equity payout is the same for both U.S. and E.U. households. Consequently, it makes no difference whether we express the equity restriction in (1.73) and (1.76) using the MRS for U.S. households or E.U. households. The optimal investment decisions of firms will be exactly the same in both cases. By the same token, it also makes no difference whether the equity issued by any firm is held by U.S. or E.U. households. When markets are complete, the problem facing each firm does not depend on the identity of the shareholders.

The second aspect concerns the presence of relative prices in the first-order conditions, (1.74) and (1.77). These equations show that firms choose investment so that the marginal utility of current consumption equals the discounted expected marginal utility of additional capital. Importantly, the latter depends on the marginal product of capital and the change in relative prices. For example, if the relative price of the U.S. good rises (i.e., P^{US}/P increases), the marginal utility of additional U.S. investment increases even when the marginal product of U.S. capital remains unchanged. Consequently, firms' investment decisions respond to variations in both productivity (which affects the marginal product of capital) and relative prices. As we shall see, variations in relative prices generate the feedback effects from the terms of trade to production.

Solving the Model

Although the structure of the model is quite straightforward, it is still too complex to examine analytically (even with the use of approximations). We must therefore study numerical solutions to the model—an approach that requires taking a stand on the time series process for productivity.

We adopt the conventional assumption that log productivity in each industry (i.e., $a_t = \ln A_t$ and $\hat{a}_t = \ln \hat{A}_t$) follows

$$\begin{bmatrix} a_t \\ \hat{a}_t \end{bmatrix} = \begin{bmatrix} \phi & 0 \\ 0 & \phi \end{bmatrix} \begin{bmatrix} a_{t-1} \\ \hat{a}_{t-1} \end{bmatrix} + \begin{bmatrix} u_t \\ \hat{u}_t \end{bmatrix}, \tag{1.78}$$

with $|\phi| < 1$, where u_t and $\hat{u}_t$ are mean-zero i.i.d. productivity shocks. To clarify how firms' decisions lead to the propagation of productivity shocks between countries, we assume that $\mathbb{CV}(u_t, \hat{u}_t) = 0$, so productivity in each industry follows an independent stationary AR(1) process.

A numerical solution to the model requires values for the parameters describing households' preferences, firms' technology, and the productivity processes. Here we face two options: The first is to choose parameter values via an estimation procedure that compares moments in the observed data with moments implied by the numerical solution of the model. Although details differ across procedures, implementing this option is computationally demanding because the model has to be solved for a great many different sets of parameter values. The second option is to calibrate the model, that is, to choose parameter values so that the distribution of observed data matches the distribution of data simulated from the numerical solution of the model. Again, the calibration procedures found in the literature differ in their details, but usually involve the following steps:

1. Choose some measurements from observed data that the model is to explain.
2. Choose functional forms and parameter values to ensure that the model's long-run (steady state) properties are consistent with the observed data, make sense, or are consistent with the estimates in other studies.
3. Find the numerical solution to the model and use it to generate time series for the variables the model is to explain.
4. Compare the simulated time series with the observed data.

Implementing these steps is much less computationally demanding than the estimation procedures because the model is only solved for the particular parameterization chosen in step 2.

Although the process just outlined appears relatively straightforward, several problems may undermine the economic relevance of a calibration exercise. For example, it may not be possible to pin down values for all the parameters by matching the steady state of the model against the long-run properties of available data. In these cases the preferred approach is to set the values for the unidentified parameters equal to appropriate estimates from microeconomic data. Unfortunately, this is often easier said than done because microeconomic studies rarely estimate models that are directly applicable (see, e.g., Browning, Hansen, and Heckman 1999). Parameter uncertainty creates further problems. Even when the parameters can be identified from long-run properties of the observed data and applicable microeconomic studies, precise parameter values are always obscured by some uncertainty. The best way to address this issue is to examine how the model simulations vary across different parameter choices. However, such sensitivity analyses are hard to conduct and report in a systematic and transparent manner for all but the simplest models. Finally, there is the issue of *how* to compare the simulated time series with the observed data. In other words, what metric should be used when comparing moments of the simulated and observed data? Should the metric take account of how parameter uncertainty affects moments of the simulated data, or how sampling uncertainty affects moments in the observed data, or both?

These issues have received much less attention than they deserve in the many papers that use calibration to study international macro models. Indeed, it is common practice to solve models with parameter values that are simply taken from earlier studies. One pedagogical advantage of this approach is that it allows the reader to easily compare the dynamic properties of models that share a common set of core features. Since our aim is to illustrate the properties of a standard model, it is the approach we follow in this chapter. More generally, the downside of this approach is that the calibrated parameter values in the original studies have been chosen to address a specific question (see step 1 above) that may only be loosely related to the focus of the current study. In short, full-blown calibration requires more than simply choosing parameter values used by other researchers.

The parameter values used to solve the model are reported in Table 1.3. Household preferences and firms' technologies are assumed symmetric across the two countries, and a single period in the model is interpreted as 1 month. Consistent with many models, households' discount factor and risk-aversion parameters are set to 0.997

TABLE 1.3
Production Economy Parameters

Parameter	Symbol	Value
Discount factor	β	0.997
Risk aversion	γ	2.000
Consumption share	λ	0.850
Consumption elasticity	θ	0.740
Depreciation rate	$\eth$	0.010
Capital share	η	0.360
Productivity AR(1)	ϕ	0.980

and 2, respectively. The share parameter, λ, and the elasticity of substitution, θ, govern preferences over the consumption of U.S. and E.U. goods. We set $\lambda = 0.74$ and $\theta = 0.85$, so the model displays home bias in consumption and imperfect substitutability between traded goods. These choices are within the wide range of values found in the literature (see Hnatkovska 2010), but are clear candidates for sensitivity analyses in a full-blown calibration exercise. Parameters on the production side of the model are chosen to be consistent with Backus, Kehoe, and Kydland (1994). The capital share in production, η, is set to 0.36 and the depreciation rate, $\eth$, is set to 0.01. Finally, we set the autoregressive coefficient in the productivity processes equal to 0.98.

Terms-of-Trade Dynamics

We now examine the implications of productivity shocks for the behavior of the U.S. terms of trade when firms make optimal investment decisions. Specifically, our task is to examine the behavior of the equilibrium terms of trade when productivity follows the process in (1.78). As a benchmark for what follows, let us first consider the implication of (1.78) in the special case where production requires no capital (i.e., when $\eta = 0$). In this case, market clearing in the markets for traded goods requires $X_t = A_t$ and $\hat{X}_t = \hat{A}_t$, where X_t and $\hat{X}_t$ are the aggregate demands for U.S. and E.U. goods derived in (1.34). We are thus back to the endowment version of the model, with the endowments following the productivity process in (1.78). The behavior of the terms of trade is determined by combining the goods market-clearing conditions with (1.78) and the relation between aggregate demand and the terms of trade implied by (1.52) and (1.65). In the absence of LOOP deviations, this gives

$$\tau_t = \phi \tau_{t-1} + \frac{\gamma}{4\gamma\lambda\theta(1-\lambda) + (2\lambda-1)^2}(u_t - \hat{u}_t).$$

Hence, the log terms of trade follow an AR(1) process with the same degree of persistence as the differential in log productivity across industries, $a_t - \hat{a}_t$. Clearly, there are no intrinsic terms-of-trade dynamics in this special case.

Let us now return to the general case where $1 > \eta > 0$. Three sets of equations hold the key to understanding how the terms of trade behave in response to productivity shocks when firms choose investment optimally. The first set comprises the goods' market-clearing conditions,

$$A_t K_t^{\eta} = Y_t = X_t + I_t \quad \text{and} \quad \hat{A}_t \hat{K}_t^{\eta} = \hat{Y}_t = \hat{X}_t + \hat{I}_t. \tag{1.79}$$

These expressions imply that each firm's choice of investment is equivalent to a choice of how much current output it will supply to satisfy the aggregate demand for its product. The second set of equations describes the implication of market clearing for the dynamics of the capital stock:

$$K_{t+1} = (1 - \eth)K_t + A_t K_t^{\eta} - X_t \quad \text{and} \quad \hat{K}_{t+1} = (1 - \eth)\hat{K}_t + \hat{A}_t \hat{K}_t^{\eta} - \hat{X}_t. \tag{1.80}$$

These equations express the intertemporal trade-off between current consumption of each good, (i.e., X_t and $\hat{X}_t$) and the accumulation of capital for future production.

The third set of equations links the expected marginal product of U.S. and E.U. capital with expected changes in the terms of trade. To derive this link, we first approximate the first-order conditions in (1.74) and (1.77) as

$$\gamma \mathbb{E}_t \Delta c_{t+1} = \mathbb{E}_t r_{t+1}^k + \mathbb{E}_t [\Delta p_{t+1}^{\text{US}} - \Delta p_{t+1}] + \varkappa_t \tag{1.81a}$$

and

$$\gamma \mathbb{E}_t \Delta c_{t+1} = \mathbb{E}_t \hat{r}_{t+1}^k + \mathbb{E}_t [\Delta p_{t+1}^{\text{EU}} - \Delta p_{t+1}] + \hat{\varkappa}_t, \tag{1.81b}$$

where

$$\varkappa_t = \ln \beta + \tfrac{1}{2} \mathbb{V}_t \left(\Delta p^{\text{US}} - \Delta p + r_{t+1}^k - \gamma \Delta c_{t+1} \right)$$

and

$$\hat{\varkappa}_t = \ln \beta + \tfrac{1}{2} \mathbb{V}_t \left(\Delta p^{\text{EU}} - \Delta p + \hat{r}_{t+1}^k - \gamma \Delta c_{t+1} \right).$$

Appendix 1.A.2 shows that these approximations hold exactly when log consumption, prices, and the marginal product of capital are jointly normally distributed. Given the symmetry of the model (in terms of productivity, production functions, and preferences), the variance terms in $\varkappa_t$ and $\hat{\varkappa}_t$ will be equal. Under these circumstances, (1.81) implies that

$$\mathbb{E}_t r_{t+1}^k - \mathbb{E}_t \hat{r}_{t+1}^k = \mathbb{E}_t [\Delta p_{t+1}^{\text{EU}} - \Delta p_{t+1}^{\text{US}}] = \mathbb{E}_t \Delta \tau_{t+1}. \tag{1.82}$$

Thus, when firms follow optimal investment policies, the difference between the expected log marginal product for U.S. and E.U. capital must equal the expected deterioration in the log U.S. terms of trade.

To describe the equilibrium dynamics of the terms of trade, we first have to identify how the aggregate consumption of each good varies in response to productivity shocks. The easiest way to do this is to conjecture that the log consumption of each good follows a particular process and then use the equilibrium conditions of the model to verify the conjecture. In this case, we conjecture that

$$
\begin{bmatrix} x_t \\ \hat{x}_t \end{bmatrix} = \begin{bmatrix} \kappa_a & \hat{\kappa}_a \\ \hat{\kappa}_a & \kappa_a \end{bmatrix} \begin{bmatrix} a_t \\ \hat{a}_t \end{bmatrix} + \begin{bmatrix} \kappa_k & \hat{\kappa}_k \\ \hat{\kappa}_k & \kappa_k \end{bmatrix} \begin{bmatrix} k_t - k \\ \hat{k}_t - k \end{bmatrix}, \tag{1.83}
$$

where k denotes the log capital stock in the steady state. At this point we do not know the values of the coefficients, κ_a, $\hat{\kappa}_a$, κ_k, and $\hat{\kappa}_k$. However, if we combine the log-linearized version of (1.80) with (1.81) and the productivity process in (1.78), we can verify that log consumption follows (1.83) and solve for the values of the coefficients. With these values in hand, we can combine (1.83) with (1.78) and the linearized version of (1.80) to describe the equilibrium dynamics of productivity, capital, and any other variable, including the terms of trade. A full description of this solution procedure is provided in Appendix 1.A.4.

We are now ready to examine how productivity shocks affect the terms of trade. Since the dynamics in this model are quite complex, we proceed in three steps: First, we consider how a U.S. productivity shock affects the behavior of U.S. output and investment in a closed-economy setting. Second, we study how the shock is transmitted between firms when U.S. and E.U. goods are perfect substitutes. This special case rules out variations in the terms of trade. Finally, we incorporate variations in the terms of trade by examining how the shock affects both firms when their goods are imperfect substitutes.

A positive productivity shock has two impacts on U.S. firms: it increases current output, and raises the expected marginal product of capital. The key choice facing each U.S. firm is how much of the additional output to allocate to investment. Here a firm faces an intertemporal trade-off. On one hand, the less output it devotes to investment, the more it can pay out in terms of current dividends to its shareholders. On the other, accumulating more capital via higher current investment will allow it to produce more in the future, and hence pay higher future dividends. Since their shareholders value both current and future dividends, firms will use some of the additional output to boost the current dividend and some to boost future dividends via increased investment. As a result, the immediate effects of a positive U.S. productivity shock in a closed economy are an increase in U.S. consumption, dividends, and investment. Thereafter, the marginal product of U.S. capital declines as capital accumulates and the effects of the productivity shock die out. As this happens, further investment becomes less attractive, so the accumulation of capital stops and output begins to fall. In the absence of further shocks, this process continues until the capital stock and productivity return to their original levels.

To understand how this transmission process differs in an open-economy setting, let us assume (for the moment) that U.S. and E.U. goods are perfect substitutes for one another. In this case, goods arbitrage implies that $P_t^{\text{US}} = P_t^{\text{EU}}$, so the equilibrium terms of trade always equal one. As a result, the expected marginal product of capital will be equalized across industries [e.g., $\mathbb{E}_t r_{t+1}^k = \mathbb{E}_t \hat{r}_{t+1}^k$ from equation (1.82)]. This implication of firms' optimal investment plans leads to the international transmission of productivity shocks. In particular, when a U.S. productivity shock raises the expected marginal product of U.S. capital, E.U. firms must adjust their investment plans to raise the expected marginal product of E.U. capital by the same amount. To do this, E.U. firms *reduce* investment because the marginal product of capital is a decreasing function of the capital stock. Consequently, the consumption of E.U.-produced goods immediately increases in response to a positive U.S. productivity shock. Thereafter, the consumption of E.U. production continues to rise until the loss

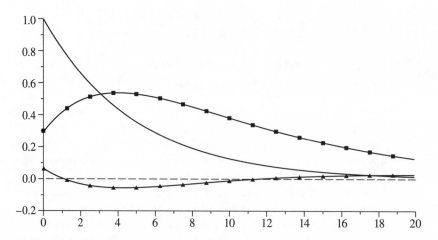

FIGURE 1.3   Impulse responses of U.S. productivity (a_t, solid) and traded goods consumption (x_t U.S., solid squares; $\hat{x}_t$ E.U., triangles).

of E.U. capital and the falling marginal product of U.S. capital makes E.U. investment attractive. From this point on, E.U. investment rises and the consumption of E.U. goods falls back toward its original level.

Now we examine the international transmission of productivity when traded goods are imperfect substitutes. For this purpose Figure 1.3 plots the impulse responses of log U.S. productivity, a_t, and the log aggregate consumption of U.S. and E.U. goods, x_t and $\hat{x}_t$, for 20 years following a one-unit productivity shock. These impulse responses are computed from the equilibrium dynamics of the model using the parameter values reported in Table 1.3.

Figure 1.3 shows that U.S. consumption rises for approximately 4 years following the productivity shock. Then, after the accumulation of U.S. capital comes to an end and the effects of the productivity shock diminish, the consumption of U.S. goods falls back toward its long-run value. The effects on E.U. consumption are quite the opposite. Consumption falls for the first 4 years before gradually returning to its long-run level. This pattern is completely different from the response of E.U. consumption when goods are perfect substitutes. To understand why, we have to consider the role played by the terms of trade in the international transmission of the U.S. productivity shock.

Figure 1.4 shows the impulse responses for the log marginal products of capital and the U.S. terms of trade. The square and triangle plots indicate the response of the log marginal product for U.S. and E.U. capital, respectively, and the solid plot depicts the log U.S. terms of trade. For comparison purposes, the figure also shows the response of the log U.S. terms of trade in the endowment economy (i.e., when $\eta = 0$) as a diamond plot. As we can see in the figure, the marginal products of U.S. and E.U. capital differ significantly in response to the productivity shock. As one would expect, a positive U.S. productivity shock immediately increases the marginal product of U.S. capital, r^k. What is more surprising is that r^k falls *below* its long-run level 4 years after the shock, and only begins to rise again after 10 years. By contrast, the productivity shock has very little impact on the marginal product of E.U. capital.

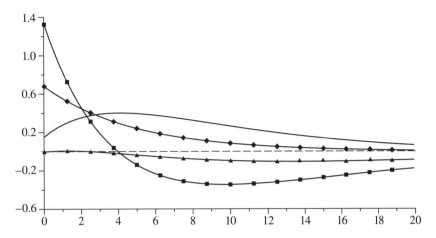

FIGURE 1.4 Impulse responses of the terms of trade (τ, solid), marginal product of capital (r^k U.S., squares; $\hat{r}^k$ E.U., triangles), and terms of trade in an endowment economy (τ, diamonds).

The terms of trade provide the key to understanding these dynamics. Figure 1.3 showed that the relative consumption of U.S. versus E.U. goods falls as the effects of the productivity shock die out. From our analysis of the endowment economy, we know that this can only happen under complete risk-sharing when there is an improvement on the U.S. terms of trade (i.e., a fall in τ). Consequently, firms must expect the U.S. terms of trade to continue to improve from some point after the productivity shock occurs. Figure 1.4 shows that this point occurs approximately 4 years after the shock. Thereafter, the expected marginal product of U.S. capital is lower than that of E.U. capital, and the slope of the terms-of-trade plot is negative. U.S. firms run down their capital stocks more rapidly than E.U. firms during this period, so the output of U.S. goods returns more quickly to its original level (see Figure 1.3).

Variations in the terms of trade also play an important role when the productivity shock hits. Figure 1.4 shows that there is an immediate deterioration in U.S. terms of trade. This has two effects. First, it changes prices so that household demand will absorb the greater supply of U.S. goods not going into investment. Second, it increases the real value of E.U. dividends. Recall that $(\hat{A}_t \hat{K}_t^\eta - \hat{I}_t)(P_t^{EU}/P_t)$ identifies the value of E.U. dividends when measured in terms of U.S. household consumption. Since a deterioration in the U.S. terms of trade raises P_t^{EU}/P_t, it also increases the real value of E.U. dividends for a given level of E.U. production and investment. In other words, a positive U.S. productivity shock benefits the holders of E.U. equity via its impact on the terms of trade. This valuation effect reduces the incentive for E.U. firms to initially cut back on investment so the consumption of E.U. goods rises. Indeed, as U.S. firms accumulate capital and the consumption of U.S. goods rises, the U.S. terms of trade continue to deteriorate so that the valuation effect on E.U. firms becomes greater. This allows E.U. firms to increase investment while their shareholders enjoy a rise in the real value of dividends. As a result, the deterioration in the U.S. terms of trade following the productivity shock is accompanied by a fall in both the marginal product of E.U. capital and the consumption of E.U. goods (see Figure 1.3).

To summarize, productivity shocks have different dynamic implications for the behavior of the terms of trade in exchange and production economies. In the former, the terms of trade change in response to the exogenously varying supplies of traded goods simply to clear markets. In the latter, variations in the terms of trade also affect the investment decisions of firms via a valuation channel and hence the supplies of traded goods available for consumption. It is this valuation channel that provides the feedback from the terms of trade to consumption that is absent in endowment economies.

Exchange-Rate Implications

The exchange-rate implications of productivity shocks in the production economy are straightforward. The equilibrium nominal exchange continues to follow (1.70):

$$s_t = f_t + \mathbb{E}_t \sum_{i=1}^{\infty} b^i \Delta f_{t+i}, \tag{1.84}$$

with fundamentals, $f_t = m_t - \hat{m}_t - \sigma \delta_t + \left(\frac{\nu-1}{\nu}\right)\xi(x_t - \hat{x}_t)$, but now x_t and $\hat{x}_t$ vary endogenously with the capital stocks and productivity according to (1.83). All the exchange-rate implications of productivity shocks are therefore captured via their effects on x_t and $\hat{x}_t$. Moreover, since $\xi(x_t - \hat{x}_t) = \varepsilon_t = (2\lambda - 1)\tau_t$, we can rewrite fundamentals using the terms of trade as

$$f_t = m_t - \hat{m}_t - \sigma \delta_t + \frac{(\nu - 1)(2\lambda - 1)}{\nu}\tau_t,$$

and hence trace the effects of productivity shocks on the spot rate via their implications for the terms of trade and fundamentals.

Productivity shocks generally induce more persistence and greater spot rate volatility in the production economy than in the endowment economy. The reason for these differences are easily understood with the aid of Figure 1.4. There we saw that U.S. productivity shocks lead to a smaller initial deterioration in the U.S. terms of trade than in the endowment economy, but that the variations are nonmonotonic and longer lasting. This means that a productivity shock has a smaller impact on current fundamentals in the production economy, but a larger impact on the present value of expected future changes in fundamentals. The balance of these effects determines how the spot rate reacts to a productivity shock. When the discount parameter, b, is close to one, the spot rate more closely reflects variations in the expected future growth of fundamentals; when b is close to zero, the spot rate more closely reflects variations in current fundamentals. In this model, the discount parameter, b, is equal to $\sigma/(1 + \sigma)$, where σ is the semi-interest elasticity of money demand. Estimates in the literature give values for σ between 20 and 60, which implies that b is very close to one. Consequently, variations in the present value term will be an important source of spot rate variation when productivity shocks have persistent effects on fundamentals via their impact on the terms of trade.

To illustrate these effects, Figure 1.5 compares the impulse response of fundamentals and the spot rate to a U.S. productivity shock in both the endowment and

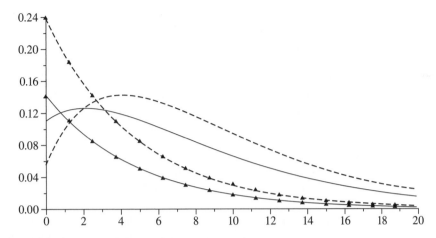

FIGURE 1.5   Impulse responses of the spot exchange rate, s_t (solid), and fundamentals, f_t (dashed), to a U.S. productivity shock in the production and endowment (with triangles) economies.

production economies. The dashed plots show the responses to fundamentals computed from the behavior of the terms of trade with $\nu = 2$. The figure shows that the U.S. productivity shock has a greater initial impact on fundamentals in the endowment economy (depicted with triangles) than in the production economy. Thereafter, fundamentals fall monotonically in the endowment economy until the effects of the productivity shock die out. In the production economy, by contrast, fundamentals rise for 4 years before slowly falling back to their original level. The difference in these response patterns simply reflects the different behavior of the terms of trade in the endowment and production economies that was illustrated in Figure 1.4.

Figure 1.5 shows a clear distinction between the effects of the productivity shock on the spot rate in the endowment and production economies. The solid and solid with triangles plots show the impulse responses for spot rates computed with $b = 40/41$, a value for the discount parameter that is consistent with a mid-range estimate of σ equal to 40. As the figure shows, productivity shocks have a smaller impact on the spot rate than on fundamentals in the endowment economy. The reason is that everyone expects fundamentals to fall following the productivity shock, so $s_t - f_t = \mathbb{E}_t \sum_{i=1}^{\infty} b^i \Delta f_{t+i}$ is negative until the effects of the shock disappear. In other words, expectations concerning the path of future fundamentals dampen the response of the spot rate. The reverse holds true in the production economy. In this case productivity shocks have a greater impact on the spot rate than fundamentals for approximately 2 years following the shock. During this period expectations regarding the near-term rise in fundamentals dominate longer-term expectations, so $s_t - f_t = \mathbb{E}_t \sum_{i=1}^{\infty} b^i \Delta f_{t+i}$ is positive and the spot rate depreciates. Thereafter, the expected future fall in fundamentals dominates so $s_t - f_t = \mathbb{E}_t \sum_{i=1}^{\infty} b^i \Delta f_{t+i}$ is negative, and the spot rate begins to appreciate.

We can now see why it is possible for productivity shocks to induce greater volatility in the spot rate in a production economy than in an endowment economy. In the former case, expectations regarding the future path of fundamentals magnify the impact of a productivity shock on the spot rate, whereas in the latter expectations act as a damper. As a result, when b is close to one, Figure 1.5 shows that there is a larger initial depreciation of the spot rate in the production economy than in the endowment economy when a positive U.S. productivity shock arrives, even though the shock induces a smaller initial rise in fundamentals. The figure also clearly shows how greater persistence in the response of fundamentals in the production economy is reflected in the response of the spot rate. In this example, the half-life of the productivity shock increases from approximately 3.5 years to 14 years.

We saw in Section 1.3.3 that it is possible to replicate the statistical features of real and nominal depreciation rates in an endowment economy with complete risk-sharing if we are free to specify the processes for money supplies and the endowments. The problem was that these specifications implied counterfactual behavior for consumption. In this section, we have seen how productivity shocks affect real and nominal exchange rates via their impact on firms' investment decisions. Since these decisions establish the supply of goods available for consumption, productivity shocks also determine the behavior of equilibrium consumption. Indeed, this model has exactly the same implications for the *joint* behavior of consumption and the real exchange rate as the endowment model. Consequently, equation (1.69) still identifies the upper bound on the variance ratio, $\mathbb{V}(\Delta\varepsilon_t)/\mathbb{V}(\Delta c_t)$, in the absence of LOOP deviations. This upper bound has a value of 3.5 for the parameters in Table 1.2, compared to the variance ratio in the data of approximately 18. Thus, although the addition of production increases the volatility of the nominal depreciation rate, it does nothing to address the counterfactual implication of complete risk-sharing for the relative volatility of the real depreciation rate and consumption growth.

1.4 Summary

- Variations in the real exchange rate can reflect changes in the relative prices of nontraded goods across countries and/or variations in the prices of traded goods across countries. Empirically, variations in the relative price of tradables at the consumer level account for the lion's share of real-exchange-rate volatility over a wide range of horizons. These variations in the relative consumer prices are attributable to the presence of distribution costs and LOOP deviations for pure traded goods.

- Monthly changes in the log spot rate, the log real exchange rate, and the log terms of trade have similar levels of volatility and are highly correlated with one another. There is very little autocorrelation in monthly real depreciation rates. Shocks to the level of the real exchange rate appear to be very persistent, with estimated half-lives ranging from 3 to 5 years.

- The high volatility and persistence of real-exchange-rate variations has proved hard to explain theoretically—a fact often referred to as the PPP Puzzle. Although stickiness in consumer prices offers a potential explanation, the degree of price-stickiness in individual traded goods appears insufficient to account for both the high volatility and the persistence of real rate variations. The PPP Puzzle may also reflect the distortions induced by the aggregation of heterogeneous dynamics for individual traded-goods prices. The question of whether these distortions, known as Aggregation Bias, are large enough to resolve the PPP Puzzle remains open.

- Access to a complete set of AD securities allows households to perfectly share risks both within and across countries. When households form optimal consumption plans, the implied nominal marginal rates of substitution between current and future consumption are equal for all households when measured in terms of a common currency. If households have time-separable isoelastic utility defined over aggregate consumption, this risk-sharing condition implies that the rate of real depreciation will be perfectly correlated with the international ratio of domestic to foreign consumption growth.

- In macro models with complete markets, the equilibrium spot exchange rate responds to changes in both current fundamentals and their expected future path. For a standard specification of household preferences, exchange-rate fundamentals comprise money supplies, the foreign exchange risk premia, and the factors driving the real exchange rate. The supplies of traded goods and LOOP deviations are the factors in an endowment economy where preferences exhibit home consumption bias. In a production economy the supplies of traded goods are linked to the capital stocks and productivity via the optimal decisions of firms.

- It is not difficult to replicate the statistical behavior of real and nominal exchange rates in either the endowment or production versions of the complete market model if we choose the exogenous processes appropriately. However, in both cases, complete risk-sharing imposes an upper bound on the variance ratio of the real depreciation rate to consumption growth that is approximately one-fifth the size of the variance ratio we estimate in the data.

1.5 Bibliography

The material in this chapter draws on two large literatures: one focusing on the behavior of real exchange rates and the other on international business cycles. Since we have only addressed the issues most relevant to the determination of nominal exchange rates, let me provide a brief perspective on the broader aspects of these literatures.

There is a very large literature examining the time series properties of real exchange rates (see Rogoff 1996 for a survey). One branch focuses on the question of whether PPP holds in the long run or, equivalently, whether real exchange rates contain a unit root. Tests on post-1973 data using single rates generally cannot reject the presence of a unit root, but when the data samples are extended, as in Lothian and Taylor (1996), the evidence supporting long-run PPP is much stronger. Recent research applying panel data analysis to the post-1973 data also rejects the presence of unit roots and supports earlier consensus estimates for the half-life of 3 years (see, e.g., Choi, Mark, and Sul 2006). Mark (2001) provides an introduction to the econometrics of these panel data methods.

The discussion of real exchange rates and relative prices has two noteworthy features. First, we have not discussed the Balassa-Samuelson model (see Balassa 1964 and Samuelson 1964 or Mark 2001 for a textbook treatment) because its focus is on the sources of long-run variation in the relative prices of nontraded to traded goods. Moreover, as the results in Engel (1999) demonstrate, variations in these relative prices at the consumer level contribute practically nothing to the variations in real exchange rates over short and medium horizons. As a consequence, the priority for any macro exchange-rate model is to explain why the international relative prices for traded goods vary in the short run, rather than why the relative prices of nontraded to traded goods vary in the long run.

The second noteworthy feature concerns the focus on consumer rather than producer prices. Betts and Kehoe (2006), Burstein, Eichenbaum, and Rebelo (2006), and others have shown that a smaller faction of real-exchange-rate variations is attributable to changes in the relative prices of traded goods when prices are measured at the producer level (or at the dock in the case of imports). These findings are important for understanding how firms in the production-distribution chain respond to changes in the spot rates (a topic we cover in Chapter 2), but they have no effect on households when markets are complete. In this setting, the demand for foreign exchange ultimately depends on the marginal utility of holding domestic versus foreign currency—a trade-off that depends on consumer rather than producer prices.

The exchange-rate models in Section 1.3 draw on the international real business cycle and open economy macro literatures. Papers in the former literature focus on the nonmonetary sources and propagation mechanisms of cross-country co-movements in business cycles (see Crucini 2006 for a recent survey). The production model we present is broadly based on Backus, Kehoe, and Kydland (1994) except that it omits the use of labor from each firm's production function. Adding labor to the model does not materially alter how productivity shocks affect the terms of trade. Models in the open economy macro literature (see Lane 2001 for a survey) specify household preferences with respect to real balances as we have done. The household demands for money implied by this specification are similar to the demand functions assumed in earlier well-known exchange-rate models, such as the Dornbusch (1976) model. Finally, our discussion of calibration relates to a large literature in macroeconomics influenced by the work of Kydland and Prescott (1982). A detailed textbook treatment of calibration and estimation methods for macro models can be found in Canova (2007).

1.6 Review Questions

1. Iceberg Trade Costs: Consider a simple two-country world comprising the U.S. and E.U. where there are only two goods, which both trade internationally. The USD prices of the U.S.- and E.U.-produced goods are P^{US} and P^{EU}, $\hat{P}^{\text{US}}$ and $\hat{P}^{\text{EU}}$ are the EUR prices, and S is the USD/EUR spot rate. There is an "iceberg" shipping cost $\mathfrak{C}$, so that for every unit of the U.S. (E.U.) good shipped abroad, only a fraction $1 - \mathfrak{C}$ arrives in Europe (United States).

   (a) Derive two no-arbitrage conditions between the USD and EUR prices of the two goods (i.e., between P^{US} and $\hat{P}^{\text{US}}$ and between P^{EU} and $\hat{P}^{\text{EU}}$).

(b) Assume that log U.S. and E.U. price indices can be written as $p = \lambda p^{\text{US}} + (1 - \lambda) p^{\text{EU}}$ and $\hat{p} = \lambda \hat{p}^{\text{US}} + (1 - \lambda) \hat{p}^{\text{EU}}$, where lowercase letters denote natural logs. Using your answer to part (a), show how the log real exchange rate between the United States and Europe is related to the shipping cost. Can Absolute PPP hold when there are shipping costs? If so, how?

2. Distribution Costs and the Terms of Trade: Suppose U.S. and E.U. households consume two traded goods; one produced in the United States and one produced in Europe. The consumer price of each good comprises a pure traded component and a distribution component. Specifically, the log dollar consumer price for good x= {US,EU} is $p_t^{\text{x}} = \gamma \wp_t^{\text{x}} + (1 - \gamma) p_t^{\text{D}}$ and the log euro price is $\hat{p}_t^{\text{x}} = \gamma \hat{\wp}_t^{\text{x}} + (1 - \gamma) \hat{p}_t^{\text{D}}$, where $\wp_t^{\text{x}}$ and $\hat{\wp}_t^{\text{x}}$ denote the wholesale prices of good x in dollars and euros, respectively. Let τ_t denote the log U.S. terms of trade computed from consumer prices, and $\tau_t^{\wp}$ the log terms of trade based on wholesale prices. Derive the relation between τ_t and $\tau_t^{\wp}$. Discuss how the presence of the distribution components affects the relationship between the real exchange rate and the terms of trade based on wholesale prices.

3. Long-Term Interest and Forward Rates: Let $P_{z_t}^n(z)$ denote the price of an n-period z-type AD security in period t when the state is $z_t \in \mathcal{Z}$ (i.e., a security that pays off \$1 in period $t + n$ if the state is z).

(a) Find an expression for the price of a two-period AD security, $P_{z_t}^2(z)$, in terms of the prices for one-period securities in periods t and $t + 1$ [i.e., $P_{z_t}^1(z)$ and $P_{z_{t+1}}^1(z)$].

(b) The price of a two-period bond in period t is $P_{z_t}^2 = \sum_{z \in \mathcal{Z}} P_{z_t}^2(z)$. Use your answer to part (a) to show that $P_{z_t}^2 = P_{z_t} \mathbb{E}_t^{\mathcal{P}} P_{z_{t+1}}$. What does this equation imply about the relationship between the yields on one- and two-period bonds? (NB: the yield on an n-period bond is related to its price by $r_t^n = -\frac{1}{n} \ln P_{z_t}^n$.)

(c) Recall that the price of a one-period type-z AD security that pays off in euros is $\hat{P}_{z_t}^1(z) = P_{z_t}^1(z) S_{t+1}(z)/S_t$, where $S_{t+1}(z)$ is the state-contingent spot rate in $t + 1$. Use this expression and your answer to part (b) to derive the relationship between the prices of two-period dollar and euro bonds, $P_{z_t}^2$ and $\hat{P}_{z_t}^2$.

(d) Using your answer from part (c), show that the dollar price of a two-period forward contract is

$$\mathcal{F}_t^2 = \frac{\mathbb{E}_t^{\mathcal{P}} \left[P_{z_{t+1}}^1 \mathcal{F}_{t+1} \right]}{\mathbb{E}_t^{\mathcal{P}} [P_{z_{t+1}}^1]}.$$

Under what circumstances will the price of a two-period forward contract, $\mathcal{F}_t^2$, be above the expected future price of a one-period contract, $\mathbb{E}_t \left[\mathcal{F}_{t+1} \right]$?

4. Spot Rates and News: Consider the special case of the endowment model where the spot rate and fundamentals are given by

$$s_t = f_t + \mathbb{E}_t \sum b^i \Delta f_{t+i},$$

with $f_t = m_t - \hat{m}_t$ and the money market conditions are

$$m_t - p_t = \kappa + c_t - \sigma r_t \quad \text{and} \quad \hat{m}_t - \hat{p}_t = \kappa + \hat{c}_t - \sigma \hat{r}_t.$$

Plot the impulse response of the spot rate and interest differential to the news in period t that there will be a permanent increase in the home money supply in period $t + 4$.

5. Exchange Rates and Demand Shocks: Suppose that the aggregate demand for U.S. and E.U. goods in the production model of Section 1.3.4 comprises the demand by households and governments. The market-clearing conditions in (1.79) are now

$$A_t K_t^{\eta} = Y_t = X_t + I_t + G_t \quad \text{and} \quad \hat{A}_t \hat{K}_t^{\eta} = \hat{Y}_t = \hat{X}_t + \hat{I}_t + \hat{G}_t,$$

where G_t and $\hat{G}_t$ denote the U.S. and E.U. government demand for domestically produced goods. Government spending is financed entirely by lump sum taxes on domestic firms so that the dividends paid by U.S. and E.U. firms are

$$D_t = P_t^{\text{US}}(A_t K_t^{\eta} - I_t - G_t) \quad \text{and} \quad \hat{D}_t = P_t^{\text{EU}}(\hat{A}_t \hat{K}_t^{\eta} - \hat{I}_t - \hat{G}_t).$$

(a) Show that these amendments have no effect on the first-order conditions governing optimal investment in (1.74) and (1.77).

(b) Using the first-order conditions and the market-clearing equations above, derive the steady state levels for the capital stocks, K and $\hat{K}$, and household aggregate demands, X and $\hat{X}$, given exogenous levels for government spending, G and $\hat{G}$, and productivity, $A = \hat{A} = 1$. Explain how a permanent increase in steady state U.S. government spending will affect the U.S. terms of trade.

(c) Now suppose that government spending, denoted by G_t and $\hat{G}_t$, follows an exogenous i.i.d. mean-zero processes. Describe how the U.S. terms of trade will respond to a positive G_t shock.

1.A Appendix

1.A.1 Dynamic Programming

Dynamic programming is a powerful tool for analyzing dynamic optimization problems. Here we illustrate its use for characterizing the consumption/portfolio choice problem facing the representative U.S. household discussed in Section 1.3.2. Readers requiring more than the very brief treatment that follows should consult a modern macroeconomics textbook, such as Ljungqvist and Sargent (2004).

Let us begin by rewriting the budget constraint in terms of the portfolio shares $\alpha_t^m = M_t / P_t W_t$, and $\alpha_t(z) = \mathcal{P}_t(z) \left(\mathcal{A}_t(z) - B_t \right) / P_t W_t$ for all $z \in \mathcal{Z}$. Combining these definitions with the budget constraint in (1.32) gives

$$A_t(z) = \frac{\alpha_t(z)}{\mathcal{P}_t(z)} P_t W_t + B_t \quad \text{and} \quad B_t \mathcal{P}_t = \left(1 - \sum_z \alpha_t(z) - \alpha_t^m\right) P_t W_t - P_t C_t.$$

Substituting these expressions into the definition of wealth, $W_{t+1} = (A_t(z_{t+1}) + M_t)/P_{t+1}$, yields

$$W_{t+1} = \frac{P_t}{\mathcal{P}_t P_{t+1}} \tag{1.85}$$

$$\times \left\{ \left(\frac{\alpha_t(z_{t+1})\mathcal{P}_t}{\mathcal{P}_t(z_{t+1})} + \alpha_t^m \mathcal{P}_t + \left(1 - \sum_z \alpha_t(z) - \alpha_t^m\right) \right) W_t - C_t \right\},$$

which is the form of the budget constraint shown in (1.35). The problem facing the household in period t is to choose the sequence of consumption and portfolio shares $\{C_{t+i}, \alpha_{t+i}^m, \alpha_{t+i}(z)\}_{i \geq 0}$ to maximize expected utility, $\mathbb{U}_t$, defined in (1.28), subject to the budget constraint in (1.85). There also has to be a lower limit on wealth, $W_t > \underline{W}$, that stops the household from accumulating debt indefinitely.

The method of dynamic programming expresses this infinite-period optimization problem as a two-period problem via the use of a value function. The value function for the household's problem is the maximized value of expected utility subject to the constraints

$$J(W_t) = \max_{\{C_{t+i}, \alpha_{t+i}^m, \alpha_{t+i}(z)\}_{i \geq 0}} \mathbb{E}_t \sum_{i=0}^{\infty} \beta^i \mathcal{U}\left(C_{t+i}, M_{t+i}/P_{t+i}\right), \tag{1.86}$$

subject to (1.85) and $W_t > \underline{W}$, where

$$\mathcal{U}\left(C_t, M_t/P_t\right) = \left\{ \frac{1}{1-\gamma} C_t^{1-\gamma} + \frac{\chi}{1-\nu} \left(M_t/P_t\right)^{1-\nu} \right\}.$$

In this case, the value function depends on wealth and the information the household has concerning future returns. We could include this information explicitly as an argument of the value function, but this is unnecessary and notationally burdensome. Next, we rewrite (1.86) as

$$J(W_t) = \max_{C_t, \alpha_t^m, \alpha_t(z)} \left\{ \mathcal{U}\left(C_t, M_t/P_t\right) \right.$$

$$\left. + \beta \mathbb{E}_t \left[\max_{\{C_{t+i}, \alpha_{t+i}^m, \alpha_{t+i}(z)\}_{i \geq 1}} \mathbb{E}_{t+1} \sum_{i=0}^{\infty} \beta \mathcal{U}\left(C_{t+1+i}, M_{t+1+i}/P_{t+1+i}\right) \right] \right\}$$

$$= \max_{C_t, \alpha_t^m, \alpha_t(z)} \left\{ \frac{1}{1-\gamma} C_t^{1-\gamma} + \frac{\chi}{1-\nu} \left(M_t/P_t\right)^{1-\nu} \right\} + \beta \mathbb{E}_t J(W_{t+1}). \tag{1.87}$$

Equation (1.87) is called the Bellman equation. It characterizes the infinite-horizon problem as a two-period problem: period t and all the remaining periods. The simplification is not costless. In order to solve the household's problem we must find the optimal choices of C_t, α_t^m, and $\alpha_t(z)$ without knowing the functional form for $J(W_t)$.

Essentially, we have to solve (1.87) given a guess for the form of $\mathcal{J}(W_{t+1})$. Then, using the "solutions" for C_t, α_t^m, and $\alpha_t(z)$, find $\mathcal{J}(W_t)$ and check that it matches the initial guess. In all but a few special cases, it is only possible to implement this method numerically. Nevertheless, we can still learn a lot about the solution by studying the first-order conditions.

To derive these conditions, we start by differentiating the value function $\mathcal{J}(W_t)$ with respect to C_t, $\alpha_t(z)$, and α_t^m:

$$C_t: \quad C_t^{-\gamma} = \beta \mathbb{E}_t \left[\mathcal{J}'(W_{t+1}) \exp(r_t - \Delta p_{t+1}) \right],$$

$$\alpha_t(z): \quad \exp(r_t) \frac{\pi_t(z) \mathcal{P}_t P_t}{\mathcal{P}_t(z) P_{t+1}} \mathcal{J}'(W_{t+1}(z)) = \mathbb{E}_t \left[\exp(r_t - \Delta p_{t+1}) \mathcal{J}'(W_{t+1}) \right],$$

$$\alpha_t^m: \quad \chi \left(M_t / P_t \right)^{-\nu} = \left(1 - \exp\left(-r_t \right) \right) \beta \mathbb{E}_t \left[\mathcal{J}'(W_{t+1}) \exp(r_t - \Delta p_{t+1}) \right],$$

where $\mathcal{J}'(W_{t+1}) = \partial \mathcal{J}(W_{t+1}) / \partial W_{t+1}$. To find an expression for $\mathcal{J}'(W_{t+1})$, we differentiate the value function in (1.87):

$$\mathcal{J}'(W_t) = \chi \alpha_t^m \left(M_t / P_t \right)^{-\nu} + \beta \mathbb{E}_t \left[\mathcal{J}'(W_{t+1}) \exp(r_t - \Delta p_{t+1}) E R_{t+1} \right].$$

Combining this equation with the definition of excess returns, $E R_{t+1}$, and the preceding first-order conditions gives

$$\mathcal{J}'(W_t) = \beta \left(1 - \sum_{z} \alpha_t(z) \right) \mathbb{E}_t \left[\mathcal{J}'(W_{t+1}) \frac{\exp\left(r_t \right) P_t}{P_{t+1}} \right]$$

$$+ \beta \sum_{z} \pi_t(z) \left[\mathcal{J}'(W_{t+1}(z)) \frac{P_t}{P_{t+1}} \frac{\alpha_t(z)}{\mathcal{P}_t(z)} \right]. \tag{1.88}$$

Since the first-order condition for $\alpha(z)$ implies that

$$\sum_{z} \pi_t(z) \left[\mathcal{J}'(W_{t+1}(z)) \frac{P_t}{P_{t+1}} \frac{\alpha_t(z)}{\mathcal{P}_t(z)} \right]$$

$$= \mathbb{E}_t \left[\mathcal{J}'(W_{t+1}) \exp(r_t - \Delta p_{t+1}) \right] \sum_{z} \alpha_t(z),$$

equation (1.88) becomes

$$\mathcal{J}'(W_t) = \beta \mathbb{E}_t \left[\mathcal{J}'(W_{t+1}) \exp(r_t - \Delta p_{t+1}) \right].$$

Comparing this expression with the first-order condition for C_t reveals that $C_t^{-\gamma} = \mathcal{J}'(W_t)$. We can therefore use this result to eliminate $\mathcal{J}'(W_{t+1})$ from the first-order conditions. The result is shown in (1.37)–(1.39).

1.A.2 Approximations

We make extensive use of log-linear and log-normal approximations. To derive the former, let $Z = X^a + Y^b$ for some variables, X, Y, and Z. The first step is to rewrite the expression in terms of logs:

$$z = ax + \ln(1 + \exp(by - ax)),$$

where $x = \ln X$, $y = \ln Y$, and $z = \ln Z$. Next, we take a first-order Taylor approximation to the second term around $y = \bar{y}$ and $x = \bar{x}$, which yields

$$z = ax + \ln(1 + \exp(b\bar{y} - a\bar{x})) + b\frac{\exp(b\bar{y} - a\bar{x})}{1 + \exp(b\bar{y} - a\bar{x})}(y - \bar{y})$$

$$- a\frac{\exp(b\bar{y} - a\bar{x})}{1 + \exp(b\bar{y} - a\bar{x})}(x - \bar{x}),$$

or, more simply,

$$z = \bar{z} + \frac{1}{c}a(x - \bar{x}) + \left(1 - \frac{1}{c}\right)b(y - \bar{y}),$$

where $c = 1 + \exp(b\bar{y} - a\bar{x})$ and $\bar{z} = a\bar{x} + \ln c$.

Log-normal approximations are based on the fact that if $x = \ln X$ is a normally distributed random variable with mean μ and variance σ^2, $\mathbb{E} \exp(x) = \exp(\mu + \frac{1}{2}\sigma^2)$.

To illustrate how they work, let us derive the expression for the foreign exchange risk premium, δ_t, in equation (1.48).

By definition, $\delta_t = \ln \mathbb{E}_t[S_{t+1}/S_t] - \ln \mathbb{E}_t^{\mathcal{P}}[S_{t+1}/S_t]$, so we begin by approximating $\ln \mathbb{E}_t[S_{t+1}/S_t]$. If $s_{t+1} = \ln S_{t+1}$ has a normal distribution conditioned on information known in period t, we can apply this result to write

$$\ln \mathbb{E}_t[S_{t+1}/S_t] = \ln\left[\exp\left(\mathbb{E}_t \Delta s_{t+1} + \tfrac{1}{2}\mathbb{V}_t(s_{t+1})\right)\right]$$

$$= \mathbb{E}_t \Delta s_{t+1} + \tfrac{1}{2}\mathbb{V}_t(s_{t+1}).$$

If s_{t+1} is not normally distributed, the second line will also contain an approximation error. This term is dropped when making a log-normal approximation. The next step is to approximate $\ln \mathbb{E}_t^{\mathcal{P}}[S_{t+1}/S_t]$. First, we use the definition of the pseudo probabilities to write

$$\mathbb{E}_t^{\mathcal{P}}\left[\frac{S_{t+1}}{S_t}\right] = \sum_{\mathcal{Z}} \pi_t(z) \frac{C_{t+1}^{-\gamma}(z)/P_{t+1}(z)}{\mathbb{E}_t\left[C_{t+1}^{-\gamma}/P_{t+1}\right]} \frac{S_{t+1}(z)}{S_t} = \frac{1}{\mathbb{E}_t\left[C_{t+1}^{-\gamma}/P_{t+1}\right]} \mathbb{E}_t\left[\frac{C_{t+1}^{-\gamma}}{P_{t+1}} \frac{S_{t+1}}{S_t}\right].$$

Second, we take log-normal approximations to the terms on the right:

$$\mathbb{E}_t\left[\frac{C_{t+1}^{-\gamma}}{P_{t+1}}\right] = \exp\left(-\mathbb{E}_t(\gamma c_{t+1} + p_{t+1}) + \tfrac{1}{2}\mathbb{V}_t(\gamma c_{t+1} + p_{t+1})\right)$$

and

$$\mathbb{E}_t\left[\frac{C_{t+1}^{-\gamma}}{P_{t+1}}\frac{S_{t+1}}{S_t}\right] = \exp\Big(-\mathbb{E}_t(\gamma c_{t+1} + p_{t+1} - \Delta s_{t+1})$$
$$+ \tfrac{1}{2}\mathbb{V}_t(\gamma c_{t+1} + p_{t+1} - \Delta s_{t+1})\Big).$$

Substituting these approximations into the definition for δ_t produces

$$\delta_t = \ln \mathbb{E}_t(S_{t+1}/S_t) - \ln \mathbb{E}_t^{\mathcal{P}}(S_{t+1}/S_t)$$
$$= \left(\mathbb{E}_t\Delta s_{t+1} + \tfrac{1}{2}\mathbb{V}_t(s_{t+1})\right)$$
$$- \left(\mathbb{E}_t\Delta s_{t+1} + \tfrac{1}{2}\mathbb{V}_t(\gamma c_{t+1} + p_{t+1} - \Delta s_{t+1}) - \tfrac{1}{2}\mathbb{V}_t(\gamma c_{t+1} + p_{t+1})\right)$$
$$= \left(\mathbb{E}_t\Delta s_{t+1} + \tfrac{1}{2}\mathbb{V}_t(s_{t+1})\right)$$
$$- \left(\mathbb{E}_t\Delta s_{t+1} + \tfrac{1}{2}\mathbb{V}_t(s_{t+1}) - \mathbb{CV}_t(s_{t+1}, \gamma c_{t+1} + p_{t+1})\right)$$
$$= \mathbb{CV}_t(s_{t+1}, \gamma c_{t+1} + p_{t+1}),$$

which is equation (1.48).

1.A.3 Labor Income

Throughout this chapter we have assumed that asset returns are the only source of household income. By contrast, most international macro models assume that households receive income from both their asset holdings and their labor in the form of wages. It is natural, then, to ask whether the presence of labor income materially affects our analysis of exchange-rate determination?

To address this question, let us first consider the budget constraint facing the representative U.S. household. In particular, suppose that the household receives exogenous labor income of $Y(z_t)$ dollars in period t when the economy is in state z. The budget constraint can now be written as

$$\sum_{\mathcal{Z}} \mathcal{P}_t(z)\left(\mathcal{A}_t(z) - B_t\right) + B_t\mathcal{P}_t + M_t = \mathcal{A}_{t-1}(z_t) + Y(z_t) + M_{t-1} - P_tC_t. \quad (1.89)$$

This expression differs from the budget constraint in (1.32) because labor income appears on the right-hand side. Nevertheless, it is still possible to write (1.89) in the form of (1.32) so that our analysis of Section 1.3 continues to apply. In particular, let

$\mathcal{Y}(z_t)$ be the present value of the stream of labor income:

$$\mathcal{Y}(z_t) = \mathbb{E}_t^P \sum_{k=0}^{\infty} \exp\left(-\sum_{j=0}^{k-1} r_{t+j}\right) \mathsf{Y}(z_{t+k}),$$

where the conditional expectations $\mathbb{E}_t^P$ are calculated using pseudo probabilities. (Recall that these expectations are defined as $\mathbb{E}_t^P \varkappa(z_{t+1}) = \sum_{\mathcal{Z}} \pi_t^P(z) \varkappa(z)$ for any variable $\varkappa$ that depends upon the state z in $t + 1$, where $\pi_t^P(z) = \mathcal{P}_t(z)/\mathcal{P}_t$.) Iterating this expression forward one period, we see that

$$\mathcal{Y}(z_t) = \mathsf{Y}(z_t) + \sum_{z_{t+1}\in\mathcal{Z}} \mathcal{P}_t(z_{t+1})\mathcal{Y}(z_{t+1}).$$

Thus, $\mathcal{Y}(z_t)$ can be interpreted as the nominal value of a claim to current and future labor income, that is, human wealth. The first term on the right is just current income, and the second is the current value of the claim in the future. Combining this expression with the budget constraint in (1.89) we obtain

$$\sum_{\mathcal{Z}} \mathcal{P}_t(z) \left(\mathcal{A}_t^*(z) - B_t\right) + B_t \mathcal{P}_t + M_t = \mathcal{A}_{t-1}^*(z_t) + M_{t-1} - \mathcal{P}_t C_t,$$

where $\mathcal{A}_t^*(z) = \mathcal{A}_t(z) + \mathcal{Y}(z_t)$. This expression has the same form as the budget constraint in (1.32) except that $\mathcal{A}_t^*(z)$ replaces $\mathcal{A}_t(z)$. This means that our analysis of household behavior under complete markets is unaffected by the presence of labor income.

The economic intuition behind this result is straightforward. Household wealth is now composed of two components: asset holdings and human wealth, $W_t = (\mathcal{A}_{t-1}(z_t) + \mathcal{Y}(z_t) + M_{t-1})/P_t$. Note that the wealth in period t depends on the number of type-z_t AD securities held from period $t - 1$ plus the value of human wealth in state z_t. This means that households can fully hedge against variations in the future stream of labor income by adjusting their portfolios of AD securities. For example, suppose there are two possible states and labor income is lower in state 1 than in state 2 so that $\mathcal{Y}(1) < \mathcal{Y}(2)$. In this case, the effects of uncertain future labor income on wealth can be completely offset if the household holds more state-1 than state-2 AD securities.

1.A.4 Derivations

Consumption and the Terms of Trade in the Endowment Economy
First, we write the log aggregate demand for each good in the form of matrix equation using (1.49), (1.50), and (1.51):

$$\begin{bmatrix} x_t \\ \hat{x}_t \end{bmatrix} = \begin{bmatrix} \lambda & 1-\lambda \\ 1-\lambda & \lambda \end{bmatrix} \begin{bmatrix} c_t \\ \hat{c}_t \end{bmatrix} + \begin{bmatrix} 1 \\ -1 \end{bmatrix} 2\lambda\theta(1-\lambda)(\tau_t + \bar{\varepsilon}_t).$$

Next, we substitute for τ_t with (1.64). After some simplification, this gives

$$
\begin{bmatrix} x_t \\ \hat{x}_t \end{bmatrix} = \frac{1}{2\lambda - 1} \begin{bmatrix} \lambda(2\lambda - 1) + 2\theta\lambda\gamma (1 - \lambda) & (1 - \lambda)(2\lambda - 1 - 2\theta\lambda\gamma) \\ (1 - \lambda)(2\lambda - 1 - 2\theta\lambda\gamma) & \lambda(2\lambda - 1) + 2\theta\lambda\gamma (1 - \lambda) \end{bmatrix} \begin{bmatrix} c_t \\ \hat{c}_t \end{bmatrix}
$$
$$
- \frac{2\lambda\theta(1 - \lambda)}{2\lambda - 1} \begin{bmatrix} 1 \\ -1 \end{bmatrix} \bar{\varepsilon}_t.
$$

Solving this equation for c_t and $\hat{c}_t$ produces

$$
\begin{bmatrix} c_t \\ \hat{c}_t \end{bmatrix} = \begin{bmatrix} \varphi & 1 - \varphi \\ 1 - \varphi & \varphi \end{bmatrix} \begin{bmatrix} x_t \\ \hat{x}_t \end{bmatrix} + \begin{bmatrix} \varsigma \\ -\varsigma \end{bmatrix} \bar{\varepsilon}_t,
$$

where

$$
\varphi = \frac{\lambda (2\lambda - 1 + 2\theta\gamma(1 - \lambda))}{(2\lambda - 1)^2 + 4\gamma\lambda\theta(1 - \lambda)} \quad \text{and} \quad \varsigma = \frac{2\lambda\theta(1 - \lambda)}{(2\lambda - 1)^2 + 4\gamma\lambda\theta(1 - \lambda)}.
$$

This is the matrix version of (1.66). Premultiplying by $[\,\gamma \quad -\gamma\,]$ gives (1.65): $\varepsilon_t = \xi(x_t - \hat{x}_t) + 2\gamma\varsigma\bar{\varepsilon}_t$, where $\xi = \gamma (2\varphi - 1)$.

To compute the upper bound in equation (1.69), we combine (1.67) and (1.68) to give

$$
\mathbb{V}(\Delta\varepsilon_t)/\mathbb{V}(\Delta c_t) = \frac{2 (\gamma (2\varphi - 1))^2}{\varphi^2 + (1 - \varphi)^2}.
$$

From the definition of φ, it follows that

$$
\gamma (2\varphi - 1) = \frac{\gamma (2\lambda - 1)}{(2\lambda - 1)^2 + 4\gamma\lambda\theta(1 - \lambda)}
$$

and

$$
1 - \varphi = -\frac{(2\theta\lambda\gamma - 2\lambda + 1)(\lambda - 1)}{(2\lambda - 1)^2 + 4\gamma\lambda\theta(1 - \lambda)}.
$$

Substituting these expressions into the equation for the variance ratio and simplifying yields

$$
\mathbb{V}(\Delta\varepsilon_t)/\mathbb{V}(\Delta c_t) = \frac{2 (\gamma (2\lambda - 1))^2}{(\lambda (2\lambda - 1 + 2\theta\gamma(1 - \lambda)))^2 + ((2\theta\lambda\gamma + 1 - 2\lambda)(\lambda - 1))^2}.
$$

Equation (1.69) is obtained by taking the limit as $\gamma \to \infty$.

Terms-of-Trade Dynamics in the Production Economy

First, we write the log-linearized firms' first-order conditions as

$$
\begin{bmatrix} \gamma \\ \gamma \end{bmatrix} \mathbb{E}_t \Delta c_{t+1} = \mathbb{E}_t \begin{bmatrix} r_{t+1}^k \\ \hat{r}_{t+1}^k \end{bmatrix} + \mathbb{E}_t \begin{bmatrix} \Delta p_{t+1}^{\mathrm{US}} - \Delta p_{t+1} \\ \Delta p_{t+1}^{\mathrm{EU}} - \Delta p_{t+1} \end{bmatrix} + \begin{bmatrix} \iota^{\mathrm{US}} \\ \iota^{\mathrm{EU}} \end{bmatrix},
$$

where $\iota^{\mathrm{US}} = \ln \beta + \frac{1}{2}\mathbb{V}_t(p_{t+1}^{\mathrm{US}} - p_{t+1} + r_{t+1}^k - \gamma c_{t+1})$ and $\iota^{\mathrm{EU}} = \ln \beta + \frac{1}{2}\mathbb{V}_t(p_{t+1}^{\mathrm{EU}} - p_{t+1} + \hat{r}_{t+1}^k - \gamma c_{t+1})$. In the absence of any LOOP deviations, $\mathbb{E}_t \Delta p_{t+1}^{\mathrm{EU}} - \mathbb{E}_t \Delta p_{t+1}^{\mathrm{US}} =$

$\mathbb{E}_t \Delta \tau_{t+1}$, so premultiplying this equation by $[\,-1 \quad 1\,]$ gives

$$\mathbb{E}_t r^k_{t+1} = \mathbb{E}_t \hat{r}^k_{t+1} + \mathbb{E}_t \Delta \tau_{t+1} + \iota^{\mathrm{EU}} - \iota^{\mathrm{US}}.$$

Next, we find expressions for log consumption of the U.S. and E.U. good, x_t and $\hat{x}_t$, that satisfy the firms' first-order conditions. We already know that $\Delta c_{t+1} = \varphi \Delta x_{t+1} + (1-\varphi)\Delta \hat{x}_{t+1}$, $\Delta p^{\mathrm{US}}_{t+1} - \Delta p_{t+1} = (\lambda - 1)\Delta \tau_{t+1}$, $\Delta p^{\mathrm{EU}}_{t+1} - \Delta p_{t+1} = \lambda \Delta \tau_{t+1}$, and $\Delta \tau_{t+1} = \zeta(\Delta x_{t+1} - \Delta \hat{x}_{t+1})$, where $\zeta = \xi/(2\lambda - 1)$. Substituting these equations into the first-order conditions gives

$$\begin{bmatrix} \gamma\varphi + (1-\lambda)\zeta & \gamma(1-\varphi) - (1-\lambda)\zeta \\ \gamma\varphi - \lambda\zeta & \lambda\zeta + \gamma(1-\varphi) \end{bmatrix} \mathbb{E}_t \begin{bmatrix} \Delta x_{t+1} \\ \Delta \hat{x}_{t+1} \end{bmatrix} = \mathbb{E}_t \begin{bmatrix} r^k_{t+1} \\ \hat{r}^k_{t+1} \end{bmatrix} + \begin{bmatrix} \iota^{\mathrm{US}} \\ \iota^{\mathrm{EU}} \end{bmatrix},$$

or more compactly,

$$\Theta \mathbb{E}_t \Delta \underline{x}_{t+1} = \mathbb{E}_t \underline{r}^k_{t+1} + \underline{\iota}. \tag{1.90}$$

Let $\underline{k}'_t = [\, k_t \quad \hat{k}_t \,]$, $\underline{a}'_t = [\, a_t \quad \hat{a}_t \,]$, and $\underline{u}'_t = [\, u_t \quad \hat{u}_t \,]$. The productivity process in (1.78) can now be written as $\underline{a}_t = \Phi \underline{a}_{t-1} + \underline{u}_t$ and the log-linearized versions of the marginal product of capital and the capital accumulation equations as

$$\underline{r}^k_{t+1} = \underline{r} + \psi \underline{a}_{t+1} - (1-\eta)\psi \left(\underline{k}_{t+1} - \underline{k} \right), \tag{1.91}$$

with $\psi = 1 - \beta(1 - \mathfrak{d}) < 1$ and

$$\underline{k}_{t+1} = \underline{k} + \left(\frac{1}{\beta} \right) (\underline{k}_t - \underline{k}) + \left(\frac{\psi}{\eta\beta} \right) \underline{a}_t - \left(\frac{\psi}{\eta\beta} - \mathfrak{d} \right) (\underline{x}_t - \underline{x}), \tag{1.92}$$

where $\underline{r}$, $\underline{k}$, and $\underline{x}$ denote the steady state values of r^k_t, k_t, and x_t.

The next step is to conjecture and verify that when firms choose investment optimally, the log consumption of each good follows

$$\underline{x}_t - \underline{x} = \kappa_a \underline{a}_t + \kappa_k \left(\underline{k}_t - \underline{k} \right) \tag{1.93}$$

for some matrices κ_a and κ_k. To verify this conjecture, we rewrite (1.90) as

$$\underline{x}_t - \underline{x} = \mathbb{E}_t \underline{x}_{t+1} - \underline{x} - \Theta^{-1} \left(\mathbb{E}_t \underline{r}^k_{t+1} - \underline{r} \right)$$

and substitute for $\mathbb{E}_t \underline{r}^k_{t+1} - \underline{r}$ with (1.91) to get

$$\underline{x}_t - \underline{x} = \mathbb{E}_t \left(\underline{x}_{t+1} - \underline{x} \right) - \psi\Theta^{-1} \mathbb{E}_t \underline{a}_{t+1} + (1-\eta)\psi\Theta^{-1} \mathbb{E}_t \left(\underline{k}_{t+1} - \underline{k} \right). \tag{1.94}$$

Next, using (1.92) with (1.93), we write

$$\begin{aligned} \mathbb{E}_t \left(\underline{k}_{t+1} - \underline{k} \right) &= \left(\frac{\psi}{\beta\eta} I - \left(\frac{\psi}{\eta\beta} - \mathfrak{d} \right) \kappa_a \right) \underline{a}_t \\ &\quad + \left(\frac{1}{\beta} I - \left(\frac{\psi}{\eta\beta} - \mathfrak{d} \right) \kappa_k \right) (\underline{k}_t - \underline{k}), \end{aligned} \tag{1.95}$$

where I is a 2×2 identity matrix. Finally, we combine (1.93) with (1.94) and (1.95) and the fact that $\mathbb{E}_t \underline{a}_{t+1} = \Phi \underline{a}_t$ to give

$$\kappa_a \underline{a}_t + \kappa_k \left(\underline{k}_t - \underline{k} \right) = \left(\kappa_a - \psi \Theta^{-1} \right) \Phi \underline{a}_t$$
$$+ \left(\kappa_k + (1-\eta)\psi\Theta^{-1} \right) \left(\frac{\psi}{\beta\eta}I - \left(\frac{\psi}{\eta\beta} - \eth \right) \kappa_a \right) \underline{a}_t$$
$$+ \left(\kappa_k + (1-\eta)\psi\Theta^{-1} \right) \left(\frac{1}{\beta}I - \left(\frac{\psi}{\eta\beta} - \eth \right) \kappa_k \right) \left(\underline{k}_t - \underline{k} \right).$$

This matrix equation must hold for all values of $\underline{a}_t$ and $\underline{k}_t - \underline{k}$ if the conjecture in (1.93) is correct. Hence, the matrices κ_a and κ_k must satisfy

$$\kappa_k = \left(\kappa_k + (1-\eta)\psi\Theta^{-1} \right) \left(\frac{1}{\beta}I - \left(\frac{\psi}{\eta\beta} - \eth \right) \kappa_k \right)$$

and

$$\kappa_a = \left(\kappa_a - \psi\Theta^{-1} \right) \Phi + \left(\kappa_k + (1-\eta)\psi\Theta^{-1} \right) \left(\frac{\psi}{\beta\eta}I - \left(\frac{\psi}{\eta\beta} - \eth \right) \kappa_a \right).$$

We find κ_a and κ_k by solving these equations numerically given the parameter values in Table 1.3.

The dynamics of the terms of trade and other variables are found from the joint dynamics of $\underline{a}_t$ and $\underline{k}_t - \underline{k}$. In particular, substituting (1.93) into (1.92) gives

$$\underline{k}_{t+1} - \underline{k} = \left(\frac{1}{\beta}I - \left(\frac{\psi}{\eta\beta} - \eth \right) \kappa_k \right) \left(\underline{k}_t - \underline{k} \right) + \left(\frac{\psi}{\beta\eta}I - \left(\frac{\psi}{\eta\beta} - \eth \right) \kappa_a \right) \underline{a}_t.$$

We can now represent the joint dynamics in matrix form as

$$\begin{bmatrix} \underline{a}_{t+1} \\ \underline{k}_{t+1} - \underline{k} \end{bmatrix} = \begin{bmatrix} \Phi & 0 \\ \frac{\psi}{\beta\eta}I - (\frac{\psi}{\eta\beta} - \eth)\kappa_a & \frac{1}{\beta}I - (\frac{\psi}{\eta\beta} - \eth)\kappa_k \end{bmatrix} \begin{bmatrix} \underline{a}_t \\ \underline{k}_t - \underline{k} \end{bmatrix} + \begin{bmatrix} \underline{u}_{t+1} \\ 0 \end{bmatrix}.$$

The dynamics of the terms of trade is then given by

$$\tau_t = [\,\zeta \quad -\zeta\,] \left(\underline{x}_{t+1} - \underline{x} \right),$$

where

$$\underline{x}_{t+1} - \underline{x} = [\,\kappa_a \quad \kappa_k\,] \begin{bmatrix} \underline{a}_{t+1} \\ \underline{k}_{t+1} - \underline{k} \end{bmatrix},$$

and the marginal products of capital by

$$\underline{r}^k_{t+1} - \underline{r} = [\,\psi I \quad -(1-\eta)\psi I\,] \begin{bmatrix} \underline{a}_{t+1} \\ \underline{k}_{t+1} - \underline{k} \end{bmatrix}.$$

CHAPTER 2

Macro Models with Frictions

This is the second of two chapters that examine the exchange-rate implications of macroeconomic models. In contrast to Chapter 1, the models studied here include frictions in product and financial markets. Frictions appear in the product markets via the presence of monopolistic competition among the producers of consumer goods. This setting allows us to study the role of price-stickiness in exchange-rate determination—an issue that has been examined extensively in the international macro literature. Frictions appear in financial markets in the form of restrictions on the set of financial assets that households can trade. In particular, we examine models where households can only trade in a limited number of equities and bonds rather than in the complete set of Arrow-Debreu securities. In this setting limits on the degree of international risk-sharing permit several new factors to affect equilibrium exchange rates.

The models we study also include two other important features. First, they introduce a distinction between the final goods consumed by households and intermediate goods that comprise international trade. This distinction is necessary to account for the dynamics of consumer prices, exchange rates, and the terms of trade. Second, we examine models where central banks control short-term nominal interest rates rather than the money supply. In so doing, our analysis of exchange-rate determination connects with the recent research on monetary policy.

We also review the empirical evidence on international risk-sharing. Standard models with complete markets make strong predictions about the joint behavior of real exchange rates and aggregate consumption that are at odds with the empirical evidence. Reconciling these findings presents an important challenge for any exchange-rate model.

2.1 The Model

2.1.1 Structure

We study the behavior of the nominal exchange rate in a canonical model with two countries, the United States and Europe. Each country is populated by a large number of identical utility-maximizing households that have access to an array of financial assets. To isolate the exchange-rate implications of price-stickiness, we initially assume that the array of assets comprises a complete set of contingent claims. We then restrict the assets to bonds and equities in order to study the exchange-rate implications of limited risk-sharing.

The production side of the model distinguishes between the intermediate goods that are traded between countries and the consumer goods that are available to households. In each country, households can choose from a continuum of different consumer goods that are produced by domestic firms in the retail sector using intermediate goods and local labor. Households cannot purchase the goods produced by foreign retail firms, so the markets for consumer goods are segmented internationally. The market for intermediate goods, by contrast, is fully integrated. Retail firms in each country can purchase domestic- or foreign-produced intermediate goods. For simplicity, there are two intermediate goods, one produced in the United States and one produced in Europe, that can be costlessly transported between countries. Thus, all international trade involves the exports and imports of intermediate goods.

The government sector in each country comprises a central bank and fiscal authority. Central banks control either the money stock or the short-term nominal interest rate, whereas the fiscal authority levies taxes, purchases intermediate goods, and issues government bonds to finance any deficit. As we shall see, the conduct of both monetary and fiscal policy has different implications for the behavior of exchange rates depending on the degree of international risk-sharing and price-stickiness.

Households

The United States is populated by a continuum of identical households distributed on the interval [0, 1] with preferences defined over a basket of final goods, real balances, and labor services. In particular, the expected utility of a representative U.S. household $n \in [0, 1]$ in period t is given by

$$\mathbb{U}_t = \mathbb{E}_t \sum_{i=0}^{\infty} \beta^i \left\{ \frac{1}{1-\gamma} C_{n,t+i}^{1-\gamma} + \frac{\chi}{1-\nu} \left(M_{n,t+i}/P_{t+i} \right)^{1-\nu} - \varkappa L_{n,t+i} \right\}, \quad (2.1)$$

where γ, ν, χ, and $\varkappa$ are positive parameters and $1 > \beta > 0$ is the subjective discount factor. As usual, $\mathbb{E}_t$ denotes expectations conditioned on period-t information, which is common to all U.S. and E.U. households. $C_{n,t}$ denotes the basket of consumption goods that takes the CES form defined over a continuum of varieties i distributed on the interval [0, 1]:

$$C_n = \left[\int_0^1 (C_n^i)^{\frac{\phi-1}{\phi}} di \right]^{\frac{\phi}{\phi-1}}, \quad (2.2)$$

where C_n^i identifies the consumption of variety i by household n. The elasticity of substitution between varieties is given by $\phi > 1$, and the corresponding U.S. retail price index is

$$P_t = \left[\int_0^1 (P_t^i)^{1-\phi} di \right]^{\frac{1}{1-\phi}}, \tag{2.3}$$

where P^i is the price of variety i. Households' utility also depends positively on their holdings of dollars, $M_{n,t}$, and negatively on the labor services they provide to firms in the U.S. retail sector, $L_{n,t}$. As in Chapter 1, we write the U.S. household's budget constraint as

$$A_{n,t} + M_{n,t} = R_{n,t}^A A_{n,t-1} + M_{n,t-1} - P_t C_{n,t} + W_t L_{n,t}, \tag{2.4}$$

where $A_{n,t}$ denotes the dollar value of financial assets held by household n at the end of period t and $R_{n,t}^A$ is the (gross) after-tax nominal return on assets held between the start of periods $t-1$ and t. Labor income during period t is identified by $W_t L_{n,t}$, where W_t is the nominal wage rate in the retail sector.

Europe is also populated by a continuum of identical households with preferences that take the form of (2.1) except that the basket of E.U. retail goods, $\hat{C}_n$, the price index, $\hat{P}_t$, holdings of euros, $\hat{M}_{n,t}$, and labor services, $\hat{L}_{n,t}$, replace $C_{n,t}$, $M_{n,t}$, P_t, and $L_{n,t}$. As in (2.2), the consumption basket is defined by the CES aggregate of $\hat{C}_n^i$, where $\hat{C}_n^i$ denotes the consumption of variety i by E.U. household n. Thus U.S. and E.U. households have the same preferences with respect to varieties of retail goods. The budget constraint of a representative E.U. household is

$$\hat{A}_{n,t} + \hat{M}_{n,t} = \hat{R}_{n,t}^A \hat{A}_{n,t-1} + \hat{M}_{n,t-1} - \hat{P}_t \hat{C}_{n,t} + \hat{W}_t \hat{L}_{n,t}, \tag{2.5}$$

where $\hat{A}_{n,t}$ denotes the euro value of financial assets held at the end of period t, $\hat{R}_{n,t}^A$ is the corresponding period-t after tax return, and $\hat{W}_t$ is the nominal wage rate in the E.U. retail sector.

Retail Firms

The retail sector in each country comprises a continuum of firms with each making a retail good of a particular variety. The firms are indexed by i, which identifies the variety of the good they produce, and are distributed on the interval [0, 1]. All firms within each country use the same technology to produce retail goods. In particular, firm i in the United States produces output of variety i in period t, Y_t^i, according to $Y_t^i = (X_t^i)^\alpha (L_t^i)^{1-\alpha}$ with $1 > \alpha > 0$, where L_t^i is the total amount of labor used in production and X_t^i is the aggregate input of intermediate goods. We assume that $X_t^i = \mathcal{F}(X_{i,t}^{US}, X_{i,t}^{EU})$, where $\mathcal{F}(.,.)$ is a CES function defined over the U.S.- and E.U.-produced intermediate goods, $X_{i,t}^{US}$ and $X_{i,t}^{EU}$, with elasticity parameter θ and share parameter λ for the U.S. good. Output of variety i in Europe is given by $\hat{Y}_t^i = (\hat{X}_t^i)^\alpha (\hat{L}_t^i)^{1-\alpha}$, where $\hat{X}_t = \mathcal{F}(X_{i,t}^{EU}, X_{i,t}^{US})$. Note that retail firms in both countries have the same production functions when the share parameter λ equals 1/2. When λ is greater (less) than 1/2, retail firms exhibit a bias toward the use of domestic (foreign) intermediate goods. We assume that $\lambda > 1/2$ in the analysis below.

Each retail firm hires domestic labor in a competitive labor market and purchases intermediate goods in a competitive world wholesale market. Let P_t^X and $\hat{P}_t^X$ denote the dollar and euro wholesale price indices associated with X_t and $\hat{X}_t$:

$$P_t^{\mathrm{X}} = \left(\lambda(P_t^{\mathrm{US}})^{1-\theta} + (1-\lambda)(P_t^{\mathrm{EU}})^{1-\theta}\right)^{\frac{1}{1-\theta}}$$

and

$$\hat{P}_t^{\mathrm{X}} = \left(\lambda(\hat{P}_t^{\mathrm{EU}})^{1-\theta} + (1-\lambda)(\hat{P}_t^{\mathrm{US}})^{1-\theta}\right)^{\frac{1}{1-\theta}},$$

where P_t^{I} and $\hat{P}_t^{\mathrm{I}}$ denote the dollar and euro prices of intermediate good $\mathrm{I}=\{\mathrm{US, EU}\}$. Cost minimization implies that the marginal cost of producing variety i in the United States and Europe is

$$MC_t = \frac{1}{\alpha^\alpha(1-\alpha)^{1-\alpha}} \left(W_t\right)^{1-\alpha} \left(P_t^{\mathrm{X}}\right)^\alpha$$

and   (2.6)

$$\widehat{MC}_t = \frac{1}{\alpha^\alpha(1-\alpha)^{1-\alpha}} (\hat{W}_t)^{1-\alpha}(\hat{P}_t^{\mathrm{X}})^\alpha,$$

where W and $\hat{W}$ are the competitively determined nominal wages in the U.S. and E.U. labor markets.[1] Note that all retail firms face the same marginal costs within each country because they have access to the same production technology, hire labor from a single national labor market, and purchase intermediate goods from a competitive wholesale market.

Cost minimization also implies that the demand for U.S.- and E.U.-produced intermediate goods by U.S. retail firm i are

$$X_{i,t}^{\mathrm{US}} = \lambda(P_t^{\mathrm{US}}/P_t^{\mathrm{X}})^{-\theta}X_t^i \quad \text{and} \quad X_{i,t}^{\mathrm{EU}} = (1-\lambda)(P_t^{\mathrm{EU}}/P_t^{\mathrm{X}})^{-\theta}X_t^i, \quad (2.7)$$

where

$$X_t^i = \left(\frac{\alpha}{1-\alpha}\right)^{1-\alpha} \left(\frac{W_t}{P_t}\right)^{\mathrm{X})^{1-\alpha}}Y_t^i \quad (2.8)$$

denotes the firm's total demand for intermediate goods.[2] The analogous demands by firm i in Europe are

$$\hat{X}_{i,t}^{\mathrm{EU}} = \lambda(\hat{P}_t^{\mathrm{EU}}/\hat{P}_t^{\mathrm{X}})^{-\theta}\hat{X}_t^i \quad \text{and} \quad \hat{X}_{i,t}^{\mathrm{US}} = (1-\lambda)(\hat{P}_t^{\mathrm{US}}/\hat{P}_t^{\mathrm{X}})^{-\theta}\hat{X}_t^i, \quad (2.9)$$

---

1. To compute the marginal cost function for U.S. firms, we first compute total cost as $\mathcal{C}(W, P^{\mathrm{X}}, Y^i) = \min WL + P^{\mathrm{X}}X$ s.t. $Y^i = X^\alpha L^{1-\alpha}$. This gives $\mathcal{C}(W, P^{\mathrm{X}}, Y^i) = \alpha^{-\alpha}(1-\alpha)^{\alpha-1}(W)^{1-\alpha}\left(P^{\mathrm{X}}\right)^\alpha Y^i$, so total cost is linear in output, and the expression for U.S. marginal cost follows immediately. Analogous calculations give the expression for the E.U. marginal cost.

2. Note that the expressions for $X_{i,t}^{\mathrm{US}}$ and $X_{i,t}^{\mathrm{EU}}$ take the standard CES form. The demand for $X_{i,t}$ is derived by combining the first-order condition from cost minimization, $\alpha W_t L_t = (1-\alpha)P_t^{\mathrm{X}}X_t$, with the production function.

where $\hat{P}_t^{\text{US}}$ and $\hat{P}_t^{\text{EU}}$ are the euro prices of U.S. and E.U. intermediate goods and

$$\hat{X}_t^i = \left(\frac{\alpha}{1-\alpha}\right)^{1-\alpha} \left(\frac{\hat{W}_t}{\hat{P}_t^{\text{x}}}\right)^{1-\alpha} \hat{Y}_t^i. \tag{2.10}$$

Unlike the labor and wholesale markets, each firm has a monopoly in the retail market because households cannot purchase variety i from a foreign retail firm. The total demand for good i is therefore the aggregate of individual domestic household demands. Since there is a unit mass of households in each country, the aggregate demand for variety i in the United States and Europe, respectively, is given by

$$C_t^i = (P_t^i / P_t)^{-\phi} C_t \quad \text{and} \quad \hat{C}_t^i = (\hat{P}_t^i / \hat{P}_t)^{-\phi} \hat{C}_t, \tag{2.11}$$

where $C_t = \int_0^1 C_{n,t} dn$ and $\hat{C}_t = \int_0^1 \hat{C}_{n,t} dn$ are aggregate U.S. and E.U. consumption. Market clearing in the U.S. and E.U. retail markets requires that $C_t^i = Y_t^i$ and $\hat{C}_t^i = \hat{Y}_t^i$ for $i \in [0, 1]$, respectively, because each retail firm enjoys a monopoly in the national market.

Each firm i hires labor, purchases intermediate goods, and sets its retail price, P^i, to maximize profits, which are then distributed as dividends to the households that hold the firm's equity. In what follows we examine the implications of different degrees of price-stickiness. Under flexible pricing, all firms choose period-t retail prices at the start of each period. In this case, retail prices reflect contemporaneous economic conditions. Under preset pricing, all firms set their period-t retail prices before the complete state of the economy in period t is known. Retail prices exhibit a minimal degree of inertia in this case. Under staggered pricing, a subset of firms is able to set retail prices each period. These firms can incorporate current conditions into their pricing decisions, but they also must accommodate the possibility that they will not be able to reset prices for some time into the future. We formulate this type of price-stickiness using the approach developed by Calvo (1983), which is used extensively in closed economy models of monetary policy.

Wholesale Firms

We model the wholesale sector of each economy in a very straightforward manner. In particular, we assume that households receive endowments of intermediate goods that they sell to retail firms on world markets. Specifically, at the start of period t, each U.S. household receives a per capita endowment of the U.S. intermediate good, EN_t^{US}, which it can sell to U.S. retail firms or the government at a dollar price of P_t^{US} or to E.U. retail firms at a euro price of $\hat{P}_t^{\text{US}}$. Similarly, each E.U. household receives a per capita endowment of the E.U. intermediate good, EN_t^{EU}, which it can sell to E.U. retail firms and the government for $\hat{P}_t^{\text{EU}}$ euros or to U.S. retail firms for P_t^{EU} dollars.

Government

The government sector in each country comprises a fiscal authority and a central bank. The fiscal authority levies lump sum taxes on dividends, chooses the level of government consumption of domestic intermediate goods, and issues one-period nominal bonds.[3] The fiscal authority budget constraints in the United States and Europe are given by

$$B_t = R_{t-1}B_{t-1} + P_t^{\text{US}}G_t - T_t \quad \text{and} \quad \hat{B}_t = \hat{R}_{t-1}\hat{B}_{t-1} + \hat{P}_t^{\text{EU}}\hat{G}_t - \hat{T}_t, \quad (2.12)$$

where B_t and $\hat{B}_t$ denote the number of dollar and euro bonds issued at the start of period t, R_t and $\hat{R}_t$ are the (gross) nominal short-term U.S. and E.U. interest rates, and G_t and $\hat{G}_t$ denote government consumption of U.S. and E.U. intermediate goods. Tax revenues in dollars and euros from the lump sum taxes on dividends are T_t and $\hat{T}_t$, respectively.

We consider the exchange-rate implications of monetary policy in two forms. First, following a long tradition in the international finance literature, we assume that each country's central bank has complete control over the money supply. Second, we consider the more realistic setting where the central banks use open market operations to control the short-term nominal interest rates. In particular, we focus on the case where the central banks use Taylor rules to set interest rates relative to the state of inflation and the gap between current GDP and its potential level.

2.1.2 Equilibrium

Equilibrium in the model is characterized by the optimality conditions governing the behavior of households and retail firms, the monetary and fiscal actions of the governments, and the market-clearing conditions in the markets for financial assets and goods. Our focus is on the equilibrium behavior of the nominal exchange rate, S, defined as the dollar price of euros, the real exchange rate, $\mathcal{E} = S\hat{P}/P$, and the U.S. terms of trade, $\mathcal{T} = P^{\text{EU}}/S\hat{P}^{\text{US}}$.

We begin in the labor market. The first-order conditions associated with U.S. and E.U. households' labor supply choices are

$$(W_t/P_t)C_{n,t}^{-\gamma} = \varkappa \quad \text{and} \quad (\hat{W}_t/\hat{P}_t)\hat{C}_{n,t}^{-\gamma} = \varkappa. \quad (2.13)$$

Equation (2.13) says that in each country households supply labor services to retail firms up to the point when the marginal utility from additional labor (i.e., $(W_t/P_t)C_{n,t}^{-\gamma}$ in the United States and $(\hat{W}_t/\hat{P}_t)\hat{C}_{n,t}^{-\gamma}$ in Europe) equals the marginal disutility, which is a constant equal to $\varkappa$. As a result, the labor market allows households to perfectly share risk within each country. For example, since all U.S. households have the same preferences and face the same nominal wage and prices, the first condition in (2.13) is only satisfied when $C_{n,t} = C_t$ for all $n \in [0, 1]$. Hence $C_{n,t}^{-\gamma}$ must equal $C_{j,t}^{-\gamma}$ for any two U.S. households n and j, as required by perfect risk-sharing. Note that this risk-sharing implication does not depend on the array of financial assets available to households. In this model the structure of financial markets determines the degree of

---

3. Alternatively, we could specify government preferences in terms of a basket of U.S. and E.U. intermediate goods so that the home bias in government consumption is less extreme. Such an extension could be important for certain calibrations of the model, but we will stick with the simpler setup here for the sake of expositional clarity.

risk-sharing among households in *different* countries not the degree of risk-sharing within each country.[4]

In the presence of complete within-country risk-sharing, there is no need to track the behavior of individual households. Instead, we can represent household behavior by the actions of representative U.S. and E.U. households with consumption $C_{n,t} = C_t$ and $\hat{C}_{n,t} = \hat{C}_t$ for all $n \in [0, 1]$. Recall that there is a unit mass of households in each country, so C_t and $\hat{C}_t$ also represent aggregate U.S. and E.U. household consumption. This feature makes it straightforward to identify the aggregate demand for real balances. In particular, the households' first-order conditions imply that

$$M_t/P_t = \chi^{1/\nu}(1 - R_t^{-1})^{-1/\nu}C_t^{\gamma/\nu}$$

and   (2.14)

$$\hat{M}_t/\hat{P}_t = \chi^{1/\nu}(1 - \hat{R}_t^{-1})^{-1/\nu}\hat{C}_t^{\gamma/\nu}.$$

Next, we consider the retail sector. Since (2.13) implies that $W_t/P_t = \varkappa C_t^{\gamma}$ and $\hat{W}_t/\hat{P}_t = \varkappa \hat{C}_t^{\gamma}$, real wages are proportional to aggregate consumption. Combining these expressions with the equations for marginal costs in (2.6) allows us to write the real marginal cost facing U.S. and E.U. retail firms as

$$RMC_t = (MC_t/P_t) = \frac{\varkappa^{1-\alpha}}{\alpha^{\alpha}(1-\alpha)^{1-\alpha}} Q_t^{\alpha} C_t^{\gamma(1-\alpha)}$$

and   (2.15)

$$\widehat{RMC}_t = (\widehat{MC}_t/\hat{P}_t) = \frac{\varkappa^{1-\alpha}}{\alpha^{\alpha}(1-\alpha)^{1-\alpha}} \hat{Q}_t^{\alpha} \hat{C}_t^{\gamma(1-\alpha)},$$

where $Q_t = P_t^{x}/P_t$ and $\hat{Q}_t = \hat{P}_t^{x}/\hat{P}_t$ denote real wholesale prices. Note that all retail firms within each country face the same real marginal costs and that those marginal costs are increasing in aggregate consumption, C_t and $\hat{C}_t$, and in the real wholesale prices.

Within-country risk-sharing also simplifies the demand for intermediate goods. Combining $W_t/P_t = \varkappa C_t^{\gamma}$ with (2.8), (2.11), and the market-clearing condition, $C_t^{i} = Y_t^{i}$; and $\hat{W}_t/\hat{P}_t = \varkappa \hat{C}_t^{\gamma}$ with (2.10), (2.11), and $\hat{C}_t^{i} = \hat{Y}_t^{i}$; we can write the demand for intermediates by each U.S. and E.U. retail firm as

---

4. One drawback of this modeling choice is that it also implies an infinitely elastic labor supply. This would be problematic if the goal was to explain the relation between employment and exchange rates. Household preferences would have to be calibrated to more reasonable estimates of the labor supply elasticity and the implications for within-country risk-sharing determined in the model's equilibrium. This task is relatively straightforward if there is a single financial asset or if markets are complete, but it is completely beyond the current state of knowledge when the available set of financial assets is insufficient to support complete risk-sharing. Fortunately, the goal here is to study the exchange-rate implications of incomplete markets and sticky prices. The specification for household preferences in (2.1) allows us to do this in Section 2.4 in a reasonably straightforward manner.

$$X_t^i = \left(\frac{\varkappa\alpha}{1-\alpha}\right)^{1-\alpha} \left(\frac{P_t^i}{P_t}\right)^{-\phi} Q_t^{\alpha-1} C_t^{\omega}$$

and

$$\hat{X}_t^i = \left(\frac{\varkappa\alpha}{1-\alpha}\right)^{1-\alpha} \left(\frac{\hat{P}_t^i}{\hat{P}_t}\right)^{-\phi} \hat{Q}_t^{\alpha-1} \hat{C}_t^{\omega},$$

with $\omega = 1 + \gamma(1-\alpha) > 0$. Substituting these expressions into (2.7) and (2.11), aggregating across firms in each country, and adding government consumption produces the following aggregate demand equations for each intermediate good:

$$X_t^{\mathrm{US}} = \lambda \left(\frac{P_t^{\mathrm{US}}}{P_t^{\mathrm{x}}}\right)^{-\theta} \Gamma_t Q_t^{\alpha-1} C_t^{\omega} + (1-\lambda)\left(\frac{\hat{P}_t^{\mathrm{US}}}{\hat{P}_t^{\mathrm{x}}}\right)^{-\theta} \hat{\Gamma}_t \hat{Q}_t^{\alpha-1} \hat{C}_t^{\omega} + G_t \quad (2.16)$$

and

$$X_t^{\mathrm{EU}} = \lambda \left(\frac{\hat{P}_t^{\mathrm{EU}}}{\hat{P}_t^{\mathrm{x}}}\right)^{-\theta} \hat{\Gamma}_t \hat{Q}_t^{\alpha-1} \hat{C}_t^{\omega} + (1-\lambda)\left(\frac{P_t^{\mathrm{EU}}}{P_t^{\mathrm{x}}}\right)^{-\theta} \Gamma_t Q_t^{\alpha-1} C_t^{\omega} + \hat{G}_t, \quad (2.17)$$

where

$$\Gamma_t = \left(\frac{\varkappa\alpha}{1-\alpha}\right)^{1-\alpha} \int_0^1 \left(\frac{P_t^i}{P_t}\right)^{-\phi} di \quad \text{and} \quad \hat{\Gamma}_t = \left(\frac{\varkappa\alpha}{1-\alpha}\right)^{1-\alpha} \int_0^1 \left(\frac{\hat{P}_t^i}{\hat{P}_t}\right)^{-\phi} di.$$

Note that the first two terms on the right-hand side of each equation identify the demand from domestic and foreign retailers, respectively. As such, the demand for intermediate goods depends on aggregate household consumption, real wholesale prices, retail price dispersion via Γ_t and $\hat{\Gamma}_t$, and the relative prices of individual intermediate goods. These relative prices are related to the terms of trade, $\mathcal{T} = P^{\mathrm{EU}}/S\hat{P}^{\mathrm{US}}$. More specifically, since intermediate goods are freely traded between countries, the Law of One Price implies that $P_t^{\mathrm{US}} = S_t\hat{P}_t^{\mathrm{US}}$ and $P_t^{\mathrm{EU}} = S_t\hat{P}_t^{\mathrm{EU}}$, so

$$\frac{P_t^{\mathrm{US}}}{P_t^{\mathrm{x}}} = \frac{1}{(\lambda + (1-\lambda)\mathcal{T}_t^{1-\theta})^{1/(1-\theta)}}, \qquad \frac{P_t^{\mathrm{EU}}}{P_t^{\mathrm{x}}} = \frac{\mathcal{T}_t}{(\lambda + (1-\lambda)\mathcal{T}_t^{1-\theta})^{1/(1-\theta)}},$$

$$\frac{\hat{P}_t^{\mathrm{EU}}}{\hat{P}_t^{\mathrm{x}}} = \frac{1}{(\lambda + (1-\lambda)\mathcal{T}_t^{\theta-1})^{1/(1-\theta)}}, \qquad \frac{\hat{P}_t^{\mathrm{US}}}{\hat{P}_t^{\mathrm{x}}} = \frac{\mathcal{T}_t}{(\lambda + (1-\lambda)\mathcal{T}_t^{\theta-1})^{1/(1-\theta)}}. \tag{2.18}$$

In equilibrium, market clearing requires that the terms of trade adjust to equate the aggregate demand for U.S. and E.U. goods defined in (2.16) and (2.17) with the available endowments given real wholesale prices, aggregate household consumption, and the dispersion of retail prices.

The equilibrium conditions in the asset and retail markets vary according to the degree of risk-sharing and price-stickiness. In Chapter 1 we showed that the intertemporal marginal rate of substitution (IMRS) must be equal for all households when they have access to a complete set of Arrow-Debreu securities. This, in turn, implies the familiar risk-sharing condition:

$$\mathcal{E}_{t+1}/\mathcal{E}_t = \left(C_{t+1}/C_t\right)^{\gamma} (\hat{C}_{t+1}/\hat{C}_t)^{-\gamma}. \tag{2.19}$$

Once again, we assume that the world economy is initially in a symmetric equilibrium with $C = \mathcal{E}\hat{C}$ and $\mathcal{E} = 1$ so that (2.19) becomes $\mathcal{E}_t = (C_t/\hat{C}_t)^{\gamma}$ or

$$\varepsilon_t = \gamma(c_t - \hat{c}_t), \tag{2.20}$$

where lowercase letters identify natural logs, for example, $\varepsilon_t = \ln \mathcal{E}_t$.

When the array of available assets makes it impossible for U.S. and E.U. households to share risk completely, the IMRSs for U.S. and E.U. households are constrained by the following set of first-order conditions:

$$1 = \mathbb{E}_t \left[\beta \left(\frac{C_{t+1}}{C_t} \right)^{-\gamma} \frac{R_{t+1}^i P_t}{P_{t+1}} \right] \quad \text{and} \quad 1 = \mathbb{E}_t \left[\beta \left(\frac{\hat{C}_{t+1}}{\hat{C}_t} \right)^{-\gamma} \frac{\hat{R}_{t+1}^j \hat{P}_t}{\hat{P}_{t+1}} \right], \tag{2.21}$$

where R_t^i and $\hat{R}_t^j$ denote the returns in dollars and euros on all assets i and j that are available to U.S. and E.U. households, respectively. The implications of these conditions for the link between the real exchange rate and the IMRS of U.S. and E.U. households depends on the number and type of financial assets available to all of them. For example, suppose both U.S. and E.U. households can hold a one-period bond with a euro return of $\hat{R}_{t+1}^j = R(\hat{P}_{t+1}/\hat{P}_t)$ and a dollar return of $R_{t+1}^j = R(\hat{P}_{t+1}/\hat{P}_t)(S_{t+1}/S_t)$. Then (2.21) implies that

$$\mathbb{E}_t[(C_{t+1}/C_t)^{-\gamma} (\mathcal{E}_{t+1}/\mathcal{E}_t)] = \mathbb{E}_t(\hat{C}_{t+1}/\hat{C}_t)^{-\gamma}.$$

Clearly, this restriction holds when the real exchange rate satisfies the risk-sharing condition in (2.19). However, it also holds true when

$$\mathcal{E}_{t+1}/\mathcal{E}_t = (C_{t+1}/C_t)^{\gamma} (\hat{C}_{t+1}/\hat{C}_t)^{-\gamma} + \zeta_{t+1},$$

where ζ_{t+1} is a nonzero "error term" that satisfies $\mathbb{E}_t[(C_{t+1}/C_t)^{-\gamma}\zeta_{t+1}] = 0$. We focus on the implications of incomplete risk-sharing in the second half of this chapter.

Equilibrium in the retail market depends on how firms set prices. Under flexible pricing, retail firms choose the profit-maximizing prices each period subject to the demand from domestic households identified in (2.11) and the market-clearing condition. The well-known solution to this problem is to choose a price that is a markup over marginal cost,

$$P_t^i = \frac{\phi}{\phi - 1} MC_t \quad \text{and} \quad \hat{P}_t^i = \frac{\phi}{\phi - 1} \widehat{MC}_t, \tag{2.22}$$

for all varieties $i \in [0, 1]$. By contrast, under preset and staggered pricing retail firms choose prices to maximize the value of expected future profits to their shareholders. We compare these pricing decisions with (2.22) in the analysis that follows.

Several aspects of the model deserve comment. First, the structure of production does not conform to the common framework of traded and nontraded goods. In particular, because retail firms are prohibited from supplying consumer goods to foreign households, there are no *pure* traded consumer goods in the model. Instead, each variety of consumer good represents a composite of traded intermediate goods and nontraded labor. This view of consumer goods is similar to that proposed by Burstein, Eichenbaum, and Rebelo (2006), except that labor stands in for the distribution costs such as wholesale and retail services, marketing, and advertising. More importantly, it allows the model to account for the variability of the real exchange rate when measured in terms of consumer prices.

The second feature concerns the distinction between consumer and wholesale prices. There is ample empirical evidence that the behavior of international relative prices differs at the retail level and at the dock. In particular, whereas the wholesale prices that importers face at the dock are quite variable, the prices of individual retail goods are so sticky that variations in the nominal exchange rate are reflected almost one-for-one in the real exchange rate. To accommodate these differences, we will examine models in which retail prices exhibit varying degrees of stickiness while the prices of intermediate goods remain completely flexible.

Finally, the model abstracts from production in the intermediate goods sector. In Chapter 1 we saw how the production/investment decisions of firms affected the behavior of the terms of trade in an economy with flexible prices. Since the prices of intermediate goods are flexible in the models we study here, adding production to the intermediate sector would have similar implications for the terms of trade. We abstract from these effects in what follows to better focus on the role of price-stickiness and incomplete markets.

2.2 Sticky Prices

We now examine the implications of price-stickiness for the behavior of the exchange rate when markets are complete. In particular, we first focus on the case where retail firms set prices one period in advance. In this setting we can easily examine how price-stickiness contributes to the dynamics of nominal and real exchange rates via overshooting. We then extend the model to incorporate staggered price-setting as found in Calvo (1983) in order to study the behavior of exchange rates in a setting where consumer prices exhibit empirically plausible dynamics.

2.2.1 Preset Price-Setting

Let us begin with the pricing problem facing U.S. retail firms. Firm i's objective is to choose P_t^i to maximize the value of period-t profits to its shareholders based on information available in period $t - 1$. This means that P_t^i is chosen to maximize

$$\mathbb{V}_{t-1}^i = \mathbb{E}_{t-1}\left[\beta\left(\frac{C_t}{C_{t-1}}\right)^{-\gamma}\left\{\left(\frac{P_t^i}{P_t} - \frac{MC_t}{P_t}\right)\left(\frac{P_t^i}{P_t}\right)^{-\phi}C_t\right\}\right]. \qquad (2.23)$$

There are two points to note here: First, the term in parentheses identifies the real period-t profit (i.e., the difference between the real price for variety i and the real marginal cost multiplied by the total demand for good i by U.S. households). Second, there is no loss of generality in using the IMRS of U.S. households to compute the real value of this profit to shareholders because under complete markets it equals the IMRS of E.U. households measured in terms of the U.S. consumption basket.

Maximizing $\mathbb{V}_{t-1}^i$ with respect to P_t^i gives

$$P_t^i = \Phi\mathbb{E}_{t-1}MC_t. \qquad (2.24)$$

Thus, firm i sets its price as a markup over expected marginal cost, $\mathbb{E}_{t-1}MC_t$. The markup, Φ, depends on $\frac{\phi}{\phi-1}$ (as in the case of flexible pricing), multiplied by a risk factor that accounts for the uncertainty the firm faces concerning future demand and marginal cost.[5] The implications of preset pricing in Europe follow in an analogous manner. In particular, in a symmetric equilibrium, each E.U. retail firm i will set prices as

$$\hat{P}_t^i = \Phi\mathbb{E}_{t-1}\widehat{MC}_t. \tag{2.25}$$

The markup, Φ, is the same as in equation (2.24) because in a symmetric equilibrium E.U. and U.S. retailers face the same conditions in their respective markets.

The implications of (2.24) and (2.25) for the behavior of U.S. and E.U. price indices are straightforward. Since firms within each country face the same marginal costs and choose the same markup, there will be no difference between the prices of different varieties within each country. Consequently, the aggregate U.S. and E.U. price indices are

$$P_t = \Phi\mathbb{E}_{t-1}MC_t \quad \text{and} \quad \hat{P}_t = \Phi\mathbb{E}_{t-1}\widehat{MC}_t.$$

Thus, preset pricing makes the price indices in period t a function of expected marginal costs based on period-$t-1$ information. This feature makes consumer prices sticky in the sense that they cannot respond to contemporaneous unanticipated events. Specifically, substituting for marginal costs in the above expressions and log-linearizing gives

$$p_t = \text{const.} + \mathbb{E}_{t-1}\left[p_t^{x} + \gamma\left(\frac{1-\alpha}{\alpha}\right)c_t \right]$$

and $\hspace{9cm}$ (2.26)

$$\hat{p}_t = \text{const.} + \mathbb{E}_{t-1}\left[\hat{p}_t^{x} + \gamma\left(\frac{1-\alpha}{\alpha}\right)\hat{c}_t \right].$$

Thus, consumer prices in period t reflect firms' prior expectations concerning household consumption and the wholesale prices.

We are now ready to examine the exchange-rate implications of price-stickiness. First, we log-linearized the definitions of the wholesale price indices to give

$$p_t^{x} = \lambda p_t^{US} + (1-\lambda)p_t^{EU} \quad \text{and} \quad \hat{p}_t^{x} = \lambda\hat{p}_t^{EU} + (1-\lambda)\hat{p}_t^{US}.$$

In the absence of trade costs, the Law of One Price applies in wholesale markets, so $p_t^{US} = s_t + \hat{p}_t^{US}$ and $p_t^{EU} = s_t + \hat{p}_t^{EU}$. Combining these restrictions with the preceding expressions yields

$$p_t^{x} - s_t - \hat{p}_t^{x} = -(2\lambda - 1)\tau_t. \tag{2.27}$$

Next, we combine the pricing equations in (2.26) with (2.27) and the definition of the real exchange rate to get

$$\varepsilon_t = s_t - \mathbb{E}_{t-1}s_t + (2\lambda - 1)\mathbb{E}_{t-1}\tau_t - \left(\frac{1-\alpha}{\alpha}\right)\gamma\mathbb{E}_{t-1}(c_t - \hat{c}_t). \tag{2.28}$$

---

5. Detailed derivations of this and other key equations are provided in the appendix.

Taking expectations on both sides of this equation and combining the result with the risk-sharing condition in (2.20) produces

$$\mathbb{E}_{t-1}(c_t - \hat{c}_t) = \frac{\alpha}{\gamma}(2\lambda - 1)\mathbb{E}_{t-1}\tau_t. \tag{2.29}$$

Thus, the expected log ratio of U.S. to E.U. consumption is proportional to the expected log terms of trade. We can now use this expression to rewrite (2.28) as

$$\varepsilon_t = s_t - \mathbb{E}_{t-1}s_t + \alpha(2\lambda - 1)\mathbb{E}_{t-1}\tau_t. \tag{2.30}$$

Equation (2.30) has two important implications: First, all *unexpected* variations in the real exchange rate come from the nominal rate (i.e., $\varepsilon_t - \mathbb{E}_{t-1}\varepsilon_t = s_t - \mathbb{E}_{t-1}s_t$) because all consumer prices are sticky. Second, the real exchange rate can be expected to vary owing to anticipated changes in the terms of trade because the production of retail goods is biased toward the use of domestic intermediates, that is, $\lambda > 1/2$.

The equilibrium terms of trade are determined in wholesale markets. Recall that wholesale prices are flexible and adjust to clear world markets given the endowments of each good, government demand, and the demand from U.S. and E.U. retail firms. To characterize the behavior of these prices, let E_t^{US} and E_t^{EU} denote the endowments of U.S. and E.U. goods net of government spending. Market clearing requires that $EN_t^{US} = X_t$ and $EN_t^{US} = X_t^{EU}$, where X_t^{US} and X_t^{EU} are the total demands for U.S. and E.U. goods identified in (2.16) and (2.17). Thus, in equilibrium, $E_t^{US} = X_t^{US} - G_t$ and $E_t^{EU} = X_t^{EU} - \hat{G}_t$. Assuming that government spending plans are always feasible (i.e., $G_t < X_t$ and $\hat{G}_t < \hat{X}_t$), we can log-linearize these equilibrium conditions to give

$$e_t^{US} = \text{const.} + \omega\left[\lambda c_t + (1 - \lambda)\hat{c}_t\right] - (1 - \alpha)\left[\lambda q_t + (1 - \lambda)\hat{q}_t\right] + 2\theta\lambda(1 - \lambda)\tau_t$$

and

$$e_t^{EU} = \text{const.} + \omega\left[(1 - \lambda)c_t + \lambda\hat{c}_t\right] - (1 - \alpha)\left[(1 - \lambda)q_t + \lambda\hat{q}_t\right] - 2\theta\lambda(1 - \lambda)\tau_t.$$

To find the equilibrium terms of trade, we first combine the equations above with the identity

$$q_t - \hat{q}_t = p_t^X - p_t + \hat{p}_t - \hat{p}_t^X = \varepsilon_t - (2\lambda - 1)\tau_t$$

to give

$$\begin{aligned} e_t^{US} - e_t^{EU} &= \left[4\theta\lambda(1 - \lambda) + (2\lambda - 1)^2(1 - \alpha)\right]\tau_t \\ &\quad + (2\lambda - 1)\omega(c_t - \hat{c}_t) - (2\lambda - 1)(1 - \alpha)\varepsilon_t. \end{aligned} \tag{2.31}$$

Next, we substitute for the real exchange rate with the risk-sharing condition in (2.20) to get

$$e_t^{US} - e_t^{EU} = \left[4\theta\lambda(1 - \lambda) + (2\lambda - 1)^2(1 - \alpha)\right]\tau_t + (2\lambda - 1)(c_t - \hat{c}_t). \tag{2.32}$$

Finally, we apply the expectations operator to both sides of (2.32) and substitute for $\mathbb{E}_{t-1}(c_t - \hat{c}_t)$ with (2.29). Rearranging the result produces the following equation for the expected terms of trade:

$$\mathbb{E}_{t-1}\tau_t = \xi\mathbb{E}_{t-1}[e_t^{\text{US}} - e_t^{\text{EU}}], \tag{2.33}$$

where

$$\xi = \frac{1}{4\theta\lambda(1 - \lambda) + (2\lambda - 1)^2[1 - \alpha + (\alpha/\gamma)]} > 0.$$

Equation (2.33) shows that the expected terms of trade vary directly with expectations concerning the relative supplies of U.S. and E.U. intermediate goods net of government spending. In particular, an expected increase in the supply of U.S. goods is associated with an anticipated deterioration in the U.S. terms of trade because it stimulates demand by lowering the relative prices of U.S. goods and increases U.S. consumption.

All that now remains is to pin down the nominal exchange rate. For this purpose, we use the log-linearized version of the interest parity condition,

$$\mathbb{E}_t\Delta s_{t+1} = r_t - \hat{r}_t + \delta_t, \tag{2.34}$$

where δ_t denotes the foreign exchange risk premium. In Chapter 1 we showed that $\delta_t = \mathbb{CV}_t(s_{t+1}, \gamma c_{t+1} + p_{t+1})$ under complete markets. Here, the presence of price-stickiness implies that $\delta_t = \gamma\mathbb{CV}_t(s_{t+1}, c_{t+1})$ because consumer prices in period $t + 1$ depend on period-t expectations. We also use the log-linearized versions of (2.14):

$$m_t - p_t = \text{const.} + \frac{\gamma}{\nu}c_t - \sigma r_t \quad \text{and} \quad \hat{m}_t - \hat{p}_t = \text{const.} + \frac{\gamma}{\nu}\hat{c}_t - \sigma\hat{r}_t, \tag{2.35}$$

where $\sigma = \frac{1}{\nu}(R - 1)^{-1} > 0$. For the present, we assume that central banks have complete control of their domestic money supplies, so (2.35) approximates the market-clearing conditions in the U.S. and E.U. money markets with m_t and $\hat{m}_t$ denoting the exogenous supplies of dollars and euros.

Exchange-Rate Overshooting

We can study the implications of price-stickiness for the behavior of the real and nominal exchange rates with the aid of a simple phase diagram. For this purpose, we use (2.30) and combine equations (2.20), (2.34), and (2.35) to give

$$\mathbb{E}_t\Delta\varepsilon_{t+1} = \alpha(2\lambda - 1)\xi\mathbb{E}_t(e_{t+1}^{\text{US}} - e_{t+1}^{\text{EU}}) - \varepsilon_t \tag{2.36a}$$

and

$$\mathbb{E}_t\Delta s_{t+1} = \frac{1}{\sigma}s_t - \frac{\nu - 1}{\sigma\nu}\varepsilon_t - \frac{1}{\sigma}\left(m_t - \hat{m}_t\right) + \delta_t. \tag{2.36b}$$

These equations govern the dynamics of the nominal and real exchange rates for given values of the money stocks, $m_t - \hat{m}_t$, the risk premium, δ_t, and the (net) endowments of intermediate goods, e_{t+1}^{US} and e_{t+1}^{EU}. When there is no change in any of these variables, the expected rates of real and nominal depreciation on the left-hand side of each equation must equal the actual rate of depreciation, so the equations will govern the actual dynamics of real and nominal rates while $m_t - \hat{m}_t$, δ_t, and $e_{t+1}^{\text{US}} - e_{t+1}^{\text{EU}}$ are constant.

Figure 2.1 shows the phase diagram associated with (2.36). The $\mathbb{E}_t\Delta\varepsilon_{t+1} = 0$ schedule is the vertical line at $\varepsilon_t = \alpha(2\lambda - 1)\xi\mathbb{E}_t[e_{t+1}^{\text{US}} - e_{t+1}^{\text{EU}}]$, and the $\mathbb{E}_t\Delta s_{t+1} = 0$

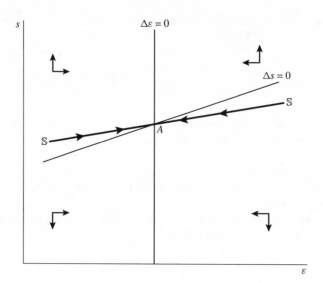

FIGURE 2.1   Phase diagram for real and nominal exchange-rate dynamics.

schedule has a slope of $1 - 1/v$, which we assume is positive. The steady state is depicted by point A. Away from the steady state, the dynamics of the model has a saddle-path property. If the point implied by the current nominal and real exchange rate is not on the saddle path $\mathbb{SS}$, the exchange rate will eventually explode or implode. Nominal and real exchange rates represented by points on $\mathbb{SS}$ will eventually attain their steady state values.

We can use the phase diagram to consider the classic example of a monetary shock—a permanent increase in the U.S. money supply at $t = 1$ from m to m'. Let us assume that at $t = 0$ the economy is in steady state at point A in Figure 2.2. In the long run, the nominal exchange rate and U.S. price level must increase in proportion to the change in the money supply. Since these movements leave the steady state real exchange rate unchanged, the new steady state for the economy will be at point C. The dynamic effects of the change in money supply are shown by the arrows. The immediate effect of the increase in the money supply is for the nominal and real exchange rate to "jump" to a point on the saddle path associated with the new steady state. Since prices are preset, the associated change in the nominal and real exchange rates must be equal, placing the economy at point B (i.e., at the intersection of $\mathbb{SS}$ and the 45° line that passes through point A). After $t = 1$, the economy moves along the saddle path toward the new steady state at point C. During this period both the real and nominal exchange rates depreciate until they reach their new steady state values of e_∞ and s_∞.

Figure 2.2 shows that the initial depreciation of the dollar from s_0 to s_1 is greater than the long-run depreciation of s_0 to s_∞. This phenomenon is known as "exchange-rate overshooting"—a term first coined by Dornbusch (1976). Overshooting occurs here because the increase in the U.S. money supply induces a fall in the spread between U.S. and E.U. interest rates. This, in turn, makes E.U. bonds relatively more attractive, so in accordance with interest parity (with a constant risk premium) there must be a compensating expected appreciation of the dollar (i.e., $\mathbb{E}_t \Delta s_{t+1} < 0$) from $t = 1$

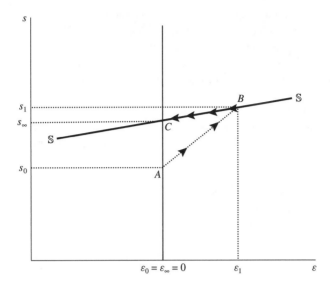

FIGURE 2.2   Exchange-rate overshooting in response to a U.S. money supply shock.

onward. The initial jump in the nominal exchange rate must therefore overshoot its long-run level to be consistent with these expectations.

We can gain a deeper understanding of this adjustment process by examining the risk-sharing and money-market-clearing conditions. In particular, if we combine (2.20) with (2.35) we obtain

$$m_t - \hat{m}_t + \hat{p}_t - p_t = \tfrac{\gamma}{\nu}(c_t - \hat{c}_t) - \sigma(r_t - \hat{r}_t) = \tfrac{1}{\nu}\varepsilon_t - \sigma(r_t - \hat{r}_t). \quad (2.37)$$

Since consumer prices are set one period in advance, this equilibrium condition implies that the initial change in the U.S. money supply, $m' - m$, must be absorbed by the real exchange rate and interest rates:

$$m' - m = \tfrac{1}{\nu}(\varepsilon_1 - \varepsilon_0) - \sigma[(r_1 - \hat{r}_1) - (r_0 - \hat{r}_0)].$$

However, since the stickiness in consumer prices also implies that $\varepsilon_1 - \varepsilon_0 = s_1 - s_0$, the nominal exchange rate cannot immediately depreciate to its new long-run level while maintaining equilibrium in the money markets when $\nu > 1$. If it did (i.e., if $s_1 - s_0 = m' - m$), then the preceding market-clearing condition implies that $(r_1 - \hat{r}_1) - (r_0 - \hat{r}_0) = -\tfrac{\nu-1}{\nu\sigma}(m' - m)$, so the spread between U.S. and E.U. rates would fall. This in turn implies that the dollar would be expected to appreciate further, so s_1 cannot be the new long-run level for the nominal exchange rate. In sum, it is the inability of the real exchange rate to immediately adjust to a level that clears the money markets without reducing the spread between U.S. and E.U. interest rates that induces overshooting.[6]

───────────────

6. Clearly, the adjustment mechanism differs when $\nu < 1$. We leave the analysis of this case as an exercise at the end of this chapter.

The overshooting mechanism described here is very similar to the one found in the Dornbusch (1976) model. In particular, money demand in the Dornbusch model is a function of income rather than consumption, but the difference between U.S. and foreign income depends positively on the real dollar exchange rate. As a consequence, the expected rate of nominal depreciation has the same form as equation (2.36b), except that the coefficients on s_t and ε_t have different interpretations. In this setting, the immediate impact of the monetary shock is a real depreciation of the dollar, which stimulates foreign income and lowers U.S. income. As a consequence, the spread between U.S. and foreign interest rates must fall to clear the money markets so the initial depreciation of the dollar must overshoot its long-run level.

Exchange-Rate Dynamics

We can gain a fuller understanding of how exchange rates behave by examining the algebraic solution to the model. For this purpose, we first rewrite (2.36b) as

$$s_t = b\mathbb{E}_t s_{t+1} + (1-b)\left\{m_t - \hat{m}_t - \sigma\delta_t + \tfrac{\nu-1}{\nu}\varepsilon_t\right\},$$

where $b = \frac{\sigma}{1+\sigma} < 1$. Solving forward under the assumption that $\lim_{j\to\infty} b^j \mathbb{E}_t s_{t+j} = 0$ gives

$$s_t = (1-b)\,\mathbb{E}_t \sum_{i=0}^{\infty} b^i \left\{m_{t+i} - \hat{m}_{t+i} - \sigma\delta_{t+i} + \tfrac{\nu-1}{\nu}\varepsilon_{t+i}\right\}. \tag{2.38}$$

Next, we use (2.38) to compute the error in forecasting the period-t exchange rate:

$$s_t - \mathbb{E}_{t-1}s_t \tag{2.39}$$

$$= (1-b) \sum_{i=0}^{\infty} b^i \left(\mathbb{E}_t - \mathbb{E}_{t-1}\right)\left\{m_{t+i} - \hat{m}_{t+i} - \sigma\delta_{t+i} + \tfrac{\nu-1}{\nu}\varepsilon_{t+i}\right\}.$$

Equations (2.30) and (2.33) together imply that

$$\varepsilon_t = s_t - \mathbb{E}_{t-1}s_t + \alpha(2\lambda - 1)\xi\mathbb{E}_{t-1}(e_t^{\mathrm{US}} - e_t^{\mathrm{EU}}). \tag{2.40}$$

It therefore follows that $\left(\mathbb{E}_t - \mathbb{E}_{t-1}\right)\varepsilon_{t+i} = \alpha(2\lambda - 1)\xi\left(\mathbb{E}_t - \mathbb{E}_{t-1}\right)(e_{t+i}^{\mathrm{US}} - e_{t+i}^{\mathrm{EU}})$ for $i > 0$ and $\left(\mathbb{E}_t - \mathbb{E}_{t-1}\right)\varepsilon_t = s_t - \mathbb{E}_{t-1}s_t$. Using these expressions to substitute for $\left(\mathbb{E}_t - \mathbb{E}_{t-1}\right)\varepsilon_{t+i}$ in (2.39) gives

$$s_t - \mathbb{E}_{t-1}s_t = (1-b)\Theta \sum_{i=0}^{\infty} b^i (\mathbb{E}_t - \mathbb{E}_{t-1})(m_{t+i} - \hat{m}_{t+i} - \sigma\delta_{t+i})$$

$$+ \alpha(2\lambda - 1)\xi(1-b)\Theta \sum_{i=1}^{\infty} b^i (\mathbb{E}_t - \mathbb{E}_{t-1})(e_{t+i}^{\mathrm{US}} - e_{t+i}^{\mathrm{EU}}), \tag{2.41}$$

where $\Theta = \frac{\nu}{\nu+(1-b)(\nu-1)}$.

Equation (2.41) shows how the nominal exchange rate initially responds to information concerning money supplies, the risk premium, and the endowments of intermediate goods. For example, in the case of an unanticipated permanent increase in the U.S. money supply of Δm, the first term on the right shows that the dollar immediately depreciates by $\Theta \Delta m$. If v is greater than one (as assumed in drawing Figures 2.1 and 2.2), then Θ is greater than one, so this initial response represents overshooting. Conversely, if v is less than one, the initial depreciation of the dollar, $\Theta \Delta m$, is less than the long-run depreciation, Δm, so there is exchange-rate undershooting. Beyond this example, equation (2.41) also shows that the exchange-rate response to monetary shocks depends on how they change the anticipated future path of the money supply. In particular shocks that have more persistent effects change the anticipated path of the future money supply farther out into the future and thereby have a larger initial impact on the exchange rate.

The second line in equation (2.41) shows how the nominal exchange rate reacts to information concerning the net endowments of intermediate goods. In particular, here we see that the dollar depreciates in response to an upward revision in the anticipated *future* endowments of U.S. goods relative to E.U. goods (net of government spending). Intuitively, these revisions must be accompanied by an expected deterioration in the future U.S. terms of trade in order to clear wholesale markets and a fall in U.S. consumption relative to E.U. consumption. As a result, the future spreads between U.S. and E.U. interest rates are expected to fall to clear the money market triggering an immediate depreciation of the dollar. Note, though, that changes in the current endowments have no exchange-rate effect. In particular, (2.40) and (2.41) imply that a temporary shock to either e_t^{US} or e_t^{EU} has no impact on either ε_t or s_t. In short, exchange rates are completely insulated from the effects of temporary real shocks.

The existence of this insulation effect nicely illustrates the role played by price-stickiness and complete markets. Recall that under preset pricing, retail firms set the prices of consumer goods one period in advance. As a result, those prices cannot incorporate the changes in marginal costs that arise from unanticipated shocks in the wholesale markets. Instead, all the effects must be borne by the terms of trade.

To see why this is so, we first use (2.37) to write

$$\left(1 - \mathbb{E}_{t-1}\right) \left(m_t - \hat{m}_t\right) - \left(1 - \mathbb{E}_{t-1}\right) \left(p_t - \hat{p}_t\right)$$

$$= \tfrac{1}{v} \left(1 - \mathbb{E}_{t-1}\right) \varepsilon_t - \sigma \left(1 - \mathbb{E}_{t-1}\right) \left(r_t - \hat{r}_t\right),$$

where $\left(1 - \mathbb{E}_{t-1}\right) \varepsilon_t = \varepsilon_t - \mathbb{E}_{t-1}\varepsilon_t$, and so on. Next, note that $\left(1 - \mathbb{E}_{t-1}\right)\left(p_t - \hat{p}_t\right) = 0$ and $\left(1 - \mathbb{E}_{t-1}\right) \varepsilon_t = \left(1 - \mathbb{E}_{t-1}\right) s_t$ with preset pricing. Thus, if there is no shock to the money stocks or risk premium,

$$s_t - \mathbb{E}_{t-1}s_t = v\sigma \left(1 - \mathbb{E}_{t-1}\right) \left(r_t - \hat{r}_t\right) = v\sigma \left(\mathbb{E}_t - \mathbb{E}_{t-1}\right) \Delta s_{t+1}.$$

This equation shows that shocks to the net endowments can only affect exchange rates if they change the expected rate of nominal depreciation. Now if the shock is purely temporary, it will have no exchange-rate effects beyond the current period. Under these circumstances, $\mathbb{E}_t s_{t+1} = \mathbb{E}_{t-1}s_{t+1}$, so the preceding expression simplifies to $s_t - \mathbb{E}_{t-1}s_t = -v\sigma \left(s_t - \mathbb{E}_{t-1}s_t\right)$. Clearly, this implication of market clearing can only be satisfied if $s_t = \mathbb{E}_{t-1}s_t$, which in turn means that $\varepsilon_t - \mathbb{E}_{t-1}\varepsilon_t = \gamma \left(1 - \mathbb{E}_{t-1}\right) \left(c_t - \hat{c}_t\right) = 0$. Thus, temporary shocks to the supplies of intermediate goods have no effect on nominal and real exchange rates or relative consumption. Equation (2.32) shows that any increase in $e_t^{US} - e_t^{EU}$ must be accompanied by either a rise in relative U.S.

consumption and/or a deterioration in the terms of trade if wholesale markets are to clear. The effects of a temporary shock to $e_t^{US} - e_t^{EU}$ must therefore be borne entirely by an adjustment in the terms of trade.

Equations (2.40) and (2.41) also provide perspective on the PPP Puzzle. Recall from Chapter 1 that shocks to the real exchange rate appear to have a half-life in the 3- to 5-year range. Since unexpected shocks to the nominal rate must be serially uncorrelated, equation (2.40) implies that variations in $\mathbb{E}_{t-1}(e_t^{US} - e_t^{EU})$ account for all of this persistence. This is unfortunate. Since variations in $\mathbb{E}_{t-1}(e_t^{US} - e_t^{EU})$ have nothing to do with price-stickiness, the model does not provide any insight into why the half-lives of real exchange rates are so long. On the other hand, price-stickiness does affect the volatility of the real exchange rate. Equations (2.40) and (2.41) show that news concerning current and future money stocks, the risk premium, and the future net endowments all contribute to the volatility of the real exchange rate. This would not be true if retail prices were flexible. When all retail firms set prices as a markup over current marginal costs as in equation (2.22), the equilibrium real exchange rate is given by $\varepsilon_t = \alpha(2\lambda - 1)\xi(e_t^{US} - e_t^{EU})$, so only shocks to the current net endowments contribute to its volatility. Price-stickiness will therefore add to the volatility of the real exchange rate if most shocks to the economy contain news about the current and future monetary policy, the risk premia, and the future net endowments of intermediate goods.

2.2.2 Staggered Price-Setting

We now amend the model to incorporate a more realistic representation of price-setting in retail markets and the conduct of monetary policy by central banks. In particular, we now assume that retail firms set prices for multiple periods in a staggered fashion as first formulated by Calvo (1983). This form of price-stickiness has been widely adopted in the macroeconomics literature because it provides empirically reasonable inflation dynamics that is grounded in the pricing decisions of individual firms. We also change the way that central banks conduct monetary policy. Instead of assuming that they control the money stock directly, we consider a more realistic setting where each central bank conducts open market operations to control short-term nominal interest rates.

The Calvo Model

In the Calvo model each retail firm has the opportunity to reset the price for its consumer good in period t with probability $\wp$. This probability is the same across firms and is independent of the time elapsed since the last adjustment. Thus, each period a fraction $1 - \wp$ of firms keeps its prices the same. In what follows we focus only on how U.S. retail firms set prices because the behavior of E.U. firms is exactly analogous.

Let $P_t^*(i)$ denote the price set by U.S. retail firm i when adjusting prices in period t. Recall that households can only buy consumer goods from domestic retailers (they cannot import consumer goods from foreign retailers). Market clearing therefore implies that the output of retailer i, Y_t^i, equals the domestic demand for good i:

$$Y_t^i = C_t^i = (P_t^i/P_t)^{-\phi}C_t, \tag{2.42}$$

where $C_t = \int_0^1 C_{n,t} \, dn$ is aggregate U.S. consumption. When firm i has the opportunity to reset its price, it chooses $P_t^*(i)$ to maximize

$$\mathbb{E}_t \sum_{j=0}^{\infty} \left\{ \Lambda_{t,t+j} \left[Y_{t+j}^i \left(P_t^*(i) - MC_{t+j}(i) \right) \right] \right\}, \tag{2.43}$$

subject to (2.42), where $MC_t(i)$ denotes the marginal cost for firm i in period t.

Equation (2.43) is the expected present value of future profits that will accrue at the new price level given the path of future marginal costs. $\Lambda_{t,t+j}$ is the stochastic discount factor between periods t and $t + j$, which is equal to $[\beta(1 - \wp)]^j$ times the IMRS between t and $t + j$ for the owners of the retail firm. Of course, under complete risk-sharing all households have the same IMRS, so $\Lambda_{t,t+j} = [\beta(1 - \wp)]^j (C_{t+j}/C_t)^{-\gamma}$. Note also that future profits are more heavily discounted when the probability of resetting prices, $\wp$, is large. When choosing $P_t^*(i)$, each firm is only concerned about future costs and demand while the price remains in effect. Larger values for $\wp$ reduce the probability that the price will be in effect in $t + j$ and so reduce the influence of output and marginal costs in $t + j$ on the period-t decision.

The first-order condition for the price-setting problem can be written as

$$P_t^*(i) = \frac{\phi}{\phi - 1} \mathbb{E}_t \sum_{j=0}^{\infty} \Psi_{t,t+j} MC_{t+i}(i), \tag{2.44}$$

where

$$\Psi_{t,t+j} = \Lambda_{t,t+j} \frac{C_{t+j}}{C_t} \left(\frac{P_{t+j}}{P_t} \right)^{\phi} \left\{ \mathbb{E}_t \sum_{j=0}^{\infty} \Lambda_{t,t+j} \frac{C_{t+j}}{C_t} \left(\frac{P_{t+j}}{P_t} \right)^{\phi} \right\}^{-1}.$$

Thus, the new price is a markup on the present value of future marginal costs. In contrast to the model of preset pricing, firms are not just concerned about current marginal costs. They recognize that they may not have the opportunity to reset prices for many periods, so the price set at t also reflects expectations of future marginal costs. Firms also set prices with regard to future demand. Expectations concerning future demand enter (2.44) via the adjusted discount factor $\Psi_{t,t+j}$. In particular, future marginal costs are discounted less (i.e., $\Psi_{t,t+i}$ is larger) when either consumption growth or inflation is higher because both imply a greater future demand while the price of the good remains fixed.

Recall that in our model all retail firms face the same marginal costs as shown in equation (2.6). This means that all U.S. retail firms resetting prices in period t face the same price-setting problem, and so will reset their prices to the same level, P_t^*. Under these circumstances, the U.S. consumer price index in (2.3) becomes

$$P_t = \left\{ (1 - \wp) P_{t-1}^{1-\phi} + \wp \left(P_t^* \right)^{1-\phi} \right\}^{\frac{1}{1-\phi}}.$$

Dividing both sides of this expression by P_{t-1} and log-linearizing the result around the point where $P_t^* = P_{t-1}$ gives

$$\Delta p_t = \wp \left(p_t^* - p_{t-1} \right). \tag{2.45}$$

Thus, U.S. inflation depends on the frequency with which individual retailers reset prices and the difference between the logs of the newly set price and last period's aggregate price level, $p_t^* - p_{t-1}$. We can express this term using a log-linear approximation to (2.44) with $P_t^*(i) = P_t^*$. Substituting the result into (2.45) gives

$$\Delta p_t = \kappa \mathbb{E}_t \sum_{i=0}^{\infty} \beta^i \left\{ rmc_{t+i} + \ln \tfrac{\phi}{\phi-1} \right\}, \tag{2.46}$$

where $\kappa = \wp \left(1 - \beta(1 - \wp)\right) / (1 - \wp) > 0$ and rmc_t denotes the log of real marginal costs facing U.S. retail firms identified in (2.15).

Equation (2.46) shows that inflation is forward looking even though individual prices may be constant for many periods. Changes in the U.S. price level are driven solely by the decisions of retailers who are currently resetting prices, and these decisions are driven by expectations concerning future real marginal costs.

We assume that all E.U. retail firms set their prices in an exactly analogous manner. E.U. inflation is therefore represented by

$$\Delta \hat{p}_t = \kappa \mathbb{E}_t \sum_{i=0}^{\infty} \beta^i \left\{ \widehat{rmc}_{t+i} + \ln \tfrac{\phi}{\phi-1} \right\}, \tag{2.47}$$

where $\widehat{rmc}_t$ is the log real marginal cost facing all E.U. retail firms identified in (2.15). Note that (2.46) and (2.47) do not include the IMRS of the retail firms' owners. The degree of risk-sharing among owners does affect inflation via the price-setting decisions of firms, but the effects are second-order and so do not show up in (2.46) and (2.47) because these equations are derived from log-linearizations of the firms' first-order conditions. Thus, although the derivation of (2.46) and (2.47) assumes complete risk-sharing, the equations also represent the approximate dynamics of inflation when markets are incomplete. We make use of this result in what follows.

Taylor Rules

The preceding analysis showed how the dynamics of real and nominal exchange rates are related to the equilibrium conditions in money markets under the assumption that central banks have complete control of the money supplies. However, modern macroeconomic models formulate monetary equilibrium rather differently. In particular, these models recognize that monetary policy is conducted with particular macroeconomic objectives, such as price stability, in mind and as a result the policy variables are endogenously determined as central banks react to changing macroeconomic conditions. Furthermore, since the mid-1980s short-term nominal interest rates have become the policy instrument used by most central banks. The assumed presence of an exogenous money supply is simply a poor representation of how actual monetary policy is conducted.

We now represent monetary policy as a policy rule that determines the short-term interest rate. In so doing, we abstract from the details of how central banks conduct open market operations or other transactions with the banking system to achieve a particular interest rate target. We simply assume that the central banks can achieve their target. This simplification is standard in modern macroeconomic models and is innocuous unless the economy is in the midst of a financial crisis that makes the banking system unstable. More specifically, we assume that central banks set short-term nominal interest rates in response to expected domestic inflation and the "output gap," where the latter is defined as the difference between the log of current GDP, y_t, and the log of GDP if prices were flexible, y_t^F:

$$r_t = r + (1 + \psi_\pi)\mathbb{E}_t \Delta p_{t+1} + \psi_y(y_t - y_t^F) + v_t, \tag{2.48a}$$

$$\hat{r}_t = r + (1 + \psi_\pi)\mathbb{E}_t \Delta \hat{p}_{t+1} + \psi_y(\hat{y}_t - \hat{y}_t^F) + \hat{v}_t, \tag{2.48b}$$

where ψ_π and ψ_y are positive coefficients, and r denotes the level of short-term interest rates if there is no output gap and (expected) inflation is at the central banks' target of zero. Following Taylor (1999), interest rate rules like those in (2.48) are commonly referred to as Taylor rules. Equations (2.48a) and (2.48b) also include "policy shocks," v_t and $\hat{v}_t$, that represent the source of unanticipated deviations in monetary policy.

The implications and efficacy of the Taylor rules in (2.48) have been extensively analyzed in closed-economy models. In particular, Woodford (2003) derives conditions under which the equilibrium behavior of both nominal and real variables is uniquely pinned down by the exogenous shocks hitting the economy. Clearly, determinacy of this type is a minimal requirement for an effective policy. Woodfood shows that determinacy can be achieved if interest rates react aggressively to variations in inflation, that is, if ψ_π is greater than zero. This condition is known as Taylor's principle. Benigno and Benigno (2008) show that this result generalizes to a two-country model with Calvo price-setting, provided both central banks are equally aggressive in responding to inflation. The Taylor rules in (2.48) assume that both central banks react in the same way to variations in inflation and the output gap.

Two further aspects of the Taylor rules in (2.48) deserve comment. First, central banks are assumed to set the current level of interest rates without regard to their prior level. This means that a sudden jump in, say, expected inflation would trigger an immediate rise in interest rates. In practice, however, central banks appear to adjust interest rates in a series of steps to achieve a target level consistent with the view of inflation and the output gap. Adding the lagged interest rate to the Taylor rules in (2.48) would allow us to model this form of interest-rate smoothing, but it would not alter the basic exchange-rate implications of the model.

The second aspect concerns the omission of the exchange rate. Clarida, Gali, and Gertler (1998) find empirical support for the notion that some central banks raise their interest rates when their currency depreciates. Despite this, the question of whether central banks *should* set their interest rate targets with respect to inflation, the output gap, *and* the real exchange rate remains open. Benigno and Benigno (2008) show that it is possible to achieve determinacy without the real exchange rate in Taylor rules. Moreover, as we will see later, variations in short-term interest rates based on (2.48) are positively correlated with the equilibrium real exchange rate. Thus, as a purely empirical matter, it is not necessary to include exchange rates in the Taylor rules to account for the findings of Clarida, Gali, and Gertler (1998).

Equilibrium Conditions

We derive the equilibrium conditions that govern the behavior of the real and nominal exchange rates in two steps. First, we identify the equilibrium real exchange rate and the terms of trade that would prevail if all prices were flexible. Second, we use the behavior of these variables to derive the equilibrium dynamics under staggered price-setting.

Characterizing the equilibrium of the model when all prices are flexible is straightforward. In this case equation (2.6) shows that all retail firms choose prices as a markup over marginal costs. Since marginal costs are the same for every firm within each country, (2.6) also implies that $P_t = \frac{\phi}{\phi-1} MC_t$ and $\hat{P}_t = \frac{\phi}{\phi-1} \widehat{MC}_t$. Substituting for marginal costs in these equations and taking logs gives

$$p_t = \text{const.} + p_t^{\text{x}} + \gamma \Big(\frac{1-\alpha}{\alpha}\Big) c_t \quad \text{and} \quad \hat{p}_t = \text{const.} + \hat{p}_t^{\text{x}} + \gamma \Big(\frac{1-\alpha}{\alpha}\Big) \hat{c}_t. \quad (2.49)$$

When these equations are combined with the identity, $\varepsilon_t \equiv s_t + \hat{p}_t - p_t$, and the risk-sharing condition in (2.20), we find that

$$\varepsilon_t = \alpha(s_t + \hat{p}_t^{\text{x}} - p_t^{\text{x}}) = \alpha(2\lambda - 1)\tau_t. \quad (2.50)$$

Thus, the real exchange rate is proportional to the terms of trade when prices are flexible and risk-sharing is complete. This means that the equilibrium terms of trade are entirely determined by the relative supplies of intermediate goods. In particular, if we use (2.50) and the risk-sharing condition to substitute for relative consumption in equation (2.32), the wholesale market-clearing condition, we find that

$$\tau_t^{\text{F}} = \xi(e_t^{\text{US}} - e_t^{\text{EU}}), \quad (2.51)$$

where

$$\xi = \frac{1}{4\theta\lambda(1-\lambda) + (2\lambda-1)^2[1-\alpha+(\alpha/\gamma)]} > 0.$$

Hence, the equilibrium real exchange rate is

$$\varepsilon_t^{\text{F}} = \alpha(2\lambda - 1)\xi(e_t^{\text{US}} - e_t^{\text{EU}}). \quad (2.52)$$

Hereafter, we will denote the flex-price log terms of trade and real exchange by τ_t^{F} and ε_t^{F}, respectively.

There are three noteworthy features of equations (2.51) and (2.52). First, they show that monetary factors play no role in the determination of the terms of trade or the real exchange rate when prices are flexible; only the (net) endowments matter. Second, the dynamics of the real exchange rate are not affected by the presence of monopolistic competition. Equation (2.52) has the same form as the equation for the real exchange rate in the flexible price model with perfect competition discussed in Chapter 1. Finally, we note from (2.46) and (2.47) that there is no U.S. or E.U. inflation when prices are fully flexible (i.e., when retail firms reset prices every period), so $\varepsilon_t^{\text{F}} = s_t - (p - \hat{p})$, where $p - \hat{p}$ is a constant. Consequently, the flex-price nominal exchange rate is given by

$$s_t^{\text{F}} = \text{const.} + \alpha(2\lambda - 1)\xi(e_t^{\text{US}} - e_t^{\text{EU}}).$$

Let us now turn to the implications of staggered price-setting. In this setting both the real exchange rate and the terms of trade depend on monetary variables insofar as they affect the price-setting decisions of firms. We therefore have to characterize the *joint* behavior of U.S. and E.U. inflation, the real exchange rate, and the terms of trade given the behavior of interest rates specified in the Taylor rules (2.48). For this purpose, we first use equations (2.46) and (2.47) to write the difference between U.S. and E.U. inflation as

$$\Delta p_t - \Delta \hat{p}_t = \kappa \mathbb{E}_t \sum_{i=0}^{\infty} \beta^i \{rmc_{t+i} - \widehat{rmc}_{t+i}\}, \qquad (2.53)$$

where rmc_t and $\widehat{rmc}_t$ are the log real marginal costs facing retail firms in the United States and Europe. Equation (2.15) implies that

$$rmc_t - \widehat{rmc}_t = \alpha(q_t - \hat{q}_t) + (1 - \alpha)\gamma(c_t - \hat{c}_t)$$

$$= \alpha[\varepsilon_t - (2\lambda - 1)\tau_t] + (1 - \alpha)\gamma(c_t - \hat{c}_t).$$

Using the risk-sharing condition in (2.20) to substitute for the difference in consumption gives

$$rmc_t - \widehat{rmc}_t = \varepsilon_t - \alpha(2\lambda - 1)\tau_t, \qquad (2.54)$$

so we can rewrite (2.53) as

$$\Delta p_t - \Delta \hat{p}_t = \kappa \mathbb{E}_t \sum_{i=0}^{\infty} \beta^i \left\{ \varepsilon_{t+i} - \alpha(2\lambda - 1)\tau_{t+i} \right\}. \qquad (2.55)$$

Equation (2.55) shows that the U.S./E.U. inflation differential depends on the current and expected future paths of the real exchange rate and the terms of trade. In particular, it implies that the inflation differential will increase in response to real depreciation of the dollar or an improvement in the U.S. terms of trade. In the case of a real depreciation, the accompanying rise in $c_t - \hat{c}_t$ under complete risk-sharing leads to a rise in U.S. real wages relative to E.U. real wages. As a consequence, the real marginal costs facing U.S. retail firms rise compared to those facing E.U. retail firms, so those U.S. firms currently adjusting prices raise them more than their E.U. counterparts. In short, the real depreciation of the dollar raises the inflation differential because its effects on real wages raise the real marginal costs facing U.S. firms relative to those facing E.U. firms.

Equation (2.55) shows that variations in the terms of trade affect inflation in a similar manner. An improvement in the U.S. terms of trade, for example, increases the U.S. marginal costs relative to E.U. marginal costs because U.S. retail firms' demands for intermediate goods exhibit home bias ($\lambda > 1/2$). Consequently, as equation (2.55) shows, a current or expected future improvement in U.S. terms of trade raises the inflation differential.

Although the real exchange rate and terms of trade affect real marginal costs through different channels, it is their combined effect that determines the behavior of the equilibrium inflation differential. To identify this effect, we combine the risk-sharing condition with the wholesale market-clearing condition in (2.32):

$$e_t^{\text{US}} - e_t^{\text{EU}} = \left[4\theta\lambda(1 - \lambda) + (2\lambda - 1)^2(1 - \alpha) \right] \tau_t + \frac{2\lambda - 1}{\gamma} \varepsilon_t.$$

This equilibrium condition must hold under both flexible and staggered price-setting. As a result, any difference between the real exchange rate under staggered and flexible pricing, $\varepsilon_t - \varepsilon_t^{\mathrm{F}}$, must be fully reflected in the difference between the terms of trade under staggered and flexible pricing, $\tau_t - \tau_t^{\mathrm{F}}$, because the endowments, e_t^{US} and e_t^{EU}, are exogenous:

$$0 = \left[4\theta\lambda(1 - \lambda) + (2\lambda - 1)^2(1 - \alpha) \right] (\tau_t - \tau_t^{\mathrm{F}}) + \frac{2\lambda - 1}{\gamma}(\varepsilon_t - \varepsilon_t^{\mathrm{F}}). \quad (2.56)$$

Under flexible pricing, $\varepsilon_t^{\mathrm{F}} = \alpha(2\lambda - 1)\tau_t^{\mathrm{F}}$, so we can rewrite (2.54) as

$$rmc_t - \widehat{rmc}_t = (\varepsilon_t - \varepsilon_t^{\mathrm{F}}) - \alpha(2\lambda - 1)(\tau_t - \tau_t^{\mathrm{F}})$$

and substitute for $\tau_t - \tau_t^{\mathrm{F}}$ from (2.56) to give

$$rmc_t - \widehat{rmc}_t = \varsigma \left(\varepsilon_t - \varepsilon_t^{\mathrm{F}} \right), \quad (2.57)$$

where

$$\varsigma = 1 + \frac{\alpha(2\lambda - 1)^2}{\gamma[4\theta\lambda(1 - \lambda) + (1 - \alpha)(2\lambda - 1)^2]} > 1.$$

Thus, U.S. retail firms will face higher real marginal costs than their E.U. counterparts when the real exchange rate is above its flex-price level. Intuitively, a real depreciation of the dollar is accompanied by a rise in U.S. real wages relative to E.U. real wages and an improvement in the U.S. terms of trade that both increase real marginal costs in the United States relative to Europe.

Next, we consider the implications of the Taylor rules. When central banks set interest rates according to equation (2.48), the spread between U.S. and E.U. interest rates is

$$r_t - \hat{r}_t = (1 + \psi_\pi)\mathbb{E}_t \left(\Delta p_{t+1} - \Delta \hat{p}_{t+1} \right) + \psi_y[(y_t - \hat{y}_t) + (\hat{y}_t^{\mathrm{F}} - y_t^{\mathrm{F}})] + v_t - \hat{v}_t.$$

Recall that the output of U.S. (E.U.) retailer i, Y_t^i ($\hat{Y}_t^i$), must equal the demand for good i, C_t^i ($\hat{C}_t^i$), in equilibrium. Aggregate U.S: and E.U. output is therefore given by $Y_t = \int_0^1 (P_t^i/P_t)C_t^i di$ and $\hat{Y}_t = \int_0^1 (\hat{P}_t^i/\hat{P}_t)\hat{C}_t^i di$, respectively. Substituting for domestic demand in these expressions and taking logs gives

$$y_t - \hat{y}_t = \ln \left(\frac{\int_0^1 (P_t^i/P_t)^{1-\phi} di}{\int_0^1 (\hat{P}_t^i/\hat{P}_t)^{1-\phi} di} \right) + c_t - \hat{c}_t. \quad (2.58)$$

When prices are flexible, there is no dispersion in retail prices within each country (i.e., $P_t^i = P_t$ and $\hat{P}_t^i = \hat{P}_t$ for all $i \in [0, 1]$), so the first term on the right of (2.58) is zero. Under these circumstances, relative GDP mirrors relative consumption, which in turn is proportional to the real exchange rate, $y_t^{\mathrm{F}} - \hat{y}_t^{\mathrm{F}} = c_t^{\mathrm{F}} - \hat{c}_t^{\mathrm{F}} = \gamma^{-1}\varepsilon_t^{\mathrm{F}}$. When firms reset prices in a staggered fashion, retail prices are dispersed because firms currently resetting prices incorporate information about marginal costs that was not available to other firms. This means that the first term in (2.58) can vary as the relative dispersion of retail prices between the United States and Europe changes. Such changes could account for a nonnegligible fraction of the variation in relative GDP during periods of very high inflation. Under normal circumstances, however, the cross-country differences in the dispersion of prices will have a negligible effect on relative GDP. This means that (2.58) is well approximated by $y_t - \hat{y}_t = c_t - \hat{c}_t$, so $y_t - \hat{y}_t = \gamma^{-1}\varepsilon_t$ under complete markets. Substituting these expressions for relative GDP into the equation for the spread produces

$$r_t - \hat{r}_t = (1 + \psi_\pi)\mathbb{E}_t\left(\Delta p_{t+1} - \Delta\hat{p}_{t+1}\right) + \psi_\varepsilon(\varepsilon_t - \varepsilon_t^{\mathrm{F}}) + v_t - \hat{v}_t, \quad (2.59)$$

where $\psi_\varepsilon = \psi_y/\gamma$.

We can now use (2.59) to pin down the expected rate of real depreciation. Combining the interest parity condition in (2.34) with the definition of the real exchange rate, we find that

$$\mathbb{E}_t\Delta\varepsilon_{t+1} = r_t - \hat{r}_t + \mathbb{E}_t\Delta\hat{p}_{t+1} - \mathbb{E}_t\Delta p_{t+1} + \delta_t,$$

or, after substituting for $r_t - \hat{r}_t$ with (2.59),

$$\mathbb{E}_t\Delta\varepsilon_{t+1} = \psi_\pi\mathbb{E}_t\left(\Delta p_{t+1} - \Delta\hat{p}_{t+1}\right) + \psi_\varepsilon(\varepsilon_t - \varepsilon_t^{\mathrm{F}}) + \delta_t + v_t - \hat{v}_t. \quad (2.60)$$

Subtracting $\mathbb{E}_t\Delta\varepsilon_{t+1}^{\mathrm{F}}$ from both sides and rearranging gives

$$(\varepsilon_t - \varepsilon_t^{\mathrm{F}}) = \frac{1}{1+\psi_\varepsilon}\mathbb{E}_t(\varepsilon_{t+1} - \varepsilon_{t+1}^{\mathrm{F}}) - \frac{\psi_\pi}{1+\psi_\varepsilon}\mathbb{E}_t\left(\Delta p_{t+1} - \Delta\hat{p}_{t+1}\right) + \frac{1}{1+\psi_\varepsilon}\mathbb{E}_t z_{t+1},$$

where $z_{t+1} \equiv \Delta\varepsilon_{t+1}^{\mathrm{F}} - \delta_t - v_t + \hat{v}_t$. Finally, iterating forward under the assumption that

$$\lim_{j\to\infty}\left(\frac{1}{1+\psi_\varepsilon}\right)^j \mathbb{E}_t(\varepsilon_{t+j} - \varepsilon_{t+j}^{\mathrm{F}}) = 0$$

gives

$$\varepsilon_t - \varepsilon_t^{\mathrm{F}} = \mathbb{E}_t\sum_{i=1}^{\infty}\left(\frac{1}{1+\psi_\varepsilon}\right)^i \left\{z_{t+i} - \psi_\pi(\Delta p_{t+i} - \Delta\hat{p}_{t+i})\right\}. \quad (2.61)$$

Equation (2.61) shows how the real exchange rate will differ from its flex-price equilibrium level. In particular, if the path of future U.S. inflation is expected to be above E.U. inflation [i.e., $\mathbb{E}_t(\Delta p_{t+1+i} - \Delta\hat{p}_{t+1+i}) > 0$], then the current real exchange rate will be below its flex-price level. Intuitively, when central banks follow Taylor rules, an expected rise in the U.S./E.U. inflation differential will be accompanied by an anticipated increase in the spread between U.S. and E.U. interest rates, so the expected future rate of nominal depreciation must rise in accordance with interest parity. Moreover, when $\psi_\pi > 0$ the rise in the spread is of sufficient magnitude that the increase in the expected nominal depreciation rate exceeds the expected increase in the inflation differential. Consequently, as equation (2.60) shows, the expected rate of real depreciation, $\mathbb{E}_t\Delta\varepsilon_{t+i}$, also rises. The current real exchange must therefore fall below the flex-price level to be consistent with these new exchange-rate expectations.

Equation (2.61) also shows how the real exchange depends on the future policy shocks, v_t and $\hat{v}_t$, the risk premium, δ_t, and the rate of real depreciation under flexible prices, $\Delta\varepsilon_{t+1}^{\mathrm{F}}$, via the forcing variable z_t. Policy shocks affect the real exchange rate in much the same way as expected inflation because they directly affect the spread between U.S. and E.U. interest rates. In the case of the risk premium, the effect comes via the interest parity condition. Equation (2.60) shows that, ceteris paribus, changes in the risk premium have a one-for-one effect on the expected real depreciation rate. Finally, recall that when prices are flexible the real exchange rate is uniquely determined by the exogenous supplies of intermediate goods net of government purchases, $\varepsilon_t^F = \alpha(2\lambda - 1)(e_t^{US} - e_t^{EU})$. Thus, any change in anticipated future paths of e_t^{US} or e_t^{EU}, such as a revision in expected future government purchases, alters the anticipated future path for ε_t^F and hence the spread between U.S. and E.U. interest rates. The current real exchange rate must therefore adjust to be consistent with the change in the expected future depreciation rate implied by interest parity.

Exchange-Rate Dynamics

The equilibrium dynamics of the model are represented by equations (2.53), (2.57), and (2.61). Writing (2.53) and (2.61) in difference form and using (2.57) to substitute for real marginal costs gives

$$\Delta p_t - \Delta \hat{p}_t = \kappa\varsigma(\varepsilon_t - \varepsilon_t^F) + \beta\mathbb{E}_t\left(\Delta p_{t+1} - \Delta \hat{p}_{t+1}\right)$$

and   (2.62)

$$\varepsilon_t - \varepsilon_t^F = \frac{1}{1+\psi_\varepsilon}\mathbb{E}_t(\varepsilon_{t+1} - \varepsilon_{t+1}^F) - \frac{\psi_\pi}{1+\psi_\varepsilon}\mathbb{E}_t\left(\Delta p_{t+1} - \Delta \hat{p}_{t+1}\right) + \frac{1}{1+\psi_\varepsilon}z_t,$$

where $z_t = \alpha(2\lambda - 1)\xi\mathbb{E}_t(\Delta e_{t+1}^{US} - \Delta e_{t+1}^{EU}) - \delta_t - v_t + \hat{v}_t$. Thus, the equilibrium of the model under staggered price-setting is characterized by two forward-looking difference equations for the inflation differential and the difference between the log real exchange rate and its flex-price level, involving the exogenous variables contained in the forcing variable, z_t. Note that these equations also implicitly identify the equilibrium rate of nominal depreciation. By definition, $\Delta s_t - \Delta\varepsilon_t = \Delta p_t - \Delta\hat{p}_t$, so

$$\Delta s_t = (\Delta p_t - \Delta\hat{p}_t) + (\Delta\varepsilon_t - \Delta\varepsilon_t^F) + \Delta\varepsilon_t^F$$

$$= (\Delta p_t - \Delta\hat{p}_t) + (\Delta\varepsilon_t - \Delta\varepsilon_t^F) + \alpha(2\lambda - 1)(\Delta e_t^{US} - \Delta e_t^{EU}).\quad (2.63)$$

The first two terms on the right come from the solution to (2.62), whereas the third is exogenous.

Our aim now is to examine how exogenous variations in the forcing variable, z_t, affect the equilibrium behavior of real and nominal exchange rates. However, in order for this exercise to make any sense, there must exist a unique bounded solution for (2.62) given the dynamics for z_t. To examine this issue we rewrite (2.62) as

$$\begin{bmatrix} \varepsilon_t - \varepsilon_t^F \\ \Delta p_t - \Delta\hat{p}_t \end{bmatrix} = \mathcal{H}\mathbb{E}_t \begin{bmatrix} \varepsilon_{t+1} - \varepsilon_{t+1}^F \\ \Delta p_{t+1} - \Delta\hat{p}_{t+1} \end{bmatrix} + \frac{1}{1+\psi_\varepsilon}\begin{bmatrix} 1 \\ \kappa\varsigma \end{bmatrix} z_t, \quad (2.64)$$

where

$$\mathcal{H} = \begin{bmatrix} \dfrac{1}{1+\psi_\varepsilon} & -\dfrac{\psi_\pi}{1+\psi_\varepsilon} \\[2mm] \dfrac{\kappa\varsigma}{1+\psi_\varepsilon} & \beta - \dfrac{\kappa\varsigma\psi_\pi}{1+\psi_\varepsilon} \end{bmatrix}.$$

Blanchard and Kahn (1980) show that a necessary and sufficient condition for the system in (2.64) to exhibit a unique and bounded solution is that the number of nonpredetermined endogenous variables (i.e., jump variables) equal the number of roots of $\mathcal{H}$ that lie inside the unit circle. Here, determinacy is ensured when

$$\psi_\pi < \frac{1+\beta}{\varsigma\kappa}\left(2 + \frac{\psi_y}{\gamma}\right). \tag{2.65}$$

This condition can be viewed as a restriction on the Taylor rule parameters, ψ_y and ψ_π. In effect, it places an upper bound on how aggressively central banks should change interest rates in response to variations in (expected) inflation. As we shall see, this restriction is not binding when the model's parameters are calibrated to standard values.

To illustrate the dynamic properties of the model, let us assume that the forcing variable follows an AR(1) process:

$$z_{t+1} = \rho z_t + u_{t+1}, \tag{2.66}$$

where $1 > \rho > 0$ and u_{t+1} are i.i.d. mean-zero shocks. We can use this specification to examine the implications of persistent variations in the net endowments, the foreign exchange risk premium, and monetary policy.

In a determinant equilibrium, $\varepsilon_t - \varepsilon_t^{\mathrm{F}}$ and $\Delta p_t - \Delta\hat{p}_t$ are uniquely determined by the anticipated path for z_t. Since equation (2.66) implies that $\mathbb{E}_t z_{t+i} = \rho^i z_t$ for all $i \geq 0$ when the value of z_t is known to agents, the equilibrium values of $\varepsilon_t - \varepsilon_t^{\mathrm{F}}$ and $\Delta p_t - \Delta\hat{p}_t$ must be proportional to z_t. In other words, in a determinant equilibrium where z_t follows the AR(1) process in (2.66), $\varepsilon_t - \varepsilon_t^{\mathrm{F}} = \pi_\varepsilon z_t$ and $\Delta p_t - \Delta\hat{p}_t = \pi_p z_t$ for some reduced-form coefficients, π_ε and π_p. To find these coefficients, we use (2.66) and the preceding equations to substitute for $\varepsilon_t - \varepsilon_t^{\mathrm{F}}$ and $\Delta p_t - \Delta\hat{p}_t$ in (2.62). This produces

$$\pi_p z_t = \kappa\varsigma\pi_\varepsilon z_t + \beta\pi_p \rho z_t$$

and

$$\pi_\varepsilon z_t = \frac{\rho\pi_\varepsilon}{1+\psi_\varepsilon}z_t - \frac{\psi_\pi\pi_p\rho}{1+\psi_\varepsilon}z_t + \frac{\rho}{1+\psi_\varepsilon}z_t.$$

Since these equations hold for all values of z_t, the coefficients π_ε and π_p must satisfy

$$\pi_p = \kappa\varsigma\pi_\varepsilon + \beta\pi_p\rho \quad \text{and} \quad \pi_\varepsilon = \frac{\rho\pi_\varepsilon}{1+\psi_\varepsilon} - \frac{\psi_\pi\pi_p\rho}{1+\psi_\varepsilon} + \frac{\rho}{1+\psi_\varepsilon}.$$

Solving for π_ε and π_p allows us to write the equilibrium real exchange rate and inflation differential as

$$\varepsilon_t - \varepsilon_t^{\mathrm{F}} = \pi_\varepsilon z_t \quad \text{and} \quad \Delta p_t - \Delta\hat{p}_t = \pi_p z_t, \tag{2.67}$$

where

$$\pi_\varepsilon = \frac{\rho(1-\beta\rho)}{(1-\beta\rho)\left(1-\rho+\psi_\varepsilon\right) + \psi_\pi\rho\kappa\varsigma} > 0$$

and

$$\pi_p = \frac{\rho \kappa \varsigma}{(1 - \beta \rho)\left(1 - \rho + \psi_\varepsilon\right) + \psi_\pi \rho \kappa \varsigma} > 0.$$

To illustrate the properties of the model, we examine the exchange-rate implications of changes in monetary policy. In particular, consider the effects of a persistent decrease in U.S. interest rates below their targeted level. In the absence of any other shocks, this loosening of monetary policy is represented by a positive u_t shock in (2.66) because z_t rises when the U.S. interest rate is pushed below target. Equation (2.67) therefore implies that a loosening of U.S. monetary policy induces an immediate real depreciation of the dollar and an increase in the U.S./E.U. inflation differential.

The economic intuition behind these results is straightforward. Consider the behavior of the spread between real interest rates in the United States and Europe implied by the Taylor rules:

$$(r_t - \mathbb{E}_t \Delta p_{t+1}) - (\hat{r}_t - \mathbb{E}_t \Delta \hat{p}_{t+1})$$
$$= \psi_\pi \mathbb{E}_t \left(\Delta p_{t+1} - \Delta \hat{p}_{t+1}\right) + \psi_\varepsilon(\varepsilon_t - \varepsilon_t^{\mathrm{F}}) + \delta_t + v_t - \hat{v}_t.$$

The change in U.S. monetary policy affects the real spread directly via the v_t term and indirectly via its effects on expected inflation and the real exchange rate. In the absence of any indirect effects, the policy change pushes down the spread, so, in accordance with interest parity, the real exchange rate is expected to appreciate (i.e., $\mathbb{E}_t \Delta \varepsilon_{t+i} < 0$ for $i > 1$). There must therefore be an immediate real depreciation of the dollar to be consistent with these expectations. In addition, the indirect effects of the policy change work via the Taylor rules. As the direct effect of the policy is to push the real exchange rate above its flex-price level, its indirect effects are to increase the difference between the U.S. and E.U. output gaps and the expected U.S./E.U. inflation differential. Under normal circumstances these developments would lead to a rise in the spread, but here they simply dampen the direct effect of the policy change. In other words, a loosening of U.S. monetary policy leads to an immediate real depreciation of the dollar and higher U.S. inflation because it induces a fall in the spread between U.S. and E.U. real interest rates.[7]

The preceding discussion refers to the behavior of the real exchange rate as a single variable. In reality, of course, the behavior of the real exchange rate is the *outcome* of the joint behavior of the nominal exchange rate and consumer prices. A more accurate way to describe how the economy adjusts to a money policy change requires a discussion of why the behavior of these variables gives rise to the real-exchange-rate dynamics described earlier.

---

7. An astute reader may wonder why the indirect effects of the policy change could not swamp the direct effects and so lead to a rise in the real spread. The answer lies in the nature of agents' long-term expectations. In the absence of any further shocks, the real exchange rate must be expected to return to its flex-price level because eventually all retail firms will have the opportunity to reset prices. Thus, if the real spread were to rise, there would have to be an immediate real appreciation of the dollar to be consistent with anticipated future depreciation required by interest parity. Obviously, the indirect effects of the policy on the spread in this case would reinforce the direct effects, so, contrary to our initial conjecture, the spread would fall.

As an aid to this discussion, Figure 2.3 plots the response of the forcing variable, z_t, the log real exchange rate, ε_t, the U.S./E.U. inflation differential, $\Delta p_t - \Delta \hat{p}_t$, and the scaled nominal rate, s_t ($\times 0.1$), following a loosening of U.S. monetary policy in which interest rates are initially pushed down by 1 percent. The behavior of the nominal exchange rate is found by using (2.67) to substitute for $\varepsilon_t - \varepsilon_t^F$ and $\Delta p_t - \Delta \hat{p}_t$ in (2.63):

$$\Delta s_t = \frac{1 - \beta\rho + \kappa\varsigma}{1 - \beta\rho} \pi_\varepsilon z_t - \pi_\varepsilon z_{t-1}, \tag{2.68}$$

where

$$\pi_\varepsilon = \frac{\rho(1 - \beta\rho)}{(1 - \beta\rho)\left(1 - \rho + \psi_\varepsilon\right) + \psi_\pi \rho\kappa\varsigma} > 0.$$

Since the response of the nominal exchange rate depends critically on the persistence of the policy change and the degree of price-stickiness, the figure includes the plots for cases where $\rho = \{0.9, 0.4\}$ and the probability of price adjustment, $\wp = \{1/4, 1/12\}$. The values for ρ imply half-lives for the policy change of approximately 6 months and 1 month. The values for price-adjustment probability imply that on average retail firms reset prices once every 4 months when $\wp = 1/4$, and once every 12 months when $\wp = 1/12$. The other parameter values used to compute the responses are reported in Table 2.1.

The preference and technology parameters are set to the same values as in Chapter 1. The values for the Taylor rule coefficients fall within the range of values estimated in the literature (see, e.g., Mark 2009) and imply that the determinacy condition in (2.65) is satisfied.

The plots in Figure 2.3 make clear that the effects of the change in monetary policy depend on both its persistence and the degree of price-stickiness. Consider, first, the responses plotted in panel A. In this case, individual retail prices are reasonably sticky (changing once a year on average), and the half-life of the policy change is

TABLE 2.1
Staggered Pricing Model Parameters

Parameter	Symbol	Value
Discount factor	β	0.997
Risk aversion	γ	1.000
Intermediate share	α	0.330
Domestic intermediate share	λ	0.850
Intermediate elasticity	θ	0.740
Taylor inflation coefficient	ψ_π	0.500
Taylor output coefficient	ψ_y	0.100
Price-setting probability	$\wp$	$\{1/4, 1/12\}$
Shock persistence	ρ	$\{0.40, 0.90\}$

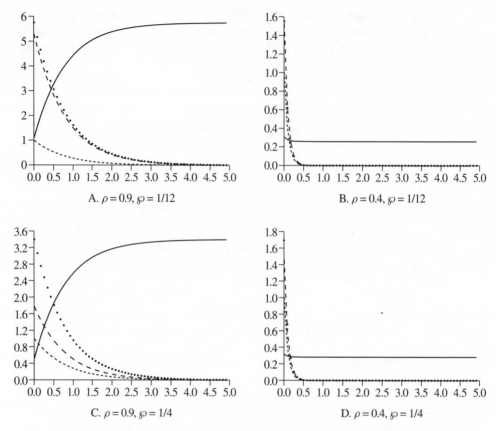

FIGURE 2.3 Impulse responses of the scaled nominal exchange rate, $0.1s_t$ (solid), the real exchange rate, ε_t (dashed), and the U.S./E.U. inflation differential, $\Delta p_t - \Delta \hat{p}_t$ (dotted), to a monetary policy change, z_t (short dashed).

approximately 6 months. As a consequence, the anticipated effects of the policy on the present value of real marginal costs lead to a sharp initial rise in the U.S./E.U. inflation differential (shown by the dotted plot), which then gradually declines back to zero over the next 3 years.

These inflationary effects have important implications for the behavior of the nominal exchange rate. We argued earlier that looser U.S. monetary policy must be characterized by a fall in the spread between real interest rates in the United States and Europe, so agents must expect a real depreciation of the dollar until policy returns to normal. This means that the nominal exchange rate must initially depreciate by more than the increase in the inflation differential so that the implied real exchange rate also depreciates. (Figure 2.3 plots the response of the log nominal exchange rate multiplied by 0.1, so the initial depreciation is 10 times larger than is shown in the plot.) Thereafter, the nominal rate must follow a path that implies a real *appreciation* of the dollar. When the policy change has large and persistent inflation effects, the nominal rate must actually depreciate further to stop the real rate from appreciating more quickly than the rate consistent with interest parity. As a consequence, the initial "jump" in the nominal rate is followed by a persistent depreciation of the dollar until U.S. monetary policy returns to normal. In short, the combination of price-stickiness and persistence of the policy change induces undershooting in the nominal exchange rate.

Let us now try to isolate the effects of persistence from those of price-stickiness. Panel B of Figure 2.3 plots the responses to a policy change with much less persistence (the half life is approximately 1 month) in an economy with the same degree of price-stickiness. In this case, the effects of the policy change are much smaller. When the change is less persistent, its effects on the present value of future real marginal costs are reduced. As a result, the policy change has less of an impact on the inflation differential and the real spread. Under these circumstances, the nominal exchange rate must initially depreciate to put the real exchange rate on the path consistent with interest parity, but there is no need for a further depreciation once the policy change has taken place. In fact, as the plots in panel B show, the nominal rate has to appreciate slightly because the inflationary impact of the policy change is too small to keep the implied real exchange rate on the path required by interest parity. Thus, in contrast to panel A, the nominal exchange rate overshoots the long-run level implied by the policy change.

Panels C and D show how the economy responds to the policy change when there is less price-stickiness. Here retail firms reset prices once every 4 months on average, rather than once every 12 months. Comparing panels B and D, we see that reducing the degree of price-stickiness has little quantitative effect on the response of the economy to policy changes with a short half-life. By contrast, a comparison of panels A and C shows that less price-stickiness significantly reduces the impact of the policy change. In particular, the initial and long-run depreciations of the nominal exchange rate are approximately half the size when price-stickiness is smaller. Intuitively, the real exchange rate is expected to return more quickly to its long-run level because more retail firms have the opportunity to reset their prices each period. This reduces the impact of the policy change on the inflation differential, so the nominal exchange rate need not depreciate by as much to put the real exchange rate on the path implied by interest parity.

Price-Setting and Pass-Through

It is useful to compare the preceding analysis with the implications of other exchange-rate models that incorporate price-stickiness. In many of these models there is no distinction between retail and wholesale markets—all goods are consumed directly by households. This means that the structure of price-setting affects the behavior of the terms of trade as well as consumer prices. For example, in the Redux model proposed by Obstfeld and Rogoff (1995), households consume baskets of domestic- and foreign-produced goods that are freely traded between countries. In this model, the Law of One Price applies to all goods, and producers set prices in their own currencies before the complete state of the economy is known. This pricing structure is known as producer currency pricing (PCP).

PCP has two important implications. First, variations in the terms of trade must be positively correlated with the nominal exchange rate. A shock inducing a depreciation of the dollar, say, increases the dollar price of U.S. imports, but has no effect on the dollar price of U.S. exports because they are preset by U.S. producers. Second, any shock that induces a depreciation (appreciation) of the nominal exchange rate will be immediately reflected in a higher (lower) domestic price for imports. In other words, shocks to the nominal exchange rate are immediately "passed through" to the domestic price index. Although the first implication appears consistent with the empirical evidence, the second does not. Betts and Devereux (1996), for example, noted that consumer price indices respond very little to monetary policy shocks that have sizable impacts on the nominal exchange rate.

Betts and Devereux (1996) proposed an alternative pricing structure, known as local currency pricing (LCP), that has been incorporated into many models (Betts and Devereux 2000; Chari, Kehoe, and McGrattan 2002; Devereux and Engel 2002; and many others). Under LCP, the segmentation of markets allows producers to set prices in the currency of consumers. More precisely, the markets for U.S. and foreign consumer goods are assumed to be segmented so that producers can set the dollar prices at which they will supply goods to U.S. households and the foreign currency price at which they will supply foreign households.

When producers preset prices, the LCP and PCP structures have strikingly different implications for the behavior of consumer prices and the terms of trade. In particular, under LCP, there is no pass-through to consumer prices from the exchange-rate reaction to a shock until producers reset prices. This implication is clearly consistent with what we observed at high frequencies. Nominal exchange rates vary day by day whereas the vast majority of individual consumer prices remain unchanged from week to week. By contrast, as Obstfeld (2001) stresses, the implications of LCP for the behavior of the terms of trade run contrary to what we observe empirically. Under LCP a nominal dollar depreciation has no effect on the dollar price of U.S. imports but increases the dollar price of U.S. exports, so the U.S. terms of trade improve. In the data, however, a depreciation of a country's currency is associated with a deterioration in its terms of trade.

The model presented earlier incorporates the LCP structure in retail markets because each firm sets the price at which it will sell goods to local households. At the same time, we avoid the counterfactual implications of LCP pricing for the behavior of the terms of trade because the latter depend on the relative prices of intermediate goods. Indeed, since the equilibrium terms of trade are entirely pinned down by the endowments of intermediate goods (net of government spending), the model implies that the correlation between the terms of trade and the nominal exchange rate is not an informative measure of whether LCP with price-stickiness can account for the observed behavior of nominal exchange rates and consumer price indices.

Measures of exchange-rate pass-through are similarly uninformative unless care is taken to control for the type of shock hitting the economy. To illustrate this point, consider the possible responses of consumer prices and the nominal exchange rate to an exogenous and persistent fall in the foreign exchange risk premium, δ_t. As we noted earlier, the effects of such a change can be represented by a positive u_t shock to the AR(1) process in (2.66), so its implications for the equilibrium depreciation rate and inflation differential are identified in equations (2.67) and (2.68). These equations imply that initial elasticity of the consumer price differential with respect to the depreciation of the dollar is

$$\frac{\Delta p - \Delta \hat{p}}{\Delta s} = \frac{\kappa \varsigma}{\kappa \varsigma + 1 - \beta \rho},$$ (2.69)

where $\kappa = \wp(1 - \beta(1 - \wp))/(1 - \wp)$.

Equation (2.69) shows that the degree of initial pass-through depends negatively on the probability of price adjustment, $\wp$, and positively on the persistence of the shock to the risk premium, ρ. When $\wp$ is small, the consumer price index is stickier because a smaller fraction of firms is resetting its prices in any period. Shocks affecting the exchange rate will therefore have a smaller impact on consumer prices, so there is little measured pass-through. The persistence of shocks also affects the degree of pass-through for a given level of price stickiness. Those firms setting prices when the shock hits adjust their prices according to how the shock affects the present value of future real marginal costs. More persistent shocks have a greater impact on this present value, so they also have a larger effect on prices that are currently being reset, thereby leading to a higher degree of pass-through. In sum, therefore, the degree of initial pass-through should not be viewed as a reliable measure of price-stickiness without regard for the persistence of shocks driving the variations in consumer prices and nominal exchange rate.

To further emphasize this point, Figure 2.4 plots the elasticity of the price differential with respect to the depreciation of the dollar over the 12 months following the shocks to the risk premium. The dashed line plots the elasticity for the case with less stickiness and more persistence (e.g., $\wp = 3/4$, $\rho = 0.9$) and the solid line plots the case with less persistence and more stickiness (e.g., $\wp = 11/12$, $\rho = 0.4$). As the figure shows, the degree of pass-through depends on the horizon. Below the 1-month horizon, the economy with stickier prices exhibits less pass-through. Above 1 month, the reverse is true. Clearly, measures of pass-through at a single horizon do not provide unambiguous information on the degree of price-stickiness.

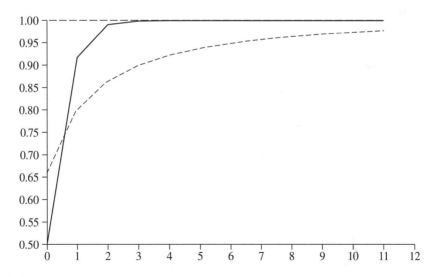

FIGURE 2.4   Exchange-rate pass-through in the 12 months following a shock to the foreign exchange risk premium.

2.3 International Risk-Sharing

In Chapter 1 we showed that when markets are complete, the optimal plans of households equalize their intertemporal marginal rates of substitution (IMRS) across the world economy. Backus and Smith (1993) first noted that the behavior of real exchange rates and aggregate consumption was inconsistent with the implications of complete markets if households had isoelastic, time-separable preferences defined over aggregate consumption. In this case, the relation between the real exchange rate and consumption is defined in equation (2.19), which we now write in log form as

$$\Delta \varepsilon_{t+1} = \gamma (\Delta c_{t+1} - \Delta \hat{c}_{t+1}). \tag{2.70}$$

Equation (2.70) implies that the rate of real depreciation should be perfectly correlated with the difference between home and foreign consumption growth. By contrast, Backus and Smith (1993) found that the actual correlation was low and often negative among many different country pairs. Subsequent research has confirmed this finding. For example, Table 2.2 reproduces the findings of Corsetti, Dedola, and Leduc (2008a) based on annual data between 1970 and 2001. The column

TABLE 2.2
Real Exchange Rate / Consumption Correlations

Country	United States	ROW
Australia	−0.09	−0.13
Austria	−0.20	−0.30
Belgium	−0.11	0.19
Canada	−0.20	0.02
Denmark	−0.20	−0.21
European Union	−0.23	−0.04
Finland	−0.40	−0.55
France	−0.21	−0.01
Germany	−0.13	0.01
Italy	−0.27	−0.31
Japan	0.04	0.08
South Korea	−0.79	−0.63
Mexico	−0.68	−0.74
Netherlands	−0.30	−0.19
New Zealand	−0.27	−0.28
Portugal	−0.48	−0.67
Sweden	−0.34	−0.29
Spain	−0.41	−0.38
Switzerland	0.09	0.32
Turkey	−0.34	−0.17
United Kingdom	−0.40	−0.04
United States	N/A	−0.31
Median	−0.26	−0.13

Source: Corsetti, Dedola, and Leduc (2008a).

headed United States reports the correlation between the real depreciation rate and relative consumption growth for individual country pairs with the U.S. Clearly, all the correlations are well below one and some are strongly negative. The column headed ROW reports the correlations for the listed country versus the "Rest-of-the-World" (computed as a trade-weighted aggregate of the other countries listed in the table). Here, again, most of the correlations are negative. These results sharply contradict the implications of risk-sharing in our model with complete markets—an observation referred to as "the Backus-Smith Puzzle." Moreover, as a consequence, they call into question whether the economic mechanisms that link the behavior of exchange rates to macroeconomic factors in the model have any empirical counterparts.

We can draw two important lessons from Table 2.2 concerning international risk sharing. First, there is no direct evidence in Table 2.2 about the actual degree of risk-sharing per se. Table 2.2 shows that the joint behavior of consumption growth and real exchange rates is inconsistent with complete risk-sharing *if* household preferences take the time-separable isoelastic form found in many models. The second lesson concerns the design of macro exchange-rate models. Clearly, models with complete markets and isoelastic preferences link consumption and the real exchange rate in a completely counterfactual way. This means that we must either drop the assumption of complete markets, or consider different preferences, or both. In the next section we examine how the exchange-rate implications of our sticky-price model change when we drop the complete-markets assumption.

2.4 Incomplete Markets

We now examine the behavior of exchange rates when financial markets are incomplete. For this purpose we amend the sticky-price model of Section 2.2.2 in two respects. First we restrict the array of financial assets households can hold to just equities and nominal bonds. In particular, U.S. households can now hold one-period dollar bonds, one-period euro bonds, and U.S. equity that is a claim on the profits of all U.S. retail firms and the endowment of the U.S. intermediate good. Analogously, E.U. households can hold dollar and euro bonds and E.U. equity that is a claim on the profits of all E.U. retail firms and the endowment of the E.U. intermediate good. Note that households cannot hold foreign equity. This restriction inhibits international risk-sharing because households cannot fully insure themselves against the effects of shocks to the foreign endowment.[8]

The second amendment concerns households' preferences. Here we set χ equal to zero so households gain no utility from holding real balances. Money supplies play no role in the determination of the exchange rate when central banks follow Taylor rules, so nothing is lost by eliminating money from the model. We also set γ equal to one so that household utility is defined with respect to the log of the consumption basket. This restriction on preferences greatly simplifies the analysis. Its implications for the behavior of exchange rates is discussed at the end of the chapter.

---

8. Obviously, this assumption is a little stark. The real objective here is to model a situation where the array of available assets provides households with greater insurance against adverse domestic shocks than foreign shocks.

2.4.1 International Solvency

When markets are incomplete, we have to ensure that any international borrowing and lending induced by a shock does not put the households in one country on the path to insolvency. In other words, if a shock induces U.S. households to borrow from E.U. households, the economy must adjust to a path that will lead U.S. households to eventually repay their international debt. As we shall see, this solvency constraint places a restriction on the behavior of the exchange rate that substitutes for the risk-sharing condition implied by complete markets.

The U.S. solvency constraint is derived by consolidating the budget constraints of U.S. households and the government. Let B_t^{US} and $\hat{B}_t^{\mathrm{US}}$ denote the number of dollar bonds and euro bonds held by U.S. households in period t and EQ_t^{US} denote the number of shares of U.S. equity. Aggregating the budget constraints of individual U.S. households gives

$$
\begin{aligned}
B_t^{\mathrm{US}} &+ P_t^{\mathrm{E}} E Q_t^{\mathrm{US}} + S_t \hat{B}_t^{\mathrm{US}} \\
&= (P_t^{\mathrm{E}} + D_t) E Q_{t-1}^{\mathrm{US}} + R_{t-1} B_{t-1}^{\mathrm{US}} + S_t \hat{R}_{t-1} \hat{B}_{t-1}^{\mathrm{US}} + W_t L_t - P_t C_t,
\end{aligned}
\tag{2.71}
$$

where $L_t = \int_0^1 L_{n,t} dn$ is the aggregate supply of U.S. labor, P_t^{E} is the (ex-dividend) price of U.S. equity, and D_t is the total period-t dividend payment.

Dividends comprise the profits of U.S. retail firms and the proceeds from the sale of U.S. intermediate goods on world markets minus taxes. Recall that $X_{i,t}^{\mathrm{US}}$ and $X_{i,t}^{\mathrm{EU}}$ identify the demand for U.S. and E.U. intermediates by U.S. firm i and that X_t^{US} denotes the world demand for U.S. intermediates. We can write period-t dividends as

$$
\begin{aligned}
D_t &= P_t C_t - W_t L_t - P_t^{\mathrm{US}} \int_0^1 X_{i,t}^{\mathrm{US}} di - S_t \hat{P}_t^{\mathrm{EU}} \int_0^1 X_{i,t}^{\mathrm{EU}} di \\
&\quad + P_t^{\mathrm{US}} (X_t^{\mathrm{US}} + G_t) - T_t.
\end{aligned}
\tag{2.72}
$$

The first four terms on the right-hand side identify the period-t profits of U.S. retail firms, and the fifth and sixth show the proceeds from selling U.S. intermediate goods net of taxes.

In this model domestic imports are equal to the real value of foreign intermediate goods demanded by all domestic retail firms. This means that U.S. imports and exports are given by

$$
\mathfrak{M}_t = \frac{S_t \hat{P}_t^{\mathrm{EU}}}{P_t} \int_0^1 X_{i,t}^{\mathrm{EU}} di \quad \text{and} \quad \mathfrak{X}_t = \frac{P_t^{\mathrm{US}}}{P_t} \int_0^1 \hat{X}_{i,t}^{\mathrm{US}} di.
\tag{2.73}
$$

Combining these expressions with (2.72) and the identity $X_t^{\mathrm{US}} = \int_0^1 X_{i,t}^{\mathrm{US}} di + \int_0^1 \hat{X}_{i,t}^{\mathrm{US}} di$ yields

$$
D_t = P_t C_t - W_t L_t + P_t \mathfrak{X}_t - P_t \mathfrak{M}_t + P_t^{\mathrm{US}} G_t - T_t.
\tag{2.74}
$$

We are now ready to derive the consolidated U.S. budget constraint. Since U.S. equity can only be held by U.S. households, market clearing ensures that EQ_t^{US} and EQ_{t-1}^{US} are equal to the total number of outstanding U.S. equity shares. Without loss of generality, we can normalize the total number of outstanding shares to one so that $EQ_t^{US} = EQ_{t-1}^{US} = 1$. Imposing this market clearing condition on (2.71) and combining the result with (2.74) and the government budget constraint in (2.12) gives

$$S_t \hat{B}_t^{US} - B_t^{EU} = P_t \mathfrak{X}_t - P_t \mathfrak{M}_t - R_{t-1} B_{t-1}^{EU} + S_t \hat{R}_{t-1} \hat{B}_{t-1}^{US}, \qquad (2.75)$$

where $B_t^{EU} = B_t - B_t^{US}$ identifies the holdings of dollar bonds by E.U. households. Equation (2.75) is the consolidated U.S. budget constraint. It shows how the evolution of the foreign assets and liabilities of the United States relate to its exports and imports. In this model, U.S. holdings of euro bonds, $\hat{B}_t^{US}$, represent foreign assets, and the E.U. holdings of dollar bonds, B_t^{EU}, represent U.S. foreign liabilities.

To derive the U.S. solvency constraint, we rewrite (2.75) in terms of real U.S. assets, FA_t, and liabilities, FL_t. In particular, let $FA_t = S_t \hat{B}_t^{US}/P_t$ and $FL_t = B_t^{EU}/P_t$ so that (2.75) becomes

$$FA_t - FL_t = \mathfrak{X}_t - \mathfrak{M}_t - R_t^{FL} FL_{t-1} + R_t^{FA} FA_{t-1}, \qquad (2.76)$$

where $R_t^{FA} = S_t \hat{R}_{t-1} P_{t-1}/(S_{t-1} P_t)$ and $R_t^{FL} = R_{t-1} P_{t-1}/P_t$ denote the real returns on foreign assets and liabilities. Rearranging this equation and iterating forward yields

$$FL_t - FA_t = \sum_{i=1}^{\infty} \mathfrak{D}_{t+i}[\mathfrak{X}_{t+i} - \mathfrak{M}_{t+i} + (R_{t+i}^{FA} - R_{t+i}^{FL})FA_{t+i-1}]$$
$$+ \lim_{i \to \infty} \mathfrak{D}_{t+i}(FL_{t+i} - FA_{t+i}), \qquad (2.77)$$

where $\mathfrak{D}_{t+i} = (\Pi_{j=1}^i R_{t+j}^{FL})^{-1}$ is the discount rate.

The first term on the right-hand side of equation (2.77) is the present value of net exports, $\mathfrak{X}_t - \mathfrak{M}_t$, and the net interest income on foreign assets, $(R_t^{FA} - R_t^{FL})FA_{t-1}$. The second term identifies the present value of the future U.S. international indebtedness as the horizon rises without limit. This term must be equal to zero to rule out Ponzi games. For example, if $\lim_{i \to \infty} \mathfrak{D}_{t+i}(FL_{t+i} - FA_{t+i}) > 0$, current U.S. indebtedness exceeds the value of the resources available for U.S. households to pay off their international debt in the future, so the U.S. would have to borrow ever larger amounts to avoid defaulting. Clearly, E.U. households would never allow such a Ponzi scheme because it amounts to providing U.S. households with free resources. Alternatively, if $\lim_{i \to \infty} \mathfrak{D}_{t+i}(FL_{t+i} - FA_{t+i}) < 0$, U.S. households would be consenting to an analogous Ponzi scheme. Thus, $\lim_{i \to \infty} \mathfrak{D}_{t+i}(FL_{t+i} - FA_{t+i})$ must equal zero to rule out Ponzi schemes by both U.S. and E.U. households.

Imposing the no-Ponzi condition and taking expectations gives us the ex ante version of equation (2.77):

$$FL_t - FA_t = \mathbb{E}_t \sum_{i=1}^{\infty} \mathfrak{D}_{t+i}[\mathfrak{X}_{t+i} - \mathfrak{M}_{t+i} + (R_{t+i}^{FA} - R_{t+i}^{FL})FA_{t+i-1}]. \qquad (2.78)$$

Here the current values of U.S. foreign assets and liabilities are linked to expectations concerning the future course of net exports and returns in a world where international debts are fully honored. Note that all the terms are endogenous. Equation (2.78) does not determine the difference between U.S. foreign liabilities and assets any more than it determines the returns, R_{t+i}^{FA} and R_{t+i}^{FL}. Instead, it describes the constraint on their joint behavior implied by national solvency.

To illustrate the economic importance of the solvency constraint, suppose for a moment that the returns on foreign assets and liabilities are equal and constant. Suppose further that some news leads everyone to anticipate that U.S. net exports will be lower going into the future. Equation (2.78) tells us that this same news must also lower the value of U.S. net foreign liabilities, $FL_t - FA_t = (S_t \hat{B}_t^{\text{US}} - B_t^{\text{EU}})/P_t$, via a combination of: (1) an appreciation in the dollar, (2) a rise in U.S. prices, and (3) a change in households' bond holdings. News concerning net exports could also lead everyone to revise their expectations concerning future returns. Under these circumstances, equation (2.78) shows that the effect of the U.S. indebtedness depends on how the anticipated interest income on foreign assets and the discount rate respond to the revision in expectations.

The nonlinear restrictions among U.S. foreign assets, liabilities, net exports, and returns in equation (2.78) cannot be easily incorporated into an exchange-rate model. We shall therefore use a log-linear approximation to (2.78):

$$fl_t - fa_t = \mathbb{E}_t \sum_{i=1}^{\infty} \mu^{i-1}[(1-\mu)\, nx_{t+i} + (r_{t+i}^{\text{FA}} - r_{t+i}^{\text{FL}})], \qquad (2.79)$$

where $nx_t = \ln(\mathfrak{X}_t/\mathfrak{M}_t)$ and $0 < \mu < 1$.[9] The derivation of (2.79) requires several steps, so the details are relegated to the appendix. Importantly, (2.79) embodies the central feature of the solvency constraint in (2.78). Any increase in the real value of U.S. foreign liabilities relative to foreign assets must be accompanied by expectations of higher future net exports and/or higher future excess returns on foreign assets. In this approximation, the rise in U.S. indebtedness is identified by an increase in the log ratio of liabilities to assets, $fl_t - fa_t = \ln(FL_t/FA_t)$; nx_t is the log ratio of exports to imports rather than net exports and $r_t^{\text{FA}} - r_t^{\text{FL}}$ denotes the log excess return on U.S. foreign assets relative to U.S. liabilities.

2.4.2 Portfolio Choice

The value of a country's foreign assets and liabilities depends, in part, on the portfolio decisions of households. In particular, in this model the real value of U.S. foreign liabilities, FL_t, depends on the number of dollar bonds E.U. households wish to hold, B_t^{EU}, while the real value of U.S. foreign assets, FA_t, depends on the holdings of euro bonds by U.S. households, $\hat{B}_t^{\text{US}}$. We now turn to the question of how households determine these asset holdings.

We concentrate on the portfolio decisions facing U.S. households. Recall that the labor market allows households to share risk completely within a country, so the aggregate household budget constraint in (2.71) also represents the budget constraint facing a representative U.S. household.

---

9. Obviously, this approximation only makes sense if FL_t and FA_t are positive in all periods. If this is not the case in the equilibrium being studied, the definitions of FL_t and FA_t can be suitably amended.

To study the portfolio problem facing this household, let A_t denote the real value of financial wealth at the start of period t: $A_t = (P_t^{EQ} E Q_{t-1}^{US} + D_t E Q_{t-1}^{US} + R_{t-1} B_{t-1}^{US} + S_t \hat{R}_{t-1} \hat{B}_{t-1}^{US})/P_t$. We can rewrite the budget constraint in (2.71) as

$$A_{t+1} = R_{t+1}^A (A_t + Y_t^L - C_t), \qquad (2.80)$$

where $Y_t^L = (W_t/P_t) L_t$ is labor income and R_{t+1}^A is the return on total savings between periods t and $t+1$. This is a portfolio return because it depends on how the household distributes its savings among dollar bonds, euro bonds, and U.S. equities. Specifically, let h_t^B and h_t^E denote the fractions of total period-t savings that the household chooses to hold in euro bonds and U.S. equities:

$$h_t^B = \frac{S_t \hat{B}_t^{US}/P_t}{A_t + Y_t^L - C_t} \quad \text{and} \quad h_t^E = \frac{P_t^E E Q_t^{US}/P_t}{A_t + Y_t^L - C_t}.$$

Then, the portfolio return is given by

$$R_{t+1}^A = \frac{R_t P_t}{P_{t+1}} \left(1 + \left[\frac{S_{t+1} \hat{R}_t}{S_t R_t} - 1 \right] h_t^B + \left[\frac{R_{t+1}^E}{R_t} - 1 \right] h_t^E \right), \qquad (2.81)$$

where $R_{t+1}^E = (P_{t+1}^E + D_{t+1})/P_t^E$ is the return on equity. The term outside the parentheses identifies the realized real return on dollar bonds and the term inside shows the contribution of equity and euro bond holdings to the overall portfolio return. This contribution depends on portfolio shares, h_t^B and h_t^E, chosen by the household in period t and the realized excess returns on euro bonds and equities identified by the terms in brackets.

The portfolio problem facing a representative U.S. household in period t amounts to the problem of choosing h_t^B and h_t^E to maximize expected utility $\mathbb{U}_t$ [defined in equation (2.1)] subject to the budget constraint in (2.80) with portfolio return defined by (2.81). The solution to this problem is characterized by the following first-order conditions:

$$1 = \mathbb{E}_t \left[\beta \left(\frac{C_{t+1}}{C_t} \right)^{-1} R_t \frac{P_t}{P_{t+1}} \right],$$

$$1 = \mathbb{E}_t \left[\beta \left(\frac{C_{t+1}}{C_t} \right)^{-1} R_{t+1}^E \frac{P_t}{P_{t+1}} \right],$$

and

$$1 = \mathbb{E}_t \left[\beta \left(\frac{C_{t+1}}{C_t} \right)^{-1} \frac{S_{t+1} \hat{R}_t}{S_t} \frac{P_t}{P_{t+1}} \right]. \qquad (2.82)$$

In principle, we would like to find expressions for the optimal values of h_t^B and h_t^E by combing these conditions with (2.80) and (2.81). Unfortunately, this is rarely possible in practice because the first-order conditions involve nonlinear functions of random variables with unknown distributions. Instead, we find expressions for h_t^B and h_t^E that well approximate the optimal portfolio choices.

To derive these expressions, we work with the log approximations to the first-order conditions and portfolio returns. As in Chapter 1, the first-order conditions in (2.82) are approximated as

$$\mathbb{E}_t \mathbf{er}_{t+1} + \tfrac{1}{2} \operatorname{diag}\left(\Sigma_t\right) = \mathbb{CV}_t \left(\mathbf{er}_{t+1}, c_{t+1} + p_{t+1}\right) \qquad (2.83a)$$

and

$$r_t - \mathbb{E}_t \Delta p_{t+1} = \mathbb{E}_t \Delta c_{t+1} - \ln \beta - \tfrac{1}{2} \mathbb{V}_t(c_{t+1} + p_{t+1}), \qquad (2.83b)$$

where $\mathbb{V}_t(\cdot)$ and $\mathbb{CV}_t(\cdot, \cdot)$ denote the variance and covariance conditioned on period-t information, $\mathbf{er}'_{t+1} = [\ \Delta s_{t+1} + \hat{r}_t - r_t \quad r^{\mathrm{E}}_{t+1} - r_t\ ]$ is a vector of log excess returns, and $\Sigma_t = \mathbb{V}_t(\mathbf{er}_{t+1})$. As usual, lowercase letters denote the logs of a variable, so r^{E}_{t+1} is the log return on U.S. equity and r^{A}_{t+1} is the log return on the portfolio. Campbell and Viceira (2002) show that the log portfolio return is well approximated by

$$r^{\mathrm{A}}_{t+1} = r_t - \Delta p_{t+1} + \mathbf{h}'_t \mathbf{er}_{t+1} + \tfrac{1}{2} \mathbf{h}'_t \left(\operatorname{diag}\left(\Sigma_t\right) - \Sigma_t \mathbf{h}_t\right), \qquad (2.84)$$

where $\mathbf{h}'_t = [\ h^{\mathrm{B}}_t \quad h^{\mathrm{E}}_t\ ]$ is the vector of portfolio shares. Note that r^{A}_{t+1} is just equal to the realized log real return on dollar bonds when $\mathbf{h}_t$ is a vector of zeros because the household does not hold any euro bonds or equity. In other cases, the portfolio return depends on the log excess returns in $\mathbf{er}_{t+1}$, and their second moments, Σ_t. The latter terms are present because we are approximating $\ln R^{\mathrm{A}}_{t+1}$, which is a nonlinear function of the portfolio shares and log excess returns.

We can now use (2.83a) and (2.84) to derive an expression for the vector of portfolio shares, $\mathbf{h}_t$. First, we combine the right-hand side of (2.83a) with the identity $c_{t+1} = a_{t+1} + c_{t+1} - a_{t+1}$ to get

$$\mathbb{CV}_t \left(\mathbf{er}_{t+1}, c_{t+1} + p_{t+1}\right) = \mathbb{CV}_t \left(\mathbf{er}_{t+1}, a_{t+1}\right) + \mathbb{CV}_t \left(\mathbf{er}_{t+1}, p_{t+1}\right)$$
$$+ \mathbb{CV}_t \left(\mathbf{er}_{t+1}, c_{t+1} - a_{t+1}\right).$$

Next, we note from (2.80) that $a_{t+1} = r^{\mathrm{A}}_{t+1} + \ln(A_t + Y^{\mathrm{L}}_t - C_t)$, so we can use (2.84) to rewrite this last expression as

$$\mathbb{CV}_t \left(\mathbf{er}_{t+1}, c_{t+1} + p_{t+1}\right) = \Sigma_t \mathbf{h}_t + \mathbb{CV}_t(\mathbf{er}_{t+1}, c_{t+1} - a_{t+1}). \qquad (2.85)$$

Finally, we combine (2.85) with (2.83a) to get

$$\mathbf{h}_t = \Sigma_t^{-1} \left\{ \mathbb{E}_t \mathbf{er}_{t+1} + \tfrac{1}{2} \operatorname{diag}\left(\Sigma_t\right) \right\} - \Sigma_t^{-1} \mathbb{CV}_t(\mathbf{er}_{t+1}, c_{t+1} - a_{t+1}). \qquad (2.86)$$

Equation (2.86) identifies two sets of factors that affect the choice of portfolio shares. The first term on the right shows the influence of expected excess returns.[10] If excess returns are uncorrelated, Σ_t is a diagonal matrix, so the portfolio share for equity and euro bonds is increasing in the expected excess return on each asset. This case confirms the conventional wisdom of investing more in assets with higher

---

10. Elements in the vector $\mathbf{er}_{t+1}$ are adjusted by the addition of one-half times the return variance, a Jensen inequality term, to account for the fact that we are working with log returns terms.

expected excess returns. If excess returns are correlated, each portfolio share depends on the expected returns on equity and euro bonds. In this case, changes in the expected excess returns on equities can be a source of variation in the desired share of euro bonds in the household's portfolio.

The second term on the right-hand side of (2.86) identifies the hedging demand for each asset. Ceteris paribus, households prefer assets that have unexpected high real returns when the marginal utility of consumption is also high. This will be the case when the covariance between the excess return and $c_{t+1} + p_{t+1}$ is negative. Equation (2.85) shows that this hedging benefit can be achieved via the choice of $\mathbf{h}_t$ and the elements of $\mathbb{CV}_t(\mathbf{er}_{t+1}, c_{t+1} - a_{t+1})$. If these elements are negative, both equities and euro bonds provide good hedges, so as (2.86) shows, households will want to hold a larger fraction of their portfolios in these assets.

One further aspect of equation (2.86) deserves note. If the joint distribution of log returns, consumption, and prices is i.i.d., none of the first and second moments on the right-hand side will vary from period to period. Under these circumstances, (2.86) says that households will want to hold constant fractions of their savings in equities, euro bonds, and (by implication) dollar bonds. This implication does not rely on any approximations. Equation (2.83a) holds exactly, and (2.86) can be derived from (2.83a) and (2.81) directly. Thus, equation (2.86) will contain an approximation error insofar as the joint distribution of log returns, consumption, and prices diverge from the i.i.d. case.

Equation (2.86) approximates the desired shares of equities and euro bonds in the U.S. household's portfolio rather than its holdings of the actual assets. We therefore have to multiply the elements of $\mathbf{h}_t$ by aggregate U.S. savings to find period-t asset holdings. In particular, combining the definitions for FA_t and h_t^{B} we obtain the following expression for U.S. foreign assets:

$$FA_t = \frac{S_t \hat{B}_t^{\mathrm{US}}}{P_t} = h_t^{\mathrm{B}}(A_t + Y_t^{\mathrm{L}} - C_t). \tag{2.87}$$

U.S. foreign liabilities are determined analogously from the portfolio decisions of E.U. households. In particular, let $\hat{\mathbf{er}}_{t+1}' = [\, r_t - \Delta s_{t+1} - \hat{r}_t \quad \hat{r}_{t+1}^{\mathrm{E}} - \hat{r}_t \,]$ be the vector of log excess returns on dollar bonds and E.U. equity relative to euro bonds, and let $\hat{\mathbf{h}}_t' = [\, \hat{h}_t^{\mathrm{B}} \quad \hat{h}_t^{\mathrm{E}} \,]$ denote the shares of dollar bonds and E.U. equity in the representative E.U. household's portfolio, $\hat{A}_t + \hat{Y}_t^{\mathrm{L}} - \hat{C}_t$. Following the preceding steps, we can approximate the desired portfolio shares by

$$\hat{\mathbf{h}}_t = \hat{\Sigma}_t^{-1} \left\{ \mathbb{E}_t \hat{\mathbf{er}}_{t+1} + \tfrac{1}{2} \operatorname{diag}(\hat{\Sigma}_t) \right\} - \hat{\Sigma}_t^{-1} \mathbb{CV}_t(\hat{\mathbf{er}}_{t+1}, \hat{c}_{t+1} - \hat{a}_{t+1}). \tag{2.88}$$

U.S. foreign liabilities can now be written as

$$FL_t = \frac{B_t^{\mathrm{EU}}}{P_t} = \frac{B_t^{\mathrm{EU}}}{S_t \hat{P}_t} \mathcal{E}_t = \hat{h}_t^{\mathrm{B}}(\hat{A}_t + \hat{Y}_t^{\mathrm{L}} - \hat{C}_t)\mathcal{E}_t. \tag{2.89}$$

We can now use these results to link U.S. indebtedness to the portfolio decisions of U.S. and E.U. households. In particular, (2.87) and (2.89) imply that

$$fl_t - fa_t = \varepsilon_t + \hat{a}_t - a_t \qquad (2.90)$$

$$+ \ln \left(\hat{h}_t^B / h_t^B \right) + \ln \left(\frac{1 - \exp(\hat{c}_t - \hat{a}_t)[1 - \exp(\hat{y}_t^L - \hat{c}_t)]}{1 - \exp(c_t - a_t)[1 - \exp(y_t^L - c_t)]} \right).$$

Here we see that variations in U.S. indebtedness can come from changes in: (1) the relative financial wealth of E.U. versus U.S. households, $\varepsilon_t + \hat{a}_t - a_t$, (2) the desired portfolio shares for foreign bonds, $\hat{h}_t^B / h_t^B$, (3) the consumption asset ratios, and (4) the labor income to consumption ratios. We examine the importance of these different channels in what follows.

2.4.3 Portfolio Balance with Flexible Prices

We are now ready to study the behavior of exchange rates when markets are incomplete. First, we examine the implications of households' portfolio choices and the international solvency constraint in an economy where retail firms reset prices every period. In this flex-price case, central banks have no reason to change short-term interest rates, so we can isolate how incomplete risk-sharing affects the behavior of exchange rates via its affects on the foreign exchange risk premium. We then reintroduce price-stickiness in the form of staggered price-setting by retail firms.

When prices are flexible, the exchange-rate implications of the model depend on the dynamics of the two key variables: the foreign exchange risk premium, $\delta_t = \mathbb{E}_t \Delta s_{t+1} + \hat{r}_t - r_t$, and the log ratio of U.S. foreign liabilities to assets or "net liabilities," $nfl_t = fl_t - fa_t$. Loosely speaking, the risk premium reflects expectations concerning the future growth in net liabilities and the returns on equities, whereas net liabilities depend on the future course of the risk premium and the endowments of intermediate goods.

We begin with the determination of log net exports, $nx_t = \ln(\mathfrak{X}_t / \mathfrak{M}_t)$. U.S. exports are determined by the aggregate demand of E.U. retail firms for U.S. intermediate goods, as shown by the second term in equation (2.16). Multiplying this term by the real price of U.S. intermediate goods, P_t^{US} / P_t, and taking logs gives

$$\ln \mathfrak{X}_t = \text{const.} - (1 - \theta)\lambda \tau_t + \hat{c}_t + \varepsilon_t + \widehat{rmc}_t.$$

U.S. imports are determined by the aggregate demand of U.S. retail firms for E.U. intermediate goods, identified by the second term in (2.17). Multiplying this term by P_t^{EU} / P_t and taking logs yields

$$\ln \mathfrak{M}_t = \text{const.} + (1 - \theta)\lambda \tau_t + c_t + rmc_t.$$

Combining these equations produces the following expression for log net exports:

$$nx_t = 2(\theta - 1)\lambda \tau_t + (\hat{c}_t + \varepsilon_t - c_t) + \widehat{rmc}_t - rmc_t. \qquad (2.91)$$

Net exports vary with the terms of trade, the difference between E.U. and U.S. consumption expenditures, and the difference between E.U. and U.S. real marginal costs. Ceteris paribus, variations in the terms of trade induce retail firms to substitute between U.S. and E.U. intermediate goods. In particular, if the elasticity of substitution, θ, is greater than one, the increase in the relative price of E.U. goods associated with a rise in τ_t induces a fall in the expenditure share of E.U. to U.S. goods across all retail firms so that net exports rise. Net exports also depend on the aggregate demand for consumer goods in each country. A rise in domestic consumption implies a higher demand for foreign intermediate goods, so net exports must rise in response to an increase in $\hat{c}_t + \varepsilon_t - c_t$. Finally, net exports vary in response to international differences in real marginal costs because these differences reflect the relative prices of nontraded inputs. In particular, higher real wages increase retail firms' demand for intermediate goods and their real marginal costs, so a rise in $\widehat{rmc}_t - rmc_t$ induces an increase in net exports.

We saw earlier that the equilibrium terms of trade were entirely determined by the endowments of intermediate goods, e_t^{US} and e_t^{EU}, when prices were flexible and markets were complete. However, when markets are incomplete this is no longer the case. In particular, when households have log preferences, the price-setting equations in (2.49) together with the definitions of the real exchange rate and the terms of trade imply that

$$\varepsilon_t = \alpha(2\lambda - 1)\tau_t + (1 - \alpha)(\varepsilon_t + \hat{c}_t - c_t). \tag{2.92}$$

Complete risk-sharing requires that $\varepsilon_t = c_t - \hat{c}_t$ when households have log preferences, so the second term on the right-hand side disappears. Under these circumstances, (2.92) and the market-clearing conditions for intermediate goods in (2.31) imply that $\tau_t = \xi(e_t^{\text{US}} - e_t^{\text{EU}})$, where $\xi = [4\theta\lambda(1 - \lambda) + (2\lambda - 1)^2]^{-1} > 0$. When markets are incomplete, (2.92) and the wholesale market-clearing condition in (2.31) imply that

$$\tau_t = \xi(e_t^{\text{US}} - e_t^{\text{EU}}) + (2\lambda - 1)\xi(\varepsilon_t + \hat{c}_t - c_t). \tag{2.93}$$

Thus the equilibrium terms of trade depend on the endowments of intermediate goods and the relative consumption expenditures of E.U. and U.S. households. Intuitively, an increase in $\varepsilon_t + \hat{c}_t - c_t$ shifts world demand toward E.U. goods and away from U.S. goods when there is home bias in the use of intermediates. As a result, there must be a rise in the relative price of E.U. goods to clear world wholesale markets or, equivalently, a deterioration in the U.S. terms of trade.

We are now ready to determine the behavior of net liabilities and the risk premium. When households have log preferences and prices are flexible, the expression for U.S. net liabilities in equation (2.90) simplifies considerably. In particular, households find it optimal to consume a constant fraction of their financial wealth and their labor income, so that (2.90) becomes

$$nfl_t = \varepsilon_t + \hat{c}_t - c_t + \ln(\hat{h}_t^{\text{B}}/h_t^{\text{B}}) \cong \varepsilon_t + \hat{c}_t - c_t + \hat{h}_t^{\text{B}} - h_t^{\text{B}}. \tag{2.94}$$

Recall that h_t^{B} and $\hat{h}_t^{\text{B}}$ denote the fraction of savings held in foreign bonds by U.S. and E.U. households. In a symmetric equilibrium where households face similar investment opportunities, these portfolio shares should be very similar, so $\ln(\hat{h}_t^{\text{B}}/h_t^{\text{B}})$ will be well approximated by $\hat{h}_t^{\text{B}} - h_t^{\text{B}}$, as shown earlier. Furthermore, h_t^{B} and $\hat{h}_t^{\text{B}}$ are determined by the portfolio share equations in (2.86) and (2.88). When households have log preferences and prices are flexible, these equations become

$$\mathbf{h}_t = \Sigma_t^{-1}\{\mathbb{E}_t \mathbf{er}_{t+1} + \tfrac{1}{2} \operatorname{diag}(\Sigma_t)\} \quad \text{and} \quad \widehat{\mathbf{h}}_t = \widehat{\Sigma}_t^{-1}\{\mathbb{E}_t \widehat{\mathbf{er}}_{t+1} + \tfrac{1}{2} \operatorname{diag}(\widehat{\Sigma}_t)\},$$

where $\mathbf{h}_t' = [\, h_t^{\mathrm{B}} \quad h_t^{\mathrm{E}}\,]$ and $\widehat{\mathbf{h}}_t' = [\, \hat{h}_t^{\mathrm{B}} \quad \hat{h}_t^{\mathrm{E}}\,]$. Note that households' portfolio choices vary with changes in both expected excess returns, $\mathbb{E}_t \mathbf{er}_{t+1}$ and $\mathbb{E}_t \widehat{\mathbf{er}}_{t+1}$, and the conditional covariance matrices, Σ_t and $\widehat{\Sigma}_t$. In principle, shocks to the economy can affect all these terms. However, here, for the sake for clarity, we focus on the role of expected log excess returns. To this end, we linearize the preceding equations for h_t^{B} and $\hat{h}_t^{\mathrm{B}}$ as

$$h_t^{\mathrm{B}} = \sigma_0 + \sigma_1 \delta_t + \sigma_2 \mathbb{E}_t[r_{t+1}^{\mathrm{E}} - r_t] + o_t \quad \text{and} \quad \hat{h}_t^{\mathrm{B}} = \hat{\sigma}_0 - \hat{\sigma}_1 \delta_t + \hat{\sigma}_2 \mathbb{E}_t[\hat{r}_{t+1}^{\mathrm{E}} - \hat{r}_t] + \hat{o}_t,$$

where the σ_i and $\hat{\sigma}_i$ are coefficients that depend on the steady state covariance matrices and $\delta_t = \mathbb{E}_t[\Delta s_{t+1} + \hat{r}_t - r_t]$. The last terms in each expression, o_t and $\hat{o}_t$, identify the effects of changes in Σ_t and $\widehat{\Sigma}_t$, respectively. Finally, combining these equations with (2.94) gives

$$nfl_t = (\varepsilon_t + \hat{c}_t - c_t) - \sigma\delta_t - \Im_t, \tag{2.95}$$

where $\Im_t = \sigma_2 \mathbb{E}_t[r_{t+1}^{\mathrm{E}} - r_t] - \hat{\sigma}_2 \mathbb{E}_t[\hat{r}_{t+1}^{\mathrm{E}} - \hat{r}_t] + o_t - \hat{o}_t$ and $\sigma = \sigma_1 + \hat{\sigma}_1$. It is straightforward to check that both σ_1 and $\hat{\sigma}_1$ are positive, so $\sigma > 0$.

Equation (2.95) is a key equation: it shows how U.S. net liabilities are linked to the three factors that affect the asset holdings of U.S. and E.U. households. First, consider the effects of a shock that shifts financial wealth from U.S. to E.U. households but has no effect on expected future excess returns. Such a shock will have no effect on the desired fraction of savings held in foreign bonds, so the shift in wealth will induce foreign households to raise their holdings of dollar bonds while U.S. households reduce their holdings of euro bonds. As a consequence, U.S. foreign liabilities rise and U.S. foreign assets fall, so nfl_t increases. The shift in wealth also induces an increase in $\varepsilon_t + \hat{c}_t - c_t$ because households consume a constant fraction of their financial wealth.

Changes in the foreign exchange risk premium also affect net U.S. liabilities because households adjust the fractions of their savings held in foreign bonds. A rise in δ_t, for example, leads U.S. households to hold a larger fraction of their savings in euro bonds and induces E.U. households to reduce the fraction of their savings in dollar bonds. These portfolio reallocations reduce E.U. holdings of U.S. bonds and increase U.S. holdings of euro bonds, so U.S. net liabilities fall. Similar portfolio reallocations can occur if there is a change in the expected excess returns on U.S. or E.U. equities, or the conditional covariance matrices, Σ_t and $\widehat{\Sigma}_t$. Equation (2.95) identifies their effect on U.S. net liabilities via the portfolio shift term, $\Im_t$.

We now use (2.95) to derive an expression for the equilibrium foreign exchange risk premium. When U.S. and E.U. households have log preferences, their first-order conditions for consumption satisfy

$$r_t - \mathbb{E}_t \Delta p_{t+1} = \text{const.} + \mathbb{E}_t \Delta c_{t+1} \quad \text{and} \quad \hat{r}_t - \mathbb{E}_t \Delta \hat{p}_{t+1} = \text{const.} + \mathbb{E}_t \Delta \hat{c}_{t+1}.$$

Using these expressions, we can rewrite the foreign exchange risk premium as

$$\delta_t = \mathbb{E}_t \Delta\varepsilon_{t+1} + \hat{r}_t - \mathbb{E}_t \Delta\hat{p}_{t+1} - (r_t - \mathbb{E}_t \Delta p_{t+1}) = \mathbb{E}_t(\Delta\varepsilon_{t+1} + \Delta\hat{c}_{t+1} - \Delta c_{t+1}).$$

Substituting for the term on the right with (2.95) and rearranging gives

$$\delta_t = \frac{1}{1+\sigma}\mathbb{E}_t(\Delta nfl_{t+1} + \Delta\Im_{t+1}) + \frac{\sigma}{1+\sigma}\mathbb{E}_t\delta_{t+1}, \qquad (2.96)$$

or after iterating forward

$$\delta_t = \frac{1}{\sigma}\mathbb{E}_t \sum_{i=1}^{\infty}\left(\frac{\sigma}{1+\sigma}\right)^i\left\{\Delta nfl_{t+i} + \Delta\Im_{t+i}\right\}. \qquad (2.97)$$

Here we see that the foreign exchange risk premium depends on the present value of future growth in net liabilities, Δnfl_{t+i}, and future changes in excess equity returns, $\Delta\Im_{t+i}$. To understand why, note that equation (2.95) implies that

$$\mathbb{E}_t(\Delta nfl_{t+1} + \Delta\Im_{t+1}) = \mathbb{E}_t\left(\Delta\varepsilon_{t+1} + \Delta\hat{c}_{t+1} - \Delta c_{t+1}\right) - \sigma\mathbb{E}_t\Delta\delta_{t+1}$$
$$= \delta_t - \sigma\mathbb{E}_t\Delta\delta_{t+1}.$$

An increase in $\mathbb{E}_t(\Delta nfl_{t+1} + \Delta\Im_{t+1})$ must be accompanied by either a rise in δ_t or a fall in $\mathbb{E}_t\Delta\delta_{t+1}$ if households are to adjust their portfolios in a consistent manner. Clearly, this can be achieved if the risk premium rises immediately and is then expected to fall back to its original level. More generally, equation (2.97) identifies the level for the current risk premium that will induce households to alter their future bond holdings in a manner that is consistent with expectations concerning $\Delta nfl_{t+i} - \Delta\Im_{t+i}$.

Finally, we turn to the solvency constraint in equation (2.79). By definition, $r^{\text{FA}}_{t+1} - r^{\text{FL}}_{t+1} = \Delta s_{t+1} + \hat{r}_t - r_t$, so iterating (2.79) forward one period gives

$$nfl_t = (1 - \mu)\,\mathbb{E}_t nx_{t+1} + \delta_t + \mu\mathbb{E}_t nfl_{t+1}. \qquad (2.98)$$

Under flexible pricing, real marginal costs are constant, so (2.91) becomes

$$nx_t = 2(\theta - 1)\lambda\tau_t + (\hat{c}_t + \varepsilon_t - c_t).$$

Combining this expression with (2.93) and (2.95) yields

$$nx_t = (1 + \varpi)\left(nfl_t + \sigma\delta_t + \Im_t\right) + \frac{\varpi}{(2\lambda - 1)}(e^{\text{US}}_t - e^{\text{EU}}_t), \qquad (2.99)$$

where $\varpi = 2(2\lambda - 1)(\theta - 1)\lambda\xi$.

Equations (2.96), (2.98), and (2.99) jointly determine the behavior of net liabilities and the risk premium in terms of $\Im_t$, e^{US}_t, and e^{EU}_t. In particular, this system of equations can be written as

$$\begin{bmatrix} \delta_t \\ nfl_t \end{bmatrix} = \mathcal{H}\mathbb{E}_t\begin{bmatrix} \delta_{t+1} \\ nfl_{t+1} \end{bmatrix} + \mathcal{G}\mathbb{E}_t\begin{bmatrix} e^{\text{US}}_{t+1} - e^{\text{EU}}_{t+1} \\ \Im_{t+1} \\ \Im_t \end{bmatrix} \qquad (2.100)$$

for some matrices, $\mathcal{H}$ and $\mathcal{G}$. This system of equations is similar to the one examined in Section 2.2.2 in the sense that δ_t and nfl_t are nonpredetermined variables. So, once again, there will be a unique and bounded solution to (2.100) if, and only if, the roots of $\mathcal{H}$ lie outside the unit circle.

Exchange-Rate Dynamics

Section 2.2.2 showed that under complete markets all variations in the flex-price spot rate, s_t^F, are driven by current changes in the endowments of U.S. and E.U. goods, e_t^{US} and e_t^{EU}. The behavior of the spot rate is very different when markets are incomplete. Here news about current and future endowments and equity returns affect the current spot rate via their impact on the foreign exchange risk premium and the international distribution of wealth.

To examine these effects, we first combine the identity $\Delta s_{t+1} = \mathbb{E}_t \Delta s_{t+1} + s_{t+1} - \mathbb{E}_t s_{t+1}$ with the definition of the risk premium to give $\Delta s_{t+1} = \delta_t + r_t - \hat{r}_t + s_{t+1} - \mathbb{E}_t s_{t+1}$. When central banks set interest rates according to the Taylor rules in (2.48) and prices are flexible, interest rates are determined entirely by policy shocks so $r_t - \hat{r}_t = v_t - \hat{v}_t$. We can therefore write the rate of nominal depreciation as

$$\Delta s_{t+1} = \delta_t + v_t - \hat{v}_t + s_{t+1} - \mathbb{E}_t s_{t+1}. \tag{2.101}$$

Recall that real marginal costs are constant when retail firms reset prices every period, so there is no incentive for individual firms to change their prices causing inflation. As a result, $s_{t+1} - \mathbb{E}_t s_{t+1} = \varepsilon_{t+1} - \mathbb{E}_t \varepsilon_{t+1}$, so (2.95) implies that

$$s_{t+1} - \mathbb{E}_t s_{t+1} = (1 - \mathbb{E}_t)(nfl_{t+1} + \sigma \delta_{t+1} + \Im_{t+1}) + (1 - \mathbb{E}_t)(c_{t+1} - \hat{c}_{t+1}).$$

Furthermore, since households consume a constant fraction of their financial wealth,

$$(1 - \mathbb{E}_t)(c_{t+1} - \hat{c}_{t+1}) = (1 - \mathbb{E}_t)(a_{t+1} - \hat{a}_{t+1}) = (1 - \mathbb{E}_t)(r_{t+1}^A - \hat{r}_{t+1}^A), \tag{2.102}$$

where r_{t+1}^A and $\hat{r}_{t+1}^A$ are the log returns on U.S. and E.U. households' financial wealth. In the absence of inflation, the excess returns on foreign bonds and domestic equity are the only sources of unexpected returns on wealth. In particular,

$$(1 - \mathbb{E}_t)(r_{t+1}^A - \hat{r}_{t+1}^A) = (h_t^B + \hat{h}_t^B)(1 - \mathbb{E}_t)s_{t+1} + h_t^E(1 - \mathbb{E}_t)r_{t+1}^E - \hat{h}_t^E(1 - \mathbb{E}_t)\hat{r}_{t+1}^E.$$

Combining this expression with the preceding equations gives

$$\begin{aligned} s_{t+1} - \mathbb{E}_t s_{t+1} = {}& \mathfrak{H}_t(1 - \mathbb{E}_t)(nfl_{t+1} + \Im_{t+1} + \sigma \delta_{t+1}) \\ & + \mathfrak{H}_t(1 - \mathbb{E}_t)(h_t^E r_{t+1}^E - \hat{h}_t^E \hat{r}_{t+1}^E), \end{aligned} \tag{2.103}$$

where $\mathfrak{H}_t = 1/(1 - h_t^B - \hat{h}_t^B)$.

Equation (2.103) shows that unexpected variations in spot rates come from two sources. The first term on the right identifies the effects of news concerning *future* endowments and excess equity returns. In particular, equation (2.100) implies that both nfl_{t+1} and δ_{t+1} will immediately change if households receive news in period $t + 1$ that leads them to revise their forecasts about future endowments and/or the excess return on equities. The second term on the right identifies the effects of *current* unexpected excess equity returns. In the absence of complete risk-sharing, unexpected equity returns change the financial wealth of U.S. and E.U. households and hence their desired holdings of dollar and euro bonds. The spot rate must adjust to offset this portfolio rebalancing because otherwise it would lead to an unsustainable change in U.S. net liabilities. In particular, if equity returns increase the real financial wealth of U.S. households relative to E.U. households, the dollar must depreciate so that the rise in U.S. holdings of euro bonds is matched by an increase in the dollar value of U.S. bonds held by E.U. households.

Equation (2.103) also shows that period-t portfolio choices affect the degree to which the spot rate responds to the arrival of new information in period $t + 1$. For example, unexpected equity returns have a larger impact on households' financial wealth in period $t + 1$ when a larger fraction of period-t savings is held in the form of equities. Period-t portfolio decisions concerning foreign bonds also have an impact. In particular, equation (2.103) shows that news in period $t + 1$ will have a bigger impact on the spot rate when foreign bonds make up a larger fraction of households' savings. The reason is that any unexpected variation in spot rates induced by the direct effects of news also has an effect on the international distribution of financial wealth. This secondary effect is larger when households hold a larger fraction of their savings in foreign bonds and serves to amplify the original effects of the news. The size of this amplification effect is given by $\mathfrak{H}_t = 1/(1 - h_t^{\mathrm{B}} - \hat{h}_t^{\mathrm{B}})$, which is increasing in $h_t^{\mathrm{B}} + \hat{h}_t^{\mathrm{B}}$.

The dynamics of the spot rate are determined by equations (2.101) and (2.103) with net liabilities and the risk premium satisfying the dynamics in (2.100). To study these dynamics, we calibrate the model using the parameter values shown in Table 2.3. These values guarantee a determinant solution to the difference equations for nfl_t and δ_t in (2.100).

The values for four of the parameters in Table 2.3 are noteworthy. The approximation for net liabilities in (2.79) involves the discount factor, μ, which is equal to one minus the steady state ratio of imports to foreign assets. This number should be close to one when imports are measured over short periods and households diversify their

TABLE 2.3
Portfolio Balance Model Parameters

Parameter	Symbol	Value
Discount factor	β	0.997
Risk-aversion	γ	1.000
Intermediate share	α	0.330
Domestic intermediate share	λ	0.850
Intermediate elasticity	θ	0.740
Net liability discount factor	μ	0.90
Portfolio share elasticity	σ	30.0
Initial foreign bond shares	$h^{\mathrm{B}}, \hat{h}^{\mathrm{B}}$	0.25
Shock persistence	ρ	0.90
Taylor inflation coefficient	ψ_π	0.500
Taylor output coefficient	ψ_y	0.100
Price-setting probability	$\wp$	1/12

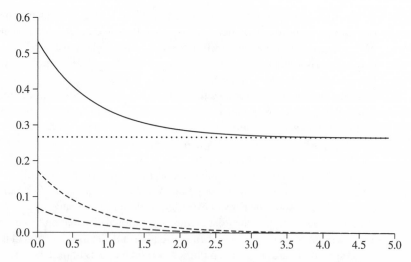

FIGURE 2.5   Impulse responses of the nominal exchange rate, s_t (solid), U.S. net liabilities, nfl_t (dashed), net exports, nx_t (short dashed), and consumption differential, $c_t - \hat{c}_t$ (dotted), to a rise in expected U.S. equities returns, $\mathbb{E}_t r^{\mathrm{E}}_{t+1} - r_t$.

bond holdings between dollar and euro bonds. Accordingly, μ is set equal to 0.9, but higher values do not materially affect the plots in Figure 2.5. In Chapter 1 we saw that the variance of the nominal depreciation rate in quarterly data was approximately 7 percent. Under log utility, the semielasticity of households' desired foreign bond holdings with respect to variation in the foreign exchange risk premium will be approximately equal to the reciprocal of this variance. Thus, since σ is the sum of these semielasticities, we set its value to 30. We also need an assumption about the composition of households' portfolios when shocks hit. In particular, equation (2.103) showed that the initial impact of any news depends on the multiplier, $\mathfrak{H} = 1/(1 - h^{\mathrm{B}} - \hat{h}^{\mathrm{B}})$. We assume that households invest 25 percent of their savings in foreign bonds, so that $\mathfrak{H}$ equals 2.

Figure 2.5 plots the responses of the log spot rate, s_t, net liabilities, nfl_t, net exports, nx_t, and the consumption differential, $c_t - \hat{c}_t$, following an increase in the expected excess return on U.S. equities over a 5-year horizon. Before the shock hits in period $t = 0$, the log spot rate is zero, the U.S. and E.U. households have equal wealth, U.S. net liabilities and net exports are zero, and there is no foreign exchange risk premium. In period $t = 1$, households receive positive news, ϵ, that leads them to revise their forecasts for future excess returns on U.S. equity upward according to $\mathbb{E}_1[r^{\mathrm{E}}_{1+i} - r_i] = \rho^{i-1}\epsilon$ for $i \geq 1$. This revision in expectations produces expected portfolio shifts of $\mathbb{E}_1\mathfrak{I}_{1+i} = \rho^{i-1}\sigma_2\epsilon$. The figure shows the effect of these shifts for the case where $\sigma_2\epsilon = 1$ so the news raises $\mathfrak{I}_t$ by 1 percent and expectations of $\mathfrak{I}_{t+i}$ by ρ^{i-1} percent.

Figure 2.5 displays several interesting features. First, the solid plot for s_t shows that the initial depreciation of the dollar overshoots its long-run response. Second, there is an immediate increase in both net exports, nx_t, and net U.S. liabilities, nfl_t. Both variables then gradually fall back to their initial value of zero. Third, the dotted line shows that there is an immediate and permanent increase in the consumption differential between U.S. and E.U. households, $c_t - \hat{c}_t$. Furthermore, the rise in the differential matches the long-run depreciation of the spot rate.

The economic explanation for these effects centers on the behavior of the foreign exchange risk premium. International solvency dictates that the news concerning expected equity returns has no anticipated long-run effect on U.S. net liabilities (i.e., $nfl_0 = \mathbb{E}_1 nfl_\infty = 0$, where $nfl_\infty = \lim_{t \to \infty} nfl_t$). This means that $\mathbb{E}_t \sum_{i=1}^{\infty} \Delta nfl_{t+i} = 0$ for $t \geq 1$, so the expression for the risk premium in equation (2.97) can be rewritten as

$$\delta_t = \frac{1}{\sigma} \mathbb{E}_t \sum_{i=1}^{\infty} \left(\tfrac{\sigma}{1+\sigma}\right)^i \Delta \Im_{t+i} - \frac{1}{\sigma} \mathbb{E}_t \sum_{i=1}^{\infty} \left[1 - \left(\tfrac{\sigma}{1+\sigma}\right)^i\right] \Delta nfl_{t+i}.$$

Since σ is large, $1 - \left(\tfrac{\sigma}{1+\sigma}\right)^i$ will be close to zero at short horizons i. Consequently, the risk premium will be primarily determined by expected future changes in $\Im_t$ unless the anticipated changes in net liabilities are very large or stretch far into the future. This is not the case in Figure 2.5. Rather, the news concerning equity returns pushes the risk premium below zero because it temporarily raises $\Im_t$ so that $\mathbb{E}_t \Delta \Im_{t+i} \leq 0$ for $t \geq 1$. In effect, the news concerning equities pushes down the risk premium to a level where households' portfolio decisions are consistent with both expected future equity returns and international solvency.

The fall in the risk premium provides the key to understanding the plots in Figure 2.5. Since interest rates and prices are constant, the risk premium governs the expected rate of real and nominal depreciation, that is, $\delta_t = \mathbb{E}_t \Delta s_{t+1} = \mathbb{E}_t \Delta \varepsilon_{t+1}$. As a consequence, once the news concerning equities arrives, households must expect the dollar to appreciate until the risk premium rises back to zero. These expectations are represented by the downward sloping plot for the spot rate in the figure. The initial reaction of the spot rate is to jump to the point at the start of this path, a point that overshoots the long-run degree of depreciation.

Figure 2.5 also shows that the news temporarily increases net exports and net liabilities. To understand these effects, note first that the news has no long-run effect on the international distribution of real wealth (i.e., wealth measured in terms of a common consumption basket). This means that when households have log preferences long-run exchange-rate expectations must match the expected long-run consumption differential, that is, $\varepsilon_\infty = c_\infty - \hat{c}_\infty$. Furthermore, since there is no spread between U.S. and E.U. interest rates, the first-order conditions for consumption imply that $c_\infty - c_t = \hat{c}_\infty - \hat{c}_t$, so $\varepsilon_\infty = c_t - \hat{c}_t$ and $\varepsilon_\infty - \varepsilon_t = c_t - \hat{c}_t - \varepsilon_t$. The figure shows ε_∞ by the horizontal dotted line. This line also identifies the long-run level of the nominal exchange rate because inflation is zero in a flex-price equilibrium. The vertical gap between the spot rate and ε_∞ identifies $\varepsilon_t + \hat{c}_t - c_t$. Thus, as the figure indicates, overshooting of the exchange rate induces an increase in E.U. consumption expenditure relative to U.S. consumption expenditure. This, in turn, increases net exports so the U.S. runs a trade surplus until the exchange rate appreciates fully to its new long-run level. It is the anticipation of higher future net exports that temporarily allows U.S. net liabilities to rise without endangering long-term solvency.

All that now remains is to explain why the temporary portfolio shift leads to a permanent depreciation of the dollar. The answer lies in households' initial foreign bond holdings, h^B and $\hat{h}^B$. When the dollar initially depreciates, it produces an unexpected change in households' financial wealth according to their foreign bond holdings. In particular, when h^B and $\hat{h}^B$ are positive, the depreciation of the dollar increases the wealth of U.S. households and reduces the wealth of E.U. households. It is this redistribution of financial wealth from Europe to the United States that immediately increases relative consumption, $c_t - \hat{c}_t$, which in turn determines the new long-run level for the real exchange rate. Indeed, if we combine (2.102) and (2.103), we find that the change in relative consumption is

$$\Delta c_1 - \Delta \hat{c}_1 = \left(\frac{h^B + \hat{h}^B}{1 - h^B - \hat{h}^B} \right) (\Delta nfl_1 + \Delta \Im_1 + \sigma \Delta \delta_1).$$

Figure 2.5 also provides a new perspective on the PPP Puzzle. In particular, the plots show that it is perfectly possible to produce permanent variations in the real exchange rate from a purely temporary shock without any price-stickiness whatsoever. The key, of course, is the degree of risk-sharing. When markets are complete, unexpected variations in the spot rates have no effect on the international distribution of financial wealth, so the real exchange rate does not have to adjust in the long run to maintain solvency. Here, by contrast, long-run adjustments are needed because unexpected variations in spot rates redistribute wealth when markets are incomplete.

2.4.4 Portfolio Balance with Sticky Prices

Finally, we examine the implications of price-stickiness and incomplete markets for the behavior of exchange rates by combining the elements of portfolio balance with the inflation dynamics implied by staggered price-setting and monetary policy in the form of Taylor rules.

The first step is to identify the behavior of real marginal costs and net exports. Equation (2.15) implies that the difference between U.S. and E.U. real marginal costs is

$$rmc_t - \widehat{rmc}_t = \alpha \varepsilon_t - \alpha(2\lambda - 1)\tau_t + (1 - \alpha)(c_t - \hat{c}_t). \tag{2.104}$$

Next, we use (2.91) and (2.31) to express the equilibrium terms of trade, τ_t, in terms of the endowments of intermediate goods and net exports:

$$\tau_t = \frac{1}{(2\lambda - 1)(2\theta\lambda - 1) + 4\theta\lambda(1 - \lambda)} (e_t^{US} - e_t^{EU})$$

$$+ \frac{(2\lambda - 1)}{(2\lambda - 1)(2\theta\lambda - 1) + 4\theta\lambda(1 - \lambda)} (nx_t + rmc_t - \widehat{rmc}_t).$$

If τ_t^F and nx_t^F denote the terms of trade and net exports under flexible prices, we can rewrite this equation as

$$\tau_t = \tau_t^F + \frac{(2\lambda - 1)}{(2\lambda - 1)(2\theta\lambda - 1) + 4\theta\lambda(1 - \lambda)} (nx_t - nx_t^F + rmc_t - \widehat{rmc}_t),$$

and combine it with the equations for net exports in (2.91) and real marginal costs in (2.104) to get

$$rmc_t - \widehat{rmc}_t = \varsigma_\varepsilon(\varepsilon_t - \varepsilon_t^{\mathrm{F}}) + \varsigma_c[(c_t - \hat{c}_t) - (c_t^{\mathrm{F}} - \hat{c}_t^{\mathrm{F}})] \qquad (2.105a)$$

and

$$nx_t - nx_t^{\mathrm{F}} = \varphi_\varepsilon(\varepsilon_t - \varepsilon_t^{\mathrm{F}}) + \varphi_c[(c_t - \hat{c}_t) - (c_t^{\mathrm{F}} - \hat{c}_t^{\mathrm{F}})] \qquad (2.105b)$$

for some coefficients, ς_i and φ_i.

The next step is to consider the behavior of inflation and the real exchange rate. When retail firms reset prices according to the Calvo model and real marginal costs take the form in (2.105a), the U.S./E.U. inflation differential follows

$$\begin{aligned}
\Delta p_t - \Delta \hat{p}_t &= \kappa\,\varsigma_\varepsilon(\varepsilon_t - \varepsilon_t^{\mathrm{F}}) + \kappa\,\varsigma_c[(c_t - \hat{c}_t) - (c_t^{\mathrm{F}} - \hat{c}_t^{\mathrm{F}})] \\
&\quad + \beta\mathbb{E}_t(\Delta\hat{p}_{t+1} - \Delta\hat{p}_{t+1}).
\end{aligned} \qquad (2.106)$$

Recall that the log ratio of U.S. to E.U. GDP, $y_t - \hat{y}_t$, is well approximated by $c_t - \hat{c}_t$ when there is little cross-country difference in the dispersion of retail prices. The spread between U.S. and E.U. interest rates implied by the Taylor rules is therefore

$$\begin{aligned}
r_t - \hat{r}_t &= (1 + \psi_\pi)\mathbb{E}_t(\Delta p_{t+1} - \Delta\hat{p}_{t+1}) \\
&\quad + \psi_y[(c_t - \hat{c}_t) - (c_t^{\mathrm{F}} - \hat{c}_t^{\mathrm{F}})] + v_t - \hat{v}_t.
\end{aligned} \qquad (2.107)$$

Combining this equation with the interest parity condition in (2.34) and the identity $\mathbb{E}_t\Delta\varepsilon_{t+1} = \mathbb{E}_t\Delta s_{t+1} + \mathbb{E}_t\Delta\hat{p}_{t+1} - \mathbb{E}_t\Delta p_{t+1}$ gives

$$\mathbb{E}_t\Delta\varepsilon_{t+1} = \psi_\pi\mathbb{E}_t\left(\Delta p_{t+1} - \Delta\hat{p}_{t+1}\right) + \psi_y[(c_t - \hat{c}_t) - (c_t^{\mathrm{F}} - \hat{c}_t^{\mathrm{F}})] + \delta_t + v_t - \hat{v}_t.$$

When prices are flexible, there is zero inflation, so $\mathbb{E}_t\Delta s_{t+1} = \mathbb{E}_t\Delta\varepsilon_{t+1}^{\mathrm{F}} = r_t - \hat{r}_t + \delta_t^{\mathrm{F}} = \delta_t^{\mathrm{F}} + v_t - \hat{v}_t$. Using this expression to substitute for the policy shocks, v_t and $\hat{v}_t$, and rearranging the result produces

$$\begin{aligned}
\varepsilon_t - \varepsilon_t^{\mathrm{F}} &= \mathbb{E}_t(\varepsilon_{t+1} - \varepsilon_{t+1}^{\mathrm{F}}) - \psi_\pi\mathbb{E}_t(\Delta p_{t+1} - \Delta\hat{p}_{t+1}) \\
&\quad - (\delta_t - \delta_t^{\mathrm{F}}) - \psi_y[(c_t - \hat{c}_t) - (c_t^{\mathrm{F}} - \hat{c}_t^{\mathrm{F}})].
\end{aligned} \qquad (2.108)$$

Equations (2.105), (2.106), and (2.108) provide the key to understanding the effects of price-stickiness. In particular, note that none of the equations contain any exogenous variables. Instead, all the variables appear as deviations from their flex-price levels. This means that endowment shocks, policy shocks, and portfolio shifts have no direct effect on the real exchange rate or on any other variables beyond those identified under flexible prices. In other words, the equilibrium behavior of the model is unaffected by the presence of sticky prices.

To understand why this is so, recall how the economy responded to a portfolio shift when prices were flexible. Figure 2.5 showed that there was an immediate and permanent rise in $c_t - \hat{c}_t$ because the portfolio shift redistributed financial wealth from E.U. to U.S. households without affecting interest rates. The presence of sticky prices does not alter this wealth effect. In equilibrium, both the real exchange rate and the consumption differential immediately jump to their new flex-price levels, which keeps real marginal costs unchanged, so retail firms have no incentive to change their prices. As a consequence, the portfolio shift has no effect on inflation or the output gap in either country, so central banks have no reason to change interest rates. In short, although the portfolio shift could *potentially* affect inflation and interest rates when prices are sticky, the economy adjusts to the redistribution of wealth induced by the portfolio shift without any inflation or changes in interest rates.

2.4.5 Monetary Policy

The exchange-rate implications of monetary policy are easily examined. As price-stickiness has no effect on the behavior of net foreign liabilities and the risk premium, the system of equations in (2.100) continues to govern the equilibrium behavior of these variables:

$$
\begin{bmatrix} \delta_t \\ nfl_t \end{bmatrix} = \mathcal{H}\mathbb{E}_t \begin{bmatrix} \delta_{t+1} \\ nfl_{t+1} \end{bmatrix} + \mathcal{G}\mathbb{E}_t \begin{bmatrix} e^{\mathrm{US}}_{t+1} - e^{\mathrm{EU}}_{t+1} \\ \Im_{t+1} \\ \Im_t \end{bmatrix},
$$

where $\Im_t = \sigma_2 \mathbb{E}_t(r^{\mathrm{E}}_{t+1} - r_t) - \hat{\sigma}_2 \mathbb{E}_t(\hat{r}^{\mathrm{E}}_{t+1} - \hat{r}_t)$. Note that the monetary policy shocks, v_t and $\hat{v}_t$, are absent from these equations. Consequently, in a determinant equilibrium neither the risk premium nor net foreign liabilities will be affected by these policy shocks unless they somehow change households' expectations concerning future excess returns on equities. This is a possibility, but not one we shall pursue here. Instead we focus on the effects of policy shocks in a determinant equilibrium where $\delta_t = nfl_t = 0$.

All the exchange-rate effects of policy shocks arise from their implications for the expected depreciation rate. In particular, because retail firms keep prices steady, $\mathbb{E}_t\Delta\varepsilon_{t+1} = \mathbb{E}_t\Delta s_{t+1}$, the interest parity condition becomes $\mathbb{E}_t\Delta\varepsilon_{t+1} = r_t - \hat{r}_t$. Substituting for $r_t - \hat{r}_t$ from (2.107), gives

$$
\mathbb{E}_t\Delta\varepsilon_{t+1} = (1 + \psi_\pi)\mathbb{E}_t(\Delta p_{t+1} - \Delta \hat{p}_{t+1}) + \psi_y[(c_t - \hat{c}_t) - (c^{\mathrm{F}}_t - \hat{c}^{\mathrm{F}}_t)] + v_t - \hat{v}_t
$$

$$
= v_t - \hat{v}_t,
$$

because $c_t - \hat{c}_t = c^{\mathrm{F}}_t - \hat{c}^{\mathrm{F}}_t$ and $\mathbb{E}_t(\Delta p_{t+1} - \Delta \hat{p}_{t+1}) = 0$. Thus the policy shocks, v_t and $\hat{v}_t$, have a one-to-one effect on the expected real rate of depreciation.

Figure 2.6 compares the exchange-rate effects of a monetary policy shock under complete and incomplete markets. The figure plots the response of the real exchange rate following a loosening of U.S. monetary policy in which interest rates are initially pushed down by 1 percent. As in Section 2.2.2, we assume that this policy shock follows an AR(1) process: $z_t = \rho z_{t-1} + \epsilon_t$ with $\rho = 0.9$, where $z_t = \hat{v}_t - v_t$. The dotted plot shows the path of z_t. The response of the real exchange rate when markets are complete is shown by the dashed plot. This response is computed from the equilibrium dynamics described in Section 2.2.2 with the risk-aversion coefficient, γ, set equal to one. Table 2.3 shows the values of all the other parameters in the model. When markets are incomplete, the path for the real exchange rate is determined by the solution to $\mathbb{E}_t\Delta\varepsilon_{t+1} = -z_t$. Rewriting this expression as a difference equation in ε_t and solving forward using the AR(1) process for z_t gives

$$
\varepsilon_t = \frac{1}{1 - \rho} z_t.
$$

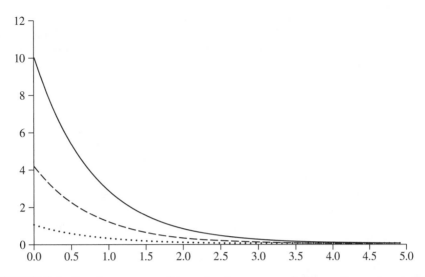

FIGURE 2.6 Impulse responses of the real exchange rate under incomplete markets (solid) and complete markets (dashed) to a monetary policy change, z_t (dotted).

The solid plot in Figure 2.6 shows the incomplete-markets response of the real exchange rate to the monetary policy shock computed from the preceding equation.

Figure 2.6 shows that the degree of risk-sharing significantly affects how the real exchange rate reacts to the monetary policy shock. In particular, the plots show that under incomplete markets the initial real depreciation of the dollar is more than twice as large as when markets are complete. The reason for this difference lies in the behavior of the spread between U.S. and E.U. interest rates. When markets are complete, the spread reacts to the direct effects of the policy change and the indirect effects induced by variations in inflation and the output gaps. In particular, the initial real depreciation of the dollar raises the U.S./E.U. inflation differential, $\Delta p_t - \Delta \hat{p}_t$, and increases the difference between the U.S. and E.U. output gaps, $(y_t - y_t^{\mathrm{F}}) - (\hat{y}_t - \hat{y}_t^{\mathrm{F}})$, so the direct effects of the policy change are dampened via central banks' adherence to the Taylor rules. This dampening effect is absent when markets are incomplete. The expected real depreciation of the dollar is associated with an immediate rise in $c_t - \hat{c}_t$, but this has no effect on inflation or the output gaps in either country because the consumption response is not affected by the presence of sticky prices. As a result, the direct effects of the policy change are not dampened via adherence to the Taylor rules. The initial real depreciation of the dollar must therefore be larger when markets are incomplete in order to be consistent with higher expected future rates of real appreciation.

Two assumptions have greatly simplified the preceding analysis. The first concerns the risk-aversion parameter, γ, which we set equal to one. If this assumption were dropped, households would no longer find it optimal to consume a constant fraction of their financial wealth. Instead, variations in current and expected future real interest rates would alter the consumption wealth ratio, which in turn would affect households' demand for foreign bonds. As a result, variations in real interest rates would generally affect the equilibrium risk premium, contrary to the foregoing analysis.

The second assumption concerns the form of the Taylor rules. Throughout we have assumed that central banks set interest rates in response to variations in the output gap measured by the log ratio of current GDP to GDP under flexible prices. Although this is a common assumption in the monetary policy literature, it has far-reaching implications when prices are sticky and markets are incomplete. In particular, our analysis in this section shows that the equilibrium behavior of the model is unaffected by the degree of price-stickiness when Taylor rules take this form because there is no incentive for firms to change prices causing inflation or central banks to vary interest rates. These incentives would change if output gaps were to be measured by the log ratio of current GDP to its long-run trend level (a constant in our model). As in the complete markets case, the direct effects of monetary policy shocks would be dampened by their effects on inflation and the output gaps. The policy shocks would also affect the foreign risk premium via their impact on household savings decisions. We study this link between monetary policy and the risk premium in Chapter 11.

2.5 Summary

- Overshooting occurs when the initial reaction of the exchange rate to a shock is larger than its long-run impact. The exchange rate undershoots when its initial reaction to a shock is smaller than the long-run effect. In either case, the shock must change the expected future rate of depreciation.

- In models where there is no distinction between retail and wholesale prices, the form of price-setting determines the joint behavior of the nominal exchange rate, inflation, and the terms of trade. Under producer currency pricing (where prices are set in the currency of the producer), variations in the nominal exchange are positively correlated with the terms of trade and are immediately passed through to the retail price of imports. Under local currency pricing (where prices are set in the currency of consumers), variations in the nominal exchange are negatively correlated with the terms of trade but are not immediately passed through to the retail price of imports. Empirically, there is a positive correlation between changes in the terms of trade and nominal exchange rates and little immediate pass-through from exchange-rate variations to retail prices.

- When retail prices are set in the staggered fashion of the Calvo (1983) model, the degree of overall price-stickiness depends on the probability that an individual firm can reset its price in any period. Varying the degree of price-stickiness does not alter the persistence of monetary policy shocks on exchange rates, but it does affect the size of the initial exchange-rate reaction. By contrast, the initial reaction of the exchange rate depends critically on the persistence of the policy shock.

- Real rates of depreciation are negatively correlated with cross-country differences in real consumption growth, a fact that contradicts the predictions of models with complete markets in which households have isoelastic, time-separable preferences defined over aggregate consumption.

- When markets are incomplete, the nominal exchange rate must maintain a level that makes the portfolio choices of households consistent with the requirements of international solvency. This portfolio balance requirement makes nominal exchange rates susceptible to shocks that: (1) affect future exports and imports, and (2) change the desired composition of households' portfolios.

- When markets are incomplete, temporary shocks can have permanent exchange-rate effects if they alter the international distribution of wealth. The presence and size of these wealth effects depends on households' existing portfolio choices, which can vary from period to period. As variations in the international distribution of wealth can occur when prices are completely flexible, their incidence can potentially explain the Purchasing Power Parity Puzzle.

- The exchange-rate implications of monetary policy shocks depend critically on the incentives firms face in setting retail prices. These incentives depend on both the degree of international risk-sharing and the form of Taylor rules governing how monetary policy reacts to changing economic conditions.

2.6 Bibliography

The models in this chapter contain many elements found in the large literature on open economy macro models with nominal rigidities that emerged in the mid-1990s. Following Svensson and van Wijnbergen (1989) and, particularly, Obstfeld and Rogoff (1995), this literature synthesized monopolistic competition with wage- and price-stickiness in a dynamic, general equilibrium setting to study a range of issues in international macroeconomics. Lane (2001) provides an early survey of this research, which has subsequently become known as New Keynesian Open-Economy Macroeconomics.

Although none of the models presented in this chapter have appeared elsewhere, they do contain a number of elements with clear antecedents in the literature. In particular, the sticky-price models with preset pricing in Section 2.2.1 exhibit local currency pricing at the retail level following Betts and Devereux (1996, 2000) and many others. Similarly, the Calvo (1983) model of staggered price-setting has been incorporated into open-economy models by Gali and Monacelli (2005) and Benigno and Benigno (2008). The distinction among retail, wholesale, and import prices has also been the focus of recent research. For example, Burstein, Neves, and Rebelo (2003) consider a model where the marketing and distribution of imported goods require the use of nontraded goods as an input, and in Obstfeld (2001) and Engel (2002) firms combine home- and foreign-produced intermediate goods into consumption goods. The models in this chapter focus on price-setting decisions of retail firms in an environment where wholesale prices freely adjust to clear world markets. This treatment of wholesale markets is clearly inadequate because import prices are not as variable as nominal exchange rates. One way to address this issue would be to introduce monopolistic competition to the wholesale markets so that price-setting decisions of producers of intermediate goods are modeled explicitly along the lines of Corsetti, Dedola, and Leduc (2008b) or Dotsey and Duarte (2008).

There are fewer antecedents for the models with incomplete markets presented in Section 2.4. To date, most open-economy models with incomplete markets assume that households can trade a single real bond that provides a payoff measured in terms of aggregate consumption (see, e.g., Corsetti, Dedola, and Leduc 2008a). As Baxter and Crucini (1995) demonstrate, these models tend to have similar quantitative properties as their complete market counterparts, particularly when subjected to temporary shocks. The models in Section 2.4 do not share this feature because they combine the international solvency constraint with the portfolio decisions of households to determine the dynamics of the foreign exchange risk premium. The resulting role of the risk premium in exchange-rate determination is foreshadowed in earlier research by Kollmann (2001), Devereux and Engel (2002), Obstfeld and Rogoff (2003), and Duarte and Stockman (2005). It also has antecedents in the literature on imperfect substitutability between domestic and foreign assets originally due to Kouri (1976) and Henderson and Rogoff (1982), and more recently revived by Blanchard, Giavazzi, and Sa (2005).

The development of general equilibrium models with portfolio choice is now an active area of research. Evans and Hnatkovska (2005a) first showed how the approximation methods developed to examine dynamic portfolio choice in partial equilibrium settings by Campbell and Viceira (2002) could be extended to solve general equilibrium models with dynamic portfolio choice and incomplete markets. The analysis in Section 2.4 draws on this approach, but for the sake of clarity stops short of providing a complete solution to the model. In particular, we treated the portfolio shift term, $\Im_t$, as an exogenous variable, when in fact it depends on expected equity returns and the conditional covariance matrices for spot rates and equities. A complete solution to the model would determine these endogenous variables in terms of the exogenous shocks to the endowments and monetary policy. This is a complex undertaking but it is feasible using the numerical methods developed in Evans and Hnatkovska (2005b). The analysis in Section 2.4 can therefore be extended to characterize the equilibrium dynamics of exchange rates in terms of strictly exogenous variables. Another method for solving general equilibrium models with portfolio choice and incomplete markets has been developed by Wincoop and Tille (2007) and Devereux and Sutherland (2010).[11]

Finally, this chapter has not touched on models with frictions that lead to segmented asset markets. Alvarez, Atkeson, and Kehoe (2002, 2009), for example, study models where agents must incur a fixed cost to transfer money between asset and goods markets. In these models asset prices (including exchange rates) are determined by the consumption of the marginal agent in asset markets, which differs from aggregate consumption. This type of model has the potential to generate volatility in real exchange rates that has little relation to aggregate consumption consistent with the statistical evidence in Table 2.2.

---

11. One complication that can arise in these models is that there is no unique steady state for the international distribution of wealth: Temporary stocks have very persistent effects on the wealth of individual households when markets are incomplete. Evans and Hnatkovska (2005b) address this by examining the equilibrium in a neighborhood around a particular initial wealth distribution. Alternatively, one can modify the model by introducing endogenous-discounting or portfolio-holding costs to induce the existence of a steady state wealth distribution along the lines investigated by Schmitt-Grohe and Uribe (2003). This is not an issue for the analysis in Section 2.4. None of the approximations used in (2.100) assume the existence of a steady state wealth distribution.

2.7 Review Questions

1. Exchange-Rate Undershooting: Consider the exchange-rate model described in equation (2.36).

   (a) Draw the phase diagram for the real- and nominal-exchange-rate dynamics in the case where $v < 1$. [Note that Figure 2.1 shows the phase diagram when $v > 1$.]

   (b) Draw a second phase diagram, analogous to Figure 2.2, to show how the real and nominal exchange rate will react to a permanent increase in the U.S. money supply. Explain why the dynamics are different from those examined in Section 2.2.1.

   (c) Draw a third phase diagram to show how the real and nominal exchange rates will react to the same permanent increases in the U.S. money supply when the increase is *announced one period in advance*. Is the initial depreciation of the dollar larger or smaller than in your answer to part (b)? Explain.

2. Duration of Overshooting: Figure 2.2 illustrates overshooting of the spot rate to a permanent increase in the U.S. money stock for the case where $v > 1$.

   (a) Suppose that the U.S. money stock follows a random walk, $m_t = m_{t-1} + u_t$, where u_t is an i.i.d. mean-zero shock. Show that the spot rate can only overshoot for one period following a u_t shock.

   (b) Draw a phase diagram, analogous to Figure 2.2, to show how the real and nominal exchange rates will react to a permanent increase in the endowment of U.S. goods. Is there under- or overshooting? Explain.

   (c) If the log U.S. endowment follows a random walk, $e_t^{US} = e_{t-1}^{US} + v_t$, where v_t is an i.i.d. mean-zero shock, how long will it take for the spot rate to fully adjust to a v_t shock?

   (d) Now suppose that the U.S. endowment follows an AR(1), $e_t^{US} = \rho_e e_{t-1}^{US} + v_t$, where v_t is an i.i.d. mean-zero shock. Explain how the spot rate response to a v_t shock differs from that in part (c). [Hint: First, identify the expected future terms of trade, the unexpected movement in the spot rate, and the behavior of the real exchange rate. Next, use these results to find the behavior of the spot rate.]

3. Sticky Prices and the Terms of Trade: Suppose that shocks to the log endowments of U.S. and E.U. intermediate goods (net of government spending) follow an AR(1) process,

$$e_t^{US} - e_t^{EU} = \rho_e(e_{t-1}^{US} - e_{t-1}^{EU}) + u_t,$$

where $1 > \rho_e > 0$ and u_t is an i.i.d. mean-zero shock.

   (a) Use the model presented in Section 2.1 to describe how a positive u_t shock will affect the terms of trade and the real exchange rate when retail prices are flexible and the production of retail goods is biased toward the use of domestic intermediates ($\lambda > 1/2$).

   (b) Exchange-rate dynamics under staggered price-setting are described by equations (2.62) and (2.63). Use these equations and your answer from part (a) to solve for the equilibrium response of the real exchange rate and the inflation differential to a positive u_t shock. Why does the response of the real exchange rate differ under staggered price-setting from the response under flexible prices? [Hint: Find a new expression for the dynamics of the forcing variable z_t and apply the solution method described in the chapter.]

(c) Use your answer to part (b) to compute the nominal-exchange-rate response. Is the implied correlation between the nominal depreciation rate and the terms of trade consistent with the empirical correlation?

4. Risk-Sharing and Incomplete Markets: Consider a special case of the incomplete markets model in Section 2.4 where the only shocks to the economy are i.i.d. endowment shocks. Further, assume that the elasticity of substitution between intermediate goods, θ, takes the limiting value of one and that prices are completely flexible.

(a) Derive expressions for U.S. imports and exports under these conditions and show that

$$\frac{\mathcal{X}_t}{\mathfrak{M}_t} = \frac{\mathcal{E}_t \hat{C}_t}{C_t}.$$

When $\theta \neq 1$ the terms of trade also affect the ratio of exports to imports. Explain why variations in the terms of trade have no effect on $\mathcal{X}_t/\mathfrak{M}_t$ when the relative consumption of E.U. and U.S. households remains constant.

(b) Use equations (2.96), (2.98), and (2.99) to determine the equilibrium behavior of net liabilities and the risk premium, nfl_t and δ_t, when shocks to the endowments of U.S. and E.U. goods are i.i.d. and the risk premia on equities are constant.

(c) Is risk-sharing complete or incomplete in this equilibrium? Explain.

(d) Suppose there is a one-period positive shock to the U.S. endowment. Explain how the terms of trade, real exchange rate, and the relative consumption of U.S. and E.U. households are affected.

5. Exogenous Portfolio Decisions: Consider a version of the Portfolio Balance model with flexible prices presented in Section 2.4 where the fractions of savings held in foreign bonds by U.S. and E.U. households, h_t^B and $\hat{h}_t^B$, are exogenous.

(a) Derive equations for the equilibrium dynamics of net liabilities, nfl_t, net exports, nx_t, and the risk premium, δ_t, when $\lambda = 1/2$.

(b) Suppose that there is a persistent exogenous portfolio shift of E.U. households moving away from U.S. bonds, that is,

$$\hat{h}_t^B = \rho \hat{h}_{t-1}^B - \epsilon_t \quad \text{with } |\rho| < 1,$$

where ϵ_t is an i.i.d. mean-zero shock. Describe the behavior of the risk premium and net exports following a positive ϵ_t shock.

(c) Use you your answer to part (b) to describe the reaction of the nominal spot rate. Explain how your answer differs from the case where the fall in $\hat{h}_t^B$ is induced by a persistent shock to the excess return on E.U. equity, $\hat{r}_{t+1}^E - \hat{r}_t$.

2.A Appendix

2.A.1 Dynamic Portfolio Choice

The Portfolio Balance models in Sections 2.4.3 and 2.4.4 embed the portfolio decisions of households in a general equilibrium setting using the approximation methods developed by John Campbell and his coauthors (see, e.g., Campbell 1993 and Campbell and Viceira 2002). This appendix provides a brief overview of how the approximations can be used to characterize optimal consumption, savings, and portfolio allocation decisions.

Campbell's approach combines log approximations of the household's first-order conditions and budget constraint. As an example, consider the representative U.S. household's problem of maximizing expected utility, $\mathbb{U}_t$ in equation (2.1), subject to the budget constraint in (2.80) with portfolio returns defined by (2.81). When there are no restrictions on the risk-aversion parameter, γ, the first-order conditions are

$$1 = \mathbb{E}_t \left[\beta \left(\frac{C_{t+1}}{C_t} \right)^{-\gamma} R_t \frac{P_t}{P_{t+1}} \right],$$

$$1 = \mathbb{E}_t \left[\beta \left(\frac{C_{t+1}}{C_t} \right)^{-\gamma} R_{t+1}^{\mathrm{E}} \frac{P_t}{P_{t+1}} \right],$$

and

$$1 = \mathbb{E}_t \left[\beta \left(\frac{C_{t+1}}{C_t} \right)^{-\gamma} \frac{S_{t+1} \hat{R}_t}{S_t} \frac{P_t}{P_{t+1}} \right].$$

Under the assumption that the joint distribution of future consumption growth and returns is log normal conditioned on period-t information, these equations can be rewritten as

$$\mathbb{E}_t \mathbf{er}_{t+1} + \tfrac{1}{2} \operatorname{diag} (\Sigma_t) = \mathbb{CV}_t \left(\mathbf{er}_{t+1}, \gamma c_{t+1} + p_{t+1} \right) \tag{2.109a}$$

and

$$r_t - \mathbb{E}_t \Delta p_{t+1} = \gamma \mathbb{E}_t \Delta c_{t+1} - \ln \beta - \tfrac{1}{2} \mathbb{V}_t(\gamma c_{t+1} + p_{t+1}), \tag{2.109b}$$

where, as before, $\mathbf{er}'_{t+1} = [\Delta s_{t+1} + \hat{r}_t - r_t \quad r_{t+1}^{\mathrm{E}} - r_t]$ and $\Sigma_t = \mathbb{V}_t(\mathbf{er}_{t+1})$. When future consumption growth and returns have a different conditional distribution, (2.109) approximates the household's first-order conditions.

The next step is to combine (2.109) with a log approximation of the household's budget constraint in (2.80). Dividing both sides of this equation by A_t and taking logs (assuming $A_t > 0$) gives

$$\Delta a_{t+1} = r_{t+1}^{\mathrm{A}} + \ln \left(1 - \exp(ca_t) \left[1 - \exp(y_t^{\mathrm{L}} - c_t) \right] \right),$$

where $ca_t = c_t - a_t$. We now log-linearize the term on the right-hand side around the points where $\exp(ca_t) = \varrho$ and $\exp(y_t^{\mathrm{L}} - c_t) = 1 - \ell$ to get

$$\Delta a_{t+1} = \text{const.} + r_{t+1}^{\mathrm{A}} - \frac{\varrho \ell}{1 - \varrho \ell} ca_t + \frac{\varrho(1 - \ell)}{1 - \varrho \ell}(y_t^{\mathrm{L}} - c_t). \tag{2.110}$$

Obviously, this approximation only makes sense if the household has positive real financial wealth, A_t, and $1 - \varrho\ell > 0$. Note that Y_t^L/C_t equals the ratio of aggregate labor costs to revenue for retail firms, $W_t L_t/P_t C_t$, and so must be less than unity. Both linearization coefficients, ϱ and ℓ, are therefore positive.

Approximations to the household's optimal consumption and portfolio choices are found by combining (2.109) with (2.110) and the equation for the log portfolio return in (2.84), which we rewrite as

$$r_{t+1}^A = r_t - \Delta p_{t+1} + er_{t+1}^A, \tag{2.111}$$

where

$$er_{t+1}^A = \mathbf{h}_t' \mathbf{er}_{t+1} + \tfrac{1}{2}\mathbf{h}_t' \left(\text{diag}\left(\Sigma_t\right) - \Sigma_t \mathbf{h}_t\right)$$

er_{t+1}^A is the excess log return on optimally invested wealth and $\mathbf{h}_t' = [\, h_t^B \quad h_t^E \,]$ is the vector of portfolio shares. To derive an equation for the portfolio shares, we first combine the right-hand side of (2.109a) with the identity $c_{t+1} = a_{t+1} + ca_{t+1}$ to give

$$\mathbb{CV}_t\left(\mathbf{er}_{t+1}, \gamma c_{t+1} + p_{t+1}\right) = \gamma\mathbb{CV}_t\left(\mathbf{er}_{t+1}, a_{t+1}\right) + \mathbb{CV}_t\left(\mathbf{er}_{t+1}, p_{t+1}\right)$$
$$+ \gamma\mathbb{CV}_t\left(\mathbf{er}_{t+1}, ca_{t+1}\right).$$

Next, note that (2.110) and (2.111) imply that $\mathbb{CV}_t(\mathbf{er}_{t+1}, a_{t+1}) = \mathbb{CV}_t(\mathbf{er}_{t+1}, r_{t+1}^A) = \Sigma_t \mathbf{h}_t - \mathbb{CV}_t\left(\mathbf{er}_{t+1}, p_{t+1}\right)$, so

$$\mathbb{CV}_t\left(\mathbf{er}_{t+1}, \gamma c_{t+1} + p_{t+1}\right) = \gamma\Sigma_t \mathbf{h}_t + (1 - \gamma)\mathbb{CV}_t\left(\mathbf{er}_{t+1}, p_{t+1}\right)$$
$$+ \gamma\mathbb{CV}_t\left(\mathbf{er}_{t+1}, ca_{t+1}\right),$$

and hence (2.109a) becomes

$$\mathbf{h}_t = \frac{1}{\gamma}\Sigma_t^{-1}\left\{\mathbb{E}_t\mathbf{er}_{t+1} + \tfrac{1}{2}\,\text{diag}\left(\Sigma_t\right)\right\}$$
$$- \Sigma_t^{-1}\left\{\gamma\mathbb{CV}_t(\mathbf{er}_{t+1}, ca_{t+1}) + (1 - \gamma)\mathbb{CV}_t\left(\mathbf{er}_{t+1}, p_{t+1}\right)\right\}. \tag{2.112}$$

This equation simplifies to (2.86) when $\gamma = 1$.

The expected excess return on optimally invested wealth is found by combining (2.111) and (2.112):

$$\mathbb{E}_t er_{t+1}^A = (\gamma - \tfrac{1}{2})\mathbf{h}_t'\Sigma_t \mathbf{h}_t$$
$$+ \mathbf{h}_t'\left\{\mathbb{CV}_t(\mathbf{er}_{t+1}, ca_{t+1}) + \left(\tfrac{1-\gamma}{\gamma}\right)\mathbb{CV}_t(\mathbf{er}_{t+1}, p_{t+1})\right\}. \tag{2.113}$$

Note that all the terms on the right-hand side depend on conditional second rather than first moments (i.e., conditional variances and covariances). When these second moments are constant, there are no variations in the expected excess return on optimally invested wealth.

All that now remains is to identify the log consumption asset ratio, ca_t. For this purpose, we combine (2.110) with (2.111) and the identity $\Delta a_{t+1} = \Delta c_{t+1} - \Delta ca_{t+1}$ to get

$$ca_t = \text{const.} + (1 - \varrho\ell)(r_t - \Delta p_{t+1} - \Delta c_{t+1}) + (1 - \varrho\ell)er^{\text{A}}_{t+1}$$
$$+ \varrho(1 - \ell)(y^{\text{L}}_t - c_t) + (1 - \varrho\ell)ca_{t+1}.$$

Taking conditional expectations on both sides of this equation produces

$$ca_t = \text{const.} + \varrho(1 - \ell)(y^{\text{L}}_t - c_t) + (1 - \varrho\ell)\mathbb{E}_t(r_t - \Delta p_{t+1} - \Delta c_{t+1})$$
$$+ (1 - \varrho\ell)\mathbb{E}_t er^{\text{A}}_{t+1} + (1 - \varrho\ell)\mathbb{E}_t ca_{t+1}. \tag{2.114}$$

Finally, note from (2.109b) that

$$\mathbb{E}_t(r_t - \Delta p_{t+1} - \Delta c_{t+1}) = \left(\frac{\gamma - 1}{\gamma}\right)\mathbb{E}_t(r_t - \Delta p_{t+1}) - \frac{1}{\gamma}\ln\beta$$
$$- \frac{1}{2\gamma}\mathbb{V}_t(\gamma ca_{t+1} + \gamma\mathbf{h}'_t er_{t+1} + (1 - \gamma)p_{t+1}). \tag{2.115}$$

Equations (2.112), (2.113), (2.114), and (2.115) jointly characterize an approximate solution to the household's consumption and portfolio problem in terms of current financial wealth, conditional second moments, expected future real interest rates, and the log ratio of labor income to consumption. Though complex, these equations can be solved numerically. For example, Evans and Hnatkovska (2005b) show how they can be solved for the case where $Y^{\text{L}}_t = 0$ in the context of a two-country general equilibrium model.

The solution to (2.112), (2.113), (2.114), and (2.115) is quite straightforward in the context of the Portfolio Balance models examined in Sections 2.4.3 and 2.4.4. Here the ratio of labor income to consumption is proportional to the real marginal costs faced by domestic retail firms, so

$$y^{\text{L}}_t - c_t = \text{const.} + rmc_t \quad \text{and} \quad \hat{y}^{\text{L}}_t - \hat{c}_t = \text{const.} + \widehat{rmc}_t.$$

Furthermore, the risk-aversion coefficient, γ, is set to one so (2.113), (2.114), and (2.115) imply that

$$ca_t = \text{const.} + \varrho(1 - \ell)(y^{\text{L}}_t - c_t) + (1 - \varrho\ell)\mathbb{E}_t(r_t - \Delta p_{t+1} - \Delta c_{t+1} + er^{\text{A}}_{t+1})$$
$$+ (1 - \varrho\ell)\mathbb{E}_t ca_{t+1},$$

and

$$\mathbb{E}_t(r_t - \Delta p_{t+1} - \Delta c_{t+1}) + \mathbb{E}_t er^{\text{A}}_{t+1} = -\ln\beta - \tfrac{1}{2}\mathbb{V}_t(ca_{t+1} + \mathbf{h}'_t er_{t+1})$$
$$+ \tfrac{1}{2}\mathbf{h}'_t \Sigma_t \mathbf{h}_t + \mathbf{h}'_t \mathbb{CV}_t(er_{t+1}, ca_{t+1})$$
$$= -\ln\beta - \tfrac{1}{2}\mathbb{V}_t(ca_{t+1}).$$

Under price flexibility, real marginal costs are constant, so the preceding equations simplify to

$$ca_t = \text{const.} - (1 - \varrho\ell)\tfrac{1}{2}\mathbb{V}_t(ca_{t+1}) + (1 - \varrho\ell)\mathbb{E}_t ca_{t+1}.$$

Clearly, a constant value for ca_t solves this equation, so (2.112) becomes

$$\mathbf{h}_t = \Sigma_t^{-1} \left\{ \mathbb{E}_t \mathbf{er}_{t+1} + \tfrac{1}{2} \operatorname{diag}\left(\Sigma_t\right) \right\} - \Sigma_t^{-1} \mathbb{CV}_t(\mathbf{er}_{t+1}, ca_{t+1})$$

$$= \Sigma_t^{-1} \left\{ \mathbb{E}_t \mathbf{er}_{t+1} + \tfrac{1}{2} \operatorname{diag}\left(\Sigma_t\right) \right\}.$$

Similar reasoning establishes that a constant value for $\widehat{ca}_t$ solves the equations governing the foreign household's decisions so that

$$\widehat{\mathbf{h}}_t = \hat{\Sigma}_t^{-1} \left\{ \mathbb{E}_t \widehat{\mathbf{er}}_{t+1} + \tfrac{1}{2} \operatorname{diag}\left(\hat{\Sigma}_t\right) \right\} - \hat{\Sigma}_t^{-1} \mathbb{CV}_t(\widehat{\mathbf{er}}_{t+1}, \widehat{ca}_{t+1})$$

$$= \hat{\Sigma}_t^{-1} \left\{ \mathbb{E}_t \widehat{\mathbf{er}}_{t+1} + \tfrac{1}{2} \operatorname{diag}\left(\hat{\Sigma}_t\right) \right\},$$

as claimed in Section 2.4.3.

Under sticky prices real marginal costs can vary so

$$ca_t = \text{const.} + \varrho(1 - \ell)rmc_t - \tfrac{1}{2}(1 - \varrho\ell)\mathbb{V}_t(ca_{t+1}) + (1 - \varrho\ell)\mathbb{E}_t ca_{t+1} \quad (2.116)$$

and

$$\widehat{ca}_t = \text{const.} + \varrho(1 - \ell)\widehat{rmc}_t - \tfrac{1}{2}(1 - \varrho\ell)\mathbb{V}_t(\widehat{ca}_{t+1}) + (1 - \varrho\ell)\mathbb{E}_t \widehat{ca}_{t+1}. \quad (2.117)$$

The terms ca_t and $\widehat{ca}_t$ now vary with changes in the present value of real marginal costs. In this case the covariance terms in the equations for h_t and $\widehat{\mathbf{h}}_t$ will generally differ from zero.

2.A.2   Derivations

Preset Price-Setting

To derive the pricing expression in (2.24), we first derive the first-order condition from maximizing $\mathbb{V}_{t-1}^i$ with respect to P_t^i as

$$\mathbb{E}_{t-1}\left[\left(\frac{C_t}{C_{t-1}}\right)^{1-\gamma} \left(\frac{P_t^i}{P_t}\right)^{-\phi-1} \left(\frac{P_t^i}{P_t}\right) \right]$$

$$= \frac{\phi}{\phi - 1} \mathbb{E}_{t-1}\left[\left(\frac{C_t}{C_{t-1}}\right)^{1-\gamma} \left(\frac{P_t^i}{P_t}\right)^{-\phi-1} \frac{MC_t}{P_t} \right]. \quad (2.118)$$

Rearranging this expression gives

$$P_t^i = \frac{\phi}{\phi - 1} \frac{\mathbb{E}_{t-1}[C_t^{1-\gamma} P_t^{\phi} MC_t]}{\mathbb{E}_{t-1}[C_t^{1-\gamma} P_t^{\phi}]\mathbb{E}_{t-1}\left[MC_t\right]} \mathbb{E}_{t-1}MC_t,$$

which is the form of equation (2.24).

Staggered Price-Setting

In order to derive the approximation in equation (2.46), we first rewrite (2.44) with $\Lambda_{t,t+j} = (\beta(1 - \wp))^j \left(C_{t+j}/C_t\right)^{-\gamma}$ and $MC_t = MC_t(i)$ as

$$P_t^* \left\{ \mathbb{E}_t \sum_{j=0}^{\infty} (\beta(1 - \wp))^j \left(\frac{C_{t+j}}{C_t}\right)^{1-\gamma} \left(\frac{P_{t+j}}{P_t}\right)^{\phi} \right\}$$

$$= \frac{\phi}{\phi - 1} \mathbb{E}_t \sum_{j=0}^{\infty} (\beta(1 - \wp))^j \left(\frac{C_{t+j}}{C_t}\right)^{1-\gamma} \left(\frac{P_{t+j}}{P_t}\right)^{\phi} MC_{t+j}.$$

or, after taking logs,

$$p_t^* + \ln \mathbb{E}_t \sum_{j=0}^{\infty} (\beta(1 - \wp))^j \mathfrak{J}_{t+j}$$

$$= \ln \frac{\phi}{\phi - 1} + \ln \mathbb{E}_t \sum_{j=0}^{\infty} (\beta(1 - \wp))^j \mathfrak{J}_{t+j} MC_{t+j},$$

(2.119)

where $\mathfrak{J}_{t+j} = \left(C_{t+j}/C_t\right)^{1-\gamma} (P_{t+j}/P_t)^{\phi}$.

Next, let $\mathfrak{B}_t = \ln(\mathbb{E}_t \sum_{j=0}^{\infty} (\beta(1 - \wp))^j \mathfrak{J}_{t+j}/\mathfrak{J}_t)$, so

$$\exp(\mathfrak{B}_t)\mathfrak{J}_t = \mathbb{E}_t \sum_{j=0}^{\infty} (\beta(1 - \wp))^j \mathfrak{J}_{t+j}.$$

Iterating this identity one period forward to obtain

$$\exp(\mathfrak{B}_t)\mathfrak{J}_t = \mathfrak{J}_t + \beta(1 - \wp)\mathbb{E}_t \exp\left(\mathfrak{B}_{t+1}\right) \mathfrak{J}_{t+1}$$

and dividing both sides by $\mathfrak{J}_t$ yields

$$\mathfrak{B}_t = \ln \left\{ 1 + \beta(1 - \wp)\mathbb{E}_t \exp\left(\mathfrak{B}_{t+1} + \Delta \ln \mathfrak{J}_{t+1}\right) \right\}.$$

Taking a first-order Taylor approximation to the right-hand side around the point where $\Delta \ln \mathfrak{J}_{t+1} = 0$ and $\mathfrak{B}_t = \mathfrak{B} = \ln(\frac{1}{1-\beta(1-\wp)})$ gives $\mathfrak{B}_t - \mathfrak{B} \cong \beta(1 - \wp) \cdot \mathbb{E}_t(\mathfrak{B}_{t+1} - \mathfrak{B} + \Delta \ln \mathfrak{J}_{t+1})$, so iterating forward,

$$\mathfrak{B}_t \cong \mathfrak{B} + \mathbb{E}_t \sum_{j=1}^{\infty} (\beta(1 - \wp))^j \Delta \ln \mathfrak{J}_{t+j}.$$

We can now approximate the left-hand side of (2.119) as

$$p_t^* + \ln \mathfrak{J}_t + \mathfrak{B} + \sum_{j=1}^{\infty} (\beta(1 - \wp))^j \Delta \ln \mathfrak{J}_{t+j}.$$

The right-hand side of (2.119) is approximated in an analogous manner:

$$\ln \frac{\phi}{\phi - 1} + \mathfrak{B} + \ln \mathfrak{I}_t + mc_t + \mathbb{E}_t \sum_{j=1}^{\infty} (\beta(1-\wp))^j \{\Delta \ln \mathfrak{I}_{t+j} + \Delta mc_{t+j}\}.$$

Equating the last two expressions and substituting for the definition of $\mathfrak{I}_{t+j}$ gives

$$p_t^* = \ln \frac{\phi}{\phi - 1} + mc_t + \mathbb{E}_t \sum_{j=1}^{\infty} \{\beta(1-\wp)\}^j \Delta mc_{t+j}.$$

The final step is to combine this equation with (2.45). For this purpose we iterate forward one period and rearrange to get

$$p_t^* = \left(1 - \beta(1 - \wp)\right) mc_t + \left(1 - \beta(1 - \wp)\right) \ln \frac{\phi}{\phi - 1} + \beta(1-\wp)\mathbb{E}_t p_{t+1}^*.$$

Subtracting p_{t-1} from both sides produces

$$p_t^* - p_{t-1} = \left(1 - \beta(1 - \wp)\right) rmc_t + \left(1 - \beta(1 - \wp)\right) \ln \frac{\phi}{\phi - 1}$$
$$+ \beta(1-\wp)\mathbb{E}_t(p_{t+1}^* - p_t) + \Delta p_t,$$

which is then substituted into (2.45) to get

$$\Delta p_t = \frac{\wp\left(1 - \beta(1-\wp)\right)}{1 - \wp} \left(rmc_t + \ln \frac{\phi}{\phi - 1}\right) + \beta \mathbb{E}_t \Delta p_{t+1}.$$

Iterating this equation forward gives us equation (2.46).

The system of equations in (2.64) has a determinant solution when both roots of matrix $\mathcal{H}$ lie inside the unit circle. This is the case when: (1) $|\det(\mathcal{H})| < 1$ and (2) $|-\text{trace}(\mathcal{H})| < 1 + \det(\mathcal{H})$. Since $\det(\mathcal{H}) = \beta/(1+\psi_\varepsilon) < 1$, only the second condition binds, that is,

$$\left| \frac{\varsigma\kappa\psi_\pi - 1}{1 + \psi_\varepsilon} - \beta \right| < 1 + \frac{\beta}{1 + \psi_\varepsilon},$$

or equivalently,

$$-(1 + \psi_\varepsilon + \beta) < \varsigma\kappa\psi_\pi - 1 - \beta(1 + \psi_\varepsilon) < 1 + \psi_\varepsilon + \beta.$$

The left-hand inequality must be true because $1 > \beta > 0$. The right-hand inequality gives the determinacy condition in equation (2.65).

International Solvency

To derive the approximate international solvency condition in equation (2.79), we first rewrite (2.76) as

$$fa_t = r_t^{\text{FA}} + fa_{t-1} + \ln\left(1 - \frac{\mathfrak{M}_t}{R_t^{\text{FA}} FA_{t-1}} + \mathfrak{R}_t\right), \tag{2.120}$$

where

$$\mathfrak{R}_t = \frac{FL_t}{R_t^{\text{FA}} FA_{t-1}} + \frac{\mathfrak{X}_t}{R_t^{\text{FA}} FA_{t-1}} - \frac{R_t^{\text{FL}}}{R_t^{\text{FA}}} \frac{FL_{t-1}}{FA_{t-1}}.$$

Approximating the right-hand side of (2.120) around the point where $1 - \frac{\mathfrak{M}_t}{R_t^{\text{FA}} FA_{t-1}} = \mu$ and $\mathfrak{R}_t = 0$ gives

$$fa_t = r_t^{\text{FA}} + fa_{t-1} + \left(1 - \frac{1}{\mu}\right)(m_t - r_t^{\text{FA}} - fa_{t-1}) + \frac{1}{\mu}\mathfrak{R}_t + k, \quad (2.121)$$

where $k \equiv \ln(\mu) + \frac{1-\mu}{\mu}\ln(1-\mu)$.

Next, we rewrite the definition of $\mathfrak{R}_t$ as

$$\frac{FL_t}{R_t^{\text{FA}} FA_{t-1}} = \left(1 - \frac{\mathfrak{X}_t}{R_t^{\text{FL}} FL_{t-1}}\right) \frac{R_t^{\text{FL}}}{R_t^{\text{FA}}} \frac{FL_{t-1}}{FA_{t-1}} + \mathfrak{R}_t,$$

and take logs:

$$fl_t - r_t^{\text{FA}} - fa_{t-1} = \ln\left\{\left(1 - \frac{\mathfrak{X}_t}{R_t^{\text{FL}} FL_{t-1}}\right) \frac{R_t^{\text{FL}}}{R_t^{\text{FA}}} \frac{FL_{t-1}}{FA_{t-1}} + \mathfrak{R}_t\right\}.$$

Approximating the right-hand side around the point where $1 - \frac{\mathfrak{X}_t}{R_t^{\text{FL}} FL_{t-1}} = \mu$, $\frac{R_t^{\text{FL}}}{R_t^{\text{FA}}} \frac{FL_{t-1}}{FA_{t-1}} = 1$, and $\mathfrak{R}_t = 0$ gives

$$\begin{aligned} fl_t = {} & r_t^{\text{FA}} + fa_{t-1} + (r_t^{\text{FL}} - r_t^{\text{FA}} + fl_{t-1} - fa_{t-1}) \\ & - \frac{1-\mu}{\mu}(x_t - r_t^{\text{FL}} - fl_{t-1}) + \frac{1}{\mu}\mathfrak{R}_t + k. \end{aligned} \quad (2.122)$$

Finally, we combine (2.121) and (2.122) to eliminate $\mathfrak{R}_t$. After some rearrangement, this produces

$$fl_t - fa_t = (1 - \mu)\,\mathbb{E}_t nx_{t+1} + \mathbb{E}_t(r_{t+1}^{\text{FA}} - r_{t+1}^{\text{FL}}) + \mu\mathbb{E}_t(fl_{t+1} - fa_{t+1}).$$

Iterating forward with $\lim_{j\to\infty}\mathbb{E}_t\mu^j(fl_{t+j} - fa_{t+j}) = 0$ leads to the approximate solvency condition in equation (2.79). This approximation does not assume the existence of a steady state where the U.S. foreign asset and liability positions are constant. To see why, we rewrite (2.76) as

$$FA_t - FL_t = \left\{\left(1 - \frac{\mathfrak{M}_t}{R_t^{\text{FA}} FA_{t-1}}\right) - \left(1 - \frac{\mathfrak{X}_t}{R_t^{\text{FL}} FL_{t-1}}\right) \frac{R_t^{\text{FL}} FL_{t-1}}{R_t^{\text{FA}} FA_{t-1}}\right\} R_t^{\text{FA}} FA_{t-1}$$

and note that the term in $\{\}$ equals zero at the linearization points used in the approximation. Here pre-existing U.S. foreign asset and liability positions, $R_t^{\text{FA}} FA_{t-1}$ ($= R_t^{\text{FL}} FL_{t-1}$), have no effect on the net foreign asset position, $FA_t - FL_t$, which must be zero.

Exports and Imports. U.S. exports are equal to the real value of U.S. intermediate goods demanded by E.U. retail firms,

$$\mathfrak{X}_t = (1 - \lambda)(P_t^{\text{US}}/P_t)(\hat{P}_t^{\text{US}}/\hat{P}_t^{\text{X}})^{-\theta}\hat{\Gamma}_t\hat{Q}_t^{\alpha-1}\hat{C}_t^{\omega},$$

and U.S. imports are equal to the value of E.U. goods demanded by U.S. retail firms,

$$\mathfrak{M}_t = (1 - \lambda)(P_t^{\text{EU}}/P_t)(P_t^{\text{EU}}/P_t^{\text{X}})^{-\theta}\Gamma_t Q_t^{\alpha-1}C_t^{\omega}.$$

These two expressions can be rewritten in terms of marginal costs as

$$\mathfrak{X}_t = \frac{(1 - \lambda)\left(\alpha^{\alpha}(1 - \alpha)^{1-\alpha}\right)}{\varkappa^{1-\alpha}}\hat{\Gamma}_t(\hat{P}_t^{\text{US}}/\hat{P}_t^{\text{X}})^{1-\theta}\widehat{RMC}_t\mathcal{E}_t\hat{C}_t$$

and

$$\mathfrak{M}_t = \frac{(1 - \lambda)\left(\alpha^{\alpha}(1 - \alpha)^{1-\alpha}\right)}{\varkappa^{1-\alpha}}\Gamma_t(P_t^{\text{EU}}/P_t^{\text{X}})^{1-\theta}RMC_t C_t.$$

Substituting these equations into the definition for log net exports, $nx_t = \ln(\mathfrak{X}_t/\mathfrak{M}_t)$, results in equation (2.91).

Portfolio Balance with Sticky Prices. When prices are sticky, the equilibrium dynamics of the Portfolio Balance model are determined by (2.106) and (2.108):

$$\Delta p_t - \Delta\hat{p}_t = \kappa\varsigma_\varepsilon(\varepsilon_t - \varepsilon_t^{\text{F}}) + \kappa\varsigma_c[(c_t - \hat{c}_t) - (c_t^{\text{F}} - \hat{c}_t^{\text{F}})]$$
$$+ \beta\mathbb{E}_t(\Delta p_{t+1} - \Delta\hat{p}_{t+1}) \tag{2.123}$$

and

$$\varepsilon_t - \varepsilon_t^{\text{F}} = \mathbb{E}_t(\varepsilon_{t+1} - \varepsilon_{t+1}^{\text{F}}) - \psi_\pi\mathbb{E}_t(\Delta p_{t+1} - \Delta\hat{p}_{t+1})$$
$$- (\delta_t - \delta_t^{\text{F}}) - \psi_y[(c_t - \hat{c}_t) - (c_t^{\text{F}} - \hat{c}_t^{\text{F}})], \tag{2.124}$$

where real marginal costs and net exports follow

$$rmc_t - \widehat{rmc}_t = \varsigma_\varepsilon(\varepsilon_t - \varepsilon_t^{\text{F}}) + \varsigma_c[(c_t - \hat{c}_t) - (c_t^{\text{F}} - \hat{c}_t^{\text{F}})] \tag{2.125a}$$

and

$$nx_t - nx_t^{\text{F}} = \varphi_\varepsilon(\varepsilon_t - \varepsilon_t^{\text{F}}) + \varphi_c[(c_t - \hat{c}_t) - (c_t^{\text{F}} - \hat{c}_t^{\text{F}})]. \tag{2.125b}$$

The remaining equations come from the solvency condition in (2.98), the portfolio balance condition in (2.90), and equations for the log consumption asset ratios of U.S. and E.U. households. We can write the former in deviation form as

$$nfl_t - nfl_t^{\text{F}} = (1 - \mu)\mathbb{E}_t(nx_{t+1} - nx_{t+1}^{\text{F}}) + (\delta_t - \delta_t^{\text{F}})$$
$$+ \mu\mathbb{E}_t(nfl_{t+1} - nfl_{t+1}^{\text{F}}). \tag{2.126}$$

To derive the latter two equations, we first combine (2.116) and (2.117) to give

$$ca_t - \widehat{ca}_t = \varrho(1 - \ell)(rmc_t - \widehat{rmc}_t) + (1 - \varrho\ell)E_t(ca_{t+1} - \widehat{ca}_{t+1}) \tag{2.127}$$

[assuming that $\mathbb{V}_t(ca_{t+1}) = \mathbb{V}_t(\widehat{ca}_{t+1})$]. We also linearize (2.90) to produce

$$nfl_t = \varepsilon_t + \hat{c}_t - c_t + \hat{h}_t^{\mathrm{B}} - h_t^{\mathrm{B}} + \frac{\varrho\ell}{1-\varrho\ell}(ca_t - \widehat{ca}_t) - \frac{\varrho(1-\ell)}{1-\varrho\ell}(rmc_t - \widehat{rmc}_t)$$

$$= \varepsilon_t + \hat{c}_t - c_t - \alpha\delta_t + \frac{\varrho\ell}{1-\varrho\ell}(ca_t - \widehat{ca}_t) - \frac{\varrho(1-\ell)}{1-\varrho\ell}(rmc_t - \widehat{rmc}_t) - \Im_t.$$

Since $ca_t = \widehat{ca}_t$ and $rmc_t = \widehat{rmc}_t$ under flexible prices, this last equation can be rewritten as

$$nfl_t - nfl_t^{\mathrm{F}} = (\varepsilon_t - \varepsilon_t^{\mathrm{F}}) - [(c_t - \hat{c}_t) - (c_t^{\mathrm{F}} - \hat{c}_t^{\mathrm{F}})] - \alpha(\delta_t - \delta_t^{\mathrm{F}})$$
$$+ \frac{\varrho\ell}{1-\varrho\ell}(ca_t - \widehat{ca}_t) - \frac{\varrho(1-\ell)}{1-\varrho\ell}(rmc_t - \widehat{rmc}_t). \tag{2.128}$$

Finally, to close the system, we note that

$$\delta_t - \delta_t^{\mathrm{F}} = \mathbb{E}_t(\Delta\varepsilon_{t+1} - \Delta\varepsilon_{t+1}^{\mathrm{F}}) + \mathbb{E}_t(\Delta\hat{c}_{t+1} - \Delta\hat{c}_{t+1}^{\mathrm{F}}) - \mathbb{E}_t(\Delta c_{t+1} - \Delta c_{t+1}^{\mathrm{F}}). \tag{2.129}$$

Inspection of (2.123)–(2.129) reveals that the flex-price values for all the variables solve the system of equations.

CHAPTER 3

Empirical Macro Models

This chapter examines the empirical performance of several macro exchange-rate models. The models we study fall into three broad classes: (1) Money-Income models based on the monetary models developed in the 1970s, (2) Taylor Rule models that incorporate more up-to-date characterizations of monetary policy, and (3) External Balance models that focus on the requirements of international solvency and international portfolio choice. Models in all three classes have been the focus of a recent resurgence in empirical exchange-rate research. In this chapter we review this research and assess the overall success of macro models in accounting for exchange-rate dynamics.

All the models we study can be written in the form of a present value relation. The Money-Income and Taylor Rule models relate the current level of the exchange rate to the expected present value of a combination of future macroeconomic variables called exchange-rate fundamentals. External Balance models, in contrast, relate the current external position of the economy to the expected present value of future depreciation rates and other variables. We therefore begin this chapter with a detailed examination of the dynamic implications of present value relations. This analysis is then used to review the empirical performance of the Money-Income, Taylor Rule, and External Balance models. The review initially focuses on in-sample model estimates and inference, that is, econometric results obtained using the entire sample of available data. There is also a strong tradition in the empirical exchange-rate literature of using out-of-sample evaluation methods. This research is reviewed at the end of the chapter.

Since the literature on empirical exchange-rate models is truly vast, this chapter does not attempt to provide a comprehensive survey of the results in every study. Nor does it provide a detailed discussion of all the econometric techniques used to estimate and test the models. We focus, instead, on recent research that is most closely related to the theoretical models presented in Chapters 1 and 2. Guidance on further reading in the empirical exchange-rate and econometrics literatures is provided in the Bibliography at the end of the chapter.

3.1 Present Value Models

Many empirical exchange-rate models fall into the class of Present Value models. These models relate the current level of the spot exchange rate to the expected present value of a combination of future macroeconomic variables called exchange-rate fundamentals. Although the identity of these variables varies from model to model, the present value relation has a number of important implications for the joint dynamics of exchange rates and fundamentals. In this section, we derive these implications for a generic Present Value model. Their relevance for specific exchange-rate models is examined in the sections that follow.

3.1.1 Present Value Equations

Present Value models formalize the idea that exchange rates are determined by equilibrium in asset markets. In particular, according to this asset market approach (see, e.g., Frenkel 1981), the log spot rate in period t is determined by

$$s_t = \lambda \mathbb{E}_t \Delta s_{t+1} + f_t, \tag{3.1}$$

with $\lambda > 0$, where $\Delta s_t \equiv s_t - s_{t-1}$ and $\mathbb{E}_t \Delta s_{t+1}$ is the expected depreciation rate between periods t and $t+1$ conditioned on period-t information, Ω_t. All the other factors affecting the demand for and the supply of foreign currency in period t are represented by exchange-rate fundamentals, f_t. These factors are assumed to be observable in period t, that is, $f_t \in \Omega_t$.

The present value relation between the spot rate and fundamentals is easily derived. First, we rewrite equation (3.1) as

$$s_t = (1 - b)f_t + b\mathbb{E}_t s_{t+1},$$

where $b = \lambda/(1 + \lambda)$. Next we solve forward for $k - 1$ periods using the Law of Iterated Expectations (i.e., $\mathbb{E}_t \mathbb{E}_{t+i} s_{t+i+1} = \mathbb{E}_t s_{t+i+1}$ for all $i > 0$), to give

$$s_t = (1 - b)\mathbb{E}_t \sum_{i=0}^{k-1} b^i f_{t+i} + b^k \mathbb{E}_t s_{t+k}. \tag{3.2}$$

Note that $f_t = \mathbb{E}_t f_t$ because $f_t \in \Omega_t$. The first term on the right is the expected present value of future fundamentals over the next k periods. The second term is the expected discounted value of the future spot rate. Finally, the Present Value model is derived from equation (3.2) under the assumption that $b^k \mathbb{E}_t s_{t+k}$ goes to zero as $k \to \infty$:

$$s_t = (1 - b)\mathbb{E}_t \sum_{i=0}^{\infty} b^i f_{t+i}. \tag{3.3}$$

The Present Value model in (3.3) combines equation (3.1) with two economic restrictions. Expectations concerning the future exchange rate must be: (1) dynamically consistent, and (2) tied to the behavior of fundamentals. The meaning of dynamic consistency is illustrated in equation (3.2). There we see that all variations in the exchange rate must originate from a change in current fundamentals, expected future fundamentals $\mathbb{E}_t f_{t+i}$ for $0 < i < k$, or the expected future exchange rate, $\mathbb{E}_t s_{t+k}$. As (3.1) shows, the first of these terms affects the spot rate directly. The second two terms affect the spot rate indirectly via their impact on the expected depreciation rate, which is consistent with equilibrium in period $t + 1$, that is, $\mathbb{E}_t \Delta s_{t+1} = \lambda \mathbb{E}_t \Delta s_{t+2} + \mathbb{E}_t f_{t+1} - s_t$. All the influence of expected future fundamentals on the current spot rate in the Present Value model comes from their effect on the expected depreciation rate.

The second economic restriction in the Present Value model concerns the long-horizon forecasts for the spot rate. Equation (3.2) shows that variations in $\mathbb{E}_t s_{t+k}$ could affect the current exchange rate independently of current and expected future fundamentals up to horizon k. The Present Value model assumes that the influence of these forecasts disappears as $k \to \infty$, so the current exchange rate depends only on the anticipated path of fundamentals. This assumption does not require that $\lim_{k\to\infty} \mathbb{E}_t s_{t+k}$ be a constant. However, it does rule out the possibility that equilibrium in the spot rate market is governed by an asset-pricing bubble. For this reason, the assumption that $\lim_{k\to\infty} b^k \mathbb{E}_t s_{t+k} = 0$ is often referred to as a "no-bubble" condition.

The dynamic implications of the Present Value model are easily derived under the assumption that fundamentals follow a particular time series process. In this case the sequence of fundamentals' forecasts (i.e., $\mathbb{E}_t f_{t+i}$ for $i > 0$) is computed from the particular process and the results substituted in (3.3) to produce an equation for the equilibrium dynamics of the exchange rate. Alternatively, we can derive the dynamic implications of the Present Value model without reference to a specific fundamentals' process. This approach turns out to be very useful in understanding the empirical performance of the exchange-rate models we examine later.

We proceed in three steps. First, we derive the implications of (3.3) for the expected depreciation rate, $\mathbb{E}_t \Delta s_{t+1}$. Second, we identify the error in forecasting next period's spot rate, $s_{t+1} - \mathbb{E}_t s_{t+1}$. This forecast error also identifies the unexpected depreciation rate because $\Delta s_{t+1} - \mathbb{E}_t \Delta s_{t+1} = s_{t+1} - \mathbb{E}_t s_{t+1}$ when $s_t \in \Omega_t$. Thus, in the last step, we compute the actual depreciation rate from the identity $\Delta s_{t+1} \equiv \mathbb{E}_t \Delta s_{t+1} + s_{t+1} - \mathbb{E}_t s_{t+1}$.

To begin, we first note that

$$(1 - b)\mathbb{E}_t \sum_{i=0}^{\infty} b^i f_{t+i} = f_t + \mathbb{E}_t \sum_{i=1}^{\infty} b^i \Delta f_{t+i}. \tag{3.4}$$

Hence, the present value equation in (3.3) can also be written as

$$s_t - f_t = \sum_{i=1}^{\infty} b^i \mathbb{E}_t \Delta f_{t+i}. \tag{3.5}$$

Next, we iterate equation (3.3) one period forward and rearrange the result to give

$$\mathbb{E}_t \Delta s_{t+1} = \frac{1-b}{b} \left(s_t - f_t \right). \tag{3.6}$$

Combining this expression with (3.5) gives the following equation for the expected depreciation rate

$$\mathbb{E}_t \Delta s_{t+1} = \frac{1-b}{b} \sum_{i=1}^{\infty} b^i \mathbb{E}_t \Delta f_{t+i}. \tag{3.7}$$

The next step is to identify the forecast error, $s_{t+1} - \mathbb{E}_t s_{t+1}$. For this we lead equation (3.3) one period forward and take expectations conditioned on period-t

information, Ω_t:

$$\mathbb{E}_t s_{t+1} = (1-b)\mathbb{E}_t \sum_{i=0}^{\infty} b^i f_{t+1+i}.$$

The actual spot rate in period $t+1$ is given by

$$s_{t+1} = (1-b)\mathbb{E}_{t+1} \sum_{i=0}^{\infty} b^i f_{t+1+i},$$

so the forecast error implied by the present value relation in (3.3) is

$$s_{t+1} - \mathbb{E}_t s_{t+1} = \tfrac{1-b}{b} \sum_{i=1}^{\infty} b^i \left(\mathbb{E}_{t+1} - \mathbb{E}_t\right) f_{t+i}. \tag{3.8}$$

Finally, we combine (3.7) and (3.8) with the identity $\Delta s_{t+1} \equiv \mathbb{E}_t \Delta s_{t+1} + s_{t+1} - \mathbb{E}_t s_{t+1}$ to get

$$\Delta s_{t+1} = \tfrac{1-b}{b} \sum_{i=1}^{\infty} b^i \mathbb{E}_t \Delta f_{t+i} + \tfrac{1-b}{b} \sum_{i=1}^{\infty} b^i \left(\mathbb{E}_{t+1} - \mathbb{E}_t\right) f_{t+i}. \tag{3.9}$$

Equation (3.9) shows that the actual depreciation rate depends on two factors: (1) expected future changes in fundamentals, $\mathbb{E}_t \Delta f_{t+i}$, and (2) the revision in forecasts of future fundamentals, $\left(\mathbb{E}_{t+1} - \mathbb{E}_t\right) f_{t+i}$, between periods t and $t+1$. The behavior of these factors provides the key to understanding the sources of exchange-rate variation, the volatility of spot rates relative to fundamentals, the predictability of spot rate changes, and the forecasting power of spot rates for future fundamentals.

3.1.2 Drivers of Depreciation Rates

According to equation (3.9), the depreciation rate varies from period to period either because forecasts for the future growth in fundamentals drive changes in the expected depreciation rate or new information induces a revision in forecasts of future fundamentals that produces an unexpected jump in the spot rate. In order to quantify these effects, we first have to identify market expectations of fundamentals.

For this purpose, let us assume that the change in fundamentals, Δf_t, follows a mean-zero covariance-stationary process and that market participants form their forecasts for Δf_{t+i} from linear projections of Δf_{t+i} on the current and past values of Δf_t, $F_t = \{\Delta f_t, \Delta f_{t-1}, \ldots\}$. From the Wold Decomposition theorem (discussed in Chapter 1), we know that the first of these assumptions implies that the time series for Δf_t can be represented by

$$\Delta f_t = \psi(L)\eta_t, \tag{3.10}$$

where $\psi(L) = 1 + \psi_1 L + \psi_2 L^2 + \cdots$ is a polynomial in the lag operator, L, and $\eta_t = \Delta f_t - \mathbb{P}(\Delta f_t | F_{t-1})$ are the projection errors in forecasting Δf_t based on F_{t-1}. Recall that these errors have the properties that $\mathbb{E}[\eta_t] = 0$, $\mathbb{E}[\eta_t, \Delta f_{t-j}] = 0$, $\mathbb{E}[\eta_t \eta_{t-j}] = 0$

for $j > 0$, and $\mathbb{E}[\eta_t^2] = \sigma^2$. The second assumption allows us to identify market participants' forecasts as

$$\mathbb{E}_t \Delta f_{t+i} = \mathbb{P}(\Delta f_{t+i}|F_t) = \left[\psi(L)/L^i \right]_+ \eta_t, \tag{3.11}$$

where $[.]_+$ denotes the annihilation operator that "removes" the negative powers in L. For example, if $\psi(L) = 1 + \psi_1 L + \psi_2 L^2$, then $\mathbb{E}_t \Delta f_{t+1} = \left[L^{-1} + \psi_1 + \psi_2 L \right]_+ \eta_t = (\psi_1 + \psi_2 L)\eta_t$.

These two assumptions are sufficient to relate market participants' forecasts, $\mathbb{E}_t \Delta f_{t+i}$, to the time series properties of fundamentals, as summarized in $\psi(L)$. Furthermore, they allow us to study the behavior of depreciation rates without taking a stand on whether the time series process for the level of fundamentals, f_t, contains a unit root. As we shall see, this degree of generality is useful in understanding the empirical literature on the exchange-rate models reviewed later.

We now use (3.10) and (3.11) to compute the two terms on the right-hand side of equation (3.9). Applying results first derived by Hansen and Sargent (1980), we show in the appendix that

$$\frac{1-b}{b} \sum_{i=1}^{\infty} b^i \mathbb{P}(\Delta f_{t+i}|F_t) = (1-b) \left(\frac{\psi(b) - \psi(L)}{b - L} \right) \eta_t \tag{3.12a}$$

and

$$\frac{1-b}{b} \sum_{i=1}^{\infty} b^i \left(\mathbb{P}(f_{t+i}|F_{t+1}) - \mathbb{P}(f_{t+i}|F_t) \right) = \psi(b)\eta_{t+1}. \tag{3.12b}$$

To illustrate the use of these formulas, consider the case where fundamentals follow a random walk. Here $\psi(L) = 1$ so $\psi(L) = \psi(b)$ and the term on the right of equation (3.12a) equals zero. In this case, the expected depreciation rate is always zero, so all the variations in the actual depreciation rate come from revisions in the forecasts of future fundamentals. Thus, $\Delta s_{t+1} = s_{t+1} - \mathbb{E}_t s_{t+1} = \eta_{t+1}$. Note that in this case, the value of b plays no role in the dynamics of the spot rate because $\mathbb{E}_t \Delta s_{t+1} = 0$, so $\Delta s_t = \Delta f_t$ from (3.1).

The expressions in (3.12) are more informative about the source of variation in the depreciation rates when there is serial correlation in Δf_t (i.e., when some of the ψ_i's in $\psi(L)$ are nonzero). For example, suppose that Δf_t follows an AR(1) process: $\Delta f_t = \phi \Delta f_{t-1} + \eta_t$ with $|\phi| < 1$. In this case $\psi(L) = (1 - \phi L)^{-1}$, so applying the formulas in (3.12) produces

$$\mathbb{E}_t \Delta s_{t+1} = \frac{\phi(1-b)}{(1-\phi b)} \frac{1}{(1-\phi L)} \eta_t \quad \text{and} \quad s_{t+1} - \mathbb{E}_t s_{t+1} = \frac{1}{1-\phi b}\eta_{t+1}. \tag{3.13}$$

Here a positive shock to fundamentals leads to an immediate unanticipated depreciation in period $t + 1$ and a rise in the expected depreciation rate, $\mathbb{E}_{t+1}\Delta s_{t+h}$, for all horizons $h > 1$. The relative contribution of these factors to the variability in the depreciation rate depends on ϕ and b. In particular, if b is close to one, variations in the expected depreciation rate will contribute very little to the variability of the actual depreciation rate unless ϕ is far from zero. This is easily seen in Figure 3.1,

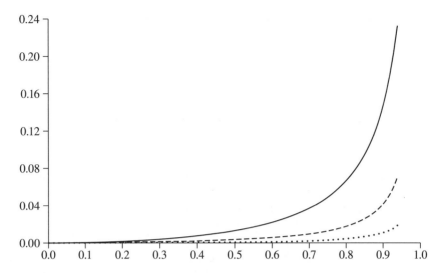

FIGURE 3.1   Plot of the variance ratio, $\mathbb{V}(\mathbb{E}_t \Delta s_{t+1})/\mathbb{V}(\Delta s_{t+1})$, against ϕ for $b = 0.8$ (solid), $b = 0.9$ (dashed), and $b = 0.95$ (dotted).

which plots the variance ratio, $\mathbb{V}(\mathbb{E}_t \Delta s_{t+1})/\mathbb{V}(\Delta s_{t+1})$, implied by (3.13), against ϕ for $b = \{0.8, 0.9, 0.95\}$. Clearly, changes in the expected depreciation rate contribute very little to the variance of the actual depreciation rate for discount factors greater than 0.8 unless ϕ is very close to one.

The implications of this example apply more generally. Engel and West (2005) show that if the process for fundamentals contains a unit root, then as b approaches one, the exchange rate will follow a process arbitrarily close to a random walk. To understand the intuition behind this result, let us rewrite the process for fundamentals in (3.10) as

$$\Delta f_t = \psi(1)\eta_t + \psi^*(L)\eta_t, \tag{3.14}$$

where $\psi^*(L) = \psi(L) - \psi(1)$. This is the first-difference form of the Beveridge-Nelson Decomposition for fundamentals presented in Chapter 1. The first term on the right identifies the change in the stochastic trend component of fundamentals, Δf_t^{T}, and the second identifies the change in the cyclical component, Δf_t^c. Recall that $f_t\ (= f_t^{\mathrm{T}} + f_t^c)$ contains a unit root if, and only if, $\psi(1) \neq 0$.

Next, consider how the trend and cycle components in fundamentals contribute to the depreciation rate. For this purpose, we first note that

$$\mathbb{P}[f_{t+i}|F_{t+1}] - \mathbb{P}[f_{t+i}|F_t] = \mathbb{P}[f_{t+i}^c|F_{t+1}] - \mathbb{P}[f_{t+i}^c|F_t] + \mathbb{P}[f_{t+i}^{\mathrm{T}}|F_{t+1}] - \mathbb{P}[f_{t+i}^{\mathrm{T}}|F_t]$$

$$= \mathbb{P}[f_{t+i}^c|F_{t+1}] - \mathbb{P}[f_{t+i}^c|F_t] + \Delta f_{t+1}^{\mathrm{T}}$$

and

$$\mathbb{P}[\Delta f_{t+i}|F_t] = \mathbb{P}[\Delta f_{t+i}^c|F_t] + \mathbb{P}[\Delta f_{t+i}^{\mathrm{T}}|F_t] = \mathbb{P}[\Delta f_{t+i}^c|F_t]$$

for all $i > 0$. Substituting these projections for the conditional expectations in equation (3.9) gives

$$\Delta s_{t+1} = \frac{1-b}{b} \sum_{i=1}^{\infty} b^i \mathbb{P}[\Delta f_{t+i}^C | F_t]$$

$$+ \frac{1-b}{b} \sum_{i=1}^{\infty} b^i \left(\mathbb{P}[f_{t+i}^C | F_{t+1}] - \mathbb{P}[f_{t+i}^C | F_t] \right) + \Delta f_{t+1}^T. \quad (3.15)$$

The first two terms on the right-hand side identify the contribution of the cyclical component forecasts to the depreciation rate. These forecasts vary less as the forecasting horizon lengthens, so shocks to fundamentals have little effect on the depreciation rate via either of these terms when b is close to one. The third term identifies the effect of changes in the trend component of fundamentals, Δf_{t+1}^T. These changes affect forecasts of the trend component at all horizons because $\mathbb{P}[f_{t+i}^T | F_{t+1}] - \mathbb{P}[f_{t+i}^T | F_t] = \Delta f_{t+1}^T$ for all $i > 0$. They therefore contribute to the unexpected jumps in the spot rate, $s_{t+1} - \mathbb{E}_t s_{t+1}$, for any value of $b \in [0, 1]$.

These observations make clear why the time series for Δs_{t+1} will be well approximated by $\Delta f_{t+1}^T = \psi(1)\eta_{t+1}$ when b is close to one, so observations on s_t will be hard to distinguish from realizations of a random walk. In effect, Engel and West identify the conditions under which revisions in forecasts of the trend in fundamentals drive unexpected changes in the spot rate, which in turn are the dominant source of variation in the depreciation rate.

The relevance of the Engel and West result depends on the size of the discount parameter b and the time series characteristics of fundamentals. Recall that $b = \lambda/(1 + \lambda)$, where the λ parameter measures the elasticity of the spot rate with respect to the expected depreciation rate. Engel and West point out that the value of λ implied by at least two important classes of macro exchange-rate models is large. As we shall see later, reasonable values for b in these models are above 0.95.

The serial correlation properties of the cyclical component in fundamentals are also important. Applying the results in (3.12) to the first two terms in (3.15) gives

$$\Delta s_{t+1} = \Delta f_{t+1}^T + \xi_{t+1},$$

where

$$\xi_{t+1} = \left[(1-b) \left(\frac{\psi^*(b) - \psi^*(L)}{b - L} \right) L + \psi^*(b) \right] \eta_{t+1}.$$

Clearly, the "approximation error," ξ_{t+1}, is zero when all the coefficients in the lag polynomial $\psi^*(L)$ equal zero. In this case there simply is no cyclical component in fundamentals, so the random walk characterization is exactly right whatever the value of b. In contrast, when Δf_t^C is serially correlated, the coefficients in $\psi^*(L)$ are nonzero, so $\mathbb{V}(\xi_{t+1}) > 0$ when $b < 1$. Many of the macro time series used to construct measures of fundamentals display some serial correlation in first-differences, but the implied estimates of the coefficients in $\psi^*(L)$ do not suggest that $\mathbb{V}(\xi_{t+1})/\mathbb{V}(\Delta f_{t+1}^T)$ is large when b is greater than 0.95. From this perspective, the Engel and West result provides an empirically relevant approximate characterization of the time series properties of the depreciation rate implied by at least two important classes of macro exchange-rate models.

3.1.3 Cointegration

Equation (3.15) also has important implications for the cointegration properties of spot exchange rates and fundamentals. Two times series, x_t and y_t, are said to be cointegrated if: (1) x_t and y_t follow nonstationary unit root processes, and (2) there exists a linear combination of x_t and y_t that follows a stationary process, that is, one without a unit root. For this to be the case, x_t and y_t must share the same trend component in their respective Beveridge-Nelson Decompositions. Shocks to the trend in x_t must be perfectly correlated with shocks to the trend in y_t; otherwise no linear combination of x_t and y_t exists without its own trend and thus a unit root.

The Present Value model implies that if fundamentals follow a unit root process, spot rates and fundamentals are cointegrated one-for-one and thus share the same trend. This is easily seen in equation (3.15). If fundamentals contain a unit root, $\Delta f_{t+1}^{\mathrm{T}} \neq 0$, so shocks to the trend in fundamentals have an immediate and one-to-one effect on the spot rate. Shocks that affect the cyclical component of fundamentals, f_t^{C}, also affect the depreciation rate via the first two terms on the right-hand side of (3.15), but their effect on the *level* of the spot rate is short-lived because they do not change the forecasts of the cyclical component at long horizons.

To see this more formally, we can apply the Beveridge-Nelson Decomposition to the process for the depreciation rate implied by (3.9), (3.12a), and (3.12b) when $\Delta f_t = \psi(L)\eta_t$:

$$\Delta s_{t+1} = \left\{ (1-b)\left(\frac{\psi(b)-\psi(L)}{b-L}\right) L + \psi(b) \right\} \eta_{t+1} = \psi_{\Delta s}(L)\eta_{t+1} + \psi(1)\eta_{t+1},$$

where

$$\psi_{\Delta s}(L) = \frac{b(1-L)\,(\psi(b)-\psi(L))}{b-L} + \psi(L) - \psi(1).$$

The $\psi_{\Delta s}(L)$ polynomial identifies how shocks to fundamentals affect the depreciation rate via their impact on the forecasts of f_t^{C}. Note that $\psi_{\Delta s}(1) = 0$, so these shocks have no long-run effect on the level of the spot rate. The second term identifies the change in the stochastic trend component of the spot rate. This term is identical to the change in the fundamentals trend, $\Delta f_{t+1}^{\mathrm{T}} = \psi(1)\eta_{t+1}$. The level of the spot rate is therefore cointegrated one for one with fundamentals because there is no trend in $s_t - f_t$.

3.1.4 Volatility

The Present Value model places restrictions on the relative volatility of spot rates versus fundamentals. These restrictions were first derived by LeRoy and Porter (1981) and Shiller (1981) in the context of a Present Value model for stock prices. To apply their insight to our exchange-rate model, we first rewrite equation (3.5) as

$$s_t - f_t = \sum_{i=1}^{\infty} b^i \Delta f_{t+i} - \sum_{i=1}^{\infty} b^i (\Delta f_{t+i} - \mathbb{E}_t \Delta f_{t+i}). \tag{3.16}$$

The first term on the right identifies the difference between the log spot rate and current fundamentals in a world where market participants have perfect foresight about future changes in fundamentals, that is, $\mathbb{E}_t \Delta f_{t+i} = \Delta f_{t+i}$ for $i > 0$. The second term is the discounted sum of the forecast errors market participants make when forecasting Δf_{t+i} based on period-t information, Ω_t. Under rational expectations, each of these forecast errors must be uncorrelated with all the elements in Ω_t, including $s_t - f_t$. Thus if we add this term to both sides of (3.16) and apply the variance operator, we obtain

$$\mathbb{V}(s_t - f_t) + \mathbb{V}\left(\sum_{i=1}^{\infty} b^i (\Delta f_{t+i} - \mathbb{E}_t \Delta f_{t+i})\right) = \mathbb{V}\left(\sum_{i=1}^{\infty} b^i \Delta f_{t+i}\right).$$

Furthermore, since the second variance on the left must be nonnegative,

$$\mathbb{V}(s_t - f_t) \le \mathbb{V}\left(\sum_{i=1}^{\infty} b^i \Delta f_{t+i}\right). \tag{3.17}$$

Hence, we have an upper bound on the volatility of the difference between the log spot rate and current fundamentals.

The volatility bound in equation (3.17) is the direct result of the simple idea than optimal forecasts for future changes in fundamentals cannot be more variable than the actual changes. It applies whatever information is available to market participants as long as $s_t - f_t \in \Omega_t$ and for any specification of fundamentals for which Δf_t is a I(0) stationary time series process.[1]

To make empirical use of the bound, we need a way to estimate $\sum_{i=1}^{\infty} b^i \Delta f_{t+i}$ from a finite data series on Δf_t. This is easily done by computing $\nabla_t = \sum_{i=1}^{T-1} b^i \Delta f_{t+i} + b^T (s_T - f_T)$. Taking conditional expectations and using equation (3.5) we find that

$$\mathbb{E}_t \nabla_t = \sum_{i=1}^{T-1} b^i \mathbb{E}_t \Delta f_{t+i} + b^T \mathbb{E}_t (s_T - f_T)$$

$$= \sum_{i=1}^{T-1} b^i \mathbb{E}_t \Delta f_{t+i} + b^T \sum_{i=1}^{\infty} b^i \mathbb{E}_t \Delta f_{T+i} = s_t - f_t.$$

We can therefore write $s_t - f_t + \left(\nabla_t - \mathbb{E}_t \nabla_t\right) = \nabla_t$ and derive the bound as

$$\mathbb{V}(s_t - f_t) \le \mathbb{V}\left(\nabla_t\right). \tag{3.18}$$

Unlike equation (3.17), estimated variances of both terms in this volatility bound can be computed in a finite data sample for a given definition of fundamentals.

---

1. Some restriction on the time series process for Δf_t is necessary to ensure that the variances in (3.17) are well defined.

The Present Value model also has implications for the volatility of the depreciation rate. Recall from (3.9) that changes in the depreciation rate depend on how market participants vary their forecasts of future fundamentals. This means that the volatility of the depreciation rate reflects changes in information available to market participants that is relevant for forecasting fundamentals rather than changes in the behavior of actual fundamentals. The importance of this distinction is most easily understood with the aid of an example.

Suppose that market participants' forecasts of future changes in fundamentals follow

$$\mathbb{E}_t \Delta f_{t+1} = \phi \mathbb{E}_{t-1} \Delta f_t + u_t, \tag{3.19}$$

with $u_t = \beta(f_t - \mathbb{E}_{t-1}f_t) + v_t$, where $1 > \phi > 0$ and v_t is an i.i.d.$(0, \sigma_v^2)$ shock that is uncorrelated with participants' forecast errors, $f_t - \mathbb{E}_{t-1}f_t$. Here u_t identifies the new period-t information used to revise forecasts of future fundamentals. In particular, applying the Law of Iterated Expectations to (3.19) gives $(\mathbb{E}_t - \mathbb{E}_{t-1})\Delta f_{t+h} = \phi^{h-1}(\mathbb{E}_t \Delta f_{t+1} - \mathbb{E}_{t-1}\Delta f_{t+1}) = \phi^{h-1}u_t$ for $h > 0$, so new period-t information changes forecasts of Δf_{t+h} when $\phi > 0$. This information can come from either current observations on fundamentals or other sources. For example, suppose fundamentals follow an AR(1) process $\Delta f_t = \phi \Delta f_{t-1} + e_t + v_t$ where e_t and v_t are i.i.d. mean-zero shocks. If participants learn the value of v_t by the start of period $t-1$ from other sources, their forecasts will take the form of (3.19) with $\beta = \phi$ and $\sigma_v^2 = \mathbb{V}(v_t)$. The specification in (3.19) does not assume that participants' information contains only the past history of fundamentals.

To derive the variance of the depreciation rate, we use (3.19) to substitute for $\mathbb{E}_t \Delta f_{t+i}$ in (3.9) and take first-differences to give

$$\Delta s_t = \frac{1-b}{1-\phi b}\mathbb{E}_{t-1}\Delta f_t + \frac{1 + b(\beta - \phi)}{1-\phi b}(f_t - \mathbb{E}_{t-1}f_t) + \frac{b}{1-\phi b}v_t.$$

Note that all three terms on the right-hand side are uncorrelated under rational expectations. The variance of the depreciation rate is therefore given by

$$\mathbb{V}(\Delta s_t) = \left(\frac{1-b}{1-\phi b}\right)^2 \mathbb{V}(\mathbb{E}_{t-1}\Delta f_t) + \left(\frac{1 + b(\beta - \phi)}{1-\phi b}\right)^2 \mathbb{V}(f_t - \mathbb{E}_{t-1}f_t)$$

$$+ \left(\frac{b}{1-\phi b}\right)^2 \sigma_v^2. \tag{3.20}$$

Next we compare $\mathbb{V}(\Delta s_t)$ with the variance of fundamentals, $\mathbb{V}(\Delta f_t)$. For this purpose, let $\mathfrak{R}^2 = \mathbb{V}(\mathbb{E}_{t-1}\Delta f_t)/\mathbb{V}(\Delta f_t)$ denote the fraction of the change in fundamentals that is predictable by market participants. With this definition we can rewrite (3.20) as

$$\frac{\mathbb{V}(\Delta s_t)}{\mathbb{V}(\Delta f_t)} = \left(\frac{1-b}{1-\phi b}\right)^2 \mathfrak{R}^2 + \left(\frac{1 + b(\beta - \phi)}{1-\phi b}\right)^2 (1 - \mathfrak{R}^2)$$

$$+ \left(\frac{b}{1-\phi b}\right)^2 \left((1-\phi^2)\mathfrak{R}^2 - \beta^2(1-\mathfrak{R}^2)\right). \tag{3.21}$$

Thus, the variance ratio of the depreciation rate to changes in fundamentals depends on the discount parameter b, the parameters governing participants' forecasts $\{\phi, \beta\}$, and the precision of their forecasts as measured by $\mathfrak{R}^2$.

To understand the implications of (3.21), let us first consider the limiting case where b approaches one. Under these circumstances variations in the expected depreciation rate disappear, so all the volatility in Δs_t reflects revisions in the present value of market participants' forecasts of future fundamentals. In terms of the variance ratio, equation (3.21) implies that

$$\lim_{b \to 1} \frac{\mathbb{V}(\Delta s_t)}{\mathbb{V}(\Delta f_t)} = 1 + \frac{2\beta}{1 - \phi} + \frac{2\,(\phi - \beta)}{1 - \phi}\,\mathfrak{R}^2.$$

The right-hand side of this expression is greater than one when $\phi > -\beta(1 - \mathfrak{R}^2)/\mathfrak{R}^2$.

Now consider a situation where market participants have access to sufficient information to perfectly predict fundamentals one period in advance; i.e., $f_t = \mathbb{E}_{t-1} f_t$. Under these circumstances, $\mathfrak{R}^2 = 1$ and equation (3.21) becomes

$$\frac{\mathbb{V}(\Delta s_t)}{\mathbb{V}(\Delta f_t)} = \left(\frac{1 - b}{1 - \phi b}\right)^2 + \left(\frac{b}{1 - \phi b}\right)^2 \left(1 - \phi^2\right).$$

Figure 3.2 plots this variance ratio against ϕ for three values of the discount factor, $b = \{0.8, 0.9, 0.95\}$. Clearly, the volatility of the depreciation rate can greatly exceed the volatility of the change in fundamentals when ϕ and b are close to one. It is important to note that in this example variations in the spot rate are driven entirely by changes in market participants' forecasts of fundamentals. Indeed, realizations of actual fundamentals do not provide any information that is used to determine spot rates, so it is hardly surprising that the depreciation rate can be many times as volatile as the change in fundamentals.

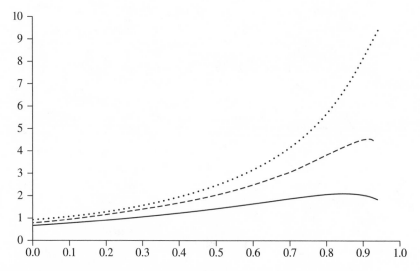

FIGURE 3.2   Plot of the variance ratio, $\mathbb{V}(\Delta s_t)/\mathbb{V}(\Delta f_t)$, against ϕ for $b = 0.8$ (solid), $b = 0.9$ (dashed), and $b = 0.95$ (dotted).

3.1.5 Joint Dynamics

The Present Value model links spot rates to market participants' forecasts of fundamentals without specifying the information available to participants beyond their observation of current fundamentals. As the preceding discussion of volatility illustrates, this feature of the Present Value model complicates the link between the behavior of the spot rate and actual fundamentals when the latter provide a very imprecise measure of participants' expectations. Nevertheless, we can still derive restrictions on the *joint* dynamics of spot rates and fundamentals without identifying all of the information available to market participants. Campbell and Shiller (1988) originally developed this insight in the context of a Present Value model for equities, but it is also applicable for Present Value exchange-rate models.

Campbell and Shiller's key idea is to consider the implications of the Present Value model for a set of expectations conditioned on less information than was available to market participants at the time. To apply this idea we return to equation (3.5):

$$s_t - f_t = \sum_{i=1}^{\infty} b^i \mathbb{E}_t \Delta f_{t+i}, \tag{3.22}$$

where the expectations on the right are conditioned on participants' period-t information, Ω_t. Let Ω_t^* denote a subset of Ω_t that comprises the history of spot rates, fundamentals, and any other variables, z_t, available to the researcher, that is, $\Omega_t^* = \{s_{t-i}, f_{t-i}, z_{t-i}\}_{i \geq 0}$. By the Law of Iterated Expectations, $\mathbb{E}[\mathbb{E}_t \Delta f_{t+i} | \Omega_t^*] = \mathbb{E}[\Delta f_{t+i} | \Omega_t^*]$ for all $i > 0$. Thus, taking expectations conditional on Ω_t^* on both sides of (3.22) produces

$$\mathbb{E}[s_t - f_t | \Omega_t^*] = \sum_{i=1}^{\infty} b^i \mathbb{E}[\Delta f_{t+i} | \Omega_t^*].$$

As s_t and f_t are elements in Ω_t^*, the expectation on the left-hand side is simply equal to $s_t - f_t$, so this expression becomes

$$s_t - f_t = \sum_{i=1}^{\infty} b^i \mathbb{E}[\Delta f_{t+i} | \Omega_t^*]. \tag{3.23}$$

Unlike (3.22), equation (3.23) relates the gap between the spot rate and fundamentals to forecasts for future fundamentals that are conditioned on a subset of market participants' information, $\Omega_t^* \subset \Omega_t$. At first glance, it may seem strange that any additional information in Ω_t has no effect on $s_t - f_t$. Surely market participants have information that is useful for forecasting future changes in fundamentals that is not available to the researcher. However, Ω_t^* is not just any subset of participants' information. As Ω_t^* contains current and past spot rates as well as the history of fundamentals, it effectively contains all the information participants are using to calculate $\mathbb{E}_t \Delta f_{t+i}$ for $i > 0$. For example, if participants have information that leads them to forecast higher growth in fundamentals 20 periods ahead than they would based on their observations of $\{f_{t-i}, z_{t-i}\}_{i \geq 0}$, this information will be reflected in a higher value for $s_t - f_t$. An information set composed of $\{s_{t-i}, f_{t-i}, z_{t-i}\}_{i \geq 0}$ will therefore capture this extra information affecting $\mathbb{E}_t \Delta f_{t+i}$. In short, we are using equation (3.22) to construct a particular subset of participants' information for which the implications of the Present Value model remain valid.

We can now use equation (3.23) to derive restrictions on the joint dynamics of spot rates and fundamentals. For this purpose we must first compute $\mathbb{E}[\Delta f_{t+i}|\Omega_t^*]$ for $i > 0$. Campbell and Shiller (1988) assume that these forecasts can be calculated from a Vector Autoregression (VAR). Let the vector $x_t = [\ \Delta f_t \quad s_t - f_t \quad z_t\ ]'$ follow a kth-order VAR:

$$x_t = a_1 x_{t-1} + a_2 x_{t-2} + \cdots a_k x_{t-k} + u_t, \tag{3.24}$$

where a_i are matrices of coefficients from each of the VAR equations and u_t is a vector of mean-zero shocks. To compute $\mathbb{E}[\Delta f_{t+i}|\Omega_t^*]$, the VAR is written in companion form:

$$\begin{bmatrix} x_t \\ \vdots \\ \vdots \\ x_{t-k+1} \end{bmatrix} = \begin{bmatrix} a_1 & \cdots & \cdots & a_k \\ I & & & \\ & \ddots & & \\ & & I & 0 \end{bmatrix} \begin{bmatrix} x_{t-1} \\ \vdots \\ \vdots \\ x_{t-k} \end{bmatrix} + \begin{bmatrix} u_t \\ 0 \\ \vdots \\ 0 \end{bmatrix},$$

or, more compactly,

$$X_t = A X_{t-1} + U_t. \tag{3.25}$$

Multiperiod forecasts are easily computed from (3.25) as $\mathbb{E}[X_{t+i}|X_t] = A^i X_t$, where A^i denotes i multiplications of the A matrix.

Next, consider the implications of equation (3.23) for the dynamics of X_t. Let the vectors $\iota_1 = [1\ 0\ \cdots\ 0]$ and $\iota_2 = [0\ 1\ 0\ \cdots\ 0]$ select Δf_t and $s_t - f_t$ from X_t. We can now compute the multiperiod forecasts of fundamentals as $\mathbb{E}[\Delta f_{t+i}|\Omega_t^*] = \iota_1 A^i X_t$ for all $i > 0$. Substituting these forecasts into (3.23) produces

$$\iota_2 X_t = s_t - f_t = \iota_1 \sum_{i=1}^{\infty} b^i A^i X_t = \iota_1 b A (I - bA)^{-1} X_t.$$

This equation must hold for all possible values of the X_t vector,[2] so the companion matrix A from the VAR must satisfy

$$\iota_2 = \iota_1 b A (I - bA)^{-1}. \tag{3.26}$$

Equation (3.26) contains a set of restrictions on the coefficients in the VAR system (3.24) that represent constraints on the joint dynamics of Δf_t, $s_t - f_t$, and the other variables in the system. They can be empirically examined for particular values of b by computing a nonlinear Wald test from estimates of the A matrix computed from Ordinary Least Squares (OLS) estimates of the VAR equations. In addition, the predicted value for $s_t - f_t$ based on the VAR estimates can be compared to its

---

2. In deriving the equation we have implicitly assumed that the eigenvalues of bA are less than one in absolute value so that $\sum_{i=1}^{\infty} b^i A^i = bA(I - bA)^{-1}$. This condition is satisfied if x_t follows a covariance-stationary time series process.

actual behavior. The predicted values are computed as $\iota_1 b\tilde{A}(I - b\tilde{A})^{-1}X_t$, where $\tilde{A}$ denotes the estimated A matrix from the VAR.

It is important to recognize that tests of the restrictions in (3.26) are really tests of a joint null hypothesis. In addition to the present value relation in (3.22) we are also testing the assumption that forecasts of future changes in fundamentals, $\mathbb{E}[\Delta f_{t+i}|\Omega_t^*]$, can be computed from the VAR as $\iota_1 A^i X_t$. This is not an innocuous assumption. Even if the dynamics of x_t can be represented by a kth-order VAR, these forecasts only represent the best forecasts of Δf_{t+i} that can be computed using *linear* combinations of the variables in X_t. It is possible that forecasts based on both linear and nonlinear combinations of the variables in X_t have a lower mean-squared forecast error. If this is the case, $\mathbb{E}[\Delta f_{t+i}|\Omega_t^*] \neq \iota_1 A^i X_t$ and the restrictions in (3.26) will not hold true even if the present value relation in (3.22) is valid.

As we will see in what follows, the restrictions in (3.26) are strongly rejected for two important exchange-rate models in the present value class. Researchers often find it useful to compare the predicted and actual values of $s_t - f_t$. These comparisons must be interpreted with care because the predicted values will be sensitive to the variables included in the VAR. If the present value relation in (3.22) does not hold, forecasts of future fundamentals based on $\Omega_t^* \subset \Omega_t$ will in general differ from market participants' forecasts, and so can vary according to how we specify Ω_t^*. In particular, if the actual and predicted values of $s_t - f_t$ look very different for a particular choice of VAR variables (i.e., a choice for z_t in $x_t = [\,\Delta f_t \quad s_t - f_t \quad z_t\,]'$), the inclusion of different variables in the VAR might well produce predicted values for $s_t - f_t$ that track the actual data much more closely. If we reject the restrictions in (3.26) but still want to assess whether the present value relation in (3.22) represents a good approximation, any analysis based on the predicted values for $s_t - f_t$ has to be robust to alternative VAR specifications.

3.1.6 Forecasting

There is a long tradition in the empirical literature of examining the forecasting power of various exchange-rate models. The Present Value model has several important implications for forecasting both depreciation rates and changes in the fundamentals.

Let us begin with forecasting the depreciation rate. By definition, the actual depreciation rate, Δs_{t+1}, comprises the expected depreciation rate, $\mathbb{E}_t \Delta s_{t+1}$, and the error market participants make when forecasting s_{t+1}, that is, $s_{t+1} - \mathbb{E}_t s_{t+1}$. Under rational expectations, the latter term is uncorrelated with the elements in participants' information set, Ω_t, so period-t variables will only have forecasting power for Δs_{t+1} if they are correlated with $\mathbb{E}_t \Delta s_{t+1}$. From the Present Value model we know that $\mathbb{E}_t \Delta s_{t+1}$ is perfectly correlated with $s_t - f_t$, so these variables should have forecasting power for Δs_{t+1}.

We can generalize this argument to long-horizon forecasts. Let $\Delta^h s_{t+h} \equiv s_{t+h} - s_t$ denote the depreciation rate over h periods. The Present Value model implies that the forecasting power of $s_t - f_t$ for $\Delta^h s_{t+h}$ varies with the forecasting horizon h. To see this formally, consider the projection of $\Delta^h s_{t+h}$ on $s_t - f_t$:

$$\Delta^h s_{t+h} = \beta_h(s_t - f_t) + \zeta_{t+h}, \qquad (3.27)$$

where $\beta_h = \mathbb{E}[(s_t - f_t)\Delta^h s_{t+h}]/\mathbb{E}[(s_t - f_t)^2]$ and $\mathbb{E}[.]$ denotes unconditional expectations. The portion of the depreciation rate that is uncorrelated with $s_t - f_t$ is identified by the projection error, ζ_{t+h}. Combining the definition for β_h with the identity, $\Delta^h s_{t+h} = \sum_{i=1}^{h} \Delta s_{t+i}$, and the fact that $\mathbb{E}[(s_t - f_t)(\Delta s_{t+i} - \mathbb{E}_{t+i-1}\Delta s_{t+i})] = 0$ for $i > 0$ gives

$$\beta_h = \frac{\sum_{i=1}^{h} \mathbb{E}[(s_t - f_t)\Delta s_{t+i}]}{\mathbb{E}[(s_t - f_t)^2]} = \frac{\sum_{i=1}^{h} \mathbb{E}[(s_t - f_t)\mathbb{E}_{t+i-1}\Delta s_{t+i}]}{\mathbb{E}[(s_t - f_t)^2]}.$$

Now the Present Value model implies that $\mathbb{E}_{t+i-1}\Delta s_{t+i} = \frac{1-b}{b}(s_{t+i-1} - f_{t+i-1})$. Using this expression to substitute for $\mathbb{E}_{t+i-1}\Delta s_{t+i}$ in the equation for β_h gives

$$\beta_h = \frac{1-b}{b}\frac{\sum_{i=1}^{h} \mathbb{E}[(s_t - f_t)(s_{t+i-1} - f_{t+i-1})]}{\mathbb{E}[(s_t - f_t)^2]} = \frac{1-b}{b}\sum_{i=0}^{h-1} \rho_i, \quad (3.28)$$

where ρ_i is the autocorrelation in $s_t - f_t$ at lag i. Recall that $b < 1$. Thus, any gap between the current spot rate and fundamentals will forecast a larger change in the future spot rate over longer horizons, h, as long as ρ_{h-1} remains positive.

The intuition behind this result is straightforward. Recall that spot rates are above current fundamentals when participants forecast positive growth in future fundamentals based on period-t information, Ω_t. These forecasts are revised as time passes, but as long as the revisions are not too large, spot rates will tend to remain above fundamentals. In other words, positive serial correlation in $s_t - f_t$ occurs when market participants have a consistent view regarding the future growth in fundamentals. Under these circumstances, the information embedded in $s_t - f_t$ has relevance for forecasting the period-by-period depreciation rates into the future, so $s_t - f_t$ has greater forecasting power for $\Delta^h s_{t+h}$ than Δs_{t+1}.

It is important to recognize that these forecasting implications of the Present Value model depend critically on the value of the discount parameter, b, and the behavior of fundamentals. To illustrate, suppose Δf_t follows the AR(1) process $\Delta f_t = \phi \Delta f_{t-1} + \eta_t$ with $|\phi| < 1$. In this case it is easy to check that

$$\beta_h = \frac{1-b}{b}\frac{1-\phi^h}{1-\phi}.$$

The left-hand panels of Figure 3.3 plot the values of β_h in this example against the horizons, h, with $\phi = \{0.1, 0.3, 0.6\}$ and $b = \{0.8, 0.95\}$. In all cases, the values of β_h are positive and rise with the horizon, but the values rise less when ϕ is smaller. These plots also clearly show that the projection coefficients are smaller at all horizons the closer the discount parameter is to one.

The right-hand panels of Figure 3.3 show how the overall forecasting power of $s_t - f_t$ changes. Here we plot 100 times the theoretical R^2 statistic from the projection (3.27), that is, $100 \times R_h^2$, where $R_h^2 = \beta_h^2 \mathbb{V}\left(s_t - f_t\right)/\mathbb{V}\left(\Delta^h s_{t+h}\right)$. These plots show that forecasts of $\Delta^h s_{t+h}$ based on $s_t - f_t$ account for a small fraction of the variance in $\Delta^h s_{t+h}$. For example, in panel B the R_h^2 statistic has a peak value of only 0.024 when $\phi = 0.6$ and $b = 0.8$. Although the projection coefficient, β_h, equals 0.4 in this case, variations in $\Delta^h s_{t+h}$ are dominated by changes in unexpected returns, $s_{t+h} - \mathbb{E}[s_{t+h}|s_t - f_t]$. The other noteworthy feature of these plots concerns the fall

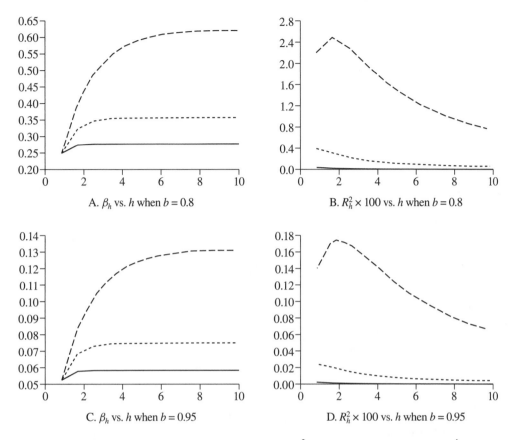

FIGURE 3.3   Projection coefficients, β_h, and R^2 statistics from projections of $\Delta^h s_{t+h}$ on $s_t - f_t$ plotted against the horizon h. The changes in fundamentals follow $\Delta f_t = \phi \Delta f_{t-1} + \eta_t$, where $\phi = 0.1$ (solid), $\phi = 0.3$ (short dashed), and $\phi = 0.6$ (long dashed).

in R_h^2 at long horizons. Although β_h is increasing in h because Δf_t is positively autocorrelated, the rise in $\beta_h^2 \mathbb{V}\left(s_t - f_t\right)$ is dominated by the increase in $\mathbb{V}\left(\Delta^h s_{t+h}\right)$ as the horizon rises. Variations in $\Delta^h s_{t+h}$ are increasingly dominated by changes in unexpected returns, $s_{t+h} - \mathbb{E}[s_{t+h}|s_t - f_t]$, as h increases.

The overall message from Figure 3.3 is clear. Although the Present Value model implies that depreciation rates can be forecast when $b < 1$, forecasts based on $s_t - f_t$ will not explain an economically significant fraction of the variations in $\Delta^h s_{t+h}$ at any horizon unless changes in fundamentals are highly autocorrelated and b is well below one. As we shall see, neither of these conditions holds true in two popular exchange-rate models.

The plots in Figure 3.3 also illustrate two more general points. First, a failure to find forecastability for future changes in spot rates using a particular set of fundamentals does not, by itself, provide much information as to whether the dynamics of spot rates are driven by those fundamentals. After all, variations in spot rates are governed entirely by the behavior of fundamentals in the Present Value model, yet the forecast power of those fundamentals can be negligible. Second, a lack of fore-castability means that spot rate dynamics are dominated by the arrival of news. In the Present Value model the news concerns the expected future path of fundamentals. Understanding the source of this news is central to understanding the source of spot rate variations.

Present Value models also have implications for forecasting fundamentals. Recall that

$$s_t - f_t = \sum_{i=1}^{\infty} b^i \mathbb{E}_t \Delta f_{t+i}, \tag{3.29}$$

so the gap between the spot rate and current fundamentals contains information on market participants' forecasts, $\mathbb{E}_t \Delta f_{t+i}$. If these forecasts only use information contained in the past history of fundamentals and other variables, $\mathcal{F}_t = \{f_{t-i}, z_{t-i}\}_{i \geq 0}$, then $s_t - f_t$ will not have any *incremental* forecasting power for Δf_{t+i} beyond that contained in $\mathcal{F}_t$. However, if market participants use additional information, then $s_t - f_t$ will have incremental forecasting power. Granger Causality tests provide a way to evaluate these forecasting implications. For example, $s_t - f_t$ is said to Granger cause Δf_{t+i} if $\mathbb{V}(\Delta f_{t+i} | s_t - f_t, \mathcal{F}_t) < \mathbb{V}(\Delta f_{t+i} | \mathcal{F}_t)$, so under these circumstances $s_t - f_t$ conveys incremental information.

As a simple example, suppose that fundamentals follow a random walk, $f_t = f_{t-1} + e_t + v_t$, where e_t and v_t are i.i.d. mean-zero errors. Let us further assume that $v_t \in \Omega_{t-1}$. Market participants' forecasts are therefore given by $\mathbb{E}_t \Delta f_{t+1} = v_{t+1}$ and $\mathbb{E}_t \Delta f_{t+i} = 0$ for $i > 1$. Substituting these forecasts into (3.29) gives $s_t - f_t = bv_{t+1}$. Forecasts of Δf_{t+i} based on the history $\{f_{t-i}\}_{i \geq 0}$ are clearly zero for all $i > 0$, but $\Delta f_{t+1} = e_{t+1} + v_{t+1} = e_{t+1} + \frac{1}{b}(s_t - f_t)$, so $s_t - f_t$ has incremental forecasting power for Δf_{t+1} relative to $\{f_{t-i}\}_{i \geq 0}$.

Depreciation rates can also have forecasting power for future fundamentals. To see why, we write the future h-period change in fundamentals as

$$\Delta^h f_{t+h} = \mathbb{E}_{t-1} \Delta^h f_{t+h} + \left(\mathbb{E}_t - \mathbb{E}_{t-1}\right) \Delta^h f_{t+h} + \left(\Delta^h f_{t+h} - \mathbb{E}_t \Delta^h f_{t+h}\right). \tag{3.30}$$

The forecasting power of the current depreciation rate, Δs_t, comes from the first two terms on the right-hand side. Recall that $\mathbb{E}_{t-1} \Delta s_t$ is proportional to $\sum_{i=0}^{\infty} b^i \mathbb{E}_{t-1} \Delta f_{t+i}$, so the first term will be correlated with Δs_t if market participants' forecasts of fundamentals generate sizable variations in the expected depreciation rate. Of course, variations in $\mathbb{E}_{t-1} \Delta s_t$ disappear as b approaches one, so this correlation is unlikely to be a source of much forecastability in specifications when the discount parameter is large. The second term on the right of (3.30) identifies the revision in participants' forecasts for $\Delta^h f_{t+h}$ due to the arrival of new information in period t. Such information is also likely to affect the depreciation rate. In particular, (3.29) implies that

$$s_t - \mathbb{E}_{t-1} s_t = \sum_{i=0}^{\infty} b^i \left(\mathbb{E}_t - \mathbb{E}_{t-1}\right) \Delta f_{t+i},$$

so an upward revision in participants' forecasts of Δf_{t+i} will induce an unexpected depreciation and a rise in $(\mathbb{E}_t - \mathbb{E}_{t-1}) \Delta^h f_{t+h}$. Note that any resulting correlation between $(\mathbb{E}_t - \mathbb{E}_{t-1})\Delta^h f_{t+h}$ and Δs_t does not disappear as b approaches one, and so can be a source of forecastability in specifications where the discount parameter is large. However, this does not mean that Δs_t will have significant *incremental* forecastable power relative to the past history of fundamentals and other variables. As before, market participants must use additional information to revise their forecasts for Δs_t to have incremental forecasting power.

3.2 Monetary Models

In this section we examine two well-known genres of exchange-rate models that fall within the Present Value class. The first are the Money-Income models based on monetary models developed in the 1970s. The second are models that describe monetary policy in terms of interest-rate-setting Taylor rules. These Taylor Rule models have been the subject of a recent resurgence in empirical exchange-rate research.

3.2.1 Money-Income Models

Money-Income models focus on the exchange-rate implications of interest parity, purchasing power parity, and money market equilibrium. Equilibrium in the home and foreign money markets is represented by

$$m_t = p_t + \gamma y_t - \alpha r_t + v_t \tag{3.31a}$$

and

$$\hat{m}_t = \hat{p}_t + \gamma \hat{y}_t - \alpha \hat{r}_t + \hat{v}_t, \tag{3.31b}$$

where m_t, p_t, and y_t denote the exogenous log money supply, the log price level, and log income level in the home country and r_t is the nominal one-period interest rate on home bonds (foreign variables are indicated by "ˆ"). The positive parameters, γ and α, respectively, identify the income elasticity and interest semielasticity of money demand, which are identical across countries. All other factors affecting money demand in each country are represented by the v_t and $\hat{v}_t$ terms.

By definition, the nominal exchange rate can be expressed as the difference between the home and foreign price levels plus the real exchange rate:

$$s_t = p_t - \hat{p}_t + \varepsilon_t. \tag{3.32}$$

Similarly, the expected rate of depreciation can be written as the sum of the interest differential and a foreign exchange risk premium:

$$\mathbb{E}_t \Delta s_{t+1} = r_t - \hat{r}_t + \delta_t. \tag{3.33}$$

Combining these equations with (3.31) produces

$$s_t = \alpha \mathbb{E}_t \Delta s_{t+1} + f_t^{\mathrm{M}}, \tag{3.34}$$

where fundamentals are given by

$$f_t^{M} = m_t - \hat{m}_t - \gamma(y_t - \hat{y}_t) + \varepsilon_t - (v_t - \hat{v}_t + \alpha\delta_t). \qquad (3.35)$$

Note that (3.34) takes the same form as equation (3.1), which was used to derive the Present Value model. Thus, in the absence of bubbles, the current spot rate can be written as the present value of future fundamentals with a discount parameter of $b = \alpha/(1 + \alpha)$. Estimates of the semielasticity parameter range between 60 in Bilson (1978) and 29 in Frankel (1979) for quarterly data, so the implied value for the discount factor in this case falls between 0.98 and 0.97.

The determinants of the variables defining exchange-rate fundamentals vary among the different versions of the monetary model. In the flexible-price versions of Frenkel (1976), Mussa (1976), and Bilson (1978), output and the real exchange rate are treated as exogenous, whereas in the sticky-price versions of Dornbusch (1976) and Frankel (1979) both variables are determined endogenously. This distinction does not affect the validity of the present value relation between spot rates and fundamentals. Variations in spot rates are driven by changing expectations of fundamentals whether or not those changes are due to changing forecasts of exogenous or endogenous macroeconomic variables. Traditional flexible- and sticky-price versions of the monetary model assume that the risk premium and money demand factors, v_t, $\hat{v}_t$, and δ_t, are absent so these terms do not appear in the definition of fundamentals. Alternatively, one could think of these terms as shocks to fundamentals.

MacDonald and Taylor (1994) provide an early assessment of the Money-Income model using the VAR techniques described in Section 3.1.5. These authors computed monthly fundamentals for the DM/USD exchange rate as $f_t^{M/Y} = m_t - \hat{m}_t - y_t + \hat{y}_t$ using $M1$ for the money stocks and industrial production for income. They then estimated a VAR for $s_t - f_t^{M/Y}$ and $\Delta f_t^{M/Y}$ with data from January 1976 to December 1990 and compared the actual behavior of $s_t - f_t^{M/Y}$ against the values predicted by the VAR estimates and the present value relation implied by the Money-Income model. This comparison produced a striking result. Whereas the time series for $s_t - f_t^{M/Y}$ varied considerably over the sample period, the predicted values for $s_t - f_t^{M/Y}$ were essentially constant. Consequently, tests of the present value restrictions on the VAR coefficients implied by the Money-Income model can be easily rejected at any reasonable level of statistical significance.

This finding turns out to be robust. Figure 3.4 plots $s_t - f_t^{M/Y}$ and its predicted values for three exchange rates {DM/USD, GBP/USD, JPY/USD} in quarterly data between 1976:I and 2008:IV (1998:IV in the case of DM/USD). The predicted values are computed from VARs that set the discount parameter b equal to 0.98 and use industrial production and money plus quasi-money in the four countries to construct $f_t^{M/Y}$. The predicted values for $s_t - f_t^{M/Y}$ are computed from a first-order VAR, but the results are not sensitive to this choice. The figure clearly shows that there are sizable and persistent variations in $s_t - f_t^{M/Y}$ over the sample period for all three currency pairs. By contrast, the predicted values for $s_t - f_t^{M/Y}$ show a much smaller amount of variation. It is therefore not surprising to find that tests on the VAR coefficients strongly reject the restrictions implied by the Present Value model in (3.26) for this definition of fundamentals.

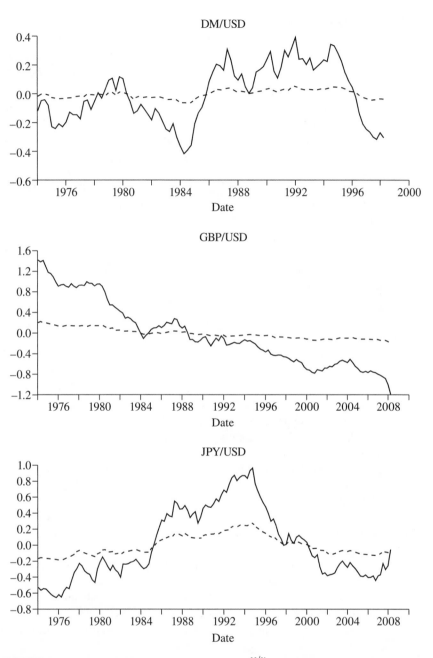

FIGURE 3.4   Actual and predicted values of $s_t - f_t^{M/Y}$. Actual values are plotted as a solid line and predicted values from a first-order VAR are plotted as a dashed line.

When viewed from the perspective of the Present Value model, the plots in Figure 3.4 strongly suggest that the definition for fundamentals is misspecified. By definition, $s_t - f_t^{M/Y} = s_t - f_t^M + (f_t^M - f_t^{M/Y})$, so the variations we observe in $s_t - f_t^{M/Y}$ must represent some combination of changes in $s_t - f_t^M$ and missing fundamentals, $f_t^M - f_t^{M/Y}$. Equation (3.35) implies that $f_t^M - f_t^{M/Y} = \varepsilon_t - (v_t - \hat{v}_t + \alpha\delta_t)$ when $\gamma = 1$, so there are several candidates for the missing fundamentals even when the income elasticity is correct. For example, the pervasive empirical evidence against PPP points to the inclusion of variables driving the real exchange rate, ε_t. Furthermore, evidence on the instability of money demand reported by Friedman and Kuttner (1992) and others suggests that the v_t and $\hat{v}_t$ factors could also play a role, whereas the well-documented failure of UIP points to the presence of variations in δ_t. In short, there are ample grounds for thinking that $f_t^{M/Y}$ is an inadequate specification for true fundamentals.

Despite these problems, a number of recent studies argue that monetary fundamentals still have some relevance for exchange-rate determination. Mark (1995) initiated this line of research by examining the predictive power of $f_t^{M/Y} - s_t$ for depreciation rates with forecasting regressions of the form

$$\Delta^h s_{t+h} = \alpha_0 + \alpha_h (f_t^{M/Y} - s_t) + u_{t+h}. \tag{3.36}$$

Mark estimated this regression in quarterly data between 1973 and 1991 for four spot rates (CAD/USD, DM/USD, JPY/USD, CHI/USD), and found positive estimates of α_h for horizons, h, ranging from 1 to 16 quarters. Furthermore, the estimates increased substantially with h across all the currency pairs. At first blush, Mark's results suggest that monetary fundamentals are relevant factors driving long-horizon depreciation rates. Unfortunately, the relatively short time span of Mark's data, combined with the high degree of dependence across overlapping observations on $\Delta^h s_{t+h}$ when h is large makes statistical inference on α_h a thorny issue. Indeed, subsequent papers by Berben and van Dijk (1998), Kilian (1999), Berkowitz and Giorgianni (2001), and Faust, Rogers, and Wright (2003) call into question whether one can make reliable inferences concerning the values of α_h (particularly at long horizons) with the available data on individual exchange rates. The appendix provides a brief overview of the econometric issues.

One potential resolution to this inference problem is to examine the forecasting power of monetary fundamentals for a set of exchange rates. The idea is to exploit the well-established fact that depreciation rates are contemporaneously correlated across different currency pairs to obtain more precise estimates of the coefficient on $f_t^{M/Y} - s_t$. Toward this end, Mark and Sul (2001) estimated the following panel forecasting equation:

$$\Delta s_{i,t+1} = \alpha_i + \alpha(f_{i,t}^{M/Y} - s_{i,t}) + u_{i,t+1}, \tag{3.37}$$

with $u_{i,t+1} = \theta_{t+1} + \epsilon_{i,t+1}$, where $s_{i,t}$ and $f_{i,t}^{M/Y}$ denote the spot rate and monetary fundamentals for currency i versus the USD in quarter t. The error term, $u_{i,t+1}$, comprises a time-specific component, θ_{t+1}, and a residual idiosyncratic component, $\epsilon_{i,t+1}$, that is uncorrelated across currencies and time.

There are two key features of this specification. First, the slope coefficient, α, is assumed to be the same across all currencies i. Second, the presence of the θ_{t+1} component introduces a degree of cross-currency dependence in the error term. Both of these features represent restrictions on the joint behavior of spot rates and monetary fundamentals that could not be exploited when estimating (3.36) currency by currency. Thus, to the extent that they represent valid restrictions, the estimates of α will be more precise. Using data from 19 countries from 1973 to 1997, Mark and Sul (2001) find small positive, but highly statistically significant, estimates of α. They also find significant out-of-sample forecasting power for $f_{i,t}^{M/Y} - s_{i,t}$. This forecasting result is supported in subsequent studies by Rapach and Wohar (2002), Groen (2005), and Engel, Mark, and West (2007). We return to the topic of out-of-sample forecasting in Section 3.4.

Ironically, these forecasting results do *not* provide support for the Money-Income model. Although that model is used to motivate the specification for fundamentals in the forecasting regressions, (3.36) and (3.37), the positive estimates of α_h and α reported in the literature are actually of the wrong sign: If variations in true fundamentals, f_t^M, are dominated by changes in monetary fundamentals, $f_t^{M/Y}$, the estimates of α_h and α should be negative. Recall from (3.29) that the current spot rate rises relative to current fundamentals in the Present Value model when market participants expect future growth in fundamentals. Under these circumstances, they must also expect a future depreciation of the spot rate [see equation (3.7)]. Thus, positive values of $f_{i,t}^{M/Y} - s_{i,t}$ should forecast an appreciation of the spot rate when $f_{i,t}^{M/Y}$ is a good measure of fundamentals, rather than the depreciation implied by positive estimates of α_h and α.

This inconsistency has been overlooked in the literature, but it is potentially important because the estimates of α_h and α contain information about missing fundamentals. In particular, we know from the Present Value model that $\Delta s_{t+1} = \frac{1-b}{b}(s_t - f_t^M) + s_{t+1} - \mathbb{E}_t s_{t+1}$. Let us further assume that $s - f_t^{M/Y}$ follows a covariance stationary process so that the limiting value of the slope coefficient is given by the standard formula: $\alpha = \mathbb{CV}(f_t^{M/Y} - s_t, \Delta s_{t+1})/\mathbb{V}(f_t^{M/Y} - s_t)$, where $\mathbb{V}(.)$ and $\mathbb{CV}(.,.)$ denote the variance and covariance. Combining these equations with the identity, $s_t - f_t^M = s_t - f_t^{M/Y} - (f_t^M - f_t^{M/Y})$, we can easily show that

$$\mathbb{CV}(s_t - f_t^{M/Y}, f_t^M - f_t^{M/Y}) > 0 \quad \text{and} \quad \mathbb{V}(f_t^M - f_t^{M/Y}) > \mathbb{V}(s_t - f_t^{M/Y}), \quad (3.38)$$

when $\alpha > 0$.[3] In words, if spot rates are driven by expectations concerning fundamentals in accordance with the Present Value model and positive values for $f_t^{M/Y} - s_t$ truly forecast future depreciations, then missing fundamentals, $f_t^M - f_t^{M/Y}$, must be positively correlated with $s_t - f_t^{M/Y}$. Furthermore, missing fundamentals must be more variable than $s_t - f_t^{M/Y}$. When one considers these implications in conjunction with the plots of $s_t - f_t^{M/Y}$ in Figure 3.4, it is hard not to conclude that the variations in missing fundamentals must be very economically significant.

---

3. The derivation of these results is left as an excercise at the end of the chapter.

Further evidence on the significance of missing fundamentals comes from the results of cointegration tests. Recall from Section 3.1.3 that in a Present Value model the log spot rate should be cointegrated one for one with fundamentals if the latter follow a unit root process. When researchers test for the presence of unit roots in the macro time series that comprise monetary fundamentals (i.e., m_t, $\hat{m}_t$, y_t, and $\hat{y}_t$), they are generally unable to reject the presence of a unit root at conventional levels of statistical significance. Thus, if missing fundamentals from the Money-Income model follow a stationary process, we would expect to reject a null hypothesis of no cointegration between s_t and $f_t^{M/Y}$. This is not the case. Engel and West (2005), for example, are unable to reject this null for six exchange rates (including those shown in Figure 3.4) in data running from 1974 to 2001. In other words, there is insufficient information in the time series for $s_t - f_t^{M/Y}$ to reject the presence of the unit root. This is hardly surprising in view of the sample paths plotted in Figure 3.4.

3.2.2 Taylor Rule Models

In Chapter 2 we noted that monetary policy is conducted with particular objectives, such as price stability, in mind so policy variables are endogenously determined as central banks react to changing macroeconomic conditions. We also noted that short-term nominal interest rates have become the policy instrument used by most central banks since the mid-1980s. Taylor Rule models consider the exchange-rate implications of central banks following monetary policy rules that relate short-term nominal interest rates to macroeconomic conditions.

The models are built on three central assumptions. First, the current policy decisions of central banks imply a stable relationship between the interest differential, $r_t - \hat{r}_t$, and macroeconomic conditions in period t. Second, market participants form their expectations concerning future interest differentials based on this same stable relationship and their forecasts of future macroeconomic conditions. Third, variations in the risk premium, δ_t, do not contribute significantly to participants' expectations about future depreciation rates.

There are two approaches to formulating a Taylor Rule exchange-rate model: one in terms of the nominal exchange rate and one in terms of the real rate. We follow the second approach. The home and foreign central banks set short-term nominal interest rates in response to expected inflation, the real exchange rate, and the output gap, y_t^G, where the last is defined as the difference between the logs of current GDP and potential GDP:

$$r_t = (1 + \psi_{\Delta p})\mathbb{E}_t \Delta p_{t+1} + \psi_y y_t^G + v_t \tag{3.39a}$$

and

$$\hat{r}_t = (1 + \psi_{\Delta p})\mathbb{E}_t \Delta \hat{p}_{t+1} + \psi_y \hat{y}_t^G - \psi \varepsilon_t + \hat{v}_t, \tag{3.39b}$$

where $\psi_{\Delta p}$, ψ_y, and ψ are positive coefficients. In this specification, the policy rules are symmetric except with respect to the real exchange rate. Both central banks react to higher expected inflation and output gaps by raising short-term interest rates in the same way. In addition, the foreign central bank also raises $\hat{r}_t$ when the real value of the foreign currency depreciates (i.e., when there is a fall in ε_t). This asymmetry accords with the empirical estimates of monetary policy reaction functions. Clarida,

Gali, and Gertler (1998) find that the German and Japanese central banks raise rates in response to a real depreciation of their domestic currency verses the USD, but there is no evidence that the Federal Reserve reacts in an analogous manner. Consistent with these findings, we follow our usual practice by considering the United States the home country. The last terms on the right of (3.39), v_t and $\hat{v}_t$, identify policy deviations, that is, the difference between the current interest rate and its target level implied by current macroeconomic conditions. These deviations may be serially correlated insofar as central banks want to smooth the adjustment of interest rates to a target level consistent with new macroeconomic conditions.

To derive the exchange-rate implications of the Taylor rules in (3.39), we first consider their effect on real interest rates. Let $rr_t = r_t - \mathbb{E}_t \Delta p_{t+1}$ and $\widehat{rr}_t = \hat{r}_t - \mathbb{E}_t \Delta \hat{p}_{t+1}$ denote the U.S. and foreign real interest rates. Combining these definitions with the Taylor rules gives the following equation for the real interest differential:

$$rr_t - \widehat{rr}_t = \psi_{\Delta p}(\mathbb{E}_t \Delta p_{t+1} - \mathbb{E}_t \Delta \hat{p}_{t+1}) + \psi_y(y_t^G - \hat{y}_t^G) + \psi \varepsilon_t + v_t - \hat{v}_t. \qquad (3.40)$$

We can also combine the interest parity condition, $\mathbb{E}_t \Delta s_{t+1} = r_t - \hat{r}_t + \delta_t$, with the identity $\varepsilon_t = s_t + \hat{p}_t - p_t$ to get

$$\mathbb{E}_t \Delta \varepsilon_{t+1} = rr_t - \widehat{rr}_t + \delta_t.$$

Finally, we substitute for $rr_t - \widehat{rr}_t$ from (3.40) and rearrange the result to produce

$$\varepsilon_t = f_t^{\text{TR}} + \frac{1}{\psi} \mathbb{E}_t \Delta \varepsilon_{t+1}, \qquad (3.41)$$

where real fundamentals are now given by

$$f_t^{\text{TR}} = \frac{1}{\psi} \left[\psi_{\Delta p} \mathbb{E}_t (\Delta \hat{p}_{t+1} - \Delta p_{t+1}) + \psi_y(\hat{y}_t^G - y_t^G) + \hat{v}_t - v_t - \delta_t \right]. \qquad (3.42)$$

Note that (3.41) takes the same form as equation (3.1) with the real exchange rate, ε_t, replacing the spot rate s_t. Thus, in the absence of bubbles, the current real rate can be written as the present value of future real fundamentals, f_t^{TR}, with a discount parameter of $b = \frac{1}{1+\psi}$:

$$\varepsilon_t = \mathbb{E}_t \sum_{i=0}^{\infty} \left(\tfrac{1}{1+\psi} \right)^{i+1} \left[\psi_{\Delta p}(\Delta \hat{p}_{t+1+i} - \Delta p_{t+1+i}) + \psi_y(\hat{y}_{t+i}^G - y_{t+i}^G) \right.$$

$$\left. + \hat{v}_{t+i} - v_{t+i} - \delta_{t+i} \right]. \qquad (3.43)$$

Alternatively, we can combine (3.41) with the identities $s_t = \varepsilon_t - \hat{p}_t + p_t$ and $\mathbb{E}_t \Delta \varepsilon_{t+1} = \mathbb{E}_t (\Delta s_{t+1} + \Delta \hat{p}_{t+1} - \Delta p_{t+1})$ to write

$$s_t = f_t^{\text{TRN}} + \frac{1}{\psi} \mathbb{E}_t \Delta s_{t+1},$$

where

$$f_t^{\text{TRN}} = f_t^{\text{TR}} + p_t - \hat{p}_t + \frac{1}{\psi} \mathbb{E}_t (\Delta \hat{p}_{t+1} - \Delta p_{t+1}).$$

This expression has the same form as equation (3.1). So the current spot rate can be written as the present value of nominal fundamentals, f_t^{TRN}, with the same discount parameter, b. Clarida, Gali, and Gertler (1998) estimated that the central banks in Germany and Japan raised interest rates in response to a 10 percent depreciation by 0.5 and 0.9 percent, respectively. These estimates translate into values for b between 0.988 and 0.978 in quarterly data. Thus the discount parameter in the present value relations for both the nominal and real exchange rate is very close to one.

Equation (3.43) makes clear how monetary policy drives the real exchange rate in a Taylor Rule model. Consider, for example, the effect of news that leads market participants to raise their forecasts for future U.S. inflation, $\mathbb{E}_t \Delta p_{t+1+i}$. If the FED follows the Taylor rule in (3.39a), these new expectations will be accompanied with an anticipated increase in future U.S. nominal interest rates. Furthermore, with $\psi_{\Delta p} > 0$, this anticipated rise in nominal interest rates will also lead to an expected rise in U.S. real interest rates. Thus, if there is no accompanying change in expected foreign real interest rates or the foreign exchange risk premium, the expected future rate of real depreciation must rise. To accommodate these expectations there must therefore be an immediate real appreciation of the dollar. In short, bad news about inflation could represent good news for the real value of the domestic currency. Clarida and Waldman (2007) report empirical evidence that supports this linkage (see Chapter 10). More generally, in a Taylor Rule model, expected changes in future macroeconomic conditions affect the current real exchange rate by changing the anticipated future real interest rate differentials implied by the policy rules and hence the expected real depreciation rate.

Several recent papers have studied the empirical implications of Taylor Rule models. Engel and West (2006) and Mark (2009) use versions of (3.43) to compare the actual and predicted values for the DM/USD real exchange rate, and Engel, Mark, and West (2007) and Molodtsova and Papell (2009) examine the forecasting power of Taylor rule fundamentals. Let us review these studies in turn.

Engel and West (2006) examine the present value relation for the DM/USD in (3.43) using monthly data from 1979:10 to 1998:12. They calibrate values for the Taylor rule parameters, $\psi_{\Delta p}$ and ψ_y, from other studies and use estimates from a VAR for $\{\Delta p_t, \Delta \hat{p}_t, y_t^{\text{G}}, \hat{y}_t^{\text{G}}, r_t, \hat{r}_t\}$ to estimate expected inflation and the output gaps. As before, their measure of fundamentals imposes equality of the Taylor rule coefficients, but it is derived from Taylor rules based on the annual rate of inflation, rather than the one-period rate shown in (3.39). They also ignore the potential roles played by policy derivations, v_t and $\hat{v}_t$, and the risk premium. Engel and West (2006) find that correlation between their predicted series for the real exchange rate, $\tilde{\varepsilon}_t$, and the actual rate, ε_t, is 0.32, but the correlation in the monthly changes, $\mathbb{CR}(\Delta \tilde{\varepsilon}_t, \Delta \varepsilon_t)$, is only 0.09. Furthermore, the time series for $\tilde{\varepsilon}_t$ is much too smooth. The sample variance of $\tilde{\varepsilon}_t$ is only 4 percent of the variance in the real DM/USD rate.

Mark (2009) undertakes a more ambitious task. He estimates Taylor rules for the FED, the Bundesbank, and European Central Bank (ECB) in quarterly data between 1962 and 2007. Unlike Engel and West, he allows for first-order serial correlation in the policy deviations and for changes in the Taylor rule parameters in 1979:III for the FED and Bundesbank and again in 1999:I when the Bundesbank ceded policymaking to the ECB. These parameter estimates are then combined with VAR forecasts for inflation and the output gap to compute the predicted values for the real DM/USD rate between 1976:I and 2007:III using the implied present value relation. Mark finds

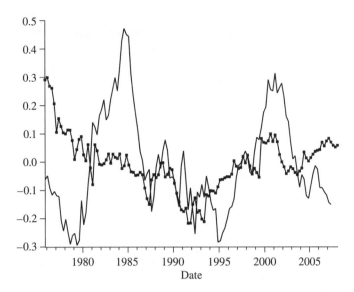

FIGURE 3.5   Actual values for the real DM/USD, ε_t (solid), and the predicted values, $\tilde{\varepsilon}_t$ (boxed), calculated by Mark (2009).

the estimates of ψ to be insignificant, so ψ is set equal to zero when he computes the present value relation.

Figure 3.5 reproduces Mark's plots of the predicted and actual DM/USD real rate. As the figure shows, the series are quite different from one another. The variations in the predicted series indicate that there are changes in the present value of future inflation and output gaps, but they are insufficient to account for the largest and most persistent swings in the actual DM/USD rate in the early 1980s and the late 1990s. Furthermore, the quarterly changes in $\tilde{\varepsilon}_t$ are essentially uncorrelated with the actual depreciation rate.

Of course the predicted values in Figure 3.5 are computed under rather strong assumptions. In particular, they are based on the idea that market participants not only knew the policy rules that central banks were currently following, but could also perfectly predict how those rules would change in the future. Furthermore, because the predicted values are computed from VARs that do not include the exchange rate, they may not be robust to the presence of additional information that market participants were using at the time to forecast future monetary policy.

Mark (2009) relaxes the first of these assumptions by using a least-squares learning procedure to compute the present value of fundamentals that define $\tilde{\varepsilon}_t$. Here market participants update their estimates of the Taylor rules, the dynamics of inflation, and the output gap every quarter in response to new observations on inflation, interest rates, and the output gaps. The predicted values calculated in this manner are better able to account for the large exchange-rate swings in the 1970s and 1980s than the plot in Figure 3.5. However, the quarterly changes in $\tilde{\varepsilon}_t$ are still essentially uncorrelated with the actual depreciation rate.

Taylor Rule and Money-Income models have potentially very different implications for forecasting the depreciation rate. Recall that in the Money-Income model $s_t - f_t^M$ loses all its forecasting power for the depreciation rate, Δs_{t+1}, as b approaches one. In contrast, in a Taylor Rule model, $\varepsilon_t - f_t^{\text{TR}}$ and $s_t - f_t^{\text{TRN}}$ retain their forecasting power for $\Delta \varepsilon_{t+1}$ and Δs_{t+1}, respectively, because the Talyor rule fundamentals, f_t^{TR} and f_t^{TRN}, become more variable as b approaches one.

To see this, recall that $\mathbb{E}_t \Delta s_{t+1} = \frac{1-b}{b}(s_t - f_t)$ in a present value model. Substituting f_t^{TRN} for f_t and setting $b = 1/(1 + \psi)$ gives

$$\mathbb{E}_t \Delta s_{t+1} = \frac{1-b}{b}(s_t - f_t^{\text{TRN}}) \tag{3.44}$$

$$= \psi \varepsilon_t + (1 + \psi_{\Delta p}) \mathbb{E}_t (\Delta p_{t+1} - \Delta \hat{p}_{t+1}) + \psi_y (y_t^G - \hat{y}_t^G) + v_t - \hat{v}_t + \delta_t.$$

Similarly, the present value relation for the real rate implies that

$$\mathbb{E}_t \Delta \varepsilon_{t+1} = \frac{1-b}{b}(\varepsilon_t - f_t^{\text{TR}})$$

$$= \psi \varepsilon_t + \psi_{\Delta p} \mathbb{E}_t (\Delta p_{t+1} - \Delta \hat{p}_{t+1}) + \psi_y (y_t^G - \hat{y}_t^G) + v_t - \hat{v}_t + \delta_t.$$

These equations clearly show that differences between expected inflation and the output gaps retain their forecasting power for the depreciation rates when $\psi = 0$.

The forecasting power of Taylor rule fundamentals has recently been studied by Engel, Mark, and West (2007); Rogoff and Stavrakeva (2008); and Molodtsova and Papell (2009). These authors focus on out-of-sample forecasting rather than the estimates of forecasting equations, but the latter are informative about the empirical performance of Taylor Rule models. The forecasting equations they study take the form

$$\Delta s_{t+1} = a_0 + a' z_t + v_{t+1}, \tag{3.45}$$

where a is a vector of coefficients and z_t is a vector of variables taken from the right-hand side of (3.44). Molodtsova and Papell (2009), for example, let $z_t' = [\pi_t, \hat{\pi}_t, y_t^G, \hat{y}_t^G, r_{t-1}, \hat{r}_{t-1}]$, where π_t and $\hat{\pi}_t$ are annual rates of inflation. Engel, Mark, and West (2007), on the other hand, use standard values for the Taylor rule parameters to get $z_t = z_t^{\text{TR}} = 0.1\varepsilon_t + 2(\pi_t - \hat{\pi}_t) + 0.5(y_t^G - \hat{y}_t^G)$. They also consider a PPP specification where $z_t = \varepsilon_t$. Rogoff and Stavrakeva (2008) consider the Molodtsova and Papell (2009) and the PPP specifications.

Table 3.1 reports estimates of the forecasting regression in (3.45) for three currency pairs in monthly data between March 1973 and December 1988 for the DM/USD and June 2006 for the GBP/USD and JPY/USD. The data series are from Molodtsova and Papell (2009). The table lists estimates of the coefficients for the variables listed at the top of each column and asymptotic standard errors that are robust to the presence of heteroskedasticity. (The table does not show the estimates of a_o.) Row (i) in each panel reports estimates of a Talyor rule specification, where U.S. and foreign variables enter symmetrically. Here we see that many of the estimated coefficients have the "wrong" sign, and most are statistically insignificantly different from zero. Row (ii) includes estimates of the Engel, Mark, and West (2007) specification with the addition of the lagged interest differential, $r_{t-1} - \hat{r}_{t-1}$. Here, the only statistically significant coefficients appear in the interest differentials. Estimates of the model based on the PPP specification are shown in row (iii). In this case there is some consistency in the estimates across the three currencies, the estimated coefficients are all negative, and two are statistically significant at the 10 percent level. This is not good news for Taylor

TABLE 3.1

Forecasting Depreciation Rates

Currency		$\pi_t - \hat{\pi}_t$	$y_t^G - \hat{y}_t^G$	ε_t	$r_{t-1} - \hat{r}_{t-1}$	z_t^{TR}	z_t^{M}	R^2
JPY/USD	(i)	1.014*	−0.073	−0.087	−2.086***			0.028
		(0.665)	(0.128)	(0.096)	(0.610)			
	(ii)				−1.64***	0.054		0.021
					(0.527)	(0.199)		
	(iii)			−0.069				0.002
				(0.081)				
	(iv)						−0.037*	0.004
							(0.026)	
GBP/USD	(i)	−0.404	−0.022	−0.033	0.795			0.017
		(0.529)	(0.308)	(0.069)	(0.617)			
	(ii)				0.913**	−0.214		0.016
					(0.540)	(0.152)		
	(iii)			−0.107**				0.011
				(0.046)				
	(iv)						−0.085**	0.009
							(0.042)	
DM/USD	(i)	0.226	0.330	−0.118**	0.555			0.016
		(1.056)	(0.387)	(0.060)	(0.946)			
	(ii)				0.990	−0.246		0.005
					(0.954)	(0.339)		
	(iii)			−0.082*				0.007
				(0.058)				
	(iv)						−0.010	< 0.001
							(0.089)	

Notes: The table reports OLS estimates of forecasting regression (3.45) together with asymptotic robust standard errors in parentheses. All specifications include a constant that is not reported. Estimates are at the monthly frequency using industrial production as the income measure, M1 for the money stocks, and detrended industrial production as the output gap. The data set comes from Molodtsova and Papell (2009). Statistical significance at the 10 percent, 5 percent, and 1 percent levels is indicated by *, **, and ***, respectively.

Rule models. As equation (3.44) shows, the real exchange rate should appear with a positive coefficient, ψ. Finally, for comparison purposes, row (iv) reports estimates of (3.45), where $z_t = z_t^M = s_t - (m_t - \hat{m}_t) + (y_t - \hat{y}_t)$. This is the specification implied by the Money-Income model discussed in Section 3.2.1. Consistent with the results reported in the literature, the estimated coefficient on z_t^M is negative.

The main message from Table 3.1 is quite clear: It is hard to find any evidence of a stable, economically significant relationship between current macroeconomic conditions, as measured by monetary, Taylor rule, or PPP fundamentals, and the nominal depreciation rate over the next month for major currencies. There are at least three ways to interpret these findings: First, there is truly no relationship between depreciation rates and fundamentals. Second, there is a relationship, but there is insufficient information in the data sample to reveal it as statistically significant. Third, the asymptotic statistical theory used as the basis for our inference is unreliable. We return to these possible explanations in Section 3.4. For the present, what is clear is that macro fundamentals appear to have little forecasting power for monthly changes in spot rates when judged by conventional statistical measures.

At first sight, the results in Table 3.1 appear hard to square with the positive correlation between ε_t and $\tilde{\varepsilon}_t$ implied by the Taylor Rule models in Engel and West (2006) and Mark (2009). However, the correlations of between 0.25 and 0.33 that these studies find do not imply that the Taylor Rule models account for much of the short-term variation in exchange rates. To see this, let ζ_t define the difference between the actual and predicted real exchange rate, $\varepsilon_t - \tilde{\varepsilon}_t$. We can now write the actual rate of real depreciation as $\Delta\varepsilon_{t+1} = \Delta\tilde{\varepsilon}_{t+1} + \Delta\zeta_{t+1}$. Multiplying both sides of this equation by $\Delta\varepsilon_{t+1}$ and taking expectations gives the following decomposition for the variance of the real depreciation rate:

$$\mathbb{V}\left(\Delta\varepsilon_{t+1}\right) = \mathbb{CV}(\Delta\tilde{\varepsilon}_{t+1}, \Delta\varepsilon_{t+1}) + \mathbb{CV}(\Delta\zeta_{t+1}, \Delta\varepsilon_{t+1}).$$

If the variations in $\Delta\tilde{\varepsilon}_{t+1}$ identified by the Taylor Rule models represent a significant portion of the news driving the unanticipated depreciation rate, $\Delta\varepsilon_{t+1} - \mathbb{E}_t\Delta\varepsilon_{t+1}$, and/or information driving the expected depreciation rate, $\mathbb{E}_t\Delta\varepsilon_{t+1}$, the first covariance term on the right should account for a significant fraction of $\mathbb{V}\left(\Delta\varepsilon_t\right)$. In fact, we can compute the contribution of the Taylor Rule models as

$$\mathfrak{N} = \frac{\mathbb{CV}(\Delta\tilde{\varepsilon}_t, \Delta\varepsilon_t)}{\mathbb{V}\left(\Delta\varepsilon_t\right)} = \mathbb{CR}(\Delta\tilde{\varepsilon}_t, \Delta\varepsilon_t)\sqrt{\frac{\mathbb{V}(\Delta\tilde{\varepsilon}_t)}{\mathbb{V}(\Delta\varepsilon_t)}}.$$

Both Engel and West (2006) and Mark (2009) report the correlations and variance ratios on the right-hand side, so we can easily compute the value for $\mathfrak{N}$ implied by their model estimates. Engel and West's estimates based on monthly data from 1979:10 to 1998:12 give a value of 0.06, whereas Mark's estimates based on quarterly data imply values for $\mathfrak{N}$ below 0.04 across all the model specifications he examines. Clearly, actual depreciation rates are largely unconnected to the factors identified by these Taylor Rule models.

3.3 External Balance Models

In Chapter 2 we studied how the requirements of international solvency placed restrictions on the joint behavior of a country's external financial position, trade flows, and the portfolio returns of domestic and foreign investors. We also showed how these restrictions could be combined with optimal portfolio decisions to derive a portfolio balance model for exchange-rate dynamics under incomplete markets. Here we empirically examine a key element of the model: the link between expected exchange-rate returns and a country's net foreign asset position. This link is the focus of an important paper by Gourinchas and Rey (2007) (henceforth G&R).

Let FA_t and FL_t, respectively, denote foreign assets held by U.S. households and U.S. foreign liabilities (i.e., U.S. assets held by foreign households), both valued in terms of U.S. consumption. The evolution of U.S. foreign assets and liabilities depends on returns and trade flows according to

$$FA_t - FL_t = \mathfrak{X}_t - \mathfrak{M}_t - R_t^{\text{FL}} FL_{t-1} + R_t^{\text{FA}} FA_{t-1}, \qquad (3.46)$$

where $\mathfrak{X}_t$ and $\mathfrak{M}_t$ represent exports and imports of goods and services during period t, R_t^{FA} denotes the (gross) return on U.S. assets held between $t-1$ and t, and R_t^{FL} denotes the analogous return on U.S. liabilities. Under the assumption that net foreign assets, $FA_t - FL_t$, satisfy the no-Ponzi condition, Chapter 2 showed that

$$FL_t - FA_t = \mathbb{E}_t \sum_{i=0}^{\infty} \mathfrak{D}_{t+i} \left\{ \mathfrak{X}_{t+i} - \mathfrak{M}_{t+i} + (R_{t+i}^{\text{FA}} - R_{t+i}^{\text{FL}}) FA_{t+i-1} \right\}, \qquad (3.47)$$

where $\mathfrak{D}_{t+i} = (\prod_{j=0}^{i} R_{t+j}^{\text{FL}})^{-1}$ is the discount factor. Thus, the current value of U.S. foreign assets and liabilities is linked to expectations concerning the future course of net exports and returns in a world where international debts are fully honored. Note that all the terms are endogenous. Equation (3.47) does not determine the difference between U.S. foreign liabilities and assets any more than it determines the returns, R_{t+i}^{FA} and R_{t+i}^{FL}. Instead, it implies that variations in current U.S. net liabilities, $FL_t - FA_t$, reflect changing expectations regarding future net exports, returns, and asset holdings.

The nonlinear restrictions between U.S. foreign assets, liabilities, net exports, and returns in equation (3.47) cannot be easily incorporated into an estimable model. Consequently, G&R work with a log-linearized version of equation (3.46). In particular, they assume that the actual data on asset holdings, returns, exports, and imports comprise cyclical and trend components and derive an approximation to the dynamics in (3.46) around a deterministic trend path where solvency is satisfied. This produces

$$nxa_{t+1}^{\text{c}} = \frac{1}{\rho} nxa_t^{\text{c}} + r_{t+1}^{\text{c}} + \Delta nx_{t+1}^{\text{c}}, \qquad (3.48)$$

where $nx_t^{\text{c}} = \mu^x \epsilon_t^x - \mu^m \epsilon_t^m$ and $nxa_t^{\text{c}} = \mu^a \epsilon_t^a - \mu^l \epsilon_t^l + \mu^x \epsilon_t^x - \mu^m \epsilon_t^m$ for positive constants μ^i and ρ is a constant between one and zero. The log deviations of assets, liabilities, exports, and imports from trend are represented by ϵ_t^a, ϵ_t^l, ϵ_t^x, and ϵ_t^m, respectively, and r_{t+1}^{c} is proportional to the log deviation of returns on net foreign assets. G&R call nx_t^{c} cyclical net exports and nxa_t^{c} the cyclical external balance. $\Delta nx_{t+1}^{\text{c}} = nx_{t+1}^{\text{c}} - nx_t^{\text{c}}$ represents detrended net export growth between periods t and $t+1$. It rises with cyclical export growth and declines with cyclical import growth. The return r_{t+1}^{c} increases with the return on foreign assets and decreases with the return on foreign liabilities. Under the no-Ponzi condition that $\lim_{i \to \infty} \rho^i nxa_{t+i}^{\text{c}} = 0$, we can iterate (3.48) forward and take conditional expectations to get

$$nxa_t^{\text{c}} = - \sum_{i=1}^{\infty} \rho^i \mathbb{E}_t [r_{t+i}^{\text{c}} + \Delta nx_{t+i}^{\text{c}}]. \qquad (3.49)$$

Thus, G&R derive a familiar present value expression that links variations in the cyclical external balance, nxa_t^c, to changing expectations regarding the cyclical components of returns and net export growth.

We can also derive an approximate present value relation from the restrictions implied by international solvency that applies to asset holdings and trade flows rather than just to their cyclical components. Let $nfa_t = \ln(FA_t/FL_t)$ denote the log ratio of U.S. assets to liabilities and $nx_t = \ln\left(\mathfrak{X}_t/\mathfrak{M}_t\right)$. From the appendix in Chapter 2 we know that the dynamics in (3.46) may be well approximated over short time periods by

$$nfa_t = (r_{t+1}^{\mathrm{FL}} - r_{t+1}^{\mathrm{FA}}) - (1 - \mu)\, nx_{t+1} + \mu nfa_{t+1}, \tag{3.50}$$

where $1 > \mu > 0$. Next, define the net external position by $nxa_t = nfa_t + nx_t$. Combining this definition with the expression above gives

$$nxa_t = r_{t+1}^{\mathrm{FL}} - r_{t+1}^{\mathrm{FA}} - \Delta nx_{t+1} + \mu nxa_{t+1}. \tag{3.51}$$

Thus, under the no-Ponzi condition, $\lim_{i \to \infty} \mu^i nxa_{t+i} = 0$, we can iterate forward and take conditional expectations to produce

$$nxa_t = -\sum_{i=1}^{\infty} \mu^{i-1} \mathbb{E}_t[r_{t+i}^{\mathrm{FA}} - r_{t+i}^{\mathrm{FL}} + \Delta nx_{t+i}]. \tag{3.52}$$

This equation is similar to the present value expression in (3.49) derived by G&R, but it applies to the comprehensive measure of the external position, nxa_t, rather than to its cyclical counterpart, nxa_t^c. Note, also, that the right-hand-side variables have simple interpretations: $r_t^{\mathrm{FA}} - r_t^{\mathrm{FL}}$ is the difference in the log returns on the portfolios of U.S. assets and liabilities, and $\Delta nx_t = \Delta \ln \mathfrak{X}_t - \Delta \ln \mathfrak{M}_t$ identifies the growth in export minus imports.[4]

Equations (3.49) and (3.52) are relevant for exchange-rate determination insofar as the adjustment channels through which external imbalances must be resolved involve anticipated future changes in exchange rates. Consider a case where nxa_t is negative, because of a net external debt position ($nfa_t < 0$), a negative trade balance ($nx_t < 0$), or both. Suppose further that the expected future returns on foreign assets and liabilities are constant. Under these circumstances, (3.52) implies that all adjustment of the U.S. external position must come through expected growth in net exports, $\mathbb{E}_t \Delta nx_{t+i} > 0$. This is the standard implication of the intertemporal approach to the current account, which G&R call the "trade channel." When this channel is operable, a fall in nxa_t will be accompanied by a rise in the expected future real depreciation rate consistent with the expected growth in net exports.

---

4. More technically, (3.52) differs from (3.49) in terms of the approximation point. G&R assume that the cyclical components of asset holdings, returns, and trade flows are small, whereas (3.50) approximates the dynamics in (3.46) around the point where the ratios $\mathfrak{X}_t/R_t^{\mathrm{FL}}FL_{t-1}$ and $\mathfrak{M}_t/R_t^{\mathrm{FA}}FA_{t-1}$ are small constants equal to $1 - \mu$. Both approximations appear to be accurate. G&R find that the approximation error in (3.48) (i.e., the difference between the LHS and RHS), has a zero mean and a standard deviation that is seven times less volatile than nxa_t^c. The approximation error in (3.51) is 16 times less volatile than nxa_t.

When expected returns on foreign assets and liabilities are variable, external adjustment may also occur through the "valuation channel." As equation (3.52) shows, the United States may adjust to a negative nxa_t position via higher expected future returns on foreign assets and/or lower expected returns on foreign liabilities, $\mathbb{E}_t(r^{\mathrm{FA}}_{t+i} - r^{\mathrm{FL}}_{t+i}) > 0$. In this case adjustment occurs via a predictable transfer of wealth from foreigners to domestic residents rather than through future trade flows. If this channel is operable, movements in nxa_t will be accompanied by changes in expected future depreciation rates that are consistent with variations in $\mathbb{E}_t(r^{\mathrm{FA}}_{t+i} - r^{\mathrm{FL}}_{t+i})$.

In Chapter 2 we examined a model in which households have access to just one foreign asset, a one-period nominal bond. In this special case $r^{\mathrm{FA}}_{t+1} - r^{\mathrm{FL}}_{t+1} = \Delta s_{t+1} + \hat{r}_t - r_t$, so the valuation channel links variations in nxa_t with revisions in expected excess returns on foreign currency, $\mathbb{E}_t(\Delta s_{t+i} + \hat{r}_{t+i-1} - r_{t+i-1})$. In reality, households have access to a wide array of foreign assets, so r^{FA}_{t+1} and r^{FL}_{t+1} represent the log return on the *portfolio* of foreign assets held by U.S. residents and the *portfolio* of U.S. assets held by foreign residents, respectively. To accommodate this fact, we write the log portfolio returns as

$$r^{\mathrm{FA}}_{t+1} = (\hat{r}_t + \Delta s_{t+1} - \Delta p_{t+1}) + er^{\mathrm{FA}}_{t+1} \tag{3.53a}$$

and

$$r^{\mathrm{FL}}_{t+1} = (r_t - \Delta p_{t+1}) + er^{\mathrm{FL}}_{t+1}. \tag{3.53b}$$

The return on the U.S. residents' foreign asset portfolios is the sum of the return on one-period foreign bonds expressed in terms of U.S. consumption, $\hat{r}_t + \Delta s_{t+1} - \Delta p_{t+1}$, plus the log excess return on all other foreign assets relative to foreign bonds, er^{FA}_{t+1}. Similarly, the return on foreign residents' U.S. assets, r^{FL}_{t+1}, is the sum of the log return on one-period U.S. bonds plus the log excess return on all other foreign-held U.S. assets relative to U.S. bonds, er^{FL}_{t+1}. The expected difference in portfolio returns is therefore

$$\mathbb{E}_t(r^{\mathrm{FA}}_{t+i} - r^{\mathrm{FL}}_{t+i}) = \mathbb{E}_t(\Delta s_{t+i} + \hat{r}_{t+i-1} - r_{t+i-1}) + \mathbb{E}_t(er^{\mathrm{FA}}_{t+i} - er^{\mathrm{FL}}_{t+i}). \tag{3.54}$$

Equation (3.54) implies that the valuation channel can operate through two mechanisms. When expected excess returns on foreign assets are constant, all the valuation effects must come via changes in the expected excess currency returns, $\mathbb{E}_t(\Delta s_{t+i} + \hat{r}_{t+i-1} - r_{t+i-1})$. The second mechanism operates via the composition of households' foreign asset portfolios. Any change in expected returns that alters how residents allocate their portfolios among different foreign assets can affect $\mathbb{E}_t(er^{\mathrm{FA}}_{t+i} - er^{\mathrm{FL}}_{t+i})$. For example, a fall in the expected excess return on U.S. equity relative to U.S. bonds may induce foreign residents to allocate a smaller fraction of their foreign asset holdings to equities so that $\mathbb{E}_t er^{\mathrm{FL}}_{t+i}$ falls. Thus, in a world with many financial assets, variations in nxa_t need not be accompanied by changes in the expected future depreciation rate even when the valuation channel is operable. Valuation effects can occur via the rebalancing of residents' portfolios among different foreign assets.

G&R compare the path for nxa^c_t against the predicted values implied by the right-hand side of (3.49) and estimates of a VAR for $\{nxa^c_t, r^c_t, \Delta nx^c_t\}$ for quarterly data between 1952:I and 2004:I. Figure 3.6 shows comparable plots for nxa_t and its predicted components computed from a third-order VAR for $\{nxa_t, r^{\mathrm{FA}}_t - r^{\mathrm{FL}}_t, \Delta nx_t\}$

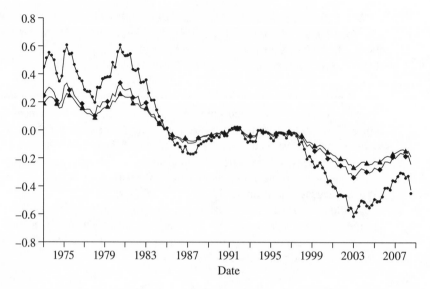

FIGURE 3.6 Decomposition of predicted nxa_t (solid) and actual nxa_t (dots) into the valuation component, nxa_t^r (solid with diamonds), and the trade component, $nxa_t^{\Delta nx}$ (solid with triangles).

with μ set to 0.99 between 1974 and 2008. The VAR is estimated with G&R's data extended to the end of the sample period. To gauge the relative importance of the two adjustment channels, the figure plots VAR-based estimates of valuation and trade components,

$$nxa_t^r = -\sum_{i=1}^{\infty} \mu^{i-1}\mathbb{E}_t(r_{t+i}^{\text{FA}} - r_{t+i}^{\text{FL}}) \quad \text{and} \quad nxa_t^{\Delta nx} = -\sum_{i=1}^{\infty} \mu^{i-1}\mathbb{E}_t\Delta nx_{t+i}.$$

Three features stand out from Figure 3.6. First, the predicted values for nxa_t closely match the actual values of nxa_t across the sample period. The Wald test for the parameter restrictions on the VAR implied by the present value relation in (3.52) has a p-value of 0.966, so is far from statistically significant. This is a test for the accuracy of the log-linear approximation used to derive (3.52) and the accuracy of the VAR forecasts for returns and net exports as measures of $\mathbb{E}_t(r_{t+i}^{\text{FA}} - r_{t+i}^{\text{FL}})$ and $\mathbb{E}_t\Delta nx_{t+i}$.

The second noteworthy feature concerns the plots of the valuation and trade components. As in G&R, the estimates of nxa_t^r and $nxa_t^{\Delta nx}$ are positively correlated, indicating that adjustments via the valuation and trade channels are mutually reinforcing. The estimates of nxa_t^r and $nxa_t^{\Delta nx}$ are also quite variable. Their contribution to the variance of nxa_t can be calculated from the variance decomposition,

$$1 = \frac{\mathbb{CV}\left(nxa_t, nxa_t^r\right)}{\mathbb{V}\left(nxa_t\right)} + \frac{\mathbb{CV}\left(nxa_t, nxa_t^{\Delta nx}\right)}{\mathbb{V}\left(nxa_t\right)} = \beta^r + \beta^{\Delta nx}.$$

The variance contributions of the estimated valuation and trade components, β^r and $\beta^{\Delta nx}$, in Figure 3.6 are 0.53 and 0.45, respectively. These estimated shares are sensitive to the value for the discount parameter, μ. When the estimates of nxa_t^r and $nxa_t^{\Delta nx}$ are computed with lower values for μ, the estimates of β^r and $\beta^{\Delta nx}$ are smaller, but the ratio, $\beta^r/\beta^{\Delta nx}$, remains largely unchanged and above one. According to these estimates, the valuation effects account for more than 50 percent of external adjustment in the United States over the sample period. By comparison, G&R find that valuation effects account for approximately 27 percent of cyclical external adjustment.

The final significant feature in Figure 3.6 concerns the long-run movement in nxa_t. There has been a persistent fall in the value of nxa_t over the past 35 years, indicating a long-term deterioration in the U.S. external position. G&R abstract from this long-term movement by focusing on their cyclical measure, nxa_{t+1}^C, but it is informative to consider the factors that could account for this prominent feature of the data. This is easily done by applying our analysis of Present Value models in Section 3.1. In particular, (3.52) implies that

$$\Delta nxa_{t+1} = -\sum_{i=1}^{\infty} \mu^{i-1} \mathbb{E}_t[\Delta r_{t+i}^{\text{FA}} - \Delta r_{t+i}^{\text{FL}} + \Delta nx_{t+i} - \Delta nx_{t+i-1}]$$

$$-\sum_{i=2}^{\infty} \mu^{i-2} \left(\mathbb{E}_{t+1} - \mathbb{E}_t\right) [r_{t+i}^{\text{FA}} - r_{t+i}^{\text{FL}} + \Delta nx_{t+i}]. \qquad (3.55)$$

The first term on the right identifies the expected change in the U.S. external position, $\mathbb{E}_t \Delta nxa_t$ and the second identifies the factors driving unexpected shocks, $nxa_{t+1} - \mathbb{E}_t nxa_{t+1}$. In principle, both terms could have contributed to the long-run deterioration in the U.S. external position. Specifically, the deterioration could have been anticipated if: (1) the future returns on foreign asset portfolios were expected to rise relative to the returns on foreign liability portfolios, and/or (2) the future growth in net exports was expected to accelerate. Alternatively, the deterioration could reflect the effects of a series of shocks that led to upward revisions in forecasts for future returns, $r_{t+i}^{\text{FA}} - r_{t+i}^{\text{FL}}$, and export growth, Δnx_{t+i}. This seems the more empirically relevant explanation because current and past values of nxa_t, returns, and net exports have had little forecasting power for Δnxa_{t+1} over the past 35 years. That said, it is unclear what economic factors could justify the ever-greater optimism concerning future returns and net export growth necessary to explain the long-term deterioration in the U.S. external position.

We now turn to the exchange-rate implications of the present value expressions in (3.49) and (3.52). G&R examine the forecasting power of nxa_t^C for future portfolio returns and FDI-weighted nominal effective depreciation rate over horizons ranging from one quarter to two years. Table 3.2 reproduces their findings at the one- and four-quarter horizons. The table also reports the estimates of forecasting equations using nxa_t and detrended nxa_t as forecasting variables, where the latter, nxa_t^{DT}, is computed as the residual from a regression of nxa_t on a linear time trend. The forecasting power of all these variables is investigated by regressing h-period returns, $\mathfrak{r}_{t,h} = (\sum_{i=1}^{h} \mathfrak{r}_{t+i})/h$, between t and $t + h$, on a constant and the period-t value of the forecasting variable, for example, nxa_t. Table 3.2 reports the estimated slope coefficient, its standard error, and the R^2 statistic from the regression. As the regressions

TABLE 3.2
Forecasting with Measures of the U.S. External Position

| | Forecasting variables | | | | | |
| | (i) nxa_t | | (ii) nxa_t^{DT} | | (iii) nxa_t^{C} | |
Horizon	1	4	1	4	1	4
Portfolio returns	−0.011**	−0.014***	−0.052***	−0.051***	−0.360***	−0.330***
	(0.006)	(0.005)	(0.014)	(0.010)	(0.070)	(0.040)
R^2	0.023	0.112	0.092	0.251	0.110	0.260
Depreciation rates						
FDI	−0.021***	−0.022***	−0.081***	−0.081***	−0.080***	−0.080***
	(0.008)	(0.006)	(0.021)	(0.016)	(0.020)	(0.010)
R^2	0.042	0.149	0.106	0.326	0.090	0.310
DM/USD	−0.019	−0.021**	−0.124***	−0.110***		
	(0.015)	(0.011)	(0.035)	(0.029)		
R^2	0.011	0.052	0.079	0.200		
GBP/USD	−0.028***	−0.031***	−0.088***	−0.095***		
	(0.011)	(0.010)	(0.031)	(0.021)		
R^2	0.035	0.149	0.058	0.226		
JPY/USD	−0.009	−0.007	−0.078***	−0.076***		
	(0.013)	(0.011)	(0.038)	(0.029)		
R^2	0.003	0.006	0.033	0.106		

Note: The table reports estimates of a_1 from regressions of the form $\mathfrak{r}_{t,h} = a_0 + a_1 z_t + \epsilon_{t+h}$, where $\mathfrak{r}_{t,h}$ is the h-period return between t and $t + h$, and the forecasting variable z_t is nxa_t in column (i), detrended nxa_t, nxa_t^{DT}, in column (ii), or the cyclical component nxa_t^{C} as computed by G&R in column (iii). Newey-West robust standard errors, reported in parentheses, account for $(h − 1)$-order serial correlation in the regression error process. Column (iii) replicates the results reported by G&R. Coefficient estimates that are significantly different from zero in one-sided t-tests at the 5 percent and 1 percent levels are indicated by ** and ***.

are estimated in quarterly data, we have to adjust the standard errors for the presence of an $(h − 1)$-order serial correlation in the regression error term. This is done using the Newey and West (1987) procedure.

The first three rows of Table 3.2 show the forecasting power of the three external balance measures for portfolio returns, that is, $\mathfrak{r}_t = r_t^{FA} − r_t^{FL}$. Here we see that the estimated slope coefficients are negative and statistically significant in all cases and that forecast power, measured by the R^2 statistics, is higher at the longer horizon. Note, also, that the forecasting power of nxa_t is less than that of the nxa_t^{DT} and nxa_t^{C} measures. A very similar picture emerges when we consider the forecasts of the FDI-weighted depreciation rate: All the slope coefficients are statistically significant and the forecasting power is highest at the 4-month horizon when nxa_t^{DT} and nxa_t^{C} are used as forecasting variables. Again, there is a remarkable degree of similarity between G&R's results and the estimates obtained using nxa_t^{DT}.

The lower portion of Table 3.2 shows the forecasting power of nxa_t and nxa_t^{DT} for the depreciation rates on individual currency pairs. Recall that both the trade and valuation channels of external adjustment may involve a change in the expected future path of individual exchange rates insofar as they are consistent with the anticipated change in future net export growth and the portfolio returns. As the table shows, the estimated slope coefficients on nxa_t and nxa_t^{DT} are negative for all the depreciation rates at both horizons. The forecasting power of nxa_t^{DT} for the three currency pairs is somewhat lower than for the FDI-weighted depreciation rate, but all the estimated slope coefficients are highly statistically significant. Thus, the forecasting power of nxa_t^{C} for FDI depreciation rates reported by G&R carries over to individual currency pairs. However, it does not extend to cases where nxa_t is the forecasting variable. The forecasting power of nxa_t for the FDI depreciation rate is mirrored by its forecasting power for the GBP/USD rate. There is some forecasting power for the DM/USD at the four quarter horizon, but none for the JPY/USD.

Overall, the results in Table 3.2 show that some measures of the U.S. external balance have forecasting power for future depreciation rates. However, the degree of forecasting power varies according to whether the depreciation rate is for a basket or a single currency pair and whether the external balance measure includes the long-term deterioration in the U.S. external position.

3.4 Predicting Exchange-Rate Movements

All of the empirical results reviewed to this point have been based on in-sample estimates and inference. That is to say, the model estimates and test statistics are computed from the entire sample period covered by the available data. Following Meese and Rogoff (1983) (hereafter M&R), there also exists a long-standing tradition in the literature of examining the out-of-sample characteristics of empirical exchange-rate models, particularly their predictive power. In what follows, we revisit M&R's analysis and discuss how it has been extended in subsequent research. We then examine the econometric arguments for using in-sample and out-of-sample methods to assess exchange-rate models empirically.

3.4.1 Meese and Rogoff

Meese and Rogoff (1983) compared time series and structural exchange-rate models on the basis of their out-of-sample accuracy during the first decade of the floating-rate period. Remarkably, they found that the structural models failed to outperform a random walk. This finding has turned out to be robust in 25 years of empirical exchange-rate research.

M&R considered structural models of the form

$$s_t = a_0 + a_1(m_t - \hat{m}_t) + a_2(y_t - \hat{y}_t) + \alpha_3(r_t - \hat{r}_t) + a_4(tb_t - \widehat{tb}_t) + u_t,$$
$$= a'z_t + u_t, \tag{3.56}$$

where u_t is a (possibly serially correlated) error term. The vector of variables, z_t, includes the log money stocks, log income, short-term interest rates, and the trade balances (tb_t and $\widehat{tb}_t$). This specification nests several 1980s vintage models, notably the flexible- and sticky-price versions of the monetary model. It also imposes the restriction that each data series appear as the difference between the home and foreign variables—a restriction that did not turn out to be consequential.

Early empirical studies, such as Frankel (1979), found that estimated versions of equation (3.56) could account for a reasonable fraction of exchange-rate variations. However, M&R argued that these in-sample results may have obscured potential problems of model misspecification and parameter instability. They therefore proposed examining the out-of-sample accuracy of the models with the following procedure: First, they estimated the structural model over a subsample of the data that ended with the initial forecast date, say period τ. They then calculated predictions for the spot rate as $\tilde{s}_{\tau+h} = \tilde{a}' z_{\tau+h}$ for several horizons, h, where $\tilde{a}$ is the estimate of a from periods $t \in [1, \tau]$ and $z_{\tau+h}$ is constructed from the data on the macro variables in $\tau + h$. This process is repeated pushing the forecasting date one period forward until the end of the sample is reached in period T. The accuracy of the h-horizon predictions is then measured by statistics computed from the prediction errors, $e_{h,\tau+h} = s_{\tau+h} - \tilde{s}_{\tau+h}$, such as the mean absolute error, the mean-squared error, and the root-mean-squared error:

$$\text{MAE} = \frac{1}{T-h-\tau} \sum_{t=\tau}^{T-h} |e_{h,t+h}|, \qquad \text{MSE} = \frac{1}{T-h-\tau} \sum_{t=\tau}^{T-h} e_{h,t+h}^2, \qquad \text{and}$$

$$\text{RMSE} = \sqrt{\text{MSE}}.$$

This procedure has two noteworthy features. First, the predictions, $\tilde{s}_{\tau+h}$, use the ex post values of the macro variables, $z_{\tau+h}$. Consequently, $\tilde{s}_{\tau+h}$ differ from the true forecasts of $s_{\tau+h}$ that could have been made using only data available at period τ. Second, the predictions can be computed from either recursive or rolling estimates of a. The former are obtained when the model is estimated using all the data up to the forecast date, that is, with an expanding subsample. The rolling estimates, in contrast, are computed using the last τ observations before the forecasting data, that is, a subsample with a fixed span. M&R and much of the subsequent literature use rolling estimates.

M&R compared the predictive accuracy of several versions of equation (3.56), univariate and multivariate time series models and a random walk for the DM/USD, JPY/USD, GBP/USD, and trade-weighted USD between November 1976 and December 1981. They found that the random walk model had a lower RMSE at the 1-, 6-, and 12-month horizons than all the other models. In other words, the random walk model was no less accurate in predicting the future exchange rate than the time series and structural models. This was quite a remarkable finding. The random walk model implies that $\tilde{s}_{\tau+h} = s_\tau$ for all $h > 0$, whereas the predictions from the structural models were computed using ex post values of the macro variables. M&R results appeared to indicate that these variables had no relevance for exchange-rate determination.

A number of factors could have contributed to M&R's findings. Their analysis used less than a decade's worth of data covering a period that witnessed considerable evolution of the world's financial markets and volatility in monetary policy. Furthermore, it is now widely recognized that log spot rates and many of the variables in z_t are well characterized by time series processes containing unit roots. Both of these factors may have adversely affected M&R's estimates of the structural models and hence their predictive accuracy.

In the past 25 years, a large literature has developed exploring these and other explanations for M&R's results. Overall, the vast majority of this research shows that their basic empirical finding continues to hold. For example, Cheung, Chinn, and Pascual (2005) studied the out-of-sample predictive accuracy of a wide set of structural models for 10 currency pairs over a forecasting period between 1983 and 2000. To account for the presence of unit roots, they estimated structural models in first differences and error-correction form:

$$\Delta s_t = a \Delta z_t + u_t \quad \text{and} \quad s_t - s_{t-h} = \gamma_0 + \gamma (s_{t-h} - a' z_{t-h}) + u_t. \quad (3.57)$$

As in M&R, predictions from the first-differenced specification on the left require ex post values of the macro variables, z_t. In contrast, predictions from the error-correction specification on the right use data available on the forecast date. These predictions are true ex ante forecasts in the sense that the parameter estimates and the predictions only use data that were available on the forecast date. Cheung, Chinn, and Pascual (2005) compare the RMSEs for the predictions of a random walk model against several different structural models over multiple forecasting horizons. They found that the predictions from the structural models had a significantly smaller RMSE than those from the random walk model in just two of 186 comparisons at the 10 percent significance level. These results clearly show that M&R's original findings are remarkably robust. The predictions from structural models concerning the future spot rates are no more accurate than the predictions of the random walk model.

3.4.2 Prediction with Panels

All out-of-sample evaluation methods require the choice of an initial forecast date that splits the available data into estimation and forecasting subsamples. This choice must balance two conflicting objectives. On one hand, the predictions from the structural models are likely to be adversely affected by significant sampling errors in the parameter estimates if the date is "too early." On the other hand, asymptotic inferences concerning the RMSEs computed from the forecasting subsample may be unreliable if the date is "too late."

One way to mitigate this trade-off is to estimate the structural models in panel data. As we noted earlier, panel estimation of forecasting equations places restrictions on the joint behavior of exchange rates and macro fundamentals that cannot be exploited when estimating structural models on a currency-by-currency basis. Thus, to the extent that they represent valid restrictions, we should be able to obtain more precise estimates of the structural models without pushing the initial forecasting date further toward the end of the available data sample. Recent research explores this possibility. Following Mark and Sul (2001), papers by Rapach and Wohar (2002), Groen (2005), Engel, Mark, and West (2007), Rogoff and Stavrakeva (2008), and Molodtsova and Papell (2009) conduct out-of-sample evaluations of exchange-rate models using panel data methods.

In these studies, the exchange-rate predictions from structural models are based on panel estimates of forecasting equations of the form

$$s_{i,t} - s_{i,t-h} = \gamma_i + \gamma(s_{i,t-h} - a_i' z_{i,t-h}) + u_{i,t}, \qquad (3.58)$$

with $u_{i,t} = \theta_t + \epsilon_{i,t}$, where $s_{i,t}$ and $z_{i,t}$ denote the spot rate and vector of macro variables for currency i versus the USD in period t. The error term, $u_{i,t}$, comprises a time-specific component, θ_t, and a residual idiosyncratic component, $\epsilon_{i,t}$, that is uncorrelated across currencies and time. Equation (3.58) includes two key features. First, the slope coefficient, γ, is assumed to be the same across all currencies i. Second, the presence of the θ_t component introduces a degree of cross-currency dependence in the error term. If θ_t were zero for all t and the slope coefficient allowed to vary across currencies, predictions based on estimates of (3.58) would be exactly the same as those derived from the error-correction specification in (3.57) currency by currency.

The evaluation of the out-of-sample prediction errors proceeds along similar lines as the currency-by-currency studies. Equation (3.58) is estimated using data from $[1, \tau]$ and the forecast for each currency, i, is computed as

$$\tilde{s}_{i,\tau+h} = s_{i,\tau} + \tilde{\gamma}_i + \tilde{\gamma}(s_{i,\tau} - \tilde{a}_i' z_{i,\tau}) + \tilde{\theta}_\tau, \qquad (3.59)$$

where $\tilde{\gamma}_i$, $\tilde{\gamma}$, and $\tilde{a}$ are the estimated parameters (vector). The last term on the right-hand side is the predicted value for the time effect θ_τ over the forecasting horizon $(\tau, \tau + h]$. This component cannot be directly computed from the panel estimates because the model in (3.58) does not specify how θ_t varies from period to period. Nevertheless, the standard approach in the literature is to compute the prediction recursively as $\tilde{\theta}_\tau = \frac{1}{\tau} \sum_{t=1}^{\tau} \tilde{\theta}_t$, where $\tilde{\theta}_t$ are panel estimates of θ_t. With these predictions for $s_{i,\tau+h}$ in hand, the prediction errors and associated statistics for each of the currencies in the data set can be computed and examined.

The results in Engel, Mark, and West (2007) are representative of the findings from the out-of-sample evaluations using panel estimation. They used quarterly data from 19 countries from 1973 until 2005 and considered choices for z_t based on the monetary, Taylor rule, and PPP fundamentals. Their results contain two noteworthy findings: First, the RMSEs from the structural models are very similar to those generated by the random walk model at the one-quarter forecasting horizon. Statistical test do reveal a few cases where the structural model outperforms the random walk model at the 10 percent significance level, but the weight of the evidence does not favor the predictive accuracy of the structural models at short horizons. Second, their results are quite different at the 4-year horizon. Here the RMSEs from the structural models based on monetary and PPP fundamentals are lower than those from the random walk for a majority of the currencies. Based on these results, Engel, Mark, and West (2007) conclude that long-horizon predictions derived from panel estimates of structure models have some power to beat the random walk.

3.4.3 Interpretation and Assessment

Meese and Rogoff (1983) compared the out-of-sample *fit* of the structural models against the random walk benchmark to assess whether existing in-sample model estimates were adversely affected by structural instability and other forms of misspecification. In other words, M&R's analysis focuses on the question of whether there was a stable contemporaneous relationship between s_t and the macro variables in z_t. Their genius was to compare the predictive accuracy of the structural models against a random walk model rather than to conduct standard tests for parameter stability. This produced a memorable and intuitively appealing result.

The subsequent literature using out-of-sample evaluation has largely departed from the focus of Meese and Rogoff (1983). In recent currency-by-currency and panel studies, the focus is on whether future depreciation rates are predictable with ex ante information. This distinction is important. In Section 3.1 we saw that there exists a stable relationship between the spot rate and fundamentals in a Present Value model, but the true forecasting power of current spot rates and fundamentals for future depreciation rates can be very limited. As a consequence, it is quite possible that tests for the null of no predictability will lack statistical power. Under these circumstances, a failure to outperform the random walk benchmark in an out-of-sample comparison is not informative regarding the existence of a stable relationship between spot rates and fundamentals. From this perspective, the currency-by-currency results reported by Cheung, Chinn, and Pascual (2005) and others do not reveal much about the identity of macro fundamentals.

How should we interpret the forecasting evidence at longer horizons? Recall from Figure 3.3 that the forecasting power of fundamentals for future depreciation rates at longer horizons will be limited in a Present Value model with a high discount parameter unless the changes in fundamentals are highly autocorrelated. This does not appear to be the case empirically. Engel and West (2005), for example, report that there is little autocorrelation in the first-differences of the macro variables that comprise monetary and PPP fundamentals. This time series evidence indicates that we should not expect these measures to have much forecasting power for depreciation rates at any horizon if they are accurate measures of the true fundamentals. The long-horizon forecasting power for monetary and PPP fundamentals reported in the literature is therefore further evidence of the importance of missing fundamentals.

The interpretation of out-of-sample evaluations using panel estimation also requires care. Here the results seem to suggest that monetary and PPP fundamentals have forecasting power for depreciation rates over longer horizons for some currency pairs. However, if we look carefully at the method used to compute the out-of-sample forecasts, it is unclear whether this interpretation of the results is correct. As equation (3.59) shows, the out-of-sample predictions use the gap between the current spot rate and estimated fundamentals, $s_{i,\tau} - \tilde{a}_i' z_{i,\tau}$, and an estimate of the time effect, $\tilde{\theta}_\tau = \frac{1}{\tau} \sum_{t=1}^{\tau} \tilde{\theta}_t$. This specification for $\tilde{\theta}_\tau$ assumes that time effects are perfectly predictable, that is, the time effect in period t is a deterministic function of the time effects in prior periods. This may be true. But if it is not, then the out-of-sample predictions are essentially ad hoc insofar as they reflect variations in $\tilde{\theta}_\tau$. Under these circumstances the out-of-sample comparisons against the random walk would tell us very little about the predictive power of the monetary and PPP fundamentals included in $z_{i,t}$. In sum, the out-of-sample predictions derived from panel data models incorporate an untested assumption about the dynamics of time effects that obscures the predictive contribution of fundamentals.

One clear goal of exchange-rate research is to develop models that provide as accurate and reliable out-of-sample forecasts as possible to policymakers contemplating the implications of alternative macroeconomic policies. This does not, however, imply that out-of-sample methods for evaluating models are necessarily superior to in-sample methods. Since a researcher can only use the available data sample, the choice of method boils down to a decision about how to combine the sample information with other theoretical restrictions in a way that is most informative for the question at hand. This point is most easily understood through a couple of examples.

In Section 3.3 we saw that future depreciation rates were strongly correlated with current measures of the U.S. external position, nxa_t, between 1974 and 2008. Although this in-sample evidence of forecasting power is consistent with the existence of an operable valuation channel over the whole period, it is perfectly possible that changes in the portfolio behavior of U.S. and foreign investors could have altered the forecasting power of nxa_t over time. An out-of-sample evaluation that assesses the predictive accuracy of nxa_t would clearly provide information on this possibility. Rogoff and Stavrakeva (2008) have undertaken this task using G&R's measure, nxa_t^c. They find that nxa_t^c has better predictive accuracy than the random walk model for the FDI-weighted exchange rate at the one-quarter horizon between the early 1990s and 2004. Prior to this period there is no significant improvement over the random walk predictions. These results clearly convey incremental information concerning future out-of-sample forecasting power beyond that provided by the in-sample estimates in Table 3.2.

As a second example, consider the out-of-sample evaluations of predictive accuracy using panel estimation and monetary fundamentals studied by Engel, Mark, and West (2007). These evaluations provide very limited information about the role of monetary fundamentals in exchange-rate determination. In particular, the results do not reveal whether monetary fundamentals have forecasting power in the "right" direction, that is, the direction consistent with the Money-Income model. This would be obvious from in-sample estimates. Moreover, the restrictions placed on the panel estimates, such as the common slope coefficient, will be inconsistent with the Money-Income model if the time series characteristics of fundamentals differ across countries. Out-performing the random walk model with monetary fundamentals under these circumstances does not provide very useful information on the actual macroeconomic drivers of exchange rates.

These examples help dispel the idea that there should be a clear preference between the use of in-sample and out-of-sample evaluation methods. This point is reinforced by Inoue and Kilian (2005). They focus on the question of how we should interpret differences between the results of in-sample and out-of-sample predictability tests. How, for example, should we interpret significant t-statistics on the estimated coefficients in a forecasting regression for the future depreciation rate, but a failure "to beat the random walk model" with the same forecasting variable in an out-of-sample evaluation? One possible explanation is that in-sample tests have a tendency to reject the no-predictability null hypothesis more often than they should at the chosen significance level. This could happen, for example, if a researcher searches over alternative forecasting models, but only reports the results for the specification with the most significant t-statistics. Such data mining will distort the true size of the test statistics. Alternatively, the in-sample tests may have higher statistical power. Inoue and Kilian (2005) show that if appropriate critical values are used, in-sample and out-of-sample tests of predictability are equally reliable against data mining under the null hypothesis of no predictability. In sum, as a purely econometric matter, there is no clear reason to prefer the use of in-sample versus out-of-sample evaluation methods.

3.5 Summary

- Present value exchange-rate models relate the current level of the spot rate to the expected present value of fundamentals. They formalize the idea that exchange rates are determined by equilibrium in asset markets.

- The rate of depreciation in a Present Value model depends on current expectations concerning the future growth in fundamentals and news concerning future fundamentals. The volatility of the depreciation rate can greatly exceed the volatility of changes in fundamentals in a Present Value model if the latter contains little of the information that drives the revisions in market participants' forecasts of future fundamentals. If the process for fundamentals contains a unit root and the discount parameter in the present value relation is close to one, news about future fundamentals will dominate variations in the depreciation rate. Under these circumstances, the time series process followed by the exchange rate will be close to a random walk.

- Money-Income models fall within the present value class, where fundamentals, $f_t^{M/Y}$, depend on income and the money stocks in each country. Estimates of these models cannot account for much of the variation in $s_t - f_t^{M/Y}$ observed during the floating-rate period. There is, however, both in-sample and out-of-sample evidence that $s_t - f_t^{M/Y}$ has forecasting power for future depreciation rates (particularly at longer horizons), but the direction of these forecasts runs contrary to the predictions of the Money-Income model.

- Taylor Rule models derive the exchange-rate implications of central banks following monetary policy rules that relate short-term nominal interest rates to macroeconomic conditions. These models imply present value relations for both real and nominal exchange rates. Estimates of the present value relation for the log level of real rates are positively correlated with actual real rates, but they can account for very little of the variation in real depreciation rates.

- Both the Money-Income and Taylor Rule models imply that fundamentals should have little forecasting power for future depreciation rates at short horizons. As a result, tests for exchange-rate predictability provide little information for or against the empirical relevance of either model. Both models also imply that spot rates should be cointegrated with fundamentals, but there is insufficient information in the available data to reject the null of no cointegration.

- External Balance models link the expected present value of future trade flows and portfolio returns to a country's current external position. These models are relevant for exchange-rate determination insofar as the adjustment channels through which external imbalances must be resolved involve anticipated future changes in exchange rates. These channels appear operable empirically. Measures of the U.S. external position have forecasting power for future depreciation rates both in-sample and out-of-sample. The degree of forecasting power varies according to whether the depreciation rate is for a basket or a single currency pair, and whether the external balance measure includes the long-term deterioration in the U.S. external position.

- In-sample and out-of-sample evaluation methods provide a complementary set of econometric techniques for evaluating the empirical exchange-rate models. Since a researcher can only use the available data sample, the choice of method boils down to a decision about how to combine the sample information with other theoretical restrictions in a way that is most informative for the question at hand.

3.6 Bibliography

There has been a long-standing consensus among researchers that macro exchange-rate models perform poorly at frequencies higher than 1 year. Indeed, surveys of the literature by Frankel and Rose (1995) and Sarno and Taylor (2002) concluded that researchers had yet to produce a model that related the behavior of exchange rates to macro variables in a reliable and robust manner. This lack of empirical success gave credence to the view that exchange rates are largely disconnected from macro fundamentals, a view Obstfeld and Rogoff (2001) call the exchange-rate Disconnect Puzzle. The research reviewed herein represents the most recent attempts to find the connection between changing macroeconomic conditions and the dynamics of exchange rates.

Are macro exchange-rate models finally gaining traction? The answer depends on one's perspective. On one hand, the positive correlation between the level of the real exchange rate and its predicted value from the Taylor Rule models in Engel and West (2006) and Mark (2009) suggests that exchange rates are not completely disconnected from the fundamentals identified by a fairly standard macro model. Furthermore, monetary fundamentals appear to have some forecasting power for depreciation rates at long horizons. On the other hand, none of the models can account for more than a small fraction of the variance in month-by-month or quarter-by-quarter depreciation rates. Nor do they identify macro fundamentals that are clearly cointegrated with the level of exchange rates. As a result, the models fail to account for much of the sustained and substantial swings in real and nominal rates over the floating-rate period.

One possible explanation for the performance of the Money-Income and Taylor Rule model concerns their reliance on uncovered interest parity (UIP). As we shall see in Chapter 11, there is overwhelming empirical evidence documenting the failure of UIP, yet these models assume that changes in interest differentials accurately reflect changes in expected depreciation rates. Insofar as changes in the risk premium lie behind the failure of UIP, they also contribute to the missing fundamentals in the Money-Income and Taylor Rule models. The theoretical models discussed in Chapter 2 show how predictable variations in the risk premium could also contribute to the forecasting power of the U.S. external position discussed in Section 3.3.

The discussion in this chapter omits one area of recent research related to the empirical performance of macro exchange-rate models, namely the estimation of open-economy macro models. This can be done with maximum likelihood methods as in Bergin (2003) or with Bayesian methods as in Lubik and Schorfheide (2005). In the latter study the system of equations comprising the equilibrium of a two-country dynamic general equilibrium model are estimated in a way that incorporates additional information on parameters through the use of Bayesian priors. One problem in this area of research is that standard specifications for the open-economy models do not produce endogenous variations in exchange rates that have the same time series properties as actual exchange rates (see, e.g., Jung 2007). In response, nonstructural stocks are included, such as PPP and UIP shocks, to isolate the model's contribution in explaining exchange-rate dynamics endogenously. These shocks typically account for a sizable fraction of the exchange-rate movements. For example, Lubik and Schorfheide (2005) find that approximately 80 percent of the variations in the real EUR/USD rate come from nonstructural PPP shocks. Thus, the strength of the connection between exchange rates and macro variables implied by the estimates of open economy macro models is broadly in line with implications of the Taylor Rule models reviewed in this chapter.

3.7 Review Questions

1. Present Value Models with News Shocks: Suppose that the growth in fundamentals follows an AR(1) process:

$$\Delta f_t = \phi \Delta f_{t-1} + e_t + v_{t-1},$$

with $f_0 = 0$ and $1 > \phi > 0$, where e_t and v_t are i.i.d. mean-zero shocks with variances σ_e^2 and σ_v^2, respectively. The v_t shocks represent news about the growth in fundamentals next period. In particular, let Ω_t denote the information available to agents in period t. We assume that agents observe e_t and v_t each period so that their information evolves according to $\Omega_t = \{e_t, v_t, \Omega_{t-1}\}$.

(a) Show that (i) $f_t - \mathbb{E}_{t-1} f_t = e_t$ and (ii) $(\mathbb{E}_t - \mathbb{E}_{t-1}) \Delta f_{t+1} = \phi e_t + v_t$.

(b) Use the Present Value model for the spot rate presented in Section 3.1.1 to compute the unexpected variation in the spot rate between periods t and $t + 1$ (i.e., $s_{t+1} - \mathbb{E}_t s_{t+1}$, where $\mathbb{E}_t$ denotes expectations condition on Ω_t). Explain why e_t and v_t shocks of the same size have different effects on $s_{t+1} - \mathbb{E}_t s_{t+1}$.

(c) By definition, the actual depreciation rate can be written as $\Delta s_{t+1} = \mathbb{E}_t \Delta s_{t+1} + s_{t+1} - \mathbb{E}_t s_{t+1}$. Derive an expression for the expected depreciation rate, $\mathbb{E}_t \Delta s_{t+1}$, and combine it with your answer in part (b) to give an equation for Δs_{t+1} in terms of the histories of the e_t and v_t shocks. Use this expression to describe and contrast how the rate of depreciation responds to a positive e_t shock and a positive v_t shock.

(d) Compute the unconditional variance of Δf_{t+1}, $\mathbb{V}(\Delta f_{t+1})$. Use your answer to part (c) to compute the variance ratio, $\mathbb{V}(\Delta s_{t+1})/\mathbb{V}(\Delta f_{t+1})$. What happens to this ratio as news shocks contribute more to the variance of fundamentals (i.e., as σ_v^2/σ_e^2 rises)?

(e) Under rational expectations, $\mathbb{V}(\Delta s_{t+1})$ is equal to $\mathbb{V}(\mathbb{E}_t \Delta s_{t+1}) + \mathbb{V}(s_{t+1} - \mathbb{E}_t s_{t+1})$. Use your answers to parts (b) and (c) to examine how the variance of the e_t and v_t shocks contribute to $\mathbb{V}(\mathbb{E}_t \Delta s_{t+1})$ and $\mathbb{V}(s_{t+1} - \mathbb{E}_t s_{t+1})$. With the aid of these results provide an economic explanation for your answer to part (d).

(f) Consider the limiting case as $b \to 1$. What happens to the correlation between Δs_t and Δf_t as σ_v^2 / σ_e^2 rises? Explain why the relative contribution of news shocks affects the correlation between depreciation rates and fundamentals in this manner.

2. Evaluating Present Value Models with Incomplete Information: Suppose that exchange-rate fundamentals, f_t, follow the process

$$f_t = z_t + e_t, \qquad z_t = z_{t-1} + u_t, \tag{3.60}$$

with $z_0 = 0$, where e_t and u_t are i.i.d. mean-zero shocks with variances σ_e^2 and σ_u^2.

(a) Assume that investors observe the history of f_t and z_t, so that their period-t information is $\Omega_t = \{f_{t-j}, z_{t-j}; j \geq 0\}$. Use the Present Value model presented in Section 3.1.1 to derive the equilibrium process for the depreciation rate. Explain why the spot rate's response to u_t and e_t shocks is different.

(b) Now suppose that agents only observe the history of fundamentals, $\Omega_t = \{f_{t-j}; j \geq 0\}$. What is the equilibrium process for the depreciation rate now? Explain why it is different from the process you computed in part (a). [Hint: Find the univariate time series representation for Δf_t and use it to identify agents' forecasts of future fundamentals growth.]

(c) Now suppose that individuals use the history of fundamentals and the log spot rate, $\Omega_t = \{s_{t-j}, f_{t-j}; j \geq 0\}$, to forecast future fundamentals. How will the process for the equilibrium spot rate compare to your answers in parts (a) and (b)? Explain.

3. Cointegration with Multiple Exchange Rates: Suppose that the Present Value model in Section 3.1.1 holds (with $b < 1$) for the log USD/EUR and log USD/GBP spot rates, denoted by $s_t^{\$/\text{€}}$ and $s_t^{\$/\text{£}}$ with respective fundamentals, $f_t^{\$/\text{€}}$ and $f_t^{\$/\text{£}}$. The time series for both fundamentals contain a unit root and are cointegrated with cointegrating vector $\Theta = [1, -\theta]$, where $\theta \neq 1$. In other words, if $f_t' = [\ f_t^{\$/\text{€}} \quad f_t^{\$/\text{£}}\ ]$, then Θf_t is a covariance-stationary process (i.e., one without a unit root).

(a) Show that $s_t^{\$/\text{€}}$ and $s_t^{\$/\text{£}}$ are cointegrated and find the cointegrating vector. [Hint: Use the Beverage-Nelson Decomposition to characterize the dynamics of fundamentals and apply the Hansen and Sargent formulas in (3.12).]

(b) Consider the behavior of the log GBP/EUR spot rate, $s_t^{\text{£}/\text{€}}$. Is $s_t^{\text{£}/\text{€}}$ cointegrated with $s_t^{\$/\text{€}}$? If so, find the cointegrating vector.

(c) How does your answer to part (b) change in the special case where $\theta = 1$?

(d) Now consider the limiting case of the Present Value model where $b \to 1$. What does cointegration between $f_t^{\$/\text{€}}$ and $f_t^{\$/\text{£}}$ now imply about the correlation between the depreciation rates for the USD/EUR and USD/GBP? Explain the economics of this special case.

4. Forecasting with Monetary Fundamentals: Section 3.2.1 reported on research that finds significant positive slope coefficients in forecasting regressions of the form

$$\Delta s_{t+1} = \alpha_0 + \alpha(f_t^{M/Y} - s_t) + u_{t+1},$$

where s_t and $f_t^{M/Y}$ denote the log spot rate and monetary fundamentals in period t. In contrast, the Present Value model implies that

$$\Delta s_{t+1} = \frac{1-b}{b}(s_t - f_t) + s_{t+1} - \mathbb{E}_t s_{t+1}.$$

(a) If the Present Value model is correct, agents hold rational expectations, and $s - f_t^{M/Y}$ follows a covariance-stationary process, show that

$$\mathbb{CV}(s_t - f_t^{M/Y}, f_t - f_t^{M/Y}) > 0,$$

when the population value of the slope coefficient α is positive.

(b) Use your answer to part (a) and the identity $s_t - f_t = s_t - f_t^{M/Y} - (f_t - f_t^{M/Y})$ to show that

$$\mathbb{V}(f_t - f_t^{M/Y}) > \mathbb{V}(s_t - f_t^{M/Y}).$$

(c) One interpretation of these results is that spot rate dynamics are consistent with the Present Value model but that variations in missing fundamentals (i.e., $f_t - f_t^{M/Y}$) are economically significant. Describe another possible interpretation of the positive estimates of α consistent with the Present Value model.

5. U.S. Net External Position Drivers: Figure 3.6 shows that there has been a steady deterioration in the U.S. net external position as measured by a persistent fall in nxa_t since 1974. By definition, $\Delta nxa_{t+1} = \mathbb{E}_t \Delta nxa_{t+1} + (nxa_{t+1} - \mathbb{E}_t nxa_{t+1})$, so we can decompose this change into an anticipated and an unanticipated component.

(a) Use the present value approximation for nxa_t in equation (3.52) to find an expression for $\mathbb{E}_t \Delta nxa_{t+1}$ in terms of the expected log returns on U.S. assets and liabilities, r_t^{FA} and r_t^{FL}, and log "net exports," nx_t.

(b) Use your answer to part (a) to identify the factors affecting the expected future changes in "net foreign assets," $\mathbb{E}_t \Delta nfa_{t+1}$.

(c) Suppose that agents' forecasts of future trade flows can be characterized by

$$\mathbb{E}_t nx_{t+1} = \phi \mathbb{E}_{t-1} nx_t + u_t,$$

with $u_t = \beta(nx_t - \mathbb{E}_{t-1} nx_t) + v_t$, where $1 > \phi > 0$ and v_t is an i.i.d. mean-zero shock. Examine how unexpected trade flows affect forecasts of future net export growth at different horizons. Then use your answer to describe how an unexpectedly large trade deficit in period t should affect forecasts of future changes in net foreign assets, $\mathbb{E}_t \Delta nfa_{t+1}$, if it has no effect on forecasts of future returns.

(d) How will the unexpected trade deficit in period t affect the expected path for the U.S. external position in the near term, that is, $\mathbb{E}_t \Delta nxa_{t+1}$?

(e) How does your answer to part (d) change if we consider the expected path for the U.S. external position beyond the near term (i.e., $\mathbb{E}_t \Delta nxa_{t+i}$ for $i > 1$)? Explain.

(f) In view of the your answers to parts (e) and (d), how likely is it that the steady deterioration in the U.S. external position over the past 25 years can be attributed to a series of shocks that have adversely affected the U.S. trade deficit?

3.A   Appendix

3.A.1   Econometric Inference in Exchange-Rate Models

The concepts of statistical size and power are central to discussions in the econometrics literature on how to conduct reliable statistical inference. The size of a test statistic is defined as the probability of falsely rejecting the null hypothesis. Tests can be under- or oversized. An undersized test is one where the probability of falsely rejecting the null is smaller than the stated or nominal size. For example, a t-statistic will be undersized if the probability of falsely rejecting the null of a zero coefficient is 4 percent when a researcher uses a 5 percent significance level. In the case of an oversized test, the probability of falsely rejecting the null is larger than the nominal size. The power of a test statistic is defined as the probability of correctly rejecting the null hypothesis for a particular level of significance. A key difficulty in determining the power of a test is that it can vary according to how the data are generated under the alternative hypothesis. The concepts of both size and power apply to tests based on asymptotic distribution theory and those derived from bootstrap simulations. They figure prominently in two areas of the econometrics literature that are particularly relevant to the exchange-rate research reviewed in this chapter.

Inference in Forecasting Regressions

The statistical significance of the coefficient estimates from the forecasting regressions in Tables 3.1 and 3.2 are based on asymptotic distribution theory. Unfortunately, there are several potential pitfalls in applying this theory to forecasting regressions of this type.

The first problem arises in cases where the forecasting horizon, h, is longer than a single period. It is now well established that the asymptotic distribution theory used to compute the standard errors poorly approximates the actual distribution of the coefficient estimates in finite samples when the horizon h is large relative to the sample size. One way around this problem is to transform the forecasting regression so that the residuals no longer contain the serial correlation structure induced by the long forecasting horizon. These methods are reviewed in Campbell, Lo, and MacKinlay (1997). Alternatively, the finite-sample distribution of the coefficient estimates can be computed by bootstrap simulations (see, e.g., Mark 1995). This issue is not a major concern for the results in Table 3.2 because the four-quarter forecasting horizon is very short compared to the sample size.

The second potential problem arises from the fact that the regressors in the fore-casting regressions are likely to be correlated with past error terms. For example, Table 3.1 reports estimates of $\Delta s_{t+1} = a' z_t + v_{t+1}$, where the v_{t+1} error term identi-fies the effect of period-$t + 1$ news on the spot rate. This news will be uncorrelated with z_t, but there is no reason why it should not affect z_{t+i} for $i > 0$. Indeed, regres-sion tests for the forecasting power of monetary fundamentals set $z_t = s_t - f_t^M$, so it is very likely that z_t is correlated with v_{t-i} for $i \geq 0$ in these tests. The presence of these correlations produces biased OLS estimates in finite samples and can lead to inference problems if one relies on standard asymptotic distribution theory. In partic-ular, a number of studies have shown that this theory provides a poor approximation to the actual finite-sample distribution of the t-statistics on the forecasting coefficients when z_t follows a persistent process and its innovations are highly correlated with the regressor (see, e.g., Stambaugh 1999). This is a particular concern for the forecasting regressions using monetary fundamentals because the lack of strong evidence on the presence of cointegration between s_t and f_t^M implies that variations in $z_t = s_t - f_t^M$ are extremely persistent. It is also a concern in the literature examining the predictability of equity returns because the log dividend-price ratio is very persistent and is often used as a forecasting variable.

Recent research in the equities literature develops forecasting tests based on an alternative asymptotic distribution theory called local-to-unit root asymptotics. This distribution theory provides an accurate approximation to the finite-sample distri-bution of test statistics when the forecasting variable is very persistent (see, e.g., Campbell and Yogo 2006 and Cavanagh, Elliott, and Stock 2009).

Out-of-Sample Evaluation

The literature contains several tests for comparing the out-of-sample predictive accu-racy of two exchange-rate models. The simplest is Theil's U test, which is computed as the ratio of the RMSEs from the two models. When the random walk model is used as a benchmark, the statistic is computed as

$$\mathrm{TU} = \mathrm{RMSE_F}/\mathrm{RMSE_{RW}},$$

where $\mathrm{RMSE_F}$ and $\mathrm{RMSE_{RW}}$ are the RMSEs from the fundamentals-based and random walk models, respectively. The fundamentals-based model is said to outperform the random walk when $\mathrm{TU} < 1$. Statistical significance for the null hypothesis that $\mathrm{TU} = 1$ is usually computed from bootstrap simulations under the null that the data follow a random walk.

In cases where the models are nonnested (i.e., when one model cannot be written as a restricted version of the other), the tests developed by West (1996) and Diebold and Mariano (2002) can be used. The test statistic for comparing models A and B with out-of-sample prediction errors $\{e_{A,t}\}_{t_0}^T$ and $\{e_{B,t}\}_{t_0}^T$ is

$$\mathrm{DMW} = \frac{d}{\sqrt{\widetilde{avar}(d)/(T - t_0)}},$$

where

$$d = \frac{1}{T - t_0} \sum_{t=t_0}^{T} d_t \quad \text{and} \quad \widetilde{avar}(d) = \widetilde{\mathbb{V}}(d_t) + 2 \sum_{j=1}^{\infty} \widetilde{\mathbb{CV}}(d_t, d_{t-j}),$$

with $d_t = e_{\text{A},t}^2 - e_{\text{B},t}^2$. The term $\widetilde{avar}(d)$ is a consistent estimate of the asymptotic long-run variance of $\sqrt{T} d$: The long-run variance is used when the prediction errors, $e_{\text{A},t}$ and $e_{\text{B},t}$, come from multiperiod horizons because this induces serial correlation in d_t. Under the null hypothesis of equal predictive accuracy, the asymptotic distribution of the DMW statistic is a standard normal, $N(0, 1)$.

Unfortunately, the asymptotic properties of the DMW statistic cannot be relied upon for comparing fundamentals-based and random walk exchange-rate models because these models are nested. Under these circumstances, the asymptotic DMW test is undersized. There are two responses to this problem in the literature. One is to compute bootstrap distributions for the DMW statistic under the null that the exchange rate follows a random walk (see, e.g., Rogoff and Stavrakeva 2008 and the references therein). Alternatively, the DMW statistic can be adjusted to take account of the fact that the models are nested and inference conducted using the asymptotic distribution (see Clark and McCracken 2005 and Clark and West 2006). West (2006) provides a summary of the recent literature on asymptotic inference about predictive accuracy.

3.A.2 Derivations

To derive the formulas in equation (3.12), we start with the following result from Hansen and Sargent (1980):

$$\sum_{i=0}^{\infty} b^i \mathbb{P}(\Delta f_{t+i} | F_t) = \left(\frac{\psi(L) - bL^{-1}\psi(b)}{1 - bL^{-1}} \right) \eta_t.$$

Subtracting $\mathbb{P}[\Delta f_t | F_t] = \Delta f_t = \psi(L)\eta_t$ from both sides produces (3.12a). Next, note that (3.6) and (3.12a) together imply that $s_t - f_t = b \left(\frac{\psi(b) - \psi(L)}{b - L} \right) \eta_t$, so taking first-differences

$$\Delta s_{t+1} = \left\{ \psi(L) + b \left(\frac{\psi(b) - \psi(L)}{b - L} \right) (1 - L) \right\} \eta_{t+1}.$$

From equation (3.9) we can therefore write

$$\frac{1-b}{b} \sum_{i=1}^{\infty} b^i \{ \mathbb{P}(f_{t+i} | F_{t+1}) - \mathbb{P}(f_{t+i} | F_t) \}$$

$$= \Delta s_{t+1} - \frac{1-b}{b} \sum_{i=0}^{\infty} b^i \mathbb{P}(\Delta f_{t+i} | F_t)$$

$$= \left\{ \psi(L) + b \left(\frac{\psi(b) - \psi(L)}{b - L} \right) (1 - L) \right\} \eta_{t+1} - (1 - b) \left(\frac{\psi(b) - \psi(L)}{b - L} \right) \eta_t$$

$$= \psi(b)\eta_{t+1},$$

as shown in (3.12b).

To derive the variance ratio in equation (3.21), we first note that $\mathbb{V}(\Delta f_t) = \mathbb{V}(\mathbb{E}_{t-1}\Delta f_t) + (f_t - \mathbb{E}_{t-1}f_t)$. It therefore follows from the definition of $\mathfrak{R}^2$ that

$$\mathbb{V}(f_t - \mathbb{E}_{t-1}f_t)/\mathbb{V}(\Delta f_t) = 1 - \mathfrak{R}^2.$$

Furthermore, (3.19) implies that

$$(1 - \phi^2)\mathbb{V}(\mathbb{E}_{t-1}\Delta f_t) = \beta^2\mathbb{V}(f_t - \mathbb{E}_{t-1}f_t) + \sigma_v^2,$$

so dividing by $\mathbb{V}(\Delta f_t)$ yields

$$(1 - \phi^2)\mathfrak{R}^2 = \beta^2(1 - \mathfrak{R}^2) + \sigma_v^2/\mathbb{V}(\Delta f_t).$$

Combining this expression with (3.20) produces equation (3.21).

PART II

MICROSTRUCTURE MODELS

CHAPTER 4

Rational Expectations Models

This is the first of five chapters that examine the microfoundations of exchange-rate dynamics. In this chapter we study the determination of exchange rates in a model where investors have heterogeneous information and rational expectations. Chapter 5 examines a model with marketmakers and investors who possess heterogeneous information. Marketmakers perform some, but not all of the functions of foreign exchange dealers, so this model serves as stepping-stone to the currency-trading model we study in Chapter 6. Chapters 7 and 8 examine the empirical implications of currency-trading models.

All the models we studied in Part I assume that households, firms, and governments have the same information about (1) the structure of the economy, and (2) its current state. This means that everyone holds the same expectations regarding future returns on risky assets, including foreign exchange. It also means that everyone faces the same degree of uncertainty concerning future returns and other variables. In this chapter, we study models where agents agree upon the structure of the economy but have different information about its current state. As we shall see, introducing informational heterogeneity presents challenges for the modeling of exchange-rate dynamics and asset prices more generally.

4.1 The Model

We study how heterogeneous information affects exchange rates in a simple two-country monetary model based on Bacchetta and van Wincoop (2006). There is a continuum of households on the unit interval [0,1] and these households are split between the home and foreign countries, which I refer to as the United States and Europe. We index U.S. households by $h \in [0, a)$ and E.U. households by $\hat{h} \in (a, 1]$, where a denotes the U.S.'s share of the world population.

There are overlapping generations of households who live for two periods. In the first period each household receives an endowment, which they invest in bonds and money. They also supply labor inelastically to a production process. In the second period each household consumes the income it receives from production and its accumulated wealth. Household preferences are defined in terms of the consumption of a single good. The only other agents in the economy are the two central banks. The Federal Reserve (FED) keeps the money supply constant, whereas the European Central Bank (ECB) changes the E.U. money supply according to a given process.

Let us begin with the problem facing U.S. household h when it is young in period t. At the start of the period the household receives an endowment W_t^h (measured in terms of the consumption good). The household then chooses how to allocate W_t^h among U.S. bonds, B_t^h, E.U. bonds, $\hat{B}_t^h$, and dollars, M_t^h, to maximize expected utility defined over next period's consumption C_{t+1}^h:

$$\mathcal{U}_t^h = \mathbb{E}_t^h \left[-\exp(-\gamma C_{t+1}^h) \right], \tag{4.1}$$

with $\gamma > 0$. Here $\mathbb{E}_t^h [.]$ denotes expectations conditioned on Ω_t^h, the information available to household h in period t. This specification for utility exhibits constant absolute risk-aversion. It appears in many models because it implies simple asset demand functions under appropriate conditions.

In period $t + 1$ household h receives income from production of Y_{t+1}^h and the return on its portfolio of bonds and money. The sequence of budget constraints facing the household is

Young: $P_t W_t^h = B_t^h + S_t \hat{B}_t^h + M_t^h$

Old: $P_{t+1} C_{t+1}^h \leq R_t B_t^h + S_{t+1} \hat{R}_t \hat{B}_t^h + M_t^h + P_{t+1} Y_{t+1}^h,$

where P_t is the price level and S_t is the USD/EUR spot exchange rate. The gross nominal interest rates on U.S. and E.U. bonds are R_t and $\hat{R}_t$, respectively. Combining these equations gives the household's dynamic budget constraint:

$$C_{t+1}^h \leq \mathcal{R}_{t+1}^B W_t^h + \mathcal{R}_{t+1}^{\hat{B}} (S_t \hat{B}_t^h / P_t) + \mathcal{R}_{t+1}^M (M_t^h / P_t) + Y_{t+1}^h, \tag{4.2}$$

where

$$\mathcal{R}_{t+1}^B = R_t \left(\frac{P_t}{P_{t+1}} \right), \quad \mathcal{R}_{t+1}^{\hat{B}} = \left(\frac{S_{t+1} \hat{R}_t}{S_t} - R_t \right) \left(\frac{P_t}{P_{t+1}} \right), \quad \text{and}$$

$$\mathcal{R}_{t+1}^M = \left(1 - R_t \right) \left(\frac{P_t}{P_{t+1}} \right). \tag{4.3}$$

$\mathcal{R}_{t+1}^{\hat{B}}$ and $\mathcal{R}_{t+1}^M$ are the excess real returns on E.U. bonds and dollars relative to U.S. bonds, $\mathcal{R}_{t+1}^B$, measured in terms of U.S. consumption.

The income household h receives when it is old depends on the future spot rate and real balances:

$$Y_{t+1}^h = \lambda_t^h \ln S_{t+1} - \frac{1}{\alpha} (M_t^h / P_t)(\ln(M_t^h / P_t) - 1), \tag{4.4}$$

with $\alpha > 0$. This particular production function contains two important features. First, the parameter λ_t^h measures the exchange-rate exposure of nonasset income to the household. As we shall see, this gives rise to a hedging demand for E.U. bonds. We index the parameter by h and time t to allow for both time-varying and cross-sectional differences in hedging demand. The second feature concerns the presence of real balances. Income is increasing in real balances provided that $M_t^h/P_t < 1$, a condition that holds in equilibrium. This form of money-in-production provides a rationale for holding real balances and ensures a simple demand for money function.

To summarize, the problem facing a young U.S. household $h \in [0, a)$ in period t is to choose M_t^h and $\hat{B}_t^h$ to maximize (4.1) subject to (4.2) and (4.4). A young E.U. household $\hat{h} \in [a, 1]$ faces an analogous problem, namely to choose its holdings of euros, $\hat{M}_t^{\hat{h}}$, and U.S. bonds, B_t^h, to maximize

$$\mathcal{U}_t^{\hat{h}} = \mathbb{E}_t^{\hat{h}} \left[- \exp(-\gamma C_{t+1}^{\hat{h}}) \right],$$

where $\gamma > 0$, subject to

$$C_{t+1}^{\hat{h}} \le \hat{\mathcal{R}}_{t+1}^{\hat{B}} W_t^{\hat{h}} + \hat{\mathcal{R}}_{t+1}^{B}(B_t^{\hat{h}}/S_t \hat{P}_t) + \hat{\mathcal{R}}_{t+1}^{\hat{M}}(\hat{M}_t^{\hat{h}}/\hat{P}_t) + Y_{t+1}^{\hat{h}},$$

with

$$Y_{t+1}^{\hat{h}} = -\lambda_t^{\hat{h}} \ln S_{t+1} - \tfrac{1}{\alpha}(\hat{M}_t^{\hat{h}}/\hat{P}_t)(\ln(\hat{M}_t^{\hat{h}}/\hat{P}_t) - 1)$$

and

$$\hat{\mathcal{R}}_{t+1}^{\hat{B}} = \hat{R}_t \left(\frac{\hat{P}_t}{\hat{P}_{t+1}} \right), \quad \hat{\mathcal{R}}_{t+1}^{B} = \left(\frac{S_t R_t}{S_{t+1}} - \hat{R}_t \right) \left(\frac{\hat{P}_t}{\hat{P}_{t+1}} \right), \quad \text{and}$$

$$\hat{\mathcal{R}}_{t+1}^{\hat{M}} = \left(1 - \hat{R}_t \right) \left(\frac{\hat{P}_t}{\hat{P}_{t+1}} \right).$$

$\hat{\mathcal{R}}_{t+1}^{B}$ and $\hat{\mathcal{R}}_{t+1}^{\hat{M}}$ are the excess real returns on U.S. bonds and euros relative to E.U. bonds, $\hat{\mathcal{R}}_{t+1}^{\hat{B}}$, measured in terms of E.U. consumption.

As in standard monetary models, the FED and ECB are assumed to have complete control over the aggregate stock of dollars and euros, M_t and $\hat{M}_t$, respectively. We further assume that the supply of dollars is fixed at M and that the log supply of euros $\hat{m}_t = \ln \hat{M}_t$ follows a simple AR(1) process:

$$\hat{m}_t = \hat{m} + \rho(\hat{m}_{t-1} - \hat{m}) + \hat{u}_t, \tag{4.5}$$

with $|\rho| < 1$, where $\hat{u}_t \sim \text{i.i.d.} N(0, \sigma^2)$.

4.2 Equilibrium with Common Information

We initially study the equilibrium of the model under the assumption that all house-holds have the same information. Although this is relatively straightforward concep-tually, there are a number of technical problems that must be addressed. Once this has been done, we move on to the case where households have different information.

Let us start with the simple case in which all households share the same constant hedging parameter, λ, and the same information. In particular we assume that at the start of period t all households observe current prices, P_t and $\hat{P}_t$, interest rates, R_t and $\hat{R}_t$, the spot exchange rate, S_t, and the foreign money stock, $\hat{M}_t$. Thus the common information set in period t is

$$\Omega_t = \left\{ P_t, \hat{P}_t, R_t, \hat{R}_t, S_t, \hat{M}_t \right\} . \tag{4.6}$$

We also assume that all households understand the structure of the world economy, namely the structure of production, preferences, and the money supply process.

An equilibrium in this economy describes a sequence of prices, interest rates, and exchange rates consistent with market clearing given the optimal portfolio decisions of households and the exogenous process for the E.U. money stock. A Walrasian auc-tioneer provides the fictional mechanism through which the equilibrium sequences are found. Specifically, the auctioneer first calls out a candidate sequence of prices, spots rates, and interest rates. Then he elicits the consumption plans and asset demands from each household. These plans represent the intentions of households if prices, exchange rates, and interest rates were to evolve as the auctioneer announced. The auctioneer then aggregates the households' plans for consumption and asset hold-ings and checks whether they are consistent with market clearing. If they are, the sequence of prices, exchange rates, and interest rates are set to their candidate values, and households execute their plans. Since these plans represent optimal decisions and their aggregate implications clear markets, we have established an equilibrium. Al-ternatively, if the aggregate implications of households' plans are inconsistent with market clearing, the auctioneer must come up with another candidate sequence and the whole process must continue.

4.2.1 The Tatomont Process

It is clear from this overview that we must be able to characterize how households optimally choose their asset holdings as a function of the prices, interest rates, and exchange rates called out by the auctioneer. In other words, we must derive the household asset demand functions. Although conceptually straightforward, this turns out to be a complex undertaking in many settings, including the one here. To get started, we therefore make two additional assumptions that permit easy derivation of the asset demands.

Asset Demands with Normal Distributed Returns
We focus on the asset demands of U.S. household $h \in [0, a)$. Let us assume that the real returns on bonds, dollars, and euros together with future income have a joint

normal distribution conditioned on information available to household h in period t, Ω_t^h. We also assume that future income is independent of current real balances (i.e., $\alpha = \infty$):

$$\{\mathcal{R}_{t+1}^B, \mathcal{R}_{t+1}^{\hat{B}}, \mathcal{R}_{t+1}^M, \hat{\mathcal{R}}_{t+1}^B, \hat{\mathcal{R}}_{t+1}^{\hat{B}}, \hat{\mathcal{R}}_{t+1}^{\hat{M}}, Y_{t+1}^h\} \tag{A1}$$

are jointly normal and

$$Y_{t+1}^h = \lambda_t \ln S_{t+1} \quad \text{and} \quad Y_{t+1}^{\hat{h}} = -\lambda_t \ln S_{t+1}. \tag{A2}$$

These assumptions imply that the household's consumption in period $t + 1$ will be normally distributed. To see why, recall that the budget constraint for the household is given by

$$C_{t+1}^h \leq \mathcal{R}_{t+1}^B W_t^h + \mathcal{R}_{t+1}^{\hat{B}}(S_t \hat{B}_t^h / P_t) + \mathcal{R}_{t+1}^M (M_t^h / P_t) + Y_{t+1}^h.$$

Since the household's utility is increasing in consumption, the optimal choice of consumption in period $t + 1$ will be equal to the right-hand side of this constraint. This also means that C_{t+1}^h is a linear combination of normally distributed random variables [with weights W_t^h, $(S_t \hat{B}_t^h / P_t)$, (M_t^h / P_t), and one] and so must also be normally distributed.

Next, we use the fact that for a normally distributed variable x, with mean μ and variance σ^2, $\mathbb{E}\left[\exp(x)\right] = \exp\left(\mu + \frac{1}{2}\sigma^2\right)$. Applying this result to the definition of $\mathcal{U}_t^h$ in (4.1) with $x = -\gamma C_{t+1}^h$ gives

$$\mathcal{U}_t^h = -\exp\left(-\gamma \mathbb{E}_t^h[C_{t+1}^h] + \frac{1}{2}\gamma^2 \mathbb{V}_t^h(C_{t+1}^h)\right) = -\exp(-\gamma u_t^h),$$

where $\mathbb{V}_t^h(\cdot)$ denotes the variance conditioned on Ω_t^h and

$$u_t^h = \mathbb{E}_t^h[C_{t+1}^h] - \frac{1}{2}\gamma \mathbb{V}_t^h(C_{t+1}^h). \tag{4.7}$$

Note that maximizing u_t^h is equivalent to maximizing $\mathcal{U}_t^h$ because the latter is simply an increasing monotonic transformation of the former. Thus, under assumptions (A1) and (A2), we can derive the household's asset demands by maximizing (4.7) subject to (4.2) and (4.4).

The first-order conditions for the bond and money holdings from this problem are

$$0 = \mathbb{E}_t^h \mathcal{R}_{t+1}^{\hat{B}} - \gamma (S_t \hat{B}_t^h / P_t) \mathbb{V}_t^h (\mathcal{R}_{t+1}^{\hat{B}})$$
$$- \gamma \mathbb{CV}_t^h \left(\mathcal{R}_{t+1}^{\hat{B}}, \mathcal{R}_{t+1}^B W_t^h + \mathcal{R}_{t+1}^M (M_t^h / P_t) + Y_{t+1}^h \right)$$

and

$$0 = \mathbb{E}_t^h \mathcal{R}_{t+1}^M - \gamma (M_t^h / P_t) \mathbb{V}_t^h (\mathcal{R}_{t+1}^M)$$
$$- \gamma \mathbb{CV}_t^h \left(\mathcal{R}_{t+1}^M, \mathcal{R}_{t+1}^B W_t^h + \mathcal{R}_{t+1}^{\hat{B}} (S_t \hat{B}_t^h / P_t) + Y_{t+1}^h \right),$$

where $\mathbb{CV}^h_t(\cdot, \cdot)$ denotes the covariance conditioned on Ω^h_t. Combining these equations and solving for $(S_t \hat{B}^h_t / P_t)$ and (M^h_t / P_t) gives

$$\begin{bmatrix} S_t \hat{B}^h_t / P_t \\ M^h_t / P_t \end{bmatrix} = \mathbb{V}^h_t \left(\mathcal{R}_{t+1} \right)^{-1} \left\{ \tfrac{1}{\gamma} \mathbb{E}^h_t \mathcal{R}_{t+1} - \mathbb{CV}^h_t (\mathcal{R}_{t+1}, \mathcal{R}^B_{t+1} W^h_t + Y^h_{t+1}) \right\}, \quad (4.8)$$

where $\mathcal{R}_{t+1} = [\, \mathcal{R}^{\hat{B}}_{t+1} \quad \mathcal{R}^M_{t+1} \,]'$.

There are several noteworthy features of these asset demand equations. First, they imply that the household's demand for bonds and real balances is independent of its endowment, W^h_t. The value of foreign bond holdings desired by rich and poor households will be the same if they have the same information about future returns and income. This is a characteristic feature of asset demands derived from specifications for utility with constant absolute risk-aversion. Second, (4.8) implies that the demand for individual assets generally depends on the conditional mean and variance of all asset returns. For example, the demand for E.U. bonds depends on both $\mathbb{E}^h_t \mathcal{R}^{\hat{B}}_{t+1}$ and $\mathbb{E}^h_t \mathcal{R}^M_{t+1}$ when the covariance between $\mathcal{R}^{\hat{B}}_{t+1}$ and $\mathcal{R}^M_{t+1}$ [i.e., the top right-hand element of $\mathbb{V}^h_t(\mathcal{R}_{t+1})$] differs from zero. This means that in general we cannot consider the demand for individual assets in isolation. The third feature concerns the last term on the right of (4.8). This term identifies the risk associated with other assets and income. In our case these risks come from the return on the endowment and future income, $\mathcal{R}^B_{t+1} W^h_t + Y^h_{t+1}$. The household can reduce the volatility of future consumption, and hence increase expected utility, by structuring its asset holdings to mitigate unexpected variations in $\mathcal{R}^B_{t+1} W^h_t + Y^h_{t+1}$.

Market Clearing

Let us consider how the Walrasian auctioneer would arrive at equilibrium prices and interest rates if household asset demands took the form of (4.8). Recall that the auctioneer first announces a *sequence* of prices, interest rates, and exchange rates, not just current values. This is necessary because asset demands depend upon the distribution of future returns and income, which are themselves functions of both current and future prices. If the auctioneer were simply to announce values for current prices, interest rates, and the spot rate, households would have insufficient information to form expectations about returns, and so could not signal their intended demands back to the auctioneer.

To describe how the Walrasian auctioneer finds the equilibrium, we have to introduce a little more notation. Let $Q_t = (P_t, \hat{P}_t, R_t, \hat{R}_t, S_t)$ denote the set of prices and interest rates for the economy at period t. The state of the economy in period t is summarized by the E.U. money stock and the distribution of endowments, $Z_t = (\hat{M}_t, \{W^h_t\}_{h \in [0,1]})$. The task for the auctioneer is to announce a candidate value for Q_t for each possible value of Z_t. In other words, in period t the auctioneer announces a value for Q_t based on the current state, Z_t, and values for Q_{t+i} based on all the possible values for Z_{t+i} for all $i > 0$. This amounts to the announcement of a candidate price function $Q_t = F^c(Z_t)$. Individual prices are computed as $\varkappa_t = F^c_\varkappa(Z_t)$ for $\varkappa = \{P, \hat{P}, R, \hat{R}, S\}$.

Once $F^c(\cdot)$ has been announced, households can formulate their asset demands. In particular, since $\mathcal{R}^B_{t+1}$, $\mathcal{R}^{\hat{B}}_{t+1}$, $\mathcal{R}^M_{t+1}$, and Y^h_{t+1} are functions of Q_{t+1} and Q_t, future returns and income can now be related to Z_{t+1} and Z_t via the $F^c(\cdot)$ function. Specifically, let $Y^h_{t+1} = G^Y(Q_{t+1}, Q_t, h)$ and $\mathcal{R}^\varkappa_{t+1} = G^\varkappa(Q_{t+1}, Q_t)$ for $\varkappa = \{B, \hat{B}, M\}$, where $G^\varkappa(\cdot, \cdot)$ and $G^Y(\cdot)$. represent the functions relating prices to returns and income. We can now write future income and returns as $Y^h_{t+1} = G^Y(F^c(Z_{t+1}), F^c(Z_t), h)$ and $\mathcal{R}^\varkappa_{t+1} = G^\varkappa(F^c(Z_{t+1}), F^c(Z_t))$. Uncertainty about future returns and income is linked to the underlying uncertainty about the future state of the economy via the $F^c(\cdot)$ function. In our setup this is uncertainty about the future E.U. money supply and endowments, which are both determined exogenously.

We may now compute the asset demands of U.S. households given $F^c(\cdot)$. Using $G^Y(F^c(Z_{t+1}), F^c(Z_t), h)$ to substitute for Y^h_{t+1} and $G^\varkappa(F^c(Z_{t+1}), F^c(Z_t))$ to substitute for $\mathcal{R}^\varkappa_{t+1}$ in (4.8) gives

$$\hat{B}^h_t = D^{\hat{B}}(Z_t, \Omega_t, F^c, h) \quad \text{and} \quad M^h_t = D^M(Z_t, \Omega_t, F^c, h). \tag{4.9}$$

Similarly, asset demands by U.S. household $\hat{h} \in [a, 1]$ can be represented as

$$\hat{B}^{\hat{h}}_t = D^{\hat{B}}(Z_t, \Omega_t, F^c, \hat{h}) \quad \text{and} \quad \hat{M}^{\hat{h}}_t = D^{\hat{M}}(Z_t, \Omega_t, F^c, \hat{h}). \tag{4.10}$$

These asset demands depend on households' information, Ω_t, and the candidate price function, $F^c(\cdot)$. They represent households' planned asset holdings given the implications of the auctioneer's announcement about future income and returns.

Household consumption plans can be represented in a similar way by substituting for returns and income in the budget constraint. In the case of U.S. household $h \in [0, a)$ this gives

$$C^h_t = G^B\left(F^c(Z_t), F^c(Z_{t-1})\right) W^h_{t-1} + G^{\hat{B}}\left(F^c(Z_t), F^c(Z_{t-1})\right)(S_{t-1}\hat{B}^h_{t-1}/P_{t-1})$$

$$+ G^M\left(F^c(Z_t), F^c(Z_{t-1})\right)(M^h_{t-1}/P_{t-1}) + G^Y(F^c(Z_t), F^c(Z_{t-1}), h).$$

Substituting for bond and money holdings from (4.9) produces

$$C^h_t = G^C\left(Z_t, Z_{t-1}, \Omega_t, F^c, h\right).$$

Consumption of E.U. households can be similarly represented by

$$C^{\hat{h}}_t = G^C(Z_t, Z_{t-1}, \Omega_t, F^c, \hat{h}).$$

The next step is for the auctioneer to check whether these planned asset demands are consistent with market clearing. There are five markets in our setup: the markets for U.S. and E.U. bonds, dollars, and euros, and the goods market. Walras' law allows us to focus on just four:

$$\text{Dollars:} \quad 0 = \int_0^a D^M(Z_t, \Omega_t, h, F^c) dh - M, \tag{4.11a}$$

$$\text{Euros:} \quad 0 = \int_a^1 D^{\hat{M}}(Z_t, \Omega_t, F^c, \hat{h}) d\hat{h} - \hat{M}_t, \tag{4.11b}$$

$$\begin{array}{l} \text{E.U.} \\ \text{Bonds:} \end{array} \quad 0 = \int_0^a D^{\hat{B}}(Z_t, \Omega_t, F^c, h) dh + \int_a^1 D^{\hat{B}}(Z_t, \Omega_t, F^c, \hat{h}) d\hat{h}, \tag{4.11c}$$

$$\text{Goods:} \quad 0 = \int_0^a \left\{ G^C\left(Z_t, Z_{t-1}, \Omega_t, F^c, h\right) - G^Y(F^c(Z_t), F^c(Z_{t-1}), h) \right\} dh$$

$$+ \int_a^1 \left\{ G^C\left(Z_t, Z_{t-1}, \Omega_t, F^c, \hat{h}\right) - G^Y(F^c(Z_t), F^c(Z_{t-1}), \hat{h}) \right\} d\hat{h}. \tag{4.11d}$$

The right-hand side of these expressions identifies the notional excess demand in each market given the plans of all households based on the candidate pricing function, $F^c(\cdot)$. If these four market-clearing conditions are satisfied, the auctioneer will adopt $F^c(\cdot)$, so equilibrium prices will satisfy $Q_t = F^c(Z_t)$. If all the market-clearing conditions are not satisfied, another candidate price function must be announced and the process repeated. In sum, therefore, the job of the Walrasian auctioneer is to come up with the pricing function $F^c(\cdot)$ that satisfies (4.11)—the market-clearing conditions that incorporate the optimizing behavior of households.

It should be clear from this description that the process of finding equilibrium prices is greatly simplified by our ability to characterize household asset demands for *any* pricing function. Here we relied on equation (4.8) to describe the demand for assets by U.S. households (and a similar equation for the asset demands of E.U. households). It is important to remember, however, that (4.8) was derived under two additional assumptions: (A1) conditional normality of income and returns, and (A2) independence of income from real balances ($\alpha = \infty$). A pricing function $F^c(\cdot)$ that satisfies the conditions in (4.11) derived from (4.8) will only give us equilibrium prices if assumptions (A1) and (A2) are valid. If they are not, we have to find another way to characterize asset demands in the market-clearing conditions.

Market Clearing without Assumptions (A1) and (A2)

Although assumptions (A1) and (A2) simplify the description of how equilibrium prices are found, they have little economic justification. Let us consider them in reverse order. When assumption A2 holds, there is no benefit to holding real balances when nominal interest rates are positive. To see why, compare the pecuniary return on dollars, $\mathcal{R}_{t+1}^M = \left(1 - R_t\right)(P_t/P_{t+1})$, with the return on U.S. bonds, $\mathcal{R}_{t+1}^B = R_t P_t/P_{t+1}$. Clearly $\mathcal{R}_{t+1}^M < \mathcal{R}_{t+1}^B$ if $R_t > 1$, so money becomes a redundant asset. By contrast, when $\alpha < \infty$, the total return from an extra dollar is $\mathcal{R}_{t+1}^M - \frac{1}{\alpha} \ln(M_t^h/P_t)$. This return can be larger than $\mathcal{R}_{t+1}^W$ even when $R_t > 1$ if $(M_t^h/P_t) < 1$, so the return on real balances need not be dominated by the return on U.S. bonds. Thus, assumption

(A2) has to be abandoned if there is to be any possible rationale for holding dollars or euros.

Under (A1) we assumed that returns and income had a joint normal distribution conditioned on Ω_t^h. There are two problems here. The first concerns the range of possible realizations for returns. If $\mathcal{R}_{t+1}^B$ is conditionally normally distributed, we can write $\mathcal{R}_{t+1}^B = \mathbb{E}_t^h \mathcal{R}_{t+1}^B + \varsigma_{t+1}$, where ς_{t+1} is the error in forecasting $\mathcal{R}_{t+1}^B$ based on Ω_t^h. Under (A1), ς_{t+1} is normally distributed, so with positive probability realizations of ς_{t+1} will be less than $\mathbb{E}_t^h \mathcal{R}_{t+1}^B$. This, in turn, means that realizations of $\mathcal{R}_{t+1}^B$ will be negative with positive probability, which is actually impossible because $\mathcal{R}_{t+1}^B = R_t P_t / P_{t+1} \geq 0$. Of course, this probability could be extremely small if $\mathbb{E}_t^h \mathcal{R}_{t+1}^B$ is large relative to the variance of ς_{t+1}, so it may be possible to view this implication of (A1) as a "technical problem" that we can live with under certain parameterizations. Indeed, this is the (implicit) view taken by many models in the literature.

The second problem with assumption (A1) is harder to ignore. It arises because we are considering a general equilibrium setting where asset prices are determined endogenously. Recall that

$$\mathcal{R}_{t+1}^B = R_t \left(\frac{P_t}{P_{t+1}} \right),$$

$$\mathcal{R}_{t+1}^{\hat{B}} = \left(\frac{S_{t+1} \hat{R}_t}{S_t} - R_t \right) \left(\frac{P_t}{P_{t+1}} \right),$$

$$\mathcal{R}_{t+1}^M = \left(1 - R_t \right) \left(\frac{P_t}{P_{t+1}} \right),$$

and

$$Y_{t+1}^h = \lambda_t^h \ln S_{t+1} - \tfrac{1}{\alpha} (M_t^h / P_t)(\ln(M_t^h / P_t) - 1),$$

so returns and income are functions of interest rates, $\hat{R}_t$ and R_t, prices, P_t, and the log spot rate, $\ln S_{t+1}$. Note that relative to the period-t information set, uncertainty about future returns and income originates from uncertainty surrounding P_{t+1} and S_{t+1}. Of course both the price level and the spot rate are endogenous variables, so we cannot simply assume that the distribution of P_{t+1} and S_{t+1} conditioned on Ω_t is such that assumption (A1) holds. Rather, the best we can do is conjecture that distribution of P_{t+1} and S_{t+1} in the equilibrium is such that the implied joint distribution of returns and income is normal. We then have to verify that equilibrium prices and the spot rate have the necessary properties. This requires showing that returns and income are conditionally normally distributed when $P_{t+1} = F_P^c(Z_{t+1})$ and $S_{t+1} = F_S^c(Z_{t+1})$ for the pricing function $F^c(\cdot)$ that solves (4.11) given the exogenous distribution of the state Z_{t+1}.

Inspection of the preceding returns and income functions quickly reveals that (A1) cannot hold in equilibria where the spot rate varies stochastically. Since Y_{t+1}^h is a linear function of $\ln S_{t+1}$, the conditional distribution of future income will only be normal if the conditional distribution of the log spot rate is normal as well. However, in this case the return on foreign bonds cannot be normally distributed because $\mathcal{R}_{t+1}^{\hat{B}}$ is a nonlinear function of $\ln S_{t+1}$. In sum, there is no (nondegenerate) distribution for the equilibrium spot rate that delivers joint normality of Y_{t+1}^h and $\mathcal{R}_{t+1}^{\hat{B}}$. Assumption (A1) cannot hold true whatever the form of the true equilibrium pricing function $F^c(\cdot)$.

4.2.2 Approximating the Equilibrium

We have shown that finding the equilibrium in our simple model is not straightforward. Although assumptions (A1) and (A2) allow us to characterize the equilibrium pricing function simply, we cannot use either assumption to find a meaningful solution to the model. At this juncture, we must therefore choose among three options: (1) reformulate the structure of the model, (2) compute a numerical approximation of the equilibrium, or (3) compute an analytical approximation of the equilibrium. Obviously, option (1) is only attractive if we think we can avoid the problems encountered earlier with a reformulation of the model. Option (2) involves finding an approximate numerical solution to the households' and auctioneer's problems simultaneously. This can be a complex task, particularly when we introduce heterogeneous information. Furthermore, it can be quite a challenge to pin down the central economic mechanisms in a model from a set of numerical results. Option (3), by contrast, offers the opportunity to develop some economic insight about the workings of the model. This is the option that Bacchetta and van Wincoop (2006) adopt and we follow.

Bacchetta and van Wincoop make three key assumptions. First, they set the population share parameter, a, arbitrarily close to one. In this setting, equilibrium conditions in the bond markets are determined entirely by U.S. households. Second, they assume that the real interest rate in the U.S. is constant. The third assumption concerns the returns on bonds. Here they employ first-order log approximations around the points where $R_t = \hat{R}_t = 1$, $P_t/P_{t-1} = \hat{P}_t/\hat{P}_{t-1} = 1$, and $S_t/S_{t-1} = 1$:

$$\mathcal{R}_{t+1}^B \cong 1 + r_t - \Delta p_{t+1}, \qquad \hat{\mathcal{R}}_{t+1}^B \cong 1 + \hat{r}_t - \Delta \hat{p}_{t+1},$$

$$\mathcal{R}_{t+1}^{\hat{B}} \cong \Delta s_{t+1} + \hat{r}_t - r_t, \qquad \hat{\mathcal{R}}_{t+1}^B \cong r_t - \hat{r}_t - \Delta s_{t+1}, \qquad (4.12)$$

$$\mathcal{R}_{t+1}^M \cong -r_t, \qquad \hat{\mathcal{R}}_{t+1}^{\hat{M}} \cong -\hat{r}_t,$$

where lowercase letters denote natural logarithms, for example, $s_t = \ln S_t$.

With these assumptions an (approximate) equilibrium comprises a process for log prices, p_t and $\hat{p}_t$, interest rates, r_t and $\hat{r}_t$, and the log spot rate, s_t, that clears markets when households choose their portfolios to maximize utility and returns follow (4.12). This equilibrium is found using the "conjecture and verify method." This method is frequently used to solve for the equilibrium in models where agents hold rational expectations. There are two steps in the procedure: First we conjecture the form of the equilibrium price processes. In our case this involves conjectures about p_t, $\hat{p}_t$, r_t, $\hat{r}_t$, and s_t. This step amounts to guessing the form of the pricing function $F^c(\cdot)$. In the second step we find the asset demands of households consistent with $F^c(\cdot)$ and verify that in aggregate they are consistent with market clearing.

To apply this procedure, we make the following conjecture:

Conjecture 1: *In equilibrium, (i) home prices are constant, and (ii) the joint distribution of the future log spot rate and E.U. price level, s_{t+1} and $\hat{p}_{t+1}$, is normal conditioned on Ω_t, with a constant covariance matrix.*

With this conjecture it is a straightforward matter to find the asset demands of households. First we combine (4.2), (4.4), and (4.12) to give

$$C_{t+1}^h = \left(1 + r_t - \Delta p_{t+1}\right) W_t^h + \left(\Delta s_{t+1} + \hat{r}_t - r_t\right)(S_t \hat{B}_t^h / P_t) - r_t (M_t^h / P_t)$$

$$+ \lambda s_{t+1} - \tfrac{1}{\alpha}(M_t^h / P_t)(\ln(M_t^h / P_t) - 1).$$

Under our conjecture, $\Delta p_{t+1} = 0$, so the distribution of C_{t+1}^h conditional on Ω_t is normal with mean and variance

$$\mathbb{E}_t^h C_{t+1}^h = (1 + r_t) W_t^h + (\mathbb{E}_t^h \Delta s_{t+1} + \hat{r}_t - r_t)(S_t \hat{B}_t^h / P_t) - r_t (M_t^h / P_t)$$

$$+ \lambda \mathbb{E}_t^h s_{t+1} - \tfrac{1}{\alpha}(M_t^h / P_t)(\ln(M_t^h / P_t) - 1) \tag{4.13}$$

and

$$\mathbb{V}_t^h(C_{t+1}^h) = [(S_t \hat{B}_t^h / P_t) + \lambda]^2 \mathbb{V}_t^h(s_{t+1}). \tag{4.14}$$

Hence maximizing expected utility $\mathcal{U}_t^h$ is equivalent to maximizing $u_t^h = \mathbb{E}_t^h C_{t+1}^h - \tfrac{1}{2}\gamma \mathbb{V}_t^h(C_{t+1}^h)$. Substituting (4.13) and (4.14) into this definition and differentiating with respect to M_t^h and $\hat{B}_t^h$ gives us two first-order conditions, which can be written as

$$m_t^h - p_t = -\alpha r_t, \tag{4.15a}$$

$$\hat{B}_t^h = \frac{P_t}{\gamma \sigma_s^2 S_t}(\mathbb{E}_t \Delta s_{t+1} + \hat{r}_t - r_t - \gamma \sigma_s^2 \lambda), \tag{4.15b}$$

where $\sigma_s^2 = \mathbb{V}_t(s_{t+1})$. Proceeding in the same way for E.U. households, we obtain

$$\hat{m}_t^{\hat{h}} - \hat{p}_t = -\alpha \hat{r}_t, \tag{4.16a}$$

$$B_t^{\hat{h}} = \frac{S_t \hat{P}_t}{\gamma \sigma_s^2}(r_t - \hat{r}_t - \mathbb{E}_t \Delta s_{t+1} + \gamma \sigma_s^2 \lambda - \gamma \sigma_{s,\hat{p}} W_t^{\hat{h}}), \tag{4.16b}$$

with $\sigma_{s,\hat{p}} = \mathbb{CV}_t(s_{t+1}, \hat{p}_{t+1})$. Since all households have the same information, the expectations in (4.15b) and (4.16b) drop the h superscript.

Equations (4.15a) and (4.16a) give us the log demand for real balances from U.S. and E.U. households, respectively. These demand functions take the same form for all households within each country. Note, also, that neither demand depends on consumption or income. This simplifying feature of the model arises from the specification of the production function in (4.4).

Equations (4.15b) and (4.16b) describe the demand for E.U. and U.S. bonds by U.S. and E.U. households. Households care about the real value of their bond holdings $(S_t \hat{B}_t^h / P_t$ and $B_t^{\hat{h}} / S_t \hat{P}_t)$, so the number of bonds demanded is decreasing in the real domestic price of the bonds (i.e., S_t / P_t for E.U. bonds purchased by U.S. households and $1/S_t \hat{P}_t$ for U.S. bonds purchased by E.U. households). Demands are also an increasing function of expected excess returns and are decreasing in the variance of the returns σ_s^2. Greater risk-aversion, γ, reduces the sensitivity of demand to expected excess returns. The demand for bonds also depends on their usefulness as a hedge against other shocks. These shocks can come from income and E.U. inflation.

The parameter λ determines the usefulness of bonds as a hedge against income shocks. To illustrate, consider the hedging role of E.U. bonds to U.S. households. If $\lambda < 0$, an unexpected depreciation of the dollar will be associated with a lower than expected future income, Y_{t+1}^h. U.S. households can offset this effect on their future consumption by structuring their bond holdings so that the value of their portfolios will offset the loss of income. As foreign bonds enjoy high returns when the spot rate depreciates, this is achieved by taking a larger position in E.U. bonds, as can be seen in the last term in (4.15b). U.S. bonds can also act as a hedge against inflation for E.U. households. If the log spot rate and E.U. inflation are negatively correlated (i.e., $\sigma_{s,\hat{p}} < 0$) unexpected returns on U.S. bonds and the E.U. endowment will also be negatively correlated [i.e., $\mathbb{CV}_t(\hat{\mathcal{R}}_{t+1}^{\hat{B}}, \hat{\mathcal{R}}_{t+1}^B) < 0$ from (4.12)], so the bonds will provide a hedge against the endowment's loss of purchasing power from inflation. The last term on the right-hand side of (4.16b) identifies this hedging effect on the demand for U.S. bonds by E.U. households.

The next step is to combine the asset demands in (4.15) and (4.16) with the market-clearing conditions in order to derive the properties of equilibrium prices, interest rates, and the spot rate. In so doing, we check the validity of Conjecture 1.

Let us begin with the U.S. money market. Recall that the U.S. real interest rate is assumed to be constant. Thus under the conjecture of zero U.S. inflation, the nominal interest rate equals the real rate, a constant, r. Under these circumstances, (4.15a) implies that the demand for dollars by all U.S. households is proportional to the price level, and hence the aggregate demand for dollars is simply $M_t = a P_t \exp(-\alpha r)$. Thus, if the U.S. money supply is fixed at M, market clearing implies that the price level satisfies $a P_t \exp(-\alpha r) = M$ or $P_t = \frac{1}{a} M \exp(-\alpha r)$, a constant, P. We have therefore verified the first part of the conjecture.

Next, consider the market for E.U. bonds. Here is where the large-country assumption comes into play. With the U.S.'s share of the world population a arbitrarily close to one, the demand for bonds by E.U. households makes no significant contribution to the aggregate demand for bonds. Since all bonds are in zero net supply, the market-clearing condition for E.U. bonds therefore simplifies to $0 = \int_0^a \hat{B}_t^h dh$. Substituting for $\hat{B}_t^h$ from (4.15b) in this condition and rearranging gives

$$\mathbb{E}_t \Delta s_{t+1} + \hat{r}_t - r_t = \lambda \gamma \sigma_s^2. \tag{4.17}$$

This equation identifies the value for the expected log return on E.U. bonds consistent with market clearing.

We can now verify the remaining part of the conjecture. First we combine the aggregate demands for dollars and euros from (4.15a) and (4.16a), $M_t = a P_t \exp(-\alpha r_t)$ and $\hat{M}_t = (1 - a) \hat{P}_t \exp(-\alpha \hat{r}_t)$, to get

$$m_t - \hat{m}_t = \ln\left(\frac{a}{1-a}\right) + p_t - \hat{p}_t - \alpha(r_t - \hat{r}_t). \tag{4.18}$$

In our simple setup there is a single good and no transport costs between countries. Therefore, the Law of One Price holds in equilibrium, that is, $P_t = S_t \hat{P}_t$, or in logs,

$$p_t = s_t + \hat{p}_t. \tag{4.19}$$

Combining this PPP condition with (4.18) and (4.17) gives

$$s_t = b\mathbb{E}_t s_{t+1} + f_t, \tag{4.20}$$

where $b = \alpha/(1 + \alpha)$ and exchange-rate fundamentals are

$$f_t = f - (1 - b)\left(\hat{m}_t - \hat{m}\right),$$

with $f = (1 - b)\left(m - \hat{m} - \ln\left(\frac{a}{1-a}\right)\right) - b\lambda\gamma\sigma_s^2$.

The final step is to solve (4.20) using the process for the money supply in (4.5). Iterating (4.20) forward with the "no bubble" assumption, $\lim_{i\to\infty} \mathbb{E}_t b^i s_{t+i} = 0$, we find that

$$s_t = \frac{1}{1-b}f + \mathbb{E}_t \sum_{i=0}^{\infty} b^i \left(f_{t+i} - f\right)$$

$$= \frac{1}{1-b}f - (1-b)\sum_{i=0}^{\infty} b^i \mathbb{E}_t \left(\hat{m}_{t+i} - \hat{m}\right)$$

$$= \frac{1}{1-b}f - \frac{1-b}{1-b\rho}\left(\hat{m}_t - \hat{m}\right). \tag{4.21}$$

Thus, under our conjecture, the log spot rate is proportional to the log E.U. money supply. Now since the distribution of $\hat{m}_{t+1}$ conditional on Ω_t is normal with variance σ^2, the distribution of s_{t+1} must also be normal with variance $\sigma_s^2 = \left(\frac{1-b}{1-b\rho}\right)^2\sigma^2$. Finally, note that with constant U.S. prices, the PPP condition in (4.19) implies that $\Delta\hat{p}_{t+1} = -\Delta s_{t+1}$. As a consequence, the conditional distribution of $\hat{p}_{t+1}$ must also be normal and the conditional covariance matrix for s_{t+1} and $\hat{p}_{t+1}$ must be constant. This completes the verification of our conjecture.

We have now shown that an approximate rational expectations equilibrium can be found under the assumptions that: (1) the U.S. real interest rate is constant, (2) the U.S. is large, and (3) returns are well characterized by the approximations in (4.12).

It is important to appreciate the role played by these assumptions. If the U.S. real interest rate varied, so too would U.S. inflation. In that case, the demand for E.U. bonds by U.S. households would contain an inflation-hedging term analogous to the last term in (4.16b). Under these circumstances, the expected log return on E.U. bonds required by market clearing would also depend on the endowments of U.S. households. Similarly, if we relaxed the large-country assumption, market clearing in the E.U. bond market would depend on the demand from both U.S. and E.U. households. In this case, the equilibrium expected log excess return would depend on the endowments of E.U. households because part of their demand for bonds is driven by the desire to hedge against inflation. Thus, assumptions (1) and (2) are both necessary to keep endowments out of the equilibrium spot rate equation.

To summarize, we have gone to some lengths to develop a simple model for the spot rate based on the optimizing decisions of many households. In particular, we have shown that it is a nontrivial problem to find the rational expectations equilibrium even when households have the same information, preferences, and access to the same technology. In other words, the fictional Walrasian auctioneer has a tough job even in relatively simple environments. It should come as no surprise that the job gets much harder when households have heterogeneous information.

4.3   Equilibrium with Heterogeneous Information

We now introduce heterogeneity into our simple model. In particular, we now assume that the income process for each U.S. household has a different hedging parameter, λ_t^h:

$$Y_{t+1}^h = \lambda_t^h s_{t+1} - \tfrac{1}{\alpha}(M_t^h/P_t)(\ln(M_t^h/P_t) - 1).$$

We further assume that λ_t^h comprises a common component, λ_t, and an idiosyncratic component, ξ_t^h:

$$\lambda_t^h = \lambda_t + \xi_t^h, \tag{4.22}$$

where $\xi_t^h \sim$ i.i.d. $N(0, \sigma_\xi^2)$, for all $h \in [0, a)$. Thus, the idiosyncratic components have a mean of zero and are uncorrelated across households. The Weak Law of Large Numbers implies that $\frac{1}{a}\int_0^a \xi_t^h dh = 0$, so the average value of λ_t^h in the United States is $\frac{1}{a}\int_0^a \lambda_t^h dh = \frac{1}{a}\int_0^a \lambda_t dh + \frac{1}{a}\int_0^a \xi_t^h dh = \lambda_t$. We assume that this average follows a random walk:

$$\lambda_t = \lambda_{t-1} + v_t,$$

where $v_t \sim$ i.i.d. $N(0, \sigma_v^2)$. Each U.S. household knows the value of its own hedging parameter, λ_t^h, but not the values for other households. We assume, however, that the average value for λ_t^h from the previous period is known by all. The evolution of household $h's$ information is therefore represented by

$$\Omega_t^h = \{P_t, \hat{P}_t, R_t, \hat{R}_t, S_t, \lambda_t^h, \hat{M}_t, \lambda_{t-1}\} \cup \Omega_{t-1}^h. \tag{4.23}$$

The remainder of the model is unchanged: (1) the U.S. money supply and real interest rate remain fixed, (2) the U.S. country is large (i.e., a is close to one), and (3) the E.U. money supply follows equation (4.5).

To solve the model we again employ the conjecture and verify method. In particular we make the following conjecture.

Conjecture 2: *In equilibrium, (i) home prices are constant, so $\hat{p}_t = -s_t$, and (ii) the equilibrium log spot rate is given by*

$$s_t = \eta_0 + \eta_1(\hat{m}_t - \hat{m}) + \eta_2\lambda_{t-1} + \eta_3 v_t, \tag{4.24}$$

for some coefficients η_i.

This conjecture is more specific than Conjecture 1. Given our assumptions about the v_t shocks and the process for the E.U. money supply, it implies that the joint distribution of $\hat{p}_{t+1}$ and s_{t+1} conditioned on Ω_t^h is indeed normal. Beyond that, equation (4.24) provides an explicit conjecture about the relationship between the equilibrium spot rate and the exogenous variables. As we shall see, we need this greater degree of specificity in order to solve the inference problem facing households as they determine their asset demands.

We now have to verify that the conjectured behavior for prices and the spot rate are consistent with market clearing given the optimal behavior of households based on their individual information sets. As before, the U.S. households' demands for money and foreign bonds are derived by maximizing u_t^h with respect to M_t^h and $\hat{B}_t^h$ subject to (4.2) and (4.4). This gives

$$m_t^h - p_t = -\alpha r_t, \tag{4.25a}$$

$$\hat{B}_t^h = \frac{P_t}{\gamma \sigma_s^2 S_t} \left(\mathbb{E}_t^h \Delta s_{t+1} + \hat{r}_t - r_t - \gamma \sigma_s^2 \lambda_t^h \right). \tag{4.25b}$$

Following the same procedure for E.U. households produces

$$\hat{m}_t^{\hat{h}} - \hat{p}_t = -\alpha \hat{r}_t, \tag{4.26a}$$

$$B_t^{\hat{h}} = \frac{S_t \hat{P}_t}{\gamma \sigma_s^2} \left(r_t - \mathbb{E}_t^{\hat{h}} \Delta s_{t+1} - \hat{r}_t - \gamma \sigma_s^2 \lambda - \gamma \sigma_{s,\hat{p}} W_t^{\hat{h}} \right). \tag{4.26b}$$

Note that the money demand equations (4.25a) and (4.26a) have the same form as they did when there was homogeneous information. The demand for real balances is the same across all households within each country, so heterogeneity plays no role in the determination of money market equilibrium. This means that we can verify part (i) of our conjecture in exactly the same way. Heterogeneity appears in the bond demand equations (4.25b) and (4.26b), via the conditional expectations terms, and in the hedging parameters.

Next, we invoke the large-country assumption. Recall that under this assumption the demand for bonds by E.U. households makes no significant contribution to the aggregate demand for bonds. Hence, market clearing in the E.U. bond market requires that $0 = \int_0^a \hat{B}_t^h dh$. Substituting for $\hat{B}_t^h$ from (4.25b), we find that

$$\frac{1}{a} \int_0^a (\mathbb{E}_t^h \Delta s_{t+1}) \, dh + \hat{r}_t - r_t = \gamma \sigma_s^2 \frac{1}{a} \int_0^a \lambda_t^h dh$$

or

$$\overline{\mathbb{E}}_t s_{t+1} - s_t + \hat{r}_t - r_t = \gamma \sigma_s^2 \lambda_t, \tag{4.27}$$

where $\overline{\mathbb{E}}_t s_{t+1} = \frac{1}{a} \int_0^a \mathbb{E}_t^h[s_{t+1}] dh$ is the average of U.S. households' expectations concerning the future spot rate. In deriving (4.27) we have used the facts that $\frac{1}{a} \int_0^a \lambda_t^h dh = \lambda_t$ and $\frac{1}{a} \int_0^a \mathbb{E}_t^h[s_t] dh = s_t$ because the current spot rate is known to all households in period t. Combining (4.27) with equations (4.25a), (4.26a), and the PPP condition as before, we find

$$s_t = b \overline{\mathbb{E}}_t s_{t+1} + f_t, \tag{4.28}$$

where exchange-rate fundamentals are now

$$f_t = f - (1 - b)(\hat{m}_t - \hat{m}) - \gamma \sigma_s^2 b \lambda_t,$$

with $f = (1 - b)\left(m - \hat{m} - \ln\left(\frac{a}{1-a}\right)\right)$.

Equation (4.28) provides the first indication of how the presence of heterogeneous information will affect the equilibrium behavior of the spot rate. It says that the current spot rate depends on fundamentals and on the average expectation concerning the future spot rate, $\overline{\mathbb{E}}_t s_{t+1}$. Since home households have private information concerning their hedging parameters, λ_t^h, and λ_t is now part of fundamentals, the model raises the possibility that households hold different expectations regarding the future spot rate.

Up to this point we have shown that under Conjecture 2, optimal behavior by households and market clearing require that the log spot rate satisfy (4.28). To complete our verification of the conjecture, and hence characterize the rational expectations equilibrium of the model, we have to show that the conjectured process in (4.24) is consistent with (4.28) given the information available to households. For this purpose, we first lead (4.24) by one period and take expectations conditioned on Ω_t^h:

$$\mathbb{E}_t^h s_{t+1} = \eta_0 + \eta_1 \mathbb{E}_t^h(\hat{m}_{t+1} - \hat{m}) + \eta_2 \mathbb{E}_t^h \lambda_t + \eta_3 \mathbb{E}_t^h v_{t+1}$$

$$= \eta_0 + \eta_1 \rho(\hat{m}_t - \hat{m}) + \eta_2 \mathbb{E}_t^h v_t + \eta_2 \lambda_{t-1}. \tag{4.29}$$

Note that if we average this equation across U.S. households, we will find an expression for $\overline{\mathbb{E}}_t s_{t+1}$ consistent with (4.24). To do this we first have to compute $\mathbb{E}_t^h v_t$. Now under our assumptions, the joint distribution of v_t and λ_t^h conditioned on λ_{t-1} is normal:

$$\begin{pmatrix} v_t \\ \lambda_t^h \end{pmatrix} \sim N \left(\begin{pmatrix} 0 \\ \lambda_{t-1} \end{pmatrix} : \begin{pmatrix} \sigma_v^2 & \sigma_v^2 \\ \sigma_v^2 & \sigma_v^2 + \sigma_\xi^2 \end{pmatrix} \right).$$

This observation allows us to compute the expectation of v_t conditioned on λ_{t-1} and λ_t^h using the properties of the bivariate normal distribution. In particular, Appendix 4.A.2 shows that

$$\mathbb{E}_t[v_t | \lambda_t^h, \lambda_{t-1}] = \beta(\lambda_t^h - \lambda_{t-1}), \tag{4.30}$$

where $\beta = \sigma_v^2/(\sigma_v^2 + \sigma_\xi^2)$. Note that λ_t^h and λ_{t-1} are known to household h in period t (i.e., $\{\lambda_t^h, \lambda_{t-1}\} \in \Omega_t^h$), so $\mathbb{E}_t[v_t | \lambda_t^h, \lambda_{t-1}]$ will equal $\mathbb{E}_t^h v_t$ *provided* there are no other elements of Ω_t^h that can be used to improve the precision of the estimates. More formally, $\mathbb{E}_t^h v_t = \mathbb{E}_t[v_t | \lambda_t^h, \lambda_{t-1}]$ if, and only if, $\mathbb{V}_t[v_t | \lambda_t^h, \lambda_{t-1}] \leq \mathbb{V}_t[v_t | \lambda_t^h, \lambda_{t-1}, \Omega_t^h]$.

For the present, we proceed under the assumption that $\mathbb{E}_t^h v_t = \mathbb{E}_t[v_t | \lambda_t^h, \lambda_{t-1}]$. Combining this equality with (4.29) and (4.30) and averaging over households gives

$$\overline{\mathbb{E}}_t s_{t+1} = \eta_0 + \eta_1 \rho(\hat{m}_t - \hat{m}) + \eta_2 \beta v_t + \eta_2 \lambda_{t-1}. \tag{4.31}$$

Substituting this expression for $\overline{\mathbb{E}}_t s_{t+1}$ and (4.24) for s_t in (4.28) yields

$$\eta_0 + \eta_1(\hat{m}_t - \hat{m}) + \eta_2 \lambda_{t-1} + \eta_3 v_t = b \left\{ \eta_0 + \eta_1 \rho(\hat{m}_t - \hat{m}) + \eta_2 \beta v_t + \eta_2 \lambda_{t-1} \right\}$$
$$+ f - (1 - b)(\hat{m}_t - \hat{m}) - \gamma \sigma_s^2 b \left(\lambda_{t-1} + v_t \right).$$

If our conjecture is valid, this equation must hold for all values of $\hat{m}_t$, v_t, and λ_{t-1}. Since the same variables appear on both sides of the equation, this requirement will be satisfied if the η_i's satisfy the following restrictions:

$$\eta_0 = b\eta_0 + f, \quad \eta_1 = b\eta_1\rho + b - 1, \quad \eta_2 = b\eta_2 - b\gamma\sigma_s^2, \quad \text{and} \quad \eta_3 = b\beta\eta_2 - \gamma\sigma_s^2 b.$$

Solving these equations and substituting the results in (4.24) gives

$$s_t = \frac{f}{1-b} - \frac{1-b}{1-b\rho}(\hat{m}_t - \hat{m}) - \frac{b\gamma\sigma_s^2}{1-b}\lambda_{t-1} + \frac{(b - \beta b - 1)b\gamma\sigma_s^2}{1-b}v_t. \quad (4.32)$$

Equation (4.32) gives us the equilibrium behavior of the log spot rate under the assumption that U.S. households form expectations with $\mathbb{E}_t[v_t|\lambda_t^h, \lambda_{t-1}] = \beta(\lambda_t^h - \lambda_{t-1})$. The first two terms on the right-hand side match our solution for the equilibrium spot rate under homogeneous information in (4.21). Thus, the presence of heterogeneous information per se does not affect the relationship between the spot rate and a traditional variable such as the money stock. Heterogeneity does, however, add two new terms, v_t and λ_{t-1}. These terms appear because the average hedging parameter λ_t is now a component of fundamentals [see (4.28)], and households' expectations concerning λ_t affect the average expectation of the future spot rate, $\overline{\mathbb{E}}_t s_{t+1}$.

4.3.1 Informational Efficiency and the Grossman Paradox

Equation (4.32) does *not* describe the equilibrium dynamics of the spot rate in a rational expectations equilibrium. This may seem surprising because we verified that Conjecture 2 is consistent with market clearing given the asset demands of households. Note, however, that our verification procedure *assumed* that $\mathbb{E}_t^h v_t = \mathbb{E}_t[v_t|\lambda_t^h, \lambda_{t-1}]$. In other words, all we have shown is that (4.32) could describe the equilibrium behavior of the spot rate if the most precise estimates of v_t available to household h depend only on λ_t^h and λ_{t-1}. If there is another variable, say, $\varkappa_t^h \in \Omega_t^h$, such that $\mathbb{V}_t[v_t|\lambda_t^h, \lambda_{t-1}] > \mathbb{V}_t[v_t|\lambda_t^h, \lambda_{t-1}, \varkappa_t^h]$, then household expectations will be different and (4.32) will not be consistent with market clearing. Candidate variables for $\varkappa_t^h$ include period-t prices, interest rates, and the spot rate. If any or all of these variables allow for more precise estimates of v_t, we need a new expression for the equilibrium spot rate.

The most obvious candidate among these variables is the spot rate. From equation (4.32) we see that the log spot rate depends on the E.U. money stock, $\hat{m}_t$, the lagged hedging parameter, λ_{t-1}, and v_t. If this relationship holds up in the true rational expectations equilibrium, then each household will be able to precisely estimate v_t as a linear combination of $\{s_t, \hat{m}_t, \lambda_{t-1}\} \in \Omega_t^h$.

To see whether this reasoning is correct, let us return to the verification of Conjecture 2 with $\mathbb{E}_t^h v_t = v_t$ replacing (4.30). Combining this equality with (4.29) and averaging over households now gives

$$\overline{\mathbb{E}}_t s_{t+1} = \eta_0 + \eta_1 \rho(\hat{m}_t - \hat{m}) + \eta_2 \lambda_{t-1} + \eta_2 v_t.$$

This equation has the same form as (4.31) with $\beta = 1$. Thus proceeding as before, we obtain

$$s_t = \frac{f}{1-b} - \frac{1-b}{1-b\rho}(\hat{m}_t - \hat{m}) - \frac{b\gamma \sigma_s^2}{1-b}\lambda_{t-1} - \frac{b\gamma \sigma_s^2}{1-b}v_t. \tag{4.33}$$

This equation does describe the equilibrium dynamics of the spot rate in the rational expectations equilibrium. Not only is it consistent with market clearing given the asset demands of households, but it also implies that v_t can be found as a linear combination of a constant, s_t, $\hat{m}_t$, and λ_{t-1}, which are all elements of Ω_t^h. Thus, $\mathbb{E}_t^h v_t = v_t$.

Equation (4.33) also describes a mapping between information and the spot rate. This mapping is a hallmark of rational expectations models and can be distinguished according to two criteria:

- Strong-, Semistrong-, and Weak-form efficiency
- Full versus partial revelation

An asset price is said to be Strong-form informationally efficient when its equilibrium value reveals a sufficient statistic for all the information in the economy. A price is Semistrong-form efficient when it reflects only public information, and Weak-form efficient when it only reflects the past history of prices. The distinction between fully and partially revealing prices depends on the inferences that can be drawn from observing prices. In cases where everyone can precisely infer all private and public information, the (set of) prices is said to be fully revealing. Asset prices are partially revealing when the inferences are imprecise.

Equation (4.33) shows that the spot rate is Strong-form efficient in our model. The spot rate reveals the value of v_t, which is a sufficient statistic for all the private information in our model. This is easily seen once we write λ_t^h as $\lambda_{t-1} + v_t + \xi_t^h$. Recall that $\lambda_{t-1} \in \Omega_t^h$, so the private information available to each household in period t is $v_t + \xi_t^h$. Although the ξ_t^h component affects the demand for bonds from each household, these idiosyncratic terms disappear from the market-clearing condition, and so have no impact on the equilibrium spot rate. Thus v_t represents the only price-relevant component of households' private information and is fully reflected by the spot rate. By contrast, the spot rate is not fully revealing about the hedging parameters. In other words, the form of the spot rate equation does not imply that $\mathbb{E}_t^h \lambda_t^j = \lambda_t^j$ for $h \neq j$. Rather, $\mathbb{E}_t^h \lambda_t^j = \lambda_t$ for all $j \neq h$, so the spot rate is partially revealing.

Equation (4.33) has one further interesting implication. Suppose that all households were given the opportunity to communicate at the start of period t and that as a result of these communications, they learned the average value for λ_t^h, that is, λ_t. Sharing information in this way would have no effect on the equilibrium spot rate (prices or interest rates). Each household would derive its demand for E.U. bonds using λ_t^h and expectations concerning the future spot rate based on $v_t = \lambda_t - \lambda_{t-1}$, so the requirements of market clearing would be exactly the same. From this perspective, it becomes clear that the equilibrium spot rate *aggregates* information. In equilibrium, households need not communicate directly in order to learn about the state of the economy; they can simply look at the current spot rate.

A presence of Strong-form informationally efficient asset prices in a rational expectations equilibrium can sometimes lead to the Grossman paradox (Grossman 1976). To see how this arises, consider the equilibrium log excess return on foreign bonds expected by household h:

$$\mathbb{E}_t^h[\Delta s_{t+1} + \hat{r}_t - r_t] = \text{const.} + \gamma \sigma_s^2 \lambda_{t-1} + \gamma \sigma_s^2 \mathbb{E}_t^h v_t.$$

Household expectations of log excess returns depend on their estimates of v_t. When the spot rate is fully revealing, $\mathbb{E}_t^h v_t = v_t$ and all households hold the same expectations regarding excess returns. Moreover, these expectations do not depend on their own private information, λ_t^h, because $\mathbb{E}_t^h v_t$ is a function of just s_t, $\hat{m}_t$, and λ_{t-1}. Now *if* the demand for E.U. bonds only differed across households because expected returns differed, the aggregate demand for bonds would be independent of the λ_t^h's, and, under these circumstances, the market-clearing spot rate could not reveal the value of v_t. In other words, if individual households lack the incentive to incorporate their private information into their asset demands because prices are informationally efficient, how can market-clearing prices aggregate the private information? In this model we avoid the Grossman paradox because household h's demand for E.U. bonds depends on both expected excess returns and the hedging parameter, λ_t^h. This means that the aggregate demand for E.U. bonds remains a function of the λ_t^h's even though all households exploit the informational efficiency of the spot rate in computing $\mathbb{E}_t^h \Delta s_{t+1} + \hat{r}_t - r_t$.

4.3.2 Higher-Order Expectations

We now consider how the presence of information heterogeneity can affect the dynamics of the spot rate. In particular we examine the role played by higher-order expectations. Recall that market clearing in the E.U. bond market requires that the log spot rate satisfy

$$s_t = b\overline{\mathbb{E}}_t s_{t+1} + f_t, \tag{4.34}$$

where f_t identifies fundamentals and $\overline{\mathbb{E}}_t$ denotes the average expectations of U.S. households. Leading this equation forward by one period to give

$$s_{t+1} = b\overline{\mathbb{E}}_{t+1}[s_{t+2}] + f_{t+1}$$

and substituting for s_{t+1} in (4.34), we find that

$$s_t = b^2 \overline{\mathbb{E}}_t \overline{\mathbb{E}}_{t+1}[s_{t+2}] + f_t + b\overline{\mathbb{E}}_t f_{t+1}.$$

Repeatedly solving for the future spot rate in this manner yields

$$s_t = f_t + \sum_{i=1}^{\infty} b^i \overline{\mathbb{E}}_t^i f_{t+i} + \lim_{i \to \infty} b^i \overline{\mathbb{E}}_t^i f_{t+i}, \tag{4.35}$$

where higher-order expectations are defined by

$$\overline{\mathbb{E}}_t^i[x_{t+1}] = \overline{\mathbb{E}}_t \left[\overline{\mathbb{E}}_{t+1}^{i-1}[x_{t+1}] \right]$$

and $\overline{\mathbb{E}}_t^1 x_{t+1} = \overline{\mathbb{E}}_t x_{t+1}$. If we further conjecture (and verify) that the second term on the right of (4.35) equals zero, we finally obtain

$$s_t = f_t + \sum_{i=1}^{\infty} b^i \overline{\mathbb{E}}_t^i f_{t+i}. \tag{4.36}$$

Equation (4.36) represents the equilibrium log spot rate as a function of all household expectations concerning fundamentals. Note that this is *not* a standard present value relation. The equation says that the period-t spot rate is a weighted sum of: (1) current fundamentals, f_t, (2) the average expectation at t of f_{t+1}, $\overline{\mathbb{E}}_t^1 f_{t+1}$, (3) the average expectation at t over the average expectation at $t+1$ concerning f_{t+2}, $\overline{\mathbb{E}}_t^2 f_{t+2} = \overline{\mathbb{E}}_t \overline{\mathbb{E}}_{t+1} f_{t+2}$, and so on. When all households hold the same expectations regarding future fundamentals, the average expectation $\overline{\mathbb{E}}_{t+1} f_{t+2}$ equals $\mathbb{E}_{t+1}^h f_{t+2}$ for all h, and so $\overline{\mathbb{E}}_t^2 f_{t+1} = \overline{\mathbb{E}}_t \mathbb{E}_{t+1}^h f_{t+2} = \mathbb{E}_t^h \mathbb{E}_{t+1}^h f_{t+2}$. But, by the Law of Iterated Expectations $\mathbb{E}_t^h \mathbb{E}_{t+1}^h f_{t+2} = \mathbb{E}_t^h f_{t+2}$, so under these circumstances $\overline{\mathbb{E}}_t^2 f_{t+1} = \overline{\mathbb{E}}_t f_{t+2}$. Applying this same logic to all the higher-order expectations in (4.36) gives

$$s_t = f_t + \overline{\mathbb{E}}_t \sum_{i=1}^{\infty} b^i f_{t+i}, \tag{4.37}$$

which is the familiar present value relation. This simplification only occurs if first-order expectations concerning all future fundamentals are equivalent to higher-order expectations. Understanding when this equivalence breaks down is the key to understanding the impact of heterogeneous information.

We can gain a better perspective on the difference between (4.36) and (4.37) by returning to difference equation (4.34). In particular, we first combine (4.34) with the identity $\overline{\mathbb{E}}_t s_{t+1} = \mathbb{E}_t^h s_{t+1} - (\mathbb{E}_t^h s_{t+1} - \overline{\mathbb{E}}_t s_{t+1})$ to get

$$s_t = b\mathbb{E}_t^h s_{t+1} + f_t - b(\mathbb{E}_t^h s_{t+1} - \overline{\mathbb{E}}_t s_{t+1}).$$

Next, we iterate forward as before, applying the Law of Iterated Expectations to the forecasts of household h (i.e., $\mathbb{E}_t^h \mathbb{E}_{t+1}^h s_{t+2} = \mathbb{E}_t^h s_{t+2}$, etc.). This yields

$$s_t = f_t + \mathbb{E}_t^h \sum_{i=1}^{\infty} b^i f_{t+i} - \mathbb{E}_t^h \sum_{i=o}^{\infty} b^{i+1} \left(s_{t+1+i} - \overline{\mathbb{E}}_{t+i} s_{t+1+i} \right)$$

$$+ \lim_{i \to \infty} b^i \mathbb{E}_t^h \left[s_{t+i} + b \left(\overline{\mathbb{E}}_{t+i} s_{t+1+i} - \mathbb{E}_{t+i}^h s_{t+1+i} \right) \right].$$

As before, we focus on the so-called "no-bubble" case in which the limit term in the second line equals zero. Imposing this constraint and averaging across the U.S.

households gives

$$s_t = f_t + \overline{\mathbb{E}}_t \sum_{i=1}^{\infty} b^i f_{t+i} - \overline{\mathbb{E}}_t \sum_{i=o}^{\infty} b^{i+1} \left(s_{t+1+i} - \overline{\mathbb{E}}_{t+i} s_{t+1+i} \right). \qquad (4.38)$$

Equation (4.38) decomposes the equilibrium log spot rate into three terms. The first two comprise current fundamentals plus the expected present value of future fundamentals averaged across households. Note that these terms are identical to the right-hand side of (4.37). The third term is the average expectation of the present value of future average forecast errors. This term equals zero when all households have the same information because

$$\overline{\mathbb{E}}_t[s_{t+1+i} - \overline{\mathbb{E}}_{t+i} s_{t+1+i}] = \mathbb{E}_t^h[s_{t+1+i} - \mathbb{E}_{t+i}^h s_{t+1+i}] = 0.$$

However, when households have different information, individual households may be able to forecast the average future forecast error $s_{t+1+i} - \overline{\mathbb{E}}_{t+i} s_{t+1+i}$, so that $\mathbb{E}_t^h[s_{t+1+i} - \overline{\mathbb{E}}_{t+i} s_{t+1+i}] \neq 0$. In other words, individual households may make private forecasts for the future spot rate that differ from their forecast of future expectations averaged across the market, $\mathbb{E}_t^h s_{t+1+i} \neq \mathbb{E}_t^h \overline{\mathbb{E}}_{t+i} s_{t+1+i}$. As we shall see, this need not happen in every case where households have different information. But when it does, it will be the reason why higher-order expectations concerning future fundamentals impact on the behavior of the spot rate.

In the next two subsections we consider two modifications to our basic model that illustrate how the presence of heterogeneous information can impact on exchange-rate behavior. The first illustrates how heterogeneity can distort the impact of shocks on the exchange rate via a process termed "rational confusion." Our second modification allows us to study the role of higher-order expectations.

4.3.3 Heterogeneous Information and Rational Confusion

Up to this point, we have assumed that differences in the hedging parameter, λ_t^h, are the only source of heterogeneity across households. We now introduce a second source of heterogeneity, private information about the future path of fundamentals. In particular we assume that each household receives a signal about the shock to the next period's E.U. money supply:

$$u_t^h = \hat{u}_{t+1} + \zeta_t^h, \qquad (4.39)$$

where $\zeta_t^h \sim \text{i.i.d.} N(0, \sigma_\zeta^2)$ for all $h \in [0, a)$. Recall that $\hat{u}_{t+1}$ is the shock to the E.U. money supply in period $t + 1$. Thus u_t^h represents private information about future monetary policy with idiosyncratic noise ζ_t^h, where $\frac{1}{a} \int_0^a \zeta_t^h dh = 0$. All other aspects of the model remain the same except for the evolution of household h's information. This is now represented by

$$\Omega_t^h = \left\{ P_t, \hat{P}_t, R_t, \hat{R}_t, S_t, \hat{M}_t, \lambda_t^h, u_t^h, \lambda_{t-1} \right\} \cup \Omega_{t-1}^h. \qquad (4.40)$$

Note that there are now two sources of heterogeneity in household information sets, the values of λ_t^h and u_t^h. As we shall see, the greater degree of heterogeneity destroys the Strong-form informational efficiency of the equilibrium spot rate, makes household inferences more complex, and is the source of rational confusion.

Once again we employ the conjecture and verify method to find the equilibrium behavior of the spot rate.

Conjecture 3: *In equilibrium, (i) home prices are constant, so $\hat{p}_t = -s_t$ and (ii) the equilibrium log spot rate is given by*

$$s_t = \eta_0 + \eta_1(\hat{m}_t - \hat{m}) + \eta_2\lambda_{t-1} + \eta_3 v_t + \eta_4\hat{u}_{t+1} \tag{4.41}$$

for some coefficients η_i.

Conjecture 3 adds $\hat{u}_{t+1}$ as a determinant of the period-t log spot rate. This may seem strange at first sight because no household knows the value of $\hat{u}_{t+1}$ in period t. Nevertheless, we include $\hat{u}_{t+1}$ in (4.41) under the conjecture that individual household demands for E.U. bonds will depend in part on u_t^h. This being the case, the aggregate demand for bonds will depend on the common component of the u_t^h's, namely $\hat{u}_{t+1}$. As a consequence, $\hat{u}_{t+1}$ will affect the market-clearing spot rate even though $\hat{u}_{t+1} \notin \Omega_t^h$ for all h. In sum, therefore, our conjecture in (4.41) is that the equilibrium spot rate *aggregates* information in the private signals concerning future fundamentals, that is, E.U. monetary policy.

The key step in verifying this conjecture is finding $\mathbb{E}_t^h \hat{u}_{t+1}$ and $\mathbb{E}_t^h \lambda_t$. Households will find it expedient to use both their private and public information to compute these expectations. In particular, note that according to (4.41), observations on s_t, $\hat{m}_t$, and λ_{t-1} provide information on a linear combination of the v_t and $\hat{u}_{t+1}$ shocks:

$$z_t = s_t - \eta_0 - \eta_1(\hat{m}_t - \hat{m}) - \eta_2\lambda_{t-1} = \eta_3 v_t + \eta_4\hat{u}_{t+1}.$$

The variable z_t provides a second signal on the values of v_t and $\hat{u}_{t+1}$ beyond the values of u_t^h and λ_t^h known to each household. As a result, estimates of v_t and $\hat{u}_{t+1}$ using u_t^h, λ_t^h, and z_t will be more precise than estimates using private information alone. In fact, under our conjecture, there is no way to combine the elements of Ω_t^h to form a third signal on the values of v_t and $\hat{u}_{t+1}$, so estimates using u_t^h, λ_t^h, and z_t will be the most precise ones available. These estimates are easily computed once we note that the joint distribution of $\{v_t, \hat{u}_{t+1}, z_t, u_t^h, \lambda_t^h\}$ is normal conditioned on Ω_t^h. In particular, applying the projection theorem in this case gives

$$\mathbb{E}_t^h \hat{u}_{t+1} = \beta_u u_t^h + \psi_u(\lambda_t^h - \lambda_{t-1}) + \kappa_u z_t \quad \text{and} \quad \mathbb{E}_t^h v_t = \beta_v u_t^h + \psi_v(\lambda_t^h - \lambda_{t-1}) + \kappa_v z_t,$$

where

$$\beta_u = \sigma_\xi^2 \sigma_v^2 \sigma_u^2 \eta_3^2 / \Xi, \qquad \psi_u = -\sigma_\xi^2 \sigma_v^2 \sigma_u^2 \eta_4 \eta_3 / \Xi, \quad \kappa_u = (\sigma_v^2 + \sigma_\xi^2)\eta_4 \sigma_u^2 \sigma_\xi^2 / \Xi,$$

$$\beta_v = -\sigma_\xi^2 \sigma_v^2 \sigma_u^2 \eta_4 \eta_3 / \Xi, \quad \psi_v = \sigma_\xi^2 \sigma_v^2 \sigma_u^2 \eta_4^2 / \Xi, \qquad \kappa_v = (\sigma_u^2 + \sigma_\xi^2)\eta_3 \sigma_v^2 \sigma_\xi^2 / \Xi,$$

and

$$\Xi = \eta_3^2 \sigma_u^2 \sigma_v^2 \sigma_\xi^2 + \eta_4^2 \sigma_u^2 \sigma_v^2 \sigma_\xi^2 + \eta_3^2 \sigma_v^2 \sigma_\xi^2 \sigma_\xi^2 + \eta_4^2 \sigma_u^2 \sigma_\xi^2 \sigma_\xi^2 > 0.$$

Substituting for $\lambda_t^h - \lambda_{t-1}$ and z_t we obtain

$$\mathbb{E}_t^h \hat{u}_{t+1} = \left(\beta_u + \eta_4\kappa_u\right)\hat{u}_{t+1} + \left(\psi_u + \eta_3\kappa_u\right)v_t + \beta_u\zeta_t^h + \psi_u\xi_t^h \tag{4.42a}$$

and

$$\mathbb{E}_t^h v_t = \left(\psi_v + \eta_3\kappa_v\right)v_t + \left(\beta_v + \eta_4\kappa_v\right)\hat{u}_{t+1} + \beta_v\zeta_t^h + \psi_v\xi_t^h. \tag{4.42b}$$

Equation (4.42) identifies how rational confusion arises in the equilbrium. Consider the case of a v_t shock that affects the hedging parameters of all households. This shock has two effects on households' information: a one-to-one impact on private information, λ_t^h, and an effect on the public information, z_t, via the coefficient η_3. Households react to this information in two ways. First they adjust their estimates of v_t by $\psi_v + \eta_3\kappa_v$: the ψ_v parameter identifies the adjustment with respect to the change in private information and $\eta_3\kappa_v$ identifies the effect of the change in z_t. Second, households adjust their estimates of $\hat{u}_{t+1}$ by $\psi_u + \eta_3\kappa_u$. This is a form of rational confusion. In an equilibrium where both η_3 and η_4 are nonzero, households cannot discern the source of the variation in z_t and λ_t^h, so they rationally attribute some weight to observations on z_t and λ_t^h when computing $\mathbb{E}_t^h \hat{u}_{t+1}$. Indeed, it is easy to check that $\psi_u + \eta_3\kappa_u = \eta_4\eta_3\sigma_u^2\sigma_\xi^2\sigma_\zeta^2 / \Xi$, so this form of rational confusion will be present when $\eta_4\eta_3 \neq 0$. Similarly, $\hat{u}_{t+1}$ shocks will affect households' estimates of v_t via rational confusion when $\beta_v + \eta_4\kappa_v = \eta_4\eta_3\sigma_v^2\sigma_\zeta^2\sigma_\xi^2 / \Xi \neq 0$.

To find whether $\eta_4\eta_3 \neq 0$ we have to verify Conjecture 3. For this purpose we first compute $\overline{\mathbb{E}}_t s_{t+1}$ from (4.41) as

$$\overline{\mathbb{E}}_t s_{t+1} = \eta_0 + \eta_1 \overline{\mathbb{E}}_t(\hat{m}_{t+1} - \hat{m}) + \eta_2 \overline{\mathbb{E}}_t \lambda_t + \eta_3 \overline{\mathbb{E}}_t v_{t+1} + \eta_4 \overline{\mathbb{E}}_t \hat{u}_{t+2}$$

$$= \eta_0 + \eta_1 \overline{\mathbb{E}}_t(\hat{m}_{t+1} - \hat{m}) + \eta_2 \overline{\mathbb{E}}_t \lambda_t.$$

Next, we use the facts that $\overline{\mathbb{E}}_t(\hat{m}_{t+1} - \hat{m}) = \rho(\hat{m}_t - \hat{m}) + \overline{\mathbb{E}}_t \hat{u}_{t+1}$, $\overline{\mathbb{E}}_t \lambda_t = \lambda_{t-1} + \overline{\mathbb{E}}_t v_t$ together with $\overline{\mathbb{E}}_t \hat{u}_{t+1} = (\beta_u + \eta_4\kappa_u)\hat{u}_{t+1} + (\psi_u + \eta_3\kappa_u)v_t$ and $\overline{\mathbb{E}}_t v_t = (\psi_v + \eta_3\kappa_v)v_t + (\beta_v + \eta_4\kappa_v)\hat{u}_{t+1}$ from (4.42) to rewrite this equation as

$$\overline{\mathbb{E}}_t s_{t+1} = \eta_0 + \eta_1\rho(\hat{m}_t - \hat{m}) + \eta_2\lambda_{t-1} + \left\{\eta_1\left(\psi_u + \eta_3\kappa_u\right) + \eta_2\left(\psi_v + \eta_3\kappa_v\right)\right\}v_t$$

$$+ \left\{\eta_1\left(\beta_u + \eta_4\kappa_u\right) + \eta_2\left(\beta_v + \eta_4\kappa_v\right)\right\}\hat{u}_{t+1}.$$

Finally, we combine our conjecture in (4.41) with (4.34) and the equation above to get

$$\eta_0 + \eta_1(\hat{m}_t - \hat{m}) + \eta_2\lambda_{t-1} + \eta_3 v_t + \eta_4\hat{u}_{t+1}$$

$$= f - (1 - b)(\hat{m}_t - \hat{m}) - \gamma\sigma_s^2 b\lambda_{t-1} - \gamma\sigma_s^2 bv_t + b\eta_0 + b\eta_1\rho(\hat{m}_t - \hat{m})$$

$$+ b\eta_2\lambda_{t-1} + b\left\{\eta_1\left(\psi_u + \eta_3\kappa_u\right) + \eta_2\left(\psi_v + \kappa_v\eta_3\right)\right\}v_t$$

$$+ b\left\{\eta_1\left(\beta_u + \eta_4\kappa_u\right) + \eta_2\left(\beta_v + \eta_4\kappa_v\right)\right\}\hat{u}_{t+1}.$$

Equating coefficients as we did before produces

$$\eta_0 = \frac{f}{1-b}, \quad \eta_1 = -\frac{1-b}{1-b\rho}, \quad \eta_2 = -\frac{b\gamma\sigma_s^2}{1-b},$$

$$\eta_3 = \frac{b(\eta_1\psi_u + \eta_2\psi_v - \gamma\sigma_s^2)}{\left(1 - b\eta_1\kappa_u - b\eta_2\kappa_v\right)}, \quad \text{and} \quad \eta_4 = \frac{b\left(\eta_1\beta_u + \eta_2\beta_v\right)}{\left(1 - b\eta_1\kappa_u - b\eta_2\kappa_v\right)}.$$

We have thus verified Conjecture 3.

The values for η_0, η_1, and η_2 are the same as in the Strong-form efficient equilibrium we studied earlier so we concentrate on η_3 and η_4. An examination of the expression for η_4 reveals that the coefficient will be zero when β_u and β_v are zero. These parameters determine how each household adjusts its estimates of $\hat{u}_{t+1}$ and v_t in response to its private signal u_t^h. If $\beta_u = \beta_v = 0$, all households ignore u_t^h when computing $\mathbb{E}_t^h \hat{u}_{t+1}$ and $\mathbb{E}_t^h v_t$, so future policy shocks, $\hat{u}_{t+1}$, have no effect on the household estimates of $\hat{u}_{t+1}$ and v_t and thus no effect on their forecasts for the future spot rate, $\mathbb{E}_t^h s_{t+1}$. The $\hat{u}_{t+1}$ shocks can only affect the current spot rate via the average of households' forecasts, $\overline{\mathbb{E}}_t s_{t+1}$, because they have no effect on current monetary policy. They will therefore have no effect on s_t under these circumstances so $\eta_4 = 0$. Now the public signal z_t fully reveals the value of v_t to all households. Thus rational confusion disappears when individual households completely ignore their private signals concerning future shocks to monetary policy.

Higher-order expectations also play a limited role in the equilibrium. To see why, consider the average error in forecasting s_{t+1}. According to (4.41), this error is

$$s_{t+1} - \overline{\mathbb{E}}_t s_{t+1} = \eta_1\left(\hat{u}_{t+1} - \overline{\mathbb{E}}_t\hat{u}_{t+1}\right) + \eta_2\left(v_t - \overline{\mathbb{E}}_t v_t\right) + \eta_3\left(v_{t+1} - \overline{\mathbb{E}}_t v_{t+1}\right)$$

$$+ \eta_4\left(\hat{u}_{t+2} - \overline{\mathbb{E}}_t\hat{u}_{t+2}\right).$$

The estimates of $\mathbb{E}_t^h \hat{u}_{t+1}$ and $\mathbb{E}_t^h v_t$ in (4.42) imply that

$$\hat{u}_{t+1} - \overline{\mathbb{E}}_t\hat{u}_{t+1} = \left(1 - \beta_u - \eta_4\kappa_u\right)\hat{u}_{t+1} - \left(\psi_u + \eta_3\kappa_u\right)v_t$$

and

$$v_t - \overline{\mathbb{E}}_t v_t = (1 - \psi_v - \kappa_v\eta_3)v_t - \left(\beta_v + \eta_4\kappa_v\right)\hat{u}_{t+1},$$

so individual households can forecast $\hat{u}_{t+1} - \overline{\mathbb{E}}_t\hat{u}_{t+1}$ and $v_t - \overline{\mathbb{E}}_t v_t$ using their estimates of $\hat{u}_{t+1}$ and v_t. By contrast, $\mathbb{E}_t^h(v_{t+1} - \overline{\mathbb{E}}_t v_{t+1}) = \mathbb{E}_t^h(\hat{u}_{t+2} - \overline{\mathbb{E}}_t\hat{u}_{t+2}) = 0$ because $\mathbb{E}_t^h\hat{u}_{t+1+i} = \mathbb{E}_t^h v_{t+i} = 0$ for $i > 0$. This means that individual households can forecast average forecast errors one period ahead [i.e., $\mathbb{E}_t^h(s_{t+1} - \overline{\mathbb{E}}_t s_{t+1}) \neq 0$], but no further [i.e., $\mathbb{E}_t^h(s_{t+1+i} - \overline{\mathbb{E}}_{t+i}s_{t+1+i}) = 0$ for $i > 0$]. Consequently, the contribution of higher-order expectations to the equilibrium spot rate is

$$\overline{\mathbb{E}}_t \sum_{i=o}^{\infty} b^{i+1}\left(s_{t+1+i} - \overline{\mathbb{E}}_{t+i}s_{t+1+i}\right) = b\overline{\mathbb{E}}_t\left(s_{t+1} - \overline{\mathbb{E}}_t s_{t+1}\right).$$

Higher-order expectations do not play a large role in this equilibrium because house-holds have private information about monetary policy only one period in advance.

4.3.4 Heterogeneous Information and Persistence

We now consider a modification of the model in which higher-order expectations play a more important role. We eliminate heterogeneity in the hedging parameter and assume that households have private information about a sequence of future monetary policy changes. In particular, we assume that $\lambda_t^h = \lambda_t$ for all $h \in [0, a)$, where $\lambda_t = \lambda_{t-1} + v_t$, with $v_t \sim$ i.i.d. $N(0, \sigma_v^2)$. Furthermore, each household now receives a private signal concerning future changes in policy over the next *two* periods:

$$u_{j,t}^h = \hat{u}_{t+j} + \zeta_{j,t}^h,$$

for $j = \{1, 2\}$. Here $u_{j,t}^h$ represents private information about monetary policy j periods ahead and $\zeta_{j,t}^h$ is the idiosyncratic noise associated with the signal $u_{j,t}^h$. As before, we assume that the noise terms are independent, mean-zero random variables, uncorrelated across households so that $\frac{1}{a} \int_0^a \zeta_{j,t}^h dh = 0$ for $j = \{1, 2\}$. All other aspects of the model remain the same. The evolution of household h's information is therefore represented by

$$\Omega_t^h = \left\{ P_t, \hat{P}_t, R_t, \hat{R}_t, S_t, \hat{M}_t, \lambda_t, u_{1,t}^h, u_{2,t}^h \right\} \cup \Omega_{t-1}^h. \tag{4.43}$$

As before there are two sources of heterogeneity in household information sets so the equilibrium spot rate will not be Strong-form informationally efficient.

Once again we use the conjecture and verify method to solve the model.

Conjecture 4: *In equilibrium, (i) home prices are constant, (ii) $\hat{p}_t = -s_t$, and (ii) the equilibrium log spot rate is given by*

$$s_t = \eta_0 + \eta_1(\hat{m}_t - \hat{m}) + \eta_2 \lambda_t + z_t, \tag{4.44}$$

where

$$z_t \equiv \sum_{i=0}^{\infty} \theta_i \hat{u}_{t+2-i}$$

for some coefficients η_i and θ_i.

Conjecture 4 adds leads and lags of the $\hat{u}_t$ policy shocks to the log spot rate via the variable z_t. As before the leads appear because the equilibrium spot rate aggregates information in the private signals concerning future fundamentals. The lagged policy shocks introduce a new source of persistence in the equilibrium dynamics of the spot rate via z_t.

The structure of information in this model is more complex than in the other equilibria we have studied, so it is useful to derive some preliminary results before attempting to verify Conjecture 4. In particular, it proves useful to represent the structure of private information in a compact form. Let $\mathbf{u}_t^h = [u_{2,t}^h, u_{1,t}^h]'$ denote the vector of the private signal received by household h, so that

$$\mathbf{u}_t^h = \hat{\mathbf{u}}_t + \boldsymbol{\zeta}_t^h, \tag{4.45}$$

where $\hat{\mathbf{u}}_t = [\hat{u}_{t+2}, \hat{u}_{t+1}]'$ and $\boldsymbol{\zeta}_t^h = [\zeta_{2,t}^h, \zeta_{1,t}^h]'$. The vector of policy shocks evolves according to

$$\begin{bmatrix} \hat{u}_{t+2} \\ \hat{u}_{t+1} \end{bmatrix} = \begin{bmatrix} 0 & 0 \\ 1 & 0 \end{bmatrix} \begin{bmatrix} \hat{u}_{t+1} \\ \hat{u}_t \end{bmatrix} + \begin{bmatrix} \hat{u}_{t+2} \\ 0 \end{bmatrix},$$

or, more compactly,

$$\hat{\mathbf{u}}_t = \mathcal{A}\hat{\mathbf{u}}_{t-1} + \boldsymbol{v}_t. \tag{4.46}$$

Note that $\mathbb{E}_{t-1}^h \boldsymbol{v}_t = 0$ for all h. Further, let ι_j be a 1×2 vector that selects the jth element of $\hat{\mathbf{u}}_t$. The identities $\hat{u}_{t+2} = \iota_1 \hat{\mathbf{u}}_t$, $\hat{u}_{t+1} = \iota_2 \hat{\mathbf{u}}_t$, and $\iota_1' \hat{u}_{t+2} = \boldsymbol{v}_t$ will all prove useful when we use (4.45) and (4.46) to compute households' expectations concerning future policy shocks later.

Next we turn to the question of how households estimate $\hat{\mathbf{u}}_t$. Given the evolution of information in (4.43) and the conjectured equation for the log spot rate in (4.44), each household receives a public signal concerning a combination of linear future policy shocks. Specifically, since $\{s_{t-i}, \hat{m}_{t-i}, \lambda_{t-i}, \hat{u}_{t-i}\} \in \Omega_t^h$ for $i \geq 0$, equation (4.44) implies that $x_t = z_t - \sum_{i=2}^{\infty} \theta_i \hat{u}_{t+2-i} = \theta_0 \hat{u}_{t+2} + \theta_1 \hat{u}_{t+1} \in \Omega_t^h$ for all h. Thus x_t provides a public signal on future policy shocks because in our conjectured equilibrium the spot rate aggregates the information in the private signals. Each household h will therefore compute its estimate of $\hat{\mathbf{u}}_t$ using x_t and its private signal $\mathbf{u}_t^h$. Since the joint distribution of $\{\hat{\mathbf{u}}_t, x_t, \mathbf{u}_t^h\}$ is normal, we can once again apply the projection theorem to get

$$\mathbb{E}_t^h \hat{\mathbf{u}}_t = \mathbb{E}_{t-1}^h \hat{\mathbf{u}}_t + \beta \left(\mathbf{u}_t^h - \mathbb{E}_{t-1}^h \mathbf{u}_t^h \right) + \kappa \left(x_t - \mathbb{E}_{t-1}^h x_t \right), \tag{4.47}$$

where the 2×2 matrix β and 2×1 vector κ depend on the conditional covariance of $\{\hat{\mathbf{u}}_t, x_t, \mathbf{u}_t^h\}$. Note that we now have to track prior expectations concerning the signals (i.e., $\mathbb{E}_{t-1}^h \mathbf{u}_t^h$ and $\mathbb{E}_{t-1}^h x_t$). In other words, household h's prior expectations concerning $\hat{\mathbf{u}}_t$ are updated using the unexpected portion of the private and public signals, $\mathbf{u}_t^h - \mathbb{E}_{t-1}^h \mathbf{u}_t^h$ and $x_t - \mathbb{E}_{t-1}^h x_t$, rather than just the signals $\mathbf{u}_t^h$ and x_t.

In order to verify Conjecture 4 we will need equations that relate $\hat{\mathbf{u}}_t$, $\mathbb{E}_t^h \hat{\mathbf{u}}_t$, and $\overline{\mathbb{E}}_t \hat{\mathbf{u}}_t$ to the sequence of $\hat{u}_t$ shocks. Deriving these equations takes a number of algebraic steps so we simply present the key results in the following lemma. (Detailed derivations are contained in the appendix.)

Lemma 1: *If the log spot rate follows the conjectured process in (4.44), and private information has the structure described by (4.45), (4.46), and (4.47), then the estimate and estimation error concerning $\hat{u}_t$ averaged across all households $h \in [0, a)$ are*

$$\overline{\mathbb{E}}_t \hat{\mathbf{u}}_t = \sum_{i=0}^{\infty} \left(\mathcal{A}^i - \mathcal{B}^i \mathcal{C} \right) \iota_1' \hat{u}_{t+2-i}, \tag{4.48}$$

$$\hat{\mathbf{u}}_t - \overline{\mathbb{E}}_t \hat{\mathbf{u}}_t = \sum_{i=0}^{\infty} \mathcal{B}^i \mathcal{C} \iota_1' \hat{u}_{t+2-i}, \tag{4.49}$$

where $B \equiv \left[(I - \beta) \, \mathcal{A} - \kappa \theta_1 \iota_1 \right]$ and $C \equiv \left[I - \beta - \kappa \theta_0 \iota_1 \right]$. Furthermore, the average expectation of the future average estimation errors is

$$\overline{\mathbb{E}}_t \left(\hat{\mathbf{u}}_{t+i} - \overline{\mathbb{E}}_{t+i} \hat{\mathbf{u}}_{t+i} \right) = \mathcal{B}^i \mathcal{D} \left(\hat{\mathbf{u}}_t - \overline{\mathbb{E}}_t \hat{\mathbf{u}}_t \right) \tag{4.50}$$

for $i \geq 0$, where $D \equiv I - \left(C\iota_1' \iota_1 + \mathcal{B} C \iota_1' \iota_2 \right)$.

Lemma 1 contains three key results. Equation (4.48) says that the average estimate of future policy shocks, $\hat{u}_{t+2}$ and $\hat{u}_{t+1}$, in general depends not only on the true values of $\hat{u}_{t+2}$ and $\hat{u}_{t+1}$, but also on the sequence of earlier shocks, that is, $\hat{u}_{t-i}$ for $i \geq 0$. This may seem surprising because the $\hat{u}_t$ shocks are serially uncorrelated. However, this dependence arises from rational confusion in household inferences. As (4.47) shows, household h's estimate of $\hat{u}_t$ depends on its prior expectation, $\mathbb{E}_{t-1}^h \hat{u}_t$, private signal, $\mathbf{u}_t^h - \mathbb{E}_{t-1}^h \mathbf{u}_t^h$, and public signal, $x_t - \mathbb{E}_{t-1}^h x_t$. It is easy to check that the last depends in part on the realizations of $\hat{u}_t$. So unless these realizations have an exactly offsetting impact on the private signal, $\mathbf{u}_t^h - \mathbb{E}_{t-1}^h \mathbf{u}_t^h$, which they generally will not, $\mathbb{E}_t^h \hat{u}_t$ will be a function of $\hat{u}_t$. Realizations of earlier shocks affect $\mathbb{E}_t^h \hat{u}_t$ through $\mathbb{E}_{t-1}^h \hat{u}_t$ via an analogous mechanism. Thus, rational confusion in the inferences drawn from public signals induces persistence in the estimates of $\mathbb{E}_t^h \hat{u}_t$, which in turn shows up in the average estimates.

Rational confusion also accounts for the behavior of the average estimation error shown in (4.49). Although $\hat{u}_t$ depends only on $\hat{u}_{t+2}$ and $\hat{u}_{t+1}$ by definition, earlier shocks can affect $\hat{u}_t - \overline{\mathbb{E}}_t \hat{u}_t$ via their impact on $\overline{\mathbb{E}}_t \hat{u}_t$. Equation (4.49) also implies that individual household estimates of the average forecast error differ from zero, that is, $\mathbb{E}_t^h (\hat{u}_t - \overline{\mathbb{E}}_t \hat{u}_t) \neq 0$ because $\mathbb{E}_t^h \hat{u}_{t+2-i} \neq 0$ for $i \geq 0$. The reason is that household h's estimate of household j's forecast differs from his own, so h's estimate of the average forecast differs from $\mathbb{E}_t^h \hat{u}_t$. Moreover, because rational confusion introduces persistence in $\hat{u}_t - \overline{\mathbb{E}}_t \hat{u}_t$, it is possible for individual households to forecast future average estimation errors so that $\mathbb{E}_t^h (\hat{u}_{t+i} - \overline{\mathbb{E}}_{t+i} \hat{u}_{t+i}) \neq 0$ for some $i > 0$. Equation (4.50) shows that the average of these forecasts depends on the current average estimate error. It should be emphasized that this latter result only holds for average expectations in the presence of heterogeneity. If all households have the same information (because they received the same private signal), then $\overline{\mathbb{E}}_t (\hat{u}_{t+i} - \overline{\mathbb{E}}_{t+i} \hat{u}_{t+i})$ $= \mathbb{E}_t^h (\hat{u}_{t+i} - \mathbb{E}_{t+i}^h \hat{u}_{t+i}) = 0$ by iterated expectations.

With Lemma 1 in hand, we can now verify Conjecture 4. Recall that the log spot rate can always be written as

$$s_t = \overline{\mathbb{E}}_t \sum_{i=0}^{\infty} b^i f_{t+i} - \overline{\mathbb{E}}_t \sum_{i=o}^{\infty} b^{i+1} \left(s_{t+1+i} - \overline{\mathbb{E}}_{t+i} s_{t+1+i} \right). \tag{4.51}$$

All we have to do is to show that our conjecture in (4.44) is a solution to this equation given the structure of information and the process for fundamentals.

To begin, consider the first term on the right-hand side, the average present value of fundamentals, f_t. Fundamentals are again equal to $f - (1 - b)(\hat{m}_t - \hat{m}) - \gamma \sigma_s^2 b \lambda_t$, so we have to compute forecasts of λ_t and $\hat{m}_t - \hat{m}$. The former is straightforward because λ_t follows a random walk and $\lambda_t \in \Omega_t^h$ for all $h \in [0, a)$, namely $\mathbb{E}_t^h \lambda_{t+i} = \lambda_t$

for $i \geq 0$. The structure of private information implies that forecasts of the future E.U. money supply are given by

$$\mathbb{E}_t^h \hat{m}_{t+1} - \hat{m} = \rho(\hat{m}_t - \hat{m}) + \mathbb{E}_t^h \hat{u}_{t+1}$$

and

$$\mathbb{E}_t^h \hat{m}_{t+i} - \hat{m} = \rho^i(\hat{m}_t - \hat{m}) + \rho^{i-1}\mathbb{E}_t^h \hat{u}_{t+1} + \rho^{i-2}\mathbb{E}_t^h \hat{u}_{t+2}$$

for $i > 1$. Substituting these forecasts into $\mathbb{E}_t^h \sum_{i=0}^\infty b^i f_{t+i}$ with the definition of fundamentals and averaging the result across households gives

$$\overline{\mathbb{E}}_t \sum_{i=0}^\infty b^i f_{t+i} = \frac{f}{1-b} - \frac{\gamma\sigma_s^2 b}{1-b}\lambda_t - \frac{1-b}{1-b\rho}(\hat{m}_t - \hat{m}) - \varphi\overline{\mathbb{E}}_t\hat{\mathbf{u}}_t, \quad (4.52)$$

where $\varphi = \frac{b^2(1-b)}{1-b\rho}\left(\iota_1 + \frac{1}{b}\iota_2\right)$.

Next we turn to the second term in (4.51), the present value of the average spot rate forecast errors. According to our conjecture in equation (4.44), the error in forecasting the log spot rate next period is

$$s_{t+1} - \mathbb{E}_t^h s_{t+1} = \eta_1(\hat{u}_{t+1} - \mathbb{E}_t^h \hat{u}_{t+1}) + (z_{t+1} - \mathbb{E}_t^h z_{t+1}) + \eta_2 v_{t+1}.$$

Computing $z_{t+1} - \mathbb{E}_t^h z_{t+1}$ from the definition of z_t and combining the result with the previous expression gives

$$s_{t+1} - \mathbb{E}_t^h s_{t+1} = (\eta_1 + \theta_2)(\hat{u}_{t+1} - \mathbb{E}_t^h \hat{u}_{t+1}) + \theta_1(\hat{u}_{t+2} - \mathbb{E}_t^h \hat{u}_{t+2}) + \theta_0 \hat{u}_{t+3} + \eta_2 v_{t+1}$$

$$= \psi(\hat{\mathbf{u}}_t - \mathbb{E}_t^h \hat{\mathbf{u}}_t) + \theta_0 \hat{u}_{t+3} + \eta_2 v_{t+1},$$

where $\psi = \left[(\eta_1 + \theta_2)\iota_2 + \theta_1\iota_1\right]$. Note that the last two terms have zero conditional expectations based on Ω_t^h, so household h's estimate of the average forecast error is simply

$$\mathbb{E}_t^h(s_{t+1} - \overline{\mathbb{E}}_t s_{t+1}) = \psi\mathbb{E}_t^h(\hat{\mathbf{u}}_t - \overline{\mathbb{E}}_t \hat{\mathbf{u}}_t). \quad (4.53)$$

Recall that the Law of Iterated Expectations still holds with respect to expectations conditioned on an individual household's information, so $\mathbb{E}_t^h(s_{t+1+i} - \overline{\mathbb{E}}_{t+i}s_{t+1+i}) = \mathbb{E}_t^h(\mathbb{E}_{t+i}^h(s_{t+1+i} - \overline{\mathbb{E}}_{t+i}s_{t+1+i}))$. Substituting for $\mathbb{E}_{t+i}^h(s_{t+1+i} - \overline{\mathbb{E}}_{t+i}s_{t+1+i})$ with (4.53), averaging the resulting expression across households, and applying (4.50) from Lemma 1 gives

$$\overline{\mathbb{E}}_t(s_{t+1+i} - \overline{\mathbb{E}}_{t+i}s_{t+1+i}) = \psi\mathcal{B}^i\mathcal{D}(\hat{\mathbf{u}}_t - \overline{\mathbb{E}}_t\hat{\mathbf{u}}_t). \quad (4.54)$$

Thus, the current average estimate of the average error in forecasting the future spot rate depends on the average error in estimating $\hat{\mathbf{u}}_t$. We can therefore write the present value of the average spot rate forecast errors as

$$\overline{\mathbb{E}}_t \sum_{i=o}^{\infty} b^{i+1}(s_{t+1+i} - \overline{\mathbb{E}}_{t+i}s_{t+1+i}) = b\psi \{I - b\mathcal{B}\}^{-1} \mathcal{D}(\hat{\mathbf{u}}_t - \overline{\mathbb{E}}_t\hat{\mathbf{u}}_t). \qquad (4.55)$$

We finally have all the elements necessary to verify Conjecture 4. Combining equations (4.44), (4.51), (4.52), and (4.55) yields

$$\eta_0 + \eta_1(\hat{m}_t - \hat{m}) + \eta_2\lambda_t + \sum_{i=0}^{\infty} \theta_i\hat{u}_{t+2-i}$$

$$= \frac{f}{1-b} - \frac{1-b}{1-b\rho}(\hat{m}_t - \hat{m}) - \frac{b\gamma\sigma_s^2}{1-b}\lambda_t - \varphi \sum_{i=0}^{\infty}(\mathcal{A}^i - \mathcal{B}^i\mathcal{C})\iota_1'\hat{u}_{t+2-i}$$

$$- b\psi \{I - b\mathcal{B}\}^{-1} \mathcal{D} \sum_{i=0}^{\infty} \mathcal{B}^i\mathcal{C}\iota_1'\hat{u}_{t+2-i}.$$

Once again this equation must hold for all possible realizations of $\hat{m}_t - \hat{m}$, λ_t, and $\{\hat{u}_{t-i}\}_{i\geq-2}$, a requirement that places restrictions on the coefficients η_i and θ_i. Substituting these parameter restrictions in (4.44) gives us the equilibrium process for the log spot rate:

$$s_t = \frac{f}{1-b} - \frac{1-b}{1-b\rho}(\hat{m}_t - \hat{m}) - \frac{b\gamma\sigma_s^2}{1-b}\lambda_t + \sum_{i=0}^{\infty} \theta_i\hat{u}_{t+2-i}, \qquad (4.56)$$

where $\theta_i = -b\psi \{I - b\mathcal{B}\}^{-1} \mathcal{D}\mathcal{B}^i\mathcal{C}\iota_1' - \varphi \left(\mathcal{A}^i - \mathcal{B}^i\mathcal{C}\right)\iota_1'$.

Our derivation of the equilibrium spot rate process has been a complex undertaking, so it worthwhile reviewing what we have learned in the process. The first point to note is that rational confusion plays an important role in the model. Individual households rationally use both private and public information to form expectations regarding future fundamentals, but inferences drawn from public information can be particularly complex. This gives rise to a rational confusion problem in which shocks affect household inferences not because they are themselves informative but because they contribute to public information that is.

The second notable feature of this model is that rational confusion affects the persistence of shocks on the equilibrium spot rate. This shows up in equation (4.56) via the θ_i coefficients for $i > 2$. These effects arise because each household receives *two* private signals concerning future policy. The first signal arrives two periods before the policy shock and the second one period before the shock. This means that inferences concerning the next period's shock depend on both the current and the last periods' private information. This serial dependence in the structure of information was absent in the models we studied earlier. Here it is the source of persistence in the equilibrium dynamics of the spot rate.

Finally, the equilibrium dynamics incorporate the effects of higher-order expectations. The effects appear because shocks have a persistent impact on the average errors in forecasting future inflation. This gives individual households the ability to forecast future average forecast errors, with the result that the equilibrium spot rate reflects more than just the average present value of future fundamentals.

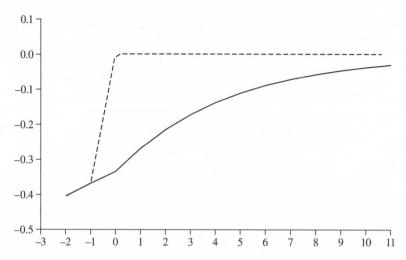

FIGURE 4.1   Impulse response of the log spot rate, s_t (solid), and z_t component (dashed) to a monetary shock, $\hat{u}_t$.

4.3.5 Dynamic Implications

How do the dynamics of the spot rate differ in this equilibrium from the others we have studied? As equation (4.56) shows, the coefficients on the money stock and hedging parameter are the same as we derived earlier in the Strong-form efficient equilibrium. This means that the θ_i coefficients contain all the dynamic implications of information heterogeneity in this equilibrium. Recall that $\mathcal{B}$, $\mathcal{C}$, and $\mathcal{D}$ are all functions of θ_1, θ_2, and θ_3, so the expression for θ_i in (4.56) for $i \le 3$ represents a set of three highly nonlinear simultaneous equations. The appendix describes how to solve these equations numerically.

Figure 4.1 illustrates the dynamic properties of the model for a particular set of parameter values. These calculations take the semi-interest elasticity of money demand, α, equal to 10, ρ equal to 0.8, and the variance of the money shocks, σ_u^2, equal to 0.01. We have also assumed that the variance of the signal noise in each household's private signal, σ_ζ^2, equals 0.01. Since our focus is on how money shocks affect the log spot rate, there is no need to specify households' risk-aversion or the variance of hedging shocks. Furthermore, none of the key features we note in what follows depend on these exact parameter values. In this sense, the dynamics implied by Figure 4.1 are reasonably representative of the model.

Figure 4.1 plots the effect of a positive one standard deviation shock to the E.U. money supply on the log spot rate. The horizontal axis indicates the number of periods *after* the shock occurs. The solid line shows the total impact of the shock through time and the dashed line shows the contribution of the shock operating via informational heterogeneity (i.e., via the θ_i coefficients). As the solid line in the figure shows, the spot rate appreciates two periods before the shock occurs and then gradually depreciates toward zero. Note, however, that the appreciation of the spot rate in periods -2 and -1 is larger than in period 0 when the shock hits. During these periods, individual households are receiving (noisy) private signals about the upcoming policy shock and are adjusting their demands for E.U. bonds. In a world with homogeneous information this anticipation effect would lead to an appreciation of the spot rate, but the effect would be smaller than at the point at which the shock hits. Everyone is anticipating a future movement in fundamentals, but its current impact on the spot rate is dampened by discounting. Here, by contrast, rational confusion in households' inferences magnify the effects of the shock so that the spot rate appreciates more in anticipation than it does when the shock hits. In this sense, rational confusion creates a form of "overshooting."

The second important feature displayed in Figure 4.1 concerns the contribution of informational heterogeneity to persistence. The dashed lines show how the money shock affects the spot rate via z_t (i.e., the line plots the θ_i coefficients). The θ_0 and θ_1 coefficients are large and negative (identifying the anticipation effects), but all the others are very close to zero. This means that once the shock has occurred, informational heterogeneity adds very little to the dynamics and the spot rate behaves essentially as it would in a completely standard model.

The lesson to be drawn from this exercise seems clear. Informational heterogeneity can generate interesting spot rate dynamics via rational confusion, but quantitatively its effects are concentrated between the time private information first arrives and the time it becomes public. This observation is supported by the findings of Bacchetta and van Wincoop (2006). They study a model where private information concerning fundamentals appears eight periods before becoming public (rather than the two periods in our model) and find that most of the quantitative effects are concentrated within this time frame.

4.4 Equilibrium Problems

The rational expectations equilibria are not without problems. First, there is no guarantee that an equilibrium price function exists; it has to be established. Second, even if an equilibrium function does exist, it may not be unique. Third, the model abstracts from the mechanics of how exactly an equilibrium is established—an abstraction that complicates deriving the empirical implications of models.

4.4.1 Existence and Uniqueness

To illustrate how the problems of existence and nonuniqueness arise, we return to the simplest version of our model. Recall that when households have homogenous information, the market-clearing spot rate satisfies

$$s_t = \frac{f}{1-b} - \frac{1-b}{1-b\rho}(\hat{m}_t - \hat{m}) - \frac{b\gamma\sigma_s^2}{1-b}\lambda_t. \tag{4.57}$$

Note that the coefficient on the hedging parameter includes the variance of the spot rate, σ_s^2. To fully describe the behavior of the equilibrium spot rate we have to find an expression for σ_s^2. In a rational expectations equilibrium, σ_s^2 equals the conditional variance of the log spot rate implied by the equilibrium process for s_t, namely (4.57). Since shocks to $\hat{m}_t$ and λ_t are independent, we have

$$\mathbb{V}(s_t|\Omega_{t-1}^h) = \left(\frac{1-b}{1-b\rho}\right)^2 \mathbb{V}(\hat{m}_t|\Omega_{t-1}^h) + \left(\frac{b\gamma\sigma_s^2}{1-b}\right)^2 \mathbb{V}(\lambda_t|\Omega_{t-1}^h)$$

$$= \left(\frac{1-b}{1-b\rho}\right)^2 \sigma_u^2 + \left(\frac{b\gamma\sigma_s^2}{1-b}\right)^2 \sigma_v^2. \tag{4.58}$$

Rearranging the last line gives us a quadratic equation in σ_s^2:

$$0 = \left(\frac{b\gamma}{1-b}\right)^2 \sigma_v^2 \left(\sigma_s^2\right)^2 - \sigma_s^2 + \left(\frac{1-b}{1-b\rho}\right)^2 \sigma_u^2,$$

so applying the standard formula

$$\sigma_s^2 = \left(\frac{1-b}{b\gamma}\right)^2 \frac{1}{2\sigma_v^2} \left\{ 1 \pm \sqrt{1 - 4\left(\frac{b\gamma}{1-b\rho}\right)^2 \sigma_v^2\sigma_u^2} \right\}. \tag{4.59}$$

The complete rational expectations solution for the equilibrium spot rate process comprises (4.57) and (4.59). Since σ_s^2 must be a nonnegative real number, no solution will exist when $\frac{1}{4}\left(\frac{1-b\rho}{b\gamma}\right)^2 < \sigma_v^2\sigma_u^2$. Alternatively, when $\frac{1}{4}\left(\frac{1-b\rho}{b\gamma}\right)^2 > \sigma_v^2\sigma_u^2$, there are two values for σ_s^2 consistent with the rational expectations, so the equilibrium spot rate is not uniquely related to fundamentals.

The situation is depicted in Figure 4.2. The three curves labeled I, II, and III plot the conditional variance of s_t as a function of σ_s^2, as shown in (4.58). The dashed 45°

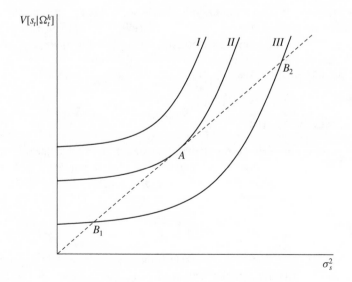

FIGURE 4.2   Rational expectations equilibria.

line represents the rational expectations restriction, $\mathbb{V}(s_t|\Omega_{t-1}^h) = \sigma_s^2$. Curve I shows $\mathbb{V}(s_t|\Omega_{t-1}^h)$ as a function of σ_s^2 when the variance of the monetary shocks is high. In this case there are no values for σ_s^2 that lie on both I and the 45° line, so there is no rational expectations equilibrium in the model. If the variance of the monetary shocks is lower so that curve III represents $\mathbb{V}(s_t|\Omega_{t-1}^h)$ as a function of σ_s^2, there are two possible rational expectations equilibria, represented by points B_1 and B_2. It is also possible that the model has a unique equilibrium. If the variance of monetary shocks implies that curve II depicts $\mathbb{V}(s_t|\Omega_{t-1}^h)$ as a function of σ_s^2, there is a unique rational expectations equilibrium where $\mathbb{V}(s_t|\Omega_{t-1}^h) = \sigma_s^2$ at point A.

Although identifying the conditions for existence and uniqueness of a rational expectations equilibrium is straightforward in our simple setup, generalizing these conditions to a broad class of models turns out to be a complex task. There are some general results in the literature (see O'Hara 1997) but existence and uniqueness often have to be established on a case by case basis.

4.4.2 Establishing an Equilibrium

Rational expectations models do not specify the mechanism through which an equilibrium is established. Rather they focus on the behavior of market participants who already know the equilibrium price function that relates market-clearing prices to fundamentals. This observation raises two questions:

1. Can market participants discover the price function that describes a rational expectations equilibrium?
2. If the rational expectations equilibrium is discoverable, how long will it take before market behavior can be accurately described by the equilibrium?

To address the first question, suppose households are initially endowed with some information about the economy, such as the history of the spot rate, but do not know the equilibrium price function. If they somehow form expectations concerning future exchange rates, a market-clearing spot rate could be found via the Tatomont process. Adding this observation to their information set, households can then form a new set of spot rate expectations, and the process can be repeated to generate a sequence of market-clearing exchange rates. This sequence will not represent realizations of a rational expectations equilibrium if household expectations differ from true conditional expectations of future market-clearing exchange rates. However, if it can be shown that household expectations converge to the true conditional expectations, the market-clearing prices in this sequence will eventually correspond to those in a rational expectations equilibrium. There is now a large literature studying this expectations formation process. For example, Evans and Honkapohja (2001) provide a comprehensive guide to models with adaptive learning in which households use statistical methods, such as least-squares learning, to modify their expectations in response to new data.

Relating the predictions of a rational expectations model to data remains a challenge even if the equilibrium is discoverable from some learning process. To see why, consider the behavior of the exchange rate in response to the arrival of public news concerning the money supply. Let us further assume that all households have dis-covered the equilibrium price function via some learning process and so form their expectations concerning the future spot rate rationally. Under these circumstances, our rational expectations model predicts that the arrival of the public news induces all households to revise their expectations simultaneously. This has an immediate effect on the aggregate demand for foreign bonds, and consequently the spot rate jumps to its new market-clearing level. In short, the impact of the public news is immediate.

The challenge for the researcher is to translate this theoretical prediction into an empirical one. In particular, does the theory mean that we can measure the spot rate impact of the public news by comparing the prenews price against the spot rate 1 second after the news arrives? This would be fine if the Tatomont process could literally take place instantaneously, but one might reasonably think that it may take a little longer before the new equilibrium spot rate is observable in the market. The question is: How long is long enough? The empirical literature considering the price impact of news seems to have settled on somewhere between 1 and 5 minutes (see Chapter 10), but these choices are largely arbitrary. Once we recognize that there is a real-world counterpart to the Tatomont process that takes more than 1 second to work, we have to consider exactly how long the process will take. This requires more than introspection.[1] We need a model that makes predictions about the adjustment process that can be compared against the data, in short a model of trading behavior. Of course such a model lies outside the realm of the rational expectations framework.

4.5 Summary

- Rational expectations models provide a theoretical framework for examining how asset prices behave in the presence of heterogeneous information without a detailed specification of how trading takes place.

- Equilibrium prices are determined via a fictional mechanism of the Walrasian auctioneer, who solicits the notional demand for assets by announcing a sequence of candidate pricing functions until market clearing is achieved. The function that emerges from this Tatomont process relates equilibrium prices to the state of the economy, or fundamentals.

- Informational heterogeneity can affect asset price dynamics via rational con-fusion and higher-order expectations. Rational confusion arises when agents make imprecise inferences based on public information, with the result that the price impact of shocks is distorted. Higher-order expectations contribute to the persistence of shocks.

---

1. Simply making an assumption about the duration of the adjustment process runs two risks. If the assumed duration is too short, the postnews price we use will not have incorporated all the impact of the news. If the assumed duration is too long, the postnews price is likely to be contaminated by the effects of other (unobservable) events.

- Rational expectations models may have no equilibria or multiple equilibria. They are silent on how an equilibrium price process is established and on the duration of the real-world counterpart of the Tatomont process.

4.6 Bibliography

The model examined in this chapter is adapted from the one developed by Bacchetta and van Wincoop (2006). Their model is part of a much larger finance literature on noisy rational expectations models in which unobserved shocks prevent equilibrium prices from being fully revealing (see Brunnermeier 2001 for a survey). Most models in this literature are static or contain just two periods, so they cannot be used to analyze how heterogeneous information affects the dynamics of asset prices. Exceptions include the multiperiod models of He and Wang (1995), Vives (1995), and Foster and Viswanathan (1996), which examine the pricing of an asset with a single payoff at a terminal date.

The concepts of rational confusion and higher-order expectations are well established in the rational expectations literature. Papers by Gennotte and Leland (1990) and Romer (1993) use rational confusion in models of the 1987 stock market crash, and Townsend (1983) showed how higher-order expectations arise in a business cycle model with heterogeneous information. Our discussion of higher-order expectations also draws on Bacchetta and van Wincoop (2008).

4.7 Review Questions

1. Information Revelation: There are N investors, indexed by n, who choose between U.S. and E.U. one-period risk-free bonds. In period $t = 0$, the USD/EUR spot rate is S_0. The unconditional distribution of the spot rate in period 1, S_1, is normal with mean μ and variance σ_s^2. Both bonds are supplied elastically with a gross return of R. The supply of euros available to investors from the foreign exchange market is $X \sim N(0, \sigma_x^2)$. Let X^n denote the number of E.U. bonds held by investor n in period 0. The problem facing investor n is to choose X^n to maximize

$$\mathbb{E}\left[-\exp(-\gamma W_1)|\Omega_0^n\right]$$

subject to

$$W_1^n = RW_0^n + R\left(S_1 - S_0\right)X^n,$$

where W_0^n is the initial wealth of investor n and Ω_0^n denotes the investor's information set.

  (a) Derive investor n's demand for euros.
  (b) Assume that each investor receives a private signal $\tilde{S}^n = S_1 + \xi^n$, where $\xi^n \sim$ i.i.d. $N(0, \sigma_\xi^2)$. What will be the aggregate demand for the

risky asset if investors only use $\tilde{S}^n$ as conditioning information (i.e., $\Omega_0^i = \{\tilde{S}^n\}$)?

(c) Using your answer to part (b), compute the market-clearing value for S_0 under the assumption that the supply of euros is $X \sim N(0, \sigma_x^2)$.

(d) Is the value for S_0 the equilibrium spot rate? Explain your reasoning.

(e) Suppose the equilibrium price takes the form

$$S_0 = \eta_0 + \eta_1 \bar{S}^n + \eta_2 X.$$

Derive investor n's demand for euros under the assumption that $\Omega_0^n = \{\tilde{S}^n, S_0\}$.

(f) Using your answer from part (e), compute the market-clearing price and solve for the coefficients η_0, η_1, and η_2.

(g) Is the equilibrium price from part (f) fully revealing?

(h) What happens to the equilibrium spot rate from part (f) as σ_x^2 tends to ∞? Explain the economics.

2. **Heterogeneous Traders:** Suppose that trade in the spot USD/EUR market takes place between a continuum of FX dealers, indexed by $d \in [0, 1]$, and two groups of investors. Dealers are risk-averse. Their aggregate demand for euros is given by

$$x_t = \frac{1}{\gamma \sigma^2} \left(\overline{\mathbb{E}}_t s_{t+1} - s_t + \hat{r}_t - r_t \right), \tag{4.60}$$

where s_t is the log USD/EUR spot rate, r_t and $\hat{r}_t$ are the U.S. and E.U. nominal interest rates, $\overline{\mathbb{E}}_t$ is the average conditional expectation of dealers given their information in period t, γ is the coefficient of risk-aversion, and σ^2 is the conditional variance of s_{t+1}.

(a) Describe how (4.60) can be derived from a utility maximization problem. [Hint: You will need an approximation at one point.]

(b) Investors come in two types. Uninformed investors supply euros to the market as b_t^U, where $b_t^U \sim N(0, \sigma_u^2)$. The supply of euros from informed customers, b_t^I, is correlated with innovations in fundamentals $f_t \equiv m_t - \hat{m}_t$, where m_t and $\hat{m}_t$ denote the log U.S. and E.U. money stocks, respectively:

$$b_t^I = -\theta \upsilon_{t+1}, \quad \text{with } \theta > 0,$$

where $f_{t+1} = \rho f_t + \upsilon_{t+1}$, and $\upsilon_{t+1} \sim \text{i.i.d.} N(0, \sigma_\upsilon^2)$. Provide an economic motivation for this specification.

(c) Market clearing in the money markets requires

$$m_t - p_t = -\alpha r_t \quad \text{and} \quad m_t^* - p_t^* = -\alpha \hat{r}_t,$$

where p_t and $\hat{p}_t$ denote the log price levels in the United States and Europe. In the USD/EUR market, clearing requires that

$$x_t = b_t \equiv b_t^U + b_t^I.$$

Under the assumption of PPP, show that the equilibrium log spot rate satisfies

$$s_t = \frac{1}{1+\alpha} \sum_{i=0}^{\infty} \left(\frac{\alpha}{1+\alpha}\right)^i \left(\overline{\mathbb{E}}_t^i f_{t+i} - \alpha\gamma\sigma^2\overline{\mathbb{E}}_t^i b_{t+i}\right),$$

where $\overline{\mathbb{E}}_t^i$ denotes ith-order expectations.

(d) Assume all dealers possess the same information and that at time t they only receive signals concerning v_{t+1}. Under these assumptions show that the log spot rate satisfies

$$s_t = \frac{1}{1+\alpha(1-\rho)} f_t + \frac{\alpha}{1+\alpha}\frac{1}{1+\alpha(1-\rho)}\mathbb{E}_t v_{t+1} - \frac{\alpha}{1+\alpha}\gamma\sigma^2 b_t,$$

where $\mathbb{E}_t$ denotes dealers' common expectations based on period t information.

(e) Now suppose that all dealers receive a signal concerning v_{t+1}, $\tilde{v}_t$, in period t; $\tilde{v}_t = v_{t+1} + \xi_t$, where $\xi_t \sim$ i.i.d.$N(0, \sigma_\xi^2)$. Further, assume that dealers observe b_t. Under these assumptions show that the equilibrium log spot rate is

$$s_t = \eta_0 f_t + \eta_1 \tilde{v}_t + \eta_2 b_t$$

and find expressions for the η_i coefficients.

(f) Compare the properties of the solution for the cases where $\theta > 0$ and $\theta = 0$. Explain the economics.

(g) By definition, the log excess returns on E.U. bonds can be written as

$$\Delta s_{t+1} + \hat{r}_t - r_t = \overline{\mathbb{E}}_t[\Delta s_{t+1} + \hat{r}_t - r_t] + s_{t+1} - \overline{\mathbb{E}}_t s_{t+1}.$$

Use this identity to compute the equilibrium log excess return when dealers observe $\tilde{v}_t$ and b_t and $\theta > 0$. Explain how excess returns vary with the supply of euros from informed investors, b_t^{I}.

3. Rational Confusion and Higher-Order Expectations: Suppose that the foreign exchange market comprises a continuum of investors, indexed by $n \in [0, 1]$. The demand for foreign currency by investor n is

$$x_t^n = \gamma^{-1}\mathbb{E}_t^n \Delta s_{t+1} + z_t^n,$$

where Δs_{t+1} is the change in the log spot rate, $s_{t+1} - s_t$, and $\mathbb{E}_t^n$ denotes expectations conditioned on investor n's period-t information, Ω_t^n, and z_t^n identifies the investor's hedging demand, which is related to the market-wide demand, z_t, by

$$z_t^n = z_t + \xi_t^n,$$

where $\xi_t^n \sim$ i.i.d.$N(0, \sigma_\xi^2)$ with the property $\int_0^1 \xi_t^n dn = 0$. Market-wide hedging demand follows an AR(1) process

$$z_t = \rho z_{t-1} + u_t$$

with $|\rho| < 1$ and $u_t \sim$ i.i.d.$N(0, \sigma_u^2)$. The supply of foreign currency is determined exogenously as $v_t \sim$ i.i.d.$N(0, \sigma_v^2)$.

(a) Derive an equation for the log spot rate that satisfies the market-clearing condition $\int_0^1 x_t^n dn = v_t$.

(b) Suppose the market-wide hedging demand is only observable to investors with a one-period lag, so that investor n's information set evolves according to

$$\Omega_t^n = \{z_t^n, s_t, z_{t-1}, \Omega_{t-1}^n\}.$$

Show that the equilibrium log spot rate follows

$$s_t = \eta_0 z_{t-1} + \eta_1 u_t + \eta_2 v_t \tag{4.61}$$

and find the values for the η_i coefficients. [Hint: Use (4.61) and the projection theorem to first compute $\mathbb{E}_t^n u_t$. Then use this expectation to verify that (4.61) satisfies the market-clearing condition for the log spot rate derived in part (a).]

(c) Compare the effect of a positive foreign currency supply shock in this equilibrium with its effect on the log spot rate in an equilibrium where investors have contemporaneous information on z_t (i.e., $\Omega_t^n = \{z_t^n, s_t, z_t, \Omega_{t-1}^n\}$ for all $n \in [0, 1]$).

(d) Show that higher-order expectations do not contribute to the dynamics of the log spot rate computed in part (b). [Hint: Show that $\mathbb{E}_t^n(s_{t+1+i} - \overline{\mathbb{E}}_{t+i}s_{t+1+i}) = 0$ for all $i > 0$.]

(e) Suppose now that z_t is observed with a two-period delay so that the evolution of each investor n's information is $\Omega_t^n = \{z_t^n, s_t, z_{t-2}, \Omega_{t-1}^n\}$. Can higher-order expectations play a role in the equilibrium dynamics of the spot rate? [Hint: There is no need to compute the new equilibrium spot rate process. Just consider its general form.]

4.A Appendix

4.A.1 The Projection Theorem

Let the $n \times 1$ vector $z = [x, y]$ have a joint multivariate normal distribution with mean vector μ and covariance matrix Σ partitioned conformably with x and y:

$$\mu = \begin{bmatrix} \mu_x \\ \mu_y \end{bmatrix} \quad \text{and} \quad \Sigma = \begin{bmatrix} \Sigma_{xx} & \Sigma_{xy} \\ \Sigma_{yx} & \Sigma_{yy} \end{bmatrix}.$$

The marginal distributions of the $n_x \times 1$ vector x and the $n_y \times 1$ vector y are given by

$$x \sim N(\mu_x, \Sigma_{xx}) \quad \text{and} \quad y \sim N(\mu_y, \Sigma_{yy}),$$

and the conditional distribution of x given y is

$$x|y \sim N(\mu_{x|y}, \Sigma_{x|y}),$$

with

$$\mu_{x|y} = \mu_x + \Sigma_{xy}\Sigma_{yy}^{-1}(y - \mu_y) \quad \text{and} \quad \Sigma_{x|y} = \Sigma_{xx} - \Sigma_{xy}\Sigma_{yy}^{-1}\Sigma_{yx}.$$

Proof: The joint density of z is

$$f(z) = (2\pi)^{-n/2}|\Sigma|^{-1/2}\exp\left(-\tfrac{1}{2}(z-\mu)'\Sigma^{-1}(z-\mu)\right).$$

Using the facts that

$$|\Sigma| = |\Sigma_{yy}||\Sigma_{xx} - \Sigma_{xy}\Sigma_{yy}^{-1}\Sigma_{yx}| \quad \text{and} \quad \Sigma^{-1} = \begin{bmatrix} \Sigma_{x|y}^{-1} & -\Sigma_{x|y}^{-1}K \\ -K'\Sigma_{x|y}^{-1} & \Sigma_{yy}^{-1} + K'\Sigma_{x|y}^{-1}K \end{bmatrix},$$

with $K = \Sigma_{xy}\Sigma_{yy}^{-1}$, to substitute for $|\Sigma|$ and Σ^{-1} in $f(z)$, we find that

$$f(z) = f(x|y)f(y),$$

where

$$f(y) = (2\pi)^{-n_y/2}|\Sigma_{yy}|^{-1/2}\exp\left(-\tfrac{1}{2}(y-\mu_y)'\Sigma_{yy}^{-1}(y-\mu_y)\right)$$

and

$$f(x|y) = (2\pi)^{-n_x/2}|\Sigma_{x|y}|^{-1/2}\exp\left(-\tfrac{1}{2}(x-\mu_{x|y})'\Sigma_{x|y}^{-1}(x-\mu_{x|y})\right).$$

Thus, the conditional distribution of x given y is normal with mean $\mu_{x|y}$ with covariance $\Sigma_{x|y}$.

The formulas for the projection theorem simplify in an important special case. Suppose that y represents a vector of n_y independent signals on the value of scalar x (i.e., $n_x = 1$),

$$y_i = x + \varepsilon_i \quad \text{for } i = \{1, 2, \ldots n_y\},$$

where y_i is the ith element in y and $\varepsilon_i \sim N(0, \Sigma_{\varepsilon\varepsilon})$. Then $\Sigma_{xy} = \Sigma_{xx}I_{n_y}$ and $\Sigma_{yy} = (\Sigma_{xx} + \Sigma_{\varepsilon\varepsilon})I_{n_y}$, where I_{n_y} is an n_y-dimensioned identity matrix. Substituting these expressions into the projection equations above gives

$$\mathbb{E}[x|y] = \mu_x + \frac{\Sigma_{xx}}{\Sigma_{xx} + \Sigma_{\varepsilon\varepsilon}} \sum_{i=1}^{n_y}(y_i - \mu_x) \quad \text{and} \quad \mathbb{V}[x|y] = \frac{\Sigma_{xx}\Sigma_{\varepsilon\varepsilon}}{\Sigma_{xx} + \Sigma_{\varepsilon\varepsilon}}.$$

4.A.2 Derivations

Budget Constraints

To derive a U.S. household's budget constraint, we first write

$$C_t^h \le R_t\left(\frac{P_t}{P_{t+1}}\right)\left(W_t^h - \frac{S_t\widehat{B}_t^h}{P_t} - \frac{M_t^h}{P_t}\right) + \frac{S_{t+1}}{P_{t+1}}\widehat{R}_t\widehat{B}_t^h + \frac{M_t^h}{P_{t+1}} + Y_{t+1}^h.$$

Next, we substitute for W_t^h:

$$C_t^h \le R_t \left(\frac{P_t}{P_{t+1}} \right) W_t^h + R_t \left(\frac{P_t}{P_{t+1}} \right) \left\{ \left(\frac{S_{t+1}\hat{R}_t}{S_t R_t} \right) - 1 \right\} \frac{S_t}{P_t} \widehat{B}_t^h$$

$$- R_t \left(\frac{P_t}{P_{t+1}} \right) (1 - R_t) \frac{M_t^h}{P_t} + Y_{t+1}^h.$$

This gives us (4.2) with the returns defined in (4.3).

The sequence of budget constraints for an E.U. household $\hat{h}$ is

$$\text{Young:} \quad \hat{P}_t W_t^{\hat{h}} = \frac{1}{S_t} B_t^{\hat{h}} + \hat{B}_t^{\hat{h}} + \hat{M}_t^{\hat{h}},$$

$$\text{Old:} \quad \hat{P}_{t+1} C_{t+1}^{\hat{h}} \le R_t \frac{1}{S_{t+1}} B_t^{\hat{h}} + \hat{R}_t \hat{B}_t^{\hat{h}} + \hat{M}_t^{\hat{h}} + \hat{P}_{t+1} Y_{t+1}^{\hat{h}}.$$

Rewriting the "old" constraint as

$$\hat{P}_{t+1} C_{t+1}^{\hat{h}} \le R_t \frac{1}{S_{t+1}} B_t^{\hat{h}} + \hat{R}_t \left(\hat{P}_t W_t^{\hat{h}} - \frac{1}{S_t} B_t^{\hat{h}} - \hat{M}_t^{\hat{h}} \right) + \hat{M}_t^{\hat{h}} + \hat{P}_{t+1} Y_{t+1}^{\hat{h}}$$

and substituting for $W_t^{\hat{h}}$ gives

$$C_{t+1}^{\hat{h}} \le \left(\frac{R_t S_t}{\hat{R}_t S_{t+1}} - 1 \right) \hat{R}_t \left(\frac{\hat{P}_t}{\hat{P}_{t+1}} \right) \frac{B_t^{\hat{h}}}{\hat{P}_t S_t} + \hat{R}_t \left(\frac{\hat{P}_t}{\hat{P}_{t+1}} \right) W_t^{\hat{h}}$$

$$+ \left(\frac{\hat{P}_t}{\hat{P}_{t+1}} \right) (1 - \hat{R}_t) \frac{\hat{M}_t^{\hat{h}}}{\hat{P}_t} + Y_{t+1}^{\hat{h}}.$$

The expression for the budget constraint and returns follows directly from this equation.

Equation (4.30): We simply apply the equation for $u_{x|y}$ from the projection theorem with $y = \lambda_t^h$, $\mu_x = 0$, $\mu_y = \lambda_{t-1}$, $\Sigma_{xy} = \sigma_v^2$, and $\Sigma_{yy} = \sigma_v^2 + \sigma_\xi^2$.

Equation (4.42): We first write the form of the joint distribution:

$$\begin{pmatrix} \hat{u}_{t+1} \\ z_t \\ u_t^h \\ v_t + \xi_t^h \end{pmatrix} \sim N \left(\begin{pmatrix} 0 \\ 0 \\ 0 \\ 0 \end{pmatrix}, \begin{pmatrix} \sigma_u^2 & \eta_4 \sigma_u^2 & \sigma_u^2 & 0 \\ \eta_4 \sigma_u^2 & \eta_3^2 \sigma_v^2 + \eta_4^2 \sigma_u^2 & \eta_4 \sigma_u^2 & \eta_3 \sigma_v^2 \\ \sigma_u^2 & \eta_4 \sigma_u^2 & \sigma_u^2 + \sigma_\xi^2 & 0 \\ 0 & \eta_3 \sigma_v^2 & 0 & \sigma_v^2 + \sigma_\xi^2 \end{pmatrix} \right).$$

Next, we apply the projection formula with $\hat{u}_{t+1} = x$, and $[z_t, u_t^h, v_t + \xi_t^h]' = y$. This gives

$$\mathbb{E}[\hat{u}_{t+1}|z_t, u_t^h, v_t + \xi_t^h]$$

$$= (\ \eta_4\sigma_u^2 \quad \sigma_u^2 \quad 0\ ) \begin{pmatrix} \eta_3^2\sigma_v^2 + \eta_4^2\sigma_u^2 & \eta_4\sigma_u^2 & \eta_3\sigma_v^2 \\ \eta_4\sigma_u^2 & \sigma_u^2 + \sigma_\zeta^2 & 0 \\ \eta_3\sigma_v^2 & 0 & \sigma_v^2 + \sigma_\xi^2 \end{pmatrix}^{-1} \begin{pmatrix} z_t \\ u_t^h \\ v_t + \xi_t^h \end{pmatrix}.$$

Multiplying out the matrices gives the equation for $\mathbb{E}_t^h \hat{u}_{t+1}$. The estimates of $\mathbb{E}_t^h v_t$ are similarly calculated from

$$\begin{pmatrix} v_t \\ z_t \\ u_t^h \\ v_t + \xi_t^h \end{pmatrix} \sim N \left(\begin{pmatrix} 0 \\ 0 \\ 0 \\ 0 \end{pmatrix}, \begin{pmatrix} \sigma_v^2 & \eta_3\sigma_v^2 & 0 & \sigma_v^2 \\ \eta_3\sigma_v^2 & \eta_3^2\sigma_v^2 + \eta_4^2\sigma_u^2 & \eta_4\sigma_u^2 & \eta_3\sigma_v^2 \\ 0 & \eta_4\sigma_u^2 & \sigma_u^2 + \sigma_\zeta^2 & 0 \\ \sigma_v^2 & \eta_3\sigma_v^2 & 0 & \sigma_v^2 + \sigma_\xi^2 \end{pmatrix} \right)$$

as

$$E\left[v_t|z_t, u_t^h, v_t + \xi_t^h\right]$$

$$= (\ \eta_3\sigma_v^2 \quad 0 \quad \sigma_v^2\ ) \begin{pmatrix} \eta_3^2\sigma_v^2 + \eta_4^2\sigma_u^2 & \eta_4\sigma_u^2 & \eta_3\sigma_v^2 \\ \eta_4\sigma_u^2 & \sigma_u^2 + \sigma_\zeta^2 & 0 \\ \eta_3\sigma_v^2 & 0 & \sigma_v^2 + \sigma_\xi^2 \end{pmatrix}^{-1} \begin{pmatrix} z_t \\ u_t^h \\ v_t + \xi_t^h \end{pmatrix}.$$

Proof of Lemma 1

First, we express $\hat{\mathbf{u}}_t$ in terms of the sequence of $\hat{u}_t$ shocks. Repeatedly substituting for the lagged values of $\hat{\mathbf{u}}_t$ in (4.46) gives

$$\hat{\mathbf{u}}_t = \sum_{i=0}^{\infty} \mathcal{A}^i v_{t-i} = \sum_{i=0}^{\infty} \mathcal{A}^i \iota_1' \hat{u}_{t+2-i}, \tag{4.62}$$

where the second equality uses the identity $\iota_1' \hat{u}_{t+2} = v_t$. Next we compute $\hat{\mathbf{u}}_t - \overline{\mathbb{E}}_t \hat{\mathbf{u}}_t$. For this purpose we first have to find expressions for $x_t - \mathbb{E}_{t-1}^h x_t$ and $u_t^h - \mathbb{E}_{t-1}^h u_t^h$. In period t all households know the entire history of the E.U. money stock [see equation (4.43)], so $\{\hat{u}_{t-i}\}_{i \geq 0} \in \Omega_t^h$. Using this fact we can compute

$$x_t - \mathbb{E}_{t-1}^h x_t = \theta_0 \left(\hat{u}_{t+2} - \mathbb{E}_{t-1}^h \hat{u}_{t+2}\right) + \theta_1 \left(\hat{u}_{t+1} - \mathbb{E}_{t-1}^h \hat{u}_{t+1}\right)$$

$$= \theta_0 \iota_1 v_t + \theta_1 \iota_1 \left(\hat{\mathbf{u}}_{t-1} - \mathbb{E}_{t-1}^h \hat{\mathbf{u}}_{t-1}\right). \tag{4.63}$$

An expression for the private signal can be found from (4.45) and (4.46):

$$u_t^h - \mathbb{E}_{t-1}^h u_t^h = \hat{\mathbf{u}}_t - \mathbb{E}_{t-1}^h \hat{\mathbf{u}}_t + \zeta_t^h$$

$$= \mathcal{A}\left(\hat{\mathbf{u}}_{t-1} - \mathbb{E}_{t-1}^h \hat{\mathbf{u}}_{t-1}\right) + v_t + \zeta_t^h. \tag{4.64}$$

Substituting (4.63) and (4.64) into (4.47) and using the fact that $\mathbb{E}_{t-1}^h \hat{\mathbf{u}}_t = \mathcal{A}\mathbb{E}_{t-1}^h \hat{\mathbf{u}}_{t-1}$ gives

$$\mathbb{E}_t^h \hat{\mathbf{u}}_t = \mathcal{A}\mathbb{E}_{t-1}^h \hat{\mathbf{u}}_{t-1} + \left[\beta\mathcal{A} + \kappa\theta_1 \iota_1\right]\left(\hat{\mathbf{u}}_{t-1} - \mathbb{E}_{t-1}^h \hat{\mathbf{u}}_{t-1}\right) + \left(\beta + \kappa\theta_0 \iota_1\right)\mathbf{v}_t + \beta\zeta_t^h.$$

Combining this equation with (4.46) yields

$$\hat{\mathbf{u}}_t - \mathbb{E}_t^h \hat{\mathbf{u}}_t = \mathcal{B}\left(\hat{\mathbf{u}}_{t-1} - \mathbb{E}_{t-1}^h \hat{\mathbf{u}}_{t-1}\right) + \mathcal{C}\mathbf{v}_t - \beta\zeta_t^h,$$

where $\mathcal{B} = \left[(I - \beta)\mathcal{A} - \kappa\theta_1 \iota_1\right]$ and $\mathcal{C} = \left(I - \beta - \kappa\theta_0 \iota_1\right)$. Averaging across households (using the fact that $\frac{1}{a}\int \zeta_t^h dh = 0$) gives us the following vector AR(1) process:

$$\hat{\mathbf{u}}_t - \overline{\mathbb{E}}_t \hat{\mathbf{u}}_t = \mathcal{B}\left(\hat{\mathbf{u}}_{t-1} - \overline{\mathbb{E}}_{t-1}\hat{\mathbf{u}}_{t-1}\right) + \mathcal{C}\mathbf{v}_t. \tag{4.65}$$

Repeated substitution in the right-hand side of this expression results in equation (4.49). To compute (4.48) we simply combine (4.62) with (4.49) and the identity $\overline{\mathbb{E}}_t \hat{\mathbf{u}}_t = \hat{\mathbf{u}}_t - (\hat{\mathbf{u}}_t - \overline{\mathbb{E}}_t \hat{\mathbf{u}}_t)$.

We begin the derivation of equation (4.50) by rewriting (4.49) as

$$\hat{\mathbf{u}}_t - \overline{\mathbb{E}}_t \hat{\mathbf{u}}_t = \left(\mathcal{C}\iota_1' \iota_1 + \mathcal{B}\mathcal{C}\iota_1' \iota_2\right)\hat{\mathbf{u}}_t + \mathcal{B}^2 \sum_{i=0}^{\infty} \mathcal{B}^i \mathcal{C}\iota_1' \hat{u}_{t-i}.$$

Note that the second term on the right only involves current and lagged values of $\hat{u}_t$ that are known to all households in period t. Consequently,

$$\overline{\mathbb{E}}_t \left(\hat{\mathbf{u}}_t - \overline{\mathbb{E}}_t \hat{\mathbf{u}}_t\right) = \left(\mathcal{C}\iota_1' \iota_1 + \mathcal{B}\mathcal{C}\iota_1' \iota_2\right)\overline{\mathbb{E}}_t \hat{\mathbf{u}}_t + \mathcal{B}^2 \sum_{i=0}^{\infty} \mathcal{B}^i \mathcal{C}\iota_1' \hat{u}_{t-i}.$$

Combining the last two equations gives

$$\hat{\mathbf{u}}_t - \overline{\mathbb{E}}_t \hat{\mathbf{u}}_t = (\mathcal{C}\iota_1' \iota_1 + \mathcal{B}\mathcal{C}\iota_1' \iota_2)(\hat{\mathbf{u}}_t - \overline{\mathbb{E}}_t \hat{\mathbf{u}}_t) + \overline{\mathbb{E}}_t(\hat{\mathbf{u}}_t - \overline{\mathbb{E}}\hat{\mathbf{u}}_t)$$

or

$$\overline{\mathbb{E}}_t \left(\hat{\mathbf{u}}_t - \overline{\mathbb{E}}_t \hat{\mathbf{u}}_t\right) = \mathcal{D}\left(\hat{\mathbf{u}}_t - \overline{\mathbb{E}}_t \hat{\mathbf{u}}_t\right),$$

where $\mathcal{D} = \left(I - \left(\mathcal{C}\iota_1' \iota_1 + \mathcal{B}\mathcal{C}\iota_1' \iota_2\right)\right)$. Now equation (4.65) implies that

$$\mathbb{E}_t^h \left(\hat{\mathbf{u}}_{t+i} - \overline{\mathbb{E}}_{t+i}\hat{\mathbf{u}}_{t+i}\right) = \mathcal{B}^i \mathbb{E}_t^h \left(\hat{\mathbf{u}}_t - \overline{\mathbb{E}}_t \hat{\mathbf{u}}_t\right)$$

because $\mathbb{E}_t^h \mathbf{v}_{t+i} = 0$ for $i > 0$. Averaging this equation across households yields

$$\overline{\mathbb{E}}_t \left(\hat{\mathbf{u}}_{t+i} - \overline{\mathbb{E}}_{t+i}\hat{\mathbf{u}}_{t+i}\right) = \mathcal{B}^i \overline{\mathbb{E}}_t \left(\hat{\mathbf{u}}_t - \overline{\mathbb{E}}_t \hat{\mathbf{u}}_t\right) = \mathcal{B}^i \mathcal{D}\left(\hat{\mathbf{u}}_t - \overline{\mathbb{E}}_t \hat{\mathbf{u}}_t\right),$$

which is equation (4.50).

4.A.3 Impulse Responses

We calculate the impulse responses shown in Figure 4.1 as follows. The dashed line shows the values of θ_{i-2} plotted against i and the solid line shows the values of θ_i for $i = \{0, 1\}$ and $\theta_{i+2} + \frac{1-b}{1-b\rho}\rho^i$ for $i \geq 0$, again plotted against i, where

$$\theta_i = -b\psi \left\{ I - b\mathcal{B} \right\}^{-1} \mathcal{D}\mathcal{B}^i \mathcal{C}\iota_1' - \varphi \left(\mathcal{A}^i - \mathcal{B}^i \mathcal{C} \right) \iota_1', \tag{4.66}$$

with $\mathcal{B} = \left[(I - \beta)\, \mathcal{A} - \kappa\theta_1\iota_1 \right]$, $\mathcal{C} = \left[I - \beta - \kappa\theta_0\iota_1 \right]$, $\mathcal{D} = I - \left(\mathcal{C}\iota_1'\iota_1 + \mathcal{B}\mathcal{C}\iota_1'\iota_2 \right)$, $\psi = \left(\theta_2 - \frac{1-b}{1-b\rho} \right)\iota_1 + \theta_1\iota_2$, $\varphi = \frac{b^2(1-b)}{1-b\rho}\left(\iota_1 + \frac{1}{b}\iota_2 \right)$, and $\mathcal{A}$ as defined in (4.46). To calculate the θ_i's we first find the values of β and κ implied by the household's inference problem. For this purpose we note that household h's observations on $\hat{\mathbf{u}}_t$ can be written as

$$\begin{bmatrix} u_{2,t} \\ u_{1,t} \\ x_t \end{bmatrix} = \begin{bmatrix} 1 & 0 \\ 0 & 1 \\ \theta_0 & \theta_1 \end{bmatrix} \hat{\mathbf{u}}_t + \begin{bmatrix} \varsigma_{2,t}^h \\ \varsigma_{2,t}^h \\ 0 \end{bmatrix}$$

or, more compactly, as

$$\hat{\mathbf{u}}_t^h = \mathcal{H}\hat{\mathbf{u}}_t + \varsigma_t^h.$$

Next we note that

$$\begin{pmatrix} \hat{\mathbf{u}}_t \\ \hat{\mathbf{u}}_t^h \end{pmatrix} \sim N \left(\begin{pmatrix} \mathbb{E}[\hat{\mathbf{u}}_t | \Omega_{t-1}^h] \\ \mathcal{H}\mathbb{E}[\hat{\mathbf{u}}_t | \Omega_{t-1}^h] \end{pmatrix}, \begin{pmatrix} \mathbb{V}\left[\hat{\mathbf{u}}_t | \Omega_{t-1}^h\right] & \mathbb{V}\left[\hat{\mathbf{u}}_t | \Omega_{t-1}^h\right]\mathcal{H}' \\ \mathcal{H}\mathbb{V}\left[\hat{\mathbf{u}}_t | \Omega_{t-1}^h\right] & \mathcal{H}\mathbb{V}\left[\hat{\mathbf{u}}_t | \Omega_{t-1}^h\right]\mathcal{H}' + \mathbb{V}\left[\varsigma_t^h\right] \end{pmatrix} \right),$$

so applying the projection theorem, we get

$$[\,\beta \quad \kappa\,] = \mathbb{V}\left[\hat{\mathbf{u}}_t | \Omega_{t-1}^h\right]\mathcal{H}' \left(\mathcal{H}\mathbb{V}\left[\hat{\mathbf{u}}_t | \Omega_{t-1}^h\right]\mathcal{H}' + \mathbb{V}\left[\varsigma_t^h\right] \right)^{-1}. \tag{4.67}$$

In order to compute β and κ we have to find $\mathbb{V}\left[\hat{\mathbf{u}}_t | \Omega_{t-1}^h\right]$. Here we use two equations. The first is from the projection theorem,

$$\mathbb{V}\left[\hat{\mathbf{u}}_t | \Omega_t^h\right] = \mathbb{V}\left[\hat{\mathbf{u}}_t | \Omega_{t-1}^h, \hat{\mathbf{u}}_t^h\right]$$

$$= \mathbb{V}\left[\hat{\mathbf{u}}_t | \Omega_{t-1}^h\right]$$

$$- \mathbb{V}\left[\hat{\mathbf{u}}_t | \Omega_{t-1}^h\right]\mathcal{H}' \left(\mathcal{H}\mathbb{V}\left[\hat{\mathbf{u}}_t | \Omega_{t-1}^h\right]\mathcal{H}' + \mathbb{V}\left[\varsigma_t^h\right] \right)^{-1} \mathcal{H}\mathbb{V}\left[\hat{\mathbf{u}}_t | \Omega_{t-1}^h\right],$$

and the second comes from (4.46):

$$\mathbb{V}\left[\hat{\mathbf{u}}_{t+1} | \Omega_t^h\right] = \mathcal{A}\mathbb{V}\left[\hat{\mathbf{u}}_t | \Omega_t^h\right]\mathcal{A}' + \mathbb{V}\left[\nu_t\right].$$

Combining these equations with the restriction that $\mathbb{V}\left[\hat{\mathbf{u}}_{t+1}|\Omega_t^h\right] = \mathbb{V}\left[\hat{\mathbf{u}}_t|\Omega_{t-1}^h\right]$ (i.e., that we are in a covariance-stationary equilibrium) gives

$$
\mathbb{V}\left[\hat{\mathbf{u}}_t|\Omega_{t-1}^h\right] = \mathcal{A}\left(\mathbb{V}\left[\hat{\mathbf{u}}_t|\Omega_{t-1}^h\right]\right.
$$

$$
- \mathbb{V}\left[\hat{\mathbf{u}}_t|\Omega_{t-1}^h\right]\mathcal{H}'\left(\mathcal{H}\mathbb{V}\left[\hat{\mathbf{u}}_t|\Omega_{t-1}^h\right]\mathcal{H}' + .\mathbb{V}\left[\varsigma_t^h\right]\right)^{-1}
$$

$$
\left.\times \mathcal{H}\mathbb{V}\left[\hat{\mathbf{u}}_t|\Omega_{t-1}^h\right]\right)\mathcal{A}' + \mathbb{V}[\nu_t]. \tag{4.68}
$$

The numerical procedure works as follows. Let Γ in $\mathbb{R}^n$ denote a vector containing candidate values of θ_0, θ_1, θ_2 and the unique elements of $\mathbb{V}\left[\hat{\mathbf{u}}_t|\Omega_t^h\right]$. Equations (4.66), (4.67), and (4.68) describe a mapping $\mathcal{F}:\mathbb{R}^n \to \mathbb{R}^n$ such that $\Gamma = \mathcal{F}(\Gamma)$. To find the fixed point of this mapping we choose Γ to minimize $(\Gamma - \mathcal{F}(\Gamma))'(\Gamma - \mathcal{F}(\Gamma))$. This, then, is a standard nonlinear minimization problem.

CHAPTER 5

Sequential Trade Models

This chapter introduces a new perspective on the determination of exchange rates. Instead of relying on the fictional Walrasian auctioneer as the mechanism through which the equilibrium exchange rate is determined, we focus instead on the decisions of a new class of economic agent—marketmakers. Marketmakers perform some, but not all, of the functions of foreign exchange dealers. In particular, they provide liquidity to other agents by quoting spot rates at which they are willing to buy or sell foreign currency. This chapter deals with the way in which marketmakers make these pricing decisions, an analysis that serves as an introduction to the more complex behavior of participants in the foreign exchange market.

The introduction of marketmakers leads to an important change in perspective regarding the determination and behavior of exchange rates. Up to this point, variations in the equilibrium exchange rate have reflected changes in the notional demand for currency across the world economy. Here we consider a model in which the equilibrium exchange rate is literally determined by the foreign currency prices quoted by marketmakers. Exchange-rate variations are therefore entirely determined by the factors that lead marketmakers to change their spot rate quotes. This change in perspective allows us to think about the origins of exchange-rate dynamics in new and important ways.

This model is also distinctive in terms of information. We study an environment in which only some agents have access to up-to-date information about exchange-rate fundamentals. A key feature of the model is that it allows us to study how this information is transmitted to marketmakers and hence into currency prices. In so doing, we replace the "black box" linking exchange rates to fundamentals with a detailed description of how information about fundamentals is transmitted via market activity into spot rates.

5.1 The Model

The model we study here is based on Glosten and Milgrom (1985) and is set in the spot foreign exchange market. There are three groups of market participants: marketmakers, informed traders, and uninformed traders. Marketmakers provide liquidity to traders by quoting spot rates at which they are willing to buy or sell a foreign currency.

We assume that there are N marketmakers (indexed by n) who seek to maximize their trading profits. Traders come in two types. Informed traders, who have access to information about the value of foreign currency and trade with marketmakers using that information, and uninformed traders, who have no information about the underlying value of the foreign currency but trade for liquidity reasons. Our focus is on how the information available to the informed traders concerning the value of foreign currency is transmitted to the spot rates quoted by the marketmakers.

The timing of events in the model is as follows: At the start of period t marketmakers quote spot rates at which they will buy and sell one unit of foreign currency. Marketmaker n will sell foreign currency at the offer or asking price of $S_{n,t}^A$ and buy at the bid price of $S_{n,t}^B$. A trader is then picked at random and allowed to trade with any marketmaker at his or her quoted spot rates. The trader may choose to buy foreign currency at the ask quote, sell at the bid quote, or decline to trade. Trading decisions are observed by all marketmakers, who then update their inferences concerning the value of foreign currency in preparation for quoting spot rates at the start of period $t + 1$.

Let us now consider the behavior of market participants in more detail. There is a continuum of traders distributed on interval [0,1]. A fraction, λ, is made up of informed (I-traders), and a fraction, $1 - \lambda$, of uninformed (U-traders). If an I-trader has the opportunity to trade, he compares the best quotes against the value of foreign currency implied by fundamentals, F_t. The best ask quote is $S_t^A = \min_n\{S_{n,t}^A\}$ and the best bid quote is $S_t^B = \max_n\{S_{n,t}^B\}$. If $S_t^A < F_t$ the trader buys foreign currency from the marketmaker quoting the best ask price. Similarly, if $S_t^B > F_t$ the trader will sell foreign currency to the marketmaker with the highest bid price. When there are multiple marketmakers offering the best quotes, the trader randomly chooses one of the marketmakers to trade with. (In equilibrium all marketmakers quote the same bid and ask prices, so the trader randomly chooses from among all the marketmakers if he wants to trade.) In cases where $S_t^A \geq F_t \geq S_t^B$, the trader declines to trade, or passes. The trading behavior of I-traders may therefore be summarized by:

State	Trade	Symbol
$Z = 1 : F_t > S_t^A$	Buy	$\mathbb{B}_t^I$
$Z = 2 : S_t^A \geq F_t \geq S_t^B$	Pass	$\mathbb{P}_t^I$
$Z = 3 : S_t^B > F_t$	Sell	$\mathbb{S}_t^I$

$$(5.1)$$

In earlier chapters we went to some lengths to determine the economic determinants of fundamentals. Here we abstract from these complications by assuming that fundamentals follow a random walk:

$$F_t \equiv F_{t-1} + U_t, \qquad (5.2)$$

where U_t is the period-t innovation to the random walk. We assume that these innovations are independently and identically distributed each period and take one of three values $\{1, 0, -1\}$ with corresponding probabilities of $\{\alpha/2, (1 - \alpha), \alpha/2\}$, where $1 \geq \alpha > 0$. This specification allows for the possibility that fundamentals may remain unchanged from one trading period to the next. The probability of a change in fundamentals is simply α.

The I-traders are assumed to observe realizations of U_t at the start of period t. This means that period-t trading decisions can be based on the value of F_t, as assumed in (5.1). Note also that U_t has a mean of zero, so the best forecast of future fundamentals based on current fundamentals is $\mathbb{E}\left[F_{t+i}|F_t\right] = F_t$ for all $i > 0$. The expected future (gross) return on buying and selling foreign currency is thus $\mathbb{E}\left[F_{t+i}|F_t\right]/S_t^{\mathrm{A}} = F_t/S_t^{\mathrm{A}}$ and $\mathbb{E}\left[F_{t+i}|F_t\right]/S_t^{\mathrm{B}} = F_t/S_t^{\mathrm{B}}$, respectively.

The trading behavior of U-traders is even more straightforward. If a U-trader has the opportunity to trade, he randomly decides to buy or sell foreign currency with probability 1/2, and then is matched with a marketmaker offering the best quotes. We use $\mathbb{B}_t^{\mathrm{U}}$ and $\mathbb{S}_t^{\mathrm{U}}$ to denote the purchase and sale of foreign currency by a U-trader in period t. It is important to note that this trading behavior is not dependent on either the spot rates quoted by the marketmaker or the value of fundamentals. As a consequence, trades by U-traders will not provide any information about the true value of foreign currency.

There are a large number of competitive marketmakers who provide liquidity to the market. This means that they stand ready to buy or sell one unit of foreign currency at the spot rates they quote each period. All marketmakers have access to the same information. They can observe both the spot rates quoted by others and the trading decisions of traders. No marketmaker observes the innovations to fundamentals, U_t, and so no one has *direct* knowledge of the true value of foreign currency each period. We denote the information set of marketmakers at the start of period t by Ω_t.

Marketmakers choose bid and ask quotes to maximize the expected profit from trading. The realized profit from selling one unit of foreign currency to a trader at the ask quote of $S_{n,t}^{\mathrm{A}}$ is $S_{n,t}^{\mathrm{A}} - F_t$, whereas the profit from buying from the trader at the bid quote of $S_{n,t}^{\mathrm{B}}$ is $F_t - S_{n,t}^{\mathrm{B}}$. Let $\mathbb{B}_t$ and $\mathbb{S}_t$ denote the purchase and sale by *any* trader (i.e., informed or uninformed) in period t. The expected profit for marketmaker n from period-t trading is then

$$(S_{n,t}^{\mathrm{A}} - \mathbb{E}[F_t|\mathbb{B}_t, \Omega_t]) \Pr\left(\mathbb{B}_t|\Omega_t\right) + (\mathbb{E}[F_t|\mathbb{S}_t, \Omega_t] - S_{n,t}^{\mathrm{B}}) \Pr\left(\mathbb{S}_t|\Omega_t\right), \quad (5.3)$$

where $\Pr\left(\mathbb{T}_t|\Omega_t\right)$ is the probability of trade $\mathbb{T}_t = \left\{\mathbb{B}_t, \mathbb{S}_t\right\}$ taking place conditioned on the marketmaker's period-t information, Ω_t. $\mathbb{E}[F_t|\mathbb{T}_t, \Omega_t]$ is the expected value of foreign currency in period t conditioned on Ω_t and the period-t trade.

At the start of period t, each marketmaker n chooses $S_{n,t}^{\mathrm{A}}$ and $S_{n,t}^{\mathrm{B}}$ to maximize his expected trading profits, taking into account the quotes of the other $N-1$ marketmakers. This constitutes a game among the marketmakers in which all N players have the same information, Ω_t. The Nash equilibrium quotes that result are given by

$$S_t^{\mathrm{A}} = S_{n,t}^{\mathrm{A}} = \mathbb{E}[F_t|\mathbb{B}_t, \Omega_t], \quad (5.4a)$$

$$S_t^{\mathrm{B}} = S_{n,t}^{\mathrm{B}} = \mathbb{E}[F_t|\mathbb{S}_t, \Omega_t], \quad (5.4b)$$

for $n = 1, 2, \ldots, N$. Thus, each marketmaker quotes the same bid and ask price and these prices are equal to the expectation of fundamentals conditioned on prior information and the type of trade that occurs.

It is easy to see why the quotes in (5.4) maximize expected trading profits for each marketmaker given the quotes of others. Suppose, for example, that marketmaker n quoted a price higher than $\mathbb{E}[F_t|\mathbb{B}_t, \Omega_t]$. Under these circumstances, the first term in (5.4) would be positive, but there would be no increase in expected trading profits because $\Pr\left(\mathbb{B}_t|\Omega_t\right)$ would fall to zero as traders wanting to purchase foreign currency would always choose to trade with other marketmakers. Alternatively, if $S_{n,t}^A < \mathbb{E}[F_t|\mathbb{B}_t, \Omega_t]$, $\Pr\left(\mathbb{B}_t|\Omega_t\right)$ remains greater than zero but the expected profit from selling foreign currency [i.e., the first term in (5.3)] becomes negative. Thus there is no benefit to marketmaker n from quoting an ask price different from $\mathbb{E}[F_t|\mathbb{B}_t, \Omega_t]$ when all others continue to quote S_t^A. Similarly, there is no benefit to quoting a bid price different from $\mathbb{E}[F_t|\mathbb{S}_t, \Omega_t]$. Quoting a bid price below $\mathbb{E}[F_t|\mathbb{S}_t, \Omega_t]$ will fail to raise expected profits and setting $S_{n,t}^B > \mathbb{E}[F_t|\mathbb{S}_t, \Omega_t]$ will result in an expected loss from foreign currency purchases.

Equation (5.4) identifies equilibrium exchange rates in the model. In macro models there is a single exchange rate for each currency pair, but here we distinguish between the price at which foreign currency can be bought, S_t^A, and the price at which it can be sold, S_t^B. The crucial point here is that these spot rates represent the optimum quote choices of marketmakers in a particular equilibrium. This is an extremely important change in perspective on the origins of exchange-rate dynamics. In the macro models presented earlier, changes in the exchange rate are driven by variations in the economy-wide notional excess demand for foreign currency via the fictional mechanism of the Walrasian auctioneer. Here, by contrast, changes in the exchange rates must reflect revisions in marketmaker expectations concerning the value of foreign currency. Understanding how developments in the economy affect marketmaker quote decisions is key to explaining exchange-rate dynamics.

The exchange-rate equations in (5.4) have two features worth noting. First they state that all marketmakers quote the same bid and ask prices. Unanimity in pricing arises here as a consequence of the trading environment. In particular, recall that a trader always has the opportunity to trade with a marketmaker offering the best bid or ask price. Of course, this only makes sense when all quotes can be costlessly observed by any trader. Under these conditions of high market transparency, marketmakers know that they will not make any trading profits by offering inferior quotes, which in turn eliminates the benefit from quoting spot rates that differ from those of others. By contrast, if the market is less transparent so that not all quotes can be costlessly observed by any trader, marketmakers can earn trading profits even when their quotes are inferior to others in the market. Under these conditions, there could be a distribution of bid and ask quotes if marketmakers had different objective functions and/or access to different information. For example, if marketmakers were risk averse or subject to capital constraints, their quote decisions would depend, in part, on their individual holdings of foreign currency. Differences in currency holdings arising from the pattern of trade would then give rise to a distribution of quotes in a market with low transparency. Differences in information would have a similar impact because individual marketmakers would not be able to perfectly predict the quotes of others.

The second noteworthy feature of (5.4) concerns the "regret-free" aspect of both the bid and ask quotes. Each quote is equal to the expected value of foreign currency (i.e., fundamentals, F_t) conditioned on information at the start of period t, Ω_t, and the fact that a trader wants to undertake the particular trade. For example, the ask quote, S_t^A, is equal to the expected value of F_t conditioned on Ω_t and the fact that a trader wants to purchase foreign currency, $\mathbb{E}[F_t|\mathbb{B}_t, \Omega_t]$. These quotes are said to be regret-free because the marketmaker is getting a fair price given that a trader wants to buy (or sell) foreign currency. One implication of regret-free pricing is that the period-t quotes incorporate information about the value of fundamentals that is contained in period-t trading.

5.2 Exchange-Rate Determination

We now consider how marketmakers determine their bid and ask quotes. Recall that optimal quotes are simply equal to marketmaker expectations concerning fundamentals. We first examine the link between quotes and marketmaker beliefs concerning fundamentals. We then study how beliefs are revised as marketmakers learn from the pattern of trading.

5.2.1 Quotes and Beliefs

Recall that innovations to fundamentals, U_t, can take one of three values, $\{1, 0, -1\}$. Since fundamentals are simply the cumulant of the innovations, $F_t = \sum_{i=0}^{t} U_i$, realizations of F_t are also discretely valued. We can therefore describe marketmaker beliefs about period-t fundamentals using the conditional probabilities $\pi_t(k) \equiv \Pr(F_t = k|\Omega_t)$, for $k = \{\ldots -3, -2, 1, 0, 1, 2, 3, \ldots\}$. The term $\pi_t(k)$ is therefore the probability that $F_t = k$ based on marketmaker's information at the start of period t.

The next task is to relate the quotes in (5.4) to marketmaker beliefs. For this purpose, we use the fact that

$$\mathbb{E}\left[F_t|\mathbb{T}_t, \Omega_t\right] = \mathbb{E}\left[F_t|\mathbb{T}_t^{\text{I}}, \mathbb{T}_t, \Omega_t\right]\Pr\left(\mathbb{T}_t^{\text{I}}|\mathbb{T}_t, \Omega_t\right)$$
$$+ \mathbb{E}\left[F_t|\mathbb{T}_t^{\text{U}}, \mathbb{T}_t, \Omega_t\right]\Pr\left(\mathbb{T}_t^{\text{U}}|\mathbb{T}_t, \Omega_t\right)$$

for $\mathbb{T} = \{\mathbb{B}, \mathbb{S}\}$. $\Pr\left(\mathbb{T}_t^{\text{J}}|\mathbb{T}_t, \Omega_t\right)$ is the probability that a type-J trader undertook trade $\mathbb{T}$ conditioned on Ω_t and the fact that a $\mathbb{T}$ trade took place. Thus $\Pr(\mathbb{B}_t^{\text{I}}|\mathbb{B}_t, \Omega_t)$ is the probability that foreign currency was purchased by an I-trader conditioned on Ω_t and the fact that foreign currency was purchased. Substituting for $\mathbb{E}\left[F_t|\mathbb{T}_t, \Omega_t\right]$ in (5.4) allows us to rewrite the equations for marketmaker quotes as

$$S_t^{\text{A}} = \mathbb{E}\left[F_t|\mathbb{B}_t^{\text{I}}, \mathbb{B}_t, \Omega_t\right]\Pr(\mathbb{B}_t^{\text{I}}|\mathbb{B}_t, \Omega_t) + \mathbb{E}\left[F_t|\mathbb{B}_t^{\text{U}}, \mathbb{B}_t, \Omega_t\right]\Pr(\mathbb{B}_t^{\text{U}}|\mathbb{B}_t, \Omega_t), \quad (5.5a)$$

and

$$S_t^{\text{B}} = \mathbb{E}\left[F_t|\mathbb{S}_t^{\text{I}}, \mathbb{S}_t, \Omega_t\right]\Pr(\mathbb{S}_t^{\text{I}}|\mathbb{S}_t, \Omega_t) + \mathbb{E}\left[F_t|\mathbb{S}_t^{\text{U}}, \mathbb{S}_t, \Omega_t\right]\Pr(\mathbb{S}_t^{\text{U}}|\mathbb{S}_t, \Omega_t). \quad (5.5b)$$

Equations 5.5 express quotes in terms of expectations conditioned on trade with a particular type of trader and the probability that the trade takes place. For example, $\mathbb{E}\left[F_t|\mathbb{B}_t^{\text{I}}, \mathbb{B}_t, \Omega_t\right]$ is the expected value of fundamentals conditioned on Ω_t and the purchase of foreign currency by an I-trader. This decomposition is useful because these conditional expectations and trade probabilities are readily computed.

Consider the expectations conditioned on the trades of U-traders. As the trading decisions of these traders are independent of the value of fundamentals, their trades convey no new information. Consequently, expectations conditioned on trades of this type are the same as expectations conditioned solely on prior information. Hence,

$$\mathbb{E}\left[F_t|\mathbb{B}_t^{\mathrm{U}}, \mathbb{B}_t, \Omega_t\right] = \mathbb{E}\left[F_t|\Omega_t\right], \tag{5.6a}$$

and

$$\mathbb{E}\left[F_t|\mathbb{S}_t^{\mathrm{U}}, \mathbb{S}_t, \Omega_t\right] = \mathbb{E}\left[F_t|\Omega_t\right]. \tag{5.6b}$$

By contrast, expectations conditioned on I-trader trades and Ω_t differ from expectations conditioned only on Ω_t because I-traders compare quotes to the value of fundamentals. In particular, since I-traders only purchase foreign currency when $S_t^{\mathrm{A}} < F_t$ and only sell when $S_t^{\mathrm{B}} > F_t$, we can rewrite the expectations in (5.5) as

$$\mathbb{E}\left[F_t|\mathbb{B}_t^{\mathrm{I}}, \mathbb{B}_t, \Omega_t\right] = \mathbb{E}\left[F_t|F_t > S_t^{\mathrm{A}}, \Omega_t\right], \tag{5.7a}$$

and

$$\mathbb{E}\left[F_t|\mathbb{S}_t^{\mathrm{I}}, \mathbb{S}_t, \Omega_t\right] = \mathbb{E}\left[F_t|F_t < S_t^{\mathrm{B}}, \Omega_t\right]. \tag{5.7b}$$

The expectations on the right-hand side of (5.6) and (5.7) are straightforwardly calculated from marketmaker beliefs as

$$\mathbb{E}\left[F_t|\Omega_t\right] = \sum_k k\pi_t(k), \tag{5.8a}$$

$$\mathbb{E}\left[F_t|F_t > S_t^{\mathrm{A}}, \Omega_t\right] = \frac{1}{\overline{\Pi}(S_t^{\mathrm{A}})} \sum_{k > S_t^{\mathrm{A}}} k\pi_t(k), \tag{5.8b}$$

and

$$\mathbb{E}\left[F_t|F_t < S_t^{\mathrm{B}}, \Omega_t\right] = \frac{1}{\underline{\Pi}(S_t^{\mathrm{B}})} \sum_{k < S_t^{\mathrm{B}}} k\pi_t(k), \tag{5.8c}$$

where $\underline{\Pi}(S_t^i) \equiv \sum_{k < S_t^i} \pi_t(k)$ and $\overline{\Pi}(S_t^i) \equiv \sum_{k > S_t^i} \pi_t(k)$ for $i = \{\mathrm{A,B}\}$.

To complete the link between marketmaker beliefs and their spot rate quotes we compute the trade probabilities. These probabilities depend on the relation between the quotes and the true value of fundamentals. Recall from (5.1) that there are three possible states of the market. State 1, where $F_t > S_t^{\mathrm{A}}$; state 2, where $S_t^{\mathrm{A}} \geq F_t \geq S_t^{\mathrm{B}}$; and state 3, where $S_t^{\mathrm{B}} > F_t$. Now suppose that $F_t > S_t^{\mathrm{A}}$. In this state I-traders will always purchase foreign currency if they are given the chance to trade. Since all N marketmakers quote the same spot rates, there is thus a $1/N$ probability that an I-trader will buy from an individual marketmaker if he is given the opportunity to trade. Since the fraction of I-traders in the market is λ and traders are chosen randomly, the probability that an I-trader will buy from a marketmaker is λ/N. By contrast, U-traders will buy with probability 1/2 when given the chance to trade, so the probability that a U-trader will buy from a marketmaker is $(1 - \lambda)/(2N)$. The probability that any trader will buy from a marketmaker is thus $(1 - \lambda)/(2N) + \lambda/N$. In states 2 and 3, I-traders will not buy, whereas U-traders will continue to purchase with probability $(1 - \lambda)/2N$. The probability of a foreign currency purchase from a marketmaker in these states is therefore $(1 - \lambda)/2N$. Proceeding in this manner we can compute the

TABLE 5.1
Trade Probabilities

	States		
	$Z = 1$	$Z = 2$	$Z = 3$
	$F_t > S_t^{\text{A}}$	$S_t^{\text{A}} \geq F_t \geq S_t^{\text{B}}$	$S_t^{\text{B}} > F_t$
$\Pr\left(Z \vert \Omega_t\right)$	$\overline{\Pi}(S_t^{\text{A}})$	$1 - \overline{\Pi}(S_t^{\text{A}}) - \underline{\Pi}(S_t^{\text{B}})$	$\underline{\Pi}(S_t^{\text{B}})$
Purchase probabilities			
$\Pr(\mathbb{B}^{\text{I}} \vert Z, \Omega_t)$	λ/N	0	0
$\Pr(\mathbb{B}^{\text{U}} \vert Z, \Omega_t)$	$(1-\lambda)/(2N)$	$(1-\lambda)/(2N)$	$(1-\lambda)/(2N)$
$\Pr(\mathbb{B} \vert Z, \Omega_t)$	$\lambda/N + (1-\lambda)/(2N)$	$(1-\lambda)/(2N)$	$(1-\lambda)/(2N)$
Sale probabilities			
$\Pr(\mathbb{S}^{\text{I}} \vert Z, \Omega_t)$	0	0	λ/N
$\Pr(\mathbb{S}^{\text{U}} \vert Z, \Omega_t)$	$(1-\lambda)/(2N)$	$(1-\lambda)/(2N)$	$(1-\lambda)/(2N)$
$\Pr(\mathbb{S} \vert Z, \Omega_t)$	$(1-\lambda)/(2N)$	$(1-\lambda)/(2N)$	$\lambda/N + (1-\lambda)/(2N)$
Pass probabilities			
$\Pr(\mathbb{P}^{\text{I}} \vert Z, \Omega_t)$	0	λ/N	0
$\Pr(\mathbb{P}^{\text{U}} \vert Z, \Omega_t)$	0	0	0
$\Pr(\mathbb{P} \vert Z, \Omega_t)$	0	λ/N	0

probability of a particular trade occurring for a given state of the market. The results of these calculation are shown in Table 5.1.

We can use the results in Table 5.1 to compute the conditional trade probabilities in the quote equations (5.5). As an example, consider the probability that a purchase was made by an I-trader, $\Pr(\mathbb{B}_t^{\text{I}} \vert \mathbb{B}_t, \Omega_t)$. The results in the table allow us to compute the probability of a purchase by any trader as

$$\Pr(\mathbb{B}_t \vert \Omega_t) = \sum_Z \Pr(\mathbb{B}_t \vert Z, \Omega_t) \Pr\left(Z \vert \Omega_t\right),$$

and the probability of a purchase by an I-trader as

$$\Pr(\mathbb{B}_t^{\text{I}} \vert \Omega_t) = \sum_Z \Pr(\mathbb{B}_t^{\text{I}} \vert Z, \Omega_t) \Pr\left(Z \vert \Omega_t\right).$$

According to Bayes' law, the probability that an I-trader will purchase foreign currency conditioned on the observation that foreign currency was purchased is

$$\Pr(\mathbb{B}_t^{\text{I}} \vert \mathbb{B}_t, \Omega_t) = \frac{\Pr(\mathbb{B}_t \vert \mathbb{B}_t^{\text{I}}, \Omega_t) \Pr(\mathbb{B}_t^{\text{I}} \vert \Omega_t)}{\Pr(\mathbb{B}_t \vert \Omega_t)},$$

where $\Pr(\mathbb{B}_t \vert \mathbb{B}_t^{\text{I}}, \Omega_t)$ is the probability that any trader purchases foreign currency conditioned on the fact that an I-trader made a purchase, and so is trivially equal to one. Making this simplification and using the results from Table 5.1 gives us

$$\Pr(\mathbb{B}_t^{\mathrm{I}}|\mathbb{B}_t, \Omega_t) = \frac{\Pr(\mathbb{B}_t^{\mathrm{I}}|\Omega_t)}{\Pr(\mathbb{B}_t|\Omega_t)} = \frac{\lambda\overline{\Pi}(S_t^{\mathrm{A}})}{(1-\lambda)/2 + \lambda\overline{\Pi}(S_t^{\mathrm{A}})}.$$

The other conditional trade probabilities in the quote equations are similarly found as

$$\Pr(\mathbb{B}_t^{\mathrm{U}}|\mathbb{B}_t, \Omega_t) = \frac{\Pr(\mathbb{B}_t^{\mathrm{U}}|\Omega_t)}{\Pr(\mathbb{B}_t|\Omega_t)} = \frac{(1-\lambda)/2}{(1-\lambda)/2 + \lambda\overline{\Pi}(S_t^{\mathrm{A}})},$$

$$\Pr(\mathbb{S}_t^{\mathrm{I}}|\mathbb{S}_t, \Omega_t) = \frac{\Pr(\mathbb{S}_t^{\mathrm{I}}|\Omega_t)}{\Pr(\mathbb{S}_t|\Omega_t)} = \frac{\lambda\underline{\Pi}(S_t^{\mathrm{B}})}{(1-\lambda)/2 + \lambda\underline{\Pi}(S_t^{\mathrm{B}})},$$

$$\Pr(\mathbb{S}_t^{\mathrm{U}}|\mathbb{S}_t, \Omega_t) = \frac{\Pr(\mathbb{S}_t^{\mathrm{U}}|\Omega_t)}{\Pr(\mathbb{S}_t|\Omega_t)} = \frac{(1-\lambda)/2}{(1-\lambda)/2 + \lambda\underline{\Pi}(S_t^{\mathrm{B}})}.$$

We now have all the results necessary to describe how marketmaker quotes are related to their beliefs about fundamentals. In particular, combining the expressions for these conditional trade probabilities with equations (5.5)–(5.8) gives us

$$S_t^{\mathrm{A}} = \frac{\lambda}{(1-\lambda)/2 + \lambda\overline{\Pi}(S_t^{\mathrm{A}})}\sum_{k>S_t^{\mathrm{A}}}k\pi_t(k) + \frac{(1-\lambda)/2}{(1-\lambda)/2 + \lambda\overline{\Pi}(S_t^{\mathrm{A}})}\sum_{k}k\pi_t(k), \quad (5.9a)$$

and

$$S_t^{\mathrm{B}} = \frac{\lambda}{(1-\lambda)/2 + \lambda\underline{\Pi}(S_t^{\mathrm{B}})}\sum_{k<S_t^{\mathrm{B}}}k\pi_t(k) + \frac{(1-\lambda)/2}{(1-\lambda)/2 + \lambda\underline{\Pi}(S_t^{\mathrm{B}})}\sum_{k}k\pi_t(k). \quad (5.9b)$$

These equations relate marketmaker beliefs about fundamentals [via the $\pi_t(k)$ probabilities] to the bid and ask quotes, S_t^{A} and S_t^{B}. Note that quotes appear on both sides of the equality sign in each expression, so neither equation provides us with an explicit formula for the bid and ask quotes. This complication arises because I-traders' decisions depend on the relation between fundamentals and quotes, so the probability of a trade with a particular trader type depends on the quotes. We examine this aspect of the model in more detail in what follows.

5.2.2 Learning from Trade

Next we turn to the issue of how marketmakers revise their beliefs about fundamentals. Recall that all marketmakers observe the trade that takes place each period, but they do not know whether the trader is informed or uninformed about the value for fundamentals.[1] The problem facing marketmakers is how to incorporate information from their observations on each trade into their beliefs about fundamentals.

---

1. This is a strong assumption because with N marketmakers quoting identical prices, the probability that a trade occurs with an individual marketmaker is only $1/N$. Consequently, it only makes sense in an enviroment where communication among marketmakers about their trades is complete and immediate.

Let $\mathbb{T}_t = \{\mathbb{B}_t, \mathbb{S}_t, \mathbb{P}_t\}$ denote the trade that takes place in period t. Since that observed period-t trade is the only new information available to marketmakers between the start of periods t and $t+1$, information at the start of period $t+1$, Ω_{t+1}, comprises $\mathbb{T}_t$ and Ω_t. Thus, period-$t+1$ beliefs can be rewritten as

$$\pi_{t+1}(k) \equiv \Pr\left(F_{t+1} = k | \Omega_{t+1}\right) = \Pr\left(F_{t+1} = k | \mathbb{T}_t, \Omega_t\right). \tag{5.10}$$

Our task is to find an expression for $\Pr\left(F_{t+1} = k | \mathbb{T}_t, \Omega_t\right)$ using observations on period-t trade, $\mathbb{T}_t$, and prior marketmakers beliefs, $\pi_t(k)$.

First we write $\Pr\left(F_{t+1} = k | \mathbb{T}_t, \Omega_t\right)$ in terms of the beliefs concerning the value of F_t. By definition,

$$\Pr(F_{t+1} = k | \mathbb{T}_t, \Omega_t) = \sum_j \Pr\left(F_{t+1} = k, F_t = j | \mathbb{T}_t, \Omega_t\right)$$

$$= \sum_j \Pr\left(F_{t+1} = k, | F_t = j, \mathbb{T}_t, \Omega_t\right) \Pr\left(F_t = j | \mathbb{T}_t, \Omega_t\right). \tag{5.11}$$

Recall that fundamentals follow a random walk with discrete innovations: that is, $F_{t+1} = F_t + U_t$, where $U_t = \{1, 0, -1\}$ with probabilities $\{\alpha/2, (1-\alpha), \alpha/2\}$. It is therefore straightforward to see that

$$\Pr\left(F_{t+1} = k, | F_t = j, \mathbb{T}_t, \Omega_t\right) = \begin{cases} 0 & j < k-1 \\ \alpha/2 & j = k-1 \\ 1-\alpha & j = k \\ a/2 & j = k+1 \\ 0 & j > k+1 \end{cases}.$$

Substituting these probabilities into (5.11) gives us

$$\Pr(F_{t+1} = k | \mathbb{T}_t, \Omega_t) = (\alpha/2) \Pr\left(F_t = k+1 | \mathbb{T}_t, \Omega_t\right)$$

$$+ (\alpha/2) \Pr(F_t = k-1 | \mathbb{T}_t, \Omega_t)$$

$$+ (1-\alpha) \Pr\left(F_t = k | \mathbb{T}_t, \Omega_t\right). \tag{5.12}$$

The last step is to compute $\Pr\left(F_t = k | \mathbb{T}_t, \Omega_t\right)$. These probabilities embody marketmaker beliefs about period-t fundamentals updated to incorporate information from period-t trades. These are easily computed from Bayes' law:

$$\Pr\left(F_t = k | \mathbb{T}_t, \Omega_t\right) = \frac{\Pr\left(\mathbb{T}_t | F_t = k, \Omega_t\right)}{\Pr\left(\mathbb{T}_t | \Omega_t\right)} \Pr\left(F_t = k | \Omega_t\right), \tag{5.13}$$

where

$$\Pr\left(\mathbb{T}_t | \Omega_t\right) = \sum_k \Pr\left(\mathbb{T}_t | F_t = k, \Omega_t\right) \Pr\left(F_t = k | \Omega_t\right).$$

The only new element in this expression is $\Pr\left(\mathbb{T}_t | F_t = k, \Omega_t\right)$, which is the probability that trade $\mathbb{T}_t$ takes place conditioned on the fact that fundamentals in t take the particular value of k. To illustrate how we find this probability, consider the case in which foreign currency is purchased (i.e., $\mathbb{T}_t = \mathbb{B}_t$). Recall that traders are selected at random and independently of either the value of fundamentals or marketmaker quotes. Thus the probability of a marketmaker trading with an I-trader or a U-trader is λ/N or $(1 - \lambda)/N$, respectively. If an I-trader is selected he will buy for sure if, and only if, $S_t^{\mathrm{A}} < F_t$, whereas a U-trader will buy with a probability of $1/2$. The conditional probability of a purchase $\Pr\left(\mathbb{B}_t | F_t = k, \Omega_t\right)$ is therefore $(1 - \lambda)/(2N) + (\lambda/N)$ if $k > S_t^{\mathrm{A}}$ and $(1 - \lambda)/(2N)$ otherwise. Proceeding analogously for the case of sales and pass trades, we obtain

$$\Pr\left(\mathbb{T}_t | F_t = k, \Omega_t\right) = \begin{cases} \frac{1}{2}(1 - \lambda) + \lambda\mathcal{I}(k > S_t^{\mathrm{A}}) & \text{if } \mathbb{T}_t = \mathbb{B}_t \\ \frac{1}{2}(1 - \lambda) + \lambda\mathcal{I}(k < S_t^{\mathrm{B}}) & \text{if } \mathbb{T}_t = \mathbb{S}_t \\ \lambda\mathcal{I}(S_t^{\mathrm{A}} \geq k \geq S_t^{\mathrm{B}}) & \text{if } \mathbb{T}_t = \mathbb{P}_t \end{cases}, \quad (5.14)$$

where $\mathcal{I}(\cdot)$ is an indicator function [i.e., equal to one when the condition in $(\cdot)$ is true and zero otherwise].

In summary, the evolution of marketmaker beliefs concerning fundamentals between the start of period t and $t + 1$ is described by (5.10)–(5.14). We can express these equations more succinctly as

$$\pi_{t+1}(k) = (\alpha/2)\Pr\left(F_t = k + 1 | \mathbb{T}_t, \Omega_t\right) + (\alpha/2)\Pr\left(F_t = k - 1 | \mathbb{T}_t, \Omega_t\right)$$

$$+ (1 - \alpha)\Pr\left(F_t = k | \mathbb{T}_t, \Omega_t\right), \quad (5.15)$$

where

$$\Pr\left(F_t = k | \mathbb{T}_t, \Omega_t\right) = \frac{\Pr\left(\mathbb{T}_t | F_t = k, \Omega_t\right)}{\sum_k \left\{\Pr\left(\mathbb{T}_t | F_t = k, \Omega_t\right)\pi_t(k)\right\}}\pi_t(k),$$

with $\Pr\left(F_t = k | \mathbb{T}_t, \Omega_t\right)$ computed from (5.14).

5.3 Exchange-Rate Dynamics

We now examine the exchange-rate implications of our model. In particular, we study how changes in the bid and ask quotes reflect the evolution of marketmaker beliefs concerning fundamentals and how these beliefs are informed by the pattern of trading. Since the equations determining optimal quotes and the evolution of beliefs are highly nonlinear, it is not possible to examine the dynamics of the model analytically. Instead, we study the results of several numerical simulations of the model.

5.3.1 Learning about Fundamentals

Case 1: Constant Fundamentals

We begin by studying a simplified version of the model in which fundamentals are a constant equal to F. In this environment, the problem facing marketmakers is

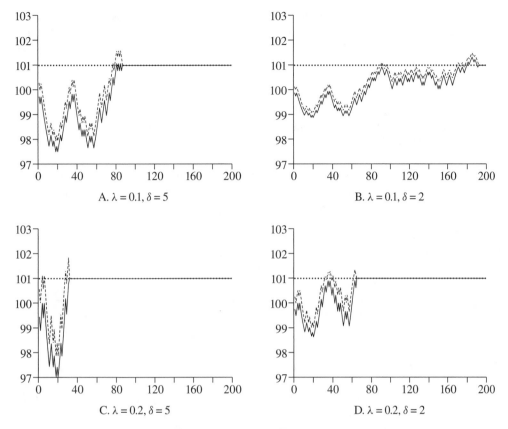

FIGURE 5.1   Learning about constant fundamentals (S_t^B, solid; S_t^A, dashed; F_t, dotted).

straightforward. They understand that given the opportunity to trade, I-traders will purchase foreign currency if their ask quote is below F and sell foreign currency if the bid quote is above F. They also understand that U-traders purchase and sell foreign currency with equal probability if they have the chance to trade, so the trades of U-traders are uninformative about F. The problem facing the marketmaker is therefore one of separating the informative trades of I-traders from the uninformative trades of U-traders. This is relatively straightforward when fundamentals are fixed. If quotes are initially below the level of F there will be more trader-initiated purchases than sales in a sequence of transactions because I-traders will always purchase when given the opportunity to trade. Similarly, there will be more trader-initiated sales than purchases in a sequence of trades if quotes are above the level of F.

We can see this intuition at work in Figure 5.1. Here we show simulations of the model for the case in which fundamentals F are fixed at 101. At the start of trading, in period $t = 0$, the marketmaker has uniform beliefs about the value of F given by

$$\pi_0(k) = \begin{cases} 0 & \text{for } k < 100 - \delta \\ \frac{1}{2\delta + 1} & \text{for } 100 - \delta \leq k \leq 100 + \delta \ . \\ 0 & \text{for } k > 100 + \delta \end{cases} \quad (5.16)$$

To examine how the dispersion of prior beliefs affects the behavior of quotes, we run simulations with δ equal to 2 and 5. Note that in both cases, the prior beliefs imply that $E\left[F|\Omega_0\right] = 100$. Thus our simulations consider a situation in which the actual level of fundamentals is 1 percent higher than marketmakers' expectations before trading starts. The only other parameters in the model are α and λ. Recall that α is the probability that fundamentals change each period, so for these simulations $\alpha = 0$; λ is the fraction of I-traders in the market. The figure presents simulations with λ equal to 0.1 and 0.2. The figure plots the bid and ask prices quoted by marketmakers over 200 periods, and the fixed level of fundamentals, $F = 101$.

Figure 5.1 depicts several noteworthy features. First, there is a good deal of variation in the time it takes marketmakers to learn the true level of fundamentals (i.e., the time it takes before the bid and ask quotes are equal to 101). In panel C, it only takes marketmakers approximately 30 periods of trading to learn about the true value of fundamentals, whereas in panel B is takes almost 200 periods. The second feature concerns the paths of the quotes. In all four cases, there is no monotonic path between the spot rates quoted in period 1 and the quotes of 101 when the true value of fundamentals is learned. In panel A, for example, we see that both the bid and ask quotes fall for several consecutive trading periods despite the fact that both spot rates are well below the true level of fundamentals. A final noteworthy feature of the figure concerns the spread between the ask and bid quotes, represented by the vertical distance between the solid and dashed plots. Although the spread changes over the learning period, these changes are much smaller than the variations in either the bid or ask quotes. In this model, time series variations in quotes dominate changes in the spread.

A closer inspection of Figure 5.1 reveals much about the economics of the model. In particular, by comparing the plots in each row we can learn something about the role of marketmaker priors. Recall that prior beliefs concerning fundamentals are more dispersed for larger values of δ, so the left-hand panels represent simulations where marketmaker priors are more dispersed than the right-hand panels. The figure clearly shows that, ceteris paribus, learning takes place more quickly when priors are dispersed. The intuition behind this observation is straightforward. If a marketmaker holds very precise beliefs about the value of fundamentals, it takes a long sequence of trades before his priors are significantly adjusted. For example, a marketmaker with precise priors will interpret initial trader-initiated purchases of foreign currency as most likely coming from U-traders, even if in fact they are from I-traders, because his ask quotes are less than F. Of course, eventually a large imbalance between the number of trader-initiated purchases and sales will be interpreted as evidence that current quotes are below true fundamentals so quotes will be revised, but this process will be slower when priors are precise. The plots also show that greater precision in marketmaker priors makes the period-by-period revision in quotes smaller. The reason is that marketmakers attach less weight to the information content of individual trades when they hold precise beliefs about fundamentals.

The composition of the trader population also affects the length of the learning period. Comparing the upper and lower panels of Figure 5.1 shows that marketmakers learn about the true value of fundamentals more quickly when the proportion of I-traders in the market is higher. This too is an intuitive finding. As trades by I-traders are the only ones that contain information about fundamentals, the greater the proportion of ɪ-traders in the market, the greater the likelihood that an individual trader-initiated purchase or sale of foreign currency is informative about the level of fundamentals (relative to current quotes). Marketmakers understand this when drawing inferences from the observed history of trades, with the result that quote revisions reach a level consistent with the true level of fundamentals more quickly.

Case 2: Learning about a Change in Fundamentals

Next, we consider how spot rates behave when there is a one-time change in fundamentals. This is a much more complex situation because marketmakers must incorporate the possibility that fundamentals are changing when they draw inferences from the observed sequence of trades.

Suppose that there is a one-time change in fundamentals, F_t, from 100 to 101 in period $t = 100$. Marketmakers understand that fundamentals can vary in the sense that their inferences incorporate a value for the probability of change, α, that is greater than zero. As before, we assume that marketmaker priors are described by (5.16), but now we set δ equal to zero. This means that marketmakers know that the period-0 value of fundamentals is 100. Figure 5.2 compares simulations of the model with the fraction of ɪ-traders in the market, λ, equal to 0.1 and 0.2.

The simulations shown in Figure 5.2 depict several important features. First, it takes some time for quotes to adjust to the change in fundamentals. In panel A, where $\lambda = 0.1$, it takes approximately 90 periods of trading before quotes are equal to the new value for fundamentals (i.e., $F_t = 101$). As before, panel B shows that this learning period is shorter when ɪ-traders make up a larger fraction of the market ($\lambda = 0.2$). The second feature concerns the lack of monotonicity in the adjustment path for quotes. In fact, a close inspection of the figure reveals that in both simulations quotes fall immediately after the rise in fundamentals. The third and most striking feature of Figure 5.2 concerns the behavior of quotes at the start and end of the simulations. Here we see periods during which quotes are revised *away* from the true (and unchanging) level of fundamentals. This feature was absent from Figure 5.1. There quotes remained constant once the true level of fundamentals became known to marketmakers.

Why would a marketmaker revise his quotes when they are currently equal to the value of fundamentals? Recall that for these simulations marketmakers know that $F_0 = 100$ in period $t = 0$, so their initial quotes are set equal to 100. This situation would continue if they believed that fundamentals were fixed. Any imbalance between purchases and sales by traders would be interpreted simply as reflecting the actions of ᴜ-traders and there would be no revision in the quotes. In these simulations there is a subtle but significant difference. Marketmakers recognize that fundamentals can change from period to period because the change probability α is greater than zero. This means that even though marketmakers start off with precise and correct beliefs about the value of F_0, as time passes their beliefs about the *current* level of fundamentals become more diffuse.

To illustrate, let us assume that very little is learned from a single period of trading, so that $\Pr(F_t = k | \mathbb{T}_t, \Omega_t)$ is well approximated by $\pi_t(k)$. Then (5.15) becomes

$$\pi_{t+1}(k) \cong (\alpha/2)\,\pi_t(k+1) + (\alpha/2)\,\pi\,(k-1) + (1-\alpha)\pi_t(k).$$

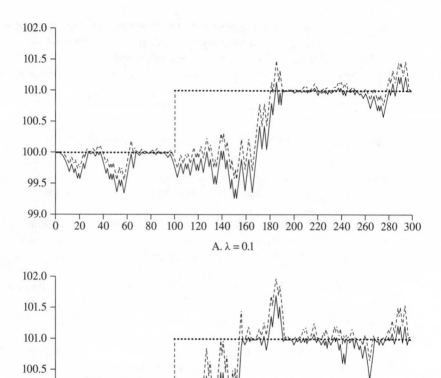

FIGURE 5.2   Learning about a change in fundamentals (S_t^B, solid; S_t^A, dashed; F_t, dotted).

Iterating this approximation forward from $\pi_0(100) = 1$ and $\pi_0(k) = 0$ for $k \neq 100$, we find that marketmaker priors evolve as

		Period	
$\pi_t(k)$	$t = 0$	$t = 1$	$t = 2$
$k = 102$	0	0	$(\alpha/2)^2$
101	0	$\alpha/2$	$(1-\alpha)(\alpha/2)$
100	1	$(1-\alpha)$	$(1-\alpha)^2$
99	0	$\alpha/2$	$(1-\alpha)(\alpha/2)$
98	0	0	$(\alpha/2)^2$

Thus, in the absence of information from trades, marketmaker priors become more diffuse about the current level of fundamentals because they recognize that fundamentals can change (i.e., when $\alpha > 0$).

It is now straightforward to understand the behavior of quotes in Figure 5.2. In these simulations marketmaker beliefs about the current value of fundamentals become more diffuse as time progresses. As a result, they place greater weight on the information content of individual trades. Now since I-traders constitute a minority of traders in our simulations, it is quite likely that trades by U-traders are misinterpreted by marketmakers as being informative. For example, if quotes are still at 100 but priors are quite diffuse, a random sale of foreign currency by a U-trader will lead to a downward revision in quotes because marketmakers understand that the trade *could* have been from an I-trader. This confusion is entirely rational. Indeed, it is very similar to the rational confusion we studied in Chapter 4. Moreover, if by chance there is a sequence of foreign currency sales by U-traders, marketmakers will continue to revise their quotes downward and away from the true value of fundamentals. Figure 5.2 shows that this process can continue for up to 20 periods of trading. Thereafter, the process is reversed. With quotes well away from fundamentals, the presence of I-traders ensures that the imbalance between the cumulative sequence of trader-initiated sales and purchases is reversed. For example, once quotes are well below the value of fundamentals, when given the opportunity to trade I-traders will always purchase, so the cumulant of purchases and sales going forward will favor purchases and lead to an upward revision in quotes. This reasoning suggests that temporary deviations of quotes from fundamentals should be shorter on average when the fraction of I-traders in the market is higher. The visual evidence in Figure 5.2 supports this intuition.

Case 3: Learning about Dynamic Fundamentals

We have seen that quotes can diverge from the true value of fundamentals for many trading periods in an environment where fundamentals undergo a one-time change. We now turn to the case in which fundamentals are truly dynamic and change at the rate implied by the change probability α. This environment adds one element that was missing earlier. Fundamentals may now change before marketmakers have a chance to learn about their past value from their trade observations. This makes the inference problem facing marketmakers even more complex, with the result that quote revisions can appear almost disconnected from the behavior of fundamentals. Figure 5.3 plots the behavior of transaction prices and fundamentals from two simulations of the model over 1000 trading periods. As before, we assume that the marketmakers initially know the value of fundamentals, $F_0 = 100$. The actual behavior of fundamentals is governed by equation (5.2) with the probability of change, α, equal to 0.05. The figure plots the realized path of fundamentals and the paths of transaction prices under alternative assumptions about the fraction of I-traders in the market: $\lambda = 0.1$ and $\lambda = 0.2$. Recall that all trades take place at either the bid or ask quote so we identify the period-t transaction price as

$$S_t = \mathcal{I}(\mathbb{T}_t = \mathbb{B}_t)S_t^A + \mathcal{I}(\mathbb{T}_t = \mathbb{S}_t)S_t^B + \mathcal{I}(\mathbb{T}_t = \mathbb{P}_t)S_{t-1}. \qquad (5.17)$$

Note that if no transaction takes place during period t (because an I-trader was given the opportunity to trade but decided to pass), we use the transaction price from the

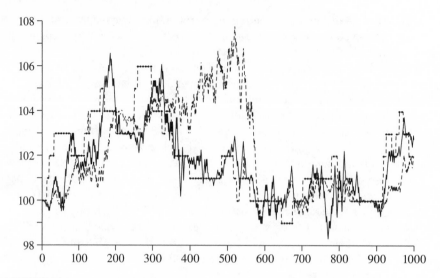

FIGURE 5.3   Transaction prices and dynamic fundamentals (transaction prices $\lambda = 0.1$, dashed; $\lambda = 0.2$, solid; F_t, dotted).

previous period. Thus, strictly speaking, S_t is the price at which the last foreign currency trade was made before the end of period t.

Variations in transaction prices are dominated by variations in quotes. To see why, we use the identity $\mathcal{I}(\mathbb{T}_t = \mathbb{B}_t) + \mathcal{I}(\mathbb{T}_t = \mathbb{S}_t) + \mathcal{I}(\mathbb{T}_t = \mathbb{P}_t) \equiv 1$ and (5.17) to write

$$S_t = S_t^{\mathrm{A}} - (S_t^{\mathrm{A}} - S_t^{\mathrm{B}})\mathcal{I}(\mathbb{T}_t = \mathbb{S}_t) + (S_{t-1} - S_t^{\mathrm{A}})\mathcal{I}(\mathbb{T}_t = \mathbb{P}_t),$$

$$S_t = S_t^{\mathrm{B}} + (S_t^{\mathrm{A}} - S_t^{\mathrm{B}})\mathcal{I}(\mathbb{T}_t = \mathbb{B}_t) + (S_{t-1} - S_t^{\mathrm{B}})\mathcal{I}(\mathbb{T}_t = \mathbb{P}_t).$$

In Figures 5.1 and 5.2 we saw that variations in the bid-ask spread are much smaller than variations in the level of quotes. We also know that I-traders will only pass when quotes are close to the true value of fundamentals. This means that variations in the first term on the right-hand side of the above expressions dominate variations in the second and third. Consequently, the path for transaction prices provides a reasonably accurate approximation to the path for both bid and ask quotes.

Two features stand out in Figure 5.3. The first concerns the volatility of spot rates relative to fundamentals. If we compare the sample variance of k-period changes in fundamentals, $F_t - F_{t-k}$, and spot rates, $S_t - S_{t-k}$, we find that the variances of spot rates and fundamentals are approximately equal for $k \in [1, 10]$ when the fraction of I-traders in the market λ equals 0.2. By contrast, the variance of price changes is approximately 25 percent higher than the variance of fundamentals when $\lambda = 0.1$. The figure also shows significant differences between the paths of fundamentals and transaction prices. Although both price plots track the level of fundamentals reasonably closely after $t = 600$, in the preceding 200 or so trading periods there is a large and persistent gap between fundamentals and spot rates when the fraction of I-traders in the market is low (e.g., $\lambda = 0.1$). Clearly, the composition of the trader population can have significant implications for how marketmakers set quotes, which is reflected in the behavior of spot rates.

The intuition for the gaps between quotes and fundamentals depicted in Figure 5.3 follows quite naturally from the cases examined earlier. We saw in Figure 5.1 that marketmakers learn about the true level of fundamentals more quickly when the fraction of I-traders in the market is higher. A faster pace of learning is critical in keeping quotes close to fundamentals when the latter are changing. This is easily seen by examining the paths in the figure for quotes and fundamentals from $t = 300$ onward. Over the next 100 trading periods fundamentals happened to fall from 104 to 101. This sizable fall was closely tracked by the downward revision in quotes in the simulation where $\lambda = 0.2$ but not at all in the case where $\lambda = 0.1$. This difference occurs for two reasons. First, a larger number of I-traders had the opportunity to trade in the $\lambda = 0.2$ case, so there was a greater imbalance between sale and purchase orders while quotes remained above the new (lower) level of fundamentals. Second, marketmakers recognized that the observed sequence of trades was more informative about the true level of fundamentals when $\lambda = 0.2$, so they revised their quotes more in response to the observed trade imbalance. In the $\lambda = 0.1$ case, the trade imbalances are smaller and marketmakers revised their quotes less in response to any imbalance. Consequently, quotes continued to drift upward after $t = 300$ despite the fall in fundamentals. It took almost 300 more periods before marketmakers received a sufficiently strong signal from the pattern of trading to revise their quotes down to the new lower level of fundamentals.

5.3.2 Market Efficiency and Volatility

Although the plots in Figure 5.3 suggest a complex link between quotes and fundamentals, we can actually describe the relationship between transaction prices and fundamentals very simply. Recall from (5.4) that marketmakers set their bid and ask quotes equal to the expected value of fundamentals conditioned on prior information and the type of trade that occurs: $S_t^A = \mathbb{E}[F_t | \mathbb{B}_t, \Omega_t]$ and $S_t^B = \mathbb{E}[F_t | \mathbb{S}_t, \Omega_t]$. Since all trades must take place at either the bid or ask quote, the transaction price for the period-t trade, S_t, must satisfy

$$S_t = \mathbb{E}[F_t | \mathbb{T}_t, \Omega_t],$$

where $\mathbb{T}_t = \{\mathbb{B}_t, \mathbb{S}_t\}$ denotes the trade that took place. Thus, the period-t transaction price is equal to the expected value of fundamentals conditioned on the information available to marketmakers *at the end* of period-t trading. In our model, trades are the only source of information for marketmakers, so $\{\mathbb{T}_t, \Omega_t\}$ constitutes the information set at the start of period $t + 1$, Ω_{t+1}. Hence, transaction prices in the model satisfy

$$S_t = \mathbb{E}\left[F_t | \Omega_{t+1}\right]. \tag{5.18}$$

Equation (5.18) has two important implications: (1) it implies that transaction prices follow a martingale, and (2) it allows us to relate the volatility of spot rates to the flow of information concerning fundamentals.

A time series process for a variable x_t is a called a martingale if $\mathbb{E}[x_{t+1}|x_t, x_{t-1}, \ldots] = x_t$. To see why this is a property of transaction prices, we first lead equation (5.18) one period forward to give

$$S_{t+1} = \mathbb{E}\left[F_{t+1}|\Omega_{t+2}\right]$$

$$= \mathbb{E}\left[F_t|\Omega_{t+2}\right] + \mathbb{E}\left[\Delta F_{t+1}|\Omega_{t+2}\right].$$

Now we take expectations conditioned on Ω_{t+1} and apply the Law of Iterated Expectations:

$$\mathbb{E}[S_{t+1}|\Omega_{t+1}] = \mathbb{E}\left[\mathbb{E}\left[F_t|\Omega_{t+2}\right]|\Omega_{t+1}\right] + \mathbb{E}\left[\mathbb{E}\left[\Delta F_{t+1}|\Omega_{t+2}\right]|\Omega_{t+1}\right]$$

$$= \mathbb{E}\left[F_t|\Omega_{t+1}\right] + \mathbb{E}\left[\Delta F_{t+1}|\Omega_{t+1}\right]$$

$$= \mathbb{E}\left[F_t|\Omega_{t+1}\right]$$

$$= S_t.$$

The third equality in this expression follows from the fact that changes in fundamentals, ΔF_{t+1}, are independent of the trades before period $t + 1$, which constitute the elements of Ω_{t+1}. Hence, $\mathbb{E}\left[\Delta F_{t+1}|\Omega_{t+1}\right] = 0$. Thus, we find that the expected transaction price in period $t + 1$ conditioned on information at the start of the period is equal to the period-t transaction price.

This martingale property implies that transaction prices are Semi-strong-form efficient. That is to say, the period-t price embodies all information known to the marketmaker (i.e., information comprising $\{\mathbb{T}_t, \Omega_t\}$) concerning the current level of fundamentals, F_t. Consequently, it is not possible to forecast future changes in transaction prices from any elements of Ω_{t+1}, including their past history of spot rates and trades.

Equation (5.18) also sheds light on the volatility of transaction prices. In particular, using (5.18) we can write the change in transaction price as

$$\Delta S_{t+1} = \mathbb{E}\left[F_{t+1}|\Omega_{t+2}\right] - \mathbb{E}\left[F_t|\Omega_{t+1}\right]$$

$$= \mathbb{E}\left[F_{t+1}|\Omega_{t+2}\right] - \mathbb{E}\left[F_{t+1}|\Omega_{t+1}\right] + \mathbb{E}\left[\Delta F_{t+1}|\Omega_{t+1}\right]$$

$$= \mathbb{E}\left[F_{t+1}|\Omega_{t+2}\right] - \mathbb{E}\left[F_{t+1}|\Omega_{t+1}\right]. \tag{5.19}$$

The change in transaction price is thus equal to the revision in marketmaker expectations concerning F_{t+1} between the start of period $t + 1$ and period $t + 2$. Since trades are the only information source for dealers, this revision is based solely on the marketmakers' observations of trade in period $t + 1$. This means that the volatility of transaction price changes depends upon how informative marketmakers view individual trades. When trades are more informative, expectations concerning fundamentals are revised more period by period, with the result that the volatility of spot rate changes is greater.

In Figure 5.3 we saw that the volatility of ΔS_{t+1} varied according to the fraction of I-traders in the market and could be significantly greater than the volatility of ΔF_{t+1}. Indeed, the plots reveal that many of the large changes in prices occur when there is no change in fundamentals or vice versa. Equation (5.19) tells us why this apparent disconnect exists. Changes in transaction prices are driven by the flow of information reaching marketmakers. Period by period this flow is conveyed by their observations on trades, which are very loosely tied to the period-by-period behavior of fundamentals. In particular, it is perfectly rational for marketmakers to revise their expectations significantly over a short period if they observe a particular sequence of trades that they deem particularly informative even though actual fundamentals remain unchanged. Conversely, it is also rational for marketmakers to pay very little attention to a sequence of trades even though fundamentals are changing if their priors concerning fundamentals are very precise. A close inspection of the plots in Figure 5.3 reveals examples of these dynamics.

5.4 Information Flows

We have shown that the period-by-period changes in transaction prices are driven by the flow of information concerning fundamentals that reaches marketmakers. In this model, marketmakers observe trades rather than fundamentals, so changes in the latter are only reflected in the behavior of prices insofar as they trigger trades that marketmakers find informative. This is a key insight because it allows for a far richer link between the behavior of fundamentals and spot rates than is present in the rational expectations models we studied in earlier chapters. Remember that one of the puzzling features of spot rates is that they can change quite dramatically without the obvious changes in fundamentals or even significant public news concerning fundamentals. The delinking of transaction price changes from fundamentals in this model represents a first theoretical step toward understanding this phenomenon.

With this in mind, we now turn to the question of how the flow of information reaching marketmakers can be measured using market data. In particular, we consider what can be learned from the behavior of the spread between the bid and ask quotes and the pattern of trading.

5.4.1 Interpreting the Quote Spread

Our earlier simulations showed that variations in the level of quotes dominated changes in the difference between the ask and bid quotes, the so-called quote spread. That is not to say that changes in the quote spread are uninformative about the state of the market. In fact, as we shall now see, in this model variations in the spread provide an empirically accurate measure of the precision of marketmakers' beliefs.

To develop the intuition behind this result, we have to return to the quote equations in (5.4). In particular, using the fact that $1 = \Pr(\mathbb{B}_t^{\mathrm{I}}|\mathbb{B}_t, \Omega_t) + \Pr(\mathbb{B}_t^{\mathrm{U}}|\mathbb{B}_t, \Omega_t)$ (because purchase trades must be made by either I-traders or U-traders), we can rewrite (5.4a) using (5.6a) and (5.7a) as

$$\left(S_t^{\mathrm{A}} - \mathbb{E}\left[F_t|\Omega_t\right]\right) \Pr(\mathbb{B}_t^{\mathrm{U}}|\mathbb{B}_t, \Omega_t) = \left(\mathbb{E}[F_t|F_t > S_t^{\mathrm{A}}, \Omega_t] - S_t^{\mathrm{A}}\right) \Pr(\mathbb{B}_t^{\mathrm{I}}|\mathbb{B}_t, \Omega_t).$$

The term on the left is the expected profit to the marketmaker from selling foreign currency to a U-trader, and that on the right is the expected loss from selling to an I-trader. By definition $\mathbb{E}[F_t|F_t > S_t^{\mathrm{A}}, \Omega_t] \geq S_t^{\mathrm{A}}$, so marketmakers cannot expect to profit from selling to I-traders. They therefore set their ask quote so as to make a compensating expected profit on currency sales to U-traders. This requires quoting an asking price with a markup over the expected value of fundamentals. In particular, rearranging the preceding expression we find

$$S_t^A = \mathbb{E}\left[F_t | \Omega_t\right] + \left(\mathbb{E}[F_t | F_t > S_t^A, \Omega_t] - S_t^A\right) \frac{\Pr(\mathbb{B}_t^I | \mathbb{B}_t, \Omega_t)}{\Pr(\mathbb{B}_t^U | \mathbb{B}_t, \Omega_t)}. \qquad (5.20)$$

Thus, the necessary markup (i.e., the second term on the right) depends on the expected size of the loss from selling to I-traders and the likelihood (i.e., the probability ratio) of selling foreign currency to an I-trader rather than a U-trader. The corresponding expression for the bid quote is

$$S_t^B = \mathbb{E}\left[F_t | \Omega_t\right] - \left(S_t^B - \mathbb{E}[F_t | F_t < S_t^B, \Omega_t]\right) \frac{\Pr(\mathbb{S}_t^I | \mathbb{S}_t, \Omega_t)}{\Pr(\mathbb{S}_t^U | \mathbb{S}_t, \Omega_t)}, \qquad (5.21)$$

where $S_t^B - \mathbb{E}[F_t | F_t < S_t^B, \Omega_t]$ is the expected loss from purchasing foreign currency from an I-trader. In this case the quote is marked down from the expected value for fundamentals. Combining (5.20) and (5.21) gives the following expression for the quote spread:

$$S_t^A - S_t^B = \left(\mathbb{E}[F_t | F_t > S_t^A, \Omega_t] - S_t^A\right) \frac{\Pr(\mathbb{B}_t^I | \mathbb{B}_t, \Omega_t)}{\Pr(\mathbb{B}_t^U | \mathbb{B}_t, \Omega_t)}$$

$$+ \left(S_t^B - \mathbb{E}[F_t | F_t < S_t^B, \Omega_t]\right) \frac{\Pr(\mathbb{S}_t^I | \mathbb{S}_t, \Omega_t)}{\Pr(\mathbb{S}_t^U | \mathbb{S}_t, \Omega_t)}. \qquad (5.22)$$

Equation (5.22) identifies two main factors affecting the quote spread: (1) the composition of traders in the market, and (2) the degree of marketmaker uncertainty concerning the true value of fundamentals. Let us consider these in turn.

In this model, the marketmaker trades with a single trader chosen at random from the population of traders in the market. Thus, the probability of trade with an I-trader is higher the larger the fraction of I-traders in the market, λ. Marketmakers recognize this fact when computing the likelihood that they will sell or purchase foreign currency from an I-trader. In particular, using our earlier calculations for the trade probabilities, we find that

$$\frac{\Pr(\mathbb{B}_t^I | \mathbb{B}_t, \Omega_t)}{\Pr(\mathbb{B}_t^U | \mathbb{B}_t, \Omega_t)} = \frac{\lambda \overline{\Pi}(S_t^A)}{(1 - \lambda)/2} \quad \text{and} \quad \frac{\Pr(\mathbb{S}_t^I | \mathbb{S}_t, \Omega_t)}{\Pr(\mathbb{S}_t^U | \mathbb{S}_t, \Omega_t)} = \frac{\lambda \underline{\Pi}(S_t^B)}{(1 - \lambda)/2}.$$

These expressions show that the likelihood of transactions with I-traders is increasing in λ, so higher values for λ will be reflected in a larger quote spread for a given set of marketmaker beliefs concerning fundamentals. In other words, marketmakers realize that they are more likely to be at an informational disadvantage when trading if λ is larger, so they increase the quote spread to compensate for the worsening adverse selection problem.

The quote spread also reflects marketmaker beliefs about fundamentals, particularly in regard to their precision. Consider the effect of less precision, or greater uncertainty. Uncertainty about the true value of fundamentals affects both the size of the expected loss from trading with I-traders and the likelihood that these trades will occur. In particular, greater dispersion in marketmaker beliefs increases the expected loss terms in (5.22): $\mathbb{E}[F_t|F_t > S_t^A, \Omega_t] - S_t^A$ and $S_t^B - \mathbb{E}[F_t|F_t < S_t^B, \Omega_t]$. The degree of dispersion also affects the trading likelihoods via $\underline{\Pi}(S_t^B) \equiv \sum_{k<S_t^B} \pi_t(k)$ and $\overline{\Pi}(S_t^A) \equiv \sum_{k>S_t^A} \pi_t(k)$. Greater dispersion increases both $\underline{\Pi}(S_t^B)$ and $\overline{\Pi}(S_t^A)$ for a given set of quotes S_t^B and S_t^A, but these effects are at least partially offset by the induced changes in the quotes, so the total impact depends on the model's parameters.

In our model simulations there is no change in the fraction of I-traders, so all the variations in the quote spread reflect changes in the precision of marketmaker beliefs. This is illustrated in Figure 5.4. Here we plot the behavior of the quote spread and the dispersion of beliefs from the $\lambda = 0.1$ simulation depicted in Figure 5.3. Panel A plots the markup on ask quotes, $S_t^A - \mathbb{E}[F_t|\Omega_t]$, and the bid quote markup, $S_t^B - \mathbb{E}[F_t|\Omega_t]$. The size of the quote spread is just the vertical difference between the two plots. Panel B compares the actual path of fundamentals with the two standard error confidence intervals for fundamentals (i.e., $\mathbb{E}[F_t|\Omega_t] \pm \sqrt{\mathbb{V}[F_t|\Omega_t]}$, where $\mathbb{V}[.|\Omega_t]$ denotes the conditional variance).

Panel A of Figure 5.4 shows a pronounced pattern in the quote spread. Starting from approximately zero, the spread increases almost monotonically over a number of trading periods before collapsing rapidly back toward zero. These cycles vary in duration between a few and several hundred trading periods and correspond closely to the fluctuations in the confidence band shown in panel B. In particular, a careful inspection of the plots shows that in every case the collapse in the spread coincides with the rapid contraction in the confidence band. This pattern confirms that changes in the quote spread closely reflect variations in the precision of marketmaker beliefs. Indeed, over the 1000 trading periods in this simulation, 97 percent of the changes in the quote spread can be accounted for by changes in $\mathbb{V}[F_t|\Omega_t]$.

Figure 5.4 displays two further noteworthy features. First, the solid and dashed plots in panel A show a high degree of symmetry around zero. This indicates that the markups on the bid and ask quotes are highly correlated. (In this simulation the correlation is higher than 0.99.) Second, the periodic collapses in the quote spread and confidence band indicate that marketmakers learn about fundamentals from particular bursts of trading activity. In other words, although marketmakers observe trades every period, there are long episodes in which trades reveal little about fundamentals so beliefs become less and less precise and other short episodes when the sequence of trades greatly increases the precision of marketmaker beliefs. Thus, although marketmakers continuously update their beliefs about fundamentals from their observations on trade, the flow of information conveyed by those trades is anything but constant.

5.4.2 Order Flow

Can we measure the information flow driving the revision in the spot rates quoted by dealers? The answer is yes. Moreover, the measure, called order flow, is surprisingly simple to construct.

Definition: *Foreign currency order flow is defined as the difference between the value of purchase and sale orders for foreign currency initiated by traders against marketmaker quotes.*

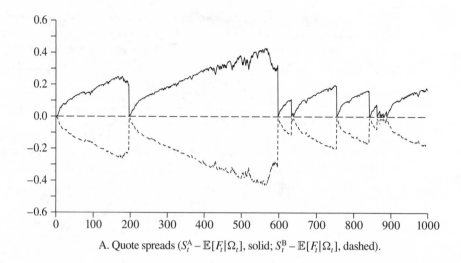

A. Quote spreads ($S_t^A - \mathbb{E}[F_t|\Omega_t]$, solid; $S_t^B - \mathbb{E}[F_t|\Omega_t]$, dashed).

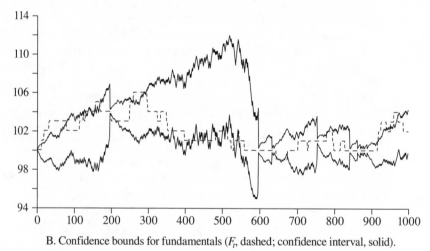

B. Confidence bounds for fundamentals (F_t, dashed; confidence interval, solid).

FIGURE 5.4   Quote spreads and the dispersion of marketmaker beliefs.

A key element in this definition is the initiator of trade. In every trade there is a buyer and a seller of foreign currency, but only one party to the trade initiates the transaction. In our model the initiator is the trader. Marketmakers quote ask and bid prices at which they stand ready to fill traders' purchase and sale orders for foreign currency, but it is the trader who decides whether to place a purchase or sale order and hence initiates the trade. Order flow provides a useful measure of the information flow hitting marketmakers precisely because it keeps track of who initiates each trade.

The period-t order flow for foreign currency is easy to calculate. Let $\Delta \mathbb{X}_t \equiv \mathbb{B}_t - \mathbb{S}_t$ denote the excess of trader-initiated purchases over sales of foreign currency, the order imbalance. Period-t order flow is

$$\Delta X_t = V_t \Delta \mathbb{X}_t, \tag{5.23}$$

where V_t is the dollar value of the period-t transaction. In our model, all orders are for one unit of foreign currency, so $V_t = S_t$. Thus, if the period-t trade is a trader-initiated purchase, $\Delta \mathbb{X}_t = 1$ and order flow is simply equal to S_t^A, which is the period-t transaction price, S_t. Conversely, if the period-t trade is a trader-initiated sale, $\Delta \mathbb{X}_t = -1$ and order flow equals $-S_t^B$, or minus the transaction price, $-S_t$.

We showed earlier that transaction prices follow a martingale. As a consequence, price changes are serially uncorrelated. The serial correlation properties of order flow are more complex and hold the key to understanding why the variable can be used to measure the flow of information. To study these properties, we focus on the behavior of the order imbalance, $\Delta \mathbb{X}_t$. As we shall see, period-by-period changes in $\Delta \mathbb{X}_t$ are the main factors driving order flow, so serial correlation in ΔX_t closely follows that in $\Delta \mathbb{X}_t$.

Recall that the relation between fundamentals and quotes in period t can be described by three states, Z_t: state 1, where $F_t > S_t^A$; state 2, where $S_t^A \geq F_t \geq S_t^B$; and state 3, where $S_t^B > F_t$. Using the trade probabilities in Table 5.1, we first note that $\mathbb{E}\left[\Delta \mathbb{X}_t | Z_t = 1\right] = \lambda/N$, $\mathbb{E}\left[\Delta \mathbb{X}_t | Z_t = 2\right] = 0$, and $\mathbb{E}\left[\Delta \mathbb{X}_t | Z_t = 3\right] = -\lambda/N$. Thus, the expected order imbalance varies across the three states of the market. By combining these results with the trade probabilities we can compute the covariance between $\Delta \mathbb{X}_{t+1}$ and $\Delta \mathbb{X}_t$ conditioned on the state in periods t and $t+1$:

$\mathrm{CV}\left[\Delta \mathbb{X}_{t+1}\Delta \mathbb{X}_t | Z_{t+1}, Z_t\right]$	$Z_t = 1$	$Z_t = 2$	$Z_t = 3$
$Z_{t+1} = 1$	$\frac{(N-1)^2\lambda^2}{N^4}$	0	$-\frac{(N-1)^2\lambda^2}{N^4}$
$Z_{t+1} = 2$	0	0	0
$Z_{t+1} = 3$	$-\frac{(N-1)^2\lambda^2}{N^4}$	0	$\frac{(N-1)^2\lambda^2}{N^4}.$

$$(5.24)$$

Here we see that the period-by-period order imbalance is positively autocorrelated if the market remains in state 1 or state 3 and negatively correlated if the market moves between states 1 and 3. Under other circumstances, order imbalance is not serially correlated. The explanation for these results is straightforward. In the case in which the ask quote remains below the true level for fundamentals, ı-traders will initiate purchases of foreign currency if they are given the opportunity to trade. This means that successive order imbalances are more likely to be positive than negative. Similarly, if the bid quote is below fundamentals, ı-traders will want to sell foreign currency so successive order imbalances are more likely to be negative. Thus in both cases, there is a high probability that order imbalances will have the same sign in successive periods, thereby creating positive autocorrelation. By similar reasoning, there is a high probability that order imbalances have different signs if the market moves between state 1 and state 3, so here the autocorrelation is negative.

The results in (5.24) provide an important perspective on how marketmakers revise their quotes in response to trade observations. In particular, they suggest that the information conveyed by an individual trade depends, in part, on the history of preceding trades. For example, consider the information contained in a trader-initiated purchase that was preceded by a sequence of 10 trades that alternated between trader-initiated sales and purchases. In this case, the new trade provides little incremental evidence against the hypothesis that order imbalances are serially uncorrelated. Hence, given the state dependency in serial correlation shown in (5.24),

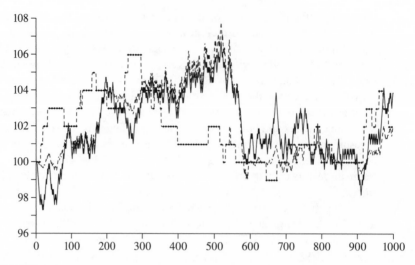

FIGURE 5.5   Transaction prices and dynamic fundamentals (X_t^s, solid; S_t, dashed; F_t, dotted).

the marketmaker has little reason to revise his view that fundamentals are close to his current bid and ask quotes (i.e., state 2). Alternatively, if eight of the last 10 trades were purchases, a further purchase provides incremental evidence that order imbalances are now positively autocorrelated. In this case, the sequence of trade observations points to state 1 with increasing precision, so marketmakers will adjust their beliefs on fundamentals accordingly.

We can further illustrate how marketmakers use the sequence of trades to revise their spot rate quotes by returning to our simulations of the model. In particular Figure 5.5 allows us to compare the path for fundamentals, transaction prices, and the cumulant of order flow. The last is computed as the sum of the period-by-period order flows from period 1 to t : $X_t = \sum_{i=1}^{t} \Delta X_i$. To facilitate comparisons among the three series, the figure plots the scaled cumulant of order flow $X_t^s \equiv 100 + 0.003 X_t$ computed as the fitted value from a regression of S_t on a constant and X_t. The plot for X_t^s shows how closely the cumulated variations in order flow can match the movements in transaction prices.

Figure 5.5 clearly shows that there is a remarkably close correspondence between changes in transaction prices and scaled order flow. Changes in prices are not perfectly correlated with changes in order flow period by period, but large and persistent movements in prices are closely matched by similar movements in X_t^s. For example, the fall in prices from 106 to 100 between $t = 500$ and $t = 600$ is almost exactly mirrored by the fall in cumulative order flow. Over all 1000 periods of trading, the correlation between transaction prices and order flow is above 0.91. This high correlation is not a simple reflection of the fact that period-t order flow ΔX_t is equal to $S_t \Delta \mathbb{X}_t$. Variations in order imbalance, $\Delta \mathbb{X}_t$, are much greater than the period-by-period changes in transaction prices, so the correlation between $\Delta \mathbb{X}_t$ and ΔX_t in our simulation is higher than 0.99.

Figure 5.5 also illustrates why order flow is a useful measure of the flow of information from I-traders to marketmakers. Consider, for example, the pattern of prices and fundamentals between $t = 100$ and 200. Initially, prices are close to the true level for fundamentals of 102. Over the next 50 or so periods fundamentals rise to 104, whereas prices remain relatively stable. Then, in the space of a few trading periods, prices rise to the new level of fundamentals, 104. What accounts for this lag in price adjustment? The answer lies in the behavior of order flow. Figure 5.5 shows that prices closely follow the movements in (scaled) order flow. This means that marketmakers only revised their quotes upward when they observed a persistent positive order imbalance. Now, ɪ-traders would have initiated foreign currency purchases as soon as fundamentals began to rise if they had been given the opportunity to trade. Under these circumstances marketmakers could have quickly seen a positive order imbalance. However, in this particular episode, too few ɪ-traders had the opportunity to trade so the order imbalances observed by marketmakers did not reflect the extent to which quotes were below fundamentals. Consequently, the pattern of trading was not informative about the rise in fundamentals for more than 50 periods of trading. This pattern of delayed price adjustment appears in several episodes of the simulation. In particular, the figure shows that the longest delay occurs after $t = 300$. In this case fundamentals fall from 104 to 100 over the next 200 trading periods, whereas transaction prices drift upward from 104 to 106 following (scaled) order flow. Once again the pattern of trading was not informative about the true level of fundamentals for many periods because there were too few trades by ɪ-traders to generate a persistently negative order imbalance.

Earlier in this chapter we saw that marketmakers learn about the true value of fundamentals more quickly when the proportion of ɪ-traders in the market is higher. This observation suggests that trader composition also affects the pace at which information about fundamentals is reflected in order flow. When the fraction of ɪ-traders is greater, there is a higher probability that they will trade each period, and since ɪ-traders only trade when quotes differ from the true level of fundamentals, this information is more likely to be reflected in order imbalances.

We can illustrate this implication by considering the regression of future order imbalance on the current difference between fundamentals and prices:

$$\Delta^k \mathbb{X}_{t+k} = \beta_k (F_t - S_t) + \omega_{t+k}, \tag{5.25}$$

where $\Delta^k \mathbb{X}_{t+k} \equiv \sum_{i=1}^{k} \Delta \mathbb{X}_{t+i}$. The term $\Delta^k \mathbb{X}_{t+k}$ identifies the aggregate order imbalance from periods $t+1$ to $t+k$, so the coefficient β_k provides a measure of how differences between fundamentals and prices affect order imbalances of the next k trading periods. In particular, if information about fundamentals is quickly revealed by the pattern of trading, β_k should be positive (and significant) for small values of k.

Figure 5.6 compares the OLS estimates of (5.25) computed from the $\lambda = 0.2$ and $\lambda = 0.1$ simulations shown in Figure 5.3. Panel A plots the estimates of β_k together with their 95 percent confidence bands (indicated by the dotted lines). In both cases the estimates of β_k are all positive and increase with the horizon, k. Panel B shows that the R^2 statistics also rise as k ranges between 1 and 35 periods. This pattern indicates that as time passes more information about the *past* value of fundamentals is reflected in the cumulated order imbalance between trader-initiated purchases and sales. The composition of traders also affects the degree to which order imbalances reflect past fundamentals. In particular, a gap between fundamentals and spot rates induces a greater order imbalance when the fraction of ɪ-traders in the market is larger.

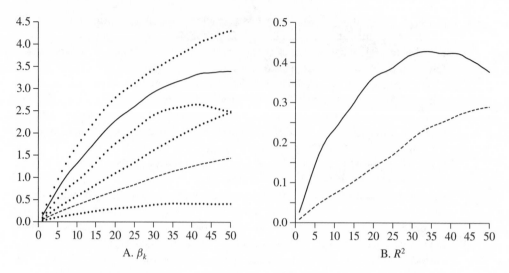

FIGURE 5.6   Estimates of regression equation (5.25) ($\lambda = 0.1$, dashed; $\lambda = 0.2$, solid; confidence bands, dotted).

For example, the estimates in panel A indicate that a unit increase in the gap between fundamentals and spot rates (roughly 1 percent) induces an aggregate order imbalance of approximately three trades on average over the next 40 periods when $\lambda = 0.2$, but only one trade when $\lambda = 0.1$. Order imbalances, and hence order flow, still contain information about fundamentals when the fraction of I-traders in the market is low, but the information is on average less precise and takes longer to accumulate.

Figure 5.6 illustrates how the composition of traders affects the transmission of information about fundamentals into order flow. This leaves us to consider how price changes are related to the behavior of order flow. Once again this is readily accomplished by a regression. In this case we consider a regression of the k-period change in ask quotes on the k-period order flow:

$$S^A_{t+k} - S^A_t = \gamma_k \left(X_{t+k-1} - X_{t-1} \right) + \nu_{t+k}. \tag{5.26}$$

Note that $X_{t+k-1} - X_{t-1} \equiv \sum_{i=0}^{k-1} \Delta X_{t+i}$ is cumulated order flow from trading in periods t to $t + k - 1$ and so represents trading activity between the times that marketmakers set the values of S^A_t and S^A_{t+k}. Thus, the coefficient γ_k measures the impact of the interim order flow on the k-period revision in ask quotes. Obviously, we could also estimate the impact of order flow on the revision in bid quotes or the change in transaction prices by making $S^B_{t+k} - S^B_t$ or $S_{t+k} - S_t$ the left-hand-side variables. The coefficient estimates from these regressions are very similar to the estimates of γ_k shown below because changes in the quote spread are much smaller than changes in either the bid or the ask quotes.

Figure 5.7 compares the estimates of (5.26) computed from the $\lambda = 0.2$ and $\lambda = 0.1$ simulations. Panel A shows that the γ_k estimates from both simulations are positive and significant at all horizons (the dotted plots denote the 95 percent confidence band). This signifies that the order flow does indeed measure the flow of information that marketmakers use in revising their quotes. Note too that the estimates of γ_k are similar

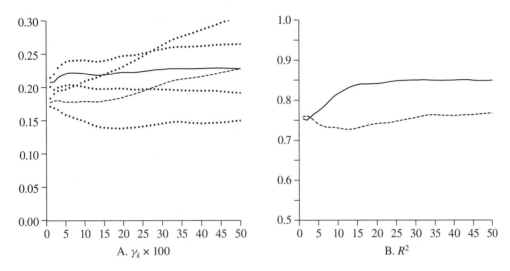

FIGURE 5.7 Estimates of regression equation (5.26) ($\lambda = 0.1$, dashed; $\lambda = 0.2$, solid; confidence bands, dotted).

across the two simulations and across different horizons. Trader composition affects the pace at which information about fundamentals becomes embedded in the pattern of trading far more than it does in the inferences marketmakers draw from trades. In terms of the model, an estimate for γ_k of 0.002 implies that on average it takes $500 of positive order flow to induce a single $1 increase in the quoted asking price for foreign currency.

Panel B of Figure 5.7 plots the R^2 statistics against horizon k. These statistics average between 0.76 for the $\lambda = 0.1$ simulation and 0.84 for the $\lambda = 0.2$ simulation. From a purely statistical perspective, these statistics imply that order flow does a remarkably good job of describing the flow of information used by marketmakers in revising their quotes. Of course, in these simulated data we know that all the information being used to revise quotes is carried by trades. From this perspective the R^2 statistics are less impressive. They imply that quote revisions based on optimal inferences from the pattern of trade are only approximately proportional to order flow.

5.5 Public versus Private Information

In our model, all information about fundamentals starts out as the private information of I-traders. This means that all the movements in spot rates reflect the process through which this private information is revealed to marketmakers. Foreign exchange markets have a more complex information structure. In particular, some information concerning fundamentals arrives in the form of public news. We now amend our model to incorporate this possibility.

Let us assume that the arrival of an announcement is governed by an exogenous process. With some probability, the current value of fundamentals, F_t, is announced at the start of period t. Announcements are observed by all traders and marketmakers, so if an announcement is made in period t, F_t becomes public information. If no announcement is made, the current value of fundamentals remains the private information of I-traders.

To understand how announcements affect the behavior of quotes and the pattern of trading, we have to return to equation (5.15), which expresses marketmakers' beliefs. Recall that beliefs are described by the probabilities $\Pr\left(F_t = k|\Omega_t\right) \equiv \pi_t(k)$. If there is no announcement at the start of period t, beliefs are determined as before by

$$\pi_t(k) = (\alpha/2) \Pr\left(F_{t-1} = k + 1|\mathbb{T}_{t-1}, \Omega_{t-1}\right) + (\alpha/2) \Pr\left(F_{t-1} = k - 1|\mathbb{T}_{t-1}, \Omega_{t-1}\right)$$

$$+ (1 - \alpha) \Pr\left(F_{t-1} = k|\mathbb{T}_{t-1}, \Omega_{t-1}\right),$$

where

$$\Pr\left(F_{t-1} = k|\mathbb{T}_{t-1}, \Omega_{t-1}\right) = \frac{\Pr\left(\mathbb{T}_{t-1}|F_{t-1} = k, \Omega_{t-1}\right)}{\sum_k \left\{\Pr\left(\mathbb{T}_{t-1}|F_{t-1} = k, \Omega_{t-1}\right) \pi_{t-1}(k)\right\}} \pi_{t-1}(k)$$

and

$$\Pr\left(\mathbb{T}_{t-1}|F_{t-1} = k, \Omega_{t-1}\right) = \begin{cases} \frac{1}{2}(1 - \lambda) + \lambda \mathcal{I}(k > S_{t-1}^{\text{A}}) & \text{if } \mathbb{T}_{t-1} = \mathbb{B}_{t-1} \\ \frac{1}{2}(1 - \lambda) + \lambda \mathcal{I}(k < S_{t-1}^{\text{B}}) & \text{if } \mathbb{T}_{t-1} = \mathbb{S}_{t-1} \\ \lambda \mathcal{I}(S_{t-1}^{\text{A}} \geq k \geq S_{t-1}^{\text{B}}) & \text{if } \mathbb{T}_{t-1} = \mathbb{P}_{t-1} \end{cases}$$

An announcement provides precise information about the current value of fundamentals. Thus, if there is an announcement that $F_t = k^*$ at the start of period t, marketmaker beliefs become

$$\pi_t(k) = \begin{cases} 1 & \text{if } k = k^* \\ 0 & \text{otherwise.} \end{cases} \tag{5.27}$$

Let us now consider what happens when an announcement arrives. Marketmakers continue to set quotes according to (5.9), but with the beliefs in (5.27) these quote equations imply

$$S_t^{\text{A}} = S_t^{\text{B}} = F_t. \tag{5.28}$$

Thus, following the arrival of an announcement, marketmakers set their quotes to fully reflect information about fundamentals. This implication of (5.9) should not come as a surprise. The arrival of an announcement removes all uncertainty about current fundamentals, so the markups on the bid and ask quotes must collapse to zero [see equations (5.20) and (5.21)].

The quotes in (5.28) have important implications for period-t trading. Recall that I-traders only wish to trade when there is a gap between quotes and the true level of fundamentals. Equation (5.28) tells us that marketmakers eliminate this gap following an announcement, so we immediately know that any trade in period-t must be initiated by U-traders. Consequently, period-t trades provide no information to marketmakers about fundamentals in period $t + 1$. This means that period-t order flow does not measure the flow of information reaching marketmakers by the start of period $t + 1$. Order flow may be positive or negative, but marketmakers know that trades are uninformative. Hence, in contrast to the results shown in Figure 5.7, there will be no relationship between order flow and quote revisions following such announcements.

It is important to emphasize why order flow does not convey any information in this setting. The arrival of an announcement makes all information concerning fundamentals public knowledge. This constitutes a significant change in the information structure of the market because it eliminates the informational asymmetry between marketmakers and traders. When announcements are absent, order flow carries information because there is asymmetric information concerning fundamentals between the I-traders and marketmakers. In our setting, announcements are both timely (i.e., they refer to current fundamentals) and fully informative. These attributes are necessary to eliminate informational asymmetry, but they are not found in actual announcements. We study how the arrival of announcements with more realistic attributes affects the foreign exchange market in Chapter 10.

5.6 Uninformed Traders

Uninformed U-traders play a vital role in the model. We saw in Section 5.4.1 that marketmakers set quotes so that the expected loss from trading with an I-trader is matched by the expected profit from trading with a U-trader. Clearly, if U-traders were absent, there would be no prospect of covering the expected losses of trading with the I-traders. Under such circumstances, marketmakers would obviously have a strong incentive to leave the market. In short, therefore, we need U-traders in the model to prevent our foreign exchange market from closing down.

The importance of U-traders can be viewed from another, more general perspective. If U-traders were absent, marketmakers would know that the counterpart to every trade knows at least as much about fundamentals as they do. Under these circumstances, the fact that a trader is willing to buy foreign currency at the ask quote indicates to the marketmaker that foreign currency is worth at least the ask quote, so he is at least as well off by keeping it. This is the intuition behind the "no trade" or "no speculation" theorems of Grossman and Stiglitz (1980) and Milgrom and Stokey (1982). It implies that marketmakers would want to renege on their commitment to trade at their quotes, so once again the market would close down.

If we need U-traders in the model to stop the market from closing down, should there not be a more explicit motivation for their trading behavior? The obvious response to this question is that U-traders are motivated by some exogenous "outside" events unrelated to the behavior of fundamentals. At one level this seems fine: the analytical clarity of a partial equilibrium model must be "purchased" with simplifying assumptions. However, the real issue is whether the behavior of prices and trades in the model is being significantly influenced by the motivations of U-traders. With this in mind, let us return to the profits of traders.

Our analysis of the model relies not only on the presence of U-traders, but also on the assumption that they comprise a constant fraction of traders in the market. We also know that marketmakers are only willing to quote spot rates because they expect to profit in their trades with U-traders. These expectations must be fulfilled on average, so in the long run U-traders must lose money in their trades with marketmakers. This implication of the model does not sit well with the assumed constant composition of the trader population. If the losses of U-traders are large and persistent, there must

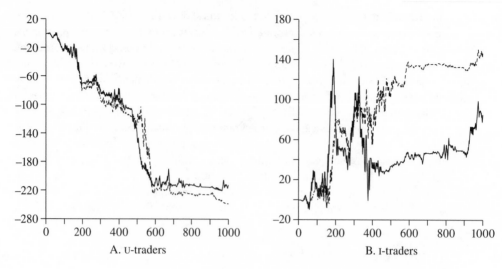

FIGURE 5.8 Trading profits ($\lambda = 0.1$, dashed; $\lambda = 0.2$, solid).

be a very strong motivation for trading or the composition of traders will change as
U-traders are driven away.

Figure 5.8 shows the extent of this problem by plotting the trader profits from the
simulations in Figure 5.3. To compute the profits we track the currency positions of
each trader type. Let z_t^J and $\hat{z}_t^J$, respectively, denote the amount in dollars and foreign
currency held by a J-trader at the end of period t. We identify profits, Λ_t^J, as the dollar
value of the closed-out position at the end of period-t trading:

$$\Lambda_t^J = z_t^J + \begin{cases} S_t^B \hat{z}_t^J & \text{if } \hat{z}_t^J > 0 \\ S_t^A \hat{z}_t^J & \text{if } \hat{z}_t^J < 0 \end{cases}.$$

Thus, a long position in foreign currency ($\hat{z}_t^j > 0$) is valued at the prevailing
bid quote, whereas a short position ($\hat{z}_t^J < 0$) must be covered at the prevailing ask
quote. Since all trades are for one unit of foreign currency, the positions evolve
as $z_t^J = z_{t-1}^J - S_t^A \mathbb{B}_t^J + S_t^B \mathbb{S}_t^J$, and $\hat{z}_t^J = \hat{z}_{t-1}^J + \mathbb{B}_t^J - \mathbb{S}_t^J$. Recall that $\mathbb{B}_t^J = 1$ when *any*
J-trader buys foreign currency and $\mathbb{S}_t^J = 1$ when *any* J-trader sells. Thus z_t^J and $\hat{z}_t^J$
represent the currency positions for the group of J-traders for $J = \{\text{I}, \text{U}\}$.

Panel A of Figure 5.8 plots the profits for the group of U-traders. As expected, U-
traders persistently lose money in both simulations. One way to gauge the significance
of these losses is to compare them to the profits of I-traders shown in panel B. The
I-traders profit in the long run, as one would expect, but their profits are less than
the losses of the U-traders. By this simple metric, the losses of the U-traders appear
significant. Another noteworthy feature of the plots concerns the volatility of profits.
During the first 600 trading periods in these simulations, the losses of U-traders
accumulated at a comparatively steady rate, whereas profits of the I-traders fluctuated
significantly. Clearly, information on fundamentals does not provide a guarantee of
profitable trading in the short run.

At the very least, the plots in Figure 5.8 should provide a note of caution before we embrace the ability of this model to explain the behavior of spot rates. Much of the analytic tractability of the model comes from the assumption that the composition of the trader population is constant. In particular, if the probability of trade between the marketmaker and an I-trader varied as the composition of the population changed, both the quote-setting and inference problems facing marketmakers would be much more complex. Nevertheless, a constant trader population becomes a rather tenuous assumption in the absence of a strong rationale for why U-traders are willing to tolerate large and persistent trading losses.

5.7 Summary

- Marketmakers provide liquidity to other agents (traders) wanting to trade a financial asset by quoting spot rates at which they are willing to buy or sell the asset. Thus, in a marketmaker model of the foreign exchange market, spot exchange rates are identified as the prices at which transactions between marketmakers and other agents take place. In this setting, all variations in the exchange rate depend on how marketmakers change their quotes.

- The model provides a detailed description of how private information about fundamentals is transmitted to marketmakers and hence into currency prices. The transmission of information occurs via transactions between marketmakers and traders. This process takes time because: (1) the holders of information (i.e., the I-traders) have to wait for the opportunity to trade, and (2) marketmakers' inferences based on the observed pattern of transactions are imprecise. As a result, the model is capable of generating significant lags between changes in fundamentals and changes in spot rates.

- The model shows that the volatility of spot rates reflects the quality of information reaching marketmakers rather than the volatility of fundamentals.

- Variations in the quote spread are dominated by changes in quotes, but nevertheless are informative about changes in the precision of marketmaker beliefs concerning fundamentals.

- Order flow is defined as the difference between the values of buyer-initiated and seller-initiated transactions. It provides an easily computable measure of the flow of information reaching marketmakers via the pattern of transactions. Private information about past fundamentals drives current order flow. This link is stronger over longer horizons and when a larger fraction of traders is informed about fundamentals.

- Order flow is a proximate driver of period-by-period changes in quotes and transaction prices in an environment of asymmetric information. If the arrival of public news in the form of an announcement eliminates the asymmetric information, order flow is no longer a proximate driver of quotes and price changes because it carries no information.

5.8 Bibliography

The model in this chapter is an extension of the classic sequential trade model developed by Glosten and Milgrom (1985). The main innovation here is that the fundamental value of the traded asset follows a random walk. The model is also related to work by Easley and O'Hara (1992), who examine a sequential trading model like that of Glosten and Milgrom (1985) with "event uncertainty." In their model, information about fundamentals arrives exogenously with some probability so marketmakers do not know for certain whether I-traders are present. Here, in contrast, marketmakers do not know whether there has been a shock to fundamentals that has changed the information carried by I-traders. Surveys by O'Hara (1997) and Brunnermeier (2001) discuss how sequential trading models fit into the larger microstructure literature.

5.9 Review Questions

1. Time Series Properties of Transaction Prices and Order Flows: In Section 5.3.2 we showed that transaction prices follow a martingale, $S_t = \mathbb{E}\left[S_{t+1}|\Omega_t\right]$.

   (a) Use this property of the model to show that $\mathbb{CV}(\Delta S_{t+1}, \Delta S_{t-i}) = 0$ for all $i > 0$.

   (b) By definition the expected order imbalance in period-t trading, $\Delta \mathbb{X}_t = \mathbb{B}_t - \mathbb{S}_t$, can be written as

   $$\mathbb{E}[\Delta \mathbb{X}_t|\Omega_t] = \sum_{z_t} \mathbb{E}[\Delta \mathbb{X}_t|Z_t, \Omega_t]\Pr(Z_t|\Omega_t).$$

   Use this expression to derive an equation for $\mathbb{E}[\Delta \mathbb{X}_t|\Omega_t]$ in terms of the likelihood ratios, $\Pr(\mathbb{B}_t^I|\mathbb{B}_t, \Omega_t)/\Pr(\mathbb{B}_t^U|\mathbb{B}_t, \Omega_t)$ and $\Pr(\mathbb{S}_t^I|\mathbb{S}_t, \Omega_t)/\Pr(\mathbb{S}_t^U|\mathbb{S}_t, \Omega_t)$.

   (c) Use your answer to part (b) to determine *the sign* of the correlation between $\Delta \mathbb{X}_t$ and ΔS_{t-1}.

   (d) In light of your answer to part (c), comment on the view that order flow cannot be a proximate driver of spot exchange-rate dynamics if it is forecastable from the history of spot rates.

2. Bias in Uninformed Trading: Consider the following variant of the model presented in the chapter. Suppose that when U-traders have the opportunity to trade they buy foreign currency with probability $\wp$ and sell foreign currency with probability $1 - \wp$.

   (a) Recalculate the trading probabilities in Table 5.1.

   (b) Use your answer to part (a) to find equations for the bid and ask quotes that marketmakers will now make.

   (c) For a given set of beliefs concerning fundamentals [i.e., the $\pi_t(k)$ probabilities], explain how marketmakers' bid and ask quotes are affected by the trading probability for U-traders. In particular, explain how their bid and ask quotes will differ from those in equation (5.9) when $\wp$ is greater than 1/2. More generally, why should the trading probability of U-traders affect marketmakers' quotes?

3. Trading and Public Announcements: Consider the effects of public announcements concerning fundamentals studied in Section 5.5.

   (a) If there is an announcement that $F_t = k^*$ at the start of period t, marketmakers' beliefs are

   $$\pi_t(k) = \begin{cases} 1 & \text{if } k = k^* \\ 0 & \text{otherwise} \end{cases}.$$

   Prove that the quote equations in (5.9) now imply that

   $$S_t^A = S_t^B = F_t.$$

   (b) If there is an announcement that $F_t = k^*$ at the start of period t and no announcement at the start of period $t + 1$, compute marketmaker beliefs $\pi_{t+1}(k)$. Show that these beliefs are independent of period-t trades and explain why this is the case.

   (c) Now suppose that announcements about the true value for current fundamentals come at the end of each period (i.e., after trading is complete). If there is an announcement that $F_t = k^*$ at the end of period t, how will marketmakers use their observations on period-t trades in determining their period-$t + 1$ quotes?

4. Dispersed Information: This chapter describes a model in which information about fundamentals is initially concentrated in the hands of a subset of traders, the I-traders. This question considers a situation where information about fundamentals is dispersed across different traders. Suppose that an asset has a random fundamental value $F = F_{\text{I}} + F_{\text{II}}$, where F_{I} and F_{II} are *independent* random variables that take the values of one or zero with equal probability:

   $$F_i = \begin{cases} 0: & \Pr = 1/2 \\ 1: & \Pr = 1/2 \end{cases} \quad i = \{\text{I, II}\}.$$

   The population of traders in the market is equally divided into two types, type I and II. Type I's know the value of the F_{I} component and type II's know the value of the F_{II} component. A marketmaker sets bid and ask prices for period-t trading, P_t^B and P_t^A, at which he is willing to buy or sell one unit of the asset according to

   $$P_t^A = E\left[F \mid \Delta \mathbb{X}_t = 1, \Omega_t\right], \tag{5.29}$$

   $$P_t^B = E\left[F \mid \Delta \mathbb{X}_t = -1, \Omega_t\right], \tag{5.30}$$

   where Ω_t denotes the information available to the marketmarker. $\Delta \mathbb{X}_t$ denotes the order imbalance in period-t trading, and is equal to 1 when a trader buys the asset and -1 when a trader sells it. The identities of the traders are not known to the marketmakers. Each period, one randomly chosen trader has the opportunity to buy or sell the asset at the quoted prices. Let Ω_t^i for $i = \{\text{I,II}\}$ denote the information available to each trader type at the start of period t.

If trader i has the opportunity to trade in period t, he will buy if $P_t^A \leq E\left[F|\Omega_t^i\right]$ and sell if $P_t^B \geq E\left[F|\Omega_t^i\right]$. All the traders and the marketmaker know the distribution of trader types and the probability distribution for the F_i components.

(a) Explain the rationale behind the price-setting equations (5.29) and (5.30).

(b) Compute $E\left[F|\Omega_t^i\right]$ for $i = \{\text{I},\text{II}\}$ in period $t = 1$ (i.e., before any trading takes place).

(c) In period 1 the marketmaker quotes prices of $P_1^A = 3/2$ and $P_1^B = 1/2$. Using your answer to part (b), calculate the probability $\Pr(\Delta\mathbb{X}_t = -1|F)$ and $\Pr(\Delta\mathbb{X}_t = 1|F)$ for each possible value of F. Be sure to explain your answer fully.

(d) Show that $P_1^A = 3/2$ and $P_1^B = 1/2$ satisfy equations (5.29) and (5.30) when $t = 1$.

(e) Suppose that the order imbalance is positive in period-1 trading. What information does this convey to type I and type II traders who did not trade with the marketmaker in period 1?

(f) How does the information conveyed to traders by the order imbalance in this model differ from the information they convey in the model presented in this chapter?

CHAPTER 6

Currency-Trading Models

This chapter introduces a model of exchange-rate determination with micro-foundations that are grounded in the institutional structure of the foreign exchange (FX) market. That is to say, agents in the model correspond to actual market participants and the environment incorporates key institutional features of currency trading. This takes us beyond the sequential trading model of Chapter 5 because the model's predictions concerning the dynamics of spot rates can be examined directly using trading data from the FX market.

We should emphasize that the modeling strategy described here does not represent a change in our goal of understanding exchange-rate dynamics. The idea is to build an exchange-rate model from microeconomic foundations that reasonably represents the key features of the market. In particular, our aims are to incorporate the institutional implications of how information is transmitted from one participant to another as trading takes place and to study how this information flow is ultimately reflected in the spot exchange rate. The fact that the model describes trading among agents does not mean that we are interested only in trading. Our focus remains on understanding exchange-rate dynamics, but we are using a model that makes detailed predictions about trading activity as well.

No model can incorporate all the institutional features of trading in the FX market—it's far too complex. Rather, we must look at the market and ask what key features should not be omitted. With this in mind, we begin with an overview of the institutional structure.

6.1 The Structure of the FX Market

The FX market is the oldest and largest financial market in the world. The origins of currency trading can be traced back to ancient times, but it was not until the advent of telecommunications that the market began to take on its current structure. This began in the 1930s with the establishment of the first currency brokers in London, but active FX trading started only in the 1960s. Since then trading has been split between the interbank market and the retail market. Neither market has a physical location, unlike, say, the New York Stock Exchange. Trading takes place by phone or electronically between participants located all around the world. That said, most trading in the

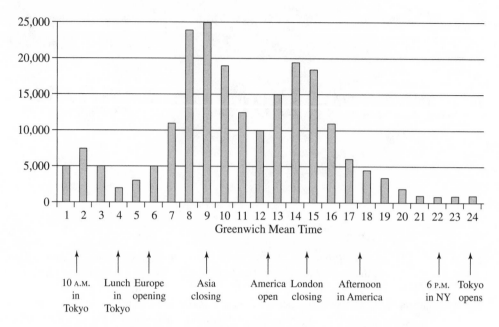

FIGURE 6.1   Average number of FX transactions per hour.

interbank market takes place among banks located in a few financial centers: Tokyo, Singapore, Frankfurt, New York, and particularly London. Trading can take place 24 hours a day, but activity is heavily concentrated during the daytime hours of the main financial centers. This gives rise to the distinct intraday trading pattern shown in Figure 6.1. Here we plot the average number of foreign exchange transactions in all currencies each hour. Note that most of the trading activity is concentrated between 7:00 A.M. and 5:00 P.M. GMT. It is important to keep this intraday trading pattern in mind when considering the results of empirical studies that use intraday data.

Global trading in foreign exchange dwafts the turnover in other financial markets. Although banks are not required to report their foreign exchange transactions, information on market activity is available through the surveys conducted every 3 years by central banks and disseminated through the Bank for International Settlements (BIS). Table 6.1 reports the results of these surveys for three segments: spot transactions, forward transactions, and foreign exchange swaps.

When many people talk of "the FX market" they are referring implicitly to spot transactions. These are agreements between two counterparties to exchange currencies at a specified exchange rate in 2 days (i.e., on the settlement day). The first row of Table 6.1 shows that turnover in the spot foreign exchange market had grown to $1 trillion on an average day in April 2007 (when the last BIS survey was conducted). Note that the growth in turnover was not steady. There was a temporary but marked decline in turnover at the time of the 2001 survey, which is attributed to the introduction of the euro and consolidation in the banking industry. Turnover in forwards and swaps has grown faster than spot market trading. Recall that in a forward trade the counterparties agree to exchange currencies at a specified exchange rate on a future date. A foreign exchange swap combines a spot and a forward transaction that go in

TABLE 6.1
Turnover in the Foreign Exchange Market

	1989	1992	1995	1998	2001	2004	2007
Spot transactions	317	394	494	568	387	621	1005
Forward transactions	27	58	97	128	131	208	362
Swap transactions	190	324	546	734	656	944	1714
Total turnover	590	820	1190	1490	1200	1880	3210
Total turnover (April 2007 rates)	na	880	1150	1650	1420	1950	3210

Notes: Daily averages in April of the survey year, in billions of U.S. dollars. Statistics are adjusted for local and cross-border double-counting. Total turnover includes an estimate of the gaps in reporting. Source: BIS (2007).

opposite directions. For example, I agree today to (1) buy €100 million in the spot market for delivery in two days, and (2) to sell €100 million forward for delivery in 1 month. Such trades allow market participants to benefit from international interest differentials, the so-called "carry trade." Much of the growth in swap turnover shown in Table 6.1 is attributed to an increase in the carry trade.

Although the BIS statistics reported in Table 6.1 represent the best quantitative information about the size and growth of the foreign exchange market, they do have limitations. First, the coverage of the surveys has changed over the years. The number of participating countries has increased with each survey as has the coverage of derivatives activity. Cross-survey comparisons are also complicated by variations in exchange rates. The last two rows of Table 6.1 report total turnover computed using average rates at the time of each survey and turnover computed with the average rates at the time of the last survey, April 2007. There are significant differences between these two measures of global turnover, particularly in the 2001 survey.

Foreign exchange trading is heavily concentrated in a few currencies. The upper panel of Table 6.2 shows the distribution of market turnover for the main currencies in the BIS surveys. Here we see that the U.S. dollar is by far the most heavily traded currency, being on one side of between 80 and 90 percent of all transactions. The next most heavily traded currencies in the 1990s were the German deutschmark (DM), Japanese yen (JPY), British pound sterling (GBP), and Swiss franc (CHI). Taken together, these five currencies were involved in approximately 78 percent of all transactions covered by the 1998 survey. This concentration of trading activity somewhat increased after the introduction of the euro (EUR). In the 2004 survey, the top five currencies (with the euro replacing the deutschmark) were on at least one side in 85 percent of all transactions. The lower panel of Table 6.2 shows that the distribution of turnover by currency pair is similarly concentrated. In the 1990s trading in USD/DM and USD/JPY dominated with turnover shares close to 20 percent. The next two most heavily traded currency pairs, USD/GBP and USD/CHI, had shares of just 8 and 5 percent, respectively. By the time of the 2004 survey, trading was heavily concentrated in just three currency pairs, USD/EUR, USD/JPY, and USD/GBP, which together accounted for 60 percent of the total turnover.

TABLE 6.2
Currency Distribution of Foreign Exchange Turnover

	1995	1998	2001	2004	2007
I: Percent shares by currency					
Dollar (USD)	83.3	87.3	90.3	88.7	86.3
Euro (EUR)			37.6	37.2	37.0
Japanese Yen (JPY)	24.1	20.2	22.7	20.3	16.5
Deutschmark (DM)	36.1	30.1			
Pound sterling (GBP)	9.4	11.0	13.2	16.9	15.0
Swiss franc (CHI)	7.3	7.1	6.1	6.1	6.8
II: Percent shares by currency pair					
USD/EUR			30	28	27
USD/DM	22	20			
USD/JPY	21	18	20	17	13
USD/GBP	7	8	11	14	12
USD/CHI	5	5	5	4	5

Notes: Daily averages in April of the survey year. As two currencies are involved in each transaction, the sum of the shares in panel I totals 200. Data are adjusted for both local and cross-border double-counting. Source: BIS (2007).

6.1.1 The Interbank Market

As the name suggests, trading in the interbank market takes place between banks. Such trading occurs in two ways: directly and indirectly. Direct interdealer trades result from "conversations" between two foreign exchange dealers working at different banks. These conversations originally took place via phone or telex, but since 1987 most take place through the Reuters Dealing 2000-1 system. This is a closed, secure electronic messaging system which provides a detailed record of each transaction.

A typical direct trade begins when the initiating dealer contacts another dealer requesting a quote. A quote request may also be accompanied by information on the size of the desired trade when it differs from the standard amount of $10 million. The initiating dealer does not disclose his interest in either buying or selling FX at this stage. By convention, dealers in the interbank market are expected to respond to quote requests very quickly (i.e., in the matter of a few seconds). They do so by quoting an ask price at which they will sell the desired amount of FX and a bid price at which they will buy. Convention also dictates that the difference between the ask and bid quotes, the spread, must be in line with the small spreads typically quoted by other dealers. Once the quotes are given, the initiating dealer must immediately decide whether to buy at the ask price, sell at the bid price, or pass.

Figure 6.2 provides a typical example of direct interdealer trade that occurred on the Reuters system on March 16, 1998, reproduced from Rime (2003). The figure shows the transaction ticket with the text of the D2000-1 conversation as it appeared on the screen of the dealer receiving the quote request. The initiating dealer, identified

```
FROM \CODE" \FULL NAME HERE" *0728GMT 160398 */7576
Our Terminal:      \CODE"   Our user  \FULL NAME HERE"

        DEM 1
#       45.47
        BA> I BUY
#       TO CONFIRM AT 1,8147 I SELL 1 MIO USD
        VAL 180398
#       MY DEM TO \FULL NAME HERE"
#       THANKS AND BYE
        TO CONFIRM AT 1,8147 I BUY 1 MIO USD
        VAL 180398
        MY USD to \FULL NAME HERE"
        THANKS DEAL FRDS. CHEERS
#
        # END REMOTE #
```

FIGURE 6.2   Example of direct interbank transaction on Reuters D2000-1.

by a code and name in the first line, begins with "DEM 1." This is a request for a spot DM/USD quote for up to $1 million. The next line shows the quoted prices of "45.47." By convention, only the last two digits of the four decimals in the two prices are quoted. The actual bid and ask quotes are therefore 1.8145 and 1.8147, respectively. The quoted spread is just 0.0002 DM/USD, or two "pips" in trading jargon. This is smaller than the spread of three "pips" typically quoted for the DM/USD in the interbank market, which suggests that the dealer was "shaving" his quotes to induce the initiating dealer to buy. The following line shows the decision of the initiating dealer: "I BUY" means that he buys $1 million at the ask price of 1.8147. The quoting dealer then confirms the exact price, quantity, valuation, settlement date (i.e., two days later), and where he wants the deutschmarks sent. The initiating dealer also confirms the terms of the transaction and says where he wants the dollars sent. Dealers sometimes use the system to exchange views concerning the market after the trade is complete, but in this case they ended the conversation with standard phrases.

There are several noteworthy aspects of "direct" interbank trading. First, the details of each conversation remain known only to the two dealers involved. The Reuters system does not report any information from a transaction (e.g., transaction price) to other dealers in the market even if they use the system. Second, at any point in time, there may be multiple pairs of dealers directly trading the same currencies. Consequently, it is perfectly possible that the same trades take place at different transaction prices. For example, while the initiating dealer in the preceding example paid the ask price of 1.81471 DM/USD, another dealer could have paid 1.81474 DM/USD to buy $10 million at the very same time. The third observation concerns the asymmetry between dealers. Although there is a buyer and seller for each currency, the dealers play different roles in the transaction. One dealer requests the quotes and decides whether and how to trade; the other quotes prices at which he is willing to trade a stated amount. This asymmetry is important when considering the information flows associated with the trade. On the one hand, the initiating dealer provides information to the quoting dealer when he decides to trade at one of the quoted trades. On the other, the quoting dealer provides information to the initiating dealer in the form of his bid and ask quotes. These information flows will figure prominently in the micro-based model we develop later.

Trading in the interbank market also takes place via foreign exchange brokers. A broker matches the desired trades of different dealers without being a party to the transactions. Dealers wishing to trade via a broker can place two types of orders: limit orders and market orders. A limit-order purchase is an instruction to buy a specified quantity up to a maximum price; a limit-order sale is an instruction to sell a specified quantity above a minimum price. By contrast, a market-purchase (sale) order is an instruction to buy (sell) a specified quantity at the best prevailing price. The job of the broker is to match market orders with limit orders. Until the 1990s, this was done by the broker announcing the best bid and ask limit-order prices over intercoms ("squawk boxes") situated in the dealing rooms of major banks. A dealer wishing to submit a market order would call the broker through a dedicated phone line and say either "mine" if he wanted to buy at the announced ask price or "yours" if he wanted to sell at the announced bid price. The broker would then match the two dealers participating in the trade and announce over the squawk box the transaction price and whether it was at the bid or the ask price.

Since the mid-1990s two electronic brokerages, the Reuters D2000-2 and EBS, have become increasingly important in the interbank market. Electronic brokerages operate in a manner similar to that of voice brokerages. The systems prioritize the limit orders submitted by dealers so that those with the best prices are matched first with incoming market orders. Market orders are processed sequentially so that each is matched with the best remaining limit order. This matching process also accounts for the credit arrangements between dealers' banks. (Credit arrangements are needed to ensure that currencies can be exchanged on the settlement date 2 days after each transaction.) The brokerage systems ensure that the counterparties of each trade have an existing credit arrangement.

There are some important informational differences between direct and indirect interbank dealing. Recall that information concerning each direct trade remains the private information of the participants; it is never collected and transmitted to the market as a whole. By contrast, indirect trading via a brokerage provides information market-wide. Voice brokers provided information on the best limit-order prices and transaction prices via the squawk boxes, but did not reveal the identity of the dealers involved in each trade. The EBS and Reuters brokerage systems provide similar information. Subscribing dealers can see the best limit-order prices on the system or the best available prices from credit-approved banks, but they cannot see the identity of the dealers behind the limit orders. They can also see the price and direction of all trades on the system, again without information on the counterparties. Thus, each dealer has continuous real-time information on the price at which he can trade (by submitting a market order) together with information on trades that have been completed across the market. Although this represents a much clearer picture of market-wide activity than was available from direct trading, it is still incomplete. In particular, the brokerage systems do not allow dealers to see the complete set of limit orders that have been submitted to the system. This means that dealers do not know the price they would pay for a market order that exhausted the quantity specified in the best limit order.

The composition of interbank trading has changed significantly in the past 20 years. Prior to the early 1990s, approximatly 60 percent of trades were direct, with the remainder taking place indirectly via voice brokers. This pattern began to change with the introduction of the electronic brokerages in the mid-1990s. Initially, they expanded at the expense of the voice brokers, but by 2001 they had become the dominant trading mechanism in the interbank market. According to the BIS, by 2001 electronic brokers accounted for 67 and 79 percent of interbank spot trades in London and New York, respectively. Since then, trading via the EBS and Reuters systems has become the dominant form of interbank trading. This is a notable institutional development and signifies a possible change in the way information is disseminated across the interbank market. We consider this possibility and its implications in what follows.

6.1.2 The Retail Market

Foreign exchange transactions between dealers and "customers" take place in the retail market. The term "customer" is used to identify anyone wanting to trade currency other than a bank: corporate treasurers, pension fund managers, hedge funds, or currency overlay firms, to name but a few.[1] Thus, customers make up a heterogeneous group.

Until recently, all trading in the retail market took place by phone. Typically, a customer would call a bank requesting quotes for a trade of a particular size. The customer trading desk at the bank would then quote an *indicative* bid and ask price at which it would try to fill the customer's order. These quotes were not firm commitments to trade at the specified prices. If prices in the interbank market moved between the time the customer agreed to trade and the time the order was passed through and executed by a dealer in the interbank market, the price paid by the customer would reflect the actual market price (plus a markup that provides a trading profit for the bank). That said, competition among banks for customer orders ensured that the indicative quotes were not a misleading indicator of the prices actually paid by customers. Indeed, although the spread between the indicative ask and bid prices is much larger than the spreads quoted in the interbank market, their midpoint seems to be reasonably accurate. Although anecdotal evidence suggests that individual customers were relatively loyal to their banks, banks' customer trading desks would also advertise for new customers by posting their indicative quotes to a Reuters information service called FXFX. This service provided customers with real-time information on the indicative quotes being offered by banks worldwide. The FXFX service was the first source of high-frequency data on currency prices used by researchers.

Like the interbank market, electronic trading has also come to the retail market. In the past few years three electronic systems—FX Connect, FXAll, and Currenex—have established themselves as the main electronic portals linking customers with the customer trading desks of banks. These systems allow customers to request quotes from several banks simultaneously, thereby intensifying the competition among banks. The systems also comprise a component of the push toward something known as Straight Through Processing (STP), a fully automated process that links customer trading decisions with electronic trading in the interbank market, trade confirmation, and settlement. STP is also beginning to blur the distinction between the interbank

---

1. A currency overlay manager is a specialist firm that implements a trading strategy that manages the risks associated with fluctuating exchange rates. They are used by many investment firms as a means to separate the management of currency risk from asset allocation and security selection.

and retail market. Some banks now offer their largest customers the ability to trade directly on the electronic brokerage systems; the bank provides the credit agreements needed to trade, with the customer submitting the market and limit orders.

Electronic Crossing Networks (ECNs) represent another form of electronic trading in the retail market. These systems match customer orders at prices obtained from the interbank market. Some systems are set up to mimic electronic brokerages, but in reality the operator of the system acts as the counterparty to market orders. As yet, ECNs account for relatively little trading volume, but their presence may add to the competitive pressure on the customer trading desks of banks.

The retail market is characterized by a distinct information structure. As in direct interdealer trading, the details of each dealer-customer trade are not disseminated across the market. Indeed, the trading decisions of customers are widely viewed by dealers as the single most important source of market-relevant information. Several large banks have developed reporting systems that provide dealers with information about the orders that are being received by their customer trading desks around the world. The aim of these systems is to provide timely information about customer demand for currencies that dealers can exploit in their own trading strategies. As such, information on customer orders is tightly held by banks and is rarely available to researchers.

6.1.3 Market Participants

Understanding the behavior of dealers and customers is key to any micro-based analysis of the foreign exchange market. Let us therefore focus on some key aspects of their behavior.

Dealers' Trading Opportunities

The trading opportunities available to a foreign exchange dealer are wider than those available to a simple marketmaker. Recall from Chapter 5 that the marketmaker quotes prices at which he is willing to trade a certain amount. Thus, all trades are initiated by the counterparty (e.g., the investor). As a consequence, if the marketmaker wants to change the composition of his asset holdings, he must adjust his quotes in order to elicit trades in the desired direction. This is just one of the trading options available to a foreign exchange dealer. As a subscriber to the Reuters D2000-1 direct trading system, a dealer will receive requests for quotes from initiating dealers that he can adjust in order to induce a trade in the desired direction. Of course, one drawback of this strategy is that it is dependent on a flow of quote requests from other dealers. Alternatively, the dealer can submit a limit order to a broker (e.g., EBS or Reuters D2000-2). If the price in the order is competitive relative to other limit orders of the system (i.e., the price is close to the best limit-order bid or ask price), the dealer is likely to quickly achieve his desired change in position as market orders arrive into the system. The dealer can also change his asset holdings by initiating trades with other dealers. This can be done directly via Reuters D2000-1 or indirectly via a market order submitted to a broker. In short, therefore, foreign exchange dealers have several trading options for controlling their asset holdings. The question of how dealers choose among these trading options has to be addressed in a micro-based model because their decisions will have important implications for the behavior of the whole market.

Dealers' Trading Constraints

Dealers face two forms of constraints: information constraints and position constraints. The former describe the information available to dealers as they make their trading decisions and the latter are the instruments used by banks to limit the risk of trading losses.

Dealers have limited information about activity in both the interbank and retail markets. In the interbank market, the best limit prices reported by voice brokers were the single most important source of market-wide price information. The best limit prices reported on the electronic brokerages now fulfill this role. Indeed, since a larger fraction of interbank trading now passes through the EBS and Reuters electronic brokers than once passed via voice brokers, the limit prices are probably a more accurate measure of market-wide prices than ever before. That said, dealers still face uncertainty about the overall state of the market. In particular, they cannot see the complete structure of limit orders on the electronic brokerages, nor do they know what is being traded directly. Information from the retail market is even more restricted. Dealers at some large banks have access to information on the customer orders received by their customer trading desks worldwide. At best, this gives them a partial picture of the aggregate currency orders hitting the market. Dealers working at other banks have no access to this information and must rely instead on their own customer orders, which may be unrepresentative of the aggregates.

Dealers also face restrictions on their asset positions. These restrictions take the form of limits on the size and duration of positions and vary across banks and among the dealers within banks. The most common restriction is on "overnight" positions. Although trading can take place 24 hours a day, Figure 6.1 showed that most trading activity is concentrated between 7:00 A.M. and 5:00 P.M. GMT. A typical dealer located in London would not be permitted to hold a net position between 3:00 P.M. (the customary end of trading by London-based dealers) and 7:00 A.M. the next day. Dealers are also restricted in the size of their intraday positions. Information on the exact restrictions is hard to come by because banks consider it proprietary, but we can gain some indirect evidence on the importance of these restrictions by looking at individual dealer positions.

Figure 6.3 shows the net position (in millions of dollars) over a single week of trading for a dealer in the USD/DM interbank market studied by Lyons (1995). The net position cumulates the trades undertaken by the dealer. When the dealer purchases (sells) dollars, his net position increases (decreases). The vertical lines represent overnight periods when the dealer did not trade.

There are several noteworthy aspects of Figure 6.3. First, the dealer had no net overnight position on any of the five trading days. Second, there are several occasions when the dealer had net positions of over \$40 million. Third, large net positions are quickly unwound. In fact, Lyons estimates the half-life of a nonzero net position to be 10 minutes over these 5 trading days. Of course none of these observations provides direct evidence on the position restrictions imposed on the dealer. It is quite possible that the formal restrictions imposed by the dealer's bank never constrained his trading decisions. Nevertheless, the speed with which net positions were unwound suggests that the dealer was acutely aware of the risks associated with large positions.

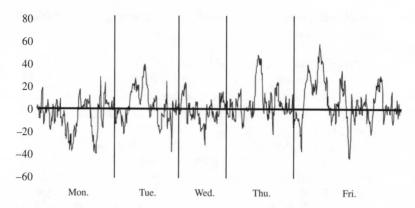

FIGURE 6.3   Net position (in millions of dollars) over one trading week in 1992 of a large bank dealer in USD/DM. Source: Lyons (1995).

There are limits to what can be safely inferred from the behavior of a single dealer over such a short time period. Indeed, Lyons notes that this dealer is atypical insofar as he has no information from the retail market. When dealers have access to such information, and it is deemed valuable in the sense that it can be used to predict the future course of spot rates, they may be given the latitude to establish and maintain sizable net positions for speculation purposes that may extend for hours and even overnight. The latitude given these dealers depends on their experience and past performance. Dealers who have been successful (or lucky) in the past are given greater latitude, whereas tighter restrictions are imposed on those who have incurred losses.

Customer Types

Broadly speaking, customer orders fall into two categories. The first relates to international trade. In simple terms, importers of foreign goods and services will generally have to purchase FX to pay exporters in their domestic currency. More realistically, corporate treasurers must manage costs and revenues from production and sales in many countries. This requires hedging against the transaction and operational risks associated with exchange-rate fluctuations through the placement of currency orders in the spot and forward markets. The second broad category relates to financial investment. Management of an internationally diversified portfolio generates currency orders for positioning and hedging reasons. In the former case, the portfolio manager undertakes currency transactions in order to change the international composition of his portfolio. In the latter case, currency orders are generated by an active currency program whose aim is to limit the exchange-rate exposure of the overall portfolio.

Customer orders can also be categorized in terms of their price-dependency. Customer orders that are generated solely in response to current and past currency prices are termed feedback orders. One simple example is a customer "stop-loss" order. This is a customer order that instructs the bank to sell a specified amount of FX if the bid price falls below a certain level. Customer orders generated by technical or chartist trading algorithms represent another more complex form of feedback. In this case, customer orders are generated when current prices reach benchmarks (e.g., trend lines) estimated from the past history of prices. Nonfeedback customer orders are driven by more than just the evolution of prices. For example, a hedge fund or currency overlay manager may interpret the implications of the latest macroeconomic data release for the value of the USD/EUR in a way that differs from the prevailing spot rate. In such a case, customer orders are generated to build a speculative position designed to profit from the anticipated future adjustment of the spot rate as the "market" adjusts to the manager's interpretation. Nonfeedback customer orders are also generated by purely allocative factors. The withdrawal of funds from an internationally diversified pension fund will necessitate FX sale orders from pension fund managers without regard to the current spot exchange rate.

6.1.4 Implications for Model Building

It should be clear from this brief overview that the institutional structure of the foreign exchange market is too complex to be accurately represented in a theoretical model. Instead, we have to focus on a small number of features that are essential for understanding the main economic mechanism at work:

1. The FX market is a two-tier market comprising the interbank and retail markets. Trading in each tier has been distinct in terms of the participants and trading mechanisms.

2. Foreign exchange dealers trade directly and indirectly in the interbank market. Unlike a simple marketmaker, dealers quote prices and initiate trades.

3. No dealer has complete information about the state of the interbank market. Brokers provide market-wide information on quotes and transaction prices, but dealers do not observe the structure of limit orders that describe market liquidity. Direct interdealer trading takes place simultaneously across the interbank market. Dealers only have information on the trades in which they themselves participate.

4. Dealers face constraints on both the duration and size of their asset positions. Dealers' overnight positions are typically small or zero.

5. Banks fill customer orders for currency in the retail tier of the market.

6. The customer orders received by banks in the retail tier of the foreign exchange market represent the most important source of private information to dealers. Dealers working at banks with a large customer base and a worldwide reporting system have a potentially important informational advantage over other market participants.

7. Customer orders come from many different agent types and may be generated by allocative, speculative, and risk-management factors. Customer orders that are purely a function of current and past currency prices are termed feedback orders.

6.2 The Portfolio Shifts Model

We are now ready to incorporate the key features of the foreign exchange market into a micro-based model of exchange-rate determination. The Portfolio Shifts model developed by Lyons (1997) and Evans and Lyons (2002a) does just that. It describes how trading activity in the interbank and retail tiers of the market relates to the evolution of the spot exchange rate. In other words, this micro-based model links exchange-rate dynamics to trading activity.

6.2.1   An Overview

The model describes trading in a single currency pair among a large number of dealers and a broker and among dealers and investors over a stylized trading day. The day begins with the arrival of news concerning the current payoff on FX. This information is learned simultaneously by all investors and dealers and so represents the arrival of public news. Individual investors also receive private information about their income. Foreign exchange trading then begins in the retail tier of the market. Dealers quote prices at which they will fill customer orders and investors place orders with individual dealers. As in the actual market, there is no public dissemination of information concerning the details of customer-dealer trades; customer orders represent a source of private information to individual dealers. Trading then takes place between dealers and the broker in the interbank tier of the market. Dealers trade directly with each other; they quote prices and initiate trades. Dealers can also trade with the broker. After interbank trading is complete, the retail tier of the market opens once more. Dealers quote prices at which they are willing to fill customer orders and investors place orders with individual dealers.

Clearly, this sequence of events represents a simplified view of trading in the actual foreign exchange market. It does, however, allow us to analyze how information pertinent to the spot exchange rate is learned by dealers via trading. In particular, the focus of the model is on how information about the aggregate demand for FX contained in the customer orders at the start of the day is learned by dealers and reflected in the FX prices they quote at the end of day. As we shall see, this information aggregation process produces an important empirical prediction linking trading activity to exchange-rate dynamics.

6.2.2   Model Details

Consider a pure exchange economy with one risky asset representing FX and one risk-free asset with a daily return of $1 + r$. The economy is populated by a continuum of risk-averse investors indexed by $n \in [0, 1]$ and D risk-averse dealers indexed by d. Each day, t, is split into three trading rounds: I, II, and III.

At the start of round I on day t, all investors and dealers observe the dividend paid to the current holders of FX. The value of the dividend, D_t, is assumed to follow a random walk,

$$D_t = D_{t-1} + V_t, \tag{6.1}$$

where $V_t \sim \text{i.i.d.} N(0, \sigma_v^2)$. Realizations of V_t represent the arrival of public macroeconomic information over time (e.g., changes in interest rates). At the start of the day each investor n also receives FX income, $Y_{n,t}$. This is private information to each investor and generates a hedging motive for the customer orders in round I trading.

The retail tier of the market opens in round I. All the dealers simultaneously and independently quote a scalar price at which they will fill customer orders to buy or sell FX. The round I price quoted by dealer d is denoted by $S^I_{d,t}$. Prices are publicly observed by all dealers and investors and are good for orders of any size. Investors then place their orders for FX. Orders may be placed with more than one dealer. If two or more dealers quote the same price, the customer order is randomly assigned among them. The customer orders received by dealer d are denoted by $Z^I_{d,t}$. Positive (negative) values of $Z^I_{d,t}$ denote net customer purchases (sales) of FX. As in the actual retail market, customer orders, $Z^I_{d,t}$, are only observed by dealer d.

Trading in the interbank tier of the market takes place in round II. The broker and all dealers simultaneously and independently quote a scalar price for FX, $S^{II}_{B,t}$, and $\{S^{II}_{d,t}\}^D_{d=1}$. The quoted prices are observed by all dealers and are good for interdealer trades of any size. All dealers then simultaneously and independently trade on other dealers' and the broker's quotes. We denote the FX orders made by dealer d as $T^{II}_{d,t}$ and orders received by dealer d as $Z^{II}_{d,t}$. Orders received by the broker are denoted by $Z^{II}_{B,t}$. When dealer d initiates a purchases (sale) of FX, $T^{II}_{d,t}$ is positive (negative). Positive values of $Z^{II}_{d,t}$ or $Z^{II}_{B,t}$ denote purchases of FX initiated by another dealer. Once again, trading with multiple dealers and the broker is feasible. If multiple agents quote the same price, trades are allocated equally among them. At the close of round II trading, all dealers and the broker observe aggregate interdealer order flow:

$$X_t = \sum_{d=1}^{D} T^{II}_{d,t}. \tag{6.2}$$

Interdealer order flow, X_t, simply aggregates the purchases of FX made by dealers initiating trades against other dealers' quotes and the broker's quote. As we will see, this variable plays a very important role in the model.

The retail tier of the market reopens in round III. The broker and dealers again simultaneously and independently quote prices, $S^{III}_{B,t}$ and $\{S^{III}_{d,t}\}^D_{d=1}$, at which they will fill dealer and customer orders, respectively. Investors observe all the prices and then place their orders with dealers. As before, orders may be placed with more than one dealer and are randomly assigned to dealers quoting the same prices. The round III customer orders received by dealer d are denoted by $Z^{III}_{d,t}$. Once each dealer has filled his customer orders, he can trade with the broker.

The complete sequence of events throughout day t is shown in Figure 6.4.

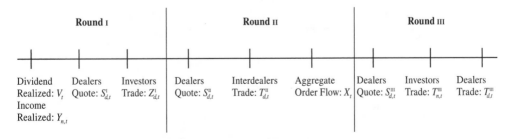

Round I			Round II			Round III		
Dividend Realized: V_t Income Realized: $Y_{n,t}$	Dealers Quote: $S^I_{d,t}$	Investors Trade: $Z^I_{d,t}$	Dealers Quote: $S^{II}_{d,t}$	Interdealers Trade: $T^{II}_{d,t}$	Aggregate Order Flow: X_t	Dealers Quote: $S^{III}_{d,t}$	Investors Trade: $T^{III}_{n,t}$	Dealers Trade: $T^{III}_{d,t}$

FIGURE 6.4   Daily timing in the portfolio shifts model.

6.2.3 Market Participants

One hallmark of a micro-based model is that the trading behavior represents optimal behavior on the part of the market participants. This means that customer orders placed by investors in rounds I and III are derived from the optimal asset demands of investors, whereas both the price quotes and interdealer trades represent the results of optimal decisionmaking by dealers and the broker. Let us therefore consider the objective and constraints facing investors, dealers, and the broker in turn.

The customer orders from investor n for FX in rounds I and III of day t are determined by their desire to maximize expected utility defined over wealth on day $t + 1$:

$$\mathcal{U}_{n,t}^i = \mathbb{E}\left[-\theta \exp(-\theta W_{n,t+1}^{\mathrm{I}})|\Omega_{n,t}^i\right], \tag{6.3}$$

with $\theta > 0$, where $W_{n,t+1}^{\mathrm{I}}$ is the wealth of investor n at the start of round I on day $t + 1$. The information available to investor n at the start of round i on day t is denoted by $\Omega_{n,t}^i$.

At the start of day t, investors receive two pieces of information. First, everyone learns the dividend paid by each unit of FX he is holding, D_t. Second, each investor n receives income $Y_{n,t}$ denominated in foreign currency. The value of $Y_{n,t}$ represents private information to each investor. We assume that the income received by investor n is

$$Y_{n,t} = Y_t + \xi_{n,t}, \tag{6.4}$$

where Y_t and $\xi_{n,t}$ are i.i.d. mean-zero normal random variables with variances of σ_Y^2 and σ_ξ^2, respectively. The income received by investor n comprises an aggregate component, Y_t, and an idiosyncratic component, $\xi_{n,t}$. Investors do not initially observe either component. However, the equilibrium behavior of currency prices will enable each investor to learn the value of Y_t by the end of day t. In the interim, the conditional distribution of Y_t will be given by the standard projection theorem. In particular,

$$Y_t|Y_{n,t} \sim N(\kappa_n Y_{n,t}, (1 - \kappa_n)\sigma_Y^2),$$

where $\kappa_n \equiv \sigma_Y^2/(\sigma_Y^2 + \sigma_\xi^2)$.

We can now describe the optimization problem facing investor n. Let $A_{n,t}^i$ denote the investor's holdings of FX at the end of round i trading (i.e., after they have traded with dealers). As we shall see, in each round dealers quote a common price for FX, i.e., $S_{d,t}^i = S_t^i$, so we need not keep track of the dealer who fills the investor's FX order. The budget constraints facing the investor are therefore

$$W_{n,t}^{\mathrm{III}} = A_{n,t}^{\mathrm{I}}(S_t^{\mathrm{III}} - S_t^{\mathrm{I}}) + W_{n,t}^{\mathrm{I}} + S_t^{\mathrm{I}}Y_{n,t} \tag{6.5a}$$

and

$$W_{n,t+1}^{\mathrm{I}} = A_{n,t}^{\mathrm{III}}(S_{t+1}^{\mathrm{I}} + D_{t+1} - (1 + r)S_t^{\mathrm{III}}) + (1 + r)W_{n,t}^{\mathrm{III}}. \tag{6.5b}$$

In round I, the investor chooses her desired holdings of FX, $A_{n,t}^{\mathrm{I}}$, to maximize $\mathcal{U}_{n,t}^{\mathrm{I}}$ subject to (6.5). At this point, her information set contains the current prices quoted by dealers $\{S^I_{d,t}\}^D_{d=1}$, knowledge of the currency dividend, D_t, and private information concerning $Y_{n,t}$. We may therefore represent her information as

$$\Omega^I_{n,t} = \left\{ \{S^I_{d,t}\}^D_{d=1}, Y_{n,t}, D_t, \Omega^{III}_{n,t-1} \right\}.$$

Round I customer orders depend on the difference between the optimal choice for $A^I_{n,t}$ and the investor's existing holdings, $A^{III}_{n,t-1}$, plus current income, $Y_{n,t}$.

In round III the investor chooses $A^{III}_{n,t}$ to maximize $\mathcal{U}^{III}_{n,t}$ subject to (6.5b). The information available to her at this point includes the round III-dealer quotes so

$$\Omega^{III}_{n,t} = \left\{ \{S^{III}_{d,t}\}^D_{d=1}, \Omega^I_{n,t} \right\}.$$

Once again, customer orders depend on the difference between the optimal choice for $A^{III}_{n,t}$ and the investor's existing holdings, $A^I_{n,t}$.

The problem facing each dealer is more complex. Like investors, each dealer d makes his day-t trading decisions to maximize expected utility defined over wealth on day $t + 1$,

$$\mathcal{U}^i_{d,t} = \mathbb{E}\left[-\theta \exp(-\theta W^I_{d,t+1}) | \Omega^i_{d,t} \right],$$

where $W^i_{d,t}$ and $\Omega^i_{d,t}$ denote the wealth and information of dealer d at the start of round i on day t. The problem for each dealer is to choose the price quotes $S^i_{d,t}$ in rounds $i = \{I,II,III\}$ and interdealer trades, $T^i_{d,t}$, in rounds II and III that will maximize expected utility given the following sequence of budget constraints:

$$W^{II}_{d,t} = W^I_{d,t} + (A^I_{d,t} - Z^I_{d,t})(S^{II}_t - S^I_t) + Z^I_{d,t}(S^I_{d,t} - S^I_t), \tag{6.6a}$$

$$W^{III}_{d,t} = W^{II}_{d,t} + (A^{II}_{d,t} + T^{II}_{d,t} - Z^{II}_{d,t})(S^{III}_t - S^{II}_t) + Z^{II}_{d,t}(S^{II}_{d,t} - S^{II}_t), \tag{6.6b}$$

and

$$W^I_{d,t+1} = (1+r)W^{III}_{d,t} + (A^{III}_{d,t} + T^{III}_{d,t} - Z^{III}_{d,t})(S^I_{t+1} + D_{t+1} - (1+r)S^{III}_t)$$
$$+ Z^{III}_{d,t}(S^{III}_{d,t} - S^{III}_t). \tag{6.6c}$$

Equations (6.6) contain important constraints on dealers' behavior, so it is worth examining their structure in detail. Dealer d enters day t with FX holdings of $A^I_{d,t-1}$ and wealth of $W^I_{d,t}$, which comprises domestic currency holdings and FX holdings, $A^I_{d,t-1}$, valued at the equilibrium spot rate quoted by other dealers, S^I_t. Equation (6.6a) says that wealth at the start of round II, $W^{II}_{d,t}$, equals $W^I_{d,t}$ plus the capital gain of FX holdings *at the end* of round I trading, $(A^I_{d,t-1} - Z^I_{d,t})(S^{II}_t - S^I_t)$, and the profit from filling customer orders. Customer orders for FX of $Z^I_{d,t}$ produce revenue of $Z^I_{d,t}S^I_{d,t}$ but reduce the dealer's FX holdings by $Z^I_{d,t}$, so the dealer's profit is $Z^I_{d,t}(S^I_{d,t} - S^I_t)$.

The evolution of wealth between the start of rounds II and III shown in equation (6.6b) takes a similar form. In this case, the dealer starts with FX holdings of $A^{II}_{d,t} = A^I_{d,t} - Z^I_{d,t}$, purchases $T^{II}_{d,t}$ from other dealers and the broker, and fills FX orders of $Z^{II}_{d,t}$. The capital gain on his FX holdings at the end of trading is therefore $(A^{II}_{d,t} + T^{II}_{d,t} - Z^{II}_{d,t})(S^{III}_t - S^{II}_t)$, whereas the profit from filling the orders from other dealers at price $S^{II}_{d,t}$ is $Z^{II}_{d,t}(S^{II}_{d,t} - S^{II}_t)$. Finally, the dealer begins round III with FX holdings of $A^{III}_{d,t} = A^{II}_{d,t} + T^{II}_{d,t} - Z^{II}_{d,t}$. Equation (6.6c) shows that the capital gain and dividend on holdings at the end of trading is $(A^{III}_{d,t} + T^{III}_{d,t} - Z^{III}_{d,t})(S^I_{t+1} + D_{t+1} - (1+r)S^{III}_t)$, where $T^{III}_{d,t}$ is the round III trade with the broker. The profit from filling customer FX orders of $Z^{III}_{d,t}$ at price $S^{III}_{d,t}$ is $Z^{III}_{d,t}(S^{III}_{d,t} - S^{III}_t)$ and FX holdings at the start of day $t+1$ are $A^I_{d,t+1} = A^{III}_{d,t} + T^{III}_{d,t} - Z^{III}_{d,t}$.

Dealers also face important information constraints. At the start of round I on day t all dealers observe the dividend D_t, but each must choose his price quote $S^I_{d,t}$ to maximize $\mathcal{U}^I_{d,t}$ subject to (6.6) before seeing the prices quoted by other dealers. The round I quote of dealer d is therefore chosen using information

$$\Omega^I_{d,t} = \{D_t, \Omega^{III}_{d,t-1}\}.$$

At the start of round II, dealer d must again choose $S^{II}_{d,t}$ before seeing other dealer quotes but his information set now contains all the round I quotes and his incoming customer FX orders, so

$$\Omega^{II}_{d,t} = \left\{ \{S^I_{d,t}\}^D_{d=1}, Z^I_{d,t}, \Omega^I_{d,t} \right\}.$$

Once these quotes are chosen, each dealer has the opportunity to initiate trade with other dealers and the broker. In particular, each dealer d chooses $T^{II}_{d,t}$ to maximize $\mathbb{E}[\mathcal{U}^{III}_{d,t} | \{S^{II}_{d,t}\}^D_{d=1}, S^{II}_{B,t}, \Omega^{II}_{d,t}]$ subject to (6.6). Note that these interdealer trading decisions are conditioned on all the price quotes in the market, but not on the incoming trades from other dealers, $Z^{II}_{d,t}$. As interdealer trading takes place simultaneously, no dealer can condition his trade on the trades initiated by other dealers.

Finally, at the start of round III, all dealers simultaneously choose $S^{III}_{d,t}$ to maximize $\mathcal{U}^{III}_{d,t}$ subject to (6.6). The information now available to the dealer d is

$$\Omega^{III}_{d,t} = \left\{ X_t, \{S^{II}_{d,t}\}^D_{d=1}, S^{II}_{B,t}, Z^{II}_{d,t}, \Omega^{II}_{d,t} \right\},$$

where $X_t \equiv \sum^D_{d=1} T_{d,t}$ is the aggregate interdealer order flow from round II trading. Once each dealer has filled his round III orders from investors, he has the opportunity to puchase FX from the broker.

The foreign exchange broker chooses quotes in rounds II and III, $S^{II}_{B,t}$ and $S^{III}_{B,t}$, to maximize expected utility defined over wealth on day $t+1$:

$$\mathcal{U}^i_{B,t} = \mathbb{E}[-\theta \exp(-\theta W^I_{B,t+1}) | \Omega^i_{B,t}],$$

where $W^i_{B,t}$ and $\Omega^i_{B,t}$ denote the wealth and information of the broker at the start of round i on day t. The broker's wealth follows the dynamics of dealer d's wealth in (6.6) except that $Z^I_{d,t} = 0$ and $T^{II}_{d,t} = T^{III}_{d,t} = 0$ because brokers do not receive customer orders in round I, nor do they initiate trades in rounds II and III. The information available to brokers evolves in the same way as that of dealer d with $Z^I_{d,t} = 0$.

Two features of the model are worth highlighting at this juncture. First, and most importantly, the model allows us to examine how both public and private information becomes embedded in currency prices via the trading decisions of FX market participants. The flow of public information is represented by the sequence of the dividend shocks, V_t, that is observed by all dealers and investors at the beginning of each day. This information will be embedded into the day-t exchange rates insofar as individual dealers find it optimal to quote prices that depend on V_t. The flow of private information originates from investors' income, $Y_{n,t}$. This information is not directly available to dealers and so can only become embedded in spot rates insofar as it can be inferred from the trading activity that dealers observe. It is this information transmission mechanism that is our central focus.

The second feature of the model concerns the trading environment. Although the model incorporates the two-tiered nature of the actual FX market and includes multiple dealers, it does not include numerous other institutional features. This makes the model tractable, but also raises the possibility that its implications are not robust to the addition of other market features. We return to this issue later in the chapter.

6.2.4 Equilibrium

An equilibrium in this model comprises: (1) a set of FX orders by investors in rounds I and III, (2) a set of FX price quotes by dealers in rounds I–III and the broker in rounds II and III, and (3) a set of dealer trading decisions in rounds II and III. All these decisions must be optimal in the sense that they maximize the expected utility of the respective agent given available information and they must be consistent with market clearing.

In rounds I and III, market clearing requires that the aggregate customer order flow equal the desired change in investors' holdings of FX:

$$\sum_{d=1}^{D} Z_{d,t}^{\mathrm{I}} = \int_{0}^{1} (A_{n,t}^{\mathrm{I}} - A_{n,t-1}^{\mathrm{III}} - Y_{n,t}) dn. \tag{6.7}$$

Recall that $A_{n,t}^{i}$ identifies the desired FX holdings of investor n in round i, so her order to purchase FX is $A_{n,t}^{\mathrm{I}} - A_{n,t-1}^{\mathrm{III}} - Y_{n,t}$ in round I. The terms on the right therefore represent aggregate customer orders for FX. Market clearing simply requires that the sum of the individual customer orders received by the D dealers equal this aggregate.

In round II market clearing requires that aggregate incoming orders for FX received by dealers and the broker equal the aggregate FX purchases initiated by dealers:

$$\sum_{d=1}^{D} Z_{d,t}^{\mathrm{II}} + Z_{\mathrm{B},t}^{\mathrm{II}} = \sum_{d=1}^{D} T_{d,t}^{\mathrm{II}}.$$

In round III, dealers receive incoming customer orders and initiate trades with the broker, so market clearing requires that

$$\sum_{d=1}^{D} Z_{d,t}^{\mathrm{III}} = \int_{0}^{1} (A_{n,t}^{\mathrm{III}} - A_{n,t}^{\mathrm{I}}) \, dn \quad \text{and} \quad Z_{\mathrm{B},t}^{\mathrm{III}} = \sum_{d=1}^{D} T_{d,t}^{\mathrm{III}}.$$

The equilibrium of the model is summarized in the following proposition.

Proposition 6.1: *In an efficient risk-sharing equilibrium: (i) all dealers quote the same price for FX in each round of trading, that is, $S_{d,t}^i = S_t^i$ for $i = \{$I, II, III$\}$; (ii) the broker quotes the same price as dealers in rounds II and III; (iii) common quotes are given by*

$$S_t^I = S_{t-1}^{III} - \lambda_A A_{t-1} + \tfrac{1}{r} V_t, \tag{6.8a}$$

$$S_t^{II} = S_t^I, \tag{6.8b}$$

and

$$S_t^{III} = S_t^{II} + \lambda_A A_{t-1} + \lambda_X (X_t - \mathbb{E}[X_t | \Omega_{D,t}^{II}]), \tag{6.8c}$$

with $A_{t-1} = \int_0^1 A_{n,t-1}^{III} dn$ and $X_t = \sum_{d=1}^D T_{d,t}^{II}$, where $\Omega_{D,t}^{II}$ denotes information common to dealers and the broker at the start of round II; (iv) the trades initiated by dealer d in round II are

$$T_{d,t}^{II} = \alpha_Z Z_{d,t}^I + \alpha_A A_{t-1}; \tag{6.9}$$

and (v) the customer orders received by dealer d in round I are

$$Z_{d,t}^I = (\beta/D)Y_t + \varepsilon_{d,t}, \tag{6.10}$$

where $\sum_{d=1}^D \varepsilon_{d,t} = 0$.

Before we verify this proposition in detail, it is worthwhile developing some intuition for why the equilibrium in the model takes this particular form. First, note that dealers and the broker quote a common price for FX, S_t^i, in trading rounds $i = \{$I, II, III$\}$. This feature of the equilibrium arises because anyone quoting a different price than S_t^i would open himself up to arbitrage trading losses. Thus, at any point in time there is a single equilibrium spot exchange rate despite the presence of multiple dealers.

The second important feature of the equilibrium concerns the impact of shocks. Recall that there are two types of shocks in the model: dividend shocks, V_t, which are public information, and shocks to income that are initially private information of individual investors. The former arrive at the start of each day and are immediately incorporated into the common quotes by dealers in round I, as (6.8a) shows. Information about income affects currency prices through a more complex process. In round I investors place FX orders with dealers that are contingent on their own foreign income. Equation (6.10) shows that these customer orders provide a noisy signal to the dealer about the aggregate component of the income shock, Y_t. (The noise, $\varepsilon_{d,t}$, comes from the fact that each dealer receives a fraction of aggregate customer orders that depend on the idiosyncratic income shocks.) Dealers act on this information when initiating interdealer trades in round II. In fact, as equation (6.9) indicates, the trades initiated by each dealer depend on the customer order he received. As a consequence, dealers learn the value of Y_t from their observation of aggregate interdealer order flow, X_t, at the end of round II. Equation (6.8c) shows that dealers incorporate this information into their round III quotes in the form of unexpected order flow, $X_t - \mathbb{E}[X_t | \Omega_{D,t}^{II}]$. It is this transmission of information via order flow that is the hallmark of a micro-based exchange-rate model.

6.2.5 Solving for the Equilibrium

To verify Proposition 6.1 we proceed in three steps: First, we describe the evolution of the broker, dealers', and investors' common information sets implied by the behavior of the exchange rate and order flows. Second, we characterize the behavior of investors given the dynamics of the exchange rate in (6.8) This allows us to verify that the customer orders received by each dealer in round ɪ take the form of (6.10). Third, we derive the optimal quote and trading strategies for the broker and dealers. These strategies give us the dynamics for the exchange rate in (6.8) and interdealer trades in (6.9).

Step 1: Information

Let $\Omega^i_{D,t} = \cap_d \Omega^i_{d,t}$ denote the common information of all dealers at the start of round i. At the start of day t, all dealers observe the dividend, D_t, so common dealer information at the start of round ɪ is

$$\Omega^{\text{I}}_{\text{D},t} = \left\{ D_t, \Omega^{\text{III}}_{\text{D},t-1} \right\}. \tag{6.11}$$

By the start of round ɪɪ, each dealer d has received new information in the form of customer orders, $Z^{\text{I}}_{d,t}$, but this information is private, so round ɪ trading does not change dealers' common information, that is, $\Omega^{\text{II}}_{\text{D},t} = \Omega^{\text{I}}_{\text{D},t}$. In round ɪɪ, the dealers' common information is augmented by their observation of aggregate interdealer order flow. In equilibrium, equations (6.9) and (6.10) imply that

$$X_t = \sum_{d=1}^{\text{D}} \alpha_z Z^{\text{I}}_{d,t} + \alpha_{\text{A}} A_{t-1} = \alpha_z \beta Y_t + \alpha_{\text{A}} A_{t-1}, \tag{6.12}$$

so aggregate interdealer order flow provides information on aggregate income, Y_t, and investors' overnight holdings of FX, $A_{t-1} \equiv \int_0^1 A^{\text{III}}_{n,t-1} dn$. We establish later in step 3 that $A_t = A_{t-1} + Y_t$ in equilibrium. Combining this result with the first difference of (6.12) and rearranging gives

$$Y_t = \frac{1}{\alpha_z \beta} \Delta X_t + \left(1 - \frac{\alpha_{\text{A}}}{\alpha_z \beta} \right) Y_{t-1}$$

$$= \frac{1}{\alpha_z \beta} \sum_{i=0}^{\infty} \left(1 - \frac{\alpha_{\text{A}}}{\alpha_z \beta} \right)^i \Delta X_{t-i}.$$

Thus, observations on the change in aggregate interdealer order flow, ΔX_{t-i}, reveal the level of aggregate income, Y_t. We may therefore write dealers' common information at the start of round ɪɪɪ as

$$\Omega^{\text{III}}_{\text{D},t} = \left\{ Y_t, \Omega^{\text{I}}_{\text{D},t} \right\}. \tag{6.13}$$

Recall that the broker also observes D_t at the start of round ɪ and X_t at the end of round ɪɪ. Hence, the broker shares the common information of dealers at the start of rounds ɪ and ɪɪɪ, that is, $\Omega^i_{\text{B},t} = \Omega^i_{\text{D},t}$ for $i = \{\text{I, III}\}$.

Let us next consider the common information of investors, $\Omega_t^i = \cap_n \Omega_{n,t}^i$. At the start of day t, all investors observe the dividend, D_t, and the common equilibrium quote, S_t^I, so common investor information in round I is

$$\Omega_t^I = \left\{ S_t^I, D_t, \Omega_{t-1}^{III} \right\}. \tag{6.14}$$

Note that Ω_t^I does not contain any information on day-t income. Individual investors know their own income, $Y_{n,t}$, but this is private information and so is not part of Ω_t^I. At the start of round III, all investors observe the common equilibrium quote of S_t^{III}, which in turn reveals the value of aggregate income, Y_t, to all investors. To see why this is so, we first note that $\mathbb{E}[Y_t | \Omega_{D,t}^{II}] = 0$ because Y_t is an i.i.d. mean-zero random variable that is uncorrelated with any elements in $\Omega_{D,t}^{II}$. Furthermore, $\mathbb{E}[A_{t-1} | \Omega_{D,t}^{II}] = A_{t-1}$ because $A_{t-1} = \sum_{i=1}^{\infty} Y_{t-i}$ and $Y_{t-i} \in \Omega_{D,t}^{II}$ for $i \geq 1$. Applying these results to (6.12) implies that

$$X_t - \mathbb{E}[X_t | \Omega_{D,t}^{II}] = \alpha_Z \beta Y_t, \tag{6.15}$$

so unexpected order flow observed by dealers is proportional to aggregate income. As a conseqence, (6.8) implies that the difference between dealers' round I and III quotes depends on investors' existing FX holdings, A_{t-1}, and aggregate income:

$$S_t^{III} - S_t^I = \lambda_A A_{t-1} + \lambda_X \alpha_Z \beta Y_t. \tag{6.16}$$

Since $A_{t-1} \in \Omega_{t-1}^I$, we may write investors' common information at the start of round III as

$$\Omega_t^{III} = \left\{ Y_t, \Omega_{t-1}^I \right\}. \tag{6.17}$$

The preceding results have several important implications: First, because dealers find it optimal to quote a common price in each trading round, the common quote must only be a function of common dealer information. This means that the value of S_t^I reveals only elements of $\Omega_{D,t}^I$ to investors at the start of round I. Thus, if investors and dealers have common information at the end of day $t-1$ (i.e., $\Omega_{D,t-1}^{III} = \Omega_{t-1}^{III}$), equations (6.11) and (6.14) imply that $\Omega_{D,t}^I = \Omega_t^I$. Further, as a consequence, (6.13) and (6.17) imply that $\Omega_{D,t}^{III} = \Omega_t^{III}$. In sum, therefore, dealers and investors share the same common information set in equilibrium, which evolves as

$$\Omega_{D,t}^I = \Omega_t^I = \left\{ D_t, \Omega_{t-1}^{III} \right\} \quad \text{and} \quad \Omega_{D,t}^{III} = \Omega_t^{III} = \left\{ Y_t, \Omega_{t-1}^I \right\}.$$

The second implication concerns investors' expectations regarding returns. Equation (6.16) implies that $\mathbb{E}[S_t^{III} - S_t^I | \Omega_{n,t}^I] = \lambda_A A_{t-1} + \lambda_X \alpha_Z \beta \mathbb{E}[Y_t | \Omega_{n,t}^I]$, so the intraday return on holding FX expected by investor n depends on his estimate of aggregate income based on private information $\Omega_{n,t}^I$. As we shall see, these expectations will generally differ from zero. As a result, customer orders in round I in part reflect the desire of investors to take speculative positions based on their private information.

The information structure also has implications for investors' overnight FX demand. In round III, investors form expectations regarding overnight excess returns, $\mathcal{R}_{t+1} \equiv S_{t+1}^I + D_{t+1} - (1+r)S_t^{III}$. We establish later that $\mathcal{R}_{t+1} = (\frac{1+r}{r})V_{t+1} + \frac{1}{\gamma}A_t$

for some positive constant γ. Since the dividend shock V_{t+1} is a mean-zero normally distributed random variable that is uncorrelated with any element in $\Omega_{n,t}^{\text{III}}$, the distribution of $\mathcal{R}_{t+1}$ conditioned on an individual investor's information, $\Omega_{n,t}^{\text{III}}$, is the same across all investors, and is equal to the distribution conditioned on common information, Ω_t^{III}. This means that the demand to hold FX overnight does not vary across investors and can be deduced from common information alone. Thus, although investors still possess private information about their own income history, by the start of round III of each day this private information does not affect future trade and quote decisions.

Step 2: Investors

Consider investor n's choice of FX holdings in round III, $A_{n,t}^{\text{III}}$. In equilibrium, the distribution of excess returns $\mathcal{R}_{t+1} \equiv S_{t+1}^{\text{I}} + D_{t+1} - (1+r)S_t^{\text{III}}$ is normal conditioned on information, $\Omega_{n,t}^{\text{III}}$. Maximizing expected utility $\mathcal{U}_{n,t}^{\text{III}}$ subject to (6.5b) is therefore equivalent to maximizing $\mathbb{E}[A_{n,t}^{\text{III}} \mathcal{R}_{t+1} | \Omega_{n,t}^{\text{III}}] - \frac{1}{2}\theta \mathbb{V}[A_{n,t}^{\text{III}} \mathcal{R}_{t+1} | \Omega_{n,t}^{\text{III}}]$. The resulting first-order condition implies that

$$A_{n,t}^{\text{III}} = \tfrac{1}{\gamma}\mathbb{E}[S_{t+1}^{\text{I}} + D_{t+1} - (1+r)S_t^{\text{III}} | \Omega_{n,t}^{\text{III}}], \tag{6.18}$$

where $\gamma = \theta \mathbb{V}[\mathcal{R}_{t+1} | \Omega_{n,t}^{\text{III}}]$. In equilibrium, all investors have the same conditional expectations concerning S_{t+1}^{I} and D_{t+1}, so their overnight FX holdings are the same, that is, $A_{n,t}^{\text{III}} = A_t^{\text{III}}$ for all $n \in [0, 1]$.

In round I, investor n chooses FX holdings of $A_{n,t}^{\text{I}}$ to maximize $\mathcal{U}_{n,t}^{\text{I}}$ subject to the sequence of budget constraints in (6.5). Combining these constraints gives

$$W_{n,t+1}^{\text{I}} = (1+r)(W_{n,t}^{\text{I}} + S_t^{\text{I}}Y_{n,t}) + (1+r)A_{n,t}^{\text{I}}(S_t^{\text{III}} - S_t^{\text{I}}) + A_{n,t}^{\text{III}}\mathcal{R}_{t+1}.$$

The first term on the right is known to investor n in round I. The second is normally distributed conditioned on the investor's information $\Omega_{n,t}^{\text{I}}$ because $S_t^{\text{III}} - S_t^{\text{I}}$ is proportional to Y_t [see equation (6.16)]. The third term contains two sources of uncertainty relative to $\Omega_{n,t}^{\text{I}}$: uncertainty about overnight excess returns, $\mathcal{R}_{t+1}$, and uncertainty about desired round III FX holdings, because $A_{n,t}^{\text{III}}$ depends on $\Omega_{n,t}^{\text{III}}$, which contains elements that are not in $\Omega_{n,t}^{\text{I}}$. We establish in what follows that both $A_{n,t}^{\text{III}}$ and $\mathcal{R}_{t+1}$ are normally distributed conditional on $\Omega_{n,t}^{\text{I}}$. As a result, the conditional distribution of $W_{n,t+1}^{\text{I}}$ is not normal because it contains the product $A_{n,t}^{\text{III}}\mathcal{R}_{t+1}$. Nevertheless, we can still evaluate expected utility, $\mathcal{U}_{n,t}^{\text{I}} \equiv \mathbb{E}[-\theta \exp(-\theta W_{n,t+1}^{\text{I}}) | \Omega_{n,t}^{\text{I}}]$, and maximize with respect to $A_{n,t}^{\text{I}}$ to give

$$A_{n,t}^{\text{I}} = \eta_{\text{A}} A_{n,t-1}^{\text{III}} + \eta_{\text{S}}\mathbb{E}[S_t^{\text{III}} - S_t^{\text{I}} | \Omega_{n,t}^{\text{I}}], \tag{6.19}$$

where η_{Y} and η_{S} are coefficients derived in the appendix. Equation (6.16) implies that

$$\mathbb{E}[S_t^{\text{III}} - S_t^{\text{I}} | \Omega_{n,t}^{\text{I}}] = \lambda_{\text{A}} A_{t-1} + \lambda_{\text{X}}\alpha_{\text{Z}}\beta \mathbb{E}[Y_t | \Omega_{n,t}^{\text{I}}] = \lambda_{\text{A}} A_{t-1} + \lambda_{\text{X}}\alpha_{\text{Z}}\beta \kappa_n Y_{n,t},$$

so substituting for $\mathbb{E}[S_t^{\text{III}} - S_t^{\text{I}} | \Omega_{n,t}^{\text{I}}]$ in (6.19) yields

$$A_{n,t}^{\text{I}} = \eta_{\text{S}}\lambda_{\text{X}}\alpha_{\text{Z}}\beta \kappa_n Y_{n,t} + (\eta_{\text{S}}\lambda_{\text{A}} + \eta_{\text{A}}) A_{t-1}^{\text{III}}.$$

We establish later that $\lambda_A = (1 - \eta_A)/\eta_s$, so this expression simplifies to

$$A_{n,t}^I = \eta_s \lambda_X \alpha_Z \beta \kappa_n Y_{n,t} + A_{t-1}^{III}. \tag{6.20}$$

Thus, desired FX holdings depend on the investors' income, $Y_{n,t}$, and existing FX holdings, $A_{n,t-1}^{III} = A_{t-1}^{III}$.

We can now derive expressions for customer orders in round I. By definition, the FX order from investor n in round I is $A_{n,t}^I - A_{n,t-1}^{III} - Y_{n,t}$. This expression simplifies to $(\eta_s \lambda_X \alpha_Z \beta \kappa_n - 1) Y_{n,t}$ after we substitute for $A_{n,t}^I$ from (6.20). Thus, the FX order of investor n provides information on his income, $Y_{n,t}$. Of course, the information obtained by each dealer depends on the orders he receives. Since all dealers quote a common round-I price in equilibrium, each dealer receives an equal share of investors' FX orders. The incoming orders received by a typical dealer d can therefore be written as

$$Z_{d,t}^I = \frac{1}{D} \left(\eta_s \lambda_X \alpha_Z \beta \kappa_n - 1 \right) Y_t + \varepsilon_{d,t}, \tag{6.21}$$

where $\varepsilon_{d,t}$ represents the idiosyncratic portion of the customer order flow with $\sum_{d=1}^{D} \varepsilon_{d,t} = 0$ [to satisfy the first market-clearing condition in (6.7)]. Note that (6.21) takes the same form as (6.10) in Proposition 6.1 with $\beta = 1/(\eta_s \lambda_X \alpha_Z \kappa_n - 1)$.

Step 3: Dealers and the Broker

We now turn to the behavior of the broker and dealers. The structure of trading in the model takes the form of a simultaneous-move game: At the start of each trading round, prices are quoted simultaneously by dealers (and the broker in rounds II and III), and in round II all dealers also simultaneously initiate a trade, $T_{d,t}^{II}$, against others' quotes. This means that the broker and the dealers cannot condition on others' quotes or trading decisions when making their own. We identify equilibrium quotes and trades using the concept of a Bayesian-Nash Equilibrium (BNE). To understand this equilibrium concept, we must first identify the quote and trading strategies of the dealers. Specifically, let $\mathcal{S} \equiv [\mathcal{S}_1, \mathcal{S}_2, \ldots \mathcal{S}_d, \ldots \mathcal{S}_D, \mathcal{S}_B]$ define the trading strategies of the broker and all the dealers in the market on day t, where $\mathcal{S}_d = (S_{d,t}^I, S_{d,t}^{II}, S_{d,t}^{III}, T_{d,t}^{II}, T_{d,t}^{III})$ and $\mathcal{S}_B = (S_{B,t}^{II}, S_{B,t}^{III})$ and let $U_j(\mathcal{S})$ denote the realized utility of agent $j = \{B, d\}$ (i.e., broker or dealer d) under the strategy $\mathcal{S}$. In a BNE, each agent j follows a strategy $\mathcal{S}_j$ such that

$$\mathbb{E}[U_j(\mathcal{S}) | \Omega_{j,t}^i] \geq \mathbb{E}[U_j(\widehat{\mathcal{S}}) | \Omega_{j,t}^i] \quad \text{for } i = \{I, II, III\}, \tag{6.22}$$

where $\widehat{\mathcal{S}}$ denotes any alternative strategy $\widehat{\mathcal{S}} = [\mathcal{S}_1, \mathcal{S}_2, \ldots \widehat{\mathcal{S}}_j, \ldots \mathcal{S}_D, \mathcal{S}_B]$. Thus, at each decision point, dealer d chooses the quote or trade that maximizes his expected utility given the equilibrium strategies of the broker and all the other dealers and the broker chooses a quote that maximizes his expected utility given the equilibrium strategies of all the dealers.

Let us now examine the implications of condition (6.22) in detail. Consider the choice of round I quotes on day t. According to Proposition 6.1, all dealers quote the same FX price, S_t^I. To see why this choice is part of the BNE strategy, suppose dealer d quotes a price of $S_{d,t}^I > S_t^I$ as part of an alternative strategy, $\widehat{\mathcal{S}}_d$. As all quotes are observable and are good for any amount, the customer orders received by dealer d will be negative as investors attempt to make arbitrage profits (i.e., investors will place FX purchase orders with the other dealers and FX sale orders with dealer d). Under these circumstances, the trading profit term, $Z_{d,t}^{\mathrm{I}}(S_{d,t}^{\mathrm{I}} - S_t^{\mathrm{I}})$, in the dealer's budget constraint (6.6a) has a limiting value of $-\infty$, so $\mathbb{E}[U_d(\mathcal{S})|\Omega_{d,t}^{\mathrm{I}}] > \mathbb{E}[U_d(\widehat{\mathcal{S}})|\Omega_{d,t}^{\mathrm{I}}]$. Similarly, if $S_{d,t}^{\mathrm{I}} < S_t^{\mathrm{I}}$, arbitrage trading will generate an incoming flow of FX orders (i.e., $Z_{d,t}^{\mathrm{I}} > 0$), so $Z_{d,t}^{\mathrm{I}}(S_{d,t}^{\mathrm{I}} - S_t^{\mathrm{I}})$ will again have a limiting value of $-\infty$. In short, quotes must be common across dealers to avoid the expected utility losses associated with arbitrage. A similar arbitrage argument applies in rounds II and III to the quotes of dealers and the broker.

Next, we turn to the determination of the common price quotes, S_t^i. We showed in step 1 that in equilibrium, investors, dealers, and the broker have common knowledge about the history of dividend and aggregate income shocks (i.e., $\{V_{t-i}, Y_{t-i}\}_{i\geq 0}$) by the time they make their round III decisions. As a result, everyone also knows that the outstanding stock of FX is equal to the sum of past aggregate income, $\sum_{i=0}^{\infty} Y_{t-i}$. The price quoted at the start of round III determines how this stock of risky assets is allocated among the broker, the dealers, and the investors.

In terms of risk-sharing, the most efficient allocation is one in which the marginal utility from holding FX is the same across all agents in every possible state of the economy. Since there are just D dealers, a broker, and a continuum of investors all with the same preferences, this can only be achieved if the round III price induces investors to hold the entire stock of FX. In other words, in an efficient risk-sharing equilibrium, dealers quote a common round III price to ensure that their (and the broker's) overnight holdings of FX are zero. This implication of the equilibrium accords well with the actual behavior of dealers. It also eliminates the incentive for further trading after round III.

To identify the round-III quote that supports an efficient risk-sharing allocation, we return to equation (6.18). Recall that the distribution of $\mathcal{R}_{t+1}$ conditioned on individual investors' information, $\Omega_{n,t}^{\mathrm{III}}$, is the same across all investors and is equal to the distribution conditioned on common information, Ω_t^{III}. Under these circumstances, (6.18) implies that the aggregate demand for FX is $A_t = \frac{1}{\gamma}\mathbb{E}[\mathcal{R}_{t+1}|\Omega_t^{\mathrm{III}}]$. Combining this expression with the definition of $\mathcal{R}_{t+1}$ gives

$$S_t^{\mathrm{III}} = \tfrac{1}{1+r}\mathbb{E}\big[S_{t+1}^{\mathrm{III}} + D_{t+1}|\Omega_t^{\mathrm{III}}\big] - \tfrac{1}{1+r}\mathbb{E}\big[S_{t+1}^{\mathrm{III}} - S_{t+1}^{\mathrm{I}}|\Omega_t^{\mathrm{III}}\big] - \tfrac{\gamma}{(1+r)}A_t.$$

Equation (6.8) of Proposition 6.1 implies that $\mathbb{E}[S_{t+1}^{\mathrm{III}} - S_{t+1}^{\mathrm{I}}|\Omega_t^{\mathrm{III}}] = \lambda_{\mathrm{A}}A_t$. Making this substitution in the preceding expression and solving forward yields

$$S_t^{\mathrm{III}} = \sum_{i=1}^{\infty} \left(\tfrac{1}{1+r}\right)^i \mathbb{E}\big[\, D_{t+i} - (\gamma + \lambda_{\mathrm{A}})A_{t+i-1}\big|\, \Omega_t^{\mathrm{III}}\big]. \tag{6.23}$$

Equation (6.23) identifies the value for the round III quote needed to induce investors to hold A_t in FX given their expectations concerning future dividends and FX holdings, D_{t+i} and A_{t+i}.

Efficient risk-sharing and market clearing imply that the aggregate investor demand for FX, A_t, is equal to aggregate holdings at the end of day $t-1$, A_{t-1}, plus foreign income received during round I, $Y_t = \int_0^1 Y_{n,t}dn$. Hence, the equilibrium dynamics of investors' FX holdings follow

$$A_t = A_{t-1} + Y_t. \tag{6.24}$$

Using this equation to forecast investor demand and (6.1) to forecast future dividends, we can rewrite (6.23) as

$$S_t^{\mathrm{III}} = \tfrac{1}{r}D_t - \tfrac{1}{r}(\gamma + \lambda_{\mathrm{A}})A_t. \tag{6.25}$$

We have thus found the value of the round III quote that achieves an efficient risk-sharing allocation of FX.

Now consider the quotes in rounds I and II. Recall that these quotes must be common across dealers to avoid arbitrage. As a consequence, they can only be a function of dealers' common information at the start of each trading round. All dealers learn of the dividend shock, V_t, at the start of day t, so they all know the value of D_t when quoting prices in rounds I and II. Dealers also receive information from the round I customer orders, $Z_{d,t}^{\mathrm{I}}$, but this information is private, so it cannot be used to set quotes in round II. Both S_t^{I} and S_t^{II} must therefore be functions of dealers' common information, $\Omega_{\mathrm{D},t}^{\mathrm{II}} = \Omega_{\mathrm{D},t}^{\mathrm{I}} = \Omega_t^{\mathrm{I}}$.

The value of S_t^{I} determines how FX is allocated among investors, dealers, and the broker. As before, efficient risk-sharing requires that investors hold the entire stock of FX throughout rounds I and II. This allocation would be feasible if all investors received the same foreign income (i.e., $Y_{n,t} = Y_t$) and the value of Y_t was known to all dealers at the start of round I. Under these circumstances, customer orders would be the same across all dealers and perfectly predictable for any given price quote, S_t^{I}, that is, $Z_t^{\mathrm{I}} = Z_{d,t}^{\mathrm{I}} = \mathbb{E}[Z_{d,t}^{\mathrm{I}}|\Omega_{\mathrm{D},t}^{\mathrm{I}}]$. Hence, the efficient risk-sharing allocation could be achieved by choosing S_t^{I} such that $Z_{d,t}^{\mathrm{I}} = 0$. When investors receive heterogeneous foreign income that is not known to dealers, it is impossible to choose a quote such that $Z_{d,t}^{\mathrm{I}} = 0$ for all d. In this case, the best dealers can do is choose S_t^{I} such that the allocation of FX holdings is ex ante efficient conditioned on common information $\Omega_{\mathrm{D},t}^{\mathrm{I}}$, that is, $\mathbb{E}[Z_{d,t}^{\mathrm{I}}|\Omega_{\mathrm{D},t}^{\mathrm{I}}] = 0$. Here, some dealers will inevitably hold open FX positions by the end of round I, but the identity and size of the positions cannot be predicted ex ante using $\Omega_{\mathrm{D},t}^{\mathrm{I}}$, so the risk cannot be shared more efficiently.

To find the value for S_t^{I}, we take expectations with respect to dealers' common information on both sides of the market-clearing condition in (6.7):

$$\sum_{d=1}^{\mathrm{D}} \mathbb{E}[Z_{d,t}^{\mathrm{I}}|\Omega_{\mathrm{D},t}^{\mathrm{I}}] = \int_0^1 E[A_{n,t}^{\mathrm{I}} - A_{n,t-1}^{\mathrm{III}} - Y_{n,t}|\Omega_{\mathrm{D},t}^{\mathrm{I}}]\,dn.$$

Substituting for $A_{n,t}^{\mathrm{I}}$ with (6.19) and noting that $\mathbb{E}[Y_{n,t}|\Omega_{\mathrm{D},t}^{\mathrm{I}}] = 0$ for all n gives

$$\sum_{d=1}^{\mathrm{D}} \mathbb{E}[Z_{d,t}^{\mathrm{I}}|\Omega_{\mathrm{D},t}^{\mathrm{I}}] = \eta_{\mathrm{S}}\mathbb{E}[S_t^{\mathrm{III}} - S_t^{\mathrm{I}}|\Omega_{\mathrm{D}t}^{\mathrm{I}}] + (\eta_{\mathrm{A}} - 1)\,A_{t-1}^{\mathrm{III}}.$$

Finally, we impose the risk-sharing restriction $\mathbb{E}[Z_{d,t}^{\mathrm{I}}|\Omega_{\mathrm{D},t}^{\mathrm{I}}] = 0$ and solve for S_t^{I}:

$$S_t^{\mathrm{I}} = \mathbb{E}[S_t^{\mathrm{III}}|\Omega_{\mathrm{D},t}^{\mathrm{I}}] - \lambda_{\mathrm{A}}A_{t-1}, \tag{6.26}$$

where $\lambda_A = (1 - \eta_A)/\eta_S$.

We are now left with the determination of the round II quote, S_t^{II}. With efficient risk-sharing in round III and common quotes within each round, the budget constraints for dealer d imply that

$$W_{d,t+1}^I = (1+r)(T_{d,t}^{II} - Z_{d,t}^{II} - Z_{d,t}^I)(S_t^{III} - S_t^{II}) - (1+r)Z_{d,t}^I(S_t^{II} - S_t^I).$$

Recall that dealers condition their round II trades, $T_{d,t}^{II}$, on their customer orders, $Z_{d,t}^I$, so the latter only affect wealth via the last term on the right-hand side. Moreover, note that this term only contributes to the conditional variance of wealth because the round I quote implies that $\mathbb{E}[Z_{d,t}^I|\Omega_{D,t}^I] = 0$. Now, since dealers' expected utility, $\mathbb{E}[\mathcal{U}_{d,t}^I|\Omega_{D,t}^I]$, is concave in wealth, the optimal choice for S_t^{II} is the value that minimizes the variance contribution of this term. Clearly, this implies that

$$S_t^{II} = S_t^I. \tag{6.27}$$

In other words, dealers will find it optimal to quote the same price in rounds I and II so as to eliminate the risk associated with unexpected customer orders.

We can now derive the quote equations in Proposition 6.1. We established earlier that $\mathbb{E}[Y_t|\Omega_{D,t}^I] = 0$, $\mathbb{E}[A_{t-1}|\Omega_{D,t}^I] = A_{t-1}$, and $X_t - \mathbb{E}[X_t|\Omega_t^I] = \alpha_Z\beta Y_t$. Combining these results with (6.25)–(6.27) implies that

$$S_t^I = S_{t-1}^{III} - \lambda_A A_{t-1} + \tfrac{1}{r}V_t, \quad S_t^{II} = S_t^I,$$

and

$$S_t^{III} = S_t^{II} + \lambda_A A_{t-1} + \lambda_X(X_t - \mathbb{E}[X_t|\Omega_t^I]),$$

where $\lambda_X = -(\gamma + \lambda_A)/(\beta r \alpha_Z)$. Recall from the customer order flow equation (6.21) that $\beta = 1/(\eta_S\lambda_X\alpha_Z\kappa_n - 1)$. Solving for λ_X and β from these expressions gives

$$\lambda_X = \frac{\gamma + \lambda_A}{r\alpha_Z + (\gamma + \lambda_A)\alpha_Z\eta_S\kappa_n} > 0 \quad \text{and} \quad \beta = -1 - \tfrac{1}{r}(\gamma + \lambda_A)\eta_S\kappa_n < 0.$$

The expression for λ_X implies that dealers revise their quotes for FX upward in round III when they observe unexpectedly high aggregate interdealer order flow from round II trading. The reason for this is quite intuitive. Unexpected order flow reveals information about the aggregate customer order flow hitting the market in round I (i.e., $X_t - \mathbb{E}[X_t|\Omega_t^I] = \alpha_Z Z_t^I$, where $Z_t^I \equiv \sum_{d=1}^D Z_{d,t}^I$). This order flow is perfectly negatively correlated with aggregate foreign income because investors hedge against their foreign income, $Z_t^I = \beta Y_t$. Thus, positive values for $X_t - \mathbb{E}[X_t|\Omega_t^I]$ imply that aggregate foreign income was negative so that the aggregate stock of FX has fallen. Consequently, efficient risk-sharing requires that the round III quote be raised so that investors will be willing to hold the smaller aggregate stock of FX overnight.

All that remains now is to confirm that interdealer trades take the form of (6.9). In round III, each dealer has the opportunity to trade with the broker after he has filled his customer orders. Now, since all dealers quote the same price in round III, each receives an equal share of aggregate customer orders, $Z_{d,t}^{III} = \frac{1}{D}\int_0^1(A_{n,t}^{III} - A_{n,t}^I)$, leaving FX holdings of $A_{d,t}^{III} - Z_{d,t}^{III}$. Dealer d can therefore eliminate his overnight holdings by initiating a trade of $T_{d,t}^{III} = Z_{d,t}^{III} - A_{d,t}^{III}$ with the broker. Hence, in equilibrium, the budget constraints in (6.6b) and (6.6c) of dealer d become

$$W^{\mathrm{I}}_{d,t+1} = (1+r)\big[W^{\mathrm{II}}_{d,t} + \hat{A}^{\mathrm{II}}_{d,t}(S^{\mathrm{III}}_t - S^{\mathrm{II}}_t) - (Z^{\mathrm{II}}_{d,t} - \mathbb{E}[Z^{\mathrm{II}}_{d,t}|\Omega^{\mathrm{II}}_{d,t}])(S^{\mathrm{III}}_t - S^{\mathrm{II}}_t)\big], \quad (6.28)$$

where $\hat{A}^{\mathrm{II}}_{d,t} \equiv A^{\mathrm{II}}_{d,t} + T^{\mathrm{II}}_{d,t} - \mathbb{E}[Z^{\mathrm{II}}_{d,t}|\Omega^{\mathrm{II}}_{d,t}]$ is the dealer's desired FX position. The problem facing dealer d in round II is to choose the trade, $T^{\mathrm{II}}_{d,t}$, implied by the utility-maximizing choice of $\hat{A}^{\mathrm{II}}_{d,t}$ given in (6.28) and the incoming orders from other dealers following BNE strategies, $Z^{\mathrm{II}}_{d,t}$. Note that dealer d cannot condition his choice for $T^{\mathrm{II}}_{d,t}$ on actual incoming orders, $Z^{\mathrm{II}}_{d,t}$, because all dealers must act simultaneously. Instead, each dealer must choose $T^{\mathrm{II}}_{d,t}$ based on his expectations regarding incoming orders $\mathbb{E}[Z^{\mathrm{II}}_{d,t}|\Omega^{\mathrm{II}}_{d,t}]$. Dealers also have to recognize that unexpected incoming orders will affect tomorrow's wealth via the last term on the right of (6.28).

In equilibrium, both $(S^{\mathrm{III}}_t - S^{\mathrm{II}}_t)$ and $Z^{\mathrm{II}}_{d,t}$ are normally distributed conditional on $\Omega^{\mathrm{II}}_{d,t}$. This means that finding the dealer's desired position involves evaluating $\mathcal{U}^{\mathrm{II}}_{d,t} \equiv \mathbb{E}[-\theta \exp(-\theta W^{\mathrm{I}}_{d,t+1})|\Omega^{\mathrm{II}}_{d,t}]$ where $W^{\mathrm{I}}_{n,t+1}$ does not have a conditional normal distribution and maximizing with respect to $\hat{A}^{\mathrm{II}}_{d,t}$. This problem is analogous to the one faced by investors in round I and can again be solved using the procedure described in the appendix. The dealer's desired FX position is given by

$$\hat{A}^{\mathrm{II}}_{d,t} = \frac{1}{1+\mathrm{D}}\varphi_{\mathrm{A}}A_{t-1} + \frac{1}{1+\mathrm{D}}\varphi_{\mathrm{Y}}\mathbb{E}[Y_t|\Omega^{\mathrm{II}}_{d,t}], \qquad (6.29)$$

where φ_{Y} and φ_{A} are coefficients given in the appendix. (We scale the coefficients by $1/(1+\mathrm{D})$ to simplify the expression that follows.)

Equation (6.29) implies that dealers' desired positions depend on their forecasts of aggregate income $\mathbb{E}[Y_t|\Omega^{\mathrm{II}}_{d,t}]$. These forecasts use the private information each dealer acquires from customer orders in round I. More specifically, when customer orders take the form of (6.10) in Proposition 6.1, $\mathbb{E}[Y_t|\Omega^{\mathrm{II}}_{d,t}] = \mathbb{E}[Y_t|Z^{\mathrm{I}}_{d,t}]$. If dealers view $\varepsilon_{d,t}$ as an i.i.d. normal random variable with mean zero and variance σ^2_ε, the projection theorem implies that

$$\mathbb{E}[Y_t|\Omega^{\mathrm{II}}_{d,t}] = \kappa_d Z^{\mathrm{I}}_{d,t}, \qquad (6.30)$$

where

$$\kappa_d = \frac{(\beta/\mathrm{D})\sigma^2_{\mathrm{Y}}}{(\beta/\mathrm{D})^2\sigma^2_{\mathrm{Y}} + \sigma^2_\varepsilon}.$$

Thus, each dealer's expectations concerning aggregate income depend on the customer orders he received in round I trading.

We can now compute the BNE trading strategies for each dealer. If all the other dealers trade according to (6.9), and orders are equally split among the broker and the dealers because they quote the same price, incoming order flow from other dealers is

$$Z^{\mathrm{II}}_{d,t} = \frac{1}{1+\mathrm{D}}\alpha_{\mathrm{Z}}\beta Y_t + \frac{\mathrm{D}}{1+\mathrm{D}}\alpha_{\mathrm{A}}A_{t-1}.$$

Dealer d's forecast of this order flow is thus

$$\mathbb{E}[Z^{\mathrm{II}}_{d,t}|\Omega^{\mathrm{II}}_{d,t}] = \frac{1}{1+\mathrm{D}}\alpha_{\mathrm{Z}}\beta E[Y_t|\Omega^{\mathrm{II}}_{d,t}] + \frac{\mathrm{D}}{1+\mathrm{D}}\alpha_{\mathrm{A}}A_{t-1}.$$

By definition, dealer d's trade is given by $T_{d,t}^{\text{II}} = \hat{A}_{d,t}^{\text{II}} - A_{d,t}^{\text{II}} + \mathbb{E}[Z_{d,t}^{\text{II}}|\Omega_{d,t}^{\text{II}}]$. Since dealers hold no overnight positions, their FX holdings at the start of round II simply reflect the customer orders they filled in round I, that is, $A_{d,t}^{\text{II}} = -Z_{d,t}^{\text{I}}$. Combining this fact with the preceding definition gives

$$T_{d,t}^{\text{II}} = \hat{A}_{d,t}^{\text{II}} + Z_{d,t}^{\text{I}} + \mathbb{E}[Z_{d,t}^{\text{II}}|\Omega_{d,t}^{\text{II}}]$$

$$= \frac{1}{1+\text{D}} \left(\varphi_{\text{Y}} + \alpha_z \beta \right) \mathbb{E}[Y_t | \Omega_{d,t}^{\text{II}}] + Z_{d,t}^{\text{I}} + \frac{1}{1+\text{D}} \left(\varphi_{\text{A}} + \text{D}\alpha_{\text{A}} \right) A_{t-1}$$

$$= \left(1 + \frac{1}{1+\text{D}} \left(\varphi_{\text{Y}} + \alpha_z \beta \right) \kappa_d \right) Z_{d,t}^{\text{I}} + \frac{1}{1+\text{D}} \left(\varphi_{\text{A}} + \text{D}\alpha_{\text{A}} \right) A_{t-1}. \quad (6.31)$$

Thus, the BNE strategy for each dealer is to initiate an interdealer trade that is a linear function of his own customer orders, $Z_{d,t}^{\text{I}}$, and the outstanding stock of FX, A_{t-1}, as shown in equation (6.9) of Proposition 6.1. Note that the coefficients on $Z_{d,t}^{\text{I}}$ and A_{t-1} in (6.31) are themselves functions of α_z and α_{A} because the trading strategies of each dealer depend on the strategy of others. The equilibrium values of α_z and α_{A} are found by equating coefficients in (6.9) and (6.31):

$$\alpha_z = \frac{1 + \text{D} + \varphi_{\text{Y}}\kappa_d}{1 + \text{D} - \beta\kappa_d} \quad \text{and} \quad \alpha_{\text{A}} = \varphi_{\text{A}}.$$

6.2.6 Features of the Equilibrium

Several features of the equilibrium deserve emphasis. To highlight them, let us consider the implications of Proposition 6.1 for the behavior of the spot exchange rate at the daily frequency:

$$S_t^{\text{III}} - S_{t-1}^{\text{III}} = \tfrac{1}{r}V_t + \lambda_{\text{X}}(X_t - \mathbb{E}[X_t|\Omega_t^{\text{I}}]). \quad (6.32)$$

Daily changes in the spot exchange rate are driven by shocks to dividends and unexpected interdealer order flow. The former reflect the effects of public news, whereas the latter conveys information that was initially dispersed across investors and was then aggregated via trading in the FX market.

Dividend shocks play a familiar role in the determination of the spot rate. Realizations of V_t are public information and affect the forecasts of future dividends by all dealers and investors in exactly the same way, that is, $\mathbb{E}[D_{t+i}|\Omega_{d,t}^{\text{I}}] - \mathbb{E}[D_{t+i}|\Omega_{d,t-1}^{\text{III}}]$ $= V_t$ and $\mathbb{E}[D_{t+i}|\Omega_{n,t}^{\text{I}}] - \mathbb{E}[D_{t+i}|\Omega_{n,t-1}^{\text{III}}] = V_t$ for all d and n. Consequently, it should come as no surprise that V_t shocks are immediately reflected in the equilibrium spot rate. That said, it is important to remember that quotes are chosen optimally in this model, so V_t shocks only affect the spot rate because dealers have an incentive to adjust their quotes once the value of V_t is known. Indeed, as equation (6.8a) shows, the BNE quote strategy of each dealer is to choose a round I quote that fully reflects the information in V_t concerning future dividends.

The role played by aggregate interdealer order flow in (6.32) is more complex. Note that it is unexpected interdealer order flow that affects the exchange rate in (6.32). The reason is that dealers adjust their quotes between rounds II and III to account for the *new* information contained in aggregate interdealer order flow. The customer orders received by each dealer reflect the difference between desired and actual FX positions of individual investors. As such, they convey information to dealers about both the current income and the overnight positions of a subset of investors. This information is effectively shared among dealers via interdealer trading in round II. As a result, X_t conveys information about aggregate income and the prior overnight FX position of all investors. Since the latter is already known to dealers, $X_t - \mathbb{E}[X_t | \Omega_t^I]$ is proportional to the new information concerning income that is incorporated into the round III quote, S_t^{III}.

Of course, the mere fact that unexpected interdealer order flow conveys new information about aggregate income to dealers does not explain why $X_t - \mathbb{E}[X_t | \Omega_t^I]$ appears in equation (6.32). For that we have to understand why dealers find it optimal to incorporate the new income information they learn into their common round III quote. In short, why is information on aggregate income, Y_t, relevant for the pricing of FX? The answer is quite simple. As in the actual market, dealers do not want to hold FX overnight—the risk of holding FX can be shared more efficiently by investors than by individual dealers. Consequently, each dealer's aim in round III is to quote a price that will induce investors to purchase all the FX currently held by dealers. In other words, the round III quote is chosen so that the excess overnight return expected by investors is such that they want to hold the entire existing stock of the FX. Obviously, this is not possible unless all dealers can calculate the existing stock of FX. However, since investors' income is the only source of FX, the existing stock can be computed from the history of aggregate income. Thus, information on Y_t is price relevant because it tells dealers what aggregate overnight FX position investors must be induced to hold. In sum, interdealer order flow conveys information about the shift in the FX portfolios of investors needed to achieve efficient risk-sharing. This is the origin of the term "portfolio shifts."

Risk-sharing also plays a role in the intraday dynamics of the exchange rate. In round I, dealers choose S_t^I so that expected customer order flow is zero conditioned on common information. This restriction ensures that the intraday allocation of FX is ex ante efficient from a risk-sharing perspective. As a result, dealers include a risk premium in their round-I quote that offsets the impact of investors' existing FX holdings on their FX orders: $\mathbb{E}[S_t^{III} - S_t^I | \Omega_{D,t}^I] = \lambda_A A_{t-1}$. This intraday risk premium accounts for the second term on the right in (6.8a) and (6.8c).

Another important feature of the model concerns timing. As we noted earlier, public news concerning currency and future dividends is immediately and fully incorporated into the spot exchange rate. By contrast, it takes time for the information concerning income to be reflected in the dealer quotes. The reason for the delay is important. Information about income is originally transmitted to dealers via the customer orders they receive in round I. Thus, each dealer has some information about Y_t at the start of round II, but the information is imprecise. At this point, each dealer could choose to use his private information on Y_t in setting his quote, but this is not optimal in the model's trading environment. Instead, his BNE strategy is to quote the same price as in round I (which is the same across all dealers and a function solely of common round-I information), because to do otherwise would expose him to arbitrage trading losses. As a result, the equilibrium spot rate remains unchanged between rounds I and II, even though dealers have information about aggregate income. The spot rate only incorporates this information when it becomes common knowledge among dealers. This process of information aggregation takes place via interdealer trading in round II. The BNE strategy of all dealers is to use their private information concerning income in determining the trade they wish to initiate with other dealers. It is for this reason that interdealer order flow provides information on aggregate income that becomes common knowledge to dealers by the start of round III.

Three further features of the model deserve comment. First, all the trading decisions of investors and dealers are motivated by the desire to maximize expected utility. Although the resulting customer and interdealer order flows convey information, neither investors nor dealers are motivated to trade for information-related reasons. This means that the information aggregation process just described may not always operate. In particular, if the speculative and hedging motives driving investors' round I orders offset one another, the customer orders received by dealers do not contain any information on aggregate income. In this case there is no information on income to aggregate via interdealer trading, and order flow X_t plays no role in the dynamics of the spot rate. The second feature concerns the dichotomy between dividend shocks and order flow. Dividend shocks represent the arrival of new public, price-relevant information that is immediately and fully incorporated into the spot rate. As such, the news has no effect on either customer or interdealer order flows because the response of dealers' quotes eliminates the incentive for anyone to adjust his desired FX position.

Finally, we turn to the role of the foreign exchange broker. It is tempting to think that the broker plays no real role in the model because he simply quotes the same price as dealers in rounds II and III, but this is not the case. In round III, the presence of the broker allows each dealer to hold no FX inventory overnight, consistent with the efficient risk-sharing allocation, even though each dealer is left with different holdings after filling customer orders. If the broker were absent, we would need further round(s) of interdealer trading to achieve the same allocation. The broker plays an even more important role in round II. Here interdealer trading is motivated by dealers' desires to take particular FX positions, $\hat{A}_{d,t}^{II}$, given customer orders from round I, $Z_{d,t}^{I}$, and expected orders from other dealers, $\mathbb{E}[Z_{d,t}^{II}|\Omega_{d,t}^{II}]$. As a result, in aggregate dealers may want to increase or decrease their holdings of FX. This is not possible if dealers only trade with each other in round II, but it can happen when they can also trade with the broker. In effect, the broker absorbs the imbalance of trades among dealers so that in aggregate dealers can achieve their desired FX holdings in round II.

6.3 Extending the Portfolio Shifts Model

Although the Portfolio Shifts model incorporates several features of the FX market, it abstracts from many others. Some of these features are unrelated to information aggregation and so have little impact on exchange-rate dynamics. Other features have important implications for how trading takes place and consequently can affect exchange-rate dynamics via their implications for information aggregation. In this section we extend the model to allow for (1) multiple currencies, and (2) lower transparency. Both extensions add features that affect trading and the process of information aggregation.

6.3.1 Multiple Currencies

The Portfolio Shifts model readily accommodates multiple currencies. In particular, suppose that $\mathbf{D}_t$ represents a $K \times 1$ vector of dividends on K risky currencies that follows

$$\mathbf{D}_t = \mathbf{D}_{t-1} + \mathbf{V}_t,$$

where $\mathbf{V}_t = [V_{t,k}]$ is a vector of mean-zero normal shocks with covariance $\mathbf{\Sigma}_v$. As before, all dealers and investors observe realizations of $\mathbf{V}_t$ at the start of day t. Each investor n also receives income in the form of K foreign currencies, denoted by the $K \times 1$ vector $\mathbf{Y}_{n,t}$. Realizations of $\mathbf{Y}_{n,t}$ represent private information to each investor and take the form

$$\mathbf{Y}_{n,t} = \mathbf{Y}_t + \xi_{n,t}, \tag{6.33}$$

where $\mathbf{Y}_t = [Y_{t,k}]$ is the vector of aggregate incomes and $\xi_{n,t}$ is the vector of idiosyncratic shocks. $\mathbf{Y}_t$ and $\xi_{n,t}$ are assumed to be vectors of independent normally distributed random variables with zero means and covariances given by $\mathbf{\Sigma}_Y$ and $\mathbf{\Sigma}_\xi$.

As before, each day is split into three trading rounds. In round I, each dealer quotes a price at which he will fill customer orders for each of the K currencies. We represent the quotes of dealer d in round i by the $K \times 1$ vector, $\mathbf{S}_{d,t}^i$. Each dealer d then receives customer orders for each currency denoted by the $K \times 1$ vector $\mathbf{Z}_{d,t}^I$. In round II, each dealer quotes prices $\mathbf{S}_{d,t}^{II}$, initiates interdealer trades in the K currencies, $\mathbf{T}_{d,t}^{II}$, and receives dealer orders in K currencies of $\mathbf{Z}_{d,t}^{II}$, where $\mathbf{T}_{d,t}^{II}$ and $\mathbf{Z}_{d,t}^{II}$ are $K \times 1$ vectors. At the close of round II, all dealers observe aggregate interdealer order flow for all K currencies,

$$\mathbf{X}_t = \sum_{d=1}^{D} \mathbf{T}_{d,t}^{II}, \tag{6.34}$$

where $\mathbf{X}_t = [X_{t,k}]$ is a vector of order flows for each of the K currencies. In round III, dealers quote prices $\mathbf{S}_{d,t}^{III}$ and receive customer orders of $\mathbf{Z}_{d,t}^{III}$. As before, all trading and quote decisions on day t maximize expected utility defined over wealth in round I of day $t + 1$.

How does the existence of multiple currencies affect the behavior of exchange rates? To address this question, let us first consider a situation in which shocks to dividends and income are uncorrelated across currencies, so $\mathbf{\Sigma}_v$, $\mathbf{\Sigma}_Y$, and $\mathbf{\Sigma}_\xi$ are all diagonal. In this special case, the daily dynamics of the spot rate for currency k take the form

$$S_{t,k}^{III} = S_{t-1,k}^{II} + \lambda_{k,k}(X_{t,k} - \mathbb{E}[X_{t,k}|\Omega_t^I]) + \tfrac{1}{r}V_{t,k}, . \tag{6.35}$$

where $S_{t,k}^i$ denotes the common quote for currency k in round i and $\lambda_{k,i}$ denotes the impact of order flow for currency i on the price quote for currency k. Thus the daily change in the spot rate for currency k responds to public news concerning own-currency dividends, $V_{t,k}$, and unexpected interdealer order flow for currency k, $X_{t,k} - \mathbb{E}[X_{t,k}|\Omega_t^I]$. These daily dynamics are exactly the same as those implied by Proposition 6.1.

The intuition behind (6.35) is straightforward. When Σ_v, Σ_Y, and Σ_ξ are all diagonal, the problem facing each investor in rounds I and III can be solved on a currency-by-currency basis. This means that the customer orders for currency k received by dealers in round I only contain information on income and overnight holdings in currency k. Consequently, the information aggregation process facilitated by interdealer trading in round II also takes place on a currency-by-currency basis, so $X_{t,k} - \mathbb{E}[X_{t,k}|\Omega_t^{\text{I}}]$ reveals aggregate income in currency k, $Y_{t,k}$. This is all the information dealers need to determine the value for their common round III quote, $S_{t,k}^{\text{III}}$, such that investors will hold the entire stock of currency k overnight.

Now suppose that shocks to dividends are correlated across currencies. Under these circumstances, the portfolio problems facing investors in rounds I and II can no longer be solved on a currency-by-currency basis. For example, in round III, the optimal portfolio position for investor n is

$$\mathbf{A}_{n,t}^{\text{III}} = \frac{1}{\theta}\Sigma_{\mathcal{R}}^{-1}\mathbb{E}[\mathcal{R}_{t+1}|\Omega_{n,t}^{\text{III}}], \tag{6.36}$$

where $\mathcal{R}_{t+1} \equiv \mathbf{S}_{t+1}^{\text{I}} + \mathbf{D}_{t+1} - (1+r)\mathbf{S}_t^{\text{III}}$ is the vector of excess overnight returns. $\mathbf{A}_{n,t}^{\text{III}}$ is now a $K \times 1$ vector that identifies the investors' desired positions in the K different currencies. If dividend shocks are correlated across currencies, the conditional covariance matrix $\Sigma_{\mathcal{R}} \equiv \mathbb{V}[\mathcal{R}_{t+1}|\Omega_{n,t}^{\text{III}}]$ will not be diagonal, so the desired position in currency k will in general depend on the expected excess returns on all K currencies. A similar argument applies to investors' desired positions in round I.

Equation (6.36) has important implications for the determination of quotes in round III. In particular, it implies that dealers must know aggregate income in all K currencies if they are to set quotes so that investors hold the entire stock of each foreign currency overnight. This information comes from the unexpected order flows for all K currencies, that is, $X_{t,k} - \mathbb{E}[X_{t,k}|\Omega_t^{\text{I}}]$ for $k = 1, 2, \ldots, K$. Indeed, investors' portfolio decisions in round I imply that the customer orders for individual currencies depend on the overnight positions and incomes in all currencies, so (6.34) implies that $X_t - \mathbb{E}[X_t|\Omega_t^{\text{I}}]$ is equal to ΨY_t for some nondiagonal matrix Ψ. As a result, dealers need information from all K order flows to determine aggregate income in each currency and hence the equilibrium round III quote. Thus, in sum, the daily dynamics of spot rate for currency k now takes the form

$$S_{t,k}^{\text{III}} = S_{t-1,k}^{\text{III}} + \sum_{i=1}^{K} \lambda_{k,i}(X_{t,k} - \mathbb{E}[X_{t,k}|\Omega_t^{\text{I}}]) + \tfrac{1}{r}V_{t,k}. \tag{6.37}$$

The conclusion from this analysis is important. Interdealer order flows act as the medium through which information about investors' income becomes known to dealers and hence incorporated into the spot exchange rates. The actual information content of individual order flows depends on how investors determine their portfolios. In special cases, customer order flows in a particular currency are sufficient (when aggregated via interdealer trading) to reveal the information necessary to achieve an efficient risk-sharing allocation of that currency. In these circumstances, only own order flow appears as a proximate determinant of exchange-rate changes. In other cases, many order flows contain information relevant for determining the efficient risk-sharing quote in any currency. Under these circumstances, many order flows appear as the proximate determinants of exchange-rate changes.

6.3.2 Lower Transparency

The Portfolio Shifts model assumes that trading in both the retail and wholesale tiers of the foreign exchange market is very transparent. Specifically, (1) all price quotes are publicly observed, (2) it is possible to trade with multiple counterparties, and (3) the broker and all dealers observe aggregate interdealer order flow at the end of round II. These assumptions imply that agents in the model have a good deal of information on market-wide activity, information that is not readily available to participants in the actual FX market. For example, investors do not have information on all price quotes of all dealers in the retail tier of the market, nor are they able to trade simultaneously with any number of dealers. Similarly, price quotes and order flows in direct interdealer trading are only known to the dealers involved in each trade, so information on dealer quotes and order flows is not known across all dealers in the market. These observations lead to the following question: Are the implications of the Portfolio Shifts model robust to lowering the degree of market transparency?

Let us first consider the role of transparency in the retail tier of the market. In round I, dealers quote a common price, S_t^I, to avoid arbitrage losses. This "fear of arbitrage" would not be present if investors could not observe all the dealers' quotes and could not trade with multiple dealers. Indeed, if each investor were randomly assigned to a single dealer who then quoted a price at which he would fill the investor's order, each dealer *could* quote a different round I price without the fear of an arbitrage loss. However, even in this case, dealers would quote a common round-I price unless they have private information about the demand for FX by their assigned subset of investors. The model's implications about round-I quotes are therefore robust to lower transparency in the retail tier provided dealers have no further information about investors when making their quote decisions. An analogous argument applies to dealers' round-III quotes.

Transparency plays a more central role in round-II trading. Here "the fear of arbitrage" induces each dealer to quote a common price—the price he quoted in round I—even though he now has private information about future prices from the customer orders he received in round I. In other words, although dealers have absorbed information from round I, the high degree of transparency in interdealer trading stops the information from being immediately reflected in the spot exchange rate.

We can gain further perspective on the role of transparency by considering a simple variant of the model. In particular, let us now assume that all interdealer trading in round II takes place via the broker. Thus, at the start of round II, the broker optimally chooses a single price, $S_{B,t}^{II}$, at which he will fill FX orders from dealers. Each dealer observes $S_{B,t}^{II}$ and then decides on the amount he wants to trade knowing that he need not fill orders from other dealers. Once trading is complete, all dealers observe aggregate order flow passing through the broker, $X_t = \sum_{d=1}^{D} T_{d,t}^{II}$.

Deriving the equilibrium in this variant of the model is straightforward. First we note that the elimination of direct interdealer trading in round II does not affect the evolution of common information because dealers still observe aggregate order flow

X_t. This means that dealers and the broker can still choose a value for S_t^{III} that supports the efficient risk-sharing allocation of FX:

$$S_t^{\mathrm{III}} = \tfrac{1}{r}D_t - \tfrac{1}{r}(\gamma + \mu_{\mathrm{A}})A_t, \tag{6.38}$$

where $\mathbb{E}[S_{t+1}^{\mathrm{III}} - S_{t+1}^{\mathrm{I}}|\Omega_t^{\mathrm{I}}] = \mu_{\mathrm{A}}A_t$ is the intraday risk premium. The value of the μ_{A} parameter is determined in the appendix.

Next, we note that the broker's choice for $S_{\mathrm{B},t}^{\mathrm{II}}$ must be a function of common round I information, Ω_t^{I}, because he does not observe the customer orders received by dealers in round I. This means that both $S_{\mathrm{B},t}^{\mathrm{II}}$ and the common round I quote made by dealers, S_t^{I}, are functions of Ω_t^{I}. As a consequence, all dealers must quote a price of $S_{\mathrm{B},t}^{\mathrm{II}}$ in round I in order to eliminate the risk associated with unexpected customer orders. Hence, in equilibrium the common round I price quoted by all dealers is

$$S_t^{\mathrm{I}} = S_{\mathrm{B},t}^{\mathrm{II}}. \tag{6.39}$$

To find the broker's optimal choice for $S_{\mathrm{B},t}^{\mathrm{II}}$, we first consider the form of the round II order flow, X_t. By definition, $X_t = \sum_{d=1}^{\mathrm{D}} T_{d,t}^{\mathrm{II}}$ where the order flow from dealer d is $T_{d,t}^{\mathrm{II}} = \hat{A}_{d,t}^{\mathrm{II}} - A_{d,t}^{\mathrm{I}}$ and $\hat{A}_{d,t}^{\mathrm{II}}$ denotes the dealer's desired FX position. The expression for $T_{d,t}^{\mathrm{II}}$ differs from the one in the original version of the model because dealers do not have to anticipate incoming orders from other dealers. The absence of interdealer orders also simplifies the determination of the dealers' desired positions. In particular, it is straightforward to establish that

$$\hat{A}_{d,t}^{\mathrm{II}} = \frac{\psi}{\mathrm{D}}\mathbb{E}[S_t^{\mathrm{III}} - S_{\mathrm{B},t}^{\mathrm{II}}|\Omega_{d,t}^{\mathrm{II}}], \tag{6.40}$$

where $\psi^{-1} = \mathrm{D}\theta\mathbb{V}[S_t^{\mathrm{III}}|\Omega_{d,t}^{\mathrm{II}}]^{-1}$. Using this result and the fact that $A_{d,t}^{\mathrm{I}} = -Z_{d,t}^{\mathrm{I}}$ (because dealers do not hold FX overnight), we can now write the order flow received by the broker as

$$X_t = \frac{\psi}{\mathrm{D}}\sum_{d=1}^{\mathrm{D}}\mathbb{E}[S_t^{\mathrm{III}} - S_{\mathrm{B},t}^{\mathrm{II}}|\Omega_{d,t}^{\mathrm{II}}] + Z_t^{\mathrm{I}}, \tag{6.41}$$

where Z_t^{I} is the aggregate customer order flow in round I.

Customer orders also depend on the broker's quote because dealers quote the same price to investors in round I. In particular, our earlier analysis of investors' round I orders implies that

$$Z_t^{\mathrm{I}} = \eta_s \int_0^1 \mathbb{E}[S_t^{\mathrm{III}} - S_{\mathrm{B},t}^{\mathrm{II}}|\Omega_{n,t}^{\mathrm{I}}]\,dn + (\eta_{\mathrm{A}} - 1)A_{t-1} - Y_t. \tag{6.42}$$

Combining (6.41) with (6.42) gives the following expression for round II order flow:

$$X_t = \left(\frac{\psi}{\mathrm{D}} + \eta_s\right)\mathbb{E}[S_t^{\mathrm{III}} - S_{\mathrm{B},t}^{\mathrm{II}}|\Omega_t^{\mathrm{I}}] + (\eta_{\mathrm{A}} - 1)A_{t-1} + \xi_t, \tag{6.43}$$

where ξ_t denotes unexpected order flow, $X_t - \mathbb{E}[X_t|\Omega_t^{\mathrm{I}}]$. As before, $\xi_t = \alpha_z\beta Y_t$, so ξ_t is a mean-zero normally distributed random variable.

We can now determine the value of the round II quote as the solution to the broker's optimization problem. Specifically, the broker chooses $S^{\text{II}}_{\text{B},t}$ to maximize expected utility, $\mathbb{E}[-\theta \exp\left(-\theta W^{\text{I}}_{\text{B},t+1}\right)|\Omega^{\text{I}}_t]$, subject to the budget constraint

$$W^{\text{I}}_{\text{B},t+1} = (1+r)W^{\text{II}}_{\text{B},t} - (1+r)X_t(S^{\text{III}}_t - S^{\text{II}}_{\text{B},t}),$$

where order flow X_t follows (6.43) and the round III price satisfies (6.38). Note, once again, that $W^{\text{I}}_{\text{B},t+1}$ depends on the product of two normally distributed random variables, so this maximization problem is a little more involved. The appendix shows that the solution is given by

$$S^{\text{II}}_{\text{B},t} = \mathbb{E}[S^{\text{III}}_t|\Omega^{\text{I}}_t] - \mu_{\text{A}}A_{t-1}. \tag{6.44}$$

We may now summarize the equilibrium dynamics of the exchange rate. Specifically, combining (6.38), (6.39), and (6.44) yields

$$S^{\text{I}}_t = S^{\text{III}}_{t-1} - \mu_{\text{A}}A_{t-1} + \tfrac{1}{r}V_t,$$
$$S^{\text{II}}_t = S^{\text{I}}_t,$$
$$S^{\text{III}}_t = S^{\text{II}}_{\text{B},t} + \mu_{\text{A}}A_{t-1} + \mu_{\text{X}}(X_t - \mathbb{E}[X_t|\Omega^{\text{I}}_t]), \tag{6.45}$$

where $\mu_{\text{X}} = -(\gamma + \mu_{\text{A}})/(r\alpha_z\beta)$.

The dynamics in (6.45) are very similar to those in Proposition 6.1. In particular, the dichotomy between the exchange-rate effects of public news and nonpublic news remain unchanged: Public information concerning dividends is immediately reflected in dealers' round I quotes, whereas information concerning foreign income only becomes reflected in the round III quotes once dealers have observed interdealer order flow. The delayed effect of income shocks on the exchange rate arises here because the broker has no more information in round II than dealers had in round I. Thus, although this version of the model eliminates arbitrage concerns from the choice of the round II price, foreign income still has no effect on the quote because it is not part of the quote-setter's information set. Speeding up the process of information aggregation requires more than simply hampering competition in the interdealer market. The quote-setters also need access to price-relevant information, that is, information on foreign income.

The other noteworthy aspect of the dynamics in (6.45) concerns the intraday risk premia. In the original version of the model, the round II price included a risk premium calibrated so that investors were expected to keep their overnight FX holdings. Here the broker chooses the round II quote to achieve a desired nonzero speculative position by the end of round II. To do that, he considers how his choice for $S^{\text{II}}_{\text{B},t}$ affects customer order flow in round I and dealer order flow in round II. As a result, quotes may be set so that investors either reduce or add to their overnight FX holdings depending on the size of the intraday risk premium $\mathbb{E}[S^{\text{III}}_t - S^{\text{II}}_{\text{B},t}|\Omega^{\text{I}}_t] = \mu_{\text{A}}A_{t-1}$. In sum, the price quotes in rounds I and II no longer support an ex ante efficient asset allocation because this is no longer optimal from the broker's point of view.

6.4 Summary

- The FX market is a two-tier market comprising the interbank and retail markets. Trading in each tier has been distinct in terms of the participants and the trading mechanisms. FX dealers trade directly and indirectly in the interbank market. No dealer has complete information about the state of the interbank market. Brokers provide market-wide information on quotes and transaction prices. Direct interdealer trading takes place simultaneously across the interbank market. Dealers face constraints on both the duration and size of their asset positions; their overnight positions are typically small or zero. Banks fill customer orders for currency in the retail tier of the market. The customer orders received by banks in the retail tier of the FX market represent the most important source of private information to dealers.

- The Portfolio Shifts model incorporates key features of the FX market in a micro-based model of exchange-rate determination. In this model the equilibrium spot exchange rate is literally the price for FX quoted by foreign exchange dealers. As such, the dynamics of the spot rate are driven by changes in the dealers' quote decisions. Public price-relevant information is immediately incorporated into the exchange rate because dealers have an incentive to change their quotes as soon as the information is known. By contrast, there is no incentive for dealers to immediately adjust their quotes to the arrival of private price-relevant information. Rather, they wait until the information becomes common knowledge via their observations on aggregate interdealer order flow before adjusting their quotes. As a result, the change in the spot rate is closely associated with unexpected aggregate interdealer order flow.

6.5 Bibliography

The overview of how trading takes place in the FX market draws on the BIS surveys, Rime (2003), Sager and Taylor (2006), Barker (2007), and discussions with market participants. Rime (2003), in particular, provides a great deal of information on how trading among dealers takes place—including screen shots of the EBS and Reuters electronic brokerage systems that now dominate interdealer trading.

The Portfolio Shifts model described in Section 6.2 extends the models developed in Lyons (1997) and Evans and Lyons (1999). The key difference here is that investors' FX orders in round 1 are derived endogenously. As a consequence, the intraday dynamics of the spot rate includes a risk premium that was not present in the orginal version of the Portfolio Shifts model. At a daily frequency, the dynamics of the spot rate and its relation to order flow are unaffected by this modification. The model presented here also demonstrates that dealers will want to take speculative intraday positions based on the private information they receive in the form of investors' FX orders. This feature of interdealer trading was first examined in Cao, Evans, and Lyons (2004). The discussion of the multicurrency version of the model draws on Evans and Lyons (2002b).

6.6 Review Questions

1. Order Flows and Portfolio Holdings: In the Portfolio Shifts model the risks of holding FX overnight are more efficiently shared by investors than by dealers, so the round III spot rate quote reflects dealers' desires to close out their existing positions.

   (a) Derive an equation that describes the daily evolution of investors' aggregate FX holdings.

   (b) Suppose a researcher has access to data on investors' aggregate FX holdings each night. Since he knows that investors initiate trades against dealers' quotes, he proposes estimating aggregate customer order flow on day t as the difference between investors' FX holdings at the end of day t and at the end of day $t - 1$. Use your answer to part (a) to determine this estimate of order flow.

   (c) Compare the estimate of customer order flow computed in part (b) with the actual aggregate customer order flow from round I trading in the Portfolio Shifts model. Does the estimate differ from actual order flow? If so, why does the difference exist?

2. Forecasting Returns: The Portfolios Shifts model implies that daily changes in spot rates are contemporaneously correlated with the unexpected interdealer order flow as shown in equation (6.32). Unexpected order flows also lead dealers to revise their forecasts for *future* excess returns.

   (a) In equilibrium, excess returns follow

$$\mathcal{R}_{t+1} = \frac{1+r}{r} V_{t+1} + \gamma A_t.$$

   Use this equation to compute dealers' expectations concerning the excess returns in rounds II and III, that is, $\mathbb{E}[\mathcal{R}_{t+1}|\Omega_{\mathrm{D},t}^{\mathrm{II}}]$ and $\mathbb{E}[\mathcal{R}_{t+1}|\Omega_{\mathrm{D},t}^{\mathrm{III}}]$.

   (b) Use your answer to part (a) to relate the revision in dealers expectations, $\mathbb{E}[\mathcal{R}_{t+1}|\Omega_{\mathrm{D},t}^{\mathrm{III}}] - \mathbb{E}[\mathcal{R}_{t+1}|\Omega_{\mathrm{D},t}^{\mathrm{II}}]$, to interdealer order flow from round II trading. Explain how and why dealers revise their expectations of future excess returns when order flow is unexpectedly high (i.e., when $X_t - \mathbb{E}[X_t|\Omega_t^{\mathrm{I}}] > 0$).

   (c) So far we have considered the revision in expectations conditioned on dealers' common information. Derive an equation for the revision in an individual dealer's expectations, that is, $\mathbb{E}[\mathcal{R}_{t+1}|\Omega_{d,t}^{\mathrm{III}}] - \mathbb{E}[\mathcal{R}_{t+1}|\Omega_{d,t}^{\mathrm{II}}]$ for dealer d. Compare your answer to part (b) with the revision in an individual dealer's expectations. Does unexpected interdealer order flow have a larger or small impact on an individual dealer's expectations? Why?

3. Properties of Order Flow: Proposition 6.1 identifies the currency trades initiated by investors and dealers in rounds I and II in equations (6.9) and (6.10). These equations determine the properties of aggregate customer and interdealer order flows.

   (a) Show that aggregate customer order flow in round I trading is serially uncorrelated. Explain why the absence of serial correlation is a necessary implication of efficient risk-sharing among dealers.

   (b) Compute the aggregate customer order flow in round III trading, Z_t^{III}. Explain how this flow is related to the round I flow.

   (c) Dealers cannot forecast customer order flows in round I, but they can forecast aggregate interdealer order flow, X_t, based on information available at the start of round II. Explain why this difference arises.

4. **Limiting Interdealer Trade:** Suppose dealers are prohibited from taking speculative positions in round II trading. In particular, each dealer d must choose his trades during round II to establish an FX position of $\hat{A}_{d,t}^{II} = 0$.

   (a) Compute the BNE trading strategies when this condition replaces the expression for $\hat{A}_{d,t}^{II}$ in equation (6.29).

   (b) Compare the volatility of aggregate customer order flow and aggregate interdealer order flow in this equilibrium. Which order flow has the greater volatility and why?

   (c) How will the equilibrium dynamics of the spot rate differ in this new equilibrium from the dynamics described in Proposition 6.1?

6.A Appendix

The solution of the Portfolio Shifts model makes use of the following lemma:

Lemma 2: *Let $\mathcal{Z} = \varkappa(a) + \Gamma'\mathcal{X} + \mathcal{X}'\Lambda\mathcal{X}$, where $\mathcal{X}$ is a $k \times 1$ vector of normally distributed random variables with zero means and covariance Σ, Λ is a symmetric $k \times k$ matrix, Γ is a $k \times 1$ vector function of the scalar a, and $\varkappa(a)$ is a function of a. Provided that $\Theta = I - 2\Lambda\Sigma$ is positive definite,*

$$\mathcal{U} = \mathbb{E}\exp(\mathcal{Z}) = |\Theta|^{-1/2}\exp\left(\delta + \Gamma'\mu + \tfrac{1}{2}\Gamma'\Theta^{-1}\Sigma\Gamma\right). \tag{6.46}$$

Differentiating $\mathcal{U}$ with respect to a gives the following first-order condition

$$\frac{\partial\varkappa}{\partial a} + \frac{\partial\Gamma}{\partial a}\left(\tfrac{1}{2}\left(\Theta^{-1}\Sigma + \left[\Theta^{-1}\Sigma\right]'\right)\Gamma\right) = 0, \tag{6.47}$$

where $\frac{\partial\Gamma}{\partial a} = \left[\frac{\partial\Gamma_1}{\partial a}, \frac{\partial\Gamma_2}{\partial a}, \ldots\right]$.

Derivations

Derivation of (6.29): In equilibrium, dealers hold no overnight FX position so wealth next day can be written as

$$W_{d,t+1}^{I} = (1+r)W_{d,t}^{II} + (1+r)\hat{A}_{d,t}^{II}(\tilde{S}_t^{III} + \overline{S}_t^{III} - S_t^{II}) - (1+r)\tilde{Z}_{d,t}^{II}(\overline{S}_t^{III} - S_t^{II})$$

$$- (1+r)\tilde{Z}_{d,t}^{II}\tilde{S}_t^{III}, \tag{6.48}$$

where tildes and bars denote forecast errors and expectations (e.g., $\tilde{Z}_{d,t}^{II} \equiv Z_{d,t}^{II} - \overline{Z}_{d,t}^{II}$ and $\overline{Z}_{d,t}^{II} \equiv \mathbb{E}[Z_{d,t}^{II}|\Omega_{d,t}^{II}]$). From Proposition 6.1 we know that all dealers and the broker quote the same round II price, so each dealer receives $\frac{1}{1+D}$ times the total order flow:

$$Z_{d,t}^{II} = \frac{1}{1+D} \sum_{d,t}^{D} \alpha_Z Z_{d,t}^{I} + \frac{D}{1+D} \alpha_A A_{t-1} = \frac{1}{1+D} \alpha_Z \beta Y_t + \frac{D}{1+D} \alpha_A A_{t-1}.$$

Consequently, unexpected order flow is $\tilde{Z}_{d,t}^{II} = \frac{1}{1+D} \alpha_Z \beta \tilde{Y}_t$. We also know from Proposition 6.1 that $S_t^{III} - S_t^{I} = \lambda_A A_{t-1} + \alpha_Z \beta Y_t$, hence $\tilde{S}_t^{III} = \alpha_Z \beta \tilde{Y}_t$. Making these substitutions into (6.48) and multiplying the result by $-\theta$ gives

$$-\theta W_{d,t+1}^{I} = -\theta(1+r)W_{d,t}^{II} - \theta(1+r)\hat{A}_{d,t}^{II}(\overline{S}_t^{III} - S_t^{II})$$

$$+ \theta(1+r)\alpha_Z \beta \left(\frac{1}{1+D}(\overline{S}_t^{III} - S_t^{II}) - \hat{A}_{d,t}^{II} \right) \tilde{Y}_t + \frac{\theta(1+r)(\alpha_Z \beta)^2}{1+D} \tilde{Y}_t^2.$$

The dealer chooses $\hat{A}_{d,t}^{II}$ to maximize $-\mathbb{E}[\exp(-\theta W_{d,t+1}^{I})|\Omega_{d,t}^{II}]$. This is equivalent to minimizing $-\mathcal{U}$ in (6.46), with

$$\varkappa = -\theta(1+r)W_{d,t}^{II} - \theta(1+r)\hat{A}_{d,t}^{II}(\overline{S}_t^{III} - S_t^{II}), \quad \mathcal{X} = \tilde{Y}_t, \quad \Lambda = \frac{\theta(1+r)(\alpha_Z \beta)^2}{1+D},$$

$$\Gamma = \theta(1+r)\alpha_Z \beta \left(\frac{1}{1+D}(\overline{S}_t^{III} - S_t^{II}) - \hat{A}_{d,t}^{II} \right), \quad \text{and}$$

$$\Theta = 1 - 2\frac{\theta(1+r)(\alpha_Z \beta)^2}{1+D} \mathbb{V}[Y_t|\Omega_{d,t}^{II}].$$

We assume that the number of dealers in the market, D, is sufficient for Θ to be positive. The first-order condition for $\hat{A}_{d,t}^{II}$ from (6.47) is therefore

$$-\theta(1+r)(\overline{S}_t^{III} - S_t^{II}) - \theta^2(1+r)^2(\alpha_Z \beta)^2 \frac{1}{\Theta} \mathbb{V}[Y_t|\Omega_{d,t}^{II}]\left(\frac{1}{1+D}(\overline{S}_t^{III} - S_t^{II}) - \hat{A}_{d,t}^{II} \right) = 0.$$

Rearranging this equation yields

$$\hat{A}_{d,t}^{II} = \frac{1+\varpi}{(D+1)\varpi}(\overline{S}_t^{III} - S_t^{II}),$$

where $\varpi \equiv \frac{\theta(1+r)(\alpha_Z \beta)^2}{\Theta(1+D)} \mathbb{V}[Y_t|\Omega_{d,t}^{II}]$. Proposition 6.1 also implies that $\overline{S}_t^{III} - S_t^{II} = \lambda_A A_{t-1} + \alpha_Z \beta \overline{Y}_t$. Combining this expression with the preceding one gives

$$\hat{A}_{d,t}^{II} = \frac{1}{1+D}\varphi_A A_{t-1} + \frac{1}{1+D}\varphi_Y \overline{Y}_t,$$

where $\varphi_A = \frac{1+\varpi}{\varpi}\lambda_A$ and $\varphi_Y = \frac{1+\varpi}{\varpi}\alpha_Z \beta$. This is the form of (6.29) with $\overline{Y}_t = \mathbb{E}[Y_t|\Omega_{d,t}^{II}]$.

Derivation of (6.19): To derive investor n's desired round II holdings, we first combine the budget constraints to give

$$W^I_{n,t+1} = (1+r)(W^I_{n,t} + S^I_t Y_{n,t}) + (1+r)(S^{III}_t - S^I_t)A^I_{n,t}$$
$$+ (S^I_{t+1} + D_{t+1} - (1+r)S^{III}_t)A^{III}_{n,t}.$$

Since investors have the same preferences and hold the entire stock of FX overnight, $A^{III}_{n,t} = A_t$ for all n, where $A_t = A_{t-1} + Y_t$. We also know from Proposition 6.1 that

$$S^{III}_t - S^I_t = \lambda_A A_{t-1} + \alpha_z \beta Y_t$$

and

$$S^I_{t+1} + D_{t+1} - (1+r)S^{III}_t = \frac{1+r}{r}V_{t+1} + \gamma A_t.$$

Using these results, we can rewrite the budget constraint as

$$W^I_{n,t+1} = (1+r)W^I_{n,t} + \gamma \overline{A}^2_t + (1+r)(\overline{S}^{III}_t - S^{II}_t)A^I_{n,t} + \frac{1+r}{r}\overline{A}_t V_{t+1}$$
$$+ 2\gamma \overline{A}_t \tilde{Y}_t + (1+r)A^I_{n,t}\alpha_z \beta \tilde{Y}_t + \frac{1+r}{r}\tilde{A}_t V_{t+1} + \gamma \tilde{Y}^2_t,$$

where tildes and bars denote forecast errors and expectations with respect to investors' information, $\Omega^I_{n,t}$.

Investor n chooses $A^I_{n,t}$ to maximize $-\mathbb{E}[\exp(-\theta W^I_{n,t+1})|\Omega^I_{n,t}]$. This is equivalent to minimizing $-\mathcal{U}$ in (6.46), with $\mathcal{Z} = -\theta W^I_{n,t+1} = \varkappa + \Gamma'\mathcal{X} + \mathcal{X}'\Lambda\mathcal{X}$, where

$$\varkappa = -\theta(1+r)W^I_{n,t} - \theta\gamma \overline{A}^2_t - \theta(1+r)(\overline{S}^{III}_t - S^{II}_t)A^I_{n,t},$$

$$\mathcal{X} = \begin{bmatrix} \tilde{Y}_t \\ V_{t+1} \end{bmatrix}, \quad \Gamma = \begin{bmatrix} -2\theta\gamma \overline{A}_t - \theta(1+r)\alpha_z\beta A^I_{n,t} \\ -\theta\frac{1+r}{r}\overline{A}_t \end{bmatrix}, \quad \text{and}$$

$$\Lambda = \begin{bmatrix} -\theta\gamma & -\theta\frac{1+r}{2r} \\ -\theta\frac{1+r}{2r} & 0 \end{bmatrix}.$$

The first-order condition for $A^I_{n,t}$ is

$$-\theta(1+r)(\overline{S}^{III}_t - S^{II}_t) + [-\theta(1+r)\alpha_z\beta \quad 0]\Psi\begin{bmatrix} -2\theta\gamma \overline{A}_t - \theta(1+r)\alpha_z\beta A^I_{n,t} \\ -\theta\frac{1+r}{r}\overline{A}_t \end{bmatrix} = 0,$$

where $\Psi = \frac{1}{2}(\Theta^{-1}\Sigma + [\Theta^{-1}\Sigma]')$. Rearranging this equation gives

$$A^I_{n,t} = \frac{1}{\theta(1+r)(\alpha_z\beta)^2 \Psi_{1,1}}(\overline{S}^{III}_t - S^{II}_t) - \frac{2\gamma r\Psi_{1,1} + (1+r)\Psi_{1,2}}{r(1+r)\alpha_z\beta\Psi_{1,1}}\overline{A}_t,$$

where $\Psi_{i,j}$ are the ij elements of Ψ. Now, since $\overline{S}^{III}_t - S^{II}_t = \lambda_A A_{t-1} + \alpha_z\beta\overline{Y}_t$ and

$\overline{A}_t = A_{t-1} + \overline{Y}_t$, it follows that $\overline{A}_t = \left(1 - \frac{\lambda_A}{\alpha_z \beta}\right) A_{t-1} + \frac{1}{\alpha_z \beta}(\overline{S}_t^{III} - S_t^{II})$. Hence,

$$A_{n,t}^I = \eta_s(\overline{S}_t^{III} - S_t^{II}) + \eta_A A_{t-1},$$

where

$$\eta_s = \frac{r - \theta 2\gamma r \Psi_{11} - \theta(1+r)\Psi_{12}}{\theta(1+r)\left(\alpha_z \beta\right)^2 \Psi_{11}} \quad \text{and} \quad \eta_A = \left(\frac{\lambda_A}{\alpha_z \beta} - 1\right) \frac{2\gamma r \Psi_{11} + (1+r)\Psi_{12}}{r(1+r)\alpha_z \beta \Psi_{11}},$$

as shown in equation (6.19).

Derivation of (6.40): If all trading takes place via the broker in round II and dealers hold no overnight FX position, the budget constraint of dealer d becomes

$$W_{d,t+1}^I = (1+r)W_{d,t}^{II} + (1+r)\hat{A}_{d,t}^{II}(\tilde{S}_t^{III} + \overline{S}_t^{III} - S_t^{II}), \tag{6.49}$$

where tildes and bars denote forecast errors and expectations with respect to $\Omega_{d,t}^{II}$. Maximizing $-\mathbb{E}[\exp(-\theta W_{d,t+1}^I)|\Omega_{d,t}^{II}]$ with respect to $\hat{A}_{d,t}^{II}$ is therefore equivalent to maximizing

$$(1+r)\hat{A}_{d,t}^{II}(\overline{S}_t^{III} - S_t^{II}) - \frac{1}{2\theta}(1+r)^2(\hat{A}_{d,t}^{II})^2 \mathbb{V}[\mathbb{S}_t^{III}|\Omega_{d,t}^{II}].$$

The first-order condition for this problem is

$$(1+r)(\overline{S}_t^{III} - S_t^{II}) = \frac{1}{\theta}(1+r)\hat{A}_{d,t}^{II}\mathbb{V}[\mathbb{S}_t^{III}|\Omega_{d,t}^{II}],$$

which can be rewritten in the form of (6.40).

Derivation of (6.44): The problem facing the broker in round II is

$$\max_{S_{B,t}^{II}} \mathbb{E}[-\theta \exp(-\theta W_{B,t+1}^I)|\Omega_t^I]$$

$$\text{s.t.} \quad W_{B,t+1}^I = (1+r)W_{B,t}^{II} - (1+r)X_t(S_t^{III} - S_{B,t}^{II}),$$

and

$$X_t = (\psi + \eta_s)(\overline{S}_t^{III} - S_{B,t}^{II}) + (\eta_A - 1)A_{t-1} + \tilde{X}_t,$$

where tildes and bars denote forecast errors and expectations with respect to the broker's information, Ω_t^I. Equation (6.45) implies that $\tilde{S}_t^{III} = \mu_X \tilde{X}_t$, so $S_t^{III} - S_{B,t}^{II} = \overline{S}_t^{III} - S_{B,t}^{II} + \mu_X \tilde{X}_t$. Combining this expression with the preceding constraints, and multiplying the result by $-\theta$ gives

$$\mathcal{Z} = -\theta W_{B,t+1}^I = \varkappa + \Gamma'\mathcal{X} + \mathcal{X}'\Lambda\mathcal{X},$$

where $\Gamma = \theta(1+r)\mu_X[(\psi + \eta_s)(\overline{S}_t^{III} - S_{B,t}^{II}) + (\eta_A - 1)A_{t-1}]$, $\mathcal{X} = \tilde{X}_t$, and $\Lambda = \theta\mu_x(1+r)$. The problem facing the broker therefore simplifies to one of minimizing

$\mathcal{U}$ with respect to $S_{B,t}^{II}$. This gives the following first-order condition:

$$0 = \theta(1+r)(\eta_A - 1)A_{t-1} + 2\theta(1+r)(\psi + \eta_s)(\overline{S}_t^{III} - S_{B,t}^{II})$$

$$+ \theta(1+r)\mu_x(\psi + \eta_s)\Psi\theta(1+r)\mu_x\left((\psi + \eta_s)(\overline{S}_t^{III} - S_{B,t}^{II}) + (\eta_A - 1)A_{t-1}\right),$$

where $\Psi = \mathbb{V}[X_t|\Omega_t^I]/(1 - 2\theta\mu_x(1+r)\mathbb{V}[X_t|\Omega_t^I])$. After some simplification we obtain

$$S_{B,t}^{II} = \overline{S}_t^{III} - \mu_A A_{t-1},$$

with

$$\mu_A = \frac{\left(1 + \mu_x^2(\psi + \eta_s)(1+r)\Psi\theta\right)(1 - \eta_A)}{\left(2 + \mu_x^2(\psi + \eta_s)(1+r)\Psi\theta\right)(\psi + \eta_s)},$$

as shown in (6.44). Note that since $\mu_x = -(\theta + \mu_A)/r a_z \beta$, we must solve for μ_A and μ_x simultaneously to completely characterize the equilibrium dynamics of the exchange rate.

CHAPTER 7

Currency-Trading Models: Empirical Evidence

This chapter examines the empirical implications of the Portfolio Shifts (PS) model. In particular we focus on the model's implications for the link between order flow and the change in the exchange rate. We consider the implications at the daily frequency for single and multiple currencies. We also move outside the structure of the model to look at the relationship between order flow and the exchange rate at higher frequencies. In particular, we consider empirical models of intraday price and trade dynamics constructed in event and clock time and models that incorporate features of centralized and decentralized trading systems.

7.1 Daily Analysis

The PS model identifies two drivers of spot exchange rates: (1) common knowledge information transmitted via macroeconomic data releases and other new announcements, and (2) dispersed information transmitted via aggregate interdealer order flow. More specifically, the model predicts that dealers will immediately and fully adjust their common price quote for FX in response to the arrival of common knowledge (CK) news, that is, new public information that has unambiguous implications for the value of foreign currency. This response of the spot rate to CK news is exactly the same as found in textbook models. The second driver, dispersed information, is novel. In the PS model, the dispersed information concerns the foreign income of investors, which is transmitted to the foreign exchange market via the customer orders received by individual dealers. This information is then disseminated across the market as dealers trade with each other. At the end of this information aggregation process, all dealers can infer the state of foreign income from their observations of aggregate interdealer order flow and adjust their price quotes accordingly. Thus, aggregate interdealer order flow provides the medium through which dispersed price-relevant information on foreign income becomes known to all dealers and is thus incorporated into the spot exchange rate.

The empirical implications of the PS model are easily summarized by the daily dynamics of the spot rate. In particular, let S_t denote the common FX price quoted by dealers at the end of day t (i.e., round III of the model). We can then write the daily change in the spot rate as

$$S_t - S_{t-1} = \lambda(X_t - \mathbb{E}_t X_t) + \xi_t, \tag{7.1}$$

where ξ_t denotes the price impact of CK news during day t and X_t is the aggregate interdealer order flow during day t. Thus, the revision in the price of FX quoted by dealers between the end of day $t-1$ and day t can be decomposed into a CK news component, ξ_t, and a dispersed information component identified by unexpected order flow, $X_t - \mathbb{E}_t X_t$, where $\mathbb{E}_t X_t$ denotes expected order flow conditioned on dealers' common information at the start of day t. The positive coefficient λ quantifies the degree to which dealers revise their quotes in response to unexpected order flow. A positive coefficient means that the quoted price for FX will be raised when there is an unexpected excess of dealer-initiated FX purchases over sales. Intuitively, unexpected positive order flow is a reflection of larger customer orders and hence lower aggregate foreign income, so dealers must raise their quotes in order for investors to hold the smaller aggregate stock of FX overnight.

One further implication of the PS model deserves special mention, namely the correlation between CK news and unexpected order flow. According to the model, the arrival of public news has no impact on order flow because dealers immediately and fully incorporate the price implications of the news into their quotes. Thus it is not the case that good CK news for the value of FX (i.e., a positive ξ_t) should induce positive order flow. The price of FX quoted by dealers will immediately adjust to incorporate the value implications of the news, so there is no change in the incentive for dealers to initiate either FX purchases or sales against the new prices being quoted by other dealers. In short, the fact that dealers choose quotes and trade optimally ensures that order flow is uncorrelated with CK news.

7.1.1 Single-Currency Results

The empirical implications of the PS model were first investigated by Evans and Lyons (2002a), who introduced three changes in equation (7.1) for estimation purposes. First, they replaced the dependent variable with the change in the log spot rate, $s_t - s_{t-1} \equiv \ln S_t - \ln S_{t-1}$, where S_t is measured in foreign currency per U.S. dollar. This substitution makes the empirical specification comparable to standard macro models but has no significant effect on the estimation results. Second, they assumed that expected interdealer order flow is zero, so that $X_t - \mathbb{E}_t X_t$ is replaced by X_t. Third, they specialize the CK information component, ξ_t, to equal the change in the nominal interest differential, $\Delta(r_t - r_t^*)$, where r_t is the nominal dollar interest rate and r_t^* is the nominal nondollar interest rate. Although ξ_t could also be correlated with other macro fundamentals, they use the interest differential because it is the main engine of exchange-rate variation in many macro models and is readily available at the daily frequency. The resulting empirical specification is therefore

$$s_t - s_{t-1} = \beta_1 X_t + \beta_2 \Delta(r_t - \hat{r}_t) + \zeta_t, \tag{7.2}$$

where ζ_t represents CK news that is uncorrelated with $\Delta(r_t - \hat{r}_t)$. This error term should also be uncorrelated with order flow, so the parameters β_1 and β_2 can be estimated by OLS.

Evans and Lyons estimate (7.2) for the DM/USD and JPY/USD spot rates between May 1 and August 31, 1996. Their data on interdealer order flow comes from the Reuters Dealing 2000-1 system. This was the dominant platform for interdealer trading at the time, accounting for approximately 90 percent of all "direct" dealer-to-dealer trades. The coverage of this order flow data closely corresponds to the measure of aggregate interdealer order flow in the PS model. Evans and Lyons use the first purchase transaction price after 4:00 P.M. GMT in London as the day-t spot rate, S_t. Recall from Chapter 6 that trading volume falls off quite sharply in the London afternoon, so the choice of 4:00 P.M. appears to be a reasonable point at which to measure the end-of-day spot rate. The change in the interest differential, $\Delta(r_t - \hat{r}_t)$, is calculated from the daily overnight interest rates for the dollar, the deutschmark, and the yen. Order flow during day t is measured as the difference between the number of buyer-initiated trades and the number of seller-initiated trades (in thousands), from 4:00 P.M. on day $t - 1$ to 4:00 P.M. on day t. Evans and Lyons do not have information on the size of each transaction and so cannot measure true interdealer order flow (i.e., the difference in *value* between buyer-initiated and seller-initiated trades). However, since there is much less variation in the size of trades than in their direction, their measure for X_t closely approximates true order flow across the market.

Evans and Lyons' (2002b) estimation results are shown in Table 7.1. The table reports the coefficient estimates and standard errors in parentheses for five versions of equation (7.2). The two right-hand columns present p-values for first-order (top) and fifth-order (bottom) residual serial correlation and conditional heteroskedasticity.

Three features of the Evans and Lyons estimation results are particularly note-worthy:

1. The coefficient on order flow, X_t, is correctly signed and significant, with t-statistics above 5 in versions I, II, and IV of the equation for both the DM/USD and JPY/USD. The positive sign indicates that net dollar purchases—a positive X_t—lead to a higher FX price for the USD. For perspective, the estimated value of 2.1 for the order flow coefficient in the DM/USD equation implies that a day with one thousand USD more purchases than sales increases the DM price of a USD by 2.1 percent. In the Evans and Lyons data set, the average size of an interdealer trade is $3.9 million. Using this as a representative figure, $1 billion of net USD purchases increases the DM price by 0.54 percent (= 2.1/3.9). At a spot rate of 1.5 DM/USD, this translates to $1 billion of net purchases increasing the DM price of a USD by 0.8 pfennigs.

2. Almost all the explanatory power in the regressions is due to order flow. In specifications III and V, where order flow is omitted, the R^2 statistics are less than 1 percent in both the DM/USD and JPY/USD equations. Moreover, the explanatory power of order flow is extraordinarily high. The R^2 statistics of 64 and 45 percent, respectively, for the DM/USD and JPY/USD equations that include order flow are an order of magnitude higher than those found in other exchange-rate models.

TABLE 7.1
Estimates of the Portfolio Shifts Model

Currencies		Regressors			Diagnostics		
		X_t	$\Delta(r_t - \hat{r}_t)$	$r_{t-1} - \hat{r}_{t-1}$	R^2	Serial	Hetero
DM/USD	I	2.14	0.51		0.64	0.77	0.07
		(0.29)	(0.26)			0.40	0.02
	II	2.15			0.63	0.73	0.05
		(0.29)				0.45	0.03
	III		0.62		0.01	0.78	0.92
			(0.77)			0.77	0.99
	IV	2.15		0.02	0.64	0.49	0.17
		(0.29)		(0.01)		0.43	0.01
	V			0.02	0.00	0.04	0.83
				(0.02)		0.24	0.98
JPY/USD	I	2.86	2.47		0.46	0.06	0.92
		(0.36)	(0.92)			0.44	0.74
	II	2.61			0.40	0.19	0.60
		(0.36)				0.33	0.83
	III		0.57		0.00	0.85	0.13
			(1.20)			0.81	0.67
	IV	2.78		0.02	0.42	0.00	0.66
		(0.38)		(0.01)		0.03	0.72
	V			(0.01)	0.00	0.12	0.18
				(0.01)		0.46	0.79

Source: Evans and Lyons (2002a).

3. The coefficient on the change in the interest differential is correctly signed, but is only significant in the JPY/USD equation. The positive sign arises in the sticky-price monetary model, for example, because an increase in the U.S. interest rate requires an immediate USD appreciation (i.e., an increase in JPY/USD) to make room for UIP-induced expected USD depreciation.

Evans and Lyons show that the results in Table 7.1 are robust to a number of modifications. For example, there is no evidence of a link between Δs_t and lagged order flow, X_{t-1}. Nor is there evidence of either state-dependency or nonlinearity between X_t and Δs_t. Although the PS model implies that unexpected order flow has a proportional effect on FX price quotes, this feature arises because the inference problem facing dealers in the model is very simple. In reality, dealers' inferences from order flow could vary with the state of the market or with the size of unexpected order flow, but there is no strong evidence to support these effects in the Evans and Lyons data at the daily frequency.

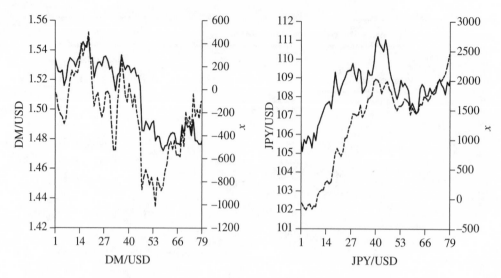

FIGURE 7.1   Exchange rates (solid) and cumulative order flow (dashed).

Figure 7.1 provides further perspective on the results in Table 7.1. Here the solid plots show the path of the spot exchange rate over the 4-month sample. The dashed plots show cumulative order flow over the same period measured against the right-hand axis. Cumulative order flow is simply the sum of daily order flow, that is, $X_{t,\infty} = \sum_{i=1}^{t} X_i$. If all the variations in spot rates reflect quote revisions driven only by order flow, the daily change in the spot rate should be proportional to daily order flow, that is, $S_t - S_{t-1} = \lambda X_t$. Under these circumstances, $S_t = \lambda X_{t,\infty}$, so the plots should coincide. The figure shows that this is not quite the case. Nevertheless, it is hard not to be impressed by the close correspondence between exchange rates and order flow over this sample period.

Figure 7.1 highlights two further important aspects of the Evans and Lyons results. First, although equation (7.2) is estimated at the daily frequency, the estimation results have implications for the behavior of spot rates over much longer periods. In particular, since there is almost no serial correlation in daily depreciation rates, the k-day change in the log spot rate is well approximated by

$$s_t - s_{t-k} \cong \beta_1 X_{t,k} + \beta_2 \Delta^k (r_t - \hat{r}_t) + \zeta_{t,k},$$

where $X_{t,k} = \sum_{i=0}^{k-1} X_{t-i}$ denotes order flow during the past k days and the terms $\beta_2 \Delta^k (r_t - \hat{r}_t) + \zeta_{t,k}$ identify the impact of public news arriving during the same period. Thus, the rate of depreciation over k days will be well approximated by the cumulative effects of order flow, $X_{t,k}$, and the arrival of public news. The figure shows that there are many instances where $s_t - s_{t-k} \cong \beta_1 X_{t,k}$ for significant horizons k.

The second feature concerns the dynamics of order flow. The plots of cumulative order flow in Figure 7.1 show no significant mean reversion because there is no detectable serial correlation in daily order flows. This feature of the data is important because the empirical specification in (7.2) assumes that realizations of daily order flow represent news to dealers. Thus daily order flow must be serially uncorrelated if the results in Table 7.1 are to be consistent with the predictions of the PS model.

It is also clear from Figure 7.1 that daily interdealer order flows can be very large. To understand why this happens it is useful to consider a simple sequence of transactions. Suppose dealer i fills a customer order to sell foreign currency. Obviously this transaction has no effect on interdealer order flow. Next, dealer i decides to unload the position by selling to another dealer j, so X_t falls by one unit. A subsequent sale by dealer j to another dealer, k, reduces X_t by a further unit. Now if a customer happens to buy dealer k's position the aggregate customer order flow from all these trades will be zero, but the aggregate interdealer order flow, X_t, remains two units below its starting point. This difference in the persistence of the two order flow measures—customer-dealer versus interdealer—is also a property of the PS model. There, aggregate customer order flow at the end of the day exactly offsets the aggregate customer order flow at the start of the day. By contrast, interdealer order flow does not net to zero.

7.1.2 Multiple Currencies

The strong empirical link between interdealer order flows and daily changes in the spot exchange rate extends across currencies. In the multicurrency version of the PS model (described in Chapter 6), interdealer order flows act as the medium through which information about investors' FX demands becomes impounded into spot exchange rates. In particular, the model shows that the information contained in individual order flows varies according to the structure of the public's portfolio demand and dealers' speculative demands. In special cases, order flows arising from trades between the home and a particular foreign currency act as a sufficient statistic for the aggregate portfolio shift that must be absorbed by investors to achieve efficient risk-sharing, and this shift can be induced by the change in just one exchange rate. In the more general case, many order flows contain information relevant for determining the aggregate portfolio shifts in any one currency, and many spot rates must be adjusted to induce the public to absorb the shift. In these circumstances, multiple order flows will appear as proximate determinants of daily exchange-rate changes.

Evans and Lyons (2002b) investigate this multicurrency implication of the PS model using interdealer order flows and spot rates from nine currencies versus the USD. Once again the order flow data come from the Reuters Dealing D2000-1 system over 4 months from May 1 to August 31, 1996. Let s_t^k denote the log of price of 1 USD in terms of currency k at the end of day-t trading (i.e., 4:00 P.M. London time). Under the assumption that dealers cannot forecast aggregate interdealer order flow, the multicurrency version of the PS model implies that

$$s_t^k - s_{t-1}^k = \lambda_{k,k} X_t^k + \sum_{j \neq k} \lambda_{k,j} X_t^j + \xi_t^k, \tag{7.3}$$

where X_t^k denotes aggregate interdealer order flow during day t for the dollar relative to currency k. The $\lambda_{k,j}$ coefficients identify the price impact of order flow j on spot rate k. The impact of the new CK information on the spot rate is represented by ξ_t^k. Theoretically speaking, ξ_t^k should be both serially uncorrelated and uncorrelated with order flows, so it can be treated as a regression error. Since CK news items may

TABLE 7.2
Multicurrency Estimates of the Portfolio Shifts Model

	Order flows									
	DM	JPY	GBP	BF	CHF	NOK	FF	LRA	GLD	R^2
DM	1.63	0.16	−0.22	−1.55	1.33	1.39	1.24	1.73	4.11	0.76
	(0.26)	(0.22)	(0.47)	(2.77)	(0.38)	(4.69)	(0.90)	(1.64)	(3.48)	0.68
JPY	−0.11	2.16	−0.88	5.49	1.34	−4.10	1.76	0.24	−0.24	0.54
	(0.28)	(0.29)	(0.68)	(3.67)	(0.57)	(6.36)	(1.38)	(2.63)	(4.73)	0.45
GBP	0.65	0.04	2.69	−4.54	0.01	−2.18	−0.27	3.17	−0.22	0.45
	(0.22)	(0.28)	(0.62)	(3.67)	(0.44)	(7.19)	(1.00)	(1.82)	(3.62)	0.33
BF	1.38	0.18	0.00	−3.26	1.42	2.79	1.87	2.31	4.32	0.78
	(0.20)	(0.18)	(0.49)	(2.24)	(0.35)	(4.34)	(0.82)	(1.64)	(2.98)	0.00
CHF	1.45	0.75	−0.53	−4.96	2.89	−8.26	0.90	2.94	4.65	0.70
	(0.33)	(0.32)	(0.72)	(4.25)	(0.59)	(7.24)	(1.35)	(2.54)	(4.62)	0.53
NOK	0.91	0.23	0.68	−2.27	2.19	0.23	1.74	1.36	7.72	0.69
	(0.30)	(0.29)	(0.62)	(3.07)	(0.49)	(5.35)	(1.16)	(1.90)	(3.88)	0.00
FF	1.13	0.11	0.06	−1.94	1.02	−6.37	2.17	4.21	5.33	0.75
	(0.19)	(0.19)	(0.51)	(2.60)	(0.35)	(4.42)	(0.79)	(1.62)	(3.12)	0.40
LRA	0.68	−0.12	−1.07	−2.40	0.11	−15.66	0.21	10.90	4.45	0.65
	(0.18)	(0.20)	(0.30)	(2.39)	(0.29)	(3.82)	(0.76)	(1.21)	(2.34)	0.37
GLD	1.36	0.18	−0.23	−1.85	1.61	1.02	1.83	3.68	6.18	0.75
	(0.22)	(0.21)	(0.54)	(2.56)	(0.37)	(5.11)	(0.87)	(1.72)	(3.45)	0.06

Notes: All currency pairs are versus USD. The currency identifiers are: DM = German deutschmark, JPY = Japanese yen, GBP = British pound, BF = Belgian franc, CHF = Swiss france, NOK = Norwegian krona, FF = French franc, LRA = Italian lira, and GLD = Dutch guilder. Source: Evans and Lyons (2002b).

contain information that is price relevant for multiple exchange rates, the ξ_t^k errors can be contemporaneously correlated across currencies. For example, CK news directly impacting the international value of the USD will affect all the exchange rates in the data set. To account for this possibility, Evans and Lyons estimate (7.3) as part of a Generalized Least-Squares (GLS) system.

Table 7.2 presents estimates of equation (7.3). The table reports the GLS estimates of the price-impact coefficients and their standard errors in parentheses. The upper entry in the right-hand column reports the associated R^2 statistic. For comparison purposes, the lower entry reports the R^2 statistic from estimating the single-currency version of (7.3) (i.e., using only the own-currency order flow X_t^k).

Three striking results emerge from the table:

1. There is a substantial degree of heterogeneity in the estimated price-impact coefficients, across both order flows and exchange-rate equations. The coefficients are not uniformly positive, and a single order flow can have different price impacts on different exchange rates. These findings should not come as a surprise for a couple of reasons. First, daily order flows are correlated across currencies, so a λ coefficient does not identify the marginal price impact of a particular order flow. Second, the price-relevant information conveyed by order flows need not be the same across currencies. If dealers are drawing different inferences in the markets for different currencies, the price impact of particular order flows λ will differ across exchange-rate equations.

2. For every exchange rate the array of order flows accounts for a substantial fraction of returns: the majority of the R^2 statistics are more than 65 percent, ranging between 45 and 78 percent. This is quite a remarkable finding when judged against the empirical performance of other empirical exchange-rate models.

3. At least two order flows have a statistically significant impact on the exchange rate in every case. For every currency save the JPY, order flows associated with the DM/USD have a positive and statistically significant price impact even after accounting for the price impact of own order flow. For some exchange rates, these cross-currency effects are economically quite significant. For example, in the case of the Norwegian krona (NOK), the price impacts of DM/USD and CHF/USD flows are highly significant and the R^2 rises from less than 1 percent to 68 percent when all order flows are introduced.

The results in Table 7.2 also provide perspective on the source of the contemporaneous correlation in daily exchange-rate changes. As is typically the case, daily exchange-rate changes are strongly positively correlated across currencies in this data sample. The standard explanation for this observation is that public news items simultaneously affect many exchange rates. The results in the table suggest that this is only a partial explanation. Insofar as different spot rates respond to the information conveyed by many order flows, order-flow-induced price movements may account for at least some of the positive cross-currency correlations. Indeed, this turns out to be the case. Using the estimates from Table 7.2, Evans and Lyons calculate that approximately 80 percent of the contemporaneous covariance in currency returns is attributable to the price impact of cross-currency order flows. Common public news does not appear to be the prime factor behind the positive contemporaneous correlation in daily exchange-rate changes.

Although the results in Tables 7.1 and 7.2 point to a strong contemporaneous link between aggregate interdealer order flow and daily changes in spot rates, they are based on a relatively short sample period and so may not be entirely representative of the link between order flows and spot rate movements over longer time spans. A growing body of research indicates that this is not the case. As more order flow data have become available, from either electronic interdealer trading systems or the trading records of individual banks, researchers have been able to study the links between exchange-rate changes and order flows over longer time spans and across many different currencies.

One important study in this regard has been undertaken by Chaboud, Chernenko, and Wright (2008). They examine the relation between interdealer order flow and

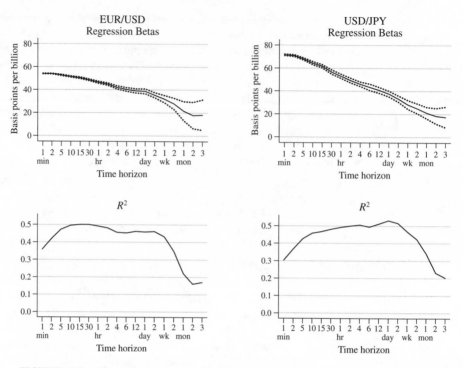

FIGURE 7.2 The exchange rate order–flow relation in EBS data. Source: Chaboud, Chernenko, and Wright (2008).

changes in the EUR/USD and JPY/USD exchange rates over a 6-year period between January 1999 and December 2004. A key feature of this research is that the order flow data come from the EBS brokerage system, which has become the dominant platform for interdealer trading in many currencies since the late 1990s. Consequently, the order flow data used by Chaboud et al. provides a good measure of interdealer trading across the entire market—as did the Evans and Lyons data from Reuters D2000-1 system in 1996.[1]

The EBS data allow Chaboud et al. to examine the relationship between interdealer order flow and spot rate changes over time periods ranging from 1 minute to 3 months (i.e., across a wide range of frequencies). These data confirm the presence of a strong contemporaneous association between exchange-rate changes and interdealer order flow at daily and intraday frequencies. At the daily frequency, estimates of the price impact coefficients are positive, highly significant, and similar in magnitude to those estimated by Evans and Lyons. Order flows also account for a sizable fraction of the daily exchange-rate changes. The R^2 statistics are approximately 0.45 for the EUR/USD and 0.50 for the YES/USD.

Figure 7.2 shows the relation between spot rate changes and order flow across the frequency spectrum estimated by Chaboud, Chernenko, and Wright (2008). The upper panels plot the estimated price impact coefficients together with a 95 percent

---

1. Breedon and Vitale (2010) estimate that the EBS system had gained more that an 80 percent share of interbank trading in the USD/EUR by 2000.

confidence band against the time horizon, and the lower panels plot the R^2 statistics. Two features stand out. First, the link between order flow and the change in the spot rate appears at least as strong at intraday frequencies as it does at daily frequencies. In fact, estimates of the price-impact coefficients rise significantly as the time horizon falls. The second feature concerns the apparent weakening of the relationship as the time horizon increases from 1 day to 1 month. The price-impact coefficients are smaller and estimated with much less precision and the R^2 statistics fall by approximately 50 percent.

7.1.3 Dealer and Customer Order Flows

According to the PS model, interdealer order flow conveys price-relevant information to dealers that initially entered the market in dispersed form via the customer orders received by individual dealers. If this is an accurate characterization of the information transmission mechanism operating in the market, customer order flows should also have some empirical explanatory power in accounting for exchange-rate changes.

Several studies have examined the relationship between exchange-rate changes and customer order flows. Rime (2001) found that customer flows accounted for approximately 33 percent of the variation in the NOK/DM spot rate at a weekly frequency over a 3-year period from January 1996 to May 1999. This figure is comparable to the EBS results of Chaboud et al. shown in Figure 7.2. Marsh and O'Rourke (2005) examine the explanatory power of customer order flows received by a large European-based bank [Royal Bank of Scotland (RBS)] between August 2002 and June 2004 for the dynamics of six exchange rates (EUR/USD, EUR/JPY, EUR/GBP, GBP/JPY, GBP/USD, USD/JPY). Their order flow data are disaggregated by customer type: nonfinancial corporates, unleveraged financials such as mutual funds, and leveraged financials including hedge funds and other financials. Distinguishing among customer types turns out to be important. Aggregate customer order flow accounts for very little of the variation in five of the six spot rates at either the 1-day or 1-week horizon—the exception is the USD/JPY, which produces a statistically significant R^2 of 0.16 at the weekly horizon.[2] By contrast, the disaggregated order flows have statistically significant price impacts at both horizons and account for a sizable fraction of the variation in exchange rates. For example, at the weekly horizon, the R^2 statistics for GBP/USD and USD/JPY are 0.19 and 0.27, respectively. Once again, these findings are comparable to those in Figure 7.2, which are based on interdealer order flow.[3]

The importance of disaggregating customer order flows according to type is further underscored by the findings in Evans and Lyons (2007). They study customer flows received by Citibank in the EUR/USD market over 6 years from April 1993 to June 1999. Like RBS, Citibank disaggregates its customers orders into three types: nonfinancial corporations (corporate), unleveraged financial institutions (investors), and leveraged financial institutions (hedge). They also distinguish between trades

---

2. Sager and Taylor (2008) find similar results using aggregate customer flow data from JP Morgan Chase and RBS.

3. Bjønnes, Rime, and Solheim (2005) also find significant explanatory power for the order flows from financial and nonfinancial customers in the SEK/EUR market.

TABLE 7.3
Exchange Rates and Customer Order Flows

Horizon	Corporate		Hedge		Investors		Aggregate	R^2 (p-value)
	U.S.	Non-U.S.	U.S.	Non-U.S.	U.S.	Non-U.S.		
1 day							0.112	0.018
							(0.028)	(<0.001)
	−0.147	−0.214	0.153	0.194	−0.029	0.353		0.078
	(0.107)	(0.064)	(0.054)	(0.056)	(0.121)	(0.059)		(<0.001)
1 week							0.173	0.054
							(0.036)	(<0.001)
	−0.167	−0.358	0.275	0.069	−0.051	0.447		0.195
	(0.133)	(0.077)	(0.064)	(0.090)	(0.143)	(0.080)		(<0.001)
1 month							0.227	0.092
							(0.066)	(<0.001)
	0.120	−0.376	0.214	−0.074	0.000	0.583		0.299
	(0.185)	(0.102)	(0.137)	(0.196)	(0.208)	(0.130)		(<0.001)

Source: Evans and Lyons (2007).

executed with Citibank in the United States, and those elsewhere within Citibank's global trading operation. It is worth noting that these data represent the customer flows to one of the largest banks operating in the foreign exchange market. Indeed, Citibank's share of customer orders in the EUR/USD market at that time was in the 10–15 percent range, a larger share than any other bank.

Table 7.3 shows the results of regressing excess returns on Citibank's customer flows at the 1-day, 1-week, and 1-month horizon. Excess returns are computed as $er_{d+h} \equiv s_{d+h} - s_d + \nabla r_d^h$, where s_d is the log of the quote at the start of day d and ∇r_d^h is the interest differential on day d for h-day deposits.[4] Order flows for each segment are aggregated from day d to day $d + h - 1$. Thus the order flows cover the same period as the revision in dealers' quotes that determine excess returns. The table reports OLS estimates at the daily frequency, with $h = 5$ and 20 for the 1-week and 1-month horizon regressions. The numbers in parentheses below the coefficient estimates are asymptotic standard errors corrected for heteroskedasticity and the $MA(h-1)$ process induced by overlapping observations. The right-hand column reports the R^2 statistics above the p-value for the null that all the coefficients on the order flows are zero.

The results in Table 7.3 contain several noteworthy features. First, they confirm that disaggregated customer order flows account for more of the variations in the

---

4. The use of excess returns rather than the change in log spot rate as the dependent variable in these regressions has no material effect on the estimation results because very little of the variability in excess returns comes from the interest differential.

foreign exchange returns than do aggregate flows. The price-impact coefficient in the aggregate customer flow is positive and significant at all three horizons, but the R^2 statistics are much smaller than when the six flow segments are included. Second, customer order flows account for a larger fraction of the variation in returns as the horizon lengthens. Although this pattern is consistent with the findings of Marsh and O'Rourke (2005) based on RBS customer flow data, it is opposite to that shown in Figure 7.2 based on the interdealer flows from EBS. Note also that the explanatory power of customer order flows at the daily frequency is much less than that reported for interdealer order flows in Tables 7.1 and 7.2. Third, the coefficients on the order flow segments are quite different from each other: Some are positive, some are negative, and some are highly statistically significant, whereas others are not.

At first sight, the coefficients on the different customer flow segments present something of a puzzle. In particular, the negative coefficients seem to indicate, rather counterintuitively, that dealers view orders to purchase the euro from some customers as an indicator that the euro is overvalued. Similarly, it seems hard to understand why orders from some customers appear to carry information at one frequency but not at others. In fact, neither observation presents much of a puzzle for two reasons: (1) customer flows are correlated across types and through time, and (2) we are not estimating a structural exchange-rate equation. It is worthwhile elaborating on both of these points.

Citibank's customer flows are strongly correlated across segments. This means that no one coefficient summarizes the total price impact of changes in a single flow segment. Thus, a negative coefficient estimate does not signify that some customer orders to purchase the euro are viewed by dealers as evidence that the euro is overvalued. Serial correlation in customer flows further complicates the interpretation of the coefficient estimates. Theoretically speaking, it is the unanticipated portion of customer orders that conveys new information to Citibank. The total flow of customer orders from a particular segment is at best an imprecise measure of the flow of information Citibank is actually receiving. As a result, the coefficient estimates do not identify the price impact of incremental customer trades.

The second point follows from the fact that we are looking at the customer orders received by a single bank rather than an aggregate measure of customer orders received by all banks across the market. The significance of this distinction is easily understood in the context of the PS model. There dealers revise their FX price quotes in response to aggregate interdealer order flow, not the flow of customer orders received by individuals. Although the trading decisions of dealers imply that interdealer order flow is driven by aggregate customer flows, the customer flows received by an individual bank have no direct effect on the FX prices that dealers quote. Consequently, the estimated price-impact coefficients in Table 7.3 should not be interpreted as structural parameters describing how FX prices are set. Of course this does not mean that exchange-rate returns should be independent of the customer flows of a large bank. Insofar as the customer flows proxy for the aggregated interdealer flow that is the driving process of quote revision, they will have some explanatory power for exchange-rate returns.

To summarize, the contemporaneous relationship between spot rate changes and order flow applies to both interdealer and customer flows. Customer flows disaggregated by customer type have more explanatory power for exchange-rate returns than the aggregate flows received by individual banks. At the daily frequency, disaggregated flows can account for less of the variation in exchange-rate returns than aggregate interdealer order flows, but the explanatory power of customer and dealer flows are comparable at lower frequencies.

7.2 Intraday Analysis

The contemporaneous correlation of spot rate changes and order flows just documented does not represent an actual test of the PS model. It is possible that the correlation we observe in many different data sets is due to an entirely different economic mechanism, one in which causation runs from exchange-rate changes to order flow. To assess this possibility, we have to examine the behavior of transactions and quotes in intraday data.

Vector Autogressions or VARs make up a popular class of econometric models for analyzing the dynamics of a set of variables. Following the work of Hasbrouck (1991), VARs have been widely utilized in the analysis of intraday data from a number of asset markets. This section first reviews key aspects of VAR modeling, and then describes how VARs have been used to examine the intraday dynamics of exchange rates and order flow.

7.2.1 Vector Autoregressions

A VAR specifies that the time series of a vector of variables, X_t, can be represented by a kth-order autoregressive process:

$$X_t = \sum_{j=1}^{k} A_j X_{t-j} + V_t, \tag{7.4}$$

where V_t is a vector of zero mean, serially uncorrelated shocks with covariance matrix $\mathbb{E}[V_t V_t'] = \Omega$. The A_j matrices contain the coefficients on the lagged values of the variables in X_t that appear in each equation of the VAR. For example, in the case where $X_t = [\, x_{1,t} \quad x_{2,t} \,]'$ and $k = 2$, equation (7.4) becomes

$$\begin{bmatrix} x_{1,t} \\ x_{2,t} \end{bmatrix} = \begin{bmatrix} a_{11}^1 & a_{12}^1 \\ a_{21}^1 & a_{22}^1 \end{bmatrix} \begin{bmatrix} x_{1,t-1} \\ x_{2,t-1} \end{bmatrix} + \begin{bmatrix} a_{11}^2 & a_{12}^2 \\ a_{21}^2 & a_{22}^2 \end{bmatrix} \begin{bmatrix} x_{1,t-2} \\ x_{2,t-2} \end{bmatrix} + \begin{bmatrix} v_{1,t} \\ v_{2,t} \end{bmatrix}. \tag{7.5}$$

Note that the equations for $x_{1,t}$ and $x_{2,t}$ contain the same variables on the right-hand side, namely the lagged values of $x_{1,t}$ and $x_{2,t}$. This feature makes estimation particularly straightforward. The coefficients, $a_{m,n}^j$, can be efficiently estimated by applying OLS to each equation in turn even when the shocks to each equation are contemporaneously correlated. The only other element in the VAR to be estimated is the covariance matrix for the shocks, Ω. This can be computed as $\hat{\Omega}_k = \frac{1}{T-k} \sum_{t=k+1}^{T} \hat{V}_t \hat{V}_t'$, where $\hat{V}_t$ is the vector of OLS residuals and T is the sample size.

What grounds are there for thinking that a VAR can adequately represent the dynamics of all the variables in X_t? The answer comes from the Wold Decomposition theorem (first discussed in Chapter 1). Recall that any covariance-stationary time series can be represented by a unique moving average process. Thus, if $\mathbb{E}X_t = \mu$ and

$\mathbb{E}[X_t X'_{t-j}] = \Gamma_j$ for all lags j and time periods t, so that X_t is covariance-stationary, without loss of generality we can write

$$X_t = \kappa_t + \Psi(L)\eta_t, \qquad (7.6)$$

where $\Psi(L) \equiv \sum_{j=0}^{\infty} \Psi_j L^j$ is a polynomial in the lag operator L, with matrices of coefficients Ψ_j and $\Psi_0 = I$. The κ_t term is a deterministic linear function of past X_t's. It will not be present in many applications so in the following discussion we will assume that $\kappa_t = 0$. We use η_t to denote the vector of white noise errors from projecting X_t on its past history, $\{X_{t-1}, X_{t-2}, \ldots\}$. (Recall that a projection is a linear regression without a constant.) These errors, or innovations as they are sometimes called, have a zero mean, are serially uncorrelated, and are homoskedastic, that is, $\mathbb{E}[\eta_t] = 0$, $\mathbb{E}[\eta_t \eta'_{t-j}] = \Sigma$ for $j = 0$ and $\mathbb{E}[\eta_t \eta'_{t-j}] = 0$ for $j > 0$. They are also uncorrelated with past values of X_t, $\mathbb{E}[\eta_t X'_{t-j}] = 0$ for $j > 0$.

One particularly important aspect of the Wold theorem concerns the properties of the moving average coefficients, Ψ_j. The theorem states that the polynomial $\Psi(L)$ is invertible, so we can also represent the dynamics of X_t in autoregressive form,

$$X_t = \sum_{j=1}^{\infty} \Phi_j X_{t-j} + \eta_t, \qquad (7.7)$$

where the autoregressive parameters Φ_j satisfy $\Psi(L)^{-1} = 1 - \sum_{j=1}^{\infty} \Phi_j L^j$.

The Wold theorem implies that any covariance-stationary time series X_t can be represented as an autoregression with white noise errors as shown in (7.7). Note, though, that (7.7) contains an infinite number of lags of X_t on the right-hand side and so cannot be directly estimated. We can, however, estimate an approximation to (7.7) that contains a finite number of lags on the right-hand side. Indeed, this is exactly the form of the VAR in (7.4). In other words, the kth-order VAR can be viewed as an approximation to the possibly infinite-order autoregressive representation implied by Wold's theorem for any covariance-stationary time series X_t.

This motivation brings to light two important aspects of using VARs. First, even if we are convinced that the time series X_t is covariance stationary, there is no guarantee that a VAR will adequately represent the dynamics of X_t. The Wold theorem tells us that an autoregressive representation for X_t exists, but it does not establish that we can well approximate this representation with a kth-order VAR for any finite k. In other words, we need assumptions beyond stationarity to ensure that $\Phi_j = 0$ for $j > k$ in (7.7). In some instances economic theory provides these assumptions, but it is far more common to choose the order of the VAR by applying a statistical criterion. Two frequently used criteria are the AIC, suggested by Akaike (1974), and the BIC, suggested by Schwarz (1978). In particular, the order of the VAR, k, is chosen to minimize

$$\text{AIC} = 2 \ln |\hat{\Omega}_k| + \frac{2n}{T} \quad \text{or} \quad \text{BIC} = 2 \ln |\hat{\Omega}_k| + \frac{n \ln T}{T},$$

where n is the number of coefficients in the VAR.

The second important aspect of working with a VAR concerns the interpretation of the VAR shocks, V_t. Let us assume that we have chosen the order of the VAR appropriately so that the estimated residuals well approximate the Wold representation innovations, that is, $\hat{V}_t \cong \eta_t$. Do the properties of the estimated residuals tell us anything about the true economic shocks driving X_t? Unfortunately, the answer is not necessarily. The Wold theorem only tells us that η_t are errors we would find in a linear regression of X_t on past X_t's. It is perfectly possible, indeed highly likely, that each element in the η_t vector reflects the impact of a combination of distinct true shocks. Another way to see this point is to remember that the moving average process in (7.6) identifies just one possible representation of the time series. The Wold theorem says that this process is unique among all linear representations where the η_t's are projection errors. It does not rule out the possibility that X_t follows a nonlinear process driven by economic shocks. If this is the case, then the estimated residuals from the VAR cannot possibly correspond to the true economic shocks.

The interpretation of shocks becomes particularly important when analyzing estimates of a VAR. In specifications with many equations and lags, interpreting the coefficient estimates in the A_j matrices is extremely difficult. Instead, researchers typically focus on the implications of the estimates for impulse responses and variance decompositions. Both are easily computed from the moving average representation of the VAR. In particular, let $\hat{A}(L) \equiv 1 - \sum_{j=1}^{k} \hat{A}_j L^j$ denote the estimated autoregressive polynomial of the kth-order VAR in (7.4), where $\hat{A}_j$ are the matrices of estimated coefficients. Hence, the VAR residuals are given by $\hat{V}_t \equiv \hat{A}(L)X_t$. Premultiplying both sides of this identity by the inverse of $\hat{A}(L)$ gives us the moving average representation implied by the VAR estimates:

$$X_t = \hat{B}(L)\hat{V}_t = \sum_{j=0}^{\infty} \hat{B}_j \hat{V}_{t-j}, \tag{7.8}$$

where $\hat{B}(L) = \hat{A}(L)^{-1}$. The impulse response function of variable n to a one-unit impulse to shock m after j periods is given by the element in row n and column m of $\hat{B}_j$. Of course, these responses only make sense if the individual shocks in $\hat{V}_t$ are orthogonal to one another. If shock m is correlated with shock $m + 1$, it simply does not make sense to consider the effects of shock m in isolation. The standard way of addressing this problem is to consider the impulse responses to a new set of orthogonal shocks.

Let $\hat{U}_t = \hat{Q}\hat{V}_t$ for some nonsingular square matrix $\hat{Q}$ with $\hat{Q}^{-1}(\hat{Q}^{-1})' = \hat{\Omega}$, where $\hat{\Omega}$ is the estimated covariance matrix for $\hat{V}_t$. By construction, the shocks in the $\hat{U}_t$ vector are orthogonal within the sample because $\frac{1}{T-k}\sum_{t=k+1}^{T} \hat{U}_t\hat{U}_t' = \hat{Q}\{\frac{1}{T-k}\sum_{t=k+1}^{T} \hat{V}_t\hat{V}_t'\}\hat{Q}' = \hat{Q}\hat{\Omega}\hat{Q}' = I$. We can now use $\hat{U}_t = \hat{Q}\hat{V}_t$ and (7.8) to write the moving average representation as

$$X_t = \hat{B}(L)\hat{Q}^{-1}\hat{Q}\hat{V}_t = \hat{C}(L)\hat{U}_t = \sum_{j=0}^{\infty} \hat{C}_j \hat{U}_{t-j}, \tag{7.9}$$

where $\hat{C}_j = \hat{B}_j\hat{Q}^{-1}$. The impulse response function of variable n to a one-unit impulse to orthogonal shock m (i.e., the mth element of $\hat{U}_t$) after j periods is given by the element in row n and column m of $\hat{C}_j$.

The orthogonalization method just described does not produce a unique set of impulse responses from the VAR estimates. The reason is that there is more than one $\hat{Q}$ matrix that can do the job. To proceed we must either: (1) choose a particular $\hat{Q}$ matrix on theoretical grounds, which pins down $\hat{C}_0 = \hat{Q}^{-1}$ because (7.8) implies that $\hat{B}_0 = I$, or (2) impose restrictions on $\hat{C}(L)$ directly that are sufficient to identify a unique value for the $\hat{Q}$ matrix.

There are several ways to compute the $\hat{C}_j$ matrices from the VAR estimates. The most straightforward is to iterate on the companion form of the VAR. To illustrate, consider the bivariate second-order VAR in (7.5). Let us further assume that economic theory uniquely identifies the $\hat{Q}$ given our estimates of $\hat{\Omega}$. The companion form of the estimated VAR is

$$
\begin{bmatrix} X_t \\ X_{t-1} \end{bmatrix} = \begin{bmatrix} \hat{A}_1 & \hat{A}_2 \\ I & 0 \end{bmatrix} \begin{bmatrix} X_{t-1} \\ X_{t-1} \end{bmatrix} + \begin{bmatrix} \hat{Q}^{-1} \\ 0 \end{bmatrix} \hat{U}_t,
$$

or, more compactly,

$$
\mathbf{X}_t = \hat{A}\mathbf{X}_{t-1} + \hat{C}\hat{U}_t. \tag{7.10}
$$

A VAR of any order can be written in the first-order form. The $\hat{C}_j$ matrices are easily computed from (7.10) as

$$
\hat{C}_j = [I \ 0]\hat{A}^j \hat{C},
$$

where $\hat{A}^j = \hat{A} \ \hat{A}^{j-1}$ and $\hat{A}^0 = I$.

Variance decompositions provide another means of analyzing VAR estimates. Let h_n be a selection vector such that $x_{n,t} = h_n \mathbf{X}_t$. The variance of $x_{n,t+\tau}$ conditioned on $\mathbf{X}_t$ implied by the companion form of the VAR is

$$
\mathbb{V}(x_{n,t+\tau}|\mathbf{X}_t) = \sum_{j=0}^{\tau-1} h_n \hat{A}^j \hat{C} \hat{C}'(\hat{A}^j)'h_n'.
$$

Note that all the $\hat{U}_t$ shocks contribute to this conditional variance. The contribution of a particular shock, say shock m, is given by

$$
\mathbb{V}(x_{n,t+\tau}|\mathbf{X}_t)_m = \sum_{j=0}^{\tau-1} h_n \hat{A}^j \hat{C} H_m \hat{C}'(\hat{A}^j)'h_n',
$$

where H_m is a matrix of zeros except for entry m on the leading diagonal, which is equal to unity. Since the $\hat{U}_t$ shocks are orthogonal by construction, $\mathbb{V}(x_{n,t+\tau}|\mathbf{X}_t) = \sum_m \mathbb{V}(x_{n,t+\tau}|\mathbf{X}_t)_m$. Thus, the ratio

$$
\mathbb{V}(x_{n,t+\tau}|\mathbf{X}_t)_m / \mathbb{V}(x_{n,t+\tau}|\mathbf{X}_t)
$$

measures the contribution of shock m to the conditional variance of variable n at horizon τ. Computing these ratios for all the variables in X_t and orthogonalized shocks provides detailed information on the sources of variation in X_t over the data sample.

7.2.2 VAR Models of Intraday Trading

VAR models of intraday FX trading fall broadly into two groups: models that characterize the dynamics of prices and trades in market time on a trade-by-trade or tic-by-tic basis and models that characterize dynamics over short time intervals of clock time such as 1 or 5 minutes. Although the econometric methods applied to both types of models are similar, the choice of whether to work in market or clock time has implications for the identification of shocks and hence the economic interpretation of the model estimates.

Market Time Models

Payne (2003) provides an early example of how a VAR can be used to examine the dynamics of FX quotes and trades on a tic-by-tic basis. His data comprise 1 week of trading activity in the DM/USD market during 1997 on the Reuters D2000-2 electronic brokerage system. The data set contains time-stamped information about all the market and limit orders passing through the system, which serves as the raw material for creating the vector of time series that will be modeled as a VAR. The vector contains: (1) the midquote defined as the average of the best limit-buy and best limit-sell prices, (2) a trade indicator, (3) a signed transaction quantity in millions of dollars, (4) the spread between the best limit-buy and limit-sell prices, referred to as the "inside spread," (5) the aggregate quantity of limit orders in millions of dollars, and (6) the number of limit orders. Payne's focus is on how the best limit-order prices change in response to market orders, with the remaining variables included to account for other aspects of trading activity.

To understand how the time series is constructed, let us focus on just the midquote and trade indicator. Our aim is to create a time series that records the evolution of quotes and trades as each market event takes place. In this application, an event takes place when: (1) the best (i.e., lowest) limit-buy price changes, or (2) the best (i.e., highest) limit-sell price changes, or (3) a market order is matched with a limit order. Let T_t denote the trade indicator generated by the arrival of a market order at t, and let S_t define the prevailing midquote. If the market order hits the best sell limit order, the dealer placing the market order is initiating a purchase of FX, and the trade indicator variable takes the value of one. If the market order hits the best buy limit order, the initiating dealer is selling FX and the indicator is set to minus one. At times when the best buy or sell limit-order price changes because dealers either add or withdraw individual limit orders, the midquote changes but there is no transaction, so T_t is set equal to zero.

The mapping from market events to a vector time series is best illustrated by an example. Suppose a sequence of market events occurs at times $t_1, t_2, \ldots$. Let $X_t = [T_t, \Delta S_{t+1}]'$ denote the vector time series we want to use in the VAR, where $\Delta S_{t+1} = S_{t+1} - S_t$. An example of the mapping from a set of market events to the time series for X_t is:

Event time	t_1	t_2	t_3	t_4
Trade: T_t	1	-1	0	0
Quote: S_t	100	101	101	99
Data: X_t	$\begin{bmatrix} 1 \\ 1 \end{bmatrix}$	$\begin{bmatrix} -1 \\ 0 \end{bmatrix}$	$\begin{bmatrix} 0 \\ -2 \end{bmatrix}$	

In this example, a market order hits a limit sell order at time t_1 when the prevailing midquote is equal to 100. As a result, the best sell limit price rises pushing up the midquote to 101. The value recorded by the X_t vector at $t = t_1$ is therefore $[1, 1]'$. Similarly at t_2 a market order hits a buy limit order when the prevailing midquote is 101, so $T_{t_2} = -1$. In this instance, the size of the market order is smaller than the quantity of limit orders at the best buy price so the midquote remains unchanged. Hence, $X_{t_2} = [-1, 0]'$. The next event takes place at t_3. Here a new buy limit order at a lower price is posted on the system so that the midquote falls from 101 to 99. Since this quote revision was not accompanied by any trade at t_3, the value recorded by the X_t vector at $t = t_3$ is $[0, -2]'$.

Payne constructs the time series for the vector X_t that includes T_t, ΔS_{t+1}, and the other variables describing the state of the electronic brokerage system at the time of each market event. He then estimates a VAR for X_t over sample periods during which most trading takes place on the Reuters system. This is an important aspect of VAR modeling with intraday data. As we noted in Chapter 6, although FX trading can take place 24 hours a day, the vast majority of transactions in most currencies occur on weekdays during European trading hours. In light of this fact, it is rather implausible to assume that X_t follows a covariance-stationary process over the full 24-hour day.[5] With few limit orders in the system outside European trading hours, a change in one limit order or the arrival of a market order will have a larger impact on the midquote than when there are a large number of limit orders. Consequently, the second moments of quote revisions and trades measured in event time will look very different between periods of little trading activity and periods when there are a large number of dealers submitting market and limit orders to the system. In sum, there are good reasons to doubt that values for X_t from any time of day represent realizations of a covariance-stationary time series suitable to be modeled as a VAR.

To address this concern, Payne estimates the VAR using observations on X_t that fall between 6:00 A.M. and 6:00 P.M. London time Monday through Friday. This does not mean that the VAR is estimated using a time series for X_t that simply excludes observations outside these time windows. Rather the VAR is estimated from consecutive values for X_t that fall within the 6:00 A.M. to 6:00 P.M. window on each day. This means that the estimates will not describe how trades and quotes behave over all 12 hours because the first observations after 6:00 A.M. must be used to account for the lags in the VAR. Since market events happen very quickly after 6:00 A.M., this is not a significant problem in practice.

---

5. Recall that this assumption is necessary if the VAR residuals are to well approximate the Wold representation innovations.

Payne identifies the impulse response functions and variance decompositions from the VAR by calculating $\hat{Q}$ (the matrix that orthogonalizes the VAR errors) from the Choleski decomposition of $\hat{\Omega}$, the estimated covariance matrix for the VAR errors. This produces a lower triangular $\hat{Q}$, so $\hat{C}_0 = \hat{Q}^{-1}$ is also lower triangular. For the case where $X_t = [T_t, \Delta S_{t+1}]'$, the moving average representation implied by the VAR estimates is therefore[6]

$$\begin{bmatrix} T_t \\ \Delta S_{t+1} \end{bmatrix} = \begin{bmatrix} \hat{c}^0_{TT} & 0 \\ \hat{c}^0_{ST} & \hat{c}^0_{SS} \end{bmatrix} \begin{bmatrix} \hat{u}^1_t \\ \hat{u}^2_t \end{bmatrix} + \begin{bmatrix} \hat{c}^1_{TT} & \hat{c}^1_{TS} \\ \hat{c}^1_{ST} & \hat{c}^1_{SS} \end{bmatrix} \begin{bmatrix} \hat{u}^1_{t-1} \\ \hat{u}^2_{t-1} \end{bmatrix} + \cdots , \qquad (7.11)$$

where, by construction, $\hat{u}^1_t$ and $\hat{u}^2_t$ are orthogonal shocks with unit variances. The important point to note here is that $\hat{u}^1_t$ shocks contemporaneously affect both the trade indicator and the revision in quotes, whereas $\hat{u}^2_t$ shocks have only a contemporaneous effect on the quote revision. The key question is: Does this response pattern allow us to identify $\hat{u}^1_t$ and $\hat{u}^2_t$ as particular *economic* shocks rather than simply orthogonalized Wold innovations?

The answer to this question is yes if we are willing to make two theoretical assumptions. The first assumption concerns the actions of dealers who have price-relevant information about the value of foreign currency that is not already fully reflected in the prevailing set of limit-order prices. The second concerns the way in which dealers react when they simultaneously learn of new information about the value of the foreign currency. These assumptions play a key role in the interpretation of empirical results concerning trade and price dynamics in many papers, so let us consider them in detail.

Consider the position of a dealer who, based on the customer order he has received, has information that leads him to believe that the value of FX is higher than the best limit sell price. The dealer can do two things to trade on this information. First, he can accumulate a larger foreign currency position by hitting the sell limit orders with market orders. Second he can submit buy limit orders at prices at or a little below the best (i.e., highest) buy limit price. This strategy will allow the dealer to accumulate a larger FX position at a lower cost than the first strategy if other dealers submit market orders to sell FX. If all dealers follow the first strategy, we can interpret the $\hat{u}^1_t$ shocks in (7.11) as representing the effects of new private information entering the trading system. With $\hat{c}^0_{TT}$ greater than zero, a positive (negative) $\hat{u}^1_t$ shock represents the effect of private information that induces dealers to submit market orders that hit the sell (buy) limit orders at time t. Insofar as these market orders induce a revision in either the best buy or sell limit prices there will also be a change in the midquote, so the $\hat{c}^0_{ST}$ coefficient will differ from zero. Alternatively, if dealers follow the second trading strategy, there will be a change in the midquote without the arrival of a market order, that is, when $T_t = 0$. In this case, the $\hat{u}^2_t$ shocks would have to represent the effects of private information because, by assumption, they have no contemporaneous effect on the trade indicator, T_t. The standard approach in the literature is to assume that

---

6. Payne estimates VAR with additional elements in the X_t vector, so the matrices of moving average coefficients will have more rows and columns and the vector of orthogonal shocks will have more shocks. Nevertheless, the matrix multiplying the contemporaneous shocks still has the lower diagonal form as shown here, so there is no loss of generality in focusing on (7.11).

dealers with private information principally follow the first trading strategy, so that the $\hat{u}_t^1$ shocks are interpreted as representing the effects of new private information.

The second assumption concerns the reaction of dealers to new public information concerning the value of foreign currency. In particular, consider the trading strategies open to a dealer when the Federal Reserve unexpectedly announces a rise of 25 basis points in the Federal Funds rate. Furthermore, suppose that in response to this information all dealers decide that the value of holding foreign currency has fallen by 0.01 per cent. Under these circumstances, dealers with limit buy orders at the best prices will immediately withdraw their orders because they will not want to accumulate large FX positions at the old limit price. As a result, the best buy limit-order price in the system will fall. The announcement also makes dealers more willing to reduce their existing FX positions, so dealers with outstanding sell limit orders will replace those orders with new ones at lower prices. As a result, both the best buy and best sell limit prices should fall immediately after dealers hear the announcement.

The key feature in the preceding example is that the limit-order prices are assumed to respond immediately to the announcement. More specifically, it is assumed that no dealer can submit a market order that hits a pre-existing limit order just after the public news arrives because *all* the limit orders at the best price are immediately withdrawn. If this is indeed the case, the $\hat{u}_t^2$ shocks in (7.11) will represent the effects of public information entering the trading system. By construction, these shocks induce a revision in the midquote when $\hat{c}_{ss}^0$ differs from zero, but have no contemporaneous effect on the trade indicator T_t. Of course, if some dealers are slow to withdraw their limit orders, a public news shock will be followed by some market orders that pick off the stale limit orders. Under these circumstances, the $\hat{u}_t^1$ shocks would better represent the effects of public news. The standard approach in the literature is to assume that dealers rarely have the opportunity to hit stale limit orders after the arrival of public news, so the $\hat{u}_t^2$ shocks are interpreted as representing the effects of new public information.

To summarize, we can identify the $\hat{u}_t^1$ and $\hat{u}_t^2$ shocks as representing the effects of new private and public information concerning the value of foreign currency under two behavioral assumptions:

1. Dealers primarily submit market orders when trading based on private information.

2. It is rarely possible to hit stale limit orders with a market order immediately following the arrival of public news.

With these identification assumptions, we can study the impact of private and public news on trades and prices by examining the impulse response functions and the variance decompositions associated with the moving average process in (7.11).

Following the work of Hasbrouck (1991), it is also common to calculate the contribution of private information to the variance of permanent price changes. To see how this statistic is computed, we rewrite (7.11) as

$$
\begin{bmatrix} T_t \\ \Delta S_{t+1} \end{bmatrix} = \begin{bmatrix} \hat{c}_{\text{TT}}(L) & \hat{c}_{\text{TS}}(L) \\ \hat{c}_{\text{ST}}(L) & \hat{c}_{\text{SS}}(L) \end{bmatrix} \begin{bmatrix} \hat{u}_t^1 \\ \hat{u}_t^2 \end{bmatrix}, \tag{7.12}
$$

where $\hat{c}_{\text{MN}}(L)$ are the estimated moving average polynomials in the lag operator L. Note that the permanent effect of a public news shock, $\hat{u}_t^2$, on the *level* of the midquote S_t is given by the sum of the coefficients in $\hat{c}_{SS}(L)$, which we denote by $\hat{c}_{SS}(1)$. Similarly, the permanent effect of a private news shock, $\hat{u}_t^1$, on the midquote is given by $\hat{c}_{ST}(1)$. Now since $\hat{u}_t^1$ and $\hat{u}_t^2$ are orthogonal serially uncorrelated shocks with unit variances, the contribution of private information to the variance of permanent changes in the midquote implied by (7.12) is given by

$$\mathcal{R} = \frac{\hat{c}_{ST}(1)^2}{\hat{c}_{ST}(1)^2 + \hat{c}_{SS}(1)^2}.$$

The $\mathcal{R}$ statistic provides a measure of what drives variations in exchange rates at low frequencies. In particular, the $\mathcal{R}$ statistic will be close to zero if all information about the value of foreign currency arrives in the form of public news and is immediately and permanently reflected in limit-order prices. The $\mathcal{R}$ statistic will also be close to zero if private information drives market orders, but the effects of these market orders on quotes are short-lived, that is, $\hat{c}_{ST}^0 \neq 0$ but $\hat{c}_{ST}(1) \cong 0$. Alternatively, if most information entering the market is in the form of private information that induces market orders and these market orders induce long-lived variations in limit-order prices, the $\mathcal{R}$ statistic should be close to one.

Payne finds that the dynamics of trades and quotes between 6:00 A.M. and 6:00 P.M. is well characterized by an eighth-order VAR. From these estimates he computes a value for the $\mathcal{R}$ statistic of 0.41 with a standard error of (0.015). This figure suggests that the private information conveyed by market orders contributes significantly to the variability of limit-order prices beyond trade-by-trade frequencies. He also computes $\mathcal{R}$ statistics from VARs estimated over various subperiods (e.g., 6:00 A.M. to 8:00 A.M.) to examine the robustness of his results to different market conditions. He computes the largest value for the $\mathcal{R}$ statistic of 0.47 between 8:00 A.M. to 10:00 A.M., when trading volume is at its highest.

Although Payne's results suggest that private information conveyed by trades contributes to exchange-rate dynamics, the size of the contribution appears smaller than that implied by the daily analyses discussed earlier. In particular, the multicurrency estimates of Evans and Lyons (2002b) reported in Table 7.2 implied that most of the variation in daily exchange rates was due to the impounding of private information conveyed by order flow. There are several possible explanations for this discrepancy. First, Payne's data cover a single week of trading on just one of the interdealer trading platforms available at the time. (Dealers could trade via the Reuters D2000-1 direct dealing system or via the electronic brokerage system run by EBS.) Dealers possessing private information need not have initiated trade with other dealers using the Reuters D2000-2 system. Second, the $\mathcal{R}$ statistic only provides meaningful information measures under the two identification assumptions listed before. If these assumptions are inaccurate, the $\mathcal{R}$ statistics are uninformative. The third reason concerns the role of feedback trading. The strong contemporaneous correlation between order flow and the daily change in exchange rates may be due, in part, to the effects of prior quote changes on trading activity at an intraday frequency. These feedback effects are captured by the estimated coefficients in the $\hat{c}_{TT}(L)$ and $\hat{c}_{TS}(L)$ polynomials in (7.12), but they are not included in the computation of the $\mathcal{R}$ statistic. It is therefore possible that some of the discrepancy between the daily estimates and Payne's results is a reflection of the presence of feedback trading. We return to this issue in what follows.

Clock Time Models

The intraday dynamics of quotes and trades on the Reuters D2000-2 system has also been studied with VARs estimated in clock time. Daníelsson and Love (2006) examine the behavior of midquote and market orders in the EUR/USD market over 8 months starting in December 1999 using observation windows of 1 and 5 minutes. As in Payne's model, the focus of their analysis is the impact of market orders on quote revisions.

When estimating a VAR in clock time, the vector time series X_t to be used is constructed from market data sampled at regular time intervals. In the Daníelsson and Love models, $X_t = [T_t, \Delta S_{t+1}]'$, where S_t is the average of the best limit buy and sell prices at the start of the tth interval in the data set and T_t is a measure of order flow defined as the difference between the number of market orders hitting sell limit orders and the number hitting buy limit orders during interval t. Thus, in the case where a 1-minute observation window is used, the X_t vector for tth window starting at 8:00 A.M. comprises T_t computed from the market orders arriving between 8:00 and 8:01 and ΔS_{t+1} calculated as the difference between the midquotes at 8:01 and 8:00.

The choice of observation window represents a key decision when estimating a model in clock time. If a very short window of a few seconds is chosen, there are likely to be a very large number of observations with no trading activity. In principle this is not a problem for the estimation of a VAR, provided that the resulting time series for X_t is covariance-stationary. However, in practice the VAR estimates are likely to have nonstandard statistical properties when the data sample contains a large number of observations with X_t equal to the null vector. For this reason, researchers rarely consider observation windows shorter than 1 minute and use only values for X_t that come from sustained periods of significant trading activity. Like Payne (2003), Daníelsson and Love estimate their VARs using observations on X_t that fall between 6:00 A.M. and 6:00 P.M. London time Monday through Friday.

The use of a longer observation window can also lead to problems. If the pace of trading is very fast with market orders and quote revisions occurring every few seconds, the identification and interpretation of VAR estimates computed from a time series for X_t constructed using a window of several minutes becomes much harder. To understand why, let us assume that trades and quotes measured in *event time,* indexed by the subscript i, follow an MA process

$$\begin{bmatrix} T_i \\ \Delta S_{i+1} \end{bmatrix} = \begin{bmatrix} c_{TT}^0 & 0 \\ c_{ST}^0 & c_{SS}^0 \end{bmatrix} \begin{bmatrix} u_i^{PRV} \\ u_i^{PUB} \end{bmatrix} + \begin{bmatrix} c_{TT}^1 & c_{TS}^1 \\ c_{ST}^1 & c_{SS}^1 \end{bmatrix} \begin{bmatrix} u_{i-1}^{PRV} \\ u_{i-1}^{PUB} \end{bmatrix} + \cdots, \quad (7.13)$$

where u_i^{PRV} and u_i^{PUB} are orthogonal shocks that denote the effects of private and public news. Now suppose that we construct a time series $X_t = [T_t, \Delta S_{t+1}]'$ with an observation window that contains two events t_i and t_{i-1}. Thus, $T_t = T_{t_i} + T_{t_i-1}$ and $\Delta S_{t+1} = \Delta S_{t_i+1} + \Delta S_{t_i}$. Under these circumstances, the economic model in (7.13) implies that the innovations in X_t are equal to

$$\begin{bmatrix} T_t - \mathcal{P}_X[T_t] \\ \Delta S_{t+1} - \mathcal{P}_X[\Delta S_{t+1}] \end{bmatrix} = \begin{bmatrix} c_{TT}^0 & 0 \\ c_{ST}^0 & c_{SS}^0 \end{bmatrix} \begin{bmatrix} u_{t_i}^{PRV} \\ u_{t_i}^{PUB} \end{bmatrix} + \begin{bmatrix} c_{TT}^1 & c_{TS}^1 \\ c_{ST}^1 & c_{SS}^1 \end{bmatrix} \begin{bmatrix} u_{t_i-1}^{PRV} \\ u_{t_i-1}^{PUB} \end{bmatrix}, \quad (7.14)$$

where $\mathcal{P}_X[\cdot]$ denotes the projection on past X_t's. Note that if the c_{TS}^1 coefficient is nonzero, an innovation in order flow is a function of both the private news shocks,

$u_{t_i}^{\text{PRV}}$ and $u_{t_i-1}^{\text{PRV}}$, and public news that occurs at the start of the window, $u_{t_i-1}^{\text{PUB}}$. In other words, even though private news is the only source of unexpected market orders in event time, shocks to order flow measured in clock time will only correctly identify the impact of new private information when $c_{\text{TS}}^1 = 0$. This condition is unlikely to hold if some dealers submit market orders in response to past quote revisions. Under these circumstances, some observation on T_i will be related to ΔS_i and hence will depend on $u_{t_i-1}^{\text{PUB}}$. Thus, if some dealers submit market orders based on earlier changes in quotes, shocks to order flow measured in clock time are likely to represent the impact of both public and private news; and, as a consequence, estimates of the MA process calculated in clock time will not be accurate.

To illustrate this point, we first compute the variance covariance of the innovations from (7.14):

$$
\begin{bmatrix}
(c_{\text{TT}}^0)^2 + (c_{\text{TT}}^1)^2 + (c_{\text{TS}}^1)^2 & c_{\text{TT}}^0 c_{\text{ST}}^0 + c_{\text{TT}}^1 c_{\text{ST}}^1 + c_{\text{TS}}^1 c_{\text{SS}}^1 \\
c_{\text{TT}}^0 c_{\text{ST}}^0 + c_{\text{TT}}^1 c_{\text{ST}}^1 + c_{\text{TS}}^1 c_{\text{SS}}^1 & (c_{\text{ST}}^0)^2 + (c_{\text{SS}}^0)^2 + (c_{\text{ST}}^1)^2 + (c_{\text{SS}}^1)^2
\end{bmatrix}. \tag{7.15}
$$

Applying the Choleski decomposition to this matrix gives us the estimated relation between the innovations in X_t and the news shocks as

$$
\begin{bmatrix}
T_t - \mathcal{P}_X[T_t] \\
\Delta S_{t+1} - \mathcal{P}_X[\Delta S_{t+1}]
\end{bmatrix}
=
\begin{bmatrix}
\hat{c}_{\text{TT}}^0 & 0 \\
\hat{c}_{\text{ST}}^0 & \hat{c}_{\text{SS}}^0
\end{bmatrix}
\begin{bmatrix}
\hat{u}_t^{\text{PRV}} \\
\hat{u}_t^{\text{PUB}}
\end{bmatrix},
$$

where the estimated coefficients are

$$
\hat{c}_{\text{TT}}^0 = \sqrt{(c_{\text{TT}}^0)^2 + (c_{\text{TT}}^1)^2 + (c_{\text{TS}}^1)^2},
$$

$$
\hat{c}_{\text{ST}}^0 = (c_{\text{TT}}^0 c_{\text{ST}}^0 + c_{\text{TT}}^1 c_{\text{ST}}^1 + c_{\text{TS}}^1 c_{\text{SS}}^1)/\hat{c}_{\text{TT}}^0,
$$

and

$$
\hat{c}_{\text{SS}}^0 = \sqrt{(c_{\text{ST}}^0)^2 + (c_{\text{SS}}^0)^2 + (c_{\text{ST}}^1)^2 + (c_{\text{SS}}^1)^2 - (\hat{c}_{\text{ST}}^0)^2}.
$$

Note that the c_{TS}^1 coefficient appears in all three coefficient estimates. Thus, feedback trading in the form of $c_{\text{TS}}^1 \neq 0$ will produce biased estimates of how public and private news affects trade and quote revisions if the VAR is estimated with data using too long an observation window.

This discussion provides an illustration of a general problem referred to as Temporal Aggregation Bias (TAB). The problem arises when agents (e.g., dealers) are acting at a higher frequency than the researcher is using to construct the empirical model. Clearly, this problem is potentially present in any clock time model of trading behavior. Indeed, given the fast pace of trading in spot FX, TAB is almost surely present to some degree in any clock time model of FX trading. The key question is: Does private information conveyed by order flow contribute significantly to the dynamics of FX quotes after allowance is made for the TAB induced by feedback trading?

Daníelsson and Love (2006) address this question with the aid of instrumental variables. To understand their approach, assume that the MA representation for X_t in *clock time* is

$$\begin{bmatrix} T_t \\ \Delta S_{t+1} \end{bmatrix} = \begin{bmatrix} c_{\mathrm{TT}}^0 & c_{\mathrm{TS}}^0 \\ c_{\mathrm{ST}}^0 & c_{\mathrm{SS}}^0 \end{bmatrix} \begin{bmatrix} u_t^{\mathrm{PRV}} \\ u_t^{\mathrm{PUB}} \end{bmatrix} + \begin{bmatrix} c_{\mathrm{TT}}^1 & c_{\mathrm{TS}}^1 \\ c_{\mathrm{ST}}^1 & c_{\mathrm{SS}}^1 \end{bmatrix} \begin{bmatrix} u_{t-1}^{\mathrm{PRV}} \\ u_{t-1}^{\mathrm{PUB}} \end{bmatrix} + \cdots. \quad (7.16)$$

Here public news, u_t^{PUB}, has a contemporaneous impact on order flow, T_t, via the c_{TS}^0 coefficient. We assume that c_{TS}^0 is nonzero as a result of temporal aggregation. The autoregressive representation corresponding to (7.16) is $C(L)^{-1} X_t = U_t$, which can also be written as

$$T_t = a_{\mathrm{TS}}^0 \Delta S_{t+1} + a_{\mathrm{TT}}^1 T_{t-1} + a_{\mathrm{TS}}^1 \Delta S_t + a_{\mathrm{TT}}^2 T_{t-2} + a_{\mathrm{TS}}^2 \Delta S_{t-1} + \cdots + u_t^{\mathrm{PRV}}, \quad (7.17a)$$

$$\Delta S_{t+1} = a_{\mathrm{ST}}^0 T_t + a_{\mathrm{ST}}^1 T_{t-1} + a_{\mathrm{SS}}^1 \Delta S_t + a_{\mathrm{ST}}^2 T_{t-2} + a_{\mathrm{SS}}^2 \Delta S_{t-1} + \cdots + u_t^{\mathrm{PUB}}. \quad (7.17b)$$

Note that ΔS_{t+1} appears on the right-hand side of (7.17a) with a coefficient of a_{TS}^0. It is a simple matter to show that this coefficient must be zero if $c_{\mathrm{TS}}^0 = 0$. Under these circumstances, all the other coefficients can be estimated by applying OLS to each equation. If $c_{\mathrm{TS}}^0 \neq 0$ as a result of temporal aggregation, (7.17) becomes a set of simultaneous equations because $a_{\mathrm{TS}}^0 \neq 0$, so OLS is no longer the appropriate estimation method.

Daníelsson and Love (2006) estimate the set of simultaneous equations in (7.17) for order flow and quotes in the USD/EUR market using lagged order flows in the USD/GBP and GBP/EUR markets to instrument for T_t in the ΔS_{t+1} equation and lagged quote revisions in the USD/GBP as instruments for ΔS_{t+1} in the T_t equation. The rationale for these instruments is based on the multicurrency results of Evans and Lyons (2002b). Recall from Table 7.2 that daily changes in spot rates are strongly correlated with order flows across many currencies. If these correlations arise from the fact that an array of order flows convey private price-relevant information for a single currency, we should be able to identify the price impact of private information conveyed by orders in USD/EUR using lagged order flows in USD/GBP and GBP/EUR as instruments for T_t in the ΔS_{t+1} equation. Similarly, since FX returns are correlated across currencies, dealers using feedback-trading strategies will condition the placement of their market orders on an array of past quote changes. We should be able to identify the extent of such trading by using lagged quote revisions in USD/GBP as instruments for ΔS_{t+1} in the T_t equation.

Daníelsson and Love compare their instrumental variable estimates of (7.17) against conventional OLS estimates computed with the $a_{\mathrm{TS}}^0 = 0$ restriction. They find that their instrumental variable estimates of a_{TS}^0 are positive and statistically significant in models estimated with both 1- and 5-minute observation windows. They then compare the impulse responses of quotes to private news computed from the estimates of (7.17) by instrumental variables and OLS (i.e., with $a_{\mathrm{TS}}^0 = 0$). According to their estimates, the presence of feedback trading amplifies the impact of private news by approximately 100 percent.

We can interpret this result with our example of the event time MA model in (7.13). In particular, let us assume that quotes respond immediately and fully to the arrival of public news. This means that the a_{SS} coefficients on lagged public news in the ΔS_{i+1} equation equal zero. Under these circumstances, the estimated response of quotes to private news from a standard VAR over the two-event observation window is given by

$$\hat{c}^0_{\text{ST}} = \frac{c^0_{\text{TT}}}{\hat{c}^0_{\text{TT}}} c^0_{\text{ST}} + \frac{c^1_{\text{TT}}}{\hat{c}^0_{\text{TT}}} c^1_{\text{ST}}, \tag{7.18}$$

where

$$\hat{c}^0_{\text{TT}} = \sqrt{(c^0_{\text{TT}})^2 + (c^1_{\text{TT}})^2 + (c^1_{\text{TS}})^2}.$$

If feedback trading is absent, $c^1_{\text{TS}} = 0$ and $\hat{c}^0_{\text{ST}}$ is a weighted average of the event time coefficients, c^0_{ST} and c^1_{ST}. When feedback is present (i.e., $c^1_{\text{TS}} \neq 0$), $\hat{c}^0_{\text{TT}}$ is larger and $\hat{c}^0_{\text{ST}}$ is smaller. Thus the estimated effect of private news on quotes is biased downward. Daníelsson and Love's estimates imply that this bias is substantial. It appears that when private news induces an initial market order in event time, the response of quotes induces further market orders in the same direction from dealers following feedback strategies, which in turn produces a larger revision in quotes.

The event time MA model in (7.13) illustrates another important property of time aggregation. Suppose that private news has no impact on quotes in event time so that the c^0_{ST} and c^1_{ST} coefficients are zero. In this case, the estimated impact of private news on quotes measured in clock time is

$$\hat{c}^0_{\text{ST}} = \frac{c^1_{\text{TS}} c^1_{\text{SS}}}{\sqrt{(c^0_{\text{TT}})^2 + (c^1_{\text{TT}})^2 + (c^1_{\text{TS}})^2}}.$$

Note that this term only differs from zero if $c^1_{\text{TS}} \neq 0$ and $c^1_{\text{SS}} \neq 0$, that is, when feedback trading is present and quotes respond to the arrival of public news with a lag. If the response of public news is immediate and complete, as any model of rational trading would imply, c^1_{SS} equals zero, so the estimated response of quotes to private news would also be zero irrespective of whether dealers are following feedback trading strategies. This means that the contemporaneous correlation between order flow and quotes measured in clock time cannot be attributed *solely* to feedback trading without a rationale for why quotes fail to fully and immediately respond to public news.

7.2.3 Decentralized Trading Models

VAR models are well suited for the empirical analyses of intraday trading in a centralized market such as an electronic brokerage because there is a natural sequencing of events: A market order arrives, a limit order is withdrawn, and so on. However, no such natural sequencing exists when trading takes place in a decentralized manner. Recall that before the late 1990s most trading in the spot FX market took place between dealers and this interdealer trade took the "direct" form of bilateral conversations between individual dealers. In this decentralized form, there might have been 50 conversations taking place simultaneously between 100 dealers in a single-currency pair, so ordering the resulting transaction prices and order flows is clearly inappropriate. Moreover, individual dealers had very little real-time information concerning market-wide trading activity: The details of each conversation, such as the quotes and transaction quantities, were only known to the counterparties. In sum, most FX trading historically took place in a decentralized manner with low transparency—features that cannot be accommodated by VAR models.

The VAR Identification Problem

The problem of using a VAR to model intraday data from decentralized trading is best explained with an example. Suppose we have data from the early 1990s on a sequence of transaction prices from "direct" interdealer trades in the DM/USD market. In particular, let S_t^a and S_t^b denote the last DM price during observation window t at which a dealer initiated a purchase and sale of USD. (Recall that in "direct" dealing there is no negotiation, so S_t^a denotes the ask price quoted to the dealer initiating a USD purchase, and S_t^b denotes the bid quote to a dealer initiating a USD sale.) With decentralized trading it is very unlikely that the same initiating dealer is involved in the sequence of trades associated with the time series for S_t^a or the time series for S_t^b. Instead, it makes far more sense to think of S_t^a and S_t^b as being drawn from the distribution of transaction prices that arise from all the "direct" interdealer trading taking place during period t.

To formalize this idea, assume that S_t^a and S_t^b are related to the market-wide average transaction price, S_t, by

$$S_t^o = S_t + v_t^o, \tag{7.19}$$

for $o = \{a, b\}$. The terms v_t^a and v_t^b are idiosyncratic components that identify the degree to which observed prices differ from the market-wide average, and their size depends on the identity of the dealers whose prices we observe. Since there are a large number of FX dealers who can execute transactions at any time, it is reasonable to assume that observed prices are drawn randomly and independently from the cross-sectional distributions of transaction prices every period. Under this assumption, we can write the components as $v_t^a = spr/2 + \omega_t^a$ and $v_t^b = -spr/2 + \omega_t^b$, where ω_t^a and ω_t^b are mean zero, serially uncorrelated, and independently distributed errors and spr is the market-wide average of the bid-ask spread.

Let us now consider the implications of (7.19) for the time series behavior of the vector of observed prices, $\Delta \mathbf{S}_t \equiv [\Delta S_t^a, \Delta S_t^b]'$, under the assumption that the market-wide average follows a random walk: $S_t = S_{t-1} + u_t$, where u_t is an i.i.d. mean-zero shock. In this example all information concerning the DM value of the USD comes in the form of CK news via the u_t shocks. Combining this random walk specification with (7.19) gives

$$\Delta \mathbf{S}_t = \begin{bmatrix} 1 \\ 1 \end{bmatrix} u_t + \begin{bmatrix} \Delta \omega_t^a \\ \Delta \omega_t^b \end{bmatrix}. \tag{7.20}$$

This reduced form equation implies that the autocovariance of $\Delta \mathbf{S}_t$ is zero beyond lag 1, that is, $\mathbb{CV}(\Delta \mathbf{S}_t, \Delta \mathbf{S}_{t-j}') = 0$ for $j > 1$. Thus the dynamics of $\Delta \mathbf{S}_t$ can also be represented by the VMA process

$$\Delta \mathbf{S}_t = \begin{bmatrix} \eta_t^a \\ \eta_t^b \end{bmatrix} + \begin{bmatrix} \psi_{aa} & \psi_{ab} \\ \psi_{ba} & \psi_{bb} \end{bmatrix} \begin{bmatrix} \eta_{t-1}^a \\ \eta_{t-1}^b \end{bmatrix}. \tag{7.21}$$

Equation (7.21) is the Wold representation for observed prices implied by our simple model. If we had a long time series on $\Delta \mathbf{S}_t$, we could compute the impulse response function for $\Delta \mathbf{S}_t$ from estimates of the moving average parameters, $\hat{\psi}$, and the Choleski decomposition, $\hat{c}$, of the residual covariance matrix as

$$\Delta \mathbf{S}_t = \begin{bmatrix} \hat{c}_{aa} & 0 \\ \hat{c}_{ba} & \hat{c}_{bb} \end{bmatrix} \begin{bmatrix} \hat{e}_t^a \\ \hat{e}_t^b \end{bmatrix} + \begin{bmatrix} \hat{c}_{aa}\hat{\psi}_{aa} + \hat{c}_{ba}\hat{\psi}_{ab} & \hat{c}_{bb}^0 \hat{\psi}_{ab} \\ \hat{c}_{aa}\hat{\psi}_{ba} + \hat{c}_{ba}\hat{\psi}_{bb} & \hat{c}_{bb}^0 \hat{\psi}_{bb} \end{bmatrix} \begin{bmatrix} \hat{e}_{t-1}^a \\ \hat{e}_{t-1}^b \end{bmatrix}, \quad (7.22)$$

where $\hat{e}_t^a$ and $\hat{e}_t^b$ are the orthogonal shocks to prices.

Do the impulse responses to the $\hat{e}_t^a$ and $\hat{e}_t^b$ shocks in (7.22) reveal anything about the role of the public news shocks, u_t, and the idiosyncratic components, v_t^o, in the dynamics of prices? Unfortunately, the answer to this question is no. Note that there are three distinct shocks in the reduced form (7.20): the public news shocks and the two idiosyncratic components. By contrast, there are just two shocks in (7.22). Obviously, there is no way that the impulse responses of prices to the $\hat{e}_t^a$ and $\hat{e}_t^b$ shocks can represent the dynamic effects of public news shocks and the two idiosyncratic components.

To reinforce this point, we can compute the impulse responses in (7.22) implied by a particular parameterization of (7.20). For example, when $\mathbb{V}(u_t) = 1$ and $\mathbb{V}(\omega_t^a) = \mathbb{V}(\omega_t^b) = 0.1$, the impulse responses are given by

$$\Delta \mathbf{S}_t = \begin{bmatrix} 1.071 & 0 \\ 0.978 & 0.437 \end{bmatrix} \begin{bmatrix} \hat{e}_t^a \\ \hat{e}_t^b \end{bmatrix} + \begin{bmatrix} -0.093 & 0.209 \\ 0 & -0.229 \end{bmatrix} \begin{bmatrix} \hat{e}_{t-1}^a \\ \hat{e}_{t-1}^b \end{bmatrix}.$$

Note that both $\hat{e}_t^a$ and $\hat{e}_t^b$ have lagged effects on observed price changes, so neither shock identifies the impact of CK news. Furthermore, both shocks have a long-run impact on ΔS_t^a and ΔS_t^b. This implication runs contrary to the effects of the ω_t shocks in (7.20), so $\hat{e}_t^a$ and $\hat{e}_t^b$ cannot represent the impact of the idiosyncratic components either.

The identification problem illustrated here is quite general; it arises because the time series of observed prices from decentralized trading contains two types of information. The first is information about the dynamics of the market-wide average transaction price. These dynamics capture the effects of both CK news and the private information conveyed by order flow. The second type of information is present because observed prices are merely representative of the distribution of transaction prices arising from simultaneous trading activity across the market. Distinguishing between the first and second type of information is critical for understanding trade and price dynamics in a market where trading is decentralized, but it is not possible with a VAR.

The Evans Intraday Trading Model

Evans (2002) presents a model designed to deal with the features of intraday decentralized trading. The model uses intraday data on transaction prices, interdealer order flow, and trade intensity from "direct" interdealer trading in the DM/USD market over 4 months in 1996. Time series observations on all the variables are constructed in clock time using a 5-minute observation window from a data feed that recorded all interdealer trades on the Reuters D2000-1 system. (This was the dominant direct interdealer trading platform at the time.) As in the earlier example, transaction prices comprise the last DM purchase and sale price for USD during period t; S^a_t and S^b_t. Interdealer order flow, x_t, is measured as the difference between the number of buyer-initiated orders and seller-initiated orders during period t. Trade intensity, n_t, is defined as the number of trades per period.

The heart of the model comprises three equations:

$$\Delta S_t = B(L, n_t)\xi_t + u_t, \tag{7.23a}$$

$$y_t = C_y(L, n_t)\xi_t, \tag{7.23b}$$

$$x_t = C_x(L, n_t)y_t, \tag{7.23c}$$

where ΔS_t is the change in the market-wide average DM price of a USD between the ends of periods $t - 1$ and t and y_t is the flow of *customer orders* received by dealers during period t. $B(L, n_t)$, $C_y(L, n_t)$, and $C_x(L, n_t)$ denote polynomials in the lag operator with coefficients that vary with trade intensity, n_t, measured in trades per 5-minute interval. The form of this state-dependency is described in what follows.

Equation (7.23a) shows how average prices respond to two types of news: CK news shocks, u_t, and dispersed information shocks, ξ_t. These shocks have zero means and are mutually independent and serially uncorrelated. As before, the u_t shocks represent unambiguous price-relevant news that is observed simultaneously by everyone and so are impounded fully and instantaneously into the prices at which all interdealer trades take place. Dispersed information shocks represent, in aggregate, the bits of information contained in the customer trades received by individual dealers. This information is first manifested in customer order flow, y_t, as shown in (7.23b). Dealers respond to the dispersed information conveyed by customer flows when quoting prices and when initiating interdealer trades. The resulting impact of dispersed information on transaction prices is captured by the first term on the right in (7.23a). Equation (7.23c) shows how interdealer order flow relates to the flow of customer orders.

Three features of this model deserve comment. First, the assumed independence between the CK and dispersed information news shocks implies that CK news has no effect on order flow. This assumption has a long history in empirical finance, dating back at least to the work of Hasbrouck (1991). Moreover, it is implied by any model in which market participants act rationally: Any revision in quotes owing to CK news should establish a new level for the average transaction price that does not systematically favor subsequent imbalances of sell orders over buy orders, or vice versa. We study this feature of currency-trading models further in Chapter 10.

The second feature concerns the dynamics of the customer order flow, y_t: The implicit assumption here is that dealers' demand for foreign currency is imperfectly elastic, so any imbalance in customer orders requires price adjustment to compensate dealers for filling the customers' orders from their own holdings. Consequently, all order flow is, at least temporarily, price relevant. Under rational expectations, this information is summarized in current and past dispersed information shocks, but remains unrelated to CK news shocks, as shown in equation (7.23b).

The third feature concerns the relation between the customer and interdealer order flows. As in the PS model, interdealer order flow depends on the flow of customer orders received by individual dealers, but equation (7.23c) allows for richer dynamics between the two flows. In particular, the model allows for the fact that dealers may react to the dispersed information contained in customer flows by first revising their quotes to other dealers before they initiate their interdealer trades. Under these circumstances, a dispersed information shock ξ_t will affect transaction prices via (7.23a) before interdealer order flow via (7.23c) and (7.23b) because the interdealer flow can respond to customer flow with a lag in (7.23b). It is worth pointing out that this trading strategy was not an optimal one for dealers in the PS model because quotes were observable to all and good for any amount. This high level of transparency never existed in "direct" interdealer trading. The dynamic relation between interdealer and customer flows in (7.23b) is needed to accommodate the fact that dealers can follow more complex trading strategies when transparency is low.

The estimable form of the model combines (7.23) with the equation linking observed transaction prices with the market-wide average in (7.19):

$$\Delta S_t^a = D(L, n_t)x_t + u_t + \Delta\omega_t^a, \tag{7.24}$$

$$\Delta S_t^b = D(L, n_t)x_t + u_t + \Delta\omega_t^b, \tag{7.25}$$

$$x_t = C(L, n_t)\xi_t, \tag{7.26}$$

where $D(L, n) = B(L, n)C(L, n)^{-1}$ and $C(L, n) = C_x(L, n)C_y(L, n)$. The polynomial $D(L, n)$ may take many forms depending on the dynamic responses of prices and interdealer order flow to dispersed information shocks. If dealers follow trading strategies in which they revise their quotes before initiating trades in response to incoming customer orders, $D(L, n)$ will include both negative and positive powers of L. Based on a series of diagnostic tests, the specification of $D(L, n)$ in the Evans model links ΔS_t^o to interdealer order flows from x_{t+4} to x_{t-1}. This implies that a dispersed information shock impacts on customer flow and prices up to 20 minutes before it affects interdealer order flow. Another series of diagnostic tests reveals that all the serial correlation in interdealer order flow can be accounted for when $C(L, n)$ is the moving average polynomial implied by an ARMA(2,2) process.

One feature that differentiates this model from the VARs considered earlier is that it allows for state-dependency in the dynamics of transaction prices and order flow. This is an important feature because, as we saw in Chapter 6, the pace of trading in the FX market varies considerably from hour to hour. As a result, it is highly unlikely that dynamic relationships between transaction prices and order flows observed over a 5-minute observation window are invariant to variations in the amount of trading activity. If the pace at which dealers assimilate and act on dispersed information changes with the arrival rate of customer orders and quote requests from other dealers in the market, variations in trade intensity will act as an indicator that the 5-minute observation window spans varying periods of "market time": the constant time scale at which dealer decisionmaking takes place. This distortion of time scales, called Time Deformation, is likely to be present in any clock time model of intraday trading.

The Evans (2002) model allows for time deformation via the presence of state-dependency in the shock variances, $\mathbb{V}(u_t) = \Sigma_u(n_t)$, $\mathbb{V}(\xi_t) = \Sigma_u(n_t)$, and $\mathbb{V}(\omega_t^a) = \mathbb{V}(\omega_t^b) = \Sigma_\omega(n_t)$, and in the $D(L, n_t)$ polynomial. (There is no evidence of state-dependency in $C(L, n_t)$.) The model specifies the lag polynomials as

$$C(L, n) = (1 - c_1 L - c_2 L)^{-1}(1 + c_3 L + c_4 L)$$

and

$$D(L, n) = d_1(n)L^{-4} + d_2(n)L^{-3} + \cdots + d_5(n) + d_6(n)L.$$

State-dependency in the coefficients and variances are modeled as

$$d_i(n) = d_i^0 \exp(-n/\gamma) + d_i^\infty(1 - \exp(-n/\gamma))$$

and

$$\Sigma_i(n) = \Sigma_i^0 \exp(-n/\gamma) + \Sigma_i^\infty(1 - \exp(-n/\gamma)),$$

where d_i^0, d_i^∞, Σ_i^0, Σ_i^∞, and γ are all parameters to be estimated. These functional forms make $d_i(n)$ and $\Sigma_i(n)$ smooth monotonic functions of the trade intensity. They bound the coefficients between d_i^0 and d_i^∞ and the variances between Σ_i^0 and Σ_i^∞ as trade intensity varies between zero and infinity. The positive scaling parameter, γ, governs the rate at which $d_i(n)$ and $\Sigma_i(n)$ vary with the trade intensity. Although these functional forms are not motivated by theoretical considerations, they do not turn out to be unduly restrictive empirically.

The model described by equations (7.24)–(7.26) is estimated using the Generalized Method of Moments (GMM). This technique exploits the orthogonality of order flow with respect to the u_t and ω_t^o shocks and the orthogonality of the ξ_t shocks to lagged order flow. As with the estimation of the VARs, the estimates are computed from data collected during European trading hours. The appendix to this chapter provides further estimation details.

With the model estimates in hand, we can examine how transaction prices respond to dispersed information shocks. For this purpose, we combine (7.24)–(7.26) to get

$$\Delta S_t^o = B(L, n_t)\xi_t + u_t + \omega_t^o - \omega_{t-1}^o, \tag{7.27}$$

where $B(L, n) = D(L, n)C(L)$ for $o = \{a, b\}$. With the estimates of $D(L, n)$ and $C(L)$ we can now compute the impulse response of the change in the average transaction price following the arrival of a one-unit dispersed information shock while trade intensity remains at n from the coefficients in $B(L, n)$. The results of these calculations based on the Evans model estimates are shown in Figure 7.3. Trade intensity varies considerably in Evans' data set; the 50, 75, and 95 percentiles for the distribution of n are 60, 105, and 220 trades per 5-minute interval. Panel A reports the effects on the period-by-period average price changes, and panel B shows the accumulated response on the average price level when n is equal to 25, 100, and 150.

Figure 7.3 displays two noteworthy features. First, the dynamic response of prices seems to vary considerably with trade intensity. When the state of the market is characterized by low trade intensity, dispersed news has small temporary effects on the average price level. In market states where trading intensity is higher, dispersed information shocks have a much larger and long-lasting effect on the level of prices. The second noteworthy feature concerns the time of the peak response. In all cases dispersed shocks have their largest (positive) effect on price changes during the third period, 15 minutes after the shock. It appears to take some time before the transmission of information from customer flows affects the price-setting decisions of a significant number of dealers. This result is not inconsistent with rational dealer behavior. Remember that transparency in "direct" interdealer trading is very low, so dealers cannot observe the initial impact of dispersed information on the average transaction price in real time. Consequently, although the impulse responses show that transaction price changes are predictable, these patterns cannot be exploited by dealers following feedback-trading strategies.

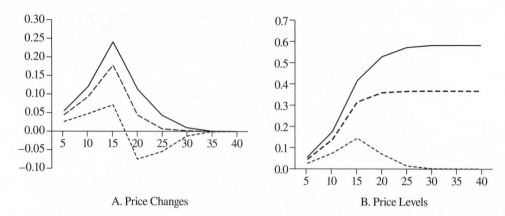

A. Price Changes   B. Price Levels

FIGURE 7.3   Impulse responses of average transaction prices to a one-unit positive shock in dispersed information at different levels of trade intensity, n: solid line, $n = 150$; dashed line, $n = 100$; short-dashed line, $n = 25$.

Equation (7.27) can also be used to decompose the variance of observed price changes into different theoretical components. In particular, consider the k-period price change, $\Delta^k S_t^o \equiv \Sigma_{i=0}^{k-1} \Delta S_{t+i}^o$, for $o = \{a, b\}$. Substituting for ΔS_t^o with (7.27) gives

$$\Delta^k S_t^o = \omega_t^o - \omega_{t-k}^o + \sum_{i=0}^{k-1} u_{t-i} + B(L, k, n_t)\xi_t, \tag{7.28}$$

where $B(L, k, n_t) = \sum_{i=0}^{k-1} B(L, L^i n_t)L^i$. Since the u_t, ξ_t, and ω_t^o shocks are mutually independent and serially uncorrelated, we can use (7.28) to write the variance of price changes as

$$\mathbb{V}(\Delta^k S_t^o) = \Sigma_\omega(n_t) + \Sigma_\omega(n_{t-k}) + \sum_{i=0}^{k-1} \Sigma_u(n_{t-i}) + \mathbb{V}\left(B(L, k, n_t)\xi_t\right). \tag{7.29}$$

The first two terms identify the contribution of the idiosyncratic sampling shocks to the variance. The contribution of CK news shocks is identified by the third term, whereas the fourth term shows the contribution of the dispersed information shocks.

Table 7.4 reports variance decompositions based on (7.29) for horizons, k (denoted in minutes), and trade intensities, n. Panel A shows the fraction of the price change variance attributable to sampling. According to these estimates, most of the short-term variability in prices is attributable to sampling unless trade intensity is high, for example, $n = 150$. Panel B reports the contribution of the dispersed information shocks. These estimates show that dispersed information is a more important source of price variation when trade intensity is high and the horizon is long.

There are two important points to take away from these findings. First, they appear consistent with the results obtained from intraday trading data passing through the electronic brokerages run by Reuters and EBS discussed earlier. In all cases, a significant fraction of the variation in FX prices is attributable to the arrival of orders. The consistency of this result across different trading platforms assures us that the underlying mechanism that links FX prices to order flows is not dependent on any one set of trading protocols—protocols that will inevitably change in the future.

TABLE 7.4
Variance Contributions

Trade intensity, n	Horizon k in minutes		
	5	60	120
A. $\mathbb{V}(\omega_t^o - \omega_{t-k}^o)/\mathbb{V}(\Delta^k S_t^o)$			
25	91.37%	47.64%	31.42%
100	69.61%	13.79%	7.33%
150	56.60%	6.88%	3.48%
B. $\mathbb{V}\left(B(L, k, n)\xi_t\right)/\mathbb{V}(\Delta^k S_t^o)$			
25	0.38%	0.74%	0.49%
100	3.25%	21.71%	24.10%
150	8.53%	42.22%	45.07%

Note: Variance contributions computed from estimates of the Evans Intraday model. Source: Evans (2002).

The second point concerns identification. Time series of trades and FX prices can be used to estimate a myriad of econometric models, from simple VARs to complex non-parametric models. The key challenge facing a researcher is not obtaining estimates that well characterize the time series properties of the data. Rather, it is developing a model in which the estimated residuals may be reasonably interpreted as estimates of particular economic shocks. This problem can only be addressed with a combination of economic theory and an understanding of how the data are generated by market activity.

7.2.4 Forecasting Order Flow and Feedback Trading

A number of recent studies have found that past changes in FX prices have forecasting power for order flows. For example, Daníelsson and Love (2006) find highly significant coefficient estimates on lagged price changes in the order flow equation of their simultaneous equation model. There is also evidence of forecastability of customer flows at the daily frequency. Sager and Taylor (2008) find that daily customer order flow data from JPMorgan Chase can be predicted with prior foreign exchange returns. Do these results establish that order flows largely reflect the actions of dealers and customers following feedback-trading strategies and, as such, convey rather little new price-relevant information?

The answer to this question is clearly no. From a theoretical perspective, changes in FX prices can be driven solely by the information conveyed by order flow which is itself forecastable using past changes in FX prices. Indeed, the PS model discussed in Chapter 6 has precisely this combination of features. Interdealer order flows are the proximate drivers of all the intraday changes in FX prices, but they depend in part on the public pre-existing FX holdings that are correlated with lagged FX price changes. The key point here is that it is the unexpected portion of order flow that conveys the price-relevant information to dealers, so the fact that order flow is to some extent forecastable does not negate its role as a conveyor of price-relevant information. In short, the fact that order flows are forecastable with prior changes in FX prices does not constitute evidence for the presence or absence of feedback trading.

To further analyze the potential significance of feedback trading, we can examine the profitability of trading rules based on forecasting equations for order flow in a particular data set. For example, using the Evans (2002) data, we can consider an intraday feedback trading rule of the form

$$\tau_t = \psi_1 \Delta S_{t-1} + \psi_2 \Delta S_{t-2} + \psi_3 \Delta S_{t-3} + \psi_4 \Delta S_{t-4} + \psi_5 \Delta S_{t-5} + \psi_6 \Delta S_{t-6}, \quad (7.30)$$

where τ_t represents the purchase of dollars during period t. The ψ_i coefficients determine the link between the history of FX price changes and the current trading decisions of a feedback trader. Our aim is to examine the profitability of following (7.30) when the values for the ψ_i coefficients are chosen to be consistent with characteristics of price changes and order flow in the data set. For the sake of simplicity, we ignore the transaction costs that arise from trading via bid-ask spreads. This means that the profitability estimates calculated in what follows *overstate* the actual profitability of following the feedback rule.

The profitability of following (7.30) can be measured in terms of DM and USD. Let $w_t^{DM} \equiv b_t^{DM} + S_t b_t^{\$}$ denote the DM value of wealth for the feedback trader at the start of period t, where S_t is defined as the DM/USD spot rate. The terms b_t^{DM} and $b_t^{\$}$ are the trader's DM and USD balances at the start of period t, which evolve according to $b_{t+1}^{DM} = b_t^{DM} - S_t \tau_t$ and $b_{t+1}^{\$} = b_t^{\$} + \tau_t$. Combining these equations with the definition of w_t^{DM} gives

$$w_{t+1}^{DM} = w_t^{DM} + \left(S_{t+1} - S_t\right)\left(b_t^{\$} + \tau_t\right) \quad (7.31)$$

and

$$w_{t+1}^{\$} = \frac{S_t}{S_{t+1}} w_t^{\$} + \frac{\left(S_{t+1} - S_t\right)}{S_{t+1}}\left(b_t^{\$} + \tau_t\right), \quad (7.32)$$

where $w_t^{\$} \equiv w_t^{DM}/S_t$ is the USD value of wealth. We measure the profitability of the trading rule in terms of the daily return on wealth in DMs, $r^{DM} = \ln w_{288}^{DM} - \ln w_1^{DM}$, and USDs, $r^{\$} = \ln w_{288}^{\$} - \ln w_1^{\$}$, and in terms of the daily profit in DMs, $\pi^{DM} = w_{288}^{DM} - w_1^{DM}$, and USDs, $\pi^{\$} = w_{288}^{\$} - w_1^{\$}$.[7]

To examine the profitability of following (7.30), we proceed as follows. First, we assume that each transaction is for $5 million and that trading intensity is constant at $n = 60$. To determine the form of the trading rule for day T, we compute the ψ_j coefficients in (7.30) as $\hat{\beta}_j(5/60)$, where $\hat{\beta}_j$ is the estimated coefficient on ΔS_{i-j} in the regression of x_t on $\{\Delta S_{t-j}\}_{j=1}^6$ estimated from day $T - 1$ order flow and price data. We then use the estimated trading rule together with price data from day T to

---

7. There are 288 5-minute observation windows in 24 hours, so differences between $t = 1$ and $t = 288$ represent daily changes.

TABLE 7.5
Profitability of Feedback Trading

	r^{DM}	π^{DM}	$r^{\$}$	$\pi^{\$}$
Median	−0.91%	−1.37m	−0.92%	−0.92m
p-Value	58.30%	58.30%	58.40%	58.40%

compute $r^{\$}$, r^{DM}, $\pi^{\$}$, and π^{DM}. This procedure is repeated for each day in the data set. Since the profitability of the trading rule varies stochastically with prices, we also compute the distribution of r^{DM}, $r^{\$}$, π^{DM}, and $\pi^{\$}$. For this purpose, we repeat our earlier calculations 1000 times using data generated from estimates of the Evans Intraday model with $n = 60$.

The upper row of Table 7.5 reports the median returns and profits measured in DMs and USD on a monthly basis from following the feedback-trading rule in (7.30). The median return and profits are all negative. The lower row of the table reports the probability of receiving a negative return or profit each day computed from distributions implied by estimates of the Evans Intraday model. Recall that these results do not take into account the transaction costs (associated with the bid-ask spread). As such, they represent an upper bound on the profitability of following such a rule in the actual market. With this perspective, it is clear that a trader would be rather fortunate to profit from following a feedback rule such as (7.30) consistent with the time series properties of order flow and prices in the Evans data set. In fact, the results show that such a strategy would most likely lead to significant trading losses.

We should emphasize that the aim of this discussion is not to refute the possibility that some dealers and customers follow feedback-trading strategies. Indeed, as we shall see in Chapter 8, there are very good reasons to believe that some dealer and customer trades are contingent on past price variations. At issue here is the interpretation of empirical findings showing that order flows are forecastable with prior prices. As a theoretical matter, forecastability in itself is uninformative about the presence of feedback trading. To go further, we need a theoretical framework to assess the profitability of feedback trading. The results in Table 7.5 show that turning the forecastability of order flows into a profitable trading strategy can be difficult.

7.3 Summary

- There is a strong positive contemporaneous correlation between daily changes in the price of FX and interdealer order flow. The correlation is robust to different forms of interdealer trading (e.g., "direct" and "indirect"), and appears across a wide cross-section of currencies. The contemporaneous relation between FX price changes and order flows is even stronger in a multicurrency setting. These results are consistent with the implications of the Portfolio Shifts model. As such, they imply that order flows are the proximate drivers of exchange rates because they convey dispersed price-relevant information that is incorporated into FX prices.

- The contribution of interdealer order flows to daily changes in exchange rates is much higher than that found for any other macroeconomic or financial variables.

- Daily changes in exchange rates are correlated with customer order flows, but the strength of this relationship is less than that found with interdealer flows. Disaggregated customer flows have more explanatory power for exchange-rate changes than aggregate flows. Their explanatory power is similar to that of interdealer flows over weekly and monthly horizons.

- The intraday analysis of FX prices and trading patterns can be examined in event time or clock time models. VAR models of FX prices and market orders from electronic brokerages imply that market orders are the proximate drivers of approximately 50 percent of the permanent variation in FX prices.

- VAR models are not well suited for analyzing decentralized trading data because there is no natural sequencing of market events. The Evans (2002) model incorporates features to account for the simultaneous trading with low transparency characteristic of "direct" interdealer trading. Estimates of this model illustrate the importance of allowing for state-dependency when studying intraday trading dynamics in clock time. They also corroborate the daily results regarding the contribution of order flow to FX price dynamics.

- The problem of Temporal Aggregation Bias arises when dealers are acting at a higher frequency than is being used in an empirical model. If dealers and/or customers follow feedback trading strategies that relate their orders to past FX price changes, temporal aggregation will bias estimates of how exchange rates respond to the information conveyed by order flow obtained from clock time models. There is evidence that this bias is significant, but it amplifies the impact of order flows on FX price changes. Feedback trading alone cannot account for the observed strong contemporaneous relation between exchange-rate changes and order flows.

7.4 Bibliography

In the past decade a large empirical literature has emerged examining spot rates and order flows. By our last count in the fall of 2009, there are now more than 250 papers that study the behavior of spot rates and order flows across many different currencies, in different trading environments, and at different frequencies. Obviously, this chapter does not present a comprehensive survey of this literature. Readers interested in more breadth and detail should consult the recent surveys by Osler (2008) and Sager and Taylor (2008).

One factor contributing to this surge in research has been the greater availability of trading data. The data used in the earliest research (e.g., Lyons 1995, Evans 2002, and Evans and Lyons 2002a) were collected by hand, which was a very time-consuming process. Fortunately, this is no longer necessary thanks to several developments in the FX market. First, since the late 1990s most interbank trading has taken place via the EBS and Reuters electronic brokerage systems. These systems now represent single electronic sources of data on interbank trading activity that simply did not exist more than a decade ago. Although data from these systems are not freely available, researchers are beginning to gain access to them (see, e.g., Chaboud, Chernenko, and Wright 2008; Chinn and Moore 2009; and Breedon, Rime, and Vitale 2010). Second, many large banks that are major participants in the FX market now collect data on their customer orders from around the world because they perceive that these data are useful for their own proprietary currency trading. These data are potentially very useful to researchers because customer order flows are the primary source of dispersed information in models of currency trading. Although banks have been (understandably) reluctant to give researchers access to these data, they are slowly becoming available (see, e.g., Marsh and O'Rourke 2005 and Evans and Lyons 2005b, 2006, and 2007). The chapters in Part III discuss how these data have been used to reveal the role order flow plays in linking spot rates to the macroeconomy. Finally, some central banks have recently begun efforts to collect FX trading data from the banks under their supervision. Unlike the customer flow data from individual banks, these data cover the entire market for some currencies. As these data-collection efforts continue, the data will become a very rich source of information on market-wide FX trading activity. In sum, although FX trading data is still not freely available, it is being collected on a much larger scale than ever before. Inevitably, researchers will gain access to these data in the future.

7.5 Review Questions

1. Designing a VAR: A researcher wishes to study the role of order flow in conveying private information in a spot FX market where trading activity varies considerably over each trading day. The researcher has 12 months of data on market orders and transaction prices from an electronic brokerage system that operates 24 hours a day, but 90 percent of the trading activity is concentrated between 7:00 and 9:00 A.M. GMT and between 1:00 and 2:00 P.M. GMT. During these periods trades take place as frequently as two to three per second. Outside these periods, there are often gaps of up to 15 minutes without a single trade. The researcher proposes estimating a VAR for the midpoint of transaction price changes and order flow.

   (a) Discuss the advantages and disadvantages of estimating the VAR in market time.

   (b) The researcher decides to estimate the VAR in clock time with a 5-minute observation window. What that are the advantages and potential drawbacks of this approach?

   (c) Another researcher suggests that the model be estimated in clock time with a 1-minute observation window, but only using data taken between 7:00 and 9:00 A.M. and between 1:00 and 2:00 P.M. What are the advantages and pitfalls of this alternative?

2. Different Data Sources: FX trading data may originate from: (i) the customer and interdealer trades of an individual bank, (ii) an electronic system recording direct interdealer trading, or (iii) an electronic limit-order book. In contrast, theoretical models of FX trading make predictions concerning aggregate customer and interdealer order flows.

(a) Can order flow constructed from the customer trades of a single bank be used to study the impact of aggregate customer order flow on spot rate dynamics? If so, why and how? If not, why not?

(b) In the equilibrium of the Portfolio Shifts model presented in Chapter 6, there is no difference between the trades initiated by dealers with other dealers and the market orders they submit to the broker. In reality there are several differences between direct and indirect interdealer trades. What are the key differences, and how should they be accounted for when estimating empirical models in intraday data?

3. Feedback Trading: Assess the veracity of the following statements.

(a) If dealers follow feedback trading strategies, past changes in transaction prices should have forecasting power for future interdealer order flow.

(b) We can test for the presence of feedback trading by examining the forecastability of order flow with past price changes.

(c) In the presence of feedback trading, estimates of the price impact of order flow carrying private information computed from a VAR containing order flow and spot price changes are biased upward.

7.A Appendix

One complication of estimating a clock time trading model is that there may be many time periods during which no market events take place. One approach to this problem is to substitute imputed values for the missing observations. These imputations can be calculated in a number of ways, from simply averaging to Bayesian estimation via the Kalman filter. Alternatively, the model can be estimated by the GMM using moments constructed without the missing observations, as in Evans (2002). This method is computationally straightforward and is applicable in cases where trading activity is concentrated in part of the day (e.g., European trading hours for spot FX). An overview of GMM can be found in Chapter 11.

To apply the GMM procedure, let us assume that the empirical model we want to estimate can be written in the state-space form:

$$\mathcal{X}_t = \mathcal{A}\mathcal{X}_{t-1} + \mathcal{E}_t, \quad \mathcal{Y}_t = \mathcal{C}\mathcal{X}_t, \tag{7.33}$$

where $\mathcal{X}_t$ is a q-dimensioned state vector and $\mathcal{Y}_t$ is a r-dimensioned vector of observed variables; $\mathcal{E}_t$ is a q-dimensioned vector of shocks with zero means that are uncorrelated with $\mathcal{X}_{t-1}$, serially uncorrelated, and have covariance matrix $\mathcal{S}$. We also assume the existence of a j-dimensioned vector of instruments, $\mathcal{Z}_t$, with the property $\mathbb{CV}(\mathcal{Y}_t, \mathcal{Z}'_{t-i}) = \mathbf{0}$ for $i \geq 0$.

Although the forms of $\mathcal{A}$, $\mathcal{C}$, and $\mathcal{S}$ vary according to the particular application, we assume that the eigenvalues of $\mathcal{A}$ lie inside the unit circle so that $\mathcal{X}_t$ and $\mathcal{Y}_t$ follow covariance-stationary processes. Thus, the unconditional means of $\mathcal{X}_t$ and $\mathcal{Y}_t$ are, respectively, equal to a q- and r-dimensioned vector of zeros. Equation (7.33) also implies that the covariance of the states, $\Gamma(k) \equiv \mathbb{CV}(\mathcal{X}_t, \mathcal{X}'_{t-k})$, is computed as

$\Gamma(k) = \mathcal{A}\Gamma(k-1)$ with $\Gamma(0) = \text{vec}^{-1}\left[(I - \mathcal{A} \otimes \mathcal{A})^{-1}\text{vec}(\mathcal{S})\right]$. The covariance of the observed variables is therefore given by

$$\mathbb{CV}(\mathcal{Y}_t'\mathcal{Y}_{t-k}') \equiv \gamma(k) = \mathcal{C}\Gamma(k)\mathcal{C}'. \tag{7.34}$$

Let θ represent the vector of parameters to be estimated. As in the standard GMM case, we consider orthogonality conditions of the form

$$E\left[\mathcal{M}_t(k;\theta)\right] = 0, \tag{7.35}$$

where

$$\mathcal{M}_t(k;\theta) = \mathcal{D}(k)\left[\begin{array}{c} \text{vec}(\mathcal{Y}_t\mathcal{Z}_{t-k}') \\ \text{vec}(\mathcal{Y}_t\mathcal{Y}_{t-k}' - \gamma(k;\theta)) \end{array}\right]$$

for $k = 0, 1, \ldots, K$. The vector $\mathcal{D}(k)$ is a vector of ones and zeros that selects the moments to be included in $\mathcal{M}_t(k;\theta)$. Equation (7.35) gives a maximum of $rj + r^2$ independent conditions when $k > 0$ and $rj + r(r+1)/2$ conditions when $k = 0$.

To compute the GMM estimates, let $\mathcal{M}_t(\theta) = [\mathcal{M}_t(0;\theta), \mathcal{M}_t(1;\theta), \ldots, \mathcal{M}_t(K;\theta)]'$ be a vector of selected moment conditions. Although all the elements of $\mathcal{M}_t(\theta)$ can be computed for any period t, if a particular element involves a value for $\mathcal{Y}_t$ or $\mathcal{Y}_{t-k}$ that has missing observations, the result is also designated as missing. This holds true irrespective of the value of θ, so the set of missing elements in $\mathcal{M}_t(\theta)$ will not vary with θ for a particular t. Let $\mathcal{T} = \{t_1^*, t_2^*, \ldots, t_T^*\}$ denote the set of observations for which none of the elements in $\mathcal{M}_t(\cdot)$ is missing. The estimates of θ are found by minimizing

$$\mathcal{Q}(\theta) = \mathcal{M}_{\mathcal{T}^*}(\theta)'\mathcal{W}^{-1}\mathcal{M}_{\mathcal{T}^*}(\theta), \tag{7.36}$$

where $\mathcal{M}_{\mathcal{T}^*}(\theta) = \frac{1}{\mathcal{T}^*}\sum_{\mathcal{T}} \mathcal{M}_t(\theta)$, with $\mathcal{T}^*$ equal to the number of observations in $\mathcal{T}$.

As in standard GMM estimation, we can obtain asymptotically efficient estimates with a two-step procedure. In the first step, we minimize $\mathcal{Q}(\theta)$ with $\mathcal{W}$ equal to the identity to obtain consistent estimates of θ, $\tilde{\theta}$. In the second step, we use $\tilde{\theta}$ to calculate a consistent estimate of the optimal weighting matrix, $\widetilde{\mathcal{W}}$. The form of this weighting matrix varies across applications according to whether elements of $\mathcal{M}_t(\theta)$ are serially correlated under the null hypothesis of a correctly specified model. The GMM estimates, $\hat{\theta}$, are then found by minimizing (7.36) with $\mathcal{W} = \widetilde{\mathcal{W}}$. The estimated asymptotic covariance matrix of $\hat{\theta}$ is given by $\widehat{\mathcal{V}} = [\widehat{\mathcal{G}}\widetilde{\mathcal{W}}^{-1}\widehat{\mathcal{G}}']^{-1}$, where $\widehat{\mathcal{G}} = \partial\mathcal{M}_{\mathcal{T}^*}(\hat{\theta})/\partial\theta'$.

Example 1: VAR Estimation

Suppose we wish to estimate a second-order VAR for order flow and quote revision from data collected over a 5-minute observation window during the hours of European trading, that is, 6:00 A.M. to 6:00 P.M. London time. The equations of the VAR are

$$\left[\begin{array}{c} T_t \\ \Delta S_{t+1} \end{array}\right] = \left[\begin{array}{cc} a_{11}^1 & a_{12}^1 \\ a_{21}^1 & a_{22}^1 \end{array}\right]\left[\begin{array}{c} T_{t-1} \\ \Delta S_t \end{array}\right] + \left[\begin{array}{cc} a_{11}^2 & a_{12}^2 \\ a_{21}^2 & a_{22}^2 \end{array}\right]\left[\begin{array}{c} T_{t-2} \\ \Delta S_{t-1} \end{array}\right] + \left[\begin{array}{c} v_{1,t} \\ v_{2,t} \end{array}\right],$$

which can be rewritten in state-space form as

$$
\mathcal{X}_t \equiv \begin{bmatrix} T_t \\ \Delta S_{t+1} \\ T_{t-1} \\ \Delta S_t \end{bmatrix} = \begin{bmatrix} a_{11}^1 & a_{12}^1 & a_{11}^2 & a_{12}^2 \\ a_{21}^1 & a_{22}^1 & a_{21}^2 & a_{22}^2 \\ 1 & 0 & 0 & 0 \\ 0 & 1 & 0 & 0 \end{bmatrix} \begin{bmatrix} T_{t-1} \\ \Delta S_t \\ T_{t-2} \\ \Delta S_{t-1} \end{bmatrix} + \begin{bmatrix} v_{1,t} \\ v_{2,t} \\ 0 \\ 0 \end{bmatrix},
$$

$$
\mathcal{Y}_t \equiv \begin{bmatrix} T_t \\ \Delta S_{t+1} \end{bmatrix} = \begin{bmatrix} 1 & 0 & 0 & 0 \\ 0 & 1 & 0 & 0 \end{bmatrix} \begin{bmatrix} T_t \\ \Delta S_{t+1} \\ T_{t-1} \\ \Delta S_t \end{bmatrix}.
$$

To compute the GMM estimates of the a_{nm}^i coefficients and the covariance of the $v_{i,t}$ shocks, we treat all values in the $\mathcal{Y}_t$ vector that fall outside 6:00 A.M. to 6:00 P.M. London time as missing observations. The GMM estimates can now be computed by minimizing (7.36) with $M_t(k;\theta) = \mathrm{vec}(\mathcal{Y}_t\mathcal{Y}_{t-k}' - \gamma(k;\theta))$ for $k = \{0, 1, \ldots, K\}$.

Example 2: Estimation of the Evans Intraday Model

The estimation method can also be applied to models with state-dependency, such as the Evans Intraday model. In particular, the state-space form for equations (7.24) and (7.25) is

$$
\mathcal{X}_t \equiv \begin{bmatrix} \omega_t^a \\ \omega_t^b \\ \omega_{t-1}^a \\ \omega_{t-1}^b \\ u_t \end{bmatrix} = \begin{bmatrix} 0 & 0 & 0 & 0 & 0 \\ 0 & 0 & 0 & 0 & 0 \\ 1 & 0 & 0 & 0 & 0 \\ 0 & 1 & 0 & 0 & 0 \\ 0 & 0 & 0 & 0 & 0 \end{bmatrix} \begin{bmatrix} \omega_{t-1}^a \\ \omega_{t-1}^b \\ \omega_{t-2}^a \\ \omega_{t-2}^b \\ u_{t-1} \end{bmatrix} + \begin{bmatrix} \omega_t^a \\ \omega_t^b \\ 0 \\ 0 \\ u_t \end{bmatrix},
$$

with

$$
\mathcal{Y}_t \equiv \begin{bmatrix} \Delta S_t^a - \sum_{i=1}^{i=-4} d_i(n_t)x_{t-i} \\ \Delta S_t^b - \sum_{i=1}^{i=-4} d_i(n_t)x_{t-i} \end{bmatrix} = \begin{bmatrix} 1 & 0 & -1 & 0 & 1 \\ 0 & 1 & 0 & -1 & 1 \end{bmatrix} \begin{bmatrix} \omega_t^a \\ \omega_t^b \\ \omega_{t-1}^a \\ \omega_{t-1}^b \\ u_t \end{bmatrix}.
$$

These equations take the form of (7.33) except that the covariance matrix of the shock vector $\mathcal{E}_t$ is state-dependent:

$$
\mathcal{S}(n_t) = \begin{bmatrix} \Sigma_\omega(n_t) & 0 & 0 & 0 & 0 \\ 0 & \Sigma_\omega(n_t) & 0 & 0 & 0 \\ 0 & 0 & 0 & 0 & 0 \\ 0 & 0 & 0 & 0 & 0 \\ 0 & 0 & 0 & 0 & \Sigma_u(n_t) \end{bmatrix}.
$$

Evans (2002) computes the GMM estimates using

$$
\mathcal{Z}_t' = [x_{t-1}, \ldots, x_{t+4}, x_{t-1}\exp(-n_t/100), \ldots, x_{t+4}\exp(-n_t/100)],
$$

as instruments, and

$$\mathcal{M}_t(0;\theta) = \begin{bmatrix} \text{vec}(\mathcal{Y}_t \mathcal{Z}_t') \\ \text{vec}(\mathcal{Y}_t \mathcal{Y}_t') - \gamma_t(0;\theta) \end{bmatrix}, \qquad \mathcal{M}_t(k;\theta) = \text{vec}(\mathcal{Y}_t \mathcal{Y}_{t-k}') - \gamma(k;\theta,n_t),$$

with $k = 1, 2$, as moments, where

$$\gamma(0;\theta,n_t) = \begin{bmatrix} \Sigma_\omega(n_t) + \Sigma_\omega(n_{t-1}) + \Sigma_\varepsilon(n_t) & \Sigma_\varepsilon(n_t) \\ \Sigma_\varepsilon(n_t) & \Sigma_\omega(n_t) + \Sigma_\omega(n_{t-1}) + \Sigma_\varepsilon(n_t) \end{bmatrix},$$

$$\gamma_t(1;\theta,n_t) = \begin{bmatrix} -\Sigma_\omega(n_{t-1}) & 0 \\ 0 & -\Sigma_\omega(n_{t-1}) \end{bmatrix},$$

and

$$\gamma_t(2;\theta,n_t) = \begin{bmatrix} 0 & 0 \\ 0 & 0 \end{bmatrix}.$$

All the values in the $\mathcal{Y}_t$ and $\mathcal{Z}_t$ vectors that fall outside 6:00 A.M. to 6:00 P.M. London time are treated as missing observations.

CHAPTER 8

Identifying Order Flow

In the preceding two chapters we saw that exchange-rate dynamics are strongly linked to the behavior of order flow, both theoretically and empirically. In this chapter we consider the wider implications of these findings. In particular, we address the following questions:

1. Can order flow be identified in traditional exchange-rate models?
2. Is it possible to construct reliable measures of order flow without the use of detailed transaction data?

Unlike traditional exchange-rate models, the Portfolio Shifts model describes the behavior of FX dealers in great detail. As a result, it is straightforward to identify order flow and examine the role it plays in driving the dynamics of the spot rate. In particular, the model shows that there should be a strong contemporaneous correlation between order flow and changes in the spot rate because order flow aggregates price-relevant information that is used by dealers to change their FX price quotes. Question 1 is motivated by the need to derive similar empirical predictions concerning information transmission in traditional exchange-rate models that do not describe the behavior of FX dealers.

Data availability motivates question 2. It is straightforward to construct an empirical measure of order flow that closely corresponds to order flow identified in a theoretical model when we have the transaction records from direct interdealer or customer-dealer trading. Unfortunately, access to such data is comparatively rare. Most trading in both the retail and interbank markets now takes place via electronic brokerages and/or crossing networks, so many newly available data do not come in a form that directly corresponds to the structure of existing micro-based models. Understanding how these data can be used to study the flow of information transmission in the FX market is critical if the empirical analysis of currency-trading models is to develop further.

8.1 Order Flow in a Rational Expectations Model

This section discusses the identification of order flow in an exchange-rate model that does not explicitly derive the behavior of FX market participants (i.e., FX dealers, brokers, and customers). Specifically, we focus on how order flow can be identified in the rational expectations exchange-rate model we described in Chapter 4. There we used the fictional mechanism of the Walrasian auctioneer to derive the equilibrium behavior of the spot exchange rate in a simple two-country setting where heterogeneous households had limited information about the state of the economy. Here we replace the Walrasian auctioneer by a trading mechanism that supports the equilibrium and allows us to identify the role of order flow as an aggregator and conveyor of information, an idea that was first suggested by Bacchetta and van Wincoop (2006).

Before we begin, it is worth noting that the exchange-rate model under consideration is populated by heterogeneous households. If this were not the case, identifying order flow would be a hopeless task because households with the same preferences, budget constraints, and information would never have any incentive to trade with one another. Clearly, there must be some underlying motive for FX trade if we are to identify order flow in any exchange-rate model.

8.1.1 Structure of the Model

Let us briefly review the structure of the model. There is a continuum of households on the unit interval [0,1] that are split between the home and foreign countries, which, once again, we refer to as the United States and Europe, respectively. U.S. households are indexed by $h \in [0, a)$ and E.U. households by $\hat{h} \in [a, 1]$, where a denotes the U.S. country's share of the world population, which we assume is close to one. There are overlapping generations of households that live for two periods. In the first period, each household receives an endowment, which it invests in bonds and money. It also supplies labor inelastically to a production process. In the second period, each household consumes the income it receives from production and its accumulated wealth. Household preferences are defined in terms of the consumption of a single good. The only other agents in the economy are the two central banks. The Federal Reserve (FED) keeps the U.S. money supply constant and the European Central Bank (ECB) changes the E.U. money supply according to a given process.

The problem facing a young U.S. household h in period t is to choose how to allocate an endowment, W_t^h, between U.S. bonds, B_t^h, E.U. bonds, $\hat{B}_t^h$, and dollars, M_t^h, to maximize expected utility defined over next period's consumption C_{t+1}^h:

$$\mathcal{U}_t^h = \mathbb{E}_t^h \big[-\exp(-\gamma C_{t+1}^h) \big], \tag{8.1}$$

with $\gamma > 0$. Here $\mathbb{E}_t^h [.]$ denotes expectations conditioned on Ω_t^h, the information available to household h in period t. The household's budget constraint is

$$C_{t+1}^h \le \mathcal{R}_{t+1}^B W_t^h + \mathcal{R}_{t+1}^{\hat{B}} \widehat{\mathfrak{B}}_t^h + \mathcal{R}_{t+1}^M \mathfrak{M}_t^h + Y_{t+1}^h, \tag{8.2}$$

where Y_{t+1}^h is the income from production, $\mathfrak{M}_t^h = M_t^h / P_t$ denotes real balances, and $\widehat{\mathfrak{B}}_t^h = S_t \hat{B}_t^h / P_t$ denotes the real value of E.U. bond holdings. The USD/EUR spot rate is S_t and the U.S. price level is P_t. The real return on U.S. bonds, $\mathcal{R}_{t+1}^B$, and the excess returns on E.U. bonds and dollars, $\mathcal{R}_{t+1}^{\hat{B}}$ and $\mathcal{R}_{t+1}^M$, are approximated by

$$\mathcal{R}_{t+1}^B \cong 1 + r_t - \Delta p_{t+1}, \quad \mathcal{R}_{t+1}^{\hat{B}} \cong s_{t+1} - s_t + \hat{r}_t - r_t, \quad \text{and} \quad \mathcal{R}_{t+1}^M \cong -r_t, \tag{8.3}$$

where r_t and $\hat{r}_t$ denote the nominal interest rates on U.S. and E.U. bonds. As usual, lowercase letters denote natural logs, for example, $s_t = \ln S_t$.

The income household h receives when it is old depends on the future exchange rate and real balances:

$$Y_{t+1}^h = \lambda_t^h s_{t+1} - \frac{1}{\alpha} \mathfrak{M}_t^h (\ln \mathfrak{M}_t^h - 1), \tag{8.4}$$

with $\alpha > 0$. The parameter λ_t^h measures the exchange-rate exposure of nonasset income to the household and gives rise to a hedging demand for E.U. bonds. This is the sole source of heterogeneity in the model. Specifically, λ_t^h comprises a common component, λ_t, and an idiosyncratic component ξ_t^h:

$$\lambda_t^h = \lambda_t + \xi_t^h, \tag{8.5}$$

where $\xi_t^h \sim \text{i.i.d.} N(0, \sigma_\xi^2)$, with $\mathbb{E}[\xi_t^h \xi_t^n] = 0$ for all $n \neq h \in [0, a)$. Thus, the idiosyncratic components are mean-zero normally distributed random variables that are uncorrelated across households. The average value of λ_t^h across all U.S. households is λ_t, which follows a random walk:

$$\lambda_t = \lambda_{t-1} + v_t, \tag{8.6}$$

where $v_t \sim \text{i.i.d.} N(0, \sigma_v^2)$.

As in standard monetary models, the FED and ECB have complete control over the money supplies, M_t and $\hat{M}_t$, respectively. We further assume that the U.S. money supply is fixed at M and that the log E.U. money supply, $\hat{m}_t = \ln \hat{M}_t$, follows an AR(1) process:

$$\hat{m}_t = \hat{m} + \rho(\hat{m}_{t-1} - \hat{m}) + \hat{u}_t, \tag{8.7}$$

where $\hat{u}_t \sim \text{i.i.d.} N(0, \sigma^2)$, with $|\rho| < 1$.

8.1.2 Walrasian Equilibrium

To establish a benchmark for what follows, let us first find the equilibrium assuming the presence of the Walrasian auctioneer. For this purpose, we must first specify the information available to each U.S. household. We assume that all households observe current prices, P_t and $\hat{P}_t$, interest rates, r_t and $\hat{r}_t$, the spot exchange rate, S_t, and the foreign money stock, $\hat{M}_t$, in period t. Each household also knows the value of its own hedging parameter, λ_t^h, but not the values for other households. It also knows the average value of the hedging parameter from last period, λ_{t-1}. With these assumptions, the evolution of household h's information between periods $t - 1$ and t is represented by

$$\Omega_t^h = \left\{ \lambda_t^h, \hat{M}_t, P_t, \hat{P}_t, r_t, \hat{r}_t, S_t, \lambda_{t-1} \right\} \cup \Omega_{t-1}^h. \tag{8.8}$$

All households also understand the structure of production, preferences, and the money supply process.

As in Chapter 4, we solve for the Walrasian equilibrium using the conjecture and verify method. Specifically, if we assume that the U.S. real interest rate is constant and that E.U. bonds are in zero net supply, it is straightforward to verify that the equilibrium log spot rate is

$$s_t = s - \frac{1-b}{1-b\rho}(\hat{m}_t - \hat{m}) - \frac{b\gamma\sigma_e^2}{1-b}\lambda_t, \tag{8.9}$$

where s is a constant, $b = \alpha/(1+\alpha)$, and $\sigma_s^2 = \mathbb{V}_t^h[s_{t+1}]$ is the conditional variance of the future log spot rate.

Two features of the equilibrium are worth noting. First, the exchange rate is Strong-form efficient. Equation (8.9) shows that all households can precisely infer the value of λ_t from observations on the foreign money stock and the equilibrium exchange rate. The second feature concerns the equilibrium asset holdings and trading patterns. The real value of E.U. bonds held by U.S. household h is

$$\widehat{\mathfrak{B}}_t^h = \frac{S_t\hat{B}_t^h}{P_t} = \frac{1}{\gamma\sigma_s^2}(\mathbb{E}_t^h\Delta s_{t+1} + \hat{r}_t - r_t) - \lambda_t^h. \tag{8.10}$$

Substituting for the log excess return implied by (8.9) and the money supply process in (8.7) in (8.10) gives

$$\widehat{\mathfrak{B}}_t^h = -(\lambda_t^h - \lambda_t) = -\xi_t^h. \tag{8.11}$$

Thus, the equilibrium bond holdings of each household depend only on the idiosyncratic component of their hedging exposure, ξ_t^h. This means that households trade with each other from one period to the next, but the resulting trading patterns contain no price-relevant information for the exchange rate. For example, (8.11) implies that household h will sell E.U. household bonds to other households when $\Delta\widehat{\mathfrak{B}}_t^h = -\Delta\xi_t^h < 0$. These transactions depend only on the values of ξ_t^h and ξ_{t-1}^h, shocks that have no effect on the equilibrium exchange rate. Consequently, it is not possible to infer *any* information from the trading patterns in this equilibrium that is relevant for the determination of the spot exchange rate.

8.1.3 Supporting the Equilibrium via Trade in a Limit-Order Market

We now examine whether the Walrasian equilibrium we have just described can be achieved if the Walrasian auctioneer is replaced by an explicit trading mechanism—a limit-order market. The use of this mechanism allows us to avoid modeling the behavior of FX dealers, but it does necessitate two modifications. First, we have to amend our assumption in (8.8) concerning the information available to each household. Second, we have to specify how households trade in the limit-order market. Let us consider these amendments in turn.

We continue to assume that each household h learns the value of the E.U. money stock, $\hat{M}_t$, and its own hedging parameter, λ_t^h, at the start of period t, together with the average value of the hedging parameter from last period, λ_{t-1}. We denote this information set by Ψ_t^h. Households also learn from the trading process that takes place during each period. In particular, all households observe aggregate order flow, Z_t, prices, interest rates, and the exchange rate that are determined by trading. We denote the information of household h at the end of period t by Φ_t^h. The evolution of household h's information is thus described by

$$\Psi_t^h = \left\{ \lambda_t^h, \hat{M}_t, \lambda_{t-1} \right\} \cup \Phi_{t-1}^h \quad \text{and} \quad \Phi_t^h = \left\{ P_t, \hat{P}_t, r_t, \hat{r}_t, S_t, Z_t \right\} \cup \Psi_t^h. \quad (8.12)$$

This information specification differs from the one used to derive the Walrasian equilibrium in (8.8) because we have to distinguish between the information available before the start of period-t trading, Ψ_t^h, and the information available after period-t trading, Φ_t^h. In particular, it makes no sense to assume that households know prices, interest rates, and the exchange rate prior to trading if the values for these variables are to be determined by the outcome of a trading process that reveals new price-relevant information. For this reason, Ψ_t^h is a subset of the information set Ω_t^h specified in (8.8). To show that trading can support the equilibrium, we establish that trades in the limit-order market based on Ψ_t^h provide the same information to households as the Walrasian auctioneer (i.e., $\Phi_t^h = \Omega_t^h$ for all h).

The second amendment to the model concerns the introduction of trading. We now assume that all households trade FX via a limit-order market. Recall that trading in a limit-order market takes place via limit and market orders. Specifically, a limit-order purchase for FX is an instruction to purchase a specific quantity of foreign currency up to a maximum price (the limit buy price); a limit-order sale for FX is an instruction to sell a specified quantity of FX above a minimum price (the limit sell price). By contrast, a market order to purchase (sell) FX is an instruction to buy (sell) a specified quantity of foreign currency at the best prevailing price.

Each period is split into multiple rounds of trading that follow a simple protocol. At the start of a round, each household has the opportunity to place a limit order to buy or sell FX. Limit orders are publicly observed. Each household then has the opportunity to submit market buy or sell orders. Market orders are submitted simultaneously and are processed as a batch: Market orders to purchase FX are aggregated, matched with the best limit sell orders, and the aggregate transaction is split equally among the participating households. Transactions initiated by market orders to sell FX are allocated in an analogous manner.

In this model one round of trading is sufficient to reveal the information necessary to support the Walrasian equilibrium. Specifically, the equilibrium exchange rate will emerge as the best limit price submitted by households at the start of the second trading round. From this point onward, the order flow induced by subsequent market orders contains no information that induces a change in the structure of limit orders, thereby establishing the equilibrium exchange rate for period t.

To implement the trading protocol, we must specify how households determine their choice of limit and market orders. Here we make two assumptions:

A1:   Each household submits limit orders consistent with its expected demand for E.U. bonds conditioned only on common prior information, $\Psi_t \equiv \cap_h \Psi_t^h$.

A2:   Each household submits market orders to fill the gap between its desired holdings of E.U. bonds based on prior private information, Ψ_t^h, and its expected holdings based on Ψ_t.

The rationale behind these assumptions is straightforward. Since limit orders are publicly observable, if a household submitted a limit order to achieve its desired portfolio based on private information, that private information would become publicly known before the household had the opportunity to trade. Alternatively, if the limit order is a function of only public information, as assumption A1 implies, the household reveals nothing about its private information until after it has had the opportunity to achieve its desired portfolio through the submission of a market order.

To show that this trading protocol can support the Walrasian equilibrium, we once again use the conjecture and verify method. First we derive the limit orders of households implied by A1 under the assumption that the exchange rate follows the equilibrium process in (8.9). Next we derive the market orders of each household and the resulting order flow, Z_t, from the first round of trading. Finally we show that the conjectured value for the equilibrium exchange rate is exactly the same as the best limit prices in the second round.

Limit Orders

We begin by deriving the limit orders submitted in round I. For this purpose, we first identify the demand for E.U. bonds by household h based on prior private information, Ψ_t^h. As before, log excess returns on E.U. bonds are conditionally normally distributed, so we can write household h's demand as

$$\widehat{\mathfrak{B}}_t^h = \frac{1}{\gamma \omega_s^2} \mathbb{E}[s_{t+1} - s_{t:1}^* + \hat{r}_t - r_t | \Psi_t^h] - \lambda_t^h, \tag{8.13}$$

where $\omega_s^2 = \mathbb{V}[s_{t+1} - s_{t:1}^* + \hat{r}_t - r_t | \Psi_t^h]$. Note that this demand function depends on the log spot exchange rate at which the household can trade in round I, $s_{t:1}^*$, rather than the Walrasian period-t rate, s_t.

Next, we split the demand for E.U. household bonds into two components:

$$\widehat{\mathfrak{B}}_t^h = \widehat{\mathfrak{B}}_t + \nabla \widehat{\mathfrak{B}}_t^h, \tag{8.14}$$

where $\widehat{\mathfrak{B}}_t = \mathbb{E}[\widehat{\mathfrak{B}}_t^h | \Psi_t]$ identifies expected demand based on prior common information and $\nabla \widehat{\mathfrak{B}}_t^h = \widehat{\mathfrak{B}}_t^h - \mathbb{E}[\widehat{\mathfrak{B}}_t^h | \Psi_t]$. We use the inverse demand function implied by $\widehat{\mathfrak{B}}_t$ in the conjectured equilibrium to identify the limit orders placed by each household. For this purpose, we take expectations conditioned on Ψ_t on both sides of (8.13). After some simple rearrangement, we get

$$s_{t:1}^* = \mathbb{E}[s_t | \Psi_t] - \gamma \omega_s^2 \lambda_{t-1} + \mathbb{E}[\Delta s_{t+1} + \hat{r}_t - r_t | \Psi_t] - \gamma \omega_s^2 \mathbb{E}[\widehat{\mathfrak{B}}_t^h | \Psi_t].$$

Note that the third term on the right-hand side identifies the expected log excess return on E.U. bonds in the Walrasian equilibrium conditioned on prior common information. Using (8.9) to evaluate this term produces $\mathbb{E}[\Delta s_{t+1} + \hat{r}_t - r_t | \Psi_t] = \gamma \sigma_s^2 \lambda_{t-1}$, so the preceding expression becomes

$$s_{t:1}^* = \mathbb{E}[s_t | \Psi_t] - \gamma (\omega_s^2 - \sigma_s^2) \lambda_{t-1} - \gamma \omega_s^2 \mathbb{E}[\widehat{\mathfrak{B}}_t^h | \Psi_t]. \tag{8.15}$$

We can use this equation to identify the prices at which the household would submit limit orders to buy and sell foreign currency. Consider the pricing of a limit order to sell Z dollars worth of E.U. bonds. If the limit order is matched with a market order, the value of the household's bond holdings will be $\widehat{\mathscr{B}}_t^h = \widehat{\mathscr{B}}_{t-1}^h - Z$. Now, equation (8.11) shows that in the Walrasian equilibrium $\widehat{\mathscr{B}}_{t-1}^h = -\xi_{t-1}^h$. Thus, if trading via the limit-order market supports this equilibrium, $\mathbb{E}[\widehat{\mathscr{B}}_{t-1}^h|\Psi_t] = 0$, $\mathbb{E}[\widehat{\mathscr{B}}_t^h|\Psi_t] = \mathbb{E}[\widehat{\mathscr{B}}_{t-1}^h|\Psi_t] - Z = -Z$, and (8.15) becomes

$$s_{t:1}^* = \mathbb{E}[s_t|\Psi_t] - \gamma(\omega_s^2 - \sigma_s^2)\lambda_{t-1} + \gamma\omega_s^2 Z. \tag{8.16}$$

Equation (8.16) identifies the log price for FX at which households will fill an incoming market order to buy Z dollars worth of E.U. bonds. Thus, the values of $s_{t:1}^*$ corresponding to positive (negative) values for Z denote limit sell (buy) prices for transactions involving $|Z|$ dollars worth of E.U. bonds. Note that the spread between the limit buy and sell prices disappears as the order size $|Z|$ tends to zero. This feature arises because $s_{t:1}^*$ identifies the price at which the household's expected demand for E.U. bonds, $\mathbb{E}[\widehat{\mathscr{B}}_t^h|\Psi_t]$, equals $-Z$. As such, the limit price does not take into account the possibility that market orders convey information about the Walrasian level of the exchange rate, s_t.

Equation (8.16) also implies that limit prices take into account the expected hedging properties of E.U. bonds. Since σ_s^2 and ω_s^2 are the variances of log excess returns conditioned on Ψ_t^h and Ψ_t, the coefficient on λ_{t-1} is positive so the limit prices are decreasing in the expected aggregate hedging parameter, $\mathbb{E}[\lambda_t|\Psi_t] = \lambda_{t-1}$. The reason is that the expected excess return necessary to compensate a household for the hedging properties of a given bond position becomes smaller as more information about the future exchange rate becomes available. Thus, if λ_{t-1} is positive, the compensating excess return must fall during period-t trading as more information becomes known. This, in turn, means that the price at which E.U. bonds can be traded must rise during period t. As a result, the limit buy and sell prices must converge (as Z tends to zero) at a level below $\mathbb{E}[s_t|\Psi_t]$, as indicated by equation (8.16).

Market Orders and Order Flow

Each household submits market orders to achieve its desired E.U. bond position, $\widehat{\mathscr{B}}_t^h$, given its holdings at the start of the period, $\widehat{\mathscr{B}}_{t-1}^h$, and its expectations concerning the incoming market orders of others. The dollar value of market orders to purchase E.U. bonds by household h is therefore given by

$$Z_{t:1}^h = \mathbb{E}[Z_{t:1}|\Psi_t^h] + \widehat{\mathscr{B}}_t^h - \widehat{\mathscr{B}}_{t-1}^h, \tag{8.17}$$

where $Z_{t:1}$ denotes the dollar value of market orders that are matched with household h's limit orders.

To evaluate the expression in (8.17), we first note that $\frac{1}{a}\int_0^a \widehat{\mathscr{B}}_t^h dh = 0$ under market clearing, so taking expectations conditioned on common prior information gives $\frac{1}{a}\int_0^a \mathbb{E}[\widehat{\mathscr{B}}_t^h|\Psi_t]\,dh = \bar{\mathscr{B}}_t = 0$. Thus, to be consistent with market clearing, equation (8.14) implies that household h's demand for E.U. household bonds is given by $\check{\mathscr{B}}_t^h = \nabla\widehat{\mathscr{B}}_t^h = \widehat{\mathscr{B}}_t^h - \mathbb{E}[\widehat{\mathscr{B}}_t^h|\Psi_t]$. Substituting for $\widehat{\mathscr{B}}_t^h$ from (8.13) in this expression gives

$$\widehat{\mathfrak{B}}_t^h = \frac{1}{\gamma \omega_s^2} \left\{ \mathbb{E}[\Delta s_{t+1} + \hat{r}_t - r_t | \Psi_t^h] - \mathbb{E}[\Delta s_{t+1} + \hat{r}_t - r_t | \Psi_t] \right\}$$

$$+ \frac{1}{\gamma \omega_s^2} \left\{ \mathbb{E}[s_t - s_{t:1}^* | \Psi_t^h] - \mathbb{E}[s_t - s_{t:1}^* | \Psi_t] \right\} - (\lambda_t^h - \lambda_{t-1}). \quad (8.18)$$

Next, we use the Walrasian equilibrium to compute the terms in brackets. Specifically, the equilibrium equation for the log spot rate in (8.16) implies that log excess returns follow

$$\Delta s_{t+1} + \hat{r}_t - r_t = -\frac{1-b}{1-b\rho} \hat{u}_{t+1} - \frac{b\gamma \sigma_s^2}{1-b} v_{t+1} + \gamma \sigma_s^2 \lambda_t. \quad (8.19)$$

Using this expression to compute the expectations in the first term of (8.18) and (8.16) to compute the expectations in the second gives

$$\widehat{\mathfrak{B}}_t^h = -\frac{2b-1}{1-b} \frac{\sigma_s^2}{\omega_s^2} \left\{ \mathbb{E}[\lambda_t | \Psi_t^h] - \mathbb{E}[\lambda_t | \Psi_t] \right\} - (\lambda_t^h - \lambda_{t-1}).$$

Now, under our assumptions about the structure of prior information, we can apply the projection theorem to show that

$$\mathbb{E}[\lambda_t | \Psi_t^h] - \mathbb{E}[\lambda_t | \Psi_t] = \beta(\lambda_t^h - \lambda_{t-1}),$$

where $\beta = \sigma_v^2 / (\sigma_v^2 + \sigma_\xi^2)$. Hence, the preceding equation becomes

$$\widehat{\mathfrak{B}}_t^h = -\left(1 + \frac{\beta(2b-1)}{1-b} \frac{\sigma_s^2}{\omega_s^2} \right) (\lambda_t^h - \lambda_{t-1}).$$

Using this expression to substitute for $\widehat{\mathfrak{B}}_t^h$ and equation (8.11) lagged one period to substitute for $\widehat{\mathfrak{B}}_{t-1}^h$, we can rewrite (8.17) as

$$Z_{t:1}^h = \mathbb{E}[Z_{t:1} | \Psi_t^h] - \left(1 + \frac{\beta(2b-1)}{1-b} \frac{\sigma_s^2}{\omega_s^2} \right) (\lambda_t^h - \lambda_{t-1}) + (\lambda_{t-1}^h - \lambda_{t-1}). \quad (8.20)$$

Equation (8.20) shows how the market orders of household h depend on its expectations regarding the incoming orders from others, together with the values of its current and past hedging parameters. Note that these orders are a function of household h's private information via Ψ_t^h and the hedging parameters, λ_t^h and λ_{t-1}^h. As a consequence, observations on the aggregate order flow induced by the submission of these market orders will provide new information that was not known at the start of period t to all households.

To see this clearly, we first have to identify a household's expectations of incoming orders, $E[Z_{t:1} | \Psi_t^h]$. Recall that under the trading protocol, all households submit their market orders simultaneously. The orders are then aggregated and matched against the best available limit orders. Since all households submit the same limit orders, this means that each household will receive a pro rata fraction of the aggregate market orders. Thus, the incoming market orders received by each household, $Z_{t:1}$, equal the average market orders, $\frac{1}{a} \int_0^a Z_{t:1}^h dh$, or aggregate order flow. Hence, if we aggregate (8.20) across all U.S. households using (8.5), (8.6), and the fact that $\frac{1}{a} \int_0^a \xi_t^h dh = 0$, we obtain

$$Z_{t:1} = \frac{1}{a} \int_0^a E[Z_{t:1}|\Psi_t^h]\,dh - \left(1 + \frac{\beta(2b-1)}{1-b}\frac{\sigma_s^2}{\omega_s^2}\right) v_t.$$

It is straightforward to solve for $Z_{t:1}$ using this equation. In particular, since $E[v_t|\Psi_t^h] = \beta(v_t + \xi_t^h)$, an application of the guess and verify method shows that

$$Z_{t:1} = -\frac{1}{1-\beta}\left(1 + \frac{\beta(2b-1)}{1-b}\frac{\sigma_s^2}{\omega_s^2}\right) v_t. \tag{8.21}$$

Equation (8.21) shows how aggregate market orders convey new information to households. Although each household knows the value of its own hedging parameter, λ_t^h, before trading takes place, it cannot precisely pin down the value of the aggregate hedging parameter, λ_t, from its prior information, Ψ_t^h. This changes when the households receive incoming market orders because $Z_{t:1}$ reveals the value of $v_t = \lambda_t - \lambda_{t-1}$ and λ_{t-1} is already known.

Exchange-Rate Dynamics and Order Flow

Are the incoming market orders received by households in round I sufficiently informative to support the Walrasian equilibrium? To address this question, consider the limit orders each household would submit at the start of round II. At this point, each household now knows the value of λ_t, so the relevant common prior information set for the determination of the limit prices is $\{\lambda_t, \Psi_t\}$. Following the steps described earlier with $\{\lambda_t, \Psi_t\}$ replacing Ψ_t produces the following equation for the limit prices in round II:

$$s_{t:II}^* = \mathbb{E}[s_t|\lambda_t, \Psi_t] + \gamma\sigma_s^2 Z$$

$$= s_t + \gamma\sigma_s^2 Z. \tag{8.22}$$

Thus, the limit buy and sell prices in round II converge at the Walrasian level of the spot rate.

The limit prices established in round II remain the limit prices for subsequent trading rounds in period t. The reason is that trading in round II and beyond does not reveal any new price-relevant information. Once households know the value of λ_t, the only sources of uncertainty affecting future exchange rates are *future* shocks to the money stock and the aggregate hedging parameter. However, since no household has private information concerning these shocks, market orders cannot provide further price-relevant information.

Another way to see this point is to compute the round II market orders. As before, household h submits market orders to fill the gap between its desired and existing E.U. bond positions net of expected incoming market orders. The former is given by (8.18) with the information sets Ψ_t and Ψ_t^h augmented with λ_t. This produces a desired position of $\widehat{\mathcal{B}}_t^h = -\xi_t^h$. The existing position comprises the *net* orders from round I trading, $Z_{t:\mathrm{I}}^h - Z_{t:\mathrm{I}}$, and the position at the start of period t, $\widehat{\mathcal{B}}_{t-1}^h = -\xi_{t-1}^h$. The market order of household h in round II is therefore

$$Z_{t:\mathrm{II}}^h = \mathbb{E}[Z_{t:\mathrm{II}}|\lambda_t, \Psi_t^h] - \xi_t^h - (Z_{t:\mathrm{I}}^h - Z_{t:\mathrm{I}} - \xi_{t-1}^h).$$

Substituting for $Z_{t:\mathrm{I}}^h - Z_{t:\mathrm{I}}$ from (8.20) and (8.21) and using the fact that $Z_{t:\mathrm{II}} = \frac{1}{a}\int_0^a Z_{t:\mathrm{II}}^h dh$, under the protocol for matching market and limit orders, we can rewrite this equation as

$$Z_{t:\mathrm{II}}^h = \left(\frac{1}{1-\beta}\left(1 + \frac{\beta(2b-1)}{1-b}\frac{\sigma_s^2}{\omega_s^2}\right) - 1\right)\xi_t^h. \tag{8.23}$$

Thus, the individual market orders submitted in round II are proportional to the idiosyncratic component of each household's hedging parameter. Since the Walrasian level of the exchange rate does not depend on these components, individual market orders in round II contain no new price-relevant information that could be incorporated into subsequent period-t limit prices. Indeed, (8.23) implies that aggregate order flow in round II is zero, so the common information available to households is $\{\lambda_t, \Psi_t\}$ for the remainder of the period. The aggregate order flow from all period-t trading, Z_t, is therefore just equal to $Z_{t:\mathrm{I}}$.

We may now summarize how trading in the limit-order market leads to the establishment of an exchange rate at the level implied by the Walrasian equilibrium. At the start of round I, households place limit orders described by the price lines labeled LB$_{\mathrm{I}}$ and LS$_{\mathrm{I}}$ in Figure 8.1. The lines converge at $s_{t:\mathrm{I}}^*$, a point that differs from household prior common expectations regarding the Walrasian rate for the period, $\mathbb{E}[s_t|\Psi_t]$. In particular, if λ_{t-1} is positive (negative) $s_{t:\mathrm{I}}^*$ will be below (above) $\mathbb{E}[s_t|\Psi_t]$ to compensate for the change in the hedging properties of E.U. bonds as more information

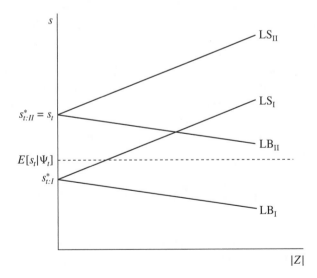

FIGURE 8.1   Limit orders supporting the Walrasian equilibrium.

becomes available. Households then submit their round I market orders. Individually, these orders depend on the aggregate and idiosyncratic shocks, v_t, ξ_t^h, and ξ_{t-1}^h. When aggregated and matched with the limit orders, the market orders produce an incoming order flow that is proportional to v_t and hence reveals the value of λ_t to all households. This new information is then incorporated into the round II limit orders, which converge at $s_{t:\mathrm{II}}^*$ as shown by $\mathrm{LB_{II}}$ and $\mathrm{LS_{II}}$ in Figure 8.1. Since further trading reveals no new price-relevant information, $\mathrm{LB_{II}}$ and $\mathrm{LS_{II}}$ also describe the limit prices for all subsequent trading rounds in period t. Hence, trading in the limit-order market establishes the Walrasian level for the exchange rate s_t as the convergence level for the limit prices, $s_{t:\mathrm{II}}^*$.

Finally, it is worth pointing out that the trading patterns described here induce a positive correlation between foreign exchange returns and the order flow observed in the data. In particular, combining the equation for log excess returns in (8.19) with the equation for aggregate order flow in (8.21), where $Z_t = Z_{t:1}$, we find that

$$\Delta s_{t+1} = r_t - \hat{r}_t + \gamma \sigma_s^2 \lambda_t - \frac{1-b}{1-b\rho} \hat{u}_{t+1} + \frac{b\gamma(1-\beta)\omega_s^2 \sigma_s^2}{(1-b)\omega_s^2 + \beta(2b-1)\sigma_s^2} Z_{t+1}.$$

The first three terms on the right identify the interest differential between U.S. and E.U. bonds and the risk premium. The next term identifies the impact of shocks to the E.U. money supply, $\hat{M}_t$. Recall that it is assumed that households learn the value of $\hat{M}_t$ before trading starts in period t, so this term identifies the impact of public news. The last term shows the impact of aggregate order flow, Z_{t+1} (i.e., the order flow from round I in period $t + 1$). The coefficient is unambiguously positive, consistent with the empirical evidence presented in Chapter 7.

In summary, we have shown that it is possible to support the exchange-rate process implied by a particular Walrasian equilibrium through trading in a limit-order market. In so doing, we were able to identify the behavior of order flow consistent with a particular set of exchange-rate dynamics. Importantly, our identification method relies on the presence of a clear dichotomy between the information contained in limit prices and market orders: Limit prices are a function of common prior information, whereas market orders submitted by each household depend only on that household's private information. These properties follow from assumptions A1 and A2 concerning the trading decisions of individual households in our analysis. If households made different trading decisions, there would be no informational dichotomy between limit prices and market orders, so order flow would not convey the new information necessary to establish new limit prices supporting the Walrasian equilibrium.

8.2 Order Flow in a Limit-Order Market

We now study the behavior of order flow in a limit-order market where the trading decisions of individual households are optimally determined. Our aim is to identify the circumstances in which order flow aggregates and conveys new price-relevant information.

The market comprises a large number of households, indexed by $h = 1, 2, \ldots, $ H, that can submit market and limit orders for a single risky asset. All market and limit orders are for one unit of the risky asset. In trading period t, the sets of prices for the existing limit sell and buy orders are denoted by $\{\mathcal{S}_t^h\}$ and $\{\mathcal{B}_t^h\}$, respectively, with the best limit ask and bid prices as

$$S_t^{\mathrm{A}} = \min_h \{\mathcal{S}_t^h\}_{h=1}^{\mathrm{H}} \quad \text{and} \quad S_t^{\mathrm{B}} = \max_h \{\mathcal{B}_t^h\}_{h=1}^{\mathrm{H}}.$$

The values of S_t^{A} and S_t^{B} are observable by all households.

Trading follows a simple protocol. At the start of period t, every household has the opportunity to withdraw or change its outstanding limit orders. If any of the revised limit orders cross (i.e., there are orders from households h and h' for which $\mathcal{S}_t^h \leq \mathcal{B}_t^{h'}$), they are matched. The market is now ready to receive new orders. First, the households are randomly sequenced. Then, each in turn has the opportunity to submit a new market or limit order. Market orders are matched with the best prevailing limit buy or sell price. As before, order flow is measured as the difference between the value of market orders to purchase the asset and the value of market orders to sell over a given trading period.

In what follows we first describe the trading problem facing a single household given the existing structure of limit orders and then discuss how the structure of the limit orders is determined from the trading decisions of individual households. We will then be in a position to examine how new information affects the behavior of order flow.

8.2.1 The Trading Problem

To simplify our analysis, we separate each household's portfolio choice problem from its trading problem. In particular, we focus on how a household chooses to trade in order to increase or reduce its risky asset position by one unit.

Consider the problem of selling one unit of the risky asset facing household h with reservation value V_t^h. We assume that the household is risk-averse with utility $\mathcal{U}^h = -\exp\left(-\theta(S_t - V_t^h)\right)$ with $\theta > 0$ if trade takes place at price S_t during period t and utility $\mathcal{U} = -1/\delta$ with $\delta < 1$ if no trade take place. Thus, the household would rather sell at price V_t^h than not trade, but would prefer to sell at a price above V_t^h.

When household h has the opportunity to trade, it has two choices. If it submits a market sell order that order will be executed at the best prevailing limit price of $S_t^{\mathrm{B}} = \max_h \{\mathcal{B}_t^h\}$. The expected utility associated with this trading strategy is

$$\mathcal{U}_{\mathrm{MSELL}}^h = -\exp\left(-\theta(S_t^{\mathrm{B}} - V_t^h)\right). \tag{8.24}$$

Alternatively, if it submits a limit order to sell one unit at the limit (asking) price of $\mathcal{S}_t^h$, its expected utility is

$$\mathcal{U}_{\mathrm{LSELL}}^h = -\exp\left(-\theta(\mathcal{S}_t^h - V_t^h)\right)\pi^{\mathrm{S}} - (1/\delta)(1 - \pi^{\mathrm{S}}), \tag{8.25}$$

where π^S is the probability that its limit order is matched with a market order from another trader. In a fully developed model, this probability would be determined endogenously from the structure of existing limit orders and probability distribution for market orders. Here we simplify matters by assuming that the probability of a match is decreasing in the gap between the proposed limit sell price, S_t^h, and the current best limit buy price, S_t^B:

$$\pi^S = \exp\left(-\frac{1}{\lambda}(S_t^h - S_t^B)\right) \tag{8.26}$$

for $S_t^h - S_t^B > 0$, where $\lambda > 1$.

To derive the optimal selling strategy for household h we compare $\mathcal{U}_{\text{MSELL}}^h$ with $\mathcal{U}_{\text{LSELL}}^h$ for an optimally chosen limit order. Combining (8.25) with (8.26) and maximizing the result gives an optimal limit sell price of $S_t^h = V_t^h + \psi$, where $\psi = \frac{1}{\theta}\ln\delta(1 + \lambda\theta)$. Clearly, if this price is below S_t^B, the optimal strategy is to submit a market sell order. If the price is above S_t^B, the household should submit a limit order with price S_t^h because, as can be seen in the appendix, $\mathcal{U}_{\text{LSELL}}^h > \mathcal{U}_{\text{MSELL}}^h$. The optimal choice of limit versus market order is therefore described by a simple trigger strategy:

$$
\begin{aligned}
&\text{Market sale at price } S_t^B &&\text{if } V_t^h \leq S_t^B - \psi, \\
&\text{Limit sale at } S_t^h = V_t^h + \psi &&\text{if } V_t^h > S_t^B - \psi.
\end{aligned}
\tag{8.27}
$$

The intuition behind this trading strategy is straightforward. When the household chooses to sell at S_t^B via a market sale, it foregoes the possibility of selling at a higher price via a limit order. Thus, it will only choose to submit a market sale order when the sale price includes a premium that compensates for this lost option. Equation (8.27) shows that $V_t^h + \psi$ is the lower bound on the bid price, so ψ represents the minimum premium necessary to compensate for the lost option value.

The choice between market and limit buy orders is determined in a symmetric fashion. In this case, the utility of a household wanting to buy at or below a reservation price of V_t^h is $\mathcal{U}^h = -\exp\left(-\theta(V_t^h - S_t)\right)$ if a trade takes place at price S_t. Thus, the expected utility from submitting a market buy order matched at the best prevailing limit price of S_t^A is

$$\mathcal{U}_{\text{MBUY}}^h = -\exp\left(-\theta(V_t^h - S_t^A)\right). \tag{8.28}$$

The expected utility from a limit buy order with a bid price of $\mathcal{B}_t^h$ is

$$\mathcal{U}_{\text{LBUY}}^h = -\exp\left(-\theta(V_t^h - \mathcal{B}_t^h)\right)\pi^B - (1/\delta)(1 - \pi^B), \tag{8.29}$$

where the probability of a limit order match is

$$\pi^B = \exp\left(-\frac{1}{\lambda}(S_t^A - \mathcal{B}_t^h)\right), \tag{8.30}$$

for $\mathcal{B}_t^h - S_t^A < 0$. Combining (8.29) with (8.30) and maximizing the result gives an expression for the optimal limit buy price together with the trigger strategy describing the optimal choice of market and limit buy orders:

$$
\begin{aligned}
&\text{Market buy at price } S_t^A && \text{if } V_t^h \geq S_t^A + \psi, \\
&\text{Limit buy at } \mathcal{B}_t^h = V_t^h - \psi && \text{if } V_t^h < S_t^A + \psi.
\end{aligned}
\tag{8.31}
$$

8.2.2 The Structure of Limit Orders

The structure of limit orders implied by the trading strategies in (8.27) and (8.31) depends on the size of the limit price premium, ψ, and the degree of heterogeneity in the reservation values, V_t^h, across households. If all households have the same reservation value (i.e., $V_t^h = V_t$ for all h), all the limit buy and sell orders will be concentrated at two prices, $S_t^B = V_t - \psi$ and $S_t^A = V_t + \psi$. In this special case the inside spread between the best bid and ask prices is just 2ψ.

The structure of limit orders is more complex when households have different reservation prices. To illustrate, Figure 8.2 plots the structure of limit orders under the assumption that the reservation values are determined by $V_t^h = \mu_t + \xi_t^h$, where $\xi_t^h \sim \text{i.i.d.} N(0, \sigma^2)$ for all h. For the purpose of this illustration, we set the mean reservation value μ_t at 100. The other parameters in the model are θ, λ, and δ. We set these equal to 0.1, 2, and 0.9, respectively. The implied size of the limit price premium, ψ, is 0.77.

Panel I of Figure 8.2 shows the percentage distribution of limit orders at the ask and bid prices computed from the reservation values of 3000 households. In this example, the standard deviation of the reservation values, σ, equals 0.25, so the dispersion of reservation prices is small relative to ψ. As a result, there are comparatively few limit orders close to the inside spread. This lack of depth close to the inside spread means that a short sequence of market buy or sell orders will lead to a significant change in the best limit prices. Panel II shows the limit-order distribution when the standard deviation of the reservation values is twice as large (i.e., $\sigma = 0.50$). Here there are many more limit orders close to the inside spread, so the best limit prices will be more stable with respect to the arrival of market orders.

Figure 8.2 also illustrates an important point about the information structure of limit orders. In this model, limit orders reveal a lot about the private price-relevant information held by households. In both panels the average limit price is very close to the mean reservation value of 100. Furthermore, the dispersion of the limit orders provides information on the dispersion of reservation values. Indeed, the standard deviation of the buy and sell limit orders in panel I closely approximates the standard deviation of the reservation values. Thus, any individual household observing the complete structure of limit orders would have an accurate picture of the distribution of price-relevant information across all households. This feature stands in stark contrast to the properties of the limit orders derived in the model of Section 8.1. Recall that limit orders in that model only reflected public information. Here

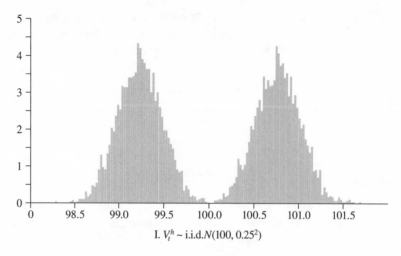

I. $V_t^h \sim$ i.i.d.$N(100, 0.25^2)$

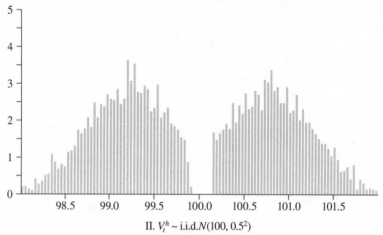

II. $V_t^h \sim$ i.i.d.$N(100, 0.5^2)$

FIGURE 8.2   The structure of limit prices (bid prices, left-hand distribution; ask prices, right-hand distribution).

households have no incentive to conceal their reservation valuations when choosing to submit a limit order.

8.2.3 Information and Order Flow

We can now examine the role of order flow as a conveyor of information in our model of the limit-order market. For this purpose, consider the trading implications of a shift in the distribution of reservation prices across households. Specifically, suppose panel II in Figure 8.2 describes the structure of outstanding limit orders at the end of period t and that the distribution of reservation values shifts to the right by one standard deviation before the start of trading period $t + 1$. Figure 8.3 shows the resulting behavior of limit prices as a sequence of 3000 households is given the opportunity to submit orders during period $t + 1$. Here the solid and dashed lines identify the best

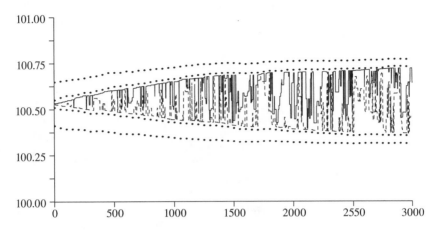

FIGURE 8.3 The evolution of limit prices (best limit ask, solid; best limit bid, dashed; inner and outer dotted lines show prices 20 and 100 orders away from the best limit prices, respectively).

ask and bid prices, and the inner and outer dotted lines show the prices that are 20 and 100 orders away from the best limit prices.

According to the trading protocol, each household with an outstanding limit order has the opportunity to revise that order before trading commences. Since there is no change in the limit price premium, ψ, the trigger strategies in (8.27) and (8.31) imply that each household with an outstanding limit order should change its limit price to match the change in its reservation value, that is, $\Delta \mathcal{S}_{t+1}^h = \Delta V_{t+1}^h$ or $\Delta \mathcal{B}_{t+1}^h = \Delta V_{t+1}^h$, where $\Delta V_{t+1}^h = 0.5 + \xi_{t+1}^h - \xi_t^h$. Consequently, the distribution of bid and ask limit prices should shift upward before trading commences. This shift in the structure of limit prices is reflected in the left-hand starting points for each of the plots in Figure 8.3. Note that both the best ask and bid limit prices are very close to the new mean valuation of 100.5. In this sense, the limit prices immediately reflect the change in reservation prices before any trading takes place.

Figure 8.3 also shows that the structure of limit orders changes further once trading begins. In particular, as more households have the opportunity to place market orders or new limit orders, the distributions of bid and ask prices begin to separate: the distribution of ask prices moves up and the distribution of bid prices moves down. As a result, there is less depth near the inside spread so that best limit prices become increasingly volatile in response to the arrival of market orders. Note, also, that trading has little impact on the overall level of limit prices. In particular, if we compare the average limit price prior to trading and after the submission of 3000 new market and limit orders, we find that they are essentially the same. Trading also has a negligible impact on order flow. Approximately 24 percent of households submit market orders when given the opportunity to trade but the orders are very evenly split between market purchases and sales. Consequently, aggregate order flow over the period is approximately zero.

It is important to recognize that the plots in Figure 8.3 do not depend upon whether the shift in the distribution of reservation values is common knowledge. Both the initial revision in limit orders and subsequent trading decisions of individual

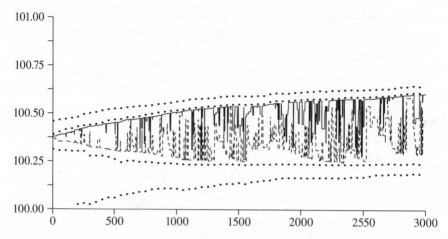

FIGURE 8.4   The evolution of limit prices with frictions (best limit ask, solid; best limit bid, dashed; inner and outer dotted lines show prices 20 and 100 orders away from the best limit prices, respectively).

households depend on their own reservation values rather than on their estimates of reservation values across the market. Consequently, the behavior of limit prices and order flow in this simulation applies equally well to the case where V_t^h represents the private information of household h or where $\{V_t^h\}_{h=1}^{\mathrm{H}}$ is common knowledge.

Up to this point we have shown how a revision in the distribution of reservation values can generate an immediate shift in the distribution of limit orders and negligible aggregate order flow. We now introduce a friction into the model so that order flow conveys price-relevant information consistent with our analysis in Section 8.1. Specifically, we now assume that there is a fixed cost to revising any outstanding limit order at the start of period $t+1$. As a consequence, only those households with outstanding orders experiencing a change in reservation value above a certain threshold will revise their orders. As before, we consider the impact of a $\sigma = 0.5$ upward shift in the reservation value distribution, but now impose a threshold of 2σ when computing the initial distribution of limit prices. The resulting behavior of limit prices is shown in Figure 8.4.

Introducing the friction has two important implications for the behavior of prices. First, the initial limit price distribution is now a mixture of old prices based on period-t reservation values and new prices based on period-$t+1$ reservation values (in those cases where the new value was sufficiently different from the old to make revising the limit price worthwhile). As a consequence, the initial limit price distribution shifts up, but as the left-hand starting point for each of the plots in Figure 8.4 shows, the shift is less than that of the reservation value distribution.

The second implication concerns the impact of trading. Figure 8.4 shows that there is a gradual but persistent upward shift in the limit price distributions as trading progresses. The reason for this shift stems from the difference between the reservation values of households' making new orders and those with existing limit orders. Households submitting new market or limit orders are making their trading decisions based on current reservation values (i.e., V_{t+1}^h), whereas some of the existing limit orders are based on old valuations (i.e., V_t^h). Now since reservation values have risen on average between t and $t + 1$, this informational asymmetry means that households wanting to buy are more likely to submit market orders than limit orders, whereas those wanting to sell are more likely to do the reverse. As a consequence, many more of the low asking prices will be matched with market purchase orders than high bid prices are matched with market sale orders. This process reduces the depth in limit sell orders and increases the depth in limit buys, so the distributions of both ask and bid prices shift upward. It also means that trading during period $t + 1$ is characterized by positive aggregate order flow. In fact, the ratio of market purchases to sales is approximately two to one in this simulation. The upward drift in the limit price distribution shown in Figure 8.4 is accompanied by strongly positive order flow.

8.2.4 Summary

We may summarize the results of our simulations as follows. If all households with outstanding limit orders have an incentive to adjust those orders upon the arrival of new information, subsequent market orders will not produce significant order flow. Under these circumstances, the price impact of new information is immediately reflected by a shift in the limit price distribution. By contrast, if a subset of pre-existing limit orders is not adjusted when new information arrives, subsequent market orders will induce a significant order flow because there exists an informational asymmetry between the counterparties in each match between a market and a limit order. In sum, therefore, the behavior of order flow depends critically on how traders with existing limit orders react to the arrival of new information.

These findings provide perspective on the analysis in Section 8.1. There we showed that order flow conveyed the information necessary to establish a level for the spot exchange rate that corresponded to the Walrasian equilibrium. In so doing, we demonstrated how to identify the order flow implications of an exchange-rate model without considering the behavior of FX dealers. A key aspect of this analysis is the restriction placed on limit orders, namely that they cannot embody new private information. In this section we have seen that this restriction does not emerge from a simple model in which market and limit orders are chosen optimally. As a consequence, order flow only responds to the arrival of new information when there is some cost to adjusting pre-existing limit orders. Understanding the source and size of these costs presents a challenge, but one that must be addressed if we want to identify the order flow implications of an exchange-rate model without FX dealers.

8.3 Estimating Order Flow

Computing order flow from the trading records of FX dealers or a limit-order market is a straightforward matter if the records are complete. All we need is information on the initiator of the trade (i.e., the buyer or the seller), the transaction price, and the quantity traded. However, in many instances, complete trading records are either unavailable to researchers for propriety or confidentiality reasons, or simple do not exist. In this section, we consider some alternative methods for estimating order flow from incomplete trading data.

8.3.1 Estimating Order Flow from Portfolio Holdings

One proposed method for estimating order flow is to use the change in the foreign currency holdings of end-users between one period and the next. For example, Froot and Ramadorai (2005) compute the daily change in foreign currency holdings of more than 10,000 mutual funds that use State Street Corporation as their custodian. They estimate aggregate order flow for currency j on day t as the USD value of net purchases of currency j between the end of days $t - 1$ and t. Froot and Ramadorai use this method to estimate order flows for 18 currencies (versus the USD) between January 1, 1994, and February 9, 2001. Note that this is a far longer time span than that covered by other data sets, such as the one used in Evans and Lyons (2002a).

There are two potential sources of error in this estimation method. The first arises from the frequency mismatch between transactions and the portfolio positions recorded in the data: A mutual fund may undertake several different transactions in currency j at different FX prices during the day, but the State Street data only provide the net daily change in its holdings of currency j. In other words, it is hard to draw reliable inferences about intraday trading patterns from daily position changes. The second problem concerns the initiator of trade. The implicit assumption in position-based estimates of order flow is that the mutual fund is the initiator of each transaction. Thus, if a mutual fund adds to its holdings of currency j during day t, it is interpreted as being the result of the fund initiating more purchases for currency j than sales during day t. This interpretation is quite standard in the literature, but it does not account for the fact that banks will accept price-contingent orders for foreign currency from end-users. Let us consider each of these problems in a little more detail.

The Frequency Mismatch Problem

One way to illustrate the problem associated with frequency mismatch is to consider the relationship between order flow and portfolio holdings in the Portfolio Shifts model we discussed in Chapter 6. In that model, the risks of holding FX overnight are more efficiently shared by investors than by dealers, so the price of FX quoted by dealers at the end of each day reflects their desire to close out their existing FX positions. Now dealers have sufficient information to precisely infer the price at which investors can be induced to hold the existing stock of FX. This means that the aggregate FX holdings of investors at the end of day t, A_t, follow

$$A_t = A_{t-1} + Y_t,$$

where Y_t is aggregate foreign income investors receive on day t. Thus if all investors used State Street as their custodian, the position-based estimate of day-t order flow would equal foreign income, Y_t.

How does this estimate compare to the order flows in the Portfolio Shifts model? Recall that at the start of day t, each dealer d receives customer orders for foreign currency equal to $Z_{d,t}^1 = (\beta/D)Y_t + \varepsilon_{d,t}$, where $\sum_d \varepsilon_{d,t} = 0$. These flows represent the difference between investors desired and existing holdings inclusive of foreign income. Since investors want to hedge against their foreign income, the β coefficient will be negative, so aggregate customer order flow, $Z_t^1 \equiv \sum_d Z_{d,t}^1 = \beta Y_t$, is perfectly *negatively* correlated with aggregate income and the position-based estimate of order flow.

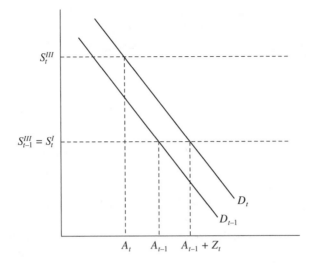

FIGURE 8.5   Order and portfolio flows in the Portfolio Shifts model.

A similar problem exists with interdealer order flow. According to the model, aggregate interdealer order flow is given by

$$X_t = \alpha_Z Z_t^{\mathrm{I}} + \alpha_A A_{t-1},$$

where α_Z and α_A are positive coefficients. As dealers seek to re-establish their FX positions after filling customer orders, interdealer order flow is positively related to customer order flow, Z_t^{I}. Consequently, the position-based estimates of order flow are negatively correlated with X_t.

We can illustrate the relationship between the portfolios and order flows in a simple diagram. Consider the situation depicted in Figure 8.5, where D_t and D_{t-1} denote investors' demand for foreign currency on days t and $t-1$. The existing stock of FX on day $t-1$ is A_{t-1}, so the efficient risk-sharing rate quoted by dealers at the end of the day is S_{t-1}^{III}. Now suppose, for the sake of clarity, that there is no public news on day t. Further let us assume that aggregate investor income is negative. In this situation the initial quote of dealers remains unchanged at $S_t^{\mathrm{I}} = S_{t-1}^{\mathrm{III}}$ whereas the demand for foreign currency shifts rightward to D_t as investors hedge against their foreign income. The net result is positive customer order flow of Z_t, which increases investors' holdings to $A_{t-1} + Z_t$. Up to this point, the change in investors' portfolios on day t correctly identifies order flow, but this is not the end of the story. Subsequent interdealer trading reveals two important pieces of information: (1) the position of D_t, and (2) the size of investors' income, Y_t. From these dealers can compute the spot rate, S_t^{III}, at which investors will hold the existing stock of foreign currency, $A_t = A_{t-1} + Y_t$, given their demand, D_t. As seen in the figure this requires a quoted price of S_t^{III} well above the initial price of S_t^{I} because dealers have to induce investors to hold a smaller FX position for efficient risk-sharing.

Figure 8.5 makes clear that order flow can only be identified by changes in portfolio holdings if those changes are measured at transaction frequencies. If the portfolio holdings are measured at lower frequencies, the changes in holdings incorporate the effects of asset demand shifts and price changes. In this example, the initial intraday change in investors' portfolio holdings from A_{t-1} to $A_{t-1} + Z_t$ correctly identifies aggregate customer order flow, but the daily change, $A_t - A_{t-1}$, includes the change induced by the revision in dealer quotes, $A_t - A_{t-1} - Z_{t-1}$. The net result is that the daily change in portfolio holdings is a very poor estimate of aggregate customer order flow.

It is important to stress that the identification problem illustrated in Figure 8.5 is quite general. It occurs whenever there is a frequency mismatch between transactions and the portfolio positions recorded in the data. As another example, consider the relation between the portfolio holdings and order flow implied by the rational expectations exchange-rate model in Section 8.1. There, the equilibrium E.U. household bond holdings of each household depend only on the idiosyncratic component of its hedging exposure; $\widehat{\mathfrak{B}}_t = -\xi_t^h$. This means that once the Walrasian equilibrium is established aggregate E.U. household bond holdings are zero. As a result, estimates of order flow using the portfolio positions measured at these points equal zero. By contrast, the aggregate order flow implied by trade in the limit-order market in (8.17) is proportional to the change in the aggregate hedging component, $\lambda_t - \lambda_{t-1} = v_t$, which is generally different from zero.

Identifying the Initiator of Trade

Accurate estimates of order flow also require information on the initiator of trade. Often this information is unavailable, but it can be inferred from institutional knowledge. For example, if the retail FX market is the data source where all transactions are known to take place bilaterally between a bank and an end-user (e.g., a mutual fund or a corporation), then it is unlikely that the bank was the initiator of the transaction. On the contrary, a typical transaction is initiated by the end-user contacting the bank to ask for some FX quotes. Such inferences about the initiator of trade are impossible in the wholesale interbank market because trade can be initiated by any bank (either directly or indirectly via a market order on an electronic brokerage system).

Although transactions in the retail FX market are typically initiated by end-users, two features of the market complicate the identification of end-user order flow. First, in the past few years some banks have given their largest customers direct access to the electronic brokerage systems that now dominate trading in the interbank market (e.g., EBS and Reuters 3000). These end-users now can submit both market and limit orders on the same terms as any bank, so it is no longer safe to assume that they are the initiators of every trade. The second complication arises from the use of stop-loss and take-profit orders by end-users. These price-contingent orders provide end-users with a close substitute to the limit orders available on the interbank brokerage systems.

We can illustrate how access to an electronic brokerage system complicates the identification of order flow from end-users' portfolio holdings with the simulations of the limit-order market model in Section 8.2. Rows (a) and (c) of Table 8.1 report the fraction of the 3000 trading opportunities that result in the submission of a market buy or market sale in the simulations depicted in Figures 8.3 and 8.4. The table also shows estimates based on the change in the portfolio holdings of the 3000 households in rows (b) and (d). The entries in the column headed Market Buys (Sales) report the faction of households that add to (reduce) their FX holdings. The right-hand column reports order flow as a fraction of 3000 trading opportunities computed as the difference between the market buy and market sale statistics.

TABLE 8.1
Estimating Order Flow from the Limit-Order Market Model

		Market buys	Market sales	Order flow
Figure 8.3	(a) Actual	11.77	12.37	−0.60
	(b) Estimates	11.57	12.57	−1.00
Figure 8.4	(c) Actual	16.43	8.83	7.60
	(d) Estimates	17.77	7.50	10.27

There is little difference between the fraction of actual and estimated transactions in rows (a) and (b) that come from the simulation in Figure 8.3. This is not to say that the change in portfolio holdings accurately tracks the submission of market orders household by household. In this simulation, approximately 30 percent of households submit limit orders when given the opportunity to trade, which are matched with subsequently submitted market orders. As a result, market orders account for approximately 70 percent of the change in portfolio holdings. Fortunately, this level of inaccuracy does not adversely affect the estimated fractions of market buys and sales. Recall that there is no significant price trend in Figure 8.3, so the portfolio changes induced by the execution of limit orders are distributed equally across households wanting to increase or reduce their FX holdings. As a result, the estimated fraction of market orders based on portfolio changes is quite accurate, as is the estimate of aggregate order flow.

Rows (c) and (d) of Table 8.1 show that portfolio changes provide less accurate estimates of market orders in the simulation shown in Figure 8.4. In this case, there is an upward trend in prices, which makes households wanting to increase their FX holdings more likely to submit a limit rather than a market buy order. Conversely, those households wanting to reduce their holdings are less likely to submit a limit than a market sale order. As a result, the number of households adding to their FX holdings overstates the number submitting market buy orders, whereas the number of households with reduced FX holdings understates the number submitting market sale orders. Taken together, these inferences concerning market orders imply that the estimate of aggregate order flow overstates true order flow by approximately 35 percent (i.e., 10.27/7.6).

The lesson to take away from these simulation results is clear. If trading takes place via a limit-order market, it is impossible to accurately identify order flow from data on portfolio holdings without further information on how traders choose between limit and market orders. This identification problem is likely to become more severe as more end-users gain direct access to the Reuters and EBS electronic brokerage systems.

A similar identification problem exists when banks and end-users trade directly with stop-loss and take-profit orders. These orders instruct a bank to either buy or sell a certain amount of currency on behalf of the end-user conditional on the spot price hitting a certain level. As the names imply, take-profit and stop-loss orders are designed to capture the profit or stop the loss associated with a particular position. For example, a take-profit order on a positive foreign currency position involves selling

TABLE 8.2
Price-Contingent Orders

	Sell	Buy
Take profit	$S^B > \bar{S}^B$	$S^A < \underline{S}^A$
Stop loss	$S^B < \underline{S}^B$	$S^A > \bar{S}^A$

foreign currency when the currency bid price, S^B, rises above a particular ceiling, $\bar{S}^B$, and a stop-loss order involves selling foreign currency when S^B falls below a particular floor, $\underline{S}^B$. Take-profit and stop-loss orders on negative foreign currency positions involve purchases of foreign currency when the current ask price, S^A, is below $\underline{S}^A$ or above $\bar{S}^A$, respectively. These features are summarized in Table 8.2.

Price-contingent orders are not equivalent to limit orders. When the current spot price reaches the trigger point (i.e., the floor or ceiling), the dealer must execute a transaction of a given size on behalf of the end-user. Thus, a take-profit buy order for €10 million with a floor of $\underline{S}^A = 1.30\$/€$ requires the dealer to purchase €10 million for the end-user if the ask price falls below 1.30$/€. Note that in this instance the order specifies the quantity of euros to be purchased rather than the price to be paid (provided the price is below $\underline{S}^A$). In general, price-contingent orders fix the amount to be traded once certain price conditions are met, but the actual transaction price is flexible. By contrast, a limit order specifies the price at which a trader is willing to transact leaving the quantity traded to be determined by the matching market orders. Thus, in a limit order the transaction price is fixed in advance but the quantity traded is flexible.

Despite these differences, price-contingent orders make the identification of order flow from changes in portfolio holdings just as difficult as when end-users can submit limit orders. The problem is that price-contingent orders induce portfolio changes that are initiated by the actions of others. For example, if trading activity in the interbank market triggers take-profit buy orders for some mutual funds, we would attribute the resulting increase in their foreign currency holdings as positive order flow from mutual funds, just as we would if the mutual funds had submitted limit buy orders that were matched by the market orders of other traders using an electronic brokerage. In short, although limit and price-contingent orders differ from a trading perspective, their implications for the identification of order flow using portfolio holdings are quite similar.

Recall from Table 8.1 that order flow estimates derived from portfolio holdings are not adversely affected by the presence of limit orders if limit purchases and sales are evenly balanced. Similarly, the presence of the price-contingent orders need not lead to inaccurate estimates of order flow if purchases and sales of foreign currency implied by take-profit and stop-loss orders are well balanced over the range for spot rates in the data sample. Unfortunately, this does not always appear to be the case. Osler (2003) examined the price-contingent orders in three currencies received by a large bank between August 1, 1999, and April 30, 2000. Although buy and sell orders were evenly balanced across the whole sample, she found two striking asymmetries: (1) Executed take-profit orders cluster more strongly at trigger points with round numbers than executed stop-loss orders.[1] (2) Stop-loss buy orders are more strongly clustered above than below trigger points with round numbers, and the opposite is true for stop-loss sell orders. Osler argued that these asymmetries could contribute to the patterns in spot rate movements predicted by technical analysis (e.g., price reversals and breakouts). For our purpose, the existence of asymmetry (2) means that the price-contingent purchases and sales of foreign currency are not always well balanced. This means that estimates of order flow derived from portfolio holdings may be less accurate when the spot rate is in the neighborhood of a trigger point with round numbers.

8.3.2 Estimating Order Flow from Transaction Prices

Estimates of order flow can also be computed from the high-frequency behavior of transaction prices. These estimates apply simple algorithms to identify the initiator of each transaction based on the change in transaction prices from one trade to another or on the relation between the current transaction price and the most recent quotes. Once the initiator of each transaction has been identified, FX order flow is estimated as the difference between the number of buyer- and seller-initiated trades for FX over a particular time period.

To understand how these algorithms work, let S_t^B and S_t^A denote the most recent bid and ask quotes for FX before a trade takes place at time t with a transaction price of S_t. The algorithms identifying whether the trade is initiated by the buyer or seller of FX are determined according to rules laid out in Table 8.3. The simplest algorithm is referred to as the Tick test. Here trades are identified as buyer-initiated if the current transaction price is higher than the previous one, and seller-initiated if it is lower. Note that this algorithm does not classify the initiators of trades that take place at the same transaction price as the last trade. This source of indeterminacy is addressed in the second algorithm proposed by Lee and Ready (1991) (hereafter LR). Here the current transaction price, S_t, is first compared against the midpoint of the prevailing quotes, $\frac{1}{2}(S_t^A + S_t^B)$. If this comparison fails to identify the initiator because $S_t = \frac{1}{2}(S_t^A + S_t^B)$, the trade is then classified using the Tick test.

One rationale for both algorithms is provided by the sequential trading model described in Chapter 5. There we considered a model in which risk-neutral market-makers quoted prices at which they were willing to buy or sell one unit of foreign currency to a population of informed and uninformed traders. In the Nash equilibrium of the model, all marketmakers quote the same bid and ask prices in each trading period t:

$$S_t^A = \mathbb{E}[F_t | \mathbb{B}_t, \Omega_t] \quad \text{and} \quad S_t^B = \mathbb{E}[F_t | \mathbb{S}_t, \Omega_t], \tag{8.32}$$

where F_t denotes exchange-rate fundamentals and Ω_t is the information common to all marketmakers at the start of period t. Trader-initiated purchases and sales of foreign

---

1. Quotations in currency markets are made with a fixed number of significant figures. For example, for USD/GBS and EUR/USD quotes contain four digits to the right of the decimal point, whereas USD/JPY quotes contain two. The spot rate is at a round number when the last two digits in the quote are 00.

TABLE 8.3
Trade Identification Algorithms

Algorithm	Condition	Inference for trade at t
Tick test	$S_t > S_{t-1}$	Buyer-initiated
	$S_t < S_{t-1}$	Seller-initiated
Lee and Ready (1991)	$S_t > \frac{1}{2}(S_t^A + S_t^B)$	Buyer-initiated
	$S_t < \frac{1}{2}(S_t^A + S_t^B)$	Seller-initiated
	$S_t = \frac{1}{2}(S_t^A + S_t^B)$ and $S_t > S_{t-1}$	Buyer-initiated
	$S_t = \frac{1}{2}(S_t^A + S_t^B)$ and $S_t < S_{t-1}$	Seller-initiated

currency are denoted by $\mathbb{B}_t$ and $\mathbb{S}_t$, respectively. Thus, equilibrium quotes are "regret-free" in the sense that they equal the expected value of fundamentals conditioned on prior information, Ω_t, and the fact that a trader wants to undertake a particular trade (i.e., $\mathbb{B}_t$ or $\mathbb{S}_t$).

Since all transactions take place at either the bid or the ask quotes, it is straightforward to access the accuracy of the algorithms in Table 8.3. Consider, for example, the implication of a trader-initiated purchase of FX in period t. In this case the transaction price is $S_t = S_t^A$, so the LR algorithm will correctly identify the initiator of the trade if $S_t^A > (S_t^A + S_t^B)/2$ or, equivalently, if $\mathbb{E}[F_t|\mathbb{B}_t, \Omega_t] > \mathbb{E}[F_t|\mathbb{S}_t, \Omega_t]$. This inequality holds true because marketmakers recognize that some traders possess superior information about the value of fundamentals than they do. Similar reasoning establishes that $S_t^B < (S_t^A + S_t^B)/2$. Hence the LR algorithm identifies the initiator of each trade with complete accuracy.

To assess the accuracy of the Tick test, we first use (8.32) to write transaction prices as $S_t = \mathbb{E}[F_t|\mathbb{T}_t, \Omega_t]$ for $\mathbb{T}_t = \{\mathbb{B}_t, \mathbb{S}_t\}$. From this expression it follows that the change in transaction prices is

$$S_t - S_{t-1} = \mathbb{E}[F_t|\mathbb{T}_t, \Omega_t] - \mathbb{E}[F_{t-1}|\mathbb{T}_{t-1}, \Omega_{t-1}]$$

$$= \mathbb{E}[F_t|\mathbb{T}_t, \Omega_t] - \mathbb{E}[F_t|\mathbb{T}_{t-1}, \Omega_{t-1}] + \mathbb{E}[\Delta F_t|\mathbb{T}_{t-1}, \Omega_{t-1}].$$

In the sequential trade model, changes in fundamentals are unforecastable, so the last term on the right-hand side disappears. More generally, any change in fundamentals over a single trading period will be negligible, so the change in transaction prices will be well approximated by

$$S_t - S_{t-1} = \mathbb{E}[F_t|\mathbb{T}_t, \Omega_t] - \mathbb{E}[F_t|\mathbb{T}_{t-1}, \Omega_{t-1}]. \tag{8.33}$$

If marketmakers obtain all their information from incoming trades $\Omega_t = \{\mathbb{T}_{t-1}, \Omega_{t-1}\}$, the change in transaction prices, $S_t - S_{t-1}$, simply reflects the revision in estimates of fundamentals given the period-t trade, $\mathbb{T}_t$. Under these circumstances, the Tick test will accurately identify the initiator of trade because marketmakers recognize that some traders possess superior information about the value of fundamentals than they do. They therefore revise their estimates of fundamentals upward (downward) in response to trader-initiated purchases (sales).

Up to this point we have shown that both algorithms accurately identify the initiator of trade in the stylized setting of the sequential trade model. We are now ready to assess whether estimates of order flow using these algorithms are likely to prove accurate when applied to FX transaction data. Recall that FX transaction data can come from three main sources: (1) direct transactions between a single bank and its customers, (2) direct interdealer transactions between banks, and (3) indirect interdealer transactions via an electronic brokerage. Let us consider these in turn.

Customer Order Flow

Although data on FX transactions between banks and their customers is rarely available on a transaction-by-transaction basis, this form of trading more closely conforms to the environment of the sequential trade model. In light of this, could transaction prices be used to construct accurate estimates of customer order flow when complete trading records are unavailable? The answer comes from equation (8.33). Suppose the bank, acting as the marketmaker in this context, obtains information from customer trades, $\mathbb{T}_t$, interdealer trades, $\mathcal{T}_t$, and macroeconomic announcements at the start of period t, $\mathcal{A}_t$, so that information evolves according to

$$\Omega_t = \left\{ \mathbb{T}_{t-1}, \mathcal{T}_{t-1}, \mathcal{A}_t, \Omega_{t-1} \right\} .$$

Under these circumstances, the change in transaction prices, $S_t - S_{t-1}$, reflects the revision in expectations concerning fundamentals from three sources: (1) period-t customer trades, $\mathbb{T}_t$, (2) period-t announcements, $\mathcal{A}_t$, and (3) interdealer trades in period $t - 1$, $\mathcal{T}_{t-1}$. Clearly, if the information contained in sources (2) and (3) dominates that contained in source (1), the change in transaction prices will not be an accurate indicator of the customer trade type. Consequently, it is possible that customer purchases (sales) of FX are associated with a fall (rise) in transaction prices.

The problem in this example is that marketmakers are using more than the flow of customer-initiated trades to revise their estimates of fundamentals. When this is the case, the Tick test will misclassify individual transactions and induce a spurious correlation between price changes and estimated customer order flow. To see why this is so, consider the extreme case where customer trades are completely uninformative. Here transaction prices are driven solely by the information in sources (2) and (3) (i.e., $\mathcal{T}_{t-1}$ and $\mathcal{A}_t$), so customer order flow will be uncorrelated with transaction price changes. By contrast, the Tick test will identify positive (negative) price changes with customer purchases (sales) so the correlation between price changes and estimated customer order flow will be positive. In cases where marketmakers obtain some information from customer trades, price changes will be more strongly correlated with estimates of customer order flow derived from the Tick test than actual order flow, leading the researcher to overestimate the importance of customer trades as a source of information.

Unfortunately, the LR algorithm does not provide an alternative for estimating customer order flow. If banks quoted firm bid and ask prices at which they were willing to fill customer orders, each customer trade could be correctly identified from the quotes and transaction prices using the LR algorithm even when banks used multiple information sources to determine quotes. However, as we noted in Chapter 6, banks only provide *indicative* quotes at which they will try to fill customer orders, so actual transaction prices can differ from either the bid or the ask quote. Thus, the

LR algorithm would not provide us with accurate estimates of the customer order flow even if data on transaction prices and quotes were available. To date, no bank has released such data to researchers.

Direct Interdealer Order Flow

Estimating order flow from direct interdealer trading poses a different set of problems. To illustrate, suppose there are just four dealers present in the market, identified by the points of the compass, {N,S,E,W}. Further, let us assume that each dealer quotes prices according to (8.32) with Ω_t replaced by private information Ω_t^i for $i = \{$N,S,E,W$\}$. Consistent with the form of actual interdealer trading, transactions are assumed to take place at quoted prices, and quotes are only observed by the dealer initiating the transaction. Now if dealer N initiates a trade with dealer E in period $t-1$ and dealer S initiates trade with dealer W in period t, the change in transaction prices will be

$$S_t - S_{t-1} = \mathbb{E}[F_t|\mathbb{T}_t, \Omega_t^W] - \mathbb{E}[F_t|\mathbb{T}_{t-1}, \Omega_{t-1}^E] + \mathbb{E}[\Delta F_t|\mathbb{T}_{t-1}, \Omega_{t-1}^E].$$

As before, the last term on the right can be safely ignored, so we can rewrite the change in prices as

$$S_t - S_{t-1} = \left\{ \mathbb{E}[F_t|\mathbb{T}_t, \Omega_t^E] - \mathbb{E}[F_t|\mathbb{T}_{t-1}, \Omega_{t-1}^E] \right\} + \left\{ \mathbb{E}[F_t|\mathbb{T}_t, \Omega_t^W] - \mathbb{E}[F_t|\mathbb{T}_t, \Omega_t^E] \right\}.$$

The first term on the right is identical to the one shown in equation (8.33). The second term identifies the difference between dealer W's and dealer E's estimates of fundamentals. If all dealers have common information the second term disappears, so the change in prices will be an accurate indicator of the period-t trade type if $\Omega_t^E = \{\mathbb{T}_{t-1}, \Omega_{t-1}^E\}$. Under other circumstances, the change in transaction prices may reveal as much about the presence of information heterogeneity across dealers as it does about the trade type. Consequently, estimates of interdealer order flow based on the Tick test are unlikely to be reliable.

A similar problem occurs if we use the LR algorithm. If data existed on the quotes and transaction prices that result from each bilateral trade between dealers, the LR algorithm would identify the initiator of each interdealer trade with complete accuracy because all transactions take place at either the bid or the ask quotes. However, in reality, no such data set matching transaction prices to quotes exists. Instead, we can compare transaction prices against prior quotes posted on an information system such as the Reuters FXFX system. Rosenberg and Traub (2009) find that estimates of order flow computed by this method are positively correlated with actual interdealer order flow in the Evans (1998) data, but that the correlations are no larger than 0.5. This low level of accuracy reflects the well-known fact that FXFX quotes are a poor proxy for the quotes offered by individual dealers in the interbank market.

Indirect Interdealer Order Flow

Estimating order flow in an electronic limit-order market is straightforward when there is complete data on transaction prices and the structure of limit prices. Since incoming market orders are matched with the best limit orders, the transaction price for an incoming market purchase must be at least as large as the best (i.e., lowest) limit sale price, whereas the transaction price for an incoming market sale must be no larger than the best (i.e., highest) limit buy price. This means that the LR algorithm will correctly identify incoming market purchases and sales as buyer- and seller-initiated trades if the quotes S_t^A and S_t^B are equated with the best limit buy and sales prices immediately prior to a transaction at time t.

When information on limit prices is unavailable, estimates of order flow can be computed using the Tick test algorithm. These estimates of order flow will not be completely accurate for two reasons. First, a sequence of market purchases or sale orders will be executed at the same transaction price while there are unfilled limit orders at the best limit price. Clearly, the Tick test algorithm would not be able to correctly identify the initiators in such a sequence of trades. The second problem arises from the submission of limit orders that change the best limit prices. To illustrate the potential problem that this can cause, suppose there is a sequence of three market purchase orders. The first is matched with the best prevailing limit order at a price of S_1^A and the second with the next best prevailing limit order at price $S_2^A (> S_1^A)$. Then, before the third market purchase arrives, a new limit sale with a price of $S_3^A (< S_1^A)$ is submitted. Thus, the third transaction then takes place at S_3^A. Under these circumstances, the Tick test would correctly identify the second transaction as buyer-initiated, but would incorrectly identify the third as seller-initiated. Changes in the structure of limit orders make the direction of transaction price changes unreliable as an indicator of incoming market orders.

8.4 Summary

- It is possible to identify the behavior of order flow consistent with a spot-exchange-rate process if that process can be supported as an equilibrium outcome of trading between agents. A limit-order market provides one trading environment in which the information necessary to support an equilibrium is revealed via trading.

- If agents trading in a limit market submit limit orders that are a function of common prior information and market orders are a function of private information, the resulting order flow will aggregate private information. This information conveyed by order flow may be sufficient to establish new limit prices that correspond to the spot rate implied by a Walrasian equilibrium.

- The behavior of order flow in a limit-order market depends critically on how agents choose between market and limit orders. If optimally chosen limit orders are a function of up-to-date private information, the arrival of new information will lead to an immediate change in the structure of limit orders and have no systematic effect on order flow. Alternatively, if there is a friction that inhibits the adjustment of outstanding limit orders when new information arrives, the order flow created by subsequent market orders will have a systematic pattern that reflects the informational asymmetry between market and limit orders.

- Order flows cannot be reliably estimated from the change in portfolio holdings *unless* the changes are measured at transaction frequencies. Changes in foreign currency holdings recorded at lower frequencies (e.g., daily or weekly) incorporate the effects of spot rate changes that are absent when order flows alter FX holdings. As a result, estimates of order flow based on the change in portfolio holdings can be negatively correlated with actual order flow. Access to electronic brokerage systems and the use of price-contingent orders further complicates the problem of identifying order flow from changes in foreign currency holdings of end-users.

- Order flow can be estimated using the high-frequency behavior of transaction prices and quotes. Estimates derived solely from transaction prices will generally be less accurate and cannot be used in cases where trading is decentralized.

8.5 Bibliography

The idea of identifying order flow in a rational expectations exchange-rate model via trading in a limit-order market was first proposed by Bacchetta and van Wincoop (2006). The analysis in Section 8.1 develops and extends the idea outlined in their paper, particularly the notion that there is an informational dichotomy between market and limit orders. Several other papers identify order flow directly from the portfolio decisions of a particular set of agents. For example, Breedon and Vitale (2010) develop a version of Bacchetta and van Wincoop's model in which FX order flow is identified by the change in the demand for foreign bonds by investors. Similarly Hau and Rey (2006), Osler (2008), and Dunne, Hau, and Moore (2010) assume that changes in the desired portfolios of investors induce order flows in equity and FX markets. All these models assume that trading takes place via a limit-order market. Thus, at a minimum, this method of identifying order flow requires that there be other agents in the economy willing to submit limit orders.

The analysis of limit-order markets has become an active area of microstructure research in equities (see Parlour and Seppi 2008 for a recent survey). Although limit and market orders are conceptually straightforward, it has proved very difficult to develop an equilibrium model of trading where the order submission strategies of individual traders are optimally determined. In particular, the integration of order submission with portfolio choice and the determination of equilibrium trading probabilities remain significant theoretical challenges. For this reason, the model of the limit-order market in Section 8.2 separated order submission from portfolio choice and used exogenously specified execution probabilities. The question of whether traders with private information will submit market or limit orders has been addressed in a number of models. For example, Angel (1994), Harris (1998), and Kaniel and Liu (2006) show that traders will submit limit orders when their private information is sufficiently persistent and Goettler and Rajan (2007) present a dynamic equilibrium model of a limit-order market with asymmetric information. There is also recent empirical evidence in Kaniel and Liu (2006) and Cao, Hansch, and Wang (2008) supporting the hypothesis that limit orders are used by informed traders in equity markets. In FX trading, Menkhoff, Osler, and Schmeling (2006) find evidence that changing market conditions significantly alter how informed traders submit orders in an electronic limit-order market for the Russian ruble.

The problem of accurately estimating order flow from incomplete transaction data has not received much attention in the literature. For example, in his recent survey, Vitale (2008) discusses the results of Froot and Ramadorai (2005) but makes no mention of the frequency mismatch problem. Similarly, the effects of price-contingent currency orders on measured order flow have yet to be examined in any detail. A number of papers have examined the accuracy of the trade classification algorithms presented in Section 8.3 in equities markets. For example, Ellis, Michaely, and O'Hara (2000) find that the algorithms have very limited success in the NASDAQ market when transactions take place at prices that differ from quotes. This source of inaccuracy is not a concern in currency markets.

8.6 Review Questions

1. Order Flow in a Rational Expectations Model: Section 8.1 showed how trading in a limit-order market could support the Walrasian equilibrium of a rational expectations model with heterogeneous information. In particular, Figure 8.1 illustrates how the structure of limit orders changes to establish the equilibrium spot rate.

    (a) Consider the change between the initial set of limit orders, LB_I and LS_I, and the new set that supports the Walrasian equilibrium, LB_{II} and LS_{II}. What accounts for the difference between these sets of limit orders? In particular, why does the best limit price, $s^*_{t,I}$, rise?

    (b) Are changes in the best limit prices, $s^*_{t,II} - s^*_{t,I}$, predictable based on households' common information before trading starts? If so, why? If not, why not?

    (c) Is there trading in the limit-order market in round II and beyond? If there is, why do these limit prices establish the Walrasian equilibrium spot rate at $s^*_{t,II} = s_t$?

    (d) What feature of the model ensures that it only takes one round of trading in the limit-order market before the Walrasian equilibrium spot rate is established?

    (e) The model assumes that all households are willing to place limit orders. Is this an innocuous assumption, or is there an incentive for individual households to only trade by placing market orders?

2. Market versus Limit Orders: In FX trading on the EBS limit-order market dealers can observe the best limit-order prices. They can also see the prices and direction of all trades. Dealers cannot see the structure of limit orders beyond the best prices, nor can they see the identity of dealers placing limit and market orders. Consider the decision facing a dealer wanting to acquire $10m worth of euros. He can summit a market purchase order for $10m worth of euros, or he can submit a limit purchase order.

    (a) Suppose that the last market order to purchase euros was matched with a limit order at a price of 1.3000$/€ and that the current best limit-order buy and sale prices are 1.2995$/€ and 1.3005$/€, respectively. Assume that the depth of these limit orders is greater than $10m. What risk does the dealer run if he submits a market purchase order?

    (b) The dealer decides to submit a purchase limit order with a price of 1.2997$/€. Initially, this order is the best limit purchase order on the system. What risk does the dealer run by submitting this order rather than the market order?

(c) At the same time, another dealer wanting to purchase $10m worth of euros submits a purchase limit order with a price of 1.2992$/€. Could the trading decisions by both dealers be rational? If so, what possible rationale could exist for their different choice of limit orders?

3. Portfolio Insurance: Price-contingent currency orders provide a form of portfolio insurance to investors taking foreign currency positions. In particular, consider the position of a U.S. investor who wants to take a long position in euros based on the belief that the USD/EUR rate will depreciate. The investor purchases €10m from a bank at 1.25$/€. At the same time he places a stop loss order to sell €10m if the USD/EUR rate falls below 1.20 $/€.

(a) As an alternative to the stop loss order, the investor could take a position in options on the USD/EUR. What options trade would provide insurance to the investor on his €10m position in the event that the USD/EUR appreciates to 1.20 $/€?

(b) Does the stop loss order provide the same portfolio insurance as the options position? If they are different, how should the investor choose between them?

8.A Appendix

On the sell side we first rewrite expected utiltiy as

$$\mathcal{U}^h_{\text{LSELL}} = \left[(1/\delta) - \exp\left(-\theta(\mathcal{S}^h_t - V^h_t)\right) \right] \pi^{\text{S}} - (1/\delta).$$

Differentiating with respect to $\mathcal{S}^h_t$ using the expression for π^{S} in (8.26) gives

$$0 = \theta \exp(-\theta(\mathcal{S}^h_t - V^h_t))\pi^{\text{S}} - \frac{1}{\lambda}\left[(1/\delta) - \exp\left(-\theta(\mathcal{S}^h_t - V^h_t)\right) \right] \pi^{\text{S}}$$

as the first-order condition, which in turn implies that

$$\mathcal{S}^h_t = V^h_t + \frac{1}{\theta} \ln \delta \,(1 + \lambda\theta).$$

Substituting this expression back into the expected utility function gives

$$\mathcal{U}^h_{\text{LSELL}} = \begin{cases} \dfrac{\lambda\theta}{\delta\,(1+\lambda\theta)}\pi^{\text{S}} - (1/\delta) & \text{for } V^h_t > S^{\text{B}}_t - \frac{1}{\theta}\ln\delta\,(1+\lambda\theta) \\ - \exp\left(-\theta(S^{\text{B}}_t - V^h_t)\right) & \text{otherwise,} \end{cases}$$

where the probability of a limit-order match is given by

$$\pi^{\text{S}} = [\delta(1+\lambda\theta)]^{-\frac{1}{\lambda\theta}} \cdot \exp\left(\frac{1}{\lambda}(S^{\text{B}}_t - V^h_t)\right).$$

Now

$$\frac{\partial \mathcal{U}^h_{\text{LSELL}}}{\partial V^h_t} = -\theta \exp\left(-\theta(\mathcal{S}^h_t - V^h_t)\right) \pi^{\text{s}} < 0$$

and

$$\frac{\partial \mathcal{U}^h_{\text{MSELL}}}{\partial V^h_t} = -\theta \exp\left(-\theta(S^{\text{B}}_t - V^h_t)\right) < 0,$$

but if $\mathcal{S}^h_t > S^{\text{B}}_t$, π^{s} is less than one, so $\partial \mathcal{U}^h_{\text{LSELL}} / \partial V^h_t$ must be greater than $\partial \mathcal{U}^h_{\text{MSELL}} / \partial V^h_t$ for any limit price above S^{B}_t. This means that $S^{\text{B}}_t - \frac{1}{\theta} \ln \delta \, (1 + \lambda \theta)$ is the minimum critical value for submitting a limit order. The derivation of trigger strategy on the buy side is analogous.

PART III

MICRO-BASED MODELS

CHAPTER 9

Order Flows and the Macroeconomy

This is the first of three chapters studying the links between activity in the foreign exchange market and the evolution of the macroeconomy. In this chapter we discuss the model developed by Evans and Lyons (2009) that bridges the gap between the macro models we studied in Part I and the microstructure models we described in Part II. Here we use the model to develop and test a set of empirical predictions concerning the role order flow plays in linking macroeconomic conditions to trading activity in the foreign exchange market. In the following chapters we use the model to examine how exchange rates react to macro data releases and the behavior of the foreign exchange risk premium.

The micro-based model we study identifies the role order flow plays in conveying macro information to the foreign exchange market. The model is micro-based in the sense that it incorporates key features of currency-trading models, such as the Portfolio Shifts model described in Chapter 6. In particular, the spot exchange rate is determined as the foreign currency price quoted by dealers who have limited information about the current state of the economy. The model also contains elements found in the macro models examined in Chapter 2. Specifically, dealers recognize that short-term interest rates are the policy instruments of central banks that react to changes in the macroeconomy. They also understand that the currency orders they receive from agents outside the foreign exchange market are driven by portfolio choices that reflect macroeconomic conditions.

A key feature of the model concerns the structure of information available to dealers and agents. In the macro models we studied in Part I, all agents had complete information about the currency state of the macroeconomy. As a consequence, transactions between agents in goods and financial markets did not convey new information to the counterparties. Here, in contrast, dealers and agents have access to quite different information concerning the macroeconomy. As in the microstructure models of Part II, dealers learn from the currency orders they receive from agents, whereas agents learn from the spot rates quoted by dealers. As we shall see, it is the properties of these information flows that opens new conceptual space for linking the behavior of spot exchange rates to the macroeconomy.

9.1 A Micro-Based Macro Model

9.1.1 Structure

The economy comprises two countries populated by a continuum of risk-averse agents, indexed by $n \in [0, 1]$, and D risk-averse dealers who act as marketmakers in the spot market for foreign currency. As usual, we refer to the home and foreign countries as the United States and Europe, so the log spot exchange rate, s_t, denotes the dollar price of euros. The only other actors in the model are the central banks (i.e., the Federal Reserve (FED) and the European Central Bank (ECB)), who conduct monetary policy by setting short-term nominal interest rates.

Dealers

The pattern of trading in actual foreign exchange markets is extremely complex. On the one hand, foreign exchange dealers quote prices at which they stand ready to buy or sell foreign currency to agents and other dealers. On the other, each dealer can initiate trades against other dealers' quotes and can submit both market and limit orders to electronic brokerages. We do not attempt to model this trading activity in any detail. Instead, we focus on the price dealers quote at the start of each trading week. In particular, we assume that the log spot price quoted by all dealers at the start of week t is given by

$$s_t = \mathbb{E}_t^{\mathrm{D}} s_{t+1} + \hat{r}_t - r_t - \delta_t, \tag{9.1}$$

where $\mathbb{E}_t^{\mathrm{D}}$ denotes expectations conditioned on the common information available to all dealers at the start of week t, Ω_t^{D}. This information set includes r_t and $\hat{r}_t$, which are the 1-week dollar and euro interest rates set by the FED and ECB, respectively. The last term on the right, δ_t, is a risk premium that dealers choose to manage risk efficiently. This risk premium is determined in what follows as a function of dealers' common information, Ω_t^{D}.

In the Portfolio Shifts model of Chapter 6, the spot exchange rate is determined by the Perfect Bayesian Equilibrium (PBE) quote strategy of a game among the dealers played over multiple trading rounds. The specification in equation (9.1) incorporates three features of these PBE quotes: First, each dealer quotes the same price to agents and other dealers. Second, quotes are common across all dealers. Third, all quotes are a function of common information, Ω_t^{D}. It is important to realize that the specification in (9.1) does not implicitly restrict all dealers to have the same information. On the contrary, dealers will generally possess heterogeneous information, which they use in forming their optimal trading strategies. However, insofar as our focus is on the behavior of the spot rate (rather than dealer trading), equation (9.1) implies that we can concentrate our attention on dealers' common information, Ω_t^{D}.

Equation (9.1) says that the price quoted by all dealers at the start of week t is equal to the expected payoff from holding foreign currency until the next week, $\mathbb{E}_t^{\mathrm{D}} s_{t+1} + \hat{r}_t - r_t$, less a premium, δ_t. In models of currency trading, the size of this premium is determined by the requirements of efficient risk-sharing. More specifically, in an economy where there is a finite number of risk-averse dealers and a continuum of risk-averse agents, dealers will choose δ_t such that their expected holdings of risky currencies at the end of week t are zero. In Chapter 6 we showed that this implication of risk-sharing accords well with the actual behavior of dealers, who are restricted as to the size of their overnight positions.

To implement this risk-sharing implication, we assume that all dealers are located in the United States. They therefore choose the risk premium, δ_t, such that their expected holdings of euros at the end of week t equal zero. These holdings are determined by the history of order flow from all agents. In particular, let x_{t+1} denote the aggregate of all orders from agents for euros received by dealers during week t, so $I_{t+1} = -\sum_{i=0}^{\infty} x_{t+1-i}$ denotes the euro holdings of all dealers at the end of week-t trading. (We identify the order flow from week-t trading with a subscript of $t+1$ to emphasize the fact that dealers cannot use the information it conveys until the start of week $t+1$.) Efficient risk-sharing requires that dealers choose a value for δ_t such that

$$\mathbb{E}_t^{\mathrm{D}} I_{t+1} = 0. \tag{9.2}$$

Clearly, this restriction makes δ_t a function of dealers' common information, Ω_t^{D}.

As we noted in Part I, recent macro exchange-rate models stress the importance of identifying expected future interest rates consistent with their use as policy instruments by central banks. With this in mind, let us assume that dealers' interest rate expectations incorporate a view on how central banks react to changes in the macroeconomy. In particular, we assume that

$$\mathbb{E}_t^{\mathrm{D}}(\hat{r}_{t+i} - r_{t+i}) = (1 + \gamma_\pi)\mathbb{E}_t^{\mathrm{D}}\left(\Delta\hat{p}_{t+1+i} - \Delta p_{t+1+i}\right)$$
$$+ \gamma_y\mathbb{E}_t^{\mathrm{D}}\left(\hat{y}_{t+i} - y_{t+i}\right) - \gamma_\varepsilon\mathbb{E}_t^{\mathrm{D}}\varepsilon_{t+i} \tag{9.3}$$

for $i > 0$, where γ_π, γ_y, and γ_ε are positive coefficients. Equation (9.3) says that dealers expect the future differential between euro and dollar rates to be higher when: (1) the future difference between E.U. and U.S. inflation, $\Delta\hat{p}_{t+1} - \Delta p_{t+1}$, is higher, (2) the difference between the E.U. and U.S. output gaps, $\hat{y}_t - y_t$, widens, or (3) when the real exchange rate, $\varepsilon_t \equiv s_t + \hat{p}_t - p_t$, depreciates. The first two terms are consistent with the widely accepted view that central banks react to higher domestic inflation and output by raising short-term interest rates. The third term captures the idea that some central banks can be expected to react to deviations in the spot rate from its purchasing power parity level.

Equation (9.3) embodies an assumption about how dealers' expectations concerning future interest rates are related to their expectations concerning macro variables (e.g., inflation and output), rather than an assumption about whether central banks actually follow particular reaction functions, such as a Taylor rule. As we shall see, the actions of central banks directly affect the spot rate via the current interest rates they set, but it is dealers' expectations about how future interest rates are related to the macroeconomy that are central to understanding the role of order flow as a source of exchange-rate dynamics.

Dealers have access to both private and public sources of information. Each dealer receives private information in the form of the currency orders from the subset of agents that trade with them and from the currency orders they receive from other dealers. In the Portfolio Shifts model, the mapping from dealers' individual information sets to the common information set for all dealers, Ω_t^{D}, is derived endogenously from the trading behavior of dealers. We do not consider this complex process here. Instead, we characterize the evolution of Ω_t^{D} directly under the assumption that a week's worth of trading is sufficient to reveal the size of the aggregate order flow from agents to all dealers. Thus, all dealers know the aggregate order flow from week-t trading, x_{t+1}, by the start of week $t + 1$. Note that this assumption is consistent with the equilibrium of the Portfolio Shifts model because there dealers could correctly infer aggregate order flow from agents after a single round of interdealer trading. The assumption also squares with the empirical evidence on the contemporaneous relationship between daily changes in spot rates and order flows, reviewed in Chapter 7. If dealers could not make reasonably precise inferences about the aggregate currency orders of agents from a day's worth of trading, order flows would not account for so much of the variation in daily spot rates that we observe.

Dealers receive public information in the form of macro data releases and their observations on short-term interest rates. To characterize this information flow, let z_t denote a vector of variables that completely describes the state of the macroeconomy in week t. This vector contains short-term interest rates, r_t and $\hat{r}_t$, prices, p_t and $\hat{p}_t$, the output gaps, y_t and $\hat{y}_t$, and other variables. A subset of the these variables, z_t^o, is contemporaneously observable to all dealers and agents. We assume that the other elements of z_t only become publicly known via macro data releases with a reporting lag of k weeks. The presence of the reporting lag is an important feature of our model and accords with reality. For example, data on the U.S. GDP in the first quarter is only released by the Bureau of Economic Analysis several weeks into the second quarter, so the reporting lag for U.S. output can run to more than 16 weeks.

With these assumptions, the evolution of dealers' common information is given by

$$\Omega_t^{\mathrm{D}} = \left\{ z_t^o, z_{t-k}, x_t, \Omega_{t-1}^{\mathrm{D}} \right\}, \qquad (9.4)$$

where $\{z_t^o, z_{t-k}\}$ identifies the source of the public information flow and x_t is the source of the information flow observed by all dealers.

Agents and the Macroeconomy

The aim of the model is to explain how the evolution of the macroeconomy is linked to activity in the foreign exchange market, so there is no need to include every aspect of agents' behavior. Instead, we focus on their demand for foreign currency. In particular, we assume that the demand for euros in week t by agent $n \in [0, 1]$ can be represented by

$$\alpha_t^n = \alpha_s \left(\mathbb{E}_t^n \Delta s_{t+1} + \hat{r}_t - r_t \right) + h_t^n, \qquad (9.5)$$

where $\alpha_s > 0$ and $\mathbb{E}_t^n$ denotes expectations conditioned on the information available to agent n after observing the spot rate at the start of week t, Ω_t^n. Equation (9.5) decomposes the demand for euros into two terms. The first is the (log) excess return expected by the agent, $\mathbb{E}_t^n \Delta s_{t+1} + \hat{r}_t - r_t$, and the second is a hedging term, h_t^n, that represents the influence of all other factors. This representation of foreign currency demand is very general. For example, it could be derived from a mean-variance portfolio choice model, or from an Overlapping Generations (OLG) portfolio model such as the Rational Expectations model in Chapter 4. In these cases, the h_t^n term identifies the expected returns on other assets and the hedging demand induced by the exposure of the agent's future income to exchange-rate risk. Alternatively, the representation in (9.5) could be derived as an approximation to the optimal currency demand implied by an intertemporal portfolio choice problem, similar to the one studied in Chapter 2.

We next relate h_t^n to the state of the macroeconomy, z_t. Without loss of generality, we assume that

$$h_t^n = \alpha_z z_t^n \qquad (9.6)$$

for some vector α_z, where z_t^n is a vector of variables that describes the observable microeconomic environment of agent n. This environment includes observable macro variables, such as interest rates, and all the micro data that influences all aspects of the agent's behavior. Equation (9.6) simply states that the agent's hedging demand for foreign currency depends on his microeconomic environment. The link between this environment and the state of the macroeconomy is given by

$$z_t^n = z_t + v_t^n, \qquad (9.7)$$

where $v_t^n = [v_{i,t}^n]$ is a vector of agent-specific shocks with the property that $\int_0^1 v_{i,t}^n dn = 0$ for all i. Together, (9.5), (9.6), and (9.7) imply that the aggregate demand for euros by agents is

$$\alpha_t \equiv \int_0^1 \alpha_t^n dn = \alpha_s (\overline{\mathbb{E}}_t^n s_{t+1} - s_t + \hat{r}_t - r_t) + h_t, \qquad (9.8)$$

where $h_t \equiv \int_0^1 h_t^n dn = \alpha_z z_t$ is the aggregate hedging demand and $\overline{\mathbb{E}}_t^n$ denotes the average of agents' expectations: $\overline{\mathbb{E}}_t^n s_{t+1} = \int_0^1 \mathbb{E}_t^n s_{t+1} dn$.

Like dealers, each agent has access to both private and public sources of information. The former comes in the form of information about the microeconomic environment, z_t^n. Each agent also receives public information about the macroeconomy from macro data releases, the short-term interest rates set by central banks, and the spot exchange rate quoted by dealers. The evolution of agent n's information can therefore be represented as

$$\Omega_t^n = \left\{ z_t^o, z_{t-k}, s_t, z_t^n, \Omega_{t-1}^n \right\} \qquad (9.9)$$

for $n \in [0, 1]$. Note that, in accordance with reality, agents do not observe aggregate order flow, x_t.

All that now remains is to characterize the behavior of the macroeconomy. In a macro model this would be done by aggregating the optimal decisions of agents with respect to consumption, savings, investment, and price-setting in a manner consistent with market clearing, given assumptions about productivity, preference shocks, and the conduct of monetary/fiscal policy. Fortunately, for our purposes, we can avoid going into all this detail. Instead, it suffices to identify a few elements of the z_t vector and to represent its dynamics in a reduced form. Specifically, we assume that the inflation, interest, price, and output differentials comprise the first four elements of z_t,

$$z_t' = [\ \Delta \hat{p}_t - \Delta p_t, \quad \hat{r}_t - r_t, \quad \hat{p}_t - p_t, \quad \hat{y}_t - y_t, \quad \ldots, \quad \ldots\ ],$$

and that the dynamics of z_t can be written as

$$z_t = A_z z_{t-1} + B_u u_t \qquad (9.10)$$

TABLE 9.1
Timing and Information Flows

Week	Event	Information flow to Dealers	Information flow to Agents
t	Data released on past macroeconomic activity and central banks set interest rates	z_{t-k} z_t^o	z_{t-k} z_t^o
	Each agent n observes her microeconomic environment		z_t^n
	Dealers quote log spot price		s_t
	Agents initiate trade against dealers' quotes producing aggregate order flow, which becomes known to all dealers via interdealer trading	x_{t+1}	
$t+1$			
$\vdots$			

for some matrices A_z and B_u, where u_t is a vector of mean-zero serially uncorrelated shocks. This representation of the macroeconomic dynamics is completely general because we have not placed any restrictions on the other variables included in the z_t vector.

To clarify how the model works, Table 9.1 summarizes the timing of events and the flows of information received by dealers and agents within each week. At the start of week t, all dealers and agents receive public information in the form of data releases on the past state of the economy, z_{t-k}, and observations on current macro variables, including the short-term interest rates set by central banks, $z_t^o = \{r_t, \hat{r}_t, \ldots\}$. Each agent n also receives private information concerning his or her current microeconomic environment, z_t^n. Next, all dealers use their common information, Ω_t^D, to quote a log spot price, s_t, that is observable by all agents. Each agent n then uses his private information, Ω_t^n, to place a foreign currency order with a dealer, who fills it at the spot rate s_t. For the remainder of the week, dealers trade among themselves. As a result of this activity (which is not modeled), all dealers learn the aggregate order flow, x_{t+1}, that resulted from the earlier week-t trades between agents and dealers.

9.1.2 Equilibrium

An equilibrium in the model comprises a sequence of spot rate quotes by dealers satisfying equation (9.1) subject to: (1) the restriction in (9.2) that identifies the risk premium, (2) dealer expectations concerning future interest rates in (9.3), and (3) the evolution of dealers' common information, Ω_t^D, in (9.4). Moreover, the evolution of Ω_t^D depends on the equilibrium currency demands of agents. Since dealers fill the foreign currency orders of agents in their capacity as marketmakers, in equilibrium the aggregate order flow received by dealers during week-t trading must equal the aggregate change in the demand for euros across all agents:

$$x_{t+1} = \alpha_t - \alpha_{t-1} = \int_0^1 \Delta \alpha_t^n \, dn. \tag{9.11}$$

This market-clearing condition implies that x_{t+1} is a function of the microeconomic environments facing all agents in weeks t and $t-1$ and their expectations concerning future excess returns which are based on agents' private information, Ω_t^n and Ω_{t-1}^n. Thus, the sequence of spot rates depends on the evolution of dealers' common information, which, in equilibrium, reflects the currency demands of agents based on microeconomic factors and their private information. At the same time, the evolution of agents' private information, Ω_t^n, depends on the equilibrium actions of dealers insofar as their spot rate quotes convey new information. In sum, equilibrium in our model is a sequence of spot rates and market-clearing order flows that support and are supported by the endogenous evolution of dealers' common information and agents' private information.

The Spot Rate Equation

Our analysis of the model's equilibrium begins with the spot rate. The spot rate quoted by dealers satisfies equation (9.1) subject to the risk-sharing restriction that identifies the risk premium and dealers' expectations concerning future interest rates in (9.3). To derive an expression for the equilibrium spot rate, we first use (9.1) to write

$$\mathbb{E}_t^{\mathrm{D}} s_{t+1} = \mathbb{E}_t^{\mathrm{D}} \left[\hat{r}_{t+1} - r_{t+1} - \delta_{t+1} \right] + \mathbb{E}_t^{\mathrm{D}} s_{t+2}.$$

Substituting for interest rate expectations with (9.3) and iterating forward under the assumption that $\mathbb{E}_t^{\mathrm{D}} \lim_{i \to \infty} \rho^i s_{t+i} = 0$ gives

$$\mathbb{E}_t^{\mathrm{D}} s_{t+1} = \mathbb{E}_t^{\mathrm{D}} \sum_{i=1}^{\infty} \rho^i (f_{t+i} - \delta_{t+i}), \tag{9.12}$$

with $\rho = 1/(1 + \gamma_\varepsilon) < 1$, where

$$f_t = (1 + \gamma_\pi) \left(\Delta \hat{p}_{t+1} - \Delta p_{t+1} \right) + \gamma_y \left(\hat{y}_t - y_t \right) + \left(\tfrac{1-\rho}{\rho} \right) \left(p_t - \hat{p}_t \right).$$

Equation (9.12) identifies dealers' expectations for next week's spot rate in terms of their forecasts for macro fundamentals, f_t, and the risk premium, δ_t. Combining (9.12) with (9.1) gives the following equation for the equilibrium spot rate:

$$s_t = (\hat{r}_t - r_t) + \mathbb{E}_t^{\mathrm{D}} \sum_{i=1}^{\infty} \rho^i f_{t+i} - \mathbb{E}_t^{\mathrm{D}} \sum_{i=0}^{\infty} \rho^i \delta_{t+i}. \tag{9.13}$$

The three terms on the right of equation (9.13) identify different factors affecting the log spot rate dealers quote at the start of week t. First, the current stance of monetary policy in the United States and Europe affects dealers' quotes via the interest differential, $\hat{r}_t - r_t$, because it contributes directly to the payoff from holding euros until week $t+1$. Second, dealers are concerned with the future course of macro fundamentals, f_t. This term embodies dealers' expectations of how central banks will react to macroeconomic conditions when setting future interest rates. The third factor arises from risk-sharing between dealers and agents as represented by the present and expected future values of the risk premium. This risk-sharing implication is not found in standard exchange-rate models, and so requires some further explanation.

Recall that dealers choose the risk premium so that $\mathbb{E}_t^D I_{t+1} = 0$, where $I_{t+1} = I_t - x_{t+1}$, and market clearing requires that the aggregate order flow received by dealers during week-t trading must equal the aggregate change in the demand for euros across all agents: $x_{t+1} = \alpha_t - \alpha_{t-1}$. These two conditions jointly imply that $I_{t+1} + \alpha_t = I_t + \alpha_{t-1} = I_1 + \alpha_0$. For clarity, we normalize $I_1 + \alpha_0$ to equal zero, so efficient risk-sharing requires that $0 = \mathbb{E}_t^D \alpha_t$. Combining this restriction with (9.5)–(9.8) and the definition of α_t gives

$$0 = \alpha_s \mathbb{E}_t^D (\overline{\mathbb{E}}_t^n s_{t+1} - s_t + \hat{r}_t - r_t) + \mathbb{E}_t^D h_t, \tag{9.14}$$

where h_t is the aggregate hedging demand for euros and $\overline{\mathbb{E}}_t^n s_{t+1} = \int_0^1 \mathbb{E}_t^n s_{t+1} dn$ is the average of agents' forecasts for next week's spot rate. Since $\mathbb{E}_t^D \Delta s_{t+1} + \hat{r}_t - r_t = \delta_t$ from equation (9.1), and $\mathbb{E}_t^D \overline{\mathbb{E}}_t^n s_{t+1} = \mathbb{E}_t^D s_{t+1} + \mathbb{E}_t^D (\overline{\mathbb{E}}_t^n s_{t+1} - s_{t+1})$ by definition, the first term on the right of (9.14) is equal to $\alpha_s \delta_t + \alpha_s \mathbb{E}_t^D (\overline{\mathbb{E}}_t^n s_{t+1} - s_{t+1})$. We may therefore rewrite equation (9.14) as

$$\delta_t = \mathbb{E}_t^D \left[s_{t+1}^e - \frac{1}{\alpha_s} h_t \right], \tag{9.15}$$

where $s_{t+1}^e = s_{t+1} - \overline{\mathbb{E}}_t^n s_{t+1}$.

Equation (9.15) shows that dealers' choices for the risk premium depend on their estimates of: (1) the aggregate hedging demand for euros, $\mathbb{E}_t^D h_t$, and (2) the average error agents make when forecasting next week's spot rate, s_{t+1}^e. Intuitively, dealers lower the risk premium when they anticipate a rise in the aggregate hedging demand for euros because the implied fall in the excess return agents expect will offset their desire to accumulate larger euro holdings. Dealers also reduce the risk premium to offset agents' desires to accumulate larger euro holdings when they are viewed as being too optimistic (on average) about the future spot rate, that is, when $\mathbb{E}_t^D s_{t+1} < \mathbb{E}_t^D \overline{\mathbb{E}}_t^n s_{t+1}$.

Combining (9.13) with (9.15) gives us the following micro-based exchange-rate equation:

$$s_t = (\hat{r}_t - r_t) + \mathbb{E}_t^D \sum_{i=1}^{\infty} \rho^i f_{t+i} + \frac{1}{\alpha_s} \mathbb{E}_t^D \sum_{i=0}^{\infty} \rho^i h_{t+i} - \frac{1}{\rho} \mathbb{E}_t^D \sum_{i=1}^{\infty} \rho^i s_{t+i}^e. \tag{9.16}$$

Two aspects of equation (9.16) differentiate the exchange-rate implications of this model from those of traditional macro models. First, the equation identifies the foreign currency price all dealers quote. As such, s_t is a function of the information available to dealers, Ω_t^D, at the time they quote prices. This information set includes contemporaneous interest rates, $\hat{r}_t$ and r_t, but not observations on the other variables that comprise the current state of the macroeconomy. Second, dealers' quotes include a risk premium that incorporates their estimates of the aggregate hedging demand and agents' forecast errors. These factors can be a source of variation in spot rates when dealers' views of current and future monetary policy remain unchanged.

The structure of equation (9.16) is similar to the spot rate equation of the rational expectations models in Chapter 4. There the market-clearing spot rate depends on

current fundamentals and higher-order expectations concerning future macro fundamentals, which can be written in terms of the average expectation of future average
forecast errors. Here, in contrast, it is dealers' expectations of the agents' average
forecast errors that affect the spot rate via their implications for efficient risk-sharing.

Information Dynamics

Equation (9.16) identifies the spot rate dealers quote in terms of current interest rates,
macro fundamentals, agents' hedging demands, and the expectations of both dealers
and agents. In equilibrium, these expectations depend on the endogenous evolution
of dealers' common information and agents' private information. We now examine
these information dynamics in detail.

The key to this endeavor is to characterize the mapping from the true state of the
economy to information available to dealers and agents. For this purpose, we introduce
a new vector, Z_t, that comprises the vectors of shocks, $\{u_t, u_{t-1}, \dots u_{t-k-1}\}$, and
z_{t-k}:

$$Z'_t = [\, u'_t, \quad u'_{t-1}, \quad \dots, \quad u'_{t-k-1}, \quad z'_{t-k} \,].$$

The dynamics of Z_t are easily derived from equation (9.10). For example, in the $k = 1$
case

$$Z_t \equiv \begin{bmatrix} u_t \\ u_{t-1} \\ u_{t-2} \\ z_{t-1} \end{bmatrix} = \begin{bmatrix} 0 & 0 & 0 & 0 \\ I & 0 & 0 & 0 \\ 0 & I & 0 & 0 \\ B_u & 0 & 0 & A_z \end{bmatrix} \begin{bmatrix} u_{t-1} \\ u_{t-2} \\ u_{t-3} \\ z_{t-2} \end{bmatrix} + \begin{bmatrix} I \\ 0 \\ 0 \end{bmatrix} u_t.$$

We write the dynamics here for the general case as

$$Z_t = AZ_{t-1} + Bu_t. \tag{9.17}$$

Note, further, that z_t can be written as a linear combination of the elements in Z_t, that
is, $z_t = \Lambda_z Z_t$ for some matrix Λ_z.

The Z_t vector contains the information that is *potentially* available to dealers and
agents about the state of the macroeconomy in week t, z_t, and about the shocks to the
economy over the past $k + 2$ weeks, $\{u_t, u_{t-1}, \dots u_{t-k-1}\}$. For example, the dealers'
estimates of z_t based on Ω^D_t must be a function of z_{t-k} and the k-period histories
of observable variables, $\{z^o_{t-i}\}_{i=0}^{k-1}$, and order flows $\{x_{t-i}\}_{i=0}^{k-1}$. Since z^o_t is a simply a
subvector of z_t, the sequence $\{z^o_{t-i}\}_{i=0}^{k-1}$ is easily represented as a function of Z_t. As
we shall see, equilibrium order flow can also be represented as a function of Z_t.

We now characterize the equilibrium mapping from Z_t to dealers' expectations
concerning Z_t based on Ω^D_t and agents' expectations based on Ω^n_t. As usual, proofs
and detailed derivations can be found in the appendix to this chapter.

Proposition 9.1: *In equilibrium, dealers' estimates of Z_t conditioned on common information, Ω_t^D, and agent n's estimates conditioned on Ω_t^n, for any $n \in [0, 1]$, can be expressed as*

$$\mathbb{E}_t^D Z_t \equiv E[Z_t | \Omega_t^D] = \Phi^D Z_t \tag{9.18a}$$

and

$$\mathbb{E}_t^n Z_t \equiv E[Z_t | \Omega_t^n] = \Phi^N Z_t + \sum_{j=0}^{\infty} \Psi_j v_{t-j}^n \tag{9.18b}$$

for some matrices Φ^D, Φ^N, and Ψ_j.

Two features of Proposition 9.1 deserve special emphasis: First, the Φ^D, Φ^N, and Ψ_j matrices depend on the equilibrium properties of spot rates and order flows. In particular, some elements of the Φ^D matrix reflect the information order flow conveys about the elements of Z_t to dealers. Similarly, some elements of Φ^N and Ψ_j reflect the information conveyed by spot rates to agents. The second feature concerns the heterogeneity of agents' estimates. Note that the Φ^N and Ψ_j matrices do not depend on the identity of the agent, n. The only sources of heterogeneity across agents' estimates are the agent-specific shocks, v_t^n. The average estimate of Z_t across all agents is therefore

$$\overline{\mathbb{E}}_t^n Z_t \equiv \int_0^1 \mathbb{E}_t^n Z_t dn = \Phi^N Z_t + \sum_{j=0}^{\infty} \Psi_j \int_0^1 v_{t-j}^n dn = \Phi^N Z_t. \tag{9.19}$$

As we shall see, the difference between $\mathbb{E}_t^D Z_t$ and $\overline{\mathbb{E}}_t^n Z_t$ plays a central role in the model.

Next, we characterize the relationship between the spot rate and dealers' estimates of Z_t.

Proposition 9.2: *In equilibrium, the log spot rate quoted by all dealers at the start of week t takes the form*

$$s_t = \Lambda_s \mathbb{E}_t^D Z_t \tag{9.20}$$

for some vector Λ_s.

Equation (9.20) plays a central role in understanding the equilibrium. It combines (9.13) with the dynamics of Z_t in (9.17) and an equation for the equilibrium risk premium (derived later) to show that the spot rate quote is linearly related to dealers' estimates of Z_t based on their common information, Ω_t^D. Two important implications follow from this representation. First, all the variations in spot rates reflect changes in dealers' estimates, $\mathbb{E}_t^D Z_t$, rather than the Z_t vector itself. Indeed, (9.18a) and (9.20) imply that $s_t = \Lambda_s \Phi^D Z_t$, so the effects of changes in Z_t on the spot rate are in effect "filtered" by the Φ^D matrix. Second, agents' expectations concerning excess returns, $\mathbb{E}_t^n \Delta s_{t+1} + \hat{r}_t - r_t$, depend on their forecasts of how dealers' estimates will change, $\mathbb{E}_t^n (\mathbb{E}_{t+1}^D Z_{t+1} - \mathbb{E}_t^D Z_t)$. As a result, agents' demands for foreign currency depend, in part, on their forecasts about what dealers will learn about the macroeconomy in the future. As we shall see, both of these implications contribute to the equilibrium dynamics of spot rates and order flow.

We are now in a position to describe the equilibrium behavior of order flow.

Proposition 9.3: *In equilibrium, the aggregate demand for foreign currency by agents in week t is*

$$\alpha_t = \alpha_s \delta_t + \alpha_s \Lambda_s \Phi^{\mathrm{D}} (\overline{\mathbb{E}}_t^n - \mathbb{E}_t^{\mathrm{D}}) Z_{t+1} + h_t, \tag{9.21}$$

which implies that the order flow from agents in week-t trading is

$$x_{t+1} = \alpha_s \Lambda_\delta (Z_t - \mathbb{E}_t^{\mathrm{D}} Z_t) - \alpha_s \Lambda_\delta (Z_{t-1} - \mathbb{E}_{t-1}^{\mathrm{D}} Z_{t-1}), \tag{9.22}$$

where $\Lambda_\delta = \Lambda_s \Phi^{\mathrm{D}} A (\Phi^{\mathrm{N}} - \Phi^{\mathrm{D}}) + \frac{\alpha_z}{\alpha_s} \Lambda_z$.

Equation (9.21) shows that the aggregate demand for foreign currency depends on three components: (1) the risk premium priced into the current spot rate quoted by dealers, (2) the difference between dealers' expectations and the average of agents' expectations concerning the state of the economy, and (3) the aggregate hedging term. The first two components identify the effects of agents' forecasts for excess returns from equation (9.8). To see why, note that $\mathbb{E}_t^{\mathrm{D}} \Delta s_{t+1} + \hat{r}_t - r_t = \delta_t$ from equation (9.1), so

$$\alpha_s (\overline{\mathbb{E}}_t^n s_{t+1} - s_t + \hat{r}_t - r_t) = \alpha_s (\mathbb{E}_t^{\mathrm{D}} \Delta s_{t+1} + \hat{r}_t - r_t) + \alpha_s (\overline{\mathbb{E}}_t^n - \mathbb{E}_t^{\mathrm{D}}) s_{t+1}$$

$$= \alpha_s \delta_t + \alpha_s \Lambda_s \Phi^{\mathrm{D}} (\overline{\mathbb{E}}_t^n - \mathbb{E}_t^{\mathrm{D}}) Z_{t+1}, \tag{9.23}$$

where the second line uses the fact that $s_{t+1} = \Lambda_s \Phi^{\mathrm{D}} Z_{t+1}$.

Equation (9.22) shows equilibrium order flow as a function of the difference between the actual state of the economy and dealers' estimates at the start of weeks t and $t-1$. This important feature of our model is an implication of (9.21) and dealers' choices for the risk premium, δ_t. In particular, recall that the risk-sharing and market-clearing conditions in (9.15) and (9.11) jointly imply that $\mathbb{E}_t^{\mathrm{D}} \alpha_t$ equals a constant, which we normalize to zero. Combining this restriction with (9.21) gives the following equation for the risk premium:

$$\delta_t = -\Lambda_s \Phi^{\mathrm{D}} \mathbb{E}_t^{\mathrm{D}} (\overline{\mathbb{E}}_t^n - \mathbb{E}_t^{\mathrm{D}}) Z_{t+1} - \frac{1}{\alpha_s} \mathbb{E}_t^{\mathrm{D}} h_t = -\Lambda_\delta \mathbb{E}_t^{\mathrm{D}} Z_t, \tag{9.24}$$

so (9.21) can be rewritten as

$$\alpha_t = \alpha_s \delta_t + \left(\alpha_s \Lambda_s \Phi^{\mathrm{D}} A (\Phi^{\mathrm{N}} - \Phi^{\mathrm{D}}) + \alpha_z \Lambda_z \right) Z_t = \alpha_s \Lambda_\delta (Z_t - \mathbb{E}_t^{\mathrm{D}} Z_t). \tag{9.25}$$

Thus, the equilibrium demand for foreign currency depends on the difference between dealers' estimates of Z_t and its actual value. Combining this expression with the market-clearing condition in (9.11) gives the equation for order flow in (9.22).

Up to this point we have described the equilibrium determination of the spot rate and order flow given the dynamics of Z_t in (9.17) and the form of dealers' and agents' expectations in Proposition 9.1. All that now remains is to establish that these expectations take the form described in (9.18). For this purpose, we first identify the flow of information reaching dealers and agents each week. Recall that the flow of information received by dealers comprises $\{z_t^o, z_{t-k}, x_t\}$, where z_t^o is the subset of variables in z_t that is publicly observable (i.e., $z_t^o = cz_t$, for some matrix c). Furthermore, equation (9.22) implies that x_t is a linear function of $Z_{t-1} - \mathbb{E}_{t-1}^{D} Z_{t-1}$ and $Z_{t-2} - \mathbb{E}_{t-2}^{D} Z_{t-2}$. These vectors of estimation errors are linear functions of $\{u_{t-1}, \ldots, u_{t-k}\}$ and $\{u_{t-2}, \ldots, u_{t-k-1}\}$, respectively, which are all elements of Z_t. Hence, (9.22) implies that $x_t = \Lambda_x Z_t$ for some vector Λ_x. We can therefore represent the flow of information to dealers at the start of week t as

$$
Z_t^{D} \equiv \begin{bmatrix} z_t^o \\ z_{t-k} \\ x_t \end{bmatrix} = \begin{bmatrix} & & & & c\Lambda_z \\ 0 & 0 & \ldots & 0 & I \\ & & & & \Lambda_x \end{bmatrix} \begin{bmatrix} u_t \\ u_{t-1} \\ \vdots \\ u_{t-1-k} \\ z_{t-k} \end{bmatrix}
$$

or, more compactly,

$$
Z_t^{D} = C Z_t. \tag{9.26}
$$

The flow of information received by individual agents comprises $\{z_t^o, z_{t-k}, s_t, z_t^n\}$. Recall from (9.7) that $z_t^n = z_t + v_t^n$, so the only endogenous source of information is the spot rate, which we can write as $s_t = \Lambda_s \Phi^{D} Z_t$ using (9.18a) and (9.20). The flow of information to agent n can now be represented by

$$
Z_t^{n} \equiv \begin{bmatrix} z_t^o \\ z_{t-k} \\ s_t \\ z_t^n \end{bmatrix} = \begin{bmatrix} & & & & c\Lambda_z \\ 0 & 0 & \ldots & 0 & I \\ & & & & \Lambda_s \Phi^{D} \\ & & & & \Lambda_z \end{bmatrix} \begin{bmatrix} u_t \\ u_{t-1} \\ \vdots \\ u_{t-1-k} \\ z_{t-k} \end{bmatrix} + \begin{bmatrix} 0 \\ 0 \\ \vdots \\ 0 \\ I \end{bmatrix} v_t^n
$$

or, more compactly,

$$
Z_t^{n} = C^{N} Z_t + D^{N} v_t^n. \tag{9.27}
$$

At the start of week t, dealers and agents use their observations on Z_t^{D} and Z_t^{n} to update their estimates of Z_t according to

$$
\mathbb{E}_t^{D} Z_t = \mathbb{E}_{t-1}^{D} Z_t + G(Z_t^{D} - \mathbb{E}_{t-1}^{D} Z_t^{D})
$$

and

$$
\mathbb{E}_t^{n} Z_t = \mathbb{E}_{t-1}^{n} Z_t + G^{N}(Z_t^{n} - \mathbb{E}_{t-1}^{n} Z_t^{n}), \tag{9.28}
$$

where G and G^{N} are the so-called gain matrices that identify how new week-t information (i.e., $Z_t^{D} - \mathbb{E}_{t-1}^{D} Z_t^{D}$ for dealers and $Z_t^{n} - \mathbb{E}_{t-1}^{n} Z_t^{n}$ for agent n) is used to revise the previous week's estimates of Z_t. The form of these matrices is determined by the Kalman filter, which is discussed in the appendix.

9.2 Empirical Implications

9.2.1 Order Flow and Macro Information

The dynamic implications of this model are quite different from those of standard exchange-rate models. We now develop these implications to explain the role order flow plays in linking the dynamics of spot rates to the evolution of the macroeconomy.

We begin with the dynamics of the spot rate. In particular, equation (9.20) in Proposition 9.2 implies that the weekly log return on foreign currency (i.e., the rate of depreciation) can be written as

$$\Delta s_{t+1} = \Lambda_s (\mathbb{E}_{t+1}^{D} Z_{t+1} - \mathbb{E}_t^{D} Z_t)$$

$$= \Lambda_s \mathbb{E}_t^{D} \Delta Z_{t+1} + \Lambda_s (\mathbb{E}_{t+1}^{D} - \mathbb{E}_t^{D}) Z_{t+1}. \qquad (9.29)$$

The first term on the second line identifies the return expected by dealers when they quote spot rates in week t: $\mathbb{E}_t^{D} \Delta s_{t+1} = r_t - \hat{r}_t + \delta_t$. The second term identifies the unexpected portion of returns, $s_{t+1} - \mathbb{E}_t^{D} s_{t+1}$, that reflects the flow of new information concerning Z_{t+1} received by dealers between the start of weeks t and $t + 1$. Using the dynamics of Z_t in (9.17), we can rewrite this term as

$$s_{t+1} - \mathbb{E}_t^{D} s_{t+1} = (\mathbb{E}_{t+1}^{D} - \mathbb{E}_t^{D}) \left(\Lambda_s A Z_t + \Lambda_s B u_{t+1} \right)$$

$$= \Lambda_s B \mathbb{E}_{t+1}^{D} u_{t+1} + \Lambda_s A (\mathbb{E}_{t+1}^{D} - \mathbb{E}_t^{D}) Z_t. \qquad (9.30)$$

The effect of contemporaneous macro information dealers receive at the start of week $t + 1$ is identified by the first term in the second line. This information must be public because dealers do not have any sources of private information concerning Z_{t+1} at the start of week $t + 1$. Any unexpected changes in short-term interest rates would affect the spot rate via this term. The second term on the right of (9.30) identifies news concerning the recent *history* of the macroeconomy. Recall that Z_t contains information on the state of the economy from week t back to $t - k - 1$, so the elements of $(\mathbb{E}_{t+1}^{D} - \mathbb{E}_t^{D}) Z_t$ identify the flow of information to dealers about past activity. This information flow is not present in standard macro models, where the current state of the macroeconomy is common knowledge, but here it comes from two sources. The first source is the macro data releases at the start of week $t + 1$. These releases provide data on *past* macroeconomic conditions and so may contribute to $(\mathbb{E}_{t+1}^{D} - \mathbb{E}_t^{D}) Z_t$. The second source of information is the aggregate order flow dealers observe at the end of week-t trading, x_{t+1}. This is a key implication of the model, and so deserves careful examination.

In equilibrium, the aggregate order flow dealers observe at the end of week-t trading reflects the change in the aggregate demand for foreign currency by agents between weeks $t - 1$ and t: $x_{t+1} = \alpha_t - \alpha_{t-1}$. Thus x_{t+1} will only be informative to dealers insofar as it aggregates information in agents' changing demands for foreign currency, $\alpha_t - \alpha_{t-1}$. Equation (9.21) in Proposition 9.3 shows that α_t contains two sources of information. The first comes from the aggregate hedging term, h_t. Although the hedging demands of individual agents may be dominated by the effects of agent-specific shocks, since these shocks have no effect on h_t, it can be a source of information concerning z_t. The second source comes from agents' forecasts for excess returns. As (9.23) shows, these forecasts embed agents' expectations concerning Z_{t+1}, specifically, the difference between the average of agents' and dealers' expectations, $\overline{\mathbb{E}}_t^n Z_{t+1} - \mathbb{E}_t^D Z_{t+1}$. As a consequence, α_t will contain an aggregation of the dispersed information individual agents use in forming their forecasts of Z_{t+1}. Although individual forecasts for Z_{t+1} based on Ω_t^n may be less precise than those of dealers, which are based on Ω_t^D, it is perfectly possible for $\overline{\mathbb{E}}_t^n Z_{t+1}$ to be more precise than $\mathbb{E}_t^D Z_{t+1}$, so the difference between these expectations can be a source of new information to dealers.

Once we recognize that the aggregate demand for foreign currency contains macro information that may not already be known to dealers, it is easy to appreciate why order flow can convey information. Recall that dealers know the history of order flow. This means that $\alpha_{t-1} \in \Omega_t^D$, so unexpected order flow from week-t trading is

$$x_{t+1} - \mathbb{E}_t^D x_{t+1} = \alpha_t - \mathbb{E}_t^D \alpha_t = \alpha_s \Lambda_\delta (Z_t - \mathbb{E}_t^D Z_t), \qquad (9.31)$$

where the term on the right follows from (9.25). Thus, order flow from week-t trading reveals information about Z_t that was not previously known to dealers, provided Λ_δ differs from a vector of zeros. Recall from (9.8) that $\alpha_t = \alpha_s (\overline{\mathbb{E}}_t^n s_{t+1} - s_t + \hat{r}_t - r_t) + h_t$. This condition will be met unless the average of agents' expectations regarding excess returns is completely offset by the aggregate hedging demand across all possible states of the macroeconomy.

9.2.2 Exchange-Rate Returns and Order Flows

In Chapter 7 we saw that the order flow data studied by Evans and Lyons (2002a,b) accounted for between 40 and 80 percent of the daily variation in the spot exchange rates of major currency pairs. Since subsequent research has established that this strong relationship between order flows and exchange-rate returns holds across different currencies, different measures of order flow, and frequencies from a few minutes to several weeks, it is important to check that the model can account for this empirical regularity. After all, if the model cannot provide a structural explanation for these empirical results, its implications for the links among spot rates, order flows, and the macroeconomy are unlikely to be of any empirical relevance.

To examine the model's implications for the return/order flow relationship, we first use (9.26), (9.28), and (9.30) to write the log excess return as

$$er_{t+1} = \Delta s_{t+1} + \hat{r}_t - r_t = \delta_t + s_{t+1} - \mathbb{E}_t^D s_{t+1}$$
$$= \delta_t + \lambda_u u_{t+1} + \lambda_z (Z_t - \mathbb{E}_t^D Z_t), \qquad (9.32)$$

where $\lambda_u = \Lambda_s GCB$ and $\lambda_z = \Lambda_s GCA$. Next, consider the projection of excess returns on unexpected order flow, $x_{t+1} - \mathbb{E}_t^D x_{t+1}$:

$$er_{t+1} = \beta_{er}(x_{t+1} - \mathbb{E}_t^D x_{t+1}) + \xi_{t+1}, \qquad (9.33)$$

where ξ_{t+1} is the projection error that identifies the portion of excess returns that is uncorrelated with order flow. By definition, the projection coefficient is given by

$$\beta_{er} = \frac{\mathbb{E}[er_{t+1}(x_{t+1} - \mathbb{E}_t^{\text{D}} x_{t+1})]}{\mathbb{E}[(x_{t+1} - \mathbb{E}_t^{\text{D}} x_{t+1})^2]},$$

where $\mathbb{E}[.]$ denotes unconditional expectations. Substituting for er_{t+1} from (9.32), we can rewrite this coefficient as

$$\beta_{er} = \lambda_u \frac{\mathbb{E}[u_{t+1}(x_{t+1} - \mathbb{E}_t^{\text{D}} x_{t+1})]}{\mathbb{E}[(x_{t+1} - \mathbb{E}_t^{\text{D}} x_{t+1})^2]} + \lambda_z \frac{\mathbb{E}[(Z_t - \mathbb{E}_t^{\text{D}} Z_t)(x_{t+1} - \mathbb{E}_t^{\text{D}} x_{t+1})]}{\mathbb{E}[(x_{t+1} - \mathbb{E}_t^{\text{D}} x_{t+1})^2]}.$$

The first term depends on the correlation between unexpected order flow during week-t trading, and the contemporaneous macro shocks at the start of week $t + 1$. This term must equal zero because, as equation (9.31) shows, order flow in week t reflects only current and prior macro conditions (i.e., the elements of Z_t). The projection coefficient is therefore determined by the second term. After substituting for unexpected order flow from (9.31), we find that

$$\beta_{er} = \frac{\lambda_z \mathbb{E}[(Z_t - \mathbb{E}_t^{\text{D}} Z_t)(x_{t+1} - \mathbb{E}_t^{\text{D}} x_{t+1})]}{\mathbb{E}[(x_{t+1} - \mathbb{E}_t^{\text{D}} x_{t+1})^2]} = \frac{\lambda_z \mathbb{V}^{\text{D}}(Z_t)\Lambda_\delta' \alpha_s}{\alpha_s \Lambda_\delta \mathbb{V}^{\text{D}}(Z_t)\Lambda_\delta' \alpha_s}, \qquad (9.34)$$

where $\mathbb{V}^{\text{D}}(Z_t) = \mathbb{E}[(Z_t - \mathbb{E}_t^{\text{D}} Z_t)(Z_t - \mathbb{E}_t^{\text{D}} Z_t)']$.

Equations (9.33) and (9.34) allow us to identify the conditions under which unexpected order flow during week-t trading contributes to the change in dealers' quotes between the beginning of week t and $t + 1$. Although the dependent variable in (9.33) is the excess return, er_{t+1}, rather than the change in the log spot rate, Δs_{t+1}, all the unanticipated variations in er_{t+1} come from unexpected revisions in dealers' quotes (i.e., $er_{t+1} - \mathbb{E}_t^{\text{D}} er_{t+1} = s_{t+1} - \mathbb{E}_t^{\text{D}} s_{t+1}$). The β_{er} coefficient therefore quantifies the extent to which dealers use new information conveyed by week-t order flow in choosing the spot price they quote at the start of week $t + 1$.

Inspection of (9.34) reveals that β_{er} will be different from zero when three conditions are satisfied: First, dealers must face some uncertainty about the current state of the macroeconomy. Otherwise $Z_t = \mathbb{E}_t^{\text{D}} Z_t$, so the covariance matrix $\mathbb{V}^{\text{D}}(Z_t)$ is a matrix of zeros. Second, dealer uncertainty about the macroeconomy must contribute to the unpredictability of order flow. Dealers may have incomplete information about some of the elements of Z_t so that $Z_t \neq \mathbb{E}_t^{\text{D}} Z_t$, but if those elements make no contribution to order flow, agents' currency orders in week t will not convey any new information to dealers. Third, even if order flows do convey new information concerning elements of Z_t, that information will only be incorporated into dealers' week-$t + 1$ quotes if it is "price relevant." In other words, the information must lead dealers to revise their forecasts concerning the future course of interest rates, aggregate hedging demands, or the average error in agents' future exchange-rate forecasts. This is the case when λ_z differs from a vector of zeros.

Equations (9.33) and (9.34) provide a structural interpretation for the contemporaneous relationship between excess returns, er_{t+1}, and *unanticipated* order flow from agents, $x_{t+1} - \mathbb{E}_t^{\text{D}} x_{t+1}$. By contrast, the studies described in Chapter 7 showed that foreign exchange returns were strongly associated with actual agent order flows. Fortunately, the model allows us to bridge this gap. Recall that dealers choose the risk premium such that $\mathbb{E}_t^{\text{D}} \alpha_t = 0$ and $x_{t+1} - \mathbb{E}_t^{\text{D}} x_{t+1} = \alpha_t - \mathbb{E}_t^{\text{D}} \alpha_t$ because $\alpha_{t-1} \in \Omega_t^{\text{D}}$. Combining these expressions with the market-clearing condition, $\alpha_t = \alpha_{t-1} + x_{t+1}$, gives $x_{t+1} - \mathbb{E}_t^D x_{t+1} = \sum_{i=0}^{\infty} \mathrm{x}_{t+1-i}$. Thus, the requirement of efficient risk-sharing on the dealers' choice of risk premium implies that unexpected agent order flows can be identified from the cumulation of current and past flows, $\mathrm{x}_{t+1} = \sum_{i=0}^{\infty} x_{t+1-i}$. This implication of the model appears consistent with the data. The results in Chapter 7 showed that changes in spot rates are more strongly linked with agent order flows when the flows are cumulated over several weeks.

9.2.3 Macro Variables and Order Flows

Let us now consider the implications of the model for the relationship between order flows and traditional macro variables. In particular, suppose we have data on a $q \times 1$ vector of macro variables, $\mathrm{Y}_t = [\mathrm{Y}_{i,t}]$, that make up a subset of the variables in the state vector, z_t, the vector that describes the true state of the macroeconomy in week t. What are the implications of the model for the link between order flows and Y_t?

To address this question, we must first recognize that order flows convey information to dealers about Z_t not Y_t, because in equilibrium dealers quote spot rates based on their current estimates of Z_t. Consequently, it is possible that the order flows convey information that is relevant to dealers' quote decisions that has nothing to do with the set of macro variables in Y_t. To allow for this possibility, consider the projection

$$Z_{i,t} - \mathbb{E}_t^D Z_{i,t} = \gamma_i(\mathrm{Y}_t - \mathbb{E}_t^D \mathrm{Y}_t) + \zeta_{i,t},$$

where $Z_{i,t}$ is the ith element of Z_t. As usual, the projection error, $\zeta_{i,t}$, has the property that $\mathbb{E}[\zeta_{i,t}(\mathrm{Y}_t - \mathbb{E}_t^D \mathrm{Y}_t)] = 0$, and the vector of projection coefficients is given by

$$\gamma_i = \mathbb{E}[(Z_{i,t} - \mathbb{E}_t^D Z_{i,t})(\mathrm{Y}_t - \mathbb{E}_t^D \mathrm{Y}_t)'](\mathbb{E}[(\mathrm{Y}_t - \mathbb{E}_t^D \mathrm{Y}_t)(\mathrm{Y}_t - \mathbb{E}_t^D \mathrm{Y}_t)'])^{-1}.$$

Stacking these projections for all the elements of Z_t allows us to write

$$Z_t - \mathbb{E}_t^D Z_t = \gamma(\mathrm{Y}_t - \mathbb{E}_t^D \mathrm{Y}_t) + \zeta_t, \tag{9.35}$$

where the ith row of the γ matrix is γ_i and $\zeta_t = [\zeta_{i,t}]$ is a vector of projection errors. Note that these errors identify the uncertainty dealers face concerning Z_t that is uncorrelated with Y_t, the vector of macro variables we are studying.

We can now use (9.35) to interpret the relation between exchange-rate returns and order flows in terms of the information that flows convey concerning Y_t. In particular, substituting for $Z_t - \mathbb{E}_t^D Z_t$ in (9.34) produces the following proposition.

Proposition 9.4: *In equilibrium, excess returns are related to order flows by*

$$er_{t+1} = \beta_{er}(x_{t+1} - \mathbb{E}_t^D x_{t+1}) + \xi_{t+1},$$

where ξ_{t+1} is a projection error. For a given vector of q macro variables, $\mathrm{Y}_t = [\mathrm{Y}_{i,t}]$, the projection coefficient can be expressed as

$$\beta_{er} = \sum_{i=1}^{q} \lambda_i \beta_i + \omega, \tag{9.36}$$

where

$$\beta_i = \frac{\mathbb{E}[(x_{t+1} - \mathbb{E}_t^D x_{t+1})(\mathrm{Y}_{i,t} - \mathbb{E}_t^D \mathrm{Y}_{i,t})]}{\mathbb{E}[(x_{t+1} - \mathbb{E}_t^D x_{t+1})^2]}$$

and

$$\omega = \lambda_z \frac{\mathbb{E}[(x_{t+1} - \mathbb{E}_t^D x_{t+1})\zeta_t]}{\mathbb{E}[(x_{t+1} - \mathbb{E}_t^D x_{t+1})^2]}.$$

The decomposition in (9.36) is reminiscent of the beta decompositions found in multifactor asset-pricing models. Here the β_i coefficients quantify the information conveyed by order flow concerning variable $\mathrm{Y}_{i,t}$. If unexpected order flow from week-t trading conveys no new information regarding the current value of $\mathrm{Y}_{i,t}$, β_i will equal zero. Note, also, that β_i is the coefficient from a projection of $\mathrm{Y}_{i,t} - \mathbb{E}_t^D \mathrm{Y}_{i,t}$ on $x_{t+1} - \mathbb{E}_t^D x_{t+1}$, a fact we use later. The λ_i coefficients in (9.36) identify the price relevance of the information conveyed by order flow concerning $\mathrm{Y}_{i,t}$. They are identified as the ith element of $\lambda_z \gamma$. If dealers do not find it optimal to incorporate the information concerning $\mathrm{Y}_{i,t}$ in their spot rate quotes at the start of week $t + 1$, λ_i will equal zero. Finally, ω identifies the price effects of information carried by order flow that is uncorrelated with the set of macro variables in Y_t.

We can use equation (9.36) to evaluate whether order flows convey macro information to dealers. Suppose, for example, that order flow only conveys information on agents' hedging demands that is uncorrelated with a set of standard macro variables, in Y_t (e.g., U.S. and E.U. output and inflation). Under these circumstances, $\beta_i = 0$ for all i, so (9.36) becomes $\beta_{er} = \omega$. Here foreign exchange returns are correlated with order flow, as we observe in the data, but this observation does not signify the presence of any connection between spot rates and standard macro variables. Alternatively, suppose that order flow aggregates dispersed information on the microeconomic environments agents face that is strongly correlated with the standard macro variables. As this information has yet to be made public via macro data releases, the β_i's will differ from zero. Under these circumstances, order flow's role as a conveyor of macro information will contribute to the observed relation between excess returns and order flow via $\sum_{i=1}^q \lambda_i \beta_i$ provided that the information is price relevant in the sense that the λ_i coefficients differ from zero.

The model also holds implications for the links among the dynamics of spot rates, order flows, and the *future* evolution of the macroeconomy. To explore these implications, we first rewrite equation (9.13) as

$$s_t = (\hat{r}_t - r_t) - \mathbb{E}_t^D f_t + \mathbb{E}_t^D \sum_{i=0}^{\infty} \rho^i \{f_{t+i} - \delta_{t+i}\}.$$

Now

$$\mathbb{E}_t^D \sum_{i=0}^{\infty} \rho^i \{f_{t+i} - \delta_{t+i}\} = \frac{1}{1-\rho}(\mathbb{E}_t^D f_t - \delta_t) + \frac{1}{1-\rho}\mathbb{E}_t^D \sum_{i=1}^{\infty} \rho^i \{\Delta f_{t+i} - \Delta \delta_{t+i}\},$$

so the equation for the spot rate becomes

$$s_t = s_t^* + \mathbb{E}_t^D \sum_{i=1}^{\infty} \rho^i \eta_{t+i}, \tag{9.37}$$

where

$$s_t^* = (\hat{r}_t - r_t) + \frac{\rho}{1-\rho} \mathbb{E}_t^D f_t - \frac{1}{1-\rho} \delta_t \quad \text{and} \quad \eta_{t+i} = \frac{1}{1-\rho}(\Delta f_{t+i} - \Delta \delta_{t+i}).$$

This equation splits the spot rate into two terms. The first, s_t^*, identifies the impact of current conditions. In particular, s_t^* depends on current interest rates, dealers' estimates of current macro fundamentals, and the risk premium. The impact of expected changes in future conditions (i.e., inflation, the output gaps, and the risk premium) is identified in the second term. It is this term that provides the link among spot rates, order flows, and the future path of macro variables.

To examine this link, consider the projection of a macro variable, $Y_{t+\tau}$, on $s_t - s_t^*$:

$$Y_{t+\tau} = \beta_Y(s_t - s_t^*) + \varsigma_{t+\tau}, \tag{9.38}$$

where $\varsigma_{t+\tau}$ is the projection error. Equation (9.37) implies that

$$\beta_Y = \sum_{i=1}^{\infty} \rho^i \mathbb{E}\Big[(\mathbb{E}_t^D \eta_{t+i})(\mathbb{E}_t^D Y_{t+\tau})\Big] \Big/ \mathbb{E}\Big[(s_t - s_t^*)^2\Big]. \tag{9.39}$$

This expression for the projection coefficient shows that the correlation between dealers' expectations $\mathbb{E}_t^D Y_{t+\tau}$ and $\mathbb{E}_t^D \eta_{t+i}$ determines the strength of the forecasting power of $s_t - s_t^*$ for $Y_{t+\tau}$.

Now we turn to the forecasting power of order flow.

Proposition 9.5: *In equilibrium, future realizations of any macro variable, $Y_{t+\tau} = \Lambda_Y Z_{t+\tau}$, can be represented by*

$$Y_{t+\tau} = \beta_Y\left(s_t - s_t^*\right) + \beta_x(x_{t+1} - \mathbb{E}_t^D x_{t+1}) + \epsilon_{t+\tau}, \tag{9.40}$$

where $\epsilon_{t+\tau}$ is a projection error, β_Y is identified in (9.39), and

$$\beta_x = \frac{\Lambda_Y A^{\tau-1} G C A \mathbb{V}^D(Z_t) \Lambda_\delta' \alpha_s}{\alpha_s \Lambda_\delta \mathbb{V}^D(Z_t) \Lambda_\delta' \alpha_s}. \tag{9.41}$$

Proposition 9.5 implies that order flow should generally have *incremental* forecasting power for future macro variables beyond that contained in $s_t - s_t^*$. To understand why, consider the following identity:

$$Y_{t+\tau} = \mathbb{E}_t^D Y_{t+\tau} + (\mathbb{E}_{t+1}^D - \mathbb{E}_t^D)Y_{t+\tau} + (1 - \mathbb{E}_{t+1}^D)Y_{t+\tau}. \tag{9.42}$$

The first term on the right identifies dealers' expectations concerning $Y_{t+\tau}$ based on the information they use to quote spot rates at the start of week t. Equation (9.38) shows that variations in this term provide $s_t - s_t^*$ with its forecasting power for $Y_{t+\tau}$. The second term identifies the revision in dealers' forecasts between the start of weeks t and $t+1$. The incremental forecasting power of order flow comes from this term, which, by construction, is uncorrelated with $\mathbb{E}_t^{\mathrm{D}} Y_{t+\tau}$. In particular, since $(\mathbb{E}_{t+1}^{\mathrm{D}} - \mathbb{E}_t^{\mathrm{D}}) Y_{t+\tau} = \Lambda_Y A^{\tau-1} (\mathbb{E}_{t+1}^{\mathrm{D}} - \mathbb{E}_t^{\mathrm{D}}) Z_{t+1}$, any information conveyed by $x_{t+1} - \mathbb{E}_t^{\mathrm{D}} x_{t+1}$ concerning Z_{t+1} will lead dealers to revise their forecasts of $Y_{t+\tau}$ if $\Lambda_Y A^{\tau-1} \neq 0$. In fact, inspection of (9.41) shows that the β_x coefficient differs from zero under exactly these circumstances.

To summarize, in this section we have derived three key implications of the model. First, unexpected order flow can convey information to dealers about current and past macroeconomic conditions. Second, the empirical relation that we observe between exchange-rate returns and order flows could arise from the fact that order flows convey information on macro variables that dealers find price relevant. Third, order flows may contain incremental forecasting power for future macro variables beyond that contained in current spot rates and dealers' estimates of current macroeconomic conditions.

9.3 Re-Examining the Disconnect Puzzle

Our review of the empirical performance of macro exchange-rate models in Chapter 3 revealed that these models are unable to reliably relate the behavior of spot exchange rates to developments in the macroeconomy at frequencies higher than a year. Indeed, the lack of empirical success of standard exchange-rate models based on macro variables has given credence to the view that exchange rates are largely disconnected from macroeconomic fundamentals, a view Obstfeld and Rogoff (2001) call the exchange-rate Disconnect Puzzle. In this section, we re-examine the Disconnect Puzzle. In particular we look at whether the links between macro variables and spot rate dynamics implied by the micro-based model are supported empirically by the high-frequency behavior of spot rates, order flows, and developments in the macroeconomy.

9.3.1 Measuring Macro Variables

In order to study whether order flow links the high-frequency behavior of spot rates to developments in the macroeconomy, we need a high-frequency measure of changing macroeconomic conditions. Standard time series data on variables such as output and inflation are not suitable for this task because they contain too little information on how dealers' views concerning the macroeconomy are changing on a day-to-day or week-to-week basis. To address this problem, Evans and Lyons (2009) and Evans (2010) use a novel measure: the real-time estimates of macro variables. As the name implies, a real-time estimate of a variable is the estimated value based on public information available on a particular date. These estimates are conceptually distinct from the values that make up standard macro time series.

A simple example clarifies the difference between a real-time estimate of a macro variable and the data series usually employed in empirical studies. Let Y denote a variable representing macroeconomic activity during month m, which ends on day $M(m)$, with value $Y_{M(m)}$. Data on the value of Y is released on day $R(m)$ after the end of month m with a reporting lag of $R(m) - M(m)$ days. Reporting lags vary from month to month because data are collected on a calendar basis, but releases issued by statistical agencies are not made on holidays and weekends. (For quarterly series, such as GDP, reporting lags can be as long as several months.) The real-time estimate of Y on day d in month m is the expected value of $Y_{M(m)}$ based on day-d information. Formally, the real-time estimate of a monthly series Y is

$$Y_{M(m)|d} = \mathbb{E}[Y_{M(m)}|\Omega_d] \quad \text{for } M(m-1) < d \leq M(m), \tag{9.43}$$

where Ω_d denotes an information set that contains only data known at the start of day d. In the case of a quarterly series such as GDP, the real-time estimate on day d is

$$Y_{Q(q)|d} = \mathbb{E}[Y_{Q(q)}|\Omega_d] \quad \text{for } Q(q-1) < d \leq Q(q), \tag{9.44}$$

where $Q(q)$ denotes the last day of quarter q.

Real-time estimates are conceptually distinct from the values for $Y_{M(m)}$ or $Y_{Q(q)}$ found in standard macro time series. To see why, let $v(m)$ denote the last day on which data on Y for month m was revised. A standard monthly time series for variable Y spanning months $m = 1, \ldots, T$ comprises the sequence $\{Y_{M(m)|v(m)}\}_{m=1}^{T}$. This latest vintage of the data series incorporates information about the value of Y that was not known during month m. We can see this more clearly by writing the difference between $Y_{M(m)|v(m)}$ and real-time estimate as

$$Y_{M(m)|v(m)} - Y_{M(m)|d} = (Y_{M(m)|v(m)} - Y_{M(m)|R(m)}) + (Y_{M(m)|R(m)} - Y_{M(m)|M(m)})$$

$$+ (Y_{M(m)|M(m)} - Y_{M(m)|d}). \tag{9.45}$$

The first term on the right-hand side represents the effects of data revisions following the initial data release. The term $Y_{M(m)|R(m)}$ denotes the value for $Y_{M(m)}$ released on day $R(m)$, so $Y_{M(m)|v(m)} - Y_{M(m)|R(m)}$ identifies the effects of all the data revisions between the day when the macro data was first released, $R(m)$, and the day when the last revision was made public, $v(m)$. Croushore and Stark (2001) and Faust, Rogers, and Wright (2003), among others, have emphasized that these revisions are significant for many series. The second term in (9.45) is the difference between the value for $Y_{M(m)}$ released on day $R(m)$ and the real-time estimate of $Y_{M(m)}$ at the end of the month. This term identifies the impact of information concerning $Y_{M(m)}$ collected by the statistical agency before the release date that was not part of the $\Omega_{M(m)}$ information set. This term is particularly important in the case of quarterly data, where the reporting lag can be several months. The third term on the right of (9.45) is the difference between the real time estimate of $Y_{M(m)}$ at the end of month m and the estimate on a day earlier in the month.

As in Evans and Lyons (2009) and Evans (2010), we use real-time estimates of GDP, consumer prices, and M1 for the United States and Germany computed with an information set based on 35 macro data series. For the U.S. estimates, the specification for Ω_d includes the three quarterly releases on U.S. GDP and the monthly releases on 18 other U.S. macro variables. The German real-time estimates are computed using a specification for Ω_d that includes the three quarterly releases on German GDP and the monthly releases on eight German macro variables. The appendix to this chapter provides an overview of the econometric method used to compute the real-time estimates of each series.

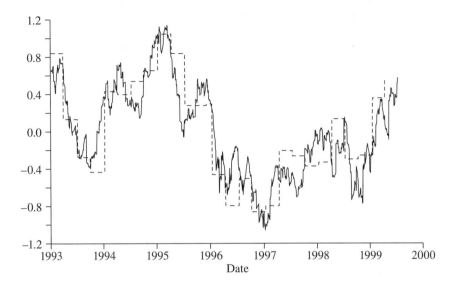

FIGURE 9.1   Real-time estimates of U.S. log GDP (solid line) and cumulant of GDP releases (dashed line). All series are detrended and multiplied by 100. Source: Evans and Lyons (2008b).

The real-time estimates have several important attributes. First the information set used to compute each real-time estimate, Ω_d, is a subset of the information available to participants in the foreign exchange market on day d. By contrast, the values for a variable Y found in either the first or final vintage of a time series (i.e., $\text{Y}_{\text{M(m)}|\text{R(m)}}$ or $\text{Y}_{\text{M(m)}|\text{V(m)}}$) contain information that was not known to participants on day d.

The second attribute of the real-time estimates concerns the frequency with which macro data are collected and released. Even though the macro variables are computed on a quarterly (GDP) or monthly (prices and money) basis, real-time estimates vary day by day as the flow of macro data releases augments the information set Ω_d. This attribute is illustrated in Figure 9.1, which plots the real-time estimates of log GDP for the United States. The real-time estimates (shown by the solid plot) clearly display a much greater degree of volatility than the cumulant of the data releases (shown by the dashed plot). This volatility reflects how inferences about current GDP change as information arrives in the form of monthly data releases during the current quarter and GDP releases referring to the previous quarter. A further noteworthy feature of the figure concerns the difference between the real-time estimates and the ex post value of log GDP represented by the vertical gap between the solid and dashed plots. This gap should be small if the current level of GDP can be precisely inferred from contemporaneously available information. However, as the figure clearly shows, there are many occasions where the real-time estimates are substantially different from the ex post values.

A third attribute of the real-time estimates concerns their variation over the sample period. Although the data cover only 6.5 years, Figure 9.1 shows that there is considerable variation in the GDP measures within this relatively short time span. The vertical axis shows that real-time estimates of U.S. GDP have a range of approximately 2.4 percent around trend.

9.3.2 Current Macro Conditions

Evans (2010) uses the real-time estimates to study whether order flows convey new price-relevant information to dealers concerning the current state of the macro-economy. Recall from Proposition 9.4 that the projection of excess returns on order flow produces a projection coefficient equal to

$$\beta_{er} = \sum_{i=1}^{q} \lambda_i \beta_i + \omega,$$

where

$$\beta_i = \frac{\mathbb{E}[(x_{t+1} - \mathbb{E}_t^D x_{t+1})(Y_{i,t} - \mathbb{E}_t^D Y_{i,t})]}{\mathbb{E}[(x_{t+1} - \mathbb{E}_t^D x_{t+1})^2]}.$$

Based on this decomposition, we can examine whether order flow conveys price-relevant macro information in two steps. First, we obtain estimates of β_i for the macro variables in $Y_t = [Y_{i,t}]$. Each of these estimates quantifies the extent to which order flow conveys new information to dealers concerning the current value of $Y_{i,t}$. Second, we estimate the λ_i parameters from a regression of excess returns on the estimates of $\beta_i(x_{t+1} - \mathbb{E}_t^D x_{t+1})$ obtained from the first step. These estimates quantify whether dealers find the macro information conveyed by order flow useful in revising their spot rate quotes.

Before we implement these steps, three data issues need addressing. Note that all the β_i coefficients contain moments involving unanticipated order flow, $x_{t+1} - \mathbb{E}_t^D x_{t+1}$. It therefore appears that we need data on both x_{t+1} and dealers' information, Ω_t^D, in order to estimate β_i in the first step. Fortunately, this is unnecessary. Recall that when dealers choose the risk premium to efficiently share risk, unexpected order flow, $x_{t+1} - \mathbb{E}_t^D x_{t+1}$, can be identified from the cumulation of current and past order flows, $X_{t+1} = \sum_{i=0}^{\infty} x_{t+1-i}$.

The second issue concerns the identification of $Y_{i,t} - \mathbb{E}_t^D Y_{i,t}$. Again, we do not have data on dealers' information, Ω_t^D, so we cannot estimate β_i directly from the sample moments involving $Y_{i,t} - \mathbb{E}_t^D Y_{i,t}$. In principle we can circumvent this problem by noting that $\mathbb{E}[x_{t+1}\mathbb{E}_t^D Y_{i,t}] = 0$, so $\beta_i = \mathbb{E}[x_{t+1}Y_{i,t}]/\mathbb{E}[x_{t+1}^2]$. This suggests that β_i could be estimated from a regression of the macro variable, $Y_{i,t}$, on the cumulation of order flow, X_{t+1}. Unfortunately, this approach is unlikely to have much statistical power in practice because the available order flow data cover 6.5 years. This is a long time span from a trading perspective, but it does not contain many observations on variables such as output, inflation, and monetary growth across a variety of macro-economic conditions. Consequently, the available time series on $Y_{i,t}$ are unlikely to be very informative about the information content of order flow.

To address this issue, Evans (2010) estimates β_i using real-time estimation errors for each macro variable, Y_i. For example, in the case of a monthly series, the real-time error is the difference between the value for $Y_{M(m)}$ released on day $R(m)$ and the real-time estimate on day d:

$$Y_{M(m)|R(m)} - Y_{M(m)|d} \quad \text{for } M(m-1) < d \leq M(m). \tag{9.46}$$

In the case of a quarterly series such as GDP, the real-time estimation error on day d is

$$Y_{Q(q)|R(q)} - Y_{Q(q)|d} \quad \text{for } Q(q-1) < d \leq Q(q). \tag{9.47}$$

Evans (2010) uses the real-time estimation error for variable Y_i at the start of each week, which we denote by $Y_{i,t}^e$.

By definition, $Y_{i,t} - \mathbb{E}_t^D Y_{i,t} = Y_{i,t}^e + \mathbb{E}[Y_{i,t}|\Omega_t] - \mathbb{E}_t^D Y_{i,t}$, where Ω_t denotes the information used to compute the real-time estimate of Y_i at the start of week t. Since Ω_t is a subset of the information available to dealers at the start of week t, Ω_t^D, it follows that

$$\mathbb{E}[x_{t+1}(Y_{i,t} - \mathbb{E}_t^D Y_{i,t})] = \mathbb{E}[x_{t+1}Y_{i,t}^e] + \mathbb{E}[x_{t+1}(\mathbb{E}[Y_{i,t}|\Omega_t] - \mathbb{E}_t^D Y_{i,t})]$$

$$= \mathbb{E}[x_{t+1}Y_{i,t}^e].$$

We can now rewrite the expression for the β_i coefficients as

$$\beta_i = \frac{\mathbb{E}[x_{t+1}(Y_{i,t} - \mathbb{E}_t^D Y_{i,t})]}{\mathbb{E}[x_{t+1}^2]} = \frac{\mathbb{E}[x_{t+1}Y_{i,t}^e]}{\mathbb{E}[x_{t+1}^2]}.$$

Estimates of β_i can therefore be obtained from the regression of the real-time estimation errors on the cumulation of order flow.

The third data issue concerns the aggregate order flow, x_t. As in the Portfolio Shifts model, it is the aggregate of agents' foreign currency orders that conveys information to dealers, so ideally we would like to use data on this aggregate order flow to examine the model's implications. Unfortunately, these data simply are not available. Nor are there enough data on interbank transactions to construct a precise proxy for aggregate order flow, as was the case in the Evans and Lyons' (1999, 2004) studies discussed in Chapter 7. Instead, Evans (2010) uses the order flows received by a single bank, Citibank, to proxy for the aggregate of agents' foreign currency orders across the entire market. Although Citibank was the single largest bank in the USD/EUR market at the time, its currency orders represented between 10 and 15 percent of the orders received by banks across the entire market. This means that the information conveyed by Citibank's order flows may not be entirely representative of the market-wide flow of information that drives spot rates. We have to be mindful of this feature when examining the empirical results that follow. At the same time, Citibank disaggregates its order flow data into six segments: trades executed between Citibank and nonfinancial corporations, investors (such as mutual funds and pension funds), and leveraged traders (such as hedge funds and proprietary traders) in the United States and trades executed among these same three groups of end-users and Citibank outside the United States. It turns out that these six end-user flows provide more information about market-wide conditions than just the total currency orders received by Citibank.

To examine whether order flows carry information on the current state of the macroeconomy, Evans (2010) estimates regressions of the real-time estimation errors on Citibank's six end-user flows, x_j:

$$Y_{i,t}^e = \sum_{j=1}^{6} b_j x_{j,t} + v_t. \qquad (9.48)$$

In these regressions, the end-user flows are cumulated between the start of weeks $t-8$ and either $t+4$ or the week before data on $Y_{i,t}$ are released, whichever period is shorter. If the Citibank's end-user flows convey no information about $Y_{i,t}$ beyond that contained in current and past data releases (i.e., the elements of Ω_t), the b_j coefficients in regression (9.48) should be close to zero and insignificant.

Table 9.2 reproduces the results from estimating (9.48) as reported in Evans (2010). The body of the table reports OLS estimates of b_j together with asymptotic standard errors corrected for heteroskedasticity. Note that the coefficient on each end-user flow is significant at the 1 percent level for at least one of the macro variables. By this metric, every end-user flow conveys some incremental macro information. A second noteworthy feature in the table concerns the level of explanatory power. In panel A, the R^2 statistics range from 13 to 20 percent. These results indicate that the flows jointly contain an economically significant amount of incremental information about the three U.S. macro variables. In the case of the German variables, the picture is

TABLE 9.2
USD/EUR Order Flows and Current Macro Information

| Real-time error | Corporate | | Hedge | | Investor | | R^2 |
	U.S.	Non-U.S.	U.S.	Non-U.S.	U.S.	Non-U.S.	
A. U.S.							
GDP	−0.530**	0.010	0.133**	0.109	0.428**	−0.256**	0.197
	(0.137)	(0.059)	(0.049)	(0.098)	(0.100)	(0.043)	
CPI	0.296	0.252**	−0.112**	−0.153	−0.572**	0.255**	0.157
	(0.181)	(0.054)	(0.048)	(0.098)	(0.107)	(0.046)	
M1	−0.243	−0.090	0.052	0.178*	0.255**	−0.242**	0.128
	(0.133)	(0.061)	(0.042)	(0.089)	(0.118)	(0.051)	
B. German							
GDP	0.106	0.100	0.120**	−0.147	−0.092	−0.065	0.029
	(0.175)	(0.064)	(0.058)	(0.093)	(0.143)	(0.052)	
CPI	−0.380**	−0.188**	0.048	0.045	−0.131	−0.068	0.018
	(0.144)	(0.049)	(0.047)	(0.109)	(0.106)	(0.048)	
M1	1.081**	0.146**	−0.122**	−0.043	0.101	0.182**	0.145
	(0.242)	(0.057)	(0.055)	(0.132)	(0.125)	(0.048)	

Notes: The table reports coefficients and standard errors from regression (9.48). The estimated coefficients on the order flows are multiplied by 1000. Estimates are calculated at the weekly frequency. The standard errors correct for heteroskedasticity. Statistical significance at the 5 percent and 1 percent level is denoted by * and **. Source: Evans (2010).

more mixed. Panel B shows that the flows only account for between 2 and 3 percent of the variations in the real-time errors for the GDP and prices, but over 14 percent in the case of M1.

The results of Clarida, Gali, and Gertler (1998) provide an interesting perspective on these findings. Their estimates of monetary policy reaction functions for the FED and the Bundesbank between 1979 and 1994 indicate that, whereas both central banks changed short-term interest rates in response to variations in inflation and output gaps, after 1982 the FED's response to the output gap was much greater than the Bundesbank's. Thus, insofar as order flows carry incremental information about the future path of interest rates, they should convey more information about U.S. GDP than German GDP. Clarida, Gali, and Gertler (1998) also note that the conventional view of the Bundesbank during the 1990s was that it simply targeted a monetary aggregate. The economically significant amount of incremental information concerning German M1 contained in the flows is certainly consistent with this view.

The results in Table 9.2 provide direct empirical evidence in support of the idea that order flows convey more timely information about the state of the macroeconomy to dealers than is available from the flow of information contained in macro data releases. By construction, the real-time estimation errors are a function of $Y_{i,t}$ and the data releases in Ω_t; they are not derived from any financial data on prices, interest rates, or order flows. Thus, we cannot attribute the results in the table to a spurious correlation between some form of measurement error in the real-time estimate and Citibank's order flows.

We now turn to the second question: Is the macro information carried by Citibank's end-user flows price relevant? Recall from the model that dealers revise their spot rate quotes in response to new information on current macroeconomic conditions insofar as it changes their view about the future course of short-term interest rates and the aggregate hedging demand for foreign currency. Clearly, information on GDP, the CPI, and M1 could qualify on both counts. What is less clear is whether the macro information available to Citibank is also transmitted to other banks (either by their own end-user flows or by Citibank's interdealer trading) in a sufficiently transparent form that it is used to revise the spot rate quotes of dealers across the market.

To address this issue, Evans (2010) estimates regressions of the form

$$er_{t+4}^4 = \lambda_0 + \sum_{i=1}^{q} \lambda_i \hat{E}[Y_{i,t}^e | X_t] + v_{t+\tau}, \tag{9.49}$$

where $\hat{E}[Y_{i,t}^e | X_t]$ is the fitted value from regression (9.48) for a set of q macro variables. The dependent variable is the excess return between the start of weeks t and $t + 4$, $er_{t+4}^4 = s_{t+\tau} - s_t + \hat{r}_t^4 - r_t^4$, where $\hat{r}_t^4$ and r_t^4 denote the 4-week euro and dollar interest rates. If there is sufficient transparency in the spot market for the macro information found in Citibank's flows to be used by dealers when revising their spot price quotes, the estimates of λ_i should be significant. Moreover, if the estimated projections $\hat{E}[Y_{i,t}^e | X_t]$ for the q macro variables well approximate the complete flow of macro information dealers use to revise their quotes, movements in $\hat{E}[Y_{i,t}^e | X_t]$ should account for the contribution of order flows to the variation in excess returns.

Estimation of (9.49) is complicated by the fact that the regressors, $\hat{E}[Y_{i,t}^e | X_t]$, are themselves estimates. Under these circumstances, OLS will not produce the correct

TABLE 9.3
Excess Returns and Real-Time Estimation Errors

	GDP		CPI		M1		
	German	U.S.	German	U.S.	German	U.S.	R^2
A							
	0.142	−0.681**					0.098
	(0.109)	(0.103)					
			0.500**	0.514**			0.112
			(0.202)	(0.112)			
					0.117	−0.704**	0.185
					(0.069)	(0.137)	
	0.137	−0.110	−1.140	0.480	1.647	0.690	0.287
	(1.904)	(0.801)	(1.452)	(0.838)	(2.284)	(1.151)	
B							
	0.427**						0.147
	(0.077)						
			−0.173**				0.044
			(0.038)				
					0.264**		0.113
					(0.042)		
	0.895**		0.517**		0.191		0.232
	(0.429)		(0.246)		(0.304)		

Notes: The table reports coefficients and standard errors from regression (9.49). Estimates are calculated at the weekly frequency. The standard errors correct for heteroskedasticity and an MA(3) error process. Statistical significance at the 1 percent level is denoted by **. Source: Evans (2010).

standard errors for the estimates of λ_i. To account for this problem, $\hat{E}[Y_{i,t}^e|X_t]$ is replaced by the real-time errors, $Y_{i,t}^e$, on the right-hand side of (9.49), and the estimates of λ_i are computed using $\hat{E}[Y_{i,t}^e|X_t]$ as an instrument for each $Y_{i,t}^e$. These instrumental variable estimates of λ_i are identical to the OLS estimates, but the standard errors correct for the fact that $\hat{E}[Y_{i,t}^e|X_t]$ are the fitted values from regression (9.48). The standard errors also have to correct for the presence of overlapping observations because (9.49) is estimated at the weekly frequency, whereas excess returns span 4 weeks. This can be done by incorporating the Newey and West (1987) covariance estimator into the instrumental variable procedure.

Table 9.3 reproduces the results from estimating (9.49) as reported in Evans (2010). The estimates in the first three rows indicate that the order flows do indeed convey price-relevant information about GDP, prices, and the money stock. The λ_i coefficients for German prices, U.S. GDP, prices, and money are all significant at the 1 percent level. However, as the fourth row of the table shows, the λ_i coefficients are no longer individually significant when all six projections are included. Panel B reports estimates of (9.49), where the estimated projections of the difference between the German and U.S. real-time errors are used as regressors. Insofar as spot rates reflect the difference between U.S. and E.U. monetary policy, order flows should carry more price-relevant information about the difference in macroeconomic conditions between countries. This seems to be the case. As the table shows, the λ_i coefficients on the GDP and CPI projections are highly significant.

The results in Table 9.3 point to an interesting pattern between the flows of macro information on GDP and the revision of dealers' spot rate quotes. Throughout the table, the λ_i estimates show that dealers revise their quotes upward when the end-user flows imply that their prior estimates of current German GDP are too low and their prior estimates of current U.S. GDP are too high. These findings map closely into the structure of the model. Recall that dealers expect the future interest differential between euro and dollar rates to be higher when their estimates of the difference between the E.U. and U.S. output gap widens. Thus, if dealers receive new information via order flow that current U.S. GDP is higher than previously estimated, they will lower their spot rate quotes in anticipation that the FED will follow a tighter monetary policy that will lower the future path of the interest differential between euro and dollar rates. Similarly, if dealers learn from order flow that their prior estimates of current German GDP are too low, they will revise their spot rate quotes upward in anticipation of tighter monetary policy in Germany. It is also interesting to note that the estimated coefficients on the U.S. GDP error projections are three to four times the absolute size of their counterparts for German GDP. It appears that dealers react more strongly to new information concerning U.S. GDP than German GDP. This difference may reflect the fact that the end-user flows carry more incremental information concerning U.S. GDP than German GDP, as shown in Table 9.2. It could also arise because dealers anticipate that the FED and Bundesbank/ECB will react differently to future macroeconomic conditions.

Another noteworthy feature of Table 9.3 concerns the R^2 statistics reported in the right-hand column. To place these statistics in perspective, let us use Proposition 9.4 to write

$$er_{t+1} = \sum_{i=1}^{q} \lambda_i E[Y_{i,t}^e | X_{t+1}] + \omega X_{t+1} + \xi_{t+1},$$

where $E[Y_{i,t}^e | X_{t+1}] = \beta_i X_{t+1}$ and $X_{t+1} = \sum_{i=0}^{\infty} x_{t+1-i}$. Recall that ω identifies the price effects of information carried by order flow that is uncorrelated with the set of q macro variables in $Y_t = [Y_{i,t}]$. If this information is absent, the preceding expression implies that the R^2 from a regression of excess returns on $E[Y_{i,t}^e | X_{t+1}]$ should be the same as the R^2 from a regression of excess returns on order flow, X_{t+1}. In other words, the information concerning the q macro variables carried by order flow will account for all of its explanatory power for excess returns. On the other hand, if most of the price-relevant information order flows convey to dealers is uncorrelated with the q macro variables, the R^2 from a regression of excess returns on $E[Y_{i,t}^e | X_{t+1}]$ will be much smaller than the R^2 from a regression of excess returns on order flow, X_{t+1}.

The R^2 statistics in Table 9.3 can be interpreted in an analogous manner. Here the real-time-error projections use Citibank's end-user flows rather than aggregate order so the regression of excess returns on these end-user flows provides the benchmark. Evans (2010) finds that the R^2 from this regression is 0.31 at the 4-week horizon. The R^2 statistic of 0.23 reported in the table therefore implies that approximately 75 percent of the explanatory power of Citibank's end-user flows for excess returns is due to the information they convey concerning current GDP, the CPI, and money stocks.

9.3.3 Future Macro Conditions

The results in Tables 9.2 and 9.3 show that Citibank's order flows carry a significant amount of timely information about current macroeconomic conditions. Furthermore, this information appears price relevant in the sense that it is reflected in how dealers revise their spot rate quotes across the market. We now turn to the related issue of whether order flow conveys information about *future* macroeconomic conditions.

Proposition 9.5 showed that order flow may contain incremental forecasting power for future macro variables, Y, beyond that contained in current spot rates and dealers' estimates of current macroeconomic conditions. In particular, the projection of $Y_{t+\tau}$ on $s_t - s_t^*$ and $x_{t+1} - \mathbb{E}_t^D x_{t+1}$,

$$Y_{t+\tau} = \beta_Y(s_t - s_t^*) + \beta_x(x_{t+1} - \mathbb{E}_t^D x_{t+1}) + \epsilon_{t+\tau}, \tag{9.50}$$

produces coefficients

$$\beta_Y = \frac{\mathbb{E}[Y_{t+\tau}(s_t - s_t^*)]}{\mathbb{E}[(s_t - s_t^*)^2]} \quad \text{and} \quad \beta_x = \frac{\mathbb{E}[Y_{t+\tau}(x_{t+1} - \mathbb{E}_t^D x_{t+1})]}{\mathbb{E}[(x_{t+1} - \mathbb{E}_t^D x_{t+1})^2]}. \tag{9.51}$$

Combining these expressions with (9.37) and the identity (9.42) gives

$$\beta_Y = \frac{\mathbb{E}[\mathbb{E}_t^D Y_{t+\tau} \sum_{i=1}^{\infty} \rho^i \mathbb{E}_t^D \eta_{t+i}]}{\mathbb{E}[(s_t - s_t^*)^2]}$$

and

$$\beta_x = \frac{\mathbb{E}[(\mathbb{E}_{t+1}^D - \mathbb{E}_t^D) Y_{t+\tau}(x_{t+1} - \mathbb{E}_t^D x_{t+1})]}{\mathbb{E}[(x_{t+1} - \mathbb{E}_t^D x_{t+1})^2]}. \tag{9.52}$$

To interpret the expressions in (9.52), recall that $\rho = 1/(1 + \gamma_\varepsilon)$, where γ_ε identifies the sensitivity of the expected interest differential, $\mathbb{E}_t^D(\hat{r}_{t+i} - r_{t+i})$, to variations in the expected real exchange rate, $\mathbb{E}_t^D \varepsilon_{t+i}$. Plausible values for γ_ε should be positive but small (see, e.g., Clarida, Gali, and Gertler 1998), so ρ should be close to one. This being the case, the expression for β_Y indicates that $s_t - s_t^*$ will have greater forecasting power when dealers' expectations, $\mathbb{E}_t^D Y_{t+\tau}$, are strongly correlated with their forecasts for expected inflation and/or output gaps over long horizons. In contrast, the expression for β_x shows that the forecasting power of order flow depends only on the information it conveys to dealers concerning $Y_{t+\tau}$. Recall that $x_{t+1} - \mathbb{E}_t^D x_{t+1} = \alpha_t - \mathbb{E}_t^D \alpha_t$, where α_t is the aggregate demand for euros that depends on the average of agents' spot rate forecasts, $\overline{\mathbb{E}}_t^n s_{t+1}$, and aggregate hedging demand, h_t. Therefore $x_{t+1} - \mathbb{E}_t^D x_{t+1}$ conveys information about h_t and $\overline{\mathbb{E}}_t^n s_{t+1}$—two factors that embed more timely information about the current state of the economy than is available to dealers from other sources. The expression for β_x shows that order flows will have incremental forecasting power when dealers find this information relevant for forecasting the future course of Y_t.

Evans and Lyons (2009) use two strategies to investigate the forecasting power of spot rates and order flows for a macro variable Y_t empirically. First they estimate β_Y and β_x from a regression of $Y_{t+\tau}$ on proxies for $s_t - s_t^*$ and $x_{t+1} - \mathbb{E}_t^D x_{t+1}$. This strategy is straightforward, but since the available order flow data covers just 6.5 years, it does not produce very precise estimates of β_Y and β_x. To address this problem, Evans and Lyons employ a novel second strategy that estimates the components of β_Y and β_x.

Let $\Omega_t \subset \Omega_t^D$ denote a subset of the information available to dealers at the start of week t that includes Y_t. Without loss of generality we can write

$$Y_{t+\tau} = \sum_{i=-t}^{\tau-1} \mathfrak{T}_{t+i} + \mathbb{E}[Y_{t+\tau}],$$

where $\mathfrak{T}_t = \mathbb{E}[Y_{t+\tau}|\Omega_{t+1}] - \mathbb{E}[Y_{t+\tau}|\Omega_t]$ is the week-t flow of information into Ω_{t+1} concerning $Y_{t+\tau}$ and $\mathbb{E}[Y_{t+\tau}] = \mathbb{E}[Y_{t+\tau}|\Omega_0]$ denotes the unconditional expectation. Substituting this expression into (9.51) gives

$$\beta_Y = \sum_{i=-t}^{\tau-1} \beta_Y^i \quad \text{and} \quad \beta_x = \sum_{i=-t}^{\tau-1} \beta_x^i, \tag{9.53}$$

where β_Y^i and β_x^i are the coefficients from the projection:

$$\mathfrak{T}_{t+i} = \beta_Y^i(s_t - s_t^*) + \beta_x^i(x_{t+1} - \mathbb{E}_t^D x_{t+1}) + \epsilon_{t+i}. \tag{9.54}$$

The strategy is to estimate this projection for different horizons i using estimates of $\mathfrak{T}_t$ obtained from the real-time estimates of macro variable Y_t. In particular, $\mathfrak{T}_t$ is estimated as the difference between the real-time estimate of $Y_{M(m)}$ at the end of week t and the end of week $t - 1$:

$$\mathfrak{T}_t = Y_{M(m)|w(t)} - Y_{M(m)|w(t-1)},$$

where $w(t)$ is the last day of week t and $w(t) \leq M(m)$. Unlike the underlying macro time series, Y, these estimates can be computed at a high enough frequency to estimate β_Y^i and β_x^i with precision in 6.5 years of data. Of course, this increase in precision comes at a cost. Statistically significant estimates of β_Y^i and β_x^i imply that $s_t - s_t^*$ and $x_{t+1} - \mathbb{E}_t^D x_{t+1}$ have forecasting power for the flow of information used to revise future expectations concerning $Y_{t+\tau}$. However, (9.53) shows that this must be true at some horizon(s), i, if $s_t - s_t^*$ and $x_{t+1} - \mathbb{E}_t^D x_{t+1}$ truly have forecasting power for $Y_{t+\tau}$. In sum, therefore, when we test the statistical significance of horizon-specific β_Y^i and β_x^i estimates, we are examining a necessary condition for the existence of forecasting power in spot rates and order flows.

Two further data issues need addressing before these strategies can be implemented. First, as in Evans (2010), the cumulants of Citibank's six end-user order flows replace unexpected order flow, $x_{t+1} - \mathbb{E}_t^D x_{t+1}$, in the regressions. As we noted before, this proxy assumes that Citibank's customer orders are reasonably representative of customer order flows across the entire market. Second, $s_t - s_t^*$ is proxied by the depreciation rate, Δs_t, and four interest rate spreads: the U.S. default, commercial paper, and term spreads and the German term spread. The term spreads are the difference between the 3-month and 5-year yields on government bonds. The U.S. default spread is the difference between Moody's AAA and BAA corporate bond yields, and the U.S. commercial paper spread is the difference between the 3-month commercial paper rate and the 3-month T-Bill rate. These interest rates represent information that was available to dealers at the start of week t: if they have forecasting power for the macro information flows, dealers should have been able to forecast these macro flows at the time.

Evans and Lyons (2009) first examine the forecasting power of the depreciation rate and spreads for the flow of information concerning GDP growth, inflation, and M1 growth in both the United States and Germany between January 1993 and June 1999. In this case the regressions take the form

$$\mathfrak{T}_{t+k}^k = \beta^k + \beta_s^k \Delta s_t + \beta_{\nabla r}^{k\prime} \nabla r_t + \xi_{t+k}, \tag{9.55}$$

where ∇r_t is the vector of spreads. The dependent variable, $\mathfrak{T}_{t+k}^k = \sum_{i=0}^{k-1} \mathfrak{T}_{t+i}$, is the flow of information between the start of weeks t and $t+k$ concerning GDP growth, inflation, or M1 growth during the quarter or month that includes week $t+k$ (measured in annual percentage terms). Evans and Lyons find that the spreads have signficant forecasting power for flows of future macro information concerning GDP and M1 growth over the next month ($k=4$) and quarter ($k=13$), but not inflation. They also find that the depreciation rate has significant forecasting power for the information flows concerning just German GDP growth and inflation. Clearly, dealers have access to much more precise information about the future course of GDP and M1 growth than is indicated by depreciation rates alone.

Next, Evans and Lyons (2009) turn to the central question: Does order flow convey new information to dealers concerning the future state of the macroeconomy? To address this question, they add the six end-user flows to the forecasting regression (9.55),

$$\mathfrak{T}_{t+k}^k = \beta^k + \beta_s^k \Delta s_t + \beta_{\nabla r}^{k\prime} \nabla r_t + \sum_{j=1}^6 \beta_j^k x_{j,t} + \xi_{t+k}, \tag{9.56}$$

where $x_{j,t}$ is the order flow from segment j in weeks $t-k$ to t. Estimates of the β_j^k coefficients reveal whether the end-user flows convey *incremental* information to dealers in week t about the future flow of macro information between weeks t and $t+k$ concerning GDP growth, inflation, and M1 growth.

Evans and Lyons find that the estimated coefficients on five of the six flows are statistically significant at the 5 percent level in at least one of the forecasting regressions and that many are significant at the 1 percent level. They also observe that the order flows collectively have more forecasting power at the one-quarter ($k=13$) than one-month ($k=4$) horizon. In every case, χ^2 tests for the joint significance of the six flow coefficients are significant at the 5 percent level at the quarterly horizon. Furthermore, the R^2 statistics in these regressions are on average about twice the size of their counterparts in (9.55) without order flows. By this measure, the flows contain an economically significant degree of incremental forecasting power for the macro information flows beyond that contained in the depreciation rates and spreads.

Evans and Lyons find that the incremental forecasting power of the six flow segments extends over a wide range of horizons. Specifically, they compute the variance contribution of the flows from the estimates of (9.56) for horizons ranging from one week to two quarters. Let $\mathfrak{T}^k_{t+k} = \tilde{\beta}^k + \widetilde{\mathfrak{T}}^k_{t,\Delta s} + \widetilde{\mathfrak{T}}^k_{t,x} + \tilde{\xi}_{t+k}$ denote estimates of (9.56), where $\widetilde{\mathfrak{T}}^k_{t,\Delta s} = \tilde{\beta}^k_s \Delta s_t + \tilde{\beta}^{k'}_{\nabla r} \nabla r_t$ and $\widetilde{\mathfrak{T}}^k_{t,x} = \sum^6_{j=1} \tilde{\beta}^k_j x_{j,t}$. Multiplying both sides of this expression by $\mathfrak{T}^k_{t+k}$ and taking expectations gives the following decomposition for the variance of the k-horizon information flow:

$$\mathbb{V}(\mathfrak{T}^k_{t+k}) = \mathbb{CV}(\widetilde{\mathfrak{T}}^k_{t,\Delta s}, \mathfrak{T}^k_{t+k}) + \mathbb{CV}(\widetilde{\mathfrak{T}}^k_{t,x}, \mathfrak{T}^k_{t+k}) + \mathbb{CV}(\hat{\xi}_{t+k}, \mathfrak{T}^k_{t+k}).$$

The contribution of the order flows is given by the second term on the right. We can calculate this contribution as the slope coefficient in the regression of $\widetilde{\mathfrak{T}}^k_{t,x}$ on $\mathfrak{T}^k_{t+k}$, that is, an estimate of $\mathbb{CV}(\widetilde{\mathfrak{T}}^k_{t,x}, \mathfrak{T}^k_{t+k})/\mathbb{V}(\mathfrak{T}^k_{t+k})$.

Figure 9.2 plots the variance contributions of the order flows together with 95 percent confidence bands for the six macro information flows for horizons $k = 1, \ldots, 26$. In five of the six cases, the contributions rise steadily with the horizon and are quite sizable beyond one quarter. The exception is U.S. GDP growth, where the contribution remains around 15 percent from the quarterly horizon onward. Recall that order flow has incremental forecasting power for a macro variable $Y_{t+\tau}$ when the projection coefficient $\beta_Y = \sum^{\tau-1}_{i=-t} \beta^i_Y$ differs from zero, where β^i_Y measures order flows' forecasting power for the flow of information at horizon i concerning $Y_{t+\tau}$. The plots in the figure show that order flows have considerable forecasting power for the future flows of information concerning GDP growth, inflation, and M1 growth at all but the shortest horizons. Clearly, then, these order flows are carrying significant information on future macroeconomic conditions.

9.3.4 Combining the Micro and Macro Evidence

The results in Evans and Lyons (2009) and Evans (2010) reviewed here point to the role order flow plays in connecting the high-frequency dynamics of spot rates to the evolution of the macroeconomy. We now ask: How do these findings square with the evidence based on the macro exchange-rate models discussed in Chapter 3? More specifically, does the micro-based evidence discussed here complement or contradict the traditional macro-based view that high-frequency movements in exchange rates are largely disconnected from the macroeconomy?

To address these questions, it is useful to consider the source of the week-by-week variations in the log spot rate implied by the micro-based model. For this purpose, we first combine (9.1) with the identity $\Delta s_{t+1} = \mathbb{E}^D_t \Delta s_{t+1} + s_{t+1} - \mathbb{E}^D_t s_{t+1}$ to give

$$\Delta s_{t+1} = r_t - \hat{r}_t + \delta_t + s_{t+1} - \mathbb{E}^D_t s_{t+1}.$$

Next, we rewrite (9.16) as

$$s_{t+1} = \hat{r}_{t+1} - r_{t+1} + \frac{\rho}{1-\rho} \mathbb{E}^D_{t+1} f_{t+1} + \frac{1}{1-\rho} \mathbb{E}^D_{t+1} \sum^\infty_{i=2} \rho^{i-1} \Delta f_{t+i} - \mathbb{E}^D_{t+1} \sum^\infty_{i=1} \rho^{i-1} \delta_{t+i}.$$

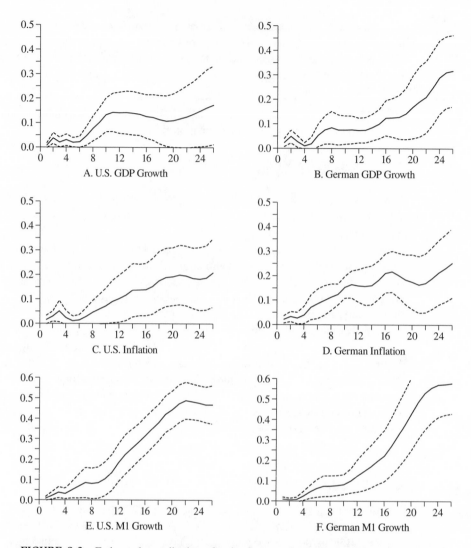

FIGURE 9.2   Estimated contribution of order flows to the variance of future information flows concerning GDP growth, inflation, and M1 growth by forecasting horizon, k, measured in weeks. Dashed lines denote 95 percent confidence bands computed as $\pm 1.96\hat{\sigma}$, where $\hat{\sigma}$ is the standard error of the estimated contribution.

Using this expression to compute $s_{t+1} - \mathbb{E}_t^D s_{t+1}$, we can rewrite the equation for the weekly depreciation rate as

$$\Delta s_{t+1} = r_t - \hat{r}_t + \delta_t$$

$$+ (1 - \mathbb{E}_t^D)(\hat{r}_{t+1} - r_{t+1}) + \frac{\rho}{1-\rho}(\mathbb{E}_{t+1}^D - \mathbb{E}_t^D)f_{t+1} - (\mathbb{E}_{t+1}^D - \mathbb{E}_t^D)\delta_{t+1}$$

$$+ \frac{1}{1-\rho}(\mathbb{E}_{t+1}^D - \mathbb{E}_t^D)\sum_{i=2}^{\infty} \rho^{i-1}\Delta f_{t+i} - (\mathbb{E}_{t+1}^D - \mathbb{E}_t^D)\sum_{i=2}^{\infty} \rho^{i-1}\delta_{t+i}. \quad (9.57)$$

This equation helps us to identify the key differences between the macro- and micro-based perspectives on the sources of high-frequency exchange-rate dynamics and their link to macro fundamentals.

In Chapter 3 we saw that interest differentials and other macro variables have very little forecasting power for the future depreciation rate (i.e., changes in the log spot rate). Thus, as a purely empirical matter, there appears to be little prospect for establishing the link between short-term variations in spot rates and macro variables known at the start of week t via interest rates and the risk premium terms, r_t, $\hat{r}_t$, and δ_t. Instead, we must focus our attention on the terms in the second and third lines of equation (9.57). The three terms in the second line identify the effects of new information concerning current macroeconomic conditions, that is, conditions at the start of week $t + 1$. The first identifies the effect of unanticipated changes in short-term interest rates. In practice, central banks change interest rates relatively rarely, and when they do, they often communicate their intentions beforehand so as not to put undue stress on the financial system. As a result, unanticipated changes in short-term interest rates are not an important source of high-frequency spot rate dynamics over long time spans—a point we return to in Chapter 10. This leaves the terms involving macro fundamentals, f_t, and the risk premium, δ_t. It is in the identification of these terms that the macro- and micro-based perspectives differ.

Macro models typically assume that Uncovered Interest Parity holds or that the drivers of the risk premium are unobservable. This means that the focus of macro-based empirical exchange-rate models is on

$$\frac{\rho}{1-\rho}(\mathbb{E}_{t+1}^D - \mathbb{E}_t^D)f_{t+1} + \frac{1}{1-\rho}(\mathbb{E}_{t+1}^D - \mathbb{E}_t^D)\sum_{i=2}^{\infty}\rho^{i-1}\Delta f_{t+i}. \qquad (9.58)$$

By definition, $(\mathbb{E}_{t+1}^D - \mathbb{E}_t^D)f_{t+1} = (\mathbb{E}_{t+1}^D - \mathbb{E}_t^D)\left(f_{t+1} - f_{t-1}\right) + (\mathbb{E}_{t+1}^D - \mathbb{E}_t^D)f_{t-1}$, where

$$f_{t-1} = (1 + \gamma_\pi)\left(\Delta\hat{p}_t - \Delta p_t\right) + \gamma_y\left(\hat{y}_{t-1} - y_{t-1}\right) + \left(\tfrac{1-\rho}{\rho}\right)\left(p_{t-1} - \hat{p}_{t-1}\right).$$

Thus, if the current state of the macroeconomy is known to all market participants (including dealers) as macro models assume, $(\mathbb{E}_{t+1}^D - \mathbb{E}_t^D)f_{t-1} = 0$ and (9.58) becomes

$$\frac{\rho}{1-\rho}(\mathbb{E}_{t+1}^D - \mathbb{E}_t^D)(f_{t+1} - f_{t-1}) + \frac{1}{1-\rho}(\mathbb{E}_{t+1}^D - \mathbb{E}_t^D)\sum_{i=2}^{\infty}\rho^{i-1}\Delta f_{t+i}. \qquad (9.59)$$

Under normal circumstances, the first term in this expression should be close to zero because macro fundamentals are unlikely to change significantly over the space of 2 weeks (i.e., between the start of weeks $t - 1$ and $t + 1$). Thus, from a macro perspective, the lion's share of the link between macro fundamentals and high-frequency spot rate dynamics must be attributable to the second term, that is, the revisions in forecasts about future changes in fundamentals, Δf_{t+i} for $i > 1$. This perspective holds true beyond the context of the micro-based model presented here. If agents observe current macro conditions that are slowly evolving, much of the short-term fluctuation in exchange rates must be driven by changes in expectations about the future.

It is a comparatively short step from this macro perspective to the Disconnect Puzzle. In Chapter 3 we saw that lagged depreciation rates have forecasting power for future changes in particular measures of macro fundamentals, $\Delta \hat{f}_t$. Although this finding is consistent with the idea that forecasts for $\Delta \hat{f}_t$ affect spot rates, empirical estimates of the present value of future changes in $\Delta \hat{f}_t$ show little short-term variation. As a result, estimates of the second term in (9.59) using $\hat{f}_t$ account for just a few percent of the variance of the depreciation rates at the monthly and quarterly horizons. By this metric, the high-frequency movements in exchange rates appear largely disconnected from the measured fundamentals.

The micro-based perspective on the Disconnect Puzzle is rather different because all the terms on the right of equation (9.57) involving fundamentals and the risk premium could link short-term variations in spot rates to the macroeconomy. Consider the terms involving fundamentals as shown in (9.58). When the weekly changes in fundamentals are negligible (i.e., $f_{t+1} \cong f_{t-1}$), the expression in (9.58) is well approximated by

$$\frac{\rho}{1-\rho}(\mathbb{E}_{t+1}^{D} - \mathbb{E}_{t}^{D})f_{t-1} + \frac{1}{1-\rho}(\mathbb{E}_{t+1}^{D} - \mathbb{E}_{t}^{D})\sum_{i=2}^{\infty}\rho^{i-1}\Delta f_{t+i}. \tag{9.60}$$

From a micro-based perspective, dealers are not assumed to have contemporaneous information on the macro variables that comprise fundamentals, so the first term in (9.60) can differ from zero. Moreover, this term appears to be significant empirically. As we saw in Section 9.3.2 order flow from week-t trading conveys significant new information concerning current GDP, prices, and money stocks, which is incorporated into spot rates. Thus, some of the high-frequency behavior of exchange rates reflects the flow of new information reaching dealers concerning the slowly evolving state of the macroeconomy.

The micro-based model also provides a new perspective on the second term in (9.60). In Section 9.3.3 we saw that Citibank's end-user flows had significant incremental forecasting power for future macro variables beyond that contained in current spot rates and other variables. Insofar as these flows proxy for the market-wide order flow that all dealers use to revise their expectations, estimates of the second term in (9.60) based on macro data will understate the degree to which revisions in dealers' expectations concerning future changes in fundamentals contribute to spot rate dynamics.

It should now be clear that the micro-based evidence complements rather than contradicts the empirical evidence derived from macro models on the link between spot rates and the macroeconomy. By concentrating on the flows of information available to dealers, micro-based models point to the role of order flow as a carrier of macroeconomic information. This information appears useful in revising forecasts of future changes in macro fundamentals, the channel emphasized by macro models. It also appears useful in revising dealers' estimates of current macroeconomic conditions.

Finally, it must be emphasized that the results reported earlier do not resolve the exchange-rate Disconnect Puzzle. Although the explanatory power of the projections for excess returns in Table 9.3 are very high relative to other models, they account for less than half the variance. The micro-based model therefore falls well short of identifying all the information dealers are using to revise their spot rate quotes.

Furthermore, empirical results always comes with caveats. The findings reported here use the worldwide flow of currency orders received by Citibank from end-users between January 1993 and June 1999. The use of these data gives rise to two potential concerns. First, the information conveyed by Citibank's flows may not be entirely representative of the market-wide flow of information that drives spot rates. If this is the case, the estimates in Table 9.3 represent a lower bound on the contribution of macro information flows to the variance of excess returns. The second concern relates to the data sample. Clearly, it is possible that order flows carried much more macro information during this period than at other times. However, in view of the well-documented empirical robustness of the relationship between spot rates and order flows over longer time spans and different currencies, there is no prima facie evidence to indicate significant instability in the underlying mechanism concerning order flow's role as a conveyor of information. Ultimately, of course, the robustness of these results will only be established by further research using longer and broader data samples.

9.4 Summary

- The micro-based approach to exchange-rate determination is based on two central ideas:
    1. Only some of the macro information relevant for the determination of the current spot exchange rate is publicly known at any point in time. Other information is present in the economy, but it exists in a dispersed microeconomic form.
    2. Spot rates are determined through the operation of the foreign exchange market. Since the spot rate is literally the price of foreign currency quoted by foreign exchange dealers, it can only impound information that is known to dealers. Consequently, the spot rate will only reflect dispersed information once it has been assimilated by dealers—a process that takes place via trading.

- To incorporate these ideas, the micro-based model presented in this chapter includes:
    1. Dealers that quote spot rates with regard to optimally sharing foreign currency risk.
    2. Agents that choose their foreign currency orders to achieve the desired composition for their portfolios.
    3. Limited information concerning the *current* state of the macro-economy is available to dealers and agents when they trade foreign currency.

- The micro-based model shows that the order flow generated by trades between dealers and agents can convey information to dealers about the current state of the macroeconomy, which they then use to revise their spot exchange-rate quotes. This implication provides a theoretical basis for the strong contemporaneous empirical link between foreign exchange rates and order flows. It also implies that order flows should have incremental forecasting power for future macro variables beyond that contained in the history of spot rates and other variables.

- The available empirical evidence strongly supports the presence of the links among the macroeconomy, order flow, and high-frequency exchange-rate returns implied by the model. Analysis of the flows generated by USD/EUR currency orders placed at Citibank indicate that between 20 and 30 percent of the variance in monthly excess returns in the USD/EUR can be linked back to developments in the macroeconomy. These transaction flows also have significant incremental forecasting power for GDP growth, money growth, and inflation in both the United States and Germany over horizons of one to two quarters.

- High-frequency variations in spot rates appear largely disconnected from macro fundamentals from a macro perspective because macro models are unable to identify significant variations in forecasts of future changes in fundamentals. Micro-based models provide a complementary perspective on the exchange-rate Disconnect Puzzle by concentrating on the role of order flow as a carrier of macroeconomic information to dealers. This information appears useful in revising dealers' forecasts of future changes in macro fundamentals and their estimates of current macroeconomic conditions.

9.5 Bibliography

This chapter is closely based on Evans and Lyons (2009) and Evans (2010), but also builds on ideas developed in a series of papers by Richard Lyons and myself. In Evans and Lyons (2004) we first showed how the gap between traditional macro- and microstructure exchange-rate models could be spanned by embedding the micro-foundations of currency trading in a standard two-country general equilibrium model. This model is based on the idea that information concerning the current state of the macroeconomy initially exists in dispersed form among individual agents, as orignally proposed by Hayek (1945). The dispersed information is aggregated and transmitted to dealers via the order flow generated by agents' currency orders, but in equilibrium it is insufficient to reveal the true state of the macroeconomy. In Evans and Lyons (2009) we developed the model further to study its implications for the forecasting power of order flows. Specifically, we identified the conditions under which order flows should have incremental forecasting power for the future path of macro variables that constitute exchange-rate fundamentals. This theoretical implication represents an extension of the work by Engel and West (2005) that we studied in Chapter 3.

The empirical results reported here relate to the findings of several other researchers, notably those of Froot and Ramadorai (2005). They examine real exchange rates, excess currency returns, real interest differentials, and the transaction flows of institutional investors across 19 country/currency areas over 7 years. Using variance decompositions from a VAR estimated at the daily frequency with pooled data, they find that innovations in transaction flows predict future changes in real interest differentials at short but not at long horizons. They also find no evidence of a long-run correlation between real interest rate differentials and the transaction flows. This result is completely consistent with the micro-based model. As question (1) in the next section demonstrates, order flows can convey information to dealers about macro variables without there being any long-run statistical relationship between order flow and the variable in question.

The results in Table 9.2 are most closely related to the findings of Rime, Sarno, and Sojli (2010). These authors consider regressions of $Y^e_{i,t}$ computed from survey estimates for individual data releases, Y_i, on aggregate interdealer order flow in the USD/EUR, USD/GBP, and USD/JPY markets over a 12-month sample starting in February 2004. They find that the coefficients on at least one of the order flows are significant at the 10 percent level for every U.S., E.U., and U.K. data release they study. These findings are based on a much shorter data sample than the results reviewed here, but they are nevertheless consistent with the idea that order flows carry information about current macroeconomy conditions.

9.6 Review Questions

1. Constructing an Equilibrium: Consider a simplified version of the micro-based model in which the interest differential is zero (i.e., $r_t - \hat{r}_t = 0$) and the hedging demand of agent $n \in [0, 1]$ is given by

$$h^n_t = h_t + v^n_t,$$

with $h_t = \rho h_{t-1} + u_t$, where $v^n_t \sim$ i.i.d.$N(0, \sigma^2_v)$ and $u_t \sim$ i.i.d.$N(0, \sigma^2_u)$. The agent-specific shock, v^n_t, has the property that $\int^1_0 v^n_t dn = 0$. Assume that information on the aggregate hedging demand, h_t, is released with a 1-week delay. Thus the value of h_{t-1} is publicly released at the beginning of week t. The evolution of the dealer's common information between the start of week $t - 1$ and t is therefore given by

$$\Omega^D_t = \{x_t, h_{t-1}, \Omega^D_t\},$$

and the evolution of agent n's information is

$$\Omega^n_t = \{s_t, h_{t-1}, h^n_t, \Omega^n_t\}.$$

(a) Suppose that the equilibrium spot rate follows $s_t = \pi h_{t-1}$ for some unknown parameter π. Compute agent n's forecast of the log excess return on euros, that is, $\mathbb{E}^n_t \Delta s_{t+1} + \hat{r}_t - r_t$.

(b) Use your answer to part (a) to compute the aggregate demand for euros in week t (i.e., $\alpha_t = \int^1_0 \alpha^n_t dn$) and hence actual and unexpected order flow from week-t trading (i.e., x_{t+1} and $x_{t+1} - \mathbb{E}^D_t x_{t+1}$).

(c) Compute the difference between dealers' forecasts for the future spot rate, $\mathbb{E}^D_t s_{t+1}$, and the average of agents' forecasts, $\overline{\mathbb{E}}^n_t s_{t+1}$. Which forecasts are more accurate? Why?

(d) Use your answer to part (c) to compute the risk premium dealers embed in their spot rate quotes, and verify that those quotes do indeed take the form of $s_t = \pi h_{t-1}$.

(e) In this model the interest differential is zero, so spot rates do not react to changes in current or expected future interest rates. Instead, spot rates react to changes in the aggregate hedging demand, h_t. Why do dealers find information about h_t price relevant and hence a determinant of their optimal quotes?

(f) Explain why the spot rate "reacts" to hedging demand shocks, u_t, with a 1-week lag.

2. Time Series Properties of the Simplified Micro-Based Model.

(a) Derive the time series process for the log spot rate, s_t, and order flow, x_t, in the equilibrium of the simplified micro-based model described in question 1.

(b) Derive the autocorrelation function for order flow. Explain why order flow is serially correlated.

(c) Can order flow be forecast from past spot rates? If yes, where does the forecasting power come from?

(d) Can past order flows be used to forecast future depreciation rates? If so why; if not why not?

3. Reporting Lags: Consider the following variants of the simplified micro-based model studied in question 1. Suppose that information on the aggregate hedging demand, h_t, is now released with a *two*-week delay. In this variant of the model the evolution of the dealers' common information between the start of week $t - 1$ and t is

$$\Omega_t^D = \{x_t, h_{t-2}, \Omega_t^D\},$$

and the evolution of agent n's information is

$$\Omega_t^n = \{s_t, h_{t-2}, h_t^n, \Omega_t^n\}.$$

All other aspects of the model remain unchanged.

(a) Prove that the equilibrium is exactly the same as the equilibrium derived in question 1. In particular, show that the equilibrium spot rate and order flow follow

$$s_t = \frac{1}{\alpha_s} \frac{\rho}{1 - \rho} h_{t-1} \quad \text{and} \quad x_{t+1} = \left(1 + \frac{\beta \rho}{1 - \rho}\right) \Delta u_t.$$

(b) Explain why increasing the reporting lag from 1 to 2 weeks has no effect on the equilibrium.

(c) In light of your answers to parts (a) and (b), how would equilibrium spot rates and order flow behave if information on the aggregate hedging demand is never released (i.e., if the reporting lag became infinite)? Explain.

4. News: Suppose that each agent n receives a signal, η_t^n, about his future hedging demand 1 week in advance:

$$\eta_t^n = h_{t+1}^n + \xi_t^n,$$

where $\xi_t^n \sim \text{i.i.d.} N(0, \sigma_\xi^2)$. All other aspects of the model remain unchanged from question 1, so the evolution of dealers' common information between the start of week $t - 1$ and t is

$$\Omega_t^D = \{x_t, h_{t-1}, \Omega_t^D\},$$

and the evolution of agent n's information is

$$\Omega_t^n = \{s_t, h_{t-1}, h_t^n, \eta_t^n, \Omega_t^n\}.$$

(a) Assume that the equilibrium spot rate, s_t, and value of last week's aggregate hedging demand, h_{t-1}, jointly allow each agent n to make a precise inference about the value of u_t. How will each agent use his signal to forecast the future shock to the aggregate hedging demand, $\mathbb{E}_t^n u_{t+1}$?

(b) If s_t and h_{t-1} jointly reveal the value of u_t to agents at the start of week t, the equilibrium log spot rate must take the form

$$s_t = \pi_1 u_t + \pi_2 h_{t-1}$$

for some unknown coefficients, π_1 and π_2. Verify that the equilibrium log spot rate satisfies this equation and find the values of π_1 and π_2.

(c) Derive the equilibrium process for order flow.

(d) Discuss how the equilibrium dynamics of the spot rate depend on the precision of agents' signals concerning their future hedging demands. In particular, how does a rise in the variance of ξ_t^n, σ_ξ^2, affect the behavior of the spot rates and order flows?

(e) Since dealers have contemporaneous knowledge of the aggregate hedging demand in this equilibrium, why do they not quote a spot rate that keeps their holdings of euros at the optimal risk-sharing level of zero?

(f) What happens to the behavior of the equilibrium spot rate and order flow in the limit as $\sigma_\xi^2 \to \infty$? How does the changing behavior affect the information flows and inferences of dealers and agents?

9.A Appendix

9.A.1 The Kalman Filter

The Kalman filter is an algorithm (or set of recursion equations) that specifies how inferences can be made concerning the state of a dynamic system based on partial observations of the system. An authoritative and comprehensive discussion of the Kalman filter can be found in Harvey (1990).

The Kalman filter can be applied to any system of equations that can be written in the following state-space form:

$$\mathcal{Z}_t = \mathbb{A}_t \mathcal{Z}_{t-1} + \mathbb{B}_t \mathcal{U}_t, \tag{9.61a}$$

$$\mathcal{Y}_t = \mathbb{C}_t \mathcal{Z}_t + \mathbb{D}_t \mathcal{V}_t, \tag{9.61b}$$

where $\mathcal{U}_t$ and $\mathcal{V}_t$ are vectors of mean-zero shocks with $\mathbb{E}[\mathcal{U}_t\mathcal{U}_t'] = \mathbb{S}_t$, $\mathbb{E}[\mathcal{V}_t\mathcal{V}_t'] = \mathbb{Q}_t$ and $\mathbb{E}[\mathcal{U}_t\mathcal{V}_t'] = 0$. Equation (9.61a) is known as the state equation. It describes the dynamics of the state vector, $\mathcal{Z}_t$, a vector of variables that completely describes the period-t state of the system. Equation (9.61b) is known as the observation equation. It relates observations on a vector of variables in $\mathcal{Y}_t$ to the current state vector and a vector of observation shocks, $\mathcal{V}_t$. Equation (9.61) describes a *time-varying* state-space system because the matrices $\mathbb{A}_t$, $\mathbb{B}_t$, $\mathbb{C}_t$, $\mathbb{D}_t$, $\mathbb{S}_t$, and $\mathbb{Q}_t$ have elements that follow *deterministic* time series processes (i.e., the elements are functions of t and are not subject to any shocks). When these matrices contain only constant coefficients, the state-space system is called *time-invariant*.

The Kalman filter is an algorithm for computing estimates of $\mathcal{Z}_t$ based on observations on $\mathcal{Y}_t$. The filter consists of two sets of equations: (1) prediction equations, and (2) updating equations. To describe the filter, let $\mathcal{F}_t$ denote the period-t history of observations on $\mathcal{Y}_t$, $\mathcal{F}_t = \{\mathcal{Y}_t, \mathcal{F}_{t-1}\}$. The mean and variance of $\mathcal{Z}_t$ conditioned on $\mathcal{F}_{t-i}$ are therefore

$$\mathcal{Z}_{t|t-i} = \mathbb{E}[\mathcal{Z}_t|\mathcal{F}_{t-i}] \text{ and } \Sigma_{t|t-i} = \mathbb{E}[(\mathcal{Z}_t - \mathbb{E}[\mathcal{Z}_t|\mathcal{F}_{t-i}])(\mathcal{Z}_t - \mathbb{E}[\mathcal{Z}_t|\mathcal{F}_{t-i}])'|\mathcal{F}_{t-i}].$$

The prediction equations of the filter produce expressions for the mean and variance of $\mathcal{Z}_{t+1}$ conditioned on $\mathcal{F}_t$ using $\mathcal{Z}_{t|t}$ and $\Sigma_{t|t}$:

$$\mathcal{Z}_{t+1|t} = \mathbb{A}_{t+1}\mathcal{Z}_{t|t} \tag{9.62}$$

and

$$\Sigma_{t+1|t} = \mathbb{A}_{t+1}\Sigma_{t|t}\mathbb{A}_{t+1}' + \mathbb{B}_{t+1}\mathbb{S}_{t+1}\mathbb{B}_{t+1}'. \tag{9.63}$$

The corresponding mean and variance of $\mathcal{Y}_{t+1}$ conditioned on $\mathcal{F}_t$ are

$$\mathcal{Y}_{t+1|t} = \mathbb{C}_{t+1}\mathcal{Z}_{t+1|t} \tag{9.64}$$

and

$$\mathcal{H}_{t+1} = \mathbb{C}_{t+1}\Sigma_{t+1|t}\mathbb{C}_{t+1}' + \mathbb{D}_{t+1}\mathbb{Q}_{t+1}\mathbb{D}_{t+1}'. \tag{9.65}$$

The prediction error in period $t + 1$ is

$$\mathcal{Y}_{t+1}^e = \mathcal{Y}_{t+1} - \mathcal{Y}_{t+1|t} = \mathbb{C}_{t+1}(\mathcal{Z}_{t+1} - \mathcal{Z}_{t+1|t}) + \mathbb{D}_{t+1}\mathcal{V}_{t+1}. \tag{9.66}$$

The prediction equations require values for $\mathcal{Z}_{t|t}$ and $\Sigma_{t|t}$ as inputs. These values are computed from the updating equations as

$$\mathcal{Z}_{t|t} = \mathcal{Z}_{t|t-1} + \mathcal{G}_t\mathcal{Y}_t^e, \tag{9.67}$$

$$\Sigma_{t|t} = (I - \mathcal{G}_t\mathbb{C}_t)\Sigma_{t|t-1}, \tag{9.68}$$

where the Kalman gain matrix, $\mathcal{G}_t$, is given by

$$\mathcal{G}_t = \Sigma_{t|t-1}\mathbb{C}_t'\mathcal{H}_t^{-1} = \Sigma_{t|t-1}\mathbb{C}_t'(\mathbb{C}_t\Sigma_{t|t-1}\mathbb{C}_t' + \mathbb{D}_t\mathbb{Q}_t\mathbb{D}_t')^{-1}. \tag{9.69}$$

These equations can be derived by applying the Projection theorem to the state-space form.

In most theoretical applications (including the micro-based model examined earlier), the state-space form for the inference problem under consideration is *time-invariant*. In this case, combining (9.63), (9.65), (9.68), and (9.69) gives

$$\Sigma_{t+1|t} = \mathbb{A}\left((I - \Sigma_{t|t-1}\mathbb{C}'\left(\mathbb{C}\Sigma_{t|t-1}\mathbb{C}' + \mathbb{D}\mathbb{Q}\mathbb{D}'\right)^{-1}\mathbb{C}\right)\Sigma_{t|t-1}\right)\mathbb{A}' + \mathbb{B}\mathbb{S}\mathbb{B}', \quad (9.70)$$

so the Kalman gain matrix, $\mathcal{G}_t$, depends on the structure of the state space form, (i.e., the form of the matrices $\mathbb{A}$, $\mathbb{B}$, $\mathbb{C}$, $\mathbb{D}$, $\mathbb{S}$, and $\mathbb{Q}$), not the sequence of observation on $\mathcal{Y}_t$. In most theoretical applications it therefore makes sense to compute the gain matrix using the steady state value of $\Sigma_{t|t-1}$, that is, the value for $\Sigma = \Sigma_{t+1|t} = \Sigma_{t|t-1}$ that solves (9.70):

$$\mathcal{G} = \Sigma\mathbb{C}'(\mathbb{C}\Sigma\mathbb{C}' + \mathbb{D}\mathbb{Q}\mathbb{D}')^{-1}.$$

9.A.2 Real-Time Estimation

The real-time estimates are computed with the aid of the Kalman filter. Complete details of this procedure are described in Evans (2005). Here we provide a brief overview for a monthly log series Y.

Let ΔY_d denote the daily increment to the monthly value for $Y_{M(m)}$, where $M(m)$ is the last day of month m. Next, define the partial sum

$$Y_d \equiv \sum_{i=M(m-1)+1}^{\min\{M(m),d\}} \Delta Y_i$$

as the cumulative daily contribution to $Y_{M(m)}$ in month m. Note that when $d = M(m)$, $Y_d = Y_{M(m)}$. The daily dynamics of Y_d are described by

$$Y_d = \left(1 - \mathfrak{D}_d\right)Y_{d-1} + \Delta Y_d, \quad (9.71)$$

where $\mathfrak{D}_d$ is a dummy variable equal to one on the first day of each month and zero otherwise.

To accommodate the presence of variable reporting lags, let Y_d^{M-1} for $d \geq M(m)$ denote the value for Y at the end of the most recently completed month. By definition,

$$Y_d^{M-1} = \left(1 - \mathfrak{D}_d\right)Y_{d-1}^{M-1} + \mathfrak{D}_d Y_{d-1}. \quad (9.72)$$

We can also track the value of $Y_{M(m)}$ K months back via the recursions

$$Y_d^{M-K} = \left(1 - \mathfrak{D}_d\right)Y_{d-1}^{M-K} + \mathfrak{D}_d Y_{d-1}^{M-K+1}. \quad (9.73)$$

Now suppose that the reporting lag for series Y is less than 1 month. If $\widehat{Y}_d$ is the value for $Y_{M(m)}$ released on day d, we have

$$\widehat{Y}_d = Y_d^{M-1}. \quad (9.74)$$

If the reporting lag is longer than 1 month (but less than 2),

$$\widehat{Y}_d = Y_d^{M-2}, \quad (9.75)$$

and so on.

The information contained in the data releases on other variables is incorporated into the real-time estimates in a similar manner. Specifically, let z_d^i denote the value of another series, released on day d, that relates to activity in the last completed month. The real-time estimates are computed under the assumption that

$$z_d^i = a_i Y_d^{M-1} + u_d^i, \tag{9.76}$$

where u_d^i is an i.i.d. $N(0, \sigma_i^2)$ shock. In cases where the reporting lag is 2 months,

$$z_d^i = a_i Y_d^{M-2} + u_d^i. \tag{9.77}$$

It is important to recognize that (9.74)–(9.77) allow for variations in the reporting lag from one data release to the next.

All that now remains is to specify the dynamics for the daily increments, ΔY_d. The real-time estimates discussed in the chapter assume that

$$\Delta Y_d = \sum_{i=1}^{\varrho} \phi_i (Y_d^{M-i} - Y_d^{M-i-1}) + u_d^Y, \tag{9.78}$$

where u_d^Y is an i.i.d. $N(0, \sigma_Y^2)$ shock.

Finding the real-time estimates of Y requires solutions to two related problems. First, there is a pure inference problem of how to compute $\mathbb{E}[Y_{M(m)} | \Omega_d]$ using the signaling equations (9.74)–(9.77), and the ΔY_d process in (9.78), given values for all the parameters in these equations. Second, we have to estimate these parameters. The Kalman filtering algorithm provides solutions to both these problems. In particular, if the state vector on day d, $\mathcal{Z}_d$, is specified as $[Y_d, Y_d^{M-1}, \ldots, Y_d^{M-2}, \Delta Y_d]'$, and the data releases on day d are included in the observation vector $\mathcal{Y}_d$, equations (9.71)–(9.78) can be written in the state-space form of (9.61) (with time periods t measured in days). The parameters of the model are then estimated by maximizing the sample likelihood function constructed from the sequence of prediction errors $\{\mathcal{Y}_d^e\}$ and covariance matrices $\{\mathcal{H}_d\}$ from the filtering equations across all days in the sample. Once these parameter estimates are obtained, the real-time estimates are computed from the elements of $\{\mathcal{Z}_{d|d}\}$ computed from the Kalman filter.

9.A.3 Derivations

The equilibrium behavior of the model depends on two key matrices, $\{\Phi^D, \Phi^N\}$, and vectors, $\{\Lambda_x, \Lambda_s\}$. To derive Φ^D and Φ^N in Proposition 9.1, we first use (9.17), (9.26), and (9.27) to characterize the behavior of $\mathbb{E}_t^D Z_t$ and $\mathbb{E}_t^n Z_t$. Applying the Kalman filter to (9.17), (9.26), and (9.27) gives

$$\mathbb{E}_t^D Z_t = A \mathbb{E}_{t-1}^D Z_{t-1} + GCA(Z_{t-1} - \mathbb{E}_{t-1}^D Z_{t-1}) + GCBu_t$$

and

$$\mathbb{E}_t^n Z_t = A \mathbb{E}_{t-1}^n Z_{t-1} + G^N C^N A(Z_{t-1} - \mathbb{E}_{t-1}^n Z_{t-1}) + G^N C^N Bu_t + G^N D^N v_t^n,$$

where G and G^N are the constant Kalman gain matrices for the dealers' and agents' inference problems. Let Σ_u and Σ_v denote the covariance matrices for u_t and v_t^n, respectively. Then these gain matrices can be written as

$$G = \Sigma^{\mathrm{D}} C' \left(C \Sigma^{\mathrm{D}} C' \right)^{-1} \quad \text{and} \quad G^{\mathrm{N}} = \Sigma^{\mathrm{N}} C^{\mathrm{N}\prime} \left(C^{\mathrm{N}} \Sigma^{\mathrm{N}} C^{\mathrm{N}\prime} + D^{\mathrm{N}} \Sigma_v D^{\mathrm{N}\prime} \right)^{-1}, \quad (9.79)$$

where $\Sigma^i = A \left((I - G^i C^i) \Sigma^i \right) A' + B \Sigma_u B'$ for $i = \{\mathrm{D}, \mathrm{N}\}$. Combining these expressions with (9.17) gives us the following expressions for the estimation errors

$$Z_t - \mathbb{E}_t^{\mathrm{D}} Z_t = \sum_{i=0}^{\infty} \{(I - GC)A\}^i \, (I - GC) B u_{t-i} \qquad (9.80)$$

and

$$Z_t - \mathbb{E}_t^n Z_t = \sum_{i=0}^{\infty} \{(I - G^{\mathrm{N}} C^{\mathrm{N}})A\}^i \{(I - G^{\mathrm{N}} C^{\mathrm{N}}) B u_{t-i} - G^{\mathrm{N}} D^{\mathrm{N}} v_{t-i}^n\}. \quad (9.81)$$

Because the inference problem facing all agents $n \in [0, 1]$ involves the same C^{N}, D^{N}, and Σ_v matrices, G^{N} is also the same across all agents. This means that the agent-specific shocks, $\{v_{t-i}^n\}$, are the only source of heterogeneity in the estimation errors, $Z_t - \mathbb{E}_t^n Z_t$.

Under the information assumptions in the model, all the elements of $(I - GC) \cdot B u_{t-i}$ for $i \geq k$ are in Ω_t^{D}, so no linear combination of these elements can affect $Z_t - \mathbb{E}_t^{\mathrm{D}} Z_t$. Therefore $\{(I - GC)A\}^i$ must be equal to the null matrices for $i \geq k$, and (9.80) becomes

$$Z_t - \mathbb{E}_t^{\mathrm{D}} Z_t = \sum_{i=0}^{k-1} \{(I - GC)A\}^i \, (I - GC) B u_{t-i} = \sum_{i=0}^{k-1} \Gamma_i u_{t-i}. \quad (9.82)$$

Since $\{u_t, u_{t-1}, \dots, u_{t-k+1}\}$ are elements of Z_t, we can rewrite this equation as $Z_t - \mathbb{E}_t^{\mathrm{D}} Z_t = \Theta^{\mathrm{D}} Z_t$. Rearranging this equation gives (9.18a) with $\Phi^{\mathrm{D}} = (I - \Theta^{\mathrm{D}})$. Similarly, since all the elements of $(I - G^{\mathrm{N}} C^{\mathrm{N}}) B u_{t-i}$ for $i \geq k$ are also in Ω_t^n, (9.81) becomes

$$Z_t - \mathbb{E}_t^n Z_t = \sum_{i=0}^{k-1} \{(I - G^{\mathrm{N}} C^{\mathrm{N}})A\}^i \, (I - G^{\mathrm{N}} C^{\mathrm{N}}) B u_{t-i}$$

$$- \sum_{i=0}^{\infty} \{(I - G^{\mathrm{N}} C^{\mathrm{N}})A\}^i \, G^{\mathrm{N}} D^{\mathrm{N}} v_{t-i}^n$$

or

$$Z_t - \mathbb{E}_t^n Z_t = \Theta^{\mathrm{N}} Z_t - \sum_{i=0}^{\infty} \{(I - G^{\mathrm{N}} C^{\mathrm{N}})A\}^i \, G^{\mathrm{N}} D^{\mathrm{N}} v_{t-i}^n.$$

Rearranging this equation gives (9.18b), where

$$\Phi^{\mathrm{D}} = (I - \Theta^{\mathrm{D}}) \quad \text{and} \quad \Psi_i = \{(I - G^{\mathrm{N}} C^{\mathrm{N}})A\}^i \, G^{\mathrm{N}} D^{\mathrm{N}}.$$

This completes the proof of Proposition 9.1.

To prove Proposition 9.2, recall that $z_t' = [\Delta \hat{p}_t - \Delta p_t, \; \hat{r}_t - r_t, \; \hat{p}_t - p_t,$ $\hat{y}_t - y_t, \; \ldots, \; \ldots]$, so $\Delta \hat{p}_t - \Delta p_t = \ell_1 z_t, \; \hat{r}_t - r_t = \ell_2 z_t$, etc., for some selection vectors, ℓ_i. Furthermore, equation (9.10) implies that

$$z_t = B_u u_t + A_z B_u u_{t-1} + A_z^2 B_u u_{t-2} + \cdots + A_z^k z_{t-k} = \Lambda_z Z_t,$$

so we can write $\Delta \hat{p}_t - \Delta p_t = \ell_1 \Lambda_z Z_t = \Lambda_{\Delta p} Z_t, \; \hat{r}_t - r_t = \ell_2 \Lambda_z Z_t = \Lambda_r Z_t$, and so on. We can therefore write dealers' estimates of fundamentals as

$$\mathbb{E}_t^D f_t = (1 + \gamma_\pi) \Lambda_{\Delta p} \mathbb{E}_t^D Z_{t+1} + \left[\gamma_y \Lambda_y - \left(\tfrac{1-\rho}{\rho} \right) \Lambda_p \right] \mathbb{E}_t^D Z_t$$

$$= \left\{ (1 + \gamma_\pi) \Lambda_{\Delta \hat{p}} A + \left[\gamma_y \Lambda_y - \left(\tfrac{1-\rho}{\rho} \right) \Lambda_p \right] \right\} \mathbb{E}_t^D Z_t$$

$$= \Lambda_f \mathbb{E}_t^D Z_t.$$

Following Proposition 9.3 we established that $\delta_t = -\Lambda_\delta \mathbb{E}_t^D Z_t$, so with the preceding expression we can now rewrite (9.13) as

$$s_t = \Lambda_r Z_t + \mathbb{E}_t^D \sum_{i=1}^{\infty} \rho^i \Lambda_f Z_{t+i} + \mathbb{E}_t^D \sum_{i=0}^{\infty} \rho^i \Lambda_\delta Z_{t+i}$$

$$= \Lambda_r Z_t + \left(\rho \Lambda_f A + \Lambda_\delta \right) (I - \rho A)^{-1} \mathbb{E}_t^D Z_t.$$

Since $\{r_t, \hat{r}_t\} \in \Omega_t^D$, $\Lambda_r Z_t = \Lambda_r \mathbb{E}_t^D Z_t$, so we can also write the second line as

$$s_t = \{ \Lambda_r + \left(\rho \Lambda_f A + \Lambda_\delta \right) (I - \rho A)^{-1} \} \mathbb{E}_t^D Z_t,$$

which is the form of equation (9.20).

Since the proof of Proposition 9.3 is presented within the text, all that remains is to show that $x_t = \Lambda_x Z_t$. We established in (9.82) that $Z_t - \mathbb{E}_t^D Z_t = \sum_{i=0}^{k-1} \Gamma_i u_{t-i}$. Substituting these estimation errors into (9.22) gives

$$x_t = \alpha_s \Lambda_\delta \Gamma_0 u_{t-1} + \alpha_s \Lambda_\delta \sum_{i=1}^{k-2} (\Gamma_i - \Gamma_{i-1}) u_{t-i-1} - \alpha_s \Lambda_\delta \Gamma_{k-1} u_{t-k-1}$$

$$= \Lambda_x Z_t, \tag{9.83}$$

because $\{u_{t-1}, u_{t-1}, \ldots, u_{t-k-1}\}$ are all elements in Z_t.

Finally, we turn to Proposition 9.5. By definition, the vector of projection coefficients in (9.40) are given by

$$\begin{bmatrix} \beta_Y \\ \beta_x \end{bmatrix} = \left(\mathbb{E} \begin{bmatrix} (s_t - s_t^*)^2 & (s_t - s_t^*)(x_{t+1} - \mathbb{E}_t^D x_{t+1}) \\ (s_t - s_t^*)(x_{t+1} - \mathbb{E}_t^D x_{t+1}) & (x_{t+1} - \mathbb{E}_t^D x_{t+1})^2 \end{bmatrix} \right)^{-1}$$

$$\times \mathbb{E} \begin{bmatrix} Y_{t+\tau}(s_t - s_t^*) \\ Y_{t+\tau}(x_{t+1} - \mathbb{E}_t^D x_{t+1}) \end{bmatrix}.$$

Since $s_t - s_t^* \in \Omega_t^D$, $\mathbb{E}[(s_t - s_t^*)(x_{t+1} - \mathbb{E}_t^D x_{t+1})] = 0$, so the solution to this equation is

$$\beta_Y = \frac{\mathbb{E}[Y_{t+\tau}(s_t - s_t^*)]}{\mathbb{E}[(s_t - s_t^*)^2]} \quad \text{and} \quad \beta_x = \frac{\mathbb{E}[Y_{t+\tau}(x_{t+1} - \mathbb{E}_t^D x_{t+1})]}{\mathbb{E}[(x_{t+1} - \mathbb{E}_t^D x_{t+1})^2]}.$$

Using (9.37) and (9.42) to substitute for $(s_t - s_t^*)$ and $Y_{t+\tau}$ in the expression for β_Y gives equation (9.39). To derive the expression for β_x, we first substitute for $Y_{t+\tau}$ with (9.42) to get

$$\beta_x = \frac{\mathbb{E}[(\mathbb{E}_{t+1}^D - \mathbb{E}_t^D)Y_{t+\tau}(x_{t+1} - \mathbb{E}_t^D x_{t+1})]}{\mathbb{E}[(x_{t+1} - \mathbb{E}_t^D x_{t+1})^2]}.$$

Next, we use the fact that

$$(\mathbb{E}_{t+1}^D - \mathbb{E}_t^D)Y_{t+\tau} = \Lambda_Y A^{\tau-1}(\mathbb{E}_{t+1}^D - \mathbb{E}_t^D)Z_{t+1}$$
$$= \Lambda_Y A^{\tau-1}(GCBu_{t+1} + GCA(Z_t - \mathbb{E}_t^D Z_t)).$$

Combining this expression with (9.31) and the equation for β_x produces

$$\beta_x = \frac{\Lambda_Y A^{\tau-1}GCA\mathbb{E}[(Z_t - \mathbb{E}_t^D Z_t)(Z_t - \mathbb{E}_t^D Z_t)']\Lambda_\delta' \alpha_s}{\alpha_s \Lambda_\delta \mathbb{E}[(Z_t - \mathbb{E}_t^D Z_t)(Z_t - \mathbb{E}_t^D Z_t)']\Lambda_\delta' \alpha_s}$$
$$= \frac{\Lambda_Y A^{\tau-1}GCA\mathbb{V}^D(Z_t)\Lambda_\delta' \alpha_s}{\alpha_s \Lambda_\delta \mathbb{V}^D(Z_t)\Lambda_\delta' \alpha_s},$$

as shown in Proposition 9.5.

CHAPTER 10

Exchange Rates, Order Flows, and Macro Data Releases

In the United States and many other countries, statistical agencies release information about the macroeconomy on an almost daily basis. These data releases constitute the main source of public information about key macro variables to participants in the FX and other financial markets. As such, the response of spot exchange rates and the prices of other financial assets to macro data releases has long been studied in order to better understand the link between financial markets and the macroeconomy.

In this chapter we examine how spot rates respond to macro data releases from two perspectives. The first is based on the traditional macro-based view of exchange-rate determination. This view provides the rationale for the long-established empirical literature using event studies. The second perspective is micro-based. Specifically, we first extend the Portfolio Shifts model from Chapter 6 to study how spot rates and order flows react to macro data releases at intraday frequencies. This analysis provides perspective on several empirical models that quantify the high-frequency effects of macro data releases. We then use the micro-based macro model from Chapter 9 to examine the effects of data releases at longer horizons. Here we will see how the risk-management activities of dealers can affect spot rates and order flows in ways that traditional macro-based models overlook.

10.1 The Macro Perspective

10.1.1 The Event-Study Rationale

Macro exchange-rate models predict that spot rates will respond immediately to the public release of macro data if it induces: (1) a change in current real interest rates and/or the foreign exchange risk premium, (2) a revision in expectations concerning future real interest rates and/or the risk premia, or (3) a revision in the expected long-run real exchange rate. The models do not predict that spot rates will respond to all data releases, or even to previously unexpected releases. Nor do they predict the size or direction of the spot rate's response to particular releases. They do, however, rule out the possibility that the spot rate's response is delayed. It is this theoretical prediction that provides the key rationale for event studies.

These theoretical implications are easily derived. We begin with the definition of the foreign exchange risk premium:

$$\delta_t = \mathbb{E}[\Delta s_{t+1}|\Omega_t] + \hat{r}_t - r_t,$$

where, as usual, r_t and $\hat{r}_t$ are the one-period dollar and euro interest rates and s_t is the log USD/EUR rate. The first term on the right is the expected rate of depreciation, which is conditioned on the common information set of all market participants at the start of period t, Ω_t. We can also write the risk premium in terms of the real exchange rate, $\varepsilon_t = s_t + \hat{p}_t - p_t$, and real interest rates, $r_t - \mathbb{E}[\Delta p_{t+1}|\Omega_t]$ and $\hat{r}_t - \mathbb{E}[\Delta \hat{p}_{t+1}|\Omega_t]$, where p_t and $\hat{p}_t$ are the log U.S. and E.U. price indices:

$$\delta_t = \mathbb{E}[\Delta \varepsilon_{t+1}|\Omega_t] + \left(\hat{r}_t - \mathbb{E}[\Delta \hat{p}_{t+1}|\Omega_t]\right) - (r_t - \mathbb{E}[\Delta p_{t+1}|\Omega_t]).$$

Rewriting this expression as

$$\varepsilon_t = \mathbb{E}[\varepsilon_{t+1}|\Omega_t] + \eta_{t,t+1},$$

where

$$\eta_{t,t+1} = \left(\hat{r}_t - \mathbb{E}[\Delta \hat{p}_{t+1}|\Omega_t]\right) - (r_t - \mathbb{E}[\Delta p_{t+1}|\Omega_t]) - \delta_t$$

and iterating forward using the Law of Iterated Expectations gives

$$\varepsilon_t = \eta_{t,t+1} + \sum_{j=1}^{\infty} \mathbb{E}[\eta_{t+j,t+j+1}|\Omega_t] + \varepsilon_t^{\infty}, \tag{10.1}$$

with $\varepsilon_t^{\infty} = \lim_{h\to\infty} \mathbb{E}[\varepsilon_{t+h}|\Omega_t]$. Note that this equation follows from the Law of Iterated Expectations and the definitions of the risk premium, real interest rates, and the real exchange rate. It contains no assumptions about the behavior of interest rates or the determinants of the expected long-run real exchange rate, ε_t^{∞}. In words, it says that the log real exchange rate must be equal to the current risk-adjusted real interest differential between t and $t+1$, $\eta_{t,t+1}$, plus the sum of expected future differentials and the expected long-run real exchange rate.

Let us now use equation (10.1) to compute the unexpected variation in the real exchange rate between the start of period t and some point before the start of period $t+1$. It proves convenient to identify variables at this point with the subscript $t+\epsilon$, for some $\epsilon < 1$. With this notation, the unexpected variation in the real exchange rate implied by equation (10.1) is

$$\varepsilon_{t+\epsilon} - \mathbb{E}[\varepsilon_{t+\epsilon}|\Omega_t] = \eta_{t+\epsilon,t+1} - \mathbb{E}[\eta_{t+\epsilon,t+1}|\Omega_t]$$

$$+ \sum_{j=1}^{\infty} \left\{\mathbb{E}[\eta_{t+j,t+j+1}|\Omega_{t+\epsilon}] - \mathbb{E}[\eta_{t+j,t+j+1}|\Omega_t]\right\}$$

$$+ \varepsilon_{t+\epsilon}^{\infty} - \varepsilon_t^{\infty}, \tag{10.2}$$

where $\eta_{t+\epsilon,t+1}$ is the risk-adjusted real interest differential between $t + \epsilon$ and $t + 1$. Like equation (10.1), this expression holds true whatever the behavior of real interest rates or the risk premium.

We can now use equation (10.2) to think through how the nominal exchange rate responds to a macro data release that takes place between t and $t + \epsilon$. For this purpose, let us assume that the interval $(t, t + \epsilon]$ covers just a few minutes. Variations in nominal and real exchange rates mirror one another over such short time periods because retail prices are effectively constant, that is, $s_{t+\epsilon} - s_t = \varepsilon_{t+\epsilon} - \varepsilon_t$. We can therefore write the change in the spot rate as

$$s_{t+\epsilon} - s_t = \varepsilon_{t+\epsilon} - \varepsilon_t$$

$$= \mathbb{E}[\varepsilon_{t+\epsilon} - \varepsilon_t | \Omega_t] + \varepsilon_{t+\epsilon} - \mathbb{E}[\varepsilon_{t+\epsilon} | \Omega_t].$$

Substituting for $\varepsilon_{t+\epsilon} - \mathbb{E}[\varepsilon_{t+\epsilon} | \Omega_t]$ with equation (10.2) gives

$$s_{t+\epsilon} - s_t = \left\{ \eta_{t+\epsilon,t+1} - \mathbb{E}[\eta_{t+\epsilon,t+1} | \Omega_t] \right\}$$

$$+ \sum_{j=1}^{\infty} \left\{ \mathbb{E}[\eta_{t+j,t+j+1} | \Omega_{t+\varepsilon}] - \mathbb{E}[\eta_{t+j,t+j+1} | \Omega_t] \right\} + u_{t+\epsilon}, \tag{10.3}$$

where $u_{t+\epsilon} = \mathbb{E}[\varepsilon_{t+\epsilon} - \varepsilon_t | \Omega_t] + \varepsilon_{t+\epsilon}^{\infty} - \varepsilon_t^{\infty}$.

Equation (10.3) provides us with a decomposition of high-frequency changes in the log spot rate that holds true in *any* model. It implies that a macro data release during $(t, t + \epsilon]$ can potentially affect the spot rate through three channels. First, if the data release leads to an unexpected rise in the current risk-adjusted real interest differential (i.e., a rise in $\eta_{t+\epsilon} - \mathbb{E}[\eta_{t+\epsilon} | \Omega_t]$), the dollar will immediately depreciate by a matching amount. The second channel operates via the forecasts of future differentials. In this case, there will be an immediate dollar depreciation if the data release leads market participants to revise their forecasts for future differentials upward. Data releases can also affect spot rates by changing long-term real-exchange-rate expectations, $\varepsilon_{t+\epsilon}^{\infty} - \varepsilon_t^{\infty}$. Obviously, this third channel will be inoperable if PPP holds in the long run. Note that the expected depreciation rate, $\mathbb{E}[\varepsilon_{t+\epsilon} - \varepsilon_t | \Omega_t]$, can also contribute to any observed change in the spot rate, but unexpected data releases during $(t, t + \epsilon]$ cannot affect this term.

Equation (10.3) makes clear why spot rates need not respond to a data release, even an unanticipated release. For example, suppose that during $(t, t + \epsilon]$ the Federal Reserve announces an increase in the FED Funds rate that was not previously anticipated by market participants. As a consequence, there is an unanticipated rise in the short-term dollar interest rate, that is, $r_{t+\epsilon} - \mathbb{E}[r_{t+\epsilon} | \Omega_t] > 0$. Clearly, it is possible that news of this change in U.S. monetary policy could lead market participants to revise their expectations for U.S. inflation upward by an exactly matching amount (i.e., $r_{t+\epsilon} - \mathbb{E}[r_{t+\epsilon} | \Omega_t] = \mathbb{E}[\Delta p_{t+1} | \Omega_{t+\epsilon}] - \mathbb{E}[\Delta p_{t+1} | \Omega_t]$), so there is no unexpected variation in the risk-adjusted interest differential, $\eta_{t+\epsilon}$. Similarly, if the revision in expectations concerning future U.S. interest rates is also mirrored by changing inflation expectations, then $\mathbb{E}[\eta_{t+i} | \Omega_{t+\varepsilon}] = \mathbb{E}[\eta_{t+i} | \Omega_t]$ for $i \geq 1$. Under these circumstances, the spot rate will not respond to the unanticipated FED Funds announcement unless it changes long-term real-exchange-rate expectations. In short, data releases may well contain new information on current and future macro variables (e.g., nominal interest rates and inflation), but they need not affect spot rates if the information they convey has offsetting effects on the risk-adjusted interest differentials.

Since the mid-1980s most central banks have conducted monetary policy by controlling short-term interest rates. In this environment, most data releases (other than policy changes) have negligible effects on current real interest rates, so any exchange-rate response occurs via changes in the risk premium and/or revisions in expectations about the future course of real interest rates. The latter effect is identified by the second term in equation (10.3). For example, a data release on GDP in the last quarter could lead market participants to believe that the FED will tighten policy relative to the ECB next year, thereby leading to a higher real interest rate in the United States than in Europe. In this case, $\mathbb{E}[\eta_{t+i}|\Omega_{t+\varepsilon}] - \mathbb{E}[\eta_{t+i}|\Omega_t] < 0$ for some $i > 0$, so the dollar should immediately appreciate when the GDP data are released. Conversely, if market participants believe that future U.S. inflation will increase more quickly than the FED will raise interest rates, their forecast for future U.S. real interest rates will fall, so $\mathbb{E}[\eta_{t+i}|\Omega_{t+\varepsilon}] - \mathbb{E}[\eta_{t+i}|\Omega_t] > 0$ for some $i > 0$, if expectations regarding future E.U. real interest rates remain unchanged. As a consequence, the release of the GDP data will induce an immediate depreciation of the dollar. Thus, even if we ignore the possible effects on the risk premium, the direction of the exchange-rate response to a GDP data release is ambiguous.

This ambiguity applies to all macro data releases. Unless we place further restrictions on the expected response of future interest rates and inflation to the new information in the data release (and are willing to ignore possible variations in the risk premia), the exchange-rate effects of a macro data release are theoretically ambiguous.

Equation (10.3) also has implications for the duration of the exchange-rate response to data releases. By definition,

$$\mathbb{E}[\Delta\varepsilon_{t+1+i}|\Omega_{t+\varepsilon}] - \mathbb{E}[\Delta\varepsilon_{t+1+i}|\Omega_t] = -(\mathbb{E}[\eta_{t+i}|\Omega_{t+\varepsilon}] - \mathbb{E}[\eta_{t+i}|\Omega_t])$$

for $i > 0$, so any data release that leads market participants to revise their forecasts for the future risk-adjusted real interest differential also changes their forecasts for the rate of real depreciation after the release takes place. Of course, actual depreciation rates may differ from these expectations. In principle, however, data releases should have some forecasting power for future depreciation rates if they do in fact change expected future differentials, η_{t+i}. Thus, spot rates may respond immediately to the release of macro data, but their initial response can differ from their total long-run response.

10.1.2 Event-Study Regressions

Event-study regressions provide estimates of the immediate exchange-rate response to data releases on a particular macro variable, such as GDP or CPI inflation. To illustrate, suppose we have data on a T observation sequence of GDP releases $\{D_{t_i}\}$ at times $\{t_1, t_2, \ldots, t_T\}$ and estimates of market participants' prior forecasts, $D^e_{t_i} = \mathbb{E}[D_{t_i}|\Omega_{t_i-h}]$ for some $h > 0$. If Δs_i denotes the change in the spot rate between t_i and $t_i + \epsilon$ for each of the T data releases, the exchange-rate response to the GDP data release is estimated by the slope coefficient in the regression

$$\Delta s_i = \beta \left(D_{t_i} - D_{t_i}^e \right) + \xi_i. \tag{10.4}$$

Note that this regression is only estimated with data during the T event windows, $[t_i, t_i + \epsilon]$, that contain the announcements. Variations in the spot rate outside these windows are not considered.

To understand the relation between regression (10.4) and the theoretical decomposition for the depreciation rate we have just derived, we use equation (10.3) to substitute for Δs_i in the least-squares formula for β:

$$\beta = \beta(\eta_{t_i + \epsilon}) + \sum_{j=1}^{\infty} \beta(\mathbb{E}[\eta_{t+j} | \Omega_{t_i + \epsilon}]) + \beta(\varepsilon_{t_i + \epsilon}^{\infty}), \tag{10.5}$$

where

$$\beta(\varkappa_{t_i + \epsilon}) = \frac{\mathbb{CV}(\varkappa_{t_i + \epsilon} - \mathbb{E}[\varkappa_{t_i + \epsilon} | \Omega_{t_i}], D_{t_i} - D_{t_i}^e)}{\mathbb{V}(D_{t_i} - D_{t_i}^e)},$$

for $\varkappa_t = \{\eta_t, \varepsilon_t^{\infty}, \mathbb{E}[\eta_{t+j} | \Omega_t]\}$. Equation (10.5) shows that the slope coefficient will differ from zero when the unexpected data release is correlated with: (1) unanticipated changes in the current risk-adjusted real interest differential, $\eta_{t_i + \epsilon}$, (2) revisions in the forecasts of future differentials, and/or (3) changes in long-run exchange-rate expectations, $\varepsilon_{t_i + \epsilon}^{\infty}$. As we noted before, the sign of these correlations is theoretically ambiguous, so there is no particular reason to expect the slope coefficient β to be positive or negative for a particular set of data releases.

We can also use equation (10.3) to identify the elements in the error term of regression (10.4). By construction, this term is uncorrelated with the unexpected data releases, $D_{t_i} - D_{t_i}^e$, so it contains the prior expected rate of depreciation, $\mathbb{E}[\varepsilon_{t+\epsilon} - \varepsilon_t | \Omega_{t_i}]$, and the effects of any other unexpected shocks that occur during the event window. Both of these terms should be negligible if the specified event window is just a few minutes in duration. Under these circumstances, the R^2 statistic from the regression should be close to one.

10.1.3 Event-Study Results

The first event studies examining the response of exchange rates to macro data releases were estimated in daily data (i.e., the event window for each release was 24 hours). These studies generally found estimates of β that were statistically significant for some data releases, such as those concerning output, inflation, and the trade balance, but the effects were quite small and only accounted for a fraction of the variation in spot rates during the event windows. For example, Klein, Mizrach, and Murphy (1991) found that between 1986 and 1988 the USD depreciated significantly against the JPY and DM when the release of trade data revealed an unexpected trade deficit, but this news explained less than half of the spot rate changes on the release days. Clearly, the event window in this and other studies based on daily data is too long to isolate the impact of the data release.

The availability of intraday exchange-rate data now allows researchers to avoid this problem. For example, Andersen, Bollerslev, Diebold, and Vega (2003) examine the response of six USD exchange rates to the unexpected components of 41 U.S. and German data releases between January 1992 and December 1998 using event windows ranging from 25 to 5 minutes. Their estimates indicate that most of the exchange-rate response to the data release is within the first 5 minutes. This finding is supported by other studies, leading many researchers to conclude that *all* the exchange-rate effects of data releases occur very quickly. As we shall see, this conclusion is not supported by more recent research.

Andersen et al. also find that exchange rates respond to the unexpected component of the data release rather than to prior expectations. As is standard in the literature, they identify prior expectations on each data release with the median forecast from a survey of professional money managers conducted at the end of the previous week by Money Market Services. Clearly, this survey measure is only a proxy for market-wide expectations immediately before a release. Aside from obvious reporting issues, managers' forecasts may be based on information that is not known to everyone, and they may change their forecasts between the time the survey is conducted and the point immediately prior to the release. The impact of these potential problems has yet to be fully examined in the literature.

Table 10.1 reproduces the results from another event study conducted by Faust, Rogers, Wang, and Wright (2007) using a 14-year span of intraday data for USD/DM(EUR) and GBP/USD from 1987 to 2002. In this case, there is a 20-minute event window that begins 5 minutes before each data release. The table reports estimates of β ($\times 10,000$) and the R^2 statistic from regression (10.4) for 10 U.S. data releases. Overall, the estimates of β show that an unexpected data release indicative of greater-than-expected U.S. growth induces an appreciation of the USD. Similarly, an unexpected tightening of U.S. monetary policy raising the FED Funds rate leads

TABLE 10.1
Event-Study Estimates

Data release	DM(EUR)		GBP	
	β	R^2	β	R^2
CPI	3.92	0.00	−5.16	0.00
FED Funds rate	−1.23***	0.20	−0.66***	0.13
GDP	−13.80***	0.18	−8.15***	0.10
Housing starts	−25.13*	0.02	−15.28	0.01
Initial unemployment claims	−0.16***	0.04	−0.09***	0.02
Nonfarm payrolls	−0.13***	0.21	−0.10***	0.21
PPI	−1.23	0.00	−8.37*	0.02
Retail sales	−14.16***	0.15	−12.12***	0.19
Trade balance	−10.09***	0.24	−7.13***	0.20
Unemployment	57.51***	0.07	48.69***	0.09

Notes: The symbols * and *** denote significance at the 10 percent and 1 percent levels, respectively. Coefficient estimates are multiplied by 10,000. Source: Faust, Rogers, Wang, and Wright (2007).

to an appreciation. These results are consistent with the idea that: (1) a tightening of monetary policy raises current and expected future real U.S. interest rates, and (2) higher-than-expected U.S. growth leads market participants to revise their forecasts for U.S. real rates upward in anticipation of tighter future monetary policy.

Although many of the β estimates in Table 10.1 are highly statistically significant, their economic importance is less clear-cut. For example, as Faust et al. note, the estimated β for nonfarm payrolls implies that if the data release is 100,000 jobs higher than expected, the USD appreciates (on average) by 13 basis points against the DM (EUR). This is not a trivial response, but it is far smaller than the daily standard deviation for changes in the spot rate of 66 basis points. Similarly, the (uncentered) R^2 statistics indicate that every data release accounts for less than 25 percent of the variance in spot rate changes over the 20-minute event windows. Recall that these statistics should be close to unity if the data release dominates market activity during the event window. Clearly, this is not the case here. Although Andersen et al. find somewhat higher R^2 statistics in their shorter data sample, they, too, are unable to account for a large fraction of spot rate movements immediately following the data releases.

Event-study results, like those in Table 10.1, are often cited as evidence supporting the existence of a link between spot rates and macro fundamentals. For example, Rogoff (2007) argues that the high-frequency response of spot rates to unexpected changes in interest rates represents the most concrete success of monetary exchange-rate models. The immediate appreciation of the dollar to an unexpected tightening of monetary policy and higher-than-expected growth is certainly *qualitatively* consistent with the predictions of monetary models with Taylor rules. However, from a quantitative perspective, the results are much less encouraging because data releases appear to account for so little of the *total* variation in spot rates.

To make this point concrete, let us return to the results of Andersen, Bollerslev, Diebold, and Vega (2003). They report R^2 statistics ranging from 0.3 to 0.6 across the 41 data releases they study. But, as they note, summing the amount of time in all of their 5-minute, postevent windows accounts for only 0.2 percent of their full sample period (e.g., roughly one 5-minute interval per day). They also find that the volatility of spot rate changes rises following announcements. In order to think about the volatility of spot rates over the whole data sample, we have to factor in higher volatility during the event windows. Let us therefore make two conservative assumptions: (1) volatility during event windows is 10 times higher than at other times, and (2) the true R^2 for all the data releases is 0.6. Now we know that there is negligible serial correlation in high-frequency spot rate changes, so the variance contribution of the data release only comes from the event windows. Thus, conservatively, the data releases account for 0.012 ($0.002 \times 0.6 \times 10$), approximately 1 percent, of the variance in spot rate changes over the sample period.

This macro-based perspective on the link between spot rate dynamics and data releases leaves us with two key questions:

1. If the information in data releases truly accounts for just 1 percent of the high-frequency variation in spot rates, what accounts for the other 99 percent?

2. Could the information in the data release actually play a larger role in spot rate determination than is captured by event studies?

10.2 Micro Perspective I: High-Frequency Dynamics

Micro-based models provide new perspectives on how the release of macro data affects the behavior of spot rates at very high intraday frequencies and at low frequencies measured in days and weeks. This section uses the Portfolio Shifts (PS) model to lay out this perspective for the intraday dynamics. It then reviews the empirical evidence on how spot rates and order flows respond to data releases at high frequencies.

10.2.1 Data Releases in the Portfolio Shifts Model

The Portfolio Shifts model presented in Chapter 6 provides a useful framework for studying the high-frequency effects of public data releases on spot rates and the FX orders of investors and dealers. In particular, it allows us to examine the channels through which the information contained in a data release becomes embedded in dealers' spot rate quotes.

Model Structure

We make one small amendment to the structure of the model in order to study the effects of data releases. Recall that the model describes a pure exchange economy with one risky asset representing FX and one risk-free asset with a daily return of $1 + r$. The economy is populated by a continuum of risk-averse investors indexed by $n \in [0, 1]$, D risk-averse FX dealers indexed by d, and an FX broker. All the actions of the risk-averse investors, dealers, and the broker during day t are chosen to maximize expected utility defined over wealth at the start of day $t + 1$. Each day is split into three trading rounds. On days without data releases, the sequence of events is exactly the same as in the original PS model. On release days, the sequence of events is depicted in Figure 10.1.

At the start of release day t everyone observes the value of the dividend, D_t, which is assumed to follow a random walk,

$$D_t = D_{t-1} + V_t, \tag{10.6}$$

where $V_t \sim$ i.i.d. $N(0, \sigma_v^2)$. Everyone also observes the data release, which contains an estimate of aggregate foreign income, Y_t^o. This estimate is related to actual foreign

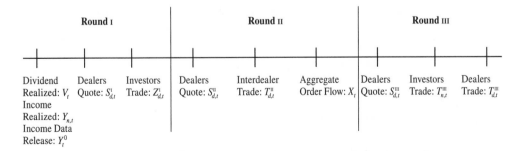

FIGURE 10.1   Daily timing in the Portfolio Shifts model on data release days.

income, Y_t, by

$$Y_t^o = Y_t + U_t, \tag{10.7}$$

where $U_t \sim$ i.i.d. $N(0, \sigma_U^2)$. Each investor, n, also receives foreign income, $Y_{n,t}$, that comprises an aggregate and idiosyncratic component:

$$Y_{n,t} = Y_t + \xi_{n,t}. \tag{10.8}$$

Investors do not initially observe either component. As in the original PS model, we assume that Y_t and ξ_t are i.i.d. mean-zero normal random variables with variances of σ_Y^2 and σ_ξ^2, respectively.

The retail tier of the FX market opens in round I. All dealers simultaneously and independently quote a scalar price at which they will fill investors' FX orders. The round I price quoted by dealer d is denoted by $S_{d,t}^I$. Prices are publicly observed by all dealers and investors and are good for orders of any size. Investors then initiate trade with dealers. Investors' net purchases of FX from dealer d are denoted by $Z_{d,t}^I$. In round II the broker and all the dealers simultaneously and independently quote scalar prices for FX, $S_{B,t}^{II}$ and $\{S_{d,t}^{II}\}_{d=1}^D$. The quoted prices are observed by all dealers and are good for interdealer trades of any size. All dealers then simultaneously and independently trade on other dealers' and the broker's quotes. The FX purchase orders made by dealer d are denoted by $T_{d,t}^{II}$ and FX purchase orders received by dealer d are $Z_{d,t}^{II}$. Purchase orders received by the broker are denoted by $Z_{B,t}^{II}$. At the close of round II trading, all dealers and the broker observe aggregate interdealer order flow:

$$X_t = \sum_{d=1}^D T_{d,t}^{II}. \tag{10.9}$$

The retail tier of the market reopens in round III. The broker and dealers again simultaneously and independently quote prices, $S_{B,t}^{III}$ and $\{S_{d,t}^{III}\}_{d=1}^D$, at which they will fill dealer and customer orders, respectively. Investors observe all the prices and then place their orders with dealers. The round III customer orders received by dealer d are denoted by $Z_{d,t}^{III}$. Once each dealer has filled his customer orders, he can trade with the broker.

The key to understanding how data releases affect spot rates and order flows in this model comes from their impact on the information sets available to investors, dealers, and the broker. Let $\Omega_{d,t}^i$, $\Omega_{n,t}^i$, and Ω_B^i, respectively, denote the information available to dealer d, investor n, and the broker before they take their first action in round $i = \{\text{I, II, III}\}$. The evolution of each dealer's information on a data release day is given by

$$\Omega_{d,t}^I = \{D_t, Y_t^o, Z_{d,t-1}^{III}, \Omega_{d,t-1}^{III}\}, \quad \Omega_{d,t}^{II} = \{Z_{d,t}^I, \Omega_{d,t}^I\},$$

and

$$\Omega_{d,t}^{III} = \{X_t, Z_{d,t}^{II}, \Omega_{d,t}^{II}\}.$$

Recall that interdealer trades in round II and the trades between dealers and investors in rounds I and III are only observed by the counterparties, so the sequence of FX orders received by dealer d is not known to other dealers. The common information of all dealers at the start of round i (i.e., $\Omega_{D,t}^i = \cap_d \Omega_{d,t}^i$) therefore evolves according to

$$\Omega^{I}_{D,t} = \{D_t, Y^o_t, \Omega^{III}_{D,t-1}\}, \quad \Omega^{II}_{D,t} = \Omega^{I}_{D,t}, \quad \text{and} \quad \Omega^{III}_{D,t} = \{X_t, \Omega^{II}_{d,t}\}. \quad (10.10)$$

The FX broker observes $\{D_t, Y^o_t\}$ at the start of round I and X_t at the end of round II. Hence, the broker shares the common information of dealers at the start of each round, that is, $\Omega^{I}_{B,t} = \Omega^i_{D,t}$ for $i = \{I, II, III\}$.

Date releases have two effects on dealers' common information. First, they augment the information available to all dealers before they choose their round I quotes. Second, they affect the *incremental* information conveyed by aggregate interdealer order flow, X_t. In the absence of data releases, X_t is the only source of common information on foreign income available to dealers. As a result, spot rates cannot incorporate any information on Y_t before round III because, in equilibrium, quotes must be a function of dealers' common information. By contrast, the information in a data release, Y^o_t, can be incorporated into dealers' round I quotes because $Y^o_t \in \Omega^{I}_{D,t}$. In this case, interdealer order flow, X_t, will convey additional information concerning foreign income that was not present in the data release.

The evolution of investor n's information is given by

$$\Omega^{I}_{n,t} = \{S^{I}_t, D_t, Y^o_t, Y_{n,t}, \Omega^{III}_{n,t-1}\} \quad \text{and} \quad \Omega^{III}_{d,t} = \{S^{III}_t, \Omega^{I}_{d,t}\}, \quad (10.11)$$

where S^i_t denotes the common equilibrium quote of dealers in round i. As in the original PS model, each investor knows more about foreign income than the dealers and the broker at the start of each day. On days without data releases, knowledge of his own income, $Y_{n,t}$, provides a private signal on aggregate foreign income to each investor in round I. Dealers, on the other hand, start each day with no information on Y_t. By contrast, the value of Y^o_t provides information on Y_t to both investors and dealers on data release days. In this case, investors' knowledge of their own income continues to provide them with an informational advantage over dealers if the data release is imprecise, but the advantage is smaller than on nonrelease days.

The differences between investors' and dealers' information are reflected in their estimates of foreign income, Y_t. On days without data releases, dealers' and investors' respective estimates are $\mathbb{E}[Y_t|\Omega^{I}_{d,t}] = 0$ and $\mathbb{E}[Y_t|\Omega^{I}_{n,t}] = \kappa_n Y_{n,t}$, where $\kappa_n = \sigma^2_Y/(\sigma^2_Y + \sigma^2_\xi) > 0$. On days with data releases, dealers' estimates in round I become

$$\mathbb{E}[Y_t|\Omega^{I}_{d,t}] = \kappa_D Y^o_t, \quad (10.12)$$

where $\kappa_D = \sigma^2_Y/(\sigma^2_Y + \sigma^2_U)$, for all d. Investors also observe the data release, so their estimates of aggregate foreign income combine the information in Y^o_t and their own income, $Y_{n,t}$. In particular, since Y^o_t and $Y_{n,t}$ are jointly normally distributed, applying the projection theorem gives

$$\mathbb{E}[Y_t|\Omega^{I}_{n,t}] = \kappa_D Y^o_t + \kappa_N(Y_{n,t} - \kappa_D Y^o_t) = (1 - \kappa_N)\kappa_D Y^o_t + \kappa_N Y_{n,t}, \quad (10.13)$$

for all $n \in [0, 1]$, where

$$\kappa_N = \frac{\sigma^2_U \sigma^2_Y}{\sigma^2_U \sigma^2_Y + \sigma^2_\xi(\sigma^2_Y + \sigma^2_U)} \geq 0.$$

Note that investors' and dealers' estimates of foreign income differ when κ_N is positive. Under these circumstances, investors' own income provides incremental information on aggregate income beyond that contained in the data release. The size of this incremental informational advantage depends on the precision of the data release. Clearly, $\kappa_N = 0$ when $\sigma_U^2 = 0$ because the data release is completely informative (i.e., $Y_t^o = Y_t$).

One final feature of the model deserves note. In the limit as $\sigma_U^2 \to \infty$, a data release does not provide any information to dealers or investors, so their behavior will be exactly the same as on a nonrelease day. In particular, (10.12) and (10.13) imply that $\mathbb{E}[Y_t | \Omega_{d,t}^I] = 0$ and $\mathbb{E}[Y_t | \Omega_{n,t}^I] = \kappa_n Y_{n,t}$ with $\kappa_n = \sigma_Y^2 / (\sigma_Y^2 + \sigma_\xi^2)$, as in the original PS model. We can therefore characterize the effect of a data release on the equilibrium behavior of spot rates and order flows as reducing σ_U^2 to a finite value. Inspection of (10.12) and (10.13) reveals that such a fall in σ_U^2 makes κ_D positive and reduces the value of κ_N. Thus, data releases not only provide dealers with some information on foreign income, they also reduce the incremental information advantage provided by investors' own income in round I.

Equilibrium

The equilibrium in this model comprises: (1) a set of FX orders by investors in rounds I and III, (2) a set of spot rate quotes by dealers in rounds I –III and by the broker in rounds II and III, and (3) a set of dealer trading decisions in rounds II and III. All these decisions must be optimal in the sense that they maximize the expected utility of the respective agent given the available information, and they must be consistent with market clearing. In rounds I and III, market clearing requires that the aggregate customer order flow equal the desired change in investors' holdings of FX:

$$\sum_{d=1}^{D} Z_{d,t}^I = \int_0^1 (A_{n,t}^I - A_{n,t-1}^{III} - Y_{n,t}) dn$$

and

$$\sum_{d=1}^{D} Z_{d,t}^{III} = \int_0^1 (A_{n,t}^{III} - A_{n,t}^I) dn, \tag{10.14}$$

where $A_{n,t}^i$ identifies the desired FX holdings of investor n in round i.

On days without data releases, all agents in the model face the same trading environment as in the original PS model. Consequently, the dynamics of spot rates and order flows on nonrelease days follow the equilibrium paths examined in Chapter 6. On release days, the equilibrium behavior of spot rates and order flows is summarized in the following proposition.

Proposition 10.1: *On data release days in an efficient risk-sharing equilibrium all dealers quote the same price for FX in each round of trading, that is, $S_{d,t}^i = S_t^i$ for $i = \{I, II, III\}$ and the broker quotes the same price as dealers in rounds II and III. The common quotes are given by*

$$S_t^I = S_{t-1}^{III} - \lambda_A A_{t-1} + \frac{1}{r} V_t - \lambda_1 Y_t^o, \tag{10.15a}$$

$$S_t^{II} = S_t^I, \tag{10.15b}$$

and

$$S_t^{III} = S_t^{II} + \lambda_A A_{t-1} + \lambda_{III} Y_t^o + \lambda_X^* (X_t - \mathbb{E}[X_t | \Omega_{D,t}^{II}]), \tag{10.15c}$$

with $\lambda_{\mathrm{I}} > 0$, $\lambda_{\mathrm{III}} > 0$ *and* $A_{t-1} \equiv \int_0^1 A_{n,t-1}^{\mathrm{III}} dn$. *The trades initiated by dealer d in round* II *are*

$$T_{d,t}^{\mathrm{II}} = \alpha_Z Z_{d,t}^{\mathrm{I}} + \alpha_A A_{t-1} + \alpha_Y Y_t^o, \qquad (10.16)$$

and the customer orders received by dealer d in round I *are*

$$Z_{d,t}^{\mathrm{I}} = \frac{\beta}{D}(Y_t - \kappa_{\mathrm{D}} Y_t^o) + \epsilon_{d,t}, \qquad (10.17)$$

where $\sum_{d=1}^D \epsilon_{d,t} = 0$.

The dynamics described in Proposition 10.1 differ in several important respects from those on nonrelease days. First, equations (10.15a) and (10.15c) show that data releases directly affect the spot rate quotes dealers make in rounds I and III via the λ_{I} and λ_{III} coefficients. Second, data releases affect the pattern of trading in rounds I and II. In round I, the effects show up in the FX orders received by each dealer. In round II, they affect the size of the trade dealers initiate with each other. Data releases also affect the price impact of interdealer order flow at the start of round III, as measured by the size of the λ_X^* coefficient in (10.15c). Let us now examine these effects in detail.

According to equation (10.15), the data release induces dealers to alter their spot rate quotes in rounds I and III. To understand why, recall that in the PS model efficient risk-sharing dictates that dealers choose their round III quotes so investors are willing to hold the entire stock of FX, A_t, overnight. Moreover, dealers are able to do so because they can all precisely infer A_t by the start of round III from their observations on order flow, X_t. These inferences are no less precise on data release days. By round III, all dealers can use their observations on X_t and Y_t^o to draw inferences about A_t, which cannot be less precise than those based solely on X_t. Consequently, the spot rate quoted by all dealers in round III of release day t is the same as in PS model:

$$S_t^{\mathrm{III}} = \frac{1}{r} D_t - \frac{1}{r}(\gamma + \lambda_A) A_t, \qquad (10.18)$$

where γ and λ_A are positive parameters derived in Chapter 6.

Next, consider the determination of the common round I quote, S_t^{I}. As in round III, dealers would like to set S_t^{I} to achieve an efficient risk-sharing allocation for FX between themselves and investors. However, at this point they have insufficient information to quote a spot rate that will induce investors to hold the entire stock of FX for rounds I and II. Under these circumstances, the best dealers can do is choose S_t^{I} such that the allocation of FX holdings is ex ante efficient conditioned on their common information, $\Omega_{\mathrm{D},t}^{\mathrm{I}}$. Since dealers' overnight holdings of FX are zero, this risk-sharing requirement implies that S_t^{I} be set such that $\mathbb{E}[Z_{d,t}^{\mathrm{I}}|\Omega_{\mathrm{D},t}^{\mathrm{I}}] = 0$ for all d, where $Z_{d,t}^{\mathrm{I}}$ is the customer order received by dealer d. Dealers also know that investors' demand for FX in round I takes the same form as in the PS model,

$$A_{n,t}^{\mathrm{I}} = \eta_S \mathbb{E}[S_t^{\mathrm{III}} - S_t^{\mathrm{I}}|\Omega_{n,t}^{\mathrm{I}}] + \eta_A A_{n,t-1}^{\mathrm{III}}, \qquad (10.19)$$

where η_S and η_A are positive parameters. To derive the round I spot rate, we first substitute this equation into the market-clearing condition in (10.14) and take expectations conditioned on $\Omega_{\mathrm{D},t}^{\mathrm{I}}$:

$$\sum_{d=1}^{\mathrm{D}} \mathbb{E}[Z_{d,t}^{\mathrm{I}}|\Omega_{\mathrm{D},t}^{\mathrm{I}}] = \int_0^1 \mathbb{E}[\eta_{\mathrm{S}}\mathbb{E}[S_t^{\mathrm{III}} - S_t^{\mathrm{I}}|\Omega_{n,t}^{\mathrm{I}}] + (\eta_{\mathrm{A}} - 1)A_{n,t-1}^{\mathrm{III}} - Y_{n,t}|\Omega_{\mathrm{D},t}^{\mathrm{I}}]\,dn$$

$$= \eta_{\mathrm{S}}\mathbb{E}[S_t^{\mathrm{III}} - S_t^{\mathrm{I}}|\Omega_{\mathrm{D},t}^{\mathrm{I}}] + (\eta_{\mathrm{A}} - 1)\,A_{t-1}^{\mathrm{III}} - \mathbb{E}[Y_t|\Omega_{\mathrm{D},t}^{\mathrm{I}}].$$

We then combine this expression with the risk-sharing restriction, $\mathbb{E}[Z_{d,t}^{\mathrm{I}}|\Omega_{\mathrm{D},t}^{\mathrm{I}}] = 0$, to produce

$$S_t^{\mathrm{I}} = \mathbb{E}[S_t^{\mathrm{III}}|\Omega_{\mathrm{D},t}^{\mathrm{I}}] - \lambda_{\mathrm{A}}A_{t-1} - \frac{1}{\eta_s}\mathbb{E}[Y_t|\Omega_{\mathrm{D},t}^{\mathrm{I}}]. \tag{10.20}$$

Equation (10.20) implies that data releases affect dealers' round I quotes through two channels. First, the information on foreign income contained in the release induces dealers to revise their spot rate forecasts, $\mathbb{E}[S_t^{\mathrm{III}}|\Omega_{\mathrm{D},t}^{\mathrm{I}}]$. Since $\mathbb{E}[A_t|\Omega_{\mathrm{D},t}^{\mathrm{I}}] = \mathbb{E}[Y_t|\Omega_{\mathrm{D},t}^{\mathrm{I}}] + A_{t-1}$ by market clearing, any information on Y_t contained in the data release will change dealers' estimates of A_t and hence their forecasts for the level of S_t^{III} consistent with efficient risk-sharing. In particular, positive values for Y_t^o will lead dealers to lower $\mathbb{E}[S_t^{\mathrm{III}}|\Omega_{\mathrm{D},t}^{\mathrm{I}}]$ because they anticipate that investors must be induced to hold a larger stock of FX overnight.

Data releases also affect dealers' round I quotes via the last term on the right of equation (10.20). Dealers recognize that the FX orders they receive in round I depend on the difference between investors' desired FX holdings, $A_{n,t}^{\mathrm{I}}$, and their existing holdings, $A_{n,t-1}^{\mathrm{III}} + Y_{n,t}$. As a consequence, they adjust their quotes so as to offset the expected hedging effect of foreign income on investors FX orders. For example, if $\mathbb{E}[Y_t|\Omega_{\mathrm{D},t}^{\mathrm{I}}]$ is positive, dealers lower their round I quotes to raise the expected FX return between rounds I and III so that their estimates of investors' desired FX holdings, $\mathbb{E}[A_{n,t}^{\mathrm{I}}|\Omega_{\mathrm{D},t}^{\mathrm{I}}]$, match their estimated current holdings, $\mathbb{E}[Y_{n,t}|\Omega_{\mathrm{D},t}^{\mathrm{I}}] + A_{t-1}$.

It is now straightforward to identify the immediate effect of a data release on dealers' round I quotes. In particular, computing $\mathbb{E}[S_t^{\mathrm{III}}|\Omega_{\mathrm{D},t}^{\mathrm{I}}]$ from (10.18) and substituting the result in (10.20) using (10.12) gives

$$S_t^{\mathrm{I}} - S_{t-1}^{\mathrm{III}} = \frac{1}{r}V_t - \lambda_{\mathrm{A}}A_{t-1} - \lambda_{\mathrm{I}}Y_t^o, \tag{10.21}$$

with $\lambda_{\mathrm{I}} = \left[\frac{1}{r}(\gamma + \lambda_{\mathrm{A}}) + \frac{1}{\eta_s}\right]\kappa_{\mathrm{D}} > 0$. Thus, the spot rate appreciates in direct response to a release indicating positive foreign income because it changes dealers' forecasts of their round III quotes and their estimates of investors' immediate demands for FX. It is this immediate effect that is the focus of event studies.

Data releases also affect the subsequent *change* in quotes. Taking the difference between (10.20) and (10.18) produces

$$S_t^{\mathrm{III}} - S_t^{\mathrm{I}} = \lambda_{\mathrm{A}}A_{t-1} + \frac{\kappa_{\mathrm{D}}}{\eta_s}Y_t^o - \frac{1}{r}(\gamma + \lambda_{\mathrm{A}})(Y_t - \kappa_{\mathrm{D}}Y_t^o). \tag{10.22}$$

The first two terms on the right of (10.22) identify the risk premium dealers embed in their round I quotes to ensure an ex ante efficient risk-sharing allocation. Data releases contribute to this premium for the reason we noted earlier. The third term on the right identifies how dealers incorporate new information concerning foreign income into their round III quotes. As in the original PS model, this information is transmitted to dealers via aggregate interdealer order flow, X_t. Here, data releases alter the trading patterns of investors and dealers, so they also affect how dealers respond to their observation of X_t when setting their round III quotes.

To see how data releases affect the transmission of information to dealers via order flow, let us first consider how they affect the customer orders received by each dealer, $Z_{d,t}^I$. Data releases change investors' desired FX holdings because they alter the informational advantage investors have over dealers in round I. This is easily seen by using (10.22) and (10.13) to compute

$$\mathbb{E}[S_t^{III} - S_t^I | \Omega_{n,t}^I] = \left(\lambda_A A_{t-1} + \frac{\kappa_D}{\eta_s} Y_t^o\right) - \frac{1}{r}(\gamma + \lambda_A)\kappa_N(Y_{n,t} - \kappa_D Y_t^o). \quad (10.23)$$

Note that the first term on the right-hand side equals dealers' expectations, $\mathbb{E}[S_t^{III} - S_t^I | \Omega_{D,t}^I]$. The second term identifies investor n's estimate of the dealers' forecast error. Since dealers choose S_t^I so that $\mathbb{E}[Z_{d,t}^I | \Omega_{D,t}^I] = 0$, it is this term that actually drives the customer orders each dealer receives after the data release. In particular, combining (10.19) with (10.23) and substituting the result into the definition of investor n's FX order, $T_{n,t}^I = A_{n,t}^I - A_{n,t-1}^{III} - Y_{n,t}$, gives

$$T_{n,t}^I = (\eta_A - 1) A_{n,t-1}^{III} + \eta_s \mathbb{E}[S_t^{III} - S_t^I | \Omega_{n,t}^I] - Y_{n,t} = \beta(Y_{n,t} - \kappa_D Y_t^o), \quad (10.24)$$

where $\beta = -1 - (\gamma + \lambda_A)\eta_s\kappa_N/r < 0$.

Thus, investor n's FX order depends on the difference between his foreign income and the dealer's estimate of aggregate income conditioned on the data release, $\kappa_D Y_t^o$. Note, also, that the strength of this relationship depends on investors' incremental information as measured by the κ_N parameter. When investors have little incremental information (i.e., when κ_N is close to zero), their forecasts for future spot rates are more similar to those of dealers, so their FX orders simply reflect their hedging demands for FX. Alternatively, if investors view their own income as a significant source of incremental information, they will want to take a speculative position that reflects the difference between their own forecasts for S_t^{III} and dealers' forecasts. Equation (10.24) shows that investors' orders are more sensitive to $Y_{n,t} - \kappa_D Y_t^o$ under these circumstances.

The information conveyed by interdealer order flow, X_t, depends on dealers' round II trading decisions. These decisions depend, in part, on the customer orders each dealer receives in round I. Since all dealers quote a common round I price in equilibrium, each dealer receives a random share of investors' aggregate FX orders. We can represent this share as the average of investors' individual orders plus a random component, $\epsilon_{d,t}$, with the property $\sum_{d=1}^{D} \epsilon_{d,t} = 0$:

$$Z_{d,t}^I = \frac{1}{D} \sum_{d=1}^{D} T_{d,t}^I + \epsilon_{d,t} = \frac{\beta}{D}(Y_t - \kappa_D Y_t^o) + \epsilon_{d,t}. \quad (10.25)$$

Equation (10.25) contains two important implications. First, it shows that the customer orders received by each dealer represent a noisy signal concerning aggregate foreign income, Y_t. Second, this signal is uncorrelated with the round I data release,

Y_t^o, because $Y_t - \kappa_{\mathrm{D}} Y_t^o = Y_t - \mathbb{E}[Y_t | \Omega_{\mathrm{D},t}^{\mathrm{I}}]$ and $Y_t^o \in \Omega_{\mathrm{D},t}^{\mathrm{I}}$. Since trades between dealers and investors are only observed by the counterparties, these implications mean that $Z_{d,t}^{\mathrm{I}}$ represents a source of *new* private information concerning foreign income that dealer d can use in forming his round II trading strategy. More specifically, if dealers view $\epsilon_{d,t}$ as an i.i.d. normal random variable with mean zero and variance σ_ϵ^2, the projection theorem implies that

$$\mathbb{E}[Y_t | \Omega_{d,t}^{\mathrm{II}}] = \kappa_{\mathrm{D}} Y_t^o + \kappa_d Z_{d,t}^{\mathrm{I}}, \qquad (10.26)$$

where

$$\kappa_d = \frac{(\beta/\mathrm{D}) \sigma_{\mathrm{U}}^2 \sigma_{\mathrm{Y}}^2}{(\beta/\mathrm{D})^2 \sigma_{\mathrm{Y}}^2 \sigma_{\mathrm{U}}^2 + \sigma_\epsilon^2 (\sigma_{\mathrm{Y}}^2 + \sigma_{\mathrm{U}}^2)} < 0.$$

Thus, dealers lower their private estimates of foreign income in response to the (net) customer purchases of FX in round I.

We can now examine how data releases affect interdealer trade. By definition, dealer d's round II trade, $T_{d,t}^{\mathrm{II}}$, is determined by the difference between his desired position $\hat{A}_{d,t}^{\mathrm{II}}$, and his current position, $A_{d,t}^{\mathrm{II}}$, plus the orders he expects to receive from other dealers, $\mathbb{E}[Z_{d,t}^{\mathrm{II}} | \Omega_{d,t}^{\mathrm{II}}]$. As in the original PS model, his desired position is proportional to the expected change in the spot rate, $\hat{A}_{d,t}^{\mathrm{II}} = \frac{1}{1+\mathrm{D}} \varphi \mathbb{E}[S_t^{\mathrm{III}} - S_t^{\mathrm{II}} | \Omega_{d,t}^{\mathrm{II}}]$, where φ is a positive parameter. Further, because dealers find it optimal to keep their quotes unchanged between rounds I and II, $\mathbb{E}[S_t^{\mathrm{III}} - S_t^{\mathrm{II}} | \Omega_{d,t}^{\mathrm{II}}] = \mathbb{E}[S_t^{\mathrm{III}} - S_t^{\mathrm{I}} | \Omega_{d,t}^{\mathrm{II}}]$. We may therefore compute dealer d's desired position with (10.22) and (10.26) as

$$\hat{A}_{d,t}^{\mathrm{II}} = \frac{1}{1+\mathrm{D}} \varphi \lambda_{\mathrm{A}} A_{t-1} + \frac{1}{1+\mathrm{D}} \frac{\varphi \kappa_{\mathrm{D}}}{\eta_s} Y_t^o - \frac{1}{1+\mathrm{D}} (\gamma + \lambda_{\mathrm{A}}) \frac{\varphi \kappa_d}{r} Z_{d,t}^{\mathrm{I}}. \quad (10.27)$$

The dealer's position at the start of round II simply depends on the customer orders he receives in round I:

$$A_{d,t}^{\mathrm{II}} = -Z_{d,t}^{\mathrm{I}}. \qquad (10.28)$$

All that now remains is to determine the dealer's forecast of incoming order flow. If all other dealers trade according to (10.16), and orders are equally split between the broker and the dealers because they quote the same price, the incoming order flow from other dealers is

$$Z_{d,t}^{\mathrm{II}} = \frac{1}{1+\mathrm{D}} \alpha_{\mathrm{Z}} \beta (Y_t - \kappa_{\mathrm{D}} Y_t^o) + \frac{\mathrm{D}}{1+\mathrm{D}} \alpha_{\mathrm{A}} A_{t-1} + \frac{\mathrm{D}}{1+\mathrm{D}} \alpha_{\mathrm{Y}} Y_t^o.$$

Taking expectations conditioned on $\Omega_{d,t}^{\mathrm{II}}$ and using (10.26) to simplify the result gives dealer d's forecast on incoming order flow:

$$\mathbb{E}[Z_{d,t}^{\mathrm{II}} | \Omega_{d,t}^{\mathrm{II}}] = \frac{1}{1+\mathrm{D}} \alpha_{\mathrm{Z}} \beta \kappa_d Z_{d,t}^{\mathrm{I}} + \frac{\mathrm{D}}{1+\mathrm{D}} \alpha_{\mathrm{A}} A_{t-1} + \frac{\mathrm{D}}{1+\mathrm{D}} \alpha_{\mathrm{Y}} Y_t^o. \quad (10.29)$$

Finally, we derive the equation for dealer d's round II trade by combining (10.27)–(10.29) with the identity, $T_{d,t}^{\mathrm{II}} = \hat{A}_{d,t}^{\mathrm{II}} + Z_{d,t}^{\mathrm{I}} + \mathbb{E}[Z_{d,t}^{\mathrm{II}} | \Omega_{d,t}^{\mathrm{II}}]$. After some simplification, this produces

$$T_{d,t}^{\mathrm{II}} = \varphi \lambda_{\mathrm{A}} A_{t-1} + \frac{\varphi \kappa_{\mathrm{D}}}{\eta_s} Y_t^o + \alpha_{\mathrm{Z}} Z_{d,t}^{\mathrm{I}}, \qquad (10.30)$$

where

$$\alpha_Z = \frac{r(1+\text{D}) - (\gamma + \lambda_\text{A})\varphi\kappa_d}{r(1+\text{D}+\kappa_d) + (\gamma + \lambda_\text{A})\eta_s\kappa_\text{N}\kappa_d}.$$

The equations for customer and dealer trades in equations (10.25) and (10.30) have three important implications. First, (10.25) implies that neither individual nor aggregate customer flows should be correlated with data releases. The reason is that dealers have a strong risk-sharing incentive to adjust their spot rate quotes immediately after the release to a level that makes customer order flows unforecastable. The idea that a data release containing bad news for the dollar should trigger positive customer order flow (i.e., customer orders to purchase FX) is simply inconsistent with dealers adjusting their quotes immediately following a data release in an efficient risk-sharing manner.

Data releases have a different impact on interdealer flows. As we can see from equation (10.30), the round II trades initiated by each dealer depend on Y_t^o and so could be forecast from public information available at the end of round I. This difference between customer and dealer order flows arises from the way dealers manage risk. As we noted above, efficient risk-sharing requires that dealers embed a risk premium in their round I quotes that depends on the data release. Efficient risk-sharing also dictates that $S_t^\text{II} = S_t^\text{I}$, so this risk premium shows up in $\mathbb{E}[S_t^\text{III} - S_t^\text{II}|\Omega_{d,t}^\text{II}]$. As a result, dealers' desired FX positions are increasing in Y_t^o, so their round II trades are forecastable with data releases. In short, interdealer order flows are forecastable because dealers have a risk-sharing incentive to make customer order flows unforecastable.

Data releases also affect the price impact of order flow as measured by the λ_x^* coefficient in (10.15c). To see why, we first use (10.25) and (10.30) to compute aggregate order flow:

$$X_t = \text{D}\frac{\varphi\kappa_\text{D}}{\eta_s}Y_t^o + \text{D}\varphi\lambda_\text{A}A_{t-1} + \alpha_Z\beta(Y_t - \kappa_\text{D}Y_t^o).$$

Next, we note that the first two terms on the right are known to dealers in round I, so unexpected order flow at start of round II is

$$X_t - \mathbb{E}[X_t|\Omega_{\text{D},t}^\text{I}] = \alpha_Z\beta(Y_t - \kappa_\text{D}Y_t^o).$$

Combining this equation with (10.22) produces (10.15c) in Proposition 10.1 with $\lambda_x^* = -(\gamma + \lambda_\text{A})/\alpha_Z\beta r$. The coefficient on order flow is found by substituting for α_Z and β:

$$\lambda_x^* = \frac{(\gamma + \lambda_\text{A})\left(r\left(1 + \text{D} + \kappa_d\right) + (\gamma + \lambda_\text{A})\eta_s\kappa_\text{N}\kappa_d\right)}{\left(r(1+\text{D}) - (\gamma + \lambda_\text{A})\varphi\kappa_d\right)\left(r + (\gamma + \lambda_\text{A})\eta_s\kappa_\text{N}\right)}. \tag{10.31}$$

In principle, data releases affect λ_x^* via their impact on both κ_d and κ_N. Recall that the κ_d parameter identifies how dealers change their private estimates of foreign income in response to the customer orders they receive in round I. Although data releases reduce the incremental information contained in *aggregate* customer orders, the effect on an individual dealer's inferences are negligible when those orders are spread across many dealers. Under these circumstances, the main effects of a data release on λ_x^* come via its impact on κ_N. In particular, an inspection of (10.31) reveals that $\partial\lambda_x^*/\partial\kappa_\text{N} < 0$, so the fall in κ_N following a data release leads to a rise in the price impact of order flow.

The intuition behind this result is straightforward. In equilibrium dealers adjust their round III quotes in response to unexpected interdealer order flow because it contains the information on foreign income necessary to achieve an efficient risk-sharing allocation of overnight FX holdings. On nonrelease days, unexpected order flow represents the first source of information on income all dealers receive, but on release days it is the second source after the round I release, Y_t^o. An unexpected order flow of a given size therefore conveys more new information to dealers on release than nonrelease days, so they adjust their round III quotes by a larger amount.

10.2.2 Empirical Evidence

The intraday dynamics of spot rates and order flows following data releases have been studied from several perspectives. We now examine whether the empirical evidence garnered from these perspectives is consistent with the theoretical predictions developed in the PS model.

A Case Study

The empirical evidence reported by Carlson and Lo (2006) provides a natural starting point. At 11:30 GMT on October 9, 1997, the Bundesbank announced a 50 basis point increase in short-term interest rates—the first tightening of monetary policy in 5 years. This was not an anticipated change in policy. Indeed, contemporary accounts by FX market participants suggest that both the size of the rate change and the timing of the Bundesbank's announcement took them completely by surprise. Consequently, this event provided Carlson and Lo with an opportunity to study precisely how FX market participants react to the surprise release of macro data.

The behavior of the spot rate and order flow from trading in the DM/USD on the Reuters electronic brokerage system around the Bundesbank announcement are shown in Figure 10.2. Recall that in this trading system transactions take place either when market orders are matched with existing limit orders or when new limit orders are matched with existing limit orders. Thus, the spot price is determined by the lowest limit ask price when a market (or new limit) purchase order arrives and by the highest limit bid price when a market (or new limit) sale order arrives. The figure also plots cumulative order flow, which is calculated as the cumulant of past market dollar purchase orders minus dollar sales orders.

Figure 10.2 reveals several interesting features about trading activity surrounding the Bundesbank's announcement. First, there is a significant appreciation of the DM/USD in the 2 minutes following the announcement. Trades were taking place at close to 1.753 DM/USD immediately before 11:30, but by 11:32 transaction prices were close to 1.740 DM/USD. This represents a 0.7 percent, or 70 basis point, fall in the price of dollars—a very sizable drop by historical norms. Second, although there is a good deal of second-by-second volatility in transaction prices, there is a clear downward trend for approximately 2 hours after the announcement followed by an upward trend until the end of the trading day. The third feature concerns the relation between transactions prices and cumulative order flow. For most of the trading day, the variations in transaction prices are closely mirrored by changes in the cumulative order flow. More precisely, minute-by-minute changes in the deutschmark transaction

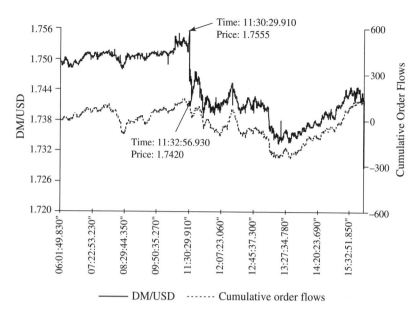

FIGURE 10.2   Spot rates and cumulative order flow on October 9, 1997. Source: Carlson and Lo (2006).

price are strongly positively correlated with positive dollar order flow *except* during the period immediately after the Bundesbank's announcement.

The first of these features appears consistent with the predictions of macro exchange-rate models: Interest parity requires that an unanticipated rise in the domestic short-term interest rate be matched by a rise in the expected depreciation rate, so the domestic currency immediately appreciates. From this perspective, all the exchange-rate effects of the Bundesbank's announcement are captured by the drop in the DM/USD transaction prices between 11:30 and 11:32. As interest is only paid on overnight DM and USD holdings, the newly established interest differential between German and U.S. interest rates should not affect the DM/USD depreciation rate between 11:32 and the end of the trading day. The variations in transaction prices and order flows during this period should not be connected to the Bundesbank's announcement.

This perspective on the events depicted in Figure 10.2 does not hold up to closer scrutiny. In particular, the immediate appreciation of the DM/USD appears to be too small to be consistent with interest parity and reasonable estimates about the expected future path of the interest differential between Germany and the United States. To see why, recall that (10.3) provides us with a decomposition of high-frequency changes in the log spot rate that holds true in any model. Under interest parity and long-run PPP with $\mathbb{E}[\varepsilon_{t+\epsilon} - \varepsilon_t | \Omega_t]$ approximately equal to zero, this equation becomes

$$s_{t+\epsilon} - s_t = \left\{ \eta_{t+\epsilon,t+1} - \mathbb{E}[\eta_{t+\epsilon,t+1} | \Omega_t] \right\}$$
$$+ \sum_{j=1}^{\infty} \left\{ \mathbb{E}[\eta_{t+j,t+j+1} | \Omega_{t+\varepsilon}] - \mathbb{E}[\eta_{t+j,t+j+1} | \Omega_t] \right\}, \tag{10.32}$$

where $\eta_{t,t+1} = \left(\hat{r}_t - \mathbb{E}[\hat{p}_{t+1} - \hat{p}_t|\Omega_t]\right) - (r_t - \mathbb{E}[p_{t+1} - p_t|\Omega_t])$. In this context, let s_t denote the log DM/USD spot rate so that r_t and $\hat{r}_t$ represent short-term German and U.S. interest rates, respectively. If the Bundesbank's announcement signaled a tightening of monetary policy, expectations about the future real interest differential should have been revised downward (i.e., $\mathbb{E}[\eta_{t+j,t+j+1}|\Omega_{t+\varepsilon}] - \mathbb{E}[\eta_{t+j,t+j+1}|\Omega_t] < 0$ for some horizon j), so the last term on the right of equation (10.32) is negative. As a consequence, the appreciation of the deutschmark will be greater than the 50 basis point fall in $\eta_{t+\epsilon,t+1} - \mathbb{E}[\eta_{t+\epsilon,t+1}|\Omega_t] = -(r_{t+\epsilon} - \mathbb{E}[r_{t+\epsilon}|\Omega_t])$. Figure 10.2 shows that this is indeed the case. But the immediate appreciation of about 70 basis points implies that agents revised their forecasts for the entire future path of the interest differential by just 20 basis points. If the Bundesbank's announcement was really viewed as the beginning of a period of policy tightening, as contemporary accounts suggest, should there not have been a larger revision in expectations concerning the future path of German real interest rates?

Our analysis of the PS model produces a different perspective. In the same way as the data release provides imprecise information on foreign income, the Bundesbank's announcement provided new but *imprecise* information on the future course of short-term interest rates. Accordingly, the depreciation of the deutschmark between 11:30 and 11:32 arose from the rapid adjustment of limit orders as dealers initially reacted to the announcement. Then, in the next 2 hours, there was a further appreciation of the DM/USD as a consensus emerged concerning the information contained in the announcement. As in the PS model, each dealer received customer orders from investors during this period, which conveyed additional information on the likely course for future interest rates. Dealers then used this information as the basis for their own trading decisions. In this particular case, the resulting interdealer order flow was predominantly negative, producing a further 40 basis point appreciation. This pattern is consistent with the development of a consensus that future real interest rates in Germany would rise by 60 basis points. In sum, therefore, the full exchange-rate effects of the Bundesbank's announcement only became evident after interdealer order flow conveyed the consensus view of the information contained in the announcement.

This interpretation of the events accounts for the major features in Figure 10.2 except for the trend reversal in transaction prices approximately 2 hours after the Bundesbank's announcement. However, it turns out that European central banks began intervening in the market when the DM/USD rate fell below 1.740 by placing dollar purchase orders with dealers. Initially, these intervention orders were unknown to most market participants and appear to have been swamped by dollar sale orders because interdealer order flow was mostly negative. However, around 14:00 a news service reported that interventions were taking place in an effort to cap the appreciation of the DM/USD. At this point it became clear to all market participants that the emerging consensus concerning higher future German interest rates was inconsistent with the Bundesbank's view. The subsequent rise in transaction prices and positive interdealer order flow likely reflect the search for a new consensus concerning the future path of interest rates that was consistent with the Bundesbank's policy view.

Econometric Evidence

The case study presented by Carlson and Lo (2006) is illustrative of the micro-based mechanisms that can determine the response of spot rates to data releases, but it hardly constitutes an empirical confirmation of the theoretical predictions we derived from the PS model. To formally examine these predictions, we must turn to some econometric models.

Love and Payne (2008) provide one of the first econometric assessments of how spot rates and interdealer order flows react to data releases. In particular, they use transaction prices and order flows from the Reuters electronic brokerage system to study the impact of data releases on trading in the EUR/USD, EUR/GBP, and GBP/USD markets over 10 months in 1999 and 2000.

The limited span of the Love and Payne data sample makes it impossible to study the impact of individual data releases with any precision, so they construct an announcement indicator that consolidates the information contained in a set of individual releases for the United States, United Kingdom, and Europe. Let $D_{k,t}$ and $D_{k,t}^e$, respectively denote the actual and expected value of the release for U.S. macro variable k in period t. Love and Payne follow the standard practice of using market surveys to identify $D_{k,t}^e$—in this case a survey conducted by Standard and Poors. Their U.S. announcement indicator in period t is constructed from the K different releases in that period:

$$\mathcal{D}_t^{\mathrm{US}} = \sum_{k=1}^{K} \mathcal{I}_k D_{k,t}^u,$$

where $D_{k,t}^u = (D_{k,t} - D_{k,t}^e)/\mathbb{V}(D_{k,t} - D_{k,t}^e)^{1/2}$ is the standardized news contained in release k. As positive news on different variables can have different directional implications for the spot rate, all the $D_{k,t}^u$ must be *signed* before they can be meaningfully combined. For this purpose, Love and Payne first estimate event-study regressions like (10.4) for each release k. They then set $\mathcal{I}_k$ equal to one or minus one depending on whether the estimated slope coefficient is positive or negative. Thus, $\mathcal{D}_t^{\mathrm{US}}$ will take on larger positive (negative) values in periods when there are a larger number of U.S. releases that individually point to a depreciation (appreciation) of the dollar. Indicators consolidating the news in U.K. and E.U. data releases are analogously defined by $\mathcal{D}_t^{\mathrm{UK}}$ and $\mathcal{D}_t^{\mathrm{EU}}$.

Love and Payne (2008) provide two sets of results concerning the effects of data releases. First, the slope coefficients in regressions of depreciation rates and order flows on $\mathcal{D}_t^i$ are statistically significant. In particular, data releases containing positive news for the value of each currency also induce positive interdealer order flow. Second, they estimate bivariate VARs for depreciation rates and order flow (in clock time) at the 1-minute frequency with $\mathcal{D}_t^i$ as additional right-hand-side variables:

$$\begin{bmatrix} A_{11}(L) & A_{12}(L) \\ A_{21}(L) & A_{22}(L) \end{bmatrix} \begin{bmatrix} X_t \\ \Delta S_{t+1} \end{bmatrix} = \begin{bmatrix} B_{11} & B_{12} \\ B_{21} & B_{22} \end{bmatrix} \begin{bmatrix} \mathcal{D}_t^i \\ \mathcal{D}_t^j \end{bmatrix} + \begin{bmatrix} u_t^x \\ u_t^s \end{bmatrix},$$

where ΔS_{t+1} is the change in the spot rate (currency i/currency j) between that start of minutes t and $t+1$ and X_t is interdealer order flow during minute t. The model estimates are then used to calculate the impulse response of spot rates to $\mathcal{D}_t^i$ and $\mathcal{D}_t^j$, which are computed from the estimated MA representation:

$$\Delta S_{t+1} = \frac{\tilde{A}_{11}(L)\tilde{B}_{21} - \tilde{A}_{12}(L)\tilde{B}_{11}}{\tilde{A}_{11}(L)\tilde{A}_{22}(L) - \tilde{A}_{12}(L)\tilde{A}_{21}(L)} \mathcal{D}_t^i$$

$$+ \frac{\tilde{A}_{11}(L)\tilde{B}_{22} - \tilde{A}_{12}(L)\tilde{B}_{12}}{\tilde{A}_{11}(L)\tilde{A}_{22}(L) - \tilde{A}_{12}(L)\tilde{A}_{21}(L)} \mathcal{D}_t^j, \tag{10.33}$$

where tildes denote estimates. Note that data releases affect spot rates directly via the B_{21} and B_{22} coefficients and indirectly through order flow via the B_{11} and B_{12} coefficients. Thus an estimate of the direct effects can be obtained from

$$\Delta S_{t+1} = \frac{\tilde{A}_{11}(L)\tilde{B}_{21}}{\tilde{A}_{11}(L)\tilde{A}_{22}(L) - \tilde{A}_{12}(L)\tilde{A}_{21}(L)} \mathcal{D}_t^i$$

$$+ \frac{\tilde{A}_{11}(L)\tilde{B}_{22}}{\tilde{A}_{11}(L)\tilde{A}_{22}(L) - \tilde{A}_{12}(L)\tilde{A}_{21}(L)} \mathcal{D}_t^j. \tag{10.34}$$

When Love and Payne use (10.33) and (10.34) to compare the total effects of data release on spot rate changes with the direct effects they find that the indirect effects contribute between 30 percent and 60 percent of the variance. In other words, a significant fraction of the price-relevant information contained in a data release becomes impounded into spot rates via order flow.

Although Love and Payne's findings are broadly consistent with some of the micro-based predictions developed in the PS model, they must also be viewed with some caution. First, as Vitale (2008) points out, their method for constructing $\mathcal{D}_t^i$ probably introduces bias into the results because it uses information from event-study regressions to sign each news item $\tilde{D}_{k,t}$. Second, there is no theoretical reason why a signed news item should always have the same effect on interdealer order flow. The indirect effects of a news item depend on the difference it produces between the initial reaction of the spot rate and private views concerning the value of the FX. For example, even if an unexpected rise in interest rates always leads to an initial appreciation in the spot rate (as it did in Figure 10.2), there is no reason to believe that the subsequent order flow will be only in one direction until a consensus emerges. Finally, Love and Payne's econometric methods do not allow the price impact of order flows to change following data releases. As (10.33) and (10.34) show, the estimated impulse response of spot rates to data releases depends on the estimates of the lag polynomials, $A_{ij}(L)$, that are computed from the whole data sample rather than from the period immediately following a release.

Evans and Lyons (2008a) developed an alternative econometric model to study the intraday response of spot rates and order flows to data releases that addresses these issues. The heart of the model comprises the following equations:

$$\Delta S_t = B(L, \Gamma_t)\xi_t + \zeta_t \tag{10.35}$$

and

$$Z_t = C_z(L, \Gamma_t)\xi_t, \tag{10.36}$$

where ΔS_t is the change in the spot rate between the end of periods $t-1$ and t and Z_t is market-wide customer order flow during period t. $B(L, \Gamma_t)$ and $C_z(L, \Gamma_t)$ denote polynomials in the lag operator with coefficients that vary with Γ_t, a vector that characterizes the period-t state of the market.

Equations (10.35) and (10.36) take that same general form as the Evans (2002) model we examined in Chapter 7. Spot rates respond to two types of shocks: common knowledge (CK) news shocks, ζ_t, and dispersed information shocks, ξ_t. These shocks have zero means, are mutually independent, and are serially uncorrelated conditioned on the state of the market in period t. The ζ_t shocks represent unambiguous price-relevant news that is simultaneously observed by everyone and impounded fully and instantaneously into dealers' spot rate quotes. Dispersed information shocks represent, in aggregate, the bits of information contained in the trades of individual investors. This information is first manifested in customer order flow, Z_t, and then subsequently impounded into dealers spot rate quotes.

Three features of this model are worthy of comment. First, CK shocks have no impact on customer order flow. Recall that efficient risk-sharing in the PS model dictates that dealers adjust their quotes so that customer orders are unforecastable conditioned on public information. This means that Z_t cannot depend on current or past CK shocks. Second, any imbalance in customer orders due to ξ_t shocks requires a spot rate adjustment. This is also true in the PS model because dealers have to adjust their prices to achieve an efficient risk-sharing allocation of FX holdings once they learn of market-wide customer orders. The final feature concerns the response of spot rates to CK news. Equation (10.35) implicitly assumes that dealers immediately and fully adjust their quotes to incorporate the price-relevant information contained in the CK news. Although this is a common empirical assumption, our analysis of the PS model shows that it may not necessarily hold true. There data releases influenced the *subsequent* change in spot rates because dealers used the CK news contained in the release to set an intraday risk premium.

Equations (10.35) and (10.36) allow us to identify three channels through which data releases might affect the dynamics of spot rates and order flows. First, when the release contains a CK component, it affects spot rates instantaneously via the ζ_t shock. This direct channel is the only operable one when everyone agrees on the price implications of the announcement. In the PS model, for example, this would be the case if the release on foreign income was completely precise. Second, when a release is viewed by different agents as having different price implications, some of its effects on prices and order flow manifest via the ξ_t shocks. In the PS model all investors observed the release, but had different estimates about actual foreign income that affected their trading decisions. Third, the arrival of a release can affect the process through which dispersed information is impounded into prices. The model allows for this by letting the polynomials $B(L, \Gamma_t)$ and $C_z(L, \Gamma_t)$ vary with the arrival of data releases.

Evans and Lyons (2008a) estimate the model using intraday data (with a 5-minute observation window) on transaction prices and order flow from "direct" interdealer trading in the spot DM/USD market over 4 months in 1996. The transaction prices comprise the last DM purchase and sale price for USD during period t, S_t^A and S_t^B. As in the Evans (2002) model, the lack of transparency in direct dealer trading is accommodated by treating S_t^A and S_t^B as random variables drawn from the respective market-wide distributions of purchase and sales prices at time t, S_t, defined in equation (10.35), by

$$S_t^o = S_t + \eta_t^o \tag{10.37}$$

for $o = \{\text{A}, \text{B}\}$, where η_t^A and η_t^B are idiosyncratic shocks that identify the degree to which observed prices differ from the market-wide average.

Estimation of (10.35) and (10.36) is also complicated by the fact that the available order flow data, X_t, comes from interdealer trades that are temporally downstream from the trades initiated by investors against dealers' quotes. As a result, a dispersed information shock, ξ_t, can affect the spot rate and customer order flow, Z_t, before it shows up in interdealer order flow, X_t. In this market it is perfectly possible for dealers to adjust their quotes in the face of an investor order induced by ξ_t before initiating trades in the interdealer market for risk-sharing or speculative motives. Thus, spot rate changes could appear temporally prior to changes in interdealer order flow even though they represent a response to earlier investor order flow. To allow for this possibility, Evans and Lyons (2008a) assume that the interdealer order flow is a distributed lag of market-wide customer order flow:

$$X_t = C_x(L, \Gamma_t) Z_{t-\ell}, \tag{10.38}$$

where, again, $C_x(L, \Gamma_t)$ is a state-dependent polynomial in the lag operator. In this specification, it takes at least ℓ periods before imbalances in customer orders for FX show up in interdealer order flow. The estimable form of the model combines (10.38) and (10.35) with (10.37) and (10.38):

$$\Delta S_t^\text{A} = D(L, \Gamma_t) X_t + \zeta_t + \Delta \eta_t^\text{A}, \tag{10.39}$$

$$\Delta S_t^\text{B} = D(L, \Gamma_t) X_t + \zeta_t + \Delta \eta_t^\text{B}, \tag{10.40}$$

$$X_t = C(L, \Gamma_t) \xi_{t-\ell}, \tag{10.41}$$

where $D(L, \Gamma) = B(L, \Gamma) L^{-\ell} C(L, \Gamma)^{-1}$ and $C(L, \Gamma) = C_x(L, \Gamma) C_z(L, \Gamma)$.

Evans and Lyons (2008a) incorporate the effects of data releases via $D(L, \Gamma)$, $C(L, \Gamma)$, and the error variances [i.e., $\mathbb{V}(\zeta_t | \Gamma_t)$, $\mathbb{V}(\xi_t | \Gamma_t)$, and $\mathbb{V}(\eta_t^o | \Gamma_t)$]. As in the PS model, data releases not only affect dealers' quotes directly, but they also change the information structure driving investors' and dealers' trades, which in turn affects the behavior of customer and interdealer order flows. To empirically accommodate such changes, the model assumes that the state of the market in period t depends on trading intensity, n_t (measured by the number of interdealer transactions during interval t) and a dummy variable, $\mathcal{N}_t$, indicating the arrival of a release in the past 15 minutes. The Reuters Money Market Headline News screen is the source of the release data. These screens are standard equipment on trading desks and are used by other market participants as a source of up-to-the-minute economic information. In particular, the screens provide information on scheduled items, such as the releases of U.S. macro data, and unscheduled items, such as the Bundesbank's announcement discussed earlier.

The estimation strategy adopted in this model is quite different from those used in event studies or other regression models, such as Love and Payne (2008). The key idea is that the arrival of a release changes: (1) the probability that spot rates will respond to

CK news shocks, (2) the probability that order flows will respond to dispersed news, and (3) the transmission of dispersed information to spot rates via order flows. For example, if releases primarily convey CK news that is directly impounded into spot rates, the variance of the ζ_t shocks should be higher at the time of a release, whereas the variance of the ξ_t shocks remains the same. Alternatively, if releases convey little CK news but lead investors to revise their trading strategies, a release should raise the variance of the ξ_t shocks but leave the variance of the ζ_t shocks unaffected. In this case, we would also expect to observe some changes in the dynamics of spot rates and order flow via $D(L, \Gamma)$ and $C(L, \Gamma)$. Importantly, this estimation strategy does not assume that every news item is equally important or that good news for the value of the dollar has a particular effect on order flows. All it requires is that variations in the number of news items identify variations in the flow and type of new information hitting the market.

Evans and Lyons (2008a) first estimate the model in (10.39)–(10.41) with specifications for $D(L, \Gamma)$, $C(L, \Gamma)$, and the error variances that do not restrict how the arrival of news items affects the dynamics of spot rates and order flows. The model estimates are then used to examine how the contribution of the ζ_t and ξ_t shocks to the variance of spot rate change as news is released. Let $\Delta^k S_t$ denote the k-period spot rate change between period $t - k$ and t. According to the model, the variance of $\Delta^k S_t$ conditioned on the state of the market during the last k periods is

$$\tilde{\mathbb{V}}(\Delta^k S_t | \Gamma) = \sum_{j=0}^{k-1} \tilde{\mathbb{V}}(\zeta_{t-j} | \Gamma_{t-j}) + \sum_{j=0}^{k-1} \tilde{B}(L, \Gamma_{t-j})^2 \tilde{\mathbb{V}}(\xi_{t-j} | \Gamma_{t-j}), \quad (10.42)$$

where $\tilde{B}(L, \Gamma) = \tilde{D}(L, \Gamma)\tilde{C}(L, \Gamma)L^{\ell}$ and tildes denote model estimates. The first component on the right-hand side is the variance contribution of CK news shocks; the second is the contribution of dispersed information shocks operating via order flow. These contributions change following news releases via $\tilde{B}(L, \Gamma)$, $\tilde{\mathbb{V}}(\zeta_t | \Gamma_t)$, and $\tilde{\mathbb{V}}(\xi_t | \Gamma_t)$.

Table 10.2, reproduced from Evans and Lyons (2008a), reports the estimated contribution of dispersed information to the variance of price changes over horizons of 5, 30, and 60 minutes (i.e., $k = \{1, 6, 12\}$) when trading intensity is at four different levels (i.e., $n = \{25, 50, 100, 150\}$ per 5-minute interval). Row (i) in each panel reports the contribution for a given trade intensity in the absence of macro news. Consistent with the results discussed in Chapter 7, these statistics show that the contribution of dispersed information to the spot rate variance rises with trade intensity and the horizon. The contribution of dispersed information in the presence of macro news is reported in row (ii). These statistics clearly show that, following the arrival of news, dispersed information contributes more to the variance of spot rates across all three horizons at different levels of trade intensity. (The statistical significance of these differences is indicated by the asterisks.) Row (iii) shows the contribution of dispersed information in the presence of scheduled news, such as the release of U.S. macro data. Recall that these data releases are the focus of event studies, so it is interesting to ask whether spot rates react differently to this subset of news items. The answer appears to be yes. In all cases, the estimated contribution of dispersed information to the variance of spot rates rises more in the presence of scheduled news than in the presence of all news items.

TABLE 10.2
Variance Decompositions

	Horizon (minutes)			Horizon (minutes)		
	5	30	60	5	30	60
	Trade intensity: $n = 25$			Trade intensity: $n = 50$		
(i) No news	0.631	0.989	0.758	1.436	2.314	2.118
(ii) News	3.895**	10.280**	11.768*	5.123**	12.137**	13.597**
(iii) Scheduled news	8.271***	16.083**	17.417*	9.868***	17.807**	19.067**
	Trade intensity: $n = 100$			Trade intensity: $n = 150$		
(i) No news	3.808	7.475	7.957	7.173	14.862	16.129
(ii) News	7.981**	15.754*	17.101*	11.214**	19.163	20.358
(iii) Scheduled news	13.231***	21.067*	22.163*	16.679**	24.053	24.980

Notes: The table reports the contribution of dispersed information shocks to variance of k-horizon spot rate changes implied by the model estimates given a constant level of trading intensity, n, and the presence or absence of macro news, $\mathcal{N}$. Cases in which the news arrival increases the contribution of dispersed information at the 10, 5, and 1 percent significance levels are indicated by *, **, and ***, respectively. Source: Evans and Lyons (2008a).

The results in Evans and Lyons (2008a) indicate that order flow contributes more to spot rate adjustment following macro data releases than at other times. This is not what one would expect if macro releases contain primarily new CK information that is directly impounded into dealers' quotes. If macro releases primarily transmit new CK information, order flow should contribute less to spot rate dynamics in the period following the release than at other times. By contrast, the preceding results strongly suggest that a macro data release triggers trading that reveals new dispersed information that affects spot rates indirectly. This finding is particularly noteworthy in the case of scheduled data releases. As these releases contain data on macro aggregates, one might have expected that they contain a greater proportion of CK to dispersed information than other releases. That order flow is at least as important in the dynamics of spot rates following scheduled data releases suggests that this common view concerning the information content of macro data releases is incorrect.

10.3   Micro Perspective II: Low-Frequency Dynamics

Up to this point we have examined how data releases can affect the behavior of spot rates and order flows in the minutes and hours following a release. We now extend our analysis to consider the effects of releases over longer horizons. First we use the implications of the PS model to examine the effects of data releases on spot rates and order flows at the daily frequency. This analysis provides a new perspective on the empirical importance of data releases as a driver of spot rates. We then use the micro-based model from Chapter 9 to study the impact of data releases on spot rates and customer order flows beyond the daily horizon.

10.3.1 Daily Effects

The implications of the PS model for the daily behavior of spot rates and order flow are easily derived from Proposition 10.1. Specifically, if S_t denotes the spot rate quoted by dealers in round III on day t, the equilibrium dynamics of spot rates and interdealer order flow can be represented by

$$\Delta S_t = \lambda_{\text{x}}^*(X_t - \mathbb{E}[X_t|\Omega_{\text{D},t}^{\text{I}}]) + \tfrac{1}{r}V_t + (\lambda_{\text{III}} - \lambda_{\text{I}})Y_t^o \tag{10.43a}$$

and

$$X_t = \mathbb{E}[X_t|\Omega_{\text{D},t}^{\text{I}}] + \alpha_{\text{z}}\beta(Y_t - \kappa_{\text{D}}Y_t^o), \tag{10.43b}$$

where $\mathbb{E}[X_t|\Omega_{\text{D},t}^{\text{I}}] = \text{D}\varphi\{\lambda_{\text{A}}A_{t-1} + (\kappa_{\text{D}}/\eta_{\text{s}})Y_t^o\}$. According to equation (10.43a), daily changes in spot rates are due to dividend news, V_t, data releases on foreign income, Y_t^o, and unexpected interdealer order flow, $X_t - \mathbb{E}[X_t|\Omega_{\text{D},t}^{\text{I}}]$. Equation (10.43b) shows that actual order flow comprises an expected component that depends on investors' known asset holdings, the data release, $\{A_{t-1}$ and $Y_t^o\}$, and an unexpected component that is proportional to dealers' estimation error after observing the data release.

To examine the effects of data releases at the daily frequency, Evans and Lyons (2008a) estimate a special case of the PS model in which expected interdealer order flow, $\mathbb{E}[X_t|\Omega_{\text{D},t}^{\text{I}}]$, is zero. This case arises when dealers are too risk-averse to try establishing speculative FX positions in round II trading. Under these circumstances, the optimal trading strategy of each dealer depends only on the customer orders he receives; and, as a result, aggregate interdealer order flow is proportional to the aggregate flow of customer orders, which must be unforecastable in an efficient risk-sharing equilibrium.

Evans and Lyons write the estimable form of the PS model as

$$\Delta S_t = \lambda_{\text{x}}X_t + \mathcal{N}_t^{\text{s}} + \varsigma_t, \tag{10.44}$$

$$X_t = \mathcal{N}_t^{\text{x}} + \zeta_t. \tag{10.45}$$

In this specification, spot rates and interdealer order flow are subject to four shocks representing different sources of information hitting the market: $\mathcal{N}_t^{\text{s}}, \varsigma_t, \mathcal{N}_t^{\text{x}},$ and ζ_t. These shocks are mean zero, serially uncorrelated, and mutually independent conditional on the day-t state of the market. The $\mathcal{N}_t^{\text{s}}$ and ς_t shocks represent information that is impounded in the spot rate directly. $\mathcal{N}_t^{\text{s}}$ identifies the CK effect of macro news arrivals on the price of FX during day t. This is the effect identified by the $-\lambda_{\text{I}}Y_t^o$ term in equation (10.43a). The term ς_t represents other factors directly impounded in spot rates, that is, factors unrelated to either order flow or macro news events, such as the dividend news term, $\tfrac{1}{r}V_t$, in (10.43a). Equation (10.45) shows order flow driven by the $\mathcal{N}_t^{\text{x}}$ and ζ_t shocks. The $\mathcal{N}_t^{\text{x}}$ shocks represent the order flow effects associated with macro news arrival. This effect is identified by $-(\lambda_{\text{I}}/\lambda_{\text{x}})(Y_t - \kappa_{\text{D}}Y_t^o)$ in equation (10.43b). Shocks to order flow that are unrelated to macro news are represented by the ζ_t shocks. They represent the effects of portfolio shifts arising from other sources, such as changing risk tolerances or hedging, that are not included in the PS model.

The $\mathcal{N}_t^{\mathrm{x}}$ shocks identify the order flow effects of dispersed information associated with macro news arrivals. In the PS model this dispersed information resides with investors in the form of their individual income, $Y_{n,t}$. Recall that investors' FX demands depend on their estimates of foreign income based on $Y_{n,t}$ and the information in the data release, Y_t^o: $\mathbb{E}[Y_t|\Omega_{n,t}^I] = \kappa_{\mathrm{D}} Y_t^o + \kappa_{\mathrm{N}}(Y_{n,t} - \kappa_{\mathrm{D}} Y_t^o)$. Thus the economy-wide distribution of individual incomes (i.e., $\{Y_{n,t}\}$ for all $n \in [0, 1]$) represents dispersed information concerning aggregate income that is first embedded in customer orders and later reflected in interdealer order flow via trading decisions of dealers.

Evans and Lyons (2008a) identify the effects of the news-related CK and dispersed-information shocks, $\mathcal{N}_t^{\mathrm{s}}$ and $\mathcal{N}_t^{\mathrm{x}}$, through state-dependency of price changes and order flow in the second moments. Specifically, they assume that the variance of $\mathcal{N}_t^{\mathrm{s}}$ and $\mathcal{N}_t^{\mathrm{x}}$ on day t is increasing in the daily flow of macro news, which is measured by the number of U.S. and German news arrivals between 5:00 P.M. on days $t-1$ and t, $\mathcal{N}_t^{\mathrm{US}}$ and $\mathcal{N}_t^{\mathrm{G}}$:

$$\mathbb{V}_t(\mathcal{N}_t^{\mathrm{s}}) = \Sigma_{\mathrm{s}}^2(\mathcal{N}_t^{\mathrm{US}}, \mathcal{N}_t^{\mathrm{G}}) \quad \text{and} \quad \mathbb{V}_t(\mathcal{N}_t^{\mathrm{x}}) = \Sigma_{\mathrm{x}}^2(\mathcal{N}_t^{\mathrm{US}}, \mathcal{N}_t^{\mathrm{G}}), \qquad (10.46)$$

where $\Sigma_{\varkappa}^2(0, 0) = 0$, with $\partial\Sigma_{\varkappa}^2/\partial\mathcal{N}_t^k > 0$ for $\varkappa = \{\mathrm{s,x}\}$ and $k = \{\mathrm{US,G}\}$. Thus, on days without news, $\mathcal{N}_t^{\mathrm{s}} = \mathcal{N}_t^{\mathrm{x}} = 0$, so price changes and order flow are driven solely by the ς_t and ζ_t shocks. These shocks are independent of news, so their variances are constant and unrelated to $\mathcal{N}_t^k$:

$$\mathbb{V}_t(\varsigma_t) = \Sigma_{\varsigma}^2 \quad \text{and} \quad \mathbb{V}_t(\zeta_t) = \Sigma_{\zeta}^2. \qquad (10.47)$$

Several features of the model in (10.44)–(10.47) deserve comment. First, the specification abstracts from the complex intraday dynamics of spot rates and order flow. Equations (10.44) and (10.45) imply that spot rate quotes fully reflect the information contained in order flow by the end of each trading day (taken to be 5:00 P.M. GMT). As a result, spot rate changes over the next 24 hours are not correlated with order flow from the past 24 hours. The specification also implies the absence of serial correlation in daily spot rate changes and interdealer order flows. Both of these implications are supported by the data. A second feature of the specification concerns the price-impact parameter, λ_{x}. As we have seen, there is empirical evidence that the price impact of order flows varies with the arrival of news in intraday data. This form of state-dependency is hard to detect at the daily frequency, so the model does not allow for state-dependency in λ_{x}. In contrast, it does allow for state-dependency in the error variances. This final feature is key to identifying the effects of macro news, so let us focus on it more closely.

Identification of the effects of macro news is achieved by the assumption that the variance of the $\mathcal{N}_t^{\mathrm{s}}$ and $\mathcal{N}_t^{\mathrm{x}}$ shocks is higher on days when there are a greater number of news arrivals, $\mathcal{N}_t^{\mathrm{US}}$ and $\mathcal{N}_t^{\mathrm{G}}$, reported on the Reuters Money Market News screen. Crucially, this assumption does not require that FX market participants view the information in each news item as equally important (which the market does not). The identifying power of this assumption does, however, depend on the absence of wild variations in the quality of Reuters' editorial judgments. For example, if the Reuters screen were flooded one day with reports containing essentially no information, but on another a few reports appeared that were of great economic significance, daily variations in the number of news reports would be a poor measure of the daily flow of macro news. This is a possibility, but it seems somewhat far-fetched.

Evans and Lyons estimate two versions of the model. Version I assumes that the variances of the $\mathcal{N}_t^s$ and $\mathcal{N}_t^x$ shocks on day t vary only with the sum of the U.S. and German news items, $\mathcal{N}_t^{ALL} \equiv \mathcal{N}_t^{US} + \mathcal{N}_t^{G}$. Under this specification, the flow of macro news is identified by the arrival rate of both U.S. and German news. It is also possible that daily variations in the flow of macro news are reflected differently in the arrival rates for U.S. and German news. Version II of the model allows the variance of $\mathcal{N}_t^s$ and $\mathcal{N}_t^x$ on day t to depend on the number of U.S. and German news items separately. The GMM estimation procedure is described in the appendix to this chapter.

With GMM estimates of both model versions in hand, Evans and Lyons examine the extent to which macro news is impounded in spot rates directly via the CK $\mathcal{N}_t^s$ shocks or indirectly via the dispersed information $\mathcal{N}_t^x$ shocks that affect spot rates via order flow. To clarify, consider the unconditional variance of spot rate changes implied by the model, $\mathbb{V}(\Delta S_t)$. By definition, this variance can be written as $\mathbb{E}[\mathbb{V}_t(\Delta S_t)] + \mathbb{V}(\mathbb{E}_t \Delta S_t)$, where $\mathbb{E}_t \Delta S_t$ and $\mathbb{V}_t(\Delta S_t)$ denote the first and second moments of spot rate changes conditioned on the day-t state of the market. Since the number of news arrivals has no implication for the direction of how spot rates will change, $\mathbb{E}_t \Delta S_t = 0$. With the aid of equation (10.44), we can therefore write the unconditional variance as

$$\mathbb{V}(\Delta S_t) = \lambda_x^2 \mathbb{E}[\mathbb{V}_t(X_t)] + \mathbb{E}[\mathbb{V}_t(\mathcal{N}_t^s + \varsigma_t)].$$

The first term on the right identifies the contribution of order flow volatility to the variance of price changes. The second term identifies the contribution of information that is directly impounded into prices. Using equations (10.45)–(10.47) to substitute for $\mathbb{V}_t(X_t)$ and $\mathbb{V}_t(\mathcal{N}_t^s + \varsigma_t)$, we obtain

$$\mathbb{V}(\Delta S_t) = \mathbb{E}[\Sigma_s^2(\mathcal{N}_t^{US}, \mathcal{N}_t^{G})] + \lambda_x^2 \mathbb{E}[\Sigma_x^2(\mathcal{N}_t^{US}, \mathcal{N}_t^{G})] + \Sigma_\varsigma^2 + \lambda_x^2 \Sigma_\zeta^2. \qquad (10.48)$$

Equation (10.48) decomposes the unconditional variance of daily price changes into four components. The first term identifies the contribution of CK shocks associated with the arrival of news via the "direct channel." The second term represents the contribution of dispersed information shocks associated with news via the "indirect channel." Note that this term includes the price-impact coefficient, λ_x, because dispersed information affects prices via order flow. The third and fourth terms identify the contribution of shocks that are not associated with the arrival of news; information embedded in the ς_t and ζ_t shocks affect spot rates via the direct and indirect channels, respectively.

Table 10.3 reproduces the variance decomposition in (10.48) based on Evans and Lyons' estimates of the model in (10.44)–(10.47). Row (i) reports the fraction of the unconditional variance attributable to the CK shocks associated with news: $\mathbb{E}[\Sigma_s^2(\mathcal{N}_t^{US}, \mathcal{N}_t^{G})]/\mathbb{V}(\Delta S_t)$. Estimates from both versions of the model indicate that the direct effect of news arrivals account for approximately 14 percent of the variance in spot rate changes. The estimates from Version II indicate that this total is split roughly 2 to 1 between German and U.S. news. Row (ii) reports the contribution of dispersed information to the variance of spot rates: $\lambda_x^2 \mathbb{E}[\Sigma_x^2(\mathcal{N}_t^{US}, \mathcal{N}_t^{G})]/\mathbb{V}(\Delta S_t)$. These statistics show that the indirect effects of news arrival account for roughly 22 percent

TABLE 10.3
Daily Variance Decompositions

	Version I combined	Version II		
		U.S.	German	Combined
(i) Direct	0.139	0.036	0.104	0.140
(ii) Indirect	0.224	0.060	0.166	0.226
(iii) Total	0.364	0.096	0.270	0.366
(iv) Ratio (indirect/direct)	1.612	1.642	1.602	1.612

Notes: The table reports elements of the variance decomposition for spot rate changes implied by the GMM estimates of the model in (10.44)–(10.47). Source: Evans and Lyons (2008a).

of the variance. Once again, the arrival of German news contributes more than twice as much as that of U.S. news through this channel. Row (iii) shows that the total contribution of news to the variance of spot rates via both channels is approximately 36 percent. These estimates are an order of magnitude larger than those found in event studies (e.g., Table 10.1). Row (iv) reports the ratio of indirect to direct effects of news arrival implied by the model estimates: $\lambda_x^2 \mathbb{E}[\Sigma_x^2(\mathcal{N}_t^{\mathrm{US}}, \mathcal{N}_t^{G})]/\mathbb{E}[\Sigma_s^2(\mathcal{N}_t^{\mathrm{US}}, \mathcal{N}_t^{G})]$. As the table shows, the contribution of news via the indirect channel is roughly 60 percent larger than the contribution via the direct channel. These estimates clearly indicate that the indirect effects of news operating via order flow are an important component of spot rate dynamics.

Evans and Lyons also examine the impact of the scheduled data release—a subset of the news items reported on the Reuters screens. These releases account for approximately 20 percent of the unconditional variance of daily spot rate changes, and their contribution is more equally balanced between the direct and indirect channels. Furthermore, approximately two thirds of the variance in daily spot rate changes can be attributed to U.S. items and one third to German items. This 2:1 ratio roughly matches the ratio of U.S. to German scheduled announcements.

The results in Table 10.3 speak directly to the question: What drives order flow? The results reported in Evans and Lyons (2002a) splits the total daily DM/USD spot rate variation into two parts: about 60 percent is due to order flow and about 40 percent to other factors. The results in the table shed light on both of these parts. They suggest that order flow's 60 percent breaks roughly into one-third (20 percent) that is induced by macro news and two-thirds (40 percent) that is not news induced. Put differently, macro news accounts for about one-third of the variance of interdealer order flow. The 40 percent of total spot rate variation due to other factors breaks into about one-third (15 percent) from the direct effect of macro news and two-thirds (25 percent) that remains unaccounted for.

10.3.2 Longer-Term Effects

Up to this point we have focused on how spot rates and order flows are affected by data releases on the release day. We now consider the effects over longer horizons. This extension is necessary for two reasons: First, most actual data releases contain data on *past* rather than current macroeconomic conditions. For example, the scheduled releases of U.S. nonfarm payrolls and the CPI are based on data collected in the previous month, whereas releases on GDP relate to the previous quarter. In contrast, our earlier analysis assumed that data releases only relate to current macroeconomic conditions. Second, the ultimate effects of a data release will be delayed until market participants reach a consensus about its spot rate implications. This process took a single round of trading in the PS model because dealers faced a relatively simple inference problem. In more complex and realistic trading environments, market participants are less able to draw precise inferences from each others' trading decisions, so reaching a consensus could take much longer. In principle, therefore, data releases could affect spot rates via their impact on order flows beyond the day of the release.

We use the micro-based model from Chapter 9 to examine how data releases conveying information on past macroeconomic conditions can have long-term effects on spot rates and order flows. Recall that in the micro-based model the economy comprises two countries populated by a continuum of risk-averse investors, indexed by $n \in [0, 1]$, and D risk-averse dealers, who act as marketmakers in the spot USD/EUR market. At the start of week t, all dealers quote a log spot price that embeds a risk premium and their forecasts of how central banks will set future short-term interest rates:

$$
s_t = (\hat{r}_t - r_t) + \mathbb{E}_t^D \sum_{i=1}^{\infty} \rho^i f_{t+i} - \mathbb{E}_t^D \sum_{i=0}^{\infty} \rho^i \delta_{t+i}, \tag{10.49}
$$

where

$$
f_t = (1 + \gamma_\pi)(\Delta \hat{p}_{t+1} - \Delta p_{t+1}) + \gamma_y (\hat{y}_t - y_t) + \left(\frac{1 - \rho}{\rho} \right) (p_t - \hat{p}_t),
$$

with $\gamma_\pi > 0$, $\gamma_y > 0$ and $1 > \rho > 0$. The term $\mathbb{E}_t^D$ denotes expectations conditioned on the common information available to all dealers at the start of week t, Ω_t^D. This information set includes r_t and $\hat{r}_t$, which are the 1-week dollar and euro interest rates set by the FED and ECB, respectively. Dealers' forecasts for future interest rates incorporate a view on how central banks will react to changes in the macroeconomy. These forecasts are reflected in exchange-rate fundamentals, f_t, that comprise the future difference between E.U. and U.S. inflation, $\Delta \hat{p}_{t+1} - \Delta p_{t+1}$, the difference between the E.U. and U.S. output gaps, $\hat{y}_t - y_t$, and the price differential, $p_t - \hat{p}_t$; δ_t is a risk premium that dealers set to manage risk efficiently.

The aggregate order flow received by dealers during week-t trading is equal to the change in aggregate demand for euros across all investors:

$$
x_{t+1} = \alpha_t - \alpha_{t-1} = \int_0^1 \Delta \alpha_t^n dn, \tag{10.50}
$$

where α_t^n denotes the demand for euros in week t by investor $n \in [0, 1]$. This demand depends on the (log) excess return expected by the investor and a hedging term,

$$
\alpha_t^n = \alpha_s \left(\mathbb{E}_t^n \Delta s_{t+1} + \hat{r}_t - r_t \right) + h_t^n, \tag{10.51}
$$

where $\alpha_s > 0$. $\mathbb{E}_t^n$ denotes expectations conditioned on the information available to investor n after observing the spot rate at the start of week t, Ω_t^n. The hedging term, $h_t^n = \alpha_z z_t^n$, depends on a vector of variables, z_t^n, that describes the observable microeconomic environment of investor n. This vector is related to the state of the macroeconomy by $z_t^n = z_t + v_t^n$, where z_t is a vector of macro variables and $v_t^n = [v_{i,t}^n]$ is a vector of investor-specific shocks with the property that $\int_0^1 v_{i,t}^n dn = 0$ for all i. The vector z_t includes the inflation, interest, price, and output differentials,

$$z_t' = [\, \Delta\hat{p}_t - \Delta p_t, \quad \hat{r}_t - r_t, \quad \hat{p}_t - p_t, \quad \hat{y}_t - y_t, \quad \ldots, \quad \ldots \,],$$

and follows an AR(1) process:

$$z_t = A_z z_{t-1} + B_u u_t, \tag{10.52}$$

where u_t is a vector of mean-zero serially uncorrelated shocks.

Data releases affect spot rates and order flow by changing the information dealers and investors have about past states of the macroeconomy. Specifically, at the start of week t, there is a set of data releases that informs all dealers and investors about the state of the macroeconomy k weeks earlier, z_{t-k}. To characterize how these data releases affect spot rates and order flows, we use a vector, Z_t, that comprises the shocks $\{u_t, u_{t-1}, \ldots, u_{t-k-1}\}$ and z_{t-k}:

$$Z_t' = [\, u_t', \quad u_{t-1}', \quad \ldots, \quad u_{t-k-1}', \quad z_{t-k}' \,].$$

The dynamics of Z_t are easily derived from equation (10.52) and can be written as

$$Z_t = AZ_{t-1} + Bu_t. \tag{10.53}$$

Note, further, that z_t can be written as a linear combination of the elements in Z_t, that is, $z_t = \Lambda_z Z_t$ for some matrix Λ_z.

The Z_t vector contains the information that is *potentially* available to dealers and investors about the state of the macroeconomy in week t, z_t, and about the shocks to the economy over the past $k + 2$ weeks, $\{u_t, u_{t-1}, \ldots, u_{t-k-1}\}$. The actual flow of information received by all dealers at the start of week t comprises a vector $Z_t^D = [z_{t-k}', (z_t^O)', x_t]'$, where z_t^O denotes a subset of the variables in z_t (e.g., interest rates) that are contemporaneously observable to dealers and investors. In Chapter 9 we established that $Z_t^D = CZ_t$ in equilibrium for some matrix C. Similarly, the flow of information to investor n comprises a vector $Z_t^n = [z_{t-k}', (z_t^O)', s_t, (z_t^n)']'$ that is related to Z_t in equilibrium by $Z_t^n = C^N Z_t + D^N v_t^n$. Based on these information flows, dealers' estimates of Z_t and the average of investors' estimates of Z_t can be represented by

$$\mathbb{E}_t^D Z_t = \Phi^D Z_t \quad \text{and} \quad \overline{\mathbb{E}}_t^n Z_t = \int_0^1 \mathbb{E}_t^n Z_t dn = \Phi^N Z_t \tag{10.54}$$

for some matrices Φ^D and Φ^N.

We are now ready to examine how the FX market responds to data releases that convey public information on past macroeconomic conditions. In particular, we address two questions: (1) Under what conditions will a macro data release that contains significant new public information have little or no immediate effect on spot rates? (2) Can data releases have persistent effects on spot rates and order flows beyond the day of the release?

Do Data Releases Contain News to Dealers?

To address the first question, consider the equilibrium behavior of spot rates and order flow:

$$s_t = \Lambda_s \mathbb{E}_t^D Z_t \tag{10.55}$$

and

$$x_{t+1} = \alpha_s \Lambda_\delta (Z_t - \mathbb{E}_t^D Z_t) - \alpha_s \Lambda_\delta (Z_{t-1} - \mathbb{E}_{t-1}^D Z_{t-1}) \tag{10.56}$$

for some vectors Λ_s and Λ_δ (derived in Chapter 9). Equation (10.55) implies that a week-t data release will only affect spot rates to the extent that it changes dealers' estimates of the elements in Z_t, and these elements are price relevant. More concretely, equation (10.49) implies that the release must change dealers' expectations concerning future monetary policy via a revision in their forecasts for future fundamentals. Alternatively, it must induce dealers to change the current risk premium and/or their forecasts for future risk premia. In either case, the key point is that dealers have to change their estimates of Z_t. If the week-t data release provides no new information to dealers concerning z_{t-k}, it will not induce the revision in dealers' estimates of Z_t necessary to produce an observable change in spot rates. Thus, the reaction of spot rates critically depends on dealers' prior information concerning z_{t-k}.

In the micro-based model, dealers' observations on past order flows provide them with potentially precise information concerning z_{t-k} before the week-t data release. To see why, we turn to the expression for equilibrium order flow in equation (10.56). In Chapter 9 we saw that $Z_t - \mathbb{E}_t^D Z_t = \sum_{i=0}^{k-1} \Gamma_i u_{t-i}$ for some matrices Γ_j. This means that order flow from week-t trading depends on the sequence of past shocks, $\{u_{t-i}\}_{i=0}^k$. In particular, we can rewrite (10.56) as

$$x_{t+1} = \alpha_s \Lambda_\delta \sum_{i=0}^{k} (\Gamma_i - \Gamma_{i-1}) u_{t-i}, \tag{10.57}$$

with $\Gamma_k = \Gamma_{-1} = 0$. Now a data release in week t at most contains new information on shocks to the economy in week $t - k$, u_{t-k}, but (10.57) implies that u_{t-k} also contributes to the order flows from weeks $t - k$ to $t - 1$. Hence a data release may contain new information on the past state of the macroeconomy relative to existing *public* information, but much of this information could already be known to dealers from their past observations on order flows.

Is there any empirical evidence to suggest that much of the macro information contained in a data release is already known to dealers? One piece of evidence comes from Rime, Sarno, and Sojli (2010). They show that interdealer order flows can explain a sizable fraction of the difference between actual data releases and estimates of expected releases based on survey responses collected earlier. Dealers must therefore have more precise information concerning up-coming releases than is contained in the survey responses. A second piece of evidence comes from Chapter 9. There we reviewed the results in Evans (2010) showing that customer order flows convey more timely information about the macroeconomy to Citibank than is available from the flow of information contained in macro data releases. Insofar as these order flows are representative of customer flows across the entire market, these results show that dealers have some information on the past macro variables before the information becomes public via a data release. The question of whether order flows provide sufficient information to justify the extent to which dealers revise their spot rate quotes in response to data releases remains open for future research.

Do Data Releases Have Persistence Effects?

Let us now turn to the question of persistence. Equation (10.56) implies that a data release in week t can at most affect the flow of customer orders in that week. To see why, suppose the release reveals new information concerning u_{t-k} to dealers at the start of week t. Efficient risk-sharing dictates that dealers use this information to revise the risk premium embedded in their spot rate quotes so that their expected euro holdings at the end of week t equal zero. To achieve this, the anticipated order flow immediately following the release must exactly offset the cumulative order flows from earlier weeks: that is, $\mathbb{E}_t^D x_{t+1} = -\sum_{i=0}^{\infty} x_{t-i}$. Combining this expression with the identity $x_t = \mathbb{E}_{t-1}^D x_t + (x_t - \mathbb{E}_{t-1}^D x_t)$ gives

$$\mathbb{E}_t^D x_{t+1} = -\mathbb{E}_{t-1}^D x_t - \sum_{i=1}^{\infty} x_{t-i} - (x_t - \mathbb{E}_{t-1}^D x_t) = -(x_t - \mathbb{E}_{t-1}^D x_t).$$

Thus, news contained in the week-t data release will be correlated with the flow of customer orders dealers anticipate immediately following the release insofar as it contains information that contributed to unanticipated order flow during the previous week's trading, that is, $x_t - \mathbb{E}_{t-1}^D x_t$. Clearly such news cannot contribute to order flows in the weeks that follow. For example, order flow in week $t + 1$ is

$$x_{t+2} = (x_{t+2} - \mathbb{E}_{t+1}^D x_{t+2}) + \mathbb{E}_{t+1}^D x_{t+2} = (x_{t+2} - \mathbb{E}_{t+1}^D x_{t+2}) - (x_{t+1} - \mathbb{E}_t^D x_{t+1}),$$

which cannot be correlated with any information in Ω_t^D, including the information in the week-t data release.

This implication of the micro-based model contrasts with the equilibrium behavior of customer order flow in the PS model. There, risk-management by dealers made customer order flow unforecastable from the information contained in the data release. The reason for this difference is subtle but important. In the PS model dealers gain enough information to achieve an efficient risk-sharing allocation for FX holdings by the end of each trading day. As a result, when the data release takes place they are not holding any unwanted FX inventory from earlier trading. Under these circumstances, there is no incentive for dealers to quote a spot rate that induces a flow of customer orders that will be correlated with their prior information, including information in the data release. In the micro-based model, by contrast, we allow for the possibility that dealers may not have sufficient information to achieve an efficient risk-sharing allocation prior to a data release. In this case dealers may have an incentive to induce a flow of customer orders that are correlated with the information in data releases.

Risk-sharing also affects the persistence of data releases on returns. In equilibrium the aggregate demand for euros depends on the risk premium priced into the current spot rate quoted by dealers, the difference between dealers' expectations and the average of investors' expectations concerning the state, and the aggregate hedging term, $h_t = \int_0^1 h_t^n dn$:

$$\alpha_t = \alpha_s \delta_t + \alpha_s \Lambda_s \mathbb{E}_t^D (\overline{\mathbb{E}}_t^n - \mathbb{E}_t^D) Z_{t+1} + h_t.$$

In recognition of this fact, dealers quote a week-t spot rate that embeds the current and expected future risk premia so that their expected future euro holdings are zero. Under market clearing this risk-sharing requirement implies that $\mathbb{E}_t^D \alpha_{t+i} = 0$ for all $i > 0$, so the risk premia satisfy

$$\delta_t = -\Lambda_\delta \mathbb{E}_t^D Z_t \quad \text{and} \quad \mathbb{E}_t^D \delta_{t+i} = -\Lambda_\delta \mathbb{E}_t^D Z_{t+i},$$

where $\Lambda_\delta = \Lambda_s \Phi^D A (\Phi^N - \Phi^D) + \frac{\alpha_z}{\alpha_s} \Lambda_z$. These risk premia describe the anticipated path for future excess returns that dealers believe is necessary to keep their future euro holdings at zero. Thus if a data release in week t changes their forecasts for $(\overline{\mathbb{E}}_{t+\tau}^n - \mathbb{E}_{t+\tau}^D) Z_{t+\tau+1}$ or h_{t+i} at some horizon i, it will also alter the path for expected excess returns at the same horizon. In sum, therefore, a data release can have persistent effects on excess returns if it induces dealers to revise their forecasts of future foreign currency demand well into the future.

Empirical evidence on the persistent effects of data releases can be found in Evans and Lyons (2005a). Here the daily change in log spot rates and Citibank's order flows from six end-user segments are modeled as a kth-order VAR:

$$
\begin{bmatrix} \Delta s_t \\ x_{1,t} \\ \vdots \\ x_{6,t} \end{bmatrix} = A_1 \begin{bmatrix} \Delta s_{t-1} \\ x_{1,t-1} \\ \vdots \\ x_{6,t-1} \end{bmatrix} + A_2 \begin{bmatrix} \Delta s_{t-2} \\ x_{1,t-2} \\ \vdots \\ x_{6,t-2} \end{bmatrix} + \cdots + A_k \begin{bmatrix} \Delta s_{t-k} \\ \Delta x_{1,t-k} \\ \vdots \\ x_{6,t-k} \end{bmatrix}
$$
$$
+ \begin{bmatrix} v_t \\ u_{1,t} \\ \vdots \\ u_{6,t} \end{bmatrix},
\tag{10.58}
$$

where $x_{j,t}$ denotes the order flow for euros from segment j during day $t - 1$. Daily innovations to the spot rate and the six order flows are identified by v_t and $u_{j,t}$. These innovations are driven, in part, by macroeconomic data releases according to

$$v_t = \sum_{i=1}^M \alpha_i D_{i,t}^u + \varsigma_t \quad \text{and} \quad u_{j,t} = \sum_{i=1}^M \beta_{j,i} D_{i,t}^u + \zeta_{j,t} \tag{10.59}$$

for $J = \{1, 2, \ldots, 6\}$, where M is the number of release types and $D_{i,t}^u = D_{i,t} - D_{i,t}^e$ is the unexpected portion of data release i on day t. The ς_t and $\zeta_{j,t}$ shocks represent the sources of spot rate and order flow innovations that are uncorrelated with the data releases. The effects of releases are identified by the α and β coefficients: α_i identifies the effect of the news in release i on the log spot rate and $\beta_{j,i}$ indicates how the news affects the jth order flow segment. Note that none of these coefficients identify the intraday transmission mechanism through which the spot rate and order flow changes take place. For example, news may impact on the spot rate directly because it induces dealers to change their quotes. News may also impact on spot rates because marketmakers change their quotes in response to induced order flow. The α_i coefficient simply identifies the total daily effect of the ith news item. Similarly, the $\beta_{j,i}$ coefficient indicates the total daily effect of news on order flow.

Evans and Lyons (2005a) use the model in (10.58) and (10.59) to study three issues: (1) If news affects order flow, do the effects persist beyond the day of the announcement? (2) If news affects spot rates, are all the effects confined to the day of the announcement? (3) Do news-induced order flows generate price movements after the announcement day?

All these questions can be readily addressed by computing impulse response functions. Specifically, we can trace out the impact of the news in release i on the spot rate and order flows using the estimates of α_i and $\beta_{j,i}$ together with the VAR coefficients in the A_k matrices. For example, let $\{\tilde{B}_k\}_{k=0}^{\infty}$ denote the sequence of matrices that define the vector moving average representation of the estimated VAR (with $\tilde{B}_0 = I$), and let $\tilde{b}_i = [\tilde{\alpha}_i, \tilde{\beta}_{1,i}, \ldots, \tilde{\beta}_{6,i}]'$ be the vector of estimated α and β coefficients for the news in release i. The estimated impact of the news in release i on the spot rate return k periods after the release is given by the first row of $\tilde{B}_k \tilde{b}_i$ and the impact on the jth order flow is given by row $j + 1$ of $\tilde{B}_k \tilde{b}_i$. Estimates of the coefficients in A_k are obtained by OLS and estimates of the b_i's are computed from regressions of the VAR residuals on the data releases.

Evans and Lyons (2005a) examine 6 years of daily data from the EUR/USD market covering data releases on 43 different U.S. and German macroeconomic variables. Ten of these releases have a significant impact on the EUR/USD spot rate at the 5 percent significance level, while 18 affect at least one of the order flow segments at the 5 percent level. Table 10.4 shows how data releases contribute to the variance of order flows and returns following each release. Panel A reports how the releases contribute to the variance of the 18 flow segments over 5 days, starting with the day of the release. The news in the data releases is a nontrivial source of daily variance in several of the order flow segments, particularly in the case of GDP and consumption expenditures. The persistence effects of news on the flow segments shows up in the variance contributions 1–4 days after the release. Though small in absolute terms, all of these contributions are all highly statistically significant. Panel B reports how releases contribute to the variance of daily spot rate returns over 5 days, starting with the day of the release. Here we see that the nonfarm payroll release makes the largest initial contribution to the variance of daily returns. In 8 of the 10 cases, the news significantly affects returns on at least 1 day after the release. However, aside from nonfarm payrolls, the news does not make a sizable contribution to the variance of returns on the days that follow.

The empirical findings in Evans and Lyons (2005a) are broadly consistent with our analysis based on the micro-based model. Data releases do indeed affect customer order flows, and the effects persist for several days beyond the day of the release. As the micro-based model shows, this behavior is quite consistent with the optimal behavior of dealers. If the release reveals new information that is correlated with investors' aggregate demand for foreign currency, dealers adjust their spot rate quotes to induce an expected flow of orders from investors consistent with an efficient risk-sharing allocation. The fact that data releases affect order flows for several days suggests that these risk-management activities take some time before being completely effective.

The persistent effects on returns are also consistent with this risk-management interpretation. Since daily interest differentials are close to zero, variations in excess returns are very closely correlated with actual spot rate returns at the daily frequency.

TABLE 10.4

Order Flow and Return Variance Contributions

		Days after announcement		
		0	1	4
A. Order flow variance				
U.S.	Capacity	6.357	2.270	3.438
	CPI	3.769	3.878	0.868
	Credit	3.608	4.626	7.038
	Durables	3.319	3.421	2.930
	Factory orders	4.403	0.606	1.090
	FED Funds	1.184	0.004	0.071
	GDP final	9.718	6.908	0.148
	GDP preliminary	13.159	6.556	12.628
	Leading	3.709	0.212	1.358
	Nonfarm payroll	3.605	8.617	6.214
	Consumption	9.189	3.369	0.116
	Unemployment	2.982	4.222	2.063
German	Employment	3.633	2.310	2.703
	Retail sales	4.237	1.247	0.158
	Current A/C	1.146	0.704	0.070
	Cost of living	4.020	0.082	0.540
	PPI	1.711	1.063	1.162
	Import prices	5.228	1.804	5.314
B. Return variance				
U.S.	Claims	0.723	0.377	0.034
	Confidence	2.532	0.412	0.054
	NAPM	3.952	0.503	6.027
	New homes	6.453	0.273	1.549
	Nonfarm payroll	26.479	2.189	10.174
	Consumption	4.203	7.534	1.304
	PPI	2.199	1.872	0.027
	Trade balance	4.573	0.919	6.511
German	Trade balance	3.276	0.577	0.184
	PPI	1.047	0.11	0.914

Notes: The table reports the variance of the order flow (panel A) and returns (panel B) owing to the news announcement (listed in the right-hand column) as a percentage of the variance that is due to all shocks impacting on order flow and returns, respectively. Source: Evans and Lyons (2005a).

Thus, if dealers adjust the risk premia embedded in the spot rate quotes for risk-sharing purposes, we should expect to see persistent effects of data releases on spot rate returns. These effects are very difficult to detect in the behavior of returns alone because dealers adjust their spot rate quotes in response to other factors in the days following a data release. However, they should be detectable in the joint behavior of order flows and returns if dealers behave in the manner of the micro-based model. With this perspective, the small but persistent effects on spot rate returns reported by Evans and Lyons (2005a) supports the idea that dealers' risk-management activities play an important role in the reaction of the foreign exchange market to data releases.

10.4 Summary

- Macro exchange-rate models predict that spot rates will respond immediately to the public release of macro data if it induces: (1) a change in current real interest rates and/or the foreign exchange risk premium, (2) a revision in expectations concerning future real interest rates and/or the risk premia, or (3) a revision in the expected long-run real exchange rate.

- Event studies provide *qualitative* empirical evidence linking variations in spot rates with the release of macroeconomic data in a manner consistent with the predictions of monetary exchange-rate models using Taylor rules. *Quantitatively*, macro data releases account for less than 1 percent of the total variation in spot rates.

- Micro-based models focus on how data releases change the structure of information concerning the macroeconomy between dealers and market participants. When a data release contains imprecise but price-relevant information, dealers adjust their spot rate quotes to accommodate the new information on payoffs and the risk of providing liquidity to the market. Efficient risk-sharing by dealers can produce predictable components in both order flows and spot rate returns following data releases. Data releases also affect the transmission of information to dealers via order flow because they alter trading patterns across the market.

- Empirical studies of intraday data indicate that data releases affect spot rates directly and indirectly via induced order flows. Furthermore, order flows appear to carry more price-relevant information that is incorporated into spot rates following macro data releases than at other times.

- More than one third of the total variance in daily spot rate changes can be related to the direct and indirect effects of macro data releases and other news sources. The indirect effects of news working via order flow contribute approximately 60 percent more to the variance of spot rate changes than do the direct effects.

- Macro data releases can affect customer order flows and spot rate returns up to a week following the releases. These persistent patterns support the idea that dealers' risk-management activities play an important role in the reaction of the foreign exchange market to data releases.

10.5 Bibliography

Although there is a large empirical literature studying the asset-pricing effects of macro news, few papers examine the possible theoretical effects of news on the trading activities of financial market participants. In particular, our analysis of how macro data releases affect dealers' quotes and order flows in the PS model has no direct antecedents in the literature. It does, however, contain some of the informational features found in Harris and Raviv (1993) and Kandel and Pearson (1995). These authors study models where public signals induce trading between agents because they use different likelihood functions to interpret the signals. Similarly, investors and dealers trade following a data release in the PS model because they draw different inferences about future spot rates based on the release and their own private information.

Most of the existing literature linking spot rates to macro news is event-study based and does not address how news affects the trading behavior of FX market participants. This literature has two branches. The first addresses the direction of exchange-rate changes (first moments) and the second, later, branch addresses exchange-rate volatility (second moments). The first branch includes studies by Cornell (1982), Engel and Frankel (1984), Hakkio and Pearce (1985), Ito and Roley (1987), Hardouvelis (1988), Klein, Mizrach, and Murphy (1991), and Ederington and Lee (2009). These studies typically find that the directional effects from scheduled macro announcements are difficult to detect at the daily frequency because they are swamped by other factors that affect spot rates. The second branch of this literature, which focuses on news effects on volatility, is partly a response to the early difficulty in finding news effects on first moments. This work finds that the arrival of scheduled announcements does indeed produce changes in spot rate volatility, but the effects are smaller than those of other market-related features such as time-of-day effects (see, e.g., Goodhart, Hall, Henry, and Pesaran 1993, DeGennaro and Shrieves 1997, and Andersen and Bollerslev 1998).

The empirical research reviewed here relates to several recent studies. In particular, the results in Evans and Lyons (2008a) concerning the intraday behavior of spot rates and order flows are echoed by Green (2004), who finds that government bond prices exhibit increased sensitivity to order flow in the 30 minutes following macro data releases. The effects of data releases on order flows have also been studied by Dominguez and Panthaki (2006), Berger et al. (2008), Gradojevic and Neely (2008), and Rime, Sarno, and Sojli (2010). These authors report that the unexpected news in data releases contributes to interdealer order flows in intraday and daily data. Such findings are often interpreted as being inconsistent with a simple efficient-market view of how public information becomes embedded into spot rates. However, as our analysis in this chapter shows, both customer and interdealer order flows can be correlated with the public news contained in a data release in equilibrium when dealers choose their spot rate quotes in an efficient risk-sharing manner.

10.6 Review Questions

1. Ambiguity and Interest Rate Smoothing: Suppose that the FED sets interest rates according to

$$r_t = r_t^* + \phi(r_{t-1} - r_{t-1}^*),$$

where $r_t^* = r + (1 + \psi)\mathbb{E}[\Delta p_{t+1}|\Omega_t]$, with $1 > \phi \geq 0$ and $\psi > 0$. The common information set of central banks and all market participants at the start of period t is Ω_t; r^* is the FED's interim interest rate target conditioned on expected inflation, $\mathbb{E}[\Delta p_{t+1}|\Omega_t]$, and r is its long-run target for the real interest rate under price stability. Expectations concerning U.S. inflation evolve according to

$$\mathbb{E}[\Delta p_{t+1}|\Omega_t] = \lambda \mathbb{E}[\Delta p_t|\Omega_{t-1}] + \beta(\Delta p_t - \mathbb{E}[\Delta p_t|\Omega_{t-1}]) + v_t,$$

with $1 > \lambda > 0$ and $\beta > 0$, where v_t is an i.i.d. mean-zero expectations shock unrelated to current unexpected inflation, $\Delta p_t - \mathbb{E}_{t-1}\Delta p_t$. During the period under consideration, the European real interest rate is constant, $\hat{r}_t - \mathbb{E}[\Delta \hat{p}_{t+1}|\Omega_t] = r$, and the foreign exchange risk premium, δ_t, is zero. All market participants expect PPP to hold in the long run.

(a) Suppose that $\phi = 0$ so the FED adjusts interests rates to their interim target immediately. Compute an expression for the log real USD/EUR exchange rate under these circumstances.

(b) Use your answer to part (a) to compute the response of the real exchange rate between t and $t + 1$ to news about inflation in period $t + 1$: $\Delta p_{t+1} - \mathbb{E}[\Delta p_{t+1}|\Omega_t]$. Explain how the response is affected by the FED's interim interest rate target.

(c) In the absence of any other news, how will the nominal USD/EUR exchange rate react to unexpectedly high U.S. inflation?

(d) Now suppose that market participants receive news unrelated to current inflation that leads them to raise their forecasts for future inflation. How will the nominal USD/EUR rate react to this news? Will the reaction be the same as the case of unexpected inflation examined in part (c)? Explain.

(e) Derive an expression for the log real USD/EUR exchange rate when the FED smooths out interest rates so that $1 > \phi > 0$.

(f) Show that the reaction of the real and nominal USD/EUR rate to news about inflation does not depend on the degree to which the FED smooths out interest rates. Explain why this is the case.

2. News about the Past: Suppose the monetary policies followed by the FED and ECB imply that the interest differential between United States and Europe follows

$$r_t - \hat{r}_t = (1 + \psi_\pi)\mathbb{E}[\Delta p_{t+1} - \Delta \hat{p}_{t+1}|\Omega_t] + \psi_y \mathbb{E}[y_t - \hat{y}_t|\Omega_t],$$

where Δp_{t+1} and $\Delta \hat{p}_{t+1}$ denote U.S. and E.U. inflation and $y_t - \hat{y}_t$ is the difference between the U.S. and E.U. output gaps. The term Ω_t denotes the common information set of central banks and all other market participants at the start of period t. U.S. and E.U. prices are contemporaneously observable, so $\{\Delta p_t, \Delta \hat{p}_t\} \in \Omega_t$ and the inflation differential follows an AR(1) process,

$$\Delta p_t - \Delta \hat{p}_t = \phi_\pi(\Delta p_{t-1} - \Delta \hat{p}_{t-1}) + v_t,$$

where $1 > \phi_\pi > 0$ and v_t are i.i.d. mean-zero shocks. The difference between the output gaps also follows an AR(1) process,

$$y_t - \hat{y}_t = \phi_y(y_{t-1} - \hat{y}_{t-1}) + e_t,$$

where $1 > \phi_y > 0$ and $e_t \sim$ i.i.d.$N(0, \sigma_e^2)$. Unlike inflation, the actual values of $y_t - \hat{y}_t$ can only be learned precisely with a one-period lag. Specifically, in period t, there is a preliminary announcement concerning the value of $y_t - \hat{y}_t$,

$$an_t = y_t - \hat{y}_t + \xi_t,$$

where $\xi_t \sim$ i.i.d.$N(0, \sigma_\xi^2)$ is a reporting error. There is also a final announcement concerning the true value of $y_{t-1} - \hat{y}_{t-1}$.

  (a) If the risk premium is zero and everyone expects that PPP will hold in the long run, derive an expression for the log real USD/EUR exchange rate in terms of the inflation differential, $\Delta p_t - \Delta \hat{p}_t$, and the estimated difference in output gaps, $\mathbb{E}[y_t - \hat{y}_t | \Omega_t]$.
  (b) Use the projection theorem to derive an expression for the estimated difference in the output gaps, $\mathbb{E}[y_t - \hat{y}_t | \Omega_t]$.
  (c) Using your answer to part (b), identify all the factors contributing to the revision in the output gap estimates between periods t and $t + 1$: $\mathbb{E}[y_{t+1} - \hat{y}_{t+1} | \Omega_{t+1}] - \mathbb{E}[y_{t+1} - \hat{y}_{t+1} | \Omega_t]$.
  (d) Use your answers to parts (a) and (c) to derive an equation for the unexpected variation in the log real USD/EUR exchange rate, $\varepsilon_{t+1} - \mathbb{E}[\varepsilon_{t+1} | \Omega_t]$. Show that news about the past difference in output gaps, $\mathbb{E}[y_t - \hat{y}_t | \Omega_{t+1}] - \mathbb{E}[y_t - \hat{y}_t | \Omega_t]$, contributes to $\varepsilon_{t+1} - \mathbb{E}[\varepsilon_{t+1} | \Omega_t]$. Explain why this news about the past is relevant.
  (e) Explain what happens to the relevance of news about the past output gaps in the limit as $\sigma_\xi^2 \to \infty$.

3. Data Releases and Order Flows: The Portfolio Shifts model examined in Section 10.2 makes precise predictions about the behavior of customer and interdealer order flows following a data release. Use the model to answer the following:

  (a) "One can always tell whether a data release represents goods news for the dollar by looking for positive dollar order flow from customers (i.e., customer orders to purchase dollars)." Assess the veracity of this statement. Does it make sense if FX dealers are managing risk efficiently?
  (b) "Interdealer order flow must be zero following a data release because all dealers observe the release and therefore value foreign currency equally." Use the Portfolio Shifts model to explain what is wrong with this statement.

4. Data Releases and Currency Holdings: In the Portfolio Shifts model, dealers hold no inventory of foreign currency when the data release takes place. To assess the importance of this feature, suppose now that the data release takes place immediately before dealers quote at the start of round II. All other aspects of the model remain unchanged.

(a) Prove that the equilibrium quotes in rounds I and III take the same form on release and nonrelease days, that is,

$$S_t^{\mathrm{I}} = S_{t-1}^{\mathrm{III}} - \lambda_{\mathrm{A}} A_{t-1} + \frac{1}{r} V_t \quad \text{and} \quad S_t^{\mathrm{III}} = \frac{1}{r} D_t - \frac{1}{r} (\gamma + \lambda_{\mathrm{A}}) A_t,$$

where γ and λ_{A} are positive parameters that were derived in Chapter 6.

(b) Derive an equation for the equilibrium round II quote, S_t^{II}, immediately following a data release, Y_t^o. Compare your answer with the value for S_t^{I} derived in Proposition 10.1. If the quotes are the same, explain why. If they differ, explain the reason for the difference.

(c) In this version of the Portfolio Shifts model, dealers have nonzero inventories of foreign currency when they quote spot rates immediately after the data release. In the original version, by contrast, their inventories were zero. In light of your answer to part (b) explain how dealers' inventories affect their quotes immediately following a data release.

10.A Appendix

Evans and Lyons (2008a) estimate two versions of the model. Version I assumes that the variances of the $\mathcal{N}_t^s$ and $\mathcal{N}_t^x$ shocks on day t vary only with the total of the U.S. and German news items, $\mathcal{N}_t^{\mathrm{ALL}} \equiv \mathcal{N}_t^{\mathrm{US}} + \mathcal{N}_t^{\mathrm{G}}$. Version II allows the variance of $\mathcal{N}_t^s$ and $\mathcal{N}_t^x$ on day t to depend on the number of U.S. and German news items separately. The variance functions are assumed to be linear in both versions of the model:

$$\text{Version I:} \quad \Sigma_\varkappa^2 (\mathcal{N}_t^{\mathrm{US}}, \mathcal{N}_t^{\mathrm{G}}) = \sigma_\varkappa \mathcal{N}_t^{\mathrm{ALL}}$$

and   (10.60)

$$\text{Version II:} \quad \Sigma_\varkappa^2 (\mathcal{N}_t^{\mathrm{US}}, \mathcal{N}_t^{\mathrm{G}}) = \sigma_\varkappa^{\mathrm{US}} \mathcal{N}_t^{\mathrm{US}} + \sigma_\varkappa^{\mathrm{G}} \mathcal{N}_t^{\mathrm{G}},$$

where $\sigma_\varkappa$, $\sigma_\varkappa^{\mathrm{US}}$, and $\sigma_\varkappa^{\mathrm{G}}$ are positive parameters for $\varkappa = \{\mathrm{s}, \mathrm{x}\}$.

The GMM estimates of the model parameters are derived from the following set of moment conditions:

$$0 = E\left[(\Delta p_t - \alpha x_t) \, x_t \right],$$ (10.61)

$$0 = E\left[\{ \mathcal{V}_t (\Delta p_t) - Var_t (\Delta p_t) \} \otimes \mathcal{Z}_t \right],$$ (10.62)

and

$$0 = E\left[\{ \mathcal{V}_t (x_t) - Var_t (x_t) \} \otimes \mathcal{Z}_t \right],$$ (10.63)

where $\mathcal{Z}_t$ is a vector of instruments. The condition in equation (10.61) follows from the assumed orthogonality between the shocks to spot rates ($\mathcal{N}_t^s$ and ς_t) and the shocks to order flow ($\mathcal{N}_t^x$ and ζ_t). Equations (10.62) and (10.63) combine the second moments of price changes and order flow implied by the model with measures of the variance of order flow, $\mathcal{V}(x_t)$, and the variance of price changes, $\mathcal{V}(\Delta p_t)$. These measures are computed for each day in the sample from the 5-minute intraday observations as

$$\mathcal{V}_t(\Delta p_t) = \sum_{i=1}^{T_t} \Delta p_{it}^2 \quad \text{and} \quad \mathcal{V}_t(x_t) = \sum_{i=1}^{T_t} x_{it}^2, \tag{10.64}$$

where the subscript it denotes the ith 5-minute observation on day t and T_t denotes the number of observations with consecutive trading. The terms $\mathcal{V}_t(\Delta p_t)$ and $\mathcal{V}_t(x_t)$ are the (uncentered) second moments of the price change and order flow process over day t, scaled by the number of 5-minute intraday observations. Andersen, Bollerslev, Diebold, and Labys (2001) show that these measures are consistent nonparametric estimates of the actual moments under mild regularity conditions.

CHAPTER 11

Exchange-Rate Risk

This chapter examines the risks associated with holding foreign currency. We begin by studying the interest parity conditions that link spot rates, forward rates, and interest rates. Empirical deviations from one of the parity conditions, Uncovered Interest Parity (UIP), represent one of the most persistent puzzles in international finance. We document the puzzle and examine how it can be exploited through currency-trading strategies known as the carry trade. Market practitioners have long known that carry-trade strategies can produce substantial returns and these returns are the focus of recent academic research.

Theoretical models explaining deviations from UIP and the returns on carry-trade strategies fall broadly within three groups: macro risk models, peso problem models, and models with financial market frictions. Section 11.2 discusses the theoretical foundations and empirical performance of recent models in the first two groups. This discussion covers asset-pricing models based on the no-arbitrage condition that links the prices of all financial assets to stochastic discount factors, Euler equation models derived from the first-order conditions of a representative investor, and peso problem models that price assets in unstable economic environments.

Section 11.3 examines foreign currency risk from the perspective of a micro-based currency-trading model. Here we use the model developed in Chapter 9 to discuss how informational frictions between dealers and other market participants contribute to the dynamics of the risk premium dealers embed in their spot rate quotes. We then review recent empirical research linking order flows to the dynamics of the risk premium and excess currency returns.

11.1 FX Returns and Interest Rates

11.1.1 Interest Parity

Interest parity conditions tie together the dynamics of spot rates, forward rates, and interest rates on Eurocurrency deposits—foreign-currency-denominated deposits held at an offshore bank. For example, a dollar deposit held at a U.K. bank is a Eurodollar deposit. Most Eurocurrency deposits are fixed interest rate time deposits with maturities that match the horizon of available forward foreign exchange contracts.

Let S_t denote the USD/GBP spot rate and $\mathcal{F}_t$ the one-period forward rate in period t. If the gross interest rates on one-period Eurodollar and Europound deposits available at a particular bank are R_t and $\hat{R}_t$, then Covered Interest Parity (CIP) requires that

$$R_t = \hat{R}_t \mathcal{F}_t / S_t. \tag{11.1}$$

We first derived this condition in Chapter 1 for an economy with complete markets, but it holds more generally in any economy where there are no arbitrage opportunities. To see why, suppose that $R_t < \hat{R}_t \mathcal{F}_t / S_t$. In this case it would be possible to make a profit by borrowing dollars at rate R_t and using the proceeds to purchase a pound deposit. The pound payoff per dollar committed would be $\hat{R}_t / S_t$ in period $t + 1$, which could be converted to dollars at the forward rate of $\mathcal{F}_t$, producing a dollar return of $\hat{R}_t \mathcal{F}_t / S_t$. Similarly, if $R_t > \hat{R}_t \mathcal{F}_t / S_t$, it would be profitable to borrow pounds to invest at the Eurodollar rate. Thus, the CIP condition in (11.1) represents a no-arbitrage condition in a world without credit risk, where anyone can borrow and lend at R_t and $\hat{R}_t$ and trade in the currency markets at prices S_t and $\mathcal{F}_t$.

In reality there are differences between borrowing and lending rates and between the bid and ask prices on FX contracts. These realities introduce transaction costs that have to be accounted for in identifying actual arbitrage opportunities. However, when this is done, the empirical evidence suggests that there are few unexploited arbitrage opportunities in major currency pairs when markets are operating normally (see Taylor 1989 and Akram, Rime, and Sarno 2008). Under these conditions, the CIP condition in (11.1) very closely approximates the actual relation we observe among spot rates, forward rates, and interest rates. We therefore proceed under the assumption that the CIP condition in (11.1) holds true.

UIP combines the CIP condition with an assumption about the relation between the forward rate and the future spot rate, namely,

$$\mathcal{F}_t = \mathbb{E}_t S_{t+1}, \tag{11.2}$$

where $\mathbb{E}_t$ denotes expectations conditioned on period-t information, Ω_t. Since the forward rate defines the price at which foreign currency can be purchased in the future, it seems intuitively reasonable to assume that $\mathcal{F}_t$ should equal the expected future price of foreign currency in the spot market. Indeed, (11.2) is often referred to as the forward market efficiency condition. That said, the theoretical rationale for (11.2) is more tenuous, as we shall now see.

In the complete-markets model of Chapter 1, the equilibrium relation between the spot and forward rates was given by

$$\mathcal{F}_t = \sum_{z \in \mathcal{Z}} \pi_t^P(z) S_{t+1}(z), \quad \text{with } \pi_t^P(z) = \mathcal{P}_t(z) \big/ \sum_{z \in \mathcal{Z}} \mathcal{P}_t(z).$$

The term $\mathcal{P}_t(z)$ is the dollar price at t of a claim to \$1 in period $t + 1$ if the state of the world is $z \in \mathcal{Z}$, where $\mathcal{Z}$ denotes the finite set of possible states. The corresponding spot rate in period $t + 1$ is $S_{t+1}(z)$. Since $\sum_{z \in \mathcal{Z}} \pi_t^P(z) = 1$ and $\pi_t^P(z) \geq 0$ for all $z \in \mathcal{Z}$, the price ratios, $\pi_t^P(z)$, can be interpreted as pseudo probabilities, so the foregoing expression becomes

$$\mathcal{F}_t = \mathbb{E}_t^P S_{t+1}. \tag{11.3}$$

Thus, when markets are complete, the forward rate is equal to the "expected" future spot rate, where expectations are computed using pseudo probabilities.

Clearly, this equilibrium relation is different from the UIP assumption when the $\pi_t^P(z)$'s differ from the actual probabilities used to compute the conditional expectation in (11.2). We showed in Chapter 1 that this will be the case when the marginal utility of \$1 for all investors differs across future states. This means that (11.2) will not generally hold even when investors are risk-neutral because variability in inflation will induce differences in the marginal utility of \$1 across future states. In other words, the UIP condition in (11.2) is not an implication of risk-neutrality even when markets are complete. When markets are incomplete, the price ratios are further restricted by the hedging attributes of the available financial assets, so (11.3) will generally differ from the UIP condition in (11.2). In sum, therefore, the term "forward market efficiency" embodies some strong theoretical assumptions that may or may not hold in actual economies.

Most empirical tests of UIP examine the implications of (11.2) for the behavior of the depreciation rate:

$$\frac{S_{t+1} - S_t}{S_t} = \left(\frac{\mathcal{F}_t}{S_t} - 1\right) + \xi_{t+1}, \tag{11.4}$$

where $\xi_{t+1} = (S_{t+1}/S_t) - \mathbb{E}_t(S_{t+1}/S_t)$. Under CIP, this expression can also be written as

$$\frac{S_{t+1} - S_t}{S_t} = \left(\frac{R_t}{\hat{R}_t} - 1\right) + \xi_{t+1}. \tag{11.5}$$

Note that both of these expressions are identities: there always exists a forecast error, ξ_{t+1}, that accounts for the difference between the actual depreciation rate and the forward premium, $(\mathcal{F}_t/S_t) - 1$, and interest differential, $(R_t/\hat{R}_t) - 1$. Consequently, it is impossible to examine UIP empirically without data on spot rate expectations, $\mathbb{E}_t S_{t+1}$, or an assumption concerning the behavior of the forecast error, ξ_{t+1}.

The typical approach in the literature is to assume the presence of rational expectations so that the forecast errors, ξ_{t+1}, are uncorrelated with any variable in the period-t information set, Ω_t. In this case, the joint null hypothesis of (11.2) and rational expectations can be examined by estimating the regression

$$\frac{S_{t+1} - S_t}{S_t} = \beta_0 + \beta_1 \left(\frac{\mathcal{F}_t}{S_t} - 1\right) + \zeta_{t+1}. \tag{11.6}$$

Clearly, this regression takes the same form as (11.4) when $\beta_0 = 0$ and $\beta_1 = 1$. Moreover, since the forecast errors, ξ_{t+1}, are uncorrelated with the forward premium under rational expectations (because $\mathcal{F}_t/S_t \in \Omega_t$), they will be represented by the regression errors, ζ_{t+1}. We can therefore test the joint null by estimating (11.6) and testing the coefficient restrictions $\beta_0 = 0$ and $\beta_1 = 1$.

Table 11.1 reproduces the estimates of regression (11.6) reported by Burnside, Eichenbaum, Kleshchelski, and Rebelo (2006) in monthly data. In this study spot and forward rates are quoted as FX/USD, so a rise in S_t corresponds to an appreciation of the dollar. Consistent with the results reported in a very large number of other studies, the estimates of β_0 are small and statistically insignificant, whereas the estimates of

TABLE 11.1

UIP Regressions

	β_0	β_1	t-Statistic	R^2	Sample
Canada	0.000	−0.632	−3.331	0.004	76:01–08:01
	(0.001)	(0.490)			
France	0.000	0.091	−1.288	0.000	76:01–98:12
	(0.003)	(0.706)			
Germany	0.003	−0.657	−1.992	0.003	76:01–98:12
	(0.002)	(0.832)			
Italy	−0.001	0.196	−2.072	0.001	76:01–98:12
	(0.003)	(0.388)			
Japan	0.010	−2.400	−5.097	0.026	78:06–08:01
	(0.003)	(0.667)			
Switzerland	0.007	−1.408	−3.495	0.014	76:01–08:01
	(0.003)	(0.689)			
United Kingdom	−0.002	−1.533	−2.945	0.014	76:01–08:01
	(0.002)	(0.860)			
Europe	0.005	−4.334	−3.223	0.048	98:12–08:01
	(0.002)	(1.655)			

Notes: OLS regression estimates of (11.6). Estimates are computed from monthly data over the sample periods listed in the right-hand column. Heteroskedastic robust standard errors are shown in parentheses. The t-statistics for the null that $\beta_1 = 1$ are reported in the column headed t-Statistic. Source: Burnside, Eichenbaum, Kleshchelski, and Rebelo (2006).

β_1 are generally negative. Furthermore, the t-statistics for the null that $\beta_1 = 1$ are generally highly statistically significant.[1] These estimates imply that low-interest-rate currencies tend to depreciate. For example, under UIP a fall in UK interest rates that lowers the forward premium on the GBP/USD should be accompanied by an expected appreciation of the GBP (i.e., a fall in S_{t+1}). Instead, the negative estimates of β_1 imply that on average the GBP depreciates against the USD.

The results in Table 11.1 are very typical of the estimates reported in the literature for major currency pairs over different sample periods. Indeed, these results are so well established that they are often referred to as the "Forward Bias" or "Forward

---

1. Statistical inference in UIP regressions can be tricky because the forward premium for many currency pairs displays a great deal of persistence. As a consequence, the asymptotic distribution for the regression coefficients may poorly approximate the actual distribution that should be used for inference in short data samples (see, e.g., Baillie and Bollerslev 2000). This is not a concern for the estimates using noneuro currencies because the data span more than 30 years.

Premium" Puzzle. At the same time, this puzzle does not appear to be a pervasive phenomenon. For example, Bansal and Dahlquist (2000) found that the puzzle is largely confined to the currency pairs of high-income economies. The forward premium on the currencies of emerging and low-income developed countries predicts future depreciation rates in a manner consistent with UIP and rational expectations. There is also much less evidence of a puzzle among industrial countries at longer investment horizons. Chinn and Meredith (2004) found that the currencies of G-7 countries with low interest rates on 5- and 10-year government bonds tend to appreciate over the long run, consistent with predictions of UIP. In sum, therefore, although the pattern of results in Table 11.1 appears to be a remarkably robust feature of the data, there is also a good deal of heterogeneity across currencies and horizons in the incidence of the Forward Premium Puzzle.

11.1.2 The Carry Trade

The results in Table 11.1 do not provide unambiguous evidence regarding the economic significance of the Forward Premium Puzzle. On the one hand, the slope coefficients are estimated with sufficient precision to easily reject the null of $\beta_1 = 1$ at standard significance levels. On the other, the R^2 statistics indicate that the forward premium accounts for very little of the variance in future depreciation rates. As a result, it is unclear whether there is sufficient predictability in the forward premium to construct a *reliably* profitable trading strategy exploiting the failure of UIP.

Recent research on the so-called "carry trade" sheds light on this issue. As we noted earlier, the results in Table 11.1 indicate that low-interest currencies tend, on average, to depreciate. This means that a trading strategy that borrows in the low-interest currency and lends in the high-interest currency will on average make a positive profit. This strategy is known as the "carry trade."

Burnside et al. (2006) provide a clear description of how the strategy works. Let b_t denote the number of dollars borrowed at the start of period t. As above, R_t and $\hat{R}_t$ are the one-period Eurodollar and Europound deposit rates. The carry-trade strategy consists of borrowing in the low-interest currency and lending in the high-interest currency, or

$$
b_t = \begin{cases} +1 & \text{if } R_t < \hat{R}_t \\ -1 & \text{if } R_t > \hat{R}_t \end{cases}.
$$

The dollar payoff on the strategy in period $t+1$ is

$$
\mathcal{X}^{\mathrm{R}}_{t+1} = b_t \left(\frac{S_{t+1}\hat{R}_t}{S_t} - R_t \right). \tag{11.7}
$$

Using the CIP condition, we can rewrite this payoff as

$$
\mathcal{X}^{\mathrm{R}}_{t+1} = b_t \left[\frac{S_{t+1} - S_t}{S_t} - \left(\frac{R_t}{\hat{R}_t} - 1 \right) \right] \hat{R}_t = b_t \left[\frac{S_{t+1} - S_t}{S_t} - \left(\frac{\mathcal{F}_t}{S_t} - 1 \right) \right] \hat{R}_t.
$$

If the dollar tends to depreciate (appreciate) when $\mathcal{F}_t < S_t$ ($\mathcal{F}_t > S_t$) as the results in Table 11.1 indicate, on average the second term in brackets will be positive when $b_t = 1$ and negative when $b_t = -1$. Thus, the strategy should produce a positive payoff on average if the regression estimates accurately characterize the behavior of spot and forward rates.

Alternatively, the carry-trade strategy can be implemented through trades in forward contracts. In this case the strategy involves purchasing the pound forward when it is at a discount ($\mathcal{F}_t < S_t$) and selling the pound forward when it is at a premium ($\mathcal{F}_t > S_t$). In particular, if the number of pounds sold forward is given by

$$a_t = \begin{cases} -R_t/\mathcal{F}_t & \text{if } \mathcal{F}_t < S_t \\ R_t/\mathcal{F}_t & \text{if } \mathcal{F}_t > S_t \end{cases},$$

the dollar payoff on the strategy is

$$\mathcal{X}^{\text{F}}_{t+1} = a_t \left(\mathcal{F}_t - S_{t+1} \right). \tag{11.8}$$

This payoff is equal to $\mathcal{X}^{\text{R}}_{t+1}$ when CIP holds. To see why, consider the case where $\mathcal{F}_t < S_t$. Under these circumstances, $b_t = 1$ because $R_t/\hat{R}_t = \mathcal{F}_t/S_t < 1$, so $\mathcal{X}^{\text{R}}_{t+1} = (S_{t+1}\hat{R}_t/S_t - R_t)$ from (11.7). At the same time, the payoff from the forward strategy in (11.8) is $(S_{t+1} - \mathcal{F}_t)R_t/\mathcal{F}_t$. Combining this expression with the CIP condition gives $\mathcal{X}^{\text{F}}_{t+1} = (S_{t+1}\hat{R}_t/S_t - R_t) = \mathcal{X}^{\text{R}}_{t+1}$.

In practice the payoff on a carry-trade strategy must account for the difference between the bid and ask prices on forward contracts and spot rate quotes. Let S^{B}_t and S^{A}_t denote bid and ask dollar spot prices for the pound, and let $\mathcal{F}^{\text{B}}_t$ and $\mathcal{F}^{\text{A}}_t$ denote the corresponding bid and ask prices for the one-period forward contract. To account for the bid-ask spreads, the number of pounds sold forward in the carry-trade strategy is now given by

$$a_t = \begin{cases} -R_t/\mathcal{F}^{\text{A}}_t & \text{if } \mathcal{F}^{\text{A}}_t < S^{\text{B}}_t \\ R_t/\mathcal{F}^{\text{B}}_t & \text{if } \mathcal{F}^{\text{B}}_t > S^{\text{A}}_t \\ 0 & \text{otherwise} \end{cases},$$

and the dollar payoff is

$$\mathcal{X}^{\text{B/A}}_{t+1} = \begin{cases} a_t(\mathcal{F}^{\text{B}}_t - S^{\text{A}}_{t+1})/S^{\text{A}}_t & \text{if } a_t > 0 \\ a_t(\mathcal{F}^{\text{A}}_t - S^{\text{B}}_{t+1})/S^{\text{B}}_t & \text{if } a_t < 0 \\ 0 & \text{otherwise} \end{cases}. \tag{11.9}$$

Actual carry-trade strategies involve multiple currencies rather than a single pair as described earlier. One simple form of multicurrency strategy is to construct a portfolio of strategies for different individual currencies versus the base currency. For example, using the dollar as the base currency, an equally weighted portfolio can be constructed by splitting each dollar of capital equally among the strategies for each of the n available currencies versus the dollar. Alternatively, the allocation of capital among the different strategies can be determined optimally to maximize some performance criteria.

TABLE 11.2
Annualized Carry-Trade Payoffs

	No transaction costs			With transaction costs		
	Mean	Standard deviation	Sharpe ratio	Mean	Standard deviation	Sharpe ratio
Canadian CAD	0.024	0.071	0.339	0.015	0.060	0.242
French FF	0.068	0.093	0.727	0.064	0.093	0.686
German DM	0.071	0.093	0.762	0.067	0.093	0.715
Italian LYA	−0.108	0.086	−1.249	−0.066	0.083	−0.797
Japanese JPY	0.026	0.112	0.235	0.021	0.112	0.187
Swiss CHP	0.002	0.095	0.017	0.015	0.088	0.169
United Kingdom GBP	0.022	0.074	0.297	0.014	0.066	0.214
Euro EUR	0.079	0.087	0.900	0.062	0.082	0.758
Portfolio	0.048	0.045	1.061	0.044	0.051	0.867
U.S. stocks	0.068	0.148	0.461			

Notes: The payoffs are measured in USD per dollar bet on an annualized basis. The portfolio payoff is computed as the equally weighted average of up to 20 individual currency carry trades against the USD. The payoff at time t on the U.S. stock market is the value-weighted excess return on all U.S. stocks divided by the U.S. gross interest rate, R_{t-1}. Source: Burnside, Eichenbaum, Kleshchelski, and Rebelo (2006).

Table 11.2 compares the payoffs on carry-trade strategies for individual currencies and for an equally weighted portfolio of currencies computed by Burnside et al. (2006). The payoffs are computed with and without transaction costs at the monthly frequency per dollar bet (i.e., the dollar is the base currency). The table reports the sample mean, $\mathbb{E}_T[\mathcal{X}]$, standard deviation, $\mathbb{V}_T(\mathcal{X})^{1/2}$, and the Sharpe ratio, $\mathbb{E}_T[\mathcal{X}]/\mathbb{V}_T(\mathcal{X})^{1/2}$ for the payoff on each strategy, $\mathcal{X}$, expressed on an annualized basis. Statistics for the excess return on the U.S. stock market are shown in the last row of the table for comparison.

Three features of Table 11.2 stand out. First, transaction costs reduce the payoffs on the carry trade, but they are too small to reduce the payoffs to zero. Second, there are large gains to diversification from adopting a multicurrency strategy. The Sharpe ratios for the equally weighted carry-trade portfolio are larger than those for the individual currencies both with and without transaction costs. This difference arises because the standard deviation for the payoff on the multicurrency strategy is much smaller than the payoffs on the individual currencies. Third, the Sharpe ratio for the multicurrency carry-trade return is substantially larger than that for the U.S. stock market because the returns on stocks are considerably more volatile than the carry-trade payoffs.

At one level the results in Table 11.2 confirm the economic significance of the Forward Premium Puzzle. A simple carry-trade strategy exploiting the puzzle produces a payoff with a much larger Sharpe ratio than a strategy of investing in the U.S. stock market. At another level the results pose their own set of puzzles. In particular, why

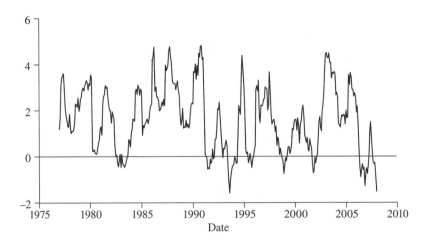

FIGURE 11.1   Realized carry-trade Sharpe ratios. Source: Burnside, Eichenbaum, Kleshchel-ski, and Rebelo (2006).

are the Sharpe ratios on the carry-trade strategies so high? Is it because the Sharpe ratio fails to reflect the true risks of executing the strategies, which are higher than the risk of holding U.S. stocks? If so, what are the risks? Alternatively, are there in-stitutional impediments that limit the capital committed to carry-trade strategies so that the (risk-adjusted) payoffs include a rent component? Again, this is a possibility, but it begs the question of what the impediments are.

Figure 11.1 provides some circumstantial evidence relevant to these issues. The figure plots the 12-month moving average of the realized Sharpe ratio for the equally weighted carry-trade portfolio (i.e., the ratio in month t is computed from the mean and standard deviation of the payoffs in months $t - 11$ to t). Note first that there is no discernible downward trend in the plot. Recall from Chapter 6 that trading in the spot and forward markets has increased dramatically in the past two decades. Against this background, it seems likely that any impediments limiting the capital committed to the carry trade in the 1970s and 1980s have now largely disappeared. Insofar as capital limits contributed to the carry-trade payoffs, there should be a downward trend in the Sharpe ratios, but this is not apparent.

The second noteworthy feature in Figure 11.1 concerns the volatility of the ratios; they range between approximately 4 and -1. According to Lyons (2001), anecdotal evidence from currency traders at banks and hedge funds indicates that Sharpe ratios are widely used as a metric to judge the performance of different trading strategies. Furthermore, these important sources of carry-trade capital only commit capital to a particular strategy when its Sharpe ratio exceeds a certain threshold, somewhere between 0.5 and 1. If the Sharpe ratios used in these decisions display at least 25 percent of the volatility of the realized Sharpe ratios shown in Figure 11.1 (a conservative estimate), the allocation of capital to various carry-trade strategies is likely to have changed considerably over time.

One reason why investors may be reluctant to commit capital to carry-trade strate-gies is that these strategies are subject to the risk associated with a currency crash, that is, the risk that the high-interest-rate currency will suddenly depreciate. A case in point occurred in October 1998 in the JPY/USD market. Panel A of Figure 11.2 plots the daily spot rate, S_t, and the 1-month forward premium, $\ln(\mathcal{F}_t/S_t) \times 1200$, for the JYP/USD in 1997 and 1998. Throughout this period the dollar was selling forward at a discount ($\mathcal{F}_t < S_t$) because Japanese interest rates were roughly 5 percent below U.S. interest rates. Figure 11.2 also shows that there was a persistent appreciation of the dollar between July 1997 and August 1998 from approximately 115 to 145 JYP/USD, a little more than 23 percent. The carry-trade strategy of purchasing dollars forward paid off handsomely during this period. This pattern came to an end in September 1998 with an initial fall in the JYP/USD rate to around 135, and then a more dramatic fall to 118 on October 7 and 8. Over these 2 months the dollar depreciated by more than 120 percent at an annualized rate—more than 20 times the expected depreciation rate implied by the forward premium under UIP.

This episode is interesting because it represents one of the most dramatic short-term movements in the spot rate of a major currency without an obvious macroeconomic cause. There were no changes in U.S. or Japanese monetary policy,[2] nor were the macro data releases in September and early October particularly noteworthy. Rather, the most newsworthy item was the collapse of the hedge fund, Long Term Capital Management. At the time, the sharp drop in the JPY/USD rate was attributed to "the unwinding of positions by hedge funds that had borrowed in cheap yen to finance purchases of higher-yielding dollar assets" (*The Economist*, 10/10/98).

Panels B, C, and D of Figure 11.2 provide some perspective on this explanation. Here we plot the daily JPY/USD rate during September and October 1998 together with the cumulative customer order flows for the dollar in the spot and forward JPY/USD markets received by Citibank. (Positive order flow denotes net orders to purchase dollars.) These order flows are disaggregated into six segments: trades executed between Citibank and nonfinancial corporate users, leveraged users (such as hedge funds and proprietary traders), and unleveraged users (such as mutual funds and pension funds) in the United States, and trades executed between these same three groups and Citibank in Asia.

If the sharp fall in the JPY/USD rate on October 7 and 8 were due to the unwinding of the carry trade, as suggested by *The Economist* and others, we should expect to see a significant drop in the cumulative customer order flow from leveraged users as they sold their forward dollar positions and/or purchased yen in the spot markets to cover their remaining forward positions. This is not what we see in panel D. It appears, instead, that most of the selling pressure from hedge funds and proprietary traders came in September, several weeks before the October crash. Indeed, at the time of the crash, these end-users were net dollar purchasers to the tune of approximately $1 billion. The order flows of the other end-users show a different pattern. In panel B we see that nonfinancial corporations were steady net purchases of the dollar in the United States whereas in Asia the orders fluctuate between net purchases and sales of the dollar. Note that these order flows are generally much smaller than those of leveraged investors, and at the time of the crash both were net purchasers of dollars. The largest difference between the U.S.- and Asian-based order flows shows up in panel C. Here we see steady selling pressure for the dollar from unleveraged investors

---

2. The Federal Reserve did cut interest rates on October 15, but contemporary accounts indicate that this was a surprise to market participants and so unrelated to the prior depreciation of the dollar.

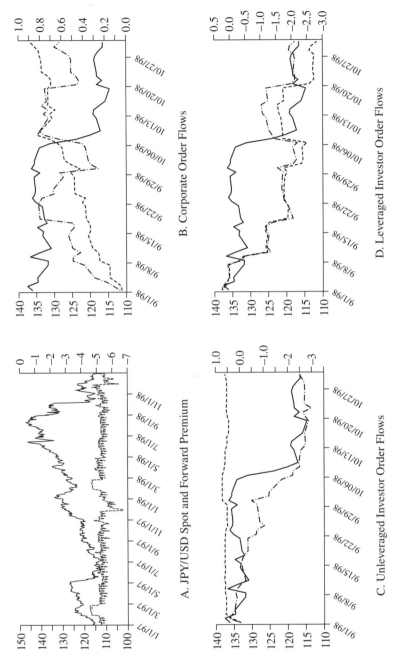

A. JPY/USD Spot and Forward Premium

B. Corporate Order Flows

C. Unleveraged Investor Order Flows

D. Leveraged Investor Order Flows

FIGURE 11.2   Crash risk and the carry trade. The solid line identifies the spot JPY/USD rate plotted against the left-hand axis in each panel. The annualized forward premium, $\ln \mathcal{F}_t / S_t \times 1200$, is plotted as the dashed line against the right-hand axis in panel A. Cumulative dollar order flow from corporate, leveraged, and unleveraged end-users based on trades executed in the United States (dashed) and in Asia (dot-dashed) are plotted in billions of dollars against the right-hand axis in panels B, C, and D.

trading in Asia during the 5 weeks preceding the crash. By contrast, there is almost no net buying or selling pressure from similar end-use trading with Citibank in the United States.

In summary, the behavior of the JPY/USD during this episode suggests that concerns about currency crashes (or equivalently, skewness in the distribution of currency returns) are a possible constraint on the amount of capital committed to carry-trade strategies. Furthermore, because the actual crash does not appear to have a clear proximate trigger either in the form of macro news, a policy change, or order flows, there is little prospect of managing the risk effectively. This is not to say that concerns about crash risk are sufficiently important to account for the returns to the carry trade or to help explain the persistence of the Forward Premium Puzzle. For that we need a model.

11.2 Macro Models

Theoretical models explaining the Forward Premium Puzzle and carry-trade payoffs fall broadly within three groups. The first group comprises models that relate the excess returns on individual currencies and carry-trade payoffs to measures of macro risk. Differences between the probability distributions used in investors' decision-making and the distributions generating the observed data on returns and payoffs are the focus of models in the second group. The third group comprises models with market frictions. This section examines models in the first two groups, which take a macroeconomic perspective insofar as they ignore the microfoundations of currency trading.

11.2.1 Stochastic Discount Factors

Macro models of exchange-rate risk build on the behavior of the Stochastic Discount Factor (SDF) that prices all financial assets in any environment that precludes arbitrage opportunities. Let $\mathcal{P}_t^i$ denote the dollar price of asset i in period t, with a dollar payoff of $\mathcal{X}_{t+1}^i$ in period $t+1$. If there are no arbitrage opportunities in the economy, there exists a positive random, $\mathcal{M}_{t+1}$, such that

$$\mathcal{P}_t^i = \mathbb{E}_t[\mathcal{M}_{t+1}\mathcal{X}_{t+1}^i] \tag{11.10}$$

for any freely traded asset i, where $\mathbb{E}_t[.]$ denotes expectations conditioned on common period-t information (that includes $\mathcal{P}_t^i$). The variable $\mathcal{M}_{t+1}$ is known as the SDF or pricing kernel.

The result in (11.10) is very general. It does not rely on the preferences of investors, the rationality of their expectations, or the completeness of financial markets. Rather it only requires that there are no restrictions on the construction of portfolios (such as short-sales constraints) and that assets with the same payoffs have the same prices.

A detailed derivation of the no-arbitrage condition in (11.10) is provided by Cochrane (2001); here we provide a little intuition. Consider first an economy with a single representative investor, who has standard time-separable utility defined over consumption, $\mathbb{E}_t \sum_{i=0}^{\infty} \beta^i U(C_{t+i})$. The first-order condition governing the investor's optimal holding of asset i is

$$1 = \mathbb{E}_t[\{\beta U'(C_{t+1})/U'(C_t)\}\mathfrak{R}^i_{t+1}], \qquad (11.11)$$

where $\mathfrak{R}^i_{t+1} = (\mathcal{X}^i_{t+1}/\mathcal{P}^i_t)(P_t/P_{t+1})$ is the real return on asset i and P_t is the price level. Clearly this first-order condition takes the same form as (11.10) with $\mathcal{M}_{t+1} = \{\beta U'(C_{t+1})/U'(C_t)\}(P_t/P_{t+1})$. Thus, in this environment, the SDF equals the nominal intertemporal marginal rate of substitution (NMRS) for the representative investor.

Next consider an economy populated by investors with different preferences and a complete set of financial markets. In this environment any asset can be represented as a portfolio of contingent claims. In particular, the price of asset i is $\mathcal{P}^i_t = \sum_{z \in \mathcal{Z}} P_t(z)\mathcal{X}^i_{t+1}(z)$, where $\mathcal{X}^i_{t+1}(z)$ is the payoff on asset i when the period-$t+1$ state of the world is z. In words, the price of the asset must be the same as the price of a portfolio of contingent claims that produces the same payoff in every possible period-$t+1$ state. If we now define $\mathcal{M}_{t+1}(z)$ as $P_t(z)/\pi_t(z)$, where $\pi_t(z)$ denotes the conditional probability of state z occurring in period $t+1$, we can rewrite this relation in the form of (11.10):

$$\mathcal{P}^i_t = \sum_{z \in \mathcal{Z}} \pi_t(z)\mathcal{M}_{t+1}(z)\mathcal{X}^i_{t+1}(z) = \mathbb{E}_t[\mathcal{M}_{t+1}\mathcal{X}^i_{t+1}].$$

Thus, when markets are complete, the SDF is equal to the ratio of the contingent claims price of future state z to the probability of state z.

Finally, consider an economy with incomplete markets populated by heterogeneous investors. In this environment (11.10) still holds but there may be more than one SDF that satisfies the no-arbitrage condition. Intuitively, the first-order condition in (11.11) holds for each investor, so each investor's NMRS works as an SDF for pricing all the freely traded assets. In Chapter 1 we saw that the NMRS is equalized across investors in every future state when markets are complete, so the NMRS of any investor produces the same, unique SDF. In contrast, when markets are incomplete there may be idiosyncratic differences among the NMRSs of different investors because they cannot completely share the risks they face. In this case we could use any one NMRS to price all the assets, so there are multiple SDFs that satisfy the no-arbitrage relation in (11.10).

Although the beauty of building a model on (11.10) comes from its general applicability, the assumed absence of arbitrage opportunities does not get us that far in accounting for the Forward Premium Puzzle. To make further progress we need a model for the SDF that identifies the stochastic process for $\mathcal{M}_{t+1}$. Here we have essentially two choices. The first is to identify $\mathcal{M}_{t+1}$ from the equilibrium of a fully specified general equilibrium model, where investors have particular preferences and access to a specific set of financial assets. This can be an extremely complex undertaking in realistic environments, where investors have access to many financial assets but markets are incomplete. The second is to follow a "reverse-engineering" approach in which we identify the properties of the SDF necessary to explain the behavior of asset prices generally and the Forward Premium Puzzle in particular. This strategy is easier to implement but leaves open the issue of how the behavior of the SDF is related to economic fundamentals.

11.2.2 Reverse Engineering the Forward Premium Puzzle

The reverse-engineering approach originates with Fama (1984), who examined what UIP regression results similar to those in Table 11.1 implied about the behavior of the foreign exchange risk premium under rational expectations. To describe his analysis, it proves useful to work with the log form of the UIP regression:

$$\Delta s_{t+1} = \beta_0 + \beta_1 f p_t + \xi_{t+1}, \tag{11.12}$$

where $\Delta s_{t+1} = s_{t+1} - s_t$ with $s_t = \ln S_t$ and $f p_t = \ln(\mathcal{F}_t / S_t)$ is the log forward premium. Estimates of this regression are very similar to estimates of (11.6). In particular, the estimates of β_1 are generally negative and the estimates of β_0 are close to zero in monthly data.

To interpret these estimates, we need a definition of the foreign exchange risk premium. For consistency with earlier chapters, the risk premium in period t is defined as the expected log excess return on foreign currency, $\delta_t = \mathbb{E}_t \Delta s_{t+1} + \hat{r}_t - r_t$. Combining this definition with the CIP condition expressed in logs, $f p_t = r_t - \hat{r}_t$, gives $\mathbb{E}_t \Delta s_{t+1} = f p_t + \delta_t$, so the actual depreciation rate can be written as

$$\Delta s_{t+1} = \mathbb{E}_t \Delta s_{t+1} + s_{t+1} - \mathbb{E}_t s_{t+1} = f p_t + \delta_t + s_{t+1} - \mathbb{E}_t s_{t+1}. \tag{11.13}$$

Note that this expression is an identity, so it must hold true for some value of the risk premium and spot rate expectations. It simply tells us that variations in the actual depreciation rate must, as a matter of logic, come from the forward premium, the risk premium, and/or the error in forecasting the future log spot rate.

Equation (11.13) implies that the population value of the slope coefficient in the regression (11.12) is

$$\beta_1 = \frac{\mathbb{CV}(\Delta s_{t+1}, f p_t)}{\mathbb{V}(f p_t)} = 1 + \frac{\mathbb{CV}(\delta_t, f p_t)}{\mathbb{V}(f p_t)} + \frac{\mathbb{CV}(s_{t+1} - \mathbb{E}_t s_{t+1}, f p_t)}{\mathbb{V}(f p_t)}. \tag{11.14}$$

Under rational expectations, the forecaster error, $s_{t+1} - \mathbb{E}_t s_{t+1}$, is uncorrelated with any elements of the period-t information set, including $f p_t$. Consequently, the right-hand term in (11.14) vanishes. Under these circumstances, a negative value for β_1 implies that

$$\mathbb{CV}(\delta_t, f p_t) < -\mathbb{V}(f p_t) < 0. \tag{11.15}$$

At the same time, we know by definition that $\mathbb{V}(\mathbb{E}_t \Delta s_{t+1}) = \mathbb{V}(f p_t) + \mathbb{V}(\delta_t) + 2\mathbb{CV}(\delta_t, f p_t) \geq 0$, so

$$\mathbb{V}(f p_t) + \mathbb{V}(\delta_t) \geq -2\mathbb{CV}(\delta_t, f p_t) > 2\mathbb{V}(f p_t),$$

or, more simply,

$$\mathbb{V}(\delta_t) > \mathbb{V}(f p_t). \tag{11.16}$$

Equations (11.15) and (11.16) identify two statistical properties of the risk premium that are necessary to account for a negative population value of the slope coefficient from regression (11.12) in the presence of rational expectations. The first condition says that the risk premium must be negatively correlated with the forward premium. In other words, the expected excess return on foreign currency must rise and fall with the interest differential between foreign and domestic interest rates, $\hat{r}_t - r_t$. This is the statistical feature exploited by carry-trade strategies. The second condition in (11.16) is more surprising. It says that the population variance of the forward premium represents a lower bound on the variance of the risk premium. Since the estimated variance for the forward premium (on an annualized basis) in major currencies is approximately 10.5 percent, the risk premium has to display a significant degree of volatility to satisfy this lower volatility bound.

It is important to recognize that the relevance of Fama's conditions rests on two key assumptions. First, (11.15) and (11.16) were derived under the assumption that $\mathbb{CV}(s_{t+1} - \mathbb{E}_t s_{t+1}, \, fp_t) = 0$. This condition is implied by rational expectations, but it need not be empirically relevant in a particular data sample. As we shall see, the sample covariance can differ from zero even when market participants hold rational expectations. Second, we can only make inferences concerning the population value of the regression coefficient β_1 based on estimates of (11.12). There is no *guarantee* that these inferences are reliable, so it is inappropriate to draw definite conclusions about the behavior of the risk premium from (11.15) and (11.16). That said, Fama's conditions are widely used as guidance in developing macro models of exchange-rate risk.

The reverse-engineering approach has been taken a step further by Backus, Foresi, and Telmer (2001). These authors use the no-arbitrage condition in (11.10) to derive restrictions on the behavior of the SDF necessary to account for the Forward Premium Puzzle. To illustrate their method, consider the price of a one-period U.K. bond with (gross) interest rate $\hat{R}_t$. The dollar price of the bond in period t is $\mathcal{P}_t^i = S_t / \hat{R}_t$ (where S_t is the USD/GBP spot rate) and the dollar payoff in period $t + 1$ is $\mathcal{X}_{t+1}^i = S_{t+1}$. The no-arbitrage condition in (11.10) can therefore be written as

$$1 = \mathbb{E}_t[\mathcal{M}_{t+1}\mathcal{X}_{t+1}^i / \mathcal{P}_t^i] = \mathbb{E}_t[\mathcal{M}_{t+1}\hat{R}_t(S_{t+1}/S_t)]. \tag{11.17}$$

The absence of arbitrage also implies the existence of a pound SDF, $\widehat{\mathcal{M}}_{t+1}$, that prices assets in pounds, that is, $\widehat{\mathcal{P}}_t^i = \mathbb{E}_t[\widehat{\mathcal{M}}_{t+1}\widehat{\mathcal{X}}_{t+1}^i]$, where $\widehat{\mathcal{P}}_t^i$ and $\widehat{\mathcal{X}}_{t+1}^i$ are the prices and payoffs for asset i in pounds. In the case of U.K. bonds, $\widehat{\mathcal{P}}_t^i = 1/\hat{R}_t$ and $\mathcal{X}_{t+1}^i = 1$, so the pound interest rate also satisfies

$$1 = \mathbb{E}_t[\widehat{\mathcal{M}}_{t+1}\hat{R}_t]. \tag{11.18}$$

Furthermore, (11.17) and (11.18) together imply that

$$\mathbb{E}_t[\mathcal{M}_{t+1}(S_{t+1}/S_t)] = \mathbb{E}_t[\widehat{\mathcal{M}}_{t+1}]. \tag{11.19}$$

This equation ties the rate of depreciation in the USD/GBP spot rate to the dollar and pound SDFs. Recall that $\mathcal{M}_{t+1}(z) = \mathcal{P}_t(z)/\pi_t(z)$ under complete markets. By analogous reasoning, we can also write $\widehat{\mathcal{M}}_{t+1}(z) = \widehat{\mathcal{P}}_t(z)/\pi_t(z)$, where $\widehat{\mathcal{P}}_t(z)$ is the pound price of a contingent claim to £1 in state z. Since the dollar cost of such a claim is $\mathcal{P}_t(z)S_{t+1}(z)/S_t$ in the absence of arbitrage, $\widehat{\mathcal{M}}_{t+1}(z)$ must equal $\mathcal{M}_{t+1}(z)S_{t+1}(z)/S_t$ for each period-$t + 1$ state z. The depreciation rate must therefore equal the difference in the log SDFs under complete markets:

$$\Delta s_{t+1} = \ln \widehat{\mathcal{M}}_{t+1} - \ln \mathcal{M}_{t+1}. \tag{11.20}$$

When markets are incomplete, there are potentially many SDFs satisfying (11.17) and (11.18), but at least one pair that also satisfies (11.20).

We can also write the forward premium in terms of the SDFs. Consider the dollar payoff on selling the pound forward in period $t + 1$. The dollar payoff is just the proceeds from the forward contract, $\mathcal{F}_t$, less the cost of purchasing pounds in the spot market at price S_{t+1}, hence $\mathcal{X}^i_{t+1} = \mathcal{F}_t - S_{t+1}$. Furthermore, since this payoff can be realized without any date-t dollar payment, the price of the claim to this payoff must equal zero. The no-arbitrage condition in (11.10) therefore implies that $\mathbb{E}_t[\mathcal{M}_{t+1}(\mathcal{F}_t - S_{t+1})] = 0$. Dividing by S_t and combining the result with (11.20) gives $(\mathcal{F}_t/S_t)\mathbb{E}_t[\mathcal{M}_{t+1}] = \mathbb{E}_t[\mathcal{M}_{t+1}(S_{t+1}/S_t)] = \mathbb{E}_t[\widehat{\mathcal{M}}_{t+1}]$, so the log forward premium is

$$fp_t = \ln \mathbb{E}_t[\widehat{\mathcal{M}}_{t+1}] - \ln \mathbb{E}_t[\mathcal{M}_{t+1}]. \tag{11.21}$$

Backus, Foresi, and Telmer (2001) use (11.20) and (11.21) to probe more deeply into the Forward Premium Puzzle. In particular, they examine whether simple time series models for the log SDF's can account for negative values of the regression coefficient β_1 in (11.12). To illustrate their approach, consider the following model for the log SDFs:

$$\begin{aligned}
-\ln \mathcal{M}_{t+1} &= \lambda m_t + \sqrt{\gamma m_t}\, u_{t+1} + \psi m_t^* + \sqrt{\varphi m_t^*}\, u_{t+1}^*, \\
-\ln \widehat{\mathcal{M}}_{t+1} &= \lambda \hat{m}_t + \sqrt{\gamma \hat{m}_t}\, \hat{u}_{t+1} + \hat{\psi} m_t^* + \sqrt{\hat{\varphi} m_t^*}\, u_{t+1}^*,
\end{aligned} \tag{11.22}$$

where λ, γ, ψ, φ, $\hat{\psi}$, and $\hat{\varphi}$ are all positive parameters. Here m_t and $\hat{m}_t$ denote country-specific factors driving the log SDFs and m_t^* is a common factor. All three factors are known (i.e., $\{m_t, \hat{m}_t, m_t^*\} \in \Omega_t$) and follow independent AR(1) processes (with restrictions on the parameters to ensure that realizations of m_t, $\hat{m}_t$, and m_t^* are always positive). The country-specific shocks, u_{t+1} and $\hat{u}_{t+1}$, and common shocks, u_{t+1}^*, are i.i.d. normally distributed with zero means and unit variances.

The specification (11.22) has three noteworthy features. First, it implies that both log SDFs will display persistent variations via the AR(1) processes for the country-specific and common factors. These factors also control the conditional variance and covariance between the log SDFs. In particular, under the assumption that $\{m_t, \hat{m}_t, m_t^*\} \in \Omega_t$, (11.22) implies that $\mathbb{V}_t(\ln \mathcal{M}_{t+1}) = \gamma m_t + \varphi m_t^*$, $\mathbb{V}_t(\ln \widehat{\mathcal{M}}_{t+1}) = \gamma \hat{m}_t + \hat{\varphi} m_t^*$, and $\mathbb{CV}_t(\ln \mathcal{M}_{t+1}, \ln \widehat{\mathcal{M}}_{t+1}) = \sqrt{\varphi \hat{\varphi}} m_t^*$. Third, the presence of the normally distributed shocks, $\{u_{t+1}, \hat{u}_{t+1}, u_{t+1}^*\}$, implies that the conditional distribution of $\ln \mathcal{M}_{t+1}$ and $\ln \widehat{\mathcal{M}}_{t+1}$ is normal, so

$$\ln \mathbb{E}_t[\mathcal{M}_{t+1}] = \mathbb{E}_t[\ln \mathcal{M}_{t+1}] + \tfrac{1}{2}\mathbb{V}_t(\ln \mathcal{M}_{t+1})$$

and

$$\ln \mathbb{E}_t[\widehat{\mathcal{M}}_{t+1}] = \mathbb{E}_t[\ln \widehat{\mathcal{M}}_{t+1}] + \tfrac{1}{2}\mathbb{V}_t(\ln \widehat{\mathcal{M}}_{t+1}).$$

The implications of (11.22) for the behavior of the expected depreciation rate and forward premium follow from (11.20) and (11.21):

$$\mathbb{E}_t \Delta s_{t+1} = \lambda(m_t - \hat{m}_t) + (\psi - \hat{\psi})m_t^*$$

and

$$fp_t = (\lambda - \tfrac{1}{2}\gamma)(m_t - \hat{m}_t) + [(\psi - \hat{\psi}) - \tfrac{1}{2}(\varphi - \hat{\varphi})]m_t^*.$$

Under rational expectations, the population value for the slope coefficient in regression (11.12) is $\beta_1 = \mathbb{CV}(\mathbb{E}_t\Delta s_{t+1}, fp_t)/\mathbb{V}(fp_t)$. Thus substituting for the depreciation rate and forward premium gives

$$\beta_1 = \frac{\lambda(\lambda - \tfrac{1}{2}\gamma) + (\psi - \hat{\psi})[(\psi - \hat{\psi}) - \tfrac{1}{2}(\varphi - \hat{\varphi})]\omega}{(\lambda - \tfrac{1}{2}\gamma)^2 + [(\psi - \hat{\psi}) - \tfrac{1}{2}(\varphi - \hat{\varphi})]^2\omega}, \qquad (11.23)$$

where $\omega = \frac{\mathbb{V}(m_t^*)}{\mathbb{V}(m_t) + \mathbb{V}(\hat{m}_t)}$.

This expression shows that the model in (11.22) can produce negative values for β_1 through two channels. The first operates via the country-specific factors. If the common factor has identical effects on both SDFs (i.e., when $\psi = \hat{\psi}$ and $\varphi = \hat{\varphi}$), it has no effect on either the expected depreciation rate or the forward premium, so (11.23) simplifies to $\beta_1 = \lambda/(\lambda - \tfrac{1}{2}\gamma)$. Clearly, we can reproduce the forward premium puzzle in this case if $0 < \lambda < \tfrac{1}{2}\gamma$. However, as Backus, Foresi, and Telmer (2001) note, this parameter restriction implies that nominal interest rates can become negative, an unappealing implication.

The second channel operates via the common factor. In the limit as $\mathbb{V}(m_t)$ and $\mathbb{V}(\hat{m}_t) \to 0$, only the common factor drives the SDFs and (11.23) simplifies to $\beta_1 = (\psi - \hat{\psi})/(\psi - \hat{\psi} - \tfrac{1}{2}(\varphi - \hat{\varphi}))$. In this case we can reproduce the Forward Premium Puzzle if the common factor has asymmetric effects on the SDFs. More specifically, rearranging the expression for β_1 gives $\varphi - \hat{\varphi} = -(\frac{1-\beta_1}{\beta_1})2(\psi - \hat{\psi})$, so negative values for β_1 imply that $\varphi - \hat{\varphi}$ and $\psi - \hat{\psi}$ must have the same sign.

This discussion makes it clear that it is possible to identify restrictions on the time series processes for the SDFs necessary to produce the Forward Premium Puzzle. Of course, reverse engineering of this form does not produce an economic explanation for the puzzle, but it does provide benchmarks for economic models of the SDFs.

11.2.3 Euler Equation Models

Euler equation models of the foreign exchange risk premia use particular specifications for preferences to identify the SDF in the no-arbitrage condition

$$0 = \mathbb{E}_t[\mathcal{M}_{t+1}(\mathcal{F}_t - S_{t+1})/S_t]. \qquad (11.24)$$

Mark (1985) provided the first example of this approach. He identified $\mathcal{M}_{t+1}$ by the NMRS of a representative U.S. investor with time-separable constant relative risk-aversion utility: $\mathcal{M}_{t+1}^c = \beta(C_{t+1}/C_t)^{-\gamma}(P_t/P_{t+1})$, where C_t is aggregate consumption. Using this specification, he then tested the restrictions implied by the no-arbitrage condition for four currencies versus the USD.

To illustrate Mark's approach, let S_t^j and $\mathcal{F}_t^j$ denote the spot and one-period forward rate for currency j versus the USD and define $\mathcal{R}_{t+1}$ as the $J \times 1$ vector of excess returns with the jth element, $\mathcal{R}_{t+1}^j \equiv (\mathcal{F}_t^j - S_{t+1}^j)/S_t^j$. (Note that $\mathcal{R}_{t+1}^j$ is the excess return on selling foreign currency j one period forward.) Since the no-arbitrage condition applies to all returns, the model implies that $\mathbb{E}_t[\mathcal{M}_{t+1}^c \mathcal{R}_{t+1}] = \mathbf{0}$, where $\mathbf{0}$ is a $J \times 1$ vector of zeros. This set of the theoretical restrictions can be estimated and tested using the Hansen (1982) GMM technique.

Generalized Method of Moments

Let $\mathcal{I}_t = [\mathcal{I}_t^i]$ denote a $1 \times K$ vector of instruments known to the investor in period t, that is, $\mathcal{I}_t^i \in \Omega_t$ for $i = 1, \ldots, K$. Applying the Law of Iterated Expectations to (11.24) gives $\mathbb{E}[\mathcal{M}_{t+1}^c \mathcal{R}_{t+1} \mathcal{I}_t^i] = 0$ for each instrument i or, more compactly,

$$\mathbb{E}[\mathcal{H}_t] = \mathbf{0}, \tag{11.25}$$

where $\mathcal{H}_t = \mathcal{M}_{t+1}^c \mathcal{R}_{t+1} \otimes \mathcal{I}_t$.[3] This expression represents $J \times K$ unconditional moment restrictions implied by the model for the J currencies using K instruments.

The preference parameters, β and γ, appear in (11.25) via $\mathcal{H}_t$. In this application, the restrictions in (11.25) can be satisfied by any value for β, so only the risk-aversion parameter γ can be estimated. In a sample with T observations, the GMM estimates of γ are found by normalizing β to one and choosing γ to minimize the quadratic form:

$$\mathcal{J} = T\mathcal{H}_T' \mathcal{W}_T \mathcal{H}_T, \tag{11.26}$$

where $\mathcal{H}_T = \frac{1}{T} \sum_{t=1}^T \mathcal{H}_t$ and $\mathcal{W}_T$ is a $JK \times JK$ weighting matrix that determines how much attention is paid to each of the JK moment conditions in (11.25). The choice of this matrix affects the precision of the GMM estimates. Hansen (1982) shows that the optimal choice that minimizes the asymptotic covariance matrix of the GMM estimates is given by the inverse of $\mathcal{S} = \lim_{T \to \infty} \mathbb{V}(\sqrt{T}\mathcal{H}_T)$. To make use of this result, consistent estimates of parameters are first computed by minimizing $\mathcal{J}$ with an arbitrary weighting matrix. These initial estimates are then used to construct consistent estimates of $\mathcal{S}$, $\mathcal{S}_T$, and a second set of parameter estimates are obtained by minimizing $\mathcal{J}$ with $\mathcal{W}_T = \mathcal{S}_T^{-1}$. This two-step procedure produces asymptotically efficient estimates. It can also be extended to test the overall fit of the model in cases where the number of coefficients being estimated, L, is less than the JK moment conditions in (11.25). Hansen (1982) shows that under the null of a correctly specified model, the value of $\mathcal{J}$ from the second step has an asymptotic χ^2 distribution with $JK - L$ degrees of freedom. Intuitively, $\mathcal{J}$ should be small if the model is correct because each of the sample averages in the $\mathcal{H}_T$ vector will be close to its theoretical value of zero.

Results

Mark (1985) implemented the GMM technique with spot and forward rates for the CAD/USD, DM/USD, NG/USD, and GBP/USD using a constant and lags of the forward premium as instruments. Using data between March 1973 and July 1983,

---

3. The notation $\otimes$ denotes the Kronecker product of two vectors; $\mathcal{H}_t$ is a $JK \times 1$ vector containing the cross product of each element in $\mathcal{M}_{t+1}^c \mathcal{R}_{t+1}$ with each element in $\mathcal{I}_t$.

he estimated the value of γ to be 48.7 with a standard error of 79.4. He also found that the $\mathcal{J}$ statistic was highly significant, so the restrictions of the model in (11.25) appear not to hold.

Mark's findings are typical of the results in most of the subsequent literature (see Engel 1996 for a survey). The large values for γ reflect the small correlation between the growth in aggregate consumption and excess currency returns. This is easily seen by taking unconditional expectations on both sides of $\mathbb{E}_t[\mathcal{M}^c_{t+1}\mathcal{R}_{t+1}] = \mathbf{0}$ and rearranging the result[4]:

$$\begin{aligned}
\mathbb{E}[\mathcal{R}_{t+1}] &= -\mathbb{CV}\big(\mathcal{M}^c_{t+1}, \mathcal{R}_{t+1}\big)/\mathbb{E}[\mathcal{M}^c_{t+1}] \\
&\cong -\mathbb{CV}\big(\ln \mathcal{M}^c_{t+1}, \mathcal{R}_{t+1}\big) \\
&= \mathbb{CV}\big(\mathcal{R}_{t+1}, \Delta p_{t+1}\big) + \gamma\mathbb{CV}\big(\mathcal{R}_{t+1}, \Delta c_{t+1}\big).
\end{aligned}$$

Thus, expected excess returns depend on the covariance between returns, inflation, and aggregate consumption growth. Over typical data periods, both sample covariances are far smaller than the average currency return, so the GMM technique chooses large values for γ—values that seem implausible from an economic standpoint.

There is also a simple explanation for the large value of the $\mathcal{J}$ statistics. We know from the UIP regression results that excess returns can be forecast with the forward premium. By definition, $\mathcal{R}^j_{t+1} \equiv \mathcal{FP}_t - (S_{t+1} - S_t)/S_t$, where $\mathcal{FP}_t \equiv (\mathcal{F}_t/S_t) - 1$. Thus the negative slope coefficients in Table 11.1 imply that a rise in $\mathcal{FP}_t$ forecasts an increase in expected excess returns. By contrast, the model implies that the forward premium has no forecasting power for $\mathcal{M}^c_{t+1}\mathcal{R}^j_{t+1}$. This is easily seen by considering the projection of $\mathcal{M}^c_{t+1}\mathcal{R}^j_{t+1}$ on the forward premium:

$$\mathcal{M}^c_{t+1}\mathcal{R}^j_{t+1} = a\mathcal{FP}_t + \xi_{t+1}.$$

Since $\mathcal{FP}_t \in \Omega_t$, (11.24) implies that $\mathbb{E}_t[\mathcal{M}^c_{t+1}\mathcal{R}^j_{t+1}\mathcal{FP}_t] = 0$, so the projection coefficient is

$$a = \frac{\mathbb{E}[\mathcal{M}^c_{t+1}\mathcal{R}^j_{t+1}\mathcal{FP}_t]}{\mathbb{E}[\mathcal{FP}_t]^2} = 0.$$

Clearly, then, there has to be a lot of variation in $\mathcal{M}^c_{t+1}$ to ensure that the forward premium can forecast $\mathcal{R}^j_{t+1}$ but not $\mathcal{M}^c_{t+1}\mathcal{R}^j_{t+1}$. Unfortunately, there are no values for γ that can produce this degree of variation from inflation and aggregate consumption growth, so the forward premium has forecasting power for $\mathcal{M}^c_{t+1}\mathcal{R}^j_{t+1}$ evaluated at the GMM estimates. It is this basic failure of the model that lies behind the large values of the $\mathcal{J}$ statistics.

---

4. The approximation in the second line disappears when $\ln \mathcal{M}^c_{t+1}$ is normally distributed.

Recent Research

Recent research on Euler equation models contains two novel twists. First, researchers derive the SDF from a richer specification for preferences. Second, they focus on the empirical implications of the model for the returns on currency portfolios rather than on individual currencies. What is striking about this research is that the overall fit of some models *appears* to be much better than that found in the earlier literature. The results of Lustig and Verdelhan (2007) (hereafter LV) are a case in point. They argue that risk associated with aggregate consumption growth can account for the differences in expected returns across different currency portfolios. This claim contrasts with the earlier literature and so warrants closer examination.

LV begin with a richer specification for the U.S. investor's preferences. One important limitation of the power utility specification used by Mark (1985) and many others is that the investor's elasticity of intertemporal substitution is equal to the reciprocal of the coefficient of relative risk-aversion. Since these are distinct concepts, it is unclear why they should be so closely linked. The elasticity of substitution measures the investors' willingness to substitute consumption over time, whereas risk-aversion describes their reluctance to substitute a plan producing uncertain consumption for one producing certain consumption.

To avoid this limitation of power utility, LV use a specification for the representative investor's preferences found in Yogo (2006) that adds durable goods to the Epstein-Zin-Weil model (Epstein and Zin 1989 and Weil 1989). In this model, the lifetime utility of the U.S. investor in period t, U_t, is recursively represented as

$$U_t = \left\{ (1-\theta)\mathfrak{u}(C_t, D_t)^{1-1/\sigma} + \theta \left[\mathbb{E}_t U_{t+1}^{1-\gamma} \right]^{(1-1/\sigma)/(1-\gamma)} \right\}^{1/(1-1/\sigma)},$$

where C_t and D_t denote the investor's consumption of nondurable and durable goods, respectively. The investor's subjective discount factor is $1 > \theta > 0$; $\sigma > 0$ denotes the elasticity of intertemporal substitution and $\gamma > 0$ determines risk-aversion. The utility from the current consumption of durables and nondurables is given by

$$\mathfrak{u}(C_t, D_t) = \left[(1-\omega)C_t^{1-1/\rho} + \omega D_t^{1-1/\rho} \right]^{1/(1-1/\rho)},$$

where $1 > \omega > 0$ and $\rho > 0$ is the elasticity of substitution between durables and nondurables. With this specification for preferences, the investor's real marginal rate of substitution is

$$MRS_{t+1} = \left\{ \theta \left(\frac{C_{t+1}}{C_t} \right)^{-1/\sigma} \left[\frac{v(D_{t+1}/C_{t+1})}{v(D_t/C_t)} \right]^{1/\rho - 1/\sigma} (R_{t+1}^w)^{1-1/\kappa} \right\}^{\kappa} \left(\frac{P_t}{P_{t+1}} \right),$$

(11.27)

where $\kappa = (1-\gamma)/(1-1/\sigma)$, R_{t+1}^w is the gross real return on wealth between periods t and $t+1$, and $v(D/C) = \left[1 - \omega + \omega(D/C)^{1-1/\rho} \right]^{1/(1-1/\rho)}$.

LV consider the pricing implications of (11.27) for a set of eight excess portfolio returns. In period t, they sort individual currencies versus the USD into portfolios according to their interest differential with the U.S., ordered from highest to lowest. The excess return on the ith portfolio in period $t+1$ is the average of the returns on the individual currencies, that is, $\mathcal{R}_{t+1}^j = ((S_{t+1}^j/S_t)\hat{R}_t^j - R_t)$ for currency j. As interest differentials vary through time, the ordering and composition of the portfolios change.

These portfolio returns are related to the returns on a multicurrency carry-trade strategy. Recall that such a strategy calls for borrowing in the low-interest currency and lending in the high-interest currency. The return on portfolio 1 contains the returns from borrowing in the USD when U.S. rates are relative low, so the return should be positively correlated with the return on carry-trade strategies. By contrast, portfolio 8 contains returns from borrowing in the USD when U.S. rates are relatively high, so the return on this portfolio will be negatively correlated with the return on carry-trade strategies.

LV work with the unconditional version of the no-arbitrage condition. Let $\mathcal{R}_{t+1}^e$ denote the vector of excess returns in dollars on the eight portfolios that satisfies $\mathbb{E}_t[\mathcal{M}_{t+1}\mathcal{R}_{t+1}^e] = \mathbf{0}$. Clearly, we can rewrite this condition as $\mathbb{E}_t[\mathfrak{M}_{t+1}\mathfrak{R}_{t+1}^e] = \mathbf{0}$, where $\mathfrak{M}_{t+1} = \mathcal{M}_{t+1}(P_{t+1}/P_t)$ is the real SDF and $\mathfrak{R}_{t+1}^e = \mathcal{R}_{t+1}^e(P_t/P_{t+1})$ is the vector of eight real excess returns (i.e., $\mathfrak{R}_{t+1}^e = [\mathfrak{R}_{1,t+1}^e, \ldots, \mathfrak{R}_{8,t+1}^e]$, where $\mathfrak{R}_{i,t+1}^e$ is the real excess return on the ith portfolio). Thus taking unconditional expectations, we obtain $\mathbb{E}[\mathfrak{M}_{t+1}\mathfrak{R}_{t+1}^e] = 0$. Combining this expression with the definition of the covariance between $\mathfrak{M}_{t+1}$ and $\mathfrak{R}_{t+1}^e$ gives

$$\mathbb{E}[\mathfrak{R}_{t+1}^e] = -\frac{\mathbb{CV}(\mathfrak{R}_{t+1}^e, \mathfrak{M}_{t+1})}{\mathbb{E}[\mathfrak{M}_{t+1}]}. \tag{11.28}$$

Next, they approximate $\mathfrak{M}_{t+1}$ with a first-order expansion of the log MRS in (11.27) in Δc_{t+1}, d_{t+1}/c_{t+1}, d_t/c_t, and $r_{w,t+1}$ around the points where $\Delta c_{t+1} = \mu_c$, $\Delta d_{t+1} = \mu_d$, and $r_{t+1}^w = \mu_r$:

$$\frac{\mathfrak{M}_{t+1}}{\mathbb{E}[\mathfrak{M}_{t+1}]} \cong \xi \left[1 - b_c(\Delta c_{t+1} - \mu_c) - b_d(\Delta d_{t+1} - \mu_d) - b_r(r_{t+1}^w - \mu_r) \right], \tag{11.29}$$

where $\xi = \{\beta \exp[-\mu_c/\sigma + (1 - 1/\kappa)\mu_r]\}^\kappa$, $b_c = \kappa[1/\sigma + (1/\rho - 1/\sigma)\omega]$, $b_d = \kappa\omega(1/\sigma - 1/\rho)$, and $b_r = 1 - \kappa$. Substituting this expression in the right-hand side of (11.28) gives

$$\mathbb{E}[\mathfrak{R}_{t+1}^e] = \mathbb{CV}(\mathfrak{R}_{t+1}^e, \Delta c_{t+1})\xi b_c + \mathbb{CV}(\mathfrak{R}_{t+1}^e, \Delta d_{t+1})\xi b_d$$
$$+ \xi\mathbb{CV}(\mathfrak{R}_{t+1}^e, r_{t+1}^w)\xi b_r. \tag{11.30}$$

Thus, expected excess returns are (approximately) governed by the covariance of the return with nondurable consumption growth, Δc_{t+1}, durable consumption growth, Δd_{t+1}, and the return on the investor's wealth, r_{t+1}^w. In the case of power utility $\gamma = 1/\sigma$, so $b_r = 0$, making the return on the investor's wealth irrelevant. If, in addition, the investor derives no utility from durables so that $\omega = 0$, the equation simplifies to $\mathbb{E}[\mathfrak{R}_{t+1}^e] = \mathbb{CV}(\mathfrak{R}_{t+1}^e, \Delta c_{t+1})\xi/\sigma$. This special case corresponds to the model in Mark (1985).

To examine the empirical implications of (11.30) for their eight portfolio returns, LV use a two-step estimation procedure first proposed by Fama and MacBeth (1973). For this purpose, they rewrite (11.30) as

$$\mathbb{E}[\mathfrak{R}_{t+1}^e] = \mathbb{CV}(\mathfrak{R}_{t+1}^e, \mathfrak{F}_{t+1}')\xi b = \underbrace{\mathbb{CV}(\mathfrak{R}_{t+1}^e, \mathfrak{F}_{t+1}')\mathbb{V}(\mathfrak{F}_{t+1})^{-1}}_{\beta} \underbrace{\mathbb{V}(\mathfrak{F}_{t+1})\xi b}_{\lambda},$$

where $\mathfrak{F}'_{t+1} = [\Delta c_{t+1},\ \Delta d_{t+1},\ r^w_{t+1}]$ and $b' = [b_c,\ b_d,\ b_r]$. The β matrix identifies the factor betas for each of the excess returns in $\mathfrak{R}^e_{t+1}$. The rows of this matrix are estimated in the first step by a time series regression of each portfolio excess return on the vector of risk factors:

$$\mathfrak{R}^e_{i,t+1} = a_i + \mathfrak{F}'_{t+1}\beta_i + \epsilon_{i,t}, \quad t = 1, \ldots, T, \ \text{for } i = 1, \ldots, 8. \quad (11.31)$$

The second step is to estimate the three factor risk premia in the 3×1 vector $\lambda = [\lambda_c,\ \lambda_d,\ \lambda_r]'$. This is done by estimating a cross-sectional regression of the average portfolio returns on a constant and the estimated betas:

$$\overline{\mathfrak{R}}^e_i = \beta_o + \tilde{\beta}_i\lambda + \zeta_i, \quad i = 1, \ldots, 8, \quad (11.32)$$

where $\overline{\mathfrak{R}}^e_i = \frac{1}{T}\sum_{t=1}^{T}\mathfrak{R}^e_{i,t}$ and $\tilde{\beta}_i$ is the estimated value of β_i from the first step. If the model is correct, both the constant, β_o, and the price errors for each portfolio return, ζ_i, should be close to zero.

LV estimate the model in annual data from 1953 to 2002 with currency returns from 81 countries (the returns on individual currencies are added as data become available). The macro risk factors are: (1) U.S. real per capita consumption of nondurables and services excluding housing, clothing, and shoes, (2) the flow of consumption services from durables per capita, and (3) the value-weighted real return on the U.S. stock market. The betas are estimated by OLS applied equation by equation to (11.31). These first-stage estimates are then used to compute the OLS estimates of the factor risk premia, λ, from (11.32).

The results from LV's estimation procedure are shown in Figure 11.3. The points show the scatter plot of the average excess returns, $\overline{\mathfrak{R}}^e_i$, against the predicted value

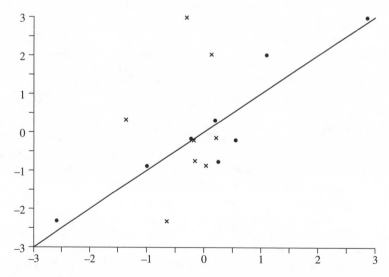

FIGURE 11.3 Portfolio excess returns. The dots show the scatter plot of average excess returns, $\mathfrak{R}^e_i$ (vertical axis), versus predicted excess returns from estimates of (11.32) (horizontal axis). The crosses plot $\mathfrak{R}^e_i$ versus the predicted excess returns from estimates of (11.32) without the constant. All data used to produce these estimates is from Lustig and Verdelhan (2007).

from the estimates of (11.32). As the figure shows, five of the returns lie very close to the 45° line, whereas the other three average returns are within 1 percent of their predicted values. This visual evidence appears to indicate that the model does a remarkably good job of explaining the pattern of average returns. Indeed, LV argue that the model accounts for 87 percent of the cross-sectional variation in returns because the R^2 statistic from estimating (11.32) is 0.87.

A closer inspection of LV's results reveals a more ambiguous picture. Burnside (2007) points to two critical features. First, the model's ability to account for the cross-sectional variation in average returns depends on how the factor risk premia are estimated in the second-step regression. LV included a constant in the regression as shown in (11.32), even though under the null hypothesis of a correctly specified model it should equal zero. Since the inclusion of the constant should not materially affect the predicted values for $\overline{\mathfrak{R}}_i^e$ if the model is indeed correct, one simple robustness test is to re-estimate (11.32) without the constant and compare the results. Figure 11.3 allows us to make this comparison. The crosses show the scatter plot of $\overline{\mathfrak{R}}_i^e$ versus the predicted values Burnside estimates from (11.32) without a constant. Clearly, this scatter plot lies further from the 45° line than the dots reported by LV. In fact the R^2 statistic indicates that the model now accounts for just 34 percent of the cross-sectional variation in $\overline{\mathfrak{R}}_i^e$.

Burnside's second observation concerns statistical inference. The two-step estimation procedure described earlier is intuitive but complicates inference because the betas used in the second step are themselves estimates. As a consequence, conventional methods for computing standard errors for the risk premia in the second step are inappropriate. One way around this problem is to combine both steps into a GMM procedure using the following moments:

$$\mathbb{E}[\mathfrak{R}_{i,t+1}^e - a_i - \beta_i'\mathfrak{F}_t] = 0, \quad i = 1, \ldots, 8,$$

$$\mathbb{E}[\left(\mathfrak{R}_{i,t+1}^e - a_i - \beta_i'\mathfrak{F}_t\right)\mathfrak{F}_t'] = 0, \quad i = 1, \ldots, 8,$$

$$\mathbb{E}[\mathfrak{R}_{i,t}^e - \beta_i'\lambda] = 0, \quad i = 1, \ldots, 8.$$

When Burnside uses these moment conditions to estimate the model by GMM, he finds that the factor betas are so imprecisely estimated that one cannot reject the null that the betas for each portfolio are jointly zero at conventional significance levels. He also finds that none of the factor risk premia in λ are statistically significant at the 5 percent level. These estimates indicate that the joint behavior of returns and the risk factors contain almost no information about the cross-sectional pattern of expected returns. In other words, when the factor betas are very imprecisely estimated, it is impossible to tell whether cross-sectional differences in portfolio returns are systematically related to the true betas as the model implies, or are unrelated to the true betas (which may be zero).

Burnside's findings are quite consistent with other results in the literature. Recall that the large estimates of the risk-aversion parameter found by Mark (1985) and others are a reflection of the small sample covariance between excess currency returns and consumption growth, which is one of the risk factors in the LV model. Furthermore, a comprehensive recent study by Burnside et al. (2006) finds that the excess returns from carry-trade strategies examined in Section 11.1.2 have no significant covariance with a wide array of risk factors. Taken together, these results are not encouraging. At their heart the models require: (1) that any expected excess currency return that differs from zero should covary with the SDF, and (2) that differences between expected returns are proportional to the difference in the covariance between returns and the SDF. In the absence of any evidence showing that excess currency returns are significantly correlated with any macro risk factors, we have yet to satisfy the first condition for specifications of the SDF based on macro variables.

11.2.4 Peso Problem Models

An implicit assumption underlying the foregoing discussion is that the moments of returns and the risk factors computed from available data samples are accurate estimates of the population moments implied by the model. If market participants have rational expectations, this assumption holds true in the limit as the span of data becomes infinite under very weak conditions. In finite data samples, however, there is plenty of scope for sample moments to significantly differ from their population counterparts, even when market participants have rational expectations. Peso problem models are designed to account for the behavior of excess currency returns by focusing on the difference between sample and population moments that can arise in finite data samples.

Peso problem models consider the behavior of asset prices in an unstable economic environment. As we have seen, any asset-pricing model based on the absence of arbitrage opportunities incorporates the expectations concerning future returns and the SDF of market participants. When these participants act in a stable economic environment, their rational expectations are based on a subjective probability distribution for future shocks hitting the economy that coincides with the distribution generating past shocks. In an unstable environment, by contrast, participants' expectations may be based on a subjective probability distribution that differs from the distribution generating past shocks if they rationally anticipate discrete shifts in the distribution of future shocks. A "peso problem" refers to the behavior of asset prices in this situation.

The potential for a peso problem to account for the behavior of excess currency returns is easily illustrated. As usual, we start with the no-arbitrage condition, $\mathbb{E}_t[\mathcal{M}_{t+1}\mathcal{R}_{t+1}^e] = 0$, for a particular excess return, $\mathcal{R}_{t+1}^e$, and SDF, $\mathcal{M}_{t+1}$, where $\mathbb{E}_t[.]$ denotes expectations conditioned on participants' information, Ω_t. For concreteness, we assume that $\mathcal{N}_{t+1} \equiv \mathcal{M}_{t+1}\mathcal{R}_{t+1}^e$ can switch between two time series processes, governed by a discrete-value variable $\mathcal{Z} = \{0, 1\}$. Let $\mathcal{N}_{t+1}(z)$ denote the realized value for $\mathcal{N}_{t+1}$ from regime $z \in \mathcal{Z}$. Without loss of generality, we can decompose realizations of $\mathcal{N}_{t+1}$ into the conditional expected value for $\mathcal{N}_{t+1}$ in regime z, $\mathbb{E}_t[\mathcal{N}_{t+1}(z)]$, and a residual, η_{t+1},

$$\mathcal{N}_{t+1} = \mathbb{E}_t[\mathcal{N}_{t+1}(0)] - \mathbb{E}_t[\nabla\mathcal{N}_{t+1}]\mathcal{Z}_{t+1} + \eta_{t+1}, \tag{11.33}$$

where $\mathbb{E}_t[\nabla\mathcal{N}_{t+1}] \equiv \mathbb{E}_t[\mathcal{N}_{t+1}(0)] - \mathbb{E}_t[\mathcal{N}_{t+1}(1)] \neq 0$.

Although the decomposition in (11.33) holds as an identity, the properties of the residuals, η_{t+1}, depend on how market participants form their expectations. When participants hold rational expectations, their forecasts, $\mathbb{E}_t[\mathcal{N}_{t+1}(z)]$, coincide with the mathematical expectation of $\mathcal{N}_{t+1}$ conditioned on Ω_t. Taking expectations on both sides of (11.33) conditioned on Ω_t for $\mathcal{Z}_{t+1} = \{0, 1\}$ implies that $\mathbb{E}_t[\eta_{t+1}] = 0$.

Thus, the residual, η_{t+1}, inherits the conventional properties of rational expectations forecast errors. It represents the forecast error participants would make if the period-$t + 1$ regime is known.

When market participants are unaware of the period-$t + 1$ regime, their forecast errors differ from the *within-regime* errors, η_{t+1}. To see this, we first identify participants' forecasts by taking conditional expectations on both sides of (11.33). Using the fact that $\mathbb{E}_t[\eta_{t+1}] = 0$, we find that

$$\mathbb{E}_t[\mathcal{N}_{t+1}] = \mathbb{E}_t[\mathcal{N}_{t+1}(0)] - \mathbb{E}_t[\nabla\mathcal{N}_{t+1}]\mathbb{E}_t[\mathcal{Z}_{t+1}]. \tag{11.34}$$

Subtracting (11.34) from (11.33) gives

$$\mathcal{N}_{t+1} - \mathbb{E}_t[\mathcal{N}_{t+1}] = \eta_{t+1} - \mathbb{E}_t[\nabla\mathcal{N}_{t+1}](\mathcal{Z}_{t+1} - \mathbb{E}_t[\mathcal{Z}_{t+1}]). \tag{11.35}$$

Equation 11.35 shows how participants' forecast errors are related to the within-regime errors. Clearly, when the future regime is known, $\mathcal{Z}_{t+1} = \mathbb{E}_t[\mathcal{Z}_{t+1}]$, so the second term vanishes. In this case there is no peso problem and participants' forecast errors inherit the conventional rational expectations properties of the within-regime errors. When the future regime is unknown, the second term in (11.35) contributes to participants' forecast errors. It is under these circumstances that a peso problem can produce significant differences between sample and population moments used to evaluate asset-pricing models.

To illustrate, suppose we compute the sample average of a sequence of values for $\mathcal{N}_{t+1}$ using a time series of excess returns, $\mathcal{R}_{t+1}^e$, and a particular specification for the SDF, $\mathcal{M}_{t+1}$. Let us further assume that this specification for the SDF is correct, in the sense that $\mathbb{E}_t[\mathcal{N}_{t+1}] = 0$. Under these circumstances, $\mathcal{N}_{t+1} = \mathbb{E}_t[\mathcal{N}_{t+1}] + \mathcal{N}_{t+1} - \mathbb{E}_t[\mathcal{N}_{t+1}] = \mathcal{N}_{t+1} - \mathbb{E}_t[\mathcal{N}_{t+1}]$, so we can use (11.35) to write the sample average of $\mathcal{N}_{t+1}$ as

$$\frac{1}{T}\sum_{t=0}^{T-1}\mathcal{N}_{t+1} = \frac{1}{T}\sum_{t=0}^{T-1}\eta_{t+1} - \frac{1}{T}\sum_{t=0}^{T-1}\mathbb{E}_t[\nabla\mathcal{N}_{t+1}](\mathcal{Z}_{t+1} - \mathbb{E}_t[\mathcal{Z}_{t+1}]). \tag{11.36}$$

Recall that $\mathbb{E}_t[\eta_{t+1}] = 0$ when market participants have rational expectations. The first term on the right-hand side should therefore be close to zero for reasonable sample sizes, T. The second term depends on the incidence of each regime within the sample. In the extreme case where only regime 0 occurs, the second term becomes $\frac{1}{T}\sum_{t=0}^{T-1}\mathbb{E}_t[\nabla\mathcal{N}_{t+1}]\mathbb{E}_t[\mathcal{Z}_{t+1}]$. This term will differ from zero so long as market participants believe that a change to regime 1 is possible, that is, when $\Pr\left(\mathcal{Z}_{t+1} = 1|\Omega_t\right) = \mathbb{E}_t[\mathcal{Z}_{t+1}] > 0$ for $t = 1, \ldots, T$. In this case, $\frac{1}{T}\sum_{t=0}^{T-1}\mathcal{N}_{t+1}$ will differ significantly from zero even though the specified SDF correctly accounts for excess returns (i.e., $\mathbb{E}_t[\mathcal{N}_{t+1}] = 0$). More generally, the second term on the right of (11.36) will be nonzero if the frequency of regime changes in the sample is unrepresentative of the underlying distribution of regime changes upon which participants base their forecasts. Under these circumstances, the presence of a peso problem would lead a researcher to incorrectly reject the specification for the SDF because the sample average, $\frac{1}{T}\sum\mathcal{N}_{t+1}$, is "too far" from zero.

First- and Second-Generation Models

Peso problem models fall into two categories. First-generation models, developed in the 1990s, focused on the implications of instability in returns. These models ignore the possibility that a change in regime could affect the SDF. Second-generation models, the subject of recent research, consider the implications of peso problems arising from instability in returns *and* the SDF.

To identify the asset-pricing implications of these models, we return to equation (11.34). In the absence of arbitrage, $\mathbb{E}_t[\mathcal{N}_{t+1}] = 0$, so the equation implies that $\mathbb{E}_t[\mathcal{N}_{t+1}(0)] = \mathbb{E}_t[\nabla \mathcal{N}_{t+1}]\mathbb{E}_t[\mathcal{Z}_{t+1}]$. Combining this expression with the identity $\mathcal{N}_{t+1}(z) = \mathcal{M}_{t+1}(z)\mathcal{R}_{t+1}^e(z)$ gives

$$\mathbb{E}_t[\mathcal{R}_{t+1}^e(0)] = \mathcal{RP}_t(0) + \mathbb{E}_t[\nabla \mathcal{N}_{t+1}]\frac{\mathbb{E}_t[\mathcal{Z}_{t+1}]}{\mathbb{E}_t[\mathcal{M}_{t+1}(0)]}, \tag{11.37}$$

where

$$\mathcal{RP}_t(z) = -\mathbb{CV}_t(\mathcal{M}_{t+1}(z), \mathcal{R}_{t+1}^e(z))/\mathbb{E}_t[\mathcal{M}_{t+1}(z)].$$

Equation 11.37 identifies the expected excess return in regime 0 at $t + 1$, conditioned on period-t information. If market participants do not expect a change in regime, then $\mathbb{E}_t[\mathcal{Z}_{t+1}] = \Pr(\mathcal{Z}_{t+1} = 1|\Omega_t) = 0$, so the second term on the right-hand side vanishes. Under these circumstances, expected excess returns differ from zero according to the within-regime risk premium, $\mathcal{RP}_t(0)$, which depends on the covariance between returns and the SDF, as is the case in standard no-arbitrage models.

Peso problems contribute to expected excess returns through the second term on the right of (11.37). In first-generation models, realizations of the SDF are assumed to be the same across regimes and uncorrelated with returns so that $\mathbb{E}_t[\mathcal{N}_{t+1}(z)] = \mathbb{E}_t[\mathcal{M}_{t+1}]\mathbb{E}_t[\mathcal{R}_{t+1}^e(z)]$ for $z = \{0, 1\}$. With this restriction and $\mathcal{RP}_t(0) = 0$, (11.37) becomes

$$\mathbb{E}_t[\mathcal{R}_{t+1}^e(0)] = \mathbb{E}_t[\nabla \mathcal{N}_{t+1}]\frac{\mathbb{E}_t[\mathcal{Z}_{t+1}]}{\mathbb{E}_t[\mathcal{M}_{t+1}(0)]} = -\mathbb{E}_t[\mathcal{R}_{t+1}^e(1)]\frac{\Pr(\mathcal{Z}_{t+1} = 1|\Omega_t)}{\Pr(\mathcal{Z}_{t+1} = 0|\Omega_t)}.$$

$$\tag{11.38}$$

Here expected excess returns in regime 0 can differ from zero even though they are uncorrelated with the SDF. Since $\mathcal{M}_{t+1}$ must be nonnegative and the no-arbitrage condition implies that $\mathbb{E}_t[\mathcal{M}_{t+1}]\mathbb{E}_t[\mathcal{R}_{t+1}^e] = 0$, expected excess returns must be zero. Thus, if market participants believe that a switch to regime 1 is possible (i.e., $\mathbb{E}_t[\mathcal{Z}_{t+1}] > 0$) and that excess returns in that regime will be negative, $\mathbb{E}_t[\mathcal{R}_{t+1}^e(1)] < 0$, the expected return in regime 0 must be positive to ensure that $\mathbb{E}_t[\mathcal{R}_{t+1}^e] = 0$. In short, expected excess returns in regime 0 must be positive to compensate for the possibility that there will be a switch to a regime in which expected excess returns are negative. Furthermore, the extent of this compensation is increasing in both $-\mathbb{E}_t[\mathcal{R}_{t+1}^e(1)]$ and the relative probability of a switch, $\Pr(\mathcal{Z}_{t+1} = 1|\Omega_t)/\Pr(\mathcal{Z}_{t+1} = 0|\Omega_t)$.

Second-generation models recognize that a change in regime could affect both excess returns and the SDF. In this case,

$$\mathbb{E}_t[\nabla \mathcal{N}_{t+1}] = \mathbb{E}_t[\mathcal{R}_{t+1}^e(0)]\mathbb{E}_t[\mathcal{M}_{t+1}(0)] + \mathbb{CV}_t(\mathcal{M}_{t+1}(0), \mathcal{R}_{t+1}^e(0))$$

$$- \mathbb{E}_t[\mathcal{M}_{t+1}(1)\mathcal{R}_{t+1}^e(1)].$$

Substituting this expression in (11.37) and simplifying gives

$$\mathbb{E}_t[\mathcal{R}^e_{t+1}(0)] = \mathcal{RP}_t(0)$$

$$- \left(\mathbb{E}_t[\mathcal{R}^e_{t+1}(1)] - \mathcal{RP}_t(1)\right) \frac{\mathbb{E}_t[\mathcal{M}_{t+1}(1)]}{\mathbb{E}_t[\mathcal{M}_{t+1}(0)]} \frac{\Pr\left(\mathcal{Z}_{t+1} = 1 | \Omega_t\right)}{\Pr\left(\mathcal{Z}_{t+1} = 0 | \Omega_t\right)}. \quad (11.39)$$

In contrast to (11.38), expected excess returns in regime 0 now depend on the within-regime risk premium, $\mathcal{RP}_t(0)$, and the risk-adjusted expected excess return in regime 1. Here market participants must be compensated for the *excess risk* associated with a switch to regime 1. Suppose, for example, that $\mathbb{E}_t[\mathcal{R}^e_{t+1}(1)] < \mathcal{RP}_t(1)$. In this case the expected excess return in regime 1 is insufficient to counterbalance the within-regime risk, $\mathcal{RP}_t(1)$, so expected excess returns in regime 0 must be greater than $\mathcal{RP}_t(0)$ to compensate. The degree of compensation not only depends on the likelihood that a regime switch will take place [i.e., $\Pr(\mathcal{Z}_{t+1} = 1 | \Omega_t) / \Pr(\mathcal{Z}_{t+1} = 0 | \Omega_t)$], but also on the value of a dollar in period $t + 1$. In particular, the compensation will have to be greater when $\mathbb{E}_t[\mathcal{M}^e_{t+1}(1)] > \mathbb{E}_t[\mathcal{M}_{t+1}(0)]$ because the value of \$1 in regime 1 is higher than in regime 0.

Empirical Evidence from First-Generation Models

Empirical evidence on the potential importance of peso problems for the behavior of foreign currency excess returns comes from two primary sources. First, there is a large literature that studies the behavior of exchange-rate expectations identified from survey data. The second source comes from studies that use switching models to investigate how peso problems affect conventional inference concerning the behavior of spot and forward rates.

Fama's (1984) interpretation of the UIP regression results, discussed in Section 11.2.2, rests on the assumption that market participants' errors in forecasting future spot rates are uncorrelated with the current forward premium. We can test this orthogonality assumption directly if we are willing to proxy participants' forecasts from survey data. In particular, let $s^e_{t,t+k}$ denote the proxy of participants' expectations conditioned on period-t information concerning the log spot rate in period $t + k$, computed from a survey conducted in period t. Further, let $fp_{t,k} = \ln(\mathcal{F}_{t,k}/S_t)$ denote the log forward premium for the k-period forward rate $\mathcal{F}_{t,k}$. We can now examine the orthogonality assumption by estimating the regression

$$s_{t+k} - s^e_{t,t+k} = \phi_0 + \phi_1 fp_{t,k} + \xi_{t+k} \quad (11.40)$$

and testing the statistical significance of the slope coefficient, ϕ_1. Clearly, under the null hypothesis that the survey forecast errors, $s_{t+k} - s^e_{t,t+k}$, are orthogonal to the forward premium, ϕ_1 should equal zero.

A large number of studies have estimated versions of regression (11.40) with different currencies, across different forecasting horizons, k, using different surveys (for a survey, see Jongen et al. 2008). The consensus to emerge from this research is that the estimates of ϕ_1 are negative and statistically significant, particularly at longer forecasting horizons.

These results do not constitute direct evidence as to the presence of peso problems. Nevertheless, the negative estimates of ϕ_1 are consistent with the idea that when the forward premium is high market participants put some weight on the possibility that a change in regime would lead to a greater depreciation in the spot rate than occurred ex post in the sample. Moreover, they provide a fresh perspective on the discussion of the Forward Premium Puzzle in Section 11.2.2.

By definition, the estimated slope from the UIP regression (11.12) is

$$\tilde{\beta}_1 = 1 + \frac{\widetilde{\mathbb{CV}}(\delta_t, fp_t)}{\widetilde{\mathbb{V}}(fp_t)} + \frac{\widetilde{\mathbb{CV}}(s_{t+1} - \mathbb{E}_t s_{t+1}, fp_t)}{\widetilde{\mathbb{V}}(fp_t)},$$

where tildes denote sample estimates. If measurement errors in the survey measures of expectations are uncorrelated with the forward premium, the estimated slope coefficient from regression (11.40) when $k = 1$ is given by the last term on the right-hand side. In this case,

$$\tilde{\beta}_1 = 1 + \phi_1 + \widetilde{\mathbb{CV}}(\delta_t, fp_t)/\widetilde{\mathbb{V}}(fp_t).$$

Thus, the negative estimates of ϕ_1 could contribute to the UIP regression estimates of β_1 reported in Table 11.1. Indeed, Froot and Frankel (1989) as well as other studies are unable to reject the null that $\beta_1 = 1 + \phi_1$ for some currencies and sample periods.

Evans and Lewis (1995) provide a more direct examination of how peso problems may contribute to the Forward Premium Puzzle. Using estimates of a switching model for the spot rate, they ran Monte Carlo experiments to look for the small sample effects of peso problems on $\tilde{\beta}_1$. In these experiments, the forward rate is driven by market participants' expectations of future spot rates (which incorporate the effects of potential switches in the spot rate process) and the risk premia:

$$\delta_t = \delta_0 + \delta_1 fp_t + v_t,$$

where v_t is an i.i.d. error. In each experiment, a sample of spot and forward rates was generated to compute the estimate of δ_1 implied by the UIP regression (11.12). Under rational expectations, (11.14) implies that the population value for δ_1 should be $\beta_1 - 1$, so the small sample estimate of δ_1 was computed to be $\tilde{\delta}_1 = \hat{\beta}_1 - 1$.

Table 11.3 reproduces the results of these Monte Carlo experiments. Columns (i) and (ii) report the OLS estimate of β_1 and the p-value for the null that $\beta_1 = 1$ based on a Wald test derived from the asymptotic distribution of the OLS estimates. The estimates are computed in monthly and quarterly data for the DM/USD, GBP/USD, and JPY/USD markets between 1975 and 1989. Column (iii) reports the mean value of $\hat{\delta}_1 - \delta_1$. This is negative for all three currencies indicating that the estimate of the UIP β_1 coefficient may indeed be biased downward by the presence of peso problems. Note, however, that the mean bias is insufficient to completely account for the negative estimates of β_1. Column (iv) reports the means and standard deviation of $\hat{\delta}_1/\delta_1$. This ratio provides a measure of how peso problems may contribute to the apparent variability of the risk premia. For all currencies, the mean value of $\hat{\delta}_1/\delta_1$ implies that the standard deviation of the measured risk premium (i.e., the risk premium implied by the estimates of the UIP regression under rational expectations) exceeds the true risk premium from the model. In the case of the GBP/USD and DM/USD markets, the standard deviations are about 20 percent higher.

It is important to keep these findings in perspective. There is no *direct* evidence from either Monte Carlo experiments or the behavior of survey proxies that partic-

TABLE 11.3
Peso Problems and the Forward Premium Puzzle

Currency	(i) $\tilde{\beta}_1$	(ii) $H_0 : \beta_1 = 1$	(iii) Bias	(iv) Ratio
Monthly data				
GBP/USD	−2.266	<0.001	−0.726	1.222
			(3.438)	(1.053)
DM/USD	−3.502	0.001	−1.068	1.237
			(3.253)	(0.722)
JPY/USD	−2.022	<0.001	−0.107	1.035
			(0.607)	(0.201)
Quarterly data				
GBP/USD	−2.347	0.001	−0.724	1.216
			(2.691)	(0.804)
DM/USD	3.448	0.004	−0.720	1.162
			(2.720)	(0.615)
JPY/USD	−2.955	<0.001	−0.124	1.031
			(0.700)	(0.177)

Source: Evans and Lewis (1995).

ipants' actual spot rate expectations were rationally influenced by the presence of a peso problem during the sample periods examined. At best the Monte Carlo studies show the potential for peso problems to affect inferences about the behavior of the risk premium from UIP regressions estimated in short data samples. They do not establish that market participants' expectations took a particular form because a peso problem was present. Similarly, the survey proxies for participants' expectations have the characteristics we would expect to see in rational forecasts when a peso problem is present, but it is also possible that they simply represent suboptimal forecasts. In sum, therefore, there is insufficient information in the time series of spot and forward rates alone to accurately identify the contribution of peso problems to the Forward Premium Puzzle.

Empirical Evidence from Second-Generation Models

Second-generation peso problem models ameliorate this identification problem by incorporating the information in options prices. The key idea is that the risks associated with a switch to a peso regime can be hedged by the addition of options to a currency portfolio. As a result, if market participants are truly concerned about a regime switch, the expected returns on this hedged portfolio should differ from those of an unhedged portfolio in the nonpeso regime. Analyzing the difference between the hedged and unhedged returns in the nonpeso regimes should therefore reveal information about the importance of peso problems for the behavior of unhedged excess currency returns.

Burnside, Eichenbaum, Kleshchelski, and Rebelo (2006) (hereafter BEKR) provide a particularly clear example of this approach. They begin with the unconditional version of (11.39):[5]

$$\mathbb{E}[\mathcal{R}_{t+1}^e(0)] = \mathcal{RP}(0) - \left(\mathbb{E}[\mathcal{R}_{t+1}^e(1)] - \mathcal{RP}(1)\right)\frac{\mathbb{E}[\mathcal{M}_{t+1}(1)]}{\mathbb{E}[\mathcal{M}_{t+1}(0)]}\frac{\wp}{1-\wp}, \quad (11.41)$$

where $\wp = \Pr(\mathcal{Z}_{t+1} = 1)$. Equation 11.41 identifies the unconditional expected excess return in regime 0, the nonpeso regime we observe in the data sample. Regime 1 is therefore considered the peso regime we do not observe. BEKR make several further simplifications to this equation. First, they assume that excess returns are uncorrelated with the SDF in regime 0, so that the within-regime risk premium, $\mathcal{RP}(0)$, equals zero. This assumption is consistent with the empirical evidence on Euler equation models discussed in Section 11.2.3. Second, they assume that the SDF in the peso regime takes on a single value, $\mathcal{M}(1)$. With these assumptions, equation (11.41) simplifies to

$$\mathbb{E}[\mathcal{R}_{t+1}^e(0)] = -\mathbb{E}[\mathcal{R}_{t+1}^e(1)]\frac{\mathcal{M}(1)}{\mathbb{E}[\mathcal{M}_{t+1}(0)]}\frac{\wp}{1-\wp}. \quad (11.42)$$

Equation (11.42) shows that the expected excess returns in the nonpeso regime can be large and positive under two sets of circumstances. First, consider the case where $\mathcal{M}(1)/\mathbb{E}[\mathcal{M}_{t+1}(0)]$ is close to one. Under these circumstances, a large positive value for $\mathbb{E}[\mathcal{R}_{t+1}^e(0)]$ reflects market participants' expectations that returns will be very negative in the peso regime because the value of the dollar next period is roughly the same across regimes. Second, if $\mathcal{M}(1)/\mathbb{E}[\mathcal{M}_{t+1}(0)]$ is much larger than one, a large positive value for $\mathbb{E}[\mathcal{R}_{t+1}^e(0)]$ need only reflect participants' anticipation of a small negative return in the peso state. Here the large values for $\mathbb{E}[\mathcal{R}_{t+1}^e(0)]$ are required to compensate for the possibility that there will be a switch to the peso regime, where the value of a dollar is much higher.

BEKR use (11.42) to compare the expected returns on two currency portfolios. The first is the return on an equally weighted portfolio of carry-trade strategies for individual currencies described in Section 11.1.2. The second is the return on an equally weighted portfolio of hedged carry-trade strategies. These strategies combine a forward position with the purchase of an option that provides insurance against possible losses in the peso regime.

To identify the payoff on the hedged carry-trade strategies, we have to describe the options contracts. Let $\mathcal{O}_t^c$ denote the dollar price in period t of a call option with a strike price of $\mathcal{K}_t$ dollars per unit of foreign currency that expires in period $t + 1$. The owner of this option contract has the right, but not the obligation, to buy foreign currency at price $\mathcal{K}_t$ in period $t + 1$.[6] In contrast, the owner of a put option, with price $\mathcal{O}_t^p$, has the right, but not the obligation, to sell foreign currency at the strike price $\mathcal{K}_t$. If R_t denotes the gross dollar interest rate, the dollar payoffs on a call and put option,

---

5. This equation is easily derived by applying the unconditional expectations operator to (11.33) and the no-arbitrage condition, $\mathbb{E}_t[\mathcal{M}_{t+1}\mathcal{R}_{t+1}^e] = 0$. For details, see the appendix.

6. For simplicity, we focus on options with one period to maturity, so there is no opportunity to exercise early.

net of option prices, are, respectively,

$$\mathcal{X}^{\text{C}}_{t+1} = \max(0, S_{t+1} - \mathcal{K}_t) - \mathcal{O}^{\text{C}}_t R_t \quad \text{and} \quad \mathcal{X}^{\text{P}}_{t+1} = \max(0, \mathcal{K}_t - S_{t+1}) - \mathcal{O}^{\text{P}}_t R_t.$$

It is easy to see how the purchase of an option can provide insurance against a forward position. Consider a situation where an investor initiates a carry-trade strategy that sells pounds one period forward at the dollar price $\mathcal{F}_t$.[7] If there is a large depreciation of the dollar against the pound, the investor will realize a significant loss because in order to fulfill the contract he must purchase pounds in the spot market at a price S_{t+1} well above $\mathcal{F}_t$. However, if the investor also purchased a call option on the pound in period t with a strike price $\mathcal{K}_t$, he can fulfill the forward contract with pounds costing $\mathcal{K}_t$ when $S_{t+1} > \mathcal{K}_t$. The minimum payoff to the hedged carry-trade strategy in this case is

$$\mathcal{X}^{\text{O}}_t = (\mathcal{F}_t - S_{t+1}) + (S_{t+1} - \mathcal{K}_t) - \mathcal{O}^{\text{C}}_t R_t = \mathcal{F}_t - \mathcal{K}_t - \mathcal{O}^{\text{C}}_t R_t. \quad (11.43)$$

Similarly, an investor can insure himself against a forward purchase of pounds, at price $\mathcal{F}_t$, by purchasing a put option at price $\mathcal{O}^{\text{P}}_t$ with a strike of $\mathcal{K}_t$. In this case the option provides insurance against an appreciation of the dollar that pushes S_{t+1} well below $\mathcal{F}_t$ because the investor can fulfill the forward contract by selling pounds at $\mathcal{K}_t$ when $S_{t+1} < \mathcal{K}_t$. The minimum payoff to this hedged strategy is

$$\mathcal{X}^{\text{O}}_t = (S_{t+1} - \mathcal{F}_t) + (\mathcal{K}_t - S_{t+1}) - \mathcal{O}^{\text{P}}_t R_t = \mathcal{K}_t - \mathcal{F}_t - \mathcal{O}^{\text{P}}_t R_t. \quad (11.44)$$

BEKR define the hedged carry-trade strategy as selling a_t pounds forward plus the purchase of an option. In particular, the strategy requires that

$$a_t = \begin{cases} 1/\mathcal{F}_t \text{ and buy } 1/\mathcal{F}_t \text{ call options on the pound} & \text{if } \mathcal{F}_t \geq S_t \\ -1/\mathcal{F}_t \text{ and buy } 1/\mathcal{F}_t \text{ put options on the pound} & \text{if } \mathcal{F}_t < S_t \end{cases}.$$

The dollar payoff on this strategy is

$$\mathcal{X}^{\text{H}}_{t+1} = \begin{cases} \mathcal{X}^{\text{F}}_{t+1} + \mathcal{X}^{\text{C}}_{t+1}/\mathcal{F}_t & \text{if } \mathcal{F}_t \geq S_t \\ \mathcal{X}^{\text{F}}_{t+1} + \mathcal{X}^{\text{P}}_{t+1}/\mathcal{F}_t & \text{if } \mathcal{F}_t < S_t \end{cases},$$

where $\mathcal{X}^{\text{F}}_{t+1} = a_t(\mathcal{F}_t - S_{t+1})$ is the payoff on the unhedged carry-trade strategy described in Section 11.1.2.

We can also write the payoffs according to whether the option is in or out of the money in period $t + 1$. That is to say, according to whether or not the investor exercises the option. For this purpose it is useful to simplify (11.43) and (11.44) using the no-arbitrage condition that links the prices of put and call options with the same strike price. Consider the payoff from buying a put and selling a call on the pound with the same strike price of $\mathcal{K}_t$:

$$\mathcal{X}^{\text{C-P}}_{t+1} = \max(0, S_{t+1} - \mathcal{K}_t) - \max(0, \mathcal{K}_t - S_{t+1}) = S_{t+1} - \mathcal{K}_t.$$

---

7. For simplicity, we ignore the difference between bid and ask prices in forward and spot contracts.

In the absence of arbitrage opportunities, the price of this payoff is $\mathcal{O}_t^c - \mathcal{O}_t^p = \mathbb{E}_t[\mathcal{M}_{t+1}\mathcal{X}_{t+1}^{c-p}]$. Combining this expression with the preceding equation gives

$$\mathcal{O}_t^c - \mathcal{O}_t^p = \mathbb{E}_t[\mathcal{M}_{t+1}(S_{t+1} - \mathcal{K}_t)] = \mathbb{E}_t[\mathcal{M}_{t+1}](\mathcal{F}_t - \mathcal{K}_t) = \frac{1}{R_t}(\mathcal{F}_t - \mathcal{K}_t).$$

The prices of put and call options are therefore linked by the put-call-forward parity condition:

$$\mathcal{O}_t^c = \mathcal{O}_t^p + \frac{1}{R_t}(\mathcal{F}_t - \mathcal{K}_t). \tag{11.45}$$

We can now find the values of $\mathcal{X}_{t+1}^c/\mathcal{F}_t$ and $\mathcal{X}_{t+1}^p/\mathcal{F}_t$ when the options are in the money by using (11.45) to substitute for $\mathcal{K}_t - \mathcal{F}_t$ in (11.43) and (11.44). This gives $\mathcal{X}_t^o = -\mathcal{O}_t^p R_t/\mathcal{F}_t$ when $\mathcal{F}_t \geq S_t$ and $\mathcal{X}_t^o = -\mathcal{O}_t^c R_t/\mathcal{F}_t$ when $\mathcal{F}_t < S_t$. The dollar payoff on the hedged carry-trade strategy can now be written as

$$\mathcal{X}_{t+1}^H = \begin{cases} \mathcal{X}_t^o & \text{if the option is in the money} \\ \mathcal{X}_{t+1}^F - \mathcal{O}_t^i R_t/\mathcal{F}_t & \text{if the option is out of the money} \end{cases},$$

where $\mathcal{O}_t^i$ denotes the cost of the put or call option purchased in period t.

BEKR compare the returns on equally weighted portfolios of hedged and unhedged carry-trade strategies for individual currencies versus the dollar, denoted by $\mathcal{R}_{t+1}^{CT}$ and $\mathcal{R}_{t+1}^{HCT}$, respectively. These portfolios are constructed by betting $1/n_t$ dollar in each individual carry trade, where n_t is the number of currencies in the sample at period t. For the case of the unhedged returns, (11.42) implies that the expected return in the nonpeso return is

$$\mathbb{E}[\mathcal{R}_{t+1}^{CT}(0)] = -\mathbb{E}[\mathcal{R}^{CT}(1)]\frac{\mathcal{M}(1)}{\mathbb{E}[\mathcal{M}_{t+1}(0)]}\frac{\wp}{1-\wp}, \tag{11.46}$$

where $\mathbb{E}[\mathcal{R}^{CT}(1)]$ denotes the expected carry-trade return in the peso regime. For the case of the hedged returns, BEKR assume that the options for all the individual currencies will be in the money in the peso regime. The expected return on the hedged carry trade in the nonpeso regime is therefore

$$\mathbb{E}[\mathcal{R}_{t+1}^{HCT}(0)] = -\mathbb{E}[\bar{\mathcal{X}}_t^o]\frac{\mathcal{M}(1)}{\mathbb{E}[\mathcal{M}_{t+1}(0)]}\frac{\wp}{1-\wp}, \tag{11.47}$$

where $\bar{\mathcal{X}}_t^o$ is the portfolio payoff when the hedged strategy for each individual currency has an option in the money. Note that $\bar{\mathcal{X}}_t^o$ can be computed from information available in the nonpeso sample because the in-the-money payoff, $\mathcal{X}_t^o$, depends on the period-t price of options, forward rates, and the risk-free rate.

We can now use these equations to find the carry-trade return in the peso regime. In particular, combining (11.46) with (11.47), we find that

$$\mathbb{E}[\mathcal{R}^{CT}(1)] = \mathbb{E}[\bar{\mathcal{X}}_t^o]\frac{\mathbb{E}[\mathcal{R}_{t+1}^{CT}(0)]}{\mathbb{E}[\mathcal{R}_{t+1}^{HCT}(0)]}.$$

BEKR use data from January 1996 to January 2008 to estimate the expectations on the right-hand side from the sample averages of $\bar{\mathcal{X}}_t^O$, $\mathcal{R}_{t+1}^{CT}$, and $\mathcal{R}_{t+1}^{HCT}$. This produces an estimate for $\mathbb{E}[\mathcal{R}^{CT}(1)]$ of -0.0154 on an annualized basis with a standard error of 0.0033. This estimate is only one standard error below the estimate for $\mathbb{E}[\mathcal{R}_{t+1}^{CT}(0)]$, the expected carry-trade return in the nonpeso regime. Fears about large negative returns in the peso regime do not appear to be the reason behind the high positive returns to the carry trade we observe in the nonpeso regime.

Of course, a peso problem may still account for the high carry-trade returns if the SDF in the peso regime is sufficiently large. To investigate this possibility, BEKR combine their estimates of $\mathbb{E}[\mathcal{R}^{CT}(1)]$ and $\mathbb{E}[\mathcal{R}_{t+1}^{CT}(0)]$ with equation (11.46) to compute

$$\frac{\mathcal{M}(1)}{\mathbb{E}[\mathcal{M}_{t+1}(0)]} = -\frac{(1-\wp)\mathbb{E}[\mathcal{R}_{t+1}^{CT}(0)]}{\wp\mathbb{E}[\mathcal{R}^{CT}(1)]}.$$

Clearly, this calculation requires a value for $\wp$, the unconditional probability that there will be a switch to the peso regime in any given month. When BEKR use a value that implies a slightly less than 2 percent probability of regime switch in any year, they obtain an estimate of $\mathcal{M}(1)/\mathbb{E}[\mathcal{M}_{t+1}(0)]$ equal to 121.7. This estimate implies that investors value \$1 next period in the peso regime by more than \$121 in the nonpeso regime. Consequently, the expected returns on the carry trade in the nonpeso regime must be large to compensate investors for the relatively small expected loss in the peso regime that they value very highly.

Are these estimates plausible? One way to address this question is to repeat the calculations for another pair of hedged and unhedged returns. BEKR do this with two equity strategies using the S&P 100 index. Remarkably, the estimate of $\mathcal{M}(1)/\mathbb{E}[\mathcal{M}_{t+1}(0)]$ from these returns (using the same value for $\wp$) is 107.8. Again, investors appear to be very concerned about the value of returns in the peso regime, rather than the returns per se.

Although the similarity between the estimates of $\mathcal{M}(1)/\mathbb{E}[\mathcal{M}_{t+1}(0)]$ from the returns on equity and carry-trade strategies is somewhat reassuring, their high values are economically implausible. To see this, consider the (gross) risk-free rate in the nonpeso regime: $R_t(0) = 1/\mathbb{E}_t[\mathcal{M}_{t+1}(0)]$. Taking unconditional expectations on both sides of this expression gives

$$\mathbb{E}[R_t(0)] = \mathbb{E}(1/\mathbb{E}_t[\mathcal{M}_{t+1}(0)]) > 1/\mathbb{E}(\mathbb{E}_t[\mathcal{M}_{t+1}(0)]) = 1/\mathbb{E}[\mathcal{M}_{t+1}(0)],$$

by iterative expectations and Jensen's inequality. In the peso regime, $R_t(1) = 1/\mathcal{M}(1)$, so combining these results we find that

$$R_t(1) < \mathbb{E}[R_t(0)]\frac{\mathbb{E}[\mathcal{M}_{t+1}(0)]}{\mathcal{M}(1)}.$$

Thus, the model estimates imply that the gross risk-free rate in the peso regime must be less than 1/100th of the expected rate in the nonpeso regime. Any reasonable estimate for $\mathbb{E}[R_t(0)]$ implies that the right-hand side of this expression is well below one, so the net risk-free rate in the peso regime must be negative!

11.3 Micro-Based Models

The micro-based model presented in Chapter 9 introduces a new perspective on the Forward Premium Puzzle. In that model the spot exchange rate is determined by the price dealers quote to achieve optimal sharing of foreign currency risk. As a consequence, foreign exchange returns include a risk premium that reflects the risk dealers face in their role as marketmakers rather than the risks faced by individual investors. This is an important change in perspective because the factors affecting the risk premium dealers implicitly include in their spot rate quotes are different from the factors determining the risk premium in the macro models discussed earlier. This section re-examines the micro-based model to see what new light it sheds on the Forward Premium Puzzle.

11.3.1 A Micro-Based Model of the Risk Premium

Model Structure

We study a simplified version of the model presented in Chapter 9. Recall that the economy comprises two countries populated by a continuum of risk-averse agents, indexed by $n \in [0, 1]$, and D risk-averse dealers, who act as marketmakers in the USD/EUR spot market.[8] At the beginning of week t all dealers quote a log USD/EUR spot price, s_t, equal to

$$s_t = \mathbb{E}_t^{\mathrm{D}} s_{t+1} + \hat{r}_t - r_t - \delta_t, \tag{11.48}$$

where $\mathbb{E}_t^{\mathrm{D}}$ denotes expectations conditioned on the common information available to all dealers at the start of week t, Ω_t^{D}. This information set includes r_t and $\hat{r}_t$, which are the 1-week dollar and euro interest rates set by the Federal Reserve (FED) and the European Central bank (ECB), respectively. The foreign exchange risk premium embedded in dealers' quotes, δ_t, is determined in what follows.

Dealers stand ready to fill the foreign currency orders of agents at their quoted price of s_t. These orders are determined by agents' demands for euros once they have observed s_t. In particular the demand for euros in week t by agent $n \in [0, 1]$ is given by

$$\alpha_t^n = \alpha_s \left(\mathbb{E}_t^n s_{t+1} - s_t + \hat{r}_t - r_t \right) + h_t^n,$$

where $\alpha_s > 0$ and $\mathbb{E}_t^n$ denotes expectations conditioned on the information available to agent n after the spot rate is quoted at the start of week t, Ω_t^n. The demand for euros depends on the log excess return expected by the agent and a hedging term, h_t^n, that represents the influence of all other factors. We assume that the hedging term comprises an aggregate and idiosyncratic components, $h_t^n = h_t + v_t^n$, where v_t^n is an i.i.d. shock with the property that $\int_0^1 v_t^n dn = 0$. The aggregate demand for euros by agents is thus given by

---

8. In this model there is no distinction between a bank and a dealer. All the support functions (e.g., the real-time collection and analysis of market news and trading data) provided by banks to their individual dealers are assumed by dealers.

$$\alpha_t = \int_0^1 \alpha_t^n dn = \alpha_s(\overline{\mathbb{E}}_t^n s_{t+1} - s_t + \hat{r}_t - r_t) + h_t, \qquad (11.49)$$

where h_t is the aggregate hedging demand and $\overline{\mathbb{E}}_t^n$ denotes the average of agents' expectations, $\overline{\mathbb{E}}_t^n s_{t+1} = \int_0^1 \mathbb{E}_t^n s_{t+1} dn$.

Let x_{t+1} denote the aggregate of all orders from agents for euros received by dealers during week t. Market clearing requires that this aggregate order flow equal the aggregate change in the demand for euros across all agents:

$$x_{t+1} = \alpha_t - \alpha_{t-1}. \qquad (11.50)$$

In models of currency trading, the risk premium embedded in dealers' spot rate quotes is determined by the requirements of efficient risk-sharing. Since there are a finite number of risk-averse dealers and a continuum of risk-averse agents, this necessitates dealers choosing δ_t such that their expected holdings of euros at the end of each week equal zero, that is $\mathbb{E}_t^D I_{t+1} = 0$, where I_{t+1} denotes the stock of euros held by all dealers at the end of week-t trading. This stock evolves according to $I_{t+1} = I_t - x_{t+1}$, so the market-clearing condition in (11.50) implies that $I_{t+1} + \alpha_t = I_t + \alpha_{t-1} = I_1 + \alpha_0$. For clarity, we normalize $I_1 + \alpha_0$ to zero, so the efficient risk-sharing condition, $\mathbb{E}_t^D I_{t+1} = 0$, implies that $\mathbb{E}_t^D \alpha_t = 0$. Combining this restriction with (11.49) gives

$$\delta_t = \mathbb{E}_t^D s_{t+1}^e - \frac{1}{\alpha_s} \mathbb{E}_t^D h_t, \qquad (11.51)$$

where $s_{t+1}^e = s_{t+1} - \overline{\mathbb{E}}_t^n s_{t+1}$.

The dealers' choice for the risk premium depends on their estimates of: (1) the average error agents make when forecasting next week's spot rate, and (2) the aggregate hedging demand for euros, h_t. Equation (11.51) implies that dealers lower the risk premium when $\mathbb{E}_t^D s_{t+1}^e < 0$ because they want to offset agents' desires to accumulate larger euro holdings when they are viewed as being too optimistic about the future spot rate. Similarly, they raise the risk premium when $\mathbb{E}_t^D s_{t+1}^e > 0$ to offset agents' desires to run down their euro holdings when they are viewed as too pessimistic. Dealers also raise (lower) the risk premium when they anticipate a lower (higher) hedging demand because the implied increase (fall) in expected excess returns will offset agents' desires to accumulate smaller (larger) euro holdings.

Differences between the information available to dealers and agents play an important role in the model. As in Chapter 9, we assume that all dealers and agents observe the interest rates at the start of each week. These rates are the only source of public information in the model. We further assume that all dealers learn the aggregate order flow that resulted from trades between dealers and agents in the previous week. The evolution of dealers' common information is therefore

$$\Omega_t^D = \{r_t, \hat{r}_t, x_t, \Omega_{t-1}^D\}. \qquad (11.52)$$

In addition to the interest differential, each agent n knows his own hedging demand, h_t^n, and the spot price quoted by all dealers. Importantly, agents do not observe order flow. The evolution of agent n's information is thus given by

$$\Omega_t^n = \{r_t, \hat{r}_t, s_t, h_t^n, \Omega_{t-1}^n\} \tag{11.53}$$

for $n \in [0, 1]$.

Up to this point, we have made one simplification to the model: we have omitted macro news announcements as a source of public information. We now make three further assumptions that allow us to study the behavior of the equilibrium risk premium in detail.

First, we assume that the interest rate decisions made by the FED and ECB give rise to the following process for the interest differential:

$$\hat{r}_t - r_t = \psi z_t + v_t \quad \text{and} \quad z_t = a z_{t-1} + u_t, \tag{A1}$$

with $\psi > 0$ and $1 > a > 0$, where v_t and u_t are i.i.d. mean-zero normally distributed shocks with variances σ_v^2 and σ_u^2, respectively. The v_t shocks represent the effects of unanticipated changes in the monetary policy that affect the interest differential for a single week. In contrast, the u_t shocks represent the effects of unanticipated policy changes that have persistent effects on the interest differential. The variable z_t identifies the long-run path for the interest differential.

Second, we assume that the aggregate hedging demand for euros is proportional to the persistent component of the interest differential:

$$h_t = \alpha_h z_t. \tag{A2}$$

This assumption captures the idea that the macroeconomic conditions affecting monetary policy also influence the aggregate hedging demand. We could also add a shock to (A2) without materially affecting the equilibrium properties of the model.

The third assumption concerns the information agents use when forming conditional expectations. Equation (11.53) and assumption (A2) jointly imply that each agent receives a private signal concerning z_t because $h_t^n = \alpha_h z_t + v_t^n$. Thus, insofar as h_t^n contains incremental information concerning z_t (i.e., information not contained in the week-t interest rates and spot rate), each agent will have a different forecast for future spot rates, $\mathbb{E}_t^n s_{t+1}$. This form of heterogeneity greatly complicates the model and obscures its implications for the behavior of the risk premium. We shall therefore assume that the variance of v_t^n dominates the variance of h_t so that each agent's forecast for the future spot rate is well approximated by the expectation condition on the current and past values of the interest differential and spot rates:

$$\mathbb{E}_t^n s_{t+1} = \mathbb{E}[s_{t+1} | \{\hat{r}_{t-i} - r_{t-i}, s_{t-i}\}_{i \geq 0}]. \tag{A3}$$

These three assumptions imply that dealers have more precise information about the behavior of the interest differential than agents. Both dealers and agents observe the interest rates set by central banks at the beginning of each week, but neither can directly observe whether the current shock to the interest differential is temporary or persistent. Dealers' informational advantage arises from the fact that equilibrium order flow, x_{t+1}, contains information on the z_t component of the interest differential. This information is not directly observed by agents. However, agents do learn about *past* shocks to the interest differential from dealers' quotes. In other words, the equilibrium we study is one in which order flow contains incremental information about the current state of the economy that dealers then pass on to agents via their spot rate quotes.[9]

Equilibrium

We can find the equilibrium of the model with the guess and verify method discussed in Chapter 4. In particular, the appendix establishes that the equilibrium spot rate follows

$$s_t = \pi_z z_{t-1} + \pi_u u_t + \pi_v v_t + \pi_e z_{t-1}^e, \qquad (11.54)$$

where $z_t^e = z_t - \overline{\mathbb{E}}_t^n z_t$ and

$$z_t^e = \eta_e z_{t-1}^e + \eta_u u_t + \eta_v v_t \qquad (11.55)$$

for some nonzero coefficients, π_i and η_i. Unanticipated order flow from week-t trading is

$$x_{t+1} - \mathbb{E}_t^{D} x_{t+1} = \alpha_h (z_t - \mathbb{E}_t^{D} z_t). \qquad (11.56)$$

In this equilibrium dealers learn the values for z_t, v_t, and u_t by the end of week-t trading because they observe both the interest differential and the order flow. In contrast, agents never fully learn the values of v_t and u_t even though they observe the interest differential and dealers' spot rate quotes. Dealers' optimal quotes do provide incremental information beyond that contained in the interest differential, but the information does not allow agents to precisely determine the past values of v_t and u_t. As a consequence, agents make persistent errors when estimating the current value for z_t. These errors show up in the AR(1) process for the average estimation error, z_t^e, shown in (11.55).

Recall that the risk premium depends on dealers' estimates of the aggregate hedging demand for euros, h_t, and the average error agents make when forecasting next week's spot rate, s_{t+1}^e. To examine these factors, we first note that dealers' estimates of z_t are

$$\mathbb{E}_t^{D} z_t = a z_{t-1} + \kappa (\psi u_t + v_t), \qquad (11.57)$$

where $\kappa = \psi \sigma_u^2 / (\psi^2 \sigma_u^2 + \sigma_v^2)$. Combining this equation with assumption (A2) gives

$$\mathbb{E}_t^{D} h_t = \alpha_h a z_{t-1} + \alpha_h \kappa (\psi u_t + v_t). \qquad (11.58)$$

To compute the average of agents' forecast errors, we next note that $\overline{\mathbb{E}}_t^n u_{t+1} = \overline{\mathbb{E}}_t^n v_{t+1} = 0$ and $\overline{\mathbb{E}}_t^n z_t^e = \overline{\mathbb{E}}_t^n z_t - \overline{\mathbb{E}}_t^n \overline{\mathbb{E}}_t^n z_t = 0$. Equation (11.54) therefore implies that

$$s_{t+1}^e = \pi_u u_{t+1} + \pi_v v_{t+1} + \left(\pi_z + \pi_e \right) z_t^e.$$

---

9. Throughout this discussion we have not drawn a distinction between dealers and the banks that employ them. A more precise statement of the model's informational structure is that each bank provides its dealers with more precise information about the interest differential (than is available to agents) by processing both public information and the information in order flow.

Like agents, dealers have no information on future shocks, so $\mathbb{E}^{D}_{t} s^{e}_{t+1} = (\pi_{z} + \pi_{e}) \cdot \mathbb{E}^{D}_{t} z^{e}_{t}$. Furthermore, because their observations on past order flow provide them with more precise information on z_{t} than is available to agents, $\mathbb{E}^{D}_{t} z^{e}_{t} = \mathbb{E}^{D}_{t} z_{t} - \mathbb{E}^{D}_{t} \overline{\mathbb{E}}^{n}_{t} z_{t} = \mathbb{E}^{D}_{t} z_{t} - \overline{\mathbb{E}}^{n}_{t} z_{t}$. Combining these results with the identity $\mathbb{E}^{D}_{t} z_{t} - \overline{\mathbb{E}}^{n}_{t} z = \mathbb{E}^{D}_{t} z_{t} - z_{t} + z^{e}_{t}$ gives

$$\mathbb{E}^{D}_{t} s^{e}_{t+1} = (\pi_{z} + \pi_{e}) \left\{ \left[\eta_{u} - (1 - \kappa \psi) \right] u_{t} + (\eta_{v} + \kappa) v_{t} + \eta_{e} z^{e}_{t-1} \right\}. \quad (11.59)$$

In equilibrium $\eta_{u} > 1 - \kappa \psi$ and $\eta_{v} + \kappa > 0$, so shocks to the current interest differential lead dealers to adjust their estimates of agents' average forecast error. Dealers also adjust their estimates to past v_{t} and u_{t} shocks via the z^{e}_{t-1} term because, as (11.55) shows, these shocks affect agents' average error in estimating z_{t}.

Finally, we combine (11.51) with (11.58) and (11.59) to produce the following equation for the risk premium:

$$\delta_{t} = (\pi_{z} + \pi_{e}) \eta_{e} z^{e}_{t-1} - \frac{\alpha_{h}}{\alpha_{s}} a z_{t-1} + \left\{ (\pi_{z} + \pi_{e}) \left[\eta_{u} - (1 - \kappa \psi) \right] - \frac{\alpha_{h}}{\alpha_{s}} \kappa \psi \right\} u_{t}$$

$$+ \left\{ (\pi_{z} + \pi_{e}) (\eta_{v} + \kappa) - \frac{\alpha_{h}}{\alpha_{s}} \kappa \right\} v_{t}. \quad (11.60)$$

Here we see that dealers adjust the risk premium in response to both u_{t} and v_{t} shocks. Since v_{t} shocks have no effect on the actual hedging demand, they only appear insofar as they affect dealers' estimates of s^{e}_{t+1} and h_{t}. Indeed, if both dealers and agents could directly observe u_{t} and v_{t} at the start of week t, the expression above would simplify to $\delta_{t} = -\frac{\alpha_{h}}{\alpha_{s}} (a z_{t-1} + u_{t})$.

11.3.2 Micro-Based Explanations for the Forward Premium Puzzle

Can the equilibrium of this micro-based model provide new insights into the Forward Premium Puzzle? We address this question in two ways. First, we examine whether the model can account for the puzzle in large data samples that are free from peso problems. Second, we consider the equilibrium dynamics of the model in a peso problem case where dealers and agents misperceive the true distribution of shocks to interest rates.

No Peso Problem Case

Recall from Section 11.2.2 that the population slope in the UIP regression (11.12) is $\beta_{1} = \mathbb{CV}(\Delta s_{t+1}, f p_{t}) / \mathbb{V}(f p_{t})$. To compute the value of β_{1} consistent with the equilibrium of the micro-based model, we first combine the identity $s_{t+1} = \mathbb{E}^{D}_{t} s_{t+1} + (s_{t+1} - \mathbb{E}^{D}_{t} s_{t+1})$ with equation (11.48) to give

$$\Delta s_{t+1} = r_{t} - \hat{r}_{t} + \delta_{t} + (s_{t+1} - \mathbb{E}^{D}_{t} s_{t+1}).$$

We then use this equation with the CIP condition, $f p_{t} = r_{t} - \hat{r}_{t}$, to write

$$\beta_1 = 1 + \frac{\mathbb{CV}(\delta_t, r_t - \hat{r}_t)}{\mathbb{V}(r_t - \hat{r}_t)} + \frac{\mathbb{CV}(s_{t+1} - \mathbb{E}_t^D s_{t+1}, r_t - \hat{r}_t)}{\mathbb{V}(r_t - \hat{r}_t)}.$$

Since dealers use their information optimally and $r_t - \hat{r}_t \in \Omega_t^D$, the right-hand term vanishes, so a negative value for β_1 implies that

$$\mathbb{V}(\delta_t) > \mathbb{V}(r_t - \hat{r}_t) \quad \text{and} \quad -\mathbb{V}(r_t - \hat{r}_t) > \mathbb{CV}(\delta_t, r_t - \hat{r}_t). \qquad (11.61)$$

These are the Fama conditions we derived in Section 11.2.2. They hold here because dealers condition on the current interest differential when forecasting the future spot rate.

Fama's first condition in (11.61) is easily met when there is a large difference between the information available to dealers and agents. In particular, consider an equilibrium where dealers' quotes provide imprecise information to agents concerning the true value of z_t. Under these circumstances, *past* v_t shocks induce significant volatility of the risk premium as dealers change their estimates of s_{t+1}^e via the z_{t-1}^e term in equation (11.60), but not the interest differential. In short, informational differences can induce volatility in the risk premium that is not present in the interest differential sufficient to satisfy Fama's first condition.

To examine the implications of Fama's second condition in (11.61), we first use (11.51) and (A1) to substitute for the risk premium and interest differential. This gives

$$-\psi^2 \mathbb{V}(z_t) - \sigma_v^2 > \mathbb{CV}(\mathbb{E}_t^D s_{t+1}^e, r_t - \hat{r}_t) - \frac{1}{\alpha_s} \mathbb{CV}(\mathbb{E}_t^D h_t, r_t - \hat{r}_t)$$

or

$$-\psi^2 \mathbb{V}(z_t) - \sigma_v^2 > -\frac{1}{\alpha_s} \mathbb{CV}\left(h_t, r_t - \hat{r}_t\right). \qquad (11.62)$$

The second expression follows because both dealers and agents condition their week-t expectations on the interest differential, $r_t - \hat{r}_t$. Specifically, since $\mathbb{E}_t^D s_{t+1}^e = s_{t+1}^e - (s_{t+1}^e - \mathbb{E}_t^D s_{t+1}^e)$ by definition, $\mathbb{CV}(\mathbb{E}_t^D s_{t+1}^e, r_t - \hat{r}_t) = \mathbb{CV}(s_{t+1}^e, r_t - \hat{r}_t) - \mathbb{CV}(s_{t+1}^e - \mathbb{E}_t^D s_{t+1}^e, r_t - \hat{r}_t) = 0$ because both s_{t+1}^e and $s_{t+1}^e - \mathbb{E}_t^D s_{t+1}^e$ must be uncorrelated with all the elements in Ω_t^n and Ω_t^D, respectively, including $r_t - \hat{r}_t$. Similarly, $\mathbb{CV}(\mathbb{E}_t^D h_t, r_t - \hat{r}_t) = \mathbb{CV}(h_t, r_t - \hat{r}_t) - \mathbb{CV}(h_t - \mathbb{E}_t^D h_t, r_t - \hat{r}_t) = \mathbb{CV}(h_t, r_t - \hat{r}_t)$ because $h_t - \mathbb{E}_t^D h_t$ must be uncorrelated with the elements of Ω_t^D. Substituting for $r_t - \hat{r}_t$ and h_t with (A1) and (A2) on the right-hand side of (11.62) produces the following bound:

$$\alpha_h < -\alpha_s(\psi^2 \mathbb{V}(z_t) + \sigma_v^2)/\psi \mathbb{V}(z_t) < 0. \qquad (11.63)$$

Since $h_t = \alpha_h z_t$, (11.63) shows that the aggregate hedging demand must be sufficiently negatively correlated with persistent variations in the interest differential if the micro-based model is to meet the second condition in (11.61).

Clearly, it is impossible to assess the plausibility of this restriction on α_h without developing agents' hedging demands from an optimizing model. That said, our discussion of the carry trade in Section 11.1.2 provides some perspective. Recall that a simple carry-trade strategy consists of purchasing foreign currency forward when

$fp_t < 0$ and selling it forward when $fp_t > 0$. Thus, if policy decisions of the FED and the ECB produce a persistent fall in z_t and $\hat{r}_t - r_t$, the accompanying rise in fp_t induced by CIP will produce forward sales of euros by agents engaged in the carry trade. Under these circumstances, the need to fulfill outstanding forward contracts will produce a higher demand for euros in the spot market. Thus, a fall in z_t produces a rise in the hedging demand for euros consistent with a negative value for α_h.

In sum, the foregoing discussion shows that the presence of informational differences between dealers and agents can be a source of variability in the risk premium. This feature of micro-based models makes them better able to meet one of Fama's conditions, but not the other. As *both* dealers and agents condition their week-t expectations on the current interest differential, informational differences cannot contribute to the correlation between the risk premium and the interest differential that is the focus of Fama's second condition. In the absence of peso problems, a micro-based model will only be able to account for the Forward Premium Puzzle if it explains why the aggregate hedging demand for foreign currency is strongly negatively correlated with the interest differential.

Peso Problem Case

Consider a situation in which both dealers and agents believe that the interest differential is subject to both persistent u_t shocks and temporary v_t shocks, with variances $\sigma_u^2 = \sigma_v^2 > 0$. Let us further assume that temporary v_t shocks do not occur in the available data sample so that the sample variance for v_t is zero. Throughout the sample a peso problem exists because both dealers and agents are expecting some of the unexpected movements in the interest differential to be short-lived, but ex post it turns out that all the shocks have persistent effects.

The potential of the micro-based model to account for the Forward Premium Puzzle in these circumstances is most easily illustrated with a numerical example. For this purpose, we assume that $\alpha_s = 10$, $\alpha_h = 0.1$, $a = 0.9$, $\psi = 0.1$, and $\sigma_v^2 = \sigma_u^2 = 1$. The aggregate demand for euros and the interest differential therefore follow

$$\alpha_t = 10(\overline{\mathbb{E}}_t^n s_{t+1} - s_t + \hat{r}_t - r_t) + 0.1z_t,$$

$$\hat{r}_t - r_t = 0.1z_t + v_t,$$

and

$$z_t = 0.9z_{t-1} + u_t,$$

where $v_t \sim$ i.i.d.$N(0, 1)$ and $u_t \sim$ i.i.d.$N(0, 1)$. Note that this calibration of the model cannot account for the Forward Premium Puzzle in large samples because the positive value for α_h clearly violates the lower bound in (11.63).

Figure 11.4 plots the equilibrium response of the calibrated model for 52 weeks following a negative u_t shock of 1 percent. Panel A shows that the shock initially raises the interest differential between dollar and euro interest rates, $r_t - \hat{r}_t$, by 10 basis points. Thereafter, the effects of the shock slowly dissipate until interest rates are equalized. According to UIP, this shock to interest rates should be accompanied by an immediate appreciation of the dollar when the u_t shock hits, followed by a slow depreciation until interest rates are equalized. This is not what happens. Panel A shows that the dollar initially appreciates by approximately 5 basis points when the u_t shock hits, but then continues to *appreciate* by a further 20 basis points over

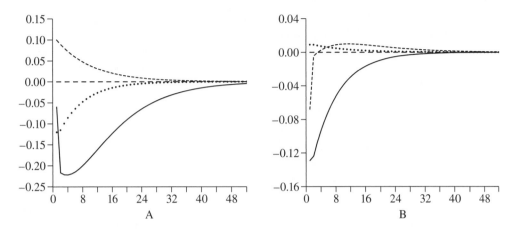

FIGURE 11.4 Peso problems in a micro-based model. Panel A shows the impulse responses of the log spot rate, s_t (solid), interest differential, $r_t - \hat{r}_t$ (dashed), and risk premium, δ_t (dotted) following a negative u_t shock. Panel B shows the impulse responses for components of the risk premium: $E_t^D s_{t+1}^e$ (solid) and $-(\alpha_h/\alpha_s)E_t^D h_t$ (dotted). The dashed plot shows dealers' expectations for the depreciation rate, $E_t^D \Delta s_{t+1}$.

the next 3 weeks. It takes until the start of the 5th week after the shock before the dollar begins to depreciate in line with the prediction of UIP. The rise in U.S. interest rates ultimately leads to a depreciation of the dollar, but the depreciation is delayed by several weeks while dealers adjust their spot rate quotes downward. Clearly, the behavior of the spot rate and interest differential during this adjustment period is consistent with the Forward Premium Puzzle.

What leads dealers to adjust their spot rate quotes downward in the weeks immediately following the u_t shock? The answer lies in the behavior of the risk premium. Panel A of Figure 11.4 shows that the risk premium, δ_t, falls by approximately 12 basis points when the u_t shock hits. It then gradually rises to zero over the following 26 weeks. This fall in the risk premium stops dealers from initially adjusting their quotes to fully reflect their new forecasts for the future interest differential. In particular, as the quote equation (11.48) shows, the fall in the risk premium leads dealers to quote higher spot prices than they would otherwise. As a consequence, dealers' initial reaction to the u_t shock induces an immediate but small appreciation of the dollar. This gradual adjustment of dealers' quotes continues until their interest rate forecasts dominate the effects of the risk premium—a process that takes 3 weeks in this calibration of the model.

Panel B of Figure 11.4 shows why the risk premium falls. Recall that dealers can learn the true value of z_t with a 1-week delay, so their estimates of the aggregate hedging component of the risk premium, $-(\alpha_h/\alpha_s)\mathbb{E}_t^D h_t$, will be accurate 1 week after the shock hits. Since a negative u_t shock *reduces* the aggregate hedging demand, this component must push the risk premium upward, as shown by the dashed plot. This means that the fall in the risk premium is entirely due to the fall in $\mathbb{E}_t^D(s_{t+1} - \overline{\mathbb{E}}_t s_{t+1})$, shown by the solid plot. Unlike dealers, agents only learn about the true value of u_t gradually from their observations on the interest differential and the spot rate. As a consequence, their estimates of z_t will be closer to the unconditional mean of zero than dealers' estimates. This means that agents' forecasts for $r_t - \hat{r}_t$, will be below dealers' forecasts following the negative u_t shock, so they are too optimistic about the future spot rate, that is, $\overline{\mathbb{E}}_t s_{t+1} > \mathbb{E}_t^D s_{t+1}$. Panel B clearly shows that dealers' desires to offset agents' unwarranted optimism dominates their estimates of the aggregate hedging demand, so their quotes following the shock embed a large negative risk premium. Note, also, that the response of the $\mathbb{E}_t^D(s_{t+1} - \overline{\mathbb{E}}_t s_{t+1})$ component dwarfs the effects of the shock on dealers' estimates of the depreciation rate, $\mathbb{E}_t^D \Delta s_{t+1}$, shown by the dot-dashed plot.

Although this is only an illustrative example, it does capture two key features of the data that have proved hard to explain in other models. Eichenbaum and Evans (1995) first documented the fact that currencies tend to appreciate for several quarters following a rise in interest rates before they depreciate. This phenomenon, often termed "delayed overshooting," is captured by the plots in Figure 11.4, albeit with a shorter duration. (The question of whether a fully developed micro-based model could produce delayed overshooting with a long duration remains open for future research.) The second feature concerns the relation between agents' average forecast error, $s_{t+1} - \overline{\mathbb{E}}_t s_{t+1}$, and the forward premium. In this example the u_t shock induces a rise in the forward premium, $fp_t = r_t - \hat{r}_t$, and a fall in $s_{t+1} - \overline{\mathbb{E}}_t s_{t+1}$. Insofar as survey data provide a reasonable proxy for the average of agents' expectations, $\overline{\mathbb{E}}_t s_{t+1}$, this co-movement is completely consistent with the empirical evidence on the correlation between survey-based measures of forecast errors and the forward premium discussed in Section 11.2.4.

This example also highlights two theoretical aspects of micro-based models. First, the variations in the risk premium have essentially nothing to do with the aggregate hedging demand. The equilibrium dynamics look very similar to those in Figure 11.4 if the value of α_h is arbitrarily close to zero. This feature of the model is very useful. In a fully developed general equilibrium setting, macro risk factors will affect spot rates via their influence on the aggregate hedging demand. If we can use a micro-based model to account for the dynamics of spot rates without strong assumptions concerning macro risks, the difficulty in estimating macro risks is no longer a roadblock to resolving the Forward Premium Puzzle.

The second aspect concerns the role of differential information. In this example, *both* dealers and agents have misperceptions about the behavior of interest rates. The dynamics displayed in Figure 11.4 do not reflect misperceptions by just one group (i.e., agents). The key feature of the equilibrium is that dealers use their observations on order flow to quickly learn about the true nature of interest rate shocks. Importantly, they also recognize that agents will be slower to draw the same precise inferences because the subsequent spot rate quotes carry less information to agents than they learned from order flow. As a result, dealers' quotes immediately following the shock are largely driven by their desire to offset agents' unwarranted optimism about future spot rates. In sum, the spot rate response is dominated by variations in the risk premium that have nothing to do with macro risk factors.

11.3.3 Excess Returns, Risk Premia, and Order Flows

Micro-based models have novel implications concerning the behavior of excess currency returns that are related to the way dealers adjust the risk premium embedded in their spot rate quotes. To illustrate these implications, let $er_{t+1} = \Delta s_{t+1} + \hat{r}_t - r_t$ denote the log excess return on euros between the start of weeks t and $t+1$. Combining this definition with identity $s_{t+1} = \mathbb{E}_t^{D} s_{t+1} + (s_{t+1} - \mathbb{E}_t^{D} s_{t+1})$ and (11.48), the equation determining dealers' quotes, gives

$$er_{t+2} = \delta_{t+1} + s_{t+2} - \mathbb{E}_{t+1}^{D} s_{t+2}$$

$$= \mathbb{E}_t^{D} \delta_{t+1} + (\delta_{t+1} - \mathbb{E}_t^{D} \delta_{t+1}) + (s_{t+2} - \mathbb{E}_{t+1}^{D} s_{t+2}). \qquad (11.64)$$

This decomposition of returns holds true in any micro-based model irrespective of what determines interest rates and the aggregate hedging demand for foreign currency. We can therefore use it to think about the possible sources of forecastability for future excess returns.

The right-hand side of (11.64) identifies two channels through which forecastability can occur. The first operates via dealers' expectations of next week's risk premium, $\mathbb{E}_t^{D} \delta_{t+1}$. Any variable known to the dealers at the start of week t could potentially be correlated with $\mathbb{E}_t^{D} \delta_{t+1}$ and hence have forecasting power for er_{t+2}. Note that this channel rules out any forecasting power for unanticipated order flow from week-t trading; $x_{t+1} - \mathbb{E}_t^{D} x_{t+1}$ cannot be correlated with $\mathbb{E}_t^{D} \delta_{t+1}$ because this estimate depends on the elements in Ω_t^{D}.

The second channel operates via the revision in dealers' estimates of the risk premium, $\delta_{t+1} - \mathbb{E}_t^{D} \delta_{t+1}$. These revisions occur because dealers change their estimates of the aggregate hedging demand and/or the average error of agents forecasting the future spot rate. They may be triggered either by the arrival of public information at the start of week $t+1$ (e.g., an unanticipated change in interest rates or a macro announcement) or by the information conveyed by order flow from week-t trading, $x_{t+1} - \mathbb{E}_t^{D} x_{t+1}$. In the latter case, order flow will have forecasting power for future excess returns.

Forecasting with Order Flows

Empirical evidence on the forecasting power of order flow for excess returns was first reported in Evans and Lyons (2005b, 2007). These papers examine the in-sample and out-of-sample forecasting power of six end-user order flows in the USD/EUR market received by Citibank between January 1993 and June 1999 (discussed in Chapter 9).

The in-sample results come from regressions of currency returns computed between the start of weeks t and $t+\tau$, $\Delta^{\tau} s_{t+\tau} = s_{t+\tau} - s_t$, on the interest differential and the order flows from the six segments between the start of weeks $t-\tau$ and t:

$$\Delta^{\tau} s_{t+\tau} = \text{const.} + b_r(r_t^{\tau} - \hat{r}_t^{\tau}) + \sum_{j=1}^{6} b_j x_{j,t} + v_{t+\tau}. \qquad (11.65)$$

The interest rates on Eurocurrency deposits with τ weeks to maturity are used to compute the interest differential, $r_t^{\tau} - \hat{r}_t^{\tau}$. Note that this regression takes the form of the UIP regressions in (11.12) with the addition of the six order flows, $x_{j,t}$.

Table 11.4 reproduces the results from estimating (11.65) at the weekly frequency as reported in Evans and Lyons (2007). The body of the table shows the OLS estimates of b_r and b_j together with asymptotic standard errors that correct for heteroskedasticity and serial correlation in specifications when the horizon τ is greater than 1 week.

TABLE 11.4
Forecasting Return Regressions

Week		Corporate		Hedge		Investors			χ^2
τ	$r - \hat{r}$	U.S.	Non-U.S.	U.S.	Non-U.S.	U.S.	Non-U.S.	R^2	(p-value)
1	0.102	0.482	−0.033	0.089	−0.153	−0.346	0.142	0.027	8.056
	(0.409)	(0.317)	(0.136)	(0.102)	(0.198)	(0.238)	(0.141)		(0.234)
2	0.147	0.509***	−0.037	0.088	−0.09	−0.449***	0.163**	0.074	17.239
	(0.324)	(0.263)	(0.104)	(0.082)	(0.148)	(0.188)	(0.096)		(0.008)
3	0.176	0.615***	−0.034	0.095*	−0.084	−0.432***	0.145**	0.121	24.500
	(0.305)	(0.215)	(0.090)	(0.073)	(0.137)	(0.177)	(0.082)		(0.001)
4	0.202	0.544***	−0.042	0.094*	−0.097	−0.517***	0.137**	0.163	30.738
	(0.302)	(0.177)	(0.084)	(0.068)	(0.125)	(0.158)	(0.072)		(<0.001)

Notes: The symbols *, **, and *** denote significance at the 10 percent, 5 percent, and 1 percent levels. Source: Evans and Lyons (2007).

The χ^2 statistics for the null hypothesis that all six b_j coefficients equal zero are shown in the right-hand column.

Three features of the results in Table 11.4 are striking. First, many of the b_j coefficients on the end-user flows are highly statistically significant, particularly the U.S. corporate and long-term investor flows. Indeed, the χ^2 statistics show that the estimated coefficients on all six flow segments are jointly significant beyond the 1-week horizon. Second, all the estimated coefficients on the interest differential are positive but statistically insignificant. This finding contrasts with the results of the UIP regressions in Table 11.1. Once we control for the influence of order flows, there is no longer any evidence that high-interest currencies depreciate. That said, all the estimates of b_r are well below unity; t-statistics for the null that $b_r = 1$ are highly significant. This means that excess returns on the euro tend to be high when $r_t - \hat{r}_t$ is negative, and vice versa. The third striking feature concerns the degree of forecastability as measured by the R^2 statistics. The forecasting power rises with the horizon, reaching 16 percent at 4 weeks. By comparison, the R^2 statistics from regressions that omit order flows are in the 2–4 percent range. Here all the forecasting power comes from the order flows. If the regressions are estimated without the interest differentials, the estimated coefficients on the flows and the R^2 statistics are essentially unchanged.

The results in Table 11.4 point to a remarkably strong within-sample relation between order flows and future exchange-rate changes. However, as we noted in Chapter 3, there is a long tradition in the exchange-rate literature of considering out-of sample forecasting performance. Evans and Lyons (2005b) examine the out-of-sample forecasting performance of the six order flows for $\Delta^{\tau} s_{t+\tau}$ as follows:

Let $\Delta^{\tau} s_{t+\tau|t}$ denote the forecast of $\Delta^{\tau} s_{t+\tau}$ computed from regression (11.65) (with const. $= b_r = 0$) estimated with sample observations ending on day t. Evans and Lyons construct the recursive τ-period out-of-sample forecasts over the forecasting period starting on day t_0 and ending on day $T - \tau$ (i.e., $\widehat{\Delta^{\tau} s_{t+\tau|t}}$ for $t_0 \leq t \leq T - \tau$).

TABLE 11.5

Forecast Comparisons

	Horizon in trading days				
	1	5	10	15	20
A. UIP					
MSE ratio	1.005	1.011	1.022	1.035	1.054
b_s	0.000	0.003	0.002	0.003	0.010
p-value	(0.533)	(0.332)	(0.457)	(0.452)	(0.359)
B. Order flows					
MSE ratio	0.961	0.876	0.848	0.810	0.806
b_s	0.027	0.057	0.102	0.122	0.157
p-value	(0.005)	(0.018)	(0.005)	(0.007)	(0.002)

Source: Evans and Lyons (2005b).

They then regress the forecasts on the realized values for $\Delta^\tau s_{t+\tau}$:

$$\widehat{\Delta^\tau s_{t+\tau|t}} = \text{const.} + b_s \Delta^\tau s_{t+\tau} + w_{t+\tau}.$$

Under the null hypothesis that s_t follows a random walk, there is no forecast change in the spot rate, so $\Delta^\tau s_{t+\tau|t} = 0$. Under these circumstances, the out-of-sample forecasts based on the regression model (11.65), $\widehat{\Delta^\tau s_{t+\tau|t}}$, differ from zero owing solely to the presence of sampling error. Furthermore, since these forecasts are calculated using data up to day t, the error cannot be correlated with $\Delta^\tau s_{t+\tau}$ under the null that the log spot rate follows a random walk (RW). Consequently, we can compare forecasting performance of the regression model (11.65) against the RW benchmark, simply by testing for the significance of the b_s coefficient. If the model in (11.65) does no better than the RW, we should find the estimates of b_s insignificantly different from zero. If the alternate model does have forecasting power, then the estimates of b_s should be positive and significant. Evans and Lyons refer to b_s as the projection statistic.

Table 11.5 reproduces the results of this out-of-sample forecasting test from Evans and Lyons (2005b). The table shows tests for two regression models: the UIP regression in (11.12) and the order flow regression in (11.65) (with const. $= b_r = 0$). These models are compared across five different forecasting horizons: 1, 5, 10, 15, and 20 trading days, using June 3, 1996, as the start of the forecasting period. Note that 20 trading days is four trading weeks, that is, roughly one calendar month. The upper row in each panel shows the ratio of mean-squared forecast errors for the regression model to the RW model. This ratio should be less than one if the variables included in the regression model have true out-of-sample forecasting power. The estimated projection statistics are reported in the middle row of each panel. Again these estimates should be positive if the variables in the regression model have forecasting power. The third row in each panel reports the p-values for the null that $b_s = 0$ computed from the asymptotic distribution of the OLS estimates.

Panel A of Table 11.5 shows that the forecasting performance of the UIP model is uniformly poor across all horizons. All the MSE ratios are greater than one and none of projection statistics are statistically significant. These findings are consistent with results of Meese and Rogoff (1983) and the voluminous literature that followed their work. In contrast, panel B shows that the forecasting performance of the order flow model is significantly better, particularly at longer horizons. According to the projection statistic, the out-of-sample forecasting power of the six order flows is significantly better than the RW model at the 1 percent level at horizons of 10 days or longer.

The estimates of b_s also provide us with a more economically meaningful measure of the forecasting performance. By definition, the τ-period change in the spot rate comprises a forecastable and unforecastable component: $\Delta^\tau s_{t+\tau} \equiv \widehat{\Delta^\tau s_{t+\tau|t}} + \widehat{\varepsilon_{t+\tau|t}}$. Multiplying both sides of this identity by $\Delta^\tau s_{t+\tau}$ and taking expectations gives us a variance decomposition for spot rate changes:

$$\mathbb{V}\left(\Delta^\tau s_{t+\tau}\right) = \mathbb{CV}(\Delta^\tau s_{t+\tau}, \widehat{\Delta^\tau s_{t+\tau|t}}) + \mathbb{CV}(\widehat{\varepsilon_{t+\tau|h}}, \Delta^\tau s_{t+\tau}).$$

Since the projection coefficient b_s is simply the ratio of the covariance between $\Delta^\tau s_{t+\tau}$ and $\widehat{\Delta^\tau s_{t+\tau|t}}$ to the variance of $\Delta^\tau s_{t+\tau}$, the values for b_s reported in Table 11.5 estimate the contribution of the regression model forecasts to the variance of spot rate changes over the forecasting period. As the table shows, the six order flows account for almost 16 percent of the sample variance in monthly spot rate changes. By this metric, the forecasting power of order flows is truly significant from an economic perspective.

How do these empirical findings relate to the micro-based model? To address this question, we first note that the forecasting power of Citibank's order flows for currency returns documented earlier carries over to excess returns. If regression (11.65) is re-estimated with the τ-week excess return, $er_{t+\tau}^\tau = \Delta^\tau s_{t+\tau} + \hat{r}_t^\tau - r_t^\tau$, as the dependent variable, the estimates of b_r are negative (and statistically significant) but the order flow coefficients and the R^2 statistics remain unchanged. Moreover, the lion's share of within-sample forecasting power continues to come from the six order flows. Similarly, repeating the out-of-sample forecasting tests with $er_{t+\tau}^\tau$ replacing $\Delta^\tau s_{t+\tau}$ has no material effects on the results reported in panel B of Table 11.5. In short, Citibank's order flows have significant forecasting power for future excess returns.

Next we use (11.64) to write the τ-week excess return as

$$er_{t+\tau}^\tau = \mathbb{E}_t^D \sum_{i=0}^{\tau-1} \delta_{t+i} + (\mathbb{E}_{t+1}^D - \mathbb{E}_t^D) \sum_{i=1}^{\tau-1} \delta_{t+i} + (s_{t+1} - \mathbb{E}_t^D s_{t+1}) + \zeta_{t+\tau}, \quad (11.66)$$

where $\zeta_{t+\tau}$ is an error term that is uncorrelated with information known to dealers at the start of week $t + 1$, Ω_{t+1}^D. (A full derivation of this equation is provided in the appendix.) Note that the second and third terms on the right-hand side identify the effects of new information dealers receive between the start of weeks t and $t + 1$. Order flows from week-t trading will have forecasting power for excess returns insofar as they convey some of this information. This occurs in the equilibrium of the micro-based model, in part because the model assumes that dealers can learn about the aggregate order flow from agents across the market by the end of each trading week. By contrast, the foregoing empirical results use the order flows received by a single (large) bank. It is therefore impossible to account for the forecasting power of Citibank's order flows within the context of the micro-based model unless some of the information conveyed by those flows was transmitted to dealers at other banks via interbank trading. In other words, the forecasting power of Citibank's order flows arises because they are a reasonably accurate proxy for the market-wide order flow that conveys information to dealers between the start of weeks t and $t + 1$.

Equation (11.66) also provides perspective on the forecasting power of order flows at different horizons, τ. As τ increases, the second term on the right includes the revision in dealers' risk premia expectations further into the future. Thus if order flow from week t conveys information relevant to dealers' expectations about the entire future path of the risk premia, the forecasting power of flows for excess returns should increase with the horizon τ. From this perspective, results in Tables 11.4 and 11.5 suggest that Citibank's order flows are conveying information to dealers that is relevant to the determination of future risk premia.

Risk Premia, Order Flows, and Macro Information

Recent research in Evans and Lyons (2009) explores the links among order flow, risk premia, and macroeconomic information in greater detail. Let $\Omega_t \subset \Omega_t^D$ denote a subset of the information available to dealers at the start of week t that includes a vector of macro variables Y_t. Without loss of generality, we can write

$$Y_{t+\tau} = \sum_{i=-t}^{\tau-1} \mathfrak{T}_{t+i} + \mathbb{E}[Y_{t+\tau}],$$

where $\mathfrak{T}_t = \mathbb{E}[Y_{t+\tau}|\Omega_{t+1}] - \mathbb{E}[Y_{t+\tau}|\Omega_t]$ is the week-t flow of information into Ω_{t+1} concerning $Y_{t+\tau}$ and $\mathbb{E}[Y_{t+\tau}] = \mathbb{E}[Y_{t+\tau}|\Omega_0]$ denotes the unconditional expectation. Evans and Lyons use a time series model to estimate six elements of $\mathfrak{T}_t$ corresponding to GDP growth, inflation, and M1 growth in the United States and Germany. From these estimates they then construct information flows for different linear combinations of the macro variables, $v_t = c\mathfrak{T}_t$: (1) the difference between U.S. and German GDP growth, $\Delta y - \Delta \hat{y}$, (2) the difference between U.S. and German inflation, $\Delta p - \Delta \hat{p}$, (3) the difference between U.S. and German M1 growth, $\Delta m - \Delta \hat{m}$, (4) the growth in the U.S. M1/GDP ratio, $\Delta m - \Delta y$, (5) the growth in the German M1/GDP ratio, $\Delta \hat{m} - \Delta \hat{y}$, and (6) the difference between the U.S. and German M1/GDP growth rates, $(\Delta m - \Delta y) - (\Delta \hat{m} - \Delta \hat{y})$.

The next step is to identify the component of these information flows conveyed by order flow. For this purpose Evans and Lyons estimate regressions of future information flows over the next quarter on Citibank's order flows, the past depreciation rate, and a set of interest rate spreads:

$$v_{t+13}^Q = \text{const.} + \sum_{j=1}^{6} b_j x_{j,t} + b_s \Delta s_t + b_{\nabla r}' \nabla \mathbf{r}_t + w_{t+13},$$

where $v_{t+13}^Q = \sum_{i=0}^{12} v_{t+i}$ and $\nabla \mathbf{r}_t$ is a vector of interest rate spreads in week t. The term v_{t+13}^Q is the flow of information about the linear combination of macro variables between the start of weeks t and $t + 13$. They then compute an estimate of the order flow component as $\tilde{v}_{t,x} = \sum_{j=1}^{6} \tilde{b}_j x_{j,t}$, where $\tilde{b}_j$ denotes the OLS estimate of b_j. This component identifies the macro information contained in Citibank's order flows concerning the future behavior of the macro variables that is not present in the interest rates, $\mathbf{r}_t$. That component is then used to estimate

$$\Delta^\tau s_{t+\tau} = \text{const.} + b_r(r_t^\tau - \hat{r}_t^\tau) + b_x \tilde{v}_{t,x} + v_{t+\tau}. \tag{11.67}$$

This regression has the same form as (11.65) except that the order flows are replaced by the order flow component. If Citibank's order flows contain incremental information about the linear combination of macro variables over the next 13 weeks that dealers use to revise the risk premium, then the estimates of b_x should be significant. As before, the interest differential is included on the right-hand side with an unrestricted coefficient, b_r, to accommodate variations in the risk premia that are unrelated to order flow.

Table 11.6 reproduces the results of estimating (11.67) for horizons $\tau = \{1, 4\}$ weeks from Evans and Lyons (2009). The body of the table reports OLS coefficients and asymptotic standard errors that account for the fact that the $\tilde{v}_{t,x}$ time series are estimates from the first-stage regression. The right-hand column reports the p-value of the χ^2 test for the null that the regression residuals are unrelated to order flow.

The results in Table 11.6 are rather striking. First, the estimates of the b_x coefficients display a similar pattern across the forecast horizons. The coefficients on the components involving the GDP growth and inflation are small and statistically insignificant. By contrast, the coefficients on the components with M1 growth, M1/GDP growth, and the M1/GDP growth differentials are all highly significant. This constitutes direct empirical evidence that the order flows convey information about the future course of the macroeconomy and that dealers use this information to revise the risk premia embedded in their spot rate quotes. More specifically, the equation for the risk premium in the micro-based model implies that

$$\delta_{t+1} - \mathbb{E}_t^D \delta_{t+1} = (\mathbb{E}_{t+1}^D - \mathbb{E}_t^D)(s_{t+2} - \overline{\mathbb{E}}_{t+1}^n s_{t+2}) - \alpha_s^{-1}(\mathbb{E}_{t+1}^D - \mathbb{E}_t^D)h_{t+1},$$

so dealers will adjust the risk premium upward when they infer from order flow that on average, agents are underestimating the future depreciation of the dollar by a larger amount, that is, when

$$(\mathbb{E}_{t+1}^D - \mathbb{E}_t^D)(s_{t+2} - \overline{\mathbb{E}}_{t+1}^n s_{t+2}) > 0.$$

This will happen, for example, when dealers raise their expectations for the future path of the interest differential, $\hat{r}_{t+i} - r_{t+i}$, *relative* to the average path expected by agents. In other words, this will occur when the information in order flow leads dealers to expect a looser (tighter) future U.S. (German) monetary policy than the average forecast outside the foreign exchange market. Under these circumstances, order flows forecasting looser (tighter) future monetary conditions in the United States (Germany) should induce dealers to raise the risk premium on the euro, with the result that the order flows forecast positive future returns on the euro. The signs of the statistically significant coefficients on the M1/GDP growth components in Table 11.6 are consistent with this explanation.

The second noteworthy feature concerns the R^2 statistics, which increase from less than 6 percent to 14 percent as we move from the 1-week to the 1-month forecasting horizon. These values are far higher than those found in UIP regression. Here all the forecasting power comes from the order flow component, $\tilde{v}_{t,x}$. If (11.67) is re-

TABLE 11.6
Forecasting with Information Flows

Horizon	$r - \hat{r}$	$\Delta y - \Delta \hat{y}$	$\Delta p - \Delta \hat{p}$	$\Delta m - \Delta \hat{m}$	$\Delta m - \Delta y$	$\Delta \hat{m} - \Delta \hat{y}$	$(\Delta m - \Delta y)$ $-(\Delta \hat{m} - \Delta \hat{y})$	R^2	χ^2 (p-value)
$\tau = 1$	−0.229 (0.369)	−0.229 (0.949)						<0.001	7.859 (0.249)
	−0.194 (0.367)		−0.290 (0.507)					0.001	8.525 (0.202)
	0.161 (0.387)			0.589** (0.218)				0.023	1.115 (0.981)
	0.04 (0.398)				0.436** (0.280)	−0.700** (0.281)		0.025	0.783 (0.993)
	0.110 (0.381)						0.585** (0.219)	0.023	1.158 (0.979)
	0.136 (0.310)						0.639** (0.184)	0.059	4.787 (0.571)
$\tau = 4$	−0.214 (0.315)	−0.094 (0.651)						<0.001	52.375 (<0.001)
	−0.200 (0.327)		−0.106 (0.383)					<0.001	53.402 (<0.001)
	0.248 (0.316)			0.709** (0.156)				0.135	8.033 (0.236)
	0.122 (0.302)				0.564** (0.193)	−0.799** (0.186)		0.138	9.129 (0.166)
	0.186 (0.307)						0.697** (0.162)	0.133	10.109 (0.120)

Notes: The symbol ** denotes significance at the 5 percent level. Source: Evans and Lyons (2009).

estimated without the interest differentials, the b_x estimates and R^2 statistics are essentially unchanged. The results are also robust to imposing $b_r = 1$ as a restriction.

Of course, a logical possibility is that dealers revise the risk premium in their spot quotes in response to order flows, but part of the reason is unrelated to future macroeconomic conditions. If this is the case, order flows should have forecasting power for future (excess) returns beyond that found in $\tilde{v}_{t,x}$. The right-hand column of Table 11.6 provides statistical evidence for this possibility. The p-values of χ^2 tests for the null that the regression residuals are unrelated to order flow are well above 5 percent in all the cases where the estimated b_x coefficients appear significant.

These findings provide a micro-based explanation for the forecasting results in Tables 11.4 and 11.5. They indicate that this forecasting power stems from the fact that order flows convey significant information about future macroeconomic conditions, specifically M1 and GDP growth, that dealers use to revise the risk premia they embed in their spot rate quotes.

11.4 Summary

- The Covered Interest Parity (CIP) condition very closely approximates the actual relationship we observe among spot rates, forward rates, and interest rates for major currencies under normal market conditions. In contrast, the empirical implications of Uncovered Interest Parity (UIP) and rational expectations are consistently at odds with the data on many major currencies. In particular, high-interest currencies tend, on average, to appreciate rather than depreciate. This phenomenon is commonly referred to as the "forward bias" or the Forward Premium Puzzle.

- Carry-trade strategies exploit the Forward Premium Puzzle by borrowing in the low-interest currency and lending in the high-interest currency. Alternatively, the strategy can be implemented by purchasing foreign currency forward when the forward rate is at a discount and selling foreign currency forward when the forward rate is at a premium. The payoffs to carry-trade strategies are large, even on a risk-adjusted basis. The Sharpe ratio for a multicurrency carry-trade strategy is much larger than the ratio from a strategy investing in U.S. equities.

- Macro models of exchange-rate risk build on the behavior of the Stochastic Discount Factor (SDF), which prices all financial assets in any environment that precludes arbitrage opportunities. We can identify the properties of the SDF necessary to explain the Forward Premium Puzzle via reverse engineering. Euler equation models identify the SDF from the preferences of a representative investor. Early models using power utility were unable to account for the excess returns on major currencies, even with very large degrees of risk-aversion. Recent research uses richer specifications for preferences that identify multiple macro risk factors driving the SDF, but none of these risk factors appear strongly correlated with excess currency returns or the returns on carry-trade strategies.

- Peso problem models are designed to account for the behavior of excess currency returns by focusing on the difference between sample and population moments that can arise in finite samples. These differences occur when market participants base their expectations on a subjective probability distribution that differs from the distribution generating past shocks because they rationally anticipate discrete shifts in the distribution of future shocks. Recent research on peso problem models considers the implications of discrete shifts that affect returns and the SDF. These models show that it is possible to account for the large returns on the carry trade if investors are concerned about a shift to a regime with small negative returns and a very high SDF.

- The foreign exchange risk premium in a micro-based model reflects the risk dealers face in their role as marketmakers rather than the risks they face as individual investors. As such, the risk premium embedded in dealers' spot rate quotes depends on their estimates of the aggregate hedging demand for foreign currency and their estimates of the average error agents will make when forecasting the future spot rate.

- In the absence of peso problems, micro-based models can account for the Forward Premium Puzzle if the aggregate hedging demand for foreign currency is negatively correlated with the interest differential between foreign and domestic interest rates. In this case informational differences between agents and dealers contribute to the volatility of the risk premium. When a peso problem is present, a micro-based model can account for the Forward Premium Puzzle because the informational differential between dealers and agents produces a negative sample correlation between the forward premium and the risk premium embedded in dealers' spot rate quotes. In this case, spot rates will exhibit delayed overshooting to interest rate shocks and the forecast errors of agents will be correlated with the forward premium.

- Micro-based models imply that order flows will have forecasting power for future excess returns when they convey information to dealers that is relevant to the determination of future risk premia. Empirically, order flows have much more forecasting power for future excess returns than other variables, both in-sample and out-of-sample. This forecasting power reflects the fact that the order flows convey new information about future output and monetary growth.

11.5 Bibliography

This chapter only touches on the vast literature that looks at the Forward Premium Puzzle. Much of the earlier research is discussed in surveys by Lewis (1995) and Engel (1996). One of the first discussions of the returns on carry-trade strategies appears in Lyons (2001). He argues that, whereas the returns to the carry trade appear sizable, they are not significant enough to induce large financial institutions to devote much of their own capital to carry-trade strategies. This may explain why transactions induced by carry-trade strategies are insufficient to immediately eliminate deviations from UIP. Recent theoretical models of the carry trade and its role in currency crashes can be found in Plantin and Shin (2008) and Brunnermeier and Pedersen (2009). Carry-trade strategies can also be devised for fixed-income instruments (see, e.g., Duarte, Longstaff, and Yu 2005).

Our discussion of the Euler equation and peso problem models draws on the work of Burnside et al. (2006) and Burnside (2007). Epstein-Zin-Weil preferences have also been used in an Euler equation model by Bansal and Shaliastovich (2007). Moore and Roche (2009) and Verdelhan (2010) build models around the habit preferences developed by Campbell and Cochrane (1999). A survey of the literature on first-generation peso problem models can be found in Evans (1996). The recent resurgence of interest in peso problem models originates from the work of Barro (2006). In addition to Burnside et al. (2006), papers by Farhi and Gabaix (2008) and Farhi et al. (2009) also examine peso problem models for excess currency returns.

The micro-based model presented in Section 11.3 is related to the work of Burnside, Eichenbaum, and Rebelo (2009). They present a model of the forward market in which a marketmaker trades with informed investors who have information about the future spot rate, and uninformed investors who follow a behavioral trading strategy. This model is similar to the sequential trade model studied in Chapter 5, except for the presence of behavioral traders that create a worse adverse selection problem for the marketmaker when the spot rate is expected to appreciate. It is this feature of the model that produces the negative correlation between the forward premium and the future depreciation rate. In contrast, the micro-based model presented here focuses on the determination of spot rates in an environment in which investors do not have better information about the future course of spot rates than dealers. On the contrary, in the equilibrium we studied, dealers have more precise information about the current state of the economy (and hence the future path of spot rates) than investors because they observe order flows. The exchange-rate dynamics in this model are therefore unrelated to the presence of adverse selection problems and how they may change through time.

A number of recent papers examine the role of informational frictions in models of the Forward Premium Puzzle. Froot and Thaler (1990) and Lyons (2001) first pointed out that if investors respond gradually to news about a higher domestic interest rate, there will be a continued appreciation of the domestic currency as portfolios are reallocated toward domestic bonds. Bacchetta and van Wincoop (2010) formalize this idea in a model where investors revise their portfolios infrequently because information is costly to acquire. Gourinchas and Tornell (2004) investigate a related model where investors' gradual response to interest rate shocks originates from misperceptions concerning the duration of the shocks. Elements of their model are present in the peso problem example discussed in Section 11.3.

11.6 Review Questions

1. Executing a Carry-Trade Strategy: Suppose that the current USD/GBP spot rate, S_t, is \$1.50/£, and the current U.S. and U.K. 1-year interest rates are 3 percent and 4 percent respectively. Over the next year there is a 60 percent probability that the dollar will depreciate against the pound by 5 percent and a 40 percent probability that it will appreciate by 5 percent.

   (a) Describe the carry-trade strategy in this situation that uses the 1-year forward rate on the USD/GBP.
   (b) Compute the payoffs per dollar invested in the strategy in both future states of the world.
   (c) An investor can also purchase at the money put and call options on the pound. Describe what options position he should take to (partially) hedge the carry-trade strategy described in your answer to part (a).
   (d) Compute the payoffs in each future state of the world to a hedged carry-trade strategy in this situation [i.e., the strategy described in your answers to parts (a) and (c)]. Remember that the payoff will have to include the cost of the option.
   (e) Show that the risk-adjusted expected payoff to the unhedged carry-trade strategy computed in your answer to part (a) is the same as the risk-adjusted expected payoff to the hedged strategy computed in your answer to part (d).

2. A Habit-Based SDF model: Verdelhan (2010) proposes a model for the domestic and foreign SDFs derived from preferences with external habits that can account for aspects of the Forward Premium Puzzle. In particular, the representative domestic agent maximizes

$$\mathbb{E}_t \sum_{i=0}^{\infty} \beta^i \frac{(C_{t+i} - H_{t+i})^{1-\gamma} - 1}{1 - \gamma}, \tag{11.68}$$

where C_t denotes consumption and H_t represents the subsistence level of consumption. The habit level is treated as exogenous by individual agents but varies with past aggregate consumption via an autoregressive process for the log consumption surplus ratio, $v_t \equiv \ln(C_t - H_t) - \ln C_t$:

$$v_{t+1} = (1 - \phi)\bar{v} + \phi v_t + \lambda(v_t)(\Delta c_{t+1} - g), \qquad (11.69)$$

where $\lambda(v_t) = (1/\bar{V})\sqrt{1 - 2(v_t - \bar{v})} - 1$ when $v \leq v_{\max}$ and 0 elsewhere. $\bar{V}$ is the steady state surplus consumption ratio and $v_{\max} = \bar{v} + (1 - \bar{V}^2)$ with $\bar{v} = \ln \bar{V}$. The representative agent in the foreign country has analogous preferences defined over foreign consumption, $\hat{C}_t$, and the foreign habit, $\hat{H}_t$, which vary via a similar autoregressive process for the log foreign consumption ratio, $\hat{v}_t = \ln(\hat{C}_t - \hat{H}_t) - \ln \hat{C}_t$. Verdelhan assumes that domestic and foreign agents have the same preference parameters, that is, β, γ, ϕ, g, and $\bar{V}$.

(a) The domestic real SDF, $\mathfrak{M}_{t+1}$, prices real payoffs on assets in terms of domestic consumption. In other words, the absence of arbitrage implies that $p_t^i = \mathbb{E}_t[\mathfrak{M}_{t+1}\mathcal{X}_{t+1}^i]$ for assets i, where p_t^i and $\mathcal{X}_{t+1}^i$ denote the price and payoff of asset i measured in terms of domestic consumption goods, C_t. Show that the real domestic SDF is

$$\mathfrak{M}_{t+1} = \beta \exp(-\gamma[g + (\phi - 1)(v_t - \bar{v}) + (1 + \lambda(v_t))(\Delta c_{t+1} - g)]).$$

(b) The no-arbitrage condition implies that the domestic real interest rate, rr_t, satisfies $1 = \mathbb{E}_t[\mathfrak{M}_{t+1} \exp(rr_t)]$. Suppose that the equilibrium process for the log of domestic consumption follows a random walk with drift, $\Delta c_{t+1} = g + u_{t+1}$, where $u_{t+1} \sim N(0, \sigma^2)$. Use your answer to part (a) to find an expression for rr_t in terms of the log consumption surplus ratio. Identify the conditions under which variations in the real rate are procyclical.

(c) Let $\widehat{\mathfrak{M}}_{t+1}$ denote the foreign real SDF that prices real payoffs in terms of foreign consumption, $\hat{C}_t$. Show that under complete markets and the absence of arbitrage

$$\mathcal{E}_{t+1}/\mathcal{E}_t = \widehat{\mathfrak{M}}_{t+1}/\mathfrak{M}_{t+1},$$

where $\mathcal{E}_t$ is the real exchange rate (the relative price of foreign consumption in terms of domestic consumption).

(d) Suppose now that the equilibrium process for the log of foreign consumption follows $\Delta \hat{c}_{t+1} = g + \hat{u}_{t+1}$, with $\hat{u}_{t+1} \sim N(0, \sigma^2)$. Find expressions for the real foreign SDF and real interest rate, $\widehat{rr}_t$. Use these expressions and your preceding answers to derive equations that relate the real depreciation rate, $\Delta \varepsilon_{t+1} \equiv \ln(\mathcal{E}_{t+1}/\mathcal{E}_t)$, and interest differential, $rr_t - \widehat{rr}_t$, to the domestic and foreign surplus ratios.

(e) Consider the projection of the real depreciation rate on a constant and the real interest differential

$$\Delta \varepsilon_{t+1} = \alpha_0 + \alpha(rr_t - \widehat{rr}_t) + \xi_{t+1}. \qquad (11.70)$$

Use your answer to part (d) to compute the population value of the slope coefficient. Explain how the cyclical properties of real interest rates affect the sign of α.

(f) In light of your answer to part (e), explain how the foreign exchange risk premium behaves over the business cycle in this model?

(g) The Forward Premium Puzzle relates to the results of regressing the nominal depreciation rate on the nominal interest:

$$\Delta s_{t+1} = \beta_0 + \beta(r_t - r_t) + \zeta_{t+1}.$$

Can specifications for the SDF that give a negative value for α also account for the negative estimates of β that we observe empirically? Explain.

3. Crash Risk and the Forward Premium Puzzle: Suppose there are two states of the world, $z \in \mathcal{Z} = \{0, 1\}$, and the depreciation rate for the USD/EUR spot rate follows

$$S_{t+1}/S_t = \mu(z_{t+1}), \quad \text{with } \mu(z) = \begin{cases} 1.03 & \text{when } z = 1 \\ 0.97 & \text{when } z = 0 \end{cases}. \quad (11.71)$$

Realizations of z_t are observed by investors and come from a Markov process with transition probabilities $\Pr(z_t = z | z_{t-1} = z) = \lambda_z$. Markets are complete, so in each period t there are two Arrow-Debreu securities with dollar prices $\mathcal{P}_t(z)$ that pay \$1 when $z_{t+1} = z$, and zero otherwise. The prices of securities are as follows:

$z_t \backslash z_{t+1}$	1	0
1	$\mathcal{P}_1(1) = 0.50$	$\mathcal{P}_1(0) = 0.45$
0	$\mathcal{P}_0(1) = 0.45$	$\mathcal{P}_0(0) = 0.50$

(a) Compute the price of a one-period forward contract in this economy when $z_t = 1$ and when $z_t = 0$. When can the euro be purchased forward at a premium or discount?

(b) Suppose that the transition probabilities for each state are the same, that is, $\lambda_1 = \lambda_0 = \lambda$. Calculate the population value of β from the projection

$$\frac{S_{t+1} - S_t}{S_t} = \beta \left(\frac{\mathcal{F}_t}{S_t} - 1 \right) + \zeta_{t+1}.$$

Show that $\beta < 0$ if λ is less than 0.5 and explain the economics behind this result.

(c) Now suppose that the spot rate process is characterized by infrequent currency crashes. In particular, the depreciation rate follows (11.71) with $\mu(1) = 1.03$ and $\mu(0) = 0.8$ and the transition probabilities governing the Markov process for z_t are $\lambda_1 = 0.97$ and $\lambda_0 = 0.8$. In this specification, the currency crash occurs when $z_t = 0$. Use the prices of the AD securities to compute the forward premia for $z_t = \{1, 0\}$ and compare the answer with the one you computed in part (a).

(d) Compute the population value for the projection coefficient β. Can this version of the model provide a resolution to the Forward Premium Puzzle?

(e) Show how your answers to parts (c) and (d) change if the AD securities prices are now given by

$z_t \backslash z_{t+1}$	1	0
1	$\mathcal{P}_1(1) = 0.40$	$\mathcal{P}_1(0) = 0.58$
0	$\mathcal{P}_0(1) = 0.45$	$\mathcal{P}_0(0) = 0.53$

(f) In light of your previous answers, comment on the likely contribution of currency crashes as explanations for the Forward Premium Puzzle.

4. Peso Problems: Suppose that there are two states of the world, $z \in \mathcal{Z} = \{0, 1\}$, and the dynamics of dollar and euro SDFs are given by

$$\ln \mathcal{M}_{t+1} = \kappa(z_{t+1}) + \phi(\ln \mathcal{M}_t - \kappa(z_t)) + v_{t+1},$$

$$\ln \widehat{\mathcal{M}}_{t+1} = \hat{\kappa}(z_{t+1}) + \phi(\ln \widehat{\mathcal{M}}_t - \hat{\kappa}(z_t)) + \hat{v}_{t+1},$$

where $v_{t+1} \sim i.d.N(0, \sigma^2(z_{t+1}))$, $\hat{v}_{t+1} \sim i.d.N(0, \hat{\sigma}^2(z_{t+1}))$, $\kappa(z) = -\mu - \frac{1}{2}\sigma^2(z_t)$, and $\hat{\kappa}(z) = -\mu - \frac{1}{2}\hat{\sigma}^2(z)$ for $z = \{1, 0\}$, with $\mu > 0$ and $1 > \phi > 0$; $\sigma(z)$ and $\hat{\sigma}(z)$ are the state-dependent standard deviations of the shock to the log SDFs. Realizations of z_t are observed by investors and come from a Markov process with transition probabilities $\Pr(z_t = z | z_{t-1} = z) = \lambda_z$.

(a) Derive an equation for the log depreciation rate, Δs_{t+1}, in the USD/EUR spot rate under the assumption of complete markets.

(b) Derive equations for the log one-period nominal interest rates in the United States and Europe, r_t and $\hat{r}_t$. Explain how changes in the state affect the dynamics of interest rates.

(c) Use your answers to parts (a) and (b) to identify the risk premium, δ_t, and forecast error, $s_{t+1} - \mathbb{E}_t s_{t+1}$, in the following identity:

$$\Delta s_{t+1} = r_t - \hat{r}_t + \delta_t + s_{t+1} - \mathbb{E}_t s_{t+1}.$$

(d) Consider the projection of the depreciation rate on the interest differential,

$$\Delta s_{t+1} = \beta(r_t - \hat{r}_t) + \xi_{t+1}.$$

Use your previous answers to compute the population value of β. Does this model reproduce the Forward Premium Puzzle? Explain.

(e) Now suppose a researcher has only T data observations from state $z = 1$, the nonpeso state. Derive an expression for the estimate of β, $\tilde{\beta}$. Discuss what happens to the value of $\tilde{\beta}$ in the limit as $T \to \infty$.

(f) Explain how the possibility of a switch to the peso state ($z = 0$) affects the behavior of the risk premium, δ_t, and the forecast errors, $s_{t+1} - \mathbb{E}_t s_{t+1}$, in the nonpeso state. How are these effects reflected in $\tilde{\beta}$?

(g) In light of your previous answers, is the presence of switching in the process for the depreciation rate and SDFs sufficient to produce a peso-problem explanation for the Forward Premium Puzzle?

11.A Appendix

11.A.1 Solving the Micro-Based Model

To verify that equations (11.54)–(11.56) describe the equilibrium of the model, we first note that dealers can precisely infer the value of z_t by the start of week $t + 1$ from their observations on order flow because (11.56) implies that $z_t = \mathbb{E}^{D}_t z_t + \alpha_h^{-1}(x_{t+1} - \mathbb{E}^{D}_t x_{t+1})$. Consequently, dealers' estimates of z_t at the start of week t can be computed from the projection theorem as

$$\mathbb{E}^{D}_t z_t = \mathbb{E}^{D}_{t-1} z_t + \kappa([\hat{r}_t - r_t] - \mathbb{E}^{D}_{t-1}[\hat{r}_t - r_t])$$

$$= a z_{t-1} + \kappa(\psi u_t + v_t), \tag{11.72}$$

where $\kappa = \psi \sigma_u^2/(\psi^2 \sigma_u^2 + \sigma_v^2)$, as shown in (11.57). When dealers have more precise information about z_t than agents, $\mathbb{E}^{D}_t z_t^e = \mathbb{E}^{D}_t z_t - \mathbb{E}^{D}_t \overline{\mathbb{E}}^{n}_t z_t = \mathbb{E}^{D}_t z_t - \overline{\mathbb{E}}^{n}_t z_t$. Their forecasts for the future spot rate are therefore

$$\mathbb{E}^{D}_t s_{t+1} = \pi_z \mathbb{E}^{D}_t z_t + \pi_e \mathbb{E}^{D}_t z_t^e = (\pi_z + \pi_e)\mathbb{E}^{D}_t z_t - \pi_e \overline{\mathbb{E}}^{n}_t z_t. \tag{11.73}$$

Agents' estimates of z_t are identified by the Kalman filtering equation

$$\mathbb{E}^{n}_t z_t = a\mathbb{E}^{n}_{t-1} z_{t-1} + \kappa_r([\hat{r}_t - r_t] - \mathbb{E}^{n}_{t-1}[\hat{r}_t - r_t]) + \kappa_s(s_t - \mathbb{E}^{n}_{t-1} s_t),$$

where κ_r and κ_s are the coefficients from the steady state gain matrix derived in what follows. Since agents are assumed to ignore the information in their own hedging demands, their estimates of z_t are the same across all agents, so $\overline{\mathbb{E}}^{n}_t z_t = \mathbb{E}^{n}_t z_t$. After substituting for the interest differential and the equilibrium spot rate from (A1) and (11.54), we can therefore write

$$\overline{\mathbb{E}}^{n}_t z_t = a z_{t-1} + \kappa_r(\psi u_t + v_t + \psi a z_{t-1}^e)$$

$$+ \kappa_s(\pi_v v_t + \pi_u u_t + (\pi_z + \pi_\eta)z_{t-1}^e) - a z_{t-1}^e. \tag{11.74}$$

Combining this expression with the equation for z_t and the definition $z_t^e = z_t - \overline{\mathbb{E}}^{n}_t z_t$ gives

$$z_t^e = \eta_e z_{t-1}^e + \eta_u u_t + \eta_v v_t,$$

where $\eta_e = a(1 - \kappa_r \psi) - \kappa_s(\pi_z + \pi_e)$, $\eta_u = 1 - \kappa_r \psi - \kappa_s \pi_u$, and $\eta_v = -\kappa_r - \kappa_s \pi_v$, as shown in (11.55). Furthermore, since $\mathbb{E}^{D}_t z_t - \overline{\mathbb{E}}^{n}_t z_t = \mathbb{E}^{D}_t z_t - z_t + z_t^e$ by definition, we can use (A1), (11.55), (11.72), and (11.74) to write

$$\mathbb{E}^{D}_t z_t - \overline{\mathbb{E}}^{n}_t z_t = \left[\eta_u - (1 - \kappa\psi)\right] u_t + (\eta_v + \kappa)v_t + \eta_e z_{t-1}^e. \tag{11.75}$$

Combining this expression with the fact that $\mathbb{E}^{D}_t s_{t+1}^e = (\pi_z + \pi_e)(\mathbb{E}^{D}_t z_t - \mathbb{E}^{n}_t z_t)$ yields (11.59).

We can now verify that the equilibrium spot rate follows equation (11.54). Substituting for $\mathbb{E}_t^D s_{t+1}$, $\hat{r}_t - r_t$ and δ_t in (11.48) using (11.72)–(11.74), (A1), and (11.60) gives

$$s_t = \pi_z z_{t-1} + \pi_u u_t + \pi_v v_t + \pi_e z_{t-1}^e,$$

with

$$\pi_z = \frac{a(\psi + \alpha_h/\alpha_s)}{1-a},$$

$$\pi_u = \frac{\psi(1 - \pi_e \kappa_r) + (\pi_z + \pi_e)(1 - \eta_u) + \alpha_h \kappa \psi/\alpha_s}{1 + \pi_e \kappa_s},$$

$$\pi_v = \frac{1 - \pi_e \kappa_r - (\pi_z + \pi_e)\eta_v + \alpha_h \kappa/\alpha_s}{1 + \pi_e \kappa_s},$$

and

$$\pi_e = -\frac{\pi_z \eta_e}{1 + \eta_e + \kappa_r \psi a + \kappa_s(\pi_z + \pi_e) - a}.$$

This is the form of equation (11.54).

To verify that unexpected order flow follows (11.56), note that $\alpha_{t-1} \in \Omega_t^D$ because dealers observe the history of order flow and that the market-clearing condition in (11.50) implies that $\alpha_{t-1} = \sum_{i=0}^{t} x_{t-i}$. Hence,

$$x_{t+1} - \mathbb{E}_t^D x_{t+1} = (\alpha_t - \alpha_{t-1}) - \mathbb{E}_t^D(\alpha_t - a_{t-1}) = \alpha_t - \mathbb{E}_t^D \alpha_t.$$

Furthermore, since dealers have at least as much information as agents, $\overline{\mathbb{E}}_t^n s_{t+1} = \mathbb{E}_t^D \overline{\mathbb{E}}_t^n s_{t+1}$. It therefore follows from (11.49) that

$$x_{t+1} - \mathbb{E}_t^D x_{t+1} = \alpha_t - \mathbb{E}_t^D \alpha_t = h_t - \mathbb{E}_t^D h_t = \alpha_h(z_t - \mathbb{E}_t^D z_t),$$

as shown in (11.56).

All that now remains is to identify the gain coefficients, κ_r and κ_s. For this purpose, let $\mathcal{Z}_t = [\, z_t \quad z_t^e \quad v_t \quad u_t \,]'$ and $\mathcal{Z}_t^n = [\, \hat{r}_t - r_t \quad s_t \,]'$, where $\mathcal{Z}_t^n$ is the vector of variables agent n observes at the start of week t. We can write the equilibrium dynamics of the $\mathcal{Z}_t$ and $\mathcal{Z}_t^n$ in state space form as

$$
\begin{bmatrix} z_t \\ z_t^e \\ v_t \\ u_t \end{bmatrix}
=
\begin{bmatrix} a & 0 & 0 & 0 \\ 0 & \eta_e & 0 & 0 \\ 0 & 0 & 0 & 0 \\ 0 & 0 & 0 & 0 \end{bmatrix}
\begin{bmatrix} z_{t-1} \\ z_{t-1}^e \\ v_{t-1} \\ u_{t-1} \end{bmatrix}
+
\begin{bmatrix} 1 & 0 \\ \eta_u & \eta_v \\ 0 & 1 \\ 1 & 0 \end{bmatrix}
\begin{bmatrix} u_t \\ v_t \end{bmatrix},
$$

or

$$\mathcal{Z}_t = \mathbb{A}\mathcal{Z}_{t-1} + \mathbb{B}\mathcal{U}_t,$$

and

$$Z_t^n = \begin{bmatrix} \hat{r}_t - r_t \\ s_t \end{bmatrix}$$

$$= \begin{bmatrix} \psi & 0 & 1 & 0 \\ \pi_z/a & \pi_e/\eta_e & \pi_v - \eta_v\pi_e/\eta_e & \pi_u - \pi_z/a - \eta_u\pi_e/\eta_e \end{bmatrix} \begin{bmatrix} z_t \\ z_t^e \\ v_t \\ u_t \end{bmatrix} = \mathbb{C}Z_t.$$

The steady state gain matrix, $\mathcal{G}$, solves the following equations from the Kalman filter:

$$\mathcal{G} = \Sigma\mathbb{C}(\mathbb{C}\Sigma\mathbb{C}')^{-1} \quad \text{and} \quad \Sigma = A(I - \mathcal{G}\mathbb{C})\Sigma A' + \mathbb{B}\mathbb{S}\mathbb{B}',$$

where $\mathbb{S} = \mathbb{E}[U_t U_t']$. The gain coefficients, κ_r and κ_s, are the elements in the first row of $\mathcal{G}$.

11.A.2 Derivations

To derive (11.41), we first take unconditional expectations on both sides of (11.33) and combine the result with the no-arbitrage condition, $\mathbb{E}[\mathcal{M}_{t+1}\mathcal{R}_{t+1}^e] = \mathbb{E}[\mathcal{N}_{t+1}] = 0$, to get

$$\mathbb{E}[\mathcal{N}_{t+1}(0)] = \mathbb{E}[\nabla\mathcal{N}_{t+1}]\wp = -\mathbb{E}[\mathcal{N}_{t+1}(1)]\frac{\wp}{1 - \wp}.$$

Next we write $\mathbb{E}[\mathcal{N}_{t+1}(z)]$ as $\mathbb{E}[\mathcal{R}_{t+1}^e(z)]\mathbb{E}[\mathcal{M}_{t+1}(z)] + \mathbb{C}\mathbb{V}(\mathcal{M}_{t+1}(z), \mathcal{R}_{t+1}^e(z))$ for $z = \{0, 1\}$. Substituting these expressions in the preceding equation and rearranging gives

$$\mathbb{E}[\mathcal{R}_{t+1}^e(0)] = \mathcal{RP}(0) - \left(\mathbb{E}[\mathcal{R}_{t+1}^e(1)] - \mathcal{RP}(1)\right)\frac{\mathbb{E}[\mathcal{M}_{t+1}(1)]}{\mathbb{E}[\mathcal{M}_{t+1}(0)]}\frac{\wp}{1 - \wp},$$

where $\mathcal{RP}(z) = -\mathbb{C}\mathbb{V}(\mathcal{M}_{t+1}(z), \mathcal{R}_{t+1}^e(z))/\mathbb{E}[\mathcal{M}_{t+1}(z)]$ as shown in equation (11.41).

To derive (11.66) we first use (11.64) to write

$$er_{t+1} = \delta_t + (s_{t+1} - \mathbb{E}_t^D s_{t+1}),$$

$$er_{t+2} = \mathbb{E}_t^D\delta_{t+1} + (\delta_{t+1} - \mathbb{E}_t^D\delta_{t+1}) + (s_{t+2} - \mathbb{E}_{t+1}^D s_{t+2}),$$

$$er_{t+3} = \mathbb{E}_t^D\delta_{t+2} + (\mathbb{E}_{t+1}^D - \mathbb{E}_t^D)\delta_{t+2} + (\delta_{t+2} - \mathbb{E}_{t+1}^D\delta_{t+2}) + (s_{t+3} - \mathbb{E}_{t+2}^D s_{t+3}),$$

and so on. Substituting these equations into the definition $er_{t+\tau}^\tau = \sum_{i=1}^\tau er_{t+i}$ produces

$$er^{\tau}_{t+\tau} = \mathbb{E}^{\mathrm{D}}_t \sum_{i=0}^{\tau-1} \delta_{t+i} + (\mathbb{E}^{\mathrm{D}}_{t+1} - \mathbb{E}^{\mathrm{D}}_t) \sum_{i=1}^{\tau-1} \delta_{t+i} + (s_{t+1} - \mathbb{E}^{\mathrm{D}}_t s_{t+1})$$

$$+ (\mathbb{E}^{\mathrm{D}}_{t+2} - \mathbb{E}^{\mathrm{D}}_{t+1}) \sum_{i=2}^{\tau-1} \delta_{t+i} + (s_{t+2} - \mathbb{E}^{\mathrm{D}}_{t+1} s_{t+2})$$

$$\vdots$$

$$+ (\mathbb{E}^{\mathrm{D}}_{t+\tau-1} - \mathbb{E}^{\mathrm{D}}_{t+\tau-2}) \delta_{t+\tau-1} + (s_{t+\tau-1} - \mathbb{E}^{\mathrm{D}}_{t+\tau-1} s_{t+\tau-1})$$

$$+ (s_{t+\tau} - \mathbb{E}^{\mathrm{D}}_{t+\tau-1} s_{t+\tau}).$$

Note that all the terms below the first line are uncorrelated with dealers' information at the start of week $t + 1$. These terms comprise $\zeta_{t+\tau}$ in equation (11.66).

References

Akaike, H. (1974). A new look at the statistical model identification. *IEEE Transactions on Automatic Control 19*(6), 716–723.

Akram, Q. F., D. Rime, and L. Sarno (2008). Arbitrage in the foreign exchange market: Turning on the microscope. *Journal of International Economics 76*(2), 237–253.

Alvarez, F., A. Atkeson, and P. Kehoe (2002). Money, interest rates, and exchange rates with endogenously segmented markets. *Journal of Political Economy 110*(1), 73–112.

Alvarez, F., A. Atkeson, and P. Kehoe (2009). Time-varying risk, interest rates, and exchange rates in general equilibrium. *Review of Economic Studies 76*(3), 851–878.

Andersen, T., and T. Bollerslev (1998, February). Deutsche mark–dollar volatility: Intraday activity patterns, macroeconomics announcements and longer run dependencies. *Journal of Finance 53*(1), 219–265.

Andersen, T., T. Bollerslev, F. Diebold, and P. Labys (2001). The distribution of realized exchange rate volatility. *Journal of the American Statistical Association 96*(453), 42–55.

Andersen, T., T. Bollerslev, F. Diebold, and C. Vega (2003). Micro effects of macro announcements: Real-time price discovery in foreign exchange. *American Economic Review 93*(1), 38–62.

Angel, J. (1994). Limit versus market orders. Working paper, Georgetown University.

Bacchetta, P., and E. van Wincoop (2006). Can information heterogeneity explain the exchange rate determination puzzle? *American Economic Review 96*(3), 552–576.

Bacchetta, P., and E. van Wincoop (2008). Higher order expectations in asset pricing. *Journal of Money, Credit and Banking 40*(5), 837–866.

Bacchetta, P., and E. van Wincoop (2010). Infrequent portfolio decisions: A solution to the forward discount puzzle. *American Economic Review 100*(3), 870–904.

Backus, D., S. Foresi, and C. Telmer (2001). Affine term structure models and the forward premium anomaly. *Journal of Finance 56*(1), 279–304.

Backus, D., P. Kehoe, and F. Kydland (1994). Dynamics of the trade balance and the terms of trade: The J-curve? *American Economic Review 84*(1), 84–103.

Backus, D., and G. Smith (1993). Consumption and real exchange rates in dynamic exchange economies with nontraded goods. *Journal of International Economics 35*(3–4), 297–316.

Baillie, R., and T. Bollerslev (2000). The forward premium anomaly is not as bad as you think. *Journal of International Money and Finance 19*(4), 471–488.

Balassa, B. (1964). The Purchasing-Power Parity doctrine: A Reappraisal. *Journal of Political Economy 72*(6), 584–596.

Bansal, R., and M. Dahlquist (2000). The forward premium puzzle: Different tales from developed and emerging economies. *Journal of International Economics 51*(1), 115–144.

Bansal, R., and I. Shaliastovich (2007). Risk and return in bond, currency, and equity markets. Working paper, Duke University.

Barker, W. (2007). The global foreign exchange market: Growth and transformation. *Bank of Canada Review 2007*(Autumn), 4–13.

Barro, R. (2006). Rare disasters and asset markets in the twentieth century. *Quarterly Journal of Economics 121*(3), 823–866.

Baxter, M., and M. Crucini (1995). Business cycles and the asset structure of foreign trade. *International Economic Review 36*(4), 821–854.

Benigno, G., and P. Benigno (2008, October). Exchange rate determination under interest rate rules. *Journal of International Money and Finance 27*(6), 971–993.

Berben, R., and D. van Dijk (1998). Does the absence of cointegration explain the typical findings in long horizon regressions? Working paper, Econometric Institute, Erasmus University.

Berger, D., A. Chaboud, S. Chernenko, E. Howorka, and J. Wright (2008). Order flow and exchange rate dynamics in electronic brokerage system data. *Journal of International Economics 75*(1), 93–109.

Bergin, P. (2003). Putting the new open economy macroeconomics to a test. *Journal of International Economics 60*(1), 3–34.

Berkowitz, J., and L. Giorgianni (2001). Long-horizon exchange rate predictability? *Review of Economics and Statistics 83*(1), 81–91.

Betts, C., and M. Devereux (1996, April). The exchange rate in a model of pricing-to-market. *European Economic Review 40*(3–5), 1007–1021.

Betts, C., and M. Devereux (2000, February). Exchange rate dynamics in a model of pricing-to-market. *Journal of International Economics 50*(1), 215–244.

Betts, C., and T. Kehoe (2006). US real exchange rate fluctuations and relative price fluctuations. *Journal of Monetary Economics 53*(7), 1297–1326.

Bilson, J. (1978). The monetary approach to the exchange rate: Some empirical evidence. *IMF Staff Papers 25*(1), 48–75.

BIS (2007, April). Triennial central bank survey of foreign exchange and derivatives market activity in April 2007.

Bjønnes, G. H., D. Rime, and H. O. A. Solheim (2005, March). Liquidity provision in the overnight foreign exchange market. *Journal of International Money and Finance 24*(2), 177–198.

Blanchard, O., F. Giavazzi, and F. Sa (2005). International investors, the U.S. current account, and the dollar. *Brookings Papers on Economic Activity 2005*(1), 1–49.

Blanchard, O., and C. Kahn (1980). The solution of linear difference models under rational expectations. *Econometrica: Journal of the Econometric Society 48*(5), 1305–1311.

Breedon, F., D. Rime, and P. Vitale (2010). A transaction data study of the forward bias puzzle. Discussion Paper 7791, CEPR.

Breedon, F., and P. Vitale (2010). An empirical study of portfolio-balance and information effects of order flow on exchange rates. *Journal of International Money and Finance 29*(3), 504–524.

Browning, M., L. P. Hansen, and J. J. Heckman (1999). Micro data and general equilibrium models. In J. B. Taylor and M. Woodford (Eds.), *Handbook of Macroeconomics*, Volume 1, Chapter 8, pp. 543–633. Elsevier.

Brunnermeier, M. (2001). *Asset Pricing Under Asymmetric Information: Bubbles, Crashes, Technical Analysis, and Herding*. Oxford University Press.

Brunnermeier, M., and L. Pedersen (2009). Market liquidity and funding liquidity. *Review of Financial Studies 22*(6), 2201–2238.

Burnside, C. (2007). The cross-section of foreign currency risk premia and consumption growth risk: A comment. Working Paper 13129, National Bureau of Economic Research.

Burnside, C., M. Eichenbaum, I. Kleshchelski, and S. Rebelo (2006, August). The returns to currency speculation. Working Paper 12489, National Bureau of Economic Research.

Burnside, C., M. Eichenbaum, and S. Rebelo (2009, July). Understanding the forward premium puzzle: A microstructure approach. *American Economic Journal: Macroeconomics 1*(2), 127–54.

Burstein, A., M. Eichenbaum, and S. Rebelo (2006). The importance of nontradable goods' prices in cyclical real exchange rate fluctuations. *Japan & the World Economy 18*(3), 247–253.

Burstein, A., J. Neves, and S. Rebelo (2003). Distribution costs and real exchange rate dynamics during exchange-rate-based stabilizations. *Journal of Monetary Economics 50*(6), 1189–1214.

Calvo, G. (1983). Staggered prices in a utility-maximizing framework. *Journal of Monetary Economics 12*(3), 383–398.

Campbell, J., (1993). Intertemporal asset pricing without consumption data. *American Economic Review 83*(3), 487–512.

Campbell, J., and J. Cochrane (1999). By force of habit: A consumption-based explanation of aggregate stock market behavior. *Journal of Political Economy 107*(2), 205–251.

Campbell, J., A. Lo, and A. MacKinlay (1997). *The Econometrics of Financial Markets*. Princeton University Press.

Campbell, J., and R. Shiller (1988). The dividend-price ratio and expectations of future dividends and discount factors. *Review of Financial Studies 1*(3), 195–228.

Campbell, J., and L. Viceira (2002). *Strategic Asset Allocation: Portfolio Choice for Long-Term Investors*. Oxford University Press.

Campbell, J., and M. Yogo (2006). Efficient tests of stock return predictability. *Journal of Financial Economics 81*(1), 27–60.

Canova, F. (2007). *Methods for Applied Macroeconomic Research*. Princeton University Press.

Cao, C., O. Hansch, and X. Wang (2008). The informational content of an open limit order book. *Journal of Futures Markets 29*, 16–41.

Cao, H. H., M. D. D. Evans, and R. K. Lyons (2004). Inventory information. *Journal of Business 79*(1), 325–364.

Carlson, J. A., and M. Lo (2006, November). One minute in the life of the DM/US$: Public news in an electronic market. *Journal of International Money and Finance 25*(7), 1090–1102.

Cavanagh, C., G. Elliott, and J. Stock (2009). Inference in models with nearly integrated regressors. *Econometric Theory 11*(5), 1131–1147.

Chaboud, A. P., S. V. Chernenko, and J. H. Wright (2008). Trading activity and exchange rates in high-frequency EBS data. *Journal of the European Economic Association 75*(1), 93–109.

Chari, V. V., P. Kehoe, and E. R. McGrattan (2002). Can sticky price models generate volatile and persistent real exchange rates? *Review of Economic Studies 69*(3), 533–563.

Chen, S., and C. Engel (2005). Does 'aggregation bias' explain the PPP puzzle? *Pacific Economic Review 10*, 49–72.

Cheung, Y., M. Chinn, and A. Pascual (2005). Empirical exchange rate models of the nineties: Are any fit to survive? *Journal of International Money and Finance 24*(7), 1150–1175.

Chinn, M., and G. Meredith (2004). Monetary policy and long-horizon uncovered interest parity. *IMF Staff Papers 51*(3), 409–431.

Chinn, M., and M. Moore (2009). Private information and the monetary model of exchange rates: Evidence from a novel data set. Working paper, Queens University.

Choi, C., N. Mark, and D. Sul (2006). Unbiased estimation of the half-life to PPP convergence in panel data. *Journal of Money, Credit and Banking 38*(4), 921–938.

Clarida, R., J. Gali, and M. Gertler (1998). Monetary policy rules in practice: Some international evidence. *European Economic Review 42*(6), 1033–1067.

Clarida, R., and D. Waldman (2007, April). Is bad news about inflation good news for the exchange rate? Working Paper 13010, National Bureau of Economic Research.

Clark, T., and M. McCracken (2005). Evaluating direct multistep forecasts. *Econometric Reviews 24*(4), 369–404.

Clark, T., and K. West (2006). Using out-of-sample mean squared prediction errors to test the martingale difference hypothesis. *Journal of Econometrics 135*(1–2), 155–186.

Cochrane, J. (2001). *Asset Pricing*. Princeton University Press.

Cornell, B. (1982). Money supply announcements, interest rates, and foreign exchange. *Journal of International Money and Finance 1*(2), 201–208.

Corsetti, G., L. Dedola, and S. Leduc (2008a, April). International risk sharing and the transmission of productivity shocks. *Review of Economic Studies 75*(2), 443–473.

Corsetti, G., L. Dedola, and S. Leduc (2008b, September). High exchange-rate volatility and low pass-through. *Journal of Monetary Economics 55*(6), 1113–1128.

Croushore, D., and T. Stark (2001). A real-time data set for macroeconomists. *Journal of Econometrics 105*(1), 111–130.

Crucini, M. (2006). International real business cycles. In S. Durlauf and L. Blume (Eds.), *The New Palgrave Dictionary of Economics*, Number 0617, pp. 494–504. Palgrave Macmillan.

Crucini, M., and M. Shintani (2008). Persistence in law of one price deviations: Evidence from micro-data. *Journal of Monetary Economics 55*(3), 629–644.

Daníelsson, J., and R. Love (2006). Feedback trading. *International Journal of Finance and Economics 11*(1), 35–53.

DeGennaro, R. P., and R. E. Shrieves (1997, December). Public information releases, private information arrival and volatility in the foreign exchange market. *Journal of Empirical Finance 4*(4), 295–315.

Devereux, M., and C. Engel (2002, July). Exchange rate pass-through, exchange rate volatility, and exchange rate disconnect. *Journal of Monetary Economics 49*(5), 913–940.

Devereux, M., and A. Sutherland (2010). Solving for country portfolios in open economy macro models. *Journal of the European Economic Association* forthcoming.

Diebold, F., and R. Mariano (2002). Comparing predictive accuracy. *Journal of Business & Economic Statistics 20*(1), 134–144.

Dominguez, K., and F. Panthaki (2006). What defines news in foreign exchange markets? *Journal of International Money and Finance 25*(1), 168–198.

Dornbusch, R. (1976). Expectations and exchange rate dynamics. *Journal of Political Economy 84*(6), 1161–1176.

Dotsey, M., and M. Duarte (2008, September). Nontraded goods, market segmentation, and exchange rates. *Journal of Monetary Economics 55*(6), 1129–1142.

Duarte, J., F. Longstaff, and F. Yu (2005). Risk and return in fixed-income arbitrage: Nickels in front of a steamroller? *Review of Financial Studies 20*(3), 769.

Duarte, M., and A. Stockman (2005). Rational speculation and exchange rates. *Journal of Monetary Economics 52*(1), 3–29.

Dunne, P., H. Hau, and M. Moore (2010). International order flows: Explaining equity and exchange rate returns. *Journal of International Money and Finance 29*(2), 358–386.

Easley, D., and M. O'Hara (1992). Time and the process of security price adjustment. *Journal of Finance 47*(2), 577–605.

Ederington, L., and J. Lee (2009). The short-run dynamics of the price adjustment to new information. *Journal of Financial and Quantitative Analysis 30*(01), 117–134.

Eichenbaum, M., and C. Evans (1995). Some empirical evidence on the effects of shocks to monetary policy on exchange rates. *Quarterly Journal of Economics*, 975–1009.

Ellis, K., R. Michaely, and M. O'Hara (2000, December). The accuracy of trade classification rules: Evidence from NASDAQ. *Journal of Financial and Quantitative Analysis 35*(4), 529–551.

Engel, C. (1996). The forward discount anomaly and the risk premium: A survey of recent evidence. *Journal of Empirical Finance 3*(2), 123–192.

Engel, C. (1999). Accounting for US real exchange rate changes. *Journal of Political Economy 107*(3), 507.

Engel, C. (2002). The responsiveness of consumer prices to exchange rates: A synthesis of some new open economy macro models. *Manchester School 70*, 1–15.

Engel, C., and J. Frankel (1984). Why interest rates react to money announcements: An answer from the foreign exchange market. *Journal of Monetary Economics 13*(1), 31–39.

Engel, C., N. Mark, and K. West (2007, August). Exchange rate models are not as bad as you think. Working Paper 13318, National Bureau of Economic Research.

Engel, C., and K. West (2005). Exchange rates and fundamentals. *Journal of Political Economy 113*(3), 485–517.

Engel, C., and K. West (2006). Taylor rules and the deutschmark–dollar real exchange rate. *Journal of Money, Credit, and Banking 38*(5), 1175–1194.

Epstein, L., and S. Zin (1989). Substitution, risk aversion, and the temporal behavior of consumption and asset returns: A theoretical framework. *Econometrica 57*(4), 937–969.

Evans, G. W., and S. Honkapohja (2001). *Learning and Expectations in Macroeconomics*. Princeton University Press.

Evans, M. D. D. (1996). Peso problems: Their theoretical and emprical implications. In G. Maddala and C. Rao (Eds.), *Handbook of Statistics*, Volume 14. North Holland.

Evans, M. D. D. (1998). The microstructure of foreign exchange dynamics. Working paper, Georgetown University.

Evans, M. D. D. (2002). FX trading and exchange rate dynamics. *Journal of Finance 57*(6), 2405–2447.

Evans, M. D. D. (2005). Where are we now? Real-time estimates of the macroeconomy. *International Journal of Central Banking 1*(6), 127–175.

Evans, M. D. D. (2010). Order flows and the exchange rate disconnect puzzle. *Journal of International Economics 80*(1), 58–71.

Evans, M. D. D., and V. Hnatkovska (2005a, October). International capital flows, returns and world financial integration. Working Paper 11701, National Bureau of Economic Research.

Evans, M. D. D., and V. Hnatkovska (2005b, October). Solving general equilibrium models with incomplete markets and many assets. Working Paper 318, National Bureau of Economic Research.

Evans, M. D. D., and K. K. Lewis (1995). Do long-term swings in the dollar affect estimates of the risk premia? *Review of Financial Studies 8*(3), 709–742.

Evans, M. D. D., and R. K. Lyons (1999, August). Order flow and exchange rate dynamics. Working Paper 7317, National Bureau of Economic Research.

Evans, M. D. D., and R. K. Lyons (2002a). Order flow and exchange rate dynamics. *Journal of Political Economy 110*(1), 170–180.

Evans, M. D. D., and R. K. Lyons (2002b). Informational integration and FX trading. *Journal of International Money and Finance 21*(6), 807–831.

Evans, M. D. D., and R. K. Lyons (2004). A new micro model of exchange rate dynamics. Working Paper 10379, National Bureau of Economic Research.

Evans, M. D. D., and R. K. Lyons (2005a). Do currency markets absorb news quickly? *Journal of International Money and Finance 24*(6), 197–217.

Evans, M. D. D., and R. K. Lyons (2005b). Meese-Rogoff redux: Micro-based exchange-rate forecasting. *American Economic Review Papers and Proceedings 95*(2), 405–414.

Evans, M. D. D., and R. K. Lyons (2006). Understanding order flow. *International Journal of Finance and Economics 11*(1), 3–23.

Evans, M. D. D., and R. K. Lyons (2007, June). Exchange rate fundamentals and order flow. Working Paper 13151, National Bureau of Economic Research.

Evans, M. D. D., and R. K. Lyons (2008a, April). How is macro news transmitted to exchange rates? *Journal of Financial Economics 88*(1), 26–50.

Evans, M. D. D., and R. K. Lyons (2008b, June). Macroeconomics and exchange rate dynamics redux. Working paper, Georgetown Unversity.

Evans, M. D. D., and R. K. Lyons (2009, July). Forecasting exchange rate fundamentals with order flow. Working paper, Georgetown University.

Fama, E. (1984). Spot and forward exchange rates. *Journal of Monetary Economics 14*(3), 319–338.

Fama, E., and J. MacBeth (1973). Risk, return, and equilibrium: Empirical tests. *Journal of Political Economy 81*(3), 607.

Farhi, E., S. P. Fraiberger, X. Gabaix, R. Ranciere, and A. Verdelhan (2009, June). Crash risk in currency markets. Working Paper 15062, National Bureau of Economic Research.

Farhi, E., and X. Gabaix (2008, February). Rare disasters and exchange rates. Working Paper 13805, National Bureau of Economic Research.

Faust, J., J. Rogers, S. Wang, and J. Wright (2007). The high-frequency response of exchange rates and interest rates to macroeconomic announcements. *Journal of Monetary Economics 54*(4), 1051–1068.

Faust, J., J. Rogers, and J. H. Wright (2003). Exchange rate forecasting: The errors we have really made. *Journal of International Economics 60*(1), 35–59.

Foster, F., and S. Viswanathan (1996). Strategic trading when agents forecast the forecasts of others. *Journal of Finance 51*(4), 1437–1478.

Frankel, J. (1979). On the mark: A theory of floating exchange rates based on real interest differentials. *American Economic Review 69*(4), 610–622.

Frankel, J., and A. K. Rose (1995). Empirical research on nominal exchange rates. In G. M. Grossman and K. Rogoff (Eds.), *Handbook of International Economics*, Volume 3, Chapter 33, pp. 1689–1729. Elsevier.

Frenkel, J. (1976). A monetary approach to the exchange rate: Doctrinal aspects and empirical evidence. *Scandinavian Journal of Economics 78*(2), 200–224.

Frenkel, J. (1981). Flexible exchange rates, prices, and the role of news: Lessons from the 1970s. *Journal of Political Economy 89*(4), 665–705.

Friedman, B., and K. Kuttner (1992). Money, income, prices, and interest rates. *American Economic Review 82*(3), 472–492.

Froot, K., and J. Frankel (1989). Forward discount bias: Is it an exchange risk premium? *Quarterly Journal of Economics 104*(1), 139–161.

Froot, K., and T. Ramadorai (2005). Currency returns, intrinsic value, and institutional-investor flows. *Journal of Finance 60*(3), 1535–1566.

Froot, K., and R. Thaler (1990). Anomalies: Foreign exchange. *Journal of Economic Perspectives 4*(3), 179–192.

Gali, J., and T. Monacelli (2005). Monetary policy and exchange rate volatility in a small open economy. *Review of Economic Studies 72*(3), 707–734.

Gennotte, G., and H. Leland (1990). Market liquidity, hedging, and crashes. *American Economic Review 80*(5), 999–1021.

Glosten, L., and P. Milgrom (1985). Bid, ask and transaction prices in a specialist market with heterogeneously informed traders. *Journal of Financial Economics 14*(1), 71–100.

Goettler, R. C., C. Parlour, and U. Rajan (2007). Microstructure effects and asset pricing. Working paper, University of California, Berkeley.

Goodhart, C., S. Hall, S. Henry, and B. Pesaran (1993). News effects in a high-frequency model of the sterling-dollar exchange rate. *Journal of Applied Econometrics 8*(1).

Gourinchas, P., and H. Rey (2007). International financial adjustment. *Journal of Political Economy 115*(4), 665–703.

Gourinchas, P., and A. Tornell (2004) Exchange rate puzzles and distorted beliefs. *Journal of International Economics 64*(2), 303–333.

Gradojevic, N., and C. Neely (2008). The dynamic interaction of order flows and the CAD/USD exchange rate. Working Paper 2008-006A, Federal Reserve Bank of St. Louis.

Green, T. (2004). Economic news and the impact of trading on bond prices. *Journal of Finance 59*(3), 1201–1233.

Groen, J. (2005). Exchange rate predictability and monetary fundamentals in a small multi-country panel. *Journal of Money, Credit & Banking 37*(3), 495–517.

Grossman, S. (1976). On the efficiency of competitive stock markets where traders have diverse information. *Journal of Finance 31*(2), 573–585.

Grossman, S., and J. Stiglitz (1980). On the impossibility of informationally efficient markets. *American Economic Review 70*(3), 393–408.

Hakkio, C., and D. Pearce (1985). The reaction of exchange rates to economic news. *Economic Inquiry 23*(4), 621–636.

Hansen, L. (1982). Large sample properties of generalized method of moments estimators. *Econometrica: Journal of the Econometric Society 50*(4), 1029–1054.

Hansen, L., and T. Sargent (1980). Formulating and estimating dynamic linear rational expectations models. *Journal of Economic Dynamics and Control 2*(1), 7–46.

Hardouvelis, G. A. (1988, March). Economic news, exchange rates and interest rates. *Journal of International Money and Finance 7*(1), 23–35.

Harris, L. (1998). Optimal dynamic order submission strategies in some stylized trading problems. *Financial Markets, Institutions & Instruments 7*(2), 1–76.

Harris, M., and A. Raviv (1993). Differences of opinion make a horse race. *Review of Financial Studies 6*(3), 473–506.

Harvey, A. (1990). *Forecasting, Structural Time Series Models and the Kalman Filter*. Cambridge University Press.

Hasbrouck, J. (1991). Measuring the information content of stock trades. *Journal of Finance 46*(1), 179–207.

Hau, H., and H. Rey (2006, April). Exchange rate, equity prices and capital flows. *Review of Financial Studies 19*(1), 273–317.

Hayek, F. (1945). The use of knowledge in society. *American Economic Review 35*(4), 519–530.

He, H., and J. Wang (1995). Differential information and dynamic behavior of stock trading volume. *Review of Financial Studies 8*(4), 919–972.

Henderson, D., and K. Rogoff (1982). Negative net foreign asset positions and stability in a world portfolio balance model. *Journal of International Economics 13*(1–2), 85–104.

Hnatkovska, V. (2010). Home bias and high turnover: Dynamic portfolio choice with incomplete markets. *Journal of International Economics 80*(1), 113–128.

Imbs, J., H. Mumtaz, M. O. Ravn, and H. Rey (2005). PPP strikes back: Aggregation and the real exchange rate. *Quarterly Journal of Economics 120*(1), 1–43.

Inoue, A., and L. Kilian (2005). In-sample or out-of-sample tests of predictability: Which one should we use? *Econometric Reviews 23*(4), 371–402.

Ito, T., and V. Roley (1987). News from the US and Japan:: Which moves the yen/dollar exchange rate? *Journal of Monetary Economics 19*(2), 255–277.

Jongen, R., W. Verschoor, and C. Wolff (2008). Foreign exchange rate expectations: Survey and synthesis. *Journal of Economic Surveys 22*(1), 140–165.

Jung, Y. (2007). Can the new open economy macroeconomic model explain exchange rate fluctuations? *Journal of International Economics 72*(2), 381–408.

Kandel, E., and N. Pearson (1995). Differential interpretation of public signals and trade in speculative markets. *Journal of Political Economy 103*(4), 831–872.

Kaniel, R., and H. Liu (2006). So what orders do informed traders use? *Journal of Business 79*, 1867–1913.

Kilian, L. (1999). Finite-sample properties of percentile and percentile-t bootstrap confidence intervals for impulse responses. *Review of Economics and Statistics 81*(4), 652–660.

Klein, M., B. Mizrach, and R. G. Murphy (1991, November). Managing the dollar: Has the Plaza agreement mattered? *Journal of Money, Credit and Banking 23*(4), 742–751.

Kollmann, R. (2001). The exchange rate in a dynamic-optimizing business cycle model with nominal rigidities: A quantitative investigation. *Journal of International Economics 55*(2), 243–262.

Kouri, P. J. K. (1976). The exchange rate and the balance of payments in the short run and in the long run: A monetary approach. *Scandinavian Journal of Economics 78*(2), 280–304.

Kydland, F., and E. Prescott (1982). Time to build and aggregate fluctuations. *Econometrica: Journal of the Econometric Society 50*(6), 1345–1370.

Lane, P. R. (2001, August). The new open economy macroeconomics: A survey. *Journal of International Economics 54*(2), 235–266.

Lee, C. M. C., and M. J. Ready (1991, June). Inferring trade direction from intraday data. *Journal of Finance 46*(2), 733–746.

LeRoy, S., and R. Porter (1981). The present-value relation: Tests based on implied variance bounds. *Econometrica: Journal of the Econometric Society 49*(3), 555–574.

Lewis, K. K. (1995). Puzzles in international financial markets. In G. M. Grossman and K. Rogoff (Eds.), *Handbook of International Economics*, Volume 3, Chapter 37, pp. 1913–1971. Elsevier.

Ljungqvist, L., and T. Sargent (2004). *Recursive Macroeconomic Theory*. MIT Press.

Lothian, J., and M. Taylor (1996). Real exchange rate behavior: The recent float from the perspective of the past two centuries. *Journal of Political Economy 104*(3), 488–509.

Love, R., and R. Payne (2008). Macroeconomic news, order flows and exchange rates. *Journal of Financial and Quantitative Analysis 43*(02), 467–488.

Lubik, T., and F. Schorfheide (2005). A Bayesian look at new open economy macroeconomics. *NBER Macroeconomics Annual 20*(1), 313–366.

Lucas, R. (1982). Interest rates and currency prices in a two-country World. *Journal of Monetary Economics 10*(3), 335–359.

Lustig, H., and A. Verdelhan (2007). The cross section of foreign currency risk premia and consumption growth risk. *American Economic Review 97*(1), 89–117.

Lyons, R. K. (1995). Tests of microstructural hypothesis in the foreign exchange market. *Journal of Financial Economics 39*(2–3), 321–351.

Lyons, R. K. (1997). A simultaneous trade model of the foreign exchange hot potato. *Journal of International Economics 42*(3–4), 275–298.

Lyons, R. K. (2001). *The Microstructure Approach to Exchange Rates*. MIT Press.

MacDonald R., and M. P. Taylor (1994). The monetary model of the exchange rate: long-run relationships, short-run dynamics and how to beat a random walk. *Journal of International Money and Finance 13*(3), 276–290.

Mark, N. (1985). On time varying risk premia in the foreign exchange market: An econometric analysis. *Journal of Monetary Economics 16*(1), 3–19.

Mark, N. (1995). Exchange rates and fundamentals: Evidence on long-horizon predictability. *American Economic Review 85*(1), 201–218.

Mark, N. (2001). *International Macroeconomics and Finance: Theory and Econometric Methods*. Blackwell.

Mark, N. (2009). Changing monetary policy rules, learning, and real exchange rate dynamics. *Journal of Money, Credit and Banking 41*(6), 1047–1070.

Mark, N., and D. Sul (2001). Nominal exchange rates and monetary fundamentals: Evidence from a small post-Bretton Woods panel. *Journal of International Economics 53*(1), 29–52.

Marsh, I. W., and C. O'Rourke (2005). Customer order flow and exchange rate movements: Is there really information content? Working paper, Cass Business School.

Meese, R., and K. Rogoff (1983). Empirical exchange rate models of the seventies: do they fit out of sample? *Journal of International Economics 14*(1–2), 3–24.

Menkhoff, L., C. L. Osler, and M. Schmeling (2006). Order-choice dynamics under asymmetric information: An empirical analysis. Typescript, University of Hannover.

Milgrom, P., and N. Stokey (1982). Information, trade and common knowledge. *Journal of Economic Theory 26*(1), 17–27.

Molodtsova, T., and D. H. Papell (2009). Out-of-sample exchange rate predictability with Taylor rule fundamentals. *Journal of International Economics 77*(2), 167–180.

Moore, M., and M. J. Roche (2009). For rich or for poor: When does uncovered interest parity hold? Working paper, Queen's University Belfast.

Mussa, M. (1976). The exchange rate, the balance of payments and monetary and fiscal policy under a regime of controlled floating. *Scandinavian Journal of Economics 78*(2), 229–248.

Newey, W., and K. West (1987). A simple, positive semi-definite, heteroskedasticity and auto-correlation consistent covariance matrix. *Econometrica: Journal of the Econometric Society 55*(3), 703–708.

Obstfeld, M. (2001, July). International macroeconomics: Beyond the Mundell-Fleming model. Working Paper 8369, National Bureau of Economic Research.

Obstfeld, M., and K. Rogoff (1995). Exchange rate dynamics redux. *Journal of Political Economy 103*(3), 624–660.

Obstfeld, M., and K. Rogoff (2000). New directions for stochastic open economy models. *Journal of International Economics 50*(1), 117–153.

Obstfeld, M., and K. Rogoff (2001). The six major puzzles in international macroeconomics: Is there a common cause? *NBER Macroeconomics Annual 2000*.

Obstfeld, M., and K. Rogoff (2003). Risk and exchange rates. In M. Obstfeld and K. S. Rogoff. *Economic Policy in the International Economy: Essays in Honor of Assaf Razin*. Cambridge University Press.

O'Hara, M. (1997). *Market Microstructure Theory*. Wiley.

Osler, C. L. (2003). Currency orders and exchange-rate dynamics: Explaining the success of technical analysis. *Journal of Finance 58*(5), 1791–1821.

Osler, C. L. (2008). *Springer Encyclopedia of Complexity and System Science*, Chapter: Foreign exchange microstructure: A survey. Springer.

Parlour, C. A., and D. J. Seppi (2008). *Handbook of Financial Intermediation and Banking*, Chapter: Limit order markets: A survey. Elsevier.

Payne, R. (2003, December). Informed trade in spot foreign exchange markets: An empirical investigation. *Journal of International Economics 61*(2), 307–329.

Plantin, G., and H. Shin (2008). Carry trades and speculative dynamics. Mimeo, Princeton University.

Rapach, D., and M. Wohar (2002). Testing the monetary model of exchange rate determination: new evidence from a century of data. *Journal of International Economics 58*(2), 359–385.

Rime, D. (2001). *Trading in Foreign Exchange Markets*. Ph.D. dissertation, Norwegian School of Management, Norway.

Rime, D. (2003). New electronic trading systems in the foreign exchange markets. In D. C. Jones (Ed.), *New Economy Handbook*, Chapter 21, pp. 471–504. Academic Press.

Rime, D., L. Sarno, and E. Sojli (2010). Exchange rate forecasting, order flow and macroeconomic information. *Journal of International Economics 80*(1), 72–88.

Rogoff, K. (1996). The Purchasing Power Parity Puzzle. *Journal of Economic Literature 34*(2), 647–668.

Rogoff, K. (2007). *NBER Macroeconomics Annual*, Chapter: Comment on exchange rate models are not as bad as you think. Chicago University Press.

Rogoff, K., and V. Stavrakeva (2008, June). The continuing puzzle of short horizon exchange rate forecasting. Working Paper 14071, National Bureau of Economic Research.

Romer, D. (1993). Rational asset-price movements without news. *American Economic Review 83*(5), 1112–1130.

Rosenberg, J., and L. Traub (2009). Price discovery in the foreign currency futures and spot market. *Journal of Derivatives 17*(2), 7–25.

Sager, M., and M. Taylor (2006). Under the microscope: The structure of the foreign exchange market. *International Journal of Finance and Economics 11*(1), 81–95.

Sager, M., and M. Taylor (2008). Commercially available order flow data and exchange rate movements: Caveat emptor. *Journal of Money, Credit and Banking 40*(4), 583–625.

Samuelson, P. (1964). Theoretical notes on trade problems. *Review of Economics and Statistics 46*(2), 145–154.

Sarno, L., and M. Taylor (2002). *The Economics of Exchange Rates*. Cambridge University Press.

Schmitt-Grohe, S., and M. Uribe (2003). Closing small open economy models. *Journal of International Economics 61*(1), 163–185.

Schwarz, G. (1978). Estimating the dimension of a model. *Annals of Statistics 6*(2), 461–464.

Shiller, R. (1981). Do stock prices move too much to be justified by subsequent changes in dividends? *American Economic Review 71*(3), 421–436.

Stambaugh, R. (1999). Predictive regressions. *Journal of Financial Economics 54*(3), 375–421.

Svensson, L., and S. van Wijnbergen (1989). Excess capacity, monopolistic competition, and international transmission of monetary disturbances. *Economic Journal 99*(397), 785–805.

Taylor, J. (1999). *Monetary Policy Rules*. University of Chicago Press.

Taylor, M. (1989). Covered interest arbitrage and market turbulence. *Economic Journal 99*(396), 376–391.

Townsend, R. (1983). Forecasting the forecasts of others. *Journal of Political Economy 91*(4), 546–588.

Verdelhan, A. (2010). A habit-based explanation of the exchange rate risk premium. *Journal of Finance 65*(1), 123–146.

Vitale, P. (2008). A guided tour of the market microstructure approach to exchange rate determination. *Journal of Economic Surveys 21*(5), 903–934.

Vives, X. (1995). Short-term investment and the information efficiency of the market. *Review of Financial Studies 8*(1), 125–160.

Weil, P. (1989). The equity premium puzzle and the risk-free rate puzzle. *Journal of Monetary Economics 24*(3), 401–421.

West, K. (1996). Asymptotic inference about predictive ability. *Econometrica: Journal of the Econometric Society 64*(5), 1067–1084.

West, K. (2006). Forecast evaluation. *Handbook of Economic Forecasting 1*, 99–134.

Wincoop, E. van, and C. Tille (2007, January). International capital flows. Working Paper 12856, National Bureau of Economic Research.

Woodford, M. (2003). *Interest and Prices: Foundations of a Theory of Monetary Policy*. Princeton University Press.

Yogo, M. (2006). A consumption-based explanation of expected stock returns. *Journal of Finance 61*(2), 539–580.

Index

Page numbers for entries occurring in figures are followed by an *f;* those for entries occurring in notes, by an *n;* and those for entries occurring in tables, by a *t.*